C# Cookbook™

Other Microsoft .NET resources from O'Reilly

Related titles

Learning C#
Programming C#
Visual C# 2005: A
    Developer's Notebook™

ASP.NET 2.0: A Developer's
    Notebook™
ASP.NET 2.0 Cookbook™
Programming ASP.NET

**.NET Books
Resource Center**

dotnet.oreilly.com is a complete catalog of O'Reilly's books on .NET and related technologies, including sample chapters and code examples.

ONDotnet.com provides independent coverage of fundamental, interoperable, and emerging Microsoft .NET programming and web services technologies.

Conferences

O'Reilly brings diverse innovators together to nurture the ideas that spark revolutionary industries. We specialize in documenting the latest tools and systems, translating the innovator's knowledge into useful skills for those in the trenches. Visit *conferences.oreilly.com* for our upcoming events.

Safari Bookshelf (*safari.oreilly.com*) is the premier online reference library for programmers and IT professionals. Conduct searches across more than 1,000 books. Subscribers can zero in on answers to time-critical questions in a matter of seconds. Read the books on your Bookshelf from cover to cover or simply flip to the page you need. Try it today for free.

SECOND EDITION

C# Cookbook™

Jay Hilyard and Stephen Teilhet

O'REILLY®

Beijing · Cambridge · Farnham · Köln · Paris · Sebastopol · Taipei · Tokyo

C# Cookbook™, Second Edition
by Jay Hilyard and Stephen Teilhet

Published by O'Reilly Media, Inc., 1005 Gravenstein Highway North, Sebastopol, CA 95472.

O'Reilly books may be purchased for educational, business, or sales promotional use. Online editions are also available for most titles (*safari.oreilly.com*). For more information, contact our corporate/institutional sales department: (800) 998-9938 or *corporate@oreilly.com*.

Editor: John Osborn	**Indexer:** Ellen Troutman Zaig
Developmental Editor: Ralph Davis	**Cover Designer:** Emma Colby
Production Editor: Mary Brady	**Interior Designer:** David Futato
Copyeditor: Norma Emory	**Illustrators:** Robert Romano, Jessamyn Read,
Proofreader: Genevieve Rajewski	and Lesley Borash

Printing History:

January 2004:	First Edition.
January 2006:	Second Edition.

ISBN-10: 0-596-10063-9
ISBN-13: 978-0-596-10063-6
[M]   [7/07]

Table of Contents

Preface

C# is a language targeted at developers for the Microsoft .NET platform who have already worked with a C-like language such as C, C++, or Java. Unlike previous versions of C or C++ for the Microsoft Windows platform, C# code runs under a *managed execution environment*. While C and C++ developers using Visual Studio .NET can write managed code using Managed C++, C# offers a middle path between C++'s overall power but sometimes difficult code and the higher-level task orientation provided by Visual Basic .NET. Microsoft portrays C# as a modern and innovative language for .NET development that will be familiar to current C++ programmers while allowing more runtime control over the executing code.

C# allows you to perform many C/C++-like functions such as direct memory access via pointers and operator overloading that are not supported in Visual Basic .NET. C# is the system-level programming language for .NET. You can still do great application-level work in C#, but it really shines when you need to build code a little closer to the Framework.

If you have seen C#, you may have noticed that it looks a lot like Java; Java programmers will feel very much at home in C# once they learn the Framework SDK. C# can also be a great language for Visual Basic .NET programmers when they need a little more control over what the code is doing and don't want to have to write C++ to gain an advantage. On the Web, you'll find a large community of people doing really neat things with C# and tons of sample code on sites such as *http://www.gotdotnet.com*, *http://www.codeproject.com*, and *http://www.4guysfromrolla.com*.

We put this book together based on programming problems we ran into when we were first learning C# as well as during our continued use of it. Since the first edition, we have encountered a whole new set of problems to overcome, and with the help of C# 2.0, we have created new solutions for them. We hope that it will help you get past some of the common (and not-so-common) pitfalls and initial questions everyone has when learning a new language as well as the slightly off-the-beaten path items that come up during a development cycle. There are recipes dealing with things we found missing from the .NET Framework Class Library (FCL), even though Microsoft has provided tons of functionality to keep folks from reinventing the wheel. Some of these solutions you might immediately use and some may never darken your door, but we hope this book helps you get the most out of C# and the .NET Framework.

The book is laid out with respect to the types of problems you will solve as you progress through your life as a C# programmer. These solutions are called *recipes*; each recipe consists of a single problem, its solution, a discussion of the solution and other relevant related information, and finally where you can look for more information about the classes used from the FCL, other books addressing this topic, related articles, and other recipes. The question-and-answer format provides complete solutions to problems, making the book easy to read and use. Nearly every recipe contains a complete, documented code sample showing you how to solve the specific problem, as well as a discussion of how the underlying technology works and a list of alternatives, limitations, and other considerations when appropriate.

Who This Book Is For

You don't have to be an experienced C# or .NET developer to use this book—it is designed for users of all levels. This book provides solutions to problems that developers face every day as well as some that may come along infrequently. The recipes are targeted at the real-world developer who needs to solve problems now, not learn lots of theory first before being able to solve the problem. While reference or tutorial books can teach general concepts, they do not generally provide the help you need in solving real-world problems. We chose to teach by example, the natural way for most people to learn.

The majority of the problems addressed in this book are frequently faced by C# developers, but some of the more advanced problems call for more intricate solutions that combine many techniques. Each recipe is designed to help you quickly understand the problem, learn how to solve it, and find out any potential trade-offs or ramifications to help you solve your problems quickly, efficiently, and with minimal effort.

To save you even the effort of typing in the solution, we provide the sample code for the book on the O'Reilly web site to facilitate the "editor inheritance" mode of development (copy and paste) as well as to help less experienced developers see good programming practice in action. The sample code provides a running test harness that exercises each of the solutions, but enough of the code is provided in each solution in the book to allow you to implement the solution without the sample code. The sample code is available from the book's catalog page: *http://www.oreilly.com/catalog/csharpckbk2*.

What You Need to Use This Book

To run the samples in this book, you need a computer running Windows 2000 or later (if you are using Windows NT 4.0, you can use many, but not all, of the examples in this book; in particular, ASP.NET and .NET Web Services do not run on NT 4.0). A few of the networking and XML solutions require Microsoft Internet Information Server (IIS) Version 5 or later.

To open and compile the samples in this book, you need Visual Studio .NET 2005. If you are proficient with the downloadable Framework SDK and its command-line compilers, you should not have any trouble following the text of this book and the code samples.

Platform Notes

The solutions in this book are developed using Visual Studio .NET 2005. The differences between Version 2.0 and Version 1.1 of the .NET Framework are significant, and the sample code has changed from the first edition to reflect that. A complete list of differences between Version 2.0 and Version 1.1 of the .NET Framework can be found at *http://www.gotdotnet.com/team/upgrade/apiChanges.aspx*.

How This Book Is Organized

This book is organized into 20 chapters, each of which focuses on a particular topic in creating C# solutions. The following paragraphs summarize each chapter to give you an overview of this book's contents:

Chapter 1, *Numbers and Enumerations*
> This chapter focuses on the numeric and enumeration data types used in C# code. Recipes cover such things as numeric conversions, using bitwise operators on numbers, and testing strings to determine whether they contain a numeric value. The display, conversion, and testing of enumeration types and recipes on using enumerations that consist of bit flags are also shown.

Chapter 2, *Strings and Characters*
> This chapter covers both the String and Char data types. Various recipes show how to compare strings in various ways, encode/decode strings, break strings apart, and put them back together again, to name a few.

Chapter 3, *Classes and Structures*
> This large chapter contains recipes dealing with both class and structure data types. This chapter covers a wide range of recipes from design patterns to converting a class to interoperating with COM.

Chapter 4, *Generics*

This is a new chapter focusing on the new generics capacity in C#, which allows you to have code operate uniformly on values of different types. There are recipes to help your general understanding of generics as well as when they are appropriate to use, what support is provided in the Framework for them, and how to create custom implementations of collections using generics.

Chapter 5, *Collections*

This chapter examines recipes that make use of collections. The collection recipes make use of—as well as extend the functionality of—the array (single, multi, and jagged), the List<T>, and the Hashtable. The new generic-based collections are explored, and the various ways to create your own strongly typed collection are also discussed.

Chapter 6, *Iterators and Partial Types*

In this chapter, two of the new features of C# are used to solve very different programming problems. We show how you can implement iterators for generic and nongeneric types and implement foreach functionality using iterators, as well as custom iterator implementations. The other feature of C# in this chapter is partial types. We show how you can use partial types to do things like better segment your code and how to generate code that is more easily extensible.

Chapter 7, *Exception Handling*

The recipes in this chapter focus on the best ways to implement exception handling in your application. Preventing unhandled exceptions, reading and displaying stack traces, and throwing/rethrowing exceptions are included recipes. In addition, specific recipes show how to overcome some tricky situations, such as exceptions from late-bound called methods, and how to build a custom exception visualizer for the debugger.

Chapter 8, *Diagnostics*

This chapter explores recipes that use data types that fall under the System. Diagnostics namespace. Recipes deal with the Trace/Debug classes, event logs, processes, performance counters, and custom debugger displays for your types.

Chapter 9, *Delegates, Events, and Anonymous Methods*

This chapter's recipes show how delegates, events, and anonymous methods can be used in your applications. Recipes allow manipulation of delegates that call more than one method, synchronous delegates, asynchronous delegates, and Windows keyboard hooks. Anonymous methods are explored and recipes show their usage in place of old-style delegates as well as their use in implementing closures and functors.

Chapter 10, *Regular Expressions*

This chapter covers a very useful set of classes that are used to run regular expressions against strings. Recipes enumerate regular expression matches, break up strings into tokens, find/replace characters, and verify the syntax of a regular expression. A recipe is also included that contains many common regular expression patterns.

Chapter 11, *Data Structures and Algorithms*

This chapter goes a bit outside of what is provided for you in the .NET Framework Class Library and implements certain data structures and algorithms that are not in the FCL, or possibly are not in existence exactly the way you would like to use them, but ones that you have used to solve problems before. Items such as queues, maps, trees, and hashes are explored.

Chapter 12, *Filesystem I/O*

This chapter deals with filesystem interactions in four distinct ways. The first way is to look at typical file interactions; the second way looks at directory- or folder-based interactions; the third way deals with paths and temporary files; and the fourth way deals with advanced filesystem I/O topics.

Chapter 13, *Reflection*

This chapter shows ways to use the built-in assembly inspection system provided by the .NET Framework to determine what types, interfaces, and methods are implemented within an assembly and how to access them in a late-bound fashion.

Chapter 14, *Web*

This chapter covers accessing a web site and its content as well as programmatically determining web site configuration. Among the recipes in this chapter are using the new web browser control and setting up caching triggers to refresh cached data when a database table changes.

Chapter 15, *XML*

If you use .NET, it is likely that you will be dealing with XML to one degree or another; in this chapter, we explore some of the uses for XML, including XPath and XSLT, and topics such as the validation of XML and transformation of XML to HTML.

Chapter 16, *Networking*

This chapter explores the connectivity options provided by the .NET Framework and how to programmatically access network resources. Recipes for using TCP/IP directly, named pipes for communication, building your own port scanner, and more are covered here.

Chapter 17, *Security*

There are many ways to write secure code and protect data using the .NET Framework, and in this chapter, we explore areas such as controlling access to types, encryption and decryption, random numbers, securely storing data, and using programmatic and declarative security.

Chapter 18, *Threading and Synchronization*

This chapter addresses the subject of using multiple threads of execution in a .NET program and issues like how to implement threading in your application, protecting resources from and allowing safe concurrent access, storing per-thread data, and the use of asynchronous delegates for processing.

Chapter 19, *Unsafe Code*

This chapter discusses how C# allows you to step outside of the safe environment of managed code and write code that is considered unsafe by the .NET Framework. The possibilities and restrictions of using unsafe code in C# are addressed by illustrating solutions to problems using unsafe code.

Chapter 20, *Toolbox*

This chapter has recipes for those random sorts of operations that developers run into over and over again, like determining locations of system resources, sending email, and working with services. It also covers some less frequently accessed but helpful application pieces like message queuing, running code in a separate AppDomain, and finding the versions of assemblies in the GAC.

In some cases, certain recipes are related. In these cases, the See Also section of the recipe as well as some text in the Discussion will note the relationships.

What Was Left Out

This book is not a reference or a primer about C#. Some good primers and reference books are *C# in a Nutshell*, *C# Language Pocket Reference*, and *Learning C#*, all titles available from O'Reilly. The MSDN Library is also invaluable. It is included with Visual Studio .NET 2005 and available online at *http://msdn.microsoft.com/library/default.asp*.

This book is not about how to use Visual Studio .NET 2005 to build, compile, and deploy applications. See *Mastering Visual Studio .NET* (O'Reilly) for excellent coverage of these topics.

Conventions Used in This Book

This book uses the following typographic conventions:

Italic

Used for URLs, names of directories and files, options, and occasionally for emphasis.

Constant width

Used for program listings and for code items such as commands, options, switches, variables, attributes, keys, functions, types, classes, namespaces, methods, modules, properties, parameters, values, objects, events, event handlers, XML tags, HTML tags, macros, the contents of files, and the output from commands.

Constant width bold

Used in program listings to highlight an important part of the code.

```
//...
```
Ellipses in C# code indicate text that has been omitted for clarity.

```
<!-- ... -->
```
Ellipses in XML Schemas and documents' code indicate text that has been omitted for clarity.

This icon indicates a tip, suggestion, or general note.

This icon indicates a warning or caution.

About the Code

Nearly every recipe in this book contains one or more code samples. These samples are included in a single solution and are pieces of code and whole projects that are immediately usable in your application. Most of the code samples are written within a class or structure, making it easier to use within your applications. In addition to this, any using directives are included for each recipe so that you will not have to search for which ones to include in your code.

Complete error handling is included only in critical areas, such as input parameters. This allows you to easily see what is correct input and what is not. Many recipes omit error handling. This makes the solution easier to understand by focusing on the key concepts.

Using Code Examples

This book is here to help you get your job done. In general, you may use the code in this book in your programs and documentation. You do not need to contact us for permission unless you're reproducing a significant portion of the code. For example, writing a program that uses several chunks of code from this book does not require permission. Selling or distributing a CD-ROM of examples from O'Reilly books *does* require permission. Answering a question by citing this book and quoting example code does not require permission. Incorporating a significant amount of example code from this book into your product's documentation *does* require permission.

We appreciate, but do not require, attribution. An attribution usually includes the title, author, publisher, and ISBN. For example: "*C# Cookbook*, Second Edition, by Jay Hilyard and Stephen Teilhet. Copyright 2006 O'Reilly Media, Inc., 0-596-10063-9."

If you feel your use of code examples falls outside fair use or the preceding permission, feel free to contact us at *permissions@oreilly.com*.

Comments and Questions

Please address any comments or questions concerning this book to the publisher:

O'Reilly Media, Inc.
1005 Gravenstein Highway North
Sebastopol, CA 95472
800-998-9938 (in the U.S. or Canada)
707-829-0515 (international or local)
707-829-0104 (fax)

We have a web page for this book, where we list errata, examples, and any additional information. You can access this page at:

http://www.oreilly.com/catalog/csharpckbk2

To comment or ask technical questions about this book, send email to:

bookquestions@oreilly.com

For more information about our books, conferences, Resource Centers, and the O'Reilly Network, see our web site at:

http://www.oreilly.com

Safari Enabled

 When you see a Safari® Enabled icon on the cover of your favorite technology book, it means the book is available online through the O'Reilly Network Safari Bookshelf.

Safari offers a solution that's better than e-books. It's a virtual library that lets you easily search thousands of top technology books, cut and paste code samples, download chapters, and find quick answers when you need the most accurate, current information. Try it for free at *http://safari.oreilly.com*.

Acknowledgments

This book started for us after a long development cycle for a new product from Compuware called DevPartner SecurityChecker. Much was learned, and some of the concepts for recipes in this edition helped to build that product. With the advent of C# 2.0 and the new features in C#, we took the opportunity to reexamine how we did things in the first edition to see how we could improve the existing recipes as well as learn better ways of accomplishing programming tasks with C#. During the process Jay moved on to other opportunities from Compuware while Steve continued to help develop the forthcoming version of SecurityChecker. We have learned an incredible amount about C# and the Framework in general while we worked hard to help bring you a better understanding of how C# has evolved and how it can help you do your job better in this edition.

This book would have been impossible without the following people and we'd like to acknowledge all of their efforts.

Ralph Davis, our editor, who helped keep us on track, refereed the technical discussions, and was a steadying influence on a stormy project. Thank you for all of your efforts during the process and for your professionalism. It was most appreciated and impressive given the circumstances.

Ian Griffiths and Nicholas Paldino, our technical editors, who gave us their honest takes on our efforts and made good suggestions on how to make the recipes even better. They helped to make this an even better book and for that we thank them.

From Jay Hilyard

Thanks to Steve Teilhet for his ideas, friendship, and generally calm demeanor, which helped me get past the challenging stages of the book. I enjoyed working with you again, even though most of it was on nights and weekends this time.

Special thanks to my wife Brooke to whom I owe an immense debt of gratitude for so many things. You are a fabulous mother and an even better wife. Who would have thought I would be the one to write the "Cookbooks"? Thank you and I love you.

My sons, Owen and Andrew, understood when Daddy couldn't go to the beach and went to bed willingly on nights when I needed them to the most. I am truly blessed to have two fine sons.

Thanks to Phil and Gail for being there to help in ways that only grandparents can.

Thanks for Matt Pietrek for helping to explain why the 2.0 Framework reacted as it did when I tried new things before there were many other resources available.

Thanks to the Compuware gang of my era that helped produce DevPartner Studio and SecurityChecker. My perspective on development using .NET was expanded greatly from my discussions and experiences with all of you and I wish you all the very best. I say thank you to Steve Munyan, Barry Tannenbaum, Craig Neth, Kit Von Sück, Bob Newton, Garry Poegel, Katie King, Alice Pizzuto, Xin Li, Charles Kekeh, Tom Wagner, Bill Holmes, Jeff Simmons, Russ Osterlund, John Lyon-Smith, Katrina Lyon-Smith, Ian Goodsell, Rich Chiodo, Andy Najberg, Bob Crowling, and everyone else.

Thanks to Patrick Hynds, Duane LaFlotte, and Naveen Kohli for helping to keep my .NET interest high.

Thanks to Tim Pelletier, Scott Cronshaw, Lance Simpson, David Bennett, Suzanne Gibson, Kate Keisling, and Shawn McGowan for helping to reignite my passion for writing software. The best is yet to come.

Thanks to Kristen Acheson for being a great friend and a fan.

Finally, thanks again to my family and friends for asking about a book they don't understand and for being excited for me.

From Steve Teilhet

I'm proud to count Jay Hilyard as a good friend, excellent coworker, and hardworking coauthor. It's not every day that you find a person who is not only a good friend, but you also work so well with. Thank you for everything.

Kandis Teilhet, my wife, was there every step of the way to give me the strength to persevere and finish this work. Words cannot express my love for you.

Patrick and Nicholas Teilhet, my two sons, made the rough patches smooth. I couldn't wish for two better sons.

My mom and dad were there to listen and give support.

Thanks to Bill Holmes, Paul Pelski, and Jeff Simmons who helped me sort through several of the newer recipes and to provide some great ideas for recipes. Thanks also to Xin Li and Tom Wagner who helped examine the code to make sure it worked in real-world applications.

Thanks to the SecurityChecker development team (and friends) who helped me expand my knowledge of C# and also helped me through the rough patches: Garry Poegel, Andrew Fournier, Katie King, Kelley-Sue LeBlanc, Xin Li, Alicia Rhoades, Tom Wagner, Tim Weaver, Dave Chestnutt, Steve Munyan, Bob Newton, Charles Kekeh, Barry Tannenbaum, and Dennis Murphy. Thanks for all your help and support—I think this calls for a celebration.

CHAPTER 1

Numbers and Enumerations

1.0   Introduction

Simple types are value types that are a subset of the built-in types in C#, although, in fact, the types are defined as part of the .NET Framework Class Library (.NET FCL). Simple types are made up of several numeric types and a bool type. These numeric types consist of a decimal type (decimal), nine integral types (byte, char, int, long, sbyte, short, uint, ulong, ushort), and two floating-point types (float, double). Table 1-1 lists the simple types and their fully qualified names in the .NET Framework.

Table 1-1. The simple data types

Fully qualified name	Alias	Value range
System.Boolean	bool	true or false
System.Byte	byte	0 to 255
System.SByte	sbyte	-128 to 127
System.Char	char	0 to 65535
System.Decimal	decimal	-79,228,162,514,264,337,593,543,950,335 to 79,228,162,514,264,337,593,543,950,335
System.Double	double	-1.79769313486232e308 to 1.79769313486232e308
System.Single	float	-3.40282347E+38 to 3.40282347E+38
System.Int16	short	-32768 to 32767
System.Uint16	ushort	0 to 65535
System.Int32	int	-2,147,483,648 to 2,147,483,647
System.UInt32	uint	0 to 4,294,967,295
System.Int64	long	-9,223,372,036,854,775,808 to 9,223,372,036,854,775,807
System.UInt64	ulong	0 to 18,446,744,073,709,551,615

The C# reserved words for the various data types are simply aliases for the fully qualified type name. Therefore, it does not matter whether you use the type name or the reserved word: the C# compiler will generate identical code.

It should be noted that the following types are not Common Language Specification-compliant (CLS-compliant): sbyte, ushort, uint, and ulong. They might not be supported by other .NET languages as a result of this. This lack of support might limit or impede the interaction between your C# code and code written in another CLS-compliant language, such as Visual Basic .NET.

Enumerations implicitly inherit from System.Enum, which in turn inherits from System.ValueType. Enumerations have a single use: to describe items of a specific group. For example, the colors red, blue, and yellow could be defined by the enumeration ValidShapeColor; likewise, square, circle, and triangle could be defined by the enumeration ValidShape. These enumerations would look like the following:

```
enum ValidShapeColor
{
    Red, Blue, Yellow
}

enum ValidShape
{
    Square = 2, Circle = 4, Triangle = 6
}
```

Each item in the enumeration receives a numeric value regardless of whether you assign one or not. Since the compiler automatically adds the numbers starting with zero and incrementing by one, for each item in the enumeration, the ValidShapeColor enumeration previously defined would be exactly the same if it were defined in the following manner:

```
enum ValidShapeColor
{
    Red = 0, Blue = 1, Yellow = 2
}
```

Enumerations are good code-documenting tools. For example, it is more intuitive to write the following:

```
ValidShapeColor currentColor = ValidShapeColor.Red;
```

instead of this:

```
int currentColor = 0;
```

Either mechanism will work, but the first method is easy to read and understand, especially for a new developer taking over someone else's code. It also has the benefit of being type-safe, which the use of raw ints does not provide.

1.1 Determining Approximate Equality Between a Fraction and Floating-Point Value

Problem

You need to compare a fraction with a value of type double or float to determine whether they are within a close approximation to each other. Take, for example, the result of comparing the expression 1/6 and the value 0.16666667. These seem to be equivalent, except that 0.16666667 is precise to only eight places to the right of the decimal point, and 1/6 is precise to the maximum number of digits to the right of the decimal point that the data type will hold.

Solution

To compare the approximate equality between a fraction and a floating-point value, verify that the difference between the two values is within an acceptable tolerance:

```
using System;

// Override that uses the System.Double.Epsilon value
public static bool IsApproximatelyEqualTo(double numerator,
                                          double denominator,
                                          double dblValue)
{
    return IsApproximatelyEqualTo(numerator,
        denominator, dblValue, double.Epsilon);
}

// Override that allows for specification of an epsilon value
// other than System.Double.Epsilon
public static bool IsApproximatelyEqualTo(double numerator,
                                          double denominator,
                                          double dblValue,
                                          double epsilon)
{
    double difference = (numerator/denominator) - dblValue;

    if (Math.Abs(difference) < epsilon)
    {
        // This is a good approximation.
        return true;
    }
    else
    {
        // This is NOT a good approximation.
        return false;
    }
}
```

Replacing the type double with float allows you to determine whether a fraction and a float value are approximately equal.

Discussion

Fractions can be expressed as a numerator over a denominator; however, storing them as a floating-point value might be necessary. Storing fractions as floating-point values introduces rounding errors that make it difficult to perform comparisons. Expressing the value as a fraction (e.g., 1/6) allows the maximum precision. Expressing the value as a floating-point value (e.g., 0.16667) can limit the precision of the value. In this case, the precision depends on the number of digits that the developer decides to use to the right of the decimal point.

You might need a way to determine whether two values are approximately equal to each other. This comparison is achieved by defining a value (epsilon), representing the smallest positive value by which two numbers can differ and still be considered equal. In other words, by taking the absolute value of the difference between the fraction (numerator/denominator) and the floating-point value (dblValue) and comparing it to a predetermined value passed to the epsilon argument, you can determine whether the floating-point value is a good approximation of the fraction.

Consider a comparison between the fraction 1/7 and its floating-point value, 0.14285714285714285. The following call to the IsApproximatelyEqualTo method indicates that there are not enough digits to the right of the decimal point in the floating-point value to be a good approximation of the fraction (there are six digits, although seven are required):

```
bool Approximate = Class1.IsApproximatelyEqualTo(1, 7, .142857, .0000001);
// Approximate == false
```

Adding another digit of precision to the third parameter of this method now indicates that this more precise number is what you require for a good approximation of the fraction 1/7:

```
bool Approximate = Class1.IsApproximatelyEqualTo(1, 7, .1428571, .0000001);
// Approximate == true
```

See Also

See the "Double.Epsilon Field" and "Single.Epsilon Field" topics in the MSDN documentation.

1.2 Converting Degrees to Radians

Problem

When using the trigonometric functions of the Math class, all units are in radians. You have one or more angles measured in degrees and want to convert these to radians in order to use them with the members of the Math class.

Solution

To convert a value in degrees to radians, multiply it by $\pi/180$:

```
using System;

public static double ConvertDegreesToRadians (double degrees)
{
    double radians = (Math.PI / 180) * degrees;
    return (radians);
}
```

Discussion

All of the static trigonometric methods in the Math class use radians as their unit of measure for angles. It is very handy to have conversion routines to convert between radians and degrees, especially when a user is required to enter data in degrees rather than radians. After all, humans understand degrees better than radians.

The equation for converting degrees to radians is shown here:

```
radians = (Math.PI / 180) * degrees
```

The static field Math.PI contains the constant π.

1.3   Converting Radians to Degrees

Problem

When using the trigonometric functions of the Math class, all units are in radians; instead, you require a result in degrees.

Solution

To convert a value in radians to degrees, multiply it by $180/\pi$:

```
using System;

public static double ConvertRadiansToDegrees(double radians)
{
    double degrees = (180 / Math.PI) * radians;
    return (degrees);
}
```

Discussion

All of the static trigonometric methods in the Math class use radians as their unit of measure for angles. It is very handy to have conversion routines to convert between radians and degrees; displaying degrees to a user is more informative than displaying radians.

The equation for converting radians to degrees is shown here:

```
degrees = (180 / Math.PI) * radians
```

The static field `Math.PI` contains the constant π.

1.4 Using the Bitwise Complement Operator with Various Data Types

Problem

The bitwise complement operator (~) is overloaded to work directly with `int`, `uint`, `long`, `ulong`, and enumeration data types consisting of the underlying types `int`, `uint`, `long`, and `ulong`. However, you need to perform a bitwise complement operation on a different numeric data type.

Solution

To use the bitwise complement operator with any data type, you must cast the resultant value of the bitwise operation to the type you wish to work with. The following code demonstrates this technique with the byte data type:

```
byte y = 1;
byte result = (byte)~y;
```

The value assigned to `result` is 254.

Discussion

The following code shows incorrect use of the bitwise complement operator on the byte data type:

```
byte y = 1;
Console.WriteLine("~y = " + ~y);
```

This code outputs the following surprising value:

```
-2
```

Clearly, the result from performing the bitwise complement of the byte variable is incorrect; it should be 254. In fact, byte is an unsigned data type, so it cannot be equal to a negative number. If you rewrite the code as follows:

```
byte y = 1;
byte result = ~y;
```

you get a compile-time error: "Cannot implicitly convert type 'int' to 'byte.'" This error message gives some insight into why this operation does not work as expected. To fix this problem, you must explicitly cast this value to a byte before you assign it to the result variable, as shown here:

```
byte y = 1;
byte result = (byte)~y;
```

This cast is required because the bitwise operators are overloaded to operate on only six specific data types: int, uint, long, ulong, bool, and enumeration data types. When one of the bitwise operators is used on another data type, that data type is converted to the supported data type that matches it most closely. Therefore, a byte data type is converted to an int before the bitwise complement operator is evaluated:

```
0x01 // byte y = 1;
0xFFFFFFFE // The value 01h is converted to an int and its
           // bitwise complement is taken.
           // This bit pattern equals -2 as an int.
0xFE // The resultant int value is cast to its original byte data type.
```

Notice that the int data type is a signed data type, unlike the byte data type. This is why you receive -2 for a result instead of the expected value 254. This conversion of the byte data type to its nearest equivalent is called *numeric promotion*. Numeric promotion also comes into play when you use differing data types with binary operators, including the bitwise binary operators.

 Numeric promotion is discussed in detail in the C# Language Specification document in section 7.2.6 (this document is available at *http://msdn.microsoft.com/vcsharp/programming/language*). It is essential to understand how numeric promotion works when using operators on differing data types and when using operators with a data type that is not overloaded to handle them. Knowing this can save you hours of debugging time.

1.5   Testing for an Even or Odd Value

Problem

You need a simple method to test a numeric value to determine whether it is even or odd.

Solution

The solution is actually implemented as two methods. To test for an even integer value, use the following method:

```
public static bool IsEven(int intValue)
{
    return ((intValue % 2) == 0);
}
```

To test for an odd integer value, use the following method:

```
public static bool IsOdd(int intValue)
{
    return ((intValue % 2) == 1);
}
```

Discussion

Every odd number always has its least-significant bit set to 1. Therefore, by checking whether this bit is equal to 1, you can tell whether it is an odd number. Conversely, testing the least-significant bit to see whether it is 0 can tell you whether it is an even number.

To test whether a value is even, you AND the value in question with 1 and then determine whether the result is equal to zero. If it is, you know that the value is an even number; otherwise, the value is odd. This operation is part of the IsEven method.

On the other hand, you can determine whether a value is odd by ANDing the value with 1, similar to how the even test operates, and then determine whether the result is 1. If so, you know that the value is an odd number; otherwise, the value is even. This operation is part of the IsOdd method.

Note that you do not have to implement both the IsEven and IsOdd methods in your application, although implementing both methods might improve the readability of your code. You can implement one in terms of the other. For example, here is an implementation of IsOdd in terms of IsEven:

```
public static bool IsOdd(int intValue)
{
    return (!IsEven(intValue));
}
```

The methods presented here accept only 32-bit integer values. To allow this method to accept other numeric data types, you can simply overload it to accept any other data types that you require. For example, if you need to also determine whether a 64-bit integer is even, you can modify the IsEven method as follows:

```
public static bool IsEven(long longValue)
{
    return ((longValue & 1) == 0);
}
```

Only the data type in the parameter list needs to be modified.

1.6   Obtaining the High Word or Low Word of a Number

Problem

You have a 32-bit integer value that contains information in both its lower and upper 16 bits. You need methods to get the high word (first 16 bits) and/or the low word (last 16 bits) of this value.

Solution

To get the high word of an integer value, perform a bitwise AND between it and the value, as shown in the following method:

```
public static int GetHighWord(int intValue)
{
    return (intValue & (0xFFFF << 16));
}
```

To get the low word of a value, use the following method:

```
public static int GetLowWord(int intValue)
{
    return (intValue & 0x0000FFFF);
}
```

This technique can easily be modified to work with other sizes of integers (e.g., 8-bit, 16-bit, or 64-bit); this trick is shown in the Discussion section.

Discussion

In order to determine the values of the high word of a number, use the following bitwise AND operation:

```
uint intValue = Int32.MaxValue;
uint MSB = intValue & (0xFFFF << 16);

// MSB == 0xFFFF0000
```

This method simply ANDs the number to another number with all of the high word set to 1. This method will zero out all of the low word, leaving the high word intact.

In order to determine the values of the low word of a number, use the following bitwise AND operation:

```
uint intValue = Int32.MaxValue;
uint LSB = intValue & 0x0000FFFF;

// LSB == 0x0000FFFF
```

This method simply ANDs the number to another number with all of the low word set to 1, which zeros out all of the high word, leaving the low word intact.

The methods presented here accept only 32-bit integer values. To allow this method to accept other numeric data types, you can simply overload this method to accept any other data types that you require. For example, if you need to also acquire the low or high byte of a 16-bit integer, you can use the same structure as the GetHighWord method as follows:

```
public static short GetHighByte(short shortValue)
{
    return (short)(shortValue & (0xFF << 8));
}
```

The GetLowWord method is modified as shown here:

```csharp
public static short GetLowByte(short shortValue)
{
    return (short)(shortValue & (short)0xFF);
}
```

1.7   Converting a Number in Another Base to Base10

Problem

You have a string containing a number in base2 (binary), base8 (octal), base10 (decimal), or base16 (hexadecimal). You need to convert this string to its equivalent integer value and display it in base10.

Solution

To convert a number in another base to base10, use the overloaded static Convert.ToInt32 method on the Convert class:

```csharp
string base2 = "11";
string base8 = "17";
string base10 = "110";
string base16 = "11FF";

Console.WriteLine("Convert.ToInt32(base2, 2) = " +
                    Convert.ToInt32(base2, 2));

Console.WriteLine("Convert.ToInt32(base8, 8) = " +
                    Convert.ToInt32(base8, 8));

Console.WriteLine("Convert.ToInt32(base10, 10) = " +
                    Convert.ToInt32(base10, 10));

Console.WriteLine("Convert.ToInt32(base16, 16) = " +
                    Convert.ToInt32(base16, 16));
```

This code produces the following output:

```
Convert.ToInt32(base2, 2) = 3
Convert.ToInt32(base8, 8) = 15
Convert.ToInt32(base10, 10) = 110
Convert.ToInt32(base16, 16) = 4607
```

Discussion

The static Convert.ToInt32 method has an overload that takes a string containing a number and an integer defining the base of this number. This method then converts the numeric string into an integer. Console.WriteLine then converts the number to base10 and displays it.

The other static methods of the Convert class, such as ToByte, ToInt64, and ToInt16, also have this same overload, which accepts a number as a string and the base in which this number is expressed. Unfortunately, these methods convert from a string value expressed in base2, base8, base10, and base16 only. They do not allow for converting a value to a string expressed in any other base types than base10. However, the ToString methods on the various numeric types do allow for this conversion.

See Also

See the "Convert Class" and "Converting with System.Convert" topics in the MSDN documentation.

1.8   Determining Whether a String Is a Valid Number

Problem

You have a string that possibly contains a numeric value. You need to know whether this string contains a valid number.

Solution

Use the static TryParse method of any of the numeric types. For example, to determine whether a string contains a double, use the following method:

```
string str = "12.5";
double result = 0;
if(double.TryParse(str,
        System.Globalization.NumberStyles.Float,
        System.Globalization.NumberFormatInfo.CurrentInfo,
        out result))
{
    // Is a double!
}
```

Discussion

This recipe shows how to determine whether a string contains only a numeric value. The TryParse method returns true if the string contains a valid number without the exception that you will get if you use the Parse method. Since TryParse does not throw exceptions, it performs better over time given a set of strings where some do not contain numbers.

See Also

See the "Parse" and "TryParse" topics in the MSDN documentation.

1.9 Rounding a Floating-Point Value

Problem

You need to round a number to a whole number or to a specific number of decimal places.

Solution

To round any number to its nearest whole number, use the overloaded static `Math.Round` method, which takes only a single argument:

```
int x = (int)Math.Round(2.5555); // x == 3
```

If you need to round a floating-point value to a specific number of decimal places, use the overloaded static `Math.Round` method, which takes two arguments:

```
decimal x = Math.Round(2.5555, 2); // x == 2.56
```

Discussion

The `Round` method is easy to use; however, you need to be aware of how the rounding operation works. The `Round` method follows the IEEE Standard 754, section 4 standard. This means that if the number being rounded is halfway between two numbers, the `Round` operation will always round to the even number. An example will show what this means to you:

```
decimal x = Math.Round(1.5); // x == 2
decimal y = Math.Round(2.5); // y == 2
```

Notice that `1.5` is rounded up to the nearest even whole number and `2.5` is rounded down to the nearest even whole number. Keep this in mind when using the `Round` method.

See Also

See Recipes 1.1 and 1.22; see the "Math Class" topic in the MSDN documentation.

1.10 Choosing a Rounding Algorithm

Problem

The `Math.Round` method will round the value 1.5 to 2; however, the value 2.5 will also be rounded to 2 using this method. You may always want to round to the greater number in this type of situation (e.g., round 2.5 to 3 instead of 2). Conversely, you might want to always round to the lesser number (e.g., round 1.5 to 1).

Solution

Use the static `Math.Floor` method to always round up when a value is halfway between two whole numbers:

```
public static double RoundUp(double valueToRound)
{
    return (Math.Floor(valueToRound + 0.5));
}
```

Use the following technique to always round down when a value is halfway between two whole numbers:

```
public static double RoundDown(double valueToRound)
{
    double floorValue = Math.Floor(valueToRound);
    if ((valueToRound - floorValue) > .5)
    {
        return (floorValue + 1);
    }
    else
    {
        return (floorValue);
    }
}
```

Discussion

The static `Math.Round` method rounds to the nearest even number (see Recipe 1.9 for more information). However, there are some times that you do not want to round a number in this manner. The static `Math.Floor` method can be used to allow for different manners of rounding.

Note that the methods used to round numbers in this recipe do not round to a specific number of decimal points; rather, they round to the nearest whole number.

See Also

See Recipes 1.9 and 1.22; see the "Math Class" topic in the MSDN documentation.

1.11 Converting Celsius to Fahrenheit

Problem

You have a temperature reading measured in Celsius and need to convert it to Fahrenheit.

Solution

```
public static double CtoF(double celsius)
{
    return (((0.9/0.5) * celsius) + 32);
}
```

To generate a double result while maintaining the same ratio (9 to 5) as the integers give, 0.9 and 0.5 are used in the calculation.

Discussion

This recipe makes use of the following Celsius-to-Fahrenheit temperature conversion equation:

```
TempFahrenheit = ((9 / 5) * TempCelsius) + 32
```

The Fahrenheit temperature scale is widely used in the United States. However, much of the rest of the world uses the Celsius temperature scale.

1.12   Converting Fahrenheit to Celsius

Problem

You have a temperature reading measured in Fahrenheit and need to convert it to Celsius.

Solution

```
public static double FtoC(double fahrenheit)
{
    return ((0.5/0.9) * (fahrenheit - 32));
}
```

Discussion

This recipe makes use of the following Fahrenheit-to-Celsius temperature conversion equation:

```
TempCelsius = (5 / 9) * (TempFahrenheit - 32)
```

The Fahrenheit temperature scale is widely used in the United States. However, much of the rest of the world uses the Celsius temperature scale.

1.13   Safely Performing a Narrowing Numeric Cast

Problem

You need to cast a value from a larger value to a smaller one, while gracefully handling conditions that result in a loss of information. For example, casting a long to an int results in a loss of information only if the long data type is greater than int.MaxSize.

Solution

The simplest way to do this check is to use the checked keyword. The following method accepts two long data types and attempts to add them together. The result is stuffed into an int data type. If an overflow condition exists, the OverflowException is thrown:

```
using System;

public void UseChecked(long lhs, long rhs)
{
    int result = 0;

    try
    {
        result =  checked((int)(lhs + rhs));
    }
    catch (OverflowException e)
    {
        // Handle overflow exception here.
    }
}
```

This is the simplest method. However, if you do not want the overhead of throwing an exception and having to wrap a lot of code in try/catch blocks to handle the overflow condition, you can use the MaxValue and MinValue fields of each type. A check using these fields can be done prior to the conversion to insure that no loss of information occurs. If this does occur, the code can inform the application that this cast will cause a loss of information. You can use the following conditional statement to determine whether sourceValue can be cast to a short without losing any information:

```
// Our two variables are declared and initialized.
int sourceValue = 34000;
short destinationValue = 0;

// Determine if sourceValue will lose information in a cast to a short.
if (sourceValue <= short.MaxValue && sourceValue >= short.MinValue)
{
    destinationValue = (short)sourceValue;
}
else
{
    // Inform the application that a loss of information will occur.
}
```

Discussion

A *narrowing conversion* occurs when a larger type is cast down to a smaller type. For instance, consider casting a value of type Int32 to a value of type Int16. If the Int32 value is smaller than or equal to the Int16.MaxValue field and the Int32 value is higher than or equal to the Int16.MinValue field, the cast will occur without error or loss of information. Loss of information occurs when the Int32 value is larger than the Int16.MaxValue field or the Int32 value is lower than the Int16.MinValue field. In either of these cases, the most significant bits of the Int32 value are truncated and discarded, changing the value after the cast.

If a loss of information occurs in an unchecked context, it will occur silently without the application noticing. This problem can cause some very insidious bugs that are hard to track down. To prevent this, check the value to be converted to determine whether it is within the lower and upper bounds of the type that it will be cast to. If the value is outside these bounds, then code can be written to handle this situation. This code could force the cast not to occur and/or possibly inform the application of the casting problem. This solution can aid in the prevention of hard-to-find arithmetic bugs from appearing in your applications.

You should understand that both techniques shown in the Solution section are valid. However, the technique you use will depend on whether you expect to hit the overflow case on a regular basis or only occasionally. If you expect to hit the overflow case quite often, you might want to choose the second technique of manually testing the numeric value. Otherwise, it might be easier to use the checked keyword, as in the first technique.

 In C#, code can run in either a *checked* or *unchecked* context; by default, the code runs in an unchecked context. In a checked context, any arithmetic and conversions involving integral types are examined to determine whether an overflow condition exists. If so, an OverflowException is thrown. In an unchecked context, no OverflowException will be thrown when an overflow condition exists.

A checked context can be set up by using the /checked{+} compiler switch, by setting the Check for Arithmetic Overflow/Underflow project property to true, or by using the checked keyword. An unchecked context can be set up using the /checked- compiler switch, by setting the Check for Arithmetic Overflow/Underflow project property to false, or by using the unchecked keyword.

Notice that floating-point and decimal types are not included in the code that handles the conversions to integral types in this recipe. The reason is that a conversion from any integral type to a float, double, or decimal will not lose any information; therefore, it is redundant to check these conversions.

In addition, you should be aware of the following when performing a conversion:

- Casting from a float, double, or decimal type to an integral type results in the truncation of the fractional portion of this number. Furthermore, if the integral portion of the number exceeds MaxValue for the target type, the result will be undefined unless the conversion is done in a checked context, in which case it will trigger an OverflowException.

- Casting from a float or double to a decimal results in the float or double being rounded to 28 decimal places.

- Casting from a double to a float results in the double being rounded to the nearest float value.

- Casting from a decimal to a float or double results in the decimal being rounded to the resulting type (float or double).

- Casting from an int, uint, or long to a float could result in the loss of precision, but never magnitude.

- Casting from a long to a double could result in the loss of precision, but never magnitude.

See Also

See the "Checked Keyword" and "Checked and Unchecked" topics in the MSDN documentation.

1.14 Finding the Length of Any Three Sides of a Right Triangle

Problem

You need to calculate the length of one side of a triangle when either the lengths of two sides are known or one angle and the length of a side are known.

Solution

Use the Math.Sin, Math.Cos, and Math.Tan methods of the Math class to find the length of one side. The equations for these methods are as follows:

```
double theta = 40;
double hypotenuse = 5;
double oppositeSide = 0;
double adjacentSide = 0;
oppositeSide = Math.Sin(theta) * hypotenuse;
oppositeSide = Math.Tan(theta) * adjacentSide;
adjacentSide = Math.Cos(theta) * hypotenuse;
adjacentSide = oppositeSide / Math.Tan(theta);
hypotenuse = oppositeSide / Math.Sin(theta);
hypotenuse = adjacentSide / Math.Cos(theta);
```

where theta (Θ) is the known angle, the oppositeSide variable is equal to the length of the side *opposite* to the angle theta, and the adjacentSide variable is equal to the length of the side *adjacent* to the angle theta. The hypotenuse variable is equal to the length of the *hypotenuse* of the triangle. See Figure 1-1.

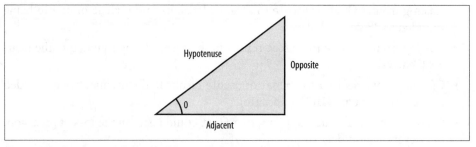

Figure 1-1. A right triangle

In addition to these three static methods, the length of the hypotenuse of a right triangle can be calculated using the Pythagorean theorem. This theorem states that the hypotenuse of a right triangle is equal to the square root of the sum of the squares of the other two sides. This equation can be realized using the `Math.Sqrt` static method, as follows:

```
double hypotenuse = Math.Sqrt((xSide * xSide) + (ySide * ySide));
```

where xSide and ySide are the lengths of the two sides that are *not* the hypotenuse of the triangle.

Discussion

Finding the length of a side of a right triangle is easy when an angle and the length of one of the sides are known. Using the trigonometric functions sine, cosine, and tangent, you can derive the lengths of either of the two unknown sides. The equations for sine, cosine, and tangent are defined here:

```
sin(Theta) = oppositeSide / hypotenuseSide
cos(Theta) = adjacentSide / hypotenuseSide
tan(Theta) = oppositeSide / adjacentSide
```

where theta is the value of the known angle. Rearranging these equations allows you to derive the following equations:

```
oppositeSide = sin(theta) * hypotenuse;
oppositeSide = tan(theta) * adjacentSide;
adjacentSide = cos(theta) * hypotenuse;
adjacentSide = oppositeSide / tan(theta);
hypotenuse = oppositeSide / sin(theta);
hypotenuse = adjacentSide / cos(theta);
```

These equations give you two methods to find the length of each side of the triangle.

When none of the angles is known but the lengths of two of the sides are known, use the Pythagorean theorem to determine the length of the hypotenuse. This theorem is defined as follows:

```
Math.Sqrt(hypotenuse * hypotenuse) = Math.Sqrt((xSide * xSide) +
                                               (ySide * ySide))
```

Simplifying this equation into a syntax usable by C#, you obtain the following code:

```
double hypotenuse = Math.Sqrt((xSide * xSide) +
                              (ySide * ySide));
```

where hypotenuse is equal to the length of the hypotenuse, and xSide and ySide are the lengths of the other two sides.

See Also

See the "Math Class" topic in the MSDN documentation.

1.15   Finding the Angles of a Right Triangle

Problem

You need to calculate an angle of a triangle when the lengths of two sides are known.

Solution

Use the Math.Atan, Math.Acos, or Math.Asin static methods of the Math class. The following code calculates the angle theta and returns the value in *radians*:

```
double theta = Math.Atan(OppositeSide / AdjacentSide);
theta = Math.Acos(AdjacentSide / Hypotenuse);
theta = Math.Asin(OppositeSide / Hypotenuse);
```

To get the angle in degrees, use the following code:

```
double theta = Math.Atan(oppositeSide / adjacentSide) * (180 / Math.PI);
theta = Math.Acos(adjacentSide / hypotenuse) * (180 / Math.PI);
theta = Math.Asin(oppositeSide / hypotenuse) * (180 / Math.PI);
```

where theta is the known angle value, oppositeSide is equal to the length of the side *opposite* to the angle, and adjacentSide is equal to the length of the side *adjacent* to the angle. The hypotenuse is the length of the *hypotenuse* of the triangle. See Figure 1-1 in Recipe 1.14 for a graphical representation of these sides of a right triangle and Recipes 1.2 and 1.3 for converting between degrees and radians.

Discussion

In some cases, you need to determine an angle of a right triangle when only the lengths of two sides are known. The three trigonometric functions arcsine, arccosine, and arctangent allow you to find any angle of a right triangle, given this information. The static methods Math.Atan, Math.Acos, and Math.Asin on the Math class provide the functionality to implement these trigonometric operations.

See Also

See Recipe 1.14; see the "Math Class" topic in the MSDN documentation.

1.16 Displaying an Enumeration Value as a String

Problem

You need to display the textual or numeric value of an enumeration member.

Solution

To display an enumeration value as a string, use the `ToString` method that each enumeration member inherits from `System.Enum`.

Using the following `ValidShape` enumeration type as an example, you can obtain the textual and numeric values so that you can display them:

```
enum ValidShape
{
    Square, Circle, Cylinder, Octagon
}
```

Using the `ToString` method of the `ValidShape` enumeration type, you can derive the value of a specific `ValidShape` enumeration value directly:

```
Console.WriteLine(ValidShape.Circle.ToString());
Console.WriteLine(ValidShape.Circle.ToString("G"));
Console.WriteLine(ValidShape.Circle.ToString("D"));
Console.WriteLine(ValidShape.Circle.ToString("F"));
Console.WriteLine(ValidShape.Circle.ToString("X"));
```

This generates the following output:

```
Circle
Circle
1
Circle
00000001
```

If you are working with a variable of type `ValidShape`, the enumeration values can be derived in the same manner:

```
ValidShape shapeStyle = ValidShape.Cylinder;

Console.WriteLine(shapeStyle.ToString());
Console.WriteLine(shapeStyle.ToString("G"));
Console.WriteLine(shapeStyle.ToString("D"));
Console.WriteLine(shapeStyle.ToString("F"));
Console.WriteLine(shapeStyle.ToString("X"));
```

The following is displayed.

```
Cylinder
Cylinder
2
Cylinder
00000002
```

Discussion

Deriving the textual or numeric representation of an enumeration value is a simple matter, using the ToString instance method on the Enum type. This method can accept a character indicating the type of formatting to place on the enumeration value. The character can be one of the following: G, g, D, d, X, x, F, or f. See Table 1-2 for a description of these formatting types.

Table 1-2. Formatting types

Formatting type	Name	Description
G or g	(General)	Displays the string representation of the enumeration value.
F or f	(Flag)	Displays the string representation of the enumeration value. The enumeration is treated as if it were a bit field.
D or d	(Decimal)	Displays decimal equivalent of the enumeration.
X or x	(Hexadecimal)	Displays hexadecimal equivalent of the enumeration.

When printing out the values of an enumeration with the Flags attribute, the information displayed takes into account that more than one of the enumeration values may have been ORed together. The output will be all of the enumerations printed out as strings separated by commas or as the ORed numeric value, depending on the formatting chosen. For example, consider if the Flags attribute was added to the ValidShape enumeration as follows:

```
[Flags]
enum ValidShape
{
    Square = 0, Circle = 1, Cylinder = 2, Octagon = 4
}
```

Now if you change the code for this recipe as follows:

```
ValidShape shapeStyle = ValidShape.Circle | ValidShape.Cylinder;

Console.WriteLine(shapeStyle.ToString());
Console.WriteLine(shapeStyle.ToString("G"));
Console.WriteLine(shapeStyle.ToString("D"));
Console.WriteLine(shapeStyle.ToString("F"));
Console.WriteLine(shapeStyle.ToString("X"));
```

you will see the following output:

```
Circle, Cylinder
Circle, Cylinder
3
Circle, Cylinder
00000003
```

This provides a flexible way of extracting the flags that you are currently using on an enumeration type.

See Also

See the "Enum.ToString Method" and the "Enumeration Format Strings" topics in the MSDN documentation.

1.17 Converting Plain Text to an Equivalent Enumeration Value

Problem

You have the textual value of an enumeration element, possibly from a database or text file. This textual value needs to be converted to a usable enumeration type.

Solution

The static Parse method on the Enum class allows the textual value of an enumeration element to be converted to a usable enumeration value. For example:

```
try
{
    Language proj1Language = (Language)Enum.Parse(typeof(Language),
                            "VBNET");
    Language proj2Language = (Language)Enum.Parse(typeof(Language),
                            "UnDefined");
}
catch (ArgumentException e)
{
    // Handle an invalid text value here
    //(such as the "UnDefined" string)
}
```

where the Language enumeration is defined as:

```
enum Language
{
    Other = 0, CSharp = 1, VBNET = 2, VB6 = 3
}
```

Discussion

The static Enum.Parse method converts text to a specific enumeration value. This technique is useful when a user is presented a list of values, with each value defined in an enumeration. When the user selects an item from this list, the text chosen can be easily converted from its string representation to its equivalent enumeration value using Enum.Parse. This method returns an object, which must then be cast to the target enum type in order to use it.

In addition to passing `Enum.Parse` a single enumeration value as a string, you can also pass the enumeration value as its corresponding numeric value. For example, consider the following line:

```
Language proj1Language = (Language)Enum.Parse(typeof(Language),
                                "VBNET");
```

You can rewrite this as follows to perform the exact same action:

```
Language proj1Language = (Language)Enum.Parse(typeof(Language), "2");
```

This is assuming that the `Language.VBNET` enumeration value is equal to 2.

Another interesting feature of the `Parse` method is that it can accept a comma-delimited list of enumeration names or values and then logically OR them together. The following example creates an enumeration with the languages `VBNET` and `CSharp` ORed together:

```
Language proj1Language = (Language)Enum.Parse(typeof(Language),
                        "CSharp, VBNET");
```

Each individual element of the comma-delimited list is trimmed of any whitespace, so it does not matter if you add any whitespace between each item in this list.

See Also

See the "Enum.Parse Method" topic in the MSDN documentation.

1.18   Testing for a Valid Enumeration Value

Problem

When you pass a numeric value to a method that accepts an enumeration type, it is possible to pass a value that does not exist in the enumeration. You want to perform a test before using this numeric value to determine if it is indeed one of the ones defined in this enumeration type.

Solution

To prevent this problem, test for the specific enumeration values that you allow for the enumeration-type parameter using a `switch` statement to list the values.

Using the following `Language` enumeration:

```
enum Language
{
    Other = 0, CSharp = 1, VBNET = 2, VB6 = 3
}
```

Suppose you have a method that accepts the Language enumeration, such as the following method:

```
public void HandleEnum(Language language)
{
    // Use language here...
}
```

You need a method to define the enumeration values you can accept in HandleEnum. The CheckLanguageEnumValue method shown here does that:

```
public static bool CheckLanguageEnumValue(Language language)
{
    switch (language)
    {
        // All valid types for the enum listed here
        // This means only the ones we specify are valid.
        // Not any enum value for this enum
        case Language.CSharp:
        case Language.Other:
        case Language.VB6:
        case Language.VBNET:
            break;
        default:
            Debug.Assert(false, language +
                " is not a valid enumeration value to pass.");
            return false;
    }
    return true;
}
```

Discussion

Although the Enum class contains the static IsDefined method, it should not be used. IsDefined uses reflection internally, which incurs a performance penalty. Also, versioning of the enumeration is not handled well. Consider the scenario in which you add the value MgdCpp (managed C++) to the Languages enum in the next version of your software. If IsDefined is used to check the argument here, it will allow MgdCpp as a valid value, since it is defined in the enumeration, even though the code for which you are validating the parameter is not designed to handle it. By being specific with the switch statement shown in CheckLanguageEnumValue, you reject the MgdCpp value and the code does not try to run in an invalid context. This, after all, is what you were after in the first place.

The enumeration check should always be used whenever the method is visible to external objects. An external object can invoke methods with public visibility, so any enumerated value passed in to this method should be screened before it is actually used.

Methods with internal, protected, and internal protected visibility have a much smaller scope than public methods, but can still suffer from the same problems as the public methods. Methods with private visibility may not need this extra level of protection. Use your own judgment on whether to use the `CheckLanguageEnumValue` method to evaluate enumeration values passed in to private methods.

The `HandleEnum` method can be called in several different ways. Three of these are shown here:

```
HandleEnum(Language.CSharp)
HandleEnum((Language)1)
HandleEnum((Language)someVar)     // Where someVar is an int type
```

Any of these method calls is valid. Unfortunately, the following method calls are also valid:

```
HandleEnum((Language)100)

int someVar = 100;
HandleEnum((Language)someVar)
```

These method calls will also compile without errors, but odd behavior will result if the code in `HandleEnum` tries to use the value passed in to it (in this case the value 100). In many cases an exception will not even be thrown; `HandleEnum` just receives the value 100 as an argument, as if it were a legitimate value of the `Language` enumeration.

The `CheckLanguageEnumValue` method prevents this from happening by screening the argument for valid `Language` enumeration values. The following code shows the modified body of the `HandleEnum` method:

```
public void HandleEnum(Language language)
{
    if (CheckLanguageEnumValue(language))
    {
        // Use language here...
    }
    else
    {
        // Deal with the invalid language value here...
    }
}
```

See Also

To test for a valid enumeration within an enumeration marked with the `Flags` attribute, see Recipe 1.19.

1.19   Testing for a Valid Enumeration of Flags

Problem

You need to determine if a given value is a valid enumeration value or a valid combination of enumeration values (i.e., bit flags ORed together in an enumeration marked with the `Flags` attribute).

Solution

To make it possible to test whether a value is a valid enumeration value or some combination of valid enumeration values, add an `All` member to the existing enumeration equal to all the members of the enumeration ORed together. Then use the `HandleFlagsEnum` method to do the test.

There is a problem with using `Enum.IsDefined` with an enumeration marked with the `Flags` attribute. Consider if the `Language` enumeration was written as follows:

```
[Flags]
enum Language
{
    CSharp = 1, VBNET = 2, VB6 = 4
}
```

Valid values for `Language` are the set of numbers {1, 2, 3, 4, 5, 6, 7}. However, the values 3, 5, 6, and 7 are not explicitly represented in this enumeration. The value 3 is equal to the `CSharp` and `VBNET` enumeration members ORed together, and the value 7 is equal to all of the enumeration members ORed together. For the values 3, 5, 6, and 7, the `Enum.IsDefined` method will return `false`, indicating that these are not valid values, when in fact they are. You need a way to determine if a correct set of flags has been passed into a method.

To fix this problem you can add a new member to the `Language` enumeration to define all values for which the `Language` enumeration is valid. In this case, the `Language` enumeration would be rewritten as:

```
[Flags]
enum Language
{
    CSharp = 1, VBNET = 2, VB6 = 4,
    All = (CSharp | VBNET | VB6)
}
```

The new `All` enumeration member is equal to all other `Language` members ORed together. Now, when you want to validate a `Language` flag, all you have to do is the following:

```
public bool HandleFlagsEnum(Language language)
{
    if ((language != 0) && ((language & Language.All) == language))
    {
        return (true);
    }
    else
    {
        return (false);
    }
}
```

Discussion

If you want to use the HandleFlagsEnum method with existing code, all that is required is to add an All member to the existing enumeration. The All member should be equal to all the members of the enumeration ORed together.

The HandleFlagsEnum method then uses this All member to determine if an enumeration value is valid. This is accomplished by ANDing the language value with Language.All, then verifying that the result equals the original language parameter.

This method can also be overloaded to handle the underlying type of the enumeration as well (in this case, the underlying type of the Language enumeration is an integer). The following code determines if an integer variable contains a valid Language enumeration value:

```
public static bool HandleFlagsEnum(int language)
{
    if ((language != 0) && ((language & (int)Language.All) == language))
    {
        return (true);
    }
    else
    {
        return (false);
    }
}
```

The overloaded HandleFlagsEnum methods return true if the language parameter is valid and false otherwise.

See Also

To test for a valid enumeration within an enumeration not marked with the Flags attribute, see Recipe 1.18.

1.20 Using Enumerated Members in a Bit Mask

Problem

An enumeration of values is needed to act as bit flags that can be ORed together to create a combination of values (flags) in the enumeration.

Solution

Mark the enumeration with the Flags attribute:

```
[Flags]
enum Language
{
    CSharp = 0x0001, VBNET = 0x0002, VB6 = 0x0004, Cpp = 0x0008
}
```

Combining elements of this enumeration is a simple matter of using the bitwise OR operator (|). For example:

```
Language lang = Language.CSharp | Language.VBNET;
```

Discussion

Adding the Flags attribute to an enumeration marks this enumeration as individual bit flags that can be ORed together. Using an enumeration of flags is no different than using a regular enumeration type. It should be noted that failing to mark an enumeration with the Flags attribute will not generate an exception or a compile-time error, even if the enumeration values are used as bit flags.

The addition of the Flags attribute provides you with two benefits. First, if the Flags attribute is placed on an enumeration, the ToString and ToString("G") methods return a string consisting of the name of the constant(s) separated by commas. Otherwise, these two methods return the numeric representation of the enumeration value. Note that the ToString("F") method returns a string consisting of the name of the constant(s) separated by commas, regardless of whether this enumeration is marked with the Flags attribute. For an indication of why this works in this manner, see the "F" formatting type in Table 1-2 in Recipe 1.16.

The second benefit is that when you examine the code and encounter an enumeration, you can better determine the developer's intention for this enumeration. If the developer explicitly defined this as containing bit flags (with the Flags attribute), you can use it as such.

An enumeration tagged with the Flags attribute can be viewed as a single value or as one or more values combined into a single enumeration value. If you need to accept multiple languages at a single time, you can write the following code:

```
Language lang = Language.CSharp | Language.VBNET;
```

The variable lang is now equal to the bit values of the two enumeration values ORed together. These values ORed together will equal 3, as shown here:

```
Language.CSharp    0001
Language.VBNET     0010
ORed bit values    0011
```

The enumeration values were converted to binary and ORed together to get the binary value 0011 or 3 in base10. The compiler views this value both as two individual enumeration values (Language.CSharp and Language.VBNET) ORed together or as a single value (3).

To determine if a single flag has been turned on in an enumeration variable, use the bitwise AND (&) operator, as follows:

```
Language lang = Language.CSharp | Language.VBNET;

if((lang & Language.CSharp) == Language.CSharp)
```

```
        Console.WriteLine("The enum contains the C# enumeration value");
    else
        Console.WriteLine("The enum does NOT contain the C# value");
```

This code will display the text "The enum contains the C# enumeration value." The ANDing of these two values either will produce zero if the variable lang does not contain the value Language.CSharp, or it will produce the value Language.CSharp if lang contains this enumeration value. Basically, ANDing these two values looks like this in binary:

```
Language.CSharp | Language.VBNET      0011
Language.CSharp                       0001
ANDed bit values                      0001
```

This is dealt with in more detail in Recipe 1.21.

In some cases the enumeration can grow quite large. You can add many other languages to this enumeration, as shown here:

```
[Flags]
enum Language
{
    CSharp = 0x0001, VBNET = 0x0002, VB6 = 0x0004, Cpp = 0x0008,
    FortranNET = 0x0010, JSharp = 0x0020, MSIL = 0x0080
}
```

When a Language enumeration value is needed to represent all languages, you would have to OR together each value of this enumeration:

```
Language lang = Language.CSharp | Language.VBNET | Language.VB6 ;
```

Instead of doing this, you can simply add a new value to this enumeration that includes all languages as follows:

```
[Flags]
enum Language
{
    CSharp = 0x0001, VBNET = 0x0002, VB6 = 0x0004, Cpp = 0x0008,
    FortranNET = 0x0010, JSharp = 0x0020, MSIL = 0x0080,
    All = (CSharp | VBNET | VB6 | Cpp | FortranNET | JSharp | MSIL)
}
```

Now there is a single enumeration value, All, that encompasses every value of this enumeration. Notice that there are two methods of creating the All enumeration value. The second method is much easier to read. Regardless of which method you use, if individual language elements of the enumeration are added or deleted, you will have to modify the All value accordingly.

Similarly, you can also add values to capture specific subsets of enumeration values as follows:

```
[Flags]
enum Language
{
    CSharp = 0x0001, VBNET = 0x0002, VB6 = 0x0004, Cpp = 0x0008,
    CobolNET = 0x000F, FortranNET = 0x0010, JSharp = 0x0020,
```

```
    MSIL = 0x0080,
    All = (CSharp | VBNET | VB6 | Cpp | FortranNET | Jsharp | MSIL),
    VBOnly = (VBNET | VB6),
    NonVB = (CSharp | Cpp | FortranNET | Jsharp | MSIL)
}
```

Now you have two extra members in the enumerations, one that encompasses VB-only languages (Languages.VBNET and Languages.VB6) and one that encompasses non-VB languages.

1.21 Determining if One or More Enumeration Flags Are Set

Problem

You need to determine if a variable of an enumeration type, consisting of bit flags, contains one or more specific flags. For example, given the following enumeration Language:

```
[Flags]
enum Language
{
    CSharp = 0x0001, VBNET = 0x0002, VB6 = 0x0004, Cpp = 0x0008
}
```

determine, using Boolean logic, if the variable lang in the following line of code contains a language such as Language.CSharp and/or Language.Cpp:

```
Language lang = Language.CSharp | Language.VBNET;
```

Solution

To determine if a variable contains a single bit flag that is set, use the following conditional:

```
if((lang & Language.CSharp) == Language.CSharp)
{
    // Lang contains at least Language.CSharp.
}
```

To determine if a variable exclusively contains a single bit flag that is set, use the following conditional:

```
if(lang == Language.CSharp)
{
    // lang contains only the Language.CSharp.
}
```

To determine if a variable contains a set of bit flags that are all set, use the following conditional:

```
if((lang & (Language.CSharp | Language.VBNET)) ==
    (Language.CSharp | Language.VBNET))
```

```
{
    // lang contains at least Language.CSharp and Language.VBNET.
}
```

To determine if a variable exclusively contains a set of bit flags that are all set, use the following conditional:

```
if((lang | (Language.CSharp | Language.VBNET)) ==
    (Language.CSharp | Language.VBNET))
{
    // lang contains only the Language.CSharp and Language.VBNET.
}
```

Discussion

When enumerations are used as bit flags and are marked with the Flags attribute, they usually will require some kind of conditional testing to be performed. This testing necessitates the use of the bitwise AND (&) and OR (|) operators.

Testing for a variable having a specific bit flag set is done with the following conditional statement:

```
if((lang & Language.CSharp) == Language.CSharp)
```

where lang is of the Language enumeration type.

The & operator is used with a bit mask to determine if a bit is set to 1. The result of ANDing two bits is 1 only when both bits are 1; otherwise, the result is 0. You can use this operation to determine if a specific bit flag is set to a 1 in the number containing the individual bit flags. If you AND the variable lang with the specific bit flag you are testing for (in this case Language.CSharp), you can extract that single specific bit flag. The expression (lang & Language.CSharp) is solved in the following manner if lang is equal to Language.CSharp:

```
Language.CSharp       0001
lang                  0001
ANDed bit values      0001
```

If lang is equal to another value such as Language.VBNET, the expression is solved in the following manner:

```
Language.CSharp       0001
lang                  0010
ANDed bit values      0000
```

Notice that ANDing the bits together returns the value Language.CSharp in the first expression and 0x0000 in the second expression. Comparing this result to the value you are looking for (Language.CSharp) tells you whether that specific bit was turned on.

This method is great for checking specific bits, but what if you want to know whether only one specific bit is turned on (and all other bits turned off) or off (and all other bits turned on)? To test if only the Language.CSharp bit is turned on in the variable lang, you can use the following conditional statement:

```
if(lang == Language.CSharp)
```

Consider if the variable lang contained only the value Language.CSharp. The expression using the OR operator would look like this:

```
lang = Language.CSharp;
if ((lang != 0) &&(Language.CSharp == (lang | Language.CSharp)))
{
    // CSharp is found using OR logic.
}
```

```
Language.CSharp      0001
lang                 0001
ORed bit values      0001
```

Now, add a language value or two to the variable lang and perform the same operation on lang:

```
lang = Language.CSharp | Language.VB6 | Language.Cpp;
if ((lang != 0) &&(Language.CSharp == (lang | Language.CSharp)))
{
    // CSharp is found using OR logic.
}
```

```
Language.CSharp      0001
lang                 1101
ORed bit values      1101
```

The first expression results in the same value as you are testing against. The second expression results in a much larger value than Language.CSharp. This indicates that the variable lang in the first expression contains only the value Language.CSharp, whereas the second expression contains other languages besides Language.CSharp (and may not contain Language.CSharp at all).

Using the OR version of this formula, you can test multiple bits to determine if they are both on and all other bits are off. This is done in the following conditional statement:

```
if((lang != 0) && ((lang | (Language.CSharp | Language.VBNET)) ==
    (Language.CSharp | Language.VBNET)))
```

Notice that to test for more than one language you simply OR the language values together. By switching the first | operator to an & operator, you can determine if at least these bits are turned on. This is done in the following conditional statement:

```
if((lang != 0) && ((lang & (Language.CSharp | Language.VBNET)) ==
    (Language.CSharp | Language.VBNET)))
```

When testing for multiple enumeration values, it may be beneficial to add a value to your enumeration, which ORs together all the values you want to test for. If you wanted to test for all languages except Language.CSharp, your conditional statement(s) would grow quite large and unwieldy. To fix this, you add a value to the Language enumeration that ORs together all languages except Language.CSharp. The new enumeration looks like this:

```
[Flags]
enum Language
{
    CSharp = 0x0001, VBNET = 0x0002, VB6 = 0x0004, Cpp = 0x0008,
    AllLanguagesExceptCSharp = VBNET | VB6 | Cpp
}
```

and your conditional statement might look similar to the following:

```
if((lang != 0) && (lang | Language.AllLanguagesExceptCSharp) ==
    Language. AllLanguagesExceptCSharp)
```

This is quite a bit smaller, easier to manage, and easier to read.

> Use the AND operator when testing if one or more bits are set to 1.
> Use the OR operator when testing if one or more bits are set to 0.

1.22 Determining the Integral Part of a Decimal or Double

Problem

You need to find the integer portion of a decimal or double number.

Solution

You can find the integer portion of a decimal or double by truncating it to the whole number closest to zero. To do so, use the overloaded static System.Math.Truncate method, which takes either a decimal or a double as an argument and returns the same type:

```
decimal pi = (decimal)System.Math.PI;
decimal decRet = System.Math.Truncate(pi);  // decRet = 3

double trouble = 5.555;
double dblRet = System.Math.Truncate(trouble);
```

Discussion

The Truncate method is new in the 2.0 version of the Framework and helps to "round" out the mathematical capabilities of the Framework. The Truncate method has the net effect of simply dropping the fractional portion of the number and returning the integral part. Once floating-point numbers get over a certain size, they do not actually have a fractional part, but have only an approximate representation of their integer portion.

See Also

See Recipe 1.9; see the "System.Math.Truncate Method" topic in the MSDN documentation.

CHAPTER 2

Strings and Characters

2.0 Introduction

String usage abounds in just about all types of applications. The System.String type does not derive from System.ValueType and is therefore considered a reference type. The string alias is built into C# and can be used instead of the full name.

The FCL does not stop with just the String class; there is also a System.Text. StringBuilder class for performing string manipulations and the System.Text. RegularExpressions namespace for searching strings. This chapter will cover the String class and the System.Text.StringBuilder class.

The System.Text.StringBuilder class provides an easy, performance-friendly method of manipulating string objects. Even though this class duplicates much of the functionality of a String class, the StringBuilder class is fundamentally different in that the string contained within the StringBuilder object can actually be modified—you cannot modify a string object. However, this duplicated functionality provides a more efficient manipulation of strings than is obtainable by using the String class.

2.1 Determining the Kind of Character a char Contains

Problem

You have a variable of type char and wish to determine the kind of character it contains—a letter, digit, number, punctuation character, control character, separator character, symbol, whitespace, or surrogate character. Similarly, you have a string variable and want to determine the kind of character in one or more positions within this string.

Solution

To determine the value of a char, use the built-in static methods on the System.Char structure shown here:

Char.IsControl   Char.IsDigit
Char.IsLetter   Char.IsNumber
Char.IsPunctuation   Char.IsSeparator
Char.IsSurrogate   Char.IsSymbol
Char.IsWhitespace

Discussion

The following examples demonstrate how to use the methods shown in the Solution section in a function to return the kind of a character. First, create an enumeration to define the various types of characters:

```
public enum CharKind
{
    Letter,
    Number,
    Punctuation,
    Unknown
}
```

Next, create a method that contains the logic to determine the type of a character and to return a CharKind enumeration value indicating that type:

```
public static CharKind GetCharKind(char theChar)
{
    if (Char.IsLetter(theChar))
    {
        return CharKind.Letter;
    }
    else if (Char.IsNumber(theChar))
    {
        return CharKind.Number;
    }
    else if (Char.IsPunctuation(theChar))
    {
        return CharKind.Punctuation;
    }
    else
    {
        return CharKind.Unknown;
    }
}
```

If, however, a character in a string needs to be evaluated, use the overloaded static methods on the char structure. The following code modifies the GetCharKind method to accept a string variable and a character position in that string. The character position determines which character in the string is evaluated.

```
public static CharKind GetCharKindInString(string theString, int charPosition)
{
    if (Char.IsLetter(theString, charPosition))
    {
        return CharKind.Letter;
    }
    else if (Char.IsNumber(theString, charPosition))
    {
        return CharKind.Number;
    }
    else if (Char.IsPunctuation(theString, charPosition))
    {
        return CharKind.Punctuation;
    }
    else
    {
        return CharKind.Unknown;
    }
}
```

The GetCharKind method accepts a character as a parameter and performs a series of tests on that character using the Char type's built-in static methods. An enumeration of all the different types of characters is defined and is returned by the GetCharKind method.

Table 2-1 describes each of the static Char methods.

Table 2-1. Char methods

Char method	Description
IsControl	A control code in the ranges \U007F, \U0000–\U001F, and \U0080–\U009F.
IsDigit	Any decimal digit in the range 0–9.
IsLetter	Any alphabetic letter.
IsNumber	Any decimal digit or hexadecimal digit.
IsPunctuation	Any punctuation character.
IsSeparator	A space separating words, a line separator, or a paragraph separator.
IsSurrogate	Any surrogate character in the range \UD800–\UDFFF.
IsSymbol	Any mathematical, currency, or other symbol character. Includes characters that modify surrounding characters.
IsWhitespace	Any space character and the following characters:
	\U0009
	\U000A
	\U000B
	\U000C
	\U000D
	\U0085
	\U2028
	\U2029

The following code example determines whether the fifth character (the charPosition parameter is zero-based) in the string is a digit:

```
if (GetCharKind("abcdefg", 4) == CharKind.Digit) {...}
```

In Version 2.0 of the .NET Framework, a few extra Is* functions were added to augment the existing methods. If the character in question is a letter (i.e., the IsLetter method returns true), you can determine if the letter is uppercase or lowercase by using the methods in Table 2-2.

Table 2-2. Upper- and lowercase Char methods

Char method	Description
IsLower	A character that is lowercase
IsUpper	A character that is uppercase

If the character in question is a surrogate (i.e., the IsSurrogate method returns true), you can use the methods in Table 2-3 to get more information on the surrogate character.

Table 2-3. Surrogate Char methods

Char method	Description
IsHighSurrogate	A character that is in the range \UD800 to \UDBFF
IsLowSurrogate	A character that is in the range \UDC00 to \UDFFF

In addition to these surrogate methods, an additional method, IsSurrogatePair, returns true only if two characters create a surrogate pair—that is, one character is a high surrogate and one character is a low surrogate.

The final addition to this group of methods is the IsLetterOrDigit method, which returns true only if the character in question is either a letter or a digit. To determine if the character is either a letter or a digit, use the IsLetter and IsDigit methods.

See Also

See the "Char Structure" topic in the MSDN documentation.

2.2 Determining Whether a Character Is Within a Specified Range

Problem

You need to determine whether a character in a char data type is within a range, such as between the numbers 1 and 5 or between the letters *A* and *M*.

Solution

Use the built-in comparison support for the char data type. The following code shows how to use the built-in comparison support:

```
public static bool IsInRange(char testChar, char startOfRange, char endOfRange)
{
    if (testChar >= startOfRange && testChar <= endOfRange)
    {
        // testChar is within the range.
        return (true);
    }
    else
    {
        // testChar is NOT within the range.
        return (false);
    }
}
```

There is only one problem with that code. If the startOfRange and endOfRange characters have different cases, the result may not be what you expect. The following code, which makes a case-insensitive comparison, can be used to solve this problem:

```
public static bool IsInRangeCaseInsensitive(char testChar,
                char startOfRange, char endOfRange)
{
    testChar = char.ToUpper(testChar);
    startOfRange = char.ToUpper(startOfRange);
    endOfRange = char.ToUpper(endOfRange);

    if (testChar >= startOfRange && testChar <= endOfRange)
    {
        // testChar is within the range.
        return (true);
    }
    else
    {
        // testChar is NOT within the range.
        return (false);
    }
}
```

Discussion

The IsInRange method accepts three parameters. The first is the testChar character that you check on, to test if it falls between the last two parameters on this method. The last two parameters are the starting and ending characters, respectively, of a range of characters. The testChar parameter must be between startOfRange and endOfRange or equal to one of these parameters for this method to return true; otherwise, false is returned.

The `IsInRange` method can be called in the following manner:

```
bool inRange = IsInRange('c', 'a', 'g');
bool inRange = IsInRange('c', 'a', 'b');
bool inRange = IsInRange((char)32, 'a', 'g');
```

The first call to this method returns true, since c is between a and g. The second method returns false, since c is not between a and b. The third method indicates how an integer value representative of a character would be passed to this method.

Note that this method tests whether the `testChar` value is inclusive between the range of characters `startOfRange` and `endOfRange`. If you wish to determine only whether `testChar` is between this range exclusive of the `startOfRange` and `endOfRange` character values, you should modify the `if` statement, as follows:

```
if (testChar > startOfRange && testChar < endOfRange)
```

2.3   Controlling Case Sensitivity When Comparing Two Characters

Problem

You need to compare two characters for equality, but you need the flexibility of performing a case-sensitive or case-insensitive comparison.

Solution

Use the `Equals` instance method on the char structure to compare the two characters:

```
public static bool IsCharEqual(char firstChar, char secondChar)
{
    return (IsCharEqual(firstChar, secondChar, false));
}

public static bool IsCharEqual(char firstChar, char secondChar,
                               bool caseSensitiveCompare)
{
    if (caseSensitiveCompare)
    {
        return (firstChar.Equals(secondChar));
    }
    else
    {
        return (char.ToUpper(firstChar).Equals(char.ToUpper(secondChar)));
    }
}
```

The first overloaded `IsCharEqual` method takes only two parameters: the characters to be compared. This method then calls the second `IsCharEqual` method with three parameters. The third parameter on this method call defaults to false so that when this method is called, you do not have to pass in a value for the `caseSensitiveCompare` parameter—it will automatically default to `false`.

Discussion

Using the `ToUpper` method in conjunction with the `Equals` method on the `String` class allows you to choose whether to take into account the case of the strings when comparing them. To perform a case-sensitive comparison of two `char` variables, simply use the `Equals` method, which, by default, performs a case-sensitive comparison. Performing a case-insensitive comparison requires that both characters be converted to their uppercase values (they could just as easily be converted to their lowercase equivalents, but for this recipe you convert them to uppercase) before the `Equals` method is invoked. Setting both characters to their uppercase equivalents removes any case sensitivity between the character values, and they can be compared using the case-sensitive `Equals` comparison method as though it were a case-insensitive comparison.

You can further extend the overloaded `IsCharEqual` methods to handle the culture of the characters passed in to it:

```
public static bool IsCharEqual(char firstChar, CultureInfo firstCharCulture,
                               char secondChar, CultureInfo secondCharCulture)
{
    return (IsCharEqual(firstChar, firstCharCulture,
            secondChar, secondCharCulture, false));
}

public static bool IsCharEqual(char firstChar, CultureInfo firstCharCulture,
                               char secondChar, CultureInfo secondCharCulture,
                               bool caseSensitiveCompare)
{
    if (caseSensitiveCompare)
    {
        return (firstChar.Equals(secondChar));
    }
    else
    {
        return (char.ToUpper(firstChar, firstCharCulture).Equals
                (char.ToUpper(secondChar, secondCharCulture)));
    }
}
```

The addition of the `CultureInfo` parameters to these methods allows you to pass in the culture information for the strings that you are calling `ToUpper` on. This information allows the `ToUpper` method to correctly uppercase the character based in the culture-specific details of the character (i.e., the language, region, etc., of the character).

Note that you must include the following using directives to compile this code:

```
using System;
using System.Globalization;
```

2.4   Finding All Occurrences of a Character Within a String

Problem

You need a way of searching a string for multiple occurrences of a specific character.

Solution

Use IndexOf in a loop to determine how many occurrences of a character exist, as well as to identify their location within the string:

```
using System;
using System.Collections;
using System.Collections.Generic;


public static int[] FindAllOccurrences(char matchChar, string source)
{
    return (FindAllOccurrences(matchChar, source, -1, false));
}

public static int[] FindAllOccurrences(char matchChar, string source,
                                       int maxMatches)
{
    return (FindAllOccurrences(matchChar, source, maxMatches, false));
}

public static int[] FindAllOccurrences(char matchChar, string source,
                                       bool caseSensitivity)
{
    return (FindAllOccurrences(matchChar, source, -1, caseSensitivity));
}

public static int[] FindAllOccurrences(char matchChar, string source,
                                       int maxMatches, bool caseSensitivity)
{
    List<int> occurrences = new List<int>();
    int foundPos = -1;    // -1 represents not found.
    int numberFound = 0;
    int startPos = 0;
    char tempMatchChar = matchChar;
    string tempSource = source;

    if (!caseSensitivity)
    {
        tempMatchChar = char.ToUpper(matchChar);
        tempSource = source.ToUpper();
    }

    do
    {
```

```
        foundPos = tempSource.IndexOf(matchChar, startPos);
        if (foundPos > -1)
        {
            startPos = foundPos + 1;
            numberFound++;

            if (maxMatches > -1 && numberFound > maxMatches)
            {
                break;
            }
            else
            {
                occurrences.Add(foundPos);
            }
        }
    } while (foundPos > -1);

    return (occurrences.ToArray());
}
```

Discussion

The FindAllOccurrences method is overloaded to allow the last two parameters (maxMatches and caseSensitivity) to be set to a default value if the developer chooses not to pass in one or both of these parameters. The maxMatches parameter defaults to -1, indicating that all matches are to be found. The caseSensitivity parameter defaults to false to allow for a case-insensitive search.

The FindAllOccurrences method starts out by determining whether case sensitivity is turned on. If false were passed in to the caseSensitivity parameter, both matchChar and source are set to all uppercase. This prevents a case-sensitive search.

The main loop in this method is a simple do loop that terminates when foundPos returns -1, meaning that no more matchChar characters can be found in the source string. You use a do loop so that the IndexOf operation is executed at least one time before the check in the while clause is performed. This check determines whether there are any more character matches to be found in the source string.

Once a match is found by the IndexOf method, the numberFound variable is incremented by one to indicate that another match was found, and startPos is moved past the previously found match to indicate where the next IndexOf operation should start. The startPos is increased to the starting position of the last match found plus one. The +1 is needed so that you do not keep matching the same character that was previously matched. Otherwise, an infinite loop will occur in the code if at least one match is found in the source string.

Finally, a check is made to determine whether you are done searching for matchChar characters. If the maxMatches parameter is set to -1, the code keeps searching until it arrives at the end of the source string. Any other number indicates the maximum number of matchChar characters to search for. The maxMatches parameter limits the number of matches that can be made in the source string. If this check indicates that you are able to keep this match, it is stored in the occurrences List<int>.

2.5   Finding the Location of All Occurrences of a String Within Another String

Problem

You need to search a string for every occurrence of a specific string. In addition, the case sensitivity, or insensitivity, of the search needs to be controlled.

Solution

Using IndexOf or IndexOfAny in a loop, you can determine how many occurrences of a character or string exist as well as their locations within the string. To find each occurrence of a string in another string using a case-sensitive search, use the following code:

```
using System;
using System.Collections;
using System.Collections.Generic;


public static int[] FindAll(string matchStr, string searchedStr, int startPos)
{
    int foundPos = -1;    // -1 represents not found.
    int count = 0;
    List<int> foundItems = new List<int>();

    do
    {
        foundPos = searchedStr.IndexOf(matchStr, startPos);
        if (foundPos > -1)
        {
            startPos = foundPos + 1;
            count++;
            foundItems.Add(foundPos);

            Console.WriteLine("Found item at position: " + foundPos.ToString());
        }
    } while (foundPos > -1 && startPos < searchedStr.Length);

    return ((int[])foundItems.ToArray());
}
```

If the FindAll method is called with the following parameters:

```
int[] allOccurrences = FindAll("Red", "BlueTealRedredGreenRedYellow", 0);
```

the string "Red" is found at locations 8 and 19 in the string searchedStr. This code uses the IndexOf method inside a loop to iterate through each found matchStr string in the searchStr string.

To find a character in a string using a case-sensitive search, use the following code:

```
public static int[] FindAll(char MatchChar, string searchedStr, int startPos)
{
    int foundPos = -1;    // -1 represents not found.
    int count = 0;
    List<int> foundItems = new List<int>();

    do
    {
        foundPos = searchedStr.IndexOf(MatchChar, startPos);
        if (foundPos > -1)
        {
            startPos = foundPos + 1;
            count++;
            foundItems.Add(foundPos);

            Console.WriteLine("Found item at position: " + foundPos.ToString());
        }
    } while (foundPos > -1 && startPos < searchedStr.Length);

    return ((int[])foundItems.ToArray());
}
```

If the FindAll method is called with the following parameters:

```
int[] allOccurrences = FindAll('r', "BlueTealRedredGreenRedYellow", 0);
```

the character 'r' is found at locations 11 and 15 in the string searchedStr. This code uses the IndexOf method inside a do loop to iterate through each found matchChar character in the searchStr string. Overloading the FindAll method to accept either a char or string type avoids the performance hit of boxing the char type to a string type.

To find each occurrence of a string in another string using a case-insensitive search, use the following code:

```
public static int[] FindAny(string matchStr, string searchedStr, int startPos)
{
    int foundPos = -1;    // -1 represents not found.
    int count = 0;
    List<int> foundItems = new List<int>();

    // Factor out case-sensitivity
    searchedStr = searchedStr.ToUpper();
    matchStr = matchStr.ToUpper();

    do
    {
        foundPos = searchedStr.IndexOf(matchStr, startPos);
        if (foundPos > -1)
        {
            startPos = foundPos + 1;
            count++;
            foundItems.Add(foundPos);
```

```
            Console.WriteLine("Found item at position: " + foundPos.ToString());
        }
    } while (foundPos > -1 && startPos < searchedStr.Length);

    return ((int[])foundItems.ToArray());
}
```

If the FindAny method is called with the following parameters:

```
int[] allOccurrences = FindAny("Red", "BlueTealRedredGreenRedYellow", 0);
```

the string "Red" is found at locations 8, 11, and 19 in the string searchedStr. This code uses the IndexOf method inside a loop to iterate through each found matchStr string in the searchStr string. The search is rendered case-insensitive by using the ToUpper method on both the searchedStr and the matchStr strings.

To find a set of characters in a string, use the following code:

```
public static int[] FindAny(char[] MatchCharArray, string searchedStr,
                            int startPos)
{
    int foundPos = -1;    // -1 represents not found.
    int count = 0;
    List<int> foundItems = new List<int>();

    do
    {
        foundPos = searchedStr.IndexOfAny(MatchCharArray, startPos);
        if (foundPos > -1)
        {
            startPos = foundPos + 1;
            count++;
            foundItems.Add(foundPos);

            Console.WriteLine("Found item at position: " + foundPos.ToString());
        }
    } while (foundPos > -1 && startPos < searchedStr.Length);

    return ((int[])foundItems.ToArray());
}
```

If the FindAll method is called with the following parameters:

```
int[] allOccurrences = FindAll(new char[]  MatchCharArray = {'R', 'r'},
                           "BlueTealRedredGreenRedYellow", 0);
```

the characters 'r' or 'R' is found at locations 8, 11, 15, and 19 in the string searchedStr. This code uses the IndexOfAny method inside a loop to iterate through each found matchStr string in the searchStr string. The search is rendered case-insensitive by using an array of char containing all characters, both uppercase and lowercase, to be searched for.

Discussion

In the example code, the foundPos variable contains the location of the found character/string within the searchedStr string. The startPos variable contains the next position at which to start the search. The IndexOf or IndexOfAny method is used to perform the actual searching. The count variable simply counts the number of times the character/string was found in the searchedStr string.

The example uses a do loop so that the IndexOf or IndexOfAny operation is executed at least one time before the check in the while clause is performed. This check determines whether there are any more character/string matches to be found in the searchedStr string. This loop terminates when foundPos returns -1 (meaning that no more character/strings can be found in the searchedStr string) or when an out-of-bounds condition exists. When foundPos equals -1, there are no more instances of the match value in the searchedStr string; therefore, you can exit the loop. If, however, the startPos overshoots the last character element of the searchedStr string, an out-of-bounds condition exists and an exception is thrown. To prevent this, always check to make sure that any positioning variables that are modified inside of the loop, such as the startPos variable, are within their intended bounds.

Once a match is found by the IndexOf or IndexOfAny method, the if statement body is executed to increment the count variable by one and to move the startPos up past the previously found match. The count variable is incremented by one to indicate that another match was found. The startPos is increased to the starting position of the last match found plus 1. Adding 1 is necessary so that you do not keep matching the same character/string that was previously matched, which will cause an infinite loop to occur in the code if at least one match is found in the searchedStr string. To see this behavior, remove the +1 from the code.

There is one potential problem with this code. Consider the case where:

```
searchedStr = "aaaa";
matchStr = "aa";
```

The code contained in this recipe will match "aa" three times.

```
(aa)aa
a(aa)a
aa(aa)
```

This situation may be fine for some applications, but not if you need it to return only the following matches:

```
(aa)aa
aa(aa)
```

To do this, change the following line in the while loop:

```
startPos = foundPos + 1;
```

to this:

```
startPos = foundPos + matchStr.Length;
```

This code moves the startPos pointer beyond the first matched string, disallowing any internal matches.

To convert this code to use a while loop rather than a do loop, the foundPos variable must be initialized to 0, and the while loop expression should be as follows:

```
while (foundPos >= 0 && startPos < searchStr.Length)
{
    foundPos = searchedStr.IndexOf(matchChar, startPos);
    if (foundPos > -1)
    {
        startPos = foundPos + 1;
        count++;
    }
}
```

See Also

See the "String.IndexOf Method" and "String.IndexOfAny Method" topics in the MSDN documentation.

2.6   Implementing a Poor Man's Tokenizer to Deconstruct a String

Problem

You need a quick method of breaking up a string into a series of discrete tokens or words.

Solution

Use the Split instance method of the String class. For example:

```
string equation = "1 + 2 - 4 * 5";
string[] equationTokens = equation.Split(new char[1]{' '});

foreach (string Tok in equationTokens)
    Console.WriteLine(Tok);
```

This code produces the following output:

```
1
+
2
-
4
*
5
```

The Split method may also be used to separate people's first, middle, and last names. For example:

```
string fullName1 = "John Doe";
string fullName2 = "Doe, John";
string fullName3 = "John Q. Doe";

string[] nameTokens1 = fullName1.Split(new char[3]{' ', ',', '.'});
string[] nameTokens2 = fullName2.Split(new char[3]{' ', ',', '.'});
string[] nameTokens3 = fullName3.Split(new char[3]{' ', ',', '.'});

foreach (string tok in nameTokens1)
{
    Console.WriteLine(tok);
}
Console.WriteLine("");

foreach (string tok in nameTokens2)
{
    Console.WriteLine(tok);
}
Console.WriteLine("");

foreach (string tok in nameTokens3)
{
    Console.WriteLine(tok);
}
```

This code produces the following output:

```
John
Doe

Doe
John

John
Q

Doe
```

Notice that a blank is inserted between the period and the space delimiters of the fullName3 name; this is correct behavior. If you do not want to process this space in your code, you can choose to ignore it.

Discussion

If you have a consistent string with parts, or tokens, that are separated by well-defined characters, the Split function can tokenize the string. Tokenizing a string consists of breaking the string down into well-defined, discrete parts, each of which is considered a token. In the two previous examples, the tokens were either parts of a mathematical equation (numbers and operators) or parts of a name (first, middle, and last).

There are several drawbacks to this approach. First, if the string of tokens is not separated by any well-defined character(s), it will be impossible to use the Split method to break up the string. For example, if the equation string looked like this:

```
string equation = "1+2-4*5";
```

you would clearly have to use a more robust method of tokenizing this string (see Recipe 10.7 for a more robust tokenizer).

A second drawback is that a string of tokenized words must be entered consistently in order to gain meaning from the tokens. For example, if you ask users to type in their names, they may enter any of the following:

```
John Doe
Doe John
John Q Doe
```

If one user enters his name the first way and another user enters it the second way, your code will have a difficult time determining whether the first token in the string array represents the first or last name. The same problem will exist for all of the other tokens in the array. However, if all users enter their names in a consistent style, such as *First Name*, space, *Last Name*, you will have a much easier time tokenizing the name and understanding what each token represents.

See Also

See Recipe 10.7; see the "String.Split Method" topic in the MSDN documentation.

2.7 Controlling Case Sensitivity When Comparing Two Strings

Problem

You need to compare the contents of two strings for equality. In addition, the case sensitivity of the comparison needs to be controlled.

Solution

Use the Compare static method on the String class to compare the two strings. Whether the comparison is case-insensitive is determined by the third parameter of one of its overloads. For example:

```
string lowerCase = "abc";
string upperCase = "AbC";
int caseInsensitiveResult = string.Compare(lowerCase, upperCase,
    StringComparison.CurrentCultureIgnoreCase);
int caseSensitiveResult = string.Compare(lowerCase,
    StringComparison.CurrentCulture);
```

The caseSensitiveResult value is -1 (indicating that lowerCase is "less than" upperCase) and the caseInsensitiveResult is zero (indicating that lowerCase "equals" upperCase).

Discussion

Using the static string.Compare method allows you the freedom to choose whether to take into account the case of the strings when comparing them. This method returns an integer indicating the lexical relationship between the two strings. A zero means that the two strings are equal, a negative number means that the first string is less than the second string, and a positive number indicates that the first string is greater than the second string.

By setting the last parameter of this method (the comparisonType parameter) to either StringComparison.CurrentCultureIgnoreCase or StringComparison.CurrentCulture, you can determine whether the Compare method takes into account the case of both strings when comparing. Setting this parameter to StringComparison.CurrentCulture forces a case-sensitive comparison; setting it to StringComparison.CurrentCulture-IgnoreCase forces a case-insensitive comparison. In the case of the overloaded version of the method with no comparisonType parameter, comparisons are always case-sensitive.

See Also

See the "String.Compare Method" topic in the MSDN documentation.

2.8   Comparing a String to the Beginning or End of a Second String

Problem

You need to determine whether a string is at the head or tail of a second string. In addition, the case sensitivity of the search needs to be controlled.

Solution

Use the EndsWith or StartsWith instance method on a string object. Comparisons with EndsWith and StartsWith are always case-sensitive. The following code compares the value in the string variable head to the beginning of the string Test:

```
string head = "str";
string test = "strVarName";
bool isFound = test.StartsWith(head);
```

The example shown next compares the value in the string variable tail to the end of the string test.

```
string tail = "Name";
string test = "strVarName";
bool isFound = test.EndsWith(tail);
```

In both examples, the isFound Boolean variable is set to true, since each string is found in test.

To do a case-insensitive comparison, employ the static string.Compare method. The following two examples modify the previous two examples by performing a case-insensitive comparison. The first is equivalent to a case-insensitive StartsWith string search:

```
string head = "str";
string test = "strVarName";
int isFound = string.Compare(head, 0, test, 0, head.Length, true);
```

The second is equivalent to a case-insensitive EndsWith string search:

```
string tail = "Name";
string test = "strVarName";
int isFound = string.Compare(tail, 0, test, (test.Length - tail.Length),
                             tail.Length, true);
```

Discussion

Use the BeginsWith or EndsWith instance methods to do a case-sensitive search for a particular string at the beginning or end of a string. The equivalent case-insensitive comparison requires the use of the static Compare method in the String class. If the return value of the Compare method is zero, a match was found. Any other number means that a match was not found.

See Also

See the "String.StartsWith Method," "String.EndsWith Method," and "String.Compare Method" topics in the MSDN documentation.

2.9   Inserting Text into a String

Problem

You have some text (either a char or a string value) that needs to be inserted at a specific location inside of a second string.

Solution

Using the Insert instance method of the String class, a string or char can easily be inserted into a string. For example, in the code fragment:

```
string sourceString = "The Inserted Text is here ->"<-";

sourceString  = sourceString.Insert(28, "Insert-This");
Console.WriteLine(sourceString);
```

the string sourceString is inserted between the > and < characters in a second string. The result is:

```
The Inserted Text is here ->Insert-This<-
```

Inserting a single character into sourceString between the > and < characters is shown here:

```
string sourceString = "The Inserted Text is here -><-";
char insertChar = '1';

sourceString  = sourceString.Insert(28, Convert.ToString(insertChar));
Console.WriteLine(sourceString);
```

There is no overloaded method for Insert that takes a char value, so converting the char to a string of length one is the next best solution.

Discussion

There are two ways of inserting strings into other strings, unless, of course, you are using the regular expression classes. The first involves using the Insert instance method on the String class. This method is also slower than the others since strings are immutable, and, therefore, a new string object must be created to hold the modified value. In this recipe, the reference to the old string object is then changed to point to the new string object. Note that the Insert method leaves the original string untouched and creates a new string object with the inserted characters.

To add flexibility and speed to your string insertions, use the Insert instance method on the StringBuilder class. This method is overloaded to accept all of the built-in types. In addition, the StringBuilder object optimizes string insertion by not making copies of the original string; instead, the original string is modified.

If you use the StringBuilder class instead of the String class to insert a string, your code appears as:

```
StringBuilder sourceString =
  new StringBuilder("The Inserted Text is here -><-");
sourceString.Insert (28, "Insert-This");
Console.WriteLine(sourceString);
```

The character insertion example changes to the following code:

```
char charToInsert = '1';
StringBuilder sourceString =
  new StringBuilder("The Inserted Text is here -><-");
sourceString.Insert (28, charToInsert);
Console.WriteLine(sourceString);
```

Note that when using the StringBuilder class, you must also use the System.Text namespace.

See Also

See the "String.Insert Method" topic in the MSDN documentation.

2.10 Removing or Replacing Characters Within a String

Problem

You have some text within a string that needs to be either removed or replaced with a different character or string. Since the replacing operation is somewhat simple, using a regular expression to aid in the replacing operation is not worth the overhead.

Solution

To remove a substring from a string, use the `Remove` instance method on the `String` class. For example:

```
string name = "Doe, John";
name = name.Remove(3, 1);
Console.WriteLine(name);
```

This code creates a new string and then sets the `name` variable to refer to it. The string contained in `name` now looks like this:

```
Doe John
```

If performance is critical, and particularly if the string removal operation occurs in a loop so that the operation is performed multiple times, you can instead use the `Remove` method of the `StringBuilder` object. The following code modifies the `str` variable so that its value becomes `12345678`:

```
StringBuilder str = new StringBuilder("1234abc5678", 12);
str.Remove(4, 3);
Console.WriteLine(str);
```

To replace a delimiting character within a string, use the following code:

```
string commaDelimitedString = "100,200,300,400,500";
commaDelimitedString = commaDelimitedString.Replace(',', ':');
Console.WriteLine(commaDelimitedString);
```

This code creates a new string and then makes the `commaDelimitedString` variable refer to it. The string in `commaDelimitedString` now looks like this:

```
100:200:300:400:500
```

To replace a placeholding string within a string, use the following code:

```
string theName = "Mary";
string theObject = "car";
string ID = "This <ObjectPlaceholder> is the property of <NamePlaceholder>.";
ID = ID.Replace("<ObjectPlaceholder>", theObject);
ID = ID.Replace("<NamePlaceholder>", theName);
Console.WriteLine(ID);
```

This code creates a new string and then makes the ID variable refer to it. The string in ID now looks like this:

```
This car is the property of Mary.
```

As when removing a portion of a string, you may, for performance reasons, choose to use the Replace method of the StringBuilder class instead. For example:

```
string newName = "John Doe";

str = new StringBuilder("name = <NAME>");
str.Replace("<NAME>", newName);
Console.WriteLine(str.ToString( ));
str.Replace('=', ':');
Console.WriteLine(str.ToString( ));

str = new StringBuilder("name1 = <FIRSTNAME>, name2 = <FIRSTNAME>");
str.Replace("<FIRSTNAME>", newName, 7, 12);
Console.WriteLine(str.ToString( ));
str.Replace('=', ':', 0, 7);
Console.WriteLine(str.ToString( ));
```

This code produces the following results:

```
name = John Doe
name : John Doe
name1 = John Doe, name2 = <FIRSTNAME>
name1 : John Doe, name2 = <FIRSTNAME>
```

Note that when using the StringBuilder class, you must use the System.Text namespace.

Discussion

The String class provides two methods that allow easy removal and modification of characters in a string: the Remove instance method and the Replace instance method. The Remove method deletes a specified number of characters starting at a given location within a string. This method returns a new string object containing the modified string.

The Replace instance method that the String class provides is very useful for removing characters from a string and replacing them with a new character or string. At any point where the Replace method finds an instance of the string passed in as the first parameter, it will replace it with the string passed in as the second parameter. The Replace method is case-sensitive and returns a new string object containing the modified string. If the string being searched for cannot be found in the original string, the method returns a reference to the original string object.

The Replace and Remove methods on a string object always create a new string object that contains the modified text. If this action hurts performance, consider using the Replace and Remove methods on the StringBuilder class.

The `Remove` method of the `StringBuilder` class is not overloaded and is straightforward to use. Simply give it a starting position and the number of characters to remove. This method returns a reference to the same instance of the `StringBuilder` object with the `Replace` method that modified the string value.

The `Replace` method of the `StringBuilder` class allows for fast character or string replacement to be performed on the original `StringBuilder` object. These methods return a reference to the same instance of the `StringBuilder` object with the `Replace` method that was called. If you are performing a replace operation that uses a format string under your control, then you should use the `AppendFormat` method of the `StringBuilder` class.

Note that this method is case-sensitive.

See Also

See the "String.Replace Method," "String.Remove Method," "StringBuilder.Replace Method," and "StringBuilder.Remove Method" topics in the MSDN documentation.

2.11   Encoding Binary Data as Base64

Problem

You have a `byte[]` representing some binary information, such as a bitmap. You need to encode this data into a string so that it can be sent over a binary-unfriendly transport such as email.

Solution

Using the static method `Convert.ToBase64String` on the `Convert` class, a `byte[]` may be encoded to its `String` equivalent:

```
using System;

public static string Base64EncodeBytes(byte[] inputBytes)
{
    return (Convert.ToBase64String(inputBytes));
}
```

Discussion

The `Convert` class makes encoding between a `byte[]` and a `String` a simple matter. The parameters for this method are quite flexible. It provides the ability to start and stop the conversion at any point in the input byte array.

To encode a bitmap file into a string that can be sent to some destination via email, you can use the following code:

```
byte[] image = null;
using (FileStream fstrm = new FileStream(@"C:\WINNT\winnt.bmp",
                                FileMode.Open, FileAccess.Read))
```

```
    {
        using (BinaryReader reader = new BinaryReader(fstrm))
        {
            byte[] image = new byte[reader.BaseStream.Length];
            for (int i = 0; i < reader.BaseStream.Length; i++)
            {
                image[i] = reader.ReadByte( );
            }
        }
    }
    string bmpAsString = Base64EncodeBytes(image);
```

The bmpAsString string can then be sent as the body of an email message.

To decode an encoded string to a byte[], see Recipe 2.12.

See Also

See Recipe 2.12; see the "Convert.ToBase64CharArray Method" topic in the MSDN documentation.

2.12   Decoding a Base64-Encoded Binary

Problem

You have a String that contains information such as a bitmap encoded as base64. You need to decode this data (which may have been embedded in an email message) from a String into a byte[] so that you can access the original binary.

Solution

Using the static method Convert.FromBase64String on the Convert class, an encoded String may be decoded to its equivalent byte[]:

```
using System;

public static byte[] Base64DecodeString(string inputStr)
{
    byte[] decodedByteArray =
      Convert.FromBase64String(inputStr);

    return (decodedByteArray);
}
```

Discussion

The static FromBase64String method on the Convert class makes decoding an encoded base64 string a simple matter. This method returns a byte[] that contains the decoded elements of the String.

If you receive a file via email, such as an image file (*.bmp*), that has been converted to a string, you can convert it back into its original bitmap file, using something like the following:

```
byte[] imageBytes = Base64DecodeString(bmpAsString);
using (FileStream fstrm = new FileStream(@"C:\winnt_copy.bmp",
                 FileMode.CreateNew, FileAccess.Write))
{
    using (BinaryWriter writer = new BinaryWriter(fstrm))
    {
        writer.Write(imageBytes);
    }
}
```

In this code, the `bmpAsString` variable was obtained from the code in the Discussion section of Recipe 2.11. The `imageBytes` byte[] is the `bmpAsString` String converted back to a byte[], which can then be written back to disk.

To encode a byte[] to a String, see Recipe 2.13.

See Also

See Recipe 2.11; see the "Convert.FromBase64CharArray Method" topic in the MSDN documentation.

2.13   Converting a String Returned as a Byte[] Back into a String

Problem

Many methods in the FCL return a byte[] because they are providing a byte stream service, but some applications need to pass strings over these byte stream services. Some of these methods include:

```
System.Diagnostics.EventLogEntry.Data
System.IO.BinaryReader.Read
System.IO.BinaryReader.ReadBytes
System.IO.FileStream.Read
System.IO.FileStream.BeginRead
System.IO.MemoryStream // Constructor
System.IO.MemoryStream.Read
System.IO.MemoryStream.BeginRead
System.Net.Sockets.Socket.Receive
System.Net.Sockets.Socket.ReceiveFrom
System.Net.Sockets.Socket.BeginReceive
System.Net.Sockets.Socket.BeginReceiveFrom
System.Net.Sockets.NetworkStream.Read
System.Net.Sockets.NetworkStream.BeginRead
System.Security.Cryptography.CryptoStream.Read
System.Security.Cryptography.CryptoStream.BeginRead
```

In many cases, this byte[] might contain ASCII- or Unicode-encoded characters. You need a way to recombine this byte[] to obtain the original string.

Solution

To convert a byte array of ASCII values to a complete string, use the following method:

```
string constructedString = Encoding.ASCII.GetString(characters);
```

To convert a byte array of Unicode values to a complete string, use the following method:

```
string constructedString = Encoding.Unicode.GetString(characters);
```

Discussion

The GetString method of the Encoding class (returned by the ASCII property) converts 7-bit ASCII characters contained in a byte array to a string. Any value larger than 127 (0x7F) will be ANDed with the value 127 (0x7F) and the resulting character value will be displayed in the string. For example, if the byte[] contains the value 200 (0xC8), this value will be converted to 72 (0x48), and the character equivalent of 72 (0x48) ('H') will be displayed. The Encoding class can be found in the System.Text namespace. The GetString method is overloaded to accept additional arguments as well. The overloaded versions of the method convert all or part of a string to ASCII and then store the result in a specified range inside a byte[].

The GetString method returns a string containing the converted byte[] of ASCII characters.

The GetString method of the Encoding class (returned by the Unicode property) converts Unicode characters into 16-bit Unicode values. The Encoding class can be found in the System.Text namespace. The GetString method returns a string containing the converted byte[] of Unicode characters.

See Also

See the "ASCIIEncoding Class" and "UnicodeEncoding Class" topics in the MSDN documentation.

2.14 Passing a String to a Method That Accepts only a Byte[ ]

Problem

Many methods in the FCL accept a byte[] consisting of characters instead of a string. Some of these methods include:

```
System.Diagnostics.EventLog.WriteEntry
System.IO.BinaryWriter.Write
System.IO.FileStream.Write
System.IO.FileStream.BeginWrite
System.IO.MemoryStream.Write
System.IO.MemoryStream.BeginWrite
System.Net.Sockets.Socket.Send
System.Net.Sockets.Socket.SendTo
System.Net.Sockets.Socket.BeginSend
System.Net.Sockets.Socket.BeginSendTo
System.Net.Sockets.NetworkStream.Write
System.Net.Sockets.NetworkStream.BeginWrite
System.Security.Cryptography.CryptoStream.Write
System.Security.Cryptography.CryptoStream.BeginWrite
```

In many cases, you might have a string that you need to pass into one of these methods or some other method that accepts only a byte[]. You need a way to break up this string into a byte[].

Solution

To convert a string to a byte[] of ASCII values, use the GetBytes method on the Encoding class:

```
byte[] retArray = Encoding.ASCII.GetBytes(characters);
```

To convert a string to a byte[] of Unicode values, use the GetBytes method on the Encoding class:

```
byte[] retArray = Encoding.Unicode.GetBytes(characters);
```

Discussion

The GetBytes method of the Encoding class (returned by the ASCII property) converts ASCII characters—contained in either a char[] or a string—into a byte[] of 7-bit ASCII values. Any value larger than 127 (0x7F) is converted to the ? character. The Encoding class can be found in the System.Text namespace. The GetBytes method is overloaded to accept additional arguments as well. The overloaded versions of the method convert all or part of a string to ASCII and then store the result in a specified range inside a byte[], which is returned to the caller.

The GetBytes method of the Encoding class (returned by the Unicode property) converts Unicode characters into 16-bit Unicode values. The Encoding class can be found in the System.Text namespace. The GetBytes method returns a byte[], each element of which contains the Unicode value of a single character of the string.

A single Unicode character in the source string or in the source char[] corresponds to two elements of the byte[]. For example, the following byte[] contains the ASCII value of the letter *S*:

```
byte[] sourceArray = {83};
```

However, for a byte[] to contain a Unicode representation of the letter *S*, it must contain two elements. For example:

```
byte[] sourceArray = {83, 0};
```

The Intel architecture uses a little-endian encoding, which means that the first element is the least-significant byte and the second element is the most-significant byte. Other architectures may use big-endian encoding, which is the opposite of little-endian encoding. The UnicodeEncoding class supports both big-endian and little-endian encodings. Using the UnicodeEncoding instance constructor, you can construct an instance that uses either big-endian or little-endian ordering. This is accomplished by using one of the two following constructors:

```
public UnicodeEncoding (bool bigEndian, bool byteOrderMark);
public UnicodeEncoding (bool bigEndian, bool byteOrderMark,
                        bool throwOnInvalidBytes);
```

The first parameter, bigEndian, accepts a Boolean argument. Set this argument to true to use big-endian or false to use little-endian.

In addition, you have the option to indicate whether a byte order mark preamble should be generated so that readers of the file will know which endianness is in use.

See Also

See the "ASCIIEncoding Class" and "UnicodeEncoding Class" topics in the MSDN documentation.

2.15 Converting Strings to Other Types

Problem

You have a string that represents the equivalent value of a number ("12"), char ("a"), bool ("true"), or a color enumeration ("Red"). You need to convert this string to its equivalent value type. Therefore, the number "12" would be converted to a numeric value such as int, short, float, and so on. The string "a" would be converted to a char value 'a', the string "true" would be converted to a bool value, and the color "Red" could be converted to an enumeration value (if an enumeration were defined that contained the element Red).

Solution

Use the Parse static method of the type that the string is to be converted to. To convert a string containing a number to its numeric type, use the following code:

```
// This code requires the use of the System and System.Globalization namespaces.

string longString = "7654321";
int actualInt = Int32.Parse(longString);      // longString = 7654321
```

```
string dblString = "-7654.321";
double actualDbl = Double.Parse(dblString, NumberStyles.AllowDecimalPoint |
    NumberStyles.AllowLeadingSign);    // dblString = "-7654.321"
```

To convert a string containing a Boolean value to a bool type, use the following code:

```
// This code requires the use of the System namespace.

string boolString = "true";
bool actualBool = Boolean.Parse(boolString);    // actualBool = true
```

To convert a string containing a char value to a char type, use the following code:

```
// This code requires the use of the System namespace.

string charString = "t";
char actualChar = char.Parse(charString);    // actualChar = 't'
```

To convert a string containing an enumeration value to an enumeration type, use the following code:

```
// This code requires the use of the System namespace.

enum Colors
{
    red, green, blue
}

string colorString = "blue";
// Note that the Parse method below is a method defined by System.Enum,
// not by Colors.
Colors actualEnum = (Colors)Colors.Parse(typeof(Colors), colorString);
    // actualEnum = blue
```

Discussion

The static Parse method available on certain data types allows easy conversion from a string value to the value of that specific value type. The Parse method is supported by the following types:

Boolean	Int64
Byte	SByte
Decimal	Single
Double	UInt16
Int16	UInt32
Int32	UInt64

Notice that these types are all ValueTypes; other types, such as IPAddress, also support the Parse method. In addition to the Parse methods that take a single string parameter and convert it to the target data type, each numeric type has a second overloaded version of the Parse method that includes a second parameter of type System.Globalization.NumberStyles. This allows the Parse method to correctly handle specific properties of numbers, such as leading or trailing signs, decimal points, currency symbols, thousands separators, and so forth. NumberStyles is marked as a flag-style enumeration, so you can bitwise OR more than one enumerated value together to allow a group of styles to be used on the string.

The NumberStyles enumeration is defined as follows:

AllowCurrencySymbol
> If the string contains a number with a currency symbol, it is parsed as currency; otherwise, it is parsed as a number.

AllowDecimalPoint
> Allows a decimal point in the number.

AllowExponent
> Allows the number to be in exponential notation format.

AllowHexSpecifier
> Allows characters that specify a hexadecimal number.

AllowLeadingSign
> Allows a leading sign symbol.

AllowLeadingWhite
> Ignores any leading whitespace.

AllowParentheses
> Allows parentheses.

AllowThousands
> Allows group separators.

AllowTrailingSign
> Allows a trailing sign symbol.

AllowTrailingWhite
> Ignores any trailing whitespace.

Any
> Applies any of the previous styles. This style simply ORs together all of the preceding styles.

Currency
> Same as the All style, except that the AllowExponent style is omitted.

Float
> Equivalent to AllowLeadingWhite, AllowTrailingWhite, AllowLeadingSign, AllowDecimalPoint, and AllowExponent.

HexNumber
> Equivalent to AllowLeadingWhite, AllowTrailingWhite, and AllowHexSpecifier.

Integer
> Equivalent to AllowLeadingWhite, AllowTrailingWhite, and AllowLeadingSign.

None
>   Applies none of the styles.

Number
>   Equivalent to AllowLeadingWhite, AllowTrailingWhite, AllowLeadingSign, Allow-TrailingSign, AllowDecimalPoint, and AllowThousands.

If the NumberStyle parameter is not supplied when it is required (as when, for example, a numeric string includes a thousands separator) or if the NumberStyle enumeration is used on a string that does not contain a number in the supplied NumberStyle format, a FormatException exception will be thrown. If the size of the number in the string is too large or too small for the data type, an OverFlowException exception will be thrown. Passing in a null for the SourceString parameter will throw an ArgumentNullException exception.

The Parse method of the two non-numeric data types, bool and char, also deserve some additional explanation. When calling Boolean.Parse, if a string value contains anything except a value equal to the static properties Boolean.FalseString, Boolean.TrueString, or the string literals "false" or "true" (which are case-insensitive), a FormatException exception is thrown. Passing in a null for the SourceString parameter throws an ArgumentNullException exception.

When invoking char.Parse, if a string value containing more than one character is passed as its single argument, a FormatException exception is thrown. Passing in a null for the string parameter throws an ArgumentNullException exception.

The static Enum.Parse method returns an Object of the same type as specified in the first parameter of this method (EnumType). This value is viewed as an Object type and must be cast to its correct enumeration type.

This method throws an ArgumentException exception if the *Value* parameter cannot be matched to a string in the enumeration. An ArgumentNullException exception is thrown if a null is passed in to the *Value* parameter.

If you do not want an exception to be thrown while attempting to convert a string to a particular type, consider using the TryParse method in types in which it is available. This method will not throw an exception if the conversion fails. Instead, it returns a Boolean true if the conversion succeeds and a false if the conversion fails.

2.16   Formatting Data in Strings

Problem

You need to format one or more embedded pieces of information inside of a string, such as a number, character, or substring.

Solution

The static `string.Format` method allows you to format strings in a variety of ways. For example:

```
int ID = 12345;
double weight = 12.3558;
char row = 'Z';
string section = "1A2C";

string output = string.Format(@"The item ID = {0:G} having weight = {1:G}
            is found in row {2:G} and section {3:G}", ID, weight, row,
            section);
Console.WriteLine(output);
output = string.Format(@"The item ID = {0:N} having weight = {1:E}
            is found in row {2:E} and section {3:E}", ID, weight, row,
            section);
Console.WriteLine(output);
output = string.Format(@"The item ID = {0:N} having weight = {1:N}
            is found in row {2:E} and section {3:D}", ID, weight, row,
            section);
Console.WriteLine(output);
output = string.Format(@"The item ID = {0:(#####)} having weight = {1:0000.00}
                lbs is found in row {2} and section {3}", ID, weight, row,
                section);
Console.WriteLine(output);
```

The output is as follows:

```
The item ID = 12345 having weight = 12.3558 is found in row Z and section 1A2C
The item ID = 12,345.00 having weight = 1.235580E+001 is found
    in row Z and section 1A2C
The item ID = 12,345.00 having weight = 12.36 is found in row Z and section 1A2C
The item ID = (12345) having weight = 0012.36 lbs is found in row Z and section 1A2C
```

To simplify things, the `string.Format` method can be discarded; all the work can be done in the `System.Console.WriteLine` method, which calls `string.Format` internally, as shown here:

```
Console.WriteLine(@"The item ID = {0,5:G} having weight = {1,10:G} " +
        "is found in row {2,-5:G} and section {3,-10:G}",
        ID, weight, row, section);
```

The output of this `WriteLine` method is:

```
The item ID = 12345 having weight =    12.3558 is found in
    row Z     and section 1A2C
```

Discussion

The `string.Format` method allows a wide range of formatting options for string data. The first parameter of this method can be passed a string that may look similar to the following:

```
"The item ID = {0,5:G}"
```

The text The item ID = will be displayed as is, with no changes. The interesting part of this string is the section enclosed in braces. This section has the following form:

```
{index, alignment:formatString}
```

Notice that this format is for numbers; different types can have differing format strings. This section can contain the following three parts:

index

A number identifying the zero-based position of the section's data in the *args* parameter array. The data is to be formatted accordingly and substituted for this section. This number is required.

alignment

The number of spaces to insert before or after this data. A negative number indicates left justification (spaces are added to the right of the data), and a positive number indicates right justification (spaces are added to the left of the data). This number is optional.

formatString

A string indicating the type of formatting to perform on this data. This section is where most of the formatting information usually resides. Tables 2-4 and 2-5 contain valid formatting codes that can be used here. This part is optional.

Table 2-4. The standard formatting strings

Formatting character(s)	Meaning
C or c	Use the currency format. A precision specifier can optionally follow, indicating the number of decimal places to use.
D or d	Use the decimal format for integral types. A precision specifier can optionally follow, which represents the minimum number of digits in the formatted number.
E or e	Use scientific notation. A precision specifier can optionally follow, indicating the number of digits to use after the decimal point.
F or f	Use fixed-point format. A precision specifier can optionally follow, which represents the number of digits to display to the right of the decimal point.
G or g	Use the general format. The number is displayed in its shortest form. A precision specifier, which represents the number of significant digits to display, can optionally follow.
N or n	Use the number format. A minus sign is added to the beginning of a negative number, and thousands separators are placed accordingly in the number. A precision specifier, which represents the number of digits to display to the right of the decimal point, can optionally follow.
P or p	Use the percent format. The number is converted to a percent representation of itself. A precision specifier, indicating the number of decimal places to use, can optionally follow.
R or r	Use the round-trip format. This format allows the number to be formatted to a representation that can be parsed back to its original form by using the Parse method. Any precision specifier is ignored.
X or x	Use the hexadecimal format. The number is converted to its hexadecimal representation. The uppercase *X* produces a hexadecimal number with all capital letters *A* through *F*. The lowercase *x* produces a hexadecimal number with all lowercase letters *a* through *f*. A precision specifier can optionally follow, which represents the minimum number of digits in the formatted number.

Table 2-5. Custom formatting strings

Formatting character(s)	Meaning
0	Use the zero placeholder format. If a digit in the original number exists in this position, display that digit. If there is no digit in the original string, display a zero.
#	Use the digit placeholder format. If a digit in the original number exists in this position, display that digit. If there is no digit in the original string, display nothing.
.	Use the decimal point format. The decimal point is matched up with the decimal point in the number that is to be formatted. Formatting to the right of the decimal point operates on the digits to the right of the decimal point in the original number. Formatting to the left of the decimal point operates in the same way.
,	Use the thousands separator format. A thousands separator will be placed after every three digits starting at the decimal point and moving to the left.
%	Use the percentage placeholder format. The original number is multiplied by 100 before being displayed.
E or e	Use the scientific notation format. A precision specifier, indicating the number of digits to use after the decimal point, can optionally follow.
\	Use the escape character format. The \ character and the next character after it are grouped into an escape sequence.
Any text within single or double quotes such as "aa" or 'aa'	Use no formatting; display as is and in the same position in which the text resides in the format string.
;	Used as a section separator between positive, negative, and zero formatting strings.
Any other character	Use no formatting; display as is and in the same position in which it resides in the format string.

In addition to the string.Format and the Console.WriteLine methods, the overloaded ToString instance method of a value type may also use the formatting characters in Table 2-5. Using ToString, the code looks like this:

```
float valueAsFloat = 122.35;
string valueAsString = valueAsFloat.ToString("[000000.####]");
```

After the ToString call, the valueAsString variable holds a formatted version of the number contained in valueAsFloat. It looks like this:

```
[000122.35]
```

The overloaded ToString method accepts a single parameter of type IFormatProvider. The IFormatProvider provided for the valueAsFloat.ToString method is a string containing the formatting for the value type plus any extra text that needs to be supplied.

See Also

See the "String.Format Method," "Standard Numeric Format Strings," and "Custom Numeric Format Strings" topics in the MSDN documentation.

2.17   Creating a Delimited String

Problem

You have an array of strings to format as delimited text and possibly to store in a text file.

Solution

Using the static `Join` method of the `String` class, the array of strings can be easily joined in as little as one line of code. For example:

```
string[] infoArray = new string[5] {"11", "12", "Checking", "111", "Savings"};
string delimitedInfo = string.Join(",", infoArray);
```

This code sets the value of `delimitedInfo` to the following:

```
11,12,Checking,111,Savings
```

Discussion

The `Join` method concatenates all the strings contained in a string array. Additionally, a specified delimiting character(s) is inserted between each string in the array. This method returns a single string object with the fully joined and delimited text.

Unlike the `Split` method of the `String` class, the `Join` method accepts only one delimiting character at a time. In order to use multiple delimiting characters within a string of values, subsequent `Join` operations must be performed on the information until all of the data has been joined together into a single string. For example:

```
string[] infoArray = new string[4] {"11", "12", "Checking", "Savings"};
string delimitedInfoBegin = string.Join(",", infoArray, 0, 2);
string delimitedInfoEnd = string.Join(",", infoArray, 2, 2);
string[] delimitedInfoTotal = new string[2] {delimitedInfoBegin,
        delimitedInfoEnd};
string delimitedInfoFinal = string.Join(":", delimitedInfoTotal);
Console.WriteLine(delimitedInfoFinal);
```

produces the following delimited string:

```
11,12:Checking,Savings
```

See Also

See the "String.Join Method" topic in the MSDN documentation.

2.18   Extracting Items from a Delimited String

Problem

You have a string, possibly from a text file, which is delimited by one or more characters. You need to retrieve each piece of delimited information as easily as possible.

Solution

Using the `Split` instance method on the `String` class, you can place the delimited information into an array in as little as a single line of code. For example:

```
string delimitedInfo = "100,200,400,3,67";
string[] discreteInfo = delimitedInfo.Split(new char[1] {','});

foreach (string Data in discreteInfo)
    Console.WriteLine(Data);
```

The string array `discreteInfo` holds the following values:

```
100
200
400
3
67
```

Discussion

The `Split` method, like most methods in the `String` class, is simple to use. This method returns a string array with each element containing one discrete piece of the delimited text split on the delimiting character(s).

In the Solution, the string `delimitedInfo` is comma-delimited. However, it can be delimited by any type of character or even by more than one character. When there is more than one type of delimiter, use code like the following:

```
string[] discreteInfo = delimitedInfo.Split(new char[3] {',', ':', ' '});
```

This line splits the `delimitedInfo` string whenever one of the three delimiting characters (comma, colon, or space character) is found.

The `Split` method is case-sensitive. To split a string on the letter *a* in a case-insensitive manner, use code like the following:

```
string[] discreteInfo = delimitedInfo.Split(new char[2] {'a', 'A'});
```

Now, anytime the letter *a* is encountered, no matter what its case, the `Split` method views that character as a delimiter.

See Also

See the "String.Join Method" topic in the MSDN documentation.

2.19 Setting the Maximum Number of Characters a StringBuilder Can Contain

Problem

You want to ensure that the data assigned to a `StringBuilder` object does not exceed a certain number of characters.

Solution

Use the overloaded constructor of the StringBuilder class, which accepts a parameter for maximum capacity. The following code creates a StringBuilder object that has a maximum size of 10 characters:

```
System.Text.StringBuilder sbMax = new System.Text.StringBuilder(10, 10);
sbMax.Append("123456789");
sbMax.Append("0");
```

This code creates a StringBuilder object, sbMax, which has a maximum length of 10 characters. Nine characters are appended to this string and then a tenth character is appended without a problem. However, if the next line of code is executed:

```
sbMax.Append("#");
```

the length of sbMax goes beyond 10 characters and an ArgumentOutOfRangeException is thrown.

Discussion

The string object is immutable and, as such, has no use for a built-in method to prevent its length from going beyond a certain point. Fortunately, the StringBuilder object contains an overloaded constructor that allows the maximum size of its string to be set. The StringBuilder constructor that you are concerned with is defined as follows:

```
public StringBuilder(int initialCapacity, int maxCapacity)
```

For most applications, the initialCapacity and maxCapacity parameters can be identical. This way gives you the best performance, overall. If these two parameters are not identical, it is critical that they can coexist. The following line of code:

```
System.Text.StringBuilder sbMax = new System.Text.StringBuilder(30, 12);
```

will throw an ArgumentOutOfRangeException. The reason is that the initialCapacity parameter is larger than maxCapacity, causing the exception. While you may not be explicitly writing these values for your application, if you are calculating them using some type of expression, you may run into these problems.

To handle an attempt to append characters to the StringBuilder string, forcing it beyond the maximum size, wrap any code to append text to the StringBuilder object in a try-catch block:

```
try
{
    sbMax.Append("New String");
}
catch(ArgumentOutOfRangeException rangeE)
{
    // Handle overrun here.
}
```

In addition to the Append method, you should also wrap any AppendFormat, Insert, and Replace methods of the StringBuilder object in a try-catch block. Any of these methods can allow characters to be added to the StringBuilder string, potentially causing its length to exceed its maximum specified length.

See Also

See the "StringBuilder.Append Method" topic in the MSDN documentation.

2.20 Iterating over Each Character in a String

Problem

You need to iterate over each character in a string efficiently in order to examine or process each character.

Solution

C# provides two methods for iterating strings. The first is the foreach loop, which can be used as follows:

```
string testStr = "abc123";
foreach (char c in testStr)
{
    Console.WriteLine(c.ToString( ));
}
```

This method is quick and easy. Unfortunately, it is somewhat less flexible than the second method, which uses the for loop instead of a foreach loop to iterate over the string. For example:

```
string testStr = "abc123";
for (int counter = 0; counter < testStr.Length; counter++)
{
    Console.WriteLine(testStr[counter]);
}
```

Discussion

The foreach loop is simpler and thus less error-prone, but it lacks flexibility. In contrast, the for loop is slightly more complex, but it makes up for that in flexibility.

The for loop method uses the indexer of the string variable testStr to get the character located at the position indicated by the counter loop index. Care must be taken not to run over the bounds of the string array when using this type of looping mechanism.

A for loop is flexible enough to change how looping over characters in a string is performed. For example, the loop can be quickly modified to start and end at a specific point in the string by simply changing the *initializer* and *conditional* expressions of the for loop. Characters can be skipped by changing the *iterator* expression to increment the counter variable by more than one. The string can also be iterated in reverse order by changing the for loop expressions, as shown:

```
for (int counter = testStr.Length - 1; counter >= 0; counter--)
{
    Console.WriteLine(testStr[counter].ToString( ));
}
```

 The compiler optimizes the use of a foreach loop iterating through a *vector array*—one that starts at zero and has only one dimension. Converting a foreach loop to another type of loop, such as a for loop, may not produce any noticeable increases in performance.

It should be noted that each of these methods was compiled using the /optimize compiler option. However, adding or removing this option has very little impact on the resulting Microsoft Intermediate Language (IL) code.

2.21 Improving String Comparison Performance

Problem

Your application consists of many strings that are compared frequently. You have been tasked with improving performance and making more efficient use of resources.

Solution

Use the intern pool to improve resource usage and, in turn, improve performance.

 In some cases string interning will not yield the performance improvements that you want. The more string comparisons made in your application, the better your chances that string interning will improve your application. There are two costs associated with string interning. The first is that the interned string is not freed until the AppDomain is shut down. The second is that the process of interning a string takes up extra time regardless of whether or not the string was previously interned.

The Intern and IsInterned instance methods of the String class allow you to use the intern pool. Use the following static methods to make use of the string intern pool:

```
using System;
using System.Text;

public class InternedStrCls
{
    public static void CreateInternedStr(char[] characters)
    {
```

```
        string NonInternedStr = new string(characters);
        String.Intern(NonInternedStr);
    }

    public static void CreateInternedStr(StringBuilder strBldr)
    {
        String.Intern(strBldr.ToString( ));
    }

    public static void CreateInternedStr(string str)
    {
        String.Intern(str);
    }

    public static void CreateInternedStr(string[] strArray)
    {
        foreach(string s in strArray)
        {
            String.Intern(s);
        }
    }
}
```

Discussion

The CLR automatically stores all string literals declared in an application in an area of memory called the *intern pool*. The intern pool contains a unique instance of each string literal found in your code, which can allow for more efficient use of resources by not storing multiple copies of strings that contain the same string literal. Another possible benefit is enhanced speed when making string comparisons. When two strings are compared using either the == operator or the Equals instance method of the String Class, a test is done to determine whether each string variable reference is the same. If they are not, then each string's length is checked. If the lengths of both strings are equal, each character is compared individually. However, if you can guarantee that the references, instead of the string contents, can be compared, much faster string comparisons can be made. String interning does just that: it guarantees that the references to equivalent string values are the same, eliminating the possibility of attempting the length and character-by-character checks. This yields better performance in situations in which the references to two equal strings are different and the length and character-by-character comparisons have to be made.

Note that the only strings automatically placed in this intern pool by the compiler are string literals—strings surrounded by double quotes—found in code by the compiler. The following lines of code will place the string "foo" into the intern pool:

```
string s = "foo";
StringBuilder sb = new StringBuilder("foo");
StringBuilder sb2 = new StringBuilder( ).Append("foo");
```

The following lines of code will not place the string "foo" into the intern pool:

```
char[] ca = new char[3] {'f','o','o'};
StringBuilder sb = new StringBuilder( ).Append("f").Append("oo");

string s1 = "f";
string s2 = "oo";
string s3 = s1 + s2;
```

You can programmatically store a new string created by your application in the intern pool using the static `string.Intern` method. This method returns a string referencing the string literal contained in the intern pool, or, if the string is not found, the string is entered into the intern pool and a reference to this newly pooled string is returned.

There is also another method used in string interning called `IsInterned`. This method operates similarly to the `Intern` method, except that it returns `null` if the string is not in the intern pool, rather than adding it to the pool. If the string is found, this method returns a string referencing the string literal contained in the intern pool, or, if the string is not found, it returns `null`.

An example of using this method is shown here:

```
string s1 = "f";
string s2 = "oo";
string s3 = s1 + s2;
if (String.IsInterned(s3) == null)
{
    Console.WriteLine("NULL");
}
```

However, if you add the following bolded line of code, the `IsInterned` test returns a non-null string object:

```
string s1 = "f";
string s2 = "oo";
string s3 = s1 + s2;
InternedStrCls.CreateInternedStr(s3);
if (String.IsInterned(s3) == null)
{
    Console.WriteLine("NULL");
}
```

The `Intern` method is useful when you need a reference to a string, even if it does not exist in the intern pool.

The `IsInterned` method can optimize the comparison of a single string to any string literal or manually interned string. Consider that you need to determine whether a string variable contains any string literal that has been defined in the application. Call the `string.IsInterned` method with the string variable as the parameter. If `null` is returned, there is no match in the intern pool, and thus there is no match between the string variable's value and any string literals:

```
string s1 = "f";
string s2 = "oo";
string s3 = s1 + s2;

if (String.IsInterned(s3) != null)
{
    // If the string "foo" has been defined in the app and placed
    // into the intern pool, this block of code executes.
}
else
{
    // If the string "foo" has NOT been defined in the app NOR been placed
    // into the intern pool, this block of code executes.
}
```

Exercise caution when using the string interning methods. Calling the Intern method for every string that your application creates will actually cause the application's performance to slow considerably, since this method must search the intern pool for the string.

Another potential problem with the IsInterned method in particular stems from the fact that every string literal in the application is stored in this intern pool at the start of the application. If you are using IsInterned to determine whether a string exists, you are comparing that string against all string literals that exist in the application, as well as any you might have explicitly interned, not just the ones in the scope in which IsInterned is used.

See Also

See the "String.Intern Method" and "String.IsInterned Method" topics in the MSDN documentation.

2.22   Improving StringBuilder Performance

Problem

In an attempt to improve string-handling performance, you have converted your code to use the StringBuilder class. However, this change has not improved performance as much as you had hoped.

Solution

The chief advantage of a StringBuilder object over a string object is that it preallocates a default initial amount of memory in an internal buffer in which a string value can expand and contract. When that memory is used, however, .NET must allocate new memory for this internal buffer. You can reduce the frequency with which this occurs by explicitly defining the size of the new memory using either of two techniques. The first approach is to set this value when the StringBuilder class constructor is called. For example, the code:

```
StringBuilder sb = new StringBuilder(200);
```

specifies that a StringBuilder object can hold 200 characters before new memory must be allocated.

The second approach is to change the value after the StringBuilder object has been created, using one of the following properties or methods of the StringBuilder object:

```
sb.Capacity = 200;
sb.EnsureCapacity(200);
```

Discussion

As noted in previous recipes in this chapter, the String class is immutable; once a string is assigned to a variable of type string, the string pointed to by that variable cannot be changed in any way. So changing the contents of a string variable entails the creation of a new string containing the modified string. The reference variable of type string must then be changed to reference this newly created string object. The old string object will eventually be marked for collection by the garbage collector, and, subsequently, its memory will be freed. Because of this busy behind-the-scenes action, code that performs intensive string manipulations using the String class suffers greatly from having to create new string objects for each string modification, and greater pressure is on the garbage collector to remove unused objects from memory more frequently.

The StringBuilder class solves this problem by preallocating an internal buffer to hold a string. The contents of this string buffer are manipulated directly. Any operations performed on a StringBuilder object do not carry the performance penalty of creating a whole new string or StringBuilder object and, consequently, filling up the managed heap with many unused objects.

There is one caveat with using the StringBuilder class, which, if not heeded, can impede performance. The StringBuilder class uses a default initial capacity to contain the characters of a string, unless you change this default initial capacity through one of the StringBuilder constructors. Once this space is exceeded, by appending characters, for instance, a new string buffer is allocated that is double the size of the original buffer. For example, a StringBuilder object with an initial size of 20 characters will be increased to 40 characters, then to 80 characters, and so on. The string contained in the original internal string buffer is then copied to this newly allocated internal string buffer along with any appended or inserted characters.

The default capacity for a StringBuilder object is 16 characters; in many cases, this is much too small. To increase this size upon object creation, the StringBuilder class has an overloaded constructor that accepts an integer value to use as the starting size of the preallocated string. Determining an initial size value that is not too large (thereby allocating too much unused space) or too small (thereby incurring a performance penalty for creating and discarding a large number of StringBuilder objects) may seem like more of an art than a science. However, determining the optimal size may prove invaluable when your application is tested for performance.

 In cases in which good values for the initial size of a StringBuilder object cannot be obtained mathematically, try running the applications under a constant load while varying the initial StringBuilder size. When a good initial size is found, try varying the load while keeping this size value constant. You may discover that this value needs to be tweaked to get better performance. Keeping good records of each run, and committing them to a graph, will be invaluable in determining the appropriate number to choose. As an added note, using Perf-Mon (Administrative Tools → Performance Monitor) to detect and graph the number of garbage collections that occur might also provide useful information in determining whether your StringBuilder initial size is causing too many reallocations of your StringBuilder objects.

The most efficient method of setting the capacity of the StringBuilder object is to set it in the call to its constructor. The overloaded constructors of a StringBuilder object that accept a capacity value are defined as follows:

```
public StringBuilder(int capacity)
public StringBuilder(string str, int capacity)
public StringBuilder(int capacity, int maxCapacity)
public StringBuilder(string str, int startPos, int length, int capacity)
```

In addition to the constructor parameters, one property of the StringBuilder object allows its capacity to be increased (or decreased). The Capacity property gets or sets an integer value that determines the new capacity of this instance of a StringBuilder object. Note that the Capacity property cannot be less than the Length property.

A second way to change the capacity is through the EnsureCapacity method, which is defined as follows:

```
public int EnsureCapacity(string capacity)
```

This method returns the new capacity for this object. If the capacity of the existing object already exceeds that of the value in the capacity parameter, the initial capacity is retained, and this value is also returned by this method.

There is one problem with using these last two members. If any of these members increases the size of the StringBuilder object by even a single character, the internal buffer used to store the string has to be reallocated. These methods are useful if they are used in exceptional cases when the StringBuilder capacity may need an extra boost, so that fewer reallocations are performed in the long run.

The StringBuilder object also contains a Length property, which, if increased, appends spaces to the end of the existing StringBuilder object's string. If the Length is decreased, characters are truncated from the StringBuilder object's string. Increasing the Length property can increase the Capacity property, but only as a side effect. If the Length property is increased beyond the size of the Capacity property, the Capacity property value is set to the new value of the Length property. This property acts similarly to the Capacity property:

```
sb.Length = 200;
```

 The String and StringBuilder objects are considered *nonblittable*, which means that they must be marshaled across any managed/ unmanaged boundaries in your code. The reason is that strings have multiple ways of being represented in unmanaged code, and there is no one-to-one correlation between these representations in unmanaged and managed code. In contrast, types such as byte, sbyte, short, ushort, int, uint, long, ulong, IntPtr, and UIntPtr are *blittable* types and do not require conversion between managed and unmanaged code. One-dimensional arrays of these blittable types, as well as structures or classes containing only blittable types, are also considered blittable and do not need extra conversion when passed between managed and unmanaged code.

The String and StringBuilder objects take more time to marshal, due to conversion between managed and unmanaged types. Performance will be improved when calling unmanaged code through Platform Invoke (P/Invoke, for short) methods if only blittable types are used. (See Recipe 2.14 for information on how to get a byte array from a string.) Consider using a byte array instead of a String or StringBuilder object, if at all possible.

Using unsafe code is also an option, since a string can be cast to a char*, which can then be passed directly to a P/Invoke or COM method. To operate correctly, the P/Invoke or COM method has to accept a WCHAR argument(s).

See Also

See the "StringBuilder Class" topic in the MSDN documentation.

2.23 Pruning Characters from the Head and/or Tail of a String

Problem

You have a string with a specific set of characters, such as spaces, tabs, escaped single/double quotes, any type of punctuation character(s), or some other character(s), at the beginning and/or end of a string. You want a simple way to remove these characters.

Solution

Use the `Trim`, `TrimEnd`, or `TrimStart` instance methods of the `String` class:

```
string foo = "--TEST--";
Console.WriteLine(foo.Trim(new char[1] {'-'}));           // Displays "TEST"

foo = ",-TEST-,-";
Console.WriteLine(foo.Trim(new char[2] {'-',','}));        // Displays "TEST"

foo = "--TEST--";
Console.WriteLine(foo.TrimStart(new char[1] {'-'}));       // Displays "TEST--"

foo = ",-TEST-,-";
Console.WriteLine(foo.TrimStart(new char[2] {'-',','}));   // Displays "TEST-,-"

foo = "--TEST--";
Console.WriteLine(foo.TrimEnd(new char[1] {'-'}));         // Displays "--TEST"

foo = ",-TEST-,-";
Console.WriteLine(foo.TrimEnd(new char[2] {'-',','}));     // Displays ",-TEST"
```

Discussion

The `Trim` method is most often used to eliminate whitespace at the beginning and end of a string. In fact, if you call `Trim` without any parameters on a string variable, this is exactly what happens. The `Trim` method is overloaded to allow you to remove other types of characters from the beginning and end of a string. You can pass in a char[] containing all the characters that you want removed from the beginning and end of a string. Note that if the characters contained in this char[] are located somewhere in the middle of the string, they are not removed.

The `TrimStart` and `TrimEnd` methods remove characters at the beginning and end of a string, respectively. These two methods are not overloaded, unlike the `Trim` method. Rather, these two methods accept only a char[]. If you pass a null into either one of these methods, only whitespace is removed from the beginning or the end of a string.

See Also

See the "String.Trim Method," "String.TrimStart Method," and "String.TrimEnd Method" topics in the MSDN documentation.

2.24 Testing a String for Null or Empty

Problem

You need a quick and easy way to check if a string is either null or of zero length.

Solution

Use the static IsNullOrEmpty method of the String class:

```
bool stringTestResult = String.IsNullOrEmpty(testString);
```

Discussion

The IsNullOrEmpty method is a very convenient method in that it allows you to test a string for null or zero length with a single method call. This method returns true if the string passed in to it is equal to one of the following:

- Null
- String.Empty

Otherwise, this method returns false.

See Also

See the "String.IsNullOrEmpty Method" topic in the MSDN documentation.

2.25 Appending a Line

Problem

You need to append a line, including a line terminator, to the current string.

Solution

Use the AppendLine method of the StringBuilder class:

```
StringBuilder sb = new StringBuilder("First line of string");

// Terminate the first line.
sb.AppendLine();

// Add a second line.
sb.AppendLine("Second line of string");
```

This code will display the following:

```
First line of string
Second line of string
```

Discussion

The AppendLine method accepts a string and returns a reference to the same instance of the StringBuilder object on which this method was called. The string that is passed in to this method has a newline character or characters automatically appended on to the end of this string. The newline character(s) is dependent on the type of platform you are running. For example, Windows uses the \r\n carriage return and line-feed characters to represent a newline; on a Unix system the newline consists of only the line-feed character \n. You do not need to worry about this, as the AppendLine method knows which newline character(s) to apply.

If you simply want to add several blank lines to your string, you can call AppendLine with no parameters. This effectively adds only a newline character to the current string in the StringBuilder object on which it was called. Calling this method with no parameter can also be used to add a newline character(s) to the current line, if the current line has no newline character(s). For example, the code in the Solution added a string with no newline character(s) to the instantiated StringBuilder object sb. You can then call sb.AppendLine() to force a newline character to be appended to this text.

See Also

See the "StringBuilder.AppendLine Method" topic in the MSDN documentation.

2.26   Encoding Chunks of Data

Problem

You need to encode some data; however, you will be receiving it in blocks of a certain size, not all at once. Your encoder needs to be able to append each block of data to the previous one to reconstitute the entire data stream.

Solution

Use the Convert method on the Encoder class. The following method, ConvertBlocksOfData, will accept character arrays and keep passing them into the Convert method until there are no more character arrays to process. The final output of the Convert method is a byte array of a particular encoding, in this case UTF7.

```
public static void ConvertBlocksOfData()
{
    // Create encoder.
    Encoding encoding = Encoding.UTF7;
    Encoder encoder = encoding.GetEncoder();

    // Set up static size byte array.
    // In your code you may want to increase this size
    // to suit your application's needs.
    byte[] outputBytes = new byte[20];

    // Set up loop to keep adding to buffer until it's full
    // or the inputBuffer is finished.
    bool isLastBuffer = false;
    int startPos = 0;
    while (!isLastBuffer)
    {
        // Get the next block of character data.
```

```
// GetInputBuffer is defined at the end of the Solution section.
char[] inputBuffer = GetInputBuffer(out isLastBuffer);

// Check to see if we will overflow the byte array.
if ((startPos + inputBuffer.Length) >= outputBytes.Length)
{
    Console.WriteLine("RESIZING ARRAY");

    // Resize the array to handle the extra data.
    byte[] tempBuffer = new byte[outputBytes.Length];
    outputBytes.CopyTo(tempBuffer, 0);
    outputBytes = new byte[tempBuffer.Length * 2];
    tempBuffer.CopyTo(outputBytes, 0);
}

// Copy the input buffer into our byte[] buffer
// where the last copy left off.
int charsUsed;
int bytesUsed;
bool completed;
encoder.Convert(inputBuffer, 0, inputBuffer.Length, outputBytes, startPos,
                inputBuffer.Length, isLastBuffer, out charsUsed,
                out bytesUsed,
                out completed);

// Increment the starting position in the byte[]
// in which to add the next input buffer.
startPos += inputBuffer.Length;
}

// Display data.
Console.WriteLine("isLastBuffer == " + isLastBuffer.ToString());
foreach (byte b in outputBytes)
{
    if (b > 0)
        Console.Write(b.ToString() + " -- ");
}
Console.WriteLine();
}
```

The following code simply creates a text string of the alphabet and returns character arrays containing incremental blocks of characters from this string. The character arrays returned are of a particular size, in this case six characters. Note that this code is used only to exercise the ConvertBlocksOfData method; in your code you may have a stream of data that originates from a network or local filesystem and arrives in chunks rather than as one long continuous stream of data.

```
const int size = 6;    // The amount of data that we will return in the char[]
static int index = 0;  // Where we are in the original text string

// Dummy method to pass data into the calling method in chunks
public static char[] GetInputBuffer(out bool isLastBuffer)
{
```

```
// The input string
string text = "abcdefghijklmnopqrstuvwxyz";

char[] inputBuffer = null;

if ((index + size) < text.Length)
{
    // Create the buffer to return (we are not finished).
    inputBuffer = text.ToCharArray(index, size);
    isLastBuffer = false;
}
else
{
    // Create the buffer to return (we are finished).
    inputBuffer = text.ToCharArray(index, text.Length - index);
    isLastBuffer = true;
}

// Increment the index to the next chunk of data in text.
index += size;

return (inputBuffer);
}
```

Discussion

In this recipe you use the GetInputBuffer method to pass chunks of data, in this case character arrays of size six, back to the ConvertBlocksOfData method. In this method the chunks of data are fed into the Convert method, which keeps accepting chunks of data until the GetInputBuffer method returns true in its isLastBuffer out parameter. This signals the Convert method that it is finished creating the byte array and it is time to clean up. The result of this is that the Convert method creates a single continuous byte array converted to a particular encoding from individual chunks of data in the form of character arrays.

The Convert method was chosen because it was designed to be used to encode data of an unspecified size, as well as data that arrives in chunks as opposed to all at once. In certain situations, such as when a server application returns data over the network in packets of a specific size and the data is too large to fit into a single packet, a data stream object will not be able to return the complete stream. Instead, the stream object will return chunks of the entire stream until there is no more to return.

The Convert method and its parameters are defined as follows:

```
public virtual void Convert(char[] chars, int charIndex, int charCount,
                byte[] bytes,
                int byteIndex, int byteCount,
                bool flush, out int charsUsed,
                out int bytesUsed, out bool completed)
```

This method's parameters are defined here:

chars
    The character array used as the input.

charIndex
    At what index to start encoding data in the chars array.

charCount
    How much data to encode in the chars array.

bytes
    The byte array that will hold the encoded chars character array.

byteIndex
    At which position in the bytes array to start storing the encoded characters.

byteCount
    The maximum allowable characters that will be converted and stored in this array.

flush
    A false value should be passed into this parameter until the last chunk of data is converted. Upon receiving the last chunk of data, a true value should be passed into this parameter.

charsUsed
    An out parameter that indicates how many characters were converted.

bytesUsed
    An out parameter that indicates how many bytes were created and stored in the bytes array as a result of the encoding process.

completed
    An out parameter returning true if all characters totaling (charCount – charIndex) were encoded and a false if they were not all encoded.

Of these parameters the flush parameter deserves a bit more discussion. This parameter is used to tell the Convert method that the current character array is the final bit of data that is being passed in. Only at this point should you pass in the value true to this parameter. This tells the Encoder object on which the Convert method was called to finish encoding the current character array that was passed in and then to clean up after itself. At this point you should not pass in any more data to the Convert method.

The Convert method will throw an ArgumentException if you accidentally overflow the inputBuffer byte array. To prevent this from happening, you can resize this inputBuffer to allow it to hold this additional data. The code to do this is in the ConvertBlocksOfData method and is shown here:

```
// Check to see if we will overflow the byte array.
if ((startPos + inputBuffer.Length) >= outputBytes.Length)
{
```

```
        Console.WriteLine("RESIZING ARRAY");

        // Resize the array to handle the extra data.
        byte[] tempBuffer = new byte[outputBytes.Length];
        outputBytes.CopyTo(tempBuffer, 0);
        outputBytes = new byte[tempBuffer.Length * 2];
        tempBuffer.CopyTo(outputBytes, 0);
    }
```

This code simply stores the original outputBytes buffer into a temporary buffer called tempBuffer and then resizes the outputBytes buffer by twice the original size. The tempBuffer data is then copied back into the outputBytes buffer, where it is eventually passed into the Convert method. We chose to double the size of the buffer since that is the normal behavior of .NET collections, such as the ArrayList. You may want to look at this code and determine for yourself if this is the optimal size for your application or if this value needs to be tweaked.

If you want to change the encoding type to another type such as Encoding.Unicode, which takes up twice as many bytes per character as UTF7, you will need to fix up the starting position and lengths for your byte array. The following code shows the changes needed to the ConvertBlocksOfData method in order for it to work with the Unicode encoding:

```
public static void ConvertBlocksOfData( )
{
    // Create encoder.
    Encoding encoding = Encoding.Unicode;
    Encoder encoder = encoding.GetEncoder( );

    // Set up static size byte array.
    // In your code you may want to increase this size
    // to suit your application's needs.
    byte[] outputBytes = new byte[20];

    // Set up loop to keep adding to buffer until it's full
    // or the inputBuffer is finished.
    bool isLastBuffer = false;
    int startPos = 0;
    while (!isLastBuffer)
    {
        // Get the next block of character data.
        char[] inputBuffer = GetInputBuffer(out isLastBuffer);

        // Check to see if we will overflow the byte array.
        if (((startPos * 2) + (inputBuffer.Length * 2)) >= outputBytes.Length)
        {
            Console.WriteLine("RESIZING ARRAY");

            // Resize the array to handle the extra data.
            byte[] tempBuffer = new byte[outputBytes.Length];
            outputBytes.CopyTo(tempBuffer, 0);
            outputBytes = new byte[tempBuffer.Length * 2];
```

```
                tempBuffer.CopyTo(outputBytes, 0);
        }

        // Copy the input buffer into our byte[] buffer
        // where the last copy left off.
        int charsUsed;
        int bytesUsed;
        bool completed;
        encoder.Convert(inputBuffer, 0, inputBuffer.Length, outputBytes,
                        startPos * 2,
                        inputBuffer.Length * 2, isLastBuffer,
                        out charsUsed,
                        out bytesUsed, out completed);

        // Increment the starting position in the byte[]
        // in which to add the next input buffer.
        startPos += inputBuffer.Length;
    }

    // Display data.
    Console.WriteLine("isLastBuffer == " + isLastBuffer.ToString());
    foreach (byte b in outputBytes)
    {
        if (b > 0)
            Console.Write(b.ToString() + " -- ");
    }
    Console.WriteLine();
}
```

The highlighted lines indicate the changes that are needed. These changes simply
take into account the larger size of the Unicode-encoded characters that will be
placed in the outputBytes buffer.

See Also

See the "Encoder.Convert Method" topic in the MSDN documentation.

CHAPTER 3

Classes and Structures

3.0 Introduction

Structures, like any other value type, implicitly inherit from System.ValueType. At first glance, a structure is similar to a class but is actually very different. Knowing when to use a structure over a class will help tremendously when designing an application. Using a structure incorrectly can result in inefficient and hard-to-modify code.

Structures have two performance advantages over reference types. First, if a structure is allocated on the stack (i.e., it is not contained within a reference type), access to the structure and its data is somewhat faster than access to a reference type on the heap. Reference type objects must follow their reference onto the heap in order to get at their data. However, this performance advantage pales in comparison to the second performance advantage of structures: namely, that cleaning up the memory allocated to a structure on the stack requires a simple change of the address to which the stack pointer points, which is done at the return of a method call. This call is extremely fast compared to allowing the garbage collector to automatically clean up reference types for you in the managed heap; however, the cost of the garbage collector is deferred so that it's not immediately noticeable.

The performance of structures falls short in comparison to that of classes when they are passed by value to other methods. Because they reside on the stack, a structure and its data have to be copied to a new local variable (the method's parameter that is used to receive the structure) when it is passed by value to a method. This copying takes more time than passing a method a single reference to an object—unless the structure is the same size as or smaller than the machine's pointer size; thus, a structure with a size of 32 bits is just as cheap to pass as a reference (which happens to be the size of a pointer) on a 32-bit machine. Keep this in mind when choosing between a class and a structure. While creating, accessing, and destroying a class's object may take longer, it also might not balance the performance hit when a structure is passed by value a large number of times to one or more methods. Keeping the size of the structure small minimizes the performance hit of passing it around by value.

Structures can also cause degradation in performance when they are passed to methods that require an object, such as any of the nongeneric collection types in the FCL. Passing a structure (or any simple type, for that matter) into a method requiring an object causes the structure to be boxed. *Boxing* is wrapping a value type in an object. This operation is time-consuming and may degrade performance.

As concerns the object-oriented capabilities of classes and structures, classes have far more flexibility. A structure cannot contain a user-defined default constructor, since the C# compiler automatically provides a default constructor that initializes all the fields in the structure to their default values. This is also why no field initializers can be added to a structure. If you need to override the default field values, a structure might not be the way to go. However, a parameterized constructor that initializes the structure's fields to any value that is necessary can be created.

Structures, like classes, can inherit from interfaces, but unlike classes, structures cannot inherit from a class or a structure. This limitation precludes creating structure hierarchies, as you can do with classes. Polymorphism as implemented through an abstract base class is also prohibited when using a structure, since a structure cannot inherit from another class.

Use a class if:

- Its identity is important. Structures get copied implicitly when being passed by value into a method.
- It will have a large memory footprint.
- Its fields need initializers.
- You need to inherit from a base class.
- You need polymorphic behavior. That is, you need to implement an abstract base class from which you will create several similar classes that inherit from this abstract base class. (Note that polymorphism can be implemented via interfaces as well, but it is usually not a good idea to place an interface on a value type, since a boxing operation will occur if the structure is converted to the interface type.) For more on polymorphism through interfaces, see Recipe 3.16.

Use a structure if:

- It will act like a primitive type (int, long, byte, etc.).
- It must have a small memory footprint.
- You are calling a P/Invoke method that requires a structure to be passed in by value. *Platform Invoke*, or P/Invoke for short, allows managed code to call out to an unmanaged method exposed from within a DLL. Many times an unmanaged DLL method requires a structure to be passed in to it; using a structure is an efficient method of doing this and is the only way if the structure is being passed by value.
- You need to avoid the overhead of garbage collection.

- Its fields need to be initialized only to their default values. This value would be zero for numeric types, `false` for Boolean types, and `null` for reference types.

- You do not need to inherit from a base class (other than `ValueType`, from which all structs inherit).

- You do not need polymorphic behavior.

3.1   Creating Union-Type Structures

Problem

You need to create a data type that behaves like a union type in C++. A union type is useful mainly in interop scenarios in which the unmanaged code accepts and/or returns a union type; we suggest that you do not use it in other situations.

Solution

Use a structure and mark it with the `StructLayout` attribute (specifying the `LayoutKind.Explicit` layout kind in the constructor). In addition, mark each field in the structure with the `FieldOffset` attribute. The following structure defines a union in which a single signed numeric value can be stored:

```
using System.Runtime.InteropServices;

[StructLayoutAttribute(LayoutKind.Explicit)]
struct SignedNumber
{
    [FieldOffsetAttribute(0)]
    public sbyte Num1;

    [FieldOffsetAttribute(0)]
    public short Num2;

    [FieldOffsetAttribute(0)]
    public int Num3;

    [FieldOffsetAttribute(0)]
    public long Num4;

    [FieldOffsetAttribute(0)]
    public float Num5;

    [FieldOffsetAttribute(0)]
    public double Num6;

    [FieldOffsetAttribute(0)]
    public decimal Num7;
}
```

The next structure is similar to the `SignedNumber` structure, except that it can contain a `String` type in addition to the signed numeric value:

```
[StructLayoutAttribute(LayoutKind.Explicit)]
struct SignedNumberWithText
{
    [FieldOffsetAttribute(0)]
    public sbyte Num1;

    [FieldOffsetAttribute(0)]
    public short Num2;

    [FieldOffsetAttribute(0)]
    public int Num3;

    [FieldOffsetAttribute(0)]
    public long Num4;

    [FieldOffsetAttribute(0)]
    public float Num5;

    [FieldOffsetAttribute(0)]
    public double Num6;

    [FieldOffsetAttribute(0)]
    public decimal Num7;

    [FieldOffsetAttribute(16)]
    public string Text1;
}
```

Discussion

Unions are structures usually found in C++ code; however, there is a way to duplicate that type of structure using a C# structure data type. A *union* is a structure that accepts more than one type at a specific location in memory for that structure. For example, the SignedNumber structure is a union-type structure built using a C# structure. This structure accepts any type of signed numeric type (sbyte, int, long, etc.), but it accepts this numeric type at only one location, or offset, within the structure.

 Since StructLayoutAttribute can be applied to both structures and classes, a class can also be used when creating a union data type.

Notice the FieldOffsetAttribute has the value zero passed to its constructor. This denotes that this field will be at the zeroth offset (this is a byte offset) within this structure. This attribute is used in tandem with the StructLayoutAttribute to manually enforce where the fields in this structure will start (that is, the offset from the beginning of this structure in memory where each field will start). The FieldOffsetAttribute can be used only with a StructLayoutAttribute set to LayoutKind.Explicit. In addition, it cannot be used on static members within this structure.

Unions can become problematic, since several types are essentially laid on top of one another. The biggest problem is extracting the correct data type from a union structure. Consider what happens if you choose to store the long numeric value long. MaxValue in the SignedNumber structure. Later, you might accidentally attempt to extract a byte data type value from this same structure. In doing so, you will get back only the first byte of the long value.

Another problem is starting fields at the correct offset. The SignedNumberWithText union overlays numerous signed numeric data types at the zeroth offset. The last field in this structure is laid out at the 16th byte offset from the beginning of this structure in memory. If you accidentally overlay the string field Text1 on top of any of the other signed numeric data types, you will get an exception at runtime. The basic rule is that you are allowed to overlay a value type on another value type, but you cannot overlay a reference type over a value type. If the Text1 field is marked with the following attribute:

```
[FieldOffsetAttribute(14)]
```

this exception is thrown at runtime (note that the compiler does not catch this problem):

```
An unhandled exception of type 'System.TypeLoadException' occurred in
Chapter_Code.exe.

Additional information: Could not load type Chapter_Code.SignedNumberWithText from
assembly 14 because it contains an object field at offset 14 that is incorrectly
aligned or overlapped by a non-object field.
```

It is imperative to get the offsets correct when using complex unions in C#.

See Also

See the "StructLayoutAttribute Class" topic in the MSDN documentation.

3.2   Allowing a Type to Represent Itself as a String

Problem

Your class or structure needs to control how its information is displayed when its ToString method is called. In addition, you need to apply different formats to this information. For example, when creating a new data type, such as a Line class, you might want to allow objects of this type to be able to display themselves in a textual format. In the case of a Line object, it might display itself as (x1, y1)(x2, y2).

Solution

Override and/or implement the IFormattable.ToString method to display numeric information, such as for a Line structure:

```csharp
using System;
using System.Text;
using System.Text.RegularExpressions;

public struct Line : IFormattable
{
    public Line(int startX, int startY, int endX, int endY)
    {
        x1 = startX;
        x2 = endX;
        y1 = startY;
        y2 = endY;
    }

    public int x1;
    public int y1;
    public int x2;
    public int y2;

    public double GetDirectionInRadians( )
    {
        int xSide = x2 - x1;
        int ySide = y2 - y1;

        if (xSide == 0)     // Prevent divide-by-zero.
            return (0);
        else
            return (Math.Atan (ySide / xSide));
    }

    public double GetMagnitude( )
    {
        int xSide = x2 - x1;
        int ySide = y2 - y1;
        return ( Math.Sqrt((xSide * xSide) + (ySide * ySide)));
    }

    // This overrides the Object.ToString method.
    // This override is not required for this recipe
    // and is included for completeness.
    public override string ToString( )
    {
        return (String.Format("({0},{1}) ({2},{3})", x1, y1, x2, y2));
    }

    public string ToString(string format)
    {
        return (this.ToString(format, null));
    }

    public string ToString(IFormatProvider formatProvider)
    {
        return (this.ToString(null, formatProvider));
    }
```

```
        public string ToString(string format, IFormatProvider formatProvider)
        {
            StringBuilder compositeStr = new StringBuilder("");

            if ((format != null) && (format.ToUpper( ).Equals("V")))
            {
                double direction = this.GetDirectionInRadians( );
                double magnitude = this.GetMagnitude( );

                string retStringD = direction.ToString("G5", formatProvider);
                string retStringM = magnitude.ToString("G5", formatProvider);

                compositeStr.Append("magnitude = ").Append(retStringM).Append
                                    ("\tDirection = ").Append(retStringD);
            }
            else
            {
                string retStringX1 = this.x1.ToString(format, formatProvider);
                string retStringY1 = this.y1.ToString(format, formatProvider);
                string retStringX2 = this.x2.ToString(format, formatProvider);
                string retStringY2 = this.y2.ToString(format, formatProvider);

                compositeStr.Append("(").Append(retStringX1).Append(",").Append
                                    (retStringY1).Append(")(").Append(retStringX2).Append
                                    (",").Append(retStringY2).Append(")");
            }

            return (compositeStr.ToString( ));
        }
    }
}
```

Discussion

The ToString method provides a convenient way to display the current contents, or state, of a structure (this recipe works equally well for reference types). The solution section of this recipe shows the various implementations of ToString for both numeric and textual data. The Line class contains two points in space that form the endpoints of a line. This line data is then fed into the ToString methods for that class to produce formatted output.

The following code exercises the ToString methods of the Line class:

```
using System.Globalization;

public static void TestLineToString( )
{
    Line V1 = new Line(0, 0, 40, 123);
    Line V2 = new Line(0, -2, 1, 11);
    Line V3 = new Line(0, 1, 0, 1);

    Console.WriteLine("\r\nTest Default ToString method");
    Console.WriteLine("V1 = " + V1);
    Console.WriteLine("V2 = " + V2);
```

```
Console.WriteLine("V1.ToString( ) = {0:V}", V1.ToString( ));
Console.WriteLine("V2.ToString( ) = {0:V}", V2.ToString( ));

Console.WriteLine("\r\nTest overloaded ToString(format) method");
Console.WriteLine("V1.ToString(\"D\") = {0:D}", V1);
Console.WriteLine("V1.ToString(\"D5\") = {0:D5}", V1);
Console.WriteLine("V1.ToString(\"F\") = {0:F}", V2);
Console.WriteLine("V1.ToString(\"N\") = {0:N}", V1);
Console.WriteLine("V2.ToString(\"n\") = {0:n}", V2);
Console.WriteLine("V1.ToString(\"E\") = {0:E}", V1);
Console.WriteLine("V2.ToString(\"X\") = {0:X}", V2);

Console.WriteLine("\r\nTest overloaded ToString(formatProvider) method");
NumberFormatInfo NullFormatter = null;
NumberFormatInfo Formatter = new NumberFormatInfo( );
Formatter.NegativeSign = "!";
Formatter.PositiveSign = "+";
Console.WriteLine("V2.ToString(Formatter) = " + V2.ToString(Formatter));
Console.WriteLine("V2.ToString(Formatter) = " + V2.ToString(Formatter));
Console.WriteLine("V2.ToString(null) = " + V2.ToString(NullFormatter));
Console.WriteLine("V2.ToString(null) = " + V2.ToString(NullFormatter));
Console.WriteLine("V2.ToString(new CultureInfo(\"fr-BE\")) = "
        + V2.ToString(new CultureInfo("fr-BE")));  //French - Belgium
Console.WriteLine("V2.ToString(new CultureInfo(\"fr-BE\")) = "
        + V2.ToString(new CultureInfo("fr-BE")));  //French - Belgium

Console.WriteLine
        ("\r\nTest overloaded ToString(format, formatProvider) method");
Console.WriteLine("V2.ToString(\"D\", Formatter) = " + V2.ToString("D",
                Formatter));
Console.WriteLine("V2.ToString(\"F\", Formatter) = " + V2.ToString("F",
                Formatter));
Console.WriteLine("V2.ToString(\"D\", null) = " + V2.ToString("D", null));
Console.WriteLine("V2.ToString(\"F\", null) = " + V2.ToString("F", null));
Console.WriteLine("V2.ToString(\"D\", new CultureInfo(\"fr-BE\")) = "
        + V2.ToString("D", new CultureInfo("fr-BE")));  //French - Belgium
Console.WriteLine("V2.ToString(\"F\", new CultureInfo(\"fr-BE\")) = "
        + V2.ToString("F", new CultureInfo("fr-BE")));  //French - Belgium

Console.WriteLine("\r\nTest overloaded ToString(\"V\", formatProvider) method");
Console.WriteLine("V2.ToString(\"V\", Formatter) = " + V2.ToString("V",
                Formatter));
Console.WriteLine("V2.ToString(\"V\", null) = " + V2.ToString("V", null));
}
```

This code displays the following results:

```
Test Default ToString method
V1 = (0,0) (40,123)
V2 = (0,-2) (1,11)
V1.ToString( ) = (0,0) (40,123)
V2.ToString( ) = (0,-2) (1,11)

Test overloaded ToString(format) method
```

```
V1.ToString("D") = (0,0)(40,123)
V1.ToString("D5") = (00000,00000)(00040,00123)
V2.ToString("F") = (0.00,-2.00)(1.00,11.00)
V1.ToString("N") = (0.00,0.00)(40.00,123.00)
V2.ToString("n") = (0.00,-2.00)(1.00,11.00)
V1.ToString("E") = (0.000000E+000,0.000000E+000)(4.000000E+001,1.230000E+002)
V2.ToString("X") = (0,FFFFFFFE)(1,B)

Test overloaded ToString(formatProvider) method
V2.ToString(Formatter) = (0,!2)(1,11)
V2.ToString(Formatter) = (0,!2)(1,11)
V2.ToString(null) = (0,-2)(1,11)
V2.ToString(null) = (0,-2)(1,11)
V2.ToString(new CultureInfo("fr-BE")) = (0,-2)(1,11)
V2.ToString(new CultureInfo("fr-BE")) = (0,-2)(1,11)

Test overloaded ToString(format, formatProvider)       method
V2.ToString("D", Formatter) = (0,!2)(1,11)
V2.ToString("F", Formatter) = (0.00,!2.00)(1.00,11.00)
V2.ToString("D", null) = (0,-2)(1,11)
V2.ToString("F", null) = (0.00,-2.00)(1.00,11.00)
V2.ToString("D", new CultureInfo("fr-BE")) = (0,-2)(1,11)
V2.ToString("F", new CultureInfo("fr-BE")) = (0,00,-2,00)(1,00,11,00)

Test overloaded ToString("V", formatProvider) method
V2.ToString("V", Formatter) = magnitude = 13.038       direction = 1.494
V2.ToString("V", null) = magnitude = 13.038       direction = 1.494
```

This method prints out the two x and y coordinates that make up the start and end points of a line for the Line class. An example output of the Line.ToString( ) method is:

```
(0,0) (40,123)
```

This output could also be displayed as the magnitude and direction of this line. This result is demonstrated in the overloaded ToString method that accepts both a format string and an IFormatProvider.

The next overloaded ToString method takes a single argument, *format*, which is a String containing the formatting information of the type. This method calls the last overloaded ToString method and passes the format information as the first parameter and a null as the second parameter. The following ToString method operates similarly to the previous ToString method, except that it accepts an IFormatProvider data type as its only parameter. The format parameter of the last ToString method is set to null when called by this method.

The final ToString method is where all the real work takes place. This method accepts two parameters, a String (format) containing formatting information and an IFormatProvider (formatProvider) containing even more specific formatting information. The format string makes use of predefined formats such as "D", "d", "F", "f", "G", "g", "X", and "x", to name a few. (See Recipe 2.16 for more information on the formatting character codes.) These formats specify whether the information will be displayed as decimal ("D" or "d"), general ("G" or "g"), hexadecimal ("X" or "x"), or one of the other types. As a note, calling ToString with no parameters always sets the format type to general. In addition, this method also takes a special format character "V" or "v". This character formatting code is not one of the predefined formatting codes; instead, it is one that we added to provide special handling of a Line object's output in vector format. This code allows the Line type to be displayed as a magnitude and a direction:

```
magnitude = 13.038       direction = 1.494
```

The second parameter accepts any data type that implements the IFormatProvider interface. Three data types in the FCL—CultureInfo, DateTimeFormatInfo, and NumberFormatInfo—implement this interface. The CultureInfo class contains formatting information specific to the various supported cultures that exist around the world. The DateTimeFormatInfo class contains formatting information specific to date and time values; similarly, the NumberFormatInfo class contains formatting information specific to numbers.

This ToString method sets up a variable, compositeStr, which will contain the final formatted value of the Line type. Next, the format parameter is checked for null. Remember, the previous ToString method that accepts the IFormatProvider parameter will call this form of the ToString method and pass in a format value of null. So you must be able to handle a null value gracefully at this point. If the format parameter passed in to the Line type is not null and is equal to the character "V", you are able to provide a string to display this line as a magnitude and a direction. The direction and magnitude values are obtained for this object and are displayed in a General format with five significant digits of precision. If, on the other hand, any other type of formatting character code was passed in—including null—each of the individual coordinates are formatted using the ToString method of the Int32 structure. These coordinates are concatenated into a string and returned to the caller to be displayed.

The method:

```
public string ToString(string format, IFormatProvider formatProvider)
```

must be implemented, since the structure implements the IFormattable interface. The IFormattable interface provides a consistent interface for this ToString method:

```
public interface IFormattable
{
    string ToString(string format, IFormatProvider formatProvider);
}
```

For the Line structure, the IFormattable.ToString method passes its parameters to the Int32 structure's ToString method with the same method signature, which provides a more uniform formatting capability for Line values.

Using the IFormattable interface forces you to implement the IFormattable.ToString method to more effectively display your type's value(s). However, you do not have to implement it, as you can see for yourself by removing this interface from the Line structure's declaration. For performance's sake, it is best to not implement this interface on structures, due to the cost of boxing the structure; however, this needs to be weighed with the design of the type. Implementing this interface on a class does not incur a performance penalty.

See Also

See Recipe 2.16; see the "IFormatProvider Interface" topic in the MSDN documentation.

3.3 Converting a String Representation of an Object into an Actual Object

Problem

You need a way of accepting a string containing a textual representation of an object and converting it to an object usable by your application. For example, if you were provided with the string representation of a line (x1, y1)(x2, y2), you would want to convert it into a Line structure.

Solution

Implement a Parse method on your Line structure:

```
using System;
using System.Text;
using System.Text.RegularExpressions;

public struct Line : IFormattable
{
    public Line(int startX, int startY, int endX, int endY)
    {
        x1 = startX;
        x2 = endX;
        y1 = startY;
        y2 = endY;
    }

    public int x1;
    public int y1;
    public int x2;
    public int y2;

    public override bool Equals(object obj)
```

```
{
    bool isEqual = false;

    if (obj == null || (this.GetType() != obj.GetType()))
    {
        isEqual = false;
    }
    else
    {
        Line theLine = (Line)obj;
        isEqual = (this.x1 == theLine.x1) &&
         (this.y1 == theLine.y1) &&
         (this.x2 == theLine.x2) &&
         (this.y2 == theLine.y2);
    }
    return (isEqual);
}

public bool Equals(Line lineObj)
{
    bool isEqual = (this.x1 == lineObj.x1) &&
     (this.y1 == lineObj.y1) &&
     (this.x2 == lineObj.x2) &&
     (this.y2 == lineObj.y2);

    return (isEqual);
}

public override int GetHashCode()
{
    return ((x1 + x2) ^ (y1 + y2));
}

public static Line Parse(string stringLine)
{
    if (stringLine == null)
    {
        throw (new ArgumentNullException(
                "stringLine",
                "A null cannot be passed into the Parse method."));
    }

    // Take this string (x1,y1)(x2,y2) and convert it to a Line object.
    int X1 = 0;
    int Y1 = 0;
    int X2 = 0;
    int Y2 = 0;

    MatchCollection MC = Regex.Matches(stringLine,
        @"\s*\(\s*(?<x1>\d+)\s*\,\s*(?<y1>\d+)\s*\)\s*\(\s*(?<x2>" +
        @"\d+)\s*\,\s*(?<y2>\d+)\s*\)" );

    if (MC.Count == 1)
    {
```

```
            Match M = MC[0];
            X1 = int.Parse(M.Groups["x1"].Value);
            Y1 = int.Parse(M.Groups["y1"].Value);
            X2 = int.Parse(M.Groups["x2"].Value);
            Y2 = int.Parse(M.Groups["y2"].Value);
        }
        else
        {
            throw (new ArgumentException("The value " + stringLine +
                                    " is not a well formed Line value."));
        }

        return (new Line(X1, Y1, X2, Y2));
    }

    public double GetDirectionInRadians()
    {
        int xSide = x2 - x1;
        int ySide = y2 - y1;

        if (xSide == 0)    // Prevent divide-by-zero.
            return (0);
        else
            return (Math.Atan (ySide / xSide));
    }

    public double GetMagnitude()
    {
        int xSide = x2 - x1;
        int ySide = y2 - y1;
        return (Math.Sqrt( Math.Sqrt((xSide * xSide) + (ySide * ySide))));
    }

    public override string ToString()
    {
        return (String.Format("({0},{1}) ({2},{3})", x1, y1, x2, y2));
    }

    public string ToString(string format)
    {
        return (this.ToString(format, null));
    }

    public string ToString(IFormatProvider formatProvider)
    {
        return (this.ToString(null, formatProvider));
    }

    public string ToString(string format, IFormatProvider formatProvider)
    {
        StringBuilder compositeStr = new StringBuilder("");

        if ((format != null) && (format.ToUpper().Equals("V")))
        {
```

```
                double direction = this.GetDirectionInRadians( );
                double magnitude = this.GetMagnitude( );

                string retStringD = direction.ToString("G5", formatProvider);
                string retStringM = magnitude.ToString("G5", formatProvider);

                compositeStr.Append(
                    "magnitude = ").Append(retStringM).Append(
                              "\tDirection = ").Append(retStringD);
        }
        else
        {
                string retStringX1 = this.x1.ToString(format, formatProvider);
                string retStringY1 = this.y1.ToString(format, formatProvider);
                string retStringX2 = this.x2.ToString(format, formatProvider);
                string retStringY2 = this.y2.ToString(format, formatProvider);

                compositeStr.Append("(").Append(retStringX1).Append(",").Append(
                     retStringY1).Append(")(").
                          Append(retStringX2).Append(",").Append(
                                retStringY2).Append(")");
        }

        return (compositeStr.ToString( ));
    }
}
```

Discussion

The Parse method is used to reconstruct one data type—in this case, a String—into the data type containing that Parse method. For example, if the string "123" were passed into the int.Parse method, the numeric data type 123 would be extracted and then returned. Many other types in the FCL use a Parse method to reconstruct an object of its own type from another data type, such as a string. Note that you are not limited as far as the type and number of parameters that can be passed into this method. As an example, see how the DateTime.Parse and DateTime.ParseExact methods are defined and overloaded.

The parsing of a string containing the start and end coordinates of a line is a little more difficult. To make things easier, use a regular expression to extract the beginning and ending x and y coordinates.

The regular expression parses out the individual coordinate values provided by the stringLine string parameter. Each found coordinate is passed on to the static int. Parse method on the int structure. This final step obtains the final parsed integer values from the matches produced by the regular expression. If the regular expression does not extract the required coordinates, you can assume that the stringLine parameter does not contain a well-formed string that can be converted to a Line object.

The following code:

```
Console.WriteLine("Line.Parse(\"(12,2)(0,45)\") = " + Line.Parse("(12,2)(0,45)"));
Console.WriteLine("Line.Parse(\"(0,0)(0,0)\") = " + Line.Parse("(0,0)(0,0)"));
```

produces this output:

```
Line.Parse("(12,2)(0,45)") = (12,2) (0,45)
Line.Parse("(0,0)(0,0)") = (0,0) (0,0)
```

 When implementing a Parse method on your own types, you need to consider the situation in which invalid data is passed to this method. When this happens, an ArgumentException should be thrown. When a null is passed in, you should instead throw an ArgumentNullException.

See Also

See the "Parse Method" topic and the parse sample under the ".NET Samples—How To: Base Data Types" topic in the MSDN documentation.

3.4   Implementing Polymorphism with Abstract Base Classes

Problem

You need to build several classes that share many common traits. These classes may share common properties, methods, events, delegates, and even indexers; however, the implementation of these may be different for each class. These classes should not only share common code but also be polymorphic in nature. That is to say, code that uses an object of the base class should be able to use an object of any of these derived classes in the same manner.

Solution

Use an abstract base class to create polymorphic code. To demonstrate the creation and use of an abstract base class, here is an example that makes use of three classes, each defining a media type: magnetic, optical, and punch card. An abstract base class, Media, is created to define what each derived class will contain, as shown in Example 3-1.

Example 3-1. Implementing an abstract base class (Media)

```
public abstract class Media
{
    public abstract void Init( );
    public abstract void WriteTo(string data);
    public abstract string ReadFrom( );
    public abstract void Close( );
```

Example 3-1. Implementing an abstract base class (Media) (continued)

```
    private IntPtr mediaHandle = IntPtr.Zero;

    public IntPtr Handle
    {
        get {return(mediaHandle);}
    }
}
```

Next, the three specialized media type classes `Magnetic`, `Optical`, and `PunchCard`, which inherit from `Media`, are defined to override each of the abstract members, as shown in Example 3-2.

Example 3-2. Implementing derived classes (Magnetic, Optical, and PunchCard)

```
public class Magnetic : Media
{
    public override void Init( )
    {
        Console.WriteLine("Magnetic Init");
    }

    public override void WriteTo(string data)
    {
        Console.WriteLine("Magnetic Write");
    }

    public override string ReadFrom( )
    {
        Console.WriteLine("Magnetic Read");

        string data = "";
        return (data);
    }

    public override void Close( )
    {
        Console.WriteLine("Magnetic Close");
    }
}

public class Optical : Media
{
    public override void Init( )
    {
        Console.WriteLine("Optical Init");
    }

    public override void WriteTo(string data)
    {
        Console.WriteLine("Optical Write");
    }
```

Example 3-2. Implementing derived classes (Magnetic, Optical, and PunchCard) (continued)

```
    public override string ReadFrom( )
    {
        Console.WriteLine("Optical Read");

        string data = "";
        return (data);
    }

    public override void Close( )
    {
        Console.WriteLine("Optical Close");
    }
}

public class PunchCard : Media
{
    public override void Init( )
    {
        Console.WriteLine("PunchCard Init");
    }

    public override void WriteTo(string data)
    {
        Console.WriteLine("PunchCard WriteTo");
    }

    public override string ReadFrom( )
    {
        Console.WriteLine("PunchCard ReadFrom");

        string data = "";
        return (data);
    }

    public override void Close( )
    {
        Console.WriteLine("PunchCard Close");
    }
}
```

In Example 3-3, the methods `TestMediaABC` and `UseMedia` show how any of the three media types can be used polymorphically from within the `UseMedia` method.

Example 3-3. Using derived classes polymorphically

```
public static void TestMediaABC( )
{
    Media x = new Magnetic( );
    UseMedia(x);

    Console.WriteLine( );
```

Example 3-3. Using derived classes polymorphically (continued)

```
    x = new Optical( );
    UseMedia(x);

    Console.WriteLine( );

    x = new PunchCard( );
    UseMedia(x);
}

private static void UseMedia(Media media)
{
    media.Init( );
    media.WriteTo("text");
    media.ReadFrom( );
    Console.WriteLine(media.Handle);
    media.Close( );

    Console.WriteLine(media.ToString( ));
}
```

The output of these methods is shown here:

```
Magnetic Init
Magnetic Write
Magnetic Read
0
Magnetic Close
Magnetic

Optical Init
Optical Write
Optical Read
0
Optical Close
Optical

PunchCard Init
PunchCard Write
PunchCard Read
0
PunchCard Close
PunchCard
```

Discussion

Polymorphism through an abstract base class is a powerful tool. With this tool, you are able to create a method (UseMedia in this solution) that accepts a parameter with a specific type that is known only at runtime. Since the use of this parameter is similar for all objects that can be passed in to this method, you do not have to worry about the specific class that is passed in; you need to know only how the abstract base class is defined. It is through this abstract base class definition that you know how to use the specific type.

There are several things to keep in mind when using an abstract base class:

- Neither this class nor its abstract members can be declared as sealed; this would defeat polymorphism.
- The abstract class cannot be instantiated using the new operator, but a variable can be declared as belonging to an abstract base class type.
- All abstract members must be overridden in a derived class unless the derived class is also abstract.
- It is implied that an abstract method is also defined as virtual.
- Only methods, properties, indexers, and events may be declared as abstract.
- Abstract methods, properties, and indexers may not be declared as static or virtual.
- If an abstract base class implements an interface, it must provide either an implementation for the interface members or an abstract definition of the interface members. A combination of the two may be applied as well.
- An abstract base class can contain abstract and nonabstract members. It is not required to contain any abstract members, but this omission may confuse those who read this code.
- An abstract class may implement any number of interfaces and may also inherit from a single class. As a note, abstract members may override virtual members in the nonabstract base class.
- A derived class can override abstract properties and must include at least one accessor method (i.e., get or set). A property in a derived class that overrides an abstract property implementing only a get or a set accessor must override that specific get or set accessor. If the abstract property implements both a get and a set accessor, the overriding class property may override one or both accessors.
- A structure cannot implement polymorphism through an abstract base class/structure. Instead, a structure should consider implementing polymorphism through interfaces (see Recipe 3.16).

It is possible to use interfaces to implement polymorphism; this is discussed at length in Recipe 3.16. There are two advantages to using an abstract base class over an interface:

- Abstract base classes allow greater flexibility in versioning. An abstract base class can add a nonabstract member without breaking existing derived classes; an interface cannot. You can also add new abstract members to the class without breaking derived classes, as long as you provide default implementations for them.
- An abstract base class can contain both abstract members and nonabstract members. An interface may contain only definitions of members with no implementation.

You should also consider using an abstract base class over an interface when a lot of disparate members need to be overridden in the derived classes. For example, if you are implementing a set of members that control searching or sorting of items, you should initially consider interfaces, since this is a focused set of members that may be implemented over a wide range of unrelated classes. If you are implementing a set of members that determines the base functionality for a complete type, such as the Media type, you will probably want to use an abstract base class. See Recipe 3.16 for the advantages of using interface polymorphism over abstract base classes.

There may be some advantages in fully implementing a base class, so that it becomes a concrete class rather than an abstract one. This is especially the case when you are adding functionality to an existing base class. Your implementations do not need to be elegant; they can do nothing at all, or they can throw a NotImplementedException. The most important advantage implementing a base class as a concrete class is that derived classes do not have to override all, or for that matter any, base class members. (Of course, it makes no sense for derived classes not to implement at least one member.) With abstract base classes, you may have a number of derived classes that provide do-nothing implementations. By moving a do-nothing implementation into the base class, you save writers of derived classes from having to implement them. Notice that the abstract Media class in this recipe could be written as a concrete class (i.e., remove the abstract keyword and implementations of its abstract methods). This will allow derived classes to ignore any members they aren't interested in and focus on only the ones they need to override.

This, of course, is also the disadvantage of concrete base classes; derived classes can ignore members that they should pay attention to. The compiler will not allow a derived class to ignore any members declared as abstract.

Example 3-4 shows the abstract Media class from earlier in this recipe (see Example 3-1) rewritten as a concrete class. All that is necessary is to remove the abstract keyword and add implementations to all abstract methods. This allows you to create objects from the Media class. If you do not wish for objects to be created from your base class (Media), you can declare it as abstract, even though all its members are fully implemented.

In this case, Init and Close are left as do-nothing methods. WriteTo and ReadFrom throw a NotImplementedException. This, in effect, requires derived classes to implement them, but it moves this requirement from compile time to runtime.

Example 3-4. Implementing a concrete base class (Media)

```
public class Media
{
    public void Init( )
    {
    }
```

Example 3-4. Implementing a concrete base class (Media) (continued)

```
    public void WriteTo(string data)
    {
        throw new NotImplementedException( );
    }

    public string ReadFrom( )
    {
        throw new NotImplementedException( );
    }

    public void Close( )
    {
    }

    private IntPtr mediaHandle = IntPtr.Zero;

    public IntPtr Handle
    {
        get {return(mediaHandle);}
    }
}
```

It is not necessary to change any of the derived classes or the driver methods
(TestMediaABC and UseMedia).

See Also

See Recipe 3.16; see section 10.1.1.1, "Abstract Classes," in the C# Language Specification.

3.5 Making a Type Sortable

Problem

You have a data type that will be stored as elements in an array or an ArrayList. You
would like to use the Array.Sort and ArrayList.Sort methods to allow custom sorting of your data types in the array. In addition, you may need to use this type in a
SortedList collection.

Solution

Implement the IComparable interface. The Square class shown in Example 3-5 implements this interface in such a way that the Array, ArrayList, and SortedList objects
can sort and search an array or collection of these Square objects.

Example 3-5. Making a type sortable by implementing IComparable

```
public class Square : IComparable
{
    public Square( ){}
    public Square(int height, int width)
    {
        this.height = height;
        this.width = width;
    }

    private int height;
    private int width;

    public int Height
    {
        get{ return (height); }
        set{ height = value; }
    }

    public int Width
    {
        get{ return (width); }
        set{ width = value; }
    }

    public int CompareTo(object obj)
    {
        if (this.GetType( ) != obj.GetType( ))
        {
            throw (new ArgumentException(
                "Both objects being compared must be of type Square."));
        }
        else
        {
            Square square2 = (Square)obj;

            long area1 = this.Height * this.Width;
            long area2 = square2.Height * square2.Width;

            if (area1 == area2)
            {
                return (0);
            }
            else if (area1 > area2)
            {
                return (1);
            }
            else
            {
                return (-1);
            }
        }
    }
```

Example 3-5. Making a type sortable by implementing IComparable (continued)

```
    public override string ToString( )
    {
        return ("Height:" + height + "  Width:" + width);
    }
}
```

Discussion

By implementing the `IComparable` interface on your class (or structure), you can take advantage of the sorting routines of the `Array`, `ArrayList`, `List<T>`, and `SortedList` classes. The algorithms for sorting are built into these classes; all you have to do is tell them how to sort your classes via the code you implement in the `IComparable.CompareTo` method.

When an array of `Square` objects is passed to the `Array.Sort` static method, the array is sorted using the `IComparable` interface of the `Square` objects. The same goes for the `ArrayList.Sort` method. The `Add` method of the `SortedList` class uses this interface to sort the objects as they are being added to the `SortedList`.

> The `Array.Sort` and `ArrayList.Sort` methods use the `QuickSort` algorithm to sort an array's elements.

`IComparer` is designed to solve the problem of allowing objects to be sorted based on different criteria in different contexts. This interface also allows you to sort types that you did not write. If you also wanted to sort the `Square` objects by height, you could create a new class called `CompareHeight`, shown in Example 3-6, which would also implement the `IComparer` interface.

Example 3-6. Making a type sortable by implementing IComparer

```
public class CompareHeight : IComparer
{
    public int Compare(object obj1, object obj2)
    {
        if (!(obj1 is Square) || !(obj2 is Square))
        {
            throw (new ArgumentException(
                    "Both parameters must be of type Square."));
        }
        else
        {
            Square square1 = (Square)obj1;
            Square square2 = (Square)obj2;

            if (square1.Height == square2.Height)
            {
                return (0);
```

```
        }
        else if (square1.Height > square2.Height)
        {
            return (1);
        }
        else
        {
            return (-1);
        }
    }
  }
}
```

This class is then passed in to the IComparer parameter of the Sort routine. Now you can specify different ways to sort your Square objects.

> For best performance, keep the CompareTo method short and efficient, since it will be called multiple times by the Sort methods. For example, in sorting an array with four items, the Compare method is called 10 times.

The TestSort method shown in Example 3-7 demonstrates how to use the Square and CompareHeight classes with the Array, ArrayList, and SortedList classes.

Example 3-7. TestSort method

```
public static void TestSort( )
{
    Square[] arrayOfSquares = new Square[4] {new Square(1,3),
                                             new Square(4,3),
                                             new Square(2,1),
                                             new Square(6,1)};

    ArrayList arrayListOfSquares = new ArrayList( );
    arrayListOfSquares.Add(new Square(1,3));
    arrayListOfSquares.Add(new Square(4,3));
    arrayListOfSquares.Add(new Square(2,1));
    arrayListOfSquares.Add(new Square(6,1));

    IComparer HeightCompare = new CompareHeight( );

    // Test an ARRAY.
    Console.WriteLine("ARRAY");
    Console.WriteLine("Original array");
    foreach (Square s in arrayOfSquares)
    {
        Console.WriteLine(s.ToString( ));
    }

    Console.WriteLine( );
```

Example 3-7. TestSort method (continued)

```csharp
Console.WriteLine("Sorted array using IComparer=HeightCompare");
Array.Sort(arrayOfSquares, HeightCompare);
foreach (Square s in arrayOfSquares)
{
    Console.WriteLine(s.ToString( ));
}

Console.WriteLine( );
Console.WriteLine("Sorted array using IComparable");
Array.Sort(arrayOfSquares);
foreach (Square s in arrayOfSquares)
{
    Console.WriteLine(s.ToString( ));
}

// Test an ARRAYLIST.
Console.WriteLine( );
Console.WriteLine( );
Console.WriteLine("ARRAYLIST");
foreach (Square s in arrayListOfSquares)
{
    Console.WriteLine(s.ToString( ));
}

Console.WriteLine( );
Console.WriteLine("Sorted ArrayList using IComparer=HeightCompare");
arrayListOfSquares.Sort(HeightCompare);
foreach (Square s in arrayListOfSquares)
{
    Console.WriteLine(s.ToString( ));
}

Console.WriteLine( );
Console.WriteLine("Sorted ArrayList using IComparable");
arrayListOfSquares.Sort( );
foreach (Square s in arrayListOfSquares)
{
    Console.WriteLine(s.ToString( ));
}

// Test a SORTEDLIST.
SortedList SortedListOfSquares = new SortedList( );
SortedListOfSquares.Add(0, new Square(1,3));
SortedListOfSquares.Add(2, new Square(4,3));
SortedListOfSquares.Add(1, new Square(2,1));
SortedListOfSquares.Add(3, new Square(6,1));

Console.WriteLine( );
Console.WriteLine( );
Console.WriteLine("SORTEDLIST");
foreach (DictionaryEntry s in SortedListOfSquares)
{
```

Example 3-7. TestSort method (continued)

```
        Console.WriteLine(s.Key + " : " + ((Square)s.Value).ToString( ));
    }
}
```

This code displays the following output:

```
ARRAY
Original array
Height:1  Width:3
Height:4  Width:3
Height:2  Width:1
Height:6  Width:1

Sorted array using IComparer=HeightCompare
Height:1  Width:3
Height:2  Width:1
Height:4  Width:3
Height:6  Width:1

Sorted array using IComparable
Height:2  Width:1
Height:1  Width:3
Height:6  Width:1
Height:4  Width:3

ARRAYLIST
Height:1  Width:3
Height:4  Width:3
Height:2  Width:1
Height:6  Width:1

Sorted ArrayList using IComparer=HeightCompare
Height:1  Width:3
Height:2  Width:1
Height:4  Width:3
Height:6  Width:1

Sorted ArrayList using IComparable
Height:2  Width:1
Height:1  Width:3
Height:6  Width:1
Height:4  Width:3

SORTEDLIST
0 : Height:1  Width:3
1 : Height:2  Width:1
2 : Height:4  Width:3
3 : Height:6  Width:1
```

See Also

See Recipe 3.6; see the "IComparable Interface" topic in the MSDN documentation.

3.6   Making a Type Searchable

Problem

You have a data type that will be stored as elements in an array or an ArrayList. You would like to use the Array.BinarySearch and ArrayList.BinarySearch methods to allow for custom searching of your data types in the array.

Solution

Use the IComparable and IComparer interfaces. The Square class, from Recipe 3.5, implements the IComparable interface in such a way that the Array, ArrayList, and SortedList objects can sort and search an array or collection of Square objects.

Discussion

By implementing the IComparable interface on your class (or structure), you can take advantage of the search routines of the Array, ArrayList, List<T>, and SortedList classes. The algorithms for searching are built into these classes; all you have to do is tell them how to search your classes via the code you implement in the IComparable. CompareTo method.

To implement the CompareTo method, see Recipe 3.5.

The Array, ArrayList, and List<T> classes provide a BinarySearch method to perform a search on the elements in that array. The elements are compared against an object passed to the BinarySearch method in the object parameter. The SortedList class does not have a BinarySearch method; instead, it has the Contains and ContainsKey methods, which perform a binary search on the key contained in the list. The ContainsValue method of the SortedList class performs a linear search when searching for values. This linear search uses the Equals method of the elements in the SortedList collection to do its work. The Compare and CompareTo methods do not have any effect on the operation of the linear search performed in the SortedList class, but they do have an effect on binary searches.

 To perform an accurate search using the BinarySearch methods of the Array and ArrayList classes, you must first sort the Array or ArrayList using its Sort method. In addition, if you pass an IComparer interface to the BinarySearch method, you must also pass the same interface to the Sort method. Otherwise, the BinarySearch method might not be able to find the object you are looking for.

The TestSort method shown in Example 3-8 demonstrates how to use the Square and CompareHeight classes with the Array, ArrayList, and SortedList classes.

Example 3-8. Making a type searchable

```
public static void TestSort( )
{
    Square[] arrayOfSquares = new Square[4] {new Square(1,3),
                                             new Square(4,3),
                                             new Square(2,1),
                                             new Square(6,1)};

    ArrayList arrayListOfSquares = new ArrayList( );
    arrayListOfSquares.Add(new Square(1,3));
    arrayListOfSquares.Add(new Square(4,3));
    arrayListOfSquares.Add(new Square(2,1));
    arrayListOfSquares.Add(new Square(6,1));

    IComparer HeightCompare = new CompareHeight( );

    // Test an ARRAY.
    Console.WriteLine("ARRAY");
    Console.WriteLine("Original array");
    foreach (Square s in arrayOfSquares)
    {
        Console.WriteLine(s.ToString( ));
    }

    Console.WriteLine( );
    Console.WriteLine("Sorted array using IComparer=HeightCompare");
    Array.Sort(arrayOfSquares, HeightCompare);
    foreach (Square s in arrayOfSquares)
    {
        Console.WriteLine(s.ToString( ));
    }

    Console.WriteLine( );
    Console.WriteLine("Search using IComparer=HeightCompare");
    int found = Array.BinarySearch(arrayOfSquares, new Square(1,3), HeightCompare);
    Console.WriteLine("found (1,3): " + found);

    Console.WriteLine( );
    Console.WriteLine("Sorted array using IComparable");
    Array.Sort(arrayOfSquares);
    foreach (Square s in arrayOfSquares)
    {
        Console.WriteLine(s.ToString( ));
    }

    Console.WriteLine("Search using IComparable");
    found = Array.BinarySearch(arrayOfSquares,
                               new Square(6,1), null);  // Use IComparable.
    Console.WriteLine("found (6,1): " + found);

    // Test an ARRAYLIST.
    Console.WriteLine( );
    Console.WriteLine( );
```

Example 3-8. Making a type searchable (continued)

```
Console.WriteLine("ARRAYLIST");
foreach (Square s in arrayListOfSquares)
{
    Console.WriteLine(s.ToString( ));
}

Console.WriteLine( );
Console.WriteLine("Sorted ArrayList using IComparer=HeightCompare");
arrayListOfSquares.Sort(HeightCompare);
foreach (Square s in arrayListOfSquares)
{
    Console.WriteLine(s.ToString( ));
}

Console.WriteLine( );
Console.WriteLine("Search using IComparer=HeightCompare");
found = arrayListOfSquares.BinarySearch(new Square(1,3), HeightCompare);
Console.WriteLine("found (1,3): " + found);

Console.WriteLine( );
Console.WriteLine("Sorted ArrayList using IComparable");
arrayListOfSquares.Sort( );
foreach (Square s in arrayListOfSquares)
{
    Console.WriteLine(s.ToString( ));
}

Console.WriteLine( );
Console.WriteLine("Search using IComparable");
found = arrayListOfSquares.BinarySearch(new Square(6,1), null);
Console.WriteLine("found (6,1): " + found);

// Test a SORTEDLIST.
SortedList SortedListOfSquares = new SortedList( );
SortedListOfSquares.Add(0, new Square(1,3));
SortedListOfSquares.Add(2, new Square(4,3));
SortedListOfSquares.Add(1, new Square(2,1));
SortedListOfSquares.Add(3, new Square(6,1));

Console.WriteLine( );
Console.WriteLine( );
Console.WriteLine("SORTEDLIST");
foreach (DictionaryEntry s in SortedListOfSquares)
{
    Console.WriteLine(s.Key + " : " + ((Square)s.Value).ToString( ));
}

Console.WriteLine( );
bool foundBool = SortedListOfSquares.Contains(2);
Console.WriteLine("SortedListOfSquares.Contains(2): " + foundBool);

foundBool = SortedListOfSquares.ContainsKey(2);
```

Example 3-8. Making a type searchable (continued)

```
Console.WriteLine("SortedListOfSquares.ContainsKey(2): " + foundBool);

// Does not use IComparer or IComparable
// -- uses a linear search along with the Equals method, which has not been
// overloaded; if the Square object were to be used as the key
// rather than the value, a binary search would be performed when searching
// for this Square object.
Square value = new Square(6,1);
foundBool = SortedListOfSquares.ContainsValue(value);
Console.WriteLine
    ("SortedListOfSquares.ContainsValue(new Square(6,1)): " + foundBool);
}
```

This code displays the following:

```
ARRAY
Original array
Height:1  Width:3
Height:4  Width:3
Height:2  Width:1
Height:6  Width:1

Sorted array using IComparer=HeightCompare
Height:1  Width:3
Height:2  Width:1
Height:4  Width:3
Height:6  Width:1

Search using IComparer=HeightCompare
found (1,3): 0

Sorted array using IComparable
Height:2  Width:1
Height:1  Width:3
Height:6  Width:1
Height:4  Width:3
Search using IComparable
found (6,1): 2

ARRAYLIST
Height:1  Width:3
Height:4  Width:3
Height:2  Width:1
Height:6  Width:1

Sorted ArrayList using IComparer=HeightCompare
Height:1  Width:3
Height:2  Width:1
Height:4  Width:3
Height:6  Width:1

Search using IComparer=HeightCompare
found (1,3): 0
```

```
Sorted ArrayList using IComparable
Height:2  Width:1
Height:1  Width:3
Height:6  Width:1
Height:4  Width:3

Search using IComparable
found (6,1): 2

SORTEDLIST
0 : Height:1  Width:3
1 : Height:2  Width:1
2 : Height:4  Width:3
3 : Height:6  Width:1

SortedListOfSquares.Contains(2): True
SortedListOfSquares.ContainsKey(2): True
SortedListOfSquares.ContainsValue(new Square(6,1)): False
```

See Also

See Recipe 3.5; see the "IComparable Interface" and "IComparer Interface" topics in
the MSDN documentation.

3.7   Indirectly Overloading the +=, −=, /=, and *= Operators

Problem

You need to control the handling of the +=, -=, /=, and *= operators within your data
type; unfortunately, these operators cannot be directly overloaded.

Solution

Overload these operators indirectly by overloading the +, -, /, and * operators, as
demonstrated in Example 3-9.

*Example 3-9. Overloading the +, −, /, and * operators*

```
public class Foo
{
    // Other class members...

    // Overloaded binary operators
    public static Foo operator +(Foo f1, Foo f2)
    {
        Foo result = new Foo( );
```

*Example 3-9. Overloading the +, –, /, and * operators (continued)*

```
    // Add f1 and f2 here...
    // place result of the addition into the result variable.

    return (result);
}

public static Foo operator +(int constant, Foo f1)
{
    Foo result = new Foo( );

    // Add the constant integer and f1 here...
    // place result of the addition into the result variable.

    return (result);
}

public static Foo operator +(Foo f1, int constant)
{
    Foo result = new Foo( );

    // Add the constant integer and f1 here...
    // place result of the addition into the result variable.

    return (result);
}

public static Foo operator -(Foo f1, Foo f2)
{
    Foo result = new Foo( );

    // Subtract f1 and f2 here...
    // place result of the subtraction into the result variable.

    return (result);
}

public static Foo operator -(int constant, Foo f1)
{
    Foo result = new Foo( );

    // Subtract the constant integer and f1 here...
    // place result of the subtraction into the result variable.

    return (result);
}

public static Foo operator -(Foo f1, int constant)
{
    Foo result = new Foo( );

    // Subtract the constant integer and f1 here...
    // place result of the subtraction into the result variable.
```

*Example 3-9. Overloading the +, –, /, and * operators (continued)*

```
        return (result);
    }

    public static Foo operator *(Foo f1, Foo f2)
    {
        Foo result = new Foo( );

        // Multiply f1 and f2 here...
        // place result of the multiplication into the result variable.

        return (result);
    }

    public static Foo operator *(int multiplier, Foo f1)
    {
        Foo result = new Foo( );

        // Multiply multiplier and f1 here...
        // place result of the multiplication into the result variable.

        return (result);
    }

    public static Foo operator *(Foo f1, int multiplier)
    {
        return (multiplier * f1);
    }

    public static Foo operator /(Foo f1, Foo f2)
    {
        Foo result = new Foo( );

        // Divide f1 and f2 here...
        // place result of the division into the result variable.

        return (result);
    }

    public static Foo operator /(int numerator, Foo f1)
    {
        Foo result = new Foo( );

        // Divide numerator and f1 here...
        // place result of the division into the result variable.

        return (result);
    }

    public static Foo operator /(Foo f1, int denominator)
    {
        return (1 / (denominator / f1));
    }
}
```

Discussion

While it is illegal to overload the +=, -=, /=, and *= operators directly, you can overload them indirectly by overloading the +, -, /, and * operators. The +=, -=, /=, and *= operators use the overloaded +, -, /, and * operators for their calculations.

The four operators +, -, /, and * are overloaded by the methods in the Solution section of this recipe. You might notice that each operator is overloaded three times. This is intentional, since a user of your object may attempt to add, subtract, multiply, or divide it by an integer value. The unknown here is: which position will the integer constant be in? Will it be in the first parameter or the second? The following code snippet shows how this might look for multiplication:

```
Foo x = new Foo( );
Foo y = new Foo( );
y *= 100;       // Uses:  operator *(Foo f1, int multiplier)
y = 100 * x;    // Uses:  operator *(int multiplier, Foo f1)
y *= x;         // Uses:  operator *(Foo f1, Foo f2)
```

The same holds true for the other overloaded operators.

If these operators were being implemented in a class, you would first check whether any were set to null. The following code for the overloaded addition operator has been modified to do this:

```
public static Foo operator +(Foo f1, Foo f2)
{
    if (f1 == null)
    {
        throw (new ArgumentNullException("f1"));
    }
    else if (f2 == null)
    {
        throw (new ArgumentNullException("f2"));
    }
    else
    {
        Foo result = new Foo( );

        // Add f1 and f2 here...
        // place result of the addition into the result variable.

        return (result);
    }
}
```

See Also

See the "Operator Overloading Usage Guidelines," "Overloadable Operators," and "Operator Overloading Tutorial" topics in the MSDN documentation.

3.8 Indirectly Overloading the &&, ||, and ?: Operators

Problem

You need to control the handling of the &&, ||, and ?: operators within your data type; unfortunately, these operators cannot be directly overloaded.

Solution

Overload these operators indirectly by overloading the &, |, true, and false operators, as shown in Example 3-10.

Example 3-10. Overloading &, |, true, and false

```
public class ObjState
{
    public ObjState(int state)
    {
        this.state = state;
    }

    public int state = 0;

    public static ObjState operator &(ObjState obj1, ObjState obj2)
    {
        if (obj1.state >= 0 && obj2.state >= 0)
            return (new ObjState(1));
        else
            return (new ObjState(-1));
    }

    public static ObjState operator |(ObjState obj1, ObjState obj2)
    {
        if (obj1.state < 0 && obj2.state < 0)
            return (new ObjState(-1));
        else
            return (new ObjState(1));
    }

    public static bool operator true(ObjState obj)
    {
        if (obj.state >= 0)
            return (true);
        else
            return (false);
    }

    public static bool operator false(ObjState obj)
    {
        if (obj.state < 0)
```

Example 3-10. Overloading &, |, true, and false (continued)

```
            return (true);
        else
            return (false);
    }

    public override string ToString( )
    {
        return (state.ToString( ));
    }
}
```

This technique gives you complete control over the operations of the &&, ||, and ?: operators.

Alternatively, you can simply add an implicit conversion to bool:

```
public class ObjState
{
    public ObjState(int state)
    {
        this.state = state;
    }

    public int state = 0;

    public static implicit operator bool(ObjState obj)
    {
        if (obj.state == 0)
        {
            throw new InvalidOperationException( );
        }

        return (obj.state > 0);
    }
}
```

This technique implements strict Boolean logic; the first technique (overriding the &&, ||, and ?: operators) gives you more freedom to stray from implementing strict Boolean logic.

Discussion

While you cannot overload the &&, ||, and ?: operators directly, you can overload them indirectly by overloading the &, |, true, and false operators. The &&, ||, and ?: operators then use the overloaded &, |, true, and false operators for their calculations.

The && operator indirectly uses the false and & operators to perform a short-circuiting AND operation. Initially, the false operator is invoked to determine whether the first object is equal to false. If so, the righthand side of the expression is not evaluated and false is returned. If the false operator returns a true, the & operator is invoked next to perform the ANDing operation on the two objects. This initial test using the false operator enables the operator to short-circuit the operation.

The || operator works the same as the && operator, except that the initial test is done using the true operator rather than the false operator.

The ?: operator requires the overloading of the true operator to be indirectly overloaded. Note that this, in turn, requires the overloading of the false operator for symmetry. The ?: operator takes a conditional expression as input and evaluates either its true or false expression. This operator can be defined as follows:

```
conditional-expression ? true-expression : false-expression
```

The ?: operator invokes the true operator to determine which expression of this operator should be evaluated. Note that if an implicit conversion to bool exists, it will be used in preference to the true operator.

When implementing these operators, you should first check to determine whether any parameters in the overloaded operator methods were set to null. The code for the overloaded & operator has been modified to do this:

```
public static ObjState operator &(ObjState obj1, ObjState obj2)
{
    if (obj1 == null || obj2 == null)
    {
        throw (new ArgumentNullException("Neither object may be null."));
    }

    if (obj1.state >= 0 && obj2.state >= 0)
        return (new ObjState(1));
    else
        return (new ObjState(-1));
}
```

See Also

See the "Operator Overloading Usage Guidelines," "Overloadable Operators," and "Operator Overloading Tutorial" topics in the MSDN documentation.

3.9   Turning Bits On or Off

Problem

You have a numeric value or an enumeration that contains bit flags. You need a method to turn on (set the bit to 1) or turn off (set the bit to 0) one or more of these bit flags. In addition, you also want a method to flip one or more bit flag values; that is, change the bit(s) to their opposite value.

Solution

The following method turns one or more bits on using a bit flag passed in to the bitToTurnOn parameter:

```
public static int TurnBitOn(int value, int bitToTurnOn)
{
    return (value | bitToTurnOn);
}
```

The following method turns one or more bits off using a bit flag passed in to the bitToTurnOff parameter:

```
public static int TurnBitOff(int value, int bitToTurnOff)
{
    return (value & ~bitToTurnOff);
}
```

The following method flips a bit to its opposite value using a bit flag passed in to the bitToFlip parameter:

```
public static int FlipBit(int value, int bitToFlip)
{
    return (value ^ bitToFlip);
}
```

The following method turns one or more bits on using a numeric bit position value passed in to the bitPosition parameter:

```
public static int TurnBitPositionOn(int value, int bitPosition)
{
    return (value | (1 << bitPosition));
}
```

The following method turns one or more bits off using a numeric bit position value passed in to the bitPosition parameter:

```
public static int TurnBitPositionOff(int value, int bitPosition)
{
    return (value & ~(1 << bitPosition));
}
```

The following method flips a bit to its opposite value using a numeric bit position value passed in to the bitPosition parameter:

```
public static int FlipBitPosition(int value, int bitPosition)
{
    return (value ^ (1 << bitPosition));
}
```

Discussion

When a large number of flags are required, and particularly when combinations of flags can be set, it becomes cumbersome and unwieldy to use Boolean variables. In this case, using the binary representation of a number, you can assign each bit to indicate a specific Boolean value. Each Boolean value is called a *bit flag*. For example, you have a number defined as a byte data type. This number is comprised of eight binary bit values, which can be either a 1 or a 0. Supposing you assign a color to each bit, your number would be defined as follows:

```
byte colorValue = 0;  // colorValue initialized to no color

// colorValue    Bit position
// red          0 (least-significant bit)
// green        1
// blue         2
// black        3
// grey         4
// silver       5
// olive        6
// teal         7 (most-significant bit)
```

By setting each bit to 0 or 1, you can define a color value for the colorValue variable. Unfortunately, the colorValue variable does not take into account all colors. You can remedy this by allowing multiple bits to be set to 1. This trick allows you to combine red (bit 0) and green (bit 1) to get the color yellow; red (bit 0) and blue (bit 2) to get violet; or red, green, and blue to get white.

 The colorValue bit mask is defined as a byte. This is because it is more convenient to use unsigned data types for bit flag variables. The other unsigned integers supported by C# are ushort, uint, and ulong. This makes it easier to create the bit mask values to use with the bit flag variable. Simply put, you do not have to worry about negative values of the data type when using unsigned data types. Be aware, though, that the ushort, uint, and ulong types are not CLS-compliant.

Now that you have your bit flags set up in the colorValue variable, you need a way to set the individual bits to a 0 or 1, as well as a way to determine whether one or more bits (colors) are turned on. To do this, you use a *bit mask*. A bit mask is a constant number, usually of the same type as the target type containing the bit flags. This bit mask value will be ANDed, ORed, or XORed with the number containing the bit flags to determine the state of each bit flag or to set each bit flag to a 0 or 1:

```
[Flags]
public enum ColorBitMask
{
    NoColorBitMask = 0,     //binary value == 00000000
    RedBitMask = 1,         //binary value == 00000001
    GreenBitMask = 2,       //binary value == 00000010
    BlueBitMask = 4,        //binary value == 00000100
    BlackBitMask = 8,       //binary value == 00001000
    GreyBitMask = 16,       //binary value == 00010000
    SilverBitMask = 32,     //binary value == 00100000
    OliveBitMask = 64,      //binary value == 01000000
    TealBitMask = 128,      //binary value == 10000000
    YellowBitMask = 3,      //binary value == 00000011
    VioletBitMask = 5,      //binary value == 00000101
    WhiteBitMask = 7,       //binary value == 00000111
}
```

One common use for the & operator is to set one or more bits in a bit flag value to 0. If you AND a binary value with 1, you always obtain the original binary value. If, on the other hand, you AND a binary value with 0, you always obtain 0. Knowing this, you can use the bit mask values to remove various colors from the colorValue variable:

```
ColorBitMask color = ColorBitMask.YellowBitMask;
ColorBitMask newColor = color & ~ColorBitMask.RedBitMask;
```

This operation removes the RedBitMask from the color value. This value is then assigned to the newColor variable. The newColor variable now contains the value 2 (00000010 in binary), which is equal to the GreenBitMask value. Essentially, you removed the color red from the color yellow and ended up with the color green, which is a constituent color of yellow.

The | operator can also be used to set one or more bits to 1. If you OR a binary value with 0, you always obtain the original binary value. If, on the other hand, you OR a binary value with 1, you always obtain 1. Using this knowledge, you can use the bit mask values to add various colors to the color variable. For example:

```
ColorBitMask color = ColorBitMask.RedBitMask;
ColorBitMask newColor = color | ColorBitMask.GreenBitMask;
```

This operation ORs the GreenBitMask to the color value, which is currently set to the value RedBitMask. This value is then assigned to the newColor variable. The newColor variable now contains the value 3 (00000011 in binary); this value is equal to the YellowBitMask value. Essentially, you added the color green to the color red and obtained the color yellow.

The ^ operator is often used to flip or invert one or more bits in a bit flag value. It returns a 1 only when either bit is set to 1. If both bits are set to 1s or 0s, this operator returns a 0. This operation provides a convenient method of flipping a bit:

```
ColorBitMask color = ColorBitMask.RedBitMask;
ColorBitMask newColor = color ^ ColorBitMask.RedBitMask;
```

The code shown here flips the least-significant bit (defined by the RedBitMask operation) to its opposite value. So if the color were red, it would become 0, or no defined color, as shown here:

```
  00000001 == Color (red)
^ 00000001 == RedBitMask
  00000000
```

If you XOR this result a second time with the bit mask RedBitMask, you get your original color (red) back again, as shown here:

```
  00000000 == Color (red)
^ 00000001 == RedBitMask
  00000001 == red
```

If this operation is performed on the color yellow, you can obtain the color other than red that makes up this color. This operation is shown next along with the code.

```
ColorBitMask color = ColorBitMask.YellowBitMask;
ColorBitMask newColor = color ^ ColorBitMask.RedBitMask;

    00000011 == Color (yellow)
  ^ 00000001 == RedBitMask
    00000010 == green
```

 Use the AND (&) operator to set one or more bits to 0.

Use the OR (|) operator to set one or more bits to 1.

Use the XOR (^) operator to flip one or more bits to their opposite values.

See Also

See Recipe 1.4; see the "C# Operators" topic in the MSDN documentation.

3.10   Making Error-Free Expressions

Problem

A complex expression in your code is returning incorrect results. For example, if you wanted to find the average area given two circles, you might write the following expression:

```
double radius1 = 2;
double radius2 = 4;
double aveArea = .5 * Math.PI * Math.Pow(radius1, 2) + Math.PI *
              Math.Pow(radius2, 2);
```

However, the result is always incorrect.

Complex mathematical and Boolean equations in your code can easily become the source of bugs. You need to write bug-free equations, while at the same time making them easier to read.

Solution

The solution is quite simple: use parentheses to explicitly define the order of operations that will take place in your equation. To fix the expression presented in the Problem section, rewrite it as follows:

```
double radius1 = 2;
double radius2 = 4;
double aveArea = .5 * (Math.PI * Math.Pow(radius1, 2) + Math.PI *
              Math.Pow(radius2, 2));
```

Notice the addition of the parentheses; these parentheses cause the area of the two circles to be calculated and added together first. Then the total area is multiplied by .5. This is the behavior you are looking for. An additional benefit is that the expression can become easier to read as the parentheses provide clear distinction of what part of the expression is to be evaluated first. This technique works equally well with Boolean equations.

Discussion

Parentheses are key to writing maintainable and bug-free equations. Not only is your intention clearly spelled out, but you also override any operator precedence rules that you might not have taken into account. In fact, the only way to override operator precedence is to use parentheses (you can use temporary variables to hold partial results, which aids in readability, but can increase the size of the IL code). Consider the following equation:

```
int x = 1 * 2 - -50 / 4 + 220 << 1;
Console.WriteLine("x = " + x);
```

The value 468 is displayed for this equation.

This is the same equation written with parentheses:

```
int y = ((1 * 2) - ((-50) / 4) + 220) << 1;
Console.WriteLine("y = " + y);
```

The same value (468) is also displayed for this equation. Notice how much easier it is to read and understand how this equation works when parentheses are used. It is possible to get carried away with the use of parentheses in an equation:

```
int z = ((((1 * 2) - ((-50) / 4)) + 220) << (1));
Console.WriteLine("z = " + z);
```

This equation also evaluates to 468, but due to the overuse of parentheses, you can get lost determining where one set of parentheses begins and where it ends. You should try to balance your placement of parentheses in strategic locations to prevent oversaturating your equation with parentheses.

Another place where you can get into trouble with operator precedence is when using a ternary operator (?:),defined as follows:

```
boolean-expression ? true-case-expression : false-case-expression
```

Each type of expression used by this operator is defined as follows:

boolean-expression
> This expression must evaluate to a Boolean value or to a value with a type that has an implicit conversion to bool or one that has a true operator. Depending on the outcome of this expression, either the *true-case-expression* or the *false-case-expression* will be executed.

true-case-expression
> This expression is evaluated when the *boolean-expression* evaluates to true.

false-case-expression
> This expression is evaluated when the *boolean-expression* evaluates to false.

Either the *true-case-expression* or the *false-case-expression* will be evaluated; never both.

The ternary operator is able to compact several lines of an if-else statement into a single expression that can fit easily on a single line. This ternary statement is also usable inline with a statement or another expression. The following code example shows the use of the ternary operator inline with an expression:

```
byte x = (byte)(8 + ((foo == 1) ? 4 : 2));
```

By examining the order of operator precedence, you can see that the == operator is evaluated first and then the ternary operator. Depending on the result of the Boolean expression foo == 1, the ternary operator will produce either the value 4 or 2. This value is then added to 8 and assigned to the variable x.

This operator is considered to have *right-associative* properties, similar to the assignment operators. Because of this, you can get into trouble using ternary expressions as expressions within other ternary expressions. Consider the following code:

```
// foo currently equals 1
// Assume that all methods will always return a Boolean true, except for Method3,
// which always returns a Boolean false.
Console.WriteLine(Method1( ) ? Method2( ) : Method3( ) ? Method4( ) : Method5( ));
```

Which methods will be called? If you started evaluating this expression from the left, your expression would essentially look like the following:

```
Console.WriteLine((Method1( ) ? Method2( ) : Method3( )) ? Method4( ) : Method5( ));
```

Notice the extra highlighted parentheses added to clarify how the expression will be evaluated in this manner. The answer that the methods Method1, Method2, and Method4 will be called is wrong. The ternary operators are evaluated from right to left, not left to right, as are most other common operators. The correct answer is that only Method1 and Method2 will be called. Extra highlighted parentheses have been added to this expression, in order to clarify how it is evaluated:

```
Console.WriteLine(Method1( ) ? Method2( ) :
        (Method3( ) ? Method4( ) : Method5( )));
```

This technique will cause Method1 and Method2 to be called in that order. If any of these methods produced side effects, the application might produce unexpected results.

 If you must use nested ternary expressions, make liberal use of parentheses around each ternary expression to clearly specify your intentions.

3.11   Minimizing (Reducing) Your Boolean Logic

Problem

Many times a Boolean equation quickly becomes large, complex, and even unmanageable. You need a way to manage this complexity while at the same time verifying that your logic works as designed.

Solution

To fix this situation, try applying the theorems shown in Table 3-1 to minimize these types of equations.

Table 3-1. Boolean theorems

Theorem ID	Theorem definition
T0	!(!x) == x
T1	x | x == x
T2	x | !x == true
T3 (DeMorgan's Theorem)	!x | !y == !(x & y)
T4	x & x == x
T5	x & !x == false
T6 (DeMorgan's Theorem)	!x & !y == !(x | y)
T7 (Commutative Law)	x | y == y | x
T8 (Associative Law)	(x | y) | z == x | (y | z)
T9 (Distributive Law)	x & y | x & z == x & (y | z)
T10	x | x & y = x
T11	x & y | x & !y = x
T12	(x & y) | (!x & z) | (y & z) == (x & y) | (!x & z)
T13 (Commutative Law)	x & y == y & x
T14 (Associative Law)	(x & y) & z == x & (y & z)
T15 (Distributive Law)	(x | y) & (x | z) == x | (y & z)
T16	x & (x | y) = x
T17	(x | y) & (x | !y) = x
T18	(x | y) & (!x | z) & (y | z) == (x | y) & (!x | z)
T19	x | x | x | ... | x == x
T20	!(x | x | x | ... | x) == !x & !x & !x & ... & !x
T21	x & x & x & ... & x == x
T22	!(x & x & x & ... & x) == !x | !x | !x | ... | !x
T23	(x | y) & (w | z) == (x & w) | (x * z) | (y & w) | (y * z)
T24	(x & y) | (w & z) == (x | w) & (x | z) & (y | w) & (y | z)

In Table 3-1, assume that w, x, y, and z are all variables of type bool. The theorem IDs allow easy identification of which theorems are being used in the Boolean equations that are being minimized in the Discussion section.

Discussion

Simplifying your Boolean logic will benefit your code by making it less cluttered and making its logic clearer and more readily understood. This simplification will lessen the number of potential locations in your logic where bugs can hide and at the same time improve maintainability.

Let's walk through several examples to show how the process of minimizing your logic works. These examples use the three Boolean variables X, Y, and Z. The names have been kept simple so that you can concentrate on minimizing the logic and not have to worry about what the code is trying to do.

The first example uses only the X and Y Boolean variables:

```
if (!X & !Y) {...}
```

From this if statement, you extract the following Boolean logic:

```
!X & !Y
```

Using theorem T6, you can eliminate one operator from this equation:

```
!(X | Y)
```

Now this equation requires only two Boolean operators to be evaluated instead of three. By the way, you might notice that this equation is a logical NOR operation.

The second example uses the X and Y Boolean variables in a seemingly complex equation:

```
if ((!X & Y) | (X & !Y) | (X & Y)){...}
```

From this if statement, you extract the Boolean logic:

```
(!X & Y) | (X & !Y) | (X & Y)
```

Using theorem T11, you can simplify the last two parenthesized expressions, yielding X, and obtain the following:

```
(!X & Y) | X
```

This equation is much simpler than the initial equation. In fact, you reduced the number of operators from seven to three, which is greater than a 2:1 ratio.

Some equations might not seem as if they can be simplified very much, but looks can be deceiving. Let's try to simplify the following equation:

```
(!X & Y) | (X & !Y)
```

Using theorem T24, you can derive the following expression:

```
(!X | X) & (!X | !Y) & (Y | X) & (Y | !Y)
```

Using theorem T2, you can remove the first and last parenthesized expressions:

```
(!X | !Y) & (Y | X)
```

Finally, using theorem T3, you can minimize the equation once again to the following form:

```
!(X & Y) & (Y | X)
```

You were able to remove only a single operator from this equation. This optimization might or might not improve the performance and readability of your code, since it is such a minor change.

You may think that this expression is in its most reduced form. However, if you examine this expression more closely, you may notice that it is the equation for the XOR operator. Knowing this, you can simplify the equation to the following:

```
X ^ Y
```

This technique really shines when you are faced with a large and complex Boolean expression, such as the one shown here:

```
(!X & !Y & !Z) | (!X & Y & Z) | (X & !Y & !Z) | (X & !Y & Z) |
(X & Y & Z)
```

Using theorem T9, you get the following equation:

```
(!X & ((!Y & !Z) | (Y & Z))) | (X & ((!Y & !Z) | (!Y & Z) |
(Y & Z)))
```

Notice that the equation (!Y & !Z) | (Y & Z) is the equivalent of the NOT XOR operation on Y and Z. So you can simplify this equation much further:

```
(!X & !(Y ^ Z)) | (X & ((!Y & !Z) | (!Y & Z) | (Y & Z)))
```

Using theorem T9, once again, you get the following equation:

```
(!X & !(Y ^ Z)) | (X & (!Y & (!Z | Z) | (Y & Z)))
```

Using theorem T2, you get the final equation:

```
(!X & !(Y ^ Z)) | (X & (!Y | (Y & Z)))
```

This equation is much simpler than the original and requires much less processing to evaluate, as well.

 While it is unnecessary in most cases to commit all of these theorems to memory, you should try to understand them all. In addition, memorizing some of the simpler theorems can come in quite handy in many circumstances.

The theorems outlined in this recipe should be complete enough to allow you to play around with minimizing your Boolean equations.

See Also

See the "C# Operators" topic in the MSDN documentation.

3.12 Converting Between Simple Types in a Language-Agnostic Manner

Problem

You need to convert between any two of the following types: bool, char, sbyte, byte, short, ushort, int, uint, long, ulong, float, double, decimal, DateTime, and string. Different languages sometimes handle specific conversions differently; you need a way to perform these conversions in a consistent manner across all .NET languages. One situation in which this recipe is needed is when VB.NET and C# components communicate within the same application.

Solution

Different languages sometimes handle casting of larger numeric types to smaller numeric types differently—these types of casts are called *narrowing conversions*. For example, consider the following Visual Basic .NET (VB.NET) code, which casts a Single to an Integer:

```
' Visual Basic .NET Code:
Dim initialValue As Single
Dim finalValue As Integer

initialValue = 13.499
finalValue = CInt(initialValue)
Console.WriteLine(finalValue.ToString( ))

initialValue = 13.5
finalValue = CInt(initialValue)
Console.WriteLine(finalValue.ToString( ))

initialValue = 13.501
finalValue = CInt(initialValue)
Console.WriteLine(finalValue.ToString( ))
```

This code outputs the following:

```
13
14
14
```

Notice that the CInt cast in VB.NET uses the fractional portion of the number to round the resulting number.

Now let's convert this code to C# using the explicit casting operator:

```
// C# Code:
float initialValue = 0;
int finalValue = 0;

initialValue = (float)13.499;
```

```
finalValue = (int)initialValue;
Console.WriteLine(finalValue.ToString( ));

initialValue = (float)13.5;
finalValue = (int)initialValue;
Console.WriteLine(finalValue.ToString( ));

initialValue = (float)13.501;
finalValue = (int)initialValue;
Console.WriteLine(finalValue.ToString( ));
```

This code outputs the following:

```
13
13
13
```

Notice that the resulting value was not rounded. Instead, the C# casting operator simply truncates the fractional portion of the number.

Consistently casting numeric types in any language can be done through the static methods on the Convert class. The previous C# code can be converted to use the ToInt32 method:

```
// C# Code:
finalValue = Convert.ToInt32((float)13.449);
Console.WriteLine(finalValue.ToString( ));

finalValue = Convert.ToInt32((float)13.5);
Console.WriteLine(finalValue.ToString( ));

finalValue = Convert.ToInt32((float)13.501);
Console.WriteLine(finalValue.ToString( ));
```

This code outputs the following:

```
13
14
14
```

Discussion

All conversions performed using methods on the Convert class are considered to be in a checked context in C#. VB.NET does not have the concept of a checked or unchecked context, so all conversions are considered to be in a checked context—an unchecked context cannot be created in VB.NET. An OverflowException will be thrown in a checked context when a narrowing conversion results in a loss of information. This exception is never thrown in an unchecked context when a narrowing conversion results in a loss of information.

The various conversion methods are listed in Table 3-2.

Table 3-2. Conversion methods on the Convert class

Method	Use
ToBoolean	Convert a type to a bool.
ToChar	Convert a type to a char.
ToString	Convert a type to a string.
ToDateTime	Convert a type to a DateTime.
ToInt16	Convert a type to a short.
ToInt32	Convert a type to an int.
ToInt64	Convert a type to a long.
ToUInt16	Convert a type to a ushort.
ToUInt32	Convert a type to a uint.
ToUInt64	Convert a type to a ulong.
ToByte	Convert a type to a byte.
ToSByte	Convert a type to an sbyte.
ToSingle	Convert a type to a float.
ToDecimal	Convert a type to a decimal.
ToDouble	Convert a type to a double.

Converting between any of the data types listed in Table 3-2 is a simple matter. All of the listed methods are static and exist on the Convert class. Converting one type to another is performed by first choosing the correct method on the Convert class. This method will be named after the type you are converting to (e.g., if you are converting to a char type, the method name would be ToChar). Next, you need to pass the type that will be cast as the parameter to the Convert method. Finally, set a variable of the resultant cast type equal to the return value of the Convert method. The following code converts the value in the variable source—defined as a short that contains a number between 0 and 9—to a char type. This char value is then returned by the Convert method and assigned to the variable destination. The variable destination must be defined as a char:

```
destination = Convert.ToChar(source);
```

Sometimes conversions will do nothing. Converting from one type to that same type will do nothing except return a result that is equivalent to the source variable's value. Take, for example, using the Convert.ToInt32 method to convert a source variable of type Int32 to a destination variable of type Int32. This method takes the value obtained from the source variable and places it in the destination variable.

Some conversions cause exceptions to occur because there is no clear way of converting between the two types; these attempted conversions are listed in Table 3-3. Because some conversions might or might not throw an exception—such as converting from an sbyte to a byte—it is good programming practice to enclose the static conversion method within a try/catch block. The following code wraps a conversion between numeric types in a try/catch block:

```
try
{
    finalValue = Convert.ToInt32(SomeFloat);
}
catch(OverflowException oe)
{
    // Handle narrowing conversions that result in a loss
    // of information here.
}
catch(InvalidCastException ice)
{
    // Handle casts that cannot be performed here.
}
```

The following code wraps a conversion from a string type to an Int32 in a try/catch block:

```
try
{
    finalValue = Convert.ToInt32(SomeString);
}
catch(OverflowException oe)
{
    // Handle narrowing conversions that result in a loss
    // of information here.
}
catch(ArgumentException ae)
{
    // Handle nulls passed into the Convert method here.
}
catch(FormatException fe)
{
    // Handle attempts to convert a string that does not contain
    // a value that can be converted to the destination type here.
}
catch(Exception e)
{
    // Handle all other exceptions here.
}
```

Table 3-3. Cases in which a source-to-destination-type conversion throws an exception

Destination	Source	Exception type
bool	Char DateTime	InvalidCastException
byte	DateTime	InvalidCastException
char	Bool DateTime decimal double float	InvalidCastException

Table 3-3. Cases in which a source-to-destination-type conversion throws an exception (continued)

Destination	Source	Exception type
DateTime	Bool byte sbyte char decimal double short int long ushort uint ulong float	InvalidCastException
decimal	Char DateTime	InvalidCastException
double	Char DateTime	InvalidCastException
short	DateTime	InvalidCastException
int	DateTime	InvalidCastException
long	DateTime	InvalidCastException
sbyte	DateTime	InvalidCastException
float	Char DateTime	InvalidCastException
ushort	DateTime	InvalidCastException
uint	DateTime	InvalidCastException
ulong	DateTime	InvalidCastException
byte	sbyte decimal double short int long ushort uint ulong float	OverFlowException (if source is out of the range of destination)
sbyte	Byte decimal double short int long ushort uint ulong float	OverFlowException (if source is out of the range of destination)

Table 3-3. Cases in which a source-to-destination-type conversion throws an exception (continued)

Destination	Source	Exception type
short	ushort	OverFlowException (if source is out of the range of destination)
ushort	short	OverFlowException (if source is out of the range of destination)
int	uint	OverFlowException (if source is out of the range of destination)
uint	sbyte short int	OverFlowException (if source is out of the range of destination)
long	ulong	OverFlowException (if source is out of the range of destination)
ulong	sbyte short int long	OverFlowException (if source is out of the range of destination)
Any type	string	ArgumentException (if source string is null) or FormatException (if source string represents an invalid value for the destination type)

Notice that the string type can be converted to any type, and that any type may be converted to a string type—assuming that the source string is not null and conforms to the destination type's range and format.

The most insidious problems can occur when a larger type is converted to a smaller type in an unchecked context; the potential exists for information to be lost. Code runs in an unchecked context if the conversion is contained in an unchecked block or if the /checked compiler option is set to false (by default, this compiler option is set to false in both debug and release builds). An example of code contained in an unchecked block is as follows:

```
short destination = 0;
int source = Int32.MaxValue;
unchecked(destination = (short)source);
```

or:

```
unchecked
{
    short destination = 0;
    int source = Int32.MaxValue;
    destination = (short)source;
}
```

A checked context is when the conversion is contained in a checked block or if the /checked compiler option is set to true. An example of code contained in a checked block is as follows:

```
short destination = 0;
int source = Int32.MaxValue;
checked(destination =(short)source);
```

or:

```
checked
{
    short destination = 0;
    int source = Int32.MaxValue;
    destination = (short)source;
}
```

This code throws an OverflowException exception if any loss of information would occur. This allows the application to be notified of the overflow condition and to handle it properly.

The Convert method is always considered to operate in a checked context, even when no other type of checked context wraps the code performing the conversion.

See Also

See the "checked Keyword," "unchecked Keyword," "Checked and Unchecked," and "Convert Class" topics in the MSDN documentation.

3.13 Determining When to Use the Cast Operator, the as Operator, or the is Operator

Problem

You need to determine which operator is best in your situation—the cast (*type*) operator, the as operator, or the is operator.

Solution

Use the information provided in the Discussion section to determine which operator is best to use.

Discussion

Use the cast operator when:

- You are casting a reference type to a reference type.
- You are casting a value type to a value type.
- You are performing a boxing or unboxing conversion.
- You are invoking a user-defined conversion. The is and as operators cannot handle this type of cast.

Use the as operator when:

- It is *not* acceptable for the InvalidCastException to be thrown. The as operator will instead return a null if the cast cannot be performed.
- You are casting a reference type to a reference type.

- You are *not* casting a value type to a value type. The cast operator must be used in this case.
- You are performing a boxing conversion.
- You are *not* performing an unboxing conversion. The cast operator must be used in this case.
- You are *not* invoking a user-defined conversion. The cast operator must be used in this case.
- You are performing a cast to a type parameter T that can be only a reference type. This is because a null may be returned after evaluating this expression.

Use the is operator when:

- You need a fast method of determining whether a cast can be performed before the actual cast is attempted.
- You do not need to actually cast a variable from one data type to another; you just need to determine if the variable can be cast to a specific type.
- It is not acceptable for the InvalidCastException to be thrown.
- You are casting a reference type to a reference type.
- You are *not* casting a value type to a value type. The cast operator must be used in this case.
- You are *not* invoking a user-defined conversion. Unlike the as operator, a compile-time error is not displayed when using the is operator with a user-defined conversion. This is operator will instead always return a false value, regardless of whether the cast can successfully be performed.

See Also

See Recipes 3.14 and 3.15; see the "( ) Operator," "as Operator," and "is Operator" topics in the MSDN documentation.

3.14   Casting with the as Operator

Problem

Ordinarily, when you attempt a casting operation, the .NET Common Language Runtime generates an InvalidCastException if the cast fails. Often, though, you cannot guarantee in advance that a cast will succeed, but you also do not want the overhead of handling an InvalidCastException.

Solution

Use the as operator. The as operator attempts the casting operation, but if the cast fails, the expression returns a null instead of throwing an exception. If the cast succeeds, the expression returns the converted value. The code that follows shows how the as operator is used.

```
public static void ConvertObj(Specific specificObj)
{
    Base baseObj = specificObj as Base;
    if (baseObj == null)
    {
        // Cast failed.
    }
    else
    {
        // Cast was successful.
    }
}
```

where the Specific type derives from the Base type:

```
public class Base {}
public class Specific : Base {}
```

In this code fragment, the as operator is used to attempt to cast the SpecificObj to the type Base. The next lines contain an if-else statement that tests the variable baseObj to determine whether it is equal to null. If it is equal to null, you should prevent any use of this variable, since it might cause a NullReferenceException to be thrown.

Discussion

The as operator has the following syntax:

expression **as** *type*

The expression and type are defined as follows:

expression
> A reference type

type
> The type to which to cast the object defined by *expression*

This operation returns *expression* cast to the type defined by *type* if the cast succeeds. If the cast fails, a null is returned, and an InvalidCastException is not thrown. Because of this, you should always check the result for null.

This operator does not work with user-defined conversions (both explicit and implicit). A user-defined conversion method extends one type to allow it to be converted to another type. This is done by adding a method, such as the following, to a class or structure:

```
public struct MyPoint
{
    public static explicit operator MyPoint(System.Drawing.Point pt)
    {
        // Convert a Point structure to a MyPoint structure type.
        return (new MyPoint( ));
    }
}
```

This method allows a `System.Drawing.Point` structure to be cast to an object of type `MyPoint`. Due to the use of the explicit keyword, the cast must be explicitly defined:

```
System.Drawing.Point systemPt = new System.Drawing.Point(0, 0);
MyPoint pt = (MyPoint)systemPt;
```

If you attempt to use the as operator in a user-defined conversion, the following compiler error is shown:

```
Cannot convert type 'MyPoint' to 'Point' via a built-in conversion
```

This type of conversion does not work with unboxing conversions, either. An unboxing conversion converts a previously boxed value type to its original value type, such as with the following code:

```
int x = 5;
object obj = x;          // Box x
int originalX = obj as int;   // Attempt to unbox obj into an integer.
```

If you attempt to use the as operator in an unboxing conversion, the following compiler error is shown:

```
The as operator must be used with a reference type ('int' is a value type)
```

This is illegal because as indicates that the cast cannot be performed by returning null, but there is no such thing as a null value for an int.

The as operator cannot be used with a type parameter T when T could be a struct, for the same reason as previously mentioned. The following code will not compile:

```
public class TestAsOp<T>
{
    public T ConvertSomething(object obj)
    {
        return (obj as T);
    }
}
```

because T could be anything since it is not constrained. If you constrain T to be only a reference type as shown here:

```
public class TestAsOp<T>
    where T: class
{
    public T ConvertSomething(object obj)
    {
        return (obj as T);
    }
}
```

your code will compile successfully, since T cannot be a struct.

See Also

See Recipes 3.13 and Recipe 3.15; see the "( ) Operator," "as Operator," and "is Operator" topics in the MSDN documentation.

3.15   Determining a Variable's Type with the is Operator

Problem

A method exists that creates an object from one of several types of classes. This object is then returned as a generic object type. Based on the type of object that was initially created in the method, you want to branch to different logic.

Solution

Use the is operator. This operator returns a Boolean true or false indicating whether the cast is legal, but the cast never actually occurs.

Suppose you have four different point classes:

```
public class Point2D {...}
public class Point3D {...}
public class ExPoint2D : Point2D {...}
public class ExPoint3D : Point3D {...}
```

Next, you have a method that accepts an integer value and, based on this value, one of the four specific point types is returned:

```
public object CreatePoint(PointTypeEnum pointType)
{
    switch (pointType)
    {
        case PointTypeEnum.Point2D:
            return (new Point2D( ));
        case PointTypeEnum.Point3D:
            return (new Point3D( ));
        case PointTypeEnum.ExPoint2D:
            return (new ExPoint2D( ));
        case PointTypeEnum.ExPoint3D:
            return (new ExPoint3D( ));
        default:
            return (null);
    }
}
```

where the PointTypeEnum is defined as:

```
public enum PointTypeEnum
{
    Point2D, Point3D, ExPoint2D, ExPoint3D
}
```

Finally, you have a method that calls the CreatePoint method. This method handles the point object type returned from the CreatePoint method based on the actual point object returned:

```
public void CreateAndHandlePoint( )
{
    // Create a new point object and return it.
    object retObj = CreatePoint(PointTypeEnum.Point2D);

    // Handle the point object based on its actual type.
    if (retObj is ExPoint2D)
    {
        Console.WriteLine("Use the ExPoint2D type");
    }
    else if (retObj is ExPoint3D)
    {
        Console.WriteLine("Use the ExPoint3D type");
    }
    else if (retObj is Point2D)
    {
        Console.WriteLine("Use the Point2D type");
    }
    else if (retObj is Point3D)
    {
        Console.WriteLine("Use the Point3D type");
    }
    else
    {
        Console.WriteLine("Invalid point type");
    }
}
```

Notice that the tests for the ExPoint2D and ExPoint3D objects are performed before the tests for Point2D and Point3D. This order will allow you to differentiate between base classes and their derived classes (ExPoint2D derives from Point2D and ExPoint3D derives from Point3D). If you had reversed these tests, the test for Point2D would evaluate to true for both the Point2D class and its derivatives (ExPoint2D).

Discussion

The is operator is a fast and easy method of predetermining whether a cast will work. If the cast fails, you have saved yourself the overhead of trying the cast and handling a thrown exception. If the is operator determines that this cast can successfully be performed, all you need to do is perform the cast.

The is operator is defined as follows:

> *expression* **is** *type*

The expression and type are defined as follows:

expression
    A reference type

type
    The type to which to cast the reference type defined by *expression*

This expression returns a Boolean value: true if the cast will succeed or `false` if the cast will fail. For example:

```
if (SpecificObj is Base)
{
    // It is of type Base.
}
else
{
    // Cannot cast SpecificObj to a Base type object.
}
```

 Never use the is operator with a user-defined conversion (either explicit or implicit). The is operator always returns `false` when used with these types of conversions, regardless of whether the cast can be performed.

This operator does not work with user-defined conversions (both explicit and implicit). Unlike the as operator, a compile-time error will not be displayed; instead, the is operator will always return `false`. This operator should never be used with user-defined conversions, since the result will always be in question. Also, unlike the as operator, the is operator will work with unboxing conversions.

The following code determines whether an unboxing operation can be performed:

```
// An int is passed in to this method and boxed.
public void SomeMethod(object o)
{
    if (o is int)
    {
        // o can be unboxed.
        // It is now possible to cast o to an int.
        int x = (int)o;
    }
    else
    {
        // Cannot unbox o.
    }
}
```

This code first declares an integer variable x and boxes it into an object variable o. The is operator is then used to determine whether o can be unboxed back into the integer variable x. This is the one case in which it is absolutely necessary to use is if you want to avoid an exception. You can't use as here because there is no such thing as a `null` int, so it cannot tell you if the unboxing fails.

See Also

See Recipes 3.13 and 3.14; see the "( ) Operator," "as Operator," and "is Operator" topics in the MSDN documentation.

3.16 Implementing Polymorphism with Interfaces

Problem

You need to implement polymorphic functionality on a set of existing classes. These classes already inherit from a base class (other than `Object`), thus preventing the addition of polymorphic functionality through an abstract or concrete base class.

In a second situation, you need to add polymorphic functionality to a structure. Abstract or concrete classes cannot be used to add polymorphic functionality to a structure.

Solution

In these circumstances, as opposed to those explored in Recipe 3.4, implement polymorphism using an interface instead of an abstract or concrete base class. The code shown here defines two different classes that inherit from `List<T>`:

```
public class InventoryItems<T> : List<T>
{
    // ...
}

public class Personnel<T> : List<T>
{
    // ...
}
```

You want to add the ability to print from either of these two objects polymorphically. To do this, create an interface called `IPrint` that defines a `Print` method to be implemented in a class:

```
public interface IPrint
{
    void Print( );
}
```

Implementing the `IPrint` interface on the `InventoryItems<T>` and `Personnel<T>` classes gives you the following code:

```
public class InventoryItems<T> : List<T>, IPrint
{
    public void Print()
    {
        foreach (T obj in this)
        {
            Console.WriteLine("Inventory Item: " + obj);
        }
    }
}
```

```
public class Personnel<T> : List<T>, IPrint
{
    public void Print()
    {
        foreach (T obj in this)
        {
            Console.WriteLine("Person: " + obj);
        }
    }
}
```

The following two methods, TestIPrintInterface and CommonPrintMethod, show how any object that implements the IPrint interface can be passed to the CommonPrintMethod polymorphically and printed:

```
public void TestIPrintInterface()
{
    // Create an InventoryItems object and populate it.
    IPrint obj = new InventoryItems<string>();
    ((InventoryItems<string>)obj).Add("Item1");
    ((InventoryItems<string>)obj).Add("Item2");

    // Print this object.
    CommonPrintMethod(obj);

    Console.WriteLine();

    // Create a Personnel object and populate it.
    obj = new Personnel<string>();
    ((Personnel<string>)obj).Add("Person1");
    ((Personnel<string>)obj).Add("Person2");

    // Print this object.
    CommonPrintMethod(obj);
}
private void CommonPrintMethod(IPrint obj)
{
    Console.WriteLine(obj.ToString());
    obj.Print();
}
```

The output of these methods is shown here:

```
CSharpRecipes.ClassAndStructs+InventoryItems`1[System.String]
Inventory Item: Item1
Inventory Item: Item2

CSharpRecipes.ClassAndStructs+Personnel`1[System.String]
Person: Person1
Person: Person2
```

Discussion

The use of interfaces is found throughout the FCL. One example is the IComparer interface: this interface requires a class to implement the Compare method, which compares two objects to determine if one is greater than, less than, or equal to another object. This method is used by the `Array`, `ArrayList`, and `List<T>` `Sort` and `BinarySearch` static methods to allow sorting and searching to be performed on the elements contained in an array. For example, if an array contains objects that implement a custom `IComparer` interface, the static `Sort` and `BinarySearch` methods will use this interface to customize their sorting/searching of elements in that array.

Another example is found in the `IEnumerable` and `IEnumerator` interfaces. These interfaces let you iterate over items in a container using the `foreach` loop. It does not matter what the contained items are or what the containing object is. The `foreach` loop can simply use these interfaces regardless of the type of objects that implement them.

In many cases, you will choose to implement polymorphism through abstract base classes, as discussed in Recipe 3.4; however, there are some cases in which interfaces are superior. Interfaces should be considered before abstract base classes in the following cases:

- When several unrelated classes need to implement a common subset of their functionality polymorphically. The Solution to this recipe demonstrates this concept.

- If one or more of the classes already inherits from a base class, an interface may be added to implement polymorphism. In the Solution for this recipe, for instance, the `InventoryItem` class could have inherited from an existing `Item` class. This would make it impossible to use an abstract base class. An interface can be added in this case to implement polymorphism.

- If, in future versions of your data type, you will want to add new polymorphic functionality without breaking the existing interface of your data type. Interface polymorphism provides better versioning than abstract or concrete base classes. To add new polymorphic functionality, implement a new interface containing this functionality on your existing data type.

- When you need to implement polymorphism on value types.

Implementing polymorphism through interfaces works not only on reference types, but also with value types. Value types cannot derive from any other type except `ValueType`; this prevents them from overriding an abstract base class. You must instead use interfaces to implement polymorphism. This can be shown by the following structure declarations:

```
public struct InventoryItems<T> : List<T>, IPrint
public struct Personnel<T> : List<T>, IPrint
```

These structures can act polymorphically on the `IPrint` interface.

These structures now can act polymorphically on the `IPrint` interface. When implementing an interface on a structure, be aware that a boxing operation will be performed whenever the value is cast to the interface type (in this case, the `IPrint` interface). The boxed object is a copy of the original structure. This means that if you modify the boxed object, using a reference to the interface, you will be modifying a copy of the original structure.

See Also

See Recipe 3.4; see the "interface Keyword" topic in the MSDN documentation.

3.17 Calling the Same Method on Multiple Object Types

Problem

You need to perform a particular action on a set of dissimilar objects contained within an array or collection, preferably without having to know each individual object's type.

Solution

Use interfaces in a polymorphic manner. The following interface contains a single method, Sort, which allows sorting to be performed on the object that implements this interface:

```
public interface IMySort
{
    void Sort( );
}
```

The next three classes implement the IMySort interface. These classes all share the same Sort method, but each class implements it in a different way:

```
public class CharContainer : IMySort
{
    public void Sort( )
    {
        // Do character type sorting here.

        Console.WriteLine("Characters sorted");
    }
}

public class NumberContainer : IMySort
{
    public void Sort( )
    {
        // Do numeric type sorting here.

        Console.WriteLine("Numbers sorted");
    }
}
```

```
public class ObjectContainer : IMySort
{
    public void Sort( )
    {
        // Do object type sorting here.

        Console.WriteLine("Objects sorted");
    }
}
```

The SortAllObjects method accepts an array of objects:

```
public void SortAllObjects(IMySort[] sortableObjects)
{
    foreach (IMySort m in sortableObjects)
    {
        m.Sort( );
    }
}
```

If this method is called as follows:

```
Obj.SortAllObjects(new IMySort[3] {new CharContainer( ),
                                   new NumberContainer( ),
                                   new ObjectContainer( )});
```

the following is displayed:

```
Characters sorted
Numbers sorted
Objects sorted
```

Discussion

The foreach loop is useful not only for iterating over individual elements in a collection or an array, but also in iterating over a specific interface implemented by each element in a collection or array. Using this technique, interface members may be used in a similar manner on each element, even if the elements are unrelated object types. Consider the following array of objects:

```
Object[] objs = new Object[6] {new CharContainer( ),
                               new NumberContainer( ),
                               new CharContainer( ),
                               new ObjectContainer( ),
                               new NumberContainer( ),
                               new ObjectContainer( )};
```

This array contains several objects of differing types. The one thread of similarity that runs through each type is the implementation of the IMySort interface, defined as follows:

```
public interface IMySort
{
    void Sort( );
}
```

Passing the Objects array in to the following method allows each Sort method to be called from each object in the Objects array:

```
public void SortAllObjects(object[] sortableObjects)
{
    foreach (IMySort m in sortableObjects)
    {
        m.Sort( );
    }
}
```

The foreach loop in this method is able to treat each object in the sortableObjects array in the same way because each object in the sortableObjects array is cast to its IMySort interface and used as such.

If the foreach loop encounters a sortableObjects array that contains one or more objects that do not implement the IMySort interface, an InvalidCastException will be thrown. To prevent an exception from being thrown, while at the same time allowing the foreach loop to iterate over all elements in the sortableObjects array, you can use the following modified code:

```
public void SortAllObjects(object[] sortableObjects)
{
    foreach (object o in sortableObjects)
    {
        IMySort sortObject = o as IMySort;
        if (sortObject!= null)
        {
            sortObject.Sort( );
        }
    }
}
```

This modified method will now test each element of the sortableObjects array to first determine whether it can be cast to an IMySort interface. If it can be cast to this interface type, the variable sortObject will not be null and the if statement will allow the Sort method on that object to be called.

See Also

See the "interface Keyword," "Base Class Usage Guidelines," and "When to Use Interfaces" topics in the MSDN documentation.

3.18   Adding a Notification Callback Using an Interface

Problem

You need a flexible, well-performing callback mechanism that does not make use of a delegate because you need more than one callback method. So the relationship between the caller and the callee is more complex than can easily be represented through the one method signature that you get with a delegate.

Solution

Use an interface to provide callback methods. The `INotificationCallbacks` interface contains two methods that will be used by a client as callback methods. The first method, `FinishedProcessingSubGroup`, is called when an amount specified in the amount parameter is reached. The second method, `FinishedProcessingGroup`, is called when all processing is complete:

```
public interface INotificationCallbacks
{
    void FinishedProcessingSubGroup(int amount);
    void FinishedProcessingGroup( );
}
```

The `NotifyClient` class shown in Example 3-11 implements the `INotificationCallbacks` interface. This class contains the implementation details for each of the callback methods.

Example 3-11. Implementing the INotificationCallbacks interface

```
public class NotifyClient : INotificationCallbacks
{
    public void FinishedProcessingSubGroup(int amount)
    {
        Console.WriteLine("Finished processing " + amount + " items");
    }

    public void FinishedProcessingGroup( )
    {
        Console.WriteLine("Processing complete");
    }
}
```

The `Task` class shown in Example 3-12 implements its callbacks through the `NotifyClient` object (see Example 3-11). The `Task` class contains a field called `notificationObj`, which stores a reference to the `NotifyClient` object that is passed to it either through construction or through the `AttachToCallback` method. The `UnAttachCallback` method removes the `NotifyClient` reference from this object. The `ProcessSomething` method invokes the callback methods.

Example 3-12. Implementing callbacks with the NotifyClient object

```
public class Task
{
    public Task(NotifyClient notifyClient)
    {
        notificationObj = notifyClient;
    }

    NotifyClient notificationObj = null;

    public void AttachToCallback(NotifyClient notifyClient)
```

Example 3-12. Implementing callbacks with the NotifyClient object (continued)

```
    {
        notificationObj = notifyClient;
    }

    public void UnAttachCallback( )
    {
        notificationObj = null;
    }

    public void ProcessSomething( )
    {
        // This method could be any type of processing.

        for (int counter = 0; counter < 100; counter++)
        {
            if ((counter % 10) == 0)
            {
                if (notificationObj != null)
                {
                    notificationObj.FinishedProcessingSubGroup(counter);
                }
            }
        }

        if (notificationObj != null)
        {
            notificationObj.FinishedProcessingGroup( );
        }
    }
}
```

The `CallBackThroughIFace` method uses callback features of the Task class as follows:

```
    public void CallBackThroughIFace( )
    {
        NotifyClient notificationObj = new NotifyClient( );
        Task t = new Task(notificationObj);
        t.ProcessSomething( );

        Console.WriteLine( );

        t.UnAttachCallback( );
        t.ProcessSomething( );

        Console.WriteLine( );

        t.AttachToCallback(notificationObj);
        t.ProcessSomething( );

        Console.WriteLine( );

        t.UnAttachCallback( );
        t.ProcessSomething( );
    }
```

This method displays the following:

```
Finished processing 0 items
Finished processing 10 items
Finished processing 20 items
Finished processing 30 items
Finished processing 40 items
Finished processing 50 items
Finished processing 60 items
Finished processing 70 items
Finished processing 80 items
Finished processing 90 items
Processing complete

Finished processing 0 items
Finished processing 10 items
Finished processing 20 items
Finished processing 30 items
Finished processing 40 items
Finished processing 50 items
Finished processing 60 items
Finished processing 70 items
Finished processing 80 items
Finished processing 90 items
Processing complete
```

The current Task class shown in Example 3-13 is designed to allow only a single notification client to be used; in many cases, this would be a severe limitation. The Task class could be modified to handle multiple callbacks, similar to a multicast delegate. The MultiTask class is a modification of the Task class to do just this.

Example 3-13. Handling multiple callbacks

```
public class MultiTask
{
    public MultiTask(NotifyClient notifyClient)
    {
        notificationObjs.Add(notifyClient);
    }

    ArrayList notificationObjs = new ArrayList( );

    public void AttachToCallback(NotifyClient notifyClient)
    {
        notificationObjs.Add(notifyClient);
    }

    public void UnAttachCallback(NotifyClient notifyClient)
    {
        notificationObjs.Remove(notifyClient);
    }

    public void UnAttachAllCallbacks( )
    {
```

Example 3-13. Handling multiple callbacks (continued)

```
        notificationObjs.Clear( );
    }

    public void ProcessSomething( )
    {
        // This method could be any type of processing.

        for (int counter = 0; counter < 100; counter++)
        {
            if ((counter % 10) == 0)
            {
                foreach (NotifyClient callback in notificationObjs)
                {
                    callback.FinishedProcessingSubGroup(counter);
                }
            }
        }

        foreach (NotifyClient callback in notificationObjs)
        {
            callback.FinishedProcessingGroup( );
        }
    }
}
```

The `MultiCallBackThroughIFace` method uses callback features of the `MultiTask` class as follows:

```
    public void MultiCallBackThroughIFace( )
    {
        NotifyClient notificationObj = new NotifyClient( );
        MultiTask t = new MultiTask(notificationObj);
        t.ProcessSomething( );

        Console.WriteLine( );

        t.AttachToCallback(notificationObj);
        t.ProcessSomething( );

        Console.WriteLine( );

        t.UnAttachCallback(notificationObj);
        t.ProcessSomething( );

        Console.WriteLine( );

        t.UnAttachAllCallbacks( );
        t.ProcessSomething( );
    }
```

This method displays the following:

```
Finished processing 0 items
Finished processing 10 items
Finished processing 20 items
Finished processing 30 items
Finished processing 40 items
Finished processing 50 items
Finished processing 60 items
Finished processing 70 items
Finished processing 80 items
Finished processing 90 items
Processing complete

Finished processing 0 items
Finished processing 0 items
Finished processing 10 items
Finished processing 10 items
Finished processing 20 items
Finished processing 20 items
Finished processing 30 items
Finished processing 30 items
Finished processing 40 items
Finished processing 40 items
Finished processing 50 items
Finished processing 50 items
Finished processing 60 items
Finished processing 60 items
Finished processing 70 items
Finished processing 70 items
Finished processing 80 items
Finished processing 80 items
Finished processing 90 items
Finished processing 90 items
Processing complete
Processing complete

Finished processing 0 items
Finished processing 10 items
Finished processing 20 items
Finished processing 30 items
Finished processing 40 items
Finished processing 50 items
Finished processing 60 items
Finished processing 70 items
Finished processing 80 items
Finished processing 90 items
Processing complete
```

Another shortcoming exists with both the Task and MultiTask classes. What if you need several types of client notification classes? For example, you already have the

NotifyClient class. What if you add a second class, `NotifyClientType2`, which also implements the INotificationCallbacks interface? This new class is shown here:

```
public class NotifyClientType2 : INotificationCallbacks
{
    public void FinishedProcessingSubGroup(int amount)
    {
        Console.WriteLine("[Type2] Finished processing " + amount + " items");
    }

    public void FinishedProcessingGroup( )
    {
        Console.WriteLine("[Type2] Processing complete");
    }
}
```

The current code base cannot handle this new client notification type. To fix this problem, you can replace all occurrences of the type `NotifyClient` with the interface type INotificationCallbacks. This allows you to use any type of notification client with your Task and MultiTask objects. The modifications to these classes are highlighted in Example 3-14.

Example 3-14. Using multiple notification clients

```
public class Task
{
    public Task(INotificationCallbacks notifyClient)
    {
        notificationObj = notifyClient;
    }

    INotificationCallbacks notificationObj = null;

    public void AttachToCallback(INotificationCallbacks notifyClient)
    {
        notificationObj = notifyClient;
    }

    ...
}

public class MultiTask
{
    public MultiTask(INotificationCallbacks notifyClient)
    {
        notificationObjs.Add(notifyClient);
    }

    ArrayList notificationObjs = new ArrayList( );

    public void AttachToCallback(INotificationCallbacks notifyClient)
    {
        notificationObjs.Add(notifyClient);
```

Example 3-14. Using multiple notification clients (continued)

```
    }

    public void UnAttachCallback(INotificationCallbacks notifyClient)
    {
        notificationObjs.Remove(notifyClient);
    }

    ...

    public void ProcessSomething( )
    {
        // This method could be any type of processing.

        for (int counter = 0; counter < 100; counter++)
        {
            if ((counter % 10) == 0)
            {
                foreach (INotificationCallbacks callback in notificationObjs)
                {
                    callback.FinishedProcessingSubGroup(counter);
                }
            }
        }

        foreach (INotificationCallbacks callback in notificationObjs)
        {
            callback.FinishedProcessingGroup( );
        }
    }
}
```

Now you can use either of the client-notification classes interchangeably. This is shown in Example 3-15 in the modified methods `MultiCallBackThroughIFace` and `CallBackThroughIFace`.

Example 3-15. Using client notification classes interchangeably

```
public void CallBackThroughIFace( )
{
    INotificationCallbacks notificationObj = new NotifyClient( );
    Task t = new Task(notificationObj);
    t.ProcessSomething( );

    Console.WriteLine( );

    t.UnAttachCallback( );
    t.ProcessSomething( );

    Console.WriteLine( );

    INotificationCallbacks notificationObj2 = new NotifyClientType2( );
    t.AttachToCallback(notificationObj2);
```

Example 3-15. Using client notification classes interchangeably (continued)

```
        t.ProcessSomething( );

        Console.WriteLine( );

        t.UnAttachCallback( );
        t.ProcessSomething( );
}

public void MultiCallBackThroughIFace( )
{
    INotificationCallbacks notificationObj = new NotifyClient( );
    MultiTask t = new MultiTask(notificationObj);
    t.ProcessSomething( );

    Console.WriteLine( );

    INotificationCallbacks notificationObj2 = new NotifyClientType2( );
    t.AttachToCallback(notificationObj2);
    t.ProcessSomething( );

    Console.WriteLine( );

    t.UnAttachCallback(notificationObj);
    t.ProcessSomething( );

    Console.WriteLine( );

    t.UnAttachAllCallbacks( );
    t.ProcessSomething( );
}
```

The highlighted code has been modified from the original code.

Discussion

Using an interface mechanism for callbacks is a simple but effective alternative to using delegates. The interface mechanism is only slightly faster than using a delegate since you are simply making a call through an interface.

This interface mechanism requires a notification client (NotifyClient) that implements a callback interface (INotificationCallbacks) to be created. This notification client is then passed to an object that is required to call back to this client. This object is then able to store a reference to the notification client and use it appropriately whenever its callback methods are used.

When using the callback methods on the notificationObj, you should test to determine whether the notificationObj is null; if so, you should not use it or else a NullReferenceException will be thrown:

```
if (notificationObj != null)
{
    notificationObj.FinishedProcessingGroup( );
}
```

Interface callbacks cannot always be used in place of delegates. The following list indicates where to use each type of callback:

- Use a delegate if you require ease of coding over performance.
- Use the interface callback mechanism if you need potentially complex callbacks. An example of this could be adding an interface with a single callback method that will be used to call back into an overloaded method. The number and types of parameters determine the method chosen.
- You need to perform a number of operations, not just a single operation (e.g., calling method1 to do some work, then calling method2 to do some more work, etc.).

See Also

See the "Interface Keyword," "Base Class Usage Guidelines," and "When to Use Interfaces" topics in the MSDN documentation.

3.19 Using Multiple Entry Points to Version an Application

Problem

Some companies reuse the same duplicated, but slightly modified, application, with each version built especially for a particular client or group of clients. Bug fixes as well as testing, adding, and modifying code in each of these code bases can get very confusing as the number of duplicated applications grows. You need a way of managing this increasing complexity.

Solution

Instead of copying the entire application to a different area, modifying the duplicated code, and creating a special build script for it, you could compile the same application (with all modifications included, of course) and use a different entry point based on the client. To do this, add a new class with a new Main entry point method, one for each client or group of clients:

```
public class ClientABC
{
    public static void Main( )
    {
        //Startup/Initialization code for client ABC
    }
}
```

```
public class ClientXYZ
{
    public static void Main( )
    {
        //Startup/Initialization code for client XYZ
    }
}
```

The build scripts can be modified to build the same application using a different entry point that matches up to one or more clients:

```
csc /out:AppABC.exe *.cs /main:ClientABC
csc /out:AppXYZ.exe *.cs /main:ClientXYZ
```

Discussion

It is very difficult to work with several slightly different copies of the same application. If a bug is found and fixed in one application, it must be fixed in all of the copies as well. This can be a time-consuming, error-prone, and arduous task. To make things easier on your coding team, consider using multiple entry points into your application, one for each client or set of clients. Using this technique, you can fix code in one place as opposed to fixing the same bug over multiple applications.

The /main compiler switch controls the class in which the compiler looks for a public static Main method that it can use as an entry point. If the compiler finds a /main switch, the Main method at the location specified in this switch is used as the entry point and all other Main methods in the application are considered as regular methods and nonentry points.

You should note that only one Main entry point method is allowed per class. If two or more are found in a single class, a compiler error will result. You can have entry points in both a nested class and its parent class, as shown here:

```
public class ClientABC
{
    public static void Main( )
    {
        //Startup/Initialization code for client ABC
    }

    public class ClientXYZ
    {
        public static void Main( )
        {
            //Startup/Initialization code for client XYZ
        }
    }
}
```

The /main compiler option would have to be modified in this case to the following:

```
csc /out:AppABC.exe *.cs /main:ClientABC
csc /out:AppXYZ.exe *.cs /main:ClientABC.Clientxyz
```

Also note that if classes `ClientABC` and `ClientXYZ` were nested in a namespace—the `MyCompany` namespace, for instance—the namespace would also have to be added to this compiler switch, as follows:

```
csc /out:AppABC.exe *.cs /main:MyCompany.ClientABC
csc /out:AppXYZ.exe *.cs /main:MyCompany.ClientABC.Clientxyz
```

The `/main` switch can be modified through the Visual Studio .NET Property Pages dialog box. Open this dialog box, then click on the Application tab. On that tab you will see a Startup object drop-down list. The fully qualified class name containing the `Main` method entry point can be entered in this drop-down list.

See Also

See the "/main Compiler Option" and the "Main" topics in the MSDN documentation.

3.20 Preventing the Creation of an Only Partially Initialized Object

Problem

You need to force a client to use an overloaded constructor, which accepts parameters to fully initialize the object, rather than a default constructor, which may not fully initialize the object. Often a default constructor cannot fully initialize an object since it may not have the necessary information to do it. Using a default constructor, the client is required to perform a multistep process; for instance, create the object and then initialize its fields through various properties and/or methods.

Solution

By removing the default constructor and strictly using parameterized constructors, the client is forced to provide the necessary initialization parameters during object creation. The following `Log<T>` class will not initialize its `logStream` field to a `StreamWriter` object on construction:

```
public class Log<T>
    where T: System.IO.TextWriter
{
    private T logStream = null;

    public T LogStream
    {
        get {return (logStream);}
        set {logStream = value;}
    }

    // Use the LogStream field...
```

```
    public void Write(string text)
    {
        logStream.Write(text);
    }
}
```

The C# compiler will automatically create a default constructor that calls the default constructor of its base class, if you omit the constructor for a class. The following modified class will prevent the default constructor from being created:

```
public class Log<T>
    where T: System.IO.TextWriter
{
    public Log(T logStream)
    {
        this.logStream = logStream;
    }

    private T logStream = null;

    public T LogStream
    {
        get {return (logStream);}
        set {logStream = value;}
    }

    // use the LogStream field...
    public void Write(string text)
    {
        logStream.Write(text);
    }
}
```

When a client creates an object from this class, the client is forced to initialize the LogStream field.

Discussion

There is a small problem with not supplying a default constructor. If a class inherits from Log<T> and does not supply a constructor of its own, the C# compiler will produce the rather cryptic error "No overload for method 'Log' takes' '0' arguments." The following class produces this error:

```
public class EnhancedLog<T> : Log<T>
    where T : System.IO.TextWriter
{
    public EnhancedLog (T logStream)
    {
        // Initialize...
    }
}
```

What this means is that Log<T> does not contain a default constructor. The C# compiler automatically adds a call to the base class's default constructor, if you do not specify otherwise. Therefore, the EnhancedLog<T> constructor contains an unseen call (this call can be seen using Ildasm) to the default constructor of the Log<T> class.

This problem can be solved in one of several ways. First, you could simply add a protected default constructor to the Log<T> class. This would prevent the creation of a Log<T> object using the default constructor, but would allow classes inheriting from Log<T> to do so without problems. A second method is to use the base keyword to direct the constructor to call a particular constructor in the base class. The following EnhancedLog<T> class uses the base keyword to call the parameterized constructor of the base Log<T> class, passing in a StreamWriter object:

```
public class EnhancedLog<T> : Log<T>
    where T : System.IO.TextWriter
{
    public EnhancedLog (T logStream) : base(logStream)
    {
        // Initialize...
    }
}
```

A third way to solve this problem is to make the Log<T> class noninheritable by adding the sealed keyword to the class declaration. While this prevents the problem of calling the default constructor, it also prevents others from inheriting from and extending the Log<T> class. For many cases, this third solution is not the best one.

3.21 Returning Multiple Items from a Method

Problem

In many cases, a single return value for a method is not enough. You need a way to return more than one item from a method.

Solution

Use the out keyword on parameters that will act as return parameters. The following method accepts an inputShape parameter and calculates height, width, and depth from that value:

```
public void ReturnDimensions(int inputShape,
                            out int height,
                            out int width,
                            out int depth)
{
    height = 0;
    width = 0;
    depth = 0;

    // Calculate height, width, and depth from the inputShape value.
}
```

This method would be called in the following manner:

```
// Declare output parameters.
int height;
int width;
int depth;

// Call method and return the height, width, and depth.
Obj.ReturnDimensions(1, out height, out width, out depth);
```

Another method is to return a class or structure containing all the return values. The previous method has been modified to return a structure instead of using out arguments:

```
public Dimensions ReturnDimensions(int inputShape)
{
    // The default ctor automatically defaults this structure's members to 0.
    Dimensions objDim = new Dimensions( );

    // Calculate objDim.Height, objDim.Width, objDim.Depth from the inputShape value.

    return (objDim);
}
```

where `Dimensions` is defined as follows:

```
public struct Dimensions
{
    int Height;
    int Width;
    int Depth;
}
```

This method would now be called in this manner:

```
// Call method and return the height, width, and depth.
Dimensions objDim = obj.ReturnDimensions(1);
```

Discussion

Marking a parameter in a method signature with the out keyword indicates that this parameter will be initialized and returned by this method. This trick is useful when a method is required to return more than one value. A method can, at most, have only one return value, but through the use of the out keyword, you can mark several parameters as a kind of return value.

To set up an out parameter, the parameter in the method signature is marked with the out keyword, shown here:

```
public void ReturnDimensions(int inputShape,
                             out int height,
                             out int width,
                             out int depth)
{
    ...
}
```

To call this method, you must also mark the calling method's arguments with the out keyword, shown here:

```
obj.ReturnDimensions(1, out height, out width, out depth);
```

The out arguments in this method call do not have to be initialized; they can simply be declared and passed in to the `ReturnDimensions` method. Regardless of whether they are initialized before the method call, they must be initialized before they are used within the `ReturnDimensions` method. Even if they are not used through every path in the `ReturnDimensions` method, they still must be initialized. That is why this method starts out with the following three lines of code:

```
height = 0;
width = 0;
depth = 0;
```

You may be wondering why you couldn't use a `ref` parameter instead of the out parameter, as both allow a method to change the value of an argument marked as such. The answer is that an out parameter makes the code somewhat self-documenting. You know that when an out parameter is encountered, this parameter is acting as a return value. In addition, an out parameter does not require the extra work to be initialized before it is passed in to the method, which a `ref` parameter does.

 The out parameter was originally designed for marshaling scenarios. An out parameter does not have to be marshaled when the method is called; rather, it is marshaled once when the method returns the data to the caller. Any other type of call (by-value or by-reference using the ref keyword) requires that the value be marshaled in both directions. Using the out keyword in marshaling scenarios improves remoting performance.

3.22 Parsing Command-Line Parameters

Problem

You require your applications to accept one or more command-line parameters in a standard format. You need to access and parse the entire command line passed to your application.

Solution

Use the `ParseCmdLine` class shown in Example 3-16 to help with parsing command-line parameters.

Example 3-16. Parsing command-line parameters

```
using System;
using System.Diagnostics;
```

Example 3-16. Parsing command-line parameters (continued)

```
public class ParseCmdLine
{
    // All args are delimited by tab or space.
    // All double-quotes are removed except when escaped '\"'.
    // All single-quotes are left untouched.

    public ParseCmdLine( ) {}

    public virtual string ParseSwitch(string arg)
    {
        arg = arg.TrimStart(new char[2] {'/', '-'});

        return (arg);
    }

    public virtual void ParseSwitchColonArg(string arg, out string outSwitch,
                                            out string outArgument)
    {
        outSwitch = "";
        outArgument = "";

        try
        {
            // This is a switch or switch/argument pair.
            arg = arg.TrimStart(new char[2] {'/', '-'});

            if (arg.IndexOf(':') >= 0)
            {
                outSwitch = arg.Substring(0, arg.IndexOf(':'));
                outArgument = arg.Substring(arg.IndexOf(':') + 1);

                if (outArgument.Trim( ).Length <= 0)
                {
                    throw (new ArgumentException(
                        "Command-Line parameter error: switch " +
                        arg +
                        " must be followed by one or more arguments.", arg));
                }
            }
            else
            {
                throw (new ArgumentException(
                        "Command-Line parameter error: argument " +
                        arg +
                        " must be in the form of a 'switch:argument}' pair.",
                        arg));
            }
        }
        catch (ArgumentException ae)
        {
            // Re-throw the exception to be handled in the calling method.
            throw;
```

Example 3-16. Parsing command-line parameters (continued)

```
        }
    catch (Exception e)
    {
        // Wrap an ArgumentException around the exception thrown.
        throw (new ArgumentException("General command-Line parameter error",
                                    arg, e));
    }
}

public virtual void ParseSwitchColonArgs(string arg, out string outSwitch,
                                         out string[] outArguments)
{
    outSwitch = "";
    outArguments = null;

    try
    {
        // This is a switch or switch/argument pair.
        arg = arg.TrimStart(new char[2] {'/', '-'});

        if (arg.IndexOf(':') >= 0)
        {
            outSwitch = arg.Substring(0, arg.IndexOf(':'));
            string Arguments = arg.Substring(arg.IndexOf(':') + 1);

            if (Arguments.Trim( ).Length <= 0)
            {
                throw (new ArgumentException(
                        "Command-Line parameter error: switch " +
                        arg +
                        " must be followed by one or more arguments.", arg));
            }

            outArguments = Arguments.Split(new char[1] {';'});
        }
        else
        {
            throw (new ArgumentException(
                "Command-Line parameter error: argument " +
                arg +
                " must be in the form of a 'switch:argument{;argument}' pair.",
                arg));
        }
    }
    catch (Exception e)
    {
        // Wrap an ArgumentException around the exception thrown.
        throw ;
    }
}

public virtual void DisplayErrorMsg( )
```

Example 3-16. Parsing command-line parameters (continued)

```
        {
            DisplayErrorMsg("");
        }

        public virtual void DisplayErrorMsg(string msg)
        {
            Console.WriteLine
                ("An error occurred while processing the command-line arguments:");
            Console.WriteLine(msg);
            Console.WriteLine( );

            FileVersionInfo version =
                        Process.GetCurrentProcess( ).MainModule.FileVersionInfo;
            if (Process.GetCurrentProcess( ).ProcessName.Trim( ).Length > 0)
            {
                Console.WriteLine(Process.GetCurrentProcess( ).ProcessName);
            }
            else
            {
                Console.WriteLine("Product Name: " + version.ProductName);
            }

            Console.WriteLine("Version " + version.FileVersion);
            Console.WriteLine("Copyright " + version.LegalCopyright);
            Console.WriteLine("TradeMarks " + version.LegalTrademarks);

            DisplayHelp( );
        }

        public virtual void DisplayHelp( )
        {
            Console.WriteLine("See help for command-line usage.");
        }
}
```

Discussion

Before command-line parameters can be parsed, a common format must first be decided upon. The format for this recipe follows the command-line format for the Visual C# .NET language compiler. The format used is defined as follows:

- All command-line arguments are separated by one or more whitespace characters.

- Each argument may start with either a - or / character, but not both. If it does not, that argument is considered a literal, such as a filename.

- Each argument that starts with either the - or / character may be divided up into a switch followed by a colon followed by one or more arguments separated with the ; character. The command-line parameter -sw:arg1;arg2;arg3 is divided up into a switch (sw) and three arguments (arg1, arg2, and arg3). Note that there should not be any spaces in the full argument; otherwise, the runtime command-line parser will split up the argument into two or more arguments.

- Strings delineated with double quotes, such as `"c:\test\file.log"` will have their double quotes stripped off. This is a function of the operating system interpreting the arguments passed in to your application.

- Single quotes are not stripped off.

- To preserve double quotes, precede the double quote character with the \ escape sequence character.

- The \ character is handled as an escape sequence character only when followed by a double quote—in which case, only the double quote is displayed.

- The ^ character is handled by the *runtime* command-line parser as a special character.

Fortunately, the runtime command-line parser (for Visual Studio .NET, this would be the CLR) handles most of this before your application receives the individual parsed arguments.

The runtime command-line parser passes a `string[]` containing each parsed argument to the entry point of your application. The entry point can take one of the following forms:

```
public static void Main( )
public static int Main( )
public static void Main(string[] args)
public static int Main(string[] args)
```

The first two accept no arguments, but the last two accept the array of parsed command-line arguments. Note that the static `Environment.CommandLine` property will also return a string containing the entire command line, and the static `Environment.GetCommandLineArgs` method will return an array of strings containing the parsed command-line arguments. The individual arguments in this array can then be passed to the various methods of the `ParseCmdLine` class. Example 3-17 shows how this can be accomplished.

Example 3-17. Passing parameters to the command-line parser

```
[STAThread]
public static void Main(string[] args)
{
    // The application should be initialized here assuming no command-line
    // parameters were found.

    ParseCmdLine parse = new ParseCmdLine( );

    try
    {
        // Create an array of all possible command-line parameters
        // and how to parse them.
        object[,] mySwitches = new object[2, 4] {
                {"file", "output", "trialmode", "debugoutput"},
                {ArgType.Simple, ArgType.Compound, ArgType.SimpleSwitch,
                 ArgType.Complex}};
```

Example 3-17. Passing parameters to the command-line parser (continued)

```
// Loop through all command-line parameters.
for (int counter = 0; counter < args.Length; counter++)
{
    args[counter] = args[counter].TrimStart(new char[2] {'/', '-'});

    // Search for the correct ArgType and parse argument according to
    // this ArgType.
    for (int index = 0; index <= mySwitches.GetUpperBound(1); index++)
    {
        string theSwitch;
        string theArgument;
        string[] theArguments;

        if (args[counter].StartsWith((string)mySwitches[0, index]))
        {
            // Parse each argument into switch:arg1;arg2...
            switch ((ArgType)mySwitches[1, index])
            {
                case ArgType.Simple:
                    theSwitch = args[counter];
                    break;

                case ArgType.SimpleSwitch:
                    theSwitch = parse.ParseSwitch(args[counter]);
                    break;

                case ArgType.Compound:
                    parse.ParseSwitchColonArg(args[counter],out theSwitch,
                                              out theArgument);
                    break;

                case ArgType.Complex:
                    parse.ParseSwitchColonArgs(args[counter],out theSwitch,
                                               out theArguments);
                    break;

                default:
                    throw (new ArgumentException(
                      "Cmd-Line parameter error: ArgType enumeration " +
                      mySwitches[1, index].ToString( ) +
                      " not recognized."));
            }

            // Implement functionality to handle each parsed
            // command-line parameter.
            switch ((string)mySwitches[0, index])
            {
                case "file":
                    // Handle this switch here...
                    break;

                case "output":
```

Example 3-17. Passing parameters to the command-line parser (continued)

```
                            // Handle this switch here...
                            break;

                    case "trialmode":
                            // Handle this switch and its argument here...
                            break;

                    case "debugoutput":
                            // Handle this switch and its arguments here...
                            break;

                    default:
                            throw (new ArgumentException(
                                "Cmd-Line parameter error: Switch " +
                                mySwitches[0, index].ToString( ) +
                                " not recognized."));
                    }
                }
            }
        }
    }
    catch (ArgumentException ae)
    {
        parse.DisplayErrorMsg(ae.ToString( ));
        return;
    }
    catch (Exception e)
    {
        // Handle other exceptions here...
    }
}
```

The ArgType enumeration is defined as follows:

```
enum ArgType
{
    Simple = 0,         // A simple file name with no preceding '/' or '-' chars
    SimpleSwitch = 1,   // A switch preceded by '/' or '-' chars
    Compound = 2,       // A 'switch:argument' pair preceded by '/' or '-' chars
    Complex = 3         // A 'switch:argument{;argument}' pair with multiple args
                        // preceded by '/' or '-' chars
}
```

Passing in the following command-line arguments to this application:

```
MyApp c:\input\infile.txt -output:d:\outfile.txt -trialmode
        /debugoutput:c:\test1.log;\\myserver\history\test2.log
```

results in the following parsed switches and arguments:

```
Literal:    c:\input\infile.txt

Switch:     output
Argument:   d:\outfile.txt
```

```
Switch:        trialmode

Switch:        debugoutput
Arguments:     c:\test1.log
               \\myserver\history\test2.log
```

If you input incorrectly formed command-line parameters, such as forgetting to add arguments to the -output switch, you get the following output:

```
An error has occurred while processing the command-line arguments:
System.ArgumentException: Command-Line parameter error: argument output must be
in the form of a 'switch:argument{;argument}' pair.
Parameter name: output
    at Chapter_Code.ParseCmdLine.ParseSwitchColonArg(String arg,
        String& outSwitch, String& outArgument)
        in c:\book cs cookbook\code\chapter3.cs:line 238
    at Chapter_Code.Class1.Main(String[] args)
        in c:\book cs cookbook\code\main.cs:line 55


CHAPTER_CODE.EXE
Version 1.0.1009.12739
Copyright
TradeMarks
See help for command-line usage.
```

This may be too much output to show to the user; for example, you might not want the entire exception to be displayed. In addition, the last line in the message indicates that you should see the help files for information on the correct command-line usage. It would be more useful to display the correct command-line arguments and some brief information on their usage. To do this, you can extend the ParseCmdLine class and make your own specialized class to use in your application. The SpecializedParseCmdLine class in Example 3-18 shows how this is accomplished.

Example 3-18. Implementing a specialized command-line parser

```
public class SpecializedParseCmdLine : ParseCmdLine
{
    public SpecializedParseCmdLine( ) {}

    public override string ParseSwitch(string arg)
    {
        if (arg.IndexOf(':') >= 0)
        {
            throw (new ArgumentException("Command-Line parameter error: switch " +
                arg + " must not be followed by one or more arguments.", arg));
        }

        return (base.ParseSwitch(arg));
    }

    public virtual void DisplayErrorMsg( )
    {
        DisplayErrorMsg("");
    }
}
```

Example 3-18. Implementing a specialized command-line parser (continued)

```
public virtual void DisplayErrorMsg(string msg)
{
    Console.WriteLine(
        "An error has occurred while processing the command-line arguments:");
    Console.WriteLine( );

    FileVersionInfo version =
            Process.GetCurrentProcess( ).MainModule.FileVersionInfo;
    if (Process.GetCurrentProcess( ).ProcessName.Trim( ).Length > 0)
    {
        Console.WriteLine(Process.GetCurrentProcess( ).ProcessName);
    }
    else
    {
        Console.WriteLine("Product Name: " + version.ProductName);
    }

    Console.WriteLine("Version " + version.FileVersion);
    Console.WriteLine("Copyright " + version.LegalCopyright);
    Console.WriteLine("TradeMarks " + version.LegalTrademarks);

    DisplayHelp( );
}
public override void DisplayHelp( )
{
    // Display correct input args.
    base.DisplayHelp( );

    Console.WriteLine("Chapter_Code [file | /output:projectfile | /trialmode |
                        /debugoutput:file{;file}]");
    Console.WriteLine( );
    Console.WriteLine("Available command-line switches:");
    Console.WriteLine("\tfile        : The file to use as input.");
    Console.WriteLine("\toutput      : The file to use as output.");
    Console.WriteLine("\ttrialmode   : Turns on the trial mode, if present.");
    Console.WriteLine("\tdebugoutput : One or more files in which to dump
                        debug information into.");
    }
}
```

This class overrides four methods of the ParseCmdLine class. The DisplayHelp method is overridden to display the relevant information needed to correctly use the command-line parameters in your application. The overloaded DisplayErrorMsg methods are overridden to prevent the lengthy exception message from being displayed. Finally, the ParseSwitch method is overridden to add some more preventive code that will disallow any arguments from being added to a switch that should not have any arguments. By overriding other methods in the ParseCmdLine class, you can modify this class to handle many other situations specific to your application.

See Also

See the "Main" and "Command-Line Arguments" topics in the MSDN documentation.

3.23 Retrofitting a Class to Interoperate with COM

Problem

An existing C# class needs to be usable by a COM object or will need to be usable sometime in the future. You need to make your class work seamlessly with COM.

Solution

Microsoft has made COM interop quite easy. In fact, you really have to complete only two minor steps to make your code visible to COM:

1. Set the Register for COM interop field in the project properties to `True`. This produces a type library that can be used by a COM client.

2. Use the *Regasm.exe* command-line tool to register the class. For example, to register the type library for the *ClassLibrary1.dll*, you would do the following:

   ```
   regasm ClassLibrary1.dll /tlb:ClassLibrary1.tlb
   ```

By default, this tool will make many decisions for you. For example, new GUIDs are created for your classes and interfaces unless you specify a particular GUID to use. This can be a bad thing; it is usually a good idea to explicitly specify which GUIDs your classes and interfaces are to use. To take control of how your C# code is viewed and used from a COM client, you need to use a few attributes. Table 3-4 contains a list of attributes and their descriptions that can be used to control these things.

Table 3-4. Attributes to control how a COM client views and uses your C# code

Attribute name	Description
`GuidAttribute`	Places a GUID on an assembly, class, struct, interface, enum, or delegate. Prevents the Tlbimp (the type library converter tool, which converts a COM type library into the equivalent metadata) from creating a new GUID for this target.
`ClassInterfaceAttribute`	Defines the class interface type that will be applied to an assembly or class. Valid interface types are:
	`AutoDispatch` An `IDispatch` interface will be exposed for this type. The interface will support only late binding. This is the default.
	`AutoDual` The interface will support both early and late binding.
	None An interface will not be explicitly provided. Therefore, only late-bound access is allowed through an `IDispatch` interface. Note that this is when other explicit interfaces are not defined.

Table 3-4. Attributes to control how a COM client views and uses your C# code (continued)

Attribute name	Description

InterfaceTypeAttribute	Defines how an interface is exposed to COM clients. This attribute may be used only on interfaces. Valid interface types are:
	
	`InterfaceIsDual`
	    The interface will be exposed as a dual interface.
	
	`InterfaceIsIDispatch`
	    The interface will be exposed as a dispinterface.
	
	`InterfaceIsIUnknown`
	    The interface will be exposed as deriving from IUnknown.
	
	If this attribute is not used, the interface will default to being exposed as a dual interface.

ProgIdAttribute	Force the ProgId of a class to a defined string. An automatically generated ProgId consists of the namespace and type name. If your ProgId may exceed 39 characters (i.e., your namespace is equal to or greater than 39 characters), you should use this attribute to manually set a ProgId that is 39 characters or less. By default the ProgId is generated from the full namespace and type name (e.g., `Namespace1.Namespace2.TypeName`).

ComVisibleAttribute	Allows fine-grained control over which C# code is visible to a COM client. To limit the exposed types, set the `ComVisibleAttribute` to `false` at the assembly level:
	
	    `[assembly: ComVisibleAttribute(false)]`
	
	and then set each type and/or member's visibility individually using the following syntax:
	
	    `[ComVisibleAttribute(true)]`
	    `public class Foo {...}`
	
	The `ComVisibleAttribute` was not specified by default in projects created in Visual Studio 2003, but in Visual Studio 2005, the attribute is specified as false in the *AssemblyInfo.cs* file. This hides all types in the assembly from COM by default.

These attributes are used in conjunction with the previous two steps mentioned to create and register the assembly's classes. Several other COM interop attributes exist in the FCL, but the ones mentioned here provide the most basic control over how your assembly is viewed and used by COM clients.

Discussion

The Foo class, defined within the Chapter_Code namespace, shows how these attributes are applied:

```
using System;

namespace Chapter_Code
{
    public class Foo
    {
        public Foo( ) {}

        private int state = 100;
```

```
            public string PrintMe( )
            {
                return("TEST SUCCESS");
            }

            public int ShowState( )
            {
                return (state);
            }

            public void SetState(int newState)
            {
                state = newState;
            }
        }
    }
```

To allow the Foo type to be exposed to a COM client, you would first add an interface, IFoo, describing the members of Foo that are to be exposed. Adding an interface in this manner is optional, especially if you are exposing classes to scripting clients. However, it is recommended since COM is interface-based and you will be able to explicitly control how it is exported. If the AutoDual interface type is used with the ClassInterfaceAttribute, early-bound clients will not need this interface either. Even though it is optional, it is still a good idea to use an interface in this manner.

Next, an unchanging GUID is added to the IFoo interface and the Foo class using the GuidAttribute. The *assembly.cs* file contains a Guid attribute attached to the assembly with a new GUID. A ProgId is also added to the Foo class. Finally, the class interface type is defined as an AutoDispatch interface, using the ClassInterfaceAttribute. The new code is shown here with the changes highlighted:

```
    using System;
    using System.Runtime.InteropServices;

    namespace Chapter_Code
    {
        [GuidAttribute("1C6CD700-A37B-4295-9CC9-D7392FDD425D")]
        public interface IFoo
        {
            string PrintMe( );
            int ShowState( );
            void SetState(int newState);
        }


        [GuidAttribute("C09E2DD6-03EE-4fef-BB84-05D3422DD3D9")]
        [ClassInterfaceAttribute(ClassInterfaceType.AutoDispatch)]
        [ProgIdAttribute("Chapter_Code.Foo")]
        public class Foo : IFoo
        {
            public Foo( ) {}
```

```
        private int state = 100;

        public string PrintMe( )
        {
            return("TEST SUCCESS");
        }

        public int ShowState( )
        {
            return (state);
        }

        public void SetState(int newState)
        {
            state = newState;
        }
    }
}
```

The code to use the exposed C# code from VB6 code using COM interop is shown here:

```
Sub TestCOMInterop( )
    'ClassLibrary1 was created using Regasm in the Solution section
    'of this recipe
    Dim x As New ClassLibrary1.Foo

    MsgBox ("Current State: " & x.ShowState( ))
    x.SetState (-1)
    MsgBox ("Current State: " & x.ShowState( ))
    MsgBox ("Print String: " & x.PrintMe( ))
End Sub
```

The first `Dim` statement creates a new instance of the `Foo` type that is usable from the VB6 code. The rest of the VB6 code exercises the exposed members of the `Foo` type.

There are some things to keep in mind when exposing C# types to COM clients:

- Only public members or explicit interface member implementations can be exposed to COM clients. Explicit interface member implementations are not public, but if the interface itself is public, it may be seen by a COM client.
- Constant fields are not exposed to COM clients.
- You must provide a default constructor in your exposed C# type.
- Parameterized constructors are not exposed to COM clients.
- Static members are not exposed to COM clients.
- Interop flattens the inheritance hierarchy so that your exposed type and its base class members are all available to the COM client. For example, the methods `ToString( )` and `GetHashCode( )`, defined in the base `Object` class, are also available to VB6 code:

    ```
    Sub TestCOMInterop( )
        Dim x As New ClassLibrary1.Foo
    ```

```
        MsgBox (x.ToString( ))
        MsgBox (x.GetHashCode( ))
    End Sub
```

- It is a good idea to explicitly state the GUIDs for any types exposed to COM clients, including any exposed interfaces, through the use of the `GuidAttribute`. This prevents Tlbexp/Regasm from creating new GUIDs every time your interface changes. A new GUID is created by the Regasm tool every time you choose the Build → Rebuild Solution or Build → Rebuild *ProjectName* menu item. These actions cause the date/time of the module (*dll* or *exe*), as well as the version number for your assembly, to change which, in turn, can cause a different GUID to be calculated. A new GUID will be calculated for a rebuilt assembly even if no code changes within that assembly. Not explicitly adding a GUID to your exposed types will cause your registry to greatly expand during the development stage as more new GUIDs are added to it.

- It is also a good idea to limit the visibility of your types/members through judicial use of the `ComVisibleAttribute`. This can prevent unauthorized use of specific types/members that could possibly corrupt data or be used to create a security hole by malicious code.

- Exposed types should implement an interface (for example, `IFoo`) that allows you to specify exactly what members of that type are exposed to COM. If such an explicit interface is not implemented, the compiler will default to exposing what it can of the type.

See Also

See the "Assembly Registration Tool (Regasm.exe)," "Type Library Exporter (Tlbexp. exe)," "Type Library Importer (Tlbimp.exe)," and "Assembly to Type Library Conversion Summary" topics in the MSDN documentation.

3.24 Initializing a Constant Field at Runtime

Problem

A field marked as const can be initialized only at compile time. You need to initialize a field to a valid value at runtime, not at compile time. This field must then act as if it were a constant field for the rest of the application's life.

Solution

You have two choices when declaring a constant value in your code. You can use a readonly field or a const field. Each has its own strengths and weaknesses. However, if you need to initialize a constant field at runtime, you must use a readonly field:

```
public class Foo
{
    public readonly int bar;

    public Foo( ) {}

    public Foo(int constInitValue)
    {
        bar = constInitValue;
    }

    // Rest of class...
}
```

This is not possible using a const field. A const field can be initialized only at compile time:

```
public class Foo
{
    public const int bar;        // This line causes a compile-time error.

    public Foo( ) {}

    public Foo(int constInitValue)
    {
        bar = constInitValue;    // This line also causes a compile-time error.
    }

    // Rest of class...
}
```

Discussion

A readonly field allows initialization to take place only in the constructor at runtime, whereas a const field must be initialized at compile time. Therefore, implementing a readonly field is the only way to allow a field that must be constant to be initialized at runtime.

There are only two ways to initialize a readonly field. The first is by adding an initializer to the field itself:

```
public readonly int bar = 100;
```

The second way is to initialize the readonly field through a constructor. This is demonstrated through the code in the Solution to this recipe.

If you look at the following class:

```
public class Foo
{
        public readonly int x;
        public const int y = 1;

        public Foo( ) {}
```

```
        public Foo(int roInitValue)
        {
            x = roInitValue;
        }

        // Rest of class...
    }
```

You'll see it is compiled into the following IL:

```
.class public auto ansi beforefieldinit Foo
    extends [mscorlib]System.Object
{
.field public static literal int32 y = int32(0x00000001)  //<<-- const field
.field public initonly int32 x                            //<<-- readonly field
.method public hidebysig specialname rtspecialname
        instance void  .ctor(int32 input) cil managed
{
    // Code size       14 (0xe)
    .maxstack  8
//001659:           }
//001660: }

//001666: public class Foo
//001667: {
//001668:           public readonly int x;
//001669:           public const int y = 1;
//001670:
//001671:           public Foo(int roInitValue)
    IL_0000:  ldarg.0
    IL_0001:  call          instance void [mscorlib]System.Object::.ctor( )
//001672:           {
//001673:                   x = input;
    IL_0006:  ldarg.0
    IL_0007:  ldarg.1
    IL_0008:  stfld         int32 Foo::x
//001674           }
    IL_000d:  ret
} // End of method Foo::.ctor

} // End of class Foo
```

Notice that a const field is compiled into a static field, and a readonly field is compiled into an instance field. Therefore, you need only a class name to access a const field.

A common argument against using const fields is that they do not version as well as readonly fields. If you rebuild a component that defines a const field and the value of that const changes in a later version, any other components that were built against the old version won't pick up the new value.

The following code shows how to use an instance readonly field:

```
Foo obj1 = new Foo(100);
Console.WriteLine(obj1.bar);
```

Those two lines compile into the following IL:

```
IL_0013:  ldc.i4      0xc8
IL_0018:  newobj      instance void Foo::.ctor(int32)
IL_001d:  stloc.1
IL_001e:  ldloc.1
IL_001f:  ldfld       int32 Foo::bar
```

Since the const field is already compiled into the application as a static member field, only one simple IL instruction is needed to use this const field at any point in the application:

```
IL_0029:  ldc.i4.1
```

Notice that the compiler compiled away the const field and uses the value it was initialized to, which is 1. This is faster than using a readonly field. However, const fields are inflexible as far as versioning is concerned.

See Also

See the "const" and "readonly" keywords in the MSDN documentation.

3.25 Writing Code That Is Compatible with the Widest Range of Managed Languages

Problem

You need to make sure your C# code will interoperate with all other managed languages that are CLS-compliant consumers, such as VB.NET.

Solution

Mark the assembly with the CLSCompliantAttribute:

```
[assembly: CLSCompliantAttribute(true)]
```

Discussion

By default, your C# assemblies created with VS.NET are not marked with the CLSCompliantAttribute. This does not mean that the assembly will not work in the managed environment. It means that this assembly may use elements that are not recognized by other CLS–compliant languages. For example, unsigned numeric types are not recognized by all managed languages, but they can be used in the C# language. The problem occurs when C# returns an unsigned data type, such as uint, through either a return value or a parameter to a calling component in another language that does not recognize unsigned data types—VB.NET is one example.

CLS compliance is enforced only on types/members marked public or protected. This makes sense because components written in other languages will be able to use only the public or protected types/members of components written in C#.

Marking your assembly as CLS-compliant means that any CLS-compliant language will be able to seamlessly interoperate with your code; that is, it enables CLS compliance checking. This makes it much easier on developers to catch problems before they manifest themselves, especially in an environment in which multiple managed languages are being used on a single project. Marking your entire assembly to be CLS-compliant is done with the following line of code:

```
[assembly: CLSCompliantAttribute(true)]
```

Sometimes you just can't be 100 percent CLS compliant, but you don't want to have to throw away the benefit of compiler checking for the 99.9 percent of your methods that are CLS compliant just so you can expose one method that is not. To mark these types or members as not being CLS compliant, use the following attribute:

```
[CLSCompliantAttribute(false)]
```

By passing a value of false to this constructor's isCompliant parameter, you prevent any type/member marked as such from causing compiler errors due to non-CLS-compliant code.

Many types/members in the FCL are not CLS compliant. This is not a problem when using C# to interact with the FCL. However, this is a problem for other languages. To solve this dilemma, the authors of the FCL usually included a CLS-compliant type/member where possible to mirror the non-CLS-compliant type/member.

The following is a list of some of the things that can be done to make code non-CLS-compliant when using the C# language:

- Two identifiers with the same name that differ only by case
- Using unsigned data types (byte, ushort, uint, ulong)
- Use of the UIntPtr type exposed through a public or protected member
- Any public or protected member that exposes boxed value types
- The use of operator overloading
- An array of non-CLS-compliant types, such as unsigned data types
- An enumeration type having a non-CLS-compliant underlying data type

See Also

See the "CLSCompliantAttribute Class" topic in the MSDN documentation.

3.26 Building Cloneable Classes

Problem

You need a method of performing a shallow cloning operation, a deep cloning operation, or both on a data type that may also reference other types.

Solution

Shallow copying means that the copied object's fields will reference the same objects as the original object. To allow shallow copying, add the following Clone method to your class:

```
using System;
using System.Collections;
using System.Collections.Generic;


public class ShallowClone : ICloneable
{
    public int data = 1;
    public List<string> listData = new List<string>();
    public object objData = new object();

    public object Clone()
    {
        return (this.MemberwiseClone());
    }
}
```

Deep copying or *cloning* means that the copied object's fields will reference new copies of the original object's fields. This method of copying is more time-consuming than the shallow copy. To allow deep copying, add the following Clone method to your class:

```
using System;
using System.Collections;
using System.Collections.Generic;
using System.Runtime.Serialization.Formatters.Binary;
using System.IO;

[Serializable]
public class DeepClone : ICloneable
{
    public int data = 1;
    public List<string> listData = new List<string>();
    public object objData = new object();

    public object Clone()
    {
        BinaryFormatter BF = new BinaryFormatter();
        MemoryStream memStream = new MemoryStream();
```

```
        BF.Serialize(memStream, this);
        memStream.Position = 0;

        return (BF.Deserialize(memStream));
    }
}
```

Add an overloaded Clone method to your class to allow for deep or shallow copying. This method allows you to decide at runtime how your object will be copied. The code might appear as follows:

```
using System;
using System.Collections;
using System.Collections.Generic;
using System.Runtime.Serialization.Formatters.Binary;
using System.IO;

[Serializable]
public class MultiClone : ICloneable
{
    public int data = 1;
    public List<string> listData = new List<string>();
    public object objData = new object();

    public object Clone(bool doDeepCopy)
    {
        if (doDeepCopy)
        {
            BinaryFormatter BF = new BinaryFormatter();
            MemoryStream memStream = new MemoryStream();

            BF.Serialize(memStream, this);
            memStream.Position = 0;

            return (BF.Deserialize(memStream));
        }
        else
        {
            return (this.MemberwiseClone());
        }
    }

    public object Clone()
    {
        return (Clone(false));
    }
}
```

Discussion

Cloning is the ability to make an exact copy (a clone) of an instance of a type. Cloning may take one of two forms: a shallow copy or a deep copy. Shallow copying is relatively easy. It involves copying the object that the Clone method was called on.

The reference type fields in the original object are copied over, as are the value-type fields. This means that if the original object contains a field of type `StreamWriter`, for instance, the cloned object will point to this same instance of the original object's `StreamWriter`; a new object is not created.

 There is no need to deal with `static` fields when performing a cloning operation. There is only one memory location reserved for each static field per class, per application domain. Besides, the cloned object will have access to the same static fields as the original.

Support for shallow copying is implemented by the `MemberwiseClone` method of the `Object` class, which serves as the base class for all .NET classes. So the following code allows a shallow copy to be created and returned by the `Clone` method:

```
public object Clone( )
{
    return (this.MemberwiseClone( ));
}
```

Making a deep copy is the second way of cloning an object. A deep copy will make a copy of the original object just as the shallow copy does. However, a deep copy will also make separate copies of each reference type field in the original object. Therefore, if the original object contains a `StreamWriter` type field, the cloned object will also contain a `StreamWriter` type field, but the cloned object's `StreamWriter` field will point to a new `StreamWriter` object, not the original object's `StreamWriter` object.

Support for deep copying is not automatically provided by the `Clone` method or the .NET Framework. Instead, the following code illustrates an easy way of implementing a deep copy:

```
BinaryFormatter BF = new BinaryFormatter( );
MemoryStream memStream = new MemoryStream( );

BF.Serialize(memStream, this);
memStream.Flush( );
memStream.Position = 0;

return (BF.Deserialize(memStream));
```

Basically, the original object is serialized out to a memory stream using binary serialization, then it is deserialized into a new object, which is returned to the caller. Note that it is important to reposition the memory stream pointer back to the start of the stream before calling the `Deserialize` method; otherwise, an exception indicating that the serialized object contains no data will be thrown.

Performing a deep copy using object serialization allows the underlying object to be changed without having to modify the code that performs the deep copy. If you performed the deep copy by hand, you'd have to make a new instance of all the instance fields of the original object and copy them over to the cloned object. This is a tedious chore in and of itself. If a change is made to the fields of the object being cloned, the deep copy code must also change to reflect this modification. Using serialization, you rely on the serializer to dynamically find and serialize all fields contained in the object. If the object is modified, the serializer will still make a deep copy without any code modifications.

One reason you might want to do a deep copy by hand is that the serialization technique presented in this recipe works properly only when everything in your object is serializable. Of course, manual cloning doesn't always help there either—some objects are just inherently noncloneable. Suppose you have a network management application in which an object represents a particular printer on your network. What's it supposed to do when you clone it? Fax a purchase order for a new printer?

One problem inherent with deep copying is performing a deep copy on a nested data structure with circular references. This recipe manages to make it possible to deal with circular references, although it's a tricky problem. So, in fact, you don't need to avoid circular references if you are using this recipe.

See Also

See the "ICloneable Interface" and "Object.MemberwiseClone Method" topics in the MSDN documentation.

3.27   Assuring an Object's Disposal

Problem

You require a way to always have the Dispose method of an object called when that object's work is done or it goes out of scope.

Solution

Use the using statement:

```
using System;
using System.IO;

// ...

using(FileStream FS = new FileStream("Test.txt", FileMode.Create))
{
    FS.WriteByte((byte)1);
    FS.WriteByte((byte)2);
    FS.WriteByte((byte)3);

    using(StreamWriter SW = new StreamWriter(FS))
    {
        SW.WriteLine("some text.");
    }
}
```

Discussion

The using statement is very easy to use and saves you the hassle of writing extra code. If the Solution had not used the using statement, it would look like this:

```
FileStream FS = new FileStream("Test.txt", FileMode.Create);
try
{
    FS.WriteByte((byte)1);
    FS.WriteByte((byte)2);
    FS.WriteByte((byte)3);

    StreamWriter SW = new StreamWriter(FS);
    try
    {
        SW.WriteLine("some text.");
    }
    finally
    {
        if (SW != null)
        {
            ((IDisposable)SW).Dispose( );
        }
    }
}
finally
{
    if (FS != null)
    {
        ((IDisposable)FS).Dispose( );
    }
}
```

Several points to note about the using statement:

- There is a using directive, such as

  ```
  using System.IO;
  ```

  which should be differentiated from the using statement. This is potentially confusing to developers first getting into this language.

- The variable(s) defined in the using statement clause must all be of the same type, and they must have an initializer. However, you are allowed multiple using statements in front of a single code block, so this isn't a significant restriction.

- Any variables defined in the using clause are considered read-only in the body of the using statement. This prevents a developer from inadvertently switching the variable to refer to a different object and causing problems when an attempt is made to dispose of the object that the variable initially referenced.

- The variable should not be declared outside of the using block and then initialized inside of the using clause.

This last point is described by the following code:

```
FileStream FS;
using(FS = new FileStream("Test.txt", FileMode.Create))
{
    FS.WriteByte((byte)1);
    FS.WriteByte((byte)2);
    FS.WriteByte((byte)3);

    using(StreamWriter SW = new StreamWriter(FS))
    {
        SW.WriteLine("some text.");
    }
}
```

For this example code, you will not have a problem. But consider that the variable FS is usable outside of the using block. Essentially, you could revisit this code and modify it as follows:

```
FileStream FS;
using(FS = new FileStream("Test.txt", FileMode.Create))
{
    FS.WriteByte((byte)1);
    FS.WriteByte((byte)2);
    FS.WriteByte((byte)3);

    using(StreamWriter SW = new StreamWriter(FS))
    {
        SW.WriteLine("some text.");
    }
}
FS.WriteByte((byte)4);
```

This code compiles but throws an `ObjectDisposedException` on the last line of this code snippet because the `Dispose` method has already been called on the `FS` object. The object has not yet been collected at this point and still remains in memory in the disposed state.

See Also

See Recipes 3.29 and 3.31; see the "IDispose Interface," "Using foreach with Collections," and "Implementing Finalize and Dispose to Clean up Unmanaged Resources" topics in the MSDN documentation.

3.28   Releasing a COM Object Through Managed Code

Problem

You need to release a COM object from managed code without forcing a garbage collection to occur.

Solution

Use the static `ReleaseComObject` method of the `Marshal` class:

```
int newRefCount = System.Runtime.InteropServices.Marshal.ReleaseComObject(COMObj);
```

where *COMObj* is a reference to the runtime callable wrapper (RCW) of a COM object.

Discussion

If the COM object is holding on to resources that need to be released in a timely manner, you will want to decrement the reference count on the COM object as soon as possible after you've finished using the COM object and have set it to `null`. The garbage collector needs to run in order to collect the unreferenced Runtime Callable Wrapper (RCW) around your COM object, thereby decrementing the reference count on the COM object. Unfortunately, there is no guarantee that the garbage collector will run in order to collect the RCW anytime in the near future.

To solve this problem, you could call `GC.Collect` yourself to try to free the RCW, but this might be overkill. Instead, use the `ReleaseComObject` method to manually force the RCW to decrement its reference count on the COM object without having to force a collection to occur.

The static `ReleaseComObject` method returns an `int` indicating the current reference count contained in the RCW object after this method has finished decrementing its reference count. Remember that this method decrements the reference count contained in the RCW, not the COM object's reference count. When the RCW reference count goes to zero, it releases its COM object.

Care must be used when calling the `ReleaseComObject` method. Misuse of this method can cause a COM object to be released by the RCW too early. Since the `ReleaseComObject` method decrements the reference count in the RCW, you should call it no more than one time for every object that contains a pointer to the RCW. Calling it multiple times might cause the RCW to release the COM object earlier than expected. Any attempt to use a reference to an RCW that has had its reference count decremented to zero results in a `NullReferenceException` exception. The RCW might not have been collected yet, but its reference to the COM object has been terminated.

See Also

See Recipes 3.28 and 3.31; see the "Marshal.ReleaseComObject Method" topic in the MSDN documentation.

3.29 Creating an Object Cache

Problem

Your application creates many objects that are expensive to create and/or have a large memory footprint—for instance, objects that are populated with data from a database or a web service upon their creation. These objects are used throughout a large portion of the application's lifetime. You need a way to not only enhance the performance of these objects—and as a result, your application—but also to use memory more efficiently.

Solution

Create an object cache to keep these objects in memory as long as possible, without tying up valuable heap space and possibly resources. Since cached objects may be reused at a later time, you also forego the process of having to create similar objects many times.

You can reuse the ASP.NET cache that is located in the `System.Web.Caching` namespace, or you can build your own lightweight caching mechanism. The See Also section at the end of this recipe provides several Microsoft resources that show you how to use the ASP.NET cache to cache your own objects. However, the ASP.NET cache is very complex and may have a nontrivial overhead associated with it, so using a lightweight caching mechanism like the one shown here is a viable alternative.

The `ObjCache<T,U>` class shown in Example 3-19 represents a type that allows the caching of any type of object defined by parameter type `U` with a key defined by parameter type `T`.

Example 3-19. Implementing a generic object cache

```
using System;
using System.Collections;
using System.Collections.Generic;


public class ObjCache<T, U>
    where U: new( )
{
    // Constructors
    public ObjCache( )
    {
        cache = new Dictionary<T, WeakReference>( );
    }

    public ObjCache(int initialCapacity)
    {
        cache = new Dictionary<T, WeakReference>(initialCapacity);
    }
```

Example 3-19. Implementing a generic object cache (continued)

```csharp
// Fields
private Dictionary<T, WeakReference> cache = null;

// Methods
public U this[T key]
{
    get
    {
        if (!cache.ContainsKey(key) || !IsObjAlive(ref key))
        {
            this[key] = new U( );
        }

        return ((U)((WeakReference)cache[key]).Target);
    }

    set
    {
        WeakReference WR = new WeakReference(value, false);
    }
}

public bool IsObjAlive(ref T key)
{
    if (cache.ContainsKey(key))
    {
        return (((WeakReference)cache[key]).IsAlive);
    }
    else
    {
        return (false);
    }
}

public int AliveObjsInCache( )
{
    int count = 0;

    foreach (KeyValuePair<T, WeakReference> item in cache)
    {
        if (((WeakReference)item.Value).IsAlive)
        {
            count++;
        }
    }

    return (count);
}

public bool DoesKeyExist(T key)
{
    return (cache.ContainsKey(key));
}
```

Example 3-19. Implementing a generic object cache (continued)

```
public bool DoesObjExist(WeakReference obj)
{
    return (cache.ContainsValue(obj));
}

public int TotalCacheSlots()
{
    return (cache.Count);
}
}
```

 The SomeComplexObj class can be replaced with any type of class you choose. For this recipe, you will use this class, but for your code, you can change it to whatever class or structure type you need.

The SomeComplexObj is defined here (realistically, this would be a much more complex object to create and use; however, for the sake of brevity, this class is written as simply as possible):

```
public class SomeComplexObj
{
    public SomeComplexObj( ) {}

    private int idcode = -1;

    public int IDCode
    {
        set{idcode = value;}
        get{return (idcode);}
    }
}
```

ObjCache<T,U>, the caching object used in this recipe, makes use of a Dictionary<T,WeakReference> object to hold all cached objects. This Dictionary<T,WeakReference> allows for fast lookup when retrieving objects and generally for fast insertion and removal times. The Dictionary<T,WeakReference> object used by this class is defined as a private field and is initialized through its overloaded constructors.

Developers using this class will mainly be adding and retrieving objects from this object. The indexer implements both the adding and retrieval mechanisms for this class. This method returns a cached object if its key exists in the Dictionary<T,WeakReference> and the WeakReference object is considered to be alive. An object that the WeakReference type refers to has not been garbage-collected. The WeakReference type can remain alive long after the object to which it referred is gone. An indication of whether this WeakReference object is alive is obtained through the read-only IsAlive property of the WeakReference object. This property returns a bool indicating whether this object is alive (true) or not (false). When an object is not alive or when its key does not exist in the Dictionary<T,WeakReference>, this method creates a new object with the same key as the one passed in to the indexer and adds it to the Dictionary<T,WeakReference>.

The indexer also implements the mechanism to add objects to the cache. This method creates a WeakReference object that will hold a weak reference to your object of type U. Each object of type U in the cache is contained within a WeakReference object. This is the core of the caching mechanism used in this recipe. A WeakReference that references an object (its target) allows that object to later be referenced. When the target of the WeakReference object is also referenced by a strong (i.e., normal) reference, the garbage collector cannot collect the target object. But if no references are made to the target stored in this WeakReference object, the garbage collector can collect this object to make room in the managed heap for new objects.

After creating the WeakReference object, the Dictionary<T,WeakReference> is searched for the same key of type T that you want to add. If an object with that key exists, it is overwritten with the new object; otherwise, the Add method of the Dictionary<T,WeakReference> class is called.

Quite a bit of extra work is required in the calling code to support a cache of heterogeneous objects. More responsibility is placed on the user of this cache object, which can quickly lead to usability and maintenance problems if not written correctly.

The code to exercise the ObjCache<T,U> class is shown in Example 3-20.

Example 3-20. Using the ObjCache class

```
// Create the cache here.
static ObjCache<string, SomeComplexObj> OC = new ObjCache<string, SomeComplexObj>();

public void TestObjCache()
{
    OC["ID1"] = new SomeComplexObj();
    OC["ID2"] = new SomeComplexObj();
    OC["ID3"] = new SomeComplexObj();
    OC["ID4"] = new SomeComplexObj();
    OC["ID5"] = new SomeComplexObj();

    Console.WriteLine("\r\n--> Add 5 weak references");
    Console.WriteLine("OC.TotalCacheSlots = " + OC.TotalCacheSlots());
    Console.WriteLine("OC.AliveObjsInCache = " + OC.AliveObjsInCache());

    ////////////// BEGIN COLLECT //////////////
    GC.Collect();
    GC.WaitForPendingFinalizers();
    //////////////  END COLLECT  //////////////


    Console.WriteLine("\r\n--> Collect all weak references");
    Console.WriteLine("OC.TotalCacheSlots = " + OC.TotalCacheSlots());
    Console.WriteLine("OC.AliveObjsInCache = " + OC.AliveObjsInCache());
```

Example 3-20. Using the ObjCache class (continued)

```
        OC["ID1"] = new SomeComplexObj();
        OC["ID2"] = new SomeComplexObj();
        OC["ID3"] = new SomeComplexObj();
        OC["ID4"] = new SomeComplexObj();
        OC["ID5"] = new SomeComplexObj();

        Console.WriteLine("\r\n--> Add 5 weak references");
        Console.WriteLine("OC.TotalCacheSlots = " + OC.TotalCacheSlots());
        Console.WriteLine("OC.AliveObjsInCache = " + OC.AliveObjsInCache());

        CreateObjLongMethod();
        Create135();
        CollectAll();
    }

    private void CreateObjLongMethod()
    {
        Console.WriteLine("\r\n--> Obtain ID1");
        string id1 = "ID1";
        if (OC.IsObjAlive(ref id1))
        {
            SomeComplexObj SCOTemp = OC["ID1"];
            SCOTemp.IDCode = 100;
            Console.WriteLine("SCOTemp.IDCode = " + SCOTemp.IDCode);
        }
        else
        {
            Console.WriteLine("Object ID1 does not exist...Creating new ID1...");
            OC["ID1"] = new SomeComplexObj();

            SomeComplexObj SCOTemp = OC["ID1"];
            SCOTemp.IDCode = 101;
            Console.WriteLine("SCOTemp.IDCode = " + SCOTemp.IDCode);
        }
    }

    private void Create135()
    {
        Console.WriteLine("\r\n--> Obtain ID1, ID3, ID5");
        SomeComplexObj SCO1 = OC["ID1"];
        SomeComplexObj SCO3 = OC["ID3"];
        SomeComplexObj SCO5 = OC["ID5"];
        SCO1.IDCode = 1000;
        SCO3.IDCode = 3000;
        SCO5.IDCode = 5000;


        ///////////// BEGIN COLLECT /////////////
        GC.Collect();
        GC.WaitForPendingFinalizers();
        /////////////  END COLLECT  /////////////
```

Example 3-20. Using the ObjCache class (continued)

```
    Console.WriteLine("\r\n--> Collect all weak references");
    Console.WriteLine("OC.TotalCacheSlots = " + OC.TotalCacheSlots());
    Console.WriteLine("OC.AliveObjsInCache = " + OC.AliveObjsInCache());

    Console.WriteLine("SCO1.IDCode = " + SCO1.IDCode);
    Console.WriteLine("SCO3.IDCode = " + SCO3.IDCode);
    Console.WriteLine("SCO5.IDCode = " + SCO5.IDCode);

    string id2 = "ID2";
    Console.WriteLine("\r\n--> Get ID2, which has been collected.  ID2 Exists ==" +
                    OC.IsObjAlive(ref id2));
    SomeComplexObj SCO2 = OC["ID2"];
    Console.WriteLine("ID2 has now been re-created.  ID2 Exists == " + OC.IsObjAlive(ref
id2));
    Console.WriteLine("OC.AliveObjsInCache = " + OC.AliveObjsInCache());
    SCO2.IDCode = 2000;
    Console.WriteLine("SCO2.IDCode = " + SCO2.IDCode);


    /////////////// BEGIN COLLECT ///////////////
    GC.Collect();
    GC.WaitForPendingFinalizers();
    ///////////////  END COLLECT  ///////////////


    Console.WriteLine("\r\n--> Collect all weak references");
    Console.WriteLine("OC.TotalCacheSlots = " + OC.TotalCacheSlots());
    Console.WriteLine("OC.AliveObjsInCache = " + OC.AliveObjsInCache());
}

private void CollectAll()
{
    /////////////// BEGIN COLLECT ///////////////
    GC.Collect();
    GC.WaitForPendingFinalizers();
    ///////////////  END COLLECT  ///////////////


    Console.WriteLine("\r\n--> Collect all weak references");
    Console.WriteLine("OC.TotalCacheSlots = " + OC.TotalCacheSlots());
    Console.WriteLine("OC.AliveObjsInCache = " + OC.AliveObjsInCache());
}
```

The output of this test code is shown here:

```
--> Add 5 weak references
OC.TotalCacheSlots = 5
OC.AliveObjsInCache = 5

--> Collect all weak references
OC.TotalCacheSlots = 5
OC.AliveObjsInCache = 0
```

```
--> Add 5 weak references
OC.TotalCacheSlots = 5
OC.AliveObjsInCache = 5

--> Obtain ID1
SCOTemp.IDCode = 100

--> Obtain ID1, ID3, ID5

--> Collect all weak references
OC.TotalCacheSlots = 5
OC.AliveObjsInCache = 3
SCO1.IDCode = 1000
SCO3.IDCode = 3000
SCO5.IDCode = 5000

--> Get ID2, which has been collected.  ID2 Exists ==False
ID2 has now been re-created.  ID2 Exists == True
OC.AliveObjsInCache = 4
SCO2.IDCode = 2000

--> Collect all weak references
OC.TotalCacheSlots = 5
OC.AliveObjsInCache = 4

--> Collect all weak references
OC.TotalCacheSlots = 5
OC.AliveObjsInCache = 0
```

Discussion

Caching involves storing frequently used objects, particularly those that are expensive to create and re-create, in memory for fast access. This technique is in contrast to recreating these objects through some time-consuming mechanism (e.g., from data in a database or from a file on disk) every time they are needed. By storing frequently used objects such as these—so that you do not have to create them nearly as much—you can further improve the performance of the application.

When deciding which types of items can be cached, you should look for objects that take a long time to create and/or initialize. For example, if an object's creation involves one or more calls to a database, to a file on disk, or to a network resource, it can be considered as a candidate for caching. In addition to selecting objects with long creation times, these objects should also be frequently used by the application. Selection depends on a combination of the frequency of use and the average time for which it is used in any given usage. Objects that remain in use for a long time when they are retrieved from the cache may work better in this cache than those that are frequently used but for only a very short period of time.

If you do not want to overwrite cached items having the same key as the object you are attempting to insert into the cache, the set accessor of the indexer must be modified. The code for the set accessor could be modified to this:

```
public U this[T key]
{
    get
    {
        if (!cache.ContainsKey(key) || !IsObjAlive(ref key))
        {
            this[key] = new U();
        }

        return ((U)((WeakReference)cache[key]).Target);
    }

    set
    {
        WeakReference WR = new WeakReference(value, false);

        if (cache.ContainsKey(key))
        {
            cache[key] = WR;
        }
        else
        {
            cache.Add(key, WR);
        }
    }
}
```

You could also add a mechanism to calculate the cache-hit ratio for this cache. The cache-hit ratio is the ratio of hits—every time an existing object is requested from the Dictionary<T,WeakReference>—to the total number of calls made to attempt a retrieval of an object. This can give you a good indication of how well your ObjCache<T,U> is working. The code to add to this class to implement calculation of a cache-hit ratio is shown highlighted in Example 3-21.

Example 3-21. Calculating a cache-hit ratio

```
private float numberOfGets = 0;
private float numberOfHits = 0;

public float HitMissRatioPercent()
{
    if (numberOfGets == 0)
    {
        return (0);
    }
    else
    {
        return ((numberOfHits / numberOfGets) * 100);
    }
}

public U this[T key]
{
```

Example 3-21. Calculating a cache-hit ratio (continued)

```
get
{
    ++numberOfGets;

    if (!cache.ContainsKey(key) || !IsObjAlive(ref key))
    {
        this[key] = new U( );
    }
    else
    {
        ++numberOfHits;
    }

    return ((U)((WeakReference)cache[key]).Target);
}

set
{
    WeakReference WR = new WeakReference(value, false);

    if (cache.ContainsKey(key))
    {
        cache[key] = WR;
    }
    else
    {
        cache.Add(key, WR);
    }
}
}
```

The numberOfGets field tracks the number of calls made to the get accessor of the indexer. The numberOfHits field tracks the number of times that an object to be retrieved exists in the cache. The HitMissRatioPercent method returns the numberOfHits divided by the numberOfGets as a percentage. The higher the percent, the better your cache is operating (100 percent is equal to a hit every time the get accessor of the indexer is called). A lower percentage indicates that this cache object is not working efficiently (zero percent is equal to a miss every time the get accessor of the indexer is called). A very low percentage indicates that the cache object may not be the correct solution to your problem or that you are not caching the correct object(s).

The WeakReference objects created for the ObjCache<T,U> class do not track objects after they are finalized. This would add much more complexity than is needed by this class.

Remember, a caching scheme adds complexity to your application. The most a caching scheme can do for your application is to enhance performance and possibly place less stress on memory resources. You should consider this when deciding whether to implement a caching scheme such as the one in this recipe.

See Also

To use the built-in ASP.NET cache object independently of a web application, see the following topics in MSDN:

- "Caching Application Data"
- "Adding Items to the Cache"
- "Retrieving Values of Cached Items"
- "Deleting Items from the Cache"
- "Notifying an Application When an Item Is Deleted from the Cache"
- "System.Web.Caching Namespace"

In addition, see the Datacache2 Sample under ".NET Samples—ASP.NET Caching" in MSDN; see the sample links to the Page Data Caching example in the ASP.NET QuickStart Tutorials.

Also see the "WeakReference Class" topic in the MSDN documentation.

3.30   Rolling Back Object Changes

Problem

You have an object that allows its state to be changed. However, you do not want these changes to become permanent if other changes to the system cannot be made at the same time. In other words, you want to be able to roll back the changes if any of a group of related changes fails.

Solution

Use the *memento design pattern* to allow your object to save its original state in order to roll back changes.

The *memento design pattern* allows object state to be saved so that it can be restored in response to a specific situation. The memento pattern is very useful for implementing undo/redo or commit/rollback actions. This pattern usually has an *originator object*—a new or existing object that needs to have an undo/redo or commit/rollback style behavior associated with it. This originator object's state—the values of its fields—will be mirrored in a *memento object*, which is an object that can store the state of an originator object. Another object that usually exists in this type of pattern is the *caretaker object*. The caretaker is responsible for saving one or more memento objects, which can then be used later to restore the state of an originator object.

The SomeDataOriginator class used in this recipe contains data that must be changed only if other system changes occur. Its source code is shown in Example 3-22.

Example 3-22. An originator object

```csharp
using System;
using System.Collections;
using System.Collections.Generic;


public class SomeDataOriginator
{
    public SomeDataOriginator() {}

    public SomeDataOriginator(int state, string id, string clsName)
    {
        this.state = state;
        this.id = id;
        this.clsName = clsName;
    }


    private int state = 1;
    private string id = "ID1001";
    private string clsName = "SomeDataOriginator";


    public string ClassName
    {
        get {return (clsName);}
        set {clsName = value;}
    }

    public string ID
    {
        get {return (id);}
        set {id = value;}
    }


    public void ChangeState(int newState)
    {
        state = newState;
    }

    public void Display()
    {
        Console.WriteLine("State: " + state);
        Console.WriteLine("Id: " + id);
        Console.WriteLine("clsName: " + clsName);
    }


    // Nested Memento class used to save outer class' state.
    public class Memento
    {
        public Memento(SomeDataOriginator data)
```

Example 3-22. An originator object (continued)

```
        {
            this.state = data.state;
            this.id = data.id;
            this.clsName = data.clsName;
            this.originator = data;
        }

        private SomeDataOriginator originator = null;
        private int state = 1;
        private string id = "ID1001";
        private string clsName = "SomeDataOriginator";


        internal void Rollback( )
        {
            originator.clsName = this.clsName;
            originator.id = this.id;
            originator.state = this.state;
        }
    }
}
```

The MementoCareTaker<T> is the caretaker object, which saves a single state that the originator object can roll back to. Its source code is:

```
    public class MementoCareTaker<T>
        where T : SomeDataOriginator.Memento
    {
        private T savedState = default(T);

        public T Memento
        {
            get {return (savedState);}
            set {savedState = value;}
        }
    }
```

MultiMementoCareTaker<T> is another caretaker object that can save multiple states to which the originator object can roll back. Its source code is:

```
    public class MultiMementoCareTaker<T>
        where T : SomeDataOriginator.Memento
    {
        private List<T> savedState = new List<T>( );

        public T this[int index]
        {
            get {return (savedState[index]);}
            set {savedState[index] = value;}
        }

        public void Add(T memento)
        {
```

```
        savedState.Add(memento);
    }

    public int Count
    {
        get {return (savedState.Count);}
    }
}
```

Discussion

This recipe makes use of two caretaker objects. The first, MementoCareTaker<T>, saves a single object state that can later be used to roll an object back. The second, MultiMementoCareTaker<T>, uses a List<T> object to save multiple object states, thereby allowing many levels of rollbacks to occur. You can also think of MultiMementoCareTaker<T> as storing multiple levels of the undo/redo state.

The originator class, SomeDataOriginator, has the state, id, and clsName fields to store information. One thing you have to add to the class, which will not affect how it behaves or how it is used, is a nested Memento class. This nested class is used to store the state of its outer class. You use a nested class so that it can access the private fields of the outer class. This allows the Memento object to get copies of all the needed fields of the originator object without having to add special logic to the originator allowing it to give this field information to the Memento object.

The Memento class contains only private fields that mirror the fields in the outer object that you want to store. Note that you do not have to store all fields of an outer type, just the ones that you want to roll back or undo. The Memento object also contains a constructor that accepts a SomeDataOriginator object. The constructor saves the pointer to this object as well as its current state. There is also a single method called Rollback. The Rollback method is central to restoring the state of the current SomeDataOriginator object. This method uses the originator pointer to this object to set the SomeDataOriginator object's fields back to the values contained in this instance of the Memento object.

The caretaker objects store any Memento objects created by the application. The application can then specify which Memento objects to use to roll back an object's state. Remember that each Memento object knows which originator object to roll back. Therefore, you need to tell the caretaker object only to use a Memento object to roll back an object, and the Memento object takes care of the rest.

There is a potential problem with the caretaker objects that is easily remedied. The problem is that the caretaker objects are not supposed to know anything about the Memento objects. The caretaker objects in this recipe see only one method, the Rollback method, that is specific to the Memento objects. So, for this recipe, this is not really a problem. However, if you decide to add more logic to the Memento class, you need a way to shield it from the caretaker. You do not want another developer to add code to the caretaker objects that may allow it to change the internal state of any Memento objects they contain.

To the caretaker objects, each Memento object should simply be an object that contains the Rollback method. To make the Memento objects appear this way to the caretaker objects, you can place an interface on the Memento class. This interface is defined as follows:

```
public interface IMemento
{
    void Rollback( );
}
```

The Memento class is then modified as follows (changes are highlighted):

```
public class Memento : IMemento
{
    public void Rollback( )
    {
        originator.clsName = this.clsName;
        originator.id = this.id;
        originator.state = this.state;
    }

    // The rest of this class does not change
}
```

The caretaker classes are modified as follows (changes are highlighted):

```
public class MementoCareTaker<T>
    where T: IMemento
{
    private T savedState = default(T);

    internal T Memento
    {
        get {return (savedState);}
        set {savedState = value;}
    }
}

public class MultiMementoCareTaker<T>
    where T: IMemento
{
    private List<T> savedState = new List<T>( );

    public T this[int index]
    {
        get {return (savedState[index]);}
        set {savedState[index] = value;}
    }

    public void Add(T memento)
    {
```

```
            savedState.Add(memento);
    }

    public int Count
    {
        get {return (savedState.Count);}
    }
}
```

Implementing the IMemento interface serves two purposes. First, it prevents the care-taker classes from knowing anything about the internals of the Memento objects they contain. Second, it allows the caretaker objects to handle any type of Memento object, so long as it implements the IMemento interface.

The following code shows how the SomeDataOriginator, Memento, and caretaker objects are used. It uses the MementoCareTaker<T> object to store a single state of the SomeDataOriginator object and then rolls the changes back after the SomeDataOriginator object is modified:

```
// Create an originator and default its internal state.
SomeDataOriginator data = new SomeDataOriginator();
Console.WriteLine("ORIGINAL");
data.Display();

// Create a caretaker object.
MementoCareTaker<SomeDataOriginator.Memento> objState =
            new MementoCareTaker<SomeDataOriginator.Memento>();

// Add a memento of the original originator object to the caretaker.
objState.Memento = new SomeDataOriginator.Memento(data);

// Change the originator's internal state.
data.ChangeState(67);
data.ID = "foo";
data.ClassName = "bar";
Console.WriteLine("NEW");
data.Display();

// Roll back the changes of the originator to its original state
objState.Memento.Rollback();
Console.WriteLine("ROLLEDBACK");
data.Display();
```

This code outputs the following:

```
ORIGINAL
State: 1
Id: ID1001
ClsName: SomeDataOriginator
NEW
State: 67
Id: foo
ClsName: bar
ROLLEDBACK
```

```
State: 1
Id: ID1001
ClsName: SomeDataOriginator
```

The use of the MultiMementoCareTaker<T> object is very similar to the MementoCareTaker object, as the following code shows:

```
SomeDataOriginator Data = new SomeDataOriginator( );
Console.WriteLine("ORIGINAL");
Data.Display( );

MultiMementoCareTaker<SomeDataOriginator.Memento> MultiObjState = new
MultiMementoCareTaker<SomeDataOriginator.Memento>( );
MultiObjState.Add(new SomeDataOriginator.Memento(Data));

Data.ChangeState(67);
Data.ID = "foo";
Data.ClassName = "bar";
Console.WriteLine("NEW");
Data.Display( );
MultiObjState.Add(new SomeDataOriginator.Memento(Data));

Data.ChangeState(671);
Data.ID = "foo1";
Data.ClassName = "bar1";
Console.WriteLine("NEW1");
Data.Display( );
MultiObjState.Add(new SomeDataOriginator.Memento(Data));

Data.ChangeState(672);
Data.ID = "foo2";
Data.ClassName = "bar2";
Console.WriteLine("NEW2");
Data.Display( );
MultiObjState.Add(new SomeDataOriginator.Memento(Data));

Data.ChangeState(673);
Data.ID = "foo3";
Data.ClassName = "bar3";
Console.WriteLine("NEW3");
Data.Display( );

for (int Index = (MultiObjState.Count - 1); Index >= 0; Index--)
{
    Console.WriteLine("\r\nROLLBACK(" + Index + ")");
    MultiObjState[Index].Rollback( );
    Data.Display( );
}
```

This code outputs the following:

```
ORIGINAL
State: 1
Id: ID1001
ClsName: SomeDataOriginator
```

```
NEW
State: 67
Id: foo
ClsName: bar
NEW1
State: 671
Id: foo1
ClsName: bar1
NEW2
State: 672
Id: foo2
ClsName: bar2
NEW3
State: 673
Id: foo3
ClsName: bar3

ROLLBACK(3)
State: 672
Id: foo2
ClsName: bar2

ROLLBACK(2)
State: 671
Id: foo1
ClsName: bar1

ROLLBACK(1)
State: 67
Id: foo
ClsName: bar

ROLLBACK(0)
State: 1
Id: ID1001
ClsName: SomeDataOriginator
```

This code creates a SomeDataOriginator object and changes its state several times. At every state change, a new Memento object is created to save the SomeDataOriginator object's state at that point in time. At the end of this code, a for loop iterates over each Memento object stored in the MultiMementoCareTaker<SomeDataOriginator. Memento> object, from the most recent to the earliest. On each iteration of this loop, the Memento object is used to restore the state of the SomeDataOriginator object.

3.31   Disposing of Unmanaged Resources

Problem

Your class references unmanaged resources such as some type of handle or manipulates a block of memory or a file via P/Invoke methods or uses a COM object that requires some cleanup method to be called before it is released. You need to make sure that the resources are released properly and in a timely manner. In a garbage-collected environment, such as that used by the Common Language Run-time (CLR), you cannot assume either will happen.

Solution

Implement the *dispose design pattern*, which is specific to .NET.

The class that contains a reference to the unmanaged resources is shown here as Foo. This object contains references to a COM object called SomeCOMObj, a FileStream object called FStream, and an ArrayList that may or may not contain references to unmanaged resources. The source code is shown in Example 3-23.

Example 3-23. Foo: A class that contains references to unmanaged code

```
using System;
using System.Collections;
using System.IO;
using System.Runtime.InteropServices;

public class Foo : IDisposable
{
    [DllImport("Kernel32.dll", SetLastError = true)]
    private static extern IntPtr CreateSemaphore(IntPtr lpSemaphoreAttributes,
        int lInitialCount, int lMaximumCount, string lpName);

    [DllImport("Kernel32.dll", SetLastError = true)]
    private static extern bool ReleaseSemaphore(IntPtr hSemaphore,
        int lReleaseCount, out IntPtr lpPreviousCount);

    public Foo( ) {}

    // Replace SomeCOMObj with your COM object type.
    private SomeCOMObj comObj = new SomeCOMObj( );
    private FileStream fileStream = new FileStream(@"c:\test.txt",
      FileMode.OpenOrCreate);
    private ArrayList aList = new ArrayList( );
    private bool hasBeenDisposed = false;
    private IntPtr hSemaphore = IntPtr.Zero;    // Unmanaged handle

    // Protect these members from being used on a disposed object.
    public void WriteToFile(string text)
    {
        if(hasBeenDisposed)
        {
            throw (new ObjectDisposedException(this.ToString( ),
                                        "Object has been disposed"));
        }

        UnicodeEncoding enc = new UnicodeEncoding( );
        fileStream.Write(enc.GetBytes(text), 0, text.Length);
    }
```

```csharp
public void UseCOMObj( )
{
    if(hasBeenDisposed)
    {
        throw (new ObjectDisposedException(this.ToString( ),
                                        "Object has been disposed"));
    }

    Console.WriteLine("GUID: " + comObj.GetType( ).GUID);
}

public void AddToList(object obj)
{
    if(hasBeenDisposed)
    {
        throw (new ObjectDisposedException(this.ToString( ),
                                        "Object has been disposed"));
    }

    aList.Add(obj);
}

public void CreateSemaphore( )
{
    // Create unmanaged handle here.
    hSemaphore = CreateSemaphore(IntPtr.Zero, 5, 5, null);
}

// The Dispose methods
public void Dispose( )
{
    Dispose(true);
}

protected virtual void Dispose(bool disposeManagedObjs)
{
    if (!hasBeenDisposed)
    {
        try
        {
            if (disposeManagedObjs)
            {
                // Dispose all items in an array or ArrayList.
                foreach (object obj in aList)
                {
                    IDisposable disposableObj = obj as IDisposable;
                    if (disposableObj != null)
                    {
                        disposableObj.Dispose( );
                    }
                }
```

```
                // Dispose managed objects implementing IDisposable.
                fileStream.Close( );

                // Reduce reference count on RCW.
                Marshal.ReleaseComObject(comObj);

                GC.SuppressFinalize(this);
            }
            // Release unmanaged handle here.
            IntPtr prevCnt = new IntPtr( );
            ReleaseSemaphore(hSemaphore, 1, out prevCnt);
        }
        catch (Exception)
        {
            hasBeenDisposed = false;
            throw;
        }

        hasBeenDisposed = true;
    }
}

// The destructor
~Foo( )
{
    Dispose(false);
}

// Optional Close method
public void Close( )
{
    Dispose( );
}
}
```

The following class inherits from Foo:

```
// Class inherits from an IDisposable class
public class Bar : Foo
{
    //...

    private bool hasBeenDisposed = false;

    protected override void Dispose(bool disposeManagedObjs)
    {
        if (!hasBeenDisposed)
        {
            try
            {
                if(disposeManagedObjs)
                {
                    // Call Dispose/Close/Clear on any managed objects here...
```

```
            }

            // Release any unmanaged objects here...

            // Call base class' Dispose method.
            base.Dispose(disposeManagedObjs);
        }
        catch (Exception)
        {
            hasBeenDisposed = false;
            throw;
        }

        hasBeenDisposed = true;
    }
  }
}
```

Whether this class directly contains any references to unmanaged resources, it should be disposed of as shown in the code.

Discussion

The *dispose design pattern* allows any unmanaged resources held by an object to be cleaned up from within the managed environment. This pattern is flexible enough to allow unmanaged resources held by the disposable object to be cleaned up explicitly (by calling the Dispose method) or implicitly (by waiting for the garbage collector to call the destructor). Finalizers are a safety net to clean up objects when you forget to do it.

 This design pattern should be used on any base class that has derived types that hold unmanaged resources. This indicates to the inheritor that this design pattern should be implemented in their derived class as well.

All the code that needs to be written for a disposable object is written within the class itself. First, all disposable types must implement the IDisposable interface. This interface contains a single method, Dispose, which accepts no parameters and returns void. The Dispose method is overloaded to accept a Boolean flag indicating whether any managed objects referenced by this object should also be disposed. If this parameter is true, managed objects referenced by this object will have their Dispose method called, and unmanaged resources are released; otherwise, only unmanaged resources are released.

The IDisposable.Dispose method will forward its call to the overloaded Dispose method that accepts a Boolean flag. This flag will be set to true to allow all managed objects to attempt to dispose of themselves as well as to release unmanaged resources held by this object.

The IDisposable interface is very important to implement. This interface allows the using statement to take advantage of the dispose pattern. A using statement that operates on the Foo object is written as follows:

```
using (Foo f = new Foo( ))
{
    f.WriteToFile("text");
}
```

Always implement the IDisposable interface on types that contain resources that need to be disposed or otherwise explicitly closed or released. This allows the use of the using keyword and aids in self-documenting the type.

A foreach loop will also make use of the IDisposable interface, but in a slightly different manner. After each iteration of this loop, the Dispose method is called via the enumerator type of the object being enumerated. The foreach loop guarantees that it will call the IDisposable.Dispose method if the object returned from the GetEnumerator method implements IDisposable.

The overloaded Dispose method that accepts a Boolean flag contains a static method call to GC.SuppressFinalize to force the garbage collector to remove this object from the *fqueue*, or finalization queue. The fqueue allows the garbage collector to run C# finalizers at a point after the object has been freed. However, this ability comes at a price: it takes many garbage collection cycles to completely collect an object with a destructor. If the object is placed on the fqueue in generation 0, the object will have to wait until generation 1 is collected, which could be some time. The GC.SuppressFinalize method removes the object from the *fqueue*, because it doesn't need specific code run for the finalizer; the memory can just be released. Calling this static method from within the Dispose method is critical to writing better performing classes.

Call the GC.SuppressFinalize method in the base class Dispose method when the overload of the Dispose method is passed true. Doing so will allow your object to be taken off of the finalization queue in the garbage collector allowing for earlier collection. This will help prevent memory retention and will help your application's performance.

A finalizer is also added to this class. The finalizer contains code to call the overloaded Dispose method, passing in false as its only argument. Note that all cleanup code should exist within the overloaded Dispose method that accepts a Boolean flag. All other methods should call this method to perform any necessary cleanup. The destructor will pass a false value into the Dispose method to prevent any managed objects from being disposed. Remember, the finalizers run in their own thread. Attempting to dispose of objects that may have already been collected or are about to be collected could have serious consequences for your code, such as resurrecting an object into an undefined state. It is best to prevent any references to other objects while the destructor is running.

It is possible to add a Close or even a Clear method to your class to be called as well as the Dispose method. Several classes in the FCL use a Close or Clear method to clean up unmanaged resources:

```
FileStream.Close( )
StreamWriter.Close( )
TcpClient.Close( )
MessageQueue.Close( )
SymmetricAlgorithm.Clear( )
AsymmetricAlgorithm.Clear( )
CryptoAPITransform.Clear( )
CryptoStream.Clear( )
```

Each of these classes also contains a Dispose method. The Clear method usually calls the Dispose method directly. There is a problem with this design. The Clear method is used extensively throughout the FCL for classes such as ArrayList, Hashtable, and other collection-type classes. However, the Clear method of the collection classes performs a much different task: it clears the collection of all its items. This Clear method has nothing to do with releasing unmanaged resources or calling the Dispose method.

The overloaded Dispose method that accepts a Boolean flag will contain all of the logic to release unmanaged resources from this object as well as possibly calling Dispose on types referenced by this object. In addition to these two actions, this method can also reduce the reference count on any COM objects that are referenced by this object. The static Marshal.ReleaseComObject method will decrement the reference count by one on the COM object reference passed in to this method:

```
Marshal.ReleaseComObject(comObj);
```

To force the reference count to go to zero, allowing the COM object to be released and its RCW to be garbage collected, you could write the following code:

```
while (Marshal.ReleaseComObject(comObj) > 0);
```

Take great care when forcing the reference count to zero in this manner. If another object is using this COM object, the COM object will be released out from under this other object. This can easily destabilize a system. For more information on using this method, see Recipe 3.28.

Any callable method/property/indexer (basically, any nonprivate method except for the Dispose and Close methods and the constructor[s] and the destructor) should throw the ObjectDisposedException exception if it is called after the object has been disposed—that is, after its Dispose method has been called. A private field called hasBeenDisposed is used as a Boolean flag to indicate whether this object has been disposed; a true confirms that it has been disposed. This flag is checked to determine whether this object has been disposed at the beginning of every method/property/indexer. If it has been disposed, the ObjectDisposedException is thrown. This prevents the use of an object after it has been disposed and potentially placed in an unknown state.

> Disposable objects should always check to see if they have been disposed in all of their public methods, properties, and indexers. If a client attempts to use your object after it has been disposed, an ObjectDisposedException should be thrown. Note that a Dispose method can be called multiple times after this object has been disposed without having any side effects (including the throwing of ObjectDisposedExceptions) on the object.

Any classes inheriting from Foo need not implement the IDisposable interface; it is implied from the base class. The inheriting class should implement the hasBeenDisposed Boolean flag field and use this flag in any methods/properties/indexers to confirm that this object has been disposed. Finally, a Dispose method is implemented that accepts a Boolean flag and overrides the same virtual method in the base class. This Dispose method does not have to call the GC.SuppressFinalize(this) static method; this is done in the base class's Dispose method.

The IDisposable.Dispose method should not be implemented in this class. When the Dispose method is called on an object of type Bar, the Foo.Dispose method will be called. The Foo.Dispose method will then call the overridden Bar.Dispose(bool) method, which, in turn, calls its base class Dispose(bool) method, Foo.Dispose(bool). The base class's finalizer is also inherited by the Bar class.

> All Dispose methods should call their base class's Dispose method.

If the client code fails to call the Dispose or Close method, the destructor will run and the Dispose(bool) method will still be called, albeit at a later time. The finalizer is the object's last line of defense for releasing unmanaged resources.

See Also

See Recipes 3.28 and 3.29; see the "Dispose Interface," "Using foreach with Collections," and "Implementing Finalize and Dispose to Clean up Unmanaged Resources" topics in the MSDN documentation.

3.32   Determining Where Boxing and Unboxing Occur

Problem

You have a project consisting of some very complex code that is a performance bot-tleneck for the entire application. You have been assigned to increase performance, but you do not know where to start looking.

Solution

A great way to start looking for performance problems is to use a profiling tool to see whether boxing is actually causing you any kind of problem in the first place. A pro-filer will show you exactly what allocations are occurring and in what volume. There are several profilers on the market; some are free and others are not.

If you have already established through profiling that boxing is definitely causing a problem but you are still having trouble working out where it's occurring, then you can use the Ildasm disassembler tool that is packaged with VS.NET. With Ildasm you can convert an entire project to its equivalent IL code and then dump the IL to a text file. To do this, Ildasm has several command-line switches, one of which is the /output switch. This switch is used as follows:

```
ildasm Proj1.dll /output:Proj1.il
```

This command will disassemble the file *Proj1.dll* and then write the disassembled IL to the file *Proj1.il*.

A second useful command-line switch is /source. This switch shows the original code (C#, VB.NET, etc.) in which this DLL was written, as well as the IL that was compiled from each of these source lines. Note that the DLL must be built with debugging enabled. This switch is used as follows:

```
ildasm Proj1.dll /output:Proj1.il /source
```

We prefer the second method of invoking Ildasm, since the original source is included, preventing you from getting lost in all of the IL code.

After running Ildasm from the command line, open the resulting IL code file into VS. NET or your favorite editor. Inside the editor, do a text search for the words *box* and *unbox*. This will find all occurrences of boxing and unboxing operations.

Using this information, you have pinpointed the problem areas. Now, you can turn your attention to them to see if there is any way to prevent or minimize the boxing/ unboxing operations.

Discussion

When a boxing or unboxing operation occurs in code, whether it was implicit or explicit, the IL generated includes the box or unbox command. For example, the fol-lowing C# code:

```
int valType = 1;
object boxedValType = valType;
valType = (int)boxedValType;
```

compiles to the following IL code:

```
//000883:          int valType = 1;
  IL_0000:  ldc.i4.1
  IL_0001:  stloc.0
//000884:          object boxedValType = valType;
  IL_0002:  ldloc.0
  IL_0003:  box       [mscorlib]System.Int32
  IL_0008:  stloc.1
//000898:          int valType = (int) boxedValType;
  IL_0061:  ldloc.1
  IL_0062:  unbox     [mscorlib]System.Int32
  IL_0067:  ldind.i4
```

Notice the box and unbox commands in the previous IL code. IL makes it very apparent when a boxing or unboxing operation occurs. You can use this to your advantage to find and hopefully prevent a boxing operation from occurring.

The following can help prevent or eliminate boxing:

- Use classes instead of structures. This usually involves simply changing the struct keyword to class in the structure definition. This change can dramatically improve performance. However, this change should be done in a very careful manner, as it can change the operation of the application.

- If you are storing value types in a collection,switch to using a generic collection. The generic collection can be instantiated for the specific value type that you will be storing in it.This allows you to create a collection that is strongly typed for that specific value type.Not only will using a generic collection alleviate the boxing/unboxing issue,but it will also speed things up since there are fewer casts to perform when adding, removing, and looking up values in this collection.

- Take care when implementing explicit interface members on structures.As the discussion shows, this causes the structure to be boxed before the call to an interface member is made through the interface.This reflects the fact that explicit implementation of a method on an interface is accessible only from the interface type. This means that the structure must be cast to that interface type before the explicitly declared methods of that interface type can be used. An interface is a reference type and therefore causes the structure to be boxed when an explicit interface method is accessed on that structure. However, in some cases this isn't true. For example, the using statement issues an IL instruction to prevent boxing when calling the Dispose method—assuming that an implicit interface implementation is used.

Note that changes to a value type that exists in both boxed and unboxed form occur independently of one another.

See Also

See the "Boxing Conversion" and "Unboxing Conversion" topics in the MSDN documentation.

Here is a list of some available profiling tools:

- Allocation Profiler (free), which can be obtained in the *UserSamples* section of the web site *http://www.gotdotnet.com/community/usersamples/*.
- DevPartner Profiler Community Edition (free), which can be obtained at *http://www.compuware.com/products/devpartner/profiler/*.
- DevPartner Studio Professional Edition (purchase), which can be purchased at *http://www.compuware.com/products/devpartner/studio/*. This package contains the code profiler tool as well as many other tools that work with .NET and other .NET code. This package also contains a memory analysis tool that can aid in debugging performance problems.

CHAPTER 4

Generics

4.0 Introduction

A long-awaited feature, generics, is finally here with the advent of Version 2.0 of the C# compiler. Generics is an extremely useful feature that allows you to write less, but more efficient, code. This aspect of generics is detailed more in Recipe 4.1. With generics comes quite a bit of programming power, but with that power comes the responsibility to use it correctly. If you are considering converting your ArrayList, Queue, Stack, and Hashtable objects to use their generic counterparts, consider reading Recipes 4.4, 4.5, and 4.10. As you will read, the conversion is not always simple and easy, and there are reasons why you might not want to do this conversion at all.

Other recipes in this chapter deal with other generic classes contained in the .NET Version 2.0 Framework, such as Recipe 4.6. Still others deal with the operation of any generic type, such as Recipes 4.2, 4.8, and 4.13.

4.1 Deciding When and Where to Use Generics

Problem

You want to use generic types in a new project or convert nongeneric types in an existing project to their generic equivalent. However, you do not really know why you would want to do this, and you do not know which nongeneric types should be converted to be generic.

Solution

In deciding when and where to use generic types, you need to consider several things:

- Will your type contain or be operating on various unspecified data types (e.g., a collection type)? If so, creating a generic type will offer several benefits over creating a nongeneric type. If your type will operate on only a single specific type, then you may not need to create a generic type.

- If your type will be operating on value types, so that boxing and unboxing operations will occur, you should consider using generics to prevent the boxing and unboxing operations.

- The stronger type checking associated with generics will aid in finding errors sooner (i.e., during compile time as opposed to runtime), thus shortening your bug-fixing cycle.

- Is your code suffering from "code bloat," with you writing multiple classes to handle different data types on which they operate (e.g., a specialized ArrayList that stores only StreamReaders and another that stores only StreamWriters)? It is easier to write the code once and have it just work for each of the data types it operates on.

- Generics allow for greater clarity of code. By eliminating code bloat and forcing stronger type checking on your types, your code will be easier to read and understand.

Discussion

In most cases your code will benefit from using a generic type. Generics allow for more efficient code reuse, faster performance, stronger type checking, and easier-to-read code.

See Also

See the "Generics Overview" and "Benefits of Generics" topics in the MSDN documentation.

4.2   Understanding Generic Types

Problem

You need to understand how the .NET types work for generics and what differences there are from regular .NET types.

Solution

A couple of quick experiments can show the differences between regular .NET types and generic .NET types. When a regular .NET type is defined, it looks like the StandardClass type defined in Example 4-1.

Example 4-1. StandardClass: a regular .NET type

```
public class StandardClass
{
    // Static counter hangs off of the Type for
    // StandardClass.
    static int _count = 0;
```

Example 4-1. StandardClass: a regular .NET type (continued)

```csharp
    // Create an array of typed items.
    int _maxItemCount;
    object[] _items;
    int _currentItem = 0;

    // Constructor that increments static counter
    public StandardClass(int items)
    {
        _count++;
        _maxItemCount = items;
        _items = new object[_maxItemCount];
    }

    /// <summary>
    /// Add an item to the class whose type
    /// is unknown as only object can hold any type.
    /// </summary>
    /// <param name="item">item to add</param>
    /// <returns>the index of the item added</returns>
    public int AddItem(object item)
    {
        if (_currentItem < _maxItemCount)
        {
            _items[_currentItem] = item;
            return _currentItem++;
        }
        else
            throw new Exception("Item queue is full");
    }

    /// <summary>
    /// Get an item from the class.
    /// </summary>
    /// <param name="index">the index of the item to get</param>
    /// <returns>an item of type object</returns>
    public object GetItem(int index)
    {
        Debug.Assert(index < _maxItemCount);
        if (index >= _maxItemCount)
            throw new ArgumentOutOfRangeException("index");

        return _items[index];
    }

    /// <summary>
    /// The count of the items the class holds
    /// </summary>
    public int ItemCount
    {
        get { return _currentItem; }
    }
```

Example 4-1. StandardClass: a regular .NET type (continued)

```
/// <summary>
/// ToString override to provide class detail
/// </summary>
/// <returns>formatted string with class details</returns>
public override string ToString()
{
    return "There are " + _count.ToString() +
        " instances of " + this.GetType().ToString() +
        " which contains " + _currentItem + " items of type " +
        _items.GetType().ToString() + "...";
}
}
```

StandardClass has a static integer member variable, _count, which is incremented in the instance constructor, and a ToString() override that prints out how many instances of StandardClass exist in this AppDomain. StandardClass also contains an array of objects (_items), the size of which is determined by the item count passed in to the constructor. It implements methods to add and retrieve items (AddItem, GetItem) and a read-only property to get the number of items in the array (ItemCount).

The GenericClass<T> type is a generic .NET type with the same static integer _count field, the instance constructor that counts the number of instantiations, and the overridden ToString() method to tell you how many instances there are of this type. GenericClass<T> also has an _items array, and methods corresponding to those in StandardClass, as you can see Example 4-2.

Example 4-2. GenericClass<T>: a generic .NET type

```
public class GenericClass<T>
{
    // Static counter hangs off of the
    // instantiated Type for
    // GenericClass.
    static int _count = 0;

    // Create an array of typed items.
    int _maxItemCount;
    T[] _items;
    int _currentItem = 0;

    // Constructor that increments static counter
    public GenericClass(int items)
    {
        _count++;
        __maxItemCount = items;
        _items = new T[_maxItemCount];
    }
```

Example 4-2. GenericClass<T>: a generic .NET type (continued)

```
/// <summary>
/// Add an item to the class whose type.
/// is determined by the instantiating type.
/// </summary>
/// <param name="item">item to add</param>
/// <returns>the zero-based index of the item added</returns>
public int AddItem(T item)
{
    if (_currentItem < _maxItemCount)
    {
        _items[_currentItem] = item;
        return _currentItem++;
    }
    else
        throw new Exception("Item queue is full");
}

/// <summary>
/// Get an item from the class.
/// </summary>
/// <param name="index">the zero-based index of the item to get</param>
/// <returns>an item of the instantiating type</returns>
public T GetItem(int index)
{
    Debug.Assert(index < _maxItemCount);
    if (index >= _maxItemCount)
        throw new ArgumentOutOfRangeException("index");

    return _items[index];
}

/// <summary>
/// The count of the items the class holds
/// </summary>
public int ItemCount
{
    get { return _currentItem; }
}

/// <summary>
/// ToString override to provide class detail
/// </summary>
/// <returns>formatted string with class details</returns>
public override string ToString()
{
    return "There are " + _count.ToString() +
        " instances of " + this.GetType().ToString() +
        " which contains " + _currentItem + " items of type " +
        _items.GetType().ToString() + "...";
}
}
```

Things start to get a little more different with GenericClass<T> when you look at the _items array implementation. The _items array is declared as:

```
T [] _items;
```

instead of:

```
object [] _items;
```

The _items array uses the type parameter of the generic class (<T>) to determine what type of items are allowed in the _items array. StandardClass uses object for the _items array type, which allows any type to be stored in the array of items (since all types derive from object), while GenericClass<T> provides type safety by allowing the type parameter to dictate what types of objects are permitted.

The next difference is visible in the method declarations of AddItem and GetItem. AddItem now takes a parameter of type T, whereas in StandardClass it took a parameter of type object. GetItem now returns a value of type T, whereas in StandardClass it returned a value of type object. These changes allow the methods in GenericClass<T> to use the instantiated type to store and retrieve the items in the array instead of having to allow any object to be stored as in StandardClass.

```
/// <summary>
/// Add an item to the class whose type
/// is determined by the instantiating type.
/// </summary>
/// <param name="item">item to add</param>
/// <returns>the zero-based index of the item added</returns>
public int AddItem(T item)
{
    if (_currentItem < _maxItemCount)
    {
        _items[_currentItem] = item;
        return _currentItem++;
    }
    else
        throw new Exception("Item queue is full");
}

/// <summary>
/// Get an item from the class.
/// </summary>
/// <param name="index">the zero-based index of the item to get</param>
/// <returns>an item of the instantiating type</returns>
public T GetItem(int index)
{
    Debug.Assert(index < _maxItemCount);
    if (index >= _maxItemCount)
        throw new ArgumentOutOfRangeException("index");

    return _items[index];
}
```

There are a few advantages this provides. First and foremost is the type safety provided by GenericClass<T> for items in the array. It was possible to write code like this in StandardClass:

```
// Regular class
StandardClass C = new StandardClass(5);
Console.WriteLine(C);

string s1 = "s1";
string s2 = "s2";
string s3 = "s3";
int i1 = 1;

// Add to the standard class (as object).
C.AddItem(s1);
C.AddItem(s2);
C.AddItem(s3);
// Add an int to the string array, perfectly OK.
C.AddItem(i1);
```

But GenericClass<T> will give a compiler error if you try the same thing:

```
// Generic class
GenericClass<string> gC = new GenericClass<string>(5);
Console.WriteLine(gC);

string s1 = "s1";
string s2 = "s2";
string s3 = "s3";
int i1 = 1;

// Add to the generic class (as string).
gC.AddItem(s1);
gC.AddItem(s2);
gC.AddItem(s3);
// Try to add an int to the string instance, denied by compiler.
// error CS1503: Argument '1': cannot convert from 'int' to 'string'
//GC.AddItem(i1);
```

Having the compiler prevent this before it can become the source of runtime bugs is a very good thing.

It may not be immediately noticeable, but the integer is actually boxed when it is added to the object array in StandardClass, as you can see in the IL for the call to GetItem on StandardClass:

```
IL_0170:  ldloc.2
IL_0171:  ldloc.s    i1
IL_0173:  box        [mscorlib]System.Int32
IL_0178:  callvirt   instance int32
                     CSharpRecipes.Generics/StandardClass::AddItem(object)
```

This boxing turns the int, which is a value type, into a reference type (object) for storage in the array. This causes extra work to be done to store value types in the object array

There is a problem when you go to get an item back from the class in the StandardClass implementation. Take a look at how StandardClass.GetItem retrieves an item:

```
// Hold the retrieved string.
string sHolder;

// Have to cast or get error CS0266:
// Cannot implicitly convert type 'object' to 'string'...
sHolder = (string)C.GetItem(1);
```

Since the item returned by StandardClass.GetItem is of type object, it needs to be cast to a string in order to get what you hope is a string for index 1. It may not be a string—all you know for sure is that it's an object—but you have to cast it to a more specific type coming out so you can assign it properly. strings are a special case, since all objects can give a string representation of themselves, but you can see how this would be a problem if the array held a double and the assignment was to a bool.

These are both fixed by the GenericClass<T> implementation. The unboxing is addressed; no unboxing is required, since the return type of GetItem is the instantiated type, and the compiler enforces this by looking at the value being returned:

```
// Hold the retrieved string.
string sHolder;
int iHolder;

// No cast necessary
sHolder = gC.GetItem(1);

// Try to get a string into an int.
// error CS0029: Cannot implicitly convert type 'string' to 'int'
//iHolder = gC.GetItem(1);
```

In order to see one other difference between the two types, instantiate a few instances of each of them like so:

```
// Regular class
StandardClass A = new StandardClass();
Console.WriteLine(A);
StandardClass B = new StandardClass();
Console.WriteLine(B);
StandardClass C = new StandardClass();
Console.WriteLine(C);

// generic class
GenericClass<bool> gA = new GenericClass<bool>();
Console.WriteLine(gA);
GenericClass<int> gB = new GenericClass<int>();
```

```
Console.WriteLine(gB);
GenericClass<string> gC = new GenericClass<string>();
Console.WriteLine(gC);
GenericClass<string> gD = new GenericClass<string>();
Console.WriteLine(gD);
```

The output from the preceding code shows this:

```
There are 1 instances of CSharpRecipes.Generics+StandardClass which contains 0
items of type System.Object[]...
There are 2 instances of CSharpRecipes.Generics+StandardClass which contains 0
items of type System.Object[]...
There are 3 instances of CSharpRecipes.Generics+StandardClass which contains 0
items of type System.Object[]...
There are 1 instances of CSharpRecipes.Generics+GenericClass`1[System.Boolean]
which contains 0 items of type System.Boolean[]...
There are 1 instances of CSharpRecipes.Generics+GenericClass`1[System.Int32]
which contains 0 items of type System.Int32[]...
There are 1 instances of CSharpRecipes.Generics+GenericClass`1[System.String]
which contains 0 items of type System.String[]...
There are 2 instances of CSharpRecipes.Generics+GenericClass`1[System.String]
which contains 0 items of type System.String[]...
```

Discussion

The type parameters in generics allow you to create type-safe code without knowing the final type you will be working with. In many instances you want the types to have certain characteristics, in which case you place constraints on the type (Recipe 4.12). Methods can also have generic type parameters when the class itself does not; Recipe 4.9 shows an example.

Notice that while StandardClass has three instances, GenericClass has one instance in which it was declared with <bool> as the type, one instance in which <int> was the type, and two instances in which <string> was the declaring type. This means that, while there is one .NET Type object created for each non-generic class, there is one .NET Type object for every type-specific instantiation of a generic class.

StandardClass has three instances in the example code because StandardClass has only one type that is maintained by the CLR. With generics, one type is maintained for each combination of the class template and the type arguments passed when constructing a type instance. To make it more clear, you get one .NET type for GenericClass<bool>, one .NET type for GenericClass<int>, and a third .NET type for GenericClass<string>.

The internal static _count member helps to illustrate this point, as static members of a class are actually connected to the type that the CLR hangs on to. The CLR creates any given only type once and then maintains it until the AppDomain unloads. This is why the output from the calls to ToString() on these objects shows that the count is three for StandardClass (as there is truly only one of these) and between one and two for the GenericClass<T> types.

See Also

See the "Generic Type Parameters" and "Generic Classes" topics in the MSDN documentation.

4.3   Getting the Type of a Generic Type

Problem

You need to get the Type object for a generic type instance at runtime.

Solution

Provide the type parameters when using the typeof operator; or instantiate the generic type using the type parameters, then use the GetType( ) method.

Given a regular type and a generic type like this:

```
public class Simple
{
    public Simple()
    {
    }
}

public class SimpleGeneric<T>
{
    public SimpleGeneric()
    {
    }
}
```

the type can be retrieved for the simple type at runtime using the typeof operator with just the name of the simple type. For the generic type, the type parameter must be provided in the call to typeof. However, the simple type instance and the generic type instance can both call GetType( ) in the same manner.

```
Simple s = new Simple();
Type t = typeof(Simple);
Type alsoT = s.GetType();


// Provide a type parameter and you can get the
// instantiated type.
Type gtInt = typeof(SimpleGeneric<int>);
Type gtBool = typeof(SimpleGeneric<bool>);
Type gtString = typeof(SimpleGeneric<string>);


// You can also use the regular old GetType call from an instance
// as it has to be of an instance of the generic class.
SimpleGeneric<int> sgI = new SimpleGeneric<int>();
Type alsoGT = sgI.GetType();
```

Discussion

The type of the generic class cannot be retrieved directly because there is no type for a generic class without a type parameter provided. (See Recipe 4.2 for more information.) Only instantiated generic classes with a type parameter provided have a Type.

If you attempt to use the typeof operator with just the generic type definition and no type parameters, you will get the following error:

```
// This produces an error:
//Error 26    Using the generic type 'CSharpRecipes.Generics.SimpleGeneric<T>'
// requires '1' type arguments
Type gt = typeof(SimpleGeneric);
```

See Also

See Recipe 4.2; see the "typeof" topic in the MSDN documentation.

4.4   Replacing the ArrayList with Its Generic Counterpart

Problem

You want to enhance the performance of your application as well as make the code easier to work with by replacing all ArrayList objects with the generic version. This is imperative when you find that structures or other value types are being stored in these data structures, resulting in boxing/unboxing operations.

Solution

Replace all occurrences of the System.Collection.ArrayList class with the more efficient generic System.Collections.Generic.List class.

Here is a simple example of using a System.Collections.ArrayList object:

```
public static void UseNonGenericArrayList()
{
    // Create and populate an ArrayList.
    ArrayList numbers = new ArrayList();
    numbers.Add(1);     // Causes a boxing operation to occur
    numbers.Add(2);     // Causes a boxing operation to occur

    // Display all integers in the ArrayList.
    // Causes an unboxing operation to occur on each iteration
    foreach (int i in numbers)
    {
        Console.WriteLine(i);
    }

    numbers.Clear();
}
```

Here is that same code using a `System.Collections.Generic.List` object:

```
public static void UseGenericList()
{
    // Create and populate a List.
    List<int> numbers = new List<int>();
    numbers.Add(1);
    numbers.Add(2);

    // Display all integers in the ArrayList.
    foreach (int i in numbers)
    {
        Console.WriteLine(i);
    }

    numbers.Clear();
}
```

Discussion

Since `ArrayLists` are used in almost all applications, it is a good place to start to enhance the performance of your application. For simple implementations of the `ArrayList` in your application, this substitution should be quite easy. However, there are some things to watch out for. For example, the generic `List` class does not implement the `ICloneable` interface while the `ArrayList` class does.

Table 4-1 shows the equivalent members that are implemented in both classes.

Table 4-1. Equivalent members in the ArrayList and the generic List classes

Members in the ArrayList class	Equivalent members in the generic List class
Capacity property	Capacity property
Count property	Count property
IsFixedSize property	((IList)myList).IsFixedSize
IsReadOnly property	((IList)myList).IsReadOnly
IsSynchronized property	((IList)myList).IsSynchronized
Item property	Item property
SyncRoot property	((IList)myList).SyncRoot
Adapter static method	N/A
Add method	Add method
AddRange method	AddRange method
N/A	AsReadOnly method
BinarySearch method	BinarySearch method
Clear method	Clear method
Clone method	GetRange(0, numbers.Count)
Contains method	Contains method
N/A	ConvertAll method
CopyTo method	CopyTo method

Table 4-1. Equivalent members in the ArrayList and the generic List classes (continued)

Members in the ArrayList class	Equivalent members in the generic List class
N/A	`Exists` method
N/A	`Find` method
N/A	`FindAll` method
N/A	`FindIndex` method
N/A	`FindLast` method
N/A	`FindLastIndex` method
N/A	`ForEach` method
`FixedSize` static method	N/A
`GetRange` method	`GetRange` method
`IndexOf` method	`IndexOf` method
`Insert` method	`Insert` method
`InsertRange` method	`InsertRange` method
`LastIndexOf` method	`LastIndexOf` method
`ReadOnly` static method	`AsReadOnly` method
`Remove` method	`Remove` method
N/A	`RemoveAll` method
`RemoveAt` method	`RemoveAt` method
`RemoveRange` method	`RemoveRange` method
`Repeat` static method	Use a `for` loop and the `Add` method
`Reverse` method	`Reverse` method
`SetRange` method	`InsertRange` method
`Sort` method	`Sort` method
`Synchronized` static method	`lock(myList.SyncRoot) {…}`
`ToArray` method	`ToArray` method
N/A	`TrimExcess` method
`TrimToSize` method	`TrimToSize` method
N/A	`TrueForAll` method

In several cases within Table 4-1 there is not a one-to-one correlation between the members of an `ArrayList` and the members of the generic `List` class. Starting with the properties, notice that only the `Capacity`, `Count`, and `Item` properties are present in both classes. To make up for the missing properties in the `List` class, you can perform a cast to an `IList`. The following code shows how to use these casts to get at the missing properties.

```
List<int> numbers = new List<int>();

Console.WriteLine(((IList)numbers).IsReadOnly);
Console.WriteLine(((IList)numbers).IsFixedSize);
```

```
Console.WriteLine(((IList)numbers).IsSynchronized);
Console.WriteLine(((IList)numbers).SyncRoot);
```

Note that due to the absence of code that returns a synchronized version of a generic List and the absence of code that returns a fixed size generic List, the IsFixedSize and IsSynchronized properties will always return false. The SyncRoot property will always return the same object on which it is called. Essentially, this property returns the this pointer. Microsoft has decided to remove the ability to create a synchronous wrapper from any of the generic collection classes. Instead, they recommend using the lock keyword to lock the entire collection or another type of synchronization object that suits your needs.

The ArrayList has several static methods to which there is no direct equivalent method in the generic List class. To fix this you have to do a little work. The closest match for the static ArrayList.ReadOnly method is the AsReadOnly instance method of the generic List class. This makes for a fairly simple substitution.

The static ArrayList.Repeat method has no direct equivalent in the generic List class. So instead, you can use the following generic method:

```
public static void Repeat<T>(List<T> list, T obj, int count)
{
    if (count < 0)
    {
        throw (new ArgumentException(
            "The count parameter must be greater or equal to zero."));
    }

    for (int index = 0; index < count; index++)
    {
        list.Add(obj);
    }
}
```

This generic method takes three parameters:

list

> The generic List object

obj

> The object that will be added to the generic List object a specified number of times

count

> The number of times to add the object contained in obj to the generic List object

Since the Clone method is also missing from the generic List class (due to the fact that this class does not implement the ICloneable interface), you can instead use the GetRange method of the generic List class.

```
List<int> oldList = new List<int>();
// Populate oldList...

List<int> newList = oldList.GetRange(0, oldList.Count);
```

The GetRange method performs a shallow copy (similar to the Clone method of the ArrayList) of a range of elements in the List object. In this case the range of elements includes all elements.

 The ArrayList has a default initial capacity of 16 elements, while the List<T> has a default initial capacity of only 4 elements. This means that the List<T> will have to be resized (and reallocated) 3 times by the time the 17th element is added, whereas the ArrayList will have to be resized only one time. This should be taken into account when evaluating the performance of your application.

See Also

See the "System.Collections.ArrayList Class" and "System.Collections.Generic.List Class" topics in the MSDN documentation.

4.5 Replacing the Stack and Queue with Their Generic Counterparts

Problem

You want to enhance the performance of your application as well as make the code easier to work with by replacing all Stack and Queue objects with their generic versions. This is imperative when you find that structures or other value types are being stored in these data structures, resulting in boxing/unboxing operations.

Solution

Replace all occurrences of the System.Collections.Stack and System.Collection.Queue objects with the System.Collections.Generic.Stack and System.Collection.Generic.Queue objects.

Here is a simple example of using a System.Collections.Queue object:

```
public static void UseNonGenericQueue()
{
    // Create a nongeneric Queue object.
    Queue numericQueue = new Queue();

    // Populate Queue (causing a boxing operation to occur).
    numericQueue.Enqueue(1);
    numericQueue.Enqueue(2);
    numericQueue.Enqueue(3);

    // De-populate Queue and display items (causing an unboxing operation to occur)
    Console.WriteLine(numericQueue.Dequeue());
    Console.WriteLine(numericQueue.Dequeue());
    Console.WriteLine(numericQueue.Dequeue().ToString());
}
```

Here is that same code using a System.Collections.Generic.Queue object:

```
public static void UseGenericQueue()
{
    // Create a generic Queue object.
    Queue<int> numericQueue = new Queue<int>();

    // Populate Queue.
    numericQueue.Enqueue(1);
    numericQueue.Enqueue(2);
    numericQueue.Enqueue(3);

    // De-populate Queue and display items.
    Console.WriteLine(numericQueue.Dequeue());
    Console.WriteLine(numericQueue.Dequeue());
    Console.WriteLine(numericQueue.Dequeue());
}
```

Here is a simple example of using a System.Collections.Stack object:

```
public static void UseNonGenericStack()
{
    // Create a nongeneric Stack object.
    Stack numericStack = new Stack();

    // Populate Stack (causing a boxing operation to occur).
    numericStack.Push(1);
    numericStack.Push(2);
    numericStack.Push(3);

    // De-populate Stack and display items (causing an unboxing operation to occur).
    Console.WriteLine(numericStack.Pop().ToString());
    Console.WriteLine(numericStack.Pop().ToString());
    Console.WriteLine(numericStack.Pop().ToString());
}
```

Here is that same code using a System.Collections.Generic.Stack object:

```
public static void UseGenericStack()
{
    // Create a generic Stack object.
    Stack<int> numericStack = new Stack<int>();

    // Populate Stack.
    numericStack.Push(1);
    numericStack.Push(2);
    numericStack.Push(3);

    // De-populate Stack and display items.
    Console.WriteLine(numericStack.Pop().ToString());
    Console.WriteLine(numericStack.Pop().ToString());
    Console.WriteLine(numericStack.Pop().ToString());
}
```

Discussion

On the surface, the generic and nongeneric Queue and Stack classes seem similar enough. However, it is a very different story underneath the surface. The basic use of the generic Queue and Stack objects are the same as with their nongeneric counterparts, except for the syntax used to instantiate the objects. The generic form requires a *type argument* in order to create the type. The type argument in this example is an int. This type argument indicates that this Queue or Stack object will be able to contain only integer types, as well as any type that implicitly converts to an integer, such as a short:

```
short s = 300;
numericQueue.Enqueue(s);     // OK, because of the implicit cast
```

However, a type that cannot be implicitly converted to an integer, such as a double, will cause a compile-time error.

```
double d = 300;
numericQueue.Enqueue(d);           // Error, no implicit case available
numericQueue.Enqueue((int)d);      // OK, because of the explicit cast
```

The nongeneric form does not require this type argument, because the nongeneric Queue and Stack objects are allowed to contain only elements of type Object.

When choosing between a generic and nongeneric Queue or Stack, you need to decide whether or not you wish to use a strongly typed Queue or Stack object (i.e., the generic Queue or Stack class) or a weakly typed Queue or Stack object (i.e., the nongeneric Queue or Stack class). Choosing the generic Queue or Stack class over its nongeneric form gives you many benefits including:

Type safety
> Each element contained in the data structure is typed to one specific type. This means no more casting of objects when they are added to or removed from the data structure. You cannot store multiple disparate types within a single data structure; you always know what type is stored within the data structure. Type checking is done at compile time rather than runtime. This boils down to writing less code, achieving better performance, and making fewer errors.

Shortened development time
> To make a type-safe data structure without using generics means having to subclass the System.Collections.Queue or System.Collections.Stack class in order to create your own. This is time-consuming and error-prone. Generics allow you to simply tell the Queue or Stack object at compile time what type it is allowed to hold.

Performance
> The generic Queue or Stack does not require a potentially time-consuming cast to occur when adding and removing elements from it. In addition, no boxing operation occurs when adding a value type to the Queue or Stack. Likewise, no unboxing operation occurs when removing a value type from the Queue or Stack.

Easier-to-read code

Your code base will be much smaller since you will not have to subclass the nongeneric Queue or Stack class to create your own strongly typed class. In addition, the type-safety features of generic code will allow you to better understand what the purpose of the Queue or Stack class is in your code.

A difference between the generic and nongeneric Queue and Stack classes, is the members implemented within each class. The members that are implemented in the nongeneric Queue and Stack classes, but not in the generic Queue and Stack class are listed here:

Clone method
IsSynchronized property
SyncRoot property
Synchronized method

The addition of the Clone method on the nongeneric Queue and Stack classes is due to the ICloneable interface being implemented only on the nongeneric Queue and Stack classes. However, all other interfaces implemented by the generic and nongeneric Queue and Stack classes are identical.

One way around the missing Clone method in the generic Queue and Stack classes is to use the constructor that accepts an IEnumerable<T> type. Since this is one of the interfaces that the Queue and Stack classes implement, it is easy to write. For the Queue object, the code is as follows:

```
public static void CloneQueue( )
{
    // Create a generic Queue object.
    Queue<int> numericQueue = new Queue<int>( );

    // Populate Queue.
    numericQueue.Enqueue(1);
    numericQueue.Enqueue(2);
    numericQueue.Enqueue(3);

    // Create a clone of the numericQueue.
    Queue<int> clonedNumericQueue = new Queue<int>(numericQueue);

    // This does a simple peek at the values not a dequeue.
    foreach (int i in clonedNumericQueue)
    {
        Console.WriteLine("foreach: " + i.ToString( ));
    }

    // De-populate Queue and display items.
    Console.WriteLine(clonedNumericQueue.Dequeue( ).ToString( ));
    Console.WriteLine(clonedNumericQueue.Dequeue( ).ToString( ));
    Console.WriteLine(clonedNumericQueue.Dequeue( ).ToString( ));
}
```

The output for this method is shown here:

```
foreach: 1
foreach: 2
foreach: 3
1
2
3
```

For the Stack object, the code is as follows.

```
public static void CloneStack( )
{
    // Create a generic Stack object.
    Stack<int> numericStack = new Stack<int>( );

    // Populate Stack.
    numericStack.Push(1);
    numericStack.Push(2);
    numericStack.Push(3);

    // Clone the numericStack object.
    Stack<int> clonedNumericStack = new Stack<int>(numericStack);

    // This does a simple peek at the values not a pop.
    foreach (int i in clonedNumericStack)
    {
        Console.WriteLine("foreach: " + i.ToString( ));
    }

    // De-populate Stack and display items.
    Console.WriteLine(clonedNumericStack.Pop( ).ToString( ));
    Console.WriteLine(clonedNumericStack.Pop( ).ToString( ));
    Console.WriteLine(clonedNumericStack.Pop( ).ToString( ));
}
```

The output for this method is shown here:

```
foreach: 1
foreach: 2
foreach: 3
1
2
3
```

This constructor creates a new instance of the Queue or Stack class containing the elements copied from the IEnumerable<T> type.

See Also

See the "System.Collections.Stack Class," "System.Collections.Generic.Stack Class," "System.Collections.Queue Class," and "System.Collections.Generic.Queue Class" topics in the MSDN documentation.

4.6 Implementing a Linked List

Problem

You need a linked data structure that allows you to easily add and remove elements.

Solution

Use the generic LinkedList<T> class. The following method creates a LinkedList<T> class, adds nodes to this linked list object, and then uses several methods to obtain information from nodes within the linked list:

```
public static void UseLinkedList()
{
    // Create a new LinkedList object.
    LinkedList<TodoItem> todoList = new LinkedList<TodoItem>();

    // Create TodoItem objects to add to the linked list.
    TodoItem i1 = new TodoItem("paint door", "Should be done third");
    TodoItem i2 = new TodoItem("buy door", "Should be done first");
    TodoItem i3 = new TodoItem("assemble door", "Should be done second");
    TodoItem i4 = new TodoItem("hang door", "Should be done last");

    // Add the items.
    todoList.AddFirst(i1);
    todoList.AddFirst(i2);
    todoList.AddBefore(todoList.Find(i1), i3);
    todoList.AddAfter(todoList.Find(i1), i4);

    // Display all items.
    foreach (TodoItem tdi in todoList)
    {
        Console.WriteLine(tdi.Name + " : " + tdi.Comment);
    }

    // Display information from the second node in the linked list.
    Console.WriteLine("todoList.First.Next.Value.Name == " +
                    todoList.First.Next.Value.Name);

    // Display information from the next to last node in the linked list.
    Console.WriteLine("todoList.Last.Previous.Value.Name == " +
                    todoList.Last.Previous.Value.Name);
}
```

The output for this method is shown here:

```
buy door : Should be done first
assemble door : Should be done second
paint door : Should be done third
hang door : Should be done last
todoList.First.Value.Name == buy door
todoList.First.Next.Value.Name == assemble door
todoList.Last.Previous.Value.Name == paint door
```

This is the `TodoItem` class, which is a simple container for two strings _name and _comment.

```
public class TodoItem
{
    public TodoItem (string name, string comment)
    {
        _name = name;
        _comment = comment;
    }

    private string _name = "";
    private string _comment = "";

    public string Name
    {
        get    {return (_name);}
        set { _name = value;}
    }

    public string Comment
    {
        get    {return (_comment);}
        set    { _comment = value;}
    }
}
```

Discussion

The `LinkedList<T>` class in the .NET framework is considered a doubly linked list. This is because each node in the linked list contains a pointer to both the previous node and the next node in the linked list. Figure 4-1 shows what a doubly linked list looks like diagrammed on paper. Each node in this diagram represents a single `LinkedListNode<T>` object.

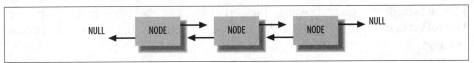

Figure 4-1. Graphical representation of a doubly linked list with three nodes

Notice that each node (i.e., the square boxes) contains a pointer to the next node (i.e., the arrows pointing to the right) and a pointer to the previous node (i.e., the arrows pointing to the left) in the linked list. In contrast, a singly linked list contains only pointers to the next node in the list. There is no pointer to the previous node.

In the `LinkedList<T>` class, the previous node is always accessed through the `Previous` property and the next node is always accessed through the `Next` property. The first node's `Previous` property in the linked list always returns a `null` value. Likewise, the last node's `Next` property in the linked list always returns a `null` value.

Each node (represented by the boxes in Figure 4-1) in the linked list is actually a generic LinkedListNode<T> object. So a LinkedList<T> object is actually a collection of LinkedListNode<T> objects. Each of these LinkedListNode<T> objects contains properties to access the next and previous LinkedListNode<T> objects, as well as the object contained within it. The object contained in the LinkedListNode<T> object is accessed through the Value property. In addition to these properties, a LinkedListNode<T> object also contains a property called List, which allows access to the containing LinkedList<T> object.

As far as performance is concerned, the List<T> class has benefits over using a LinkedList<T> class. Adding and removing nodes within a List<T> is, in general, faster than the same operation using a LinkedList<T> class. Comparing the List<T>. Add method to the Add* methods of the LinkedList<T> class, the performance hit isn't due to the actual add operation, but due to the pressure that the LinkedList<T> puts on the garbage collector. A List<T> stores its data essentially in one big array on the managed heap, whereas the LinkedList<T> can potentially store its nodes all over the managed heap. This forces the garbage collector to work that much harder to manage LinkedList<T> node objects on the managed heap. Note that the List<T>.Insert* methods can be slower than adding a node anywhere within a LinkedList<T> using one of its Add* methods. However, this is dependent on where the object is inserted into the List<T>. An Insert method must shift all the elements within the List<T> object, at the point where the new element is inserted, up by one position. If the new element is inserted at or near the end of the List<T>, the overhead of shifting the existing elements is negligible compared to the garbage collector overhead of managing the LinkedList<T> nodes objects.

Another area where the List<T> can outperform the LinkedList<T> is when you're doing an indexed access. With the List<T>, you can use the indexer to do an indexed lookup of the element at the specified position. However, with a LinkedList<T> class, you do not have that luxury. With a LinkedList<T> class, you must navigate the LinkedListNode<T> objects using the Previous and Next properties on each LinkedListNode<T>, running through the list until you find the one at the specified position.

A List<T> class also has performance benefits over a LinkedList<T> class when searching for an element or node. The List<T>.BinarySearch method is faster at finding elements within a List<T> object than its comparable methods within the LinkedList<T> class, namely the Contains, Find, and FindLast methods. This is due to the fact that the LinkedList<T> methods perform a linear search whereas the List<T>. BinarySearch method performs a binary search. In simple terms, a binary search takes advantage of the fact that the elements within the List<T> are sorted. This entails calling the Sort method before the BinarySearch (note that if any new elements are added, the Sort method must again be called before the BinarySearch method). Using this, the binary search will examine the middle element in the list and ask the question: is the object you're looking for greater than the object at the current point in the list? If so, you know the target object is at an index somewhere in the list above the current index. If not, the object is at an index somewhere in the list below the current index. The binary search algorithm keeps asking this question until the object is found. In contrast, a linear search starts at the first element in a list and determines if that object is the one you are looking for. If not, the search continues to the next element in the list. This operation keeps repeating until the object is found in the list.

See Also

See the "LinkedList<T> Class" topic in the MSDN documentation.

4.7   Creating a Value Type That Can be Initialized to Null

Problem

You have a variable that is a numeric type, which will hold a numeric value obtained from a database. The database may return this value as a null. You need a simple clean way to store this numeric value, even if it is returned as a null.

Solution

Use a *nullable* value type. There are two ways of creating a nullable value type. The first way is to use the ? type modifier:

```
int? myDBInt = null;
```

The second way is to use the Nullable<T> generic type:

```
Nullable<int> myDBInt = new Nullable<int>();
```

Discussion

Essentially both of the following statements are equivalent:

```
int? myDBInt = null;
Nullable<int> myDBInt = new Nullable<int>();
```

In both cases, myDBInt is considered a nullable type and is initialized to null. A nullable type implements the INullableValue interface, which has two read-only property members, HasValue and Value. The HasValue property returns false if the nullable type is set to null; otherwise it returns true. If HasValue returns true, you can access the Value property, which contains the currently stored value in the nullable data type. If HasValue returns false and you attempt to read the Value property, you will get an InvalidOperationException thrown. This is because the Value property is undefined at this point.

In addition, testing the nullable type can be done in one of two ways. First, by using the HasValue property as shown here:

```
if (myDBInt.HasValue)
    Console.WriteLine("Has a value:  " + myDBInt.Value);
else
    Console.WriteLine("Does not have a value (NULL)");
```

and, second, by comparing it to null:

```
if (myDBInt != null)
    Console.WriteLine("Has a value:  " + myDBInt.Value);
else
    Console.WriteLine("Does not have a value (NULL)");
```

Either method is acceptable.

When casting a nullable type to a non-nullable type, the cast operates as it would normally, except when the nullable type is set to null. In this case, an InvalidOperationException is thrown. When casting a non-nullable type to a nullable type, the cast operates as it would normally. No InvalidOperationException will be thrown, as the non-nullable type can never be null.

The tricky thing to watch out for with nullable types is when comparisons are performed. For example if the following code is executed:

```
if (myTempDBInt < 100)
    Console.WriteLine("myTempDBInt < 100");
else
    Console.WriteLine("myTempDBInt >= 100");
```

The text "myTempDBInt >= 100" is displayed, which is obviously incorrect. To fix this code, you have to check if myTempDBInt is null. If it is not, you can execute the if statement in the previous code block:

```
if (myTempDBInt != null)
{
    if (myTempDBInt < 100)
        Console.WriteLine("myTempDBInt < 100");
    else
        Console.WriteLine("myTempDBInt >= 100");
}
else
{
    // Handle the null here.
}
```

Another interesting thing about nullable types is that you can use them in expressions similar to normal numeric types, for example:

```
int? DBInt = 10;
int Value = 2;
int? Result = DBInt + Value;    // Result == 12
```

The result of using a nullable type in an expression is a null if any nullable type is null. However, if none of the nullable types is null, the operation is evaluated as it normally would be. If DBInt, for example, is set to null, the value placed in Result will also be null.

See Also

See the "Nullable<T> Generic Class" and "Using Nullable Types" topics in the MSDN documentation.

4.8 Reversing the Contents of a Sorted List

Problem

You want to be able to reverse the contents of a sorted list of items while also maintaining the ability to access them in both array and list styles like SortedList and the generic SortedList<T> classes provide. Neither SortedList nor SortedList<T> provides a direct way to accomplish this without reloading the list.

Solution

Use the ReversibleSortedList<TKey,TValue> class provided for you here. Reversible-SortedList<TKey,TValue> is based on the original SortedList<TKey,TValue> class so that all of the same functionality is preserved, with the additional bonus of being able to reverse the order of the list easily.

After instantiating a ReversibleSortedList<TKey,TValue>, the key of which is an int and the value of which is a string, a series of unordered numbers and their text representations are inserted into the list. Those items are then displayed.

```
ReversibleSortedList<int, string> rsl = new ReversibleSortedList<int, string>();
rsl.Add(2, "2");
rsl.Add(5, "5");
rsl.Add(3, "3");
rsl.Add(1, "1");

foreach (KeyValuePair<int, string> kvp in rsl)
{
    Debug.WriteLine("\t" + kvp.Key + "\t" + kvp.Value);
}
```

The output for the list is shown sorted in ascending order (the default):

```
1    1
2    2
3    3
5    5
```

Now the sort order is reversed by setting the SortDirection property of the ReversibleSortedList to Descending. Then the Sort() method is called to resort the list in the new order. The results are then displayed.

```
// Switch sort directions.
rsl.Comparer.SortDirection = ListSortDirection.Descending;

// Re-sort the list.
rsl.Sort( );

foreach (KeyValuePair<int, string> kvp in rsl)
{
    Debug.WriteLine("\t" + kvp.Key + "\t" + kvp.Value);
}
```

This time the output is in descending order:

```
5    5
3    3
2    2
1    1
```

When a new item is added to the list, it is added in the current sort order, but by quickly reversing the order after adding all of the items, you keep the ordering of the list intact:

```
rsl.Add(4, "4");

foreach (KeyValuePair<int, string> kvp in rsl)
{
    Debug.WriteLine("\t" + kvp.Key + "\t" + kvp.Value);
}

// Switch sort directions.
rsl.Comparer.SortDirection = ListSortDirection.Ascending;

// Re-sort the list.
rsl.Sort( );

foreach (KeyValuePair<int, string> kvp in rsl)
{
    Debug.WriteLine("\t" + kvp.Key + "\t" + kvp.Value);
}
```

It can be seen that the output has both descending and ascending orders with the new item:

```
5    5
4    4
3    3
2    2
1    1
1    1
2    2
3    3
4    4
5    5
```

This is accomplished in the ReversibleSortedList<TKey,TValue> by a nested class called SortDirectionComparer<T> that implements the IComparer<T> interface. This class can be seen in the Discussion section where the ReversibleSorted-List<TKey,TValue> is listed. A class that implements the IComparer<T> interface can be taken as a parameter to the ReversibleSortedList<TKey,TValue> to override the default sorting. Within that IComparer<T> implementation is the Compare method:

```
public int Compare(T lhs, T rhs)
{
    int compareResult =
        lhs.ToString().CompareTo(rhs.ToString());

    // If order is DESC, reverse this comparison.
    if (SortDirection == ListSortDirection.Descending)
        compareResult *= -1;
    return compareResult;
}
```

The Compare method uses the SortDirection property of the SortDirectionComparer<T> to determine the ordering of the items. This property is set on an internal instance of SortDirectionComparer<T> by the ReversibleSortedList<TKey,TValue> class. This happens when its own SortDirection property is set in the constructor shown here:

```
public ReversibleSortedList()
{
    this.keys = ReversibleSortedList<TKey, TValue>.emptyKeys;
    this.values = ReversibleSortedList<TKey, TValue>.emptyValues;
    this._size = 0;
    this._sortDirectionComparer = new SortDirectionComparer<TKey>();
    this._currentSortDirection = this._sortDirectionComparer.SortDirection;
}
```

This allows it to reverse the sort order at any given time but does not take care of reordering the list for items already in the list. To do that, the Reversible-SortedList<TKey,TValue> class adds a new Sort() method that takes care of reordering the list like so:

```
public void Sort()
{
    // Check if we are already sorted the right way.
    if (this._currentSortDirection != this._sortDirectionComparer.SortDirection)
    {
        // Reverse the arrays as they were already sorted on insert.
        Array.Reverse(this.keys, 0, this._size);
        Array.Reverse(this.values, 0, this._size);
        // Set our current order.
        this._currentSortDirection = this._sortDirectionComparer.SortDirection;
    }
}
```

Discussion

ReversibleSortedList<TKey,TValue> is shown in its entirety in Example 4-3.

Example 4-3. ReversibleSortedList class

```
[Serializable, ComVisible(false), DebuggerDisplay("Count = {Count}")]
public class ReversibleSortedList<TKey, TValue> :
        IDictionary<TKey, TValue>, ICollection<KeyValuePair<TKey, TValue>>,
        IEnumerable<KeyValuePair<TKey, TValue>>,
        IDictionary, ICollection, IEnumerable
{
    #region SortDirectionComparer class definition
    public class SortDirectionComparer<T> : IComparer<T>
    {
        private System.ComponentModel.ListSortDirection _sortDir;

        public SortDirectionComparer()
        {
            _sortDir = ListSortDirection.Ascending;
        }

        public SortDirectionComparer(ListSortDirection sortDir)
        {
            _sortDir = sortDir;
        }

        public System.ComponentModel.ListSortDirection SortDirection
        {
            get { return _sortDir; }
            set { _sortDir = value; }
        }

        public int Compare(T lhs, T rhs)
        {
            int compareResult =
                lhs.ToString().CompareTo(rhs.ToString());

            // If order is DESC, reverse this comparison.
            if (SortDirection == ListSortDirection.Descending)
                compareResult *= -1;
            return compareResult;
        }
    }
    #endregion // SortDirectionComparer

    #region CTORS
    static ReversibleSortedList()
    {
        ReversibleSortedList<TKey, TValue>.emptyKeys = new TKey[0];
        ReversibleSortedList<TKey, TValue>.emptyValues = new TValue[0];
    }

    public ReversibleSortedList()
```

Example 4-3. ReversibleSortedList class (continued)

```
{
    this.keys = ReversibleSortedList<TKey, TValue>.emptyKeys;
    this.values = ReversibleSortedList<TKey, TValue>.emptyValues;
    this._size = 0;
    this._sortDirectionComparer = new SortDirectionComparer<TKey>();
    this._currentSortDirection = this._sortDirectionComparer.SortDirection;
}

public ReversibleSortedList(SortDirectionComparer<TKey> comparer)
    : this()
{
    if (comparer != null)
    {
        this._sortDirectionComparer = comparer;
        this._currentSortDirection = _sortDirectionComparer.SortDirection;
    }
}

public ReversibleSortedList(IDictionary<TKey, TValue> dictionary)
    : this(dictionary, (SortDirectionComparer<TKey>)null)
{
}

public ReversibleSortedList(int capacity)
{
    if (capacity < 0)
    {
        throw new ArgumentOutOfRangeException(
            "capacity", "Non-negative number required");
    }
    this.keys = new TKey[capacity];
    this.values = new TValue[capacity];
    this._sortDirectionComparer = new SortDirectionComparer<TKey>();
    this._currentSortDirection = _sortDirectionComparer.SortDirection;
}

public ReversibleSortedList(IDictionary<TKey, TValue> dictionary,
                            SortDirectionComparer<TKey> comparer)
    : this((dictionary != null) ? dictionary.Count : 0, comparer)
{
    if (dictionary == null)
    {
        throw new ArgumentNullException("dictionary");
    }
    dictionary.Keys.CopyTo(this.keys, 0);
    dictionary.Values.CopyTo(this.values, 0);
    Array.Sort<TKey, TValue>(this.keys, this.values,
                            this._sortDirectionComparer);
    this._size = dictionary.Count;
}

public ReversibleSortedList(int capacity, SortDirectionComparer<TKey> comparer)
    : this(comparer)
```

Example 4-3. ReversibleSortedList class (continued)

```
    {
        this.Capacity = capacity;
    }
    #endregion //CTORS

    #region Public Methods
    public void Add(TKey key, TValue value)
    {
        if (key.Equals(null))
        {
            throw new ArgumentNullException("key");
        }
        int num1 = Array.BinarySearch<TKey>(this.keys, 0, this._size, key,
                                        this._sortDirectionComparer);
        if (num1 >= 0)
        {
            throw new ArgumentException("Attempting to add duplicate");
        }
        this.Insert(~num1, key, value);
    }

    public void Clear()
    {
        this.version++;
        Array.Clear(this.keys, 0, this._size);
        Array.Clear(this.values, 0, this._size);
        this._size = 0;
    }

    public bool ContainsKey(TKey key)
    {
        return (this.IndexOfKey(key) >= 0);
    }

    public bool ContainsValue(TValue value)
    {
        return (this.IndexOfValue(value) >= 0);
    }

    public IEnumerator<KeyValuePair<TKey, TValue>> GetEnumerator()
    {
        return new ReversibleSortedList<TKey, TValue>.Enumerator<TKey, TValue>(
                this);
    }
    public int IndexOfKey(TKey key)
    {
        if (key.Equals(null))
        {
            throw new ArgumentNullException("key");
        }
        int num1 = Array.BinarySearch<TKey>(this.keys, 0, this._size, key,
                                        this._sortDirectionComparer);
```

Example 4-3. ReversibleSortedList class (continued)

```
        if (num1 < 0)
        {
            return -1;
        }
        return num1;
    }

    public int IndexOfValue(TValue value)
    {
        return Array.IndexOf<TValue>(this.values, value, 0, this._size);
    }

    public bool Remove(TKey key)
    {
        int num1 = this.IndexOfKey(key);
        if (num1 >= 0)
        {
            this.RemoveAt(num1);
        }
        return (num1 >= 0);
    }

    public void RemoveAt(int index)
    {
        if ((index < 0) || (index >= this._size))
        {
            throw new ArgumentOutOfRangeException("index", "Index out of range");
        }
        this._size--;
        if (index < this._size)
        {
            Array.Copy(this.keys, (int)(index + 1), this.keys, index,
                    (int)(this._size - index));
            Array.Copy(this.values, (int)(index + 1), this.values, index,
                    (int)(this._size - index));
        }
        this.keys[this._size] = default(TKey);
        this.values[this._size] = default(TValue);
        this.version++;
    }

    public void Sort()
    {
        // Check if we are already sorted the right way.
        if (this._currentSortDirection !=
            this._sortDirectionComparer.SortDirection)
        {
            // Reverse the arrays as they were already sorted on insert.
            Array.Reverse(this.keys, 0, this._size);
            Array.Reverse(this.values, 0, this._size);
            // Set our current order.
            this._currentSortDirection = this._sortDirectionComparer.SortDirection;
```

Example 4-3. ReversibleSortedList class (continued)

```
        }
    }

    public void TrimExcess()
    {
        int num1 = (int)(this.keys.Length * 0.9);
        if (this._size < num1)
        {
            this.Capacity = this._size;
        }
    }

    public bool TryGetValue(TKey key, out TValue value)
    {
        int num1 = this.IndexOfKey(key);
        if (num1 >= 0)
        {
            value = this.values[num1];
            return true;
        }
        value = default(TValue);
        return false;
    }

    #endregion // Public Methods

    #region Private Methods
    private void EnsureCapacity(int min)
    {
        int num1 = (this.keys.Length == 0) ? 4 : (this.keys.Length * 2);
        if (num1 < min)
        {
            num1 = min;
        }
        this.InternalSetCapacity(num1, false);
    }

    private TValue GetByIndex(int index)
    {
        if ((index < 0) || (index >= this._size))
        {
            throw new ArgumentOutOfRangeException("index", "Index out of range");
        }
        return this.values[index];
    }

    private TKey GetKey(int index)
    {
        if ((index < 0) || (index >= this._size))
        {
            throw new ArgumentOutOfRangeException("index", "Index out of range");
        }
}
```

Example 4-3. ReversibleSortedList class (continued)

```
        return this.keys[index];
    }

    private KeyList<TKey, TValue> GetKeyListHelper( )
    {
        if (this.keyList == null)
        {
            this.keyList = new KeyList<TKey, TValue>(this);
        }
        return this.keyList;
    }

    private ValueList<TKey, TValue> GetValueListHelper( )
    {
        if (this.valueList == null)
        {
            this.valueList = new ValueList<TKey, TValue>(this);
        }
        return this.valueList;
    }

    private void Insert(int index, TKey key, TValue value)
    {
        if (this._size == this.keys.Length)
        {
            this.EnsureCapacity(this._size + 1);
        }
        if (index < this._size)
        {
            Array.Copy(this.keys, index, this.keys, (int)(index + 1),
                        (int)(this._size - index));
            Array.Copy(this.values, index, this.values, (int)(index + 1),
                        (int)(this._size - index));
        }
        this.keys[index] = key;
        this.values[index] = value;
        this._size++;
        this.version++;
    }

    private void InternalSetCapacity(int value, bool updateVersion)
    {
        if (value != this.keys.Length)
        {
            if (value < this._size)
            {
                throw new ArgumentOutOfRangeException(
                    "value", "Too small capacity");
            }
            if (value > 0)
            {
                TKey[] localArray1 = new TKey[value];
```

Example 4-3. ReversibleSortedList class (continued)

```
                    TValue[] localArray2 = new TValue[value];
                    if (this._size > 0)
                    {
                        Array.Copy(this.keys, 0, localArray1, 0, this._size);
                        Array.Copy(this.values, 0, localArray2, 0, this._size);
                    }
                    this.keys = localArray1;
                    this.values = localArray2;
                }
                else
                {
                    this.keys = ReversibleSortedList<TKey, TValue>.emptyKeys;
                    this.values = ReversibleSortedList<TKey, TValue>.emptyValues;
                }
                if (updateVersion)
                {
                    this.version++;
                }
            }
        }

        private static bool IsCompatibleKey(object key)
        {
            if (key.Equals(null))
            {
                throw new ArgumentNullException("key");
            }
            return (key is TKey);
        }

        void ICollection<KeyValuePair<TKey, TValue>>.Add(
                                    KeyValuePair<TKey, TValue> keyValuePair)
        {
            this.Add(keyValuePair.Key, keyValuePair.Value);
        }

        bool ICollection<KeyValuePair<TKey, TValue>>.Contains(
                                      KeyValuePair<TKey, TValue> keyValuePair)
        {
            int num1 = this.IndexOfKey(keyValuePair.Key);
            if ((num1 >= 0) && EqualityComparer<TValue>.Default.Equals(
                                            this.values[num1],
                                            keyValuePair.Value))
            {
                return true;
            }
            return false;
        }

        void ICollection<KeyValuePair<TKey, TValue>>.CopyTo(
                                       KeyValuePair<TKey, TValue>[] array,
                                       int arrayIndex)
```

Example 4-3. ReversibleSortedList class (continued)

```
{
    if (array == null)
    {
        throw new ArgumentNullException("array");
    }
    if ((arrayIndex < 0) || (arrayIndex > array.Length))
    {
        throw new ArgumentOutOfRangeException(
                "arrayIndex", "Need a non-negative number");
    }
    if ((array.Length - arrayIndex) < this.Count)
    {
        throw new ArgumentException("ArrayPlusOffTooSmall");
    }
    for (int num1 = 0; num1 < this.Count; num1++)
    {
        KeyValuePair<TKey, TValue> pair1;
        pair1 = new KeyValuePair<TKey, TValue>(
                    this.keys[num1], this.values[num1]);
        array[arrayIndex + num1] = pair1;
    }
}

bool ICollection<KeyValuePair<TKey, TValue>>.Remove(
                            KeyValuePair<TKey, TValue> keyValuePair)
{
    int num1 = this.IndexOfKey(keyValuePair.Key);
    if ((num1 >= 0) && EqualityComparer<TValue>.Default.Equals(
                            this.values[num1],
                            keyValuePair.Value))
    {
        this.RemoveAt(num1);
        return true;
    }
    return false;
}

IEnumerator<KeyValuePair<TKey, TValue>>
    IEnumerable<KeyValuePair<TKey, TValue>>.GetEnumerator()
{
    return new ReversibleSortedList<TKey, TValue>.Enumerator<TKey, TValue>(
                this);
}

void ICollection.CopyTo(Array array, int arrayIndex)
{
    if (array == null)
    {
        throw new ArgumentNullException("array");
    }
    if (array.Rank != 1)
    {
```

Example 4-3. ReversibleSortedList class (continued)

```
            throw new ArgumentException(
                    "MultiDimensional array copies are not supported");
        }
        if (array.GetLowerBound(0) != 0)
        {
            throw new ArgumentException("A non-zero lower bound was provided");
        }
        if ((arrayIndex < 0) || (arrayIndex > array.Length))
        {
            throw new ArgumentOutOfRangeException(
                    "arrayIndex", "Need non negative number");
        }
        if ((array.Length - arrayIndex) < this.Count)
        {
            throw new ArgumentException("Array plus the offset is too small");
        }
        KeyValuePair<TKey, TValue>[] pairArray1 =
            array as KeyValuePair<TKey, TValue>[];
        if (pairArray1 != null)
        {
            for (int num1 = 0; num1 < this.Count; num1++)
            {
                pairArray1[num1 + arrayIndex] =
                    new KeyValuePair<TKey, TValue>(this.keys[num1],
                                                    this.values[num1]);
            }
        }
        else
        {
            object[] objArray1 = array as object[];
            if (objArray1 == null)
            {
                throw new ArgumentException("Invalid array type");
            }
            try
            {
                for (int num2 = 0; num2 < this.Count; num2++)
                {
                    objArray1[num2 + arrayIndex] =
                        new KeyValuePair<TKey, TValue>(this.keys[num2],
                                                        this.values[num2]);
                }
            }
            catch (ArrayTypeMismatchException)
            {
                throw new ArgumentException("Invalid array type");
            }
        }
    }

    void IDictionary.Add(object key, object value)
    {
```

Example 4-3. ReversibleSortedList class (continued)

```
        ReversibleSortedList<TKey, TValue>.VerifyKey(key);
        ReversibleSortedList<TKey, TValue>.VerifyValueType(value);
        this.Add((TKey)key, (TValue)value);
    }

    bool IDictionary.Contains(object key)
    {
        if (ReversibleSortedList<TKey, TValue>.IsCompatibleKey(key))
        {
            return this.ContainsKey((TKey)key);
        }
        return false;
    }

    IDictionaryEnumerator IDictionary.GetEnumerator()
    {
        return new ReversibleSortedList<TKey, TValue>.Enumerator<TKey, TValue>(
                this);
    }

    void IDictionary.Remove(object key)
    {
        if (ReversibleSortedList<TKey, TValue>.IsCompatibleKey(key))
        {
            this.Remove((TKey)key);
        }
    }

    IEnumerator IEnumerable.GetEnumerator()
    {
        return new ReversibleSortedList<TKey, TValue>.Enumerator<TKey, TValue>(
                this);
    }


    private static void VerifyKey(object key)
    {
        if (key.Equals(null))
        {
            throw new ArgumentNullException("key");
        }
        if (!(key is TKey))
        {
            throw new ArgumentException(
                    "Argument passed is of wrong type", "key");
        }
    }

    private static void VerifyValueType(object value)
    {
        if (!(value is TValue) && ((value != null) || typeof(TValue).IsValueType))
        {
```

Example 4-3. ReversibleSortedList class (continued)

```
            throw new ArgumentException(
                    "Argument passed is of wrong type", "value");
    }
}
#endregion // Private methods

#region Public Properties
public int Capacity
{
    get
    {
        return this.keys.Length;
    }
    set
    {
        this.InternalSetCapacity(value, true);
    }
}

public SortDirectionComparer<TKey> Comparer
{
    get
    {
        return this._sortDirectionComparer;
    }
}

public int Count
{
    get
    {
        return this._size;
    }
}

public TValue this[TKey key]
{
    get
    {
        TValue local1;
        int num1 = this.IndexOfKey(key);
        if (num1 >= 0)
        {
            return this.values[num1];
        }
        else
        {
            //throw new KeyNotFoundException( );
            local1 = default(TValue);
            return local1;
        }
    }
```

Example 4-3. ReversibleSortedList class (continued)

```
    set
    {
        if (key == null)
        {
            throw new ArgumentNullException("key");
        }
        int num1 = Array.BinarySearch<TKey>(this.keys, 0, this._size, key,
                                    this._sortDirectionComparer);
        if (num1 >= 0)
        {
            this.values[num1] = value;
            this.version++;
        }
        else
        {
            this.Insert(~num1, key, value);
        }
    }
}

public IList<TKey> Keys
{
    get
    {
        return this.GetKeyListHelper();
    }
}

public IList<TValue> Values
{
    get
    {
        return this.GetValueListHelper();
    }
}
#endregion // Public Properties

#region Private Properties
bool ICollection<KeyValuePair<TKey, TValue>>.IsReadOnly
{
    get
    {
        return false;
    }
}

ICollection<TKey> IDictionary<TKey, TValue>.Keys
{
    get
    {
        return this.GetKeyListHelper();
    }
```

Example 4-3. ReversibleSortedList class (continued)

```
    }

    ICollection<TValue> IDictionary<TKey, TValue>.Values
    {
        get
        {
            return this.GetValueListHelper();
        }
    }

    bool ICollection.IsSynchronized
    {
        get
        {
            return false;
        }
    }

    object ICollection.SyncRoot
    {
        get
        {
            return this;
        }
    }

    bool IDictionary.IsFixedSize
    {
        get
        {
            return false;
        }
    }

    bool IDictionary.IsReadOnly
    {
        get
        {
            return false;
        }
    }

    object IDictionary.this[object key]
    {
        get
        {
            if (ReversibleSortedList<TKey, TValue>.IsCompatibleKey(key))
            {
                int num1 = this.IndexOfKey((TKey)key);
                if (num1 >= 0)
                {
                    return this.values[num1];
```

Example 4-3. ReversibleSortedList class (continued)

```
                }
            }
            return null;
        }
        set
        {
            ReversibleSortedList<TKey, TValue>.VerifyKey(key);
            ReversibleSortedList<TKey, TValue>.VerifyValueType(value);
            this[(TKey)key] = (TValue)value;
        }
    }


    ICollection IDictionary.Keys
    {
        get
        {
            return this.GetKeyListHelper();
        }
    }


    ICollection IDictionary.Values
    {
        get
        {
            return this.GetValueListHelper();
        }
    }
    #endregion // Private properties

    #region Fields
    private const int _defaultCapacity = 4;
    private int _size;
    //private IComparer<TKey> comparer;
    private static TKey[] emptyKeys;
    private static TValue[] emptyValues;
    private KeyList<TKey, TValue> keyList;
    private TKey[] keys;
    private ValueList<TKey, TValue> valueList;
    private TValue[] values;
    private int version;
    // Declare comparison object.
    private SortDirectionComparer<TKey> _sortDirectionComparer = null;
    // Default to ascending.
    private ListSortDirection _currentSortDirection = ListSortDirection.Descending;
    #endregion

    #region Nested Types

    #region Enumerator <K, V>
    [Serializable, StructLayout(LayoutKind.Sequential)]
    private struct Enumerator<K, V> : IEnumerator<KeyValuePair<K, V>>, IDisposable,
                                      IDictionaryEnumerator, IEnumerator
```

Example 4-3. ReversibleSortedList class (continued)

```
{
    private ReversibleSortedList<K, V> _ReversibleSortedList;
    private K key;
    private V value;
    private int index;
    private int version;
    internal Enumerator(ReversibleSortedList<K, V> ReversibleSortedList)
    {
        this._ReversibleSortedList = ReversibleSortedList;
        this.index = 0;
        this.version = this._ReversibleSortedList.version;
        this.key = default(K);
        this.value = default(V);
    }
    public void Dispose()
    {
        this.index = 0;
        this.key = default(K);
        this.value = default(V);
    }
    object IDictionaryEnumerator.Key
    {
        get
        {
            if ((this.index == 0) ||
                (this.index == (this._ReversibleSortedList.Count + 1)))
            {
                throw new InvalidOperationException(
                        "Enumeration operation cannot occur.");
            }
            return this.key;
        }
    }
    public bool MoveNext()
    {
        if (this.version != this._ReversibleSortedList.version)
        {
            throw new InvalidOperationException(
                    "Enumeration failed version check");
        }
        if (this.index < this._ReversibleSortedList.Count)
        {
            this.key = this._ReversibleSortedList.keys[this.index];
            this.value = this._ReversibleSortedList.values[this.index];
            this.index++;
            return true;
        }
        this.index = this._ReversibleSortedList.Count + 1;
        this.key = default(K);
        this.value = default(V);
        return false;
    }
```

Example 4-3. ReversibleSortedList class (continued)

```csharp
DictionaryEntry IDictionaryEnumerator.Entry
{
    get
    {
        if ((this.index == 0) ||
            (this.index == (this._ReversibleSortedList.Count + 1)))
        {
            throw new InvalidOperationException(
                "Enumeration operation cannot happen.");
        }
        return new DictionaryEntry(this.key, this.value);
    }
}
public KeyValuePair<K, V> Current
{
    get
    {
        return new KeyValuePair<K, V>(this.key, this.value);
    }
}

object IEnumerator.Current
{
    get
    {
        if ((this.index == 0) ||
            (this.index == (this._ReversibleSortedList.Count + 1)))
        {
            throw new InvalidOperationException(
                "Enumeration operation cannot occur");
        }
        return new DictionaryEntry(this.key, this.value);
    }
}
object IDictionaryEnumerator.Value
{
    get
    {
        if ((this.index == 0) ||
            (this.index == (this._ReversibleSortedList.Count + 1)))
        {
            throw new InvalidOperationException(
                "Enumeration operation cannot occur");
        }
        return this.value;
    }
}
void IEnumerator.Reset()
{
    if (this.version != this._ReversibleSortedList.version)
    {
        throw new InvalidOperationException(
            "Enumeration version check failed");
```

Example 4-3. ReversibleSortedList class (continued)

```
            }
            this.index = 0;
            this.key = default(K);
            this.value = default(V);
        }
    }
    #endregion //  Enumerator <K, V>

    #region KeyList<K,V>
    [Serializable]
    private sealed class KeyList<K, V> : IList<K>, ICollection<K>,
                                    IEnumerable<K>, ICollection, IEnumerable
    {
        // Methods
        internal KeyList(ReversibleSortedList<K, V> dictionary)
        {
            this._dict = dictionary;
        }

        public void Add(K key)
        {
            throw new NotSupportedException("Add is unsupported");
        }

        public void Clear()
        {
            throw new NotSupportedException("Clear is unsupported");
        }

        public bool Contains(K key)
        {
            return this._dict.ContainsKey(key);
        }

        public void CopyTo(K[] array, int arrayIndex)
        {
            Array.Copy(this._dict.keys, 0, array, arrayIndex, this._dict.Count);
        }

        public IEnumerator<K> GetEnumerator()
        {
            return new
                ReversibleSortedList<K, V>.ReversibleSortedListKeyEnumerator(
                                    this._dict);
        }

        public int IndexOf(K key)
        {
            if (key == null)
            {
                throw new ArgumentNullException("key");
            }
```

Example 4-3. ReversibleSortedList class (continued)

```
        int num1 = Array.BinarySearch<K>(this._dict.keys, 0,
                                 this._dict.Count, key,
                                 this._dict._sortDirectionComparer);
        if (num1 >= 0)
        {
            return num1;
        }
        return -1;
    }

    public void Insert(int index, K value)
    {
        throw new NotSupportedException("Insert is unsupported");
    }

    public bool Remove(K key)
    {
        //throw new NotSupportedException("Remove is unsupported");
        return false;
    }

    public void RemoveAt(int index)
    {
        throw new NotSupportedException("RemoveAt is unsupported");
    }

    void ICollection.CopyTo(Array array, int arrayIndex)
    {
        if ((array != null) && (array.Rank != 1))
        {
            throw new ArgumentException(
                "MultiDimensional arrays are not unsupported");
        }
        try
        {
            Array.Copy(this._dict.keys, 0, array, arrayIndex,
                    this._dict.Count);
        }
        catch (ArrayTypeMismatchException atme)
        {
            throw new ArgumentException("InvalidArrayType", atme);
        }
    }

    IEnumerator IEnumerable.GetEnumerator()
    {
        return new
            ReversibleSortedList<K, V>.ReversibleSortedListKeyEnumerator(
                                                this._dict);
    }
```

Example 4-3. ReversibleSortedList class (continued)

```
    // Properties
    public int Count
    {
        get
        {
            return this._dict._size;
        }
    }

    public bool IsReadOnly
    {
        get
        {
            return true;
        }
    }

    public K this[int index]
    {
        get
        {
            return this._dict.GetKey(index);
        }
        set
        {
            throw new NotSupportedException("Set is an unsupported operation");
        }
    }

    bool ICollection.IsSynchronized
    {
        get
        {
            return false;
        }
    }

    object ICollection.SyncRoot
    {
        get
        {
            return this._dict;
        }
    }


    // Fields
    private ReversibleSortedList<K, V> _dict;
}
#endregion // KeyList<K,V>

#region ReversibleSortedListKeyEnumerator definition
```

Example 4-3. ReversibleSortedList class (continued)

```
[Serializable]
private sealed class ReversibleSortedListKeyEnumerator : IEnumerator<TKey>,
                                                          IDisposable,
                                                          IEnumerator
{
    // Methods
    internal ReversibleSortedListKeyEnumerator(
            ReversibleSortedList<TKey, TValue> ReversibleSortedList)
    {
        this._ReversibleSortedList = ReversibleSortedList;
        this.version = ReversibleSortedList.version;
    }

    public void Dispose()
    {
        this.index = 0;
        this.currentKey = default(TKey);
    }

    public bool MoveNext()
    {
        if (this.version != this._ReversibleSortedList.version)
        {
            throw new InvalidOperationException(
                "Enumeration failed version check");
        }
        if (this.index < this._ReversibleSortedList.Count)
        {
            this.currentKey = this._ReversibleSortedList.keys[this.index];
            this.index++;
            return true;
        }
        this.index = this._ReversibleSortedList.Count + 1;
        this.currentKey = default(TKey);
        return false;
    }

    void IEnumerator.Reset()
    {
        if (this.version != this._ReversibleSortedList.version)
        {
            throw new InvalidOperationException(
                "Enumeration failed version check");
        }
        this.index = 0;
        this.currentKey = default(TKey);
    }


    // Properties
    public TKey Current
    {
```

Example 4-3. ReversibleSortedList class (continued)

```
        get
        {
            return this.currentKey;
        }
    }

    object IEnumerator.Current
    {
        get
        {
            if ((this.index == 0) || (this.index ==
                    (this._ReversibleSortedList.Count + 1)))
            {
                throw new InvalidOperationException(
                        "Enumeration operation could not occur");
            }
            return this.currentKey;
        }
    }


    // Fields
    private ReversibleSortedList<TKey, TValue> _ReversibleSortedList;
    private TKey currentKey;
    private int index;
    private int version;
}
#endregion //ReversibleSortedListKeyEnumerator definition

#region ReversibleSortedListValueEnumerator definition
[Serializable]
private sealed class ReversibleSortedListValueEnumerator : IEnumerator<TValue>,
                                                           IDisposable,
                                                           IEnumerator
{
    // Methods
    internal ReversibleSortedListValueEnumerator(
                ReversibleSortedList<TKey, TValue> ReversibleSortedList)
    {
        this._ReversibleSortedList = ReversibleSortedList;
        this.version = ReversibleSortedList.version;
    }

    public void Dispose()
    {
        this.index = 0;
        this.currentValue = default(TValue);
    }

    public bool MoveNext()
    {
        if (this.version != this._ReversibleSortedList.version)
```

Example 4-3. ReversibleSortedList class (continued)

```
    {
        throw new InvalidOperationException(
            "Enumeration failed version check");
    }
    if (this.index < this._ReversibleSortedList.Count)
    {
        this.currentValue = this._ReversibleSortedList.values[this.index];
        this.index++;
        return true;
    }
    this.index = this._ReversibleSortedList.Count + 1;
    this.currentValue = default(TValue);
    return false;
}

void IEnumerator.Reset()
{
    if (this.version != this._ReversibleSortedList.version)
    {
        throw new InvalidOperationException(
            "Enumeration failed version check");
    }
    this.index = 0;
    this.currentValue = default(TValue);
}


// Properties
public TValue Current
{
    get
    {
        return this.currentValue;
    }
}

object IEnumerator.Current
{
    get
    {
        if ((this.index == 0) || (this.index ==
                (this._ReversibleSortedList.Count + 1)))
        {
            throw new InvalidOperationException(
                    "Enumeration operation could not occur");
        }
        return this.currentValue;
    }
}
```

Example 4-3. ReversibleSortedList class (continued)

```
    // Fields
    private ReversibleSortedList<TKey, TValue> _ReversibleSortedList;
    private TValue currentValue;
    private int index;
    private int version;
}
#endregion //ReversibleSortedListValueEnumerator

#region ValueList <K, V> definition
[Serializable]
private sealed class ValueList<K, V> : IList<V>, ICollection<V>,
                                  IEnumerable<V>, ICollection, IEnumerable
{
    // Methods
    internal ValueList(ReversibleSortedList<K, V> dictionary)
    {
        this._dict = dictionary;
    }

    public void Add(V key)
    {
        throw new NotSupportedException("Add is not supported");
    }

    public void Clear()
    {
        throw new NotSupportedException("Clear is not supported");
    }

    public bool Contains(V value)
    {
        return this._dict.ContainsValue(value);
    }

    public void CopyTo(V[] array, int arrayIndex)
    {
        Array.Copy(this._dict.values, 0, array, arrayIndex, this._dict.Count);
    }

    public IEnumerator<V> GetEnumerator()
    {
        return new
                ReversibleSortedList<K, V>.ReversibleSortedListValueEnumerator(
                                                    this._dict);
    }

    public int IndexOf(V value)
    {
        return Array.IndexOf<V>(this._dict.values, value, 0, this._dict.Count);
    }

    public void Insert(int index, V value)
    {
```

Example 4-3. ReversibleSortedList class (continued)

```
        throw new NotSupportedException("Insert is not supported");
    }

    public bool Remove(V value)
    {
        //throw new NotSupportedException("Remove is not supported");
        return false;
    }

    public void RemoveAt(int index)
    {
        throw new NotSupportedException("RemoveAt is not supported");
    }

    void ICollection.CopyTo(Array array, int arrayIndex)
    {
        if ((array != null) && (array.Rank != 1))
        {
            throw new ArgumentException(
                "MultiDimensional arrays not supported");
        }
        try
        {
            Array.Copy(this._dict.values, 0, array, arrayIndex,
                        this._dict.Count);
        }
        catch (ArrayTypeMismatchException atme)
        {
            throw new ArgumentException("Invalid array type", atme);
        }
    }

    IEnumerator IEnumerable.GetEnumerator( )
    {
        return new
            ReversibleSortedList<K, V>.ReversibleSortedListValueEnumerator(
                                                    this._dict);
    }


    // Properties
    public int Count
    {
        get
        {
            return this._dict._size;
        }
    }

    public bool IsReadOnly
```

Example 4-3. ReversibleSortedList class (continued)

```
    {
        get
        {
            return true;
        }
    }

    public V this[int index]
    {
        get
        {
            return this._dict.GetByIndex(index);
        }
        set
        {
            throw new NotSupportedException("Set by indexer is not supported");
        }
    }

    bool ICollection.IsSynchronized
    {
        get
        {
            return false;
        }
    }

    object ICollection.SyncRoot
    {
        get
        {
            return this._dict;
        }
    }


    // Fields
    private ReversibleSortedList<K, V> _dict;
    }
    #endregion // ValueList <TKey, TValue> definition

    #endregion // Nested types
}
```

A SortedList blends array and list syntax to allow for accessing the data in either format, which can be a handy thing to do. The data is accessible as key/value pairs or directly by index. Like the SortedList, the ReversibleSortedList<T> will not allow duplicate keys to be added. In addition, values that are reference or nullable types can be null, but keys cannot. The default capacity of a ReversibleSortedList<T> is 16, like the current default capacity of the SortedList. The items can be iterated using a foreach loop, with KeyValuePair being the type returned. While accessing elements of the ReversibleSortedList<T>, they may only be read from. The usual iterator syntax prohibits updating or deleting elements of the list while reading, as it will invalidate the iterator.

See Also

See Recipe 6.3; see the "SortedList," "Generic KeyValuePair Structure," and "Generic SortedList" topics in the MSDN documentation.

4.9   Making Read-Only Collections the Generic Way

Problem

You have a collection of information that you want to expose from your class, but you don't want any users modifying the collection.

Solution

Use the ReadOnlyCollection<T> wrapper to easily support collection classes that cannot be modified. For example, a Lottery class that contained the winning lottery numbers should make the winning numbers accessible, but not allow them to be changed:

```
public class Lottery
{
    // Make a list.
    List<int> _numbers = null;

    public Lottery()
    {
        // Make the internal list
        _numbers = new List<int>(5);
        // Add values
        _numbers.Add(17);
        _numbers.Add(21);
        _numbers.Add(32);
        _numbers.Add(44);
        _numbers.Add(58);
    }

    public ReadOnlyCollection<int> Results
    {
        // Return a wrapped copy of the results.
        get { return new ReadOnlyCollection<int>(_numbers); }
    }
}
```

Lottery has an internal List<int> of winning numbers that it fills in the constructor. The interesting part is that it also exposes a property called Results, which returns a

ReadOnlyCollection typed as <int> for seeing the winning numbers. Internally, a new ReadOnlyCollection wrapper is created to hold the List<int> that has the numbers in it, and then this instance is returned for use by the user.

If users then attempt to set a value on the collection, they get a compile error:

```
Lottery tryYourLuck = new Lottery();
// Print out the results.
for (int i = 0; i < tryYourLuck.Results.Count; i++)
{
    Console.WriteLine("Lottery Number " + i + " is " + tryYourLuck.Results[i]);
}

// Change it so we win!
tryYourLuck.Results[0]=29;

//The above line gives // Error    26 //   Property or indexer
// 'System.Collections.ObjectModel.ReadOnlyCollection<int>.this[int]'
// cannot be assigned to -- it is read only
```

Discussion

The main advantage ReadOnlyCollection provides is the flexibility to use it with any collection that supports IList or IList<T> as an interface. ReadOnlyCollection can be used to wrap a regular array like this:

```
int [] items = new int[3];
items[0]=0;
items[1]=1;
items[2]=2;
    new ReadOnlyCollection<int>(items);
```

This provides a way to standardize the read-only properties on classes to make it easier for consumers of the class to recognize which properties are read-only simply by the return type.

See Also

See the "IList" and "Generic IList" topics in the MSDN documentation.

4.10 Replacing the Hashtable with Its Generic Counterpart

Problem

You want to enhance the performance of your application as well as make the code easier to work with by replacing all Hashtable objects with the generic version. This is imperative when you find that structures or other value types are being stored in these data structures, resulting in boxing/unboxing operations.

Solution

Replace all occurrences of the System.Collections.Hashtable class with the faster generic System.Collections.Generic.Dictionary class.

Here is a simple example of using a System.Collections.Hashtable object:

```
public static void UseNonGenericHashtable( )
{
    // Create and populate a Hashtable.
    Hashtable numbers = new Hashtable();
    numbers.Add(1, "one");    // Causes a boxing operation to occur for the key
    numbers.Add(2, "two");    // Causes a boxing operation to occur for the key

    // Display all key/value pairs in the Hashtable.
    // Causes an unboxing operation to occur on each iteration for the key
    foreach (DictionaryEntry de in numbers)
    {
        Console.WriteLine("Key: " + de.Key + "\tValue: " + de.Value);
    }

    numbers.Clear( );
}
```

Here is that same code using a System.Collections.Generic.Dictionary<T,U> object:

```
public static void UseGenericDictionary( )
{
    // Create and populate a Dictionary.
    Dictionary<int, string> numbers = new Dictionary<int, string>( );
    numbers.Add(1, "one");
    numbers.Add(2, "two");

    // Display all key/value pairs in the Dictionary.
    foreach (KeyValuePair<int, string> kvp in numbers)
    {
        Console.WriteLine("Key: " + kvp.Key + "\tValue: " + kvp.Value);
    }

    numbers.Clear( );
}
```

Discussion

For simple implementations of the Hashtable in your application, this substitution should be quite easy. However, there are some things to watch out for. For example, the generic Dictionary class does not implement the ICloneable interface, while the Hashtable class does.

Table 4-2 shows the equivalent members that are implemented in both classes.

Table 4-2. Equivalent members in the Hashtable and the generic Dictionary classes

Members in the Hashtable class	Equivalent members in the generic Dictionary class
N/A	`Comparer` property
`Count` property	`Count` property
`IsFixedSize` property	`((IDictionary)myDict).IsFixedSize`
`IsReadOnly` property	`((IDictionary)myDict).IsReadOnly`
`IsSynchronized` property	`((IDictionary)myDict).IsSynchronized`
`Item` property	`Item` property
`Keys` property	`Keys` property
`SyncRoot` property	`((IDictionary)myDict).SyncRoot`
`Values` property	`Values` property
`Add` method	`Add` method
`Clear` method	`Clear` method
`Clone` method	Use overloaded constructor which accepts an `IDictionary<T,U>` type
`Contains` method	`ContainsKey` method
`ContainsKey` method	`ContainsKey` method
`ContainsValue` method	`ContainsValue` method
`CopyTo` method	`((ICollection)myDict).CopyTo(arr,0)`
`Remove` method	`Remove` method
`Synchronized` static method	`lock(myDictionary.SyncRoot) {…}`
N/A	`TryGetValue` method

In several cases within Table 4-2, there is not a one-to-one correlation between the members of a `Hashtable` and the members of the generic `Dictionary` class. Starting with the properties, notice that only the `Count`, `Keys`, `Values`, and `Item` properties are present in both classes. To make up for the missing properties in the `Dictionary` class, you can perform a cast to an `IDictionary`. The following code shows how to use these casts to get at the missing properties:

```
Dictionary<int, string> numbers = new Dictionary<int, string>();

Console.WriteLine(((IDictionary)numbers).IsReadOnly);
Console.WriteLine(((IDictionary)numbers).IsFixedSize);
Console.WriteLine(((IDictionary)numbers).IsSynchronized);
Console.WriteLine(((IDictionary)numbers).SyncRoot);
```

Note that due to the absence of code to be able to return a synchronized version of a generic `Dictionary`, the `IsSynchronized` property will always return `false`. The `SyncRoot` property will always return the same object on which it is called. Essentially, this property returns the `this` pointer. Microsoft has decided to remove the ability to create a synchronous wrapper from any of the generic collection classes.

Instead, they recommend using the lock keyword to lock the entire collection or another type of synchronization object that suits your needs.

Since the Clone method is also missing from the generic Dictionary class (due to the fact that this class does not implement the ICloneable interface), you can instead use the overloaded constructor, which accepts an IDictionary<T,U> type:

```
// Create and populate a Dictionary.
Dictionary<int, string> numbers = new Dictionary<int, string>();
numbers.Add(1, "one");
numbers.Add(2, "two");

// Display all key/value pairs in the original Dictionary.
foreach (KeyValuePair<int, string> kvp in numbers)
{
    Console.WriteLine("Original Key: " + kvp.Key + "\tValue: " + kvp.Value);
}

// Clone the Dictionary object.
Dictionary<int, string> clonedNumbers = new Dictionary<int, string>(numbers);

// Display all key/value pairs in the cloned Dictionary.
foreach (KeyValuePair<int, string> kvp in numbers)
{
    Console.WriteLine("Cloned Key: " + kvp.Key + "\tValue: " + kvp.Value);
}
```

There are two more methods that are missing from the Dictionary class, the Contains and CopyTo methods. The Contains method is easy to reproduce in the Dictionary class. In the Hashtable class, the Contains method and the ContainsKey method both exhibit the same behavior, therefore you can simply use the ContainsKey method of the Dictionary class to simulate the Contains method of the Hashtable class:

```
// Create and populate a Dictionary.
Dictionary<int, string> numbers = new Dictionary<int, string>();
numbers.Add(1, "one");
numbers.Add(2, "two");

Console.WriteLine("numbers.ContainsKey(1) == " + numbers.ContainsKey(1));
Console.WriteLine("numbers.ContainsKey(3) == " + numbers.ContainsKey(3));
```

The CopyTo method is also easy to simulate in the Dictionary class, but it involves a little more work:

```
// Create and populate a Dictionary.
Dictionary<int, string> numbers = new Dictionary<int, string>();
numbers.Add(1, "one");
numbers.Add(2, "two");

// Display all key/value pairs in the Dictionary.
foreach (KeyValuePair<int, string> kvp in numbers)
{
    Console.WriteLine("Key: " + kvp.Key + "\tValue: " + kvp.Value);
}
```

```
// Create object array to hold copied information from Dictionary object.
KeyValuePair<int, string>[] objs = new KeyValuePair<int, string>[numbers.Count];

// Calling CopyTo on a Dictionary
// Copies all KeyValuePair objects in Dictionary object to objs[]
((IDictionary)numbers).CopyTo(objs, 0);

// Display all key/value pairs in the objs[].
foreach (KeyValuePair<int, string> kvp in objs)
{
    Console.WriteLine("Key: " + kvp.Key + "\tValue: " + kvp.Value);
}
```

Calling CopyTo on the Dictionary object involves setting up an array of KeyValuePair<T,U> objects, which will end up holding all the KeyValuePair<T,U> objects within the Dictionary object after the CopyTo method is called. Next, the numbers Dictionary object is cast to an IDictionary type so that the CopyTo method may be called. Once the CopyTo method is called, the objs array will contain copies of all the KeyValuePair<T,U> objects that are in the original numbers object. Note that iteration of the objs array, using a foreach loop, is done in the same fashion as with the numbers object.

See Also

See the "System.Collections.Hashtable Class" and "System.Collections.Generic.Dictionary Class" topics in the MSDN documentation.

4.11 Using foreach with Generic Dictionary Types

Problem

You need to enumerate the elements within a type that implements System.Collections.Generic.IDictionary, such as System.Collections.Generic.Dictionary or System.Collections.Generic.SortedList.

Solution

The simplest way is to use the KeyValuePair structure in a foreach loop as shown here:

```
// Create a Dictionary object and populate it.
Dictionary<int, string> myStringDict = new Dictionary<int, string>();
myStringDict.Add(1, "Foo");
myStringDict.Add(2, "Bar");
myStringDict.Add(3, "Baz");

// Enumerate and display all key and value pairs.
foreach (KeyValuePair<int, string> kvp in myStringDict)
```

```
{
    Console.WriteLine("key   " + kvp.Key);
    Console.WriteLine("Value " + kvp.Value);
}
```

Discussion

The nongeneric System.Collections.Hashtable (the counterpart to the System.Collections.Generic.Dictionary class), System.Collections.CollectionBase, and System.Collections.SortedList classes support foreach using the DictionaryEntry type as shown here:

```
foreach (DictionaryEntry de in myDict)
{
    Console.WriteLine("key   " + de.Key);
    Console.WriteLine("Value " + de.Value);
}
```

However, the Dictionary object supports the KeyValuePair<T,U> type when using a foreach loop. This is due to the fact that the GetEnumerator method returns an IEnumerator, which in turn returns KeyValuePair<T,U> types, not DictionaryEntry types.

The KeyValuePair<T,U> type is well suited to be used when enumerating the generic Dictionary class with a foreach loop. The DictionaryEntry object contains key and value pairs as objects, whereas the KeyValuePair<T,U> type contains key and value pairs as their original types, defined when creating the Dictionary object. This boosts performance and can reduce the amount of code you have to write, as you do not have to cast the key and value pairs to their original types.

See Also

See the "System.Collections.Generic.Dictionary Class," "System.Collections.Generic.SortedList Class," and "System.Collections.Generic.KeyValuePair Structure" topics in the MSDN documentation.

4.12   Constraining Type Arguments

Problem

Your generic type needs to be created with a type argument that must support the members of a particular interface such as the IDisposable interface.

Solution

Use constraints to force the type arguments of a generic type to be of a type that implements one or more particular interfaces:

```
public class DisposableList<T> : IList<T>
    where T : IDisposable
```

```
{
    private List<T> _items = new List<T>();

    // Private method that will dispose of items in the list
    private void Delete(T item)
    {
        item.Dispose();
    }
}
```

This DisposableList class allows only an object that implements IDisposable to be passed in as a type argument to this class. The reason for this is that whenever an object is removed from a DisposableList object, the Dispose method is always called on that object. This allows you to transparently handle the management of any object stored within this DisposableList object.

The following code exercises a DisposableList object:

```
public static void TestDisposableListCls()
{
    DisposableList<StreamReader> dl = new DisposableList<StreamReader>();

    // Create a few test objects.
    StreamReader tr1 = new StreamReader("c:\\boot.ini");
    StreamReader tr2 = new StreamReader("c:\\autoexec.bat");
    StreamReader tr3 = new StreamReader("c:\\config.sys");

    // Add the test object to the DisposableList.
    dl.Add(tr1);
    dl.Insert(0, tr2);
    dl.Add(tr3);

    foreach(StreamReader sr in dl)
    {
        Console.WriteLine("sr.ReadLine() == " + sr.ReadLine());
    }

    // Call Dispose before any of the disposable objects are
    // removed from the DisposableList.
    dl.RemoveAt(0);
    dl.Remove(tr1);
    dl.Clear();
}
```

Discussion

The where keyword is used to constrain a type parameter to accept only arguments that satisfy the given constraint. For example, the DisposableList has the constraint that any type argument T must implement the IDisposable interface:

```
public class DisposableList<T> : IList<T>
    where T : IDisposable
```

This means that the following code will compile successfully:

```
DisposableList<StreamReader> dl = new DisposableList<StreamReader>();
```

but the following code will not:

```
DisposableList<string> dl = new DisposableList<string>();
```

This is because the string type does not implement the IDisposable interface, and the StreamReader type does.

Other constraints on the type argument are allowed, in addition to requiring one or more specific interfaces to be implemented. You can force a type argument to be inherited from a specific base class, such as the TextReader class:

```
public class DisposableList<T> : IList<T>
    where T : System.IO.TextReader, IDisposable
```

You can also determine if the type argument is narrowed down to only value types or only reference types. The following class declaration is constrained to using only value types:

```
public class DisposableList<T> : IList<T>
    where T : struct
```

This class declaration is constrained to only reference types:

```
public class DisposableList<T> : IList<T>
    where T : class
```

In addition, you can also require any type argument to implement a public default constructor:

```
public class DisposableList<T> : IList<T>
    where T : IDisposable, new()
```

Using constraints allows you to write generic types that accept a narrower set of available type arguments. If the IDisposable constraint is omitted in the solution for this recipe, a compile-time error will occur. This is because not all of the types that can be used as the type argument for the DisposableList class will implement the IDisposable interface. If you skip this compile-time check, a DisposableList object may contain objects that do not have a public no-argument Dispose method. In this case, a runtime exception will occur. Generics and constraints in particular force strict type checking of the class-type arguments and allow you to catch these problems at compile time rather than at runtime.

See Also

See the "where Keyword" topic in the MSDN documentation.

4.13 Initializing Generic Variables to Their Default Values

Problem

You have a generic class that contains a variable of the same type as the type parameter defined by the class itself. Upon construction of your generic object, you want that variable to be initialized to its default value.

Solution

Simply use the `default` keyword to initialize that variable to its default value:

```
public class DefaultValueExample<T>
{
    T data = default(T);

    public bool IsDefaultData( )
    {
        T temp = default(T);

        if (temp.Equals(data))
        {
            return (true);
        }
        else
        {
            return (false);
        }
    }

    public void SetData(T val)
    {
        data = val;
    }
}
```

The code to use this class is shown here:

```
public static void ShowSettingFieldsToDefaults( )
{
    DefaultValueExample<int> dv = new DefaultValueExample<int>();

    // Check if the data is set to its default value; true is returned.
    bool isDefault = dv.IsDefaultData( );
    Console.WriteLine("Initial data: " + isDefault);

    // Set data.
    dv.SetData(100);
```

```
        // Check again, this time a false is returned.
        isDefault = dv.IsDefaultData( );
        Console.WriteLine("Set data: " + isDefault);
    }
```

The first call to IsDefaultData returns true, while the second returns false. The output is shown here:

```
Initial data: True
Set data: False
```

Discussion

When initializing a variable of the same type parameter as the generic class, you cannot just set that variable to null. What if the type parameter is a value type such as an int or char? This will not work since value types cannot be null. You may be thinking that a *nullable* type such as long? or Nullable<long> can be set to null (see Recipe 4.7 for more on nullable types). However, the compiler has no way of knowing what type argument the user will use to construct the type.

The default keyword allows you to tell the compiler that at compile time the default value of this variable should be used. If the type argument supplied is a numeric value (e.g., int, long, decimal), then the default value is zero. If the type argument supplied is a reference type, then the default value is null. If the type argument supplied is a struct, then the default value of the struct is determined by initializing each member field of the struct to zero for numeric types or null for reference types.

See Also

See Recipe 4.7; see the "default Keyword in Generic Code" topic in the MSDN documentation.

CHAPTER 5

Collections

5.0 Introduction

Collections are groups of items; in .NET, collections contain objects (including boxed value types). Each object contained in a collection is called an *element*. Some collections contain a straightforward list of elements, while others (*dictionaries*) contain a list of key and value pairs. The following collection types consist of a straightforward list of elements:

```
System.Collections.ArrayList
System.Collections.BitArray
System.Collections.Queue
System.Collections.Stack
System.Collections.Generic.LinkedList<T>
System.Collections.Generic.List<T>
System.Collections.Generic.Queue<T>
System.Collections.Generic.Stack<T>
```

The following collection types are dictionaries:

```
System.Collections.Hashtable
System.Collections.SortedList
System.Collections.Generic.Dictionary<T,U>
System.Collections.Generic.SortedList<T,U>
```

These collection classes are organized under the System.Collections and the System.Collections.Generic namespaces. In addition to these namespaces, another namespace called System.Collections.Specialized contains a few more useful collection classes. These classes might not be as well known as the previous classes, so here is a short explanation of the collection classes under the System.Collections.Specialized namespace:

ListDictionary

This class operates very similarly to the Hashtable. However, this class beats out the Hashtable on performance when it contains 10 or fewer elements.

HybridDictionary

This class consists of two internal collections, the ListDictionary and the Hashtable. Only one of these classes is used at any one time. The ListDictionary is used while the collection contains 10 or fewer elements, and then a switch is made to use a Hashtable when the collection grows beyond 10 elements. This switch is made transparently to the developer. Once the Hashtable is used, this collection cannot revert to using the ListDictionary even if the elements number 10 or fewer. Also note that, when using strings as the key, this class supports both case-sensitive (with respect to the invariant culture) and case-insensitive string searches through setting a Boolean value in the constructor.

CollectionsUtil

This class contains two static methods: one to create a case-insensitive Hashtable and another to create a case-insensitive SortedList. When you directly create a Hashtable and SortedList object, you always create a case-sensitive Hashtable or SortedList, unless you use one of the constructors that take an IComparer and pass CaseInsensitiveComparer.Default to it.

NameValueCollection

This collection consists of key and value pairs, which are both of type String. The interesting thing about this collection is that it can store multiple string values with a single key. The multiple string values are comma-delimited. The String.Split method is useful when breaking up multiple strings in a value.

StringCollection

This collection is a simple list containing string elements. This list accepts null elements as well as duplicate strings. This list is case-sensitive.

StringDictionary

This is a Hashtable that stores both the key and value as strings. Keys are converted to all-lowercase letters before being added to the Hashtable, allowing for case-insensitive comparisons. Keys cannot be null, but values may be set to null.

The C# compiler also supports a fixed-size array. Arrays of any type may be created using the following syntax:

```
int[] foo = new int[2];
T[] bar = new T[2];
```

where foo is an integer array containing exactly two elements and bar is an array of unknown type T.

Arrays come in several styles as well: multidimensional, jagged, and even multidimensional jagged. Multidimensional arrays are defined as shown here:

```
int[,] foo = new int[2,3];    // A 2-dimensional array
                              // containing 6 elements
```

```
int[,,] bar = new int[2,3,4];    // A 3-dimensional array
                                 // containing 24 elements
```

A two-dimensional array is usually described as a table with rows and columns. The foo array would be described as a table of two rows, each containing three columns of elements. A three-dimensional array can be described as a cube with layers of tables. The bar array could be described as four layers of two rows, each containing three columns of elements.

Jagged arrays are arrays of arrays. If you picture a jagged array as a one-dimensional array with each element in that array containing another one-dimensional array, it could have a different number of elements in each row. A jagged array is defined as follows:

```
int[][] baz = new int[2][] {new int[2], new int[3]};
```

The baz array consists of a one-dimensional array containing two elements. Each of these elements consists of another array, the first array having two elements and the second array having three.

The rest of this chapter contains recipes dealing with arrays and the various collection types.

5.1   Swapping Two Elements in an Array

Problem

You want an efficient method to swap two elements that exist within a single array.

Solution

Use the generic SwapElementsInArray<T> method:

```
public static void SwapElementsInArray<T>(T[] theArray, int index1, int index2)
{
    if (index1 >= theArray.Length ||
        index2 >= theArray.Length ||
        index1 < 0 || index2 < 0)
    {
        throw(new ArgumentOutOfRangeException(
            "index passed in to this method is out of bounds."));    }
    else
    {
        T tempHolder = theArray[index1];
        theArray[index1] = theArray[index2];
        theArray[index2] = tempHolder;
    }
}
```

Discussion

There is no specific method in the .NET Framework that allows you to swap only two specific elements within an array. The SwapElementsInArray method presented in this recipe allows for only two specified elements of an array (specified in the index1 and index2 arguments to this method).

The following code uses the SwapElementsInArray<T> method to swap the zeroth and fourth elements in an array of integers:

```
public static void TestSwapArrayElements()
{
    int[] someArray = new int[5] {1,2,3,4,5};

    for (int counter = 0; counter < someArray.Length; counter++)
    {
        Console.WriteLine("Element " + counter + " = " + someArray[counter]);
    }

    SwapElementsInArray(someArray, 0, 4);

    for (int counter = 0; counter < someArray.Length; counter++)
    {
        Console.WriteLine("Element " + counter + " = " + someArray[counter]);
    }
}
```

This code produces the following output:

```
Element 0 = 1    ← The original array
Element 1 = 2
Element 2 = 3
Element 3 = 4
Element 4 = 5

Element 0 = 5    ← The array with elements swapped
Element 1 = 2
Element 2 = 3
Element 3 = 4
Element 4 = 1
```

5.2   Reversing an Array Quickly

Problem

You want an efficient method to reverse the order of elements within an array.

Solution

You can use the static Reverse method, as in this snippet of code:

```
int[] someArray = new int[5] {1,2,3,4,5};
Array.Reverse(someArray);
```

or you can write your own reversal method:

```
public static void DoReversal<T>(T[] theArray)
{
    T tempHolder = default(T);

    if (theArray.Length > 0)
    {
        for (int counter = 0; counter < (theArray.Length / 2); counter++)
        {
            tempHolder = theArray[counter];
            theArray[counter] = theArray[theArray.Length - counter - 1];
            theArray[theArray.Length - counter - 1] = tempHolder;
        }
    }
    else
    {
        Trace.WriteLine("Nothing to reverse");
    }
}
```

While there is more code to write, the benefit of the DoReversal<T> method is that it
is about twice as fast as the Array.Reverse method. In addition, you can tailor the
DoReversal<T> method to a specific situation. For example, the DoReversal<T>
method accepts a value type array (int), whereas the Array.Reverse method accepts
only a reference type (System.Array). This means that a boxing operation will occur
for the int value types. The DoReversal<T> method removes any boxing operations.

Discussion

The following TestArrayReversal method creates a test array of five integers and displays the elements in their initial order. Next, the DoReversal<T> method is called to
reverse the elements in the array. After this method returns, the array is then displayed a second time as a reversed array:

```
public static void TestArrayReversal( )
{
    int[] someArray = new int[5] {1,2,3,4,5};

    for (int counter = 0; counter < someArray.Length; counter++)
    {
        Console.WriteLine("Element " + counter + " = " + someArray[counter]);
    }

    DoReversal(someArray);

    for (int counter = 0; counter < someArray.Length; counter++)
    {
        Console.WriteLine("Element " + counter + " = " + someArray[counter]);
    }
}
```

This code displays the following:

```
Element 0 = 1    ← The original array
Element 1 = 2
Element 2 = 3
Element 3 = 4
Element 4 = 5

Element 0 = 5    ← The reversed array
Element 1 = 4
Element 2 = 3
Element 3 = 2
Element 4 = 1
```

Reversing the elements in an array is a fairly common routine. The algorithm here swaps elements in the array until it is fully reversed. The DoReversal<T> method accepts a single parameter, *theArray*, which is a pointer to the first element in the array that is to be reversed.

The array is actually reversed inside of the for loop. The for loop counts from zero (the first element in the array) to a value equal to the array's length divided by two:

```
for (int counter = 0; counter < (theArray.Length / 2); counter++)
```

Note that this is *integer division*, so if the array length is an odd number, the remainder is discarded. Since your array length is five, the for loop counts from zero to one.

Inside of the loop are three lines of code:

```
tempHolder = theArray[counter];
theArray[counter] = theArray[theArray.Length - counter - 1];
theArray[theArray.Length - counter - 1] = tempHolder;
```

These three lines swap the first half of the array with the second half. As the for loop counts from zero, these three lines swap the first and last elements in the array. The loop increments the counter by one, allowing the second element and the next to last element to be swapped. This continues until all elements in the array have been swapped.

There is one element in the array that cannot be swapped; this is the middle element of an array with an odd number for the length. For example, in this code, there are five elements in the array. The third element should not be swapped. Put another way, all of the other elements pivot on this third element when they are swapped. This does not occur when the length of the array is an even number.

By dividing the array length by two, you can compensate for even or odd array elements. Since you get back an integer number from this division, you can easily skip over the middle element in an array with an odd length.

See Also

See Recipes 5.3 and 5.4; see the "Array.Reverse Method" topic in the MSDN documentation.

5.3 Reversing a Two-Dimensional Array

Problem

You need to reverse each row in a two-dimensional array. The Array.Reverse method does not support this operation.

Solution

Use the following Reverse2DimArray<T> method:

```
public static void Reverse2DimArray<T>(T[,] theArray)
{
    for (int rowIndex = 0; rowIndex <= (theArray.GetUpperBound(0)); rowIndex++)
    {
        for (int colIndex = 0;
            colIndex <= (theArray.GetUpperBound(1) / 2);
            colIndex++)
        {
            T tempHolder = theArray[rowIndex, colIndex];
            theArray[rowIndex, colIndex] =
                    theArray[rowIndex, theArray.GetUpperBound(1) - colIndex];
            theArray[rowIndex, theArray.GetUpperBound(1) - colIndex] = tempHolder;
        }
    }
}
```

Discussion

The following TestReverse2DimArray method shows how the Reverse2DimArray<T> method is used:

```
public static void TestReverse2DimArray()
{
    int[,] someArray =
        new int[5,3] {{1,2,3},{4,5,6},{7,8,9},{10,11,12},{13,14,15}};

    // Display the original array.
    foreach (int i in someArray)
    {
        Console.WriteLine(i);
    }
    Console.WriteLine();

    Reverse2DimArray(someArray);

    // Display the reversed array.
    foreach (int i in someArray)
    {
        Console.WriteLine(i);
    }
}
```

This method displays the following:

```
1
2
3
4
5
6
7
8
9
10
11
12
13
14
15

3     ← Note that each row of 3 elements are reversed
2
1
6     ← This is the start of the next row
5
4
9
8
7
12
11
10
15
14
13
```

The `Reverse2DimArray<T>` method uses the same logic presented in the previous recipe to reverse the array; however, a nested for loop is used instead of a single for loop. The outer for loop iterates over each row of the array (there are five rows in the `someArray` array). The inner for loop is used to iterate over each column of the array (there are three columns in the `someArray` array). The reverse logic is then applied to the elements handled by the inner for loop, which allows each row in the array to be reversed.

See Also

See Recipes 5.2 and 5.4.

5.4   Reversing a Jagged Array

Problem

The `Array.Reverse` method does not provide a way to reverse each subarray in a jagged array. You need this functionality.

Solution

Use the ReverseJaggedArray<T> method:

```
public static void ReverseJaggedArray<T>(T[][] theArray)
{
    for (int rowIndex = 0; rowIndex <= (theArray.GetUpperBound(0)); rowIndex++)
    {
        for (int colIndex = 0;
              colIndex <= (theArray[rowIndex].GetUpperBound(0) / 2);
              colIndex++)
        {
            T tempHolder = theArray[rowIndex][colIndex];
            theArray[rowIndex][colIndex] =
                    theArray[rowIndex][theArray[rowIndex].GetUpperBound(0) -
colIndex];
            theArray[rowIndex][theArray[rowIndex].GetUpperBound(0) - colIndex] =
                    tempHolder;
        }
    }
}
```

Discussion

The following TestReverseJaggedArray method shows how the ReverseJaggedArray<T>
method is used:

```
public static void TestReverseJaggedArray()
{
    int[][] someArray =
        new int[][] {new int[3] {1,2,3}, new int[6]{10,11,12,13,14,15}};

    // Display the original array.
    for (int rowIndex = 0; rowIndex < someArray.Length; rowIndex++)
    {
        for (int colIndex = 0; colIndex < someArray[rowIndex].Length; colIndex++)
        {
            Console.WriteLine(someArray[rowIndex][colIndex]);
        }
    }
    Console.WriteLine();

    ReverseJaggedArray(someArray);

    // Display the reversed array.
    for (int rowIndex = 0; rowIndex < someArray.Length; rowIndex++)
    {
        for (int colIndex = 0; colIndex < someArray[rowIndex].Length; colIndex++)
        {
            Console.WriteLine(someArray[rowIndex][colIndex]);
        }
    }
}
```

This method displays the following:

```
1
2
3
10
11
12
13
14
15

3     ← The first reversed subarray
2
1
15    ← The second reversed subarray
14
13
12
11
10
```

The logic used to reverse each subarray of a jagged array is very similar to the reversal logic discussed in the previous recipe. The ReverseJaggedArray<T> method uses the same basic logic presented in Recipe 5.2 to reverse each element in the array; however, a nested for loop is used instead of a single for loop. The outer for loop iterates over each element of the first dimensioned array of the jagged array (there are two elements in this array). The inner for loop is used to iterate over each element contained within the second dimensioned array of the jagged array. The reverse logic is then applied to the elements handled by the inner for loop. This allows each array contained by the first dimensioned array in the jagged array to be reversed.

See Also

See Recipes 5.2 and 5.3.

5.5   Writing a More Flexible StackTrace Class

Problem

You have a StackTrace object that contains a listing of stack frames. You need to iterate through these stack frames as if you were using a Collection-type object.

Solution

Wrap the public interface of a StackTrace object to look like a Collection-type object. The StackTraceList class shown in Example 5-1 implements this design pattern.

Example 5-1. Writing a more flexible StackTrace class

```
using System;
using System.Collections;
using System.Diagnostics;
using System.Reflection;
using System.Text;
using System.Threading;

public class StackTraceList : StackTrace, IList
{
    public StackTraceList( ) : base( )
    {
        InitInternalFrameArray( );
    }

    public StackTraceList(bool needFileInfo) : base(needFileInfo)
    {
        InitInternalFrameArray( );
    }

    public StackTraceList(Exception e) : base(e)
    {
        InitInternalFrameArray( );
    }

    public StackTraceList(int skipFrames) : base(skipFrames)
    {
        InitInternalFrameArray( );
    }

    public StackTraceList(StackFrame frame) : base(frame)
    {
        InitInternalFrameArray( );
    }

    public StackTraceList(Exception e, bool needFileInfo) : base(e, needFileInfo)
    {
        InitInternalFrameArray( );
    }

    public StackTraceList(Exception e, int skipFrames) : base(e, skipFrames)
    {
        InitInternalFrameArray( );
    }

    public StackTraceList(int skipFrames, bool needFileInfo) :
        base(skipFrames, needFileInfo)
    {
        InitInternalFrameArray( );
    }

    public StackTraceList(Thread targetThread, bool needFileInfo) :
        base(targetThread, needFileInfo)
```

Example 5-1. Writing a more flexible StackTrace class (continued)

```
{
    InitInternalFrameArray( );
}

public StackTraceList(Exception e, int skipFrames, bool needFileInfo) :
        base(e, skipFrames, needFileInfo)
{
    InitInternalFrameArray( );
}

private StackFrame[] internalFrameArray = null;

private void InitInternalFrameArray( )
{
    internalFrameArray = new StackFrame[base.FrameCount];

    for (int counter = 0; counter < base.FrameCount; counter++)
    {
        internalFrameArray[counter] = base.GetFrame(counter);
    }
}

public string GetFrameAsString(int index)
{
    StringBuilder str = new StringBuilder("\tat ");
    str.Append(GetFrame(index).GetMethod( ).DeclaringType.FullName);
    str.Append(".");
    str.Append(GetFrame(index).GetMethod( ).Name);
    str.Append("(");
    foreach (ParameterInfo PI in GetFrame(index).GetMethod( ).GetParameters( ))
    {
        str.Append(PI.ParameterType.Name);
        if (PI.Position <
            (GetFrame(index).GetMethod( ).GetParameters( ).Length - 1))
        {
            str.Append(", ");
        }
    }
    str.Append(")");

    return (str.ToString( ));
}

// IList properties/methods
public bool IsFixedSize
{
    get {return (internalFrameArray.IsFixedSize);}
}

public bool IsReadOnly
{
    get {return (true);}
```

Example 5-1. Writing a more flexible StackTrace class (continued)

```csharp
    }

    // Note that this indexer must return an object to comply
    // with the IList interface for this indexer.
    public object this[int index]
    {
        get {return (internalFrameArray[index]);}
        set {throw (new NotSupportedException(
          "The set indexer method is not supported on this object."));}
    }

    public int Add(object value)
    {
        return (((IList)internalFrameArray).Add(value));
    }

    public void Insert(int index, object value)
    {
        ((IList)internalFrameArray).Insert(index, value);
    }

    public void Remove(object value)
    {
        ((IList)internalFrameArray).Remove(value);
    }

    public void RemoveAt(int index)
    {
        ((IList)internalFrameArray).RemoveAt(index);
    }

    public void Clear( )
    {
        // Throw an exception here to prevent the loss of data.
        throw (new NotSupportedException(
                "The Clear method is not supported on this object."));
    }

    public bool Contains(object value)
    {
        return (((IList)internalFrameArray).Contains(value));
    }

    public int IndexOf(object value)
    {
        return (((IList)internalFrameArray).IndexOf(value));
    }

    // IEnumerable method
    public IEnumerator GetEnumerator( )
    {
        return (internalFrameArray.GetEnumerator( ));
```

Example 5-1. Writing a more flexible StackTrace class (continued)

```
    }

    // ICollection properties/methods
    public int Count
    {
        get {return (internalFrameArray.Length);}
    }

    public bool IsSynchronized
    {
        get {return (internalFrameArray.IsSynchronized);}
    }

    public object SyncRoot
    {
        get {return (internalFrameArray.SyncRoot);}
    }

    public void CopyTo(Array array, int index)
    {
        internalFrameArray.CopyTo(array, index);
    }
}
```

Discussion

This recipe uses the System.Diagnostics.StackTrace object to obtain a list of stack frames, which it then provides to the user. The StackTrace class provides a convenient way to obtain a stack trace, an exception object, or a specific thread from the current point in code. Unfortunately, the StackTrace provides only a very simplified way to get at each stack frame. It would be much better if the StackTrace object operated like a collection. To make this happen, you can create an intermediate object called StackTraceList that inherits from StackTrace and implements the ICloneable, IList, ICollection, and IEnumerable interfaces.

The constructors for the StackTraceList class mimic the StackTrace constructors. Each StackTraceList constructor passes its work along to the base class using the base keyword:

```
    public StackTraceList( ) : base( )
```

Each StackTraceList constructor contains a call to the private method, Init-InternalFrameArray. This private method copies all of the individual StackFrame objects from the base StackTrace object into a private field of type StackFrame[] called internalFrameArray. The StackTraceList uses the internalFrameArray field as a convenient storage mechanism for each individual StackFrame object; in addition, you get a free implementation of the IEnumerator interface. It also makes it easier to make the StackTraceList class look and feel more like an array than a StackTrace object.

Another useful method added to the `StackTraceList` class is the public `GetFrame-AsString` method. This method accepts an index of a specific `StackFrame` object in the `internalFrameArray` field. From this `StackFrame` object, it constructs a string similar to the string output for each `StackFrame`.

The methods implemented from the `IList`, `ICollection`, and `IEnumerable` interfaces forward their calls on to the `internalFrameArray` field, which implements the same interfaces—throwing the `NotSupportedException` for most of these interface methods.

The `StackTrace` object can now be used as if it were a collection, through the intermediate `StackTraceList` object. To obtain a `StackTraceList` object for the current point in code, use the following code:

```
StackTraceList arrStackTrace = new StackTraceList( );
```

To display a portion or all of the stack trace, use the following code:

```
// Display the first stack frame.
Console.WriteLine(arrStackTrace[0].ToString( ));

// Display all stack frames.
foreach (StackFrame SF in arrStackTrace)
{
    Console.WriteLine("stackframe: " + SF.ToString( ));
}
```

To obtain a `StackTraceList` object from a thrown exception, use the following code:

```
...
catch (Exception e)
{
    StackTraceList EST = new StackTraceList(e, true);

    Console.WriteLine("TOSTRING: " + Environment.NewLine + EST.ToString( ));
    foreach (StackFrame SF in EST)
    {
        Console.WriteLine(SF.ToString( ));
    }
}
```

To copy the `StackFrame` objects to a new array, use the following code:

```
StackFrame[] myNewArray = new StackFrame[arrStackTrace.Count];
arrStackTrace.CopyTo(myNewArray, 0);
```

You will notice that the first `StackFrame` object in the stack trace contains something like the following:

```
at AdapterPattern.StackTraceList..ctor( )
```

This is actually the constructor call to the `StackTraceList` object. This information is usually not necessary to display and can be removed quite easily. When creating the `StackTraceList` object, pass in an integer one as an argument to the constructor. This will force the first stack frame (the one containing the call to the `StackTraceList` constructor) to be discarded:

```
StackTraceList arrStackTrace = new StackTraceList(1);
```

You should note that the Add, Insert, Remove, and RemoveAt methods on the IList interface of an Array type throw the NotSupportedException, because an array is fixed in length and these methods will alter the length of the array.

See Also

See the "StackTrace Class" and "IList Interface" topics in the MSDN documentation. Also see the "Adapter Design Pattern" chapter in *Design Patterns* (Addison-Wesley).

5.6   Determining the Number of Times an Item Appears in a List<T>

Problem

You need the number of occurrences of one type of object contained in a List<T>. The List<T> contains methods, such as Contains and BinarySearch to find a single item. Unfortunately, these methods cannot find all duplicated items at one time—essentially, there is no *count all* functionality. If you want to find multiple items, you need to implement your own routine.

Solution

Use the ListEx<T> generic class shown in Example 5-2, which inherits from the List<T> class in order to extend its functionality. Two methods—CountAll and BinarySearchCountAll—are added to return the number of times a particular object appears in a sorted and an unsorted List<T>.

Example 5-2. Determining the number of times an item appears in a List <T>

```
using System;
using System.Collections;
using System.Collections.Generic;


public class ListEx<T> : List<T>
{
    // Count the number of times an item appears in this
    //   unsorted or sorted List<T>
    public int CountAll(T searchValue)
    {
        int foundCounter = 0;

        for (int index = 0; index < this.Count; index++)
        {
            if (this[index].Equals(searchValue))
            {
                foundCounter++;
```

```
        }
    }

    return (foundCounter);
}

// Count the number of times an item appears in this sorted List<T>.
public int BinarySearchCountAll(T searchValue)
{
    // Search for first item.
    int center = this.BinarySearch(searchValue);
    int left = center;
    while (left > 0 && this[left-1].Equals(searchValue))
    {
        left -= 1;
    }

    int right = center;
    while (right < (this.Count - 1) && this[right+1].Equals(searchValue))
    {
        right += 1;
    }

    return (right - left) + 1;
    }
}
```

Discussion

The CountAll method accepts a search value (searchValue) of type object. This method then proceeds to count the number of times the search value appears in the ListEx<T> class. This method may be used when the ListEx<T> is sorted or unsorted. If the ListEx<T> is sorted (a ListEx<T> is sorted by calling the Sort method), the BinarySearchCountAll method can be used to increase the efficiency of the searching. This is done by making use of the BinarySearch method on the ListEx<T> class, which is much faster than iterating through the entire ListEx<T>x. This is especially true as the ListEx<T> grows in size.

The following code exercises these two new methods of the ListEx<T> class:

```
class Test
{
    static void Main()
    {
        ListEx<int> arrayExt = new ListEx<int>();
        arrayExt.Add(-2);
        arrayExt.Add(-2);
        arrayExt.Add(-1);
        arrayExt.Add(-1);
        arrayExt.Add(1);
        arrayExt.Add(2);
```

```
            arrayExt.Add(2);
            arrayExt.Add(2);
            arrayExt.Add(2);
            arrayExt.Add(3);
            arrayExt.Add(100);
            arrayExt.Add(4);
            arrayExt.Add(5);

            Console.WriteLine("--CONTAINS TOTAL--");
            int count = arrayExt.CountAll(2);
            Console.WriteLine("Count2: " + count);

            count = arrayExt.CountAll(3);
            Console.WriteLine("Count3: " + count);

            count = arrayExt.CountAll(1);
            Console.WriteLine("Count1: " + count);

            Console.WriteLine("\r\n--BINARY SEARCH COUNT ALL--");
            arrayExt.Sort();
            count = arrayExt.BinarySearchCountAll(2);
            Console.WriteLine("Count2: " + count);

            count = arrayExt.BinarySearchCountAll(3);
            Console.WriteLine("Count3: " + count);

            count = arrayExt.BinarySearchCountAll(1);
            Console.WriteLine("Count1: " + count);
    }
}
```

This code outputs the following:

```
--CONTAINS TOTAL--
Count2: 4
Count3: 1
Count1: 1

--BINARY SEARCH COUNT ALL--
Count2: 4
Count3: 1
Count1: 1
```

The CountAll method uses a sequential search that is performed in a for loop. A linear search must be used since the List<T> is not sorted. The if statement determines whether each element in the List<T> is equal to the search criterion (searchValue). If the element is found to be a match, the counter (foundCounter) is incremented by one. This counter is returned by this method to indicate the number of items matching the search criteria in the List<T>.

The BinarySearchCountAll method implements a binary search to locate an item matching the search criteria (searchValue) in the List<T>. If one is found, a while loop is used to find the very first matching item in the sorted List<T>, and the position of that element is recorded in the left variable. A second while loop is used to find the very last matching item, and the position of this element is recorded in the right variable. The value in the left variable is subtracted from the value in the right variable and then one is added to this result in order to get the total number of matches.

Recipe 5.7 contains a variation of this recipe that returns the actual items found, rather than a count.

See Also

See Recipe 5.7; see the "ArrayList Class" topic in the MSDN documentation.

5.7 Retrieving All Instances of a Specific Item in a List<T>

Problem

You need to retrieve every object contained in a List<T> that matches a search criterion. The List<T> contains the BinarySearch method to find a single item—essentially, there is no *find all* functionality. If you want to find all items duplicated in a List<T>, you must write your own routine.

Solution

Use the ListEx<T> class shown in Example 5-3, which inherits from the List<T> class in order to extend its functionality. Two methods—GetAll and BinarySearchGetAll—are added to return an array of all the matching objects found in this sorted or unsorted List<T>.

Example 5-3. Retrieving all instances of a specific item in a List<T>

```
using System;
using System.Collections;
using System.Collections.Generic;

public class ListEx<T> : List<T>
{
    // The method to retrieve all matching objects in a
    // sorted or unsorted ListEx<T>
    public T[] GetAll(T searchValue)
    {
        List<T> foundItem = new List<T>();

        for (int index = 0; index < this.Count; index++)
        {
            if (this[index].Equals(searchValue))
            {
                foundItem.Add(this[index]);
```

```
            }
        }

        return (foundItem.ToArray( ));
    }

    // The method to retrieve all matching objects in a sorted ListEx<T>
    public T[] BinarySearchGetAll(T searchValue)
    {
        bool done = false;
        List<T> RetObjs = new List<T>( );

        // Search for first item.
        int center = this.BinarySearch(searchValue);
        if (center > 0)
        {
            RetObjs.Add(this[center]);

            int left = center;
            while (left > 0 && this[left - 1].Equals(searchValue))
            {
                left -= 1;
                RetObjs.Add(this[left]);
            }

            int right = center;
            while (right < (this.Count - 1) &&
                    this[right + 1].Equals(searchValue))
            {
                right += 1;
                RetObjs.Add(this[right]);
            }
        }

        return (RetObjs.ToArray( ));
    }
}
```

Discussion

The GetAll and BinarySearchGetAll methods used in this recipe are very similar to
those used in Recipe 5.6. The main difference is that these methods return the actual
items found in an object array instead of a count of the number of times an item was
found. The main thing to keep in mind when choosing a method is whether you are
going to be searching a List<T> that is sorted. Choose the GetAll method to obtain an
array of all found items from an unsorted List<T>, and choose the BinarySearchGetAll
method to get all items in a sorted List<T>.

The following code exercises these two new methods of the ListEx<T> class:

```
    class Test
    {
```

```csharp
static void Main()
{
    ListEx<int> arrayExt = new ListEx<int>();
    arrayExt.Add(-1);
    arrayExt.Add(-1);
    arrayExt.Add(1);
    arrayExt.Add(2);
    arrayExt.Add(2);
    arrayExt.Add(2);
    arrayExt.Add(2);
    arrayExt.Add(3);
    arrayExt.Add(100);
    arrayExt.Add(4);
    arrayExt.Add(5);

    Console.WriteLine("--GET All--");
    int[] objects = arrayExt.GetAll(2);
    foreach (object o in objects)
    {
        Console.WriteLine("obj2: " + o);
    }

    Console.WriteLine();
    objects = arrayExt.GetAll(-2);
    foreach (object o in objects)
    {
        Console.WriteLine("obj-2: " + o);
    }

    Console.WriteLine();
    objects = arrayExt.GetAll(5);
    foreach (object o in objects)
    {
        Console.WriteLine("obj5: " + o);
    }

    Console.WriteLine("\r\n--BINARY SEARCH GET ALL--");
    arrayExt.Sort();
    objects = arrayExt.BinarySearchGetAll(-2);
    foreach (object o in objects)
    {
        Console.WriteLine("obj-2: " + o);
    }

    Console.WriteLine();
    objects = arrayExt.BinarySearchGetAll(2);
    foreach (object o in objects)
    {
        Console.WriteLine("obj2: " + o);
    }

    Console.WriteLine();
    objects = arrayExt.BinarySearchGetAll(5);
    foreach (object o in objects)
```

```
        {
            Console.WriteLine("obj5: " + o);
        }
    }
}
```

This code outputs the following:

```
--GET All--
obj2: 2
obj2: 2
obj2: 2
obj2: 2


obj5: 5

--BINARY SEARCH GET ALL--

obj2: 2
obj2: 2
obj2: 2
obj2: 2

obj5: 5
```

The BinarySearchGetAll method is faster than the GetAll method, especially if the array has already been sorted. If a BinarySearch is used on an unsorted List<T>, it is highly likely that the results returned by the search will be incorrect.

See Also

See Recipe 5.6; see the "List<T> Class" topic in the MSDN documentation.

5.8   Inserting and Removing Items from an Array

Problem

You need the ability to insert and remove items from a standard System.Array type. When an item is inserted, it should not overwrite the item where it is being inserted; instead, it should be inserted between the element at that index and the previous index. When an item is removed, the void left by the element should be closed by shifting the other elements in the array. However, the Array type has no usable method to perform these operations.

Solution

If possible, switch to a List<T> instead. If this is not possible (for example, if you're not in control of the code that creates the Array or ArrayList in the first place), use the approach shown in the following class. Two methods insert and remove items from the array. The InsertIntoArray method will insert an item into the array without overwriting any data that already exists in the array. The RemoveFromArray will remove an element from the array:

```
using System;

public class ArrayUtilities
{
    public void InsertIntoArray(Array target,
      object value, int index)
    {
        if (index < target.GetLowerBound(0) ||
            index > target.GetUpperBound(0))
        {
            throw (new ArgumentOutOfRangeException("index", index,
              "Array index out of bounds."));
        }
        else
        {
            Array.Copy(target, index, target, index + 1,
                    target.Length - index - 1);
        }

        target.SetValue(value, index);
    }

    public void RemoveFromArray(Array target, int index)
    {
        if (index < target.GetLowerBound(0) ||
            index > target.GetUpperBound(0))
        {
            throw (new ArgumentOutOfRangeException("index", index,
              "Array index out of bounds."));
        }
        else if (index < target.GetUpperBound(0))
        {
            Array.Copy(target, index + 1, target, index,
                    target.Length - index - 1);
        }

        target.SetValue(null, target.GetUpperBound(0));
    }
}
```

Discussion

The InsertIntoArray and RemoveFromArray methods make use of the Array.Copy static method to perform their operations. Initially, both methods test to see whether an item is being added or removed within the bounds of the array target. If the item passes this test, the Array.Copy method is used to shift items around to either make room for an element to be inserted or to overwrite an element being removed from the array.

The RemoveFromArray method accepts two parameters. *target* is the array from which an element is to be removed; the second parameter, *index*, is the zero-based position of the element to be removed in the array. Elements at and above the inserted element are shifted down by one. The last element in the array is set to the default value for the array type.

The InsertIntoArray method accepts three parameters. The first parameter, *target*, is the array that is to have an element added; *value* is the element to be added; and *index* is the zero-based position at which *value* is to be added. Elements at and above the inserted element are shifted up by one. The last element in the array is discarded.

The following code illustrates the use of the InsertIntoArray and RemoveFromArray methods:

```
class CTest
{
    static void Main( )
    {
        ArrayUtilities arrlib = new ArrayUtilities ( );
        string[] numbers = {"one", "two", "four", "five", "six"} ;

        arrlib.InsertIntoArray(numbers, "three", 2);
        foreach (string number in numbers)
        {
            Console.WriteLine(number);
        }

        Console.WriteLine( );
        arrlib.RemoveFromArray(numbers, 2);
        foreach (string number in numbers)
        {
            Console.WriteLine(number);
        }
    }
}
```

This code displays the following:

```
one
two
three
four
five

one
two
four
five
```

See Also

See the "Array Class" and "List<T> Class" topics in the MSDN documentation.

5.9   Keeping Your List<T> Sorted

Problem

You will be using the BinarySearch method of the List<T> to periodically search the List<T> for specific elements. The addition, modification, and removal of elements will be interleaved with the searches. The BinarySearch method, however, presupposes a sorted array; if the List<T> is not sorted, the BinarySearch method will possibly return incorrect results. You do not want to have to remember to always call the List<T>.Sort method before calling the List<T>.BinarySearch method, not to mention incurring all the overhead associated with this call. You need a way of keeping the List<T> sorted without always having to call the List<T>.Sort method.

Solution

The following SortedList generic class enhances the adding and modifying of elements within a List<T>. These methods keep the array sorted when items are added to it and modified. Note that a DeleteSorted method is not required since deleting an item does not disturb the sorted order of the remaining items:

```
using System;
using System.Collections;
using System.Collections.Generic;


public class SortedList<T> : List<T>
{
    public void AddSorted(T item)
    {
        int position = this.BinarySearch(item);
        if (position < 0)
        {
            // This bit of code will be described in detail later.
            position = ~position;
        }

        this.Insert(position, item);
    }

    public void ModifySorted(T item, int index)
    {
        this.RemoveAt(index);

        int position = this.BinarySearch(item);
        if (position < 0)
        {
            position = ~position;
        }

        this.Insert(position, item);
    }
}
```

Discussion

Instead of calling `List<T>.Add` directly to add elements, use the `AddSorted` method to add elements while at the same time keeping the `List<T>` sorted. The `AddSorted` method accepts a generic type (T) to add to the sorted list.

Likewise, instead of using the `List<T>` indexer directly to modify elements, use the `ModifySorted` method to modify elements while at the same time keeping the `List<T>` sorted. Call this method, passing in the generic type *T* to replace the existing object (*item*), and the index of the object to modify (*index*).

The following code exercises the `SortedList<T>` class:

```
class CTest
{
    static void Main()
    {
        // Create a SortedList and populate it with
        // randomly chosen numbers.
        SortedList<int> sortedAL = new SortedList<int>();
        sortedAL.AddSorted(200);
        sortedAL.AddSorted(20);
        sortedAL.AddSorted(2);
        sortedAL.AddSorted(7);
        sortedAL.AddSorted(10);
        sortedAL.AddSorted(0);
        sortedAL.AddSorted(100);
        sortedAL.AddSorted(-20);
        sortedAL.AddSorted(56);
        sortedAL.AddSorted(55);
        sortedAL.AddSorted(57);
        sortedAL.AddSorted(200);
        sortedAL.AddSorted(-2);
        sortedAL.AddSorted(-20);
        sortedAL.AddSorted(55);
        sortedAL.AddSorted(55);

        // Display it.
        foreach (int i in sortedAL)
        {
            Console.WriteLine(i);
        }

        // Now modify a value at a particular index.
        sortedAL.ModifySorted(0, 5);
        sortedAL.ModifySorted(1, 10);
        sortedAL.ModifySorted(2, 11);
        sortedAL.ModifySorted(3, 7);
        sortedAL.ModifySorted(4, 2);
        sortedAL.ModifySorted(2, 4);
        sortedAL.ModifySorted(15, 0);
        sortedAL.ModifySorted(0, 15);
        sortedAL.ModifySorted(223, 15);
```

```
            // Display it.
            Console.WriteLine( );
            foreach (int i in sortedAL)
            {
                Console.WriteLine(i);
            }
        }
    }
```

This method automatically places the new item in the List<T> while keeping its sort order; this is done without having to explicitly call List<T>.Sort. The reason this works is because the AddSorted method first calls the BinarySearch method and passes it the object to be added to the ArrayList. The BinarySearch method will either return the index where it found an identical item or a negative number that you can use to determine where the item that you are looking for should be located. If the BinarySearch method returns a positive number, you can use the List<T>. Insert method to insert the new element at that location, keeping the sort order within the List<T>. If the BinarySearch method returns a negative number, you can use the bitwise complement operator ~ to determine where the item should have been located, had it existed in the sorted list. Using this number, you can use the List<T>.Insert method to add the item to the correct location in the sorted list while keeping the correct sort order.

You can remove an element from the sorted list without disturbing the sort order, but modifying an element's value in the List<T> most likely will cause the sorted list to become unsorted. The ModifySorted method alleviates this problem. This method works similarly to the AddSorted method, except that it will initially remove the element from the List<T> and then insert the new element into the correct location.

See Also

See the "List<T> Class" topic in the MSDN documentation.

5.10   Sorting a Dictionary's Keys and/or Values

Problem

You want to sort the keys and/or values contained in a Hashtable in order to display the entire Hashtable to the user, sorted in either ascending or descending order.

Solution

Use the Keys and Values properties of a Dictionary<T,U> object to obtain an ICollection of its key and value objects. The methods shown here return a List<T> of objects containing the keys or values of a Dictionary<T,U>:

```
using System;
using System.Collections;
```

```
using System.Collections.Generic;


public static List<T> GetKeys<T,U>(Dictionary<T,U> table)
{
    return (new List<T>(table.Keys));
}
```

The method shown here returns a List<U> of objects containing the values in a Dictionary<T,U>:

```
using System;
using System.Collections;
using System.Collections.Generic;


public static List<U> GetValues<T,U>(Dictionary<T,U> table)
{
    return (new List<U>(table.Values));
}
```

The following code creates a Dictionary<T,U> object and displays it sorted in ascending and descending order:

```
public static void TestSortKeyValues()
{
    // Define a Dictionary<T,U> object.
    Dictionary<string, string> hash = new Dictionary<string, string>();
    hash.Add(2, "two");
    hash.Add(1, "one");
    hash.Add(5, "five");
    hash.Add(4, "four");
    hash.Add(3, "three");

    // Get all the keys in the Dictionary<T,U> and sort them.
    List<string> keys = GetKeys(hash);
    keys.Sort();

    // Display sorted list.
    foreach (object obj in keys)
        Console.WriteLine("Key: " + obj + "    Value: " + hash[obj]);

    // Reverse the sorted list.
    Console.WriteLine();
    keys.Reverse();

    // Display reversed list.
    foreach (object obj in keys)
        Console.WriteLine("Key: " + obj + "    Value: " + hash[obj]);
    Console.WriteLine();
    Console.WriteLine();

    // Get all the values in the Dictionary<T,U> and sort them.
    List<string> values = GetValues(hash);
    values.Sort();
```

```
// Display sorted list.
foreach (string obj in values)
    Console.WriteLine("Value: " + obj);

// Reverse the sorted value list.
Console.WriteLine( );
values.Reverse( );

// Display sorted list.
foreach (string obj in values)
    Console.WriteLine("Value: " + obj);}
```

The key/value pairs are displayed as shown:

```
Key: 1    Value: one
Key: 2    Value: two
Key: 3    Value: three
Key: 4    Value: four
Key: 5    Value: five

Key: 5    Value: five
Key: 4    Value: four
Key: 3    Value: three
Key: 2    Value: two
Key: 1    Value: one


Value: five       ← Notice that the values are sorted alphabetically
Value: four
Value: one
Value: three
Value: two

Value: two
Value: three
Value: one
Value: four
Value: five
```

Discussion

The Dictionary<T,U> object exposes two useful properties for obtaining a collection of its keys or values. The Keys property returns an ICollection containing all the keys currently in the Dictionary<T,U>. The Values property returns the same for all values currently contained in the Dictionary<T,U>.

The GetKeys method uses the Keys property. Once the ICollection of keys is returned through this property, a new List<T> is created to hold the keys. This List<T> is then returned to the caller. The GetValues method works in a similar manner except that it uses the Values property.

The GetValues method uses the Values property. Once the ICollection of values is returned through this property, a new List<U> is created of the same size to hold the values. This List<U> is then returned to the caller.

The ICollection object returned from either the Keys or Values property of a Dictionary<T,U> object contains direct references to the key and value collections within the Dictionary<T,U>. This means that if the keys and/or values change in a Dictionary<T,U>, the key and value collections will be altered accordingly.

See Also

See the "Dictionary<T,U> Class" and "List<T> Class" topics in the MSDN documentation.

5.11 Creating a Dictionary with Max and Min Value Boundaries

Problem

You need to use a generic Dictionary object in your project that stores only numeric data in its value (the key can be of any type) between a set maximum and minimum value.

Solution

Create a class with accessors and methods that enforce these boundaries. The class shown in Example 5-4, MaxMinValueDictionary, allows only integers that fall between a maximum and minimum value to be stored.

Example 5-4. Creating a dictionary with max and min value boundaries

```
using System;
using System.Collections;
using System.Collections.Generic;
using System.Runtime.Serialization;


[Serializable]
public class MaxMinValueDictionary<T>
{
    protected Dictionary<T,int> internalDictionary = null;

    public MaxMinValueDictionary(int minValue, int maxValue)
    {
        this.minValue = minValue;
        this.maxValue = maxValue;
        internalDictionary = new Dictionary<T,int>();
    }
```

Example 5-4. Creating a dictionary with max and min value boundaries (continued)

```
    protected int minValue = int.MinValue;
    protected int maxValue = int.MaxValue;

    public int Count
    {
        get { return (internalDictionary.Count); }
    }

    public Dictionary<T,int>.KeyCollection Keys
    {
        get { return (internalDictionary.Keys); }
    }

    public Dictionary<T,int>.ValueCollection Values
    {
        get { return (internalDictionary.Values); }
    }

    public int this[T key]
    {
        get
        {
            return (internalDictionary[key]);
        }
        set
        {
            if (value >= minValue && value <= maxValue)
            {
                internalDictionary[key] = value;
            }
            else
            {
                throw (new ArgumentOutOfRangeException("value", value,
                "Value must be within the range " + minValue + " to " + maxValue));
            }
        }
    }

    public void Add(T key, int value)
    {
        if (value >= minValue && value <= maxValue)
        {
            internalDictionary.Add(key, value);
        }
        else
        {
            throw (new ArgumentOutOfRangeException("value", value,
            "Value must be within the range " + minValue + " to " + maxValue));
        }
    }

    public bool ContainsKey(T key)
    {
```

```
        return (internalDictionary.ContainsKey(key));
    }

    public bool ContainsValue(int value)
    {
        return (internalDictionary.ContainsValue(value));
    }

    public override bool Equals(object obj)
    {
        return (internalDictionary.Equals(obj));
    }

    public IEnumerator GetEnumerator()
    {
        return (internalDictionary.GetEnumerator());
    }

    public override int GetHashCode()
    {
        return (internalDictionary.GetHashCode());
    }

    public void GetObjectData(SerializationInfo info, StreamingContext context)
    {
        internalDictionary.GetObjectData(info, context);
    }

    public void OnDeserialization (object sender)
    {
        internalDictionary.OnDeserialization(sender);
    }

    public override string ToString()
    {
        return (internalDictionary.ToString());
    }

    public bool TryGetValue(T key, out int value)
    {
        return (internalDictionary.TryGetValue(key, out value));
    }

    public void Remove(T key)
    {
        internalDictionary.Remove(key);
    }

    public void Clear()
    {
        internalDictionary.Clear();
    }
}
```

Discussion

The `MaxMinValueDictionary` class wraps the `Dictionary<T,U>` class so it can restrict the range of allowed values. The overloaded constructor for the `MaxMinValueDictionary` class is defined here:

```
public MaxMinValueDictionary(int minValue, int maxValue)
```

This constructor allows the range of values to be set. Its parameters are:

minValue
> The smallest integer value that can be added as a value in a key/value pair

maxValue
> The largest integer value that can be added as a value in a key/value pair

The overridden indexer has both get and set. The get returns the value that matches the provided *key*. The set checks the *value* parameter to determine whether it is within the boundaries of the `minValue` and `maxValue` fields before it is set.

The `Add` method accepts an integer for its *value* parameter and performs the same tests as the set accessor on the indexer. If the test passes, the integer is added to the `MaxMinValueDictionary`.

To modify the `MaxMinValueDictionary<T>` class to accept numeric values other than an integer, simply change all instances of the `int` value parameter to another numeric type, such as a double or a long. Anytime you see `Dictionary<T,int>`, you will need to change the `int` type to the numeric type of your choosing. In addition, the `minValue` and `maxValue` fields will need to be changed to that type, as will the parameters to the constructor and the return type of the indexer.

See Also

See the "Hashtable Class" topic in the MSDN documentation.

5.12   Displaying an Array's Data as a Delimited String

Problem

You have an array or type that implements `ICollection`, and you wish to display or store it as a string delimited by commas or some other delimiting character. This ability will allow you to easily save data stored in an array to a text file as delimited text.

Solution

The `ConvertCollectionToDelStr` method will accept any object that implements the `ICollection` interface. This collection object's contents are converted into a delimited string:

```
public static string ConvertCollectionToDelStr(ICollection theCollection,
    char delimiter)
{
    StringBuilder delimitedData = new StringBuilder( );

    foreach (string strData in theCollection)
    {
        if (strData.IndexOf(delimiter) >= 0)
        {
            throw (new ArgumentException(
            "Cannot have a delimiter character in an element of the array.",
            "theCollection"));
        }

        delimitedData.Append(strData).Append(delimiter);
    }

    // Return the constructed string minus the final
    // appended delimiter char.
    return (delimitedData.ToString( ).TrimEnd(delimiter));
}
```

Discussion

The following TestDisplayDataAsDelStr method shows how to use the Convert-CollectionToDelStr method to convert an array of strings to a delimited string:

```
public static void TestDisplayDataAsDelStr( )
{
    string[] numbers = {"one", "two", "three", "four", "five", "six"} ;

    string delimitedStr = ConvertCollectionToDelStr(numbers, ',');
    Console.WriteLine(delimitedStr);
}
```

This code creates a delimited string of all the elements in the array and displays it as follows:

```
one,two,three,four,five,six
```

Of course, instead of a comma as the delimiter, you could also have used a semicolon, dash, or any other character. The delimiter type was made a char because it is best to use only a single delimiting character if you are going to use the String.Split method to restore the delimited string to an array of substrings. String.Split works only with delimiters that consist of one character.

See Also

See the "ICollection Interface" topic in the MSDN documentation.

5.13   Storing Snapshots of Lists in an Array

Problem

You have an ArrayList, Queue, or Stack object and you want to take a snapshot of its current state. (Note that this recipe also works for any other data type that implements the ICollection interface.)

Solution

Use the CopyTo method declared in the ICollection interface. The following method, TakeSnapshotOfList, accepts any type that implements the ICollection interface and takes a snapshot of the entire object's contents. This snapshot is returned as an object array:

```
public static T[] TakeSnapshotOfList<T>(ICollection theList)
{
    T[] snapshot = new T[theList.Count];
    theList.CopyTo(snapshot, 0);
    return (snapshot);
}
```

Discussion

The following method creates a Queue<int> object, enqueues some data, and then takes a snapshot of it:

```
public static void TestListSnapshot()
{
    Queue<int> someQueue = new Queue<int>();
    someQueue.Enqueue(1);
    someQueue.Enqueue(2);
    someQueue.Enqueue(3);

    int[] queueSnapshot = TakeSnapshotOfList<int>(someQueue);
}
```

The TakeSnapshotOfList<T> is useful when you want to record the state of an object that implements the ICollection interface. This "snapshot" can be compared to the original list later on to determine what, if anything, has changed in the list. Multiple snapshots can be taken at various points in an application's run to show the state of the list or lists over time.

The TakeSnapshotOfList<T> method could easily be used as a logging/debugging tool for developers. Take, for example, a List<T> that is being corrupted at some point in the application. You can take snapshots of the List<T> at various points in the application using the TakeSnapshotOfList<T> method and then compare the snapshots to narrow down the list of possible places where the List<T> is being corrupted.

See Also

See the "ICollection Interface" and "Array Class" topics in the MSDN documentation.

5.14 Persisting a Collection Between Application Sessions

Problem

You have a collection such as an `ArrayList`, `List<T>`, `Hashtable`, or `Dictionary<T,U>` in which you are storing application information. You can use this information to tailor the application's environment to the last known settings (e.g., window size, window placement, currently displayed toolbars). You can also use it to allow the user to start the application at the same point where it was last shut down. In other words, if the user is editing an invoice and needs to shut down the computer for the night, the application will know exactly which invoice to initially display when the application is started next time.

Solution

Serialize the object(s) to and from a file:

```
public static void SaveObj<T>(T obj, string dataFile)
{
    FileStream FS = File.Create(dataFile);
    BinaryFormatter binSerializer = new BinaryFormatter( );
    binSerializer.Serialize(FS, obj);
    FS.Close( );
}

public static T RestoreObj<T>(string dataFile)
{
    FileStream FS = File.OpenRead(dataFile);
    BinaryFormatter binSerializer = new BinaryFormatter( );
    T obj = (T)binSerializer.Deserialize(FS);
    FS.Close( );

    return (obj);
}
```

Discussion

The `dataFile` parameter accepts a string value to use as a filename. The `SaveObj<T>` method accepts an object and attempts to serialize it to a file. Conversely, the `RestoreObj<T>` method removes the serialized object from the file created in the `SaveObj<T>` method.

The `TestSerialization` utility shown in Example 5-5 demonstrates how to use these methods to serialize a `Hashtable` object and a `List<int>` object (note that this will work for any type that is marked with the `SerializableAttribute`).

Example 5-5. Persisting a collection between application sessions

```
public static void TestSerialization( )
{
    // Create a Hashtable object to save/restore to/from a file.
    Hashtable HT = new Hashtable( );
    HT.Add(0, "Zero");
    HT.Add(1, "One");
    HT.Add(2, "Two");

    // Display this object's contents and save it to a file.
    foreach (DictionaryEntry DE in HT)
        Console.WriteLine(DE.Key + " : " + DE.Value);
    SaveObj(HT);

    // Restore this object from the same file and display its contents.
    Hashtable HTNew = new Hashtable( );
    HTNew = (Hashtable)RestoreObj( );
    foreach (DictionaryEntry DE in HTNew)
        Console.WriteLine(DE.Key + " : " + DE.Value);


    // Create a List<int> object to save/restore to/from a file.
    Console.WriteLine( );
    List<int> test = new List<int>( );
    test.Add(1);
    test.Add(2);

    // Display this object's contents and save it to a file.
    foreach (int i in test)
        Console.WriteLine(i.ToString( ));
    SaveObj<List<int>>(test, "TEST.DATA");

    // Restore this object from the same file and display its contents.
    List<int> testNew = new List<int>( );
    testNew = RestoreObj<List<int>>("TEST.DATA");
    foreach (int i in testNew)
        Console.WriteLine(i.ToString( ));
}
```

If you serialize your objects to disk at specific points in your application, you can then deserialize them and return to a known state, for instance, in the event of an unintended shutdown.

If you rely on serialized objects to store persistent information, you need to figure out what you are going to do when you deploy a new version of the application. You should plan ahead with either a strategy for making sure the types you serialize don't get changed or a technique for dealing with changes. Otherwise you are going to have big problems when you deploy an update.

See Also

See the "ArrayList Class," "Hashtable Class," "List<T> Class," "Dictionary<T,U> Class," "File Class," and "BinaryFormatter Class" topics in the MSDN documentation.

5.15   Testing Every Element in an Array or List<T>

Problem

You need an easy way to test every element in an Array or List<T>. The results of this test should indicate that the test passed for all elements in the collection or it failed for at least one element in the collection.

Solution

Use the TrueForAll method as shown here:

```
// Create a List of strings.
List<string> strings = new List<string>();
strings.Add("one");
strings.Add(null);
strings.Add("three");
strings.Add("four");

// Determine if there are no null values in the List.
string str = strings.TrueForAll(delegate(string val)
{
    if (val == null)
        return false;
    else
        return true;
}).ToString();

// Display the results.
Console.WriteLine(str);
```

Discussion

The addition of the TrueForAll method on the Array and List<T> classes allows you to easily set up tests for all elements in these collections. The code in the Solution for this recipe tests all elements to determine if any are null. You could just as easily set up tests to determine...

- If any numeric elements are above a specified maximum value
- If any numeric elements are below a specified minimum value
- If any string elements contain a specified set of characters
- If any data objects have all of their fields filled in

...as well as any others you may come up with.

The `TrueForAll` method accepts a generic delegate `Predicate<T>` called match and returns a Boolean value:

```
public bool TrueForAll(Predicate<T> match)
```

The match parameter determines whether or not a true or false should be returned by the `TrueForAll` method.

The `TrueForAll` method basically consists of a loop that iterates over each element in the collection. Within this loop, a call to the match delegate is invoked. If this delegate returns true, the processing continues on to the next element in the collection. If this delegate returns false, processing stops and a false is returned by the `TrueForAll` method. When the `TrueForAll` method is finished iterating over all the elements of the collection and the match delegate has not returned a false value for any element, the `TrueForAll` method returns a true.

See Also

See the "Array Class," "List<T> Class," and "TrueForAll Method" topics in the MSDN documentation.

5.16 Performing an Action on Each Element in an Array or List<T>

Problem

You need an easy way to iterate over all the elements in an Array or List<T>, performing an operation on each element as you go.

Solution

Use the ForEach method of the Array or List<T> classes:

```
// Create and populate a List of Data objects.
List<Data> numbers = new List<Data>();
numbers.Add(new Data(1));
numbers.Add(new Data(2));
numbers.Add(new Data(3));
numbers.Add(new Data(4));

// Display them.
foreach (Data d in numbers)
    Console.WriteLine(d.val);

// Add 2 to all Data.val integer values.
numbers.ForEach(delegate(Data obj)
{
    obj.val += 2;
});
```

```
    // Display them.
    foreach (Data d in numbers)
        Console.WriteLine(d.val);

    // Total val integer values in all Data objects in the List.
    int total = 0;
    numbers.ForEach(delegate(Data obj)
    {
        total += obj.val;
    });

    // Display total.
    Console.WriteLine("Total: " + total);
```

This code outputs the following:

```
1
2
3
4
3
4
5
6
Total: 18
```

The Data class is defined as follows:

```
public class Data
{
    public Data(int v)
    {
        val = v;
    }

    public int val = 0;
}
```

Discussion

The ForEach method of the Array and List<T> collections allows you to easily perform an action on every element within these collections. This is accomplished through the use of the Action<T> delegate, which is passed in as a parameter to the ForEach method:

```
public void ForEach (Action<T> action)
```

The action parameter is a delegate of type Action<T> that contains the code that will be invoked for each element of the collection.

The ForEach method basically consists of a loop that iterates over each element in the collection. Within this loop, a call to the action delegate is invoked. Processing continues on to each element in the collection until the last element is finished processing. When this occurs, the ForEach method is finished and returns to the calling method.

This recipe uses the ForEach method of a List<T> object in two different ways. The first is to actually modify the values of each element of the List<T> object:

```
// Add 2 to all Data.val integer values.
numbers.ForEach(delegate(Data obj)
{
    obj.val += 2;
});
```

This call to ForEach will iterate over each Data element within the numbers List<Data> object. On every iteration, the value val contained in the current Data object obj has its value incremented by two.

The second way is to collect a total of all the values val contained in each Data object obj in the numbers List<Data> object:

```
// Total val integer values in all Data objects in the List.
int total = 0;
numbers.ForEach(delegate(Data obj)
{
    total += obj.val;
});
```

This code uses the total variable to build a running total of the values contained in each element. In this instance you do not modify any values in any of the Data objects; instead, you examine each Data object and record information about its value.

See Also

See the "Array Class," "List<T> Class," and "ForEach Method" topics in the MSDN documentation.

5.17 Creating a Read-Only Array or List<T>

Problem

You need a way to create a read-only Array or List<T>, where the Array or List<T> itself is read-only.

Solution

Use the AsReadOnly method of the Array or List<T> class as shown here:

```
// Create and populate a List of strings.
List<string> strings = new List<string>();
strings.Add("1");
strings.Add("2");
strings.Add("3");
strings.Add("4");
```

```
// Create a read-only strings List.
IList<string> readOnlyStrings = strings.AsReadOnly( );

// Display them.
foreach (string s in readOnlyStrings)
    Console.WriteLine(s);
```

Discussion

The AsReadOnly method accepts no parameters and returns a read-only wrapper around the collection on which it is called. For example, the following statement:

```
IList<string> readOnlyStrings = strings.AsReadOnly( );
```

returns a read-only IList<string> type from the original strings List<string> type. This read-only readOnlyStrings variable behaves similarly to the original strings object, except that you cannot add, modify, or delete elements from this object. If you attempt one of these actions, a System.NotSupportedException will be thrown along with the message "Collection is read-only". Any of the following lines of code will cause this exception to be thrown:

```
readOnlyStrings.Add("5");
readOnlyStrings.Remove("1");
readOnlyStrings[0] = "1.1";
```

While you cannot modify the data within the readOnlyStrings object, you can point this object to refer to a different object of type IList<string>, for example:

```
readOnlyStrings = new List<string>( );
```

On the other hand, if you add, modify, or delete elements from the original strings object, the changes will be reflected in the new readOnlyStrings object. For example, the following code creates a List<string>, populates it, and then creates a read-only object readOnlyStrings from this original List<string> object. Next, the readOnlyStrings object elements are displayed; the original List<string> object is modified and then the readOnlyStrings object elements are again displayed. Notice that they have changed.

```
// Create and populate a List of strings.
List<string> strings = new List<string>( );
strings.Add("1");
strings.Add("2");
strings.Add("3");
strings.Add("4");

// Create a read-only strings List.
IList<string> readOnlyStrings = strings.AsReadOnly( );

// Display them.
foreach (string s in readOnlyStrings)
    Console.WriteLine(s);

// Change the value in the original array.
strings[0] = "one";
```

```
    strings[1] = null;

    // Display them again.
    Console.WriteLine( );
    foreach (string s in readOnlyStrings)
        Console.WriteLine(s);
```

This code outputs the following:

```
1
2
3
4

one
        ← The null value
3
4
```

For an alternate method to making read-only collections, see Recipe 4.9.

See Also

See the "Array Class," "List<T> Class," "IList<T> Interface," and "AsReadOnly Method" topics in the MSDN documentation.

CHAPTER 6

Iterators and Partial Types

6.0   Introduction

Two of the four main new features in C# 2.0 are iterators and partial types. *Iterators* allow for a block of code to yield an ordered sequence of values. *Partial types* allow for different parts of classes to be placed in different locations.

Iterators are a mechanism whereby a class can enumerate data using the foreach loop construct. However, iterators are much more flexible than this. You can easily generate a sequence of data returned by the enumerator; it does not have to be hardcoded up front. For example, you could easily write an enumerator that generates the Fibonacci sequence on demand. Another flexible feature of iterators is that you do not have to set a limit on the number of values returned by the iterator, so in this example you could choose when to stop producing the Fibonacci sequence.

Previous versions of the .NET Framework required you to perform several steps to allow the foreach construct to operate on your type. First, you had to implement the IEnumerable interface on your type, then you had to implement the IEnumerator interface on another type. This second type performed the actual work to enable foreach functionality. The methods MoveNext and Reset, along with the Current property, then had to be written by hand inside this type.

Iterators allow you to hand the work of writing this class off to the C# compiler. With Version 2.0 of the C# compiler, the ability for a type to be used by a foreach loop requires much less work. Now you need to add only an iterator to your type. An iterator is a member within your type (e.g., a method, an operator overload, or the get accessor of a property) that returns either a System.Collections.IEnumerator, a System.Collections.Generic.IEnumerator<T>, a System.Collections.IEnumerable, or a System.Collections.Generic.IEnumerable<T> and that contains at least one yield statement. This simplicity allows you to more easily write types that can be used by foreach loops.

Partial types allow the developer to split pieces of a type across several areas where the type is defined. The type can be in multiple files, multiple areas in the same file, or a combination of the two. Declaring a type as partial is an indicator to the C# compiler that this type may not be fully represented in this location and that it cannot be fully compiled until the other parts are found or the end of the list of modules to compile is found. Partial types are purely a compiler-implemented feature with no impact to the underlying Microsoft Intermediate Language that is generated for the class. The main examples of using partial types are in the Visual Studio IDE, where the designer uses them to keep designer-generated code separate from UI logic the developer creates, and in the DataSet creation code, which is based on an XML Schema Definition of the data. Even though partial types are only a compiler-level feature, you can use them to your advantage in a few situations that are pointed out in Recipes 6.10 and 6.11.

6.1 Implementing Nested foreach Functionality in a Class

Problem

You need a class that contains a list of objects; each of these objects in turn contains a list of objects. You want to use a nested foreach loop to iterate through all objects in both the outer and inner arrays in the following manner:

```
foreach (SubGroup sg in group)
{
    foreach (Item i in sg)
    {
        // Operate on Item objects contained in the innermost object collection sg,
        // which in turn is contained in another outer collection called group.
    }
}
```

Solution

Implement the IEnumerable interface on the class. The Group class shown in Example 6-1 contains a List of SubGroup objects; each SubGroup object contains a List of Item objects. Implement IEnumerable on the top-level class (Group) and on each of the objects returned (SubGroup) by this top-level enumeration.

Example 6-1. Implementing for each functionality in a class

```
using System;
using System.Collections;

//----------------------------------------
// The top-level class
//----------------------------------------
```

Example 6-1. Implementing for each functionality in a class (continued)

```
public class Group : IEnumerable
{
    //CONSTRUCTORS
    public Group( ) {}

    //FIELDS
    private List<SubGroup> innerArray = new List<SubGroup>( );

    //PROPERTIES
    public int Count
    {
        get{return(innerArray.Count);}
    }

    //METHODS
    public void AddGroup(string name)
    {
        SubGroup subGroup = new SubGroup(name);
        innerArray.Add(subGroup);
    }

    public SubGroup GetGroup(int setIndex)
    {
        return(innerArray[setIndex]);
    }

    IEnumerator IEnumerable.GetEnumerator( )
    {
        for (int index = 0; index < Count; index++)
        {
            yield return (innerArray[index]);
        }
    }
}

//-----------------------------------------
//  The inner class
//-----------------------------------------
public class SubGroup : IEnumerable
{
    //CONSTRUCTORS
    public SubGroup( ) {}

    public SubGroup(string name)
    {
        subGroupName = name;
    }

    //FIELDS
    private string subGroupName = "";
    private List<Item> itemArray = new List<Item>( );
```

Example 6-1. Implementing for each functionality in a class (continued)

```
//PROPERTIES
public string SubGroupName
{
    get{return(subGroupName);}
}

public int Count
{
    get{return(itemArray.Count);}
}

//METHODS
public void AddItem(string name, int location)
{
    Item itm = new Item(name, location);
    itemArray.Add(itm);
}

public Item GetSubGroup(int index)
{
    return(itemArray[index]);
}

IEnumerator IEnumerable.GetEnumerator( )
{
    for (int index = 0; index < Count; index++)
    {
        yield return (itemArray[index]);
    }
}
}

//-----------------------------------------
// The lowest-level class
//-----------------------------------------
public class Item
{
    //CONSTRUCTOR
    public Item(string name, int location)
    {
        itemName = name;
        itemLocation = location;
    }

    private string itemName = "";
    private int itemLocation = 0;

    public string ItemName
    {
        get {return(itemName);}
        set {itemName = value;}
```

Example 6-1. Implementing for each functionality in a class (continued)

```
    }

    public int ItemLocation
    {
        get {return(itemLocation);}
        set {itemLocation = value;}
    }
}
```

Discussion

Building functionality into a class to allow it to be iterated over using the foreach loop is much easier now that iterators are available in Version 2.0 of the C# language. In previous versions of the .NET Framework, you not only had to implement the IEnumerable interface on the type that you wanted to make enumerable, but you also had to implement the IEnumerator interface on a nested class. The methods MoveNext and Reset along with the property Current then had to be written by hand in this nested class. Iterators allow you to hand the work of writing this nested class off to the C# compiler.

The ability for a class to be used by the foreach loop requires the inclusion of an iterator. An iterator can be a method, an operator overload, or the get accessor of a property that returns either a System.Collections.IEnumerator, a System.Collections.Generic.IEnumerator<T>, a System.Collections.IEnumerable, or a System.Collections.Generic.IEnumerable<T> and that contains at least one yield statement.

Here are two examples of iterator members implemented using the GetEnumerator method:

```
    IEnumerator IEnumerable.GetEnumerator( )
    {
        for (int index = 0; index < Count; index++)
        {
            yield return (someArray[index]);
        }
    }
    IEnumerator<T> IEnumerable<T>.GetEnumerator( )
    {
        for (int index = 0; index < Count; index++)
        {
            yield return (someArray[index]);
        }
    }
```

The code for this recipe is divided among three classes. The top-level class is the Group class, which contains a List of SubGroup objects. The SubGroup object also contains a List, but this List contains Item objects. To enumerate their contained lists, both the Group and SubGroup implement the IEnumerable interface. They therefore contain a GetEnumerator iterator method, which returns an IEnumerator. The class structure looks like this:

```
Group (Implements IEnumerable)
    SubGroup (Implements IEnumerable)
        Item
```

By examining the Group class, you can see how classes usable by a foreach loop are constructed. This class contains:

- A simple List, which will be iterated over by the class's enumerator.
- A property, Count, that returns the number of elements in the List.
- An iterator method, GetEnumerator, which is defined by the IEnumerable interface. This method yields a specific value on each iteration of the foreach loop.
- A method, AddGroup, which adds a SubGroup object to the List.
- A method, GetGroup, which returns a SubGroup object in the List.

To create the SubGroup class, you follow the same pattern as with the Group class—except the SubGroup class contains a List of Item objects.

The final class is the Item class. This class is the lowest level of this structure and contains data. It has been grouped within the SubGroup objects, all of which are contained in the Group object. There is nothing out of the ordinary with this class; it simply contains data and the means to set and retrieve this data.

Using these classes is quite simple. The following method shows how to create a Group object that contains multiple SubGroup objects, which in turn contain multiple Item objects:

```
public void CreateNestedObjects()
{
    Group topLevelGroup = new Group();

    // Create two groups under the TopLevelSet object.
    topLevelGroup.AddGroup("sg1");
    topLevelGroup.AddGroup("sg2");

    // For each SubGroup object in the topLevelGroup object add two Item objects.
    foreach (SubGroup SG in topLevelGroup)
    {
        SG.AddItem("item1", 100);
        SG.AddItem("item2", 200);
    }
}
```

The CreateNestedObjects method first creates a topLevelGroup object of the Group class, then creates two SubGroups within it called sg1 and sg2. Each of these SubGroup objects in turn is filled with two Item objects called item1 and item2.

The next method shows how to read all of the Item objects contained within the Group object that was created in the CreateNestedObjects method:

```
public void ReadNestedObjects(Set topLevelGroup)
{
    Console.WriteLine("topLevelGroup.Count: " + topLevelGroup.Count);

    // Outer foreach to iterate over all SubGroup objects
    // in the topLevelGroup object
    foreach (SubGroup SG in topLevelGroup)
    {
        Console.WriteLine("\tSG.SubGroupName:  " + SG.SubGroupName);
        Console.WriteLine("\tSG.Count: " + SG.Count);

        // Inner foreach to iterate over all Item objects
        // in the current SubGroup object
        foreach (Item i in SG)
        {
            Console.WriteLine("\t\ti.ItemName:      " + i.ItemName);
            Console.WriteLine("\t\ti.ItemLocation: " + i.ItemLocation);
        }
    }
}
```

This method displays the following:

```
topLevelGroup.Count: 2
        SG.SubGroupName:  sg1
        SG.Count: 2
                I.ItemName:      item1
                I.ItemLocation: 100
                I.ItemName:      item2
                I.ItemLocation: 200
        SG.SubGroupName:  sg2
        SG.Count: 2
                I.ItemName:      item1
                I.ItemLocation: 100
                I.ItemName:      item2
                I.ItemLocation: 200
```

As you see here, the outer foreach loop is used to iterate over all SubGroup objects that are stored in the top-level Group object. The inner foreach loop is used to iterate over all Item objects that are stored in the current SubGroup object.

See Also

See the "Iterators," "yield," "IEnumerator Interface," and "IEnumerable Interface" topics in the MSDN documentation.

6.2   Creating Custom Enumerators

Problem

You need to add foreach support to a class, but the normal way of adding an iterator (i.e, implementing IEnumerable on a type and returning a reference to this

IEnumerable from a member function) is not flexible enough. Instead of simply iterating from the first element to the last, you also need to iterate from the last to the first, and you need to be able to step over, or skip, a predefined number of elements on each iteration. You want to make all of these types of iterators available to your class.

Solution

The Container<T> class shown in Example 6-2 acts as a container for a private List<T> called internalList. Container is implemented so you can use it in a foreach loop to iterate through the private internalList.

Example 6-2. Creating custom iterators

```
public class Container<T>
{
    public Container() {}

    private List<T> internalList = new List<T>();

    public List<T> List
    {
        set    {internalList = value;}
    }

    // This iterator iterates over each element from first to last.
    public IEnumerator<T> GetEnumerator()
    {
        for (int index = 0; index < internalList.Count; index++)
        {
            yield return (internalList[index]);
        }
    }

    // This iterator iterates over each element from last to first.
    public IEnumerable<T> ReverseOrder
    {
        get
        {
            for (int index = internalList.Count - 1; index >= 0; index--)
            {
                yield return (internalList[index]);
            }
        }
    }

    // This iterator iterates over each element from first to last stepping
    // over a predefined number of elements.
    public IEnumerable<T> ForwardOrderStep(int step)
    {
        for (int index = 0; index < internalList.Count; index += step)
        {
            yield return (internalList[index]);
```

Example 6-2. Creating custom iterators (continued)

```
        }
    }

    // This iterator iterates over each element from last to first stepping
    // over a predefined number of elements.
    public IEnumerable<T> ReverseOrderStep(int step)
    {
        for (int index = internalList.Count - 1; index >= 0; index -= step)
        {
            yield return (internalList[index]);
        }
    }
}
```

Discussion

Iterators provide an easy method of moving from item to item within an object using the familiar foreach loop construct. The object can be an array, a collection, or some other type of container. This is similar to using a for loop to manually iterate over each item contained in an array. In fact, an iterator can be set up to use a for loop, or any other looping construct for that matter, as the mechanism for yielding each item in the object. In fact, you do not even have to use a looping construct. The following code is perfectly valid:

```
public static IEnumerable<int> GetValues()
{
    yield return 10;
    yield return 20;
    yield return 30;
    yield return 100;
}
```

With the foreach loop, you do not have to worry about moving the current element pointer to the beginning of the list or even about incrementing this pointer as you move through the list. In addition, you do not have to watch for the end of the list, since you cannot go beyond the bounds of the list. The best part about the foreach loop and iterators is that you do not have to know how to access the list of elements within its container—indeed, you do not even have to have access to the list of elements; the iterator member(s) implemented on the container do this for you.

The Container class contains a private List of items called internalList. There are four iterator members within this class:

```
GetEnumerator
ReverseOrder
ForwardOrderStep
ReverseOrderStep
```

The GetEnumerator method is implemented to return an IEnumerable<T>. This method iterates over each element in the internalList from the first to the last element. This iterator, similar to the others, uses a for loop to yield each element in the internalList.

The ReverseOrder property implements an iterator in its get accessor (set accessors cannot be iterators). This iterator is very similar in design to the GetEnumerator method, except that the for loop works on the internalList in the reverse direction. Notice that even though this iterator is implemented as a property, there is no reason why it cannot be implemented as a method that takes no parameters.

The last two iterators, ForwardOrderStep and ReverseOrderStep, are similar in design to GetEnumerator and ReverseOrder, respectively. The main difference (besides the fact that ReverseOrder is a property) is that the for loop uses the step parameter to skip over the specified number of items in the internalList. Notice also that only the GetEnumerator method must return an IEnumerator<T> interface; the other three iterators must return IEnumerable<T> interfaces.

Using each of these iterators is extremely simple. To iterate over each element in the Container object from first to last, use the following code:

```
Container<int> cntnr = new Container<int>();
//... Add data to cntnr here ...
foreach (int i in cntnr)
{
    Console.WriteLine(i);
}
```

To iterate over each element in the Container object from last to first, use the following code:

```
Container<int> cntnr = new Container<int>();
//... Add data to cntnr here ...
foreach (int i in cntnr.ReverseOrder)
{
    Console.WriteLine(i);
}
```

To iterate over each element in the Container object from first to last while skipping every other element, use the following code:

```
Container<int> cntnr = new Container<int>();
//... Add data to cntnr here ...
foreach (int i in cntnr.ForwardOrderStep(2))
{
    Console.WriteLine(i);
}
```

To iterate over each element in the Container object from last to first while skipping to every third element, use the following code:

```
Container<int> cntnr = new Container<int>();
//... Add data to cntnr here ...
```

```
foreach (int i in cntnr.ReverseOrderStep(3))
{
    Console.WriteLine(i);
}
```

In each of the last two examples, the iterator method accepts an integer value, step, that determines how many items will be skipped.

See Also

See the "Iterators," "yield," "IEnumerator Interface," and "IEnumerable Interface" topics in the MSDN documentation.

6.3   Creating an Iterator on a Generic Type

Problem

You want elements contained in your generic type to be enumerated using the foreach statement.

Solution

Add an iterator to your generic type, as shown here:

```
public class ShoppingList<T>
{
    public ShoppingList() {}

    private List<T> _items = new List<T>();

    public void AddItem(T item)
    {
        _items.Add(item);
    }

    // Iterator
    public IEnumerator<T> GetEnumerator()
    {
        for (int index = 0; index < _items.Count; index++)
        {
            yield return (_items[index]);
        }
    }
}
```

The following code creates a new ShoppingList<T> object and fills it with strings; it then proceeds to use a foreach loop to enumerate and display each string:

```
public static void TestShoppingCart()
{
    // Create ShoppingList object and fill it with data.
    ShoppingList<string> scart = new ShoppingList<string>();
```

```
    scart.AddItem("item1");
    scart.AddItem("item2");
    scart.AddItem("item3");
    scart.AddItem("item4");
    scart.AddItem("item5");
    scart.AddItem("item6");

    // Display all data in ShoppingCart object.
    foreach(string s in scart)
    {
        Console.WriteLine(s);
    }
}
```

Discussion

Adding an iterator to a type is fairly straightforward. You simply add a GetEnumerator method that accepts no arguments and returns an IEnumerator<T> type. In addition to this, the enumerator must have public accessibility. The GetNext method on the object returned by this GetEnumerator method is called by the foreach loop to determine what object is returned on every iteration.

The code that you write inside of the GetEnumerator method is what actually does the work of determining the next object to be returned by the foreach loop. This is accomplished through the use of the yield return statement. For example, in this recipe you simply use a for loop to iterate over each item in the _items List<T> and display each item in turn from the first to the last.

This is all the work that the developer has to do; the rest is performed by the C# compiler. The compiler takes this code and from it creates a class that is nested within the ShoppingList<T> class, which contains a simple state machine. This state machine is based on the code within the GetEnumerator method.

Notice that the IEnumerable<T> interface was not explicitly implemented on the ShoppingList<T> class. It is optional for you to explicitly implement this interface. Whether you choose to implement this interface or not, the final behavior of the ShoppingList<T> class iterator is the same.

If you choose to implement the IEnumerator<T> interface on the ShoppingList<T> class, the code will change to look like this:

```
public class ShoppingList<T> : IEnumerable<T>
{
    public ShoppingList() {}

    private List<T> _items = new List<T>();

    public void AddItem(T item)
    {
        _items.Add(item);
    }
```

```
// Iterator
IEnumerator<T> IEnumerable<T>.GetEnumerator()
{
    for (int index = 0; index < _items.Count; index++)
    {
        yield return (_items[index]);
    }
}

IEnumerator IEnumerable.GetEnumerator()
{
    for (int index = 0; index < _items.Count; index++)
    {
        yield return (_items[index]);
    }
}
```

This makes it more apparent that this class supports enumeration. You can also specify a concrete type in place of T in IEnumerable<T>, such as IEnumerable<string>, if you wish that class to enumerate values only of type string. Regardless of the method you choose, the operation of the iterator and the foreach loop is identical.

See Also

See the "Iterators," "IEnumerator Interface," and "IEnumerable Interface" topics in the MSDN documentation.

6.4   Creating an Iterator on a Non-generic Type

Problem

You want elements contained in your non-generic type to be enumerated using the foreach statement.

Solution

Add an iterator to your non-generic type, as shown here:

```
public class NGShoppingList
{
    public NGShoppingList() {}

    private List<string> _items = new List<string>();

    public void AddItem(string item)
    {
        _items.Add(item);
    }

    public IEnumerator<string> GetEnumerator()
```

```
        {
            for (int index = 0; index < _items.Count; index++)
            {
                yield return (_items[index]);
            }
        }
    }
}
```

The following code creates a new NGShoppingList object and fills it with strings; it then proceeds to use a foreach loop to enumerate and display each string:

```
public static void TestShoppingCart()
{
    // Create NGShoppingList object and fill it with data.
    NGShoppingList scart = new NGShoppingList();
    scart.AddItem("item1");
    scart.AddItem("item2");
    scart.AddItem("item3");
    scart.AddItem("item4");
    scart.AddItem("item5");
    scart.AddItem("item6");

    // Display all data in NGShoppingCart object.
    foreach(string s in scart)
    {
        Console.WriteLine(s);
    }
}
```

Discussion

Adding an iterator to a type is fairly straightforward. You simply add a GetEnumerator method that accepts no arguments and returns an IEnumerator<string> type. In addition to this, the enumerator must have public accessibility. This GetEnumerator method is called by the foreach loop to determine what object is returned by this loop on every iteration.

The code that you write inside of the GetEnumerator method is what actually does the work of determining the next object to be returned by the foreach loop. This is accomplished through the use of the yield return statement. For example, in this recipe you simply use a for loop to iterate over each item in the _items List<string> and display each item in turn from the first to the last.

This is all the work that the developer has to do; the rest is performed by the C# compiler. The compiler takes this code and from it creates a class that is nested within the NGShoppingList class, which contains a simple state machine. This state machine is based on the code within the GetEnumerator method.

Notice that the IEnumerable interface was not explicitly implemented on the NGShoppingList class. It is optional for you to explicitly implement this interface. Whether you choose to implement this interface or not, the final behavior of the NGShoppingList class iterator is the same.

If you choose to implement the IEnumerator interface on the NGShoppingList class, the class declaration will change to look like this:

```
public class NGShoppingList : IEnumerable
```

Regardless of the method you choose, the operation of the iterator and the foreach loop is identical.

See Also

See the "Iterators," "IEnumerator Interface," and "IEnumerable Interface" topics in the MSDN documentation.

6.5   Creating Iterators That Accept Parameters

Problem

You need to add a new iterator that accepts parameters to a type in order for the iterator to do special processing during the looping operation.

Solution

Add a method that is public, returns an IEnumerable, and uses the yield return statement, as shown in Example 6-3.

Example 6-3. Creating iterators that accept parameters

```
public class Foo
{
    private List<string> _items = new List<string>();

    public void AddItem(string item)
    {
        _items.Add(item);
    }

    public IEnumerator GetEnumerator()
    {
        for (int index = 0; index < _items.Count; index++)
        {
            yield return (_items[index]);
        }
    }

    // An iterator that accepts a starting index and an ending index to iterate over
    public IEnumerable GetRange(int start, int end)
    {
        if (start < 0)
        {
            throw (new IndexOutOfRangeException
                ("the start index cannot be less than zero."));
```

Example 6-3. Creating iterators that accept parameters (continued)

```
        }

        if (end < start)
        {
            throw (new IndexOutOfRangeException(
                "the end index cannot be less than the start parameter."));
        }

        if (end >= _items.Count)
        {
            throw (new IndexOutOfRangeException(
              "the end index cannot be greater than or equal to the length of the list."));
        }

        for (int index = start; (index < _items.Count) && (index <= end); index++)
        {
            yield return (_items[index]);
        }
    }
}
```

Discussion

Adding a default iterator to a type via the GetEnumerator method is easy and straight-forward. However, this forces you to give up some flexibility. For example, using the GetEnumerator method prevents you from passing in any parameters. If you can pass in parameters, you can more easily control the way the foreach loop iterates over the items in this type.

The GetRange iterator accepts both a starting and ending index value. These values indicate the index value at which to start iterating (start) and the index value at which the iterations will cease (end). The following code shows how this iterator is used:

```
public static void TestIteratorMethod()
{
    //Create Foo object and fill it with data.
    Foo f = new Foo();
    f.AddItem("item1");
    f.AddItem("item2");
    f.AddItem("item3");
    f.AddItem("item4");
    f.AddItem("item5");
    f.AddItem("item6");

    // Display all data in Foo object.
    foreach (string s in f.GetRange(3, 4))
    {
        Console.WriteLine(s);
    }
}
```

This code displays the following:

```
item4
item5
```

which are the string elements at the third and fourth index in the _items list in the object.

Two out-of-bounds situations can occur. The first is when the end parameter is set to a value that is past the end of the _items list. The following code shows this:

```
foreach (string s in f.GetRange(0, 50))
{
    Console.WriteLine(s);
}
```

This foreach loop will display all items in the _items list. This is because you have set up the for loop in the GetRange iterator method to handle this situation. The for loop's conditional expression is shown here:

```
for (int index = start; (index < _items.Count) && (index <= end); index++)
```

The for loop will stop looping either when the index loop counter is greater than the end parameter or when it goes past the end of the _items list. Another out-of-bounds situation is when the start parameter is less than the initial index in the _items list, which is zero. The following code starts iterating at a negative start index:

```
foreach (string s in f.GetRange(-3, 5))
{
    Console.WriteLine(s);
}
```

This causes an IndexOutOfRangeException to be thrown.

See Also

See the "Iterators," "IEnumerator Interface," and "IEnumerable Interface" topics in the MSDN documentation.

6.6   Adding Multiple Iterators on a Single Type

Problem

You need to add an iterator to a type that already implements the GetEnumerator iterator method; however, the iterators that you need to add are simple enough that they do not require parameters to be passed in to them as in Recipe 6.5. for example, the existing GetEnumerator iterator yields all elements in a forward-only order, but you also need to add an iterator that yields all elements in reverse order, an iterator that yields only the first half of the elements, and one that yields only the second half of the elements.

Solution

To add simple iterators that do not require parameters to be passed in to them, you can add properties with a get accessor. The get accessor must return an IEnumerable type and make use of the yield return statement. Example 6-4 shows one way to implement the solution.

Example 6-4. Adding multiple iterators that do not require parameters on a single type

```
public class SimpleListIterator
{
    private List<string> _items = new List<string>();

    public void AddItem(string item)
    {
        _items.Add(item);
    }

    public IEnumerator GetEnumerator()
    {
        for (int index = 0; index < _items.Count; index++)
        {
            yield return (_items[index]);
        }
    }

    // Additional iterators implemented as property get accessors
    public IEnumerable ReverseOrder
    {
        get
        {
            for (int index = _items.Count - 1; index >= 0; index--)
            {
                yield return (_items[index]);
            }
        }
    }

    public IEnumerable FirstHalf
    {
        get
        {
            for (int index = 0; index < (_items.Count / 2); index++)
            {
                yield return (_items[index]);
            }
        }
    }

    public IEnumerable SecondHalf
    {
        get
        {
```

Example 6-4. Adding multiple iterators that do not require parameters on a single type (continued)

```
        for (int index = (_items.Count / 2); index < _items.Count; index++)
        {
            yield return (_items[index]);
        }
    }
  }
}
```

Discussion

The SimpleListIterator class contains the typical GetEnumerator iterator method that yields all items in the _items list. In addition to this iterator method, the class contains three additional iterators: ReverseOrder, FirstHalf, and SecondHalf. The ReverseOrder iterator simply yields the elements in the _items list in reverse-index order, whereas the GetEnumerator method yields all elements in forward-index order. This is accomplished by setting up a for loop to start at either the zeroth element, for the GetEnumerator iterator method, or at the last element, as with the ReverseOrder iterator property.

The FirstHalf iterator property starts at the zeroth index of the _items list and yields all elements in the list up to the middle index. At this point iteration stops. The SecondHalf iterator property starts where the FirstHalf iterator property left off and continues yielding elements of the _items list until the end of this list.

The following code shows how the GetEnumerator iterator method is used, as well as the three iterator properties:

```
public static void TestIteratorProperties()
{
    //Create SimpleListIterator object and fill it with data.
    SimpleListIterator b = new SimpleListIterator();
    b.AddItem("item1");
    b.AddItem("item2");
    b.AddItem("item3");
    b.AddItem("item4");
    b.AddItem("item5");
    b.AddItem("item6");
    b.AddItem("item7");

    // Display all data in SimpleListIterator object.
    Console.WriteLine("\r\nGetEnumerator iterator");
    foreach (string s in b)
    {
        Console.WriteLine(s);
    }

    Console.WriteLine("\r\nReverseOrder iterator");
    foreach (string s in b.ReverseOrder)
    {
        Console.WriteLine(s);
```

```
        }

        Console.WriteLine("\r\nFirstHalf iterator");
        foreach (string s in b.FirstHalf)
        {
            Console.WriteLine(s);
        }

        Console.WriteLine("\r\nSecondHalf iterator");
        foreach (string s in b.SecondHalf)
        {
            Console.WriteLine(s);
        }
    }
}
```

This code produces the following output:

```
GetEnumerator iterator
item1
item2
item3
item4
item5
item6
item7

ReverseOrder iterator
item7
item6
item5
item4
item3
item2
item1

FirstHalf iterator
item1
item2
item3

SecondHalf iterator
item4
item5
item6
item7
```

Notice that when using the GetEnumerator iterator, the foreach loop is set up as a typical foreach loop. However, when one of the iterator properties is used, the foreach loop is set up slightly differently. In this case, the iterator property's get accessor is actually called:

```
foreach (string s in b.ReverseOrder)
```

The iterator property returns an IEnumerable, which in turn is used by the foreach loop to obtain an IEnumerator.

See Also

See the "Iterators," "IEnumerator Interface," and "IEnumerable Interface" topics in the MSDN documentation.

6.7 Implementing Iterators as Overloaded Operators

Problem

You need the ability to iterate over two or more collections and enumerate all elements in each set using a foreach loop construct. In addition to this, you also want to be able to iterate over the unique elements in each set and the duplicate elements in each set.

Solution

Create overloaded operators that act as iterators. The following code shows how to set up an iterator on an overloaded + operator:

```
public static IEnumerable<T> operator +(IEnumerable<T> lhs, IEnumerable<T> rhs)
{
    foreach (T t in lhs)
    {
        yield return (t);
    }

    foreach (T t in rhs)
    {
        yield return (t);
    }
}
```

We will use the previous code example in creating a Set class, shown in Example 6-5, which makes use of the familiar GetEnumerator iterator method, but also overloads the +, |, and & operators for use as iterators.

Example 6-5. Implementing iterators as overloaded operators (+, |, and &)

```
public class Set<T>
{
    private List<T> _items = new List<T>();

    public void AddItem(T name)
    {
        if (!_items.Contains(name))
            _items.Add(name);
        else
            throw (new ArgumentException("This value can only be added to a set once.",
                "name"));
    }
```

Example 6-5. Implementing iterators as overloaded operators (+, |, and &) (continued)

```
public int Count
{
    get {return (_items.Count);}
}

public T this[int index]
{
    get {return (_items[index]);}
    set {_items[index] = value;}
}

public void AddRange(Set<T> original)
{
    foreach(T t in original)
    {
        AddItem(t);
    }
}

public bool Contains(T t)
{
    if (_items.Contains(t))
        return (true);
    else
        return (false);
}


// Iterators
public IEnumerator<T> GetEnumerator()
{
    for (int index = 0; index < _items.Count; index++)
    {
        yield return (_items[index]);
    }
}

public static IEnumerable<T> operator +(Set<T> lhs, Set<T> rhs)
{
    for (int index = 0; index < lhs.Count; index++)
    {
        yield return (lhs[index]);
    }

    for (int index = 0; index < rhs.Count; index++)
    {
        yield return (rhs[index]);
    }
}

public static IEnumerable<T> operator +(IEnumerable<T> lhs, Set<T> rhs)
{
```

```
        foreach (T t in lhs)
        {
            yield return (t);
        }

        for (int index = 0; index < rhs.Count; index++)
        {
            yield return (rhs[index]);
        }
    }

    public static IEnumerable<T> operator +(Set<T> lhs, IEnumerable<T> rhs)
    {
        foreach (T t in rhs)
        {
            yield return (t);
        }

        for (int index = 0; index < lhs.Count; index++)
        {
            yield return (lhs[index]);
        }
    }

    public static IEnumerable<T> operator |(Set<T> lhs, Set<T> rhs)
    {
        // Strip out duplicates from lhs Set object.
        Set<T> tempSet = new Set<T>();
        for (int index = 0; index < lhs.Count; index++)
        {
            if (!tempSet.Contains(lhs[index]))
            {
                tempSet.AddItem(lhs[index]);
            }
        }

        for (int index = 0; index < tempSet.Count; index++)
        {
            yield return (tempSet[index]);
        }

        for (int index = 0; index < rhs.Count; index++)
        {
            if (!tempSet.Contains(rhs[index]))
            {
                yield return (rhs[index]);
            }
        }
    }

    public static IEnumerable<T> operator |(IEnumerable<T> lhs, Set<T> rhs)
    {
```

Example 6-5. Implementing iterators as overloaded operators (+, |, and &) (continued)

```
    // Strip out duplicates from lhs Set object.
    Set<T> tempSet = new Set<T>( );
    foreach (T t in lhs)
    {
        if (!tempSet.Contains(t))
        {
            tempSet.AddItem(t);
        }
    }

    for (int index = 0; index < tempSet.Count; index++)
    {
        yield return (tempSet[index]);
    }

    for (int index = 0; index < rhs.Count; index++)
    {
        if (!tempSet.Contains(rhs[index]))
        {
            yield return (rhs[index]);
        }
    }
}

public static IEnumerable<T> operator |(Set<T> lhs, IEnumerable<T> rhs)
{
    // Strip out duplicates from lhs Set object.
    Set<T> tempSet = new Set<T>( );
    foreach (T t in lhs)
    {
        if (!tempSet.Contains(t))
        {
            tempSet.AddItem(t);
        }
    }

    for (int index = 0; index < tempSet.Count; index++)
    {
        yield return (tempSet[index]);
    }

    foreach (T t in rhs)
    {
        if (!tempSet.Contains(t))
        {
            yield return (t);
        }
    }
}

public static IEnumerable<T> operator &(Set<T> lhs, Set<T> rhs)
{
```

```
    // Strip out duplicates from lhs Set object.
    Set<T> tempSet = new Set<T>( );
    for (int index = 0; index < lhs.Count; index++)
    {
        if (!tempSet.Contains(lhs[index]))
        {
            tempSet.AddItem(lhs[index]);
        }
    }

    for (int index = 0; index < tempSet.Count; index++)
    {
        if (rhs.Contains(tempSet[index]))
        {
            yield return (tempSet[index]);
        }
    }
}

public static IEnumerable<T> operator &(IEnumerable<T> lhs, Set<T> rhs)
{
    // Strip out duplicates from lhs Set object.
    Set<T> tempSet = new Set<T>( );
    foreach (T t in lhs)
    {
        if (!tempSet.Contains(t))
        {
            tempSet.AddItem(t);
        }
    }

    for (int index = 0; index < tempSet.Count; index++)
    {
        if (rhs.Contains(tempSet[index]))
        {
            yield return (tempSet[index]);
        }
    }
}

public static IEnumerable<T> operator &(Set<T> lhs, IEnumerable<T> rhs)
{
    // Strip out duplicates from lhs Set object.
    Set<T> tempSet = new Set<T>( );
    for (int index = 0; index < lhs.Count; index++)
    {
        if (!tempSet.Contains(lhs[index]))
        {
            tempSet.AddItem(lhs[index]);
        }
    }
```

Example 6-5. Implementing iterators as overloaded operators (+, |, and &) (continued)

```
        foreach (T t in rhs)
        {
            if (tempSet.Contains(t))
            {
                yield return (t);
            }
        }
    }
}
```

The following code makes use of the overloaded operator iterators in Example 6-5:

```
public static void TestOperatorIterator()
{
    //Create a Set<string> object and fill it with data.
    Set<string> set1 = new Set<string>();
    set1.AddItem("item1");
    set1.AddItem("item11");
    set1.AddItem("item2");
    set1.AddItem("item2");
    set1.AddItem("item3");
    set1.AddItem("XYZ");

    //Create a second Set<string> object and fill it with data.
    Set<string> set2 = new Set<string>();
    set2.AddItem("item30");
    set2.AddItem("item11");
    set2.AddItem("item11");
    set2.AddItem("item2");
    set2.AddItem("item12");
    set2.AddItem("item1");

    // Display all data in both set objects.
    Console.WriteLine("\r\nDisplay all data in both sets");
    foreach (string s in (set1 + set2))
    {
        Console.WriteLine(s);
    }

    // Display all unique data in both set objects.
    Console.WriteLine("\r\nDisplay only unique data in both sets");
    foreach (string s in (set1 | set2))
    {
        Console.WriteLine(s);
    }

    // Display all duplicate data in both set objects.
    Console.WriteLine("\r\nDisplay only duplicate data in both sets");
    foreach (string s in (set1 & set2))
    {
        Console.WriteLine(s);
    }
}
```

This code produces the following output:

```
Display all data in both sets
item1
item11
item2
item2
item3
XYZ
item30
item11
item11
item2
item12
item1

Display only unique data in both sets
item1
item11
item2
item3
XYZ
item30
item12

Display only duplicate data in both sets
item1
item11
item2
```

Discussion

In addition to allowing methods and property get accessors to be iterator methods, operator overloads can also be made into iterator methods. To become an iterator method, the operator overload method simply has to return a System.Collections. IEnumerable or a System.Collections.Generic.IEnumerable<T> type and implement the yield return statement.

The + operator is overloaded to yield every element of each Set object, both the lhs and rhs Set objects. From the foreach loop's perspective, this effectively allows the loop to iterate over every Set object that is added together as if it were one big Set object. The foreach loop is able to make use of this overloaded operator since the return value of this method is an IEnumerable<T> type. Therefore, a simple foreach loop can be set up as follows to return all elements of two Set objects:

```
foreach (string s in (set1 + set2))
```

The | operator is overloaded to return only unique items from both Set objects in the expression. It does this by first creating a temporary Set object (tempSet), which contains all values of the lhs Set object after the duplicate values have been stripped out of it. Once this is completed, all of the `tempSet` object elements are yielded. Finally, the `rhs` Set object is examined for any elements that are not already contained within the `tempSet` object. All of the unique values from the `rhs` are also yielded.

The & operator is overloaded to return only the items from the `lhs` Set object that are duplicated in the `rhs` Set object. It does this by first creating a temporary Set object (`tempSet`), which contains all values of the `lhs` Set object after the duplicate values have been stripped out of it. Once this is completed, the `rhs` Set object is examined for any duplicate elements that are contained within the `tempSet` Set object. If a duplicate is found, that element is yielded.

This code works fine if we are constructing `foreach` loops that contain only one of these operators in the expression. For example, this works fine:

```
foreach (string s in (set1 + set2))
```

However, the following code will cause problems:

```
foreach (string s in (set1 + set2 + set3))
```

The reason for this is that the expression is evaluated as ((set1 + set2) + set3). Therefore the result of the inner equation is an IEnumerable<T>, which is then added to set3. In order for this equation to work, we also need to overload the + operator to accept a Set<T> object and an IEnumerable<T> object as shown here:

```
public static IEnumerable<T> operator +(Set<T> lhs, IEnumerable<T> rhs) (...)
public static IEnumerable<T> operator +(IEnumerable<T> lhs, Set<T> rhs) (...)
```

These two extra overloads will allow more complex equations to be evaluated properly for foreach statements.

See Also

See the "Iterators," "IEnumerator Interface," and "IEnumerable Interface" topics in the MSDN documentation.

6.8   Forcing an Iterator to Stop Iterating

Problem

You have a requirement that if an iterator encounters malformed or out-of-bounds data that the iterations are to stop immediately.

Solution

It is possible to throw an exception from an iterator, which terminates the iterator and the foreach loop. However, there is a more performance-friendly technique. You can use the `yield break` statement within your iterator:

```
public class Foo
{
    private List<T> _items = new List<T>();

    public IEnumerator GetEnumerator()
    {
        for (int index = 0; index < _items.Count; index++)
        {
            if (/*perform some test on the data here*/)
            {
                // There was a problem with the data, stop.
                yield break;
            }
            else
            {
                // The data was fine, continue.
                yield return (_items[index]);
            }
        }
    }
}
```

Discussion

It is possible to stop iterations using a throw statement to throw an exception. However, you cannot place a catch block within an iterator body to handle the thrown exception. The try/catch block must be around the foreach loop as shown here:

```
Foo test = new Foo();
// Add elements to the test class...

try
{
    foreach ( object o in test) {...}
}
catch (Exception e)
{
    // Handle exception from iterator method here...
    Console.WriteLine("In outer finally block");
}
```

When an exception occurs inside the foreach block, the following string will be displayed:

```
In outer finally block
```

For more on how iterators deal with exceptions, see Recipe 6.9.

Another way of terminating an iterator, and thus terminating the foreach loop, is to use the yield break statement. This statement has the same effect as simply exiting from the function. This yield break statement can be used only within an iterator block. This means any method, property get accessor, or operator overload member that is set up as an iterator (i.e., is public and returns an IEnumerable or IEnumerable<T> type).

See Also

See Recipe 6.9; see the "Iterators," "yield," "IEnumerator Interface," and "IEnumerable Interface" topics in the MSDN documentation.

6.9 Dealing with Finally Blocks and Iterators

Problem

You have added a try/finally block to your iterator and you notice that the `finally` block is not being executed when you think it should.

Solution

Wrap a try block around the iteration code in the `GetEnumerator` iterator with a finally block following this try block:

```
public class StringSet
{
    private List<string> _items = new List<string>();

    public void AddString(string str)
    {
        _items.Add(str);
    }

    public IEnumerator GetEnumerator()
    {
        try
        {
            for (int index = 0; index < _items.Count; index++)
            {
                yield return (_items[index]);
            }
        }
        finally
        {
            Console.WriteLine("In iterator finally block");
        }
    }
}
```

The foreach code that calls this iterator looks like this:

```
// Create a new StringSet object.
StringSet strSet = new StringSet();

// Store string data in the strSet object...

// Use the GetEnumerator iterator.
foreach (string s in strSet)
```

```
    {
        Console.WriteLine(s);
    }
```

When this code is run, the following output is displayed:

```
String data1
String data2
...
String dataN
In iterator finally block
```

Move the try/finally block around the yield return statement within the iterator.
The new iterator code will look like this:

```
public IEnumerator GetEnumerator( )
{
    for (int index = 0; index < _items.Count; index++)
    {
        try
        {
            yield return (_items[index]);
        }
        finally
        {
            Console.WriteLine("In iterator finally block");
        }
    }
}
```

When this code is run, the following output is displayed:

```
String data1
In foreach finally block
String data2
In foreach finally block
...
String dataN
In foreach finally block
In iterator finally block
```

Discussion

You may have thought that the output would display the "In iterator finally block"
string after displaying each item in the strSet object. However, this is not the way
that finally blocks are handled in iterators. If you had a normal function that was
structured in exactly the same way (but did something other than a yield return
inside the loop), you wouldn't expect the finally block to run once per iteration.
You'd expect it to run once. Iterators go out of their way to preserve these semantics. All finally blocks inside the iterator member body are called only after the iterations are complete, code execution leaves the foreach loop (such as when a break,
return, or throw statement is encountered), or when a yield break statement is executed, effectively terminating the iterator.

To see how iterators deal with catch and finally blocks (note that there can be no catch blocks inside of an iterator member body), consider the following code:

```
public static void TestFinallyAndIterators()
{
    // Create a StringSet object and fill it with data.
    StringSet strSet = new StringSet();
    strSet.AddString("item1");
    strSet.AddString("item2");

    // Display all data in StringSet object.
    try
    {
        foreach (string s in strSet)
        {
            try
            {
                Console.WriteLine(s);
            }
            catch (Exception)
            {
                Console.WriteLine("In foreach catch block");
            }
            finally
            {
                Console.WriteLine("In foreach finally block");
            }
        }
    }
    catch (Exception)
    {
        Console.WriteLine("In outer catch block");
    }
    finally
    {
        Console.WriteLine("In outer finally block");
    }
}
```

Assuming that your original StringSet.GetEnumerator method is used (i.e., the one that contained the try/finally block), you will see the following behaviors.

If no exception occurs, you see this:

```
item1
In foreach finally block
item2
In foreach finally block
In iterator finally block
In outer finally block
```

We see that the finally block that is within the foreach loop is executed on each iteration. However, the finally block within the iterator is executed only after all iterations are finished. Also notice that the iterator's finally block is executed before the finally block that wraps the foreach loop.

If an exception occurs in the iterator itself, during processing of the second element, the following is displayed:

```
item1
In foreach finally block
(Exception occurs here...)
In iterator finally block
In outer catch block
In outer finally block
```

Notice that immediately after the exception is thrown, the finally block within the iterator is executed. This can be useful if you need to clean up only after an exception occurs. If no exception happens, then the finally block is not executed. After the iterator's finally block executes, the exception is caught by the catch block outside the foreach loop. At this point, the exception could be handled or rethrown. Once this catch block is finished processing, the outer finally block is executed. Notice that the catch block within the foreach loop was never given the opportunity to handle the exception. This is due to the fact that the corresponding try block does not contain a call to the iterator.

If an exception occurs in the foreach loop, during processing of the second element, the following is displayed:

```
item1
In foreach finally block
(Exception occurs here...)
In foreach catch block
In foreach finally block
In iterator finally block
In outer finally block
```

Notice in this situation that the catch and finally blocks within the foreach loop are executed first, then the iterator's finally block. Lastly, the outer finally block is executed.

Understanding the way catch and finally blocks operate inside iterators will allow you to add catch and finally blocks in the correct location. If you need a finally block to execute once, immediately after the iterations are finished, add this finally block to the iterator method. If, however, you want the finally block to execute on each iteration, you need to place the finally block within the foreach loop body.

If you need to catch iterator exceptions immediately after they occur, you should consider wrapping the foreach loop in a try/catch block. Any try/catch block within the foreach loop body will miss exceptions thrown from the iterator.

See Also

See the "Iterators," "yield," "IEnumerator Interface," and "IEnumerable Interface" topics in the MSDN documentation.

6.10 Organizing Your Interface Implementations

Problem

You have a class that implements an interface with many methods. These methods support only the interface functionality and don't necessarily relate well to the other code in your class. You would like to keep the interface implementation code separate from the main class code.

Solution

Use partial classes to separate the interface implementation code into a separate file. For example, you have a class called `TriValue` that takes three decimal values and performs some operations on them, like getting the average, the sum, and the product. This code is currently in a file called *TriValue.cs*, which contains:

```csharp
public partial class TriValue
{
    decimal first;
    decimal second;
    decimal third;

    public TriValue(decimal val1, decimal val2,decimal val3)
    {
        this.first = val1;
        this.second = val2;
        this.third = val3;
    }

    public TypeCode GetTypeCode()
    {
        return TypeCode.Object;
    }

    public decimal GetAverage()
    {
        return (GetSum() / 3);
    }

    public decimal GetSum()
    {
        return first + second + third;
    }

    public decimal GetProduct()
    {
```

```
        return first * second * third;
    }
}
```

Now you want to add support for the IConvertible interface to the TriValue class so that it can be converted to other data types. We could just add all 16 method implementations to the class definition in *TriValue.cs* and hide the code using a #region statement. Instead, you can now use the partial keyword on the TriValue class and store the IConvertible implementation code in a separate file. Once a class begins to be defined in multiple files, it is important to have a naming convention for those files, so that it is easy to find implementation code and for other developers to understand where to put new code when it is added to this class. We will use the [BaseClass].[Interface].cs naming convention here. This will give you a new file called *TriValue.IConvertible.cs* that contains the IConvertible interface implementation code, shown in Example 6-6.

Example 6-6. Using partial classes to organize your interface implementations

```
/// Partial class that implements IConvertible
public partial class TriValue : IConvertible
{
    bool IConvertible.ToBoolean(IFormatProvider provider)
    {
        if (GetAverage( ) > 0)
            return true;
        else
            return false;
    }

    byte IConvertible.ToByte(IFormatProvider provider)
    {
        return Convert.ToByte(GetAverage( ));
    }

    char IConvertible.ToChar(IFormatProvider provider)
    {
        decimal val = GetAverage( );
        if (val > char.MaxValue)
            val = char.MaxValue;
        if (val < char.MinValue)
            val = char.MinValue;
        return Convert.ToChar((ulong)val);
    }

    DateTime IConvertible.ToDateTime(IFormatProvider provider)
    {
        return Convert.ToDateTime(GetAverage( ));
    }

    decimal IConvertible.ToDecimal(IFormatProvider provider)
    {
        return GetAverage( );
```

```csharp
    }

    double IConvertible.ToDouble(IFormatProvider provider)
    {
        return Convert.ToDouble(GetAverage());
    }

    short IConvertible.ToInt16(IFormatProvider provider)
    {
        return Convert.ToInt16(GetAverage());
    }

    int IConvertible.ToInt32(IFormatProvider provider)
    {
        return Convert.ToInt32(GetAverage());
    }

    long IConvertible.ToInt64(IFormatProvider provider)
    {
        return Convert.ToInt64(GetAverage());
    }

    sbyte IConvertible.ToSByte(IFormatProvider provider)
    {
        return Convert.ToSByte(GetAverage());
    }

    float IConvertible.ToSingle(IFormatProvider provider)
    {
        return Convert.ToSingle(GetAverage());
    }

    string IConvertible.ToString(IFormatProvider provider)
    {
        return string.Format("({0},{1},{2})",
            first.ToString(),second.ToString(),third.ToString());
    }

    object IConvertible.ToType(Type conversionType, IFormatProvider provider)
    {
        return Convert.ChangeType(GetAverage(), conversionType);
    }

    ushort IConvertible.ToUInt16(IFormatProvider provider)
    {
        return Convert.ToUInt16(GetAverage());
    }

    uint IConvertible.ToUInt32(IFormatProvider provider)
    {
        return Convert.ToUInt32(GetAverage());
    }
```

Example 6-6. Using partial classes to organize your interface implementations (continued)

```
    ulong IConvertible.ToUInt64(IFormatProvider provider)
    {
        return Convert.ToUInt64(GetAverage());
    }
}
```

Now you have the interface implemented and your original class definition is still straightforward. For classes that implement many interfaces, this approach will allow for a more tightly organized implementation.

Discussion

It should be noted that there is *no* Microsoft intermediate language (MSIL) indicator that these are partial classes if you look at your class in Ildasm or Reflector. It will look just like a normal class by the time it gets to MSIL. Intellisense handles the merge as well. Since partial types are a language trick, they cannot span assemblies, as the class needs to be resolved by the compiler. Partial types can be declared in the same file as well as in separate files, but still must be in the same namespace so the compiler can resolve it before generating the MSIL.

You can use the partial type support for classes, nested classes, structures, and interfaces, but you cannot have a partial enum definition. Partial types can declare support for different interfaces per partial type. However, single inheritance is still in force and must be the same or omitted from the secondary partial type. You can see that in the Solution the partial TriValue class definition in *TriValue.cs* you created does not specify the inheritance from IConvertible, only the one in *TriValue. IConvertible.cs* does.

The previous TriValue class can be exercised with the following code:

```
class Program
{
    static void Main(string[] args)
    {
        TriValue tv = new TriValue(3, 4, 5);
        Console.WriteLine("Average: {0}",tv.GetAverage());
        Console.WriteLine("Sum: {0}", tv.GetSum());
        Console.WriteLine("Product: {0}", tv.GetProduct());
        Console.WriteLine("Boolean: {0}", Convert.ToBoolean(tv));
        Console.WriteLine("Byte: {0}", Convert.ToByte(tv));
        Console.WriteLine("Char: {0}", Convert.ToChar(tv));
        Console.WriteLine("Decimal: {0}", Convert.ToDecimal(tv));
        Console.WriteLine("Double: {0}", Convert.ToDouble(tv));
        Console.WriteLine("Int16: {0}", Convert.ToInt16(tv));
        Console.WriteLine("Int32: {0}", Convert.ToInt32(tv));
        Console.WriteLine("Int64: {0}", Convert.ToInt64(tv));
        Console.WriteLine("SByte: {0}", Convert.ToSByte(tv));
        Console.WriteLine("Single: {0}", Convert.ToSingle(tv));
```

```
            Console.WriteLine("String: {0}", Convert.ToString(tv));
            Console.WriteLine("Type: {0}", Convert.GetTypeCode(tv));
            Console.WriteLine("UInt16: {0}", Convert.ToUInt16(tv));
            Console.WriteLine("UInt32: {0}", Convert.ToUInt32(tv));
            Console.WriteLine("UInt64: {0}", Convert.ToUInt64(tv));
        }
    }
```

The preceding code produces the following output:

```
Average: 4
Sum: 12
Product: 60
Boolean: True
Byte: 4
Char: _
Decimal: 4
Double: 4
Int16: 4
Int32: 4
Int64: 4
SByte: 4
Single: 4
String: (3,4,5)
Type: Object
UInt16: 4
UInt32: 4
UInt64: 4
```

See Also

See the "Partial Class Definitions" and "partial Keyword" topics in the MSDN documentation.

6.11 Generating Code That Is No Longer in Your Main Code Paths

Problem

Occasionally as a developer you run into a situation in which it would be handy to be able to regenerate your class based on a set of data that can change. You need to be able to do this without destroying all of the logic you have already created or causing yourself a painful merge between an old and a new class file.

Solution

Write a utility that can regenerate the code that is dependent on external data and keep the generated code in a separate file that defines a partial class. To demonstrate this, we have created a Visual Studio 2005 add-in called PartialClassAddin in the sample code that will allow you to enter a class name and then select which attributes to apply to the class. This is a standard add-in generated by selecting the add-in template from the project wizard. Its main dialog box is shown in Figure 6-1.

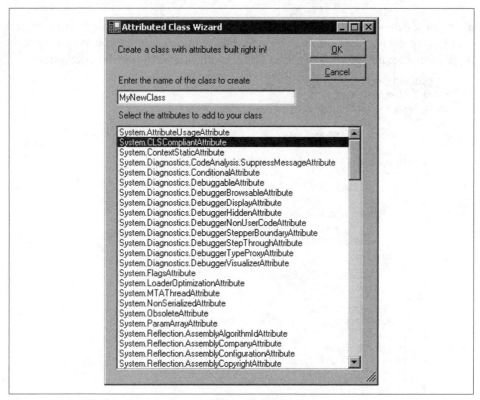

Figure 6-1. Attributed Class Wizard from partial class add-in

Enter a class name MyNewClass, select the System.CLSCompliantAttribute and the System.SerializeableAttribute from the list, and click the OK button. This generates the *MyNewClass_Attributes.cs* file with the following in it:

```
// Using directives
using System;

namespace NamespaceForMyNewClass
{
    #region Attributes
    [System.CLSCompliant(true)]
    [System.Serializable()]
    #endregion // Attributes

    public partial class MyNewClass
    {
```

```
        public MyNewClass()
        {
        }
    }
}
```

By making MyNewClass a partial class, you can add this generated file to your project and replace it when the class attributes need to be updated, while you store your main logic in another file (perhaps *MyNewClass.cs*) with a partial MyNewClass definition:

```
// Using directives
using System;
using System.Diagnostics;

namespace NamespaceForMyNewClass
{
    public partial class MyNewClass : BaseClass
    {
        public DoSomeWork ()
        {
            for(int i=0;i<10;i++)
            {
                Debug.WriteLine(i);
            }
        }
    }

    // Declare base class...
    public BaseClass
    {
        public BaseClass()
        {
        }
    }
}
```

Notice that in the file you hold the logic in (*MyNewClass.cs* as shown before), the class can declare its inheritance from BaseClass as well as define some functionality (DoSomeWork method).

Discussion

Generating code is not something to do lightly. But in certain circumstances building a tool can save you a lot of time over the course of maintaining a project. Partial classes provide a nice way to separate your mainstream code from the "noise" that changes only in response to external pieces. Windows Forms and Windows Forms controls are both now declared as partial, as are the DataSets generated from an XSD schema to help facilitate the generated code model.

This add-in was created using the Visual Studio 2005 add-in wizard, and the project has the form added to it. The form loads all types derived from System.Attribute to populate the listbox, then uses reflection to figure out the parameters. Once the code has been built, run the project from the debugger. When VS2005 comes up, you can access the Tools menu and the PartialClassAddin menu item to get to this wizard. You can unregister this add-in by going to the Tools menu in VS2005 and selecting the Add-In Manager option. The Add-In Manager dialog is shown in Figure 6-2.

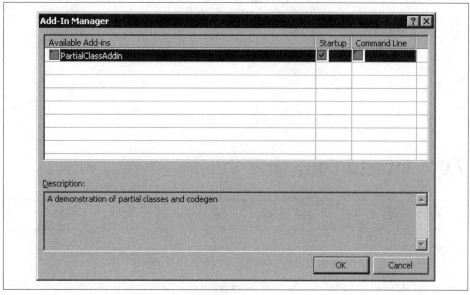

Figure 6-2. Visual Studio 2005 Add-In Manager

Uncheck the PartialClassAddin to remove this from your main environment.

See Also

See the "Partial Class Definitions," "Creating Automation Objects," and "Attribute" topics in the MSDN documentation.

CHAPTER 7

Exception Handling

7.0 Introduction

This chapter contains recipes covering the exception-handling mechanism, including the try, catch, and finally blocks. Along with these recipes are others covering the mechanisms used to throw exceptions manually from within your code. The final types of recipes include those dealing with the Exception classes and their uses, as well as subclassing them to create new types of exceptions.

Often the design and implementation of exception handling is performed later in the development cycle. But with the power and complexities of C# exception handling, you need to plan and even implement your exception-handling scheme much earlier. Doing so will increase the reliability and robustness of your code while minimizing the impact of adding exception handling after most or all of the application is coded.

Exception handling in C# is very flexible. It allows you to choose a fine- or coarse-grained approach to error handling and any level between. This means that you can add exception handling around any individual line of code (the fine-grained approach) or around a method that calls many other methods (the coarse-grained approach), or you can use a mix of the two, with mainly a coarse-grained approach and a more fine-grained approach in specific critical areas of the code. When using a fine-grained approach, you can intercept specific exceptions that might be thrown from just a few lines of code. The following method sets an object's property to a numeric value using fine-grained exception handling:

```
protected void SetValue(object value)
{
    try
    {
        myObj.Property1 = value;
    }
    catch (Exception e)
    {
        // Handle potential exceptions arising from this call here.
    }
}
```

Consequently, this approach can add a lot of extra baggage to your code if used throughout your application. This fine-grained approach to exception handling should be used when you have a single line or just a few lines of code and you need to handle that exception in a specific manner. If you do not have specific handling for errors at that level, you should let the exception bubble up the stack. For example, using the previous SetValue method, you may have to inform the user that an exception occurred and provide a chance to try the action again. If a method exists on myObj that needs to be called whenever an exception is thrown by one of its methods, you should make sure that this method is called at the appropriate time.

Coarse-grained exception handling is quite the opposite; it uses fewer try/catch or try/catch/finally blocks. One example would be to place a try/catch block around all of the code in every public method in an application or component. Doing this allows exceptions to be handled at the highest level in your code. If an exception is thrown at any location in your code, it will be bubbled up the call stack until a catch block is found that can handle it. If try/catch blocks are placed on all public methods, then all exceptions will be bubbled up to these methods and handled. This allows for much less exception-handling code to be written, but your ability to handle specific exceptions that may occur in particular areas of your code is diminished. You must determine how best to add exception-handling code to your application. This means applying the right balance of fine- and coarse-grained exception handling in your application.

C# allows catch blocks to be written without any parameters. An example of this is shown here:

```
public void CallCOMMethod( )
{
    try
    {
        // Call a method on a COM object.
        myCOMObj.Method1( );
    }
    catch
    {
        // Handle potential exceptions arising from this call here.
    }
}
```

The catch with no parameters is a holdover from C++, where exception objects did not have to be derived from the Exception class. Writing a catch clause in this manner in C++ allows any type of object thrown as an exception to be caught. However, in C#, only objects derived from the Exception base class may be thrown as an exception. Using the catch block with no parameters allows all exceptions to be caught, but you lose the ability to view the exception and its information. A catch block written in this manner:

```
catch
{
```

```
    // NOT Able to write the following line of code
    //Console.WriteLine(e.ToString);
}
```

is equivalent to this:

```
catch (Exception e)
{
    // Able to write the following line of code
    Console.WriteLine(e.ToString);
}
```

except that the Exception object can now be accessed.

 If you are catching an exception that was thrown from C++, it may not have originally derived from System.Exception, as C++ can throw integers, strings, and custom exception classes as exceptions. Similarly, the Win32 API function RaiseError allows for raising an exception as well, but ultimately all of these types are mapped by the CLR back to an instance of a class derived from System.Exception.

Avoid writing a catch block without any parameters. Doing so will prevent you from accessing the actual Exception object that was thrown.

When catching exceptions in a catch block, you should determine up front when exceptions need to be rethrown, when exceptions need to be wrapped in an outer exception and thrown, and when exceptions should be handled immediately and not rethrown.

Wrapping an exception in an outer exception is a good practice when the original exception would not make sense to the caller. When wrapping an exception in an outer exception, you need to determine what exception is most appropriate to wrap the caught exception. As a rule of thumb, the wrapping exception should always aid in tracking down the original problem by not obscuring the original exception with an unrelated or vague wrapping exception.

Another useful practice when catching exceptions is to provide catch blocks to handle specific exceptions in your code. When using specific catch blocks, consider adding a generic catch block that handles all other exceptions (Exception). This will ensure that all other exceptions are handled at some point in your code. Also, remember that base class exceptions—when used in a catch block—catch not only that type but also all of its subclasses.

The following code uses specific catch blocks to handle different exceptions in the appropriate manner:

```
public void CallCOMMethod( )
{
    try
    {
        // Call a method on a COM object.
```

```
        myCOMObj.Method1( );
    }
    catch (System.Runtime.InteropServices.ExternalException exte)
    {
        // Handle potential COM exceptions arising from this call here.
    }
    catch (InvalidOperationException ae)
    {
        // Handle any potential method calls to the COM object which are
        // not valid in its current state.
    }
}
```

In this code, ExternalException and its derivatives are handled differently than InvalidOperationException and its derivatives. If any other types of exceptions are thrown from the myCOMObj.Method1, they are not handled here, but are bubbled up until a valid catch block is found. If no valid catch block is found, the exception is considered unhandled and the application terminates.

At times, cleanup code must be executed regardless of whether an exception is thrown. Any object must be placed in a stable known state when an exception is thrown. In these situations when code must be executed, use a finally block. The following code has been modified (see boldface lines) to use a finally block:

```
public void CallCOMMethod( )
{
    try
    {
        // Call a method on a COM object.
        myCOMObj.Method1( );
    }
    catch (System.Runtime.InteropServices.ExternalException exte)
    {
        // Handle potential COM exceptions arising from this call here.
    }
    finally
    {
        // Clean up and free any resources here.
        // For example, there could be a method on myCOMObj to allow us to clean
        // up after using the Method1 method.
    }
}
```

The finally block will always execute, no matter what happens in the try and catch blocks. The finally block executes even if a return, break, or continue statement is executed in the try or catch blocks or if a goto is used to jump out of the exception handler. This allows for a reliable method of cleaning up after the try (and possibly catch) block code executes. The finally block is also very useful for final resource cleanup when no catch blocks are specified. This pattern would be used if the code being written can't handle exceptions from calls it is making but wants to make sure that resources it uses are cleaned up properly before moving up the stack. The following example makes sure that the SqlConnection and SqlCommand are cleaned up properly in the finally block:

```
public void RunCommand( string connection, string command )
{
    SqlConnection sqlConn =  null;
    SqlCommand sqlComm = null;

    try
    {
        sqlConn = new SqlConnection(connection);
            sqlComm = new SqlCommand(command, sqlConn);
        sqlConn.Open( );
            sqlComm.ExecuteNonQuery( );
    }
    finally
    {
        if (null != sqlComm);
                sqlComm.Dispose( );
            if (null != sqlConn)
                sqlConn.Dispose( );
    }
}
```

When determining how to structure exception handling in your application or component, consider doing the following:

- Use a single try-catch or try-catch-finally exception handler at locations higher up in your code. These exception handlers can be considered coarse-grained.

- Code farther down the call stack should contain try-finally exception handlers. These exception handlers can be considered fine-grained.

The fine-grained try-finally exception handlers allow for better control over cleaning up after an exception occurs. The exception is then bubbled up to the coarser-grained try-catch or try-catch-finally exception handler. This technique allows for a more centralized scheme of exception handling and minimizes the code that you have to write to handle exceptions.

To improve performance, you should handle the case when an exception could be thrown, rather than catch the exception after it is thrown, if you know the code will be run in a single-threaded environment. If the code will run on multiple threads, there is still the potential that the initial check could succeed but the object value change (perhaps to null) in another thread before the actions following the check can be taken.

For example, in a single-threaded environment, if a method has a good chance of returning a null value, you should test the returned value for null before that value is used, as opposed to using a try-catch block and allowing the NullReferenceException to be thrown. Remember that throwing an exception has a negative impact on performance, whereas exception-handling code has a minimal impact on performance, as long as an exception is not thrown.

To illustrate this, here is a method that uses exception-handling code to process the NullReferenceException:

```
public void SomeMethod( )
{
    try
    {
        Stream s = GetAnyAvailableStream( );
        Console.WriteLine("This stream has a length of " + s.Length);
    }
    catch (Exception e)
    {
        // Handle a null stream here.
    }
}
```

Here is the method implemented to use an if-else conditional instead:

```
public void SomeMethod( )
{
    Stream s = GetAnyAvailableStream( );

    if (s != null)
    {
        Console.WriteLine("This stream has a length of " + s.Length);
    }
    else
    {
        // Handle a null stream here.
    }
}
```

Additionally, you should also make sure that this stream is closed by using the finally block in the following manner:

```
public void SomeMethod( )
{
    Stream s = null;
    try
    {
        s = GetAnyAvailableStream( );

        if (s != null)
        {
            Console.WriteLine("This stream has a length of " + s.Length);
        }
        else
        {
            // Handle a null stream here.
        }
    }
```

```
    finally
    {
        if (s != null)
        {
            s.Close( );
        }
    }
}
```

The `finally` block contains the method call that will close the stream, ensuring that there is no data loss.

Consider throwing exceptions instead of returning error codes. With well-placed exception-handling code, you should not have to rely on methods that return error codes such as a Boolean `true-false` to correctly handle errors, which makes for much cleaner code. Another benefit is that you do not have to look up any values for the error codes to understand the code. However, the biggest advantage is that when an exceptional situation arises, you cannot just ignore it as you can with error codes.

This technique is especially useful when writing a managed C# component that is called by one or more COM objects. Throwing an exception is much cleaner and easier to read than returning an `HRESULT`. The managed wrapper that the runtime creates for your managed object will convert the `HRESULT` to the nearest equivalent managed exception type.

Throw specific exceptions, not general ones. For example, throw an `Argument-NullException` instead of an `ArgumentException`, which is the base class of `ArgumentNullException`. Throwing an `ArgumentException` just tells you that there was a problem with a parameter value to a method. Throwing an `ArgumentNullException` tells you more specifically what the problem with the parameter really is. Another potential problem is that a more general exception may not be caught if the catcher of the exception is looking for a more specific type derived from the thrown exception.

The FCL provides several exception types that you will find very useful to throw in your own code. Many of these exceptions are listed here with a definition of where and when they should be thrown:

- Throw an `InvalidOperationException` in a property, indexer, or method when it is called with the object in an inappropriate state. This state could be caused by calling an indexer on an object that has not yet been initialized or calling methods out of sequence.

- Throw `ArgumentException` if invalid parameters are passed into a method, property, or indexer. The `ArgumentNullException`, `ArgumentOutOfRangeException`, and `InvalidEnumArgumentException` are three subclasses of the `ArgumentException` class. It is more appropriate to throw one of these subclassed exceptions since they are more indicative of the root cause of the problem. The `ArgumentNullException` indicates that a parameter was passed in as `null` and that this parameter cannot be null under any circumstance. The `ArgumentOutOfRangeException` indicates that an argument was passed in that was outside of a valid acceptable range. This exception is used mainly with numeric values. The `InvalidEnumArgumentException` indicates that an enumeration value was passed in that does not exist in that enumeration type.

- Throw a `FormatException` when an invalid formatting parameter is passed in as a parameter to a method. This technique is mainly used when overriding/overloading methods such as `ToString` that can accept formatting strings, as well as in the parse methods on the various numeric types.

- Throw `ObjectDisposedException` when a property, indexer, or method is called on an object that has already been disposed.

- Many exceptions that derive from the `SystemException` class, such as `NullReferenceException`, `ExecutionEngineException`, `StackOverflowException`, `OutOfMemoryException`, and `IndexOutOfRangeException` are thrown only by the CLR and should not be explicitly thrown with the `throw` keyword in your code.

7.1 Verifying Critical Parameters

Problem

You have a method, property, or indexer that requires the correct value or set of values to be passed in to it (e.g., cannot be `null`, must be within a numeric range or a set of numeric ranges, the enumeration value must be a valid value in the enumeration). If an incorrect value is passed in to the method, it must inform the application and handle the invalid value gracefully.

Solution

The parameters passed in to a public method should always be tested for correctness before they are used; however, it may be more appropriate to use `Debug.Assert` or even to use no tests when checking parameters to nonpublic methods. If one or more fail the test, an `ArgumentException`, or one of its derivatives, should be thrown to ensure that the application is notified that critical data has possibly been corrupted. (Note that an `IndexOutOfRangeException` could instead be thrown from within an indexer.)

When a numeric parameter that is out of a specified range is passed, the `ArgumentOutOfRangeException` should be thrown. The following code checks whether the `numberOfItems` parameter is greater than an upper bound of 100:

```
public static void TestParams(int numberOfItems, object myObject, Language language)
{

    Debug.Assert(numberOfItems <= 100);
    if (numberOfItems > 100)
    {
```

```
        throw (new ArgumentOutOfRangeException("numberOfItems", numberOfItems,
            "The number of items has exceeded the defined limits."));
    }

    //...trailing code
}
```

Many parameters passed to methods may produce strange results when they are null. To prevent this from happening, test the parameters. If any of them is null, throw the ArgumentNullException.

The following code checks the myObject object variable to see whether it is null:

```
public static void TestParams(int numberOfItems, object myObject, Language language)
{
    //... previous code

    Debug.Assert(myObject != null);
    if (myObject == null
    {
        throw (new ArgumentNullException("myObject",
            "The object passed may not be null."));
    }

    //...trailing code
}
```

If a method accepts an enumeration value, a caller may pass a numeric value in lieu of an enumeration value of the parameter's type. This is dangerous since the caller can easily pass in a number that does not exist in the enumeration. To prevent this problem, test for the specific enumeration values that are allowed for the enumeration-type parameter using a switch statement to list the values. There is a static IsDefined method on the Enum class, which you should avoid. IsDefined uses reflection internally, thereby incurring a performance penalty, and does not handle versioning of the enumeration well. Consider if the value MgdCpp (for managed C++) is added to the Languages enum in the next version of your software. If you use IsDefined to check the argument here, it will allow MgdCpp as a valid value as it is defined in the enumeration, even though the code for which you are validating the parameter is not designed to handle it. By being specific with the switch statement, the MgdCpp value will be rejected, and the code will not try to run in an invalid context. If the parameter contains a bad value (falls through to the default case in the switch), throw the InvalidEnumArgumentException. The following code shows how to test for a bad enumeration value:

```
public static void TestParams(int numberOfItems, object myObject, Language language)
{
    //... previous code

    switch (language)
    {
```

```
        // All valid types for the enum listed here.
        // This means only the ones we specify are valid
        // not any enum value for this enum.
        // NOTE: All and VB6 enum types are not valid for this method....
        case Language.CSharp:
        case Language.Other:
        case Language.VBNET:
            break;
        default:
            Debug.Assert(false, language +
                    " is not a valid enumeration value to pass.");
            throw (new
                    System.ComponentModel.InvalidEnumArgumentException("language",
                        (int)language, typeof(Language)));
            break;
    }

        //...trailing code
}
```

Discussion

Testing parameters in this way does not have to be done on every method. Instead, you should test the parameters that are passed in to all public methods of public classes and throw an exception only if they are in error. For nonpublic methods, you can add `Debug.Assert` statements to test these parameters.

Being in control of the code within your assembly makes it much easier for you to know which valid parameters, their ranges, and so on, you need to pass. Someone who is unfamiliar with your assembly has a much higher chance of passing in bad arguments to the parameters in the assembly's public interface. Therefore, you should guard against other developers passing bad parameters to methods in your assembly by having both a `Debug.Assert` statement checking the condition *and* code to handle the problem if the condition is not met at runtime. The `Assert` will help developers figure out what is going wrong faster, and the handling code will protect you when running.

The more general exceptions, such as `ArgumentException`, were designed this way, so that the more specific exceptions, such as `ArgumentNullException`, can be wrapped with the more general exceptions, such as `ArgumentException`. This specificity gives a much clearer picture of how and where the exception occurred.

See Also

See the "ArgumentException Class" topic in the MSDN documentation.

7.2   Knowing When to Catch and Rethrow Exceptions

Problem

You want to establish when it is appropriate to catch and rethrow an exception.

Solution

It is appropriate if you have a section of code where you want to perform some action if an exception occurs, but not perform any actions to actually handle the exception. In order to get the exception so that you can perform the initial action on it, establish a catch block to catch the exception. Then once the action has been performed, rethrow the exception from the catch block in which the original exception was handled. Use the throw keyword, followed by a semicolon, to rethrow an exception:

```
try
{
    Console.WriteLine("In inner try");
    int z2 = 9999999;
    checked{z2 *= 999999999;}
}
catch(DivideByZeroException dbze)
{
    // Record the fact that the divide-by-zero exception occurred.
    EventLog.WriteEntry("MyApplication", dbze.Message, EventLogEntryType.Error);
    throw;
}
```

Here, you create an EventLog entry that records the occurrence of a divide-by-zero exception. Then the exception is propagated up the call stack by the throw statement.

Discussion

Establishing a catch block for an exception is essentially saying that you want to do something about that exceptional case. If you do not rethrow the exception, or create a new exception to wrap the original exception and throw it, the expectation is that you have handled the condition that caused the exception and that the program can continue normal operation. By choosing to rethrow the exception, you are indicating that there is still an issue to be dealt with and that you are counting on code farther up the stack to handle the condition. If you need to perform an action based on a thrown exception *and* need to allow the exception to continue after your code executes, then rethrowing is the mechanism to handle this. If both of those conditions are not met, don't rethrow the exception; just handle it or remove the catch block.

Remember that throwing exceptions is expensive. Try not to needlessly throw and rethrow exceptions since this might bog down your application.

7.3   Identifying Exceptions and Their Usage

Problem

There are many exceptions to choose from in the FCL. You need an easily accessible list of these exceptions that indicates when and where to use them. By throwing exceptions in a consistent manner (e.g., throwing an `ArgumentNullException` when an an argument is null), you and others on your team will be able to debug problems more easily.

Solution

Use the list of exceptions and their definitions in Table 7-1 to determine which exception to employ when throwing or catching exceptions.

Discussion

Table 7-1. The built-in exception types

Exception name	Derives from	Description
System.ApplicationException	Exception	Thrown when a nonfatal application error occurs.
System.ArgumentNullException	ArgumentException	Thrown when a parameter value for a method is null and null is not allowed.
System.ArgumentOutOfRangeException	ArgumentException	Thrown when a parameter value for a method is out of the range of expected values.
System.ArrayTypeMismatchException	SystemException	Thrown when an incompatible data type is assigned to an element in an array.
System.Runtime.InteropServices.COMException	ExternalException	Thrown when an unknown HRESULT is returned from a COM object.
System.Configuration.ConfigurationException	SystemException	Thrown when an invalid configuration setting is encountered.
System.Reflection.CustomAttributeFormatException	FormatException	Thrown when a custom attribute format is incorrect.
System.IO.DirectoryNotFoundException	IOException	Thrown when a file or directory cannot be found.
System.Exception	Object	Base class of all exceptions; you should always throw a more derived exception.
System.FormatException	SystemException	Thrown when a string is not in the expected format.
System.IndexOutOfRangeException	SystemException	Thrown when you attempt to access an array element with an index value outside the valid range for that array.
System.Configuration.Install.InstallException	SystemException	Thrown during software installation when an error is encountered during uninstall, committing of data, or rolling back of data.

Table 7-1. The built-in exception types (continued)

Exception name	Derives from	Description
System.ComponentModel. InvalidEnumArgumentException	ArgumentException	Thrown when an invalid enumeration value is passed to a method.
System. InvalidOperationException	SystemException	Thrown when a method is called while the object it resides in is in a state that makes it illegal to call this method.
System.IO.IOException	SystemException	Thrown when a general I/O exception occurs; you should throw a more derived exception.
System.MemberAccessException	SystemException	Thrown when a general error occurs while using a class member; you should throw a more derived exception.
System.MethodAccessException	MemberAccessException	Thrown when a general error occurs while using a method member.
System. NotFiniteNumberException	ArithmeticException	Thrown when a double or single data type is expected to have a finite number and instead it contains NaN, +infinity, or - infinity.
System. NotImplementedException	SystemException	Thrown when a member is accessed that is not yet implemented.
System.NotSupportedException	SystemException	Thrown when a member is accessed that is not supported.
System. NullReferenceException	SystemException	Thrown when a reference set to null is used.
System. ObjectDisposedException	InvalidOperation- Exception	Thrown when a disposed object is accessed.
System.ServiceProcess. TimeoutException	SystemException	Thrown when a service times out.
System.ComponentModel. WarningException	SystemException	Thrown when a warning message needs to be displayed. This exception does not imply a serious failure of the application or system.
System.Net.WebException	InvalidOperation- Exception	Thrown when a pluggable protocol causes an error.
System.Xml.XmlException	SystemException	Thrown due to a general error in the XML.

See Also

See the "Exception Class" topic in the MSDN documentation; also see the classes that derive from the Exception class.

7.4   Handling Derived Exceptions Individually

Problem

You have an exception hierarchy that consists of a base exception class and multiple derived exception classes. At some point in your code, you want to handle only one or two of these derived exceptions in a specific manner. All other derived exceptions should be handled in a more generic manner. You need a clean way to indicate that certain exceptions in an exception class hierarchy should be handled differently from the rest.

Solution

The exception handlers for C# allow for multiple catch clauses to be implemented. Each of these catch clauses can take a single parameter—a type derived from the Exception class. An exception handler that uses multiple catch clauses is shown here:

```
try
{
    int d = 0;
    int z = 1/d;
}
catch(DivideByZeroException dbze)
{
    Console.WriteLine("A divide by zero exception occurred. Error message == "
        + dbze.Message);
}
catch(OverflowException ofe)
{
    Console.WriteLine("An Overflow occurred. Error message == " + ofe.Message);
}
catch(Exception e)
{
    Console.WriteLine("Another type of error occurred. Error message == "
        + e.Message);
}
```

This code produces the following output:

```
A divide by zero exception occurred. Error message == Attempted to divide by zero.
```

Discussion

Notice the exception types that each catch clause handles in this try-catch block. These specific exception types will be handled on an individual basis within their own catch block. Suppose the try block looks like this:

```
try
{
    int z2 = 9999999;
    checked{z2 *= 999999999;}
}
```

You will get the following message:

```
An Overflow occurred. Error message == Arithmetic operation resulted in an overflow.
```

Now, since the OverflowException is being thrown, it is handled in a totally different catch block.

You could do the same thing in a single catch block using an if-else statement. An example of this is shown here:

```
catch(Exception e)
{
    if (e is OverflowException)
        Console.WriteLine("An Overflow occurred. Error message == " + e.Message);
    else if (e is DivideByZeroException)
        Console.WriteLine("A divide by zero exception occurred. Error message == " +
                    e.Message);
    else
        Console.WriteLine("Another type of error occurred. Error message == " +
                    e.Message);
}
```

The if-else statements are used to check the type of this exception and then execute the appropriate code. This structure has two flaws. The first is that the compiler does not check whether the exceptions are listed in the correct order in the if-else statements. If a derived exception class is placed in the if-else conditional structure after the exception class that it inherits from (Arthimetic Exception), then the derived exception class will never be checked. Consider the following modified catch clause:

```
try
{
    int d = 0;
    int z = 1/d;
}
catch(Exception e)
{
    if (e is ArithmeticException)
        Console.WriteLine("The base class exception was chosen.");
    else if (e is OverflowException)
        Console.WriteLine("An Overflow occurred. Error message == " + e.Message);
    else if (e is DivideByZeroException)
        Console.WriteLine("A divide by zero exception occurred. Error message == " +
                    e.Message);
    else
        Console.WriteLine("Another type of error occurred. Error message == " +
                    e.Message);
}
```

This code produces the following output:

```
The base class exception was chosen.
```

Even though the DivideByZeroException was thrown, the ArithmeticException is always found first, as the DivideByZeroException and OverflowException both have the ArithmeticException class as their base class.

The second flaw is one of appearance. Using multiple catch clauses is much easier to read thanks to its natural and consistent structure. This is the way the language should be used, and, therefore, this is what many developers are going to look for.

Other developers reading your code may find it more natural to read the multiple catch classes rather than the single catch clause with a decision structure inside of it. There is one case in which you might consider using the single catch clause with the decision structure: when large amounts of code would have to be duplicated in each catch clause and there is no way to put the duplicated code in a finally clause after the try-catch block. Even this scenario offers the alternative of structuring the code in a nested try-catch fashion like this:

```
try
{
    try
    {
        ...code here...
    }
    catch
    {
        ...put the code that is common to handling all exceptions here
        throw;
    }
}
catch (ExceptionTypeA a)
{
    ...  do specific exception A handling here
}
catch (ExceptionTypeB b)
{
    ...  do specific exception B handling here
}
```

See Also

See the "Error Raising and Handling Guidelines" topic in the MSDN documentation.

7.5   Assuring Exceptions Are Not Lost When Using Finally Blocks

Problem

You have multiple nested try-catch, try-finally, and try-catch-finally blocks. If a catch block attempts to throw an exception, it is possible that the thrown exception will get discarded and that a new and unexpected exception will be caught by an outer exception handler. You want to prevent this situation from occurring.

Solution

Add an inner try-catch block in the finally block of the outer exception handler:

```
private void PreventLossOfException( )
{
```

```
    try
    {
        //...
    }
    catch(Exception e)
    {
        Console.WriteLine("Error message == " + e.Message);
        throw;
    }
    finally
    {
        try
        {
            //...
        }
        catch(Exception e)
        {
            Console.WriteLine(@"An unexpected error occurred in the finally block.
                            Error message == " + e.Message);
        }
    }
}
```

This block will prevent the original exception from being lost.

Discussion

Consider what would happen if an error were thrown from the inner `finally` block contained in the `ThrowException` method, as is instigated by the code shown in Example 7-1.

Example 7-1. Throwing an error from the inner finally block of the ThrowExceptionMethod

```
private void ThrowException( )
{
    try
    {
        Console.WriteLine("In inner try");
        int z2 = 9999999;
        checked{z2 *= 999999999;}
    }
    catch(OverflowException ofe)
    {
        Console.WriteLine("An Overflow occurred.   Error message == " +
                        ofe.Message);
        throw;
    }
    catch(Exception e)
    {
        Console.WriteLine("Another type of error occurred.   " +
                        "Error message == " + e.Message);
        throw;
    }
    finally
```

```
    {
        try
        {
            Console.WriteLine("In inner finally");
            throw(new Exception("Oops"));
        }
        catch(Exception e)
        {
            Console.WriteLine(@"An error occurred in the finally block. " +
                                "Error message == " + e.Message);
        }
    }
}

public void PreventLossOfException( )
{
    try
    {
        Console.WriteLine("In outer try");
        ThrowException( );
    }
    catch(Exception e)
    {
        Console.WriteLine("In outer catch.   ReThrown error == " + e.Message);
    }
    finally
    {
        Console.WriteLine("In outer finally");
    }
}
```

The following output would be displayed:

```
In outer try
In inner try
An Overflow occurred.   Error message == Arithmetic operation resulted in an
overflow.
In inner finally
In outer catch.   ReThrown error == Oops
In outer finally
```

If you modify the inner `finally` block to handle its own errors (changes are highlighted), similarly to the following code:

```
public void PreventLossOfException( )
{
    try
    {
        Console.WriteLine("In outer try");
        ThrowException( );
    }
    catch(Exception e)
```

```
        {
            Console.WriteLine("In outer catch.   ReThrown error == " + e.Message);
        }
        finally
        {
            Console.WriteLine("In outer finally");
        }
    }
```

you will get the following output:

```
In outer try
In inner try
An Overflow occurred.   Error message == Arithmetic operation resulted in an
overflow.
In inner finally
An error occurred in the finally block.   Error message == Oops
In outer catch.   ReThrown error == Arithmetic operation resulted in an overflow.
In outer finally
```

By handling exceptions within the inner finally block, you assure that the correct
rethrown exception bubbles up to the outer exception handler.

> When writing a finally block, consider placing a separate try-catch
> around the code.

See Also

See the "Error Raising and Handling Guidelines" topic and the "throw," "try,"
"catch," and "finally" keywords in the MSDN documentation.

7.6   Handling Exceptions Thrown from Methods Invoked via Reflection

Problem

Using reflection, you invoke a method that generates an exception. You want to
obtain the real exception object and its information in order to diagnose and fix the
problem.

Solution

The real exception and its information can be obtained through the InnerException
property of the TargetInvocationException that is thrown by MethodInfo.Invoke.

Discussion

The following example shows how an exception that occurs within a method
invoked via reflection is handled. The Reflect class contains a ReflectionException

---

method that invokes the static `TestInvoke` method using the reflection classes as shown in Example 7-2.

Example 7-2. Obtaining information on an exception invoked by a method accessed through reflection

```csharp
using System;
using System.Reflection;

public class Reflect
{
    public void ReflectionException( )
    {
        Type reflectedClass = typeof(Reflect);
        try
        {
            MethodInfo methodToInvoke = reflectedClass.GetMethod("TestInvoke");

            if (methodToInvoke != null)
            {
                object oInvoke = methodToInvoke.Invoke(null, null);
            }
        }
        catch(TargetInvocationException e)
        {
            Console.WriteLine("MESSAGE: " + e.Message);
            Console.WriteLine("SOURCE: " + e.Source);
            Console.WriteLine("TARGET: " + e.TargetSite);
            Console.WriteLine("STACK: " + e.StackTrace + "\r\n");

            if(e.InnerException != null)
            {
                Console.WriteLine( );
                Console.WriteLine("\t**** INNEREXCEPTION START ****");
                Console.WriteLine("\tINNEREXCEPTION MESSAGE: " +
                                    e.InnerException.Message);
                Console.WriteLine("\tINNEREXCEPTION SOURCE: " +
                                    e.InnerException.Source);
                Console.WriteLine("\tINNEREXCEPTION STACK: " +
                                    e.InnerException.StackTrace);
                Console.WriteLine("\tINNEREXCEPTION TARGETSITE: " +
                                    e.InnerException.TargetSite);
                Console.WriteLine("\t****  INNEREXCEPTION END  ****");
            }

            Console.WriteLine( );

            // Shows fusion log when assembly cannot be located
            Console.WriteLine(e.ToString( ));
        }
    }
}
```

Example 7-2. Obtaining information on an exception invoked by a method accessed through reflection (continued)

```
    // Method to invoke via reflection
    public static void TestInvoke( )
    {
        throw (new Exception("Thrown from invoked method."));
    }
}
```

This code displays the following text:

```
MESSAGE: Exception has been thrown by the target of an invocation.
SOURCE: mscorlib
TARGET: System.Object _InvokeMethodFast(System.Object, System.Object[], System.
SignatureStruct ByRef, System.Reflection.MethodAttributes, System.RuntimeTypeHandle)
STACK:    at System.RuntimeMethodHandle._InvokeMethodFast(Object target, Object[]
arguments, SignatureStruct& sig, MethodAttributes methodAttributes, RuntimeTypeHandle
typeOwner)
    at System.RuntimeMethodHandle.InvokeMethodFast(Object target, Object[] arguments,
SignatureStruct sig, MethodAttributes methodAttributes, RuntimeTypeHandle typeOwner)
    at System.Reflection.RuntimeMethodInfo.Invoke(Object obj, BindingFlags invokeAttr,
Binder binder, Object[] parameters, CultureInfo culture, Boolean
skipVisibilityChecks)
    at System.Reflection.RuntimeMethodInfo.Invoke(Object obj, BindingFlags invokeAttr,
Binder binder, Object[] parameters, CultureInfo culture)
    at System.Reflection.MethodBase.Invoke(Object obj, Object[] parameters)
    at CSharpRecipes.ExceptionHandling.ReflectionException( ) in
        C:\C#Cookbook2\CSharpRecipes\07_ExceptionHandling.cs:line 195


**** INNEREXCEPTION START ****
INNEREXCEPTION MESSAGE: Thrown from invoked method.
INNEREXCEPTION SOURCE: CSharpRecipes
INNEREXCEPTION STACK:    at CSharpRecipes.ExceptionHandling.TestInvoke( ) in
    C:\C#Cookbook2\CSharpRecipes\07_ExceptionHandling.cs:line 226
INNEREXCEPTION TARGETSITE: Void TestInvoke( )
****   INNEREXCEPTION END   ****
```

When the `methodToInvoke.Invoke` method is called, the `TestInvoke` method is called. It throws an exception. The outer exception is the `TargetInvocationException`; this is the generic exception thrown when a method invoked through reflection throws an exception. The CLR automatically wraps the original exception thrown by the invoked method inside of the `TargetInvocationException` object's `InnerException` property. In this case, the exception thrown by the invoked method is of type `System.Exception`. This exception is shown after the section that begins with the text **** INNEREXCEPTION START ****.

In addition to this text, the code also calls `e.ToString` to print out the exception text. The text output from `ToString` is:

```
System.Reflection.TargetInvocationException: Exception has been thrown by the target
of an invocation. ---> System.Exception: Thrown from invoked method.
    at ClassLibrary1.Reflect.TestInvoke( ) in
```

```
        C:\BOOK CS CookBook\Code\Test.cs:line 49
    at ClassLibrary1.Reflect.TestInvoke( ) in
        C:\BOOK CS CookBook\Code\Test.cs:line 49
    --- End of inner exception stack trace ---
    at System.Reflection.RuntimeMethodInfo.InternalInvoke(Object obj, BindingFlags
       invokeAttr, Binder binder, Object[] parameters, CultureInfo culture, Boolean
       isBinderDefault, Assembly caller, Boolean verifyAccess)
    at System.Reflection.RuntimeMethodInfo.InternalInvoke(Object obj, BindingFlags
       invokeAttr, Binder binder, Object[] parameters, CultureInfo culture, Boolean
       verifyAccess)
    at System.Reflection.RuntimeMethodInfo.Invoke(Object obj, BindingFlags invokeAttr,
       Binder binder, Object[] parameters, CultureInfo culture)
    at System.Reflection.MethodBase.Invoke(Object obj, Object[] parameters)
    atReflect.ReflectionException( ) in c:\book cs cookbook
       \code\test.cs:line 22
```

Using the ToString method is a quick and simple way of displaying the most relevant outer exception information along with the most relevant information for each inner exception.

See Also

See the "Type Class" and "MethodInfo Class" topics in the MSDN documentation.

7.7   Debugging Problems When Loading an Assembly

Problem

You want to use a reflection-based technique, such as the static Assembly.LoadFrom method, to load an assembly. If this method fails, you want to collect as much useful information as you can as to why the assembly failed to load.

Solution

Either call the ToString method on the exception object or use the FusionLog property on BadImageFormatException, FileLoadException, or FileNotFoundException. When an exception occurs while using a file, the exception contains extra information that is taken from the fusion log. To see this in action, run the following code:

```
public static void LoadMissingDLL( )
{
    // Load the DLL.
    try
    {
        Assembly reflectedAssembly = Assembly.LoadFrom("BadFileName.dll");
    }
    catch (FileNotFoundException fnf)
    {
        // This displays the fusion log information only.
        Console.WriteLine(fnf.FusionLog);
    }
```

```
        catch (Exception e)       // Note that you would use one catch block or the other,
        {                         //  not both.
            // This displays the exception information along
            // with any fusion log information.
            Console.WriteLine(e.ToString( ));
        }
    }
```

Discussion

Use this technique to debug problems when loading an assembly from a file. When using the ToString method of the Exception object, notice the bottom part of the error message that starts with "Fusion log follows." This is the section that can provide some clue as to why the reflection APIs could not find your assembly. If you want just the fusion information, you can use the FusionLog property of one of the aforementioned exception objects. The Assembly Binding Log Viewer (*fuslogvw.exe*) is another place where the load failure information can be retrieved. In order for this log to be filled, the HKEY_LOCAL_MACHINE\SOFTWARE\Microsoft\Fusion|ForceLog and LogFailures entries should be specified as type DWORD with a value of 1 for each entry. Without these entries, the log will not record failure information, and it will only be available from the FusionLog property.

See Also

See the "BadImageFormatException Class," "FileLoadException Class," and "File-NotFoundException Class" topics in the MSDN documentation.

7.8   Mapping Back and Forth Between Managed Exceptions and HRESULTs

Problem

You need a reference table that maps each managed exception to its COM HRESULT counterpart. This mapping will allow you to determine the relative mapping between managed exceptions and COM HRESULTs in unmanaged code.

Solution

There can be multiple managed exceptions for a given HRESULT. Every managed exception maps to an HRESULT. Table 7-2 lists the managed exception classes and their equivalent HRESULT values. Use this table to determine what type of managed exception to use when throwing an exception back to unmanaged code, as well as what type of exception object to use when handling returned COM/COM+ HRESULT values. When there are multiple managed exceptions for a single HRESULT, use the one that most closely matches the condition being represented in managed code. The Marshal.ThrowExceptionForHR method will also create and throw the correctly mapped managed exception given an HRESULT, while Marshal.GetHRForException will determine the proper HRESULT given a managed exception.

Table 7-2. Mapping between managed exceptions and HRESULTs

.NET exception class name	HRESULT name (hex value of HRESULT)
AccessException	COR_E_MEMBERACCESS (0x8013151A)
AmbiguousMatchException	COR_E_AMBIGUOUSMATCH (0X80138000211D)
AppDomainUnloadedException	MSEE_E_APPDOMAINUNLOADED (0x80131015)
ApplicationException	COR_E_APPLICATION (0x80131600)
ArgumentException	COR_E_ARGUMENT (0x80070057)
ArgumentNullException	E_POINTER (0x80004003)
ArgumentOutOfRangeException	COR_E_ARGUMENTOUTOFRANGE (0x80131502)
ArithmeticException	COR_E_ARITHMETIC (0x80070216)
ArrayTypeMismatchException	COR_E_ARRAYTYPEMISMATCH (0x80131503)
BadImageFormatException	COR_E_BADIMAGEFORMAT (0x8007000B)
CannotUnloadAppDomainException	COR_E_CANNOTUNLOADAPPDOMAIN (0x80131015)
COMException	Any other HRESULT defaults to this .Net Exception
ContextMarshalException	COR_E_CONTEXTMARSHAL (0x80090020)
CryptographicException	NTE_FAIL (0x80004001)
CryptographicUnexpectedOperationException	CORSEC_E_CRYPTO_UNEX_OPER (0x80131431)
CustomAttributeFormatException	COR_E_FORMAT (0x80131537)
DirectoryNotFoundException	COR_E_DIRECTORYNOTFOUND (0x80070003) STG_E_PATHNOTFOUND (0x80030003)
DivideByZeroException	COR_E_DIVIDEBYZERO (0x80020012)
DllNotFoundException	COR_E_DLLNOTFOUND (0x80131524)
DuplicateWaitObjectException	COR_E_DUPLICATEWAITOBJECT (0x80131529)
EndOfStreamException	COR_E_ENDOFSTREAM (0x801338)
EntryPointNotFoundException	COR_E_TYPELOAD (0x80131522)
Exception	COR_E_EXCEPTION (0x80131500)
ExecutionEngineException	COR_E_EXECUTIONENGINE (0x80131506)
ExternalException	E_FAIL (0x80004005)
FieldAccessException	COR_E_FIELDACCESS (0x80131507)
FileLoadException	COR_E_FILELOAD (0x80131621 or 0x80131018)
FileNotFoundException	COR_E_FILENOTFOUND (0x80070002)
FormatException	COR_E_FORMAT (0x80131537)
IndexOutOfRangeException	COR_E_INDEXOUTOFRANGE (0x80131508)
InvalidCastException	COR_E_INVALIDCAST (0x80004002)
InvalidComObjectException	COR_E_INVALIDCOMOBJECT (0x80131527)

Table 7-2. Mapping between managed exceptions and HRESULTs (continued)

.NET exception class name	HRESULT name (hex value of HRESULT)
InvalidFilterCriteriaException	COR_E_INVALIDFILTERCRITERIA (0x80131601)
InvalidOleVariantTypeException	COR_E_INVALIDOLEVARIANTTYPE (0x80131531)
InvalidOperationException	COR_E_INVALIDOPERATION (0x80131509)
InvalidProgramException	COR_E_INVALIDPROGRAM (0x8013153A)
IOException	COR_E_IO (0x80131620)
IsolatedStorageException	ISS_E_ISOSTORE (0x80131450)
MarshalDirectiveException	COR_E_MARSHALDIRECTIVE (0x80131535)
MethodAccessException	COR_E_METHODACCESS (0x80131510)
MissingFieldException	COR_E_MISSINGFIELD (0x80131511)
MissingManifestResourceException	COR_E_MISSINGMANIFESTRESOURCE (0x80131532)
MissingMemberException	COR_E_MISSINGMEMBER (0x80131512)
MissingMethodException	COR_E_MISSINGMETHOD (0x80131513)
MulticastNotSupportedException	COR_E_MULTICASTNOTSUPPORTED (0x80131514)
NotFiniteNumberException	COR_E_NOTFINITENUMBER (0x80131528)
NotImplementedException	E_NOTIMPL (0x80004001)
NotSupportedException	COR_E_NOTSUPPORTED (0x80131515)
NullReferenceException	COR_E_NULLREFERENCE (0x80004003)
OutOfMemoryException	COR_E_OUTOFMEMORY (0x8007000E)
OverflowException	COR_E_OVERFLOW (0x80131516)
PathTooLongException	COR_E_PATHTOOLONG (0x8013206)
PlatformNotSupportedException	COR_E_PLATFORMNOTSUPPORTED (0x80131539)
PolicyException	CORSEC_E_POLICY_EXCEPTION
RankException	COR_E_RANK (0x80131517)
ReflectionTypeLoadException	COR_E_REFLECTIONTYPELOAD (0x80131602)
RemotingException	COR_E_REMOTING (0x8013150B)
RemotingTimeoutException	COR_E_REMOTING (0x8013150B)
SafeArrayTypeMismatchException	COR_E_SAFEARRAYTYPEMISMATCH (0x80131533)
SafeArrayRankMismatchException	COR_E_SAFEARRAYRANKMISMATCH (0x80131538)
SecurityException	COR_E_SECURITY (0x8013150A)
SEHException	E_FAIL (0x80004005)
SerializationException	COR_E_SERIALIZATION (0x8013150C)
ServerException	COR_E_SERVER (0x8013150E)
StackOverflowException	COR_E_STACKOVERFLOW (0x800703E9)
SUDSGeneratorException	COR_E_EXCEPTION (0x80131500)
SUDSParserException	COR_E_EXCEPTION (0x80131500)

Table 7-2. Mapping between managed exceptions and HRESULTs (continued)

.NET exception class name	HRESULT name (hex value of HRESULT)
SynchronizationLockException	COR_E_SYNCHRONIZATIONLOCK (0x80131518)
SystemException	COR_E_SYSTEM (0x80131501)
TargetException	COR_E_TARGET
TargetInvocationException	COR_E_TARGETINVOCATION (0x80131604)
TargetParameterCountException	COR_E_TARGETPARAMCOUNT (0x80138002)
ThreadAbortException	COR_E_THREADABORTED (0x80131530)
ThreadInterruptedException	COR_E_THREADINTERRUPTED (0x80131519)
ThreadStateException	COR_E_THREADSTATE (0x80131520)
ThreadStopException	COR_E_THREADSTOP
TypeInitializationException	COR_E_TYPEINITIALIZATION (0x80131534)
TypeLoadException	COR_E_TYPELOAD (0x80131522)
TypeUnloadedException	COR_E_TYPEUNLOADED (0x80131013)
UnauthorizedAccessException	COR_E_UNAUTHORIZEDACCESS (0x80070005)
VerificationException	COR_E_VERIFICATION
WeakReferenceException	COR_E_WEAKREFERENCE

Discussion

Handling exceptions generated by COM/COM+ components involves the following two steps:

1. Handle any specific exceptions to which the .NET Common Language Runtime maps the COM/COM+ HRESULTs you're interested in. The table in the Solution section lists the managed exceptions and the standard HRESULT values returned by COM/COM+ objects to which they are mapped.

2. Handle any user-defined exceptions that are unique to a specific COM/COM+ component by trapping the COMException exception. The COMException class reflects COM/COM+ HRESULTs that have no mapping to managed exceptions.

The following code fragment illustrates this handling of COM/COM+ exceptions:

```
try
{
    CallCOMMethod( );
}
catch (UnauthorizedAccessException uae)
{
    // Handle COM/COM+ access exceptions here.
}
catch (System.Runtime.InteropServices.COMException ce)
{
    // Handle user-defined COM/COM+ exceptions here.
}
```

```
catch (Exception e)
{
    // Handle all other exceptions here.
}
```

See Recipe 7.9 for more information on handling user-defined HRESULTs.

See Also

See Recipe 7.9; see the "Error Raising and Handling Guidelines," "HRESULTs and Exceptions," and "Handling COM Interop Exceptions" topics in the MSDN documentation.

7.9   Handling User-Defined HRESULTs

Problem

A COM object can return a user-defined HRESULT or an HRESULT that has no mapping to a managed exception type. You wish to handle these returned HRESULTs in a more specific manner.

Solution

The following code fragment illustrates the handling of user-defined COM/COM+ exceptions:

```
try
{
    CallCOMMethod( );
}
catch (System.Runtime.InteropServices.COMException ce)
{
    switch ((uint)ce.ErrorCode)
    {
        case 0x80042000:
            // Handle specific user-defined COM/COM+ exception here.
            break;
        case 0x80042001:
            // Handle specific user-defined COM/COM+ exception here.
            break;
        default:
            // Handle any other specific user-defined COM/COM+
            // exceptions here.
            break;
    }
}
catch (Exception e)
{
    // Handle all other exceptions here.
}
```

Discussion

Handle any user-defined exceptions that are unique to a specific COM/COM+ component by trapping the COMException exception. This class reflects COM/COM+ HRESULTs that have no mapping to managed exceptions.

The COMException has a property, ErrorCode, in addition to those properties in the base Exception class. This property contains the HRESULT value that the COM/COM+ object returned. Another difference between COMException and Exception is that the InnerException property of a COMException object will always be null.

See Also

See the "Error Raising and Handling Guidelines" and "Handling COM Interop Exceptions" topics in the MSDN documentation.

7.10 Preventing Unhandled Exceptions

Problem

You need to make absolutely sure that every exception thrown by your application is handled and that no exception is bubbled up past the outermost exception handler. Hackers often use these types of exceptions to aid in their analysis of the vulnerabilities of a web application for instance.

Solution

Place try-catch or try-catch-finally blocks in strategic places in your application. In addition, use the exception event handler as a final line of defense against unhandled exceptions.

Discussion

If an exception occurs and is not handled, it will cause your application to shut down prematurely. This can leave data in an unstable state, possibly requiring manual intervention—meaning that you could be spending a long night cleaning up the data by hand. To minimize the damage, you can place exception handlers in strategic locations throughout your code.

The most obvious location to place exception-handling code is inside of the Main method. The Main method is the entry point to executables (files with an *.exe* extension). Therefore, if any exceptions occur inside your executable, the CLR starts looking for an exception handler, starting at the location where the exception occurred. If none is found, the CLR walks the stack until one is found; each method on the stack is examined in turn to determine whether an exception handler exists. If no exception handlers are found in the final method in the stack, the exception is considered unhandled and the application is terminated. In an executable, this final method is the Main method.

In addition to or in place of using try-catch or try-catch-finally blocks at the entry point of your application, you can use the exception event handler to capture unhandled exceptions. Note that Windows Forms applications provide their own unhandled exception trap around exception handlers. To see how to deal with this in a WinForms application, review Recipe 7.20. There are two steps to setting up an exception event handler. The first is to create the actual event handler. This is done as follows:

```
static void LastChanceHandler(object sender, UnhandledExceptionEventArgs args)
{
    try
    {
        Exception e = (Exception) args.ExceptionObject;

        Console.WriteLine("Unhandled exception == " + e.ToString( ));
        if (args.IsTerminating)
        {
            Console.WriteLine("The application is terminating");
        }
        else
        {
            Console.WriteLine("The application is not terminating");
        }
    }
    catch(Exception e)
    {
        Console.WriteLine("Unhandled exception in unhandled exception handler == " +
                        e.ToString( ));
    }
    finally
    {
        // Add other exception logging or cleanup code here.
    }
}
```

Next, you should add code to your application to wire up this event handler. The code to wire up the event handler should be executed as close to the start of the application as possible. For example, by placing this code in the Main method:

```
public static void Main( )
{
    AppDomain.CurrentDomain.UnhandledException +=
            new UnhandledExceptionEventHandler(LastChanceHandler);

    //...
}
```

you are assured of being able to clean up after any unhandled exception.

The exception event handler takes two parameters. The first is the sender object, which is the AppDomain object that threw the exception. The second argument is an UnhandledExceptionEventArgs object. This object contains all the relevant information on the unhandled exception. Using this object, you can obtain the actual exception object that was thrown as well as a Boolean flag that indicates whether the application will terminate.

Exception event handlers are a great help when used in multithreaded code. In the 1.x versions of the Framework, if an unhandled exception were thrown in a thread other than the main thread, that thread would abort. However, only the worker thread, and not the application as a whole, would terminate. But you were not clearly notified when the CLR aborted this thread, which could cause some interesting debugging problems. In Version 2.0 of the Framework, any unhandled exception will now propagate and cause the application to terminate. However, when an exception event handler is used, you can be notified of any unhandled exceptions that occur in any worker thread and that cause it to abort.

The exception event handler captures unhandled exceptions for only the primary application domain. Any application domains created from the primary application domain do not fire this event for unhandled exceptions. These secondary AppDomains must be registered with as well for the UnhandledException event individually to receive their exception events. Note that if the exception is thrown on the main thread, the system will bring up an error dialog before running the exception event handler.

See Also

See the "Error Raising and Handling Guidelines" and "UnhandledException-EventHandler Delegate" topics in the MSDN documentation.

7.11 Getting Exception Information

Problem

There are several different methods of getting exception information. You need to choose the best one to use.

Solution

The .NET platform supports several mechanisms for displaying exception information, depending on the specific type of information that you want to show. The easiest method is to use the ToString method of the thrown exception object, usually in the catch block of an exception handler:

```
catch(Exception e)
{
    Console.WriteLine(e.ToString( ));
}
```

Another mechanism is to manually display the individual properties of the exception and iterate through each inner exception, if any exist. The default Exception.ToString method will iterate over the inner exceptions as well, so if you want to make sure you get all of that information, you need to roll over them when examining the properties directly. For example, the custom method shown in Example 7-3 is called from a catch block. It takes a single exception object as a parameter and proceeds to display its information, including information on all inner exceptions and the exception data block.

Example 7-3. Displaying exception information, including information on all inner exceptions and the exception data block

```
public static int exceptionLevel = 0;
public static void DisplayException(Exception e)
{
    // Increment exception level.
    exceptionLevel++;
    // Make spacer for level.
    string indent = new string('\t',exceptionLevel-1);
    // Write out exception level data.
    Console.WriteLine(indent + "*** Exception Level {0} " +
                    "**************************************", exceptionLevel);
    Console.WriteLine(indent + "ExceptionType: " + e.GetType( ).Name.ToString( ));
    Console.WriteLine(indent + "HelpLine: " + e.HelpLink);
    Console.WriteLine(indent + "Message: " + e.Message);
    Console.WriteLine(indent + "Source: " + e.Source);
    Console.WriteLine(indent + "StackTrace: " + e.StackTrace);
    Console.WriteLine(indent + "TargetSite: " + e.TargetSite);
    Console.WriteLine(indent + "Data:");
    foreach (DictionaryEntry de in e.Data)
    {
        Console.WriteLine(indent + "\t{0} : {1}",de.Key,de.Value);
    }

    // Get the inner exception for this exception.
    Exception ie = e.InnerException;

    // Print out the inner exceptions recursively.
    while(ie != null)
    {
        DisplayException(ie);
        // Check to see if we are doing the inner exceptions.
        if(exceptionLevel>1)
            ie = ie.InnerException;
        else // back to main level
            ie = null;
    }
    // Decrement exception level.
    exceptionLevel--;
}
```

Discussion

A typical exception object of type Exception displays the following information if its ToString method is called:

```
System.Exception: Exception of type System.Exception was thrown.
    at Chapter_Code.Chapter7.TestSpecializedException( ) in c:\book cs cookbook\code\
        test.cs:line 286
```

Three pieces of information are shown here:

- The exception type (Exception in this case) followed by a colon
- The string contained in the exception's Message property
- The string contained in the exception's StackTrace property

The great thing about the ToString method is that information about any exception contained in the InnerException property is automatically displayed as well. The following text shows the output of an exception that wraps an inner exception:

```
System.Exception: Exception of type System.Exception was thrown.
---> System.Exception: The Inner Exception
   at Chapter_Code.Chapter7.TestSpecializedException( )
      in c:\book cs cookbook\code\
      test.cs:line 306
   --- End of inner exception stack trace ---
   at Chapter_Code.Chapter7.TestSpecializedException( )
      in c:\book cs cookbook\code\
      test.cs:line 310
```

The same three pieces of information are displayed for each exception. The output is broken down into the following format:

```
Outer exception type: Outer exception Message property
---> Inner Exception type: Inner exception Message property
Inner Exception StackTrace property
      --- End of inner exception stack trace ---
Outer exception StackTrace property
```

If the inner exception contains an exception object in its InnerException property, that exception is displayed as well. In fact, information for all inner exceptions is displayed in this format.

Calling the ToString method is a quick, useful way of getting the most pertinent information out of the exception and displaying it in a formatted string. However, not all of the exception's information is displayed. There might be a need to display the HelpLine or Source properties of the exception. In fact, if this is a user-defined exception, there could be custom fields that need to be displayed or captured in an error log. Also, you might not like the default formatting that the ToString method offers, or you may want to see the information in the Data collection of items. In these cases, consider writing your own method to display the exception's information based on the DisplayException method shown in the Solution.

To illustrate the custom method presented in the Solution section (the DisplayException method), consider the following code, which throws an exception wrapping two inner exceptions:

```
Exception InnerInner = new Exception("The InnerInner Exception.");
InnerInner.Data.Add("Key1 for InnerInner", "Value1 for InnerInner");

ArgumentException Inner = new ArgumentException("The Inner Exception.", InnerInner);
Inner.Data.Add("Key1 for Inner", "Value1 for Inner");
```

```
NullReferenceException se = new NullReferenceException("A Test Message.", Inner);
se.HelpLink = "MyComponent.hlp";
se.Source = "MyComponent";
se.Data.Add("Key1 for Outer", "Value1 for Outer");
se.Data.Add("Key2 for Outer", "Value2 for Outer");
se.Data.Add("Key3 for Outer", "Value3 for Outer");


try
{
    throw (se);
}
catch(Exception e)
{
    DisplayException(e);
}
```

If this code were executed, DisplayException would display the following:

```
*** Exception Level 1 ***************************************
ExceptionType: NullReferenceException
HelpLine: MyComponent.hlp
Message: A Test Message.
Source: MyComponent
StackTrace:    at CSharpRecipes.ExceptionHandling.TestDisplayException() in C:\PRJ32\
Book_2_0\C#Cookbook2\Code\CSharpRecipes\07_ExceptionHandling.cs:line 371
TargetSite: Void TestDisplayException()
Data:
    Key1 for Outer : Value1 for Outer
    Key2 for Outer : Value2 for Outer
    Key3 for Outer : Value3 for Outer
    *** Exception Level 2 ***************************************
    ExceptionType: ArgumentException
    HelpLine:
    Message: The Inner Exception.
    Source:
    StackTrace:
    TargetSite:
    Data:
        Key1 for Inner : Value1 for Inner
        *** Exception Level 3 ***************************************
        ExceptionType: Exception
        HelpLine:
        Message: The InnerInner Exception.
        Source:
        StackTrace:
        TargetSite:
        Data:
            Key1 for InnerInner : Value1 for InnerInner
```

The outermost exception is displayed first, followed by all of its properties. Next, each inner exception is displayed in a similar manner.

The while loop of the DisplayException method is used to iterate through each inner exception until the innermost exception is reached. The indent variable is used to create the staggered display of inner exception information based on the level of the exception.

See Also

See the "Error Raising and Handling Guidelines" and "Exception Class" topics in the MSDN documentation.

7.12 Getting to the Root of a Problem Quickly

Problem

A thrown and caught exception can contain one or more inner exceptions. The innermost exception usually indicates the origin of the problem. You want to be able to view the original thrown exception and skip all of the outer exceptions and to view the initial problem.

Solution

The GetBaseException instance method of the Exception class displays information on only the innermost (original) exception; no other exception information is displayed. This method accepts no parameters and returns the innermost exception. For example:

```
Console.WriteLine(e.GetBaseException( ).ToString( ));
```

Discussion

Calling the GetBaseException( ).ToString( ) method on an exception object that contains an inner exception produces the same error information as if the ToString method were called directly on the inner exception. However, if the exception object does not contain an inner expression, the information on the provided exception object is displayed. For the following code:

```
Exception innerInner = new Exception("The innerInner Exception.");
ArgumentException inner = new ArgumentException("The inner Exception.", innerInner);
NullReferenceException se = new NullReferenceException("A Test Message.", inner);

try
{
    throw (se);
}
catch(Exception e)
{
    Console.WriteLine(e.GetBaseException( ).ToString( ));
}
```

something similar to this would be displayed:

```
System.Exception: The innerInner Exception.
    at Chapter_Code.EH.MyMethod( ) in c:\book cs cookbook\code\test.cs:line 286
```

Notice that no exception other than the innerInner exception is displayed. This useful technique gets to the root of the problem while filtering out all of the other outer exceptions that you are not interested in.

See Also

See the "Error Raising and Handling Guidelines" and "Exception Class" topics in the MSDN documentation.

7.13   Creating a New Exception Type

Problem

None of the built-in exceptions in the .NET Framework provide the implementation details that you require for an exception that you need to throw. You need to create your own exception class that operates seamlessly with your application, as well as other applications. Whenever an application receives this new exception, it can inform the user that a specific error occurred in a specific component. This report will greatly reduce the time required to debug the problem.

Solution

Create your own exception class. To illustrate, let's create a custom exception class, RemoteComponentException, that will inform a client application that an error has occurred in a remote server assembly.

Discussion

The exception hierarchy starts with the Exception class; from this are derived two classes: ApplicationException and SystemException. The SystemException class and any classes derived from it are reserved for the developers of the FCL. Most of the common exceptions, such as the NullReferenceException or the OverflowException, are derived from SystemException. The FCL developers created the ApplicationException class for other developers using the .NET languages to derive their own exceptions from. This partitioning allows for a clear distinction between user-defined exceptions and the built-in system exceptions. However, Microsoft now recommends deriving directly from Exception, rather than ApplicationException. Nothing actively prevents you from deriving a class from either SystemException or ApplicationException. But it is better to be consistent and use the convention of always deriving from the Exception class for user-defined exceptions.

You should follow the naming convention for exceptions when determining the name of your exception. The convention is very simple. Whatever you decide on for the exception's name, add the word Exception to the end of the name (e.g., use UnknownException as the exception name instead of just Unknown). Every user-defined exception should include *at least* three constructors, described next. This is not a requirement, but it makes your exception classes operate similarly to every other exception class in the FCL and minimizes the learning curve for other developers using your new exception. These three constructors are:

The default constructor
> This constructor takes no arguments and simply calls the base class's default constructor.

A constructor with a parameter that accepts a message string
> This message string overwrites the default contents of the Message field of this exception. Like the default constructor, this constructor also calls the base class's constructor, which also accepts a message string as its only parameter.

A constructor that accepts a message string and an inner exception as parameters
> The object contained in the *innerException* parameter is added to the InnerException property of this exception object. Like the other two constructors, this constructor calls the base class's constructor of the same signature.

If this exception will be caught in unmanaged code, such as a COM object, you can also set the HRESULT value for this exception. An exception caught in unmanaged code becomes an HRESULT value. If the exception does not alter the HRESULT value, it defaults to the HRESULT of the base class exception, which, in the case of a user-defined exception object that inherits from ApplicationException, is COR_E_APPLICATION (0x80131600). To change the default HRESULT value, simply set the value of this field in the constructor. The following code demonstrates this technique:

```
public class RemoteComponentException : Exception
{
    public RemoteComponentException( ) : base( )
    {
        HResult = 0x80040321;
    }

    public RemoteComponentException(string message) : base(message)
    {
        HResult = 0x80040321;
    }

    public RemoteComponentException(string message, Exception innerException)
        : base(message, innerException)
    {
        HResult = 0x80040321;
    }
}
```

Now the HResult that the COM object will see is the value 0x80040321. See Table 7-2 in Recipe 7.8 for more information on the mapping of HRESULT values to their equivalent managed exception classes.

 It is usually a good idea to override the Message property in order to incorporate any new fields into the exception's message text. Always remember to include the base class's message text along with any additional text you add to this property.

Fields and their accessors should be created to hold data specific to the exception. Since this exception will be thrown as a result of an error that occurs in a remote server assembly, you will add a private field to contain the name of the server or service. In addition, you will add a public read-only property to access this field. Since you're adding this new field, you should add two constructors that accept an extra parameter used to set the value of the serverName field.

If necessary, override any base class members whose behavior is inherited by the custom exception class. For example, since you have added a new field, you need to determine whether it will need to be added to the default contents of the Message field for this exception. If it does, you must override the Message property.

```
public override string Message
{
    get
    {
        if (this.ServerName.Length == 0)
            return (base.Message + Environment.NewLine +
                    "An unnamed server has encountered an error.");
        else
            return (base.Message + Environment.NewLine +
                    "The server " + this.ServerName +
                    " has encountered an error.");
    }
}
```

Notice that the Message property in the base class is displayed on the first line and your additional text is displayed on the next line. This organization takes into account that a user might modify the message that will appear in the Message property by using one of the overloaded constructors that takes a message string as a parameter.

In certain cases (such as remoting), your exception object should be serializable and deserializable. This involves performing the following two additional steps:

1. Add the Serializable attribute to the class definition. This attribute specifies that this class can be serialized or deserialized. A SerializationException is thrown if this attribute does not exist on this class and an attempt is made to serialize this class.

2. The class should implement the ISerializable interface if you want control over how serialization and deserialization are performed, and it should provide an implementation for its single member, GetObjectData. Here you implement it because the base class implements it, which means that you have no choice but to reimplement it if you want the fields you added (e.g., serverName) to get serialized.

```
// Used during serialization to capture information about extra fields
public override void GetObjectData(SerializationInfo exceptionInfo,
                                   StreamingContext exceptionContext)
{
    base.GetObjectData(exceptionInfo, exceptionContext);
    exceptionInfo.AddValue("ServerName", this.ServerName);
}
```

In addition, a new overridden constructor is needed that accepts information to deserialize this object:

```
// Serialization ctor
public RemoteComponentException(SerializationInfo exceptionInfo,
        StreamingContext exceptionContext)
        : base(exceptionInfo, exceptionContext)
{
    this.serverName = exceptionInfo.GetString("ServerName");
}
```

 Even though it is not required, you should make all user-defined exception classes serializable and deserializable. That way, the exceptions can be propagated properly over remoting and AppDomain boundaries.

At this point, the RemoteComponentException class contains everything you need for a complete user-defined exception class. You could stop at this point, but let's continue a bit farther and override some default functionality that deals with the hash code, equality, and inequality.

Overriding the GetHashCode method

Since you have overridden the Equals method, you should override the GetHashCode method, which overrides the hash code generation algorithm:

```
// GetHashCode
public override int GetHashCode( )
{
    return (ServerName.GetHashCode( ));
}
```

Overriding the == and != operators

When overriding the Equals method, both the == and != operators should be overloaded as well. Notice that both operators ultimately use the Equals method to determine equality. Therefore, they are simple to write.

```
// == operator
public static bool operator ==(RemoteComponentException v1,
    RemoteComponentException v2)
{
    return (v1.Equals(v2));
}

// != operator
public static bool operator !=(RemoteComponentException v1,
   RemoteComponentException v2)
{
    return (!(v1 == v2));
}
```

As a final note, it is generally a good idea to place all user-defined exceptions in a separate assembly, which allows for easier reuse of these exceptions in other applications and, more importantly, allows other application domains and remotely executing code to both throw and handle these exceptions correctly no matter where they are thrown. The assembly that holds these exceptions should be signed with a strong name and added to the Global Assembly Cache (GAC), so that any code that uses or handles these exceptions can find the assembly that defines them. See Recipe 17.10 for more information on how to do this.

If you are sure that the exceptions being defined won't ever be thrown or handled outside of your assembly, then you can leave the exception definitions there. But if for some reason an exception that you throw finds its way out of your assembly, the code that ultimately catches it will not be able to resolve it.

The complete source code for the RemoteComponentException class is shown in Example 7-4.

Example 7-4. RemoteComponentException class

```
using System;
using System.IO;
using System.Runtime.Serialization;
using System.Runtime.Serialization.Formatters.Binary;

[SerializableAttribute]
public class RemoteComponentException :
  Exception, ISerializable
{
    // New exception field
    private string serverName = "";

    // Normal exception ctors
    public RemoteComponentException( ) : base( )
    {
    }

    public RemoteComponentException(string message) : base(message)
    {
```

Example 7-4. RemoteComponentException class (continued)

```
}

public RemoteComponentException(string message,
  Exception innerException)
    : base(message, innerException)
{
}

// Exception ctors that accept the new ServerName parameter
public RemoteComponentException(string message,
  string serverName) : base(message)
{
    this.serverName = serverName;
}

public RemoteComponentException(string message,
  Exception innerException, string serverName)
        : base(message, innerException)
{
    this.serverName = serverName;
}

// Serialization ctor
public RemoteComponentException(SerializationInfo exceptionInfo,
        StreamingContext exceptionContext)
        : base(exceptionInfo, exceptionContext)
{
    this.serverName = exceptionInfo.GetString("ServerName");
}

// Read-only property
public string ServerName
{
    get{return (serverName.Trim( ));}
}

public override string Message
{
    get
    {
        if (this.ServerName.Length == 0)
            return (base.Message + Environment.NewLine +
                    "An unnamed server has encountered an error.");
        else
            return (base.Message + Environment.NewLine +
                    "The server " + this.ServerName +
                    " has encountered an error.");
    }
}

// Overridden methods
// ToString method
```

Example 7-4. RemoteComponentException class (continued)

```csharp
public override string ToString( )
{
    string errorString = "An error has occured in a server " +
        "component of this client.";
    errorString += Environment.NewLine + "Server Name: " +
        this.ServerName;
    if (this.InnerException == null)
    {
        errorString += Environment.NewLine +
            "Server component failed to provide an " +
            "underlying exception!";
    }
    else
    {
        string indent = "\t";
        Exception ie = this;
        while(ie.InnerException != null)
        {
            ie = ie.InnerException;
            errorString += Environment.NewLine + indent +
                "inner exception type thrown by server component: " +
                ie.GetType( ).Name.ToString( );
            errorString += Environment.NewLine + indent + "Message: "
                + ie.Message;
            errorString += Environment.NewLine + indent +
                "StackTrace: " + ie.StackTrace;

            indent += "\t";
        }
    }
    errorString += Environment.NewLine + "StackTrace of client " +
                "component: " + this.StackTrace;

    return (errorString);
}

// Call base.ToString method.
public string ToBaseString( )
{
    return (base.ToString( ));
}

// GetHashCode
public override int GetHashCode( )
{
    return (ServerName.GetHashCode( ));
}

// Equals
public override bool Equals(object obj)
{
    bool isEqual = false;
```

Example 7-4. RemoteComponentException class (continued)

```
        if (obj == null || (this.GetType( ) != obj.GetType( )))
        {
            isEqual = false;
        }
        else
        {
            RemoteComponentException se = (RemoteComponentException)obj;
            if ((this.ServerName.Length == 0)
              && (se.ServerName.Length == 0))
                isEqual = false;
            else
                isEqual = (this.ServerName == se.ServerName);
        }

        return (isEqual);
    }

    // == operator
    public static bool operator ==(RemoteComponentException v1,
        RemoteComponentException v2)
    {
        return (v1.Equals(v2));
    }

    // != operator
    public static bool operator !=(RemoteComponentException v1,
        RemoteComponentException v2)
    {
        return (!(v1 == v2));
    }

    // Used during serialization to capture information about extra fields
    public override void GetObjectData(SerializationInfo exceptionInfo,
                                      StreamingContext exceptionContext)
    {
        base.GetObjectData(exceptionInfo, exceptionContext);
        exceptionInfo.AddValue("ServerName", this.ServerName);
    }
}
```

The code to test the RemoteComponentException class is shown in Example 7-5.

Example 7-5. Testing the RemoteComponentException class

```
public void TestSpecializedException( )
{
    // Generic inner exception used to test the
    // RemoteComponentException's inner exception.
    Exception inner = new Exception("The inner Exception");

    // Test each ctor.
    Console.WriteLine(Environment.NewLine + Environment.NewLine +
```

Example 7-5. Testing the RemoteComponentException class (continued)

```
  "TEST EACH CTOR");
RemoteComponentException se1 = new RemoteComponentException ( );
RemoteComponentException se2 =
  new RemoteComponentException ("A Test Message for se2");
RemoteComponentException se3 =
  new RemoteComponentException ("A Test Message for se3", inner);
RemoteComponentException se4 =
  new RemoteComponentException ("A Test Message for se4",
                               "MyServer");
RemoteComponentException se5 =
  new RemoteComponentException ("A Test Message for se5", inner,
                               "MyServer");

// Test new ServerName property.
Console.WriteLine(Environment.NewLine +
  "TEST NEW SERVERNAME PROPERTY");
Console.WriteLine("se1.ServerName == " + se1.ServerName);
Console.WriteLine("se2.ServerName == " + se2.ServerName);
Console.WriteLine("se3.ServerName == " + se3.ServerName);
Console.WriteLine("se4.ServerName == " + se4.ServerName);
Console.WriteLine("se5.ServerName == " + se5.ServerName);

// Test overridden Message property.
Console.WriteLine(Environment.NewLine +
  "TEST -OVERRIDDEN- MESSAGE PROPERTY");
Console.WriteLine("se1.Message == " + se1.Message);
Console.WriteLine("se2.Message == " + se2.Message);
Console.WriteLine("se3.Message == " + se3.Message);
Console.WriteLine("se4.Message == " + se4.Message);
Console.WriteLine("se5.Message == " + se5.Message);

// Test -overridden- ToString method.
Console.WriteLine(Environment.NewLine +
  "TEST -OVERRIDDEN- TOSTRING METHOD");
Console.WriteLine("se1.ToString( ) == " + se1.ToString( ));
Console.WriteLine("se2.ToString( ) == " + se2.ToString( ));
Console.WriteLine("se3.ToString( ) == " + se3.ToString( ));
Console.WriteLine("se4.ToString( ) == " + se4.ToString( ));
Console.WriteLine("se5.ToString( ) == " + se5.ToString( ));

// Test ToBaseString method.
Console.WriteLine(Environment.NewLine +
  "TEST TOBASESTRING METHOD");
Console.WriteLine("se1.ToBaseString( ) == " + se1.ToBaseString( ));
Console.WriteLine("se2.ToBaseString( ) == " + se2.ToBaseString( ));
Console.WriteLine("se3.ToBaseString( ) == " + se3.ToBaseString( ));
Console.WriteLine("se4.ToBaseString( ) == " + se4.ToBaseString( ));
Console.WriteLine("se5.ToBaseString( ) == " + se5.ToBaseString( ));

// Test -overridden- == operator.
Console.WriteLine(Environment.NewLine +
  "TEST -OVERRIDDEN- == OPERATOR");
```

Example 7-5. Testing the RemoteComponentException class (continued)

```
Console.WriteLine("se1 == se1 == " + (se1 == se1));
Console.WriteLine("se2 == se1 == " + (se2 == se1));
Console.WriteLine("se3 == se1 == " + (se3 == se1));
Console.WriteLine("se4 == se1 == " + (se4 == se1));
Console.WriteLine("se5 == se1 == " + (se5 == se1));
Console.WriteLine("se5 == se4 == " + (se5 == se4));

// Test -overridden- != operator.
Console.WriteLine(Environment.NewLine +
  "TEST -OVERRIDDEN- != OPERATOR");
Console.WriteLine("se1 != se1 == " + (se1 != se1));
Console.WriteLine("se2 != se1 == " + (se2 != se1));
Console.WriteLine("se3 != se1 == " + (se3 != se1));
Console.WriteLine("se4 != se1 == " + (se4 != se1));
Console.WriteLine("se5 != se1 == " + (se5 != se1));
Console.WriteLine("se5 != se4 == " + (se5 != se4));

// Test -overridden- GetBaseException method.
Console.WriteLine(Environment.NewLine +
  "TEST -OVERRIDDEN- GETBASEEXCEPTION METHOD");
Console.WriteLine("se1.GetBaseException( ) == " + se1.GetBaseException( ));
Console.WriteLine("se2.GetBaseException( ) == " + se2.GetBaseException( ));
Console.WriteLine("se3.GetBaseException( ) == " + se3.GetBaseException( ));
Console.WriteLine("se4.GetBaseException( ) == " + se4.GetBaseException( ));
Console.WriteLine("se5.GetBaseException( ) == " + se5.GetBaseException( ));

// Test -overridden- GetHashCode method.
Console.WriteLine(Environment.NewLine +
  "TEST -OVERRIDDEN- GETHASHCODE METHOD");
Console.WriteLine("se1.GetHashCode( ) == " + se1.GetHashCode( ));
Console.WriteLine("se2.GetHashCode( ) == " + se2.GetHashCode( ));
Console.WriteLine("se3.GetHashCode( ) == " + se3.GetHashCode( ));
Console.WriteLine("se4.GetHashCode( ) == " + se4.GetHashCode( ));
Console.WriteLine("se5.GetHashCode( ) == " + se5.GetHashCode( ));

// Test serialization.
Console.WriteLine(Environment.NewLine +
  "TEST SERIALIZATION/DESERIALIZATION");
BinaryFormatter binaryWrite = new BinaryFormatter( );
Stream ObjectFile = File.Create("se1.object");
binaryWrite.Serialize(ObjectFile, se1);
ObjectFile.Close( );
ObjectFile = File.Create("se2.object");
binaryWrite.Serialize(ObjectFile, se2);
ObjectFile.Close( );
ObjectFile = File.Create("se3.object");
binaryWrite.Serialize(ObjectFile, se3);
ObjectFile.Close( );
ObjectFile = File.Create("se4.object");
binaryWrite.Serialize(ObjectFile, se4);
ObjectFile.Close( );
ObjectFile = File.Create("se5.object");
```

Example 7-5. Testing the RemoteComponentException class (continued)

```
        binaryWrite.Serialize(ObjectFile, se5);
        ObjectFile.Close( );

        BinaryFormatter binaryRead = new BinaryFormatter( );
        ObjectFile = File.OpenRead("se1.object");
        object Data = binaryRead.Deserialize(ObjectFile);
        Console.WriteLine("----------" + Environment.NewLine + Data);
        ObjectFile.Close( );
        ObjectFile = File.OpenRead("se2.object");
        Data = binaryRead.Deserialize(ObjectFile);
        Console.WriteLine("----------" + Environment.NewLine + Data);
        ObjectFile.Close( );
        ObjectFile = File.OpenRead("se3.object");
        Data = binaryRead.Deserialize(ObjectFile);
        Console.WriteLine("----------" + Environment.NewLine + Data);
        ObjectFile.Close( );
        ObjectFile = File.OpenRead("se4.object");
        Data = binaryRead.Deserialize(ObjectFile);
        Console.WriteLine("----------" + Environment.NewLine + Data);
        ObjectFile.Close( );
        ObjectFile = File.OpenRead("se5.object");
        Data = binaryRead.Deserialize(ObjectFile);
        Console.WriteLine("----------" + Environment.NewLine +
           Data + Environment.NewLine + "----------");
        ObjectFile.Close( );

        Console.WriteLine(Environment.NewLine + "END TEST" + Environment.NewLine);
    }
```

The output from Example 7-5 is presented in Example 7-6.

Example 7-6. Output displayed by the RemoteComponentException class

```
TEST EACH CTOR

TEST NEW SERVERNAME PROPERTY
se1.ServerName ==
se2.ServerName ==
se3.ServerName ==
se4.ServerName == MyServer
se5.ServerName == MyServer

TEST -OVERRIDDEN- MESSAGE PROPERTY
se1.Message == Error in the application.
An unnamed server has encountered an error.
se2.Message == A Test Message for se2
An unnamed server has encountered an error.
se3.Message == A Test Message for se3
An unnamed server has encountered an error.
se4.Message == A Test Message for se4
The server MyServer has encountered an error.
se5.Message == A Test Message for se5
The server MyServer has encountered an error.
```

Example 7-6. Output displayed by the RemoteComponentException class (continued)

```
TEST -OVERRIDDEN- TOSTRING METHOD
se1.ToString( ) == An error has occurred in a server component of this client.
Server Name:
Server component failed to notify of the underlying exception!
StackTrace of client component:
se2.ToString( ) == An error has occured in a server component of this client.
Server Name:
Server component failed to notify of the underlying exception!
StackTrace of client component:
se3.ToString( ) == An error has occurred in a server component of this client.
Server Name:
    Inner exception type thrown by server component: Exception
    Message: The Inner Exception
    StackTrace:
StackTrace of client component:
se4.ToString( ) == An error has occured in a server component of this client.
Server Name: MyServer
Server component failed to notify of the underlying exception!
StackTrace of client component:
se5.ToString( ) == An error has occurred in a server component of this client.
Server Name: MyServer
    Inner exception type thrown by server component: Exception
    Message: The Inner Exception
    StackTrace:
StackTrace of client component:


TEST TOBASESTRING METHOD
se1.ToBaseString( ) == CSharpRecipes.ExceptionHandling+RemoteComponentException: Error in
the application.
An unnamed server has encountered an error.
se2.ToBaseString( ) == CSharpRecipes.ExceptionHandling+RemoteComponentException: A Test
Message for se2
An unnamed server has encountered an error.
se3.ToBaseString( ) == CSharpRecipes.ExceptionHandling+RemoteComponentException: A Test
Message for se3
An unnamed server has encountered an error. ---> System.Exception: The Inner Exception
    --- End of inner exception stack trace ---
se4.ToBaseString( ) == CSharpRecipes.ExceptionHandling+RemoteComponentException: A Test
Message for se4
The server MyServer has encountered an error.
se5.ToBaseString( ) == CSharpRecipes.ExceptionHandling+RemoteComponentException: A Test
Message for se5
The server MyServer has encountered an error. ---> System.Exception: The Inner Exception
    --- End of inner exception stack trace ---


TEST -OVERRIDDEN- == OPERATOR
se1 == se1 == False
se2 == se1 == False
se3 == se1 == False
se4 == se1 == False
se5 == se1 == False
se5 == se4 == True
```

Example 7-6. Output displayed by the RemoteComponentException class (continued)

```
TEST -OVERRIDDEN- != OPERATOR
se1 != se1 == True
se2 != se1 == True
se3 != se1 == True
se4 != se1 == True
se5 != se1 == True
se5 != se4 == False


TEST -OVERRIDDEN- GETBASEEXCEPTION METHOD
se1.GetBaseException() == An error has occurred in a server component of this client.
Server Name:
Server component failed to notify of the underlying exception!
StackTrace of client component:
se2.GetBaseException() == An error has occurred in a server component of this client.
Server Name:
Server component failed to notify of the underlying exception!
StackTrace of client component:
se3.GetBaseException() == System.Exception: The Inner Exception
se4.GetBaseException() == An error has occurred in a server component of this client.
Server Name: MyServer
Server component failed to notify of the underlying exception!
StackTrace of client component:
se5.GetBaseException() == System.Exception: The Inner Exception


TEST -OVERRIDDEN- GETHASHCODE METHOD
se1.GetHashCode() == 757602046
se2.GetHashCode() == 757602046
se3.GetHashCode() == 757602046
se4.GetHashCode() == -1303092675
se5.GetHashCode() == -1303092675


TEST SERIALIZATION/DESERIALIZATION
----------
An error has occurred in a server component of this client.
Server Name:
Server component failed to notify of the underlying exception!
StackTrace of client component:
----------
An error has occurred in a server component of this client.
Server Name:
Server component failed to notify of the underlying exception!
StackTrace of client component:
----------
An error has occurred in a server component of this client.
Server Name:
    Inner exception type thrown by server component: Exception
    Message: The Inner Exception
    StackTrace:
StackTrace of client component:
----------
An error has occurred in a server component of this client.
Server Name: MyServer
Server component failed to notify of the underlying exception!
```

Example 7-6. Output displayed by the RemoteComponentException class (continued)

```
StackTrace of client component:
----------
An error has occurred in a server component of this client.
Server Name: MyServer
    Inner exception type thrown by server component: Exception
    Message: The Inner Exception
    StackTrace:
StackTrace of client component:
----------

END TEST
```

See Also

See Recipe 17.10; see the "Using User-Defined Exceptions" and "Exception Class" topics in the MSDN documentation.

7.14 Obtaining a Stack Trace

Problem

You need a view of what the stack looks like at any particular point in your application. However, you do not have an exception object from which to obtain this stack trace.

Solution

Use the following line of code to obtain a stack trace at any point in your application:

```
    string currentStackTrace = System.Environment.StackTrace;
```

The variable currentStackTrace now contains the stack trace at the location where this line of code was executed.

Discussion

A good use of the Solution is tracking down stack overflow problems. You can obtain the current stack trace at various points in your application and then calculate the stack depth. This depth calculation can then be logged to determine when and why the stack is overflowing or potential trouble spots where the stack may grow very large.

It is very easy to obtain a stack trace using the System.Environment.StackTrace property. Unfortunately, this stack trace also lists three methods defined in the System. Environment class that are called when you use the Environment.StackTrace property. The returned stack trace, using this method, will look something like following:

```
    at System.Environment.GetStackTrace(Exception e)
    at System.Environment.GetStackTrace(Exception e)
```

```
at System.Environment.get_StackTrace( )
at Chapter_Code.Class1.ObtainingStackTrace( ) in c:\book cs cookbook\test.cs:line 260
at Chapter_Code.Class1.Main(String[] args) in c:\book cs cookbook\main.cs:line 78
```

The first three items in the stack trace are method calls that you are not interested in. To fix this, you can write the following method to find and remove these items from the stack trace:

```
public static string GetStackTraceInfo(string currentStackTrace)
{
    string firstStackTraceCall = "System.Environment.get_StackTrace( )";
    int posOfStackTraceCall = currentStackTrace.IndexOf(firstStackTraceCall);
    return (currentStackTrace.Substring(posOfStackTraceCall +
            firstStackTraceCall.Length));
}
```

This method is called using the following line of code:

```
string stackTraceInfo = GetStackTraceInfo(System.Environment.StackTrace);
```

The second line in the GetStackTraceInfo method creates and initializes a string variable to the first called StackTrace method—which is actually a call to the get portion of the StackTrace property. This variable is used in the third line to obtain its starting position in the complete stack trace string. The final line of code grabs the end of the complete stack trace string, starting at the ending of the first called StackTrace method. The FinalStackTrace variable now contains the following string:

```
at Chapter_Code.Class1.ObtainingStackTrace( ) in c:\book cs cookbook\test.cs:line 260
at Chapter_Code.Class1.Main(String[] args) in c:\book cs cookbook\main.cs:line 78
```

This is the current stack trace at the point in the code where the Environment. StackTrace method was called.

Now that you have a stack trace of your code, you can calculate the stack depth at the point where you call Environment.StackTrace. The following code uses a regular expression to determine the depth of a stack trace:

```
using System;
using System.Text.RegularExpressions;

public static int GetStackTraceDepth(string currentStackTrace)
{
    string firstStackTraceCall = "System.Environment.get_StackTrace( )";
    int posOfStackTraceCall = currentStackTrace.IndexOf(firstStackTraceCall);
    string finalStackTrace = currentStackTrace.Substring(posOfStackTraceCall +
            firstStackTraceCall.Length);

    MatchCollection methodCallMatches = Regex.Matches(finalStackTrace,
            @"\sat\s.*(\sin\s.*\:line\s\d*)?");
    return (methodCallMatches.Count);
}
```

This regular expression captures every method call in the stack trace string. Note that, if the correct symbols are located for your assembly, the stack trace might look like this:

```
at Chapter_Code.Class1.ObtainingStackTrace( ) in c:\book cs cookbook\test.cs:line 260
at Chapter_Code.Class1.Main(String[] args) in c:\book cs cookbook\main.cs:line 78
```

However, if the correct symbols cannot be found, the stack trace string will look similar to the following:

```
at Chapter_Code.Class1.ObtainingStackTrace( )
at Chapter_Code.Class1.Main(String[] args)
```

The file and line numbers are not displayed in this case, and the regular expression must take this into account.

To get a count of the stack depth, use the Count property of the MatchCollection object to give the total number of method calls in the stack. In addition, you can obtain each individual method call as an independent string by iterating through the MatchCollection object. The code to do this is:

```
Console.WriteLine("-------------");
foreach(Match m in MethodCallMatches)
{
    Console.WriteLine(m.Value + System.Environment.NewLine + "-------------");
}
```

This code will display the following:

```
-------------
at Chapter_Code.Class1.ObtainingStackTrace( ) in
  c:\book cs cookbook\test.cs:line 260
-------------
at Chapter_Code.Class1.Main(String[] args) in
  c:\book cs cookbook\main.cs:line 78
-------------
```

Each method and its information are contained within a Match object within the MatchCollection object.

The Environment.StackTrace method can be useful as a debugging tool. You can see at various points in your application which methods have been called and their calling order. This can come in very handy when creating and debugging an application that uses recursion. In addition, you can also keep track of the stack depth by using the Environment.StackTrace property.

See Also

See the "Environment.StackTrace Property" topic in the MSDN documentation.

7.15 Breaking on a First-Chance Exception

Problem

You need to fix a problem with your code that is throwing an exception. Unfortunately, an exception handler is trapping the exception, and you are having a tough time pinpointing where and when the exception is being thrown.

Forcing the application to break on an exception before the application has a chance to handle it is very useful in situations in which you need to step through the code at the point where the exception is first being thrown. If this exception were thrown and not handled by your application, the debugger would intervene and break on the line of code that caused the unhandled exception. In this case, you can see the context in which the exception was thrown. However, if an exception handler is active when the exception is thrown, the exception handler will handle it and continue on, preventing you from being able to see the context at the point where the exception was thrown. This is the default behavior for all exceptions.

Solution

Select Debug → Exceptions within Visual Studio 2005 to display the Exceptions dialog box (see Figure 7-1). Select the exception from the tree that you want to modify and then click on the checkbox in the Thrown column in the list view. Click the OK button and then run your application. Any time the application throws a System.ArgumentOutOfRangeException, the debugger will break on that line of code before your application has a chance to handle it.

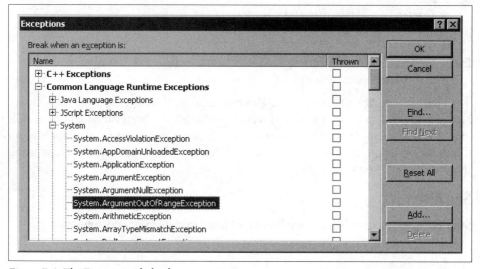

Figure 7-1. The Exceptions dialog box

Using the Exceptions dialog box, you can target specific exceptions or sets of exceptions for which you wish to alter the default behavior. This dialog has three main sections. The first is the TreeView control, which contains the list of categorized exceptions. Using this TreeView, you can choose one or more exceptions or groups of exceptions whose behavior you wish to modify.

The next section on this dialog is the column Thrown in the list next to the Tree-View. This column contains a checkbox for each exception that will enable the debugger to break when that type of exception is first thrown. At this stage, the exception is considered a *first-chance exception*. Checking the checkbox in the Thrown column forces the debugger to intervene when a first-chance exception of the type chosen in the TreeView control is thrown. Unchecking the checkbox allows the application to attempt to handle the first-chance exception.

This dialog contains two helpful buttons, Find and Find Next, to allow you to search for an exception rather than dig into the TreeView control and search for it on your own. In addition, three other buttons—Reset All, Add, and Delete—are used to reset to the original state and to add and remove user-defined exceptions, respectively. For example, you can create your own exception, as you did in Recipe 7.13, and add this exception to the TreeView list. You must add any managed exception such as this to the TreeView node entitled Common Language Runtime Exceptions. This setting tells the debugger that this is a managed exception and should be handled as such.

To add a user-defined exception to the TreeView, click the Add button. The dialog box shown in Figure 7-2 appears.

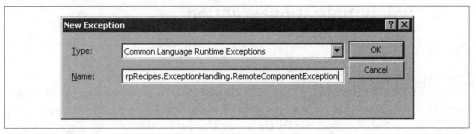

Figure 7-2. Adding a user-defined exception to the TreeView

Type the name of the exception—exactly as its class name is spelled with the full namespace scoping—into the Name field of this dialog box. Do not append any other information to this name, such as the namespace it resides in or a class name that it is nested within. Doing so will cause the debugger to fail to see this exception when it is thrown. Clicking the OK button places this exception into the TreeView under the Common Language Runtime Exceptions node. The Exceptions dialog box will look something like the one in Figure 7-3 after you add this user-defined exception.

The Delete button deletes any selected user-defined exception that you added to the TreeView. The Reset All button deletes any and all user-defined exceptions that have been added to the TreeView. Check the Thrown column to have the debugger stop when that exception type is thrown.

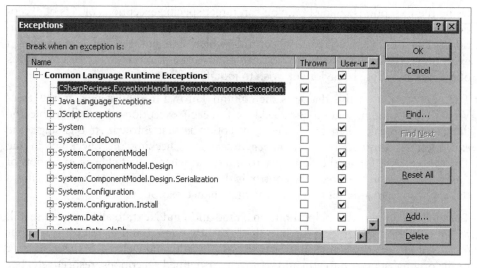

Figure 7-3. The Exceptions dialog box after adding a user-defined exception to the TreeView

See Also

See the "Exception Handling (Debugging)" topic in the MSDN documentation.

7.16 Preventing the Nefarious TypeInitializationException

Problem

Problems can occur when initializing a class's or a structure's static fields. Some of these problems are serious enough to raise a TypeInitializationException exception. Unfortunately, this exception can be hard to track down and can potentially shut down your application. You want to prevent this from occurring.

Solution

To demonstrate how to handle a TypeInitializationException, take the following example that initializes static fields to a value, null, or does not initialize them at all (not initializing is not recommended, of course), as is the case with the following class:

```
public class TestInit
{
    public static object one;
    public static string two = one.ToString( );
}
```

You should consider rewriting the class to include a static constructor that performs the initialization of the static fields. This will aid in the debugging of your static fields:

```
public class TestInit
{
    static TestInit( )
    {
        try
        {
            one = null;
            two = one.ToString( );
        }
        catch (Exception e)
        {
            Console.WriteLine("CAUGHT EXCEPTION IN .CCTOR: " + e.ToString( ));
        }
    }

    public static object one;
    public static string two;
}
```

Discussion

To see this exception in action, run the following method:

```
public static void Main( )
{
    // Causes TypeInitializationException
    TestInit c = new TestInit( );

    // Replacing this method's code with the following line
    // will produce similar results.
    //TestInit.one.ToString( );
}
```

This code creates an instance of the TestInit class. You are assured that any static fields of the class will be initialized before this class is created, and any static constructors on the TestInit class will be called as well. The TestInit class is written as follows:

```
public class TestInit
{
    public static object one = null;
    public static string two = one.ToString( );
}
```

As you can see, a NullReferenceException should be thrown on the second static field, since it is trying to call ToString on an object set to null. If run from the development environment, you will see the exception dialog pop up. The exception dialog shown is depicted in Figure 7-4. The application is blocked until shut down manually through the IDE.

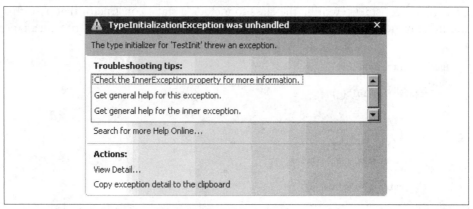

Figure 7-4. An unhandled TypeInitializationException dialog

However, if this executable is run from outside the development environment, the message box shown in Figure 7-5 is displayed and the application can either be shut down or debugged.

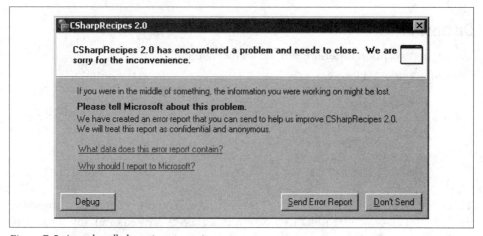

Figure 7-5. An unhandled runtime exception

Now, let's wrap a try-catch block around the Main method, as shown here:

```
public static void Main( )
{
    try
    {
        // Causes TypeInitializationException
        TestInit c = new TestInit( );
    }
    catch(Exception e)
    {
        Console.WriteLine("CAUGHT EXCEPTION IN CREATING METHOD: " + e.ToString( ));
    }
}
```

When this code is run inside the development environment, the TypeInitializationException is caught by the new exception handler that you added to the Main method. The text displayed by the exception handler is shown here:

```
CAUGHT EXCEPTION IN CREATING METHOD: System.TypeInitializationException: The type
initializer for 'TestInit' threw an exception. ---> System.NullReferenceException:
Object reference not set to an instance of an object.
   at CSharpRecipes.ExceptionHandling.TestInit..cctor() in C:\Book_2_0\Code\
CSharpRecipes\07_ExceptionHandling.cs:line 729
   --- End of inner exception stack trace ---
   at CSharpRecipes.ExceptionHandling.TestInit..ctor()
   at CSharpRecipes.ExceptionHandling.TestTypeInitFailure() in C:\ \Book_2_0\Code\
CSharpRecipes\07_ExceptionHandling.cs:line 708
```

The TypeInitializationException wraps the NullReferenceException that was the original exception thrown. The runtime provides the TypeInitializationException wrapper automatically.

A third method of trapping this exception is to use the exception event handler. This exception event handler is described in detail in Recipe 7.10. When only this exception handler is employed with no supporting try-catch or try-catch-finally blocks, the following events occur when running the executable in the development environment:

1. The exception dialog shown in Figure 7-4 is displayed.

2. The event exception handler intercepts the exception before the application is terminated. When the executable is run standalone, the message box in Figure 7-5 is displayed first. Then, the event exception handler intercepts the exception, and, finally, the application is terminated.

The second method seems to work best; use try-catch blocks at a minimum around code that will potentially cause static fields to initialize.

There is a way to eliminate the TypeInitializationException from the picture. You can simply initialize your class's or structure's static fields within the appropriate static constructor(s), first presented in the Solution section of this recipe and shown again here:

```
public class TestInit
{
    static TestInit( )
    {
        try
        {
            one = null;
            two = one.ToString( );
        }
        catch (Exception e)
        {
            Console.WriteLine("CAUGHT EXCEPTION IN .CCTOR: " + e.ToString( ));
        }
```

```
        }

        public static object one;
        public static string two;
    }
```

When this code is executed, the catch block captures the real exception and there is no fear of the application shutting down. The text displayed by the catch block is as follows:

```
CAUGHT EXCEPTION IN .CCTOR: System.NullReferenceException: Object reference not set
to an instance of an object.
    at Chapter_Code.TestInit..cctor( ) in c:\book cs cookbook\code\test.cs:line 191
```

This is much cleaner and more elegant than the other solutions. In addition, tracking down the source of the bug is much easier. As a note, this exception now operates in the same manner regardless of whether the application is being run in the development environment.

See Also

See the "Error Raising and Handling Guidelines" and "TypeInitializationException Class" topics in the MSDN documentation.

7.17 Handling Exceptions Thrown from an Asynchronous Delegate

Problem

When using a delegate asynchronously, you want to be notified if the delegate has thrown any exceptions.

Solution

Wrap the EndInvoke method of the delegate in a try/catch block:

```
using System;
using System.Threading;

public class AsyncAction
{
    public void PollAsyncDelegate( )
    {
        // Create the async delegate to call Method1 and call its BeginInvoke method.
        AsyncInvoke MI = new AsyncInvoke(TestAsyncInvoke.Method1);
        IAsyncResult AR = MI.BeginInvoke(null, null);

        // Poll until the async delegate is finished.
        while (!AR.IsCompleted)
        {
```

```
            System.Threading.Thread.Sleep(100);
            Console.Write('.');
        }
        Console.WriteLine("Finished Polling");

        // Call the EndInvoke method of the async delegate.
        try
        {
            int RetVal = MI.EndInvoke(AR);
            Console.WriteLine("RetVal: " + RetVal);
        }
        catch (Exception e)
        {
            Console.WriteLine(e.ToString( ));
        }
    }
}
```

The following code defines the AsyncInvoke delegate and the asynchronously invoked static method TestAsyncInvoke.Method1:

```
public delegate int AsyncInvoke( );

public class TestAsyncInvoke
{
    public static int Method1( )
    {
        throw (new Exception("Method1"));    // Simulate an exception being thrown.
    }
}
```

Discussion

If the code in the PollAsyncDelegate method did not contain a call to the delegate's EndInvoke method, the exception thrown in Method1 either would simply be discarded and never caught or, if the application had the top, level exception handlers wired up (Recipes 7.10 and 7.20) it would be caught. If EndInvoke is called, then this exception would occur when EndInvoke is called and could be caught there. This behavior is by design; for all unhandled exceptions that occur within the thread, the thread immediately returns to the thread pool and the exception is lost.

If a method that was called asynchronously through a delegate throws an exception, the only way to trap that exception is to include a call to the delegate's EndInvoke method and wrap this call in an exception handler. The EndInvoke method must be called to retrieve the results of the asynchronous delegate; in fact, the EndInvoke method must be called even if there are no results. These results can be obtained through a return value or any ref or out parameters of the delegate.

See Also

For more on calling delegates asynchronously, see Recipe 9.4.

For information about wiring up top-level exception handlers in your application, see Recipes 7.10 and 7.20.

7.18   Giving Exceptions the Extra Info They Need with Exception.Data

Problem

You want to send some additional information along with an exception.

Solution

Use the Data property on the System.Exception object to store key-value pairs of information relevant to the exception.

For example, say there is a System.ArgumentException being thrown from a section of code and you want to include the underlying cause and the length of time it took. The code would add two key-value pairs to the Exception.Data property by specifying the key in the indexer and then assigning the value.

In the example that follows, the Data for the irritable exception uses "Cause" and "Length" for its keys. Once the items have been set in the Data collection, the exception can be thrown and caught, and more data can be added in subsequent catch blocks for as many levels of exception handling as the exception is allowed to traverse.

```
try
{
    try
    {
        try
        {
            try
            {
                ArgumentException irritable =
                    new ArgumentException("I'm irritable!");
                irritable.Data["Cause"]="Computer crashed";
                irritable.Data["Length"]=10;
                throw irritable;
            }
            catch (Exception e)
            {
                // See if I can help...
                if(e.Data.Contains("Cause"))
                    e.Data["Cause"]="Fixed computer";
                throw;
            }
        }
        catch (Exception e)
```

```
        {
            e.Data["Comment"]="Always grumpy you are";
            throw;
        }
    }
    catch (Exception e)
    {
        e.Data["Reassurance"]="Error Handled";
        throw;
    }
}
```

The final catch block can then iterate over the Exception.Data collection and display all of the supporting data that has been gathered in the Data collection since the initial exception was thrown:

```
catch (Exception e)
{
    Console.WriteLine("Exception supporting data:");
    foreach(DictionaryEntry de in e.Data)
    {
        Console.WriteLine("\t{0} : {1}",de.Key,de.Value);
    }
}
```

Discussion

Exception.Data is an object that supports the IDictionary interface. This allows you to:

- Add and remove name-value pairs
- Clear the contents
- Search the collection to see if it contains a certain key
- Get an IDictionaryEnumerator for rolling over the collection items
- Index into the collection using the key
- Access an ICollection of all of the keys and all of the values separately

It is a very handy thing to be able to tack on code-specific data to the system exceptions, as it provides the ability to give a more complete picture of what happened in the code when the error occurred. The more information available to the poor soul (probably yourself) who is trying to figure out why the exception was thrown in the first place, the better the chance of it being fixed. Do yourself and your team a favor and give a little bit of extra information when throwing exceptions; you won't be sorry you did.

See Also

See the "Exception.Data Property" topic in the MSDN documentation.

7.19   Looking at Exceptions in a New Way Using Visualizers

Problem

You want to see all of the exception data laid out differently from Visual Studio's presentation, as your exceptions usually have multiple inner exceptions showing the root cause.

Solution

Create a debugger visualizer by deriving a class from `Microsoft.VisualStudio.DebuggerVisualizers.DialogDebuggerVisualizer` that can be plugged in to Visual Studio for all exception types. The easiest way to create one of these is to create a class library project and then add a class that derives from `DialogDebuggerVisualizer`. You will create the `ExceptionVisualizer` to show exceptions with a focus on getting right to the inner exception information. The `ExceptionDisplay` class is implemented as the presentation for the `ExceptionVisualizer`.

First, add a reference to the `Microsoft.VisualStudio.DebuggerVisualizers` namespace in the class library project that was created. Now add the using directive like this:

```
using Microsoft.VisualStudio.DebuggerVisualizers;
```

Next declare the `ExceptionVisualizer` class. The only method you must implement is `Show`, which passes in the `IDialogVisualizerService` and `IVisualizerObjectProvider` interfaces. To get the exception object that the visualizer is being asked to display, call the `GetObject` method on the `IVisualizerObjectProvider` interface and cast it to `System.Exception`. This exception is assigned to a WinForm called `ExceptionDisplay` by setting the `CurrentException` property. `ExceptionDisplay` is the display piece of the visualizer and will be described in detail shortly. The second method provided here is the `TestShowVisualizer` method. This is simply a test method to make it easier to develop the visualizer. It is rather challenging to develop the visualizer while running inside of Visual Studio (and the target program); by implementing this test method, you can create a simple test application to feed the exception directly to the visualizer through the use of the `VisualizerDevelopmentHost`. The `VisualizerDevelopmentHost` class allows you to "sandbox" your visualizer outside of Visual Studio while still providing it with the interfaces it expects from Visual Studio for data that can be provided to the host. `TestShowVisualizer` takes in an exception object and sets up the host, then calls `ShowVisualizer` to invoke the visualizer code with the given exception object:

```
namespace ExceptionalVisualizer
{
    public class ExceptionVisualizer : DialogDebuggerVisualizer
    {
        override protected void Show(IDialogVisualizerService windowService,
```

```
                IVisualizerObjectProvider objectProvider)
    {
        ExceptionDisplay display = new ExceptionDisplay( );
        display.CurrentException = (Exception)objectProvider.GetObject( );
        display.ShowDialog( );
    }

    public static void TestShowVisualizer(object exception)
    {
      VisualizerDevelopmentHost visualizerHost =
        new VisualizerDevelopmentHost(exception,
         typeof(ExceptionVisualizer));
      visualizerHost.ShowVisualizer( );
    }
  }
}
```

ExceptionDisplay is a Windows Form that allows for displaying an exception in a more
tabular format that shows very quickly the inner exception information, as shown in
Figure 7-6. The code for the ExceptionDisplay is found in the sample code in the
ExceptionDisplay.cs file.

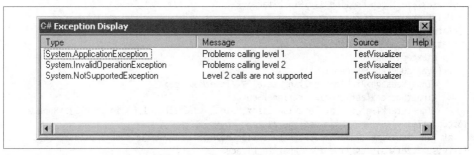

Figure 7-6. ExceptionDisplay window showing exception details

The context menu provides access to the Message Box shown in Figure 7-7 when you
right-click on one of the exception types. It allows you to see the call stack for the
exception.

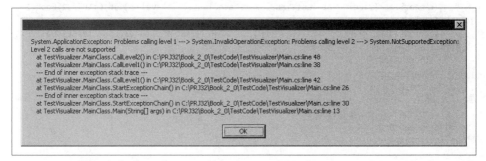

Figure 7-7. Call stack display information from ExceptionDisplay

Or the exception data can be copied to the clipboard, as shown in Figure 7-8.

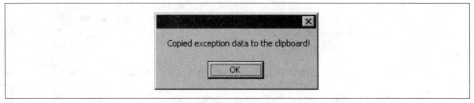

Figure 7-8. Result from copying exception data to the clipboard

The clipboard data appears in XML format, as shown in Example 7-7.

Example 7-7. Exception data in XML format

```
<ApplicationException_0>
  <Message>Problems calling level 1</Message>
  <Source>TestVisualizer</Source>
  <StackTrace>   at TestVisualizer.MainClass.StartExceptionChain() in C:\PRJ32\Book_2_0\
TestCode\TestVisualizer\Main.cs:line 30
   at TestVisualizer.MainClass.Main(String[] args) in C:\PRJ32\Book_2_0\TestCode\
TestVisualizer\Main.cs:line 13</StackTrace>
  <HelpLink />
  <TargetSite />
  <Data />
  <InnerExceptions>
    <InvalidOperationException_1>
      <InnerMessage>Problems calling level 2</InnerMessage>
      <InnerSource>TestVisualizer</InnerSource>
      <InnerStackTrace>   at TestVisualizer.MainClass.CallLevel1() in C:\PRJ32\Book_2_0\
TestCode\TestVisualizer\Main.cs:line 42
   at TestVisualizer.MainClass.StartExceptionChain() in C:\PRJ32\Book_2_0\TestCode\
TestVisualizer\Main.cs:line 26</InnerStackTrace>
      <InnerHelpLink />
      <InnerTargetSite />
      <InnerData />
      <NotSupportedException_2>
        <InnerMessage>Level 2 calls are not supported</InnerMessage>
        <InnerSource>TestVisualizer</InnerSource>
        <InnerStackTrace>   at TestVisualizer.MainClass.CallLevel2() in C:\PRJ32\Book_2_
0\TestCode\TestVisualizer\Main.cs:line 48
   at TestVisualizer.MainClass.CallLevel1() in C:\PRJ32\Book_2_0\TestCode\TestVisualizer\
Main.cs:line 38</InnerStackTrace>
        <InnerHelpLink />
        <InnerTargetSite />
        <InnerData />
      </NotSupportedException_2>
    </InvalidOperationException_1>
  </InnerExceptions>
</ApplicationException_0>
```

The other important part of setting up the visualizer infrastructure is that the class library needs to display the System.Diagnostics.DebuggerVisualizerAttribute for each object type it is going to support. To support System.Exception, the following attribute is necessary:

```
[assembly: System.Diagnostics.DebuggerVisualizer(
typeof(ExceptionalVisualizer.ExceptionVisualizer),
typeof(VisualizerObjectSource),
Target = typeof(System.Exception),
Description = "Exception Visualizer")]
```

The DebuggerVisualizerAttribute can have the properties listed in Table 7-3.

Table 7-3. DebuggerVisualizerAttribute properties

Property	Description
Description	Description of the visualizer
Target	The target type for the visualizer to be available for when the attribute is applied at the assembly level
TargetTypeName	Specifies the fully qualified type name when the attribute is applied at the assembly level
VisualizerObjectSourceTypeName	The fully qualified type name of the visualizer object
VisualizerTypeName	The fully qualified name of the visualizer type

Once the Visualizer is built, it needs to be deployed to one or both of the following locations:

- *Visual Studio Install Directory>\Common7\Packages\Debugger\Visualizers* (for all users)
- *My Documents>\Visual Studio\Visualizers* (for the current user)

This is where Visual Studio 2005 looks for the visualizers on debugging startup so that they can be loaded into the processes. The visualizer is accessed through a magnifying glass icon when the mouse hovers over an exception object in the debugger, as shown in Figure 7-9. Select the down arrow and choose the type of visualizer to use. These type names are taken from the Description property of the DebuggerVisualizerAttribute.

Figure 7-9. DebuggerVisualizer selection window in Visual Studio

Discussion

There is one big gotcha when building a debugger visualizer. If you pick a common base type (like System.Exception) and register the visualizer for that base type, you get only the base type occurrences. For System.Exception this means that the

ExceptionVisualizer would be brought up only in the visualizer list for System.
Exception exceptions. This being less than ideal for a more general purpose viewer
such as we're creating here, there is a bit more automation code to help create the
attributes to place on the ExceptionVisualizer.

Since the DebuggerVisualizerAttribute is at assembly scope, it is possible to have a
separate C# file (*.cs) that holds nothing but the attributes for the exception types
that the ExceptionVisualizer should support. To create this file with all of the exception types in the framework, the code enumerates the assemblies in the current
framework directory and creates a DebuggerVisualizerAttribute for each type with
System.Exception as the base class. To do this, a bit of code from Recipes 13.8, 20.4,
and 20.6 is borrowed to get the exception types as shown in GetExceptionTypes in
Example 7-8, which returns a List<Type>.

Example 7-8. GetExceptionTypes class

```
public static List<Type> GetExceptionTypes( )
{
    // Init our list
    List<Type> exceptionTypes = new List<Type>(100);
    List<string> typeFullNames = new List<string>(100);

    // Get the System.Exception type to reflect on.
    Type type = Type.GetType("System.Exception");
    // Get the framework directory (20.5).
    string frameworkDir = GetCurrentFrameworkPath( );
    string[] asmFiles = Directory.GetFiles(frameworkDir, "*.dll",
                        SearchOption.AllDirectories);
    foreach (string asmFile in asmFiles)
    {
        // Check the current module for subclasses of System.Exception.
        List<Type> subClasses = null;
        try
        {
            // Get the subclasses in this assembly for System.Exception
            // from Recipe 13.8.
            subClasses = GetSubClasses(asmFile, type);
        }
        catch (FileLoadException)
        {
            // Might not be a .NET assembly so skip it
            continue;
        }

        // Write out the subclasses for this type.
        if (subClasses.Count > 0)
        {
            // Store the new types from this assembly.
            foreach (Type t in subClasses)
            {
                if (!exceptionTypes.Contains(t))
```

Example 7-8. GetExceptionTypes class (continued)

```
            {
                // Skip crt exceptions.
                if ((t.FullName.IndexOf("<CrtImplementationDetails>") == -1)&&
                    (t.FullName.IndexOf("com.") == -1))
                {
                    // Some types have different AQNs but same FullName.
                    // Filter them out.
                    if (!typeFullNames.Contains(t.FullName))
                    {
                        // No nested exception classes as they are
                        // usually private
                        if (!t.FullName.Contains("+"))
                        {
                            typeFullNames.Add(t.FullName);

                            // Just work on public exceptions.
                            if ((t.Attributes & TypeAttributes.Public) != 0)
                                exceptionTypes.Add(t);
                        }
                    }
                }
            }
        }
    }
    return exceptionTypes;
}
```

Once you have the list of exceptions, then you can crank out the attributes in the C# file by rolling over the types and calling the `WriteDebuggerVisualizerAttribute` method for each exception we want the `ExceptionVisualizer` to support:

```
static void Main(string[] args)
{
    try
    {
        // Get all of the exception types.
        List<Type> exceptionTypes = GetExceptionTypes();
        List<Assembly> assembliesReferenced = new List<Assembly>(100);

        FileStream fs =
        new FileStream(@"..\..\..\ExceptionSupport.cs",
                FileMode.OpenOrCreate, FileAccess.Write);
        StreamWriter writer = new StreamWriter(fs);

        // Add the initial using statement.
        writer.WriteLine("// Generated on " + DateTime.Now.ToString("F") +
                " by ExceptionSupportCreator");
        writer.WriteLine("using Microsoft.VisualStudio.DebuggerVisualizers;");
        writer.WriteLine("");
        foreach (Type t in exceptionTypes)
        {
```

```
                if (!ignoreAssemblies.Contains(t.Assembly.FullName))
                {
                    if (!assembliesReferenced.Contains(t.Assembly))
                    {
                        writer.WriteLine("//Adding for assembly " +
                            t.Assembly.FullName);
                        assembliesReferenced.Add(t.Assembly);
                    }
                    WriteDebuggerVisualizerAttribute(t, writer);
                }
            }
            writer.WriteLine("");
            writer.WriteLine("");
            writer.WriteLine("// Add references for these assemblies");
            foreach (Assembly assm in assembliesReferenced)
            {
                writer.WriteLine("// {0}", assm.FullName);
            }
            writer.Flush();
            writer.Close();
        }
        catch (Exception ex)
        {
            Console.WriteLine(ex.ToString());
        }
    }
```

The `WriteDebuggerVisualizerAttribute` method is shown here:

```
public static void WriteDebuggerVisualizerAttribute(Type t, StreamWriter writer)
{
    // Write out the debugger visualizer attrib for this exception type
    writer.WriteLine("");
    writer.WriteLine("[assembly: System.Diagnostics.DebuggerVisualizer(");
    writer.WriteLine("typeof(ExceptionalVisualizer.ExceptionVisualizer),");
    writer.WriteLine("typeof(VisualizerObjectSource),");
    writer.WriteLine("Target = typeof(" + t.FullName + "),");
    writer.WriteLine("Description = \"Exception Visualizer\")]");
    writer.WriteLine("");
}
```

Once the *ExceptionSupport.cs* file is created, it is built into the class library containing the visualizer, and then the visualizer will support all of the various exception types. In order for this to compile correctly, the references to the framework assemblies with the exceptions must be added.

See Also

See Recipes 13.8, 20.4, and 20.6; see the "DebuggerVisualizerAttribute" topic in the MSDN documentation.

7.20   Dealing with Unhandled Exceptions in WinForms Applications

Problem

You have a WinForms-based application in which you want to catch and log any unhandled exceptions on any thread.

Solution

You need to hook up handlers for both the `System.Windows.Forms.Application.ThreadException` event *and* the `System.AppDomain.UnhandledException` event. Both of these events need to be hooked up, as the WinForms support in the Framework does a lot of exception trapping itself. It exposes the `System.Windows.Forms.Application.ThreadException` event to allow you to get any unhandled exceptions that happen on the UI thread that the WinForms and their events are running on. In spite of its deceptive name, the `System.Windows.Forms.Application.ThreadException` event handler will *not* catch unhandled exceptions on worker threads constructed by the program or from `ThreadPool` threads. In order to catch all of those possible routes for unhandled exceptions in a WinForms application, you need to hook up a handler for the `System.AppDomain.UnhandledException` event that does catch those (but not the UI thread ones that `System.Windows.Forms.Application.ThreadException` does).

To hook up the necessary event handlers to catch all of your unhandled exceptions in a WinForms application, add the following code to the `Main` function in your application:

```
static void Main( )
{
    // Adds the event handler to catch any exceptions that happen
    // in the main UI thread.
    Application.ThreadException +=
        new ThreadExceptionEventHandler(OnThreadException);

    // Add the event handler for all threads in the AppDomain except
    // for the main UI thread.
    AppDomain.CurrentDomain.UnhandledException +=
        new UnhandledExceptionEventHandler(CurrentDomain_UnhandledException);

    Application.EnableVisualStyles( );
    Application.Run(new Form1( ));
}
```

The `System.AppDomain.UnhandledException` event handler is hooked up to the current `AppDomain` by using the `AppDomain.CurrentDomain` property, which gives access to the current `AppDomain`. The `ThreadException` handler for the application is accessed through the `Application.ThreadException` property.

The event handler code is established in the `CurrentDomain_UnhandledException` and `OnThreadException` handler methods. See Recipe 7.10 for more information on the `UnhandledExceptionEventHandler`. The `ThreadExceptionEventHandler` is passed the sender object and a `ThreadExceptionEventArgs` object. `ThreadExceptionEventArgs` has an Exception property that contains the unhandled exception from the WinForms UI thread.

```
// Handles the exception event for all other threads
static void CurrentDomain_UnhandledException(object sender,
                             UnhandledExceptionEventArgs e)
{
    // Just show the exception details.
    MessageBox.Show("CurrentDomain_UnhandledException: " +
            e.ExceptionObject.ToString());
}

// Handles the exception event from a UI thread
static void OnThreadException(object sender, ThreadExceptionEventArgs t)
{
    // Just show the exception details.
    MessageBox.Show("OnThreadException: " + t.Exception.ToString());
}
```

Discussion

Exceptions are the primary way to convey errors in .NET, so when you build an application it is imperative that there be a final line of defense against unhandled exceptions. An unhandled exception will crash the program (even if it looks a bit nicer in .NET); this is not the impression you wish to make on your customers. It would have been nice to have one event to hook up to for all unhandled exceptions. The `AppDomain.UnhandledException` event comes pretty close to that, but having to do handle one extra event isn't the end of the world either. In coding event handlers for both `AppDomain.UnhandledException` and `Application.ThreadException`, you can easily call a single handler that writes the exception information to the event log, the debug stream, or custom trace logs or even sends you an email with the information. The possibilities are limited only by how you want to handle errors that can happen to any program given enough exposure.

See Also

See Recipe 7.10; see the "Error Raising and Handling Guidelines," "Thread-ExceptionEventHandler Delegate," and "UnhandledExceptionEventHandler Delegate" topics in the MSDN documentation.

CHAPTER 8

Diagnostics

8.0   Introduction

The FCL contains many classes to obtain diagnostic information about your application, as well as the environment it is running in. In fact, there are so many classes that a namespace, System.Diagnostics, was created to contain all of them. This chapter contains recipes for instrumenting your application with debug/trace information, obtaining process information, using the built-in event log, and taking advantage of performance counters.

Debugging (using the Debug class) is turned on by default in debug builds only, and tracing (using the Trace class) is turned on by default in both debug and release builds. These defaults allow you to ship your application instrumented with tracing code using the Trace class. You ship your code with tracing compiled in but turned off in the configuration so that the tracing code is not called (for performance reasons) unless it is a server-side application (where the value of the instrumentation may outweigh the performance hit). If a problem that you cannot re-create on your development computer occurs on a production machine, you can enable tracing and allow the tracing information to be dumped to a file. This file can be inspected to help pinpoint the real problem. This usage is discussed at length in Recipes 8.1 and 8.2.

Since both the Debug and Trace classes contain the same members with the same names, they can be interchanged in your code by renaming Debug to Trace and vice versa. Most of the recipes in this chapter use the Trace class; you can modify those recipes so that they use the Debug class by replacing each Trace with Debug in the code.

8.1   Controlling Tracing Output in Production Code

Problem

Mysterious bugs often appear at the client's site, even after the application is thoroughly tested. Most of the time these bugs are difficult, if not impossible, to reproduce on your development machine. Knowing this, you want an application with built-in instrumentation that's off by default but can easily be turned on when you need it.

Solution

Use the Trace class for any tracing code that you might need to turn on after your application has been deployed. To turn on tracing at a client's site, provide the client with an application configuration file such as this one:

```
<?xml version="1.0" encoding="utf-8" ?>
<configuration>
    <system.diagnostics>
        <switches>
            <add name="DatabaseSwitch" value="4"/>
            <!-- 4 == TraceLevel.Verbose -->
        </switches>

        <trace autoflush = "true" indentsize = "2">
            <listeners>
                <add name = "MyListener"
                    type = "System.Diagnostics.TextWriterTraceListener"
                    initializeData = " MyFileName.log"/>
            </listeners>
        </trace>
    </system.diagnostics>
</configuration>
```

Discussion

Allowing tracing code to be enabled and used at a client site can be extremely useful when debugging problems in release code. This technique is even more useful when the problem cannot easily be reproduced in-house. For this reason, it is—in some cases—a wise practice to use the Trace class instead of the Debug class when adding tracing code to your application.

To control the trace output at a client site, you can use an XML config file. This XML file must have the same base name as the executable that is to use these switches, followed by an extension of *.exe.config*. For example, if the executable name were *Accounting.exe*, the configuration file would be named *Accounting.exe.config*. This file should be placed in the same directory as the executable *Accounting.exe*.

The application configuration file always consists of the following two outer elements for diagnostic information:

```
<configuration>
    <system.diagnostics>
        ...
    </system.diagnostics>
</configuration>
```

(The configuration element may contain other child elements besides the system. diagnostics element.)

Within these elements, the switches and trace elements may be added. These two elements contain information specific to switches and listeners. If your code contains a TraceSwitch (as shown in the next example) or BooleanSwitch object—or any other type derived from the Switch class—you can control this object's trace-level setting through the <switches> element in the configuration file:

```
private static TraceSwitch ts = new TraceSwitch("DatabaseSwitch",
        "Only allow database transactions to be logged");
```

The listeners element shown in the Solution adds a new TraceListener-derived object to the listeners collection. Learn more about TraceListener in Recipe 8.2. Any Trace or Debug statements will use this new listener.

The switches element of the Solution can contain the three elements defined here:

> Clears any previously added switch. In the world of ASP.NET, where *web.config* files are nested, this can be useful to clear settings that are inherited from previous configuration files.

<add name="*Switch_Name*" value="*Number*"/>
> Adds new switch initialization information to be used at runtime. The name attribute defines the name of the switch that is used in your code. The value attribute is set to a number that turns the switch either on or off, in the case of a BooleanSwitch class, or defines the switch level (e.g., the amount of output you wish to receive), in the case of a TraceSwitch class. To turn on a BooleanSwitch, use a nonzero value (negative numbers work here, too); to turn it off, use zero.

<remove name="*Switch_Name*"/>
> Removes switch initialization information at runtime. The name attribute defines the name of the switch that is used in your code.

Immediately after the switches tags in the Solution are the trace tags, although the ordering of these tags is up to you. The trace tags can contain the following two optional attributes:

autoflush = true|false
> Indicates whether the listener automatically flushes its buffer after every write (true) or not (false)

indentsize = "4"
> Specifies the number of indent characters to use when indenting the output

Within the trace tags are the listeners tags, which, in turn, can contain any of the following defined tags:

> Clears any previously added listeners. This tag also removes the DefaultTraceListener from the listeners collection.

```
<add name= "Listener_Name" type="Listener_Fully_Scoped_Type_Name"
initializeData="String_Passed_Into_CTOR"/>
```

Adds a new listener to any Trace and Debug classes used in your application. The name attribute defines the name of the listener that is used in your code. The type attribute is set to the listener's class name. The optional initializeData attribute allows a string to be passed in to the constructor of this listener. If you are using a custom listener, you will need to include a constructor that accepts a string as the only argument to prevent an exception from being thrown.

```
<remove name = "MyListener"/>
```

Removes a listener at runtime. The name attribute defines the name of the listener to be removed. This could be useful if another configuration file, such as the *machine.config* file, has already added a listener or if any listeners were created through your application's code. If more than one listener is added, the output will be written out twice—once for each listener.

Regardless of whether your code defines TRACE and/or DEBUG, the code will attempt to access this file for switch initialization information if a class derived from Switch is instantiated. The Switch class is discussed in Recipe 8.3. If you wish to prevent this behavior, place any code that instantiates a switch class inside of a method decorated with the ConditionalAttribute attribute:

```
public class Traceable
{
    BooleanSwitch DBSwitch = null;
    BooleanSwitch UISwitch = null;
    BooleanSwitch exceptionSwitch = null;

    [System.Diagnostics.ConditionalAttribute("TRACE")]
    public void EnableTracing( )
    {
        DBSwitch = new BooleanSwitch("DatabaseSwitch",
                "Switch for database tracing");
        UISwitch = new BooleanSwitch("UISwitch",
                "Switch for user interface tracing");
        exceptionSwitch = new BooleanSwitch("ExceptionSwitch",
                    "Switch for tracing thrown exceptions");
    }
}
```

The ConditionalAttribute attribute prevents your application from calling the EnableTracing method when TRACE is undefined and thereby keeps the switches from being used.

In addition to the application configuration file (*MyApp.exe.config*), a *machine.config* file is also located in the directory *<Common Language Runtime install path>\ CONFIG*. The configuration tags and all of their containing elements may be placed in this file as well. However, doing so will enable these switches and listeners on a machinewide level. This can cause applications that define their own listeners to behave strangely, especially if the listeners are duplicated. Additionally, the application will look for configuration information in the application configuration file first and the *machine.config* file second.

The application configuration file and the machine configuration file are both case-sensitive. Be sure that your tag names and their attributes are in the correct case. However, the string assigned to the name attribute does not seem to be case-sensitive, while other strings assigned to attributes are.

See Also

See the "Trace and Debug Settings Schema" topic in the MSDN documentation.

8.2 Providing Fine-Grained Control over Debugging/Tracing Output

Problem

Your application consists of multiple components. You need, at specific times, to turn on debug/trace output for a select few components, while leaving all other debug/trace output turned off. In addition, you need control over the type and amount of information that is produced by the Trace/Debug statements.

Solution

Use the BooleanSwitch class with an application configuration file (*.config*). The following method creates three switches for your application: one that controls tracing for database calls, one that controls tracing for UI components, and one that controls tracing for any exceptions that are thrown by the application:

```
public class Traceable
{
    BooleanSwitch DBSwitch = null;
    BooleanSwitch UISwitch = null;
    BooleanSwitch exceptionSwitch = null;

    [System.Diagnostics.ConditionalAttribute("TRACE")]
    public void EnableTracing( )
    {
        DBSwitch = new BooleanSwitch("DatabaseSwitch",
                "Switch for database tracing");
        Console.WriteLine("DBSwitch Enabled = " + DBSwitch.Enabled);

        UISwitch = new BooleanSwitch("UISwitch",
                "Switch for user interface tracing");
        Console.WriteLine("UISwitch Enabled = " + UISwitch.Enabled);

        exceptionSwitch = new BooleanSwitch("ExceptionSwitch",
```

```
                                    "Switch for tracing thrown exceptions");
            Console.WriteLine("ExceptionSwitch Enabled = " + exceptionSwitch.Enabled);
    }
}
```

After creating each switch, the Enabled property is displayed, indicating whether the switch is on or off.

Creating these switches without an application configuration file results in every switch being disabled. To control what state each switch is set to, use an application configuration file, shown here:

```
<?xml version="1.0" encoding="utf-8" ?>
<configuration>
    <system.diagnostics>
        <switches>
            <clear/>
            <add name="DatabaseSwitch" value="1" />
            <add name="UISwitch" value="0" />
            <add name="ExceptionSwitch" value="0" />
        </switches>
    </system.diagnostics>
</configuration>
```

The TraceSwitch class can also be used with an application configuration file (*AppName.exe.config*). The following method creates a new TraceSwitch object with a level assigned by the application configuration file:

```
public class Traceable
{
    TraceSwitch DBFilterSwitch = null;
    TraceSwitch UIFilterSwitch = null;
    TraceSwitch exceptionFilterSwitch = null;

    public void SetTracingFilter( )
    {
        DBFilterSwitch = new TraceSwitch("DatabaseFilter",
                        "Filter database output");
        Console.WriteLine("DBFilterSwitch Level = " + DBFilterSwitch.Level);

        UIFilterSwitch = new TraceSwitch("UIFilter",
                        "Filter user interface output");
        Console.WriteLine("UIFilterSwitch Level = " + UIFilterSwitch.Level);

        exceptionFilterSwitch = new TraceSwitch("ExceptionFilter",
                            "Filter exception output");
        Console.WriteLine("exceptionFilterSwitch Level = "
                            + exceptionFilterSwitch.Level);
    }
}
```

After creating each filter switch, the Level property is displayed to indicate the switch's level.

Creating these switches at this point results in every switch's level being set to zero. To turn them on, use an application configuration file, shown here:

```xml
<?xml version="1.0" encoding="utf-8" ?>
<configuration>
    <system.diagnostics>
        <switches>
            <clear/>
            <add name="DatabaseFilter" value="4" />
            <add name="UIFilter" value="0" />
            <add name="ExceptionFilter" value="1" />
        </switches>
    </system.diagnostics>
</configuration>
```

This XML file contains a nested tag called switches. This tag defines switch names and sets a value indicating the level of the switch. The TraceSwitch class accepts the five predefined trace levels shown in Table 8-1. The level of the TraceSwitch can be set through code, but that defeats the flexibility of using a configuration file.

Table 8-1. The TraceSwitch class's tracing levels

Level name	Value	Default
Off	0	Yes
Error	1	No
Warning	2	No
Info	3	No
Verbose	4	No

For more information on the application configuration file, see Recipe 8.1.

Discussion

Turning tracing on or off involves the BooleanSwitch class. When the BooleanSwitch is created, it attempts to locate a switch with the same name as the *displayName* parameter in either the *machine.config* or application configuration file. If it cannot locate this name in either file, BooleanSwitch.Enabled is set to false.

The application configuration file for a WinForms- or Console-based application is an XML file named with the assembly's name followed by *.exe.config*. An ASP.NET-based web application can have multiple *web.config* files (one in each directory of the application). An application will automatically use the configuration file(s) that is (are) appropriate; however, the top-level configuration file must be in the same main directory as the application. Notice the switches tag nested inside the system. diagnostics element. This tag allows switches to be added and their values set. For Boolean switches, a zero turns the switch off, and any other positive or negative number turns it on. The Enabled property of the BooleanSwitch can be set through code or by setting the value in the config file.

This XML file must have the same name as the executable using these switches, followed by *.config*. For example, if the executable name were *Accounting.exe*, the configuration file would be named *Accounting.exe.config*. This file should be placed in the same directory as the executable *Accounting.exe*. For more information on this file, see Recipe 8.1.

The application configuration file can also set trace and debug output levels in this same switches tag. These levels identify the scope of the output, for example, if the output will contain only warnings, only errors, only informational messages, or some combination thereof. The level specified is the maximum trace level for the switch so it includes all levels below it up through that level. Of course, this is only an example; you may define your own levels as well. For more information on controlling these output levels, see Recipe 8.3.

The TraceSwitch class operates similarly to the BooleanSwitch class, except that the TraceSwitch class encapsulates the available levels that control the type and amount of debug/trace output. The BooleanSwitch class is simply an on/off switch used to enable or disable debugging/tracing.

When the TraceSwitch is created, it attempts to locate a switch with the same name as the *displayName* parameter in either the *machine.config* or application configuration files. If it cannot locate this name in either file, the TraceSwitch.Level property is set to zero.

The application configuration file can also enable or disable trace and debug output in this same switches tag. For more information on this topic, see Recipe 8.1.

See Also

See Recipes 8.1 and 8.3; see the "BooleanSwitch Class" and "Trace and Debug Settings Schema" topics in the MSDN documentation.

8.3   Creating Your Own Custom Switch Class

Problem

The BooleanSwitch and TraceSwitch classes defined in the FCL may not always have the required flexibility or fine-grained control that you need. You want to create a switch class that provides more control and flexibility. For example, you might want to create a class that allows you to set more precise trace levels than those supported by the TraceSwitch class, which are:

```
TraceError
TraceWarning
TraceInfo
TraceVerbose
```

However, you need a finer-grained set of levels, such as those shown in Table 8-2.

Table 8-2. A set of custom trace levels

Disable	MinorError
Note	MediumError
Warning	CriticalError

Solution

You can create your own switch class that inherits from System.Diagnostics.Switch and provides the level of control that you need. For example, creating a class that allows you to set more precise trace levels than those supported by the TraceSwitch class involves the following steps:

1. Define a set of enumerated values that represent the levels to be supported by your switch class. The following definition implements the levels listed in Table 8-2:

```
public enum AppSpecificSwitchLevel
{
    Disable = 0,
    Note = 1,
    Warning = 2,
    MinorError = 3,
    MediumError = 4,
    CriticalError = 5
}
```

2. Define a class, such as AppSpecificSwitch (shown in Example 8-1), that inherits from System.Diagnostics.Switch and sets your own levels.

Example 8-1. AppSpecificSwitch, a custom switch class

```
public class AppSpecificSwitch : Switch
{
    protected AppSpecificSwitchLevel level = 0;

    public AppSpecificSwitch(string displayName, string description)
        : base(displayName, description)
    {
        Level = (AppSpecificSwitchLevel)base.SwitchSetting;
    }

    // Read/write Level property
    public AppSpecificSwitchLevel Level
    {
        get
        {
            return level;
        }
```

Example 8-1. AppSpecificSwitch, a custom switch class (continued)

```
    set
    {
        if (value < AppSpecificSwitchLevel.Disable)
        {
            level = AppSpecificSwitchLevel.Disable;
        }
        else if (value > AppSpecificSwitchLevel.CriticalError)
        {
            level = AppSpecificSwitchLevel.CriticalError;
        }
        else
        {
            level = value;
        }
    }
}

// Read-only properties for the AppSpecificSwitchLevel enum
public bool Disable
{
    get
    {
        if (level <= AppSpecificSwitchLevel.Disable)
        {
            return (true);
        }
        else
        {
            return (false);
        }
    }
}

public bool Note
{
    get
    {
        if (level <= AppSpecificSwitchLevel.Note)
        {
            return (true);
        }
        else
        {
            return (false);
        }
    }
}

public bool Warning
{
    get
    {
```

Example 8-1. AppSpecificSwitch, a custom switch class (continued)

```
                if (level <= AppSpecificSwitchLevel.Warning)
                {
                    return (true);
                }
                else
                {
                    return (false);
                }
            }
        }

        public bool MinorError
        {
            get
            {
                if (level <= AppSpecificSwitchLevel.MinorError)
                {
                    return (true);
                }
                else
                {
                    return (false);
                }
            }
        }

        public bool MediumError
        {
            get
            {
                if (level <= AppSpecificSwitchLevel.MediumError)
                {
                    return (true);
                }
                else
                {
                    return (false);
                }
            }
        }

        public bool CriticalError
        {
            get
            {
                if (level <= AppSpecificSwitchLevel.CriticalError)
                {
                    return (true);
                }
                else
                {
                    return (false);
```

Example 8-1. AppSpecificSwitch, a custom switch class (continued)

```
        }
    }
  }
}
```

3. In code, you can instantiate this custom class by invoking its constructor:

```
AppSpecificSwitch appSwitch = new AppSpecificSwitch("MyApplication",
                          "My Application Specific Switch");
```

4. Set the switch in the application configuration file. For example, the following configuration file sets the level of your custom switch to `AppSpecificSwitchLevel.CriticalLevel`:

```
<?xml version="1.0" encoding="utf-8" ?>
<configuration>
    <system.diagnostics>
        <switches>
            <add name="MyApplication" value="5" />
        </switches>
    </system.diagnostics>
</configuration>
```

More information on configuration files can be found in Recipes 8.1 and 8.2.

Discussion

The `BooleanSwitch` and `TraceSwitch` classes defined in the FCL might not always have the flexibility that you need. In these cases, you can create a class that inherits from the `Switch` class—the abstract base class of all switch type classes.

The critical part of creating a custom switch class is the constructor. The constructor must call its base class constructor using the `:base()` syntax. If this syntax is omitted, a compiler error will appear, indicating that there is no default constructor to call on the base class `Switch`. You might notice that the `Switch` class contains a single public constructor that accepts two string parameters. This is designed so that you must use this constructor when building an object of this type or any type derived from it. Calling the base class's constructor also allows the application configuration file to be searched, if one exists, for any initialization value for this switch object.

You can circumvent the configuration file search by writing the constructor as follows:

```
public AppSpecificSwitch(string displayName, string description)
    : base("", description)
{
    this.Level = (AppSpecificSwitchLevel)base.SwitchSetting;
}
```

The other item of interest in this constructor is the one line of code in its body. This line of code grabs the level information acquired from the application configuration file and sets this inherited class's `Level` property to this value. This line is required because the base class is the one that receives the initialization information from a configuration file, not the inherited class.

This class contains several other properties. The first is the Level property, which gets and sets the current level of this object. The levels are defined in the AppSpecificSwitchLevel enumeration. This class also contains a read-only property for each element in the AppSpecificSwitchLevel enumeration. These can be used to query this object to determine whether its various levels are set.

See Also

See Recipes 8.1 and 8.2; see the "Switch Class" and "Trace and Debug Settings Schema" topics in the MSDN documentation.

8.4   Compiling Blocks of Code Conditionally

Problem

Specific blocks of code will be used only in a certain build configuration for your application. These blocks of code should not be compiled into other builds of the application. You need a way to conditionally compile specific blocks of code based on the type of build.

Solution

There are two devices for allowing or preventing code from being compiled. The first is to use the C# preprocessor directives. The available preprocessor directives are:

```
#define
#undef
#if
#elif
#else
#endif
```

The #define and #undef preprocessor directives define and undefine symbols. These symbols are then used by the #if and #elif preprocessor directives to determine whether the blocks of code they wrap are to be compiled. While it is possible to use this device, it is more likely that the second one (discussed next) would be used to support multiple build configurations.

The second device for allowing or preventing code from being compiled is to use the ConditionalAttribute attribute. This allows a method to be compiled based on a defined symbol. This attribute specifies a method as conditionally compiled in the following manner:

```
#define TRACE

...

[ConditionalAttribute("TRACE")]
```

```
public void TraceHelp(string message)
{
    ...
}
```

The TraceHelp method is compiled only when the TRACE preprocessing identifier is defined.

Discussion

The ConditionalAttribute attribute can be used only on methods. It prevents them from being compiled and called at runtime when the preprocessor identifier passed to the ConditionalAttribute constructor is undefined. Properties, indexers, and other members cannot have this attribute.

Another limitation of this attribute is that it can be placed only on a method that returns void. This makes sense, since code that invokes this method doesn't expect a return value and will run successfully whether or not the method is invoked. For example, in the code:

```
int retValue = Car.GetModelNumber( );
```

if the GetModelNumber method is not compiled, then this code will not be able to function correctly.

Along these same lines, a method marked as override cannot be marked with the ConditionalAttribute attribute. However, the virtual method that a method overrides may be marked with the ConditionalAttribute attribute. If the virtual method is marked with this attribute, all methods overriding it are compiled and called based on whether the virtual method is compiled. In other words, the overriding methods are implicitly marked with the same ConditionalAttribute attribute as the virtual method. While this is an interesting side effect of marking the base virtual method, it could cause confusion among developers debugging assemblies that override this method. If they are not familiar with this, the method may simply appear to be missing for them in certain builds depending on what the conditional attribute is specified as. As such, it is not recommended that you do this in practice.

#define and #undef apply only to preprocessor identifiers within a file scope, whereas the /define: compiler option defines preprocessor identifiers for all files in a project. #define and #undef also take precedence over the /define: compiler option. For instance, if the project's /define: compiler option defined TRACE, and one of the files that project contains has the code:

```
#undef TRACE
```

then TRACE will be defined for all files except the one containing the #undef TRACE directive.

To set the project's /define: compiler option in Visual Studio .NET, right-click on the project name in the Solution Explorer tool window, then click the Properties menu item. This step will display the Property Pages dialog box for this project. Next, click the Configuration Properties node in the tree on the left side of this dialog box. In the control to the right of this tree, find the line entitled Conditional Compilation Constants. On this line, you may add or remove any preprocessor identifiers that you want.

The #if and #elif directives determine what code within a member is to be compiled. For example:

```
public void MyMethod( )
{
    #if (TRACE)
        Method1( );
    #elif (DEBUG)
        Method2( );
    #else
        Method3( );
    #endif
}
```

MyMethod will call Method1 when TRACE is defined, Method2 if TRACE is undefined and DEBUG is defined, and Method3 if both TRACE and DEBUG are undefined.

See Also

See the "C# Preprocessor Directives" and "ConditionalAttribute Class" topics in the MSDN documentation.

8.5   Determining Whether a Process Has Stopped Responding

Problem

You need to watch one or more processes to determine whether the user interface has stopped responding to the system. This functionality is similar to the column in the Task Manager that displays the text Responding or Not Responding, depending on the state of the application.

Solution

Use the method and enumeration shown in Example 8-2 to determine whether a process has stopped responding.

Example 8-2. Determining whether a process has stopped responding

```
public static ProcessRespondingState IsProcessResponding(Process process)
{
    if (process.MainWindowHandle == IntPtr.Zero)
    {
```

```
            Trace.WriteLine("{0} does not have a MainWindowHandle",
                process.ProcessName);
            return ProcessRespondingState.Unknown;
        }
        else
        {
            // This process has a MainWindowHandle.
            if (!process.Responding)
            {
                Trace.WriteLine("{0} is not responding.",process.ProcessName);
                return ProcessRespondingState.NotResponding;
            }
            else
            {
                Trace.WriteLine("{0} is responding.",process.ProcessName);
                return ProcessRespondingState.Responding;
            }
        }
    }
}

public enum ProcessRespondingState
{
    Responding,
    NotResponding,
    Unknown
}
```

Discussion

The IsProcessResponding method accepts a single parameter, *process*, identifying a process. The Responding property is then called on the Process object represented by the *process* parameter. This property returns a ProcessRespondingState enumeration value to indicate that a process is currently responding (Responding), that it is not currently responding (NotResponding), or that response cannot be determined for this process as there is no main window handle (Unknown)...

The Responding property always returns true if the process in question does not have a MainWindowHandle. Processes such as Idle, spoolsv, Rundll32, and svchost do not have a main window handle and therefore the Responding property always returns true for them. To weed out these processes, you can use the MainWindowHandle property of the Process class, which returns the handle of the main window for a process. If this property returns zero, the process has no main window.

To determine whether all processes on a machine are responding, you can call the IsProcessResponding method as follows:

```
MyObject.ProcessRespondingState state;
foreach (Process proc in Process.GetProcesses())
```

```
        {
            state = MyObject.IsProcessResponding(proc);
            if (state == MyObject.ProcessRespondingState.NotResponding)
            {
                Console.WriteLine("{0} is not responding.",proc.ProcessName);
            }
        }
    }
```

This code snippet iterates over all processes currently running on your system. The static `GetProcesses` method of the `Process` class takes no parameters and returns an array of `Process` objects with information for all processes running on your system. Each `Process` object is then passed in to your `IsProcessResponding` method to determine whether it is responding. Other static methods on the `Process` class that retrieve `Process` objects are `GetProcessById`, `GetCurrentProcess`, and `GetProcessesByName`.

See Also

See the "Process Class" topic in the MSDN documentation.

8.6   Using Event Logs in Your Application

Problem

You need to add the ability for your application to log events that occur in your application, such as startup, shutdown, critical errors, and even security breaches. Along with reading and writing to a log, you need the ability to create, clear, close, and remove logs from the event log.

Your application might need to keep track of several logs at one time. For example, your application might use a custom log to track specific events, such as startup and shutdown, as they occur in your application. To supplement the custom log, your application could make use of the security log already built into the event log system to read/write security events that occur in your application.

Support for multiple logs comes in handy when one log needs to be created and maintained on the local computer and another duplicate log needs to be created and maintained on a remote machine. This remote machine might contain logs of all running instances of your application on each user's machine. An administrator could use these logs to quickly find any problems that occur or discover if security is breached in your application. In fact, an application could be run in the background on the remote administrative machine that watches for specific log entries to be written to this log from any user's machine. Recipe 8.9 uses an event mechanism to watch for entries written to an event log and could easily be used to enhance this recipe.

Solution

Use the event log built into the Microsoft Windows operating system to record specific events that occur infrequently. The AppEvents class shown in Example 8-3 contains all the methods needed to create and use an event log in your application.

Example 8-3. Creating and using an event log

```
using System;
using System.Diagnostics;

public class AppEvents
{
    // Constructors
    public AppEvents(string logName) :
        this(logName, Process.GetCurrentProcess( ).ProcessName, ".") {}

    public AppEvents(string logName, string source) : this(logName, source, ".") {}

    public AppEvents(string logName, string source, string machineName)
    {
        this.logName = logName;
        this.source = source;
        this.machineName = machineName;

        if (!EventLog.SourceExists(source, machineName))
        {
            EventSourceCreationData sourceData =
                new EventSourceCreationData(source, logName);
            sourceData.MachineName = machineName;

            EventLog.CreateEventSource(sourceData);
        }

        log = new EventLog(logName, machineName, source);
        log.EnableRaisingEvents = true;
    }


    // Fields
    private EventLog log = null;
    private string source = "";
    private string logName = "";
    private string machineName = ".";


    // Properties
    public string Name
    {
        get{return (logName);}
    }

    public string SourceName
```

Example 8-3. Creating and using an event log (continued)

```
{
    get{return (source);}
}

public string Machine
{
    get{return (machineName);}
}


// Methods
public void WriteToLog(string message, EventLogEntryType type,
    CategoryType category, EventIDType eventID)
{
    if (log == null)
    {
        throw (new ArgumentNullException("log",
            "This Event Log has not been opened or has been closed."));
    }

    log.WriteEntry(message, type, (int)eventID, (short)category);
}

public void WriteToLog(string message, EventLogEntryType type,
    CategoryType category, EventIDType eventID, byte[] rawData)
{
    if (log == null)
    {
        throw (new ArgumentNullException("log",
            "This Event Log has not been opened or has been closed."));
    }

    log.WriteEntry(message, type, (int)eventID, (short)category, rawData);
}

public EventLogEntryCollection GetEntries( )
{
    if (log == null)
    {
        throw (new ArgumentNullException("log",
            "This Event Log has not been opened or has been closed."));
    }

    return (log.Entries);
}

public void ClearLog( )
{
    if (log == null)
    {
        throw (new ArgumentNullException("log",
            "This Event Log has not been opened or has been closed."));
```

Example 8-3. Creating and using an event log (continued)

```
        }

        log.Clear( );
    }

    public void CloseLog( )
    {
        if (log == null)
        {
            throw (new ArgumentNullException("log",
                "This Event Log has not been opened or has been closed."));
        }

        log.Close( );
        log = null;
    }

    public void DeleteLog( )
    {
        if (EventLog.SourceExists(source, machineName))
        {
            EventLog.DeleteEventSource(source, machineName);
        }

        if (logName != "Application" &&
            logName != "Security" &&
            logName != "System")
        {
            if (EventLog.Exists(logName, machineName))
            {
                EventLog.Delete(logName, machineName);
            }
        }

        if (log != null)
        {
            log.Close( );
            log = null;
        }
    }
}
```

The EventIDType and CategoryType enumerations used in this class are defined as follows:

```
    public enum EventIDType
    {
        NA = 0,
        Read = 1,
        Write = 2,
        ExceptionThrown = 3,
        BufferOverflowCondition = 4,
```

```
    SecurityFailure = 5,
    SecurityPotentiallyCompromised = 6
}

public enum CategoryType : short
{
    None = 0,
    WriteToDB = 1,
    ReadFromDB = 2,
    WriteToFile = 3,
    ReadFromFile = 4,
    AppStartUp = 5,
    AppShutDown = 6,
    UserInput = 7
}
```

Discussion

The `AppEvents` class created for this recipe provides applications with an easy-to-use interface for creating, using, and deleting single or multiple event logs in your application. Support for multiple logs comes in handy when one log needs to be created and maintained on the local computer and another duplicate log needs to be created and maintained on a remote machine. This remote machine might contain logs of all running instances of your application on each user's machine. An administrator could use these logs to quickly discover if any problems occur or security is breached in your application. In fact, an application could be run in the background on the remote administrative machine that watches for specific log entries to be written to this log from any user's machine. Recipe 8.9 uses an event mechanism to watch for entries written to an event log and could easily be used to enhance this recipe.

The methods of the `AppEvents` class are described as follows:

`WriteToLog`
:   This method is overloaded to allow an entry to be written to the event log with or without a byte array containing raw data.

`GetEntries`
:   Returns all the event log entries for this event log in an `EventLogEntryCollection`.

`ClearLog`
:   Removes all the event log entries from this event log.

`CloseLog`
:   Closes this event log, preventing further interaction with it.

`DeleteLog`
:   Deletes this event log and the associated event log source.

An `AppEvents` object can be added to an array or collection containing other `AppEvents` objects; each `AppEvents` object corresponds to a particular event log. The following code creates two `AppEvents` classes and adds them to a `ListDictionary` collection:

```
public void CreateMultipleLogs( )
{
    AppEvents AppEventLog = new AppEvents("AppLog", "AppLocal");
    AppEvents GlobalEventLog = new AppEvents("System", "AppGlobal");

    ListDictionary LogList = new ListDictionary( );
    LogList.Add(AppEventLog.Name, AppEventLog);
    LogList.Add(GlobalEventLog.Name, GlobalEventLog);
}
```

To write to either of these two logs, obtain the `AppEvents` object by name from the `ListDictionary` object, cast the resultant object type to an `AppEvents` type, and call the `WriteToLog` method:

```
((AppEvents)LogList[AppEventLog.Name]).WriteToLog("App startup",
    EventLogEntryType.Information, CategoryType.AppStartUp,
    EventIDType.ExceptionThrown);

((AppEvents)LogList[GlobalEventLog.Name]).WriteToLog("App startup security check",
    EventLogEntryType.Information, CategoryType.AppStartUp,
    EventIDType.BufferOverflowCondition);
```

Containing all `AppEvents` objects in a `ListDictionary` object allows you to easily iterate over all the `AppEvents` that your application has instantiated. Using a `foreach` loop, you can write a single message to both a local and a remote event log:

```
foreach (DictionaryEntry Log in LogList)
{
    ((AppEvents)Log.Value).WriteToLog("App startup",
        EventLogEntryType.FailureAudit,
        CategoryType.AppStartUp, EventIDType.SecurityFailure);
}
```

To delete each log in the `logList` object, you can use the following `foreach` loop:

```
foreach (DictionaryEntry Log in LogList)
{
    ((AppEvents)Log.Value).DeleteLog( );
}
LogList.Clear( );
```

You should be aware of several key points. The first concerns a small problem with constructing multiple `AppEvents` classes. If you create two `AppEvents` objects and pass in the same source string to the `AppEvents` constructor, an exception will be thrown. Consider the following code, which instantiates two `AppEvents` objects with the same source string:

```
AppEvents appEventLog = new AppEvents("AppLog", "AppLocal");
AppEvents globalEventLog = new AppEvents("Application", "AppLocal");
```

The objects are instantiated without errors, but when the WriteToLog method is called on the globalEventLog object, the following exception is thrown:

```
An unhandled exception of type 'System.ArgumentException' occurred in system.dll.

Additional information: The source 'AppLocal' is not registered in log 'Application'.
(It is registered in log 'AppLog'.) " The Source and Log properties must be matched,
or you may set Log to the empty string, and it will automatically be matched to the
Source property.
```

This exception occurs because the WriteToLog method internally calls the WriteEntry method of the EventLog object. The WriteEntry method internally checks to see whether the specified source is registered to the log you are attempting to write to. In this case, the AppLocal source was registered to the first log it was assigned to—the AppLog log. The second attempt to register this same source to another log, Application, failed silently. You do not know that this attempt failed until you try to use the WriteEntry method of the EventLog object.

Another key point about the AppEvents class is the following code, placed at the beginning of each method (except for the DeleteLog method):

```
if (log == null)
{
    throw (new ArgumentNullException("log",
        "This Event Log has not been opened or has been closed."));
}
```

This code checks to see whether the private member variable log is a null reference. If so, an ArgumentException is thrown, informing the user of this class that a problem occurred with the creation of the EventLog object. The DeleteLog method does not check the log variable for null since it deletes the event log source and the event log itself. The EventLog object is not involved in this process except at the end of this method, where the log is closed and set to null, if it is not already null. Regardless of the state of the log variable, the source and event log should be deleted in this method.

The DeleteLog method makes a critical choice when determining whether to delete a log. The following code prevents the application, security, and system event logs from being deleted from your system:

```
if (logName != "Application" &&
    logName != "Security" &&
    logName != "System")
{
    if (EventLog.Exists(logName, machineName))
    {
        EventLog.Delete(logName, machineName);
    }
}
```

If any of these logs is deleted, so are the sources registered with the particular log. Once the log is deleted, it is permanent; believe us, it is not fun to try and re-create the log and its sources without a backup.

As a last note, the EventIDType and CategoryType enumerations are designed mainly to log security-type breaches as well as potential attacks on the security of your application. Using these event IDs and categories, the administrator can more easily track down potential security threats and do postmortem analysis after security is breached. These enumerations can easily be modified or replaced with your own to allow you to track different events that occur as a result of your application running.

 You should minimize the number of entries written to the event log from your application. The reason for this is that writing to the event log causes a performance hit. Writing too much information to the event log can noticeably slow your application. Pick and choose the entries you write to the event log wisely.

See Also

See Recipe 8.9; see the "EventLog Class" topic in the MSDN documentation.

8.7   Changing the Maximum Size of a Custom Event Log

Problem

Custom event logs are created with a default maximum size of 512K. For some applications, this default may be too small or even too large. You need a way of programmatically modifying this size. If you are a system administrator, you might need to write a utility to modify this value.

Solution

There is no direct way to modify the maximum size of an event log. However, the following method makes use of the registry to circumvent this limitation:

```
using System;
using Microsoft.Win32;

public void SetCustomLogMaxSize(string logName, int maxSize)
{
    RegistryKey key = Registry.LocalMachine.OpenSubKey
      (@"SYSTEM\CurrentControlSet\Services\Eventlog\" + logName, true);
    if (key == null)
    {
        Console.WriteLine(
            "Registry key for this Event Log does not exist.");
```

```
        }
        else
        {
            key.SetValue("MaxSize", maxSize);
            Registry.LocalMachine.Close( );
        }
    }
}
```

Discussion

The FCL classes devoted to making use of the event log contain most of the functionality that a developer will ever need. Yet there are some small items that are not directly accessible using the event log API in the FCL. One of these is the manipulation of the maximum size of an event log. Event logs are initialized to a maximum size of 512K, after which the event log entries are overwritten by default.

There are cases in which an application may produce many or very few entries in an event log. In these cases, it would be nice to manipulate the maximum size of an event log so that memory is used most efficiently and critical entries are not lost or overwritten because the event log fills up too fast.

It is possible to set the maximum size of an event log manually through the Event Viewer application. Unfortunately, you might not always have access to the machine to do this. In addition, this is a tedious and time-consuming process. You can programmatically set the maximum size by changing the value of a registry entry. If an event log were named MyLog, the properties of this log would reside in the following registry location:

```
HKEY_LOCAL_MACHINE\SYSTEM\CurrentControlSet\Services\Eventlog\MyLog
```

This location contains several value entries containing properties of this event log. The value entry you are interested in is MaxSize. Using the static methods of the Registry class, you can add or modify this value to one of your choosing with code like the following:

```
Microsoft.Win32.RegistryKey lm = Registry.LocalMachine;
Microsoft.Win32.RegistryKey logKey = lm.OpenSubKey(
            @"SYSTEM\CurrentControlSet\Services\Eventlog\RegistryLog", true);
logKey.SetValue("MaxSize", (int) 1024);
logKey.Close;
```

To access this registry value, you first call the RegistryKey.OpenSubKey method. This method returns a RegistryKey object, which in this case represents the key containing the MaxSize value entry. The SetValue method of the RegistryKey object is called next to change the value of the MaxSize entry. If this value entry does not exist, it is created with the desired value. This information is then flushed to the registry and the RegistryKey class is closed. Both of these actions are performed though the Close method on the RegistryKey class.

While it is possible to adjust this registry value programmatically, in most instances, only highly privileged accounts would have the security access necessary for this code to run successfully, such as when the application is being installed or in a utility run by an administrator. This should not be attempted as part of normal application operations since it does require such a high level of access.

See Also

See the "Registry.LocalMachine Field" and "RegistryKey.Open Method" topics in the MSDN documentation.

8.8   Searching Event Log Entries

Problem

Your application might have added many entries to the event log. To perform an analysis of how the application operated, how many errors were encountered, and so on, you need to be able to perform a search through all of the entries in an event log. Unfortunately, there are no good built-in search mechanisms for event logs.

Solution

You will eventually have to sift through all the entries your application writes to an event log in order to find the entries that allow you to perhaps fix a bug or improve your application's security system. Unfortunately, there are no good search mechanisms for event logs. This recipe contains an EventLogSearch class, to which you'll add static methods allowing you to search for entries in an event log based on various criteria. In addition, this search mechanism allows complex searches involving multiple criteria to be performed on an event log at one time. The code for the EventSearchLog class is shown in Example 8-4.

Example 8-4. EventSearchLog class

```
using System;
using System.Collections;
using System.Diagnostics;

public sealed class EventLogSearch
{
    private EventLogSearch( ) {}     // Prevent this class from being instantiated.

    public static EventLogEntry[] FindTimeGeneratedAtOrBefore(
        IEnumerable logEntries, DateTime timeGeneratedQuery)
    {
        ArrayList entries = new ArrayList( );

        foreach (EventLogEntry logEntry in logEntries)
        {
            if (logEntry.TimeGenerated <= timeGeneratedQuery)
            {
```

Example 8-4. EventSearchLog class (continued)

```
                entries.Add(logEntry);
            }
        }

        EventLogEntry[] entriesArray = new EventLogEntry[entries.Count];
        entries.CopyTo(entriesArray);
        return (entriesArray);
    }

    public static EventLogEntry[] FindTimeGeneratedAtOrAfter(
        IEnumerable logEntries, DateTime timeGeneratedQuery)
    {
        ArrayList entries = new ArrayList();

        foreach (EventLogEntry logEntry in logEntries)
        {
            if (logEntry.TimeGenerated >= timeGeneratedQuery)
            {
                entries.Add(logEntry);
            }
        }

        EventLogEntry[] entriesArray = new EventLogEntry[entries.Count];
        entries.CopyTo(entriesArray);
        return (entriesArray);
    }
}
```

Discussion

Other searchable criteria can be added to this class by following the same coding pattern for each search method. For instance, the following example shows how to add a search method to find all entries that contain a particular username:

```
    public static EventLogEntry[] FindUserName(IEnumerable logEntries,
        string userNameQuery)
    {
        ArrayList entries = new ArrayList();

        foreach (EventLogEntry logEntry in logEntries)
        {
            if (logEntry.UserName == userNameQuery)
            {
                entries.Add(logEntry);
            }
        }

        EventLogEntry[] entriesArray = new EventLogEntry[entries.Count];
        entries.CopyTo(entriesArray);
        return (entriesArray);
    }
```

The methods shown in Table 8-3 list other search methods that could be included in this class and describe which property of the event log entries they search on. (All of these methods are implemented on the code for this book, which can be found at *http://www.oreilly.com/catalog/csharpckbk2.*)

Table 8-3. Other possible search methods

Search method name	Entry property searched
FindCategory (overloaded to accept a string type category name)	Category == CategoryNameQuery
FindCategory (overloaded to accept a short type category number)	Category == CategoryNumberQuery
FindEntryType	EntryType == EntryTypeQuery
FindInstanceID	InstanceID == InstanceIDQuery
FindMachineName	MachineName == MachineNameQuery
FindMessage	Message == Message.Query
FindSource	Source == SourceQuery

The FindCategory method can be overloaded to search on either the category name or category number.

The following method makes use of the EventLogSearch methods to find and display entries that are marked as Error log entries:

```
public void FindAnEntryInEventLog( )
{
    EventLog Log = new EventLog("System");

    EventLogEntry[] Entries = EventLogSearch.FindEntryType(Log.Entries,
        EventLogEntryType.Error);

    foreach (EventLogEntry Entry in Entries)
    {
        Console.WriteLine("Message:      " + Entry.Message);
        Console.WriteLine("InstanceId:   " + Entry.InstanceId);
        Console.WriteLine("Category:     " + Entry.Category);
        Console.WriteLine("EntryType:    " + Entry.EntryType.ToString( ));
        Console.WriteLine("Source:       " + Entry.Source);
    }
}
```

The following method finds and displays entries generated at or after 8/3/2003, marked as Error type logs, and containing an event ID of 7000:

```
public void FindAnEntryInEventLog( )
{
    EventLog Log = new EventLog("System");

    EventLogEntry[] Entries = EventLogSearch.FindTimeGeneratedAtOrAfter(Log.Entries,
        DateTime.Parse("8/3/2003"));
```

```
Entries = EventLogSearch.FindEntryType(Entries, EventLogEntryType.Error);
Entries = EventLogSearch.FindInstanceId(Entries, 7000);

foreach (EventLogEntry Entry in Entries)
{
    Console.WriteLine("Message:       " + Entry.Message);
    Console.WriteLine("InstanceId:    " + Entry.InstanceId);
    Console.WriteLine("Category:      " + Entry.Category);
    Console.WriteLine("EntryType:     " + Entry.EntryType.ToString());
    Console.WriteLine("Source:        " + Entry.Source);
}
}
```

Note that this search mechanism can search within only one event log at a time.

To illustrate how searching works, let's assume that you are using the FindInstanceID method to search on the InstanceID. Initially, you would call the FindInstanceID search method, passing in a collection that implements the IEnumerable interface, such as the EventLogEntryCollection collection (that contains all entries in that event log) or an array of EventLogEntry objects. The EventLogEntryCollection is returned by the Entries property of the EventLog class. The FindInstanceID method will return an array of EventLogEntry objects that match the search criteria (the value passed in to the second argument of the FindInstanceID method).

The real power of this searching method design is that the initial search on the EventLogEntryCollection returns an array of EventLogEntry objects. This EventLogEntry array may then be passed back into another search method to be searched again, effectively narrowing down the search query. For example, the EventLogEntry array returned from the FindInstanceID method may be passed into another search method such as the FindEntryType method to narrow down the search to all entries that are a specific entry type (informational, error, etc.).

See Also

See the "EventLog Class" and "EventLogEntry Class" topics in the MSDN documentation.

8.9   Watching the Event Log for a Specific Entry

Problem

You may have multiple applications that write to a single event log. For each of these applications, you want a monitoring application to watch for one or more specific log entries to be written to the event log. For example, you might want to watch for a log entry that indicates that an application encountered a critical error or shut down unexpectedly. These log entries should be reported in real time.

Solution

Monitoring an event log for a specific entry requires the following steps:

1. Create the following method to set up the event handler to handle event log writes:

```
public void WatchForAppEvent(EventLog log)
{
    log.EnableRaisingEvents = true;
    // Hook up the System.Diagnostics.EntryWrittenEventHandler.
    log.EntryWritten += new EntryWrittenEventHandler(OnEntryWritten);
}
```

2. Create the event handler to examine the log entries and determine whether further action is to be performed. For example:

```
public static void OnEntryWritten(object source,
                                  EntryWrittenEventArgs entryArg)
{
    if (entryArg.Entry.EntryType == EventLogEntryType.Error)
    {
        Console.WriteLine(entryArg.Entry.Message);
        Console.WriteLine(entryArg.Entry.Category);
        Console.WriteLine(entryArg.Entry.EntryType.ToString( ));
        // Do further actions here as necessary...
    }
}
```

Discussion

This recipe revolves around the `EntryWrittenEventHandler` delegate, which calls back a method whenever any new entry is written to the event log. The `EntryWrittenEventHandler` delegate accepts two arguments: a *source* of type object and an *entryArg* of type `EntryWrittenEventArgs`. The *entryArg* parameter is the most interesting of the two. It contains a property called `Entry` that returns an `EventLogEntry` object. This `EventLogEntry` object contains all the information you need concerning the entry that was written to the event log.

This event log that you are watching is passed as the `WatchForAppEvent` method's *log* parameter. This method performs two actions. First, it sets log's `EnableRaisingEvents` property to `true`. If this property were set to `false`, no events would be raised for this event log when an entry is written to it. The second action this method performs is to add the `OnEntryWritten` callback method to the list of event handlers for this event log.

To prevent this delegate from calling the `OnEntryWritten` callback method, you can set the `EnableRaisingEvents` property to `false`, effectively turning off the delegate.

Note that the `Entry` object passed to the *entryArg* parameter of the `OnEntryWritten` callback method is read-only, so the entry cannot be modified before it is written to the event log.

See Also

See the "Handling the EntryWritten Event" and "EventLog.EntryWritten Event" topics in the MSDN documentation.

8.10 Finding All Sources Belonging to a Specific Event Log

Problem

You need to determine which sources are attached to a particular event log before the log is examined and/or deleted. A source is a component or application that has registered itself to a particular event log as a source of events.

Solution

Use the following method to extract all of the source names registered to a log (pass the log's name in as the logName argument):

```
public static List<string> FindSourceNamesFromLog(string logName)
{
    List<string> sourceNamesList = new List<string>();

    // Get the registry key for the specific log.
    RegistryKey keyLog = Registry.LocalMachine.OpenSubKey
        (@"SYSTEM\CurrentControlSet\Services\Eventlog\" + logName);
    if (keyLog != null && keyLog.SubKeyCount>0)
    {
        // Get the sources from the log key.
        string[] sourceNames = keyLog.GetSubKeyNames();

        // Set capacity for the list.
        sourceNamesList.Capacity = keyLog.SubKeyCount;

        // Add all of the sources into the list.
        sourceNamesList.AddRange(sourceNames);
    }

    // Return the list.
    return sourceNamesList;
}
```

To obtain a listing of *all* logs and their registered sources, use the following method:

```
public static Hashtable FindSourceNamesFromAllLogs()
{
    // Make a hashtable to store the logs and their sources.
    Hashtable logsAndSources = new Hashtable();
```

```
// Get a list of all logs on the box.
string[] eventLogNames = Registry.LocalMachine.OpenSubKey
    (@"SYSTEM\CurrentControlSet\Services\Eventlog").GetSubKeyNames();

foreach (string log in eventLogNames)
{
    // Get all the source names for this log.
    List<string> sourceNamesList = FindSourceNamesFromLog(log)

    // Add the source name list with the log name
    // as the key to the hashtable.
    logsAndSources.Add(log, sourceNamesList);
}

return logsAndSources;
}
```

This method returns a Hashtable with the log name as the key and a List<string> of source names as the Hashtable's value. The information in the Hashtable of List<string>s can be accessed using the following code:

```
foreach (DictionaryEntry DE in logsAndSources)
{
    Console.WriteLine("Log: " + DE.Key);                // Display the log.
    foreach (string source in ((List<string>)DE.Value))
    {
        // Display all sources for this log.
        Console.WriteLine("\tSource: " + source);
    }
}
```

Discussion

This recipe is similar to Recipe 8.7 in that you need to find information concerning an event log that can be obtained only through the registry. If you need to find the sources associated with a log called MyLog, you would look up all of the subkeys contained in the following location:

```
HKEY_LOCAL_MACHINE\SYSTEM\CurrentControlSet\Services\Eventlog\MyLog\
```

If MyLog were associated with two sources called AppSource and MonitorSource, the following keys would exist under the MyLog key:

```
\AppSource
\MonitorSource
```

The full registry path for both keys would be:

```
HKEY_LOCAL_MACHINE\SYSTEM\CurrentControlSet\Services\Eventlog\MyLog\AppSource
HKEY_LOCAL_MACHINE\SYSTEM\CurrentControlSet\Services\Eventlog\MyLog\MonitorSource
```

This recipe makes use of the Registry and RegistryKey classes to look up the subkeys under the event log's key in the registry. See Recipe 8.7 for more information dealing with opening registry keys using the Registry and RegistryKey classes.

The read-only `SubKeyCount` property and `GetSubKeyNames` method of the `RegistryKey` class are used to obtain the number of subkeys that reside under a particular key and a string array containing their names.

The `FindSourceNamesFromLog` method uses the `GetSubKeyNames` method to obtain a list of event logs from the `EventLog` registry key. It then searches these log names until the log name passed to this method through the *logName* parameter is found. Once the correct log is found, its subkeys—representing all of the sources tied to that log—are saved to the `sourceNamesList` array. This array is then passed back to the caller.

See Also

See Recipe 8.7; see the "Registry.LocalMachine Field" and "RegistryKey.Open Method" topics in the MSDN documentation.

8.11 Implementing a Simple Performance Counter

Problem

You need to use a performance counter to track application-specific information. The simpler performance counters find, for example, the change in a counter value between successive samplings or just count the number of times an action occurs. Other, more complex counters exist but are not dealt with in this recipe. For example, a custom counter could be built to keep track of the number of database transactions, the number of failed network connections to a server, or even the number of users connecting to your web service per minute.

Solution

Create a simple performance counter that finds, for example, the change in a counter value between successive samplings or that just counts the number of times an action occurs. Use the following method (`CreateSimpleCounter`) to create a simple custom counter:

```
public PerformanceCounter CreateSimpleCounter(string counterName, string counterHelp,
    System.Diagnostics.PerformanceCounterType counterType, string categoryName,
    string categoryHelp)
{
    CounterCreationDataCollection counterCollection =
            new CounterCreationDataCollection( );

    // Create the custom counter object and add it to the collection of counters.
    CounterCreationData counter = new CounterCreationData(counterName, counterHelp,
            counterType);
    counterCollection.Add(counter);

    // Create category.
    if (PerformanceCounterCategory.Exists(categoryName))
    {
```

```
        PerformanceCounterCategory.Delete(categoryName);
    }

    PerformanceCounterCategory appCategory =
        PerformanceCounterCategory.Create(categoryName, categoryHelp,
            PerformanceCounterCategoryType.SingleInstance, counterCollection);

    // Create the counter and initialize it.
    PerformanceCounter appCounter =
        new PerformanceCounter(categoryName, counterName, false);

    appCounter.RawValue = 0;

    return (appCounter);
}
```

Discussion

The first action this method takes is to create the `CounterCreationDataCollection` object and `CounterCreationData` object. The `CounterCreationData` object is created using the *counterName*, *counterHelp*, and *countertype* parameters passed to the `CreateSimpleCounter` method. The `CounterCreationData` object is then added to the `counterCollection`.

 The `ASPNET` user account, as well as many other user accounts by default, prevent performance counters from being read. You can either increase the permissions allowed for these accounts or use impersonation with an account that has access to enable this functionality. However, this then becomes a deployment requirement of your application. Decreasing security for the `ASPNET` account or other user accounts may very well be frowned upon by IT folks deploying your application.

If *categoryName*—a string containing the name of the category that is passed as a parameter to the method—is not registered on the system, a new category is created from a `PerformanceCounterCategory` object. If one is registered, it is deleted and created anew. Finally, the actual performance counter is created from a `PerformanceCounter` object. This object is initialized to zero and returned by the method. `PerformanceCounterCategory` takes a `PerformanceCounterCategoryType` as a parameter. The possible settings are shown in Table 8-4.

Table 8-4. PerformanceCounterCategoryType enumeration values

Name	Description
MultiInstance	There can be multiple instances of the performance counter.
SingleInstance	There can be only one instance of the performance counter.
Unknown	Instance functionality for this performance counter is unknown.

The `CreateSimpleCounter` method returns a `PerformanceCounter` object that will be used by an application. The application can perform several actions on a `PerformanceCounter` object. An application can increment or decrement it using one of these three methods:

```
long value = appCounter.Increment( );
long value = appCounter.Decrement( );
long value = appCounter.IncrementBy(i);

// Additionally, a negative number may be passed to the
// IncrementBy method to mimic a DecrementBy method
// (which is not included in this class). For example:
long value = appCounter.IncrementBy(-i);
```

The first two methods accept no parameters, while the third accepts a `long` containing the number by which to increment the counter. All three methods return a `long` type indicating the new value of the counter.

In addition to incrementing or decrementing this counter, you can also take samples of the counter at various points in the application. A sample is a snapshot of the counter and all of its values at a particular instance in time. A sample may be taken using the following line of code:

```
CounterSample counterSampleValue = appCounter.NextSample( );
```

The `NextSample` method accepts no parameters and returns a `CounterSample` structure.

At another point in the application, a counter can be sampled again, and both samples can be passed in to the static `Calculate` method on the `CounterSample` class. These actions may be performed on a single line of code as follows:

```
float calculatedSample = CounterSample.Calculate(counterSampleValue,
                                         appCounter.NextSample( ));
```

The calculated sample `calculatedSample` may be stored for future analysis.

The simpler performance counters already available in the .NET Framework are:

`CounterDelta32/CounterDelta64`
Determines the difference (or change) in value between two samplings of this counter. The `CounterDelta64` counter can hold larger values than `CounterDelta32`.

`CounterTimer`
Calculates the percentage of the `CounterTimer` value change over the `CounterTimer` time change. Tracks the average active time for a resource as a percentage of the total sample time.

`CounterTimerInverse`
Calculates the inverse of the `CounterTimer` counter. Tracks the average inactive time for a resource as a percentage of the total sample time.

CountPerTimeInterval32/CountPerTimeInterval64

> Calculates the number of items waiting within a queue to a resource over the time elapsed. These counters give the delta of the queue length for the last two sample intervals divided by the interval duration.

ElapsedTime

> Calculates the difference in time between when this counter recorded the start of an event and the current time, measured in seconds.

NumberOfItems32/NumberOfItems64

> These counters return their value in decimal format. The NumberOfItems64 counter can hold larger values than NumberOfItems32. This counter does not need to be passed to the static Calculate method of the CounterSample class; there are no values that must be calculated. Instead, use the RawValue property of the PerformanceCounter object (i.e., in this recipe, the appCounter.RawValue property would be used).

NumberOfItemsHEX32/NumberOfItemsHEX64

> These counters return their value in hexadecimal format. The NumberOfItemsHEX64 counter can hold larger values than NumberOfItemsHEX32. This counter does not need to be passed to the static Calculate method of the CounterSample class; there are no values that must be calculated. Instead, use the RawValue property of the PerformanceCounter object (i.e., in this recipe, the appCounter.RawValue property would be used).

RateOfCountsPerSecond32/RateOfCountsPerSecond64

> Calculates the RateOfCountsPerSecond* value change over the RateOfCounts-PerSecond* time change, measured in seconds. The RateOfCountsPerSecond64 counter can hold larger values than the RateOfCountsPerSecond32 counter.

Timer100Ns

> Percentage counter showing the active component time as a percentage of the total elapsed time of the sample interval measured in 100 nanoseconds (ns) units. Processor\ % User Time is an example of this type of counter.

Timer100nsInverse

> Percentage-based counter showing the average active percentage of time tracked during the sample interval. Processor\ % Processor Time is one example of this type of counter.

See Also

See Recipe 8.12; see the "PerformanceCounter Class," "PerformanceCounterType Enumeration," "PerformanceCounterCategory Class," "ASP.NET Impersonation," and "Monitoring Performance Thresholds" topics in the MSDN documentation.

8.12 Implementing Performance Counters That Require a Base Counter

Problem

You need to use some of the more advanced performance counters to accurately track information about your application. The performance counters exist as two counters used together. The first counter is the *main counter*, which is divided by the second counter, called the *base counter*. Essentially, the first counter is the numerator and the second counter is the denominator; the *custom counter* reports the result of this division operation. The main counter is used in tandem with its base counter type to calculate, for example, the average amount of time it takes for an action (e.g., connecting to a server) to complete or the average number of actions that occur during a single process (e.g., database timeouts).

Solution

Create a complex performance counter, which is used in tandem with the base counter type to calculate, for example, the average amount of time it takes for an action to complete or the average number of actions that occur during a single process. Use the `CreateComplexCounter` method shown in Example 8-5 to create a complex custom counter.

Example 8-5. Creating a complex counter

```
public void CreateComplexCounter(string counterName, string counterHelp,
    PerformanceCounterType counterType, string baseCounterName,
    string baseCounterHelp,  PerformanceCounterType baseCounterType,
    string categoryName, string categoryHelp,
    out PerformanceCounter appCounter,
    out PerformanceCounter appBaseCounter)
{
    CounterCreationDataCollection counterCollection =
      new CounterCreationDataCollection( );

    // Create the custom counter object and its base counter object
    // and add them to the collection of counters (they must be
    // added successively).
    CounterCreationData counter = new CounterCreationData(counterName,
      counterHelp, counterType);
    counterCollection.Add(counter);
    CounterCreationData BaseCounter =
      new CounterCreationData(baseCounterName,
          baseCounterHelp, baseCounterType);
    counterCollection.Add(BaseCounter);

    // Create category.
    if (PerformanceCounterCategory.Exists(categoryName))
    {
```

Example 8-5. Creating a complex counter (continued)

```
        PerformanceCounterCategory.Delete(categoryName);
    }

    PerformanceCounterCategory appCategory =
        PerformanceCounterCategory.Create(categoryName, categoryHelp,
                PerformanceCounterCategoryType.SingleInstance,
                counterCollection);

    // Create the counter and initialize it.
    PerformanceCounter newAppCounter =
        new PerformanceCounter(categoryName, counterName, false);
    PerformanceCounter newAppBaseCounter =
        new PerformanceCounter(categoryName, baseCounterName, false);

    newAppCounter.RawValue = 0;
    newAppBaseCounter.RawValue = 0;

    appCounter = newAppCounter;
    appBaseCounter = newAppBaseCounter;
}
```

Discussion

The `CreateComplexCounter` method returns two `PerformanceCounter` objects as out parameters; one is the counter, the other is the base counter. These two counters are used in tandem; the base counter controls some aspect of the denominator in the calculation relating these two counters. Since the value of the `appCounter` parameter, returned from this method, depends on the value in the `appBaseCounter` parameter, we are considering these types of counters as complex counters.

> The `ASPNET` user account, as well as many other user accounts by default, prevent performance counters from being read. You can either increase the permissions allowed for these accounts or use impersonation with an account that has access to enable this functionality. However, this then becomes a deployment requirement of your application. Decreasing security for the `ASPNET` account or other user accounts may very well be frowned upon by IT folks deploying your application.

This method operates similarly to the `CreateSimpleCounter` method described in Recipe 8.11. The one major difference is that two `CounterCreationData` objects are created and added to the `CounterCreationDataCollection` object. This first `CounterCreationData` object is the main counter used in the calculation for this counter. The second is the base counter, used in the denominator of the calculation for this counter. These counters must be added, in order, to the `CounterCreation-DataCollection` object. In addition, the counter defined by the *counterName* parameter must be added before the counter defined by the *baseCounterName* parameter.

The application can perform several actions on these `PerformanceCounter` objects. An application can increment or decrement a `PerformanceCounter` object using one of these three methods:

```
long value = newAppCounter.Increment( );
long value = newAppCounter.Decrement( );
long value = newAppCounter.IncrementBy(i);

long value = newAppBaseCounter.Increment( );
long value = newAppBaseCounter.Decrement( );
long value = newAppBaseCounter.IncrementBy(i);

// Additionally, a negative number may be passed in to the IncrementBy method
// to mimic a DecrementBy method (which is not included in this class).
long value = newAppCounter.IncrementBy(-i);
long value = newAppBaseCounter.IncrementBy(-i);
```

The first two methods accept no parameters, while the third accepts a `long` containing the number by which to increment the counter. All three methods return a `long` type indicating the new value of the counter.

In addition to incrementing or decrementing these counters, you can also take samples of these counters at various points in the application. A sample is a snapshot of the counter and all of its values at a particular instance in time. A sample may be taken using the following lines of code:

```
CounterSample counterSampleValue = newAppCounter.NextSample( );
CounterSample counterSampleBaseValue = newAppBaseCounter.NextSample( );
```

The `NextSample` method accepts no parameters and returns a `CounterSample` object.

At another point in the application, a counter may be sampled again, and the samples can be passed in to the static `Calculate` method on the `CounterSample` class. These actions may be performed in a single line of code as follows:

```
float calculatedSample = CounterSample.Calculate(counterSampleValue,
                                    newAppCounter.NextSample( ));
```

Note that you need to pass only the `newAppCounter` samples; the `newAppBaseCounter` samples are handled for you. The calculated sample `calculatedSample` may be stored for future analysis. See Recipe 8.11 for a definition of the `Calculate` method.

The complex performance counters defined in the .NET Framework are defined here:

AverageCount64

> Calculates the `AverageTimer64` value change over the `AverageBase` value change. This counter uses `AverageBase` as its base counter type.

AverageTimer32

> Calculates the `AverageTimer32` value change over the number of ticks per second, all over the `AverageBase` value change. This counter uses `AverageBase` as its base counter type.

`CounterMultiTimer`

Calculates the percentage of `CounterMultiTimer` value change over the `CounterMultiTimer` time change divided by `CounterMultiBase`. This counter uses `CounterMultiBase` as its base counter type.

`CounterMultiTimerInverse`

A percentage counter that shows the active time of one or more components as a percentage of the total time of the sample interval. These counters are known as *inverse multitimer counters*, as multitimers monitor multiple component instances (like a volume or processor), and inverse counters measure nonactive time and derive active time from that measure. Measures time in system ticks.

`CounterMultiTimer100Ns`

Measures active time of one or more components in 100ns increments.

`CounterMultiTimer100NsInverse`

Measures active time of one or more components in 100ns increments by tracking the nonactive time and deriving the active time from that (inverse timer).

`RawFraction`

Calculates a percentage of the `RawFraction` counter value over the `RawBase` counter value. This counter uses `RawBase` as its base counter type.

`SampleCounter`

Calculates the `SampleCounter` value change over the corresponding `SampleBase` value change per second. This counter uses `SampleBase` as its base counter type.

`SampleFraction`

Calculates the percentage of `SampleCounter` value change over the `SampleBase` value change. This counter uses `SampleBase` as its base counter type.

See Also

See Recipe 8.11; see the "PerformanceCounter Class," "PerformanceCounterType Enumeration," "PerformanceCounterCategory Class," "ASP.NET Impersonation," and "Monitoring Performance Thresholds" topics in the MSDN documentation.

8.13 Enabling and Disabling Complex Tracing Code

Problem

You have an object that contains complex tracing/debugging code. In fact, there is so much tracing/debugging code that to turn it all on would create an extremely large amount of output. You want to be able to generate objects at runtime that contain all of the tracing/debugging code, only a specific portion of this tracing/debugging code, or no tracing/debugging code. The amount of tracing code generated could depend on the state of the application or the environment in which it is running. The tracing code needs to be generated during object creation.

Solution

Use the `TraceFactory` class shown in Example 8-6, which implements the factory design pattern to allow creation of an object that either generates tracing information or does not.

Example 8-6. TraceFactory class

```
#define TRACE
#define TRACE_INSTANTIATION
#define TRACE_BEHAVIOR

using System.Diagnostics;

public class TraceFactory
{
    public TraceFactory( ) {}

    public Foo CreateObj( )
    {
        Foo obj = null;

        #if (TRACE)
            #if (TRACE_INSTANTIATION)
                obj = new BarTraceInst( );
            #elif (TRACE_BEHAVIOR)
                obj = new BarTraceBehavior( );
            #else
                obj = new Bar( );
            #endif
        #else
            obj = new Bar( );
        #endif

        return (obj);
    }
}
```

The class hierarchy for the `Bar`, `BarTraceInst`, and `BarTraceBehavior` classes is shown next. The `BarTraceInst` class contains only the constructor tracing code, the `BarTraceBehavior` class contains tracing code only within specific methods, and the `Bar` class contains no tracing code:

```
public abstract class Foo
{
    public virtual void SomeBehavior( )
    {
        //...
    }
}

public class Bar : Foo
{
```

```
        public Bar( ) {}

        public override void SomeBehavior( )
        {
            base.SomeBehavior( );
        }
    }

    public class BarTraceInst : Foo
    {
        public BarTraceInst( )
        {
            Trace.WriteLine("BarTraceInst object instantiated");
        }

        public override void SomeBehavior( )
        {
            base.SomeBehavior( );
        }
    }

    public class BarTraceBehavior : Foo
    {
        public BarTraceBehavior( ) {}

        public override void SomeBehavior( )
        {
            Trace.WriteLine("SomeBehavior called");
            base.SomeBehavior( );
        }
    }
```

Discussion

The *factory design pattern* is designed to abstract away the creation of objects within
a system. This pattern allows code to create objects of a particular type by using an
intermediate object called a factory. In its simplest form, a factory pattern consists of
some client code that uses a factory object to create and return a specific type of
object. The factory pattern allows changes to be made in the way objects are created, independent of the client code. This design prevents code changes to the way
an object is constructed from permeating throughout the client code.

Consider that you could have a class that contained numerous lines of tracing code.
If you ran this code to obtain the trace output, you would be inundated with reams
of information. This setup is hard to manage and even harder to read to pinpoint
problems in your code. One solution to this problem is to use a factory to create an
object based on the type of tracing code you wish to output.

To do this, create an abstract base class called Foo that contains all of the base behavior. The Foo class is subclassed to create the Bar, BarTraceInst, and BarTraceBehavior

classes. The Bar class contains no tracing code, the BarTraceInst class contains tracing code only in its constructor (and potentially in its destructor), and the BarTraceBehavior class contains tracing code only in specific methods. (The class hierarchy provided in the Solution section is much simpler than classes that you would create; this allows you to focus more on the design pattern and less on the class hierarchy from which the factory creates classes.)

A TraceFactory class that will act as your factory to create objects inheriting from the abstract Foo class is created. The TraceFactory class contains a single public method called CreateObj. This method attempts to instantiate an object that inherits from Foo based on the preprocessor symbols defined in your application. If the following line of code exists:

```
#define TRACE_BEHAVIOR
```

the BarTraceBehavior class is created. If this line exists:

```
#define TRACE_INSTANTIATION
```

the BarTraceInst class is created. If neither of these exists, the Bar class is created. Once the correct class is created, it is returned to the caller. The caller never needs to know which exact object is instantiated, only that it is of type Foo. This allows you to add even more classes to handle varying types and amounts of tracing code.

To instantiate a TraceFactory class, use the following code:

```
TraceFactory factory = new TraceFactory( );
```

Using this factory object, you can create a new object of type Foo:

```
Foo obj = factory.CreateObj( );
Console.WriteLine(obj.ToString( ));
obj.SomeBehavior( );
```

Now you can use the Foo object without regard to the trace output that it will produce. To create and use a different Foo object, all you have to do is define a different preprocessor symbol that controls which subclass of Foo is created.

See Also

See the "C# Preprocessor Directives" and "ConditionalAttribute Class" topics in the MSDN documentation.

8.14 Capturing Standard Output for a Process

Problem

You need to be able to capture standard output for a process you are launching.

Solution

Use the `RedirectStandardOutput` property of the `Process.StartInfo` class to capture the output from the process. By redirecting the standard output stream of the process, you read it when the process terminates. `UseShellExecute` is a property on the `ProcessInfo` class that tells the runtime whether or not to use the Windows shell to start the process or not. By default, it is turned on (true) and the shell runs the program, which means that the output cannot be redirected. This needs to be set to off and then the redirection can occur. The `UseShellExecute` property is set to `false` to ensure this is not started using the Windows shell for your purposes here.

In this example, a `Process` object for *cmd.exe* is set up with arguments to perform a directory listing, and then the output is redirected. A logfile is created to hold the resulting output and the `Process.Start` method is called.

```
// See 12.21 for more info on redirection...
Process application = new Process();
// Run the command shell.
application.StartInfo.FileName = @"cmd.exe";

// Get a directory listing from the current directory.
application.StartInfo.Arguments = @"/Cdir " + Environment.CurrentDirectory;
Console.WriteLine("Running cmd.exe with arguments: {0}",
                  application.StartInfo.Arguments);

// Redirect standard output so we can read it.
application.StartInfo.RedirectStandardOutput = true;
application.StartInfo.UseShellExecute = false;

// Create a logfile to hold the results in the current EXE directory.
using (StreamWriter logger = new StreamWriter("cmdoutput.log"))
{
    // Start it up.
    application.Start();
```

Once the process is started, the `StandardOutput` stream can be accessed and a reference to it held. The code then reads in the information from the output stream while the application runs and writes it to the logfile that was set up previously. Once the application finishes, the logfile is closed.

```
    // Get stdout.
    StreamReader output = application.StandardOutput;

    // Dump the output stream while the app runs.
    do
    {
        using (output)
        {
            char[] info = null;
            while (output.Peek() >= 0)
            {
                info = new char[4096];
```

```
                output.Read(info, 0, info.Length);
                // Write to the logger.
                logger.Write(info, 0, info.Length);
            }
        }
    }
    while (!application.HasExited);
}

// Close the process object.
application.Close();
```

cmdoutput.log holds information similar to the following output:

```
Volume in drive C has no label.
 Volume Serial Number is DDDD-FFFF

 Directory of C:\C#Cookbook2\Code\CSharpRecipes\bin\Debug

08/28/2005  12:25 PM    <DIR>          .
08/28/2005  12:25 PM    <DIR>          ..
08/28/2005  12:25 PM                 0 cmdoutput.log
08/15/2005  09:46 PM           489,269 CSharpCookbook.zip
08/28/2005  12:24 PM           450,560 CSharpRecipes.exe
08/28/2005  12:24 PM         1,031,680 CSharpRecipes.pdb
07/22/2005  08:28 AM             5,120 CSharpRecipes.vshost.exe
04/12/2005  10:15 PM               432 CSharpRecipes.vshost.xml
05/10/2005  10:14 PM               998 CSharpRecipes.vshost.xsd
03/29/2005  10:27 AM               432 CSharpRecipes.xml
05/10/2005  10:14 PM               998 CSharpRecipes.xsd
03/29/2005  10:27 AM               155 data.txt
04/12/2005  10:15 PM               134 HT.data
12/10/2003  10:11 PM            12,288 REGEX_Test.dll
08/20/2005  09:27 PM            16,384 SampleClassLibrary.dll
08/20/2005  09:27 PM            11,776 SampleClassLibrary.pdb
08/02/2005  08:56 PM               483 se1.object
08/02/2005  08:56 PM               480 se2.object
08/02/2005  08:56 PM               767 se3.object
08/02/2005  08:56 PM               488 se4.object
08/02/2005  08:56 PM               775 se5.object
04/12/2005  10:15 PM             1,369 TEST.DATA
04/12/2005  10:14 PM               327 TestBinSerXML.txt
              21 File(s)      2,024,915 bytes
               2 Dir(s)  98,005,683,712 bytes free
```

Discussion

Redirecting standard output is a common task that can sometimes be of great use for tasks like automated build scenarios or test harnesses. While not quite as easy as simply placing > after the command line for a process at the command prompt, this approach is more flexible, as the stream output can be reformatted as XML or HTML for posting to a web site. This also provides the opportunity to send the data to multiple locations at once, which the simple command-line redirect function as provided by Windows is incapable of.

Waiting to read from the stream until the application has finished ensures that there will be no deadlock issues. If the stream is accessed synchronously before this time, then the possibility exists for the parent to block the child. At a minimum, the child will wait until the parent has finished reading from the stream before it continues writing to it. So by postponing the read until the end, you allow the child to have less performance degradation at the cost of some additional time at the end.

See Also

See Recipe 12.21; see the "ProcessStartInfo.RedirectStandardOutput Property" and "ProcessStartInfo.UseShellExecute Property" topics in the MSDN documentation.

8.15 Creating Custom Debugging Displays for Your Classes

Problem

You have a set of classes that are used in your application. You would like to see at a glance in the debugger what a particular instance of the class holds. The default debugger display doesn't show any useful information for your class today.

Solution

Add a DebuggerDisplayAttribute to your class to make the debugger show you something you consider useful about your class. For example, if you had a Citizen class that held the honorific and name information, you could add a DebuggerDisplayAttribute like this one:

```
[DebuggerDisplay("Citizen Full Name = {_honorific}{_first}{_middle}{_last}")]
public class Citizen
{
    private string _honorific;
    private string _first;
    private string _middle;
    private string _last;

    public Citizen(string honorific, string first, string middle, string last)
    {
        _honorific = honorific;
        _first = first;
        _middle = middle;
        _last = last;
    }
}
```

Now when instances of the Citizen class are instantiated, the debugger will show the information the way the DebuggerDisplayAttribute on the class directs it to. To see this, instantiate two Citizens, Mrs. Alice G. Jones and Mr. Robert Frederick Jones like this:

```
Citizen mrsJones = new Citizen("Mrs.","Alice","G.","Jones");
Citizen mrJones = new Citizen("Mr.", "Robert", "Frederick", "Jones");
```

When this code is run under the debugger, the custom display is used, as shown in Figure 8-1.

Figure 8-1. Debugger display controlled by DebuggerDisplayAttribute

Discussion

It is nice to be able to see the pertinent information for classes you write quickly. But the more powerful part of this feature is the ability for your team members to quickly understand what this class instance holds. The this pointer is accessible from the DebuggerDisplayAttribute declaration, but any properties accessed using the this pointer will not evaluate the property attributes before processing. Essentially, if you access a property on the current object instance as part of constructing the display string, if that property has attributes, they will not be processed, and therefore you may not get the value you thought you would. If you have custom ToString() overrides in place already, the debugger will use these as the DebuggerDisplayAttribute without your specifying it, provided the correct option is enabled under Tools\Options\Debugging as shown in Figure 8-2.

See Also

See the "Using DebuggerDisplayAttribute" and "DebuggerDisplayAttribute" topics in the MSDN documentation.

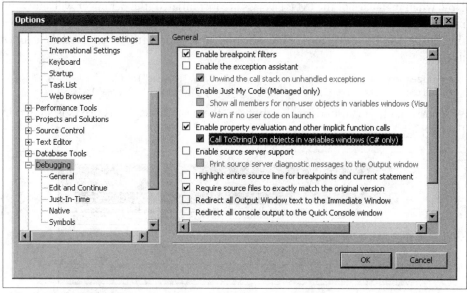

Figure 8-2. Setting the debugger to call ToString( ) for object display

8.16 Determining Current AppDomain Settings Information

Problem

You want to know about the current settings for the AppDomain your code is executing in to help in debugging various issues with assembly loading, authorization issues, and startup problems.

Solution

Examine the properties of the AppDomain.CurrentDomain.SetupInformation class to see the activation settings, the security information for the AppDomain, associated file paths like code base and configuration files, assembly binding and policy settings, and load optimization and shadow copy settings. Get the AppDomainSetup object with the current AppDomain settings information like this:

```
AppDomainSetup info = AppDomain.CurrentDomain.SetupInformation;
```

Now the ActivationArguments can be examined to find out things like the code base and full name of the AppDomain as well as the corresponding ActivationData and ActivationContext information:

```
Console.WriteLine("Current AppDomain Properties:");
if (info.ActivationArguments != null)
{
```

```
if (info.ActivationArguments.ApplicationIdentity != null)
{
    Console.WriteLine("\tAppDomain CodeBase: {0}",
        info.ActivationArguments.ApplicationIdentity.CodeBase);
    Console.WriteLine("\tAppDomain Full Name: {0}",
        info.ActivationArguments.ApplicationIdentity.FullName);
}
foreach (string data in info.ActivationArguments.ActivationData)
{
    Console.WriteLine("\tActivation Data: {0}", data);
}
if (info.ActivationArguments.ActivationContext != null)
{
    Console.WriteLine("\tAppDomain Identity: {0}",
        info.ActivationArguments.ActivationContext.Identity);
}
}
```

The current values for the application base and name are available from their respective properties:

```
Console.WriteLine("\tCurrent Application Base: {0}",
    info.ApplicationBase);
Console.WriteLine("\tCurrent Application Name: {0}",
    info.ApplicationName);
```

To look at the security information for the application, see if the ApplicationTrust property of the AppDomainSetup object is available. If it is, the identity full name, code base, granted permission set, and level of trust are available.

```
if (info.ApplicationTrust != null)
{
    Console.WriteLine("\tSecurity Info for the Application:");
    Console.WriteLine("\t\tApplication Identity CodeBase: {0}",
        info.ApplicationTrust.ApplicationIdentity.CodeBase);
    Console.WriteLine("\t\tApplication Identity FullName: {0}",
        info.ApplicationTrust.ApplicationIdentity.FullName);
    Console.WriteLine("\t\tDefaultGrantSet: {0}",
        info.ApplicationTrust.DefaultGrantSet.ToXml());
    Console.WriteLine("\t\tIs the application trusted to run: {0}",
        info.ApplicationTrust.IsApplicationTrustedToRun);
}
```

Some of the more general properties of the AppDomain, like the shadow copy path, the path to the configuration file, and the path to the license file, are also available directly from the AppDomainSetup object:

```
Console.WriteLine("\tApplication Shadow Copy Path : {0}",
    info.CachePath);
Console.WriteLine("\tConfig File : {0}",
    info.ConfigurationFile);
Console.WriteLine("\tThe license file for this appdomain is located here: {0}",
    info.LicenseFile);
```

Information about the assembly-loading constraints for the AppDomain is also available, such as if the AppDomain should probe the appbase or private bin path for assemblies when loading and what those paths are. It can be determined if the AppDomain is allowing binding redirection, if it is allowing code to be downloaded, if it uses a publisher policy, and where dynamically generated assemblies are stored by looking at the DisallowBindingRedirects, DisallowCodeDownload, DisallowPublisherPolicy, and DynamicBase properties, respectively.

```
Console.WriteLine("\tAssembly loading parameters:");
Console.WriteLine("\t\tIs probing allowed in appbase and private bin path? : {0}",
    !info.DisallowApplicationBaseProbing);
Console.WriteLine("\t\tPrivate Bin Path: {0}",
    info.PrivateBinPath);
if (info.PrivateBinPathProbe != null)
{
    if (info.PrivateBinPathProbe.Length > 0)
        Console.WriteLine("\t\tExclude AppBase from search path");
    else
        Console.WriteLine("\t\tInclude AppBase in search path");
}

Console.WriteLine("\t\tIs binding redirection allowed?: {0}",
    !info.DisallowBindingRedirects);
Console.WriteLine("\t\tIs code downloading allowed : {0}",
    !info.DisallowCodeDownload);
Console.WriteLine("\t\tIs publisher policy used? : {0}",
    !info.DisallowPublisherPolicy);
Console.WriteLine("\t\tDynamically generated files are stored at: {0}",
    info.DynamicBase);
```

Finally, the loader optimization and shadow copy information can be retrieved from the LoaderOptimization, ShadowCopyDirectories, and ShadowCopyFiles properties:

```
Console.WriteLine("\t\tLoader optimization: {0}",
    info.LoaderOptimization.ToString());
Console.WriteLine("\t\tShadow Copy Dirs: {0}",
    info.ShadowCopyDirectories);
Console.WriteLine("\t\tShadow Copy Files: {0}",
    info.ShadowCopyFiles);
```

Discussion

The Common Language Runtime is a very flexible and configurable environment, which is a good thing in most cases. But when debugging, it can be helpful to see the actual runtime settings that the program is dealing with, instead of trying to piece them together from multiple configuration files and policy settings. The AppDomainSetup type provides a wealth of information about where the AppDomain is storing things, what access it has been given, and where it is looking for assemblies. Debugging assembly-load problems can be frustrating at best, and having an extra arrow in your quiver to figure out what is happening will help with faster bug resolution.

See Also

See the "AppDomainSetup class," "AppDomainSetup.ApplicationTrust Property," and "AppDomainSetup.ActivationArguments Property" topics in the MSDN documentation.

8.17 Boosting the Priority of a Process Programmatically

Problem

You want a specific program to run at a higher priority than most of the other processes on the machine to help it complete a time-critical task.

Solution

Use the `ProcessStartInfo` and `Process` classes to launch the program and then adjust it to a higher priority like this:

```
// Run recursive dir operation on the c:\ drive
ProcessStartInfo psi = new ProcessStartInfo("cmd.exe","/C\"dir c:\\ /S\"");
// Don't show the window.
psi.CreateNoWindow = true;
// Start the process.
Process p = Process.Start(psi);
// Raise the process priority to AboveNormal.
p.PriorityClass = ProcessPriorityClass.AboveNormal;
```

Discussion

The `Process.PriorityClass` property takes one of the `ProcessPriorityClass` enumeration values to indicate what priority the process should have. The enumeration values and descriptions are listed in Table 8-5.

Table 8-5. ProcessPriorityClass enumeration values

Name	Description
Idle	Run only when the system is idle. Preempted by any action.
BelowNormal	Will run with a light load on the CPU but will be preempted by any normal or higher process.
Normal	This is the default priority processes run at.
AboveNormal	A boost in scheduling priority from a normal process.
High	Used for time-critical tasks. Use carefully as it can eat most of the processor time and starve other applications.
RealTime	The highest possible priority. This should be used only when the process being altered is the only task that needs to occur on the machine.

Setting the priority above AboveNormal should be done in only very specialized situations for short durations of time, as it can starve other processes on the machine. The operating system uses the priority level to determine scheduling for the processors, and if one process is set to a higher priority for a long time, the processes with lesser priority may never finish.

See Also

See the "Process Class," "ProcessStartInfo Class," and "ProcessPriorityClass Enumeration" topics in the MSDN documentation.

8.18   Looking at Your Runtime Environment and Seeing What You Can Do About It

Problem

You want a way to easily gather information about the environment your program is running under to assist in troubleshooting customer issues.

Solution

Write a utility function that can gather this information for the process using the System.Environment class members. To view and manipulate the environment variables, use the GetEnvironmentVariables, GetEnvironmentVariable, and SetEnvironmentVariable methods:

```
Console.WriteLine("Current environment settings:");
foreach (DictionaryEntry de in Environment.GetEnvironmentVariables())
{
    Console.WriteLine("\t\tEnvironment Variable {0}: Value {1}", de.Key, de.Value);
}
Console.WriteLine("\tSetting environment variable MYENVVAR to {0}", "FOO");
Environment.SetEnvironmentVariable("MYENVVAR", "FOO");
Console.WriteLine("\tGetting Environment Variable MYENVVAR: Value {0}", Environment.
GetEnvironmentVariable("MYENVVAR"));
```

The command-line parameters, current working directory, and system directory are available from the CommandLine, CurrentDirectory, and SystemDirectory properties, respectively:

```
Console.WriteLine("\tCommand Line: {0}",Environment.CommandLine);
Console.WriteLine("\tCurrent Directory: {0}",Environment.CurrentDirectory);
Console.WriteLine("\tSystem Directory: {0}",Environment.SystemDirectory);
```

For machine-specific information, the machine name (MachineName), operating system version (OSVersion), and number of processors (ProcessorCount) are easily accessed:

```
Console.WriteLine("\tMachine NetBIOS Name: {0}",Environment.MachineName);
Console.WriteLine("\tOS Version Information: {0}",Environment.OSVersion.
VersionString);
Console.WriteLine("\tNumber of processors: {0}",Environment.ProcessorCount);
```

To see the current call stack, use the StackTrace property:

```
Console.WriteLine("\tCurrent Stack Trace: {0}",Environment.StackTrace);
```

For information about the current user and thread, the UserDomainName, UserInteractive, and UserName properties do the job:

```
Console.WriteLine("\tCurrent User Domain Name: {0}",Environment.UserDomainName);
Console.WriteLine("\tIs this an interactive user process?: {0}",Environment.
UserInteractive);
Thread.CurrentThread.Name = "Main thread";
Console.WriteLine("\tUser who started Thread ({0}): {1}",Thread.CurrentThread.Name,
    Environment.UserName);
```

Finally, the CLR version and amount of physical memory being used by the process are available in the Version and WorkingSet properties:

```
Console.WriteLine("\tCLR Version this code is running in: {0}",Environment.Version);
Console.WriteLine("\tAmount of physical memory used by this working set: {0}",
Environment.WorkingSet);
```

Discussion

Adding code to your programs for troubleshooting potential customer issues may seem like a hassle when you are coding, but it can be a lifesaver when you get that call on Friday morning that threatens to ruin your weekend. Having additional information about the environment the customer is running your code in can lead to the discovery of bad settings, interaction conflicts with other third-party software, or the uncovering of the source of the issue itself. System.Environment has a lot of valuable information that is worth making available for your support folks; they will thank you for it.

See Also

See the "System.Environment Class" topic in the MSDN documentation.

CHAPTER 9

Delegates, Events, and Anonymous Methods

9.0   Introduction

Delegates contain all that is needed to allow a method, with a specific signature and return type, to be invoked by your code. A delegate can be passed to methods and a reference to it can be stored in a structure or class. A delegate is used when, at design time, you do not know which method you need to call and the information to determine this is available only at runtime.

Another scenario is when the code calling a method is being developed independently of the code that will supply the method to be called. The classic example is a Windows Forms control. If you create a control, you are unlikely to know what method should be called in the application when the control raises an event, so you must provide a delegate to allow the application to hook up a handler to the event. When other developers use your control, they will typically decide when they are adding the control (through the designer or programmatically) and which method should be called to handle the event published by the control. (For example, it's common to connect a Button's click handler to a delegate at design time.)

Anonymous methods are delegates without the full delegate syntax. They are a feature of the C# compiler and not a CLR type. An anonymous method is ultimately created as a delegate instance by the compiler, but the syntax for declaring an anonymous method can be more concise than declaring a regular delegate. Anonymous methods also permit you to capture variables in the same scope and use programming techniques such as closures and functors (explained later in this chapter).

This chapter's recipes make use of delegates, events, and anonymous methods. Among other topics, these recipes cover:

- Handling each method invoked in a multicast delegate separately
- Synchronous delegate invocation versus asynchronous delegate invocation
- Enhancing an existing class with events
- Various uses of anonymous methods, closures, and functors

If you are not familiar with delegates, events, or anonymous methods, you should read the MSDN documentation on these topics. There are also good tutorials and example code showing you how to set up and use them in a basic fashion.

9.1 Controlling When and If a Delegate Fires Within a Multicast Delegate

Problem

You have combined multiple delegates to create a multicast delegate. When this multicast delegate is fired, each delegate within it is fired in turn. You need to exert more control over such things as the order in which each delegate is fired, firing only a subset of delegates, or firing each delegate based on the success or failure of previous delegates.

Solution

Use the GetInvocationList method to obtain an array of Delegate objects. Next, iterate over this array using a for (or foreach if order is irrelevant) loop. You can then invoke each Delegate object in the array individually and optionally retrieve its return value.

In .NET, all delegate types support multicast—that is, any delegate instance can invoke multiple methods each time it is itself invoked if it has been set up to do so. In this recipe, we use the term *multicast* to describe a delegate that has been set up to invoke multiple methods. The following delegate defines the MyDelegate delegate type:

```
public delegate int MyDelegate( );
```

The following method creates a multicast delegate called allInstances and then uses GetInvocationList to allow each delegate to be fired individually, in reverse order:

```
public static void InvokeInReverse( )
{
    MyDelegate myDelegateInstance1 = new MyDelegate(TestInvoke.Method1);
    MyDelegate myDelegateInstance2 = new MyDelegate(TestInvoke.Method2);
    MyDelegate myDelegateInstance3 = new MyDelegate(TestInvoke.Method3);

    MyDelegate allInstances =
            myDelegateInstance1 +
            myDelegateInstance2 +
            myDelegateInstance3;

    Console.WriteLine("Fire delegates in reverse");
    Delegate[] delegateList = allInstances.GetInvocationList( );
    for (int counter = delegateList.Length - 1; counter >= 0; counter--)
    {
        ((MyDelegate)delegateList[counter])( );
    }
}
```

As the following methods demonstrate by firing every other delegate, you don't have to invoke all of the delegates in the list. Note that, in this example, the multicast delegate is constructed in one method (InvokeEveryOtherSetup) and used in another method (InvokeEveryOtherImpl). You might be wondering what would happen if the MyDelegate parameter passed to InvokeEveryOtherImpl were a unicast delegate and you called GetInvocationList on it. Have no fear: GetInvocationList will happily give you a list of one delegate instance:

```
public static void InvokeEveryOtherSetup( )
{
    MyDelegate myDelegateInstance1 = new MyDelegate(TestInvoke.Method1);
    MyDelegate myDelegateInstance2 = new MyDelegate(TestInvoke.Method2);
    MyDelegate myDelegateInstance3 = new MyDelegate(TestInvoke.Method3);

    MyDelegate allInstances =
            myDelegateInstance1 +
            myDelegateInstance2 +
            myDelegateInstance3;

    InvokeEveryOtherImpl(allInstances);
}

public static void InvokeEveryOtherImpl(MyDelegate delegateInstance)
{
    Delegate[] delegateList = delegateInstance.GetInvocationList( );

    // See if there are any delegates hooked up.
    if (delegateList.Length > 0)
    {
        Console.WriteLine("Invoke every other delegate");
        for (int counter = 0; counter < delegateList.Length; counter += 2)
        {
            // Invoke the delegate.
            int retVal = ((MyDelegate)delegateList[counter])( );
        }
    }
}
```

The following class contains each of the methods that will be called by the MyDelegate multicast delegate allInstances:

```
public class TestInvoke
{
    public static int Method1( )
    {
        Console.WriteLine("Invoked Method1");
        return (1);
    }

    public static int Method2( )
    {
        Console.WriteLine("Invoked Method2");
        return (2);
```

```
    }

    public static int Method3( )
    {
        Console.WriteLine("Invoked Method3");
        return (3);
    }
}
```

The following delegate defines the `MyDelegate` delegate:

```
public delegate bool MyDelegateTF( );
```

It is also possible to decide whether to continue firing delegates in the list based on the return value of the currently firing delegate. The following method fires each delegate, stopping only when a delegate returns a `false` value:

```
public static void InvokeWithTest( )
{
    MyDelegateTF myDelegateInstanceTF1 =
        new MyDelegateTF(TestInvokeTF.Method1);
    MyDelegateTF myDelegateInstanceTF2 =
        new MyDelegateTF(TestInvokeTF.Method2);
    MyDelegateTF myDelegateInstanceTF3 =
        new MyDelegateTF(TestInvokeTF.Method3);

    MyDelegateTF allInstancesTF =
            myDelegateInstanceTF1 +
            myDelegateInstanceTF2 +
            myDelegateInstanceTF3;

    Console.WriteLine(
        "Invoke individually (Call based on previous return value):");
    foreach (MyDelegateTF instance in allInstancesTF.GetInvocationList( ))
    {
        // This break is not required; it is an optimization to prevent the
        // loop from continuing to execute.
        if (!instance( ))
            break;
    }
}
```

The following class contains each of the methods that will be called by the `MyDelegateTF` multicast delegate `allInstancesTF`:

```
public class TestInvokeTF
{
    public static bool Method1( )
    {
        Console.WriteLine("Invoked Method1");
        return (true);
    }

    public static bool Method2( )
    {
```

```
        Console.WriteLine("Invoked Method2");
        return (false);
    }

    public static bool Method3( )
    {
        Console.WriteLine("Invoked Method3");
        return (true);
    }
}
```

Discussion

A delegate, when called, will invoke all delegates stored within its *invocation list*. These delegates are usually invoked sequentially from the first to the last one added. With the use of the GetInvocationList method of the MulticastDelegate class, you can obtain each delegate in the invocation list of a multicast delegate. This method accepts no parameters and returns an array of Delegate objects that corresponds to the invocation list of the delegate on which this method was called. The returned Delegate array contains the delegates of the invocation list in the order in which they would normally be called; that is, the zeroth element in the Delegate array contains the Delegate object that is normally called first.

This application of the GetInvocationList method gives you the ability to control exactly when and how the delegates in a multicast delegate are invoked and allows you to prevent the continued invocation of delegates when one delegate fails. This ability is important if each delegate is manipulating data and one of the delegates fails in its duties but does not throw an exception. If one delegate fails in its duties and the remaining delegates rely on all previous delegates to succeed, you must quit invoking delegates at the point of failure. Note that an exception will force the invocation of delegates to cease, but throwing an exception is an expensive process. This recipe handles a delegate failure more efficiently and also provides more flexibility in dealing with these errors. For example, you can write logic to specify which delegates are to be invoked, based on the performance of previously invoked delegates.

See Also

See Recipes 9.2 and 9.3; see the "Delegate Class" and "Delegate.GetInvocationList Method" topics in the MSDN documentation.

9.2 Obtaining Return Values from Each Delegate in a Multicast Delegate

Problem

You have added multiple delegates to a single multicast delegate. Each of these individual delegates returns a value that is required by your application. Ordinarily, the values returned by individual delegates in a multicast delegate are lost—all except the value from the last delegate to fire, the return value of which is returned to the calling application. You need to be able to access the return value of each delegate that is fired in the multicast delegate.

Solution

Use the `GetInvocationList` method as in Recipe 9.1. This method returns each individual delegate from a multicast delegate. In doing so, you can invoke each delegate individually and get its return value. The following method creates a multicast delegate called `All` and then uses `GetInvocationList` to fire each delegate individually. After firing each delegate, the return value is captured:

```
public static void TestIndividualInvokesRetVal()
{
    MyDelegate myDelegateInstance1 = new MyDelegate(TestInvoke.Method1);
    MyDelegate myDelegateInstance2 = new MyDelegate(TestInvoke.Method2);
    MyDelegate myDelegateInstance3 = new MyDelegate(TestInvoke.Method3);

    MyDelegate allInstances =
            myDelegateInstance1 +
            myDelegateInstance2 +
            myDelegateInstance3;

    Console.WriteLine("Invoke individually (Obtain each return value):");
    foreach (MyDelegate instance in allInstances.GetInvocationList())
    {
        int retVal = instance();
        Console.WriteLine("\tOutput: " + retVal);
    }
}
```

The following delegate defines the `MyDelegate` delegate type:

```
public delegate int MyDelegate( );
```

The following class contains each of the methods that will be called by the `MyDelegate` multicast delegate instances:

```
public class TestInvoke
{
    public static int Method1( )
    {
        Console.WriteLine("Invoked Method1");
        return (1);
    }

    public static int Method2( )
    {
        Console.WriteLine("Invoked Method2");
        return (2);
    }
}
```

```
        public static int Method3( )
        {
            Console.WriteLine("Invoked Method3");
            return (3);
        }
    }
```

Discussion

One quirk with multicast delegates is that if any or all delegates within its invocation list return a value, only the value of the last invoked delegate is returned; all others are lost. This loss can become annoying, or worse, if your code requires these return values. Consider a case in which the allInstances delegate was invoked normally, as in the following code:

```
    retVal = allInstances( );
    Console.WriteLine(retVal);
```

The value 3 would be displayed since Method3 was the last method invoked by the allInstances delegate. None of the other return values would be captured.

By using the GetInvocationList method of the MulticastDelegate class, you can get around this limitation. This method returns an array of Delegate objects that can each be invoked separately. Note that this method does not invoke each delegate; it simply returns an array of them to the caller. By invoking each delegate separately, you can retrieve each return value from each fired delegate. (More information on the GetInvocationList method is presented in Recipe 9.1.)

Note that any out or ref parameters will also be lost when a multicast delegate is invoked. This recipe allows you to obtain the out and/or ref parameters of each invoked delegate within the multicast delegate.

However, you still need to be aware that any unhandled exceptions emanating from one of these invoked delegates will be bubbled up to the method Test-IndividualInvokesRetVal, presented in this recipe. To better handle this situation, see Recipe 9.3.

See Also

See Recipes 9.1 and 9.3; see the "Delegate Class" and "Delegate.GetInvocationList Method" topics in the MSDN documentation.

9.3 Handling Exceptions Individually for Each Delegate in a Multicast Delegate

Problem

You have added multiple delegates to a single multicast delegate. Each of these individual delegates must be invoked, regardless of whether an unhandled exception is thrown within one of the delegates. But once a delegate in a multicast delegate throws an unhandled exception, no more delegates are fired. You need a way to trap unhandled exceptions within each individual delegate while still allowing the rest of the delegates to fire.

Solution

Use the `GetInvocationList` method as shown in Recipe 9.1. This method returns each individual delegate from a multicast delegate and, by doing so, allows you to invoke each delegate within the try block of an exception handler.

The following delegate defines the `MyDelegate` delegate type:

```
public delegate int MyDelegate( );
```

The method shown in Example 9-1 creates a multicast delegate called `allInstances` and then uses `GetInvocationList` to retrieve each delegate individually. Each delegate is then fired within the try block of an exception handler.

Example 9-1. Handling exceptions individually for each delegate in a multicast delegate

```
public static void TestIndividualInvokesExceptions( )
{
    MyDelegate myDelegateInstance1 = new MyDelegate(TestInvoke.Method1);
    MyDelegate myDelegateInstance2 = new MyDelegate(TestInvoke.Method2);
    MyDelegate myDelegateInstance3 = new MyDelegate(TestInvoke.Method3);

    MyDelegate allInstances =
            myDelegateInstance1 +
            myDelegateInstance2 +
            myDelegateInstance3;

    Console.WriteLine("Invoke individually (handle exceptions):");

    // Create an instance of a wrapper exception to hold any exceptions
    // encountered during the invocations of the delegate instances.
    MyExceptionHolderException holderEx = new MyExceptionHolderException( );

    foreach (MyDelegate instance in allInstances.GetInvocationList( ))
    {
        try
        {
            int retVal = instance( );
            Console.WriteLine("\tOutput: " + retVal);
        }
        catch (SecurityException se)
        {
            // Stop everything; malicious code may be attempting to
            // access privileged data.

            // Create an EventLog instance and assign its source.
            EventLog myLog = new EventLog( );
            myLog.Source = "MyApplicationSource";
```

```
            // Write an entry to the event log.
            myLog.WriteEntry("Security Failure in MyApplication! " +
                se.ToString(),
                    EventLogEntryType.Error);
            // Rethrow the exception to stop things since it was a
            // security failure.
            throw;
        }
        catch (Exception e)
        {
            // Display (or log) the exception and continue.
            Console.WriteLine(e.ToString());
            // Add this exception to the exception holder.
            holderEx.Add(e);
        }
    }
    // If we caught any exceptions along the way, throw our
    // wrapper exception with all of them in it.
    if (holderEx.Exceptions.Count > 0)
        throw holderEx;
}
```

The `MyExceptionHolderException` class is able to have multiple exceptions added to it. It exposes a `List<Exception>` through the `Exceptions` property, as shown in Example 9-2.

Example 9-2. MyExceptionHolderException class

```
public class MyExceptionHolderException : Exception
{
    private List<Exception> _exceptions = null;

    public MyExceptionHolderException()
    {
        _exceptions = new List<Exception>();
    }

    public List<Exception> Exceptions
    {
        get { return _exceptions; }
    }

    public void Add(Exception ex)
    {
        if (ex == null)
            throw new ArgumentNullException("ex");

        _exceptions.Add(ex);
    }

    public void AddRange(Exception [] exceptions)
    {
```

Example 9-2. MyExceptionHolderException class (continued)

```
        if (exceptions == null)
            throw new ArgumentNullException("ex");

        _exceptions.AddRange(exceptions);
    }
}
```

The following class contains each of the methods that will be called by the MyDelegate multicast delegate instances:

```
public class TestInvoke
{
    public static int Method1( )
    {
        Console.WriteLine("Invoked Method1");
        return (1);
    }

    public static int Method2( )
    {
        Console.WriteLine("Invoked Method2");
        return (2);
    }

    public static int Method3( )
    {
        // Simulate an exception being thrown.
        throw (new Exception("Method3"));
        Console.WriteLine("Invoked Method3");
        return (3);
    }
}
```

Discussion

If an exception occurs in a delegate that is invoked from within a multicast delegate and that exception is unhandled, any remaining delegates are not invoked. This is the expected behavior of a multicast delegate. However, in some circumstances, you'd like to be able to handle exceptions thrown from individual delegates and then determine at that point whether to continue invoking the remaining delegates.

In the TestIndividualInvokesExceptions method of this recipe, if an exception SecurityException is caught, it is logged to the event log and the exception is rethrown. However, if another type of Exception object is thrown, you just display or log it and continue invoking delegates. This strategy allows for as fine-grained handling of exceptions as you need. Note that, if you rethrow an exception, the exception will be bubbled up to the next enclosing exception handler. If the next outer exception handler is outside of the loop used to iterate through each delegate object returned by the GetInvocationList method, any remaining delegates will not be invoked. One way to deal with this is to store all of the exceptions that occur during delegate processing, then wrap all of the exceptions encountered during processing in a custom exception. After processing completes, throw the custom exception. See the MyExceptionHoldingException class in the Solution.

By adding a finally block to this try-catch block, you can be assured that code within this finally block is executed after every delegate returns. This technique is useful if you want to interleave code between calls to delegates, such as code to clean up objects that are not needed or code to verify that each delegate left the data it touched in a stable state.

See Also

See Recipes 9.1 and 9.2; see the "Delegate Class" and "Delegate.GetInvocationList Method" topics in the MSDN documentation.

9.4   Converting Delegate Invocation from Synchronous to Asynchronous

Problem

You have determined that one or more delegates invoked synchronously within your application are taking a long time to execute. This delay is making the user interface less responsive to the user. The invocation of these delegates should be converted from synchronous to asynchronous mode.

Solution

A typical synchronous delegate type and supporting code that invokes the delegate are shown here:

```
public delegate void SyncDelegateTypeSimple();

// The class and method that are invoked through the SyncDelegateTypeSimple delegate
public class TestSyncDelegateTypeSimple
{
    public static void Method1()
    {
        Console.WriteLine("Invoked Method1");
    }
}
```

The code to use this delegate is:

```
public static void TestSimpleSyncDelegate()
{
    SyncDelegateTypeSimple sdtsInstance =
        new SyncDelegateTypeSimple(TestSyncDelegateTypeSimple.Method1);
    sdtsInstance();
}
```

This delegate can be called asynchronously on a thread obtained from the thread pool by modifying the code as follows:

```
public static void TestSimpleAsyncDelegate( )
{
    AsyncCallback callBack = new AsyncCallback(DelegateSimpleCallback);

    SyncDelegateTypeSimple sdtsInstance =
        new SyncDelegateTypeSimple(TestSyncDelegateTypeSimple.Method1);

    IAsyncResult asyncResult =
        sdtsInstance.BeginInvoke(callBack, null);

    Console.WriteLine("WORKING...");
}

// The callback that gets called when TestSyncDelegateTypeSimple.Method1
// is finished processing
private static void DelegateSimpleCallback(IAsyncResult iResult)
{
    AsyncResult result = (AsyncResult)iResult;
    SyncDelegateTypeSimple sdtsInstance =
        (SyncDelegateTypeSimple)result.AsyncDelegate;

    sdtsInstance.EndInvoke(result);
    Console.WriteLine("Simple callback run");
}
```

 AsyncResult can be found in the System.Runtime.Remoting.Messaging namespace in *mscorlib*.

Of course you might also want to change the TestSyncDelegateTypeSimple class name to TestAsyncDelegateTypeSimple and the SyncDelegateTypeSimple delegate name to AsyncDelegateTypeSimple just to be consistent with your naming.

The previous example shows how to call a delegate that accepts no parameters and returns void. The next example shows a synchronous delegate that accepts parameters and returns an integer:

```
public delegate int SyncDelegateType(string message);

public class TestSyncDelegateType
{
    public static int Method1(string message)
    {
        Console.WriteLine("Invoked Method1 with message: " + message);
        return (1);
    }
}
```

The code to use this delegate is:

```
public static void TestComplexSyncDelegate()
{
    SyncDelegateType sdtInstance =
        new SyncDelegateType(TestSyncDelegateType.Method1);

    int retVal = sdtInstance("Synchronous call");

    Console.WriteLine("Sync: " + retVal);
}
```

The synchronous invocation of the delegate can be converted to asynchronous invocation in the following manner:

```
public static void TestCallbackAsyncDelegate()
{
    AsyncCallback callBack =
        new AsyncCallback(DelegateCallback);

    SyncDelegateType sdtInstance =
        new SyncDelegateType(TestSyncDelegateType.Method1);

    IAsyncResult asyncResult =
        sdtInstance.BeginInvoke("Asynchronous call", callBack, null);

    Console.WriteLine("WORKING...");
}

// The callback that gets called when TestSyncDelegateType.Method1
// is finished processing
private static void DelegateCallback(IAsyncResult iResult)
{
    AsyncResult result = (AsyncResult)iResult;
    SyncDelegateType sdtInstance =
        (SyncDelegateType)result.AsyncDelegate;

    int retVal = sdtInstance.EndInvoke(result);
    Console.WriteLine("retVal (Callback): " + retVal);
}
```

Discussion

Converting the invocation of a delegate from being synchronous to asynchronous is not an overly complicated procedure. You need to add calls to both `BeginInvoke` and `EndInvoke` on the delegate that is being called synchronously. A callback method, `DelegateCallback`, is added, which gets called when the delegate is finished. This callback method then calls the `EndInvoke` method on the delegate invoked using `BeginInvoke`.

You must always call EndInvoke when invoking delegates asynchronously, even when the delegate returns void, to ensure proper cleanup of resources in the CLR.

The notification callback method specified in the *callback* parameter accepts a single parameter of type IAsyncResult. This parameter can be cast to an AsyncResult type and used to set up the call to the EndInvoke method. If you want to handle any exceptions thrown by the asynchronous delegate in the notification callback, wrap the EndInvoke method in a try/catch exception handler.

See Also

See the "Delegate Class" and "Asynchronous Delegates" topics in the MSDN documentation.

9.5   Wrapping Sealed Classes to Add Events

Problem

Through the use of inheritance, adding events to a nonsealed class is fairly easy. For example, inheritance is used to add events to a Hashtable object. However, adding events to a sealed class, such as System.IO.DirectoryInfo, requires a technique other than inheritance.

Solution

To add events to a sealed class, such as the DirectoryInfo class, wrap it using another class, such as the DirectoryInfoNotify class defined in Example 9-3.

 You can use the FileSystemWatcher class (see Recipes 12.23 and 12.24) to monitor the filesystem changes asynchronously due to activity outside of your program, or you can use the DirectoryInfoNotify class defined here to monitor your program's activity when using the filesystem.

Example 9-3. Adding events to a sealed class

```
using System;
using System.IO;

public class DirectoryInfoNotify
{
    public DirectoryInfoNotify(string path)
    {
        internalDirInfo = new DirectoryInfo(path);
    }

    private DirectoryInfo internalDirInfo = null;
    public event EventHandler AfterCreate;
    public event EventHandler AfterCreateSubDir;
    public event EventHandler AfterDelete;
    public event EventHandler AfterMoveTo;
```

Example 9-3. Adding events to a sealed class (continued)

```
protected virtual void OnAfterCreate( )
{
    EventHandler afterCreate = AfterCreate;
    if (afterCreate!= null)
    {
        afterCreate (this, new EventArgs( ));
    }
}

protected virtual void OnAfterCreateSubDir( )
{
    EventHandler afterCreateSubDir = AfterCreateSubDir;
    if (afterCreateSubDir != null)
    {
        afterCreateSubDir(this, new EventArgs( ));
    }
}

protected virtual void OnAfterDelete( )
{
    EventHandler afterDelete = AfterDelete;
    if (afterDelete != null)
    {
        afterDelete(this, new EventArgs( ));
    }
}

protected virtual void OnAfterMoveTo( )
{
    EventHandler afterMoveTo = AfterMoveTo;
    if (afterMoveTo != null)
    {
        afterMoveTo(this, new EventArgs( ));
    }
}

// Event firing members
public void Create( )
{
    internalDirInfo.Create( );
    OnAfterCreate( );
}

public DirectoryInfoNotify CreateSubdirectory(string path)
{
    DirectoryInfo subDirInfo = internalDirInfo.CreateSubdirectory(path);
    OnAfterCreateSubDir( );

    return (new DirectoryInfoNotify(subDirInfo.FullName));
}

public void Delete(bool recursive)
```

Example 9-3. Adding events to a sealed class (continued)

```
    {
        internalDirInfo.Delete(recursive);
        OnAfterDelete( );
    }

    public void Delete( )
    {
        internalDirInfo.Delete( );
        OnAfterDelete( );
    }

    public void MoveTo(string destDirName)
    {
        internalDirInfo.MoveTo(destDirName);
        OnAfterMoveTo( );
    }

    // Nonevent firing members
    public string FullName
    {
        get {return (internalDirInfo.FullName);}
    }
    public string Name
    {
        get {return (internalDirInfo.Name);}
    }
    public DirectoryInfoNotify Parent
    {
        get {return (new DirectoryInfoNotify(internalDirInfo.Parent.FullName));}
    }
    public DirectoryInfoNotify Root
    {
        get {return (new DirectoryInfoNotify(internalDirInfo.Root.FullName));}
    }

    public override string ToString( )
    {
        return (internalDirInfo.ToString( ));
    }
}
```

The DirectoryInfoObserver class, shown in Example 9-4, allows you to register any
DirectoryInfoNotify objects with it. This registration process allows the
DirectoryInfoObserver class to listen for any events to be raised in the registered
DirectoryInfoNotify object(s). The only events that are raised by the Directory-
InfoNotify object are after a modification has been made to the directory structure
using a DirectoryInfoNotify object that has been registered with a Directory-
InfoObserver object.

Example 9-4. DirectoryInfoObserver class

```
public class DirectoryInfoObserver
{
    public DirectoryInfoObserver( ) {}

    public void Register(DirectoryInfoNotify dirInfo)
    {
        dirInfo.AfterCreate += new EventHandler(AfterCreateListener);
        dirInfo.AfterCreateSubDir +=
                new EventHandler(AfterCreateSubDirListener);
        dirInfo.AfterMoveTo += new EventHandler(AfterMoveToListener);
        dirInfo.AfterDelete += new EventHandler(AfterDeleteListener);
    }

    public void UnRegister(DirectoryInfoNotify dirInfo)
    {
        dirInfo.AfterCreate -= new EventHandler(AfterCreateListener);
        dirInfo.AfterCreateSubDir -=
                new EventHandler(AfterCreateSubDirListener);
        dirInfo.AfterMoveTo -= new EventHandler(AfterMoveToListener);
        dirInfo.AfterDelete -= new EventHandler(AfterDeleteListener);
    }

    public void AfterCreateListener(object sender, EventArgs e)
    {
        Console.WriteLine("Notified after creation of directory--sender: " +
                        ((DirectoryInfoNotify)sender).FullName);
    }

    public void AfterCreateSubDirListener(object sender, EventArgs e)
    {
        Console.WriteLine("Notified after creation of SUB-directory--sender: " +
                        ((DirectoryInfoNotify)sender).FullName);
    }

    public void AfterMoveToListener(object sender, EventArgs e)
    {
        Console.WriteLine("Notified of directory move--sender: " +
                        ((DirectoryInfoNotify)sender).FullName);
    }

    public void AfterDeleteListener(object sender, EventArgs e)
    {
        Console.WriteLine("Notified of directory deletion--sender: " +
                        ((DirectoryInfoNotify)sender).FullName);
    }
}
```

Discussion

Wrapping is a very useful technique with many different applications (proxies, facades, etc.). However, if you use it, all classes in your application have to use the wrapped version of the class, or your wrapper code will not execute for cases when the sealed class is used directly.

In some situations this technique might be useful even when a class is not sealed. For example, if you want to raise notifications when methods that have not been declared as virtual are called, you'll need this technique to wrap those methods and supply the notifications. So even if DirectoryInfo were not sealed, you would still need this technique because you can't override its Delete, Create, and other methods. And hiding them with the new keyword is unreliable because someone might use your object through a reference of type DirectoryInfo instead of type DirectoryInfoNotify, in which case the original methods and not your new methods will be used. So the delegation approach presented here is the only reliable technique when methods in the base class are not virtual methods, regardless of whether the base class is sealed.

The TestDirectoryInfoObserver method shown in Example 9-5 creates two DirectoryInfoObserver objects along with two DirectoryInfoNotify objects, and then it proceeds to create a directory, *C:\testdir,* and a subdirectory under *C:\testdir* called *new*.

Example 9-5. TestDirectoryInfoObserver method

```
public void TestDirectoryInfoObserver( )
{
    // Create two observer objects.
    DirectoryInfoObserver observer1 = new DirectoryInfoObserver( );
    DirectoryInfoObserver observer2 = new DirectoryInfoObserver( );

    // Create a notification object for the directory c:\testdir.
    DirectoryInfoNotify dirInfo = new DirectoryInfoNotify(@"c:\testdir");

    // Register the notification object under both observers.
    observer1.Register(dirInfo);
    observer2.Register(dirInfo);

    // Create the directory c:\testdir.
    dirInfo.Create( );

    // Have the first observer watch the new subdirectory as well.
    DirectoryInfoNotify subDirInfo = dirInfo.CreateSubdirectory("new");
    observer1.Register(subDirInfo);

    // Delete the subdirectory first and then the parent directory.
    subDirInfo.Delete(true);
    dirInfo.Delete(false);

    // Unregister notification objects with their observers.
    observer2.UnRegister(dirInfo);
    observer1.UnRegister(dirInfo);
}
```

This code outputs the following:

```
Notified after creation of directory--sender: c:\testdir
Notified after creation of directory--sender: c:\testdir
Notified after creation of SUB-directory--sender: c:\testdir
Notified after creation of SUB-directory--sender: c:\testdir
Notified of directory deletion--sender: c:\testdir\new
Notified of directory deletion--sender: c:\testdir
Notified of directory deletion--sender: c:\testdir
```

Rather than using inheritance to override members of a sealed class (i.e., the DirectoryInfo class), the sealed class is wrapped by a notification class (i.e., the DirectoryInfoNotify class).

The main drawback to wrapping a sealed class is that each method available in the underlying DirectoryInfo class might have to be implemented in the outer DirectoryInfoNotify class, which can be tedious if the underlying class has many visible members. The good news is that if you know you will not be using a subset of the wrapped class's members, you do not have to wrap each of those members. Simply do not make them visible from your outer class, which is what you have done in the DirectoryInfoNotify class. Only the methods you intend to use are implemented on the DirectoryInfoNotify class. If more methods on the DirectoryInfo class will later be used from the DirectoryInfoNotify class, they can be added with minimal effort.

For a DirectoryInfoNotify object to wrap a DirectoryInfo object, the DirectoryInfoNotify object must have an internal reference to the wrapped DirectoryInfo object. This reference is in the form of the internalDirInfo field. Essentially, this field allows all wrapped methods to forward their calls to the underlying DirectoryInfo object. For example, the Delete method of a DirectoryInfoNotify object forwards its call to the underlying DirectoryInfo object as follows:

```
public void Delete( )
{
    // Forward the call.
    internalDirInfo.Delete( );

    // Raise an event.
    OnAfterDelete( );
}
```

You should make sure that the method signatures are the same on the outer class as they are on the wrapped class. This convention will make it much more intuitive and transparent for another developer to use. You could also make it completely different to differentiate the wrapper from the contained class. The key is not to have it look very similar to the contained class but with slight differences, as that would be the most confusing for your consumers.

There is one method, CreateSubdirectory, that requires further explanation:

```
public DirectoryInfoNotify CreateSubdirectory(string path)
{
    DirectoryInfo subDirInfo = internalDirInfo.CreateSubdirectory(path);
    OnAfterCreateSubDir( );

    return (new DirectoryInfoNotify(subDirInfo.FullName));
}
```

This method is unique since it returns a DirectoryInfo object in the wrapped class. However, if you also returned a DirectoryInfo object from this outer method, you might confuse the developer attempting to use the DirectoryInfoNotify class. If a developer is using the DirectoryInfoNotify class, she will expect that class to also return objects of the same type from the appropriate members rather than returning the type of the wrapped class.

To fix this problem and make the DirectoryInfoNotify class more consistent, a DirectoryInfoNotify object is returned from the CreateSubdirectory method. The code that receives this DirectoryInfoNotify object might then register it with any available DirectoryInfoObserver object(s). This technique is shown here:

```
// Create a DirectoryInfoObserver object and a DirectoryInfoNotify object.
DirectoryInfoObserver observer = new DirectoryInfoObserver( );
DirectoryInfoNotify dirInfo = new DirectoryInfoNotify(@"c:\testdir");

// Register the DirectoryInfoNotify object with the DirectoryInfoObserver object.
observer.Register(dirInfo);

// Create the c:\testdir directory and then create a subdirectory within that
// directory; this will return a new DirectoryInfoNotify object, which is
// registered with the same DirectoryInfoObserver object as the dirInfo object.
dirInfo.Create( );
DirectoryInfoNotify subDirInfo = dirInfo.CreateSubdirectory("new");
observer.Register(subDirInfo);

// Delete this subdirectory.
subDirInfo.Delete(true);

// Clean up.
observer.UnRegister(dirInfo);
```

The observer object will be notified of the following events in this order:

1. When the dirInfo.Create method is called

2. When the dirInfo.CreateSubdirectory method is called

3. When the subDirInfo.Delete method is called

If the second observer.Register method were not called, the third event (subDirInfo.Delete) would not be caught by the observer object.

The `DirectoryInfoObserver` class contains methods that listen for events on any `DirectoryInfoNotify` objects that are registered with it. The *Xxx*`Listener` methods are called whenever their respective event is raised on a registered `DirectoryInfoNotify` object. Within these *Xxx*`Listener` methods, you can place any code that you wish to execute whenever a particular event is raised.

These *Xxx*`Listener` methods accept a *sender* object parameter, which is a reference to the `DirectoryInfoNotify` object that raised the event. This *sender* object can be cast to a `DirectoryInfoNotify` object and its members may be called if needed. This parameter allows you to gather information and take action based on the object that raised the event.

The second parameter to the *Xxx*`Listener` methods is of type `EventArgs`, which is a rather useless class for your purposes. Recipe 9.6 shows a way to use a class derived from the `EventArgs` class to pass information from the object that raised the event to the *Xxx*`Listener` method on the observer object and then back to the object that raised the event.

See Also

See Recipe 9.6; see the "Event Keyword" and "Handling and Raising Events" topics in the MSDN documentation.

9.6 Passing Specialized Parameters to and from an Event

Problem

You have implemented Recipe 9.5, but you want to allow an event listener to cancel an action that raised a particular event. For example, if a class attempts to create a new directory, you want to be able to verify that the directory is being created in the correct location. If the directory is not being created in the correct location (perhaps an insecure location), you want to be able to prevent the directory's creation.

Solution

Use a class derived from `EventArgs` as the second parameter to the event handler. In this example, you use `CancelEventArgs`, a class defined in the .NET Framework Class Library. The Solution for Recipe 9.5 has been modified to include an event that is raised before the `Create` method of the `DirectoryInfoNotify` object actually creates a new path. An object of type `CancelEventArgs` is passed to this new event to allow any listeners of this event to cancel the `Create` method action. The modified class is shown in Example 9-6 with the modifications highlighted.

Example 9-6. Passing specialized parameters to and from an event

```
using System;
using System.ComponentModel;
using System.IO;

public class DirectoryInfoNotify
{
    public DirectoryInfoNotify(string path)
    {
        internalDirInfo = new DirectoryInfo(path);
    }

    private DirectoryInfo internalDirInfo = null;
    public event CancelEventHandler BeforeCreate;
    public event EventHandler AfterCreate;
    public event EventHandler AfterCreateSubDir;
    public event EventHandler AfterDelete;
    public event EventHandler AfterMoveTo;

    protected virtual void OnBeforeCreate(CancelEventArgs e)
    {
        CancelEventHandler beforeCreate = BeforeCreate;
        if (beforeCreate != null)
        {
            beforeCreate (this, e);
        }
    }

    protected virtual void OnAfterCreate( )
    {
        EventHandler afterCreate = AfterCreate;
        if (afterCreate!= null)
        {
            afterCreate (this, new EventArgs( ));
        }
    }

    protected virtual void OnAfterCreateSubDir( )
    {
        EventHandler afterCreateSubDir = AfterCreateSubDir;
        if (afterCreateSubDir != null)
        {
            afterCreateSubDir(this, new EventArgs( ));
        }
    }

    protected virtual void OnAfterDelete( )
    {
        EventHandler afterDelete = AfterDelete;
        if (afterDelete != null)
        {
            afterDelete(this, new EventArgs( ));
        }
```

```csharp
    }

    protected virtual void OnAfterMoveTo( )
    {
        EventHandler afterMoveTo = AfterMoveTo;
        if (afterMoveTo != null)
        {
            afterMoveTo(this, new EventArgs( ));
        }
    }

    // Event firing members
    public void Create( )
    {
        CancelEventArgs args = new CancelEventArgs(false);
        OnBeforeCreate(args);

        if (!args.Cancel)
        {
            internalDirInfo.Create( );
            OnAfterCreate( );
        }
    }

    public DirectoryInfoNotify CreateSubdirectory(string path)
    {
        DirectoryInfo subDirInfo = internalDirInfo.CreateSubdirectory(path);
        OnAfterCreateSubDir( );

        return (new DirectoryInfoNotify(subDirInfo.FullName));
    }

    public void Delete(bool recursive)
    {
        internalDirInfo.Delete(recursive);
        OnAfterDelete( );
    }

    public void Delete( )
    {
        internalDirInfo.Delete( );
        OnAfterDelete( );
    }

    public void MoveTo(string destDirName)
    {
        internalDirInfo.MoveTo(destDirName);
        OnAfterMoveTo( );
    }

    // Nonevent firing members
    public virtual string FullName
```

```
{
    get {return (internalDirInfo.FullName);}
}
public string Name
{
    get {return (internalDirInfo.Name);}
}
public DirectoryInfoNotify Parent
{
    get {return (new DirectoryInfoNotify(internalDirInfo.Parent.FullName));}
}
public DirectoryInfoNotify Root
{
    get {return (new DirectoryInfoNotify(internalDirInfo.Root.FullName));}
}

public override string ToString( )
{
    return (internalDirInfo.ToString( ));
}
}
```

The DirectoryInfoObserver class contains each of the event listeners and is shown in Example 9-7 with the modifications highlighted.

Example 9-7. Modified DirectoryInfoOberver class

```
public class DirectoryInfoObserver
{
    public DirectoryInfoObserver( ) {}

    public void Register(DirectoryInfoNotify dirInfo)
    {
        dirInfo.BeforeCreate += new CancelEventHandler(BeforeCreateListener);
        dirInfo.AfterCreate += new EventHandler(AfterCreateListener);
        dirInfo.AfterCreateSubDir +=
                new EventHandler(AfterCreateSubDirListener);
        dirInfo.AfterMoveTo += new EventHandler(AfterMoveToListener);
        dirInfo.AfterDelete += new EventHandler(AfterDeleteListener);
    }

    public void UnRegister(DirectoryInfoNotify dirInfo)
    {
        dirInfo.BeforeCreate -= new CancelEventHandler(BeforeCreateListener);
        dirInfo.AfterCreate -= new EventHandler(AfterCreateListener);
        dirInfo.AfterCreateSubDir -=
                new EventHandler(AfterCreateSubDirListener);
        dirInfo.AfterMoveTo -= new EventHandler(AfterMoveToListener);
        dirInfo.AfterDelete -= new EventHandler(AfterDeleteListener);
    }

    public void BeforeCreateListener(object sender, CancelEventArgs e)
```

Example 9-7. Modified DirectoryInfoOberver class (continued)

```
{
    if (!e.Cancel)
    {
        if (!((DirectoryInfoNotify)sender).Root.FullName.Equals(@"d:\"))
        {
            e.Cancel = true;
        }
        else
        {
            Console.WriteLine(
                    "Notified BEFORE creation of directory--sender: " +
                    ((DirectoryInfoNotify)sender).FullName);
        }
    }
}

public void AfterCreateListener(object sender, EventArgs e)
{
    Console.WriteLine("Notified after creation of directory--sender: " +
                    ((DirectoryInfoNotify)sender).FullName);
}

public void AfterCreateSubDirListener(object sender, EventArgs e)
{
    Console.WriteLine("Notified after creation of SUB-directory--sender: " +
                    ((DirectoryInfoNotify)sender).FullName);
}

public void AfterMoveToListener(object sender, EventArgs e)
{
    Console.WriteLine("Notified of directory move--sender: " +
                    ((DirectoryInfoNotify)sender).FullName);
}

public void AfterDeleteListener(object sender, EventArgs e)
{
    Console.WriteLine("Notified of directory deletion--sender: " +
                    ((DirectoryInfoNotify)sender).FullName);
}
}
```

Discussion

The code for the modified DirectoryInfoNotify class contains a new event called BeforeCreate, which is raised from the OnBeforeCreate method. The OnBeforeCreate method is initially called by the Create method immediately before calling the Create method of the wrapped DirectoryInfo object. This setup allows the event listener for the BeforeCreate event to decide whether the directory creation operation should be canceled.

The DirectoryInfoObserver class contains a new method, BeforeCreateListener, which listens for the BeforeCreate event. In addition, the Register and UnRegister methods of this class contain logic to add/remove this event to/from the list of events that will be listened for on any registered DirectoryInfoNotify objects.

The OnBeforeCreate method of the DirectoryInfoNotify class is passed a parameter of a type called CancelEventArgs, which exists in the .NET FCL. This type derives from EventArgs and contains one useful property, called Cancel. This property will be used by the BeforeCreateListener method of the DirectoryInfoObserver class to determine whether the Create method should be canceled before it has a chance to create a new directory.

The CancelEventArgs object will be created in a DirectoryInfoNotify object, and when the BeforeCreate event is raised, the CancelEventArgs object will be passed to the BeforeCreateListener method on the DirectoryInfoObserver object. This method will then determine whether the creation of the directory should proceed or be canceled. The determination is made by comparing the root drive of the directory to see if it is anything but the *D:* drive; if so, the operation is canceled. This prevents any registered DirectoryInfoNotify objects from creating a directory on any drive other than the *D:* drive.

If multiple DirectoryInfoObserver objects are listening to the BeforeCreate event and one of those observer objects decides to cancel the operation, the entire operation is canceled unless you take some action to prevent this, as shown in Recipe 9.1.

The same CancelEventArgs object is referenced by each observer as well as each object that raised the event. This allows you to read the value of the Cancel property on the returned CancelEventArgs object in the Create method of the DirectoryInfoNotify object. If this property returns true, the operation cannot proceed; otherwise, the operation is permitted.

You are not confined to merely passing EventArgs objects or any of its subclasses found in the FCL; you can subclass the EventArgs class to create a specialized EventArgs type. This would be beneficial if the object passed in to the *sender* parameter of the event does not include all of the information that the *Xxx*Listener methods will need. For example, you could create the following specialized EventArgs class:

```
public class UserEventArgs : EventArgs
{
    public UserEventArgs(string userName)
    {
        this.userName = userName;
    }

    private string userName = "";

    public string UserName
    {
        get {return (userName);}
    }
}
```

This class passes the name of the logged-on user to the *Xxx*Listener methods to allow them to determine whether the operation should continue based on that user's privileges. This is just one example of creating a specialized EventArgs class. You can create others to pass in whatever information your listeners need.

See Also

See Recipe 9.5; see the "Event Keyword," "EventHandler Delegate," and "Handling and Raising Events" topics in the MSDN documentation.

9.7 An Advanced Interface Search Mechanism

Problem

You are searching for an interface using the Type class. However, complex interface searches are not available through the GetInterface and GetInterfaces methods of a Type object. The GetInterface method searches for an interface only by name (using a case-sensitive or case-insensitive search), and the GetInterfaces method returns an array of all the interfaces implemented on a particular type. You want a more focused searching mechanism that might involve searching for interfaces that define a method with a specific signature or implemented interfaces that are loaded from the GAC. You need more flexible and more advanced searching for interfaces that does not involve creating your own interface search engine. This capability might be used for applications like a code generator or reverse engineering tool.

Solution

The FindInterfaces method of a Type object can be used along with a callback to perform complex searches of interfaces on a type. The method shown in Example 9-8 will call a custom interface searching method, SearchInterfacesOfType.

Example 9-8. Performing complex searches of interfaces on a type

```
using System;
using System.Reflection;

public class SearchType
{
    public void FindSpecificInterfaces( )
    {
        Type[] types = new Type[3] {Type.GetType("System.ICloneable"),
                    Type.GetType("System.Collections.ICollection"),
                    Type.GetType("System.IAppDomainSetup")};
        Type[] interfaces = SearchInterfacesOfType(Type.GetType(
                        "System.Collections.ArrayList"), types);

        if (interfaces.Length > 0)
        {
            Console.WriteLine("Matches found:");
```

```
        for(int counter =0; counter < interfaces.Length; counter++)
        {
            Console.WriteLine("\tIFace Name: " +
                                interfaces[counter].ToString( ));
            Console.WriteLine("\tIFace Base Type: " +
                                interfaces[counter].BaseType);
            foreach (object attr in
                    interfaces[counter].GetCustomAttributes(false))
            {
                Console.WriteLine("\t\tIFace attr: " + attr.ToString( ));
            }
        }
    }
    else
    {
        Console.WriteLine("\t\tNo matches found");
    }
}

public static Type[] SearchInterfacesOfType(Type searchedType,
                                Type[] interfaceNames)
{
    TypeFilter filter = new TypeFilter(InterfaceFilterCallback);
    Type[] interfaces =  searchedType.FindInterfaces(filter, interfaceNames);

    return (interfaces);
}


public static bool InterfaceFilterCallback(Type type, object criteria)
{
    foreach (Type interfaceName in (Type[])criteria)
    {
        if (type.IsInstanceOfType(interfaceName))
        {
            return (true);
        }
    }

    return (false);
}
```

The `FindSpecificInterfaces` method searches for any of the three interface types contained in the `Names` array that are implemented by the `System.Collections.ArrayList` type.

The `SearchInterfacesOfType` method accepts a type (*searchedType*) on which to search for interfaces and an array of types (*interfaceNames*) that contains criteria for the search. For this method, the criterion is a `Type` array of interfaces. This method then calls the `FindInterfaces` method on the *searchedType* parameter, passing in a delegate and the `Type` array criteria of interfaces. (The delegate will be invoked for each interface found.) This method then returns an array of interface types that match the criterion.

The TypeFilter delegate, filter, defines the IfaceFilterCallback method to be called for each interface found on the *searchedType* object. The real power of this search mechanism lies in the IfaceFilterCallback callback method.

This callback searches for each of the interface types in the *criteria* array that is implemented by the *searchedType* parameter of the SearchInterfacesOfType method.

Discussion

The FindInterfaces method of a Type object makes use of the TypeFilter delegate, which is passed to the *filter* parameter. This delegate is supplied by the FCL and allows an extra layer of filtering (of any type that you want) to occur. This delegate returns a Boolean value, where true indicates that the *ifaceType* object passed to this delegate should be included in the Type array that the FindInterfaces method returns; false indicates that this *ifaceType* object should not be included.

The FindInterfaces method will take into account all interfaces implemented by the type being searched as well as all of its base types when performing a search. In addition, if any of the interfaces implemented by any of these types also implements one or more interfaces, those interfaces are included in the search.

There are many ways to use this TypeFilter delegate to search for interfaces implemented on a type—here are just a few other searches that can be performed:

- A filter to search for all implemented interfaces that are defined within a particular namespace (in this case, the System.Collections namespace):

```
public bool IfaceFilterCallback(Type type, object criteria)
{
    return (type.Namespace == "System.Collections");
}
```

- A filter to search for all implemented interfaces that contain a method called Add, which returns an Int32 value:

```
public bool IfaceFilterCallback(Type type, object criteria)
{
    MethodInfo mi = type.GetMethod("Add");
    if (mi != null &&
        mi.ReturnType == Type.GetType("System.Int32"))
    {
        return (true);
    }
    else
    {
        return (false);
    }
}
```

- A filter to search for all implemented interfaces that are loaded from the GAC:

```
public bool IfaceFilterCallback(Type type, object criteria)
{
    if (type.Assembly.GlobalAssemblyCache)
    {
        return (true);
    }
    else
    {
        return (false);
    }
}
```

- A filter to search for all implemented interfaces that are defined within an assembly with the version number 1.0.3300.0:

```
public bool IfaceFilterCallback(Type type, object criteria)
{
    if (type.Assembly.FullName.IndexOf("Version=1.0.3300.0") >= 0)
    {
        return (true);
    }
    else
    {
        return (false);
    }
}
```

See Also

See Recipe 9.8; see the "Delegate Class" and "Type.FindInterfaces Method" topics in the MSDN documentation.

9.8 An Advanced Member Search Mechanism

Problem

You are searching for a member within a type using the Type class. However, complex member searches are not available through the GetMember and GetMembers methods of a Type object. The GetMember method searches for a member name only within a type limited by the set of BindingFlags used, and the GetMembers method searches for all members limited by the set of BindingFlags used. BindingFlags is an enumeration of various member types that can be searched. The BindingFlags related to this recipe are defined here:

DeclaredOnly
    Include members declared at the same level of the Type's hierarchy in the search. No inherited members.

Default
    Use no binding flags.

FlattenHierarchy

Include all static members in the inheritance hierarchy in the search (do not include static members of nested types in the search).

IgnoreCase

Perform a case-insensitive search.

Instance

Include instance members in the search.

NonPublic

Include nonpublic members in the search.

Public

Include public members in the search.

Static

Include static members in the search.

You need to create more flexible and advanced searches for members that do not involve creating your own member search engine, such as a code generation tool that uses preexisting assemblies as an input might need.

Solution

The FindMembers method of a Type object can be used, along with a callback, to create your own complex searches. The TestSearchMembers method shown in Example 9-9 will call your custom member-searching method, SearchMembers.

Example 9-9. Performing advanced member searches on a type

```
using System;
using System.Reflection;

public class SearchType
{
    public void TestSearchMembers( )
    {
        MemberInfo[] members = SearchMembersByReturnType(this.GetType( ),
                                        Type.GetType("System.Int32"));

        if (members.Length > 0)
        {
            Console.WriteLine("Matches found:");

            // Display information for each match.
            for(int counter = 0; counter < members.Length; counter++)
            {
                Console.WriteLine("\tMember Name: " +
                                members[counter].ToString( ));
                Console.WriteLine("\tMember Type: " +
                                members[counter].MemberType);
                foreach (object attr in
```

Example 9-9. Performing advanced member searches on a type (continued)

```
                          members[counter].GetCustomAttributes(false))
                {
                    Console.WriteLine("\t\tMember attr: " +
                      attr.ToString( ));
                }
            }
        }
        else
        {
            Console.WriteLine("\t\tNo matches found");
        }
    }

    public MemberInfo[] SearchMembersByReturnType(Type searchedType,
                                                  Type returnType)
    {
        // Delegate that compares the member's return type
        // against the returnType parameter.
        MemberFilter filterCallback = new MemberFilter(ReturnTypeFilter);

        MemberInfo[] members = searchedType.FindMembers(MemberTypes.All,
                    BindingFlags.Instance | BindingFlags.Public |
                    BindingFlags.NonPublic | BindingFlags.Static,
                    filterCallback,
                    returnType);

        return (members);
    }

    private bool ReturnTypeFilter(MemberInfo member, object criteria)
    {
        // Obtain the return type of either a method or property.
        Type returnType = null;
        if (member is MethodInfo)
            returnType = ((MethodInfo)member).ReturnType;
        else if (member is PropertyInfo)
            returnType = ((PropertyInfo)member).PropertyType;
        else
            return (false);

        // Match return type
        if (returnType == ((Type)criteria))
            return (true);
        else
            return (false);
    }
```

This method will search for any member in the current type that has a return value of
System.Int32.

The SearchMembersByReturnType method accepts a Type object in which to search and
a string representation of the full name of a return type. This method simply calls the

FindMembers method of the *searchType* object passed to it. Notice that the *returnType* parameter is passed to the FindMembers method as the last parameter.

The MemberFilter delegate, filterCallback, defines the ReturnTypeFilter method to be called for each member that meets the specified criteria of the FindMembers method (i.e., MemberTypes.All, BindingFlags.Instance, BindingFlags.Public, Binding-Flags.NonPublic, and BindingFlags.Static). The real power of this search mechanism lies in the ReturnTypeFilter callback method.

This callback method casts the member parameter to the correct member type (i.e., MethodInfo or PropertyInfo), obtains the return type, and compares that return type to the one passed in to the *returnType* parameter of the SearchMembersByReturnType method. A return value of true indicates that the return types matched; a false indicates they did not match.

Discussion

Most complex member searches can be made easier through the use of the FindMembers method of a Type object. This method returns an array of MemberInfo objects that contain all members that match the *memberType*, *bindingAttr*, and *filterCriteria* parameters.

This method makes use of the MemberFilter delegate, which is passed in to the *filter* parameter. This delegate is supplied by the FCL and allows an extra layer of member filtering to occur. This filtering can be anything you want. This delegate returns a Boolean value, where true indicates that the *member* object passed in to this delegate should be included in the MemberInfo array that the FindMembers method returns, and false indicates that this *member* object should not be included.

There are many ways to use this MemberFilter delegate to search for members within a type. Here are just a few other items that can be searched for:

* A filter callback to search for fields marked as const:

```
private bool ReturnTypeFilter(MemberInfo member, object criteria)
{
    if (member is FieldInfo)
    {
        if (((FieldInfo)member).IsLiteral)
        {
            return (true);
        }
        else
        {
            return (false);
        }
    }

    return (false);
}
```

- A filter callback to search for fields marked as readonly:

```
private bool ReturnTypeFilter(MemberInfo member, object criteria)
{
    if (member is FieldInfo)
    {
        if (((FieldInfo)member).IsInitOnly)
        {
            return (true);
        }
        else
        {
            return (false);
        }
    }

    return (false);
}
```

- A filter to search for a read-only property:

```
private bool ReturnTypeFilter(MemberInfo member, object criteria)
{
    if (member is PropertyInfo)
    {
        if (((PropertyInfo)member).CanRead && !((PropertyInfo)member).CanWrite)
        {
            return (true);
        }
        else
        {
            return (false);
        }
    }

    return (false);
}
```

- A filter to search for any methods that contain out parameters:

```
private bool ReturnTypeFilter(MemberInfo member, object criteria)
{
    if (member is MethodInfo)
    {
        ParameterInfo[] params = ((MethodInfo)member).GetParameters( );
        foreach (ParameterInfo param in params)
        {
            if (param.IsOut)
            {
                return (true);
            }
        }
```

```
            return (false);
        }

        return (false);
    }
```

- A filter to search for any members that are marked with the `System.`
  `ObsoleteAttribute` attribute:

```
private bool ReturnTypeFilter(MemberInfo member, object criteria)
{
    object[] attrs = member.GetCustomAttributes(false);
    foreach (object attr in attrs)
    {
        if (attr.ToString( ).Equals("System.ObsoleteAttribute"))
        {
            return (true);
        }
    }

    return (false);
}
```

See Also

See Recipe 9.7; see the "Delegate Class" and "Type.FindMembers Method" topics in
the MSDN documentation.

9.9   Observing Additions and Modifications
to a Hashtable

Problem

You have multiple objects that need to observe modifications to a `Hashtable`. When
an item is added or modified in the `Hashtable`, each of these observer objects should
be able to vote to allow or disallow the action. In order for an action to be allowed to
complete, all observer objects must vote to allow the action. If even one observer
object votes to disallow the action, the action is prevented.

Solution

To observe additions and modifications to the `ObservableHashtable` class (shown in
Example 9-10) object that is registered with this object, use the `HashtableObserver`
class implemented in Example 9-11. The `ObservableHashtable` class is an extension of
the regular `Hashtable` class and allows itself to be observed by the `HashtableObserver`
class.

Example 9-10. ObservableHashtable class

```
public class ObservableHashtable : Hashtable
{
    public event HashtableEventHandler BeforeAddItem;
    public event HashtableEventHandler AfterAddItem;
    public event HashtableEventHandler BeforeChangeItem;
    public event HashtableEventHandler AfterChangeItem;

    protected virtual bool OnBeforeAdd(HashtableEventArgs e)
    {
        HashtableEventHandler beforeAddItem = BeforeAddItem;
        if (beforeAddItem != null)
        {
            beforeAddItem(this, e);
            return (e.KeepChanges);
        }

        return (true);
    }

    protected virtual void OnAfterAdd(HashtableEventArgs e)
    {
        HashtableEventHandler afterAddItem = AfterAddItem;
        if (afterAddItem != null)
        {
            afterAddItem(this, e);
        }
    }

    protected virtual bool OnBeforeChange(HashtableEventArgs e)
    {
        HashtableEventHandler beforeChangeItem = BeforeChangeItem;
        if (beforeChangeItem != null)
        {
            beforeChangeItem(this, e);
            return (e.KeepChanges);
        }

        return (true);
    }

    protected virtual void OnAfterChange(HashtableEventArgs e)
    {
        HashtableEventHandler afterChangeItem = AfterChangeItem;
        if (afterChangeItem != null)
        {
            afterChangeItem(this, e);
        }
    }

    public override void Add(object key, object value)
    {
        HashtableEventArgs hashArgs =
```

Example 9-10. ObservableHashtable class (continued)

```
            new HashtableEventArgs(key, value);
        if(OnBeforeAdd(hashArgs))
        {
            base.Add(key, value);
        }
        else
        {
            Debug.WriteLine("Addition of key/value cannot be performed");
        }

        OnAfterAdd(hashArgs);
    }

    public override object this[object key]
    {
        get
        {
            return (base[key]);
        }
        set
        {
            // See if this key is there to be changed; if not, add it.
            if (base.ContainsKey(key))
            {
                HashtableEventArgs hashArgs = new HashtableEventArgs(key, value);

                if (OnBeforeChange(hashArgs))
                {
                    base[key] = value;
                }
                else
                {
                    Debug.WriteLine("Change of value cannot be performed");
                }

                OnAfterChange(hashArgs);
            }
            else
            {
                Debug.WriteLine("Item did not exist, adding");
                Add(key, value);
            }
        }
    }
}
```

The HashtableEventHandler is defined as follows:

```
[Serializable]
public delegate void HashtableEventHandler(object sender,
                            HashtableEventArgs args);
```

Example 9-11 shows the code for the HashtableObserver class.

Example 9-11. HashtableObserver class

```
// The observer object that will observe a registered
// ObservableHashtable object
public class HashtableObserver
{
    public HashtableObserver( ) {}

    // Set up delegate/events for approving an addition or change.
    public delegate bool Approval(HashtableEventArgs args);
    public event Approval ApproveAdd;
    public event Approval ApproveChange;

    public void Register(ObservableHashtable hashtable)
    {
        // Hook up to the ObservableHashTable instance events.
        hashtable.BeforeAddItem +=
            new HashtableEventHandler(BeforeAddListener);
        hashtable.AfterAddItem +=
            new HashtableEventHandler(AfterAddListener);
        hashtable.BeforeChangeItem +=
            new HashtableEventHandler(BeforeChangeListener);
        hashtable.AfterChangeItem +=
            new HashtableEventHandler(AfterChangeListener);
    }

    public void Unregister(ObservableHashtable hashtable)
    {
        // Unhook from the ObservableHashTable instance events.
        hashtable.BeforeAddItem -=
            new HashtableEventHandler(BeforeAddListener);
        hashtable.AfterAddItem -=
            new HashtableEventHandler(AfterAddListener);
        hashtable.BeforeChangeItem -=
            new HashtableEventHandler(BeforeChangeListener);
        hashtable.AfterChangeItem -=
            new HashtableEventHandler(AfterChangeListener);
    }

    private void CheckApproval(Approval approval,
                    HashtableEventArgs args)
    {
        // Check everyone who wants to approve.
        foreach (Approval approvalInstance in approval.GetInvocationList( ))
        {
            if (!approvalInstance(args))
            {
                // If any of the concerned parties
                // refuse, then no add.  Adds by default.
                args.KeepChanges = false;
                break;
            }
        }
    }
```

Example 9-11. HashtableObserver class (continued)

```csharp
    public void BeforeAddListener(object sender, HashtableEventArgs args)
    {
        // See if anyone is hooked up for approval.
        Approve approveAdd = ApproveAdd;
        if (approveAdd != null)
        {
            CheckApproval(approveAdd, args);
        }

        Debug.WriteLine("[NOTIFY] Before Add...: Add Approval = " +
                        args.KeepChanges.ToString( ));
    }

    public void AfterAddListener(object sender, HashtableEventArgs args)
    {
        Debug.WriteLine("[NOTIFY] ...After Add:  Item approved for adding: " +
                        args.KeepChanges.ToString( ));
    }

    public void BeforeChangeListener(object sender, HashtableEventArgs args)
    {
        // See if anyone is hooked up for approval.
        Approve approveChange = ApproveChange;
        if (approveChange != null)
        {
            CheckApproval(approveChange, args);
        }

        Debug.WriteLine("[NOTIFY] Before Change...: Change Approval = " +
                        args.KeepChanges.ToString( ));
    }

    public void AfterChangeListener(object sender, HashtableEventArgs args)
    {
        Debug.WriteLine("[NOTIFY] ...After Change:  Item approved for change: " +
                        args.KeepChanges.ToString( ));
    }
}
```

The HashtableEventArgs class is a specialization of the EventArgs class, which provides the Hashtable key and value being added or modified to the HashtableObserver object, as well as a Boolean property, KeepChanges. This flag indicates whether the addition or modification in the ObservableHashtable object will succeed or be rolled back. The source code for the HashtableEventArgs class is:

```csharp
// Event arguments for ObservableHashtable
public class HashtableEventArgs : EventArgs
{
    public HashtableEventArgs(object key, object value)
    {
```

```
            this.key = key;
            this.value = value;
        }

        private object key = null;
        private object value = null;
        private bool keepChanges = true;

        public bool KeepChanges
        {
            get {return (keepChanges);}
            set {keepChanges = value;}
        }

        public object Key
        {
            get {return (key);}
        }

        public object Value
        {
            get {return (value);}
        }
    }
```

Discussion

The *observer design pattern* allows one or more observer objects to act as spectators over one or more subjects. Not only do the observer objects act as spectators, but they can also induce change in the subjects. According to this pattern, any subject is allowed to register itself with one or more observer objects. Once this is done, the subject can operate as it normally does. The key feature is that the subject doesn't have to know what it is being observed by—this allows the coupling between subjects and observers to be minimized. The observer object(s) will then be notified of any changes in state to the subjects. When the subject's state changes, the observer object(s) can change the state of other objects in the system to bring them into line with changes that were made to the subject(s). In addition, the observer could even make changes or refuse changes to the subject(s) themselves.

The observer pattern is best implemented with events in C#. The event object provides a built-in way of implementing the observer design pattern. This recipe implements this pattern on a Hashtable. The Hashtable object must raise events for any listening observer objects to handle. But the Hashtable class found in the FCL does not raise any events. In order to make a Hashtable raise events at specific times, you must derive a new class, ObservableHashtable, from the Hashtable class. This ObservableHashtable class overrides the Add and indexer members of the base Hashtable. In addition, four events (BeforeAddItem, AfterAddItem, BeforeChangeItem, and AfterChangeItem) are created; they will be raised before and after items are added or modified in the `ObservableHashtable` object. To raise these events, the following four methods are created, one to raise each event:

- The `OnBeforeAdd` method raises the `BeforeAddItem` event.
- The `OnAfterAdd` method raises the `AfterAddItem` event.
- The `OnBeforeChange` method raises the `BeforeChangeItem` event.
- The `OnAfterChange` method raises the `AfterChangeItem` event.

The `Add` method calls the `OnBeforeAdd` method, which then raises the event to any listening observer objects. The `OnBeforeAdd` method is called before the `base.Add` method—which adds the key/value pair to the `Hashtable`—is called. After the key/value pair has been added, the `OnAfterAdd` method is called. This operation is similar to the indexer set method.

 The `Onxxx` methods that raise the events in the `ObservableHashtable` class are marked as `protected virtual` to allow classes to subclass this class and implement their own method of dealing with the events. Note that this statement is not applicable to sealed classes. In those cases, you can simply make the methods `public`.

The `HashtableEventArgs` class contains three private fields defined as follows:

key
> The key that is to be added to the `Hashtable`.

value
> The value that is to be added to the `Hashtable`.

keepChanges
> A flag indicating whether the key/value pair should be added to the `Hashtable`. `true` indicates that this pair should be added to the `Hashtable`.

The `keepChanges` field is used by the observer to determine whether an add or change operation should proceed. This flag is discussed further when you look at the `HashtableObserver` observer object.

The `HashtableObserver` is the observer object that watches any `ObservableHashtable` objects it is told about. Any `ObservableHashtable` object can be passed to the `HashtableObserver.Register` method in order to be observed. This method accepts an `ObservableHashtable` object (hashtable) as its only parameter. This method then hooks up the event handlers in the `HashtableObserver` object to the events that can be raised by the `ObservableHashtable` object passed in through the hashtable parameter. Therefore, the following events and event handlers are bound together:

- The `ObservableHashtable.BeforeAddItem` event is bound to the `HashtableObserver.BeforeAddListener` event handler.
- The `ObservableHashtable.AfterAddItem` event is bound to the `HashtableObserver.AfterAddListener` event handler.

- The `ObservableHashtable.BeforeChangeItem` event is bound to the `Hashtable-Observer.BeforeChangeListener` event handler.

- The `ObservableHashtable.AfterChangeItem` event is bound to the `Hashtable-Observer.AfterChangeListener` event handler.

The `BeforeAddListener` and `BeforeChangeListener` methods watch for additions and changes to the key/value pairs of the watched `ObservableHashtable` object(s). Since you have an event firing before and after an addition or modification occurs, you can determine whether the addition or change should occur.

Two events are published by the `HashtableObserver` to allow for an external entity to approve or deny the addition or changing of a hashtable entry. These events are named `ApproveAdd` and `ApproveChange`, respectively, and are of delegate type `Approval` as shown below:

```
public delegate bool Approval(HashtableEventArgs args);
```

This is where the `keepChanges` field of the `HashtableEventArgs` object comes into play. If an external source wants to block the addition or change, it can simply return false from its event handler implementation of the appropriate `Approve*` event.

The `HashtableObserver` object will set this flag according to whether it determines that the action should proceed or be prematurely terminated. The `Hashtable-EventArgs` object is passed back to the `OnBeforeAdd` and `OnBeforeChange` methods. These methods then return the value of the `KeepChanges` property to either the calling `Add` method or indexer. The `Add` method or indexer then uses this flag to determine whether the base `Hashtable` object should be updated.

The code in Example 9-12 shows how to instantiate `ObservableHashtables` and `HashtableObservers`, and how to register, set up approval, use, and unregister them.

Example 9-12. Using the ObservableHashTable and HashTableObserver classes

```
public static void TestObserverPattern( )
{
    // Create three observable hashtable instances.
    ObservableHashtable oh1 = new ObservableHashtable( );
    ObservableHashtable oh2 = new ObservableHashtable( );
    ObservableHashtable oh3 = new ObservableHashtable( );

    // Create an observer for the three subject objects.
    HashtableObserver observer = new HashtableObserver( );

    // Register the three subjects with the observer.
    observer.Register(oh1);
    observer.Register(oh2);
    observer.Register(oh3);

    // Hook up the approval events for adding or changing.
    observer.ApproveAdd +=
        new HashtableObserver.Approval(SeekApproval);
```

Example 9-12. Using the ObservableHashTable and HashTableObserver classes (continued)

```
    observer.ApproveChange +=
        new HashtableObserver.Approval(SeekApproval);

    // Use the observable instances.
    oh1.Add(1,"one");
    oh2.Add(2,"two");
    oh3.Add(3,"three");

    // Unregister the observable instances.
    observer.Unregister(oh3);
    observer.Unregister(oh2);
    observer.Unregister(oh1);
}

public static bool SeekApproval(HashtableEventArgs args)
{
    // Allow only strings of no more than 3 characters in
    // our hashtable.
    string value = (string)args.Value;
    if (value.Length <= 3)
        return true;
    return false;
}
```

Note that if the ObservableHashtables are used without registering them, no events will be raised. Since no events are raised, the observer cannot do its job, and values may be added to the unregistered subjects that are out of bounds for the application.

When using the observer design pattern in this fashion, keep in mind that fine-grained events, such as the ones in this recipe, could possibly drag down performance, so profile your code. If you have many subjects raising many events, your application could fail to meet performance expectations. If this occurs, you need to either minimize the number of actions that cause events to be raised or remove some events.

See Also

See the "Event Keyword," "EventHandler Delegate," "EventArgs Class," and "Handling and Raising Events" topics in the MSDN documentation.

9.10   Using the Windows Keyboard Hook

Problem

You need to watch and respond to specific user keyboard input, and, based on the input, you want to perform one or more actions. For example, pressing the Windows key and the E key at the same time launches Windows Explorer. You would like to add other Windows key combinations for your own applications. In addition, you could prevent the user from using specific keys (such as the Windows key) from within your application.

Solution

The Windows Forms application shown in Example 9-13 uses the WH_KEYBOARD Windows hook.

Example 9-13. Using the Windows keyboard hook

```
using System;
using System.Windows.Forms;
using System.Runtime.InteropServices;

namespace WindowsApplication2
{
    public class Form1 : System.Windows.Forms.Form
    {
        // Required designer variable
        private System.ComponentModel.Container components = null;

        private System.Windows.Forms.Button button1;
        private System.Windows.Forms.Button button2;
        private System.Windows.Forms.TextBox textBox1;

        public Form1( )
        {
            // Required for Windows Form Designer support
            InitializeComponent( );
        }

        protected override void Dispose( bool disposing )
        {
            if( disposing )
            {
                if (components != null)
                {
                    components.Dispose( );
                }
            }
            base.Dispose( disposing );
        }

        #region Windows Form Designer generated code
        /// <summary>
        /// Required method for Designer support - do not modify
        /// the contents of this method with the code editor.
        /// </summary>
        private void InitializeComponent( )
        {
            this.button1 = new System.Windows.Forms.Button( );
            this.button2 = new System.Windows.Forms.Button( );
            this.textBox1 = new System.Windows.Forms.TextBox( );
```

Example 9-13. Using the Windows keyboard hook (continued)

```
            this.SuspendLayout( );
            //
            // button1
            //
            this.button1.Name = "button1";
            this.button1.TabIndex = 0;
            this.button1.Text = "Start";
            this.button1.Click +=
              new System.EventHandler(this.button1_Click);
            //
            // button2
            //
            this.button2.Location = new System.Drawing.Point(0, 48);
            this.button2.Name = "button2";
            this.button2.TabIndex = 1;
            this.button2.Text = "End";
            this.button2.Click +=
              new System.EventHandler(this.button2_Click);
            //
            // textBox1
            //
            this.textBox1.Location = new System.Drawing.Point(80, 0);
            this.textBox1.Multiline = true;
            this.textBox1.Name = "textBox1";
            this.textBox1.ScrollBars =
              System.Windows.Forms.ScrollBars.Vertical;
            this.textBox1.Size = new System.Drawing.Size(752, 504);
            this.textBox1.TabIndex = 2;
            this.textBox1.Text = "";
            this.textBox1.WordWrap = false;
            //
            // Form1
            //
            this.AutoScaleBaseSize = new System.Drawing.Size(5, 13);
            this.ClientSize = new System.Drawing.Size(832, 509);
            this.Controls.AddRange(new System.Windows.Forms.Control[] {
                                       this.textBox1,
                                       this.button2,
                                       this.button1});
        this.Name = "Form1";
        this.Text = "Form1";
        this.ResumeLayout(false);
    }
    #endregion

    [STAThread]
    static void Main( )
    {
        Application.Run(new Form1( ));
    }

    // Declare Windows API calls used to access Windows hooks
```

Example 9-13. Using the Windows keyboard hook (continued)

```csharp
[DllImport("user32.dll")]
public static extern int SetWindowsHookEx(int hookType,
                                          HookProc callback,
                                          int instance,
                                          int threadID);
[DllImport("user32.dll")]
public static extern int CallNextHookEx(int hookHandle, int code,
                                        int wparam, int lparam);
[DllImport("user32.dll")]
public static extern bool UnhookWindowsHookEx(int hookHandle);
[DllImport("user32.dll")]
public static extern int GetKeyState(int vKey);

// Fields, constants, and structures used by the keyboard hook.
int hookHandle = 0;
HookProc cb = null;

public const int WH_KEYBOARD = 2;

public const int HC_ACTION = 0;
public const int HC_NOREMOVE = 3;

public const int VK_CONTROL = 0x11;
public const int VK_LWIN = 0x5B;
public const int VK_RWIN = 0x5C;
public const int VK_APPS = 0x5D;
public const int VK_LSHIFT = 0xA0;
public const int VK_RSHIFT = 0xA1;
public const int VK_LCONTROL = 0xA2;
public const int VK_RCONTROL = 0xA3;
public const int VK_LMENU = 0xA4;
public const int VK_RMENU = 0xA5;
public const int VK_BROWSER_BACK = 0xA6;
public const int VK_BROWSER_FORWARD = 0xA7;
public const int VK_BROWSER_REFRESH = 0xA8;
public const int VK_BROWSER_STOP = 0xA9;
public const int VK_BROWSER_SEARCH = 0xAA;
public const int VK_VOLUME_MUTE = 0xAD;
public const int VK_VOLUME_DOWN = 0xAE;
public const int VK_VOLUME_UP = 0xAF;
public const int VK_MEDIA_NEXT_TRACK = 0xB0;
public const int VK_MEDIA_PREV_TRACK = 0xB1;
public const int VK_MEDIA_STOP = 0xB2;
public const int VK_MEDIA_PLAY_PAUSE = 0xB3;
public const int KF_UP = 0x8000;
public const long KB_TRANSITION_FLAG = 0x80000000;
public const int VK_W = 0x57;


// Keyboard hook delegate
public delegate int HookProc(int code, int wparam, int lparam);
```

Example 9-13. Using the Windows keyboard hook (continued)

```csharp
public int Proc(int code, int wparam, int lparam)
{
    if (code == HC_ACTION)
    {
        switch (wparam)
        {
            case VK_BROWSER_BACK:
                // Handle Back keyboard button here.
                textBox1.Text += "Browser Back key caught" +
                                Environment.NewLine;
                break;
            case VK_BROWSER_FORWARD:
                // Handle Forward keyboard button here.
                textBox1.Text += "Browser Forward key caught" +
                                Environment.NewLine;
                break;
            case VK_BROWSER_REFRESH:
                // Handle Refresh keyboard button here.
                textBox1.Text += "Browser Refresh key caught" +
                                Environment.NewLine;
                break;
            case VK_BROWSER_STOP:
                // Handle Stop keyboard button here.
                textBox1.Text += "Browser Stop key caught" +
                                Environment.NewLine;
                break;
            case VK_BROWSER_SEARCH:
                // Handle Search keyboard button here.
                textBox1.Text += "Browser Search key caught" +
                                Environment.NewLine;
                break;
            case VK_VOLUME_MUTE:
                // Handle Mute keyboard button here.
                textBox1.Text += "Volume Mute key caught" +
                                Environment.NewLine;
                break;
            case VK_VOLUME_DOWN:
                // Handle Volume - keyboard button here.
                textBox1.Text += "Volume Down key caught" +
                                Environment.NewLine;
                break;
            case VK_VOLUME_UP:
                // Handle Volume + keyboard button here.
                textBox1.Text += "Volume Up key caught" +
                                Environment.NewLine;
                break;
            case VK_MEDIA_NEXT_TRACK:
                // Handle Next Track keyboard button here.
                textBox1.Text += "Media Next Track key caught" +
                                Environment.NewLine;
                break;
            case VK_MEDIA_PREV_TRACK:
```

Example 9-13. Using the Windows keyboard hook (continued)

```
                        // Handle Previous Track keyboard button here.
                        textBox1.Text += "Media Previous Track key caught" +
                                            Environment.NewLine;
                        break;
                    case VK_MEDIA_STOP:
                        // Handle Stop keyboard button here.
                        textBox1.Text += "Media Stop key caught" +
                                            Environment.NewLine;
                        break;
                    case VK_MEDIA_PLAY_PAUSE:
                        // Handle Play keyboard button here.
                        textBox1.Text += "Media Play/Pause key caught" +
                                            Environment.NewLine;
                        break;
                }
            }
            return (CallNextHookEx(hookHandle, code, wparam, lparam));
        }

        // Click event handlers for button1 and button2.
        private void button1_Click(object sender, System.EventArgs e)
        {
            // Set the keyboard hook.
            if (hookHandle == 0)
            {
                cb = new HookProc(Proc);
                hookHandle = SetWindowsHookEx(WH_KEYBOARD, cb, 0,
                                    AppDomain.GetCurrentThreadId( ));
            }
            else
            {
                textBox1.Text += "Hook already set" + Environment.NewLine;
            }
            textBox1.Text += "Start: " + hookHandle + Environment.NewLine;
        }

        private void button2_Click(object sender, System.EventArgs e)
        {
            // Unhook the keyboard hook.
            textBox1.Text += "End: " + UnhookWindowsHookEx(hookHandle) +
                        Environment.NewLine;
            hookHandle = 0;
        }
    }
}
```

Discussion

The hooks provided by the Windows operating system allow for very powerful code to be written with a minimum of work. The hook used in this recipe is the WH_KEYBOARD hook, which watches messages that are generated by the keyboard.

The WH_KEYBOARD hook allows keyboard messages to be watched or discarded. To discard a keyboard message, return a 1 from the Proc hook callback method. The HookProc delegate is used as the method to which the keyboard hook calls back whenever a keyboard message is received. This hook does not allow the message to be modified.

To use a hook, as the code in the Solution section shows, you first need to declare the following three Windows API functions:

SetWindowsHookEx

> This API creates the hook specified by the first parameter and attaches it to the callback method specified in the second parameter. The return value of this function is the handle to the newly created hook. This handle needs to be stored so that it can later be used to remove the hook.

CallNextHookEx

> This API calls the next hook in the hook chain if SetWindowsHookEx has been called multiple times for a single type of hook. The return value is dependent on the type of hook that is installed.

UnhookWindowsHookEx

> This API removes the callback to the hook specified by the hook handle passed as its only parameter. This hook handle is returned by the SetWindowHookEx function.

Once these functions are declared, the next step is to declare the delegate for the hook callback method. This hook callback method is automatically invoked whenever a keyboard message is sent. The return value of both the delegate and callback methods is the return value of the CallNextHookEx API method.

The keyboard hook used in this recipe will intercept only messages that are sent to the message queue of the thread on which the hook is installed. The thread on which to install the hook is passed as the fourth argument of the SetWindowsHookEx API method. For this recipe, the current thread is passed as an argument using the static AppDomain.GetCurrentThreadId method. Therefore, if you have a multithreaded application and you want each thread to intercept messages sent by the keyboard, you will have to call SetWindowsHookEx on each thread to set up the WH_KEYBOARD hook.

The keyboard hook can also be used to capture keys pressed in combination. For example, if the Windows Menu key is pressed along with the V key, a keyboard hook callback procedure can be implemented to capture this action:

```
// Hook callback method
public int Proc(int code, int wparam, int lparam)
{
    if (code == HC_ACTION)
    {
        // Check the state of the Window's keyboard Pop-Up Menu key.
        int state = GetKeyState(VK_APPS);

        // Is the Menu key already down?
```

```
        if ((state & KF_UP) == KF_UP)
        {
            // Is the key up?
            if ((lparam & KB_TRANSITION_FLAG) == KB_TRANSITION_FLAG)
            {
                // Is this the V key?
                if (wparam == VK_V)
                {
                    // Handle AppMenu-v key combination here...
                    textBox1.Text += "AppMenu-v action caught" +
                                    Environment.NewLine;
                }
            }
        }
    }
    return (CallNextHookEx(hookHandle, code, wparam, lparam));
}
```

This callback gets the state of the Menu key and determines whether it is depressed
((state & KF_UP) == KF_UP). If it is depressed, the V key is checked to see if it is being
released ((lparam & KB_TRANSITION_FLAG) == KB_TRANSITION_FLAG). If these conditions are true, a message is displayed. (Of course, you could add your own code here
to do something more interesting.)

See Also

See Recipe 9.11; see *Subclassing & Hooking with Visual Basic* (O'Reilly); and see the
"Delegate Class" and "Hooks" topics in the MSDN documentation.

9.11   Tracking and Responding to the Mouse

Problem

Many new mice have more than just a left and right button. Nowadays, mice come
with several additional buttons and a mouse wheel. You need to allow your application to take advantage of these new mice features. Additionally, you might need to
know the mouse's current location on a particular window, whether it is on the client area of the window (where your menus, toolbars, and controls are placed in the
window), whether it is on the nonclient area of the window (window border, title-
bar, close button, etc.), or the *x* and *y* coordinates of the mouse pointer.

Solution

Use the mouse events that are built into the System.Windows.Forms.Form class.

Discussion

Seven mouse events exist in the `System.Windows.Forms.Form` class. These are, in the order in which they occur:

- `MouseEnter`
- `MouseMove`
- `MouseHover, MouseDown,` or `MouseWheel`
- `MouseUp` (if `MouseDown` was the previously raised event)
- `MouseLeave`

Most of these events accept a `MouseEventArgs` object that contains all the information about the mouse when the event is raised. The `MouseEventArgs` class contains the following data:

- Which button the user is acting on
- The number of times the mouse button was clicked
- The direction and speed of the mouse wheel
- The *x* and *y* coordinates of the mouse pointer

Your code can make use of any one or more of these events on the `Form` class along with the `MouseEventArgs` object.

See Also

See the "Form Class," "MouseEventArgs Class," "Control.MouseDown Event," "Control.MouseEnter Event," "Control.MouseHover Event," "Control.MouseLeave Event," "Control.MouseMove Event," "Control.MouseWheel Event," "Control.MouseUp Event," and "Control.MouseMove Event" topics in the MSDN documentation.

9.12   Using Anonymous Methods

Problem

There is a new feature in C# 2.0 called anonymous methods. While anonymous methods can be viewed as syntactic sugar for making delegate calls less difficult, you want to understand all of the different ways that they can be used to help you in your daily programming chores as well as understand the ramifications of those uses.

Solution

Anonymous methods can be implemented and used in a variety of ways:

- Using return values and parameters
- Written inline or through delegate inference (explained shortly)
- Using generic type parameters

Let's start with the original way to use delegates. First you would declare a delegate type, DoWork in this case, and then you would create an instance of it (as shown here in the WorkItOut method). Declaring the instance of the delegate requires that you specify a method to execute when the delegate is invoked, and here the DoWorkMethodImpl method has been connected. The delegate is fired and the text is written to the console via the DoWorkMethodImpl method.

```
// Declare delegate.
class OldWay
{
    // Declare delegate.
    delegate int DoWork(string work);

    // Have a method to create an instance of and call the delegate.
    public void WorkItOut()
    {
        // Create instance.
        DoWork dw = new DoWork(DoWorkMethodImpl);
        // Invoke delegate
        int i = dw("DoWorkMethodImpl1");
    }

    // Have a method that the delegate is tied to with a matching signature
    // so that it is invoked when the delegate is called.
    public int DoWorkMethodImpl(string s)
    {
        Console.WriteLine(s);
        return s.GetHashCode();
    }
}
```

Anonymous methods allow you to set up code to run when a delegate is invoked but there does not need to be a formal method declaration that is given to the delegate. For example, you could have written the preceding code using an anonymous method like this:

```
class NewWay
{
    // Declare delegate.
    delegate int DoWork(string work);

    // Have a method to create an instance of and call the delegate.
    public void WorkItOut()
    {
        // Declare instance.
        DoWork dw = delegate(string s)
        {
            Console.WriteLine(s);
            return s.GetHashCode();
        };
```

```
        // Invoke delegate.
        int i = dw("DoWorkMethodImpl1");
    }
}
```

Notice that instead of having a method called DoWorkMethodImpl, you use the
delegate keyword to directly assign the code from that method inline to the DoWork
delegate. The assignment looks like this:

```
DoWork dw = delegate(string s)
{
    Console.WriteLine(s);
    return s.GetHashCode( );
};
```

You also provide the parameter required by the DoWork delegate (string) and your
code returns an int (s.GetHashCode( )) as the delegate requires. When setting up an
anonymous method, the code must match the delegate signature or you will get a
compiler error.

There is yet another way you can set up the delegate using anonymous methods and
that is through the magic of delegate inference. Delegate inference allows you to
assign the method name directly to the delegate instance without having to write the
code for creating a new delegate object. Under the covers, C# actually writes the IL
for creating the delegate object, but you don't have to do it explicitly here. Using delegate inference instead of writing out new delegate( ) everywhere helps to unclutter
the code involved in the usage of delegates, as shown here:

```
class DirectAssignmentWay
{
    // Declare delegate.
    delegate int DoWork(string work);

    // Have a method to create an instance of and call the delegate.
    public void WorkItOut( )
    {
        // Declare instance and assign method.
        DoWork dw = DoWorkMethodImpl;
        // invoke delegate
        int i = dw("DoWorkMethodImpl1");
    }
    // Have a method that the delegate is tied to with a matching signature
    // so that it is invoked when the delegate is called.
    public int DoWorkMethodImpl(string s)
    {
        Console.WriteLine(s);
        return s.GetHashCode( );
    }
}
```

Notice that all that is assigned to the DoWork delegate instance dw is the method name DoWorkMethodImpl. There is no "new DoWork(DoWorkMethodImpl)" call as there was in older C# code.

 Remember, the underlying delegate wrapper does not go away, delegate inference just simplifies the syntax a bit by hiding some of it.

Alternatively, you can also set up anonymous methods that take generic type parameters to enable working with generic delegates as you do here in the GenericWay class:

```csharp
class GenericWay
{
    // Declare generic delegate.
    delegate T DoGenericWork<T>(T t);

    // Have a method to create two instances of and call the delegates.
    public void WorkItOut()
    {
        DoGenericWork<string> dwString = delegate(string s)
        {
            Console.WriteLine(s);
            return s;
        };

        // Invoke string delegate.
        string retStr = dwString("DoWorkMethodImpl1");

        DoGenericWork<int> dwInt = delegate(int i)
        {
            Console.WriteLine(i);
            return i;
        };

        // Invoke int delegate.
        int j = dwInt(5);
    }
}
```

The DoGenericWork delegate is defined with one type parameter, T, which is used to specify the type of the returned value as well as the single parameter passed. Setting up the delegate this way allows the WorkItOut method to create two instances of DoGenericWork, one using string and the other using int as the type.

Discussion

One of the most useful things about anonymous methods is the concept of outer variables. The official definition of outer variables is that they are any local variable, value parameter, or parameter array with a scope that contains the anonymous method.

What does this mean? It means that, inside of the code of the anonymous method, you can touch variables outside of the scope of that method. There is a concept of "capturing" the variables that occurs when an anonymous method actually makes reference to one of the outer variables. In the following example, the count variable is captured and incremented by the anonymous method. The count variable is not part of the original scope of the anonymous method but part of the outer scope. It is incremented and then the incremented value is returned and totaled.

```
delegate int Count();

int count = 0;
int total = 0;
Count countUp = delegate { return count++; };
for(int i=0;i<10;i++)
{
    total += countUp();
}
Debug.WriteLine("Total = " + total);
```

What capturing actually does is extend the lifetime of the outer variable to coincide with the lifetime of the underlying delegate instance that represents the anonymous method. This should encourage you to be careful about what you touch from inside an anonymous method. You could be causing things to hang around a lot longer than you originally planned on. The garbage collector won't get a chance to clean up those outer variables until later once they are used in the anonymous method. Capturing outer variables has another garbage-collector effect: when locals or value parameters are captured, they are no longer considered to be fixed but are now movable, so any unsafe code must now fix that variable before use by using the fixed keyword.

Outer variables can affect how the compiler generates the internal IL for the anonymous method. If the anonymous method uses outer variables, it is generated as a nested class, rather than as another private method of the class it is declared in, as it otherwise would be. If the outer method is a static, then the anonymous method can access only static variables, as the nested class will also be generated as a static.

A few last things to remember about anonymous methods:

- They can't use break, goto, or continue to jump from the anonymous method to a target outside the anonymous method block.
- No unsafe code can be executed inside of an anonymous method.

See Also

See the "Anonymous Methods" topic in the MSDN documentation.

9.13 Set Up Event Handlers Without the Mess

Problem

In versions of the .NET Framework previous to 2.0, the System.EventHandler delegate could be used on events in which the arguments were always of type System.EventArgs. This was great if you really didn't care about any data that went along with an event. But as you are all fine programmers and can see the possibilities of passing data along with the event, you had to set up a delegate and an event for every event you wanted. Example 9-14 demonstrates an old newspaper class that sends news to subscribers using the pre-.NET 2.0 event and event-handling methodology.

Example 9-14. Using pre-.NET 2.0 event and event-handling methods

```
class IWannaKnowThen
{
    // Show the client talking to the newspaper class.
    public static void TryMe( )
    {
        // Make a newspaper class.
        OldNewsPaper DailyPaperFlash = new OldNewsPaper( );

        // Hook up the news event to our handler (StaleNews).
        DailyPaperFlash.NewsEvent +=
            new OldNewsPaper.NewsEventHandler(StaleNews);

        // Send news.
        DailyPaperFlash.TransmitNews("Patriots win first super bowl!");
        DailyPaperFlash.TransmitNews("W takes office amongst recount.");
        DailyPaperFlash.TransmitNews("VS2003 is sooo passe");
    }

    // Write out news to debug stream
    private static void StaleNews(object src, OldNewsEventArgs nea)
    {
        System.Diagnostics.Debug.WriteLine(nea.LatestNews);
    }
}

// EventArgs derived class to hold our news data
public class OldNewsEventArgs : EventArgs
{
    private string _latestNews;

    public OldNewsEventArgs(string latestNews)
    {
        _latestNews = latestNews;
    }
    public string LatestNews
    {
        get { return _latestNews; }
```

```
    }
}

// OldNewsPaper class
public class OldNewsPaper
{
    // Allow clients to get the news.
    public delegate void NewsEventHandler(Object sender, OldNewsEventArgs nea);
    public event NewsEventHandler NewsEvent;

    // Provide nice wrapper for sending news to clients.
    public void TransmitNews(string news)
    {
        NewsEventHandler newsEvent = NewsEvent;
        if (newsEvent != null)
            newsEvent(this, new OldNewsEventArgs(news));
    }
}
```

This code sets up an event that will report the news to subscribers as it comes in. It passes them the news data as an argument of type OldNewsEventArgs that has a LatestNews property.

As you can see from this example, whenever you had to set up multiple event handlers, it became an exercise in copy-and-paste and changing the event argument class type over and over again. It would be nice to not have to define lots of delegates and events just to change the event arguments, as all events (and corresponding handlers) are supposed to look like this:

```
void [EventHandler](object sender, [EventArgs] args)
{
    // Do something about this event firing.
}
```

Solution

EventHandler<T> takes a type parameter that represents the type of the System. EventArgs derived class to use in your event handlers. The beauty of this is that you no longer have to keep creating a delegate and an event for every event you wish to publish from your class. Even better, the Framework has to have only one event delegate instead of one for every event that passes custom data! Using the example shown in the Problem section, you can now rewrite the declaration of the event handler like this:

```
// Old way
public delegate void NewsEventHandler(Object sender, OldNewsEventArgs nea);
public event NewsEventHandler NewsEvent;

// New way
public event EventHandler<OldNewsEventArgs> NewsEvent;
```

Now you set up the nice wrapper function to allow the user to easily trigger the event:

```
// Old way
public void TransmitNews(string news)
{
    // Copy to a temporary variable to be thread-safe.
    NewsEventHandler newsEvent = NewsEvent;
    if (newsEvent != null)
        newsEvent(this, new NewsEventArgs(news));
}

// New way
public void TransmitNews(string news)
{
    // Copy to a temporary variable to be thread-safe.
    EventHandler<OldNewsEventArgs> oldNews = NewsEvent;
    if (oldNews != null)
        oldNews(this, new OldNewsEventArgs(news));
}
```

The client can then hook up to the OldNewsPaper class like this:

```
// Old way
class IWannaKnowThen
{
    // Show the client talking to the newspaper class.
    public static void TryMe()
    {
        // Make a newspaper class.
        OldNewsPaper DailyPaperFlash = new OldNewsPaper();

        // Hook up the news event to our handler (StaleNews).
        DailyPaperFlash.NewsEvent +=
            new OldNewsPaper.NewsEventHandler(StaleNews);

        // Send news.
        DailyPaperFlash.TransmitNews("Patriots win first super bowl!");
        DailyPaperFlash.TransmitNews("W takes office amongst recount.");
        DailyPaperFlash.TransmitNews("VS2003 is sooo passe");
    }

    // Write out news to debug stream.
    private static void StaleNews(object src, OldNewsEventArgs nea)
    {
        System.Diagnostics.Debug.WriteLine(nea.LatestNews);
    }
}

// New way
class IWannaKnowNow
{
    public static void TryMe()
    {
```

```
      // Make a newspaper class.
      OldNewsPaper DailyPaperFlash = new OldNewsPaper( );

      // Hook up the news event to our handler (BreakingNews).
      DailyPaperFlash.NewsEvent +=
          new EventHandler<OldNewsEventArgs>(BreakingNews);

      // Send news.
      DailyPaperFlash.TransmitNews("Patriots win again!");
      DailyPaperFlash.TransmitNews("4 more years for W.");
      DailyPaperFlash.TransmitNews("VS2005 & .NET 2.0 Rocks LA");
    }

    private static void BreakingNews(object src, NewsEventArgs nea)
    {
        System.Diagnostics.Debug.WriteLine(nea.LatestNews);
    }
  }
}
```

Discussion

The main benefit of using the generic EventHandler instead of System.EventHandler is that you write less code. Being able to declare a generic delegate allows you to have one delegate definition for multiple types. Why is this interesting, you might ask? Previously, when a delegate or event was declared by a class that wanted to publish information and allow multiple client classes to subscribe to it, if any data were to be passed along to the client classes, the convention was that a new class that derived from System.EventArgs had to be created. Then the class would be instantiated, filled with the data, and passed to the client. If the publishing class had only one event to notify people of, this wasn't too bad. If the publishing class had a lot of events, say like a class derived from a UserControl, there would have to be a separate class derived from System.EventArgs and a separate event defined for every event that needed different data passed to it. Now with a generic delegate, you can simply declare one delegate/event for each list of parameters you deal with, then declare the type-specific events you need. Since events are supposed to have this signature:

```
    void eventname( object sender, System.EventArgs args)
```

the kind folks at Microsoft gave you System.EventHandler<T> to deal with the case of most events. If your code does have events defined that have more than two parameters, there would need to be a new delegate created to be the base of those events. Since most events do not have more than two parameters, this is a bit nonstandard but not out of the question.

See Also

See Recipes 9.5, 9.6, and 9.9; see the "Generic EventHandler" and "System. EventHandler" topics in the MSDN documentation.

9.14 Using Different Parameter Modifiers in Anonymous Methods

Problem

You know you can pass parameters to anonymous methods but you need to figure out what parameter modifiers are valid with anonymous methods.

Solution

Anonymous methods can use out and ref parameter modifiers but not the params modifier in their parameter list. However, this does not prevent the creation of delegates with any of these modifiers as shown here:

```
// Declare out delegate.
delegate int DoOutWork(out string work);

// Declare ref delegate.
delegate int DoRefWork(ref string work);

// Declare params delegate.
delegate int DoParamsWork(params string[] workItems);
```

Even though the DoParamsWork delegate is defined with the params keyword on the parameter, it can still be used as a type for an anonymous method, as you'll see in a bit. To use the DoOutWork delegate, create an anonymous method inline using the out keyword and assign it to the DoOutWork delegate instance. Inside the anonymous method body, the out variable s is assigned a value first (as it doesn't have one by definition as an out parameter), writes it to the console, and returns the string hash code.

```
// Declare instance and assign method.
DoOutWork dow = delegate(out string s)
{
    s = "WorkFinished";
    Console.WriteLine(s);
    return s.GetHashCode();
};
```

To run the anonymous method code, invoke the delegate with an out parameter and then print out the result to the console:

```
// Invoke delegate.
string work;
int i = dow(out work);
Console.WriteLine(work);
```

To use the ref parameter modifier in an anonymous method, you create an inline method to hook up to the DoRefWork delegate with a ref parameter. In the method, you show you can write the original value out, reassign the value, and get the hash code of the new value:

```
// Declare instance and assign method.
DoRefWork drw = delegate(ref string s)
{
    Console.WriteLine(s);
    s = "WorkFinished";
    return s.GetHashCode( );
};
```

To run the anonymous method, you assign a value to the string work and then pass it as a ref parameter to the DoRefWork delegate that is instantiated. Upon return from the delegate call, you write out the new value for the work string:

```
// Invoke delegate.
work = "WorkStarted";
i = drw(ref work);
Console.WriteLine(work);
```

Even though it is possible to declare a delegate with the params modifier, you cannot hook up the delegate using an anonymous method with the params keyword in the parameter list. You get the CS1670 "params is not valid in this context" compiler error on the DoParamsWork line.

```
// "params is not valid in this context"
//DoParamsWork dpw = delegate(params object[] workItems)
//{
//    foreach (object o in workItems)
//    {
//        Console.WriteLine(o.ToString( ));
//    }
//    return o.GetHashCode( );
//};
```

You can, however, omit the params keyword and still call the delegate as shown here:

```
// All we have to do is omit the params keyword.
DoParamsWork dpw = delegate(string[] workItems)
{
    foreach (object o in workItems)
    {
        Console.WriteLine(o.ToString( ));
    }
    return workItems.GetHashCode( );
};
```

Notice that although you've removed the params keyword from the anonymous method, this doesn't stop you from using the same syntax. The params keyword is present on the delegate type, so you can invoke it thusly:

```
int i = dpw("Hello", "42", "bar");
```

So this illustrates that you can bind an anonymous method to a delegate declared using params, and once you've done that, you can call it passing in any number of parameters you like just as you'd expect.

Discussion

Anonymous methods cannot access the ref or out parameters of an outer scope. This means any out or ref variables that were defined as part of the containing method are off-limits for use inside the body of the anonymous method.

```
// Declare delegate.
delegate int DoWork(string work);

public void TestOut(out string outStr)
{
    // Declare instance.
    DoWork dw = delegate(string s)
    {
        Console.WriteLine(s);
        // Causes error CS1628:
        // "Cannot use ref or out parameter 'outStr' inside an
        // anonymous method block"
        //outStr = s;
        return s.GetHashCode( );
    };
    // Invoke delegate.
    int i = dw("DoWorkMethodImpl1");
}

public void TestRef(ref string refStr)
{
    // Declare instance.
    DoWork dw = delegate(string s)
    {
        Console.WriteLine(s);
        // Causes error CS1628:
        // "Cannot use ref or out parameter 'refStr' inside an
        // anonymous method block"
        // refStr = s;
        return s.GetHashCode( );
    };
    // Invoke delegate
    int i = dw("DoWorkMethodImpl1");
}
```

Interestingly enough, anonymous methods can access outer variables with the params modifier.

```
// Declare delegate.
delegate int DoWork(string work);

public void TestParams(params string[] items)
{
```

```
// Declare instance.
DoWork dw = delegate(string s)
{
    Console.WriteLine(s);
    foreach (string item in items)
    {
        Console.WriteLine(item);
    }
    return s.GetHashCode();
};
// Invoke delegate.
int i = dw("DoWorkMethodImpl1");
}
```

Since the params modifier is there for the benefit of the calling site (so the compiler knows to make this a method call that supports variable-length argument lists) and since anonymous methods are never called directly (always called via a delegate), then it makes no sense for an anonymous method to be decorated with something there for the benefit of the calling site—there is no calling site. This is why it doesn't matter that you can't use the params keyword on an anonymous method. For anonymous methods, the calling site is always calling through the delegate, so what matters is whether that delegate has the params keyword or not.

See Also

See Recipe 9.12; see the "CS1670," "CS1628," "out," "ref," "params," and "System. ParamArrayAttribute" topics in the MSDN documentation.

9.15   Using Closures in C#

Problem

You want to associate a small amount of state with some behavior without going to the trouble of building a new class.

Solution

Use anonymous methods to implement closures. Closures can be defined as functions that capture the state of the environment that is in scope where they are declared. Put more simply, they are current state plus some behavior that can read and modify that state. Anonymous methods have the capacity to capture external variables and extend their lifetime, which makes closures possible in C# now.

To show an example of this, you will build a quick reporting system that tracks sales personnel and their revenue production versus commissions. The closure behavior is that you can build one bit of code that does the commission calculations per quarter and works on every salesperson.

First, you have to define your sales personnel:

```
class SalesWeasel
{
    ...
    #region Private members
    private string _name;
    private decimal _annualQuota;
    private decimal _commissionRate;
    private decimal _commission = 0m;
    private decimal _totalCommission = 0m;
    #endregion // Private members
    ...
}
```

Sales personnel have a name, an annual quota, a commission rate for sales, and some
storage for holding a quarterly commission and a total commission. Now that you
have something to work with, let's write a bit of code to do the work of calculating
the commissions:

```
delegate void CalculateEarnings(SalesWeasel weasel);

static CalculateEarnings GetEarningsCalculator(decimal quarterlySales,
                              decimal bonusRate,
                                int weaselCount)
{
    return delegate(SalesWeasel weasel)
    {
        // Assume all weasels contributed equally to quarterly revenue.
        decimal weaselSalesPortion = quarterlySales / weaselCount;
        // Figure out the weasel's quota for the quarter.
        decimal quarterlyQuota = (weasel.AnnualQuota / 4);
        // Did he make quota for the quarter?
        if (quarterlySales < quarterlyQuota)
        {
            // Didn't make quota, no commission
            weasel.Commission = 0;
        }
        // Check for bonus-level performance (200% of quota).
        else if (quarterlySales > (quarterlyQuota * 2.0m))
        {
          decimal baseCommission = quarterlyQuota *
              weasel.CommissionRate;
         weasel.Commission = (baseCommission +
                    ((quarterlySales - quarterlyQuota) *
                    (weasel.CommissionRate * (1 + bonusRate)))));
        }
        else // Just regular commission
        {
            weasel.Commission = weasel.CommissionRate * quarterlySales;
        }
    };
}
```

You've declared the delegate type as CalculateEarnings, and it takes a SalesWeasel. You have a factory method to construct an instance of this delegate for you called GetEarningsCalculator, which creates an anonymous method to do the calculation of the SalesWeasel's commission and returns a CalculateEarnings instantiation.

To get set up, you have to create your SalesWeasels:

```
// Set up the sales weasels...
SalesWeasel[] weasels = new SalesWeasel[3];
weasels[0] = new SalesWeasel("Chas",100000m, 0.10m);
weasels[1] = new SalesWeasel("Ray",200000m, 0.025m);
weasels[2] = new SalesWeasel("Biff",50000m, 0.001m);
```

Then set up earnings calculators based on quarterly earnings:

```
decimal q1Earnings = 65000m;
decimal q2Earnings = 20000m;
decimal q3Earnings = 37000m;
decimal q4Earnings = 110000m;

// Set up earnings calculators for each quarter.
CalculateEarnings eCalcQ1 =
    GetEarningsCalculator(q1Earnings, 0.10m, weasels.Length);
CalculateEarnings eCalcQ2 =
    GetEarningsCalculator(q2Earnings, 0.10m, weasels.Length);
CalculateEarnings eCalcQ3 =
    GetEarningsCalculator(q3Earnings, 0.10m, weasels.Length);
CalculateEarnings eCalcQ4 =
    GetEarningsCalculator(q4Earnings, 0.15m, weasels.Length);
```

And finally run the numbers for each quarter for all SalesWeasels:

```
// Figure out Q1.
WriteQuarterlyReport("Q1", q1Earnings, eCalcQ1, weasels);
// Figure out Q2.
WriteQuarterlyReport("Q2", q2Earnings, eCalcQ2, weasels);
// Figure out Q3.
WriteQuarterlyReport("Q3", q3Earnings, eCalcQ3, weasels);
// Figure out Q4.
WriteQuarterlyReport("Q4", q4Earnings, eCalcQ4, weasels);
```

WriteQuarterlyReport invokes the CalculateEarnings anonymous method implementation (eCalc) for every SalesWeasel and modifies the state to assign quarterly commission values based on the commission rates for each one:

```
static void WriteQuarterlyReport(string quarter,
                                 decimal quarterlySales,
                                 CalculateEarnings eCalc,
                                 SalesWeasel[] weasels)
{
    Console.WriteLine("{0} Sales Earnings on Quarterly Sales of {1}:",
        quarter, quarterlySales.ToString("C"));
    foreach (SalesWeasel weasel in weasels)
    {
        // Calc commission
```

```
        eCalc(weasel);
        // Report
        Console.WriteLine("    SalesWeasel {0} made a commission of : {1}",
            weasel.Name, weasel.Commission.ToString("C"));
    }
}
```

You can finally generate the annual report from this data, which will tell the executives which sales personnel are worth keeping by calling WriteCommissionReport:

```
decimal annualEarnings = q1Earnings + q2Earnings +
                         q3Earnings + q4Earnings;
// Let's see who is worth keeping...
WriteCommissionReport(annualEarnings,weasels);
```

WriteCommissionReport checks the revenue earned by the individual sales personnel against their commission, and if their commission is more than 20 percent of the revenue they generated, you recommend action be taken:

```
static void WriteCommissionReport(decimal annualEarnings,
                        SalesWeasel[] weasels)
{
    decimal revenueProduced = ((annualEarnings) / weasels.Length);
    Console.WriteLine("");
    Console.WriteLine("Annual Earnings were {0}",
        annualEarnings.ToString("C"));
    Console.WriteLine("");
    foreach(SalesWeasel weasel in weasels)
    {
        Console.WriteLine("    Paid {0} {1} to produce {2}",
            weasel.Name,
            weasel.TotalCommission.ToString("C"),
            revenueProduced.ToString("C"));

        // If his commission is more than 20% of what he produced
        // can him.
        if ((revenueProduced * 0.2m) < weasel.TotalCommission)
        {
            Console.WriteLine("        FIRE {0}!",weasel.Name);
        }
    }
}
```

The output for your revenue and commission tracking program is listed here for your enjoyment:

```
Q1 Sales Earnings on Quarterly Sales of $65,000.00:
        SalesWeasel Chas made a commission of : $6,900.00
        SalesWeasel Ray made a commission of : $1,625.00
        SalesWeasel Biff made a commission of : $70.25
Q2 Sales Earnings on Quarterly Sales of $20,000.00:
        SalesWeasel Chas made a commission of : $0.00
        SalesWeasel Ray made a commission of : $0.00
        SalesWeasel Biff made a commission of : $20.00
Q3 Sales Earnings on Quarterly Sales of $37,000.00:
```

```
                SalesWeasel Chas made a commission of : $3,700.00
                SalesWeasel Ray made a commission of : $0.00
                SalesWeasel Biff made a commission of : $39.45
  Q4 Sales Earnings on Quarterly Sales of $110,000.00:
                SalesWeasel Chas made a commission of : $12,275.00
                SalesWeasel Ray made a commission of : $2,975.00
                SalesWeasel Biff made a commission of : $124.63

  Annual Earnings were $232,000.00

     Paid Chas $22,875.00 to produce $77,333.33
        FIRE Chas!
     Paid Ray $4,600.00 to produce $77,333.33
     Paid Biff $254.33 to produce $77,333.33
```

Discussion

One of the best ways we've heard of to describe closures in C# is to think of an object as a set of methods associated with data and to think of a closure as a set of data associated with a function. If you need to have several different operations on the same data, an object approach may make more sense. These are two different angles on the same problem, and the type of problem you are solving will help you decide which is the right approach. It just depends on your inclination as to which way to go. There are times when 100 percent pure object-oriented programming can get tedious and unnecessary, and closures are a nice way to solve some of those problems. The SalesWeasel commission example presented here is a demonstration of what you can do with closures. It could have been done without them, but at the expense of writing more class and method code.

Closures have been defined as stated earlier, but there is a stricter definition that essentially implies that the behavior associated with the state should not be able to modify the state in order to be a true closure. We tend to agree more with the first definition as it defines what a closure should be, not how it should be implemented, which seems too restrictive. Whether you choose to think of this as a neat side feature of anonymous methods or you feel it is worthy of being called a closure, it is another programming trick for your toolbox and should not be dismissed.

See Also

See Recipe 9.12; see the "Anonymous Methods" topic in the MSDN documentation.

9.16 Performing Multiple Operations on a List Using Functors

Problem

You want to be able to perform multiple operations on an entire collection of objects at once, while keeping the operations functionally segmented.

Solution

Use a functor (or *function object* as it is also known) as the vehicle for transforming the collection. A *functor* is any object that can be called as a function. Examples of this are a function, a function pointer, or even an object that defines operator () for us C/C++ converts.

Needing to perform multiple operations on a collection is a reasonably common thing in software. Let's say that you have a stock portfolio with a bunch of stocks in it. Your StockPortfolio class would have a List of Stock objects. It would be able to be created with an initial capacity, and it would have the ability to add stocks.

```
public class StockPortfolio
{
    List<Stock> _stocks;

    public StockPortfolio(int capacity)
    {
        _stocks = new List<Stock>(capacity);
    }

    public void AddStock(string ticker, double gainLoss)
    {
        _stocks.Add(new Stock(ticker, gainLoss));
    }

    More methods down here...
}
```

The Stock class is rather simple. You just need a ticker symbol for the stock and its percentage of gain or loss:

```
public class Stock
{
    string _tickerSymbol;
    double _gainLoss;

    public Stock(string ticker, double gainLoss)
    {
        _tickerSymbol = ticker;
        _gainLoss = gainLoss;
    }

    public double GainLoss    {get { return _gainLoss; }    }
    public string Ticker      {get { return _tickerSymbol; }}
}
```

To use this StockPortfolio, you add a few stocks to it with gain/loss percentages and print out your starting portfolio. Once you have the portfolio, you want to get a list of the three best performing stocks, so you can cash in by selling them, and print out your portfolio again.

```
StockPortfolio tech = new StockPortfolio(10);
tech.AddStock("OU81", -10.5);
tech.AddStock("C#4VR", 2.0);
tech.AddStock("PCKD", 12.3);
tech.AddStock("BTML", 0.5);
tech.AddStock("NOVB", -35.2);
tech.AddStock("MGDCD", 15.7);
tech.AddStock("GNRCS", 4.0);
tech.AddStock("FNCTR", 9.16);
tech.AddStock("ANYMS", 9.12);
tech.AddStock("PCLS", 6.11);

tech.PrintPortfolio("Starting Portfolio");
// Cash in by selling the best performers.
List<Stock> best = tech.GetBestPerformers(3);
tech.SellStocks(best);
tech.PrintPortfolio("After Selling Best 3 Performers");
```

So far nothing terribly interesting is happening. Let's take a look at how you figured out what the three best performers were by looking at the internals of the GetBestPerformers method:

```
public List<Stock> GetWorstPerformers(int bottomNumber)
{
    int foundItems = 0;

    // Sort the stocks by performance using a binary functor.
    _stocks.Sort(delegate(Stock lhs, Stock rhs)
    {
        // Reverse parameters to sort highest to lowest.
        return Comparer<double>.Default.Compare(rhs.GainLoss, lhs.GainLoss);
    });

    // Return stock that match criteria using a unary functor.
    return _stocks.FindAll(delegate(Stock s)
    {
        // If we have accepted no more than how many were asked for
        // then keep accepting.
        if (foundItems < bottomNumber)
        {
            string result = "gain";
            if (s.GainLoss < 0)
                result = "loss";
            Console.WriteLine(
                string.Format("Best stock added ({0}) with {1} of {2}%",
                    s.Ticker, result, System.Math.Abs(s.GainLoss)));
            // Increment count.
            foundItems++;
            return true;
        }
        else // Have all we need
```

```
            return false;
    });
}
```

The first thing you do is make sure the list is sorted so that the best performing stocks are at the front of the list by calling the Sort method on List<T>. One of the overloads of the Sort method is defined to take a Comparison<T> which is defined like this:

```
public delegate int Comparison<T>(T x, T y)
```

You create the Comparison you need by using the Comparer<T> class passing a double as the argument and using the default comparison method, while passing the gain/loss percentage for each stock as it is iterated over by the Sort function. The stocks being compared (rhs, lhs) are reversed to place the best performing stocks at the front of the list:

```
return Comparer<double>.Default.Compare(rhs.GainLoss, lhs.GainLoss);
```

Your comparison tells Sort which object should be placed ahead of the other. This is a simple callback from Sort that allows you to control the algorithm to determine sort order. You wrapped this up in an anonymous method by using the delegate keyword and now you have your Comparison delegate that the Sort function needs.

Now that your list is sorted, you use the FindAll function from List<T>, which takes a Predicate<T> as the parameter. Again you use the delegate keyword to create an anonymous method to determine if the item FindAll passes to the anonymous method should be returned in the list that FindAll is building. In your functor, you take the first n items in the list (n is the total number of stocks performing the best) represented by bottomNumber, and once you have taken that many, you return false to FindAll so that no more items are returned.

GetBestPerformers returns a List<Stock> full of the three best performers. As they are making money, it is time to cash in and sell them. For your purposes, selling is simply removing them from the list of stocks in StockPortfolio. To accomplish this, you use yet another functor to iterate over the list of stocks handed to the SellStocks function (the list of worst-performing ones in your case) and then remove that stock from the internal list that the StockPortfolio class maintains:

```
public void SellStocks(List<Stock> stocks)
{
    stocks.ForEach(delegate(Stock s)
    {
        _stocks.Remove(s);
    });
}
```

Discussion

Functors come in a few different flavors that are known as a *generator* (a function with no parameters), a unary function (a function with one parameter), and a binary function (a function with two parameters). Before you ask, yes, you could keep going, but the STL (Standard Template Library from C++) didn't bother so we won't either at this point. If the functor happens to return a Boolean value, then it gets an even more special naming convention: a unary function that returns a Boolean is called a *predicate*, and a binary function with a Boolean return is called a *binary predicate*. You will now notice in the Framework that there are both Predicate<T> and BinaryPredicate<T> delegates defined to facilitate these uses of functors.

The List<T> and System.Array classes have been enhanced in the 2.0 version of the .NET Framework to take predicates (Predicate<T>, BinaryPredicate<T>), actions (Action<T>), comparisons (Comparison<T>), and converters (Converter<T,U>). This allows these collections to be operated on in a much more general way than was previously possible and brings some of the richness of the C++ STL to C#.

Thinking in terms of functors can be a bit of a challenge at first, but once you put a bit of time into it, you can start to see powerful possibilities open up before you. Any code you can write once, debug once, and use many times is a useful thing, and functors can help you get to that place.

See Also

See the "System.Collections.Generic.List<T>" and "System.Array" topics in the MSDN documentation.

CHAPTER 10

Regular Expressions

10.0 Introduction

The .NET Framework Class Library includes the System.Text.RegularExpressions namespace, which is devoted to creating, executing, and obtaining results from regular expressions executed against a string.

Regular expressions take the form of a pattern that can be matched to zero or more characters within a string. The simplest of these patterns, such as .* (match anything and everything) and [A-Za-z] (match any letter) are easy to learn, but more advanced patterns can be difficult to learn and even more difficult to implement correctly. Learning and understanding regular expressions can take considerable time and effort, but the work will pay off.

Regular expression patterns can take a simple form—such as a single word or character—or a much more complex pattern. The more complex patterns can recognize and match such things as the year portion of a date, all of the <SCRIPT> tags in an ASP page, or a phrase in a sentence that varies with each use. The .NET regular expression classes provide a very flexible and powerful way to do such things as recognize text, replace text within a string, and split up text into individual sections based on one or more complex delimiters.

Despite the complexity of regular expression patterns, the regular expression classes in the FCL are easy to use in your applications. Executing a regular expression consists of the following steps:

1. Create an instance of a Regex object that contains the regular expression pattern along with any options for executing that pattern.

2. Retrieve a reference to an instance of a Match object by calling the Match instance method if you want only the first match found. Or retrieve a reference to an instance of the MatchesCollection object by calling the Matches instance method if you want more than just the first match found. If, however, you want to know only whether the input string was a match and do not need the extra details on the nature of the match, you can use the Regex.IsMatch method.

3. If you've called the `Matches` method to retrieve a `MatchCollection` object, iterate over the `MatchCollection` using a foreach loop. Each iteration will allow access to every `Match` object that the regular expression produced.

10.1 Enumerating Matches

Problem

You need to find one or more substrings corresponding to a particular pattern within a string. You need to be able to inform the searching code to return either all matching substrings or only the matching substrings that are unique within the set of all matched strings.

Solution

Call the `FindSubstrings` method shown in Example 10-1, which executes a regular expression and obtains all matching text. This method returns either all matching results or only the unique matches; this behavior is controlled by the `findAllUnique` parameter. Note that if the `findAllUnique` parameter is set to `true`, the unique matches are returned sorted alphabetically.

Example 10-1. FindSubstrings method

```
using System;
using System.Collections;
using System.Text.RegularExpressions;

public static Match[] FindSubstrings(string source, string matchPattern,
                                     bool findAllUnique)
{
    SortedList uniqueMatches = new SortedList( );
    Match[] retArray = null;

    Regex RE = new Regex(matchPattern, RegexOptions.Multiline);
    MatchCollection theMatches = RE.Matches(source);

    if (findAllUnique)
    {
        for (int counter = 0; counter < theMatches.Count; counter++)
        {
            if (!uniqueMatches.ContainsKey(theMatches[counter].Value))
            {
                uniqueMatches.Add(theMatches[counter].Value,
                                  theMatches[counter]);
            }
        }

        retArray = new Match[uniqueMatches.Count];
        uniqueMatches.Values.CopyTo(retArray, 0);
    }
```

Example 10-1. FindSubstrings method (continued)

```
    else
    {
        retArray = new Match[theMatches.Count];
        theMatches.CopyTo(retArray, 0);
    }

    return (retArray);
}
```

The TestFindSubstrings method shown in Example 10-2 searches for any tags in an XML string; it does this by searching for a block of text that begins with the < character and ends with the > character.

This method first displays all unique tag matches present in the XML string and then displays all tag matches within the string.

Example 10-2. The TestFindSubstrings method

```
public static void TestFindSubstrings( )
{
    string matchPattern = "<.*>";

    string source = @"<?xml version='1.0' encoding='UTF-8'?>
            <!-- My comment -->
            <![CDATA[<escaped> <><chars>>>>>]]>
            <Window ID='Main'>
              <Control ID='TextBox'>
                <Property Top='0' Left='0' Text='BLANK'/>
              </Control>
              <Control ID='Label'>
                <Property Top='0' Left='0' Caption='Enter Name Here'/>
              </Control>
              <Control ID='Label'>
                <Property Top='0' Left='0' Caption='Enter Name Here'/>
              </Control>
            </Window>";

    Console.WriteLine("UNIQUE MATCHES");
    Match[] x1 = FindSubstrings(source, matchPattern, true);
    foreach(Match m in x1)
    {
        Console.WriteLine(m.Value);
    }

    Console.WriteLine( );
    Console.WriteLine("ALL MATCHES");
    Match[] x2 = FindSubstrings(source, matchPattern, false);
    foreach(Match m in x2)
    {
        Console.WriteLine(m.Value);
    }
}
```

The following text will be displayed:

```
UNIQUE MATCHES
<!-- My comment -->
<![CDATA[<escaped> <><chars>>>>>]]>
</Control>
</Window>
<?xml version="1.0\" encoding=\"UTF-8\"?>
<Control ID="Label">
<Control ID="TextBox">
<Property Top="0" Left="0" Caption="Enter Name Here"/>
<Property Top="0" Left="0" Text="BLANK"/>
<Window ID="Main">

ALL MATCHES
<?xml version="1.0\" encoding=\"UTF-8\"?>
<!-- my comment -->
<![CDATA[<escaped> <><chars>>>>>]]>
<Window ID="Main">
<Control ID="TextBox">
<Property Top="0" Left="0" Text="BLANK"/>
</Control>
<Control ID="Label">
<Property Top="0" Left="0" Caption="Enter Name Here"/>
</Control>
<Control ID="Label">
<Property Top="0" Left="0" Caption="Enter Name Here"/>
</Control>
</Window>
```

Discussion

As you can see, the regular expression classes in the FCL are quite easy to use. The first step is to create an instance of the Regex object that contains the regular expression pattern, along with any options for running this pattern. The second step is to get a reference to an instance of the Match object, if you need only the first found match, or a MatchCollection object, if you need more than just the first found match. To get a reference to this object, the two instance methods Match and Matches can be called from the Regex object that was created in the first step. The Match method returns a single match object (Match) and Matches returns a collection of match objects (MatchCollection).

The FindSubstrings method returns an array of Match objects that can be used by the calling code. You may have noticed that the unique elements are returned sorted, and the nonunique elements are not sorted. A SortedList, which is used by the FindSubstrings method to store unique strings that match the regular expression pattern, automatically sorts its items when they are added.

The regular expression used in the TestFindSubstrings method is very simplistic and will work in most—but not all—conditions. For example, if two tags are on the same line, as shown here:

```
<tagData></tagData>
```

the regular expression will catch the entire line, not each tag separately. You could change the regular expression from <.*> to <[^>]*> to match only up to the closing > ([^>]* matches everything that is *not* a >). However, this will fail in the CDATA section, matching <![CDATA[<escaped>, <>, and <chars> instead of <![CDATA[<escaped> <> <chars>>>>>]]>. The more complicated @"(<!\[CDATA.*>|<[^>]*>)" will match either <!\[CDATA.*> (a greedy match for everything within the CDATA section) or <[^>]*>, described previously.

See Also

See the ".NET Framework Regular Expressions" and "SortedList Class" topics in the MSDN documentation.

10.2 Extracting Groups from a MatchCollection

Problem

You have a regular expression that contains one or more named groups, such as the following:

```
\\\\(?<TheServer>\w*)\\(?<TheService>\w*)\\
```

where the named group TheServer will match any server name within a UNC string, and TheService will match any service name within a UNC string.

You need to store the groups that are returned by this regular expression in a keyed collection (such as a Dictionary<string, Group>) in which the key is the group name.

Solution

The ExtractGroupings method shown in Example 10-3 obtains a set of Group objects keyed by their matching group name.

Example 10-3. ExtractGroupings method

```
using System;
using System.Collections;
using System.Collections.Generics;
using System.Text.RegularExpressions;


public static List<Dictionary<string, Group>> ExtractGroupings(string source,
                                       string matchPattern,
                                       bool wantInitialMatch)
{
    List<Dictionary<string, Group>> keyedMatches =
        new List<Dictionary<string, Group>>();
    int startingElement = 1;
    if (wantInitialMatch)
    {
```

Example 10-3. ExtractGroupings method (continued)

```
        startingElement = 0;
    }

    Regex RE = new Regex(matchPattern, RegexOptions.Multiline);
    MatchCollection theMatches = RE.Matches(source);

    foreach(Match m in theMatches)
    {
        Dictionary<string, Group> groupings = new Dictionary<string, Group>();

        for (int counter = startingElement; counter < m.Groups.Count; counter++)
        {
            // If we had just returned the MatchCollection directly, the
            // GroupNameFromNumber method would not be available to use.
            groupings.Add(RE.GroupNameFromNumber(counter), m.Groups[counter]);
        }

        keyedMatches.Add(groupings);
    }

    return (keyedMatches);
}
```

The ExtractGroupings method can be used in the following manner to extract named groups and organize them by name:

```
public static void TestExtractGroupings()
{
    string source = @"Path = ""\\MyServer\MyService\MyPath;
                        \\MyServer2\MyService2\MyPath2""";
    string matchPattern = @"\\\\(?<TheServer>\w*)\\(?<TheService>\w*)\\";

    foreach (Dictionary<string, Group> grouping in
                ExtractGroupings(source, matchPattern, true))
    {
        foreach (KeyValuePair kvp in grouping)
            Console.WriteLine("Key / Value = " + kvp.Key + " / " + kvp.Value);
        Console.WriteLine("");
    }
}
```

This test method creates a source string and a regular expression pattern in the MatchPattern variable. The two groupings in this regular expression are highlighted here:

```
string matchPattern = @"\\\\(?<TheServer>\w*)\\(?<TheService>\w*)\\";
```

The names for these two groups are: TheServer and TheService. Text that matches either of these groupings can be accessed through these group names.

The source and matchPattern variables are passed in to the ExtractGroupings method, along with a Boolean value, which is discussed shortly. This method

returns a `List<T>` that contains `Dictionary<string,Group>` objects. These Dictionary-
ary`<string,Group>` objects contain the matches for each of the named groups in the
regular expression, keyed by their group name.

This test method, `TestExtractGroupings`, returns the following:

```
Key / Value = 0 / \\MyServer\MyService\
Key / Value = TheService / MyService
Key / Value = TheServer / MyServer

Key / Value = 0 / \\MyServer2\MyService2\
Key / Value = TheService / MyService2
Key / Value = TheServer / MyServer2
```

If the last parameter to the `ExtractGroupings` method were to be changed to `false`,
the following output would result:

```
Key / Value = TheService / MyService
Key / Value = TheServer / MyServer

Key / Value = TheService / MyService2
Key / Value = TheServer / MyServer2
```

The only difference between these two outputs are that the first grouping is not displayed when the last parameter to `ExtractGroupings` is changed to `false`. The first
grouping is always the complete match of the regular expression.

Discussion

Groups within a regular expression can be defined in one of two ways. The first way
is to add parentheses around the subpattern that you wish to define as a grouping.
This type of grouping is sometimes labeled as *unnamed*. This grouping can later be
easily extracted from the final text in each `Match` object returned by running the regular expression. The regular expression for this recipe could be modified, as follows,
to use a simple unnamed group:

```
string matchPattern = @"\\\\(\w*)\\(\w*)\\";
```

After running the regular expression, you can access these groups using a numeric
integer value starting with 1.

The second way to define a group within a regular expression is to use one or more
named groups. A named group is defined by adding parentheses around the subpattern that you wish to define as a grouping and, additionally, adding a name to each
grouping, using the following syntax:

```
(?<Name>\w*)
```

The *Name* portion of this syntax is the name you specify for this group. After executing this regular expression, you can access this group by the name *Name*.

To access each group, you must first use a loop to iterate each Match object in the MatchCollection. For each Match object, you access the GroupCollection's indexer, using the following unnamed syntax:

```
string group1 = m.Groups[1].Value;
string group2 = m.Groups[2].Value;
```

or the following named syntax where m is the Match object:

```
string group1 = m.Groups["Group1_Name"].Value;
string group2 = m.Groups["Group2_Name"].Value;
```

If the Match method was used to return a single Match object instead of the MatchCollection, use the following syntax to access each group:

```
// Unnamed syntax
string group1 = theMatch.Groups[1].Value;
string group2 = theMatch.Groups[2].Value;

// Named syntax
string group1 = theMatch.Groups["Group1_Name"].Value;
string group2 = theMatch.Groups["Group2_Name"].Value;
```

where theMatch is the Match object returned by the Match method.

See Also

See the ".NET Framework Regular Expressions" and "Hashtable Class" topics in the MSDN documentation.

10.3   Verifying the Syntax of a Regular Expression

Problem

You have constructed a regular expression dynamically, either from your code or based on user input. You need to test the validity of this regular expression's syntax before you actually use it.

Solution

Use the VerifyRegEx method shown in Example 10-4 to test the validity of a regular expression's syntax.

Example 10-4. VerifyRegEx method

```
using System;
using System.Text.RegularExpressions;

public static bool VerifyRegEx(string testPattern)
{
    bool isValid = true;
```

Example 10-4. VerifyRegEx method (continued)

```
    if ((testPattern != null) && (testPattern.Trim( ).Length > 0))
    {
        try
        {
            Regex.Match("", testPattern);
        }
        catch (ArgumentException)
        {
            // BAD PATTERN: syntax error
            isValid = false;
        }
    }
    else
    {
        //BAD PATTERN: pattern is null or blank
        isValid = false;
    }

    return (isValid);
}
```

To use this method, pass it the regular expression that you wish to verify:

```
public static void TestUserInputRegEx(string regEx)
{
    if (VerifyRegEx(regEx))
        Console.WriteLine("This is a valid regular expression.");
    else
        Console.WriteLine("This is not a valid regular expression.");
}
```

Discussion

The VerifyRegEx method calls the static Regex.Match method, which is useful for running regular expressions on the fly against a string. The static Regex.Match method returns a single Match object. By using this static method to run a regular expression against a string (in this case a blank string), you can determine whether the regular expression is invalid by watching for a thrown exception. The Regex.Match method will throw an ArgumentException if the regular expression is not syntactically correct. The Message property of this exception contains the reason the regular expression failed to run, and the ParamName property contains the regular expression passed to the Match method. Both of these properties are read-only.

Before testing the regular expression with the static Match method, the regular expression is tested to see if it is null or blank. A null regular expression string returns an ArgumentNullException when passed in to the Match method. On the other hand, if a blank regular expression is passed in to the Match method, no exception is thrown (as long as a valid string is also passed to the first parameter of the Match method).

10.4   Quickly Finding Only the Last Match in a String

Problem

You need to find the last pattern match in a string, but you do not want the overhead of finding all matches in a string and having to move to the last match in the collection of matches.

Solution

Using the `RegexOptions.RightToLeft` option, the match starts at the end of the string and proceeds toward the beginning. The first found match is the last match in the string. You supply the `RegexOptions.RightToLeft` constant as an argument to the `Match` method. The instance `Match` method can be used as follows:

```
Regex RE = new Regex(Pattern, RegexOptions.RightToLeft);
Match theMatch = RE.Match(Source);
```

or use the static `Regex.Match` method:

```
Match theMatch = Regex.Match(Source, Pattern, RegexOptions.RightToLeft);
```

where *Pattern* is the regular expression pattern and *Source* is the string against which to run the pattern.

Discussion

The `RegexOptions.RightToLeft` regular expression option will force the regular expression engine to start searching for a pattern starting with the end of the string and proceeding backward toward the beginning of the string. The first match encountered will be the match closest to the end of the string—in other words, the last match in the string.

See Also

See the ".NET Framework Regular Expressions" topic in the MSDN documentation.

10.5   Replacing Characters or Words in a String

Problem

You are given a string in which a complex pattern of characters needs to be replaced with a new string.

Solution

Using the `Replace` instance method on the `Regex` class allows for easy replacement of text within a string. The overloaded `Replace` methods shown in Example 10-5 accept a *source* string that contains characters or words to be replaced, a *matchPattern* to

---

match the replaceable text in the *source* parameter, and a *replaceStr* string to replace the text matched by *matchPattern*. In addition two parameters, *count* and *startPos*, control the number of replacements allowed and where the replacements start from in the *source* string, respectively.

Example 10-5. Overloaded Replace methods

```
using System;
using System.Text.RegularExpressions;

public class RegexUtils
{
    public static string ReplaceStrWithChar(string source, char matchPattern,
                                            string replaceStr)
    {
        return (ReplaceStrWithStr(source, matchPattern.ToString( ),
                        replaceStr, -1, 0));
    }

    public static string ReplaceStrWithChar(string source, char matchPattern,
                        string replaceStr, int count)
    {
        return (ReplaceStrWithStr(source, matchPattern.ToString( ),
                replaceStr, count, 0));
    }

    public static string ReplaceStrWithChar(string source, char matchPattern,
                        string replaceStr, int count, int startPos)
    {
        return (ReplaceStrWithStr(source, matchPattern.ToString( ),
                replaceStr, count, startPos));
    }

    public static string ReplaceStrWithStr(string source, string matchPattern,
                        string replaceStr)
    {
        return (ReplaceStrWithStr(source, matchPattern, replaceStr, -1, 0));
    }

    public static string ReplaceStrWithStr(string source, string matchPattern,
                        string replaceStr, int count)
    {
        return (ReplaceStrWithStr(source, matchPattern, replaceStr, count, 0));
    }

    public static string ReplaceStrWithStr(string source, string matchPattern,
                        string replaceStr, int count, int startPos)
    {
        Regex RE = new Regex(matchPattern);
        string newString = RE.Replace(source, replaceStr, count, startPos);

        return (newString);
    }
}
```

To use the overloaded Replace methods to replace the word "FOO" with the word "BAR" in a sentence, you could write the following:

```
public static void TestReplace( )
{
    string source = "Replace the FOO in this text block of text FOO.";
    string matchPattern = "FOO";
    string replaceStr = "BAR";

    Console.WriteLine(Replace(source, matchPattern, replaceStr));
    Console.WriteLine(Replace(source, matchPattern, replaceStr, -1));
    Console.WriteLine(Replace(source, matchPattern, replaceStr, -1, 0));
    Console.WriteLine(Replace(source, matchPattern, replaceStr, 1));
    Console.WriteLine(Replace(source, matchPattern, replaceStr, 1, 0));
    Console.WriteLine(Replace(source, matchPattern, replaceStr, 1));
    Console.WriteLine(Replace(source, matchPattern, replaceStr, 1, 20));

    Console.WriteLine(Replace(source, matchPattern, replaceStr, -1, 0));
    Console.WriteLine(Replace(source, matchPattern, replaceStr, 1, 0));
    Console.WriteLine(Replace(source, matchPattern, replaceStr, 1, 20));
}
```

which would produce the following output:

```
Replace the BAR in this text block of text BAR.
Replace the BAR in this text block of text BAR.
Replace the BAR in this text block of text BAR.
Replace the BAR in this text block of text FOO.
Replace the BAR in this text block of text FOO.
Replace the BAR in this text block of text FOO.
Replace the FOO in this text block of text BAR.
Replace the BAR in this text block of text BAR.
Replace the BAR in this text block of text FOO.
Replace the FOO in this text block of text BAR.
```

This code looks for the word "FOO", and each time this pattern is found, the string "BAR" is substituted for the matched string ("FOO").

Discussion

Using the overloaded instance Replace method on the Regex class, you can easily substitute a string for a pattern in a second string each time that pattern is found. Several overloads of this method provide even more flexibility in determining where to replace matches and how many matches will be replaced.

An overloaded static Replace method is also provided on the Regex class. This method is somewhat different than its instance method counterpart. This static Replace method does not allow for the flexibility of a *startPos* or a *count* parameter. In lieu of these parameters, an *options* parameter is used. This parameter allows for modification of the *RegexOptions* options. If you require that the regular expression options (RegexOptions) be controllable, rather than using the less flexible static Regex.Replace method, you can modify the overloaded Replace methods as shown in Example 10-6.

Example 10-6. Modifying overloaded Replace methods to accept a RegexOptions parameter

```
public class RegexUtils
{
    // Constant to provide a default set of options for the regular expression
    const RegexOptions defaultOptions = RegexOptions.IgnorePatternWhitespace |
                                        RegexOptions.Multiline;

    public static string ReplaceStrWithChar(string source, char matchPattern,
                            string replaceStr)
    {
        return (ReplaceStrWithStr(source, matchPattern.ToString( ), replaceStr, -1, 0,
                    defaultOptions));
    }

    public static string ReplaceStrWithChar(string source, char matchPattern,
                            string replaceStr, int count)
    {
        return (ReplaceStrWithStr(source, matchPattern.ToString( ), replaceStr,
                    count, 0, defaultOptions));
    }

    public static string ReplaceStrWithChar(string source, char matchPattern,
                            string replaceStr, int count, int startPos)
    {
        return (ReplaceStrWithStr(source, matchPattern.ToString( ), replaceStr,
                    count, startPos, defaultOptions));
    }

    public static string ReplaceStrWithChar(string source, char matchPattern,
                            string replaceStr, int count, int startPos,
                            RegexOptions options)
    {
        return (ReplaceStrWithStr(source, matchPattern.ToString( ), replaceStr,
                    count, startPos, options));
    }

    public static string ReplaceStrWithStr(string source, string matchPattern,
                            string replaceStr)
    {
        return (ReplaceStrWithStr(source, matchPattern, replaceStr, -1, 0,
                    defaultOptions));
    }

    public static string ReplaceStrWithStr(string source, string matchPattern,
                            string replaceStr, int count)
    {
        return (ReplaceStrWithStr(source, matchPattern, replaceStr, count, 0,
                    defaultOptions));
    }

    public static string ReplaceStrWithStr(string source, string matchPattern,
                            string replaceStr, int count, int startPos)
```

```
    {
        return (ReplaceStrWithStr(source, matchPattern, replaceStr, count,
                            startPos, defaultOptions));
    }

    public static string ReplaceStrWithStr(string source, string matchPattern,
                            string replaceStr, int count, int startPos,
                            RegexOptions options)
    {
        Regex RE = new Regex(matchPattern, options);
        string newString = RE.Replace(source, replaceStr, count, startPos);

        return (newString);
    }
}
```

An *options* parameter of type RegexOptions has been added to the end of the last method's parameter list. This Replace method uses this *options* parameter to define how the Regex object will use the regular expression. Note also that a constant defaultOptions of type RegexOptions has been defined to provide a uniform way to represent the default set of options in each overloaded method.

See Also

See the ".NET Framework Regular Expressions" topic in the MSDN documentation.

10.6 Augmenting the Basic String Replacement Function

Problem

You need to replace character patterns within the target string with a new string. However, in this case, each replacement operation has a unique set of conditions that must be satisfied in order to allow the replacement to occur. Consider, for example, that you receive a string containing information and you need to make global modifications that will depend on a specific criterion.

Solution

Use the overloaded instance Replace method shown in Example 10-7 that accepts a MatchEvaluator delegate along with its other parameters. The MatchEvaluator delegate is a callback method that overrides the default behavior of the Replace method.

Example 10-7. Overloaded Replace method that accepts a MatchEvaluator delegate

```
using System;
using System.Text.RegularExpressions;

public static string MatchHandler(Match theMatch)
{
    // Handle all ControlID_ entries.
    if (theMatch.Value.StartsWith("ControlID_"))
    {
        long controlValue = 0;

        // Obtain the numeric value of the Top attribute.
        Match topAttribiteMatch = Regex.Match(theMatch.Value, "Top=([-]*\\d*)");
        if (topAttribiteMatch.Success)
        {
            if (topAttribiteMatch.Groups[1].Value.Trim( ).Equals(""))
            {
                // If blank, set to zero.
                return (theMatch.Value.Replace(
                        topAttribiteMatch.Groups[0].Value.Trim( ),
                        "Top=0"));
            }
            else if (topAttribiteMatch.Groups[1].Value.Trim( ).StartsWith("-"))
            {
                // If only a negative sign (syntax error), set to zero.
                return (theMatch.Value.Replace(
                        topAttribiteMatch.Groups[0].Value.Trim( ), "Top=0"));
            }
            else
            {
                // We have a valid number.
                // Convert the matched string to a numeric value.
                controlValue = long.Parse(topAttribiteMatch.Groups[1].Value,
                            System.Globalization.NumberStyles.Any);

                // If the Top attribute is out of the specified range,
                // set it to zero.
                if (controlValue < 0 || controlValue > 5000)
                {
                    return (theMatch.Value.Replace(
                            topAttribiteMatch.Groups[0].Value.Trim( ),
                            "Top=0"));
                }
            }
        }
    }
}
```

The callback method for the Replace method is shown here:

```
public static void ComplexReplace(string matchPattern, string source)
{
    MatchEvaluator replaceCallback = new MatchEvaluator(MatchHandler);
    Regex RE = new Regex(matchPattern, RegexOptions.Multiline);
```

```
        string newString = RE.Replace(source, replaceCallback);

        Console.WriteLine("Replaced String = " + newString);
    }
```

To use this callback method with the static Replace method, modify the previous ComplexReplace method as follows:

```
public void ComplexReplace(string matchPattern, string source)
{
    MatchEvaluator replaceCallback = new MatchEvaluator(MatchHandler);
    string newString = Regex.Replace(source, matchPattern,
                                     replaceCallback);

    Console.WriteLine("Replaced String = " + newString);
}
```

where *source* is the original string to run the replace operation against, and *matchPattern* is the regular expression pattern to match in the *source* string.

If the ComplexReplace method is called from the following code:

```
public static void TestComplexReplace( )
{
    string matchPattern = "(ControlID_.*)";
    string source = @"WindowID=Main
ControlID_TextBox1 Top=-100 Left=0 Text=BLANK
ControlID_Label1 Top=9999990 Left=0 Caption=Enter Name Here
ControlID_Label2 Top= Left=0 Caption=Enter Name Here";

    ComplexReplace(matchPattern, source);
}
```

only the Top attributes of the ControlID_* lines are changed from their original values to 0.

The result of this replace action will change the Top attribute value of a ControlID_* line to zero if it is less than zero or greater than 5000. Any other tag that contains a Top attribute will remain unchanged. The following three lines of the source string will be changed from:

```
ControlID_TextBox1 Top=-100 Left=0 Text=BLANK
ControlID_Label1 Top=9999990 Left=0 Caption=Enter Name Here
ControlID_Label2 Top= Left=0 Caption=Enter Name Here";
```

to:

```
ControlID_TextBox1 Top=0 Left=0 Text=BLANK
ControlID_Label1 Top=0 Left=0 Caption=Enter Name Here
ControlID_Label2 Top=0 Left=0 Caption=Enter Name Here";
```

Discussion

The MatchEvaluator delegate, which is automatically invoked when it is supplied as a parameter to the Regex class's Replace method, allows for custom replacement of each string that conforms to the regular expression pattern.

If the current Match object is operating on a ControlID_* line with a Top attribute that is out of the specified range, the code within the MatchHandler callback method returns a new modified string. Otherwise, the currently matched string is returned unchanged. This ability allows you to override the default Replace functionality by replacing only that part of the source string that meets certain criteria. The code within this callback method gives you some idea of what can be accomplished using this replacement technique.

To make use of this callback method, you need a way to call it from the ComplexReplace method. First, a variable of type System.Text.RegularExpressions. MatchEvaluator is created. This variable (replaceCallback) is the delegate that is used to call the MatchHandler method:

```
MatchEvaluator replaceCallback = new MatchEvaluator(MatchHandler);
```

Finally, the Replace method is called with the reference to the MatchEvaluator delegate passed in as a parameter:

```
string newString = RE.Replace(source, replaceCallback);
```

See Also

See the ".NET Framework Regular Expressions" topic in the MSDN documentation.

10.7 Implementing a Better Tokenizer

Problem

A simple method of *tokenizing*—or breaking up a string into its discrete elements—was presented in Recipe 2.6. However, this is not powerful enough to handle all your string-tokenizing needs. You need a tokenizer—also referred to as a *lexer*—that can split up a string based on a well-defined set of characters.

Solution

Using the Split method of the Regex class, you can use a regular expression to indicate the types of tokens and separators that you are interested in gathering. This technique works especially well with equations, since the tokens of an equation are well defined. For example, the code:

```
using System;
using System.Text.RegularExpressions;

public static string[] Tokenize(string equation)
{
    Regex RE = new Regex(@"([\+\-\*\(\)\^\\])");
    return (RE.Split(equation));
}
```

will divide up a string according to the regular expression specified in the Regex constructor. In other words, the string passed in to the Tokenize method will be divided up based on the delimiters +, -, *, (,), ^, and \. The following method will call the Tokenize method to tokenize the equation (y - 3)(3111*x^21 + x + 320):

```
public void TestTokenize( )
{
    foreach(string token in Tokenize("(y - 3)(3111*x^21 + x + 320)"))
        Console.WriteLine("String token = " + token.Trim( ));
}
```

which displays the following output:

```
String token =
String token = (
String token = y
String token = -
String token = 3
String token = )
String token =
String token = (
String token = 3111
String token = *
String token = x
String token = ^
String token = 21
String token = +
String token = x
String token = +
String token = 320
String token = )
String token =
```

Notice that each individual operator, parenthesis, and number has been broken out into its own separate token.

Discussion

The tokenizer created in Recipe 2.6 would be useful in specific controlled circumstances. However, in real-world projects, you do not always have the luxury of being able to control the set of inputs to your code. By making use of regular expressions, you can take the original tokenizer and make it flexible enough to allow it to be applied to any type or style of input you desire.

The key method used here is the Split instance method of the Regex class. The return value of this method is a string array with elements that include each individual token of the source string—the equation, in this case.

Notice that the static method allows RegexOptions enumeration values to be used, while the instance method allows for a starting position to be defined and a maximum number of matches to occur. This may have some bearing on whether you choose the static or instance method.

See Also

See Recipe 2.6; see the ".NET Framework Regular Expressions" topic in the MSDN documentation.

10.8   Compiling Regular Expressions

Problem

You have a handful of regular expressions to execute as quickly as possible over many different strings. Performance is of the utmost importance.

Solution

The best way to do this task is to use compiled regular expressions. However, there are some drawbacks to using this technique, which we will examine.

There are two ways to compile regular expressions. The easiest way is to use the `RegexOptions.Compiled` enumeration value in the `Options` parameter of the static `Match` or `Matches` methods on the `Regex` class:

```
Match theMatch = Regex.Match(source, pattern, RegexOptions.Compiled);

MatchCollection theMatches = Regex.Matches(source, pattern, RegexOptions.Compiled);
```

If more than a few expressions will be compiled and/or the expressions need to be shared across applications, consider precompiling all of these expressions into their own assembly. Do this by using the static `CompileToAssembly` method on the `Regex` class. The following method accepts an assembly name and compiles two simple regular expressions into this assembly:

```
public static void CreateRegExDLL(string assmName)
{
    RegexCompilationInfo[] RE = new RegexCompilationInfo[2]
        {new RegexCompilationInfo("PATTERN", RegexOptions.Compiled,
                                  "CompiledPATTERN", "Chapter_Code", true),
            new RegexCompilationInfo("NAME", RegexOptions.Compiled,
                                  "CompiledNAME", "Chapter_Code", true)};

    System.Reflection.AssemblyName aName =
        new System.Reflection.AssemblyName( );
    aName.Name = assmName;

    Regex.CompileToAssembly(RE, aName);
}
```

Now that the expressions are compiled to an assembly, the assembly can be added as a reference to your project and used as follows:

```
Chapter_Code.CompiledNAME CN = new Chapter_Code.CompiledNAME( );
Match mName = CN.Match("Get the NAME from this text.");
Console.WriteLine("mName.Value = " + mName.Value);
```

This code displays the following text:

```
mName.Value = NAME
```

Note that this code can be used as part of your build process. The resulting assembly can then be shipped with your application.

Discussion

Compiling regular expressions allows the expression to run faster. To understand how, you need to examine the process that an expression goes through as it is run against a string. If an expression is not compiled, the regular expression engine converts the expression to a series of internal codes that are recognized by the regular expression engine; it is not converted to MSIL. As the expression runs against a string, the engine interprets the series of internal codes. This can be a slow process, especially as the source string becomes very large and the expression becomes much more complex.

There is a class of scenarios for which performance of uncompiled regex is unacceptable, but for which compiled regex performs acceptably. To mitigate this performance problem, you can compile the expression so that it gets converted directly to a series of MSIL instructions, which performs the pattern matching for the specific regular expression. Once the Just-In-Time (JIT) compiler is run on this MSIL, the instructions are converted to machine code. This allows for an extremely fast execution of the pattern against a string.

There are two drawbacks to using the `RegexOptions.Compiled` enumerated value to compile regular expressions. The first is that the first time an expression is used with the `Compiled` flag, it performs very slowly, due to the compilation process. Fortunately, this is a one-time expense since every unique expression is compiled only once. The second drawback is that an in-memory assembly gets generated to contain the IL, which can never be unloaded. An assembly can never be unloaded from an `AppDomain`. The garbage collector cannot remove it from memory. If large numbers of expressions are compiled, the amount of heap resources that will be used up and not released will be large. So use this technique wisely.

Compiling regular expressions into their own assembly immediately gives you two benefits. First, precompiled expressions do not require any extra time to be compiled while your application is running. Second, they are in their own assembly and therefore can be used by other applications.

 Consider precompiling regular expressions and placing them in their own assembly rather than using the `RegexOptions.Compiled` flag.

To compile one or more expressions into an assembly, the static `CompileToAssembly` method of the `Regex` class must be used. To use this method, a `RegexCompilationInfo`

array must be created and filled with RegexCompilationInfo objects. The next step is to create the assembly in which the expression will live. An instance of the AssemblyName class is created using the default constructor. Next, this assembly is given a name (do not include the *.dll* file extension in the name; it is added automatically). Finally, the CompileToAssembly method can be called with the RegexCompilationInfo array and the AssemblyName object supplied as arguments.

 In our example, this assembly is placed in the same directory that the executable was launched from.

See Also

See the ".NET Framework Regular Expressions" and "AssemblyName Class" topics in the MSDN documentation.

10.9   Counting Lines of Text

Problem

You need to count lines of text within a string or within a file.

Solution

Use the LineCount method shown in Example 10-8 to read in the entire file and count the number of line feeds.

Example 10-8. LineCount method

```
using System;
using System.Text.RegularExpressions;
using System.IO;

public static long LineCount(string source, bool isFileName)
{
    if (source != null)
    {
        string text = source;

        if (isFileName)
        {
            using (FileStream FS = new FileStream(source, FileMode.Open,
                                        FileAccess.Read, FileShare.Read))
            {
                using (StreamReader SR = new StreamReader(FS))
                {
                    text = SR.ReadToEnd( );
                }
            }
```

Example 10-8. LineCount method (continued)

```
                }
            }

            Regex RE = new Regex("\n", RegexOptions.Multiline);
            MatchCollection theMatches = RE.Matches(text);

            if (isFileName)
            {
                return (theMatches.Count);
            }
            else
            {
                return (theMatches.Count) + 1;
            }
        }
        else
        {
            // Handle a null source here.
            return (0);
        }
}
```

LineCount2, a better performing alternate version of this method uses the StreamReader.ReadLine method to count lines in a file and a regular expression to count lines in a string, as shown in Example 10-9.

Example 10-9. LineCount2 method

```
public static long LineCount2(string source, bool isFileName)
{
    if (source != null)
    {
        string text = source;
        long numOfLines = 0;

        if (isFileName)
        {
            using (FileStream FS = new FileStream(source, FileMode.Open,
                                    FileAccess.Read, FileShare.Read))
            {
                using (StreamReader SR = new StreamReader(FS))
                {
                    while (text != null)
                    {
                        text = SR.ReadLine( );

                        if (text != null)
                        {
                            ++numOfLines;
                        }
                    }
                }
            }
```

Example 10-9. LineCount2 method (continued)

```
            }

            return (numOfLines);
        }
        else
        {
            Regex RE = new Regex("\n", RegexOptions.Multiline);
            MatchCollection theMatches = RE.Matches(text);

            return (theMatches.Count + 1);
        }
    }
    else
    {
        // Handle a null source here.
        return (0);
    }
}
```

The following method counts the lines within a specified text file and a specified string:

```
public static void TestLineCount( )
{
    // Count the lines within the file TestFile.txt.
    LineCount(@"C:\TestFile.txt", true);

    // Count the lines within a string.
    // Notice that the \r\n characters start a new line
    // as well as just the \n character.
    LineCount("Line1\r\nLine2\r\nLine3\nLine4", false);
}
```

Discussion

Every line ends with a special character. For Windows files, the line-terminating characters are a carriage return followed by a line-feed. This sequence of characters is described by the regular expression pattern \r\n. Unix files terminate their lines with just the line-feed character (\n). The regular expression "\n" is the lowest common denominator for both sets of line-terminating characters. Consequently, this method runs a regular expression that looks for the pattern "\n" in a string or file.

Macintosh files usually end with a carriage-return character (\r). To count the number of lines in this type of file, the regular expression should be changed to the following in the constructor of the Regex object:

```
    Regex RE = new Regex("\r", RegexOptions.Multiline);
```

Simply running this regular expression against a string returns the number of lines minus one because the last line does not have a line-terminating character. To account for this, one is added to the final count of line feeds in the string.

The LineCount method accepts two parameters. The first is a string that either contains the actual text that will have its lines counted or the path and name of a text file whose lines are to be counted. The second parameter, isFileName, determines whether the first parameter (source) is a string or a file path. If this parameter is true, the source parameter is a file path; otherwise, it is simply a string.

See Also

See the ".NET Framework Regular Expressions," "FileStream Class," and "Stream-Reader Class" topics in the MSDN documentation.

10.10 Returning the Entire Line in Which a Match Is Found

Problem

You have a string or file that contains multiple lines. When a specific character pattern is found on a line, you want to return the entire line, not just the matched text.

Solution

Use the StreamReader.ReadLine method to obtain each line in a file in which to run a regular expression against, as shown in Example 10-10.

Example 10-10. Returning the entire line in which a match is found

```
public static List<string> GetLines(string source, string pattern, bool isFileName)
{
    string text = source;
    List<string> matchedLines = new List<string>();

    // If this is a file, get the entire file's text.
    if (isFileName)
    {
        using (FileStream FS = new FileStream(source, FileMode.Open,
            FileAccess.Read, FileShare.Read))
        {
            using (StreamReader SR = new StreamReader(FS))
            {
                Regex RE = new Regex(pattern, RegexOptions.Multiline);
                while (text != null)
                {
                    text = SR.ReadLine();

                    if (text != null)
```

```
                    {
                        // Run the regex on each line in the string.
                        MatchCollection theMatches = RE.Matches(text);

                        if (theMatches.Count > 0)
                        {
                            // Get the line if a match was found.
                            matchedLines.Add(text);
                        }
                    }
                }
            }
        }
    }
    else
    {
        // Run the regex once on the entire string.
        Regex RE = new Regex(pattern, RegexOptions.Multiline);
        MatchCollection theMatches = RE.Matches(text);

        // Use these vars to remember the last line added to matchedLines
        // so that we do not add duplicate lines.
        int lastLineStartPos = -1;
        int lastLineEndPos = -1;

        // Get the line for each match.
        foreach (Match m in theMatches)
        {
            int lineStartPos = GetBeginningOfLine(text, m.Index);
            int lineEndPos = GetEndOfLine(text, (m.Index + m.Length - 1));

            // If this is not a duplicate line, add it.
            if (lastLineStartPos != lineStartPos &&
                lastLineEndPos != lineEndPos)
            {
                string line = text.Substring(lineStartPos,
                                    lineEndPos - lineStartPos);
                matchedLines.Add(line);

                // Reset line positions.
                lastLineStartPos = lineStartPos;
                lastLineEndPos = lineEndPos;
            }
        }
    }

    return (matchedLines);
}

public static int GetBeginningOfLine(string text, int startPointOfMatch)
{
    if (startPointOfMatch > 0)
```

Example 10-10. Returning the entire line in which a match is found (continued)

```
    {
        --startPointOfMatch;
    }

    if (startPointOfMatch >= 0 && startPointOfMatch < text.Length)
    {
        // Move to the left until the first '\n char is found.
        for (int index = startPointOfMatch; index >= 0; index--)
        {
            if (text[index] == '\n')
            {
                return (index + 1);
            }
        }

        return (0);
    }

    return (startPointOfMatch);
}

public static int GetEndOfLine(string text, int endPointOfMatch)
{
    if (endPointOfMatch >= 0 && endPointOfMatch < text.Length)
    {
        // Move to the right until the first '\n char is found.
        for (int index = endPointOfMatch; index < text.Length; index++)
        {
            if (text[index] == '\n')
            {
                return (index);
            }
        }

        return (text.Length);
    }

    return (endPointOfMatch);
}
```

The following method shows how to call the GetLines method with either a filename or a string:

```
public static void TestGetLine( )
{
    // Get each line within the file TestFile.txt as a separate string.
    Console.WriteLine( );
    List<string> lines = GetLines(@"C:\TestFile.txt", "\n", true);
    foreach (string s in lines)
        Console.WriteLine("MatchedLine: " + s);

    // Get the lines matching the text "Line" within the given string.
```

```
        Console.WriteLine( );
        lines = GetLines("Line1\r\nLine2\r\nLine3\nLine4", "Line", false);
        foreach (string s in lines)
            Console.WriteLine("MatchedLine: " + s);
    }
```

Discussion

The GetLines method accepts three parameters:

source
> The string or filename in which to search for a pattern

pattern
> The regular expression pattern to apply to the *source* string

isFileName
> Pass in true if the *source* is a filename or false if *source* is a string

This method returns a List<string> of strings that contains each line in which the regular expression match was found.

The GetLines method can obtain the lines on which matches occur, within a string or a file. When running a regular expression against a file with a name that is passed in to the *source* parameter (when *isFileName* equals true) in the GetLines method, the file is opened and read line by line. The regular expression is run against each line and, if a match is found, that line is stored in the matchedLines List<string>. Using the ReadLine method of the StreamReader object saves you from having to determine where each line starts and ends. Determining where a line starts and ends in a string requires some work, as you shall see.

Running the regular expression against a string passed in to the *source* parameter (when *isFileName* equals false) in the GetLines method produces a MatchCollection. Each Match object in this collection is used to obtain the line on which it is located in the *source* string. The line is obtained by starting at the position of the first character of the match in the *source* string and moving one character to the left until either an '\n' character is found or the beginning of the *source* string is found (this code is found in the GetBeginningOfLine method). This gives you the beginning of the line, which is placed in the variable LineStartPos. Next, the end of the line is found by starting at the last character of the match in the *source* string and moving to the right until either an '\n' character is found or the end of the *source* string is found (this code is found in the GetEndOfLine method). This ending position is placed in the LineEndPos variable. All of the text between the LineStartPos and LineEndPos will be the line in which the match is found. Each of these lines is added to the matchedLines List<string> and returned to the caller.

Something interesting you can do with the GetLines method is to pass in the string "\n" in the pattern parameter of this method. This trick will effectively return each line of the string or file as a string in the List<string>.

Note that if more than one match is found on a line, each matching line will be added to the List<string>.

See Also

See the ".NET Framework Regular Expressions," "FileStream Class," and "Stream-Reader Class" topics in the MSDN documentation.

10.11 Finding a Particular Occurrence of a Match

Problem

You need to find a specific occurrence of a match within a string. For example, you want to find the third occurrence of a word or the second occurrence of a social security number. In addition, you may need to find every third occurrence of a word in a string.

Solution

To find a particular occurrence of a match in a string, simply subscript the array returned from Regex.Matches:

```
public static Match FindOccurrenceOf(string source, string pattern,
                                     int occurrence)
{
    if (occurrence < 1)
    {
        throw (new ArgumentException("Cannot be less than 1",
                                     "occurrence"));
    }

    // Make occurrence zero-based.
    --occurrence;

    // Run the regex once on the source string.
    Regex RE = new Regex(pattern, RegexOptions.Multiline);
    MatchCollection theMatches = RE.Matches(source);

    if (occurrence >= theMatches.Count)
    {
        return (null);
    }
    else
    {
        return (theMatches[occurrence]);
    }
}
```

To find each particular occurrence of a match in a string, build a List<Match> on the fly:

```
public static List<Match> FindEachOccurrenceOf(string source, string pattern,
                                               int occurrence)
{
    List<Match> occurrences = new List<Match>();

    // Run the regex once on the source string.
    Regex RE = new Regex(pattern, RegexOptions.Multiline);
    MatchCollection theMatches = RE.Matches(source);

    for (int index = (occurrence - 1); index < theMatches.Count; index += occurrence)
    {
        occurrences.Add(theMatches[index]);
    }

    return (occurrences);
}
```

The following method shows how to invoke the two previous methods:

```
public static void TestOccurrencesOf()
{
    Match matchResult = FindOccurrenceOf
                        ("one two three one two three one two three one"
                        + " two three one two three one two three", "two", 2);
    if (matchResult != null)
        Console.WriteLine(matchResult.ToString() + "\t" + matchResult.Index);

    Console.WriteLine();
    List<Match> results = FindEachOccurrenceOf
                        ("one one two three one two three one "
                        + " two three one two three", "one", 2);
    foreach (Match m in results)
        Console.WriteLine(m.ToString() + "\t" + m.Index);
}
```

Discussion

This recipe contains two similar but distinct methods. The first method, FindOccurrenceOf, returns a particular occurrence of a regular expression match. The occurrence you want to find is passed in to this method via the occurrence parameter. If the particular occurrence of the match does not exist—for example, you ask to find the second occurrence, but only one occurrence exists—a null is returned from this method. Because of this, you should check that the returned object of this method is not null before using that object. If the particular occurrence exists, the Match object that holds the match information for that occurrence is returned.

The second method in this recipe, FindEachOccurrenceOf, works similarly to the FindOccurrenceOf method, except that it continues to find a particular occurrence of a regular expression match until the end of the string is reached. For example, if you ask to find the second occurrence, this method would return a List<Match> of zero or more Match objects. The Match objects would correspond to the second, fourth, sixth, and eighth occurrences of a match and so on until the end of the string is reached.

See Also

See the ".NET Framework Regular Expressions" and "ArrayList Class" topics in the MSDN documentation.

10.12 Using Common Patterns

Problem

You need a quick list from which to choose regular expression patterns that match standard items. These standard items could be a social security number, a zip code, a word containing only characters, an alphanumeric word, an email address, a URL, dates, or one of many other possible items used throughout business applications.

These patterns can be useful in making sure that a user has input the correct data and that it is well formed. These patterns can also be used as an extra security measure to keep hackers from attempting to break your code by entering strange or malformed input (e.g., SQL injection or cross-site-scripting attacks). Note that these regular expressions are not a silver bullet that will stop all attacks on your system; rather, they are an added layer of defense.

Solution

- Match only alphanumeric characters along with the characters -, +, ., and any whitespace:

  `^([\w\.+-]|\s)*$`

 Be careful using the - character within a character class—a regular expression enclosed within [and]. That character is also used to specify a range of characters, as in a-z for a through z inclusive. If you want to use a literal - character, either escape it with \ or put it at the end of the expression, as shown in the previous and next examples.

- Match only alphanumeric characters along with the characters -, +, ., and any whitespace, with the stipulation that there is at least one of these characters and no more than 10 of these characters:

  `^([\w\.+-]|\s){1,10}$`
- Match a person's name, up to 55 characters:

  `^[a-zA-Z\'\-\s]{1,55}$`
- Match a positive or negative integer:

  `^((\+|-)\d)?\d*$`
- Match a date in the form ##/##/#### where the day and month can be a one- or two-digit value and year can either be a two- or four-digit value:

  `^\d{1,2}\/\d{1,2}\/\d{2,4}$`

- Match a time to be entered with an optional am or pm extension (note that this regular expression also handles military time):

    `^\d{1,2}:\d{2}\s?([ap]m)?$`

- Verify if the input is a social security number of the form ###-##-####:

    `^\d{3}-\d{2}-\d{4}$`

- Match an IPv4 address:

    `^([0-2]?[0-5]?[0-5]\.){3}[0-2]?[0-5]?[0-5]$`

- Verify that an email address is in the form *name@address* where *address* is not an IP address:

    `^[A-Za-z0-9_\-\.]+@(([A-Za-z0-9\-])+\.)+([A-Za-z\-])+$`

- Verify that an email address is in the form *name@address* where *address* is an IP address:

    `^[A-Za-z0-9_\-\.]+@([0-2]?[0-5]?[0-5]\.){3}[0-2]?[0-5]?[0-5]$`

- Match or verify a URL that uses either the HTTP, HTTPS, or FTP protocol. Note that this regular expression will not match relative URLs.

    `^(http|https|ftp)\://[a-zA-Z0-9\-\.]+\.[a-zA-Z]{2,3}(:[a-zA-Z0-9]*)?/?([a-zA-Z0-9\-\._\?\,\'/\\+&%\$#\=~])*$`

- Match only a dollar amount with the optional $ and + or - preceding characters (note that any number of decimal places may be added):

    `^\$?[+-]?[\d,]*(\.\d*)?$`

  This is similar to the previous regular expression except that no more than two decimal places are allowed:

    `^\$?[+-]?[\d,]*\.?\d{0,2}$`

- Match a credit card number to be entered as four sets of four digits separated with a space, -, or no character at all:

    `^((\d{4}[- ]?){3}\d{4})$`

- Match a zip code to be entered as five digits with an optional four-digit extension:

    `^\d{5}(-\d{4})?$`

- Match a North American phone number with an optional area code and an optional - character to be used in the phone number and no extension:

    `^(\(?[0-9]{3}\)?)?\-?[0-9]{3}\-?[0-9]{4}$`

- Match a phone number similar to the previous regular expression but allow an optional five-digit extension prefixed with either ext or extension:

    `^(\(?[0-9]{3}\)?)?\-?[0-9]{3}\-?[0-9]{4}(\s*ext(ension)?[0-9]{5})?$`

- Match a full path beginning with the drive letter and optionally match a filename with a three-character extension (note that no .. characters signifying to move up the directory hierarchy are allowed, nor is a directory name with a . followed by an extension):

    `^[a-zA-Z]:[\\/]([_a-zA-Z0-9]+[\\/]?)*([_a-zA-Z0-9]+\.[_a-zA-Z0-9]{0,3})?$`

- Verify if the input password string matches some specific rules for entering a password (i.e., the password is between 6 and 25 characters in length and contains alphanumeric characters):

  `^(?=.*\d)(?=.*[a-z])(?=.*[A-Z]).{6,25}$`

- Determine if any malicious characters were input by the user. Note that this regular expression will not prevent all malicious input, and it also prevents some valid input, such as last names that contain a single quote.

  `^([^\)\(\<\>\"\'\%\&\+\;][(-{2})])*$`

Discussion

Regular expressions are effective at finding specific information, and they have a wide range of uses. Many applications use them to locate specific information within a larger range of text, as well as to filter out bad input. The filtering action is very useful in tightening the security of an application and preventing an attacker from attempting to use carefully formed input to gain access to a machine on the Internet or a local network. By using a regular expression to allow only good input to be passed to the application, you can reduce the likelihood of many types of attacks, such as SQL injection or cross-site-scripting.

The regular expressions presented in this recipe provide only a minute cross-section of what can be accomplished with them. By taking these expressions and manipulating parts of them, you can easily modify them to work with your application. Take, for example, the following expression, which allows only between 1 and 10 alphanumeric characters, along with a few symbols as input:

  `^([\w\.+-]|\s){1,10}$`

By changing the {1,10} part of the regular expression to {0,200}, this expression will now match a blank entry or an entry of the specified symbols up to and including 200 characters.

Note the use of the ^ character at the beginning of the expression and the $ character at the end of the expression. These characters start the match at the beginning of the text and match all the way to the end of the text. Adding these characters forces the regular expression to match the entire string or none of it. By removing these characters, you can search for specific text within a larger block of text. For example, the following regular expression matches only a string containing nothing but a U.S. zip code (there can be no leading or trailing spaces):

  `^\d{5}(-\d{4})?$`

This version matches only a zip code with leading or trailing spaces (notice the addition of the \s* to the start and end of the expression):

  `^\s*\d{5}(-\d{4})?\s*$`

However, this modified expression matches a zip code found anywhere within a string (including a string containing just a zip code):

```
\d{5}(-\d{4})?
```

Use the regular expressions in this recipe and modify them to suit your needs.

See Also

Two good books that cover regular expressions are *Regular Expression Pocket Reference* and *Mastering Regular Expressions*, Second Edition (both from O'Reilly).

10.13 Documenting Your Regular Expressions

Problem

You have one or more complex regular expressions that may exist in a file outside of your code. You need a way to place comments within the regular expression itself. These comments will aid others in being able to read and maintain your regular expressions later on.

Solution

Add comments to the regular expression using the # comment character:

```
string matchPattern = @"\\\\          # Find this:  \\
                (?<TheServer>\w*)      # Server name
                \\                     # Find this:  \
                (?<TheService>\w*)\\   # Service name";
```

When using this expression in a Regex object, the RegexOptions.Ignore-PatternWhitespace enumeration value must be added to the options parameter of the Regex object constructor:

```
Regex RE = new Regex(matchPattern,
    RegexOptions.Multiline | RegexOptions.IgnorePatternWhitespace);
MatchCollection theMatches = RE.Matches("The source text goes here...");
```

or add C#-style comments outside of the regular expression string:

```
string matchPattern = @"\\\\" +            // Find this:  \\
                @"(?<TheServer>\w*)" +     // Server name
                @"\\" +                    // Find this:  \
                @"(?<TheService>\w*)\\";   // Service name
```

Discussion

With large and complex regular expressions, it is desirable to break up the expression into manageable pieces and to identify what each piece does. For example, the regular expression in the Solution section will pull the server and service pieces out of a UNC string. By breaking up the regular expression onto separate lines and adding comments to each line, you have allowed other developers (who might not be familiar with regular expressions) to more quickly and easily read and maintain your regular expression.

Typically, you would use the string concatenation and C#-style commenting to comment a regular expression string. However, if you are retrieving the regular expression from an external source, such as a text file, regular expression–style commenting (#) is the type to use.

With simpler regular expressions, you can get away with adding a C# comment outside of the regular expression string to indicate what it does. But adding comments to the regular expression itself greatly aids in understanding it.

10.14 Using Built-in Regular Expressions to Parse ASP.NET Pages

Problem

You need to build a tool that parses ASP.NET pages in order to extract specific bits of information. This tool could possibly be used to detect whether specific meta tags are being used or if there are any comments that could expose information useful to a hacker.

Solution

Use the classes in the System.Web.RegularExpressions namespace. In this recipe you will focus on mapping out the start and end tags on a page, as shown in Example 10-11.

 In order to make use of any of the classes in the System.Web. RegularExpressions namespace, you need to manually import the *System.Web.RegularExpressions.dll* file into your project.

Example 10-11. Parsing a web page

```
public static void ASPNETStartEndTagParsing(string html)
{
    int index = 0;
    while (index < html.Length)
    {
        Match m = null;

        // Display the start tag.
        TagRegex aspTag = new TagRegex();
        m = aspTag.Match(html, index);
        if (m.Success)
        {
```

Example 10-11. Parsing a web page (continued)

```
            index = m.Index + m.Length;
            Console.WriteLine("ASP.NET Start Tag");
            Console.WriteLine(m.Value);
            continue;
        }


        // Display the end tag.
        EndTagRegex aspEndTag = new EndTagRegex();
        m = aspEndTag.Match(html, index);
        if (m.Success)
        {
            index = m.Index + m.Length;
            Console.WriteLine("ASP.NET End Tag");
            Console.WriteLine(m.Value);
            continue;
        }

        index++;
    }
}
```

When the ASPNETStartEndTagParsing method is called in the following manner:

```
public static void TestASPNETParsing()
{
    string testHTML = "<%-- Comment --%>  <%@ Page Language=\"CS\" " +
                      "AutoEventWireup=\"false\" CodeFile=\"Default.aspx.cs\" " +
                      "Inherits=\"Default_aspx\" %>" +
                      "<!DOCTYPE html PUBLIC \"-//W3C//DTD XHTML 1.1//EN\" " +
                      "\"http://www.w3.org/TR/xhtml11/DTD/xhtml11.dtd\">" +
                      "<html xmlns=\"http://www.w3.org/1999/xhtml\">  " +
                      "<head runat=\"server\"> " +
                      "<title>Untitled Page</title>  " +
                      "</head><body><form id=\"form1\" runat=\"server\"><div> " +
                      "<asp:Login ID=\"Login1\" runat=\"server\"></asp:Login>" +
                      "</div></form></body></html>";

    ASPNETStartEndTagParsing(testHTML);
}
```

the following is displayed:

```
ASP.NET Start Tag
<html xmlns="http://www.w3.org/1999/xhtml">
ASP.NET Start Tag
<head runat="server">
ASP.NET Start Tag
<title>
ASP.NET End Tag
</title>
ASP.NET End Tag
</head>
ASP.NET Start Tag
```

```
<body>
ASP.NET Start Tag
<form id="form1" runat="server">
ASP.NET Start Tag
<div>
ASP.NET Start Tag
<asp:Login ID="Login1" runat="server">
ASP.NET End Tag
</asp:Login>
ASP.NET End Tag
</div>
ASP.NET End Tag
</form>
ASP.NET End Tag
</body>
ASP.NET End Tag
</html>
```

Discussion

There are 15 classes within the System.Web.RegularExpressions namespace that give you the ability to parse existing aspx pages and HTML pages as well as other types of web pages. You can even parse XML to some extent. Each of these classes inherits from the System.Text.RegularExpressions.Regex class. What makes these classes unique is that each contains one regular expression that allows them to parse different aspects of a web page. For example, the CommentRegex class contains the following regular expressions:

```
\G<%--(([^-]*)-)*?-%>
```

which look for a comment within a web page in the following format:

```
<%-- this is a comment -->
```

Table 10-1 lists each class and its associated regular expression along with its description.

Table 10-1. Descriptions of the System.Web.RegularExpressions classes

Class name	Regular expression	Description
AspCodeRegex	\G<%(?!@)(?<code>.*?)%>	Parses a code block of the form <% code %>.
AspExprRegex	\G<%\s*?=(?<code>.*?)?%>	Parses an expression block of the form <%= expression %>.
CommentRegex	\G<%--(([^-]*)-)*?-%>	Parses a comment of the form <%-- comment --%>.
DatabindExprRegex	\G<%#(?<code>.*?)?%>	Parses a data binding expression of the form <%# expressions %>.
DataBindRegex	\G\s*<%\s*?#(?<code>.*?)?%>\s*\z	Parses a data binding of the form <%# expressions %>.

Class name	Regular expression	Description
DirectiveRegex	\G<%\s*@(\s*(?<attrname>\w[\w:]*(?=\W))(\s*(?<equal>=)\ s*"(?<attrval>[^"]*)"|\ s*(?<equal>=)\s*'(?<attrval> [^']*)'|\s*(?<equal>=)\ s*(?<attrval>[^\s%>]*)|(?<equal>)(?<attrval>\s*?)))*\s*?%>	Parses a directive of the form <%@ directive %>.
EndTagRegex	\G</(?<tagname>[\w:\.]+)\s*>	Parses an end tag of the form </tagname>.
GTRegex	[^%]>	Parses a greater-than character that is not part of a tag.
IncludeRegex	\G<!--\s*#(?i:include)\ s*(?<pathtype>[\w]+)\s*=\ s*["']?(?<filename>[^\ "']*?)["']?\s*-->	Parses an #include directive of the form <!-- #include file="myfile.txt" -->.
LTRegex	<[^%]	Parses a less-than character that is not part of a tag.
RunatServerRegex	runat\W*server	Parses the runat attribute of the form runat="server".
ServerTagsRegex	<%(?![#$])(([^%]*)%)*?>	Parses server tags of the form <% data %>.
SimpleDirectiveRegex	<%\s*@(\s*(?<attrname>\w[\w:]*(?=\W))(\s*(?<equal>=)\ s*"(?<attrval>[^"]*)"|\ s*(?<equal>=)\s*'(?<attrval> [^']*)'|\s*(?<equal>=)\ s*(?<attrval>[^\s%>]*)|(?<equal>)(?<attrval>\s*?)))*\s*?%>	Parses a directive of the form <%@ directive %>. Note that the only difference between this regex and the one used by the DirectiveRegex is the lack of the \G, which forces the next match to start where the last match ended.
TagRegex	\G<(?<tagname>[\w:\.]+)(\ s+(?<attrname>\w[-\w:]*)(\s*=\ s*"(?<attrval>[^"]*)"|\s*=\ s*'(?<attrval>[^']*)'|\s*=\ s*(?<attrval><%#.*?%>)|\s*=\ s*(?!'|")(?<attrval>[^\s=/>]*)(?!'|")|(?<attrval>\s*?)))*\ s*(?<empty>/)?>	Parses a beginning tag of the form <tagname> or <asp:tagname>, including any attributes and their values.
TextRegex	\G[^<]+	Can be used to parse the text between two tags. Use TagRegex to find the ending of a beginning tag and then use this class to find any text between it and the next tag.

You will notice that some of these classes are designed to operate on the matches of another class. For example the RunatServerRegex class can determine if a particular tag is written to be executed on the server or not. The following code displays all start tags and whether or not they are written to be executed on the server:

```
public static void ASPNETStartTagParsing(string html)
{
    int index = 0;
    while (index < html.Length)
    {
        Match m = null;

        // Display the start tag and whether it contains a runat="server" attribute.
        TagRegex aspTag = new TagRegex( );
        m = aspTag.Match(html, index);
        if (m.Success)
        {
            index = m.Index + m.Length;
            Console.WriteLine("ASP.NET Start Tag");
            Console.WriteLine(m.Value);

            RunatServerRegex aspRunAt = new RunatServerRegex( );
            Match mInner = aspRunAt.Match(m.Value, 0);
            if (mInner.Success)
            {
                Console.WriteLine("\tASP.NET RunAt");
                Console.WriteLine("\t" + mInner.Value);
            }

            continue;
        }

        index++;
    }
}
```

Nesting these ASP.NET parsing classes in this manner will allow you to tear apart a web page quite easily.

CHAPTER 11

Data Structures and Algorithms

11.0 Introduction

In this chapter, you will look at certain data structures and algorithms that are not available for you in the FCL through Version 2.0. Examples are provided for algorithms like hash-code creation and string balancing. The FCL does not support every data structure you might need, so this chapter provides solutions for priority and double queues, binary and *n*-ary trees, sets, and a multimap, as well as many other things.

11.1 Creating a Hash Code for a Data Type

Problem

You have created a class or structure that will be used as a key in a Hashtable or Dictionary<T,U>. You need to overload the GetHashCode method in order to return a good distribution of hash values (the Discussion section defines a good distribution of hash values). You also need to choose the best hash-code algorithm to use in the GetHashCode method of your object.

Solution

The following procedures implement hash-code algorithms and can be used to override the GetHashCode method. Included in the discussion of each method are the pros and cons of using it, as well as why you would want to use one instead of another.

In addition, it is desirable, for performance reasons, to use the return value of the GetHashCode method to determine whether the data contained within two objects is equal. Calling GetHashCode to return a hash value of two objects and comparing their hash values can be faster than calling the default implementation of Equals on the Object type, which individually tests the equality of all pertinent data within two objects. In fact, some developers even opt to compare hash-code values returned from GetHashCode within their overloaded Equals method. Using a custom implementation of the Equals method in this fashion is faster than the default implementation of the Object.Equals method.

The simple hash

This hash accepts a variable number of integer values and XORs each value to obtain a hash code. This simple algorithm has a good chance of producing an adequate distribution and good performance. Remember to profile and measure it to confirm that it works as well for your particular data set. It fails when you need to integrate values greater in size than an integer. Its code is:

```
public int SimpleHash(params int[] values)
{
    int hashCode = 0;
    if (values != null)
    {
        foreach (int val in values)
        {
            hashCode ^= val;
        }
    }

    return (hashCode);
}
```

The folding hash

This hash allows you to integrate the long data type into a hash algorithm. It takes the upper 32 bits of the long value and folds them over the lower 32 bits of this value. The actual process of folding the two values is implemented by XORing them and using the result. Once again, this is a good performing algorithm with good distribution properties, but, again, it fails when you need to go beyond the long data type. A sample implementation is:

```
public int FoldingHash(params long[] values)
{
    int hashCode = 0;
    if (values != null)
    {
        int tempLowerVal = 0;
        int tempUpperVal = 0;
        foreach (long val in values)
        {
            tempLowerVal = (int)(val & 0x000000007FFFFFFF);
            tempUpperVal = (int)((val >> 32) & 0xFFFFFFFF);
            hashCode^= tempLowerVal ^ tempUpperVal;
        }
    }

    return (hashCode);
}
```

The contained object cache

This hash obtains the hash codes from a variable number of object types. The only types that should be passed in to this method are reference-type fields contained within your object. This method XORs all the values returned by the GetHashCode method of each object. Its source code is:

```
public int ContainedObjHash(params object[] values)
{
    int hashCode = 0;
    if (values != null)
    {
        foreach (object val in values)
        {
            hashCode ^= val.GetHashCode( );
        }
    }

    return (hashCode);
}
```

The CryptoHash method

Potentially the best method of obtaining a hash value for an object is to use the hashing classes built in to the FCL. The CryptoHash method returns a hash value for some input using the MACTripleDES class. This method returns a very good distribution for the hash value, although you may pay for it in performance. If you do not require a near-perfect hash value and are looking for an excellent distribution, consider using this approach to calculate a hash value:

```
private readonly byte[] Key = new byte[16] {1,122,3,11,65,7,9,45,42,98,
                                            77,34,99,45,167,211};

public int CryptoHash(string strValue)
{
    int hashCode = 0;
    if (strValue != null)
    {
        byte[] encodedUnHashedString =
                Encoding.Unicode.GetBytes(strValue);

        // Replace the following key with your own
        // key value.
        MACTripleDES hashingObj = new MACTripleDES(Key);
        byte[] code =
                hashingObj.ComputeHash(encodedUnHashedString);

        // Use the BitConverter class to take the
        // first 4 bytes, fold them over the last 4 bytes
        // and use them as an int for the hash code.
        int hashCodeStart = BitConverter.ToInt32(code, 0);
        int hashCodeEnd = BitConverter.ToInt32(code, 4);
```

```
        hashCode = hashCodeStart ^ hashCodeEnd;
    }

    return (hashCode);
}
```

The CryptoHash method using a nonstring

This method shows how other, nonstring data types can be used with the built-in hashing classes to obtain a hash code. This method converts a numeric value to a string and then to a byte array. The array is then used to create the hash value using the SHA256Managed class. Finally, the first four values in the byte array are concatenated together to obtain a hash code. The code is:

```
private readonly byte[] Key = new byte[16] {1,122,3,11,65,7,9,45,42,98,
                                            77,34,99,45,167,211};

public int CryptoHash(long longValue)
{
    int hashCode = 0;
    byte[] encodedUnHashedString =
                Encoding.Unicode.GetBytes(longValue.ToString( ));

    MACTripleDES hashingObj = new MACTripleDES(Key);
    byte[] code = hashingObj.ComputeHash(encodedUnHashedString);

    // Use the BitConverter class to take the
    // first 4 bytes, fold them over the last 4 bytes
    // and use them as an int for the hash code.
    int hashCodeStart = BitConverter.ToInt32(code, 0);
    int hashCodeEnd = BitConverter.ToInt32(code, 4);

    hashCode = hashCodeStart ^ hashCodeEnd;

    return (hashCode);
}
```

The shift and add hash

This method uses each character in the input string, strValue, to determine a hash value. This algorithm produces a good distribution of hash codes even when it is fed similar strings. However, it will break down when long strings that end with the same characters are passed. While this may not happen many times with your applications, it is something to be aware of. If performance is critical, this is an excellent method to use. Its code is:

```
public int ShiftAndAddHash (string strValue)
{
    int hashCode = 0;
    long workHashCode = 0;

    if (strValue != null)
```

```
    {
        for (int counter=0; counter<strValue.Length; counter++)
        {
            workHashCode = (workHashCode << (counter % 4)) +
                    (int)strValue[counter];
        }
        workHashCode = workHashCode % (127);
    }
    hashCode = (int)workHashCode;

    return (hashCode);
}
```

The calculated hash

This method is a rather widely accepted method of creating a good hash value that
accepts several different data types and uses a different algorithm to compute the
hash value for each. It calculates the hash code as follows:

- It assigns an arbitrary odd primary number to the HashCode variable. This variable will eventually contain the final hash code. Good primary numbers to use
  are 3, 5, 7, 11, 13, 17, 19, 23, 29, 31, 37, 41, 43, 47, 53, 59, 61, or 67. Obviously, others exist beyond this set, but this should give you a good starting point.

- For numeric types equal to or less than the size of an int and char data types, it
  multiplies the current HashCode by the primary number selected and then adds to
  this value the value of the numeric type cast to an integer.

- For numeric types greater than the size of an int, it multiplies the current
  HashCode by the primary number selected and then adds to this the folded version of this numeric value. (For more information on folding, see "The folding
  hash" method earlier in this recipe.)

- For char, floating-point, or decimal data types, it multiplies the current HashCode
  by the primary number selected, casts the numeric value to an integer, and then
  uses the folding method to calculate its value.

- For bool data types, it multiplies the current HashCode by the primary number
  selected and then adds a 1 for true and 0 for false (you can reverse this behavior
  if you wish).

- For object data types, it multiplies the current HashCode by the primary number
  selected and then adds the return value of GetHashCode called on this object. If an
  object is set to null, use the value 0 in your calculations.

- For an array or collection, it determines the contained type(s) and uses each element of the array or collection to calculate the hash value, as follows (in the case
  of an integer array named MyArray):

  ```
  foreach (int element in myArray)
  {
      hashCode = (hashCode * 31) + element;
  }
  ```

This algorithm will produce a good distributed hash code for your object and has the added benefit of being able to employ any data type. This is a high-performing algorithm for simple, moderately complex, and even many complex objects. However, for extremely complex objects—ones that contain many large arrays, large Hashtables, or other objects that use a slower hash-code algorithm—this algorithm will start performing badly. In this extreme case, you may want to consider switching to another hash-code algorithm to speed performance or simply paring down the amount of fields used in the calculation. Be careful if you choose this second method to increase performance; you could inadvertently cause the algorithm to produce similar values for differing objects. The code for the calculated hash method is:

```
public int CalcHash(short someShort, int someInt, long someLong,
                    float someFloat, object someObject)
{
    int hashCode = 7;
    hashCode = hashCode * 31 + (int)someShort;
    hashCode = hashCode * 31 + someInt;
    hashCode = hashCode * 31 +
                        (int)(someLong ^ (someLong >> 32));
    long someFloatToLong = (long)someFloat;
    hashCode = hashCode * 31 +
            (int)(someFloatToLong ^ (someFloatToLong >> 32));

    if (someObject != null)
    {
        hashCode = hashCode * 31 +
                        someObject.GetHashCode( );
    }

    return (hashCode);
}
```

The string-concatenation hash

This technique converts its input into a string and then uses that string's GetHashCode method to automatically generate a hash code for an object. It accepts an integer array, but you can substitute any type that can be converted into a string. You can also use several different types of arguments as input to this method. This method iterates through each integer in the array passed as an argument to the method. The ToString method is called on each value to return a string. The ToString method of an int data type returns the value contained in that int. Each string value is appended to the string variable HashString. Finally, the GetHashCode method is called on the HashString variable to return a suitable hash code.

This method is simple and efficient, but it does not work well with objects that have not overridden the ToString method to return something other than their data type. It may be best to simply call the GetHashCode method on each of these objects individually. You should use your own judgment and the rules found in this recipe to make your decision.

```csharp
public int ConcatStringGetHashCode(int[] someIntArray)
{
    int hashCode = 0;
    StringBuilder hashString = new StringBuilder( );

    if (someIntArray != null)
    {
        foreach (int i in someIntArray)
        {
            hashString.Append(i.ToString( ) + "^");
        }
    }
    hashCode = hashString.GetHashCode( );

    return (hashCode);
}
```

The following using directives must be added to any file containing this code:

```csharp
using System;
using System.Text;
using System.Security.Cryptography;
```

Discussion

The GetHashCode method is called when you are using an instance of this class as the key in a Hashtable or Dictionary<T,U> object. Whenever your object is added to a Hashtable or Dictionary<T,U> as a key, its GetHashCode method is. A hash code is also obtained from your object when a search is performed for it in the Hashtable or Dictionary<T,U>.

The following class implements the SimpleHash algorithm for the overloaded GetHashCode method:

```csharp
public class SimpleClass
{
    private int x = 0;
    private int y = 0;

    public override int GetHashCode( )
    {
        return(SimpleHash(x, y));
    }

    private static int SimpleHash(params int[] values)
    {
        int hashCode = 0;
        if (values != null)
        {
            foreach (int val in values)
            {
                hashCode ^= val;
            }
        }
```

```
            return (hashCode);
        }
    }
```

This class can then be used as a key in a Hashtable or Dictionary<T,U> in code like the following:

```
SimpleClass simpleClass = new SimpleClass( );

Hashtable hashTable = new Hashtable( );
hashTable.Add(simpleClass, 100);

Dictionary<SimpleClass, int> dict = new Dictionary<SimpleClass, int>( );
dict.Add(simpleClass, 100);
```

There are several rules for writing a good GetHashCode method and a good hash-code algorithm:

- This method should return the same value for two different objects that have value equality. Value equality means that two objects contain the same data.

- The hash algorithm should return a good distribution of values for the best performance in a Hashtable or Dictionary<T,U>. A good distribution of values means that the hash values returned by the GetHashCode method are usually different for objects of the same type, unless those objects have value equality. Note that objects containing very similar data should also return a unique hash value. This distribution allows the Hashtable or Dictionary<T,U> to work more efficiently and thus perform better.

- This method should not throw an exception.

- Both the Equals method and GetHashCode method should be overridden together.

- The GetHashCode method should compute the hash code using the exact set of variables that the overridden Equals method uses when calculating equality.

- The hash algorithm should be as fast as possible to speed up the process of adding and searching for keys in a Hashtable or Dictionary<T,U>.

- Use the GetHashCode values of any contained objects when calculating the hash code of the parent object.

- Use the GetHashCode values of all elements of an array when calculating the array's hash code.

The System.Int32, System.UInt32, and System.IntPtr data types in the FCL use an additional hash-code algorithm not covered in the Solution section. Basically, these data types return the value that they contain as a hash code. Most likely, your objects will not be so simple as to contain a single numeric value, but if they are, this method works extremely well.

You may also want to combine specific algorithms to suit your purposes. For instance, if your object contains one or more string types and one or more long data types, you can combine the ContainedObjHash method and the FoldingHash method to create a hash value for your object. The return values from each method can either be added or XORed together.

Once an object is in use as a key in a Hashtable or Dictionary<T,U>, it should never return a different value for the hash code. Originally, it was documented that hash codes must be immutable, as the authors of Hashtable or Dictionary<T,U> thought that this should be dealt with by whoever writes GetHashCode. It doesn't take much thought to realize that for mutable types, if you require both that the hash code never changes *and* that Equals represents the equality of the mutable objects *and* that if a.Equals(b), then a.GetHashCode( ) == b.GetHashCode( ), then the only possible implementation of GetHashCode is one that returns the same integer constant for all values.

The GetHashCode method is called when you are using this object as the key in a Hashtable or Dictionary<T,U> object. Whenever your object is added to a Hashtable or Dictionary<T,U> as a key, the GetHashCode method is called on your object to obtain a hash code. This hash code must not change while your object is a key in the Hashtable or Dictionary<T,U>. If it does, the Hashtable or Dictionary<T,U> will not be able to find your object.

See Also

See the "GetHashCode Method," "Dictionary<T,U> Class," and "Hashtable Class" topics in the MSDN documentation.

11.2   Creating a Priority Queue

Problem

You need a data structure that operates similarly to a Queue but that returns objects based on a specific order. When objects are added to this queue, they are located in the queue according to their priority. When objects are retrieved from the queue, the queue simply returns the highest or lowest priority element based on which one you ask for.

Solution

Create a generic priority queue that orders items as they are added to the queue and returns items based on their priority. The PriorityQueue<T> class of Example 11-1 shows how this can be accomplished.

Example 11-1. Generic PriorityQueue class

```
using System;
using System.Collections;
using System.Collections.Generic;
```

Example 11-1. Generic PriorityQueue class (continued)

```csharp
public class PriorityQueue<T> : IEnumerable<T>, ICloneable
{
    public PriorityQueue( ) {}
    public PriorityQueue(IComparer<T> icomparer)
    {
        specialComparer = icomparer;
    }


    protected List<T> internalQueue = new List<T>( );
    protected IComparer<T> specialComparer = null;


    public int Count
    {
        get {return (internalQueue.Count);}
    }

    public void Clear( )
    {
        internalQueue.Clear( );
    }

    public object Clone( )
    {
        // Make a new PQ and give it the same comparer.
        PriorityQueue<T> newPQ = new PriorityQueue<T>(specialComparer);
        newPQ.CopyTo(internalQueue.ToArray( ),0);
        return newPQ;
    }

    public int IndexOf(T item)
    {
        return (internalQueue.IndexOf(item));
    }

    public bool Contains(T item)
    {
        return (internalQueue.Contains(item));
    }

    public int BinarySearch(T item)
    {
        return (internalQueue.BinarySearch(item, specialComparer));
    }

    public bool Contains(T item, IComparer<T> specialComparer)
    {
        return (internalQueue.BinarySearch(item, specialComparer) >= 0);
    }

    public void CopyTo(T[] array, int index)
```

Example 11-1. Generic PriorityQueue class (continued)

```
    {
        internalQueue.CopyTo(array, index);
    }

    public virtual T[] ToArray( )
    {
        return (internalQueue.ToArray( ));
    }

    public virtual void TrimToSizeTrimExcess( )
    {
        internalQueue.TrimExcess( );
    }

    public void Enqueue(T item)
    {
        internalQueue.Add(item);
        internalQueue.Sort(specialComparer);
    }

    public T DequeueSmallest( )
    {
        T item = internalQueue[0];
        internalQueue.RemoveAt(0);

        return (item);
    }

    public T DequeueLargest( )
    {
        T item = internalQueue[internalQueue.Count - 1];
        internalQueue.RemoveAt(internalQueue.Count - 1);

        return (item);
    }

    public T PeekSmallest( )
    {
        return (internalQueue[0]);
    }

    public T PeekLargest( )
    {
        return (internalQueue[internalQueue.Count - 1]);
    }

    public IEnumerator GetEnumerator( )
    {
        return (internalQueue.GetEnumerator( ));
    }

    IEnumerator<T> System.Collections.Generic.IEnumerable<T>.GetEnumerator( )
```

Example 11-1. Generic PriorityQueue class (continued)

```
    {
        return (internalQueue.GetEnumerator( ));
    }
}
```

For example, perhaps your application or component needs to send packets of data of differing sizes across a network. The algorithm for sending these packets of data states that the smallest (or perhaps the largest) packets will be sent before the larger (or smaller) ones. An analogous programming problem involves queuing up specific jobs to be run. Each job could be run based on its type, order, or size.

This priority queue is designed so that items—in this case, string values—may be added in any order; but when they are removed from the head or tail of the queue, they are dequeued in a specific order. The IComparer<T> type object, a specialComparer that is passed in through the constructor of this object, determines this order. The queued string objects are stored internally in a field called internalQueue of type List<T>. This was the simplest way to construct this type of queue, since a List<T> has most of the functionality built into it that we wanted to implement for this type of queue.

Many of the methods of this class delegate to the internalQueue in order to perform their duties. These types of methods include Count, Clear, TrimExcess, and many others. Some of the more important methods of the PriorityQueue<T> class are Enqueue, DequeueSmallest, DequeueLargest, PeekSmallest, and PeekLargest.

The Enqueue method accepts a type T as an argument and adds it to the end of the internalQueue. Next, this List<T> is sorted according to the specialComparer object. If the specialComparer object is null, the comparison defaults to the IComparer of the string object. By sorting the List<T> after each item is added, you do not have to perform a sort before every search, dequeue, and peek method. A small performance hit will occur when an item is added, but this is a one-time-only penalty. Keep in mind that when items are removed from the head or tail of this queue, the internal List<T> does not have to be resorted.

There are two dequeue methods: DequeueSmallest and DequeueLargest. These methods remove items from the head (index equals 0) of the internalQueue and from the tail (index equals internalQueue.Count - 1), respectively. Before returning the string, these methods will remove that string from the queue. The PeekSmallest and PeekLargest methods work in a similar manner, except that they do not remove the string from the queue.

Two other methods of interest are the overloaded Contains methods. The only real difference between these two methods is that one of the Contains methods uses the IComparer interface of the string object, whereas the other overloaded Contains method uses the specialComparer interface when searching for a string in the internalQueue, if one is provided.

The `PriorityQueue<T>` class members are listed in Table 11-1.

Table 11-1. PriorityQueue class members

Member	Description
Count property	Returns an `int` indicating the number of items in the queue. Calls the `internalQueue.Count` method.
Clear method	Removes all items from the queue. Calls the `internalQueue` method.
Clone method	Returns a copy of the `PriorityQueue<T>` object.
IndexOf method	Returns the zero-based index of the queue item that contains a particular search string. Its syntax is: `IndexOf(T item)` where *item* is the string to be found in the queue. Calls the `internalQueue` method.
Contains method	Returns a `bool` indicating whether a particular search string is found in the queue. Its syntax is: `Contains(T item)` where *item* is the string to be found in the queue. Calls the `internalQueue` method.
BinarySearch method	Returns the zero-based index of the queue item that contains a particular search type T. Its syntax is: `BinarySearch(T item)` where *item* is the type T to be found in the queue. The comparison of *item* with the type T found in the queue is handled by the `IComparer<T>` implementation, if one was passed as an argument to one of the overloads of the `PriorityQueue<T>` class constructor. Calls the `internalQueue` method.
Contains method	Returns a `bool` indicating whether a particular search type T is found in the queue. Its syntax is: `Contains(T item, IComparer<T> specialComparer)` where *item* is the string to be found in the queue. The comparison of *item* with the strings found in the queue is handled by the `IComparer<T>` implementation, if one was passed as an argument to one of the overloads of the `PriorityQueue<T>` class constructor. Calls the `internalQueue` method.
CopyTo method	Copies the queue items to a one-dimensional array starting at a particular position in the queue. Its syntax is: `CopyTo(T[] array, int arrayIndex)` where *array* is the array to receive the copy of the queue items and *arrayIndex* is the position in the queue from which to begin copying items. Calls the `internalQueue` method.
ToArray method	Copies the items in the queue to an object array. Calls the `internalQueue` method.
TrimExcess method	Sets the capacity of the queue to the current count of its items. If the `TrimExcess` method is called when no items are in the queue, its capacity is set to a default value. Calls the `internalQueue` method.
Enqueue method	Adds an item to the queue. It then sorts the queue based on either the default sort behavior of each item or the `IComparer<T>` implementation passed as an argument to one of the `PriorityQueue<T>` class constructors. Its syntax is: `Enqueue(T item)` where *item* is the type T to be added to the queue.

Table 11-1. PriorityQueue class members (continued)

Member	Description
DequeueLargest method	Returns and removes the item at the tail of the queue (i.e., the last item in the queue).
DequeueSmallest method	Returns and removes the item at the head of the queue (i.e., the first item in the queue).
PeekSmallest method	Returns the item at the head of the queue (i.e., the first item in the queue).
PeekLargest method	Returns the item at the tail of the queue (i.e., the last item in the queue).
GetEnumerator method	Returns an enumerator that allows iteration of the items in the queue. Calls the internalQueue method.

The `PriorityQueue<T>` can be instantiated and filled with strings using code like the Test class shown in Example 11-2.

Example 11-2. Testing the PriorityQueue class

```
class Test
{
    static void Main()
    {
        // Create ArrayList of messages.
        List<string> msgs = new List<string>();
        msgs.Add("foo");
        msgs.Add("This is a longer message.");
        msgs.Add("bar");
        msgs.Add(@"Message with odd characters
                    !@#$%^&*()_+=-0987654321~|}{[]\\;:?/>.<,");
        msgs.Add(@"<
                    >");
        msgs.Add("<text>one</text><text>two</text><text>three</text>" +
                    "<text>four</text>");
        msgs.Add("");
        msgs.Add("1234567890");

        // Create a Priority Queue with the appropriate comparer.
        // The comparer is created from the CompareLen type
        // defined in the Discussion section.
        CompareLen<string> comparer = new CompareLen<string>();
        PriorityQueue<string> pqueue = new PriorityQueue<string>(comparer);

        // Add all messages from the List to the priority queue.
        foreach (string msg in msgs)
        {
            pqueue.Enqueue(msg);
        }

        // Display messages in the queue in order of priority.
        foreach (string msg in pqueue)
        {
            Console.WriteLine("Msg: " + msg);
        }
```

Example 11-2. Testing the PriorityQueue class (continued)

```
        Console.WriteLine("pqueue.IndexOf('bar') == " + pqueue.IndexOf("bar"));
        Console.WriteLine("pqueue.IndexOf('_bar_') == " + pqueue.IndexOf("_bar_"));

        Console.WriteLine("pqueue.Contains('bar') == " + pqueue.Contains("bar"));
        Console.WriteLine("pqueue.Contains('_bar_') == " +
            pqueue.Contains("_bar_"));

        Console.WriteLine("pqueue.BinarySearch('bar') == " +
            pqueue.BinarySearch("bar"));
        Console.WriteLine("pqueue.BinarySearch('_bar_') == " +
                        pqueue.BinarySearch("_bar_"));

        // Dequeue messages starting with the smallest.
        int currCount = pqueue.Count;
        for (int index = 0; index < currCount; index++)
        {
            // In order to dequeue messages starting with the largest, uncomment
            // the following line and comment the following lines that
            // dequeue starting with the smallest message.
            //Console.WriteLine("pqueue.DequeueLargest(): " +
            //                    pqueue.DequeueLargest().ToString());

            Console.WriteLine("pqueue.DequeueSmallest(): " +
                            pqueue.DequeueSmallest().ToString());
        }
    }
}
```

The output of this method is shown here:

```
Msg:
Msg: foo
Msg: bar
Msg: 1234567890
Msg: This is a longer message.
Msg: <text>one</text><text>two</text><text>three</text><text>four</text>
Msg: Message with odd characters
                 !@#$%^&*()_+=-0987654321~|}{[]\\;:?/>.<,
Msg: <
                     >
pqueue.IndexOf('bar') == 2
pqueue.IndexOf('_bar_') == -1
pqueue.Contains('bar') == True
pqueue.Contains('_bar_') == False
pqueue.BinarySearch('bar') == 1
pqueue.BinarySearch('_bar_') == -4
pqueue.DequeueSmallest():
pqueue.DequeueSmallest(): foo
pqueue.DequeueSmallest(): bar
pqueue.DequeueSmallest(): 1234567890
pqueue.DequeueSmallest(): This is a longer message.
pqueue.DequeueSmallest(): <text>one</text><text>two</text><text>three
</text><text>four</text>
```

```
pqueue.DequeueSmallest( ): Message with odd characters
                    !@#$%^&*( )_+=-0987654321~|}{[]\\;:?/>.<,
pqueue.DequeueSmallest( ): <
                     >
```

A List<T> of string messages is created that will be used to fill the queue. A new CompareLen IComparer<T> type object is created and passed in to the constructor of the PriorityQueue<T>. If you did not pass in this IComparer<T> object, the output would be much different: instead of items being retrieved from the queue based on length, they would be retrieved based on their alphabetical order. (The IComparer<T> interface is covered in detail in the Discussion section.) Finally, a foreach loop is used to enqueue all messages into the PriorityQueue<T> object.

At this point, the PriorityQueue<T> object can be used in a manner similar to the Queue<T> class contained in the FCL, except for the ability to remove items from both the head and tail of the queue.

Discussion

You can instantiate the PriorityQueue<T> class with or without a special comparer object. The special comparer object used in this recipe is defined in Example 11-3.

Example 11-3. Special CompareLen comparer class

```
public class CompareLen<T> : IComparer<T>
    where T: IComparable<T>
{
    public int Compare(T obj1, T obj2)
    {
        int result = 0;
        if (typeof(T) == typeof(string))
        {
            result = CompareStrings(obj1 as string, obj2 as string);
        }
        else
        {
            // Default to the object type's comparison algorithm.
            result = Comparer<T>.Default.Compare(obj1, obj2);
        }
        return (result);
    }

    private int CompareStrings(string str1, string str2)
    {
        if (str1 == null || str2 == null)
        {
            throw(new ArgumentNullException(
                "The strings being compared may not be null."));
        }

        if (str1.Length == str2.Length)
        {
            return (0);
```

Example 11-3. Special CompareLen comparer class (continued)

```
        }
        else if (str1.Length > str2.Length)
        {
            return (1);
        }
        else
        {
            return (-1);
        }
    }

    public bool Equals(T item1, T item2)
    {
        if (item1 == null || item2 == null)
        {
            throw(new ArgumentNullException(
                "The objects being compared may not be null."));
        }

        return (item1.Equals(item2));
    }

    public int GetHashCode(T obj)
    {
        if (obj == null)
        {
            throw(new ArgumentNullException(
                "The obj parameter may not be null."));
        }

        return (obj.GetHashCode( ));
    }
}
```

This special comparer is required because you want to prioritize the elements in the queue by size. The default string IComparer<string> interface compares strings alphabetically. Implementing the IComparer<T> interface requires that you implement a single method, Compare, with the following signature:

```
    int Compare(T x, T y);
```

where *x* and *y* are the objects being compared. When implementing custom Compare methods, the method is to return 0 if *x* equals *y*, less than 0 if *x* is less than *y*, and greater than 0 if *x* is greater than *y*. This method is called automatically by the .NET runtime whenever the custom IComparer<T> implementation is used.

See Also

See the "List<T> Class," "IEnumerable Interface," "ICloneable Interface," "IComparer<T> Interface," and "IComparable<T> Interface" topics in the MSDN documentation.

11.3   Creating a Double Queue

Problem

You need a queue object in which you can explicitly control the adding and removing of objects to either the head (top) or tail (bottom), also known as a double queue.

Solution

A queue that allows explicit removal of items from the head and the tail is called a *double queue*.

Example 11-4 shows one way you can implement a double queue.

Example 11-4. DblQueue class

```
using System;
using System.Collections;
using System.Collections.Generic;


[Serializable]
public class DblQueue<T> : ICollection<T>, ICloneable
{
    public DblQueue( )
    {
        internalList = new List<T>( );
    }

    public DblQueue(ICollection<T> coll)
    {
        internalList = new List<T>(coll);
    }


    protected List<T> internalList = null;


    public virtual int Count
    {
        get {return (internalList.Count);}
    }

    public virtual bool IsSynchronized
    {
        get {return (false);}
    }

    public virtual object SyncRoot
    {
        get {return (this);}
    }
```

Example 11-4. DblQueue class (continued)

```csharp
public virtual void Clear()
{
    internalList.Clear();
}

public object Clone()
{
    // Make a new DblQueue.
    DblQueue<T> newDQ = new DblQueue<T>();
    newDQ.CopyTo(internalList.ToArray(), 0);
    return newDQ;
}

public virtual bool Contains(T obj)
{
    return (internalList.Contains(obj));
}

public virtual void CopyTo(Array array, int index)
{
    for (int cntr = 0; cntr < internalList.Count; cntr++)
    {
        array.SetValue((object)internalList[cntr], cntr);
    }
}

public virtual T DequeueHead()
{
    T retObj = internalList[0];
    internalList.RemoveAt(0);
    return (retObj);
}

public virtual T DequeueTail()
{
    T retObj = internalList[internalList.Count - 1];
    internalList.RemoveAt(internalList.Count - 1);
    return (retObj);
}

public virtual void EnqueueHead(T obj)
{
    internalList.Insert(0, obj);
}

public virtual void EnqueueTail(T obj)
{
    internalList.Add(obj);
}

public virtual T PeekHead()
{
```

Example 11-4. DblQueue class (continued)

```
        return (internalList[0]);
    }

    public virtual T PeekTail()
    {
        return (internalList[internalList.Count - 1]);
    }

    public virtual IEnumerator GetEnumerator()
    {
        return (internalList.GetEnumerator());
    }

    public virtual T[] ToArray()
    {
        return (internalList.ToArray());
    }

    public virtual void TrimExcess()
    {
        internalList.TrimExcess();
    }

    void System.Collections.Generic.ICollection<T>.Add(T item)
    {
        throw (new NotSupportedException(
                "Use the EnqueueHead or EnqueueTail methods."));
    }

    void System.Collections.Generic.ICollection<T>.CopyTo(T[] item, int index)
    {
        for (int cntr = index; cntr < internalList.Count; cntr++)
        {
            item[cntr - index] = internalList[cntr];
        }
    }

    bool System.Collections.Generic.ICollection<T>.Remove(T item)
    {
        throw (new NotSupportedException(
                "Use the DequeueHead or DequeueTail methods."));
    }

    bool System.Collections.Generic.ICollection<T>.IsReadOnly
    {
        get {throw (new NotSupportedException("Not Supported."));}
    }

    IEnumerator<T> System.Collections.Generic.IEnumerable<T>.GetEnumerator()
    {
        return (internalList.GetEnumerator());
    }
}
```

The double queue class created for this recipe was developed in a fashion similar to the PriorityQueue<T> in Recipe 11.2. It exposes most of the List<T> members through wrapper methods. For instance, the DblQueue<T>.Count and DblQueue<T>.Clear methods, among others, simply delegate their calls to the List<T>.Count and List<T>.Clear methods, respectively.

The methods defined in Table 11-2 are of particular interest to constructing a double queue.

Table 11-2. Members of the DblQueue class

Member	Description
Count property	Returns an int indicating the number of items in the queue.
Clear method	Removes all items from the queue.
Clone method	Returns a copy of the DblQueue<T> object.
Contains method	Returns a bool indicating whether the queue contains a particular search object. Its syntax is: `Contains(T obj)` where *obj* is the object to be found in the queue.
CopyTo method	Copies a range of items from this queue into an array. Its syntax is: `CopyTo(Array array, int index)` where *array* is the array into which the queue will be copied and *index* is the index in the queue at which to start copying items. The head of the queue is at index 0.
DequeueHead method	Removes and returns the object at the head (i.e., position 0) of the queue. This method makes use of the indexer and RemoveAt methods of the internal List<T> to return the first (zeroth) element in the List<T>. Its syntax is: `DequeueHead( )`
DequeueTail method	Removes and returns the object at the tail (i.e., position (List<T>.Count - 1)) of the queue. This method makes use of the indexer and RemoveAt methods of the internal List<T> to return the last element in the List<T>. Its syntax is: `DequeueTail( )`
EnqueueHead method	Accepts an object type to add to the head of the queue. This method makes use of the Insert method of the internal List<T> to add an element to the start (zeroth position) in the List<T>. Its syntax is: `EnqueueHead(T obj)` where *obj* is the object to add to the head of the queue.
EnqueueTail method	Accepts an object type to add to the tail of the queue. This method makes use of the Add method of the internal List<T> to add an element to the end of the List<T>. Its syntax is: `EnqueueTail(T obj)` where *obj* is the object to add to the tail of the queue.
PeekHead method	Returns, but does not remove, the object at the head of the queue. This method makes use of the indexer of the internal List<T> to obtain the first (zeroth) element in the List<T>. Its syntax is: `PeekHead( )`

Table 11-2. Members of the DblQueue class (continued)

Member	Description
PeekTail method	Returns, but does not remove, the object at the tail of the queue. This method makes use of the indexer of the internal List<T> to obtain the last element in the List<T>. Its syntax is: PeekTail( )
ToArray method	Returns the entire queue as an object array. Its syntax is: ToArray( ) The first element in the object array (index 0) is the item at the head object in the queue and the last element in the array is the tail object in the queue.
TrimExcess method	Sets the capacity of the queue to the number of elements currently in the queue. Its syntax is: TrimExcess( )

The code in Example 11-5 exercises the DblQueue<T> class.

Example 11-5. Testing the DblQueue class

```
class Test
{
    static void Main( )
    {
        DblQueue<int> dqueue = new DblQueue<int>( );

        // Count should be zero.
        Console.WriteLine("dqueue.Count: " + dqueue.Count);
        try
        {
            // Attempt to remove an item from an empty queue.
            object o = dqueue.DequeueHead( );
        }
        catch (Exception e)
        {
            Console.WriteLine("THIS EXCEPTION IS ON PURPOSE!");
            Console.WriteLine(e.ToString( ));
            Console.WriteLine("THIS EXCEPTION IS ON PURPOSE!");
        }

        // Add items to queue.
        dqueue.EnqueueHead(1);
        dqueue.EnqueueTail(2);
        dqueue.EnqueueHead(0);
        dqueue.EnqueueTail(3);

        dqueue.TrimExcess( );

        // Display all items in original queue.
        foreach (int i in dqueue)
        {
            Console.WriteLine("Queued Item: " + i.ToString( ));
        }
```

Example 11-5. Testing the DblQueue class (continued)

```
        // Find these items in original queue.
        Console.WriteLine("dqueue.Contains(1): " + dqueue.Contains(1));
        Console.WriteLine("dqueue.Contains(10): " + dqueue.Contains(10));

        // Peek at head and tail values without removing them.
        Console.WriteLine("dqueue.PeekHead(): " + dqueue.PeekHead( ).ToString( ));
        Console.WriteLine("dqueue.PeekTail(): " + dqueue.PeekTail( ).ToString( ));

        // Copy this queue to an array.
        Array arr = Array.CreateInstance(typeof(object), dqueue.Count);
        dqueue.CopyTo(arr, 0);
        foreach (object o in arr)
        {
            Console.WriteLine("Queued Item (CopyTo): " + o.ToString( ));
        }

        // Remove one item from the queue's head and two items from the tail.
        Console.WriteLine("dqueue.DequeueHead( ): " + dqueue.DequeueHead( ));
        Console.WriteLine("dqueue.DequeueTail( ): " + dqueue.DequeueTail( ));
        Console.WriteLine("dqueue.DequeueTail( ): " + dqueue.DequeueTail( ));

        // Display the count of items and the items themselves.
        Console.WriteLine("dqueue.Count: " + dqueue.Count);
        foreach (int i in dqueue)
        {
            Console.WriteLine("Queued Item: " + i.ToString( ));
        }
    }
}
```

The output for this method is shown here:

```
dqueue.Count: 0
THIS EXCEPTION IS ON PURPOSE!
System.ArgumentOutOfRangeException: Index was out of range. Must be non-negative and
less than the size of the collection.
Parameter name: index
   at System.ThrowHelper.ThrowArgumentOutOfRangeException(ExceptionArgument argument,
ExceptionResource resource)
   at System.ThrowHelper.ThrowArgumentOutOfRangeException( )
   at System.Collections.Generic.List`1.get_Item(Int32 index)
   at CSharpRecipes.DataStructsAndAlgorithms.DblQueue`1.DequeueHead( ) in C:\Documents
and Settings\Admin\Desktop\CSharp Recipes 2nd Edition\Code\CSharpRecipes\11_
DataStructsAndAlgorithms.cs:line 570
   at CSharpRecipes.DataStructsAndAlgorithms.CreatingAMoreVersatileQueue( ) in C:\
Documents and Settings\Admin\Desktop\CSharp Recipes 2nd Edition\Code\CSharpRecipes\
11_DataStructsAndAlgorithms.cs:line 456
THIS EXCEPTION IS ON PURPOSE!
Queued Item: 0
Queued Item: 1
Queued Item: 2
Queued Item: 3
dqueue.Contains(1): True
```

```
dqueue.Contains(10): False
dqueue.PeekHead( ): 0
dqueue.PeekTail( ): 3
Queued Item (CopyTo): 0
Queued Item (CopyTo): 1
Queued Item (CopyTo): 2
Queued Item (CopyTo): 3
dqueue.DequeueHead( ): 0
dqueue.DequeueTail( ): 3
dqueue.DequeueTail( ): 2
dqueue.Count: 1
Queued Item: 1
```

Discussion

The DblQueue<T> class implements the same three interfaces as the Queue<T> class found in the System.Collections.Generic namespace of the FCL. These are the ICollection, IEnumerable, and ICloneable interfaces. The IEnumerable interface forces the DblQueue<T> to implement the GetEnumerator method. The implementation of the DblQueue<T>.GetEnumerator method returns the IEnumerator object for the internal List<T>, used to store the queued items.

The ICollection interface forces three properties and a method to be implemented by the DblQueue<T> class. The IsSynchronized property returns false, and the SyncRoot method returns the DblQueue<T> object on which it was called. These synchronization properties and methods will be discussed at length in Recipes 4.4, 4.10, and 18.2.

The ICollection interface also forces the Count property and the CopyTo method to be implemented by the DblQueue<T> class. Both of these delegate to the corresponding List<T> property and method for their implementations.

The Enqueue and Dequeue methods of the Queue<T> class found in the FCL operate in only one direction, enqueuing to the tail and dequeuing from the head of the queue. The DblQueue<T> class allows these operations to be performed on both the head and tail of a queue. The DblQueue<T> class has the flexibility of being used as a first-in, first-out (FIFO) queue, which is similar in operation to the Queue<T> class, or of being used as a first-in, last-out (FILO) stack, which is similar in operation to the Stack<T> class. In fact, with a DblQueue<T>, you can start off using it as a FIFO queue and then change in midstream to using it as a FILO stack. This can be done without having to do anything special, such as creating a new class.

See Also

See the "List<T> Class," "IEnumerable Interface," "ICloneable Interface," and "ICollection Interface" topics in the MSDN documentation.

11.4   Determining Where Characters or Strings Do Not Balance

Problem

It is not uncommon to accidentally create strings that contain unbalanced parentheses. For example, a user might enter the following equation in your calculator application:

```
(((a) + (b)) + c * d
```

This equation contains four (characters while matching them with only three) characters. You cannot solve this equation, since the user did not supply the fourth) character. Likewise, if a user enters a regular expression, you might want to do a simple check to see that all the (, {, [, and < characters match up to every other), },], and > character.

In addition to determining whether the characters/strings/tags match, you should know where the unbalanced character/string/tag exists in the string.

Solution

Use the various Check methods of the Balance class shown in Example 11-6 to determine whether and where the character/string is unbalanced.

Example 11-6. Balance class with overloaded Check methods

```
using System;
using System.Collections;


public class Balance
{
    public Balance() {}

    private Stack<int> bookMarks = new Stack<int>();

    public int Check(string source, char openChar, char closeChar)
    {
        return (Check(source.ToCharArray(), openChar, closeChar));
    }

    public int Check(char[] source, char openChar, char closeChar)
    {
        bookMarks.Clear();

        for (int index = 0; index < source.Length; index++)
        {
            if (source[index] == openChar)
            {
                bookMarks.Push(index);
```

Example 11-6. Balance class with overloaded Check methods (continued)

```
        }
        else if (source[index] == closeChar)
        {
            if (bookMarks.Count <= 0)
            {
                return (index);
            }
            else
            {
                bookMarks.Pop( );
            }
        }
    }

    if (bookMarks.Count > 0)
    {
        return ((int)bookMarks.Pop( ));
    }
    else
    {
        return (-1);
    }
}

public int Check(string source, string openChars, string closeChars)
{
    return (Check(source.ToCharArray( ), openChars.ToCharArray( ),
            closeChars.ToCharArray( )));
}

public int Check(char[] source, char[] openChars, char[] closeChars)
{
    bookMarks.Clear( );

    for (int index = 0; index < source.Length; index++)
    {
        if (source[index] == openChars[0])
        {
            if (CompareArrays(source, openChars, index))
            {
                bookMarks.Push(index);
            }
        }

        if (source[index] == closeChars[0])
        {
            if (CompareArrays(source, closeChars, index))
            {
                if (bookMarks.Count <= 0)
                {
                    return (index);
                }
```

Example 11-6. Balance class with overloaded Check methods (continued)

```
                else
                {
                    bookMarks.Pop( );
                }
            }
        }
    }

    if (bookMarks.Count > 0)
    {
        return ((int)bookMarks.Pop( ));
    }
    else
    {
        return (-1);
    }
}

public bool CompareArrays(char[] source, char[] targetChars, int startPos)
{
    bool isEqual = true;

    for (int index = 0; index < targetChars.Length; index++)
    {
        if (targetChars[index] != source[startPos + index])
        {
            isEqual = false;
            break;
        }
    }

    return (isEqual);
}
}
```

The Check method determines whether there is one closing element for every opening element. There are four overloaded Check methods, and each takes three parameters of varying types. These methods return an integer indicating where the offending
character is located or a negative number if each *openChar* has a matching *closeChar*.

The code to exercise the Balance class is shown in Example 11-7.

Example 11-7. Testing the Balance class

```
class Test
{
    static void Main( )
    {
        Balance balanceUtil = new Balance( );

        // A string with an unbalanced } char. This unbalanced char is the final
        // } char in the string.
```

Example 11-7. Testing the Balance class (continued)

```
            string unbalanced = @"{namespace Unbalanced
                    {
                        public class Tipsy
                        {
                            public Tipsy()
                            {
                    }}}}}
                ";

        // Use the various overloaded Check methods
        // to check for unbalanced } chars.
        Console.WriteLine("Balance {}: " +
                balanceUtil.Check(unbalanced, '{', '}'));
        Console.WriteLine("Balance {}: " +
                balanceUtil.Check(unbalanced.ToCharArray(), '{', '}'));
    }
}
```

This code produces the following output:

```
    Balance {}: 268
    Balance {}: 268
```

where a -1 means that the items are balanced and a number greater than -1 indicates the character position that contains the unbalanced character.

Discussion

Determining whether characters have a matching character is actually quite easy when a Stack<T> object is used. A stack works on a FILO principle. The first item added to a stack is always the last one to be removed; conversely, the last item added to a stack is always the first removed.

To see how the stack is used in matching characters, let's see how you'd use it to handle the following equation:

```
    ((a + (b)) + c) * d
```

The algorithm works like this: you iterate through all characters in the equation, then any time you come upon a left or right parenthesis, you push or pop an item from the stack. If you see a left parenthesis, you know to push it onto the stack. If you see a right parenthesis, you know to pop a left parenthesis from the stack. In fact, the left parenthesis that was popped off the stack is the matching left parenthesis to the current right parenthesis. If all parentheses are balanced, the stack will be empty after iterating through all characters in the equation. If the stack is not empty, the top left parenthesis on the stack is the one that does not have a matching right parenthesis. If there are two or more items in the stack, there is more than one unbalanced parenthesis in the equation.

For the previous equation, starting at the lefthand side, you push one left parenthesis on the stack and then immediately push a second one. You consume the a and + characters and then come upon a third left parenthesis; your stack now contains three left parentheses. You consume the b character and come upon two right parentheses in a row. For each right parenthesis, you will pop one matching left parenthesis off the stack. Your stack now contains only one left parenthesis. You consume the + and c characters and come upon the last right parenthesis in the equation. You pop the final left parenthesis off the stack and then check the rest of the equation for any other parentheses. Since the stack is empty and you are at the end of the equation, you know that each left parenthesis has a matching right parenthesis.

For the Check methods in this recipe, the location in the string where each left parenthesis is located is pushed onto the stack. This allows you to immediately locate the offending parenthesis.

See Also

See the "Stack<T> Class" topic in the MSDN documentation.

11.5   Creating a One-to-Many Map (MultiMap)

Problem

A Hashtable or a Dictionary<T,U> can map only a single key to a single value, but you need to map a key to one or more values. In addition, it may also be possible to map a key to null.

Solution

Use a Dictionary<T,U> with values that are a List<U>. This structure allows you to add multiple values (in the List<U>) for each key of the Dictionary<T,U>. The MultiMap<T,U> class shown in Example 11-8, which is used in practically the same manner as a Dictionary<T,U> class, does this.

Example 11-8. MultiMap class

```
using System;
using System.Collections;
using System.Collections.Generic;


public class MultiMap<TKey, UValue> : IDictionary<TKey, IList<UValue>>
{
    private Dictionary<TKey, IList<UValue>> map =
        new Dictionary<TKey, IList<UValue>>();


    public IList<UValue> this[TKey key]
```

Example 11-8. MultiMap class (continued)

```
{
    get {return (map[key]);}
    set {map[key] = value;}
}

public void Add(TKey key, UValue item)
{
    AddSingleMap(key, item);
}

public void Add(TKey key, IList<UValue> items)
{
    foreach (UValue val in items)
        AddSingleMap(key, val);
}

public void Add(KeyValuePair<TKey, IList<UValue>> keyValuePair)
{
    foreach (UValue val in keyValuePair.Value)
        AddSingleMap(keyValuePair.Key, val);
}

public void Clear()
{
    map.Clear();
}

public int Count
{
    get {return (map.Count);}
}

public bool IsReadOnly
{
    get {throw(new NotSupportedException(
        "This operation is not supported."));}
}

public bool Contains(TKey key)
{
    return (map.ContainsKey(key));
}

public bool Contains(KeyValuePair<TKey, IList<UValue>> keyValuePair)
{
    return (map.ContainsKey(keyValuePair.Key) &&
            map.ContainsValue(keyValuePair.Value));
}

public bool ContainsKey (TKey key)
{
    return (map.ContainsKey(key));
```

Example 11-8. MultiMap class (continued)

```csharp
    }

    public bool ContainsValue(UValue item)
    {
        if (item == null)
        {
            foreach (KeyValuePair<TKey, IList<UValue>> kvp in map)
            {
                if (((List<UValue>)kvp.Value).Count == 0)
                {
                    return (true);
                }
            }

            return (false);
        }
        else
        {
            foreach (KeyValuePair<TKey, IList<UValue>> kvp in map)
            {
                if (((List<UValue>)kvp.Value).Contains(item))
                {
                    return (true);
                }
            }

            return (false);
        }
    }

    IEnumerator<KeyValuePair<TKey, IList<UValue>>> IEnumerable<KeyValuePair<TKey,
                        IList<UValue>>>.GetEnumerator()
    {
        return (map.GetEnumerator());
    }

    IEnumerator System.Collections.IEnumerable.GetEnumerator()
    {
        return (map.GetEnumerator());
    }

    public bool Remove(TKey key)
    {
        return (RemoveSingleMap(key));
    }

    public bool Remove(KeyValuePair<TKey, IList<UValue>> keyValuePair)
    {
        return (Remove(keyValuePair.Key));
    }

    protected virtual void AddSingleMap(TKey key, UValue item)
    {
```

Example 11-8. MultiMap class (continued)

```
        // Search for key in map Hashtable.
        if (map.ContainsKey(key))
        {
            // Add value to List in map.
            List<UValue> values = (List<UValue>)map[key];

            // Add this value to this existing key.
            values.Add(item);
        }
        else
        {
            if (item == null)
            {
                // Create new key and mapping to an empty List.
                map.Add(key, new List<UValue>());
            }
            else
            {
                List<UValue> values = new List<UValue>();
                values.Add(item);

                // Create new key and mapping to its value.
                map.Add(key, values);
            }
        }
    }

    protected virtual bool RemoveSingleMap(TKey key)
    {
        if (this.ContainsKey(key))
        {
            // Remove the key from KeysTable.
            return (map.Remove(key));
        }
        else
        {
            throw (new ArgumentOutOfRangeException("key", key,
                    "This key does not exists in the map."));
        }
    }

    public bool TryGetValue(TKey key, out UValue item)
    {
        throw (new NotSupportedException(
                "This operation is not supported, use " +
                "TryGetValue(TKey, out IList<UValue>) instead."));
    }

    public bool TryGetValue(TKey key, out IList<UValue> items)
    {
        return (map.TryGetValue(key, out items));
    }
```

Example 11-8. MultiMap class (continued)

```
    public ICollection<TKey> Keys
    {
        get { return (map.Keys); }
    }

    public ICollection<IList<UValue>> Values
    {
        get { return (map.Values); }
    }

    public void CopyTo(TKey[] arr, int index)
    {
        int cntr = 0;
        foreach (KeyValuePair<TKey, IList<UValue>> keyValuePair in map)
        {
            arr[cntr + index] = keyValuePair.Key;
            cntr++;
        }
    }

    public void CopyTo(KeyValuePair<TKey, IList<UValue>>[] arr, int index)
    {
        CopyTo(arr, index);
    }
}
```

The methods defined in Table 11-3 are of particular interest to using a `MultiMap<T,U>` object.

Table 11-3. Members of the MultiMap class

Member	Description
Indexer	The get accessor obtains a List<U> of all values that are associated with a key. The set accessor adds an entire List<U> of values to a key. Its syntax is: `public List<U> this[T key]` where *key* is the key to be added to the MultiMap<T,U> through the set accessor, or it is the key with values that you want to retrieve via the get accessor.
Add method	Adds a key to the Dictionary<T,List<U>> and its associated value. Its syntax is: `Add(T key, T value)` where *key* is the key to be added to the MultiMap<T,U> and *value* is the value to add to the internal List<U> of the private map field.
Clear method	Removes all items from the MultiMap<T,U> object.
Count method	Returns a count of all keys in the MultiMap<T,U> object.
Clone method	Returns a deep copy of the MultiMap<T,U> object.
ContainsKey method	Returns a bool indicating whether the MultiMap<T,U> contains a particular value as its key. Its syntax is: `ContainsKey(T key)` where *key* is the key to be found in the MultiMap<T,U>.

Table 11-3. Members of the MultiMap class (continued)

Member	Description
ContainsValue method	Returns a `bool` indicating whether the `MultiMap<T,U>` contains a particular value. Its syntax is: `ContainsValue(T value)` where *value* is the object to be found in the `MultiMap<T,U>`.
Remove method	Removes a key from the `MultiMap<T,U>` and all its referent values in the internal map `Dictionary<T, List<U>>`. Its syntax is: `Remove(T key)` where *key* is the key to be removed.

Items may be added to a `MultiMap<T,U>` object by running the code shown in Example 11-9.

Example 11-9. Testing the MultiMap class

```
public static void TestMultiMap( )
{
    string s = "foo";

    // Create and populate a MultiMap object.
    MultiMap<int, string> myMap = new MultiMap<int, string>( );
    myMap.Add(0, "zero");
    myMap.Add(1, "one");
    myMap.Add(2, "two");
    myMap.Add(3, "three");
    myMap.Add(3, "duplicate three");
    myMap.Add(3, "duplicate three");
    myMap.Add(4, "null");
    myMap.Add(5, s);
    myMap.Add(6, s);

    // Display contents.
    foreach (KeyValuePair<int, List<string>> entry in myMap)
    {
        Console.Write("Key: " + entry.Key.ToString( ) + "\tValue: ");
        foreach (string str in myMap[entry.Key])
        {
            Console.Write(str + " : ");
        }
        Console.WriteLine( );
    }

    // Obtain values through the indexer.
    Console.WriteLine( );
    Console.WriteLine("((ArrayList) myMap[3])[0]: " + myMap[3][0]);
    Console.WriteLine("((ArrayList) myMap[3])[1]: " + myMap[3][1]);

    // Add items to MultiMap using a List.
    List<string> testArray = new List<string>( );
    testArray.Add("BAR");
```

Example 11-9. Testing the MultiMap class (continued)

```
    testArray.Add("BAZ");
    myMap[10] = testArray;
    myMap[10] = testArray;

    // Remove items from MultiMap.
    myMap.Remove(0);
    myMap.Remove(1);

    // Display MultiMap.
    Console.WriteLine();
    Console.WriteLine("myMap.Count: " + myMap.Count);
    foreach (KeyValuePair<int, List<string>> entry in myMap)
    {
        Console.Write("entry.Key: " + entry.Key.ToString() +
                      "\tentry.Value(s): ");
        foreach (string str in myMap[entry.Key])
        {
            if (str == null)
            {
                Console.Write("null : ");
            }
            else
            {
                Console.Write(str + " : ");
            }
        }
        Console.WriteLine();
    }

    // Determine if the map contains the key or the value.
    Console.WriteLine();
    Console.WriteLine("myMap.ContainsKey(2): " + myMap.ContainsKey(2));
    Console.WriteLine("myMap.ContainsValue(two): " +
    myMap.ContainsValue("two"));

    Console.WriteLine("Contains Key 2: " + myMap.ContainsKey(2));
    Console.WriteLine("Contains Key 12: " + myMap.ContainsKey(12));

    Console.WriteLine("Contains Value two: " + myMap.ContainsValue("two"));
    Console.WriteLine("Contains Value BAR: " + myMap.ContainsValue("BAR"));

    // Clear all items from MultiMap.
    myMap.Clear();
}
```

This code displays the following:

```
Key: 0    Value: zero :
Key: 1    Value: one :
Key: 2    Value: two :
Key: 3    Value: three : duplicate three : duplicate three :
Key: 4    Value:
Key: 5    Value: foo :
```

```
Key: 6    Value: foo :

((ArrayList) myMap[3])[0]: three
((ArrayList) myMap[3])[1]: duplicate three

myMap.Count: 6
entry.Key: 2     entry.Value(s): two :
entry.Key: 3     entry.Value(s): three : duplicate three : duplicate three :
entry.Key: 4     entry.Value(s):
entry.Key: 5     entry.Value(s): foo :
entry.Key: 6     entry.Value(s): foo :
entry.Key: 10    entry.Value(s): BAR : BAZ :

myMap.ContainsKey(2): True
myMap.ContainsValue(two): True
Contains Key 2: True
Contains Key 12: False
Contains Value two: True
Contains Value BAR: True
```

Discussion

A one-to-many map, or multimap, allows one object, a key, to be associated, or *mapped*, to zero or more objects. The MultiMap<T,U> class presented here operates similarly to a Dictionary<T,U>. The MultiMap<T,U> class contains a Dictionary<T, List<U>> field called map that contains the actual mapping of keys to values. Several of the MultiMap<T,U> methods are delegated to the methods on the map Dictionary<T, List<U>> object.

A Dictionary<T,U> operates on a one-to-one principle: only one key may be associated with one value at any time. However, if you need to associate multiple values with a single key, you must use the approach used by the MultiMap<T,U> class. The private map field associates a key with a single List<U> of values, which allows multiple mappings of values to a single key and mappings of a single value to multiple keys. As an added feature, a key can also be mapped to a null value.

Here's what happens when key-value pairs are added to a MultiMap<t,U> object:

1. The MultiMap<T,U>.Add method is called with a *key* and *value* provided as parameters.

2. The Add method checks to see whether *key* exists in the map Dictionary<T, List<U>> object.

3. If *key* does not exist, it is added as a key in the map Dictionary<T, List<U>> object. This key is associated with a new List<U> as the value associated with *key* in this Hashtable.

4. If the *key* does exist, the *key* is looked up in the map Dictionary<T, List<U>> object and the *value* is added to the *key*'s List<U>.

To remove a key using the Remove method, the key and List<U> pair are removed from the map Dictionary<T, List<U>>. This allows removal of all values associated with a single key. The MultiMap<T,U>.Remove method calls the RemoveSingleMap method, which encapsulates this behavior. Removal of key "0", and all values mapped to this key, is performed with the following code:

```
myMap.Remove(1);
```

To remove all keys and their associated values, use the MultiMap<T,U>.Clear method. This method removes all items from the map Dictionary<T, List<U>>.

The other major member of the MultiMap<T,U> class needing discussion is its indexer. The indexer returns the List<U> of values for a particular key through its get accessor. The set accessor simply adds the List<U> provided to a single key. This code creates an array of values and attempts to map them to key "5" in the myMap object:

```
List<string> testArray = new List<string>();
testArray.Add("BAR");
testArray.Add("BAZ");
myMap["5"] = testArray;
```

The following code makes use of the get accessor to access each value associated with key "3":

```
Console.WriteLine(myMap[3][0]);
Console.WriteLine(myMap[3][1]);
Console.WriteLine(myMap[3][2]);
```

This looks somewhat similar to using a jagged array. The first indexer ([3] in the preceding examples) is used to pull the List<U> from the map Dictionary<T, List<U>>, and the second indexer is used to obtain the value in the List<U>. This code displays the following:

```
three
duplicate three
duplicate three
```

This MultiMap<T,U> class also allows the use of the foreach loop to enumerate its key-value pairs. The following code displays each key-value pair in the MyMap object:

```
foreach (KeyValuePair<int, List<string>> entry in myMap)
{
    Console.Write("Key: " + entry.Key.ToString() + "\tValue: ");
    foreach (string str in myMap[entry.Key])
    {
        Console.Write(str + " : ");
    }
    Console.WriteLine();
}
```

The outer foreach loop is used to retrieve all the keys and the inner foreach loop is used to display each value mapped to a particular key. This code displays the following for the initial MyMap object:

```
Key: 0  Value: zero :
Key: 1  Value: one :
Key: 2  Value: two :
Key: 3  Value: three : duplicate three : duplicate three :
Key: 4  Value:
Key: 5  Value: foo :
Key: 6  Value: foo :
```

Two methods that allow searching of the MultiMap<T,U> object are ContainsKey and ContainsValue. The ContainsKey method searches for the specified key in the map Dictionary<T, List<U>>. The ContainsValue method searches for the specified value in a List<U> in the map Dictionary<T, List<U>>. Both methods return true if the key-value was found or false otherwise:

```
Console.WriteLine("Contains Key 2: " + myMap.ContainsKey(2));
Console.WriteLine("Contains Key 12: " + myMap.ContainsKey(12));

Console.WriteLine("Contains Value two: " + myMap.ContainsValue("two"));
Console.WriteLine("Contains Value BAR: " + myMap.ContainsValue("BAR"));
```

Note that the ContainsKey and ContainsValue methods are both case-sensitive.

See Also

See the "List<T> Class," "Dictionary<T,U> Class," and "IEnumerator Interface" topics in the MSDN documentation.

11.6   Creating a Binary Tree

Problem

You need to store information in a tree structure, where the left node is less than its parent node and the right node is greater than or equal to (in cases in which the tree can contain duplicates) its parent. The stored information must be easily inserted into the tree, removed from the tree, and found within the tree.

Solution

To implement a binary tree of the type described in the Problem statement, each node must be an object that inherits from the IComparable<T> interface. This means that every node that wishes to be included in the binary tree must implement the CompareTo method. This method will allow one node to determine whether it is less than, greater than, or equal to another node.

Use the BinaryTree<T> class shown in Example 11-10, which contains all of the nodes in a binary tree and lets you traverse it.

Example 11-10. Generic BinaryTree class

```csharp
using System;
using System.Collections;
using System.Collections.Generic;


public class BinaryTree<T> : IEnumerable<T>
    where T: IComparable<T>
{
    public BinaryTree( ) {}

    public BinaryTree(T value)
    {
        BinaryTreeNode<T> node = new BinaryTreeNode<T>(value);
        root = node;
        counter = 1;
    }


    protected int counter = 0;                  // Number of nodes in tree
    protected BinaryTreeNode<T> root = null;  // Pointer to root node in this tree


    public void AddNode(T value)
    {
        BinaryTreeNode<T> node = new BinaryTreeNode<T>(value);
        ++counter;

        if (root == null)
        {
            root = node;
        }
        else
        {
            root.AddNode(node);
        }
    }

    public BinaryTreeNode<T> SearchDepthFirst(T value)
    {
        return (root.DepthFirstSearch(value));
    }

    public void Print( )
    {
        root.PrintDepthFirst( );
    }

    public BinaryTreeNode<T> Root
    {
```

Example 11-10. Generic BinaryTree class (continued)

```
        get {return (root);}
    }

    public int Count
    {
        get {return (counter);}
    }

    IEnumerator<T> System.Collections.Generic.IEnumerable<T>.GetEnumerator()
    {
        List<T> nodes = new List<T>();

        nodes = root.IterateDepthFirst();
        nodes.Add(root.Value);

        foreach (T t in nodes)
            yield return (t);
    }

    IEnumerator System.Collections.IEnumerable.GetEnumerator()
    {
        throw (new NotSupportedException("This operation is not " +
 "supported use the GetEnumerator() that returns an IEnumerator<T>."));
    }
}
```

The BinaryTreeNode<T> shown in Example 11-11 encapsulates the data and behavior
of a single node in the binary tree.

Example 11-11. Generic BinaryTreeNode class

```
public class BinaryTreeNode<T>
    where T: IComparable<T>
{
    public BinaryTreeNode() {}

    public BinaryTreeNode(T value)
    {
        nodeValue = value;
    }


    protected T nodeValue = default(T);
    protected BinaryTreeNode<T> leftNode = null;   //  leftNode.nodeValue < Value
    protected BinaryTreeNode<T> rightNode = null;  //  rightNode.nodeValue >= Value


    public int Children
    {
        get
        {
            int currCount = 0;
```

Example 11-11. Generic BinaryTreeNode class (continued)

```
            if (leftNode != null)
            {
                ++currCount;
                currCount += leftNode.Children( );
            }

            if (rightNode != null)
            {
                ++currCount;
                currCount += rightNode.Children( );
            }

            return (currCount);
        }
    }


public BinaryTreeNode<T> Left
{
    get {return (leftNode);}
}

public BinaryTreeNode<T> Right
{
    get {return (rightNode);}
}

public T Value
{
    get {return (nodeValue);}
}

public void AddNode(BinaryTreeNode<T> node)
{
    if (node.nodeValue.CompareTo(nodeValue) < 0)
    {
        if (leftNode == null)
        {
            leftNode = node;
        }
        else
        {
            leftNode.AddNode(node);
        }
    }
    else if (node.nodeValue.CompareTo(nodeValue) >= 0)
    {
        if (rightNode == null)
        {
            rightNode = node;
        }
        else
        {
```

Example 11-11. Generic BinaryTreeNode class (continued)

```
                rightNode.AddNode(node);
            }
        }
    }

    public bool AddUniqueNode(BinaryTreeNode<T> node)
    {
        bool isUnique = true;

        if (node.nodeValue.CompareTo(nodeValue) < 0)
        {
            if (leftNode == null)
            {
                leftNode = node;
            }
            else
            {
                leftNode.AddNode(node);
            }
        }
        else if (node.nodeValue.CompareTo(nodeValue) > 0)
        {
            if (rightNode == null)
            {
                rightNode = node;
            }
            else
            {
                rightNode.AddNode(node);
            }
        }
        else   //node.nodeValue.CompareTo(nodeValue) = 0
        {
            isUnique = false;
            // Could throw exception here as well...
        }

        return (isUnique);
    }

    public BinaryTreeNode<T> DepthFirstSearch(T targetObj)
    {
        // NOTE: foo.CompareTo(bar) == -1   -->   (foo < bar)
        BinaryTreeNode<T> retObj = null;
        int comparisonResult = targetObj.CompareTo(nodeValue);

        if (comparisonResult  == 0)
        {
            retObj = this;
        }
        else if (comparisonResult > 0)
        {
```

Example 11-11. Generic BinaryTreeNode class (continued)

```
            if (rightNode != null)
            {
                retObj = rightNode.DepthFirstSearch(targetObj);
            }
        }
        else if (comparisonResult < 0)
        {
            if (leftNode != null)
            {
                retObj = leftNode.DepthFirstSearch(targetObj);
            }
        }

        return (retObj);
    }

    public void PrintDepthFirst()
    {
        if (leftNode != null)
        {
            leftNode.PrintDepthFirst();
        }

        Console.WriteLine(this.nodeValue.ToString());

        if (leftNode != null)
        {
            Console.WriteLine("\tContains Left: " +
            leftNode.nodeValue.ToString());
        }
        else
        {
            Console.WriteLine("\tContains Left:  NULL");
        }

        if (rightNode != null)
        {
            Console.WriteLine("\tContains Right: " +
            rightNode.nodeValue.ToString());
        }
        else
        {
            Console.WriteLine("\tContains Right: NULL");
        }

        if (rightNode != null)
        {
            rightNode.PrintDepthFirst();
        }
    }

    public List<T> IterateDepthFirst()
    {
```

Example 11-11. Generic BinaryTreeNode class (continued)

```
        List<T> tempList = new List<T>();

        if (leftNode != null)
        {
            tempList.AddRange(leftNode.IterateDepthFirst());
        }

        if (leftNode != null)
        {
            tempList.Add(leftNode.nodeValue);
        }

        if (rightNode != null)
        {
            tempList.Add(rightNode.nodeValue);
        }

        if (rightNode != null)
        {
            tempList.AddRange(rightNode.IterateDepthFirst());
        }

        return (tempList);
    }

    public void RemoveLeftNode()
    {
        leftNode = null;
    }

    public void RemoveRightNode()
    {
        rightNode = null;
    }
}
```

The methods defined in Table 11-4 are of particular interest to using a BinaryTree<T> object.

Table 11-4. Members of the BinaryTree<T> class

Member	Description
Overloaded constructor	This constructor creates a BinaryTree<T> object with a root node. Its syntax is: `BinaryTree(T value)` where *value* is the root node for the tree. Note that this tree may not be flattened.
AddNode method	Adds a node to the tree. Its syntax is: `AddNode(T value, int id)` where *value* is the object to be added and *id* is the node index. Use this method if the tree will be flattened.

Table 11-4. Members of the BinaryTree<T> class (continued)

Member	Description
AddNode method	Adds a node to the tree. Its syntax is: `AddNode(T value)` where *value* is the object to be added. Use this method if the tree will not be flattened.
SearchDepthFirst method	Searches for and returns a `BinaryTreeNode<T>` object in the tree, if one exists. This method searches the depth of the tree first. Its syntax is: `SearchDepthFirst(T value)` where *value* is the object to be found in the tree.
Print method	Displays the tree in depth-first format. Its syntax is: `Print( )`
Root property	Returns the `BinaryTreeNode<T>` object that is the root of the tree. Its syntax is: `Root`
TreeSize property	A read-only property that gets the number of nodes in the tree. Its syntax is: `int TreeSize {get;}`

The methods defined in Table 11-5 are of particular interest to using a Binary-TreeNode<T> object.

Table 11-5. Members of the BinaryTreeNode<T> class

Member	Description
Overloaded constructor	This constructor creates a `BinaryTreeNode<T>` object. Its syntax is: `BinaryTreeNode(T value)` where *value* is the object contained in this node, which will be used to compare to its parent.
NumOfChildren property	A read-only property to retrieve the number of children below this node. Its syntax is: `int NumOfChildren {get;}`
Left property	A read-only property to retrieve the left child node below this node. Its syntax is: `BinaryTreeNode<T> Left {get;}`
Right property	A read-only property to retrieve the right child node below this node. Its syntax is: `BinaryTreeNode<T> Right {get;}`
Children method	Retrieves the number of child nodes below this node. Its syntax is: `Children( )`
GetValue method	Returns the `IComparable<T>` object that this node contains. Its syntax is: `GetValue( )`
AddNode method	Adds a new node recursively to either the left or right side. Its syntax is: `AddNode(BinaryTreeNode<T> node)` where *node* is the node to be added. Duplicate nodes may be added using this method.
AddUniqueNode method	Adds a new node recursively to either the left side or the right side. Its syntax is: `AddUniqueNode(BinaryTreeNode<T> node)` where *node* is the node to be added. Duplicate nodes may not be added using this method. A Boolean value is returned: `true` indicates a successful operation; `false` indicates an attempt to add a duplicate node.

Table 11-5. Members of the BinaryTreeNode<T> class (continued)

Member	Description
DepthFirstSearch method	Searches for and returns a BinaryTreeNode<T> object in the tree, if one exists. This method searches the depth of the tree first. Its syntax is: `DepthFirstSearch(T targetObj)` where *targetObj* is the object to be found in the tree.
PrintDepthFirst method	Displays the tree in depth-first format. Its syntax is: `PrintDepthFirst( )`
RemoveLeftNode method	Removes the left node and any child nodes of this node. Its syntax is: `RemoveLeftNode( )`
RemoveRightNode method	Removes the right node and any child nodes of this node. Its syntax is: `RemoveRightNode( )`

The code in Example 11-12 illustrates the use of the BinaryTree<T> and BinaryTreeNode<T> classes when creating and using a binary tree.

Example 11-12. Using the BinaryTree and Binary TreeNode classes

```
public static void TestBinaryTree( )
{
    BinaryTree<string> tree = new BinaryTree<string>("d");
    tree.AddNode("a");
    tree.AddNode("b");
    tree.AddNode("f");
    tree.AddNode("e");
    tree.AddNode("c");
    tree.AddNode("g");

    tree.Print( );
    tree.Print( );

    Console.WriteLine("tree.TreeSize: " + tree.Count);
    Console.WriteLine("tree.Root.DepthFirstSearch(b).Children: " +
                    tree.Root.DepthFirstSearch("b").Children);
    Console.WriteLine("tree.Root.DepthFirstSearch(a).Children: " +
                    tree.Root.DepthFirstSearch("a").Children);
    Console.WriteLine("tree.Root.DepthFirstSearch(g).Children: " +
                    tree.Root.DepthFirstSearch("g").Children);

    Console.WriteLine("tree.SearchDepthFirst(a): " +
                    tree.SearchDepthFirst("a").Value);
    Console.WriteLine("tree.SearchDepthFirst(b): " +
                    tree.SearchDepthFirst("b").Value);
    Console.WriteLine("tree.SearchDepthFirst(c): " +
                    tree.SearchDepthFirst("c").Value);
    Console.WriteLine("tree.SearchDepthFirst(d): " +
                    tree.SearchDepthFirst("d").Value);
```

```
Console.WriteLine("tree.SearchDepthFirst(e): " +
                    tree.SearchDepthFirst("e").Value);
Console.WriteLine("tree.SearchDepthFirst(f): " +
                    tree.SearchDepthFirst("f").Value);

tree.Root.RemoveLeftNode();
tree.Print();

tree.Root.RemoveRightNode();
tree.Print();
}
```

The output for this method is shown here:

```
a
    Contains Left:  NULL
    Contains Right: b
b
    Contains Left:  NULL
    Contains Right: c
c
    Contains Left:  NULL
    Contains Right: NULL
d
    Contains Left: a
    Contains Right: f
e
    Contains Left:  NULL
    Contains Right: NULL
f
    Contains Left: e
    Contains Right: g
g
    Contains Left:  NULL
    Contains Right: NULL
a
    Contains Left:  NULL
    Contains Right: b
b
    Contains Left:  NULL
    Contains Right: c
c
    Contains Left:  NULL
    Contains Right: NULL
d
    Contains Left: a
    Contains Right: f
e
    Contains Left:  NULL
    Contains Right: NULL
f
```

```
        Contains Left: e
        Contains Right: g
g
        Contains Left:  NULL
        Contains Right: NULL
tree.TreeSize: 7
tree.Root.DepthFirstSearch(a).Children: 1
tree.Root.DepthFirstSearch(a).Children: 2
tree.Root.DepthFirstSearch(g).Children: 0
tree.SearchDepthFirst(a): a
tree.SearchDepthFirst(b): b
tree.SearchDepthFirst(c): c
tree.SearchDepthFirst(d): d
tree.SearchDepthFirst(e): e
tree.SearchDepthFirst(f): f
d
        Contains Left:  NULL
        Contains Right: f
e
        Contains Left:  NULL
        Contains Right: NULL
f
        Contains Left: e
        Contains Right: g
g
        Contains Left:  NULL
        Contains Right: NULL
d
        Contains Left:  NULL
        Contains Right: NULL
```

Discussion

Trees are data structures in which each node has exactly one parent and possibly many children. The root of the tree is a single node that branches out into one or more child nodes. A *node* is the part of the tree structure that contains data and contains the branches (or in more concrete terms, *references*) to its children node(s).

A tree can be used for many things, such as to represent a management hierarchy with the president of the company at the root node and the various vice presidents as child nodes of the president. The vice presidents may have managers as child nodes, and so on. A tree can be used to make decisions, where each node of the tree contains a question, and the answer given depends on which branch is taken to a child node. The tree described in this recipe is called a *binary tree*. A binary tree can have zero, one, or two child nodes for every node in the tree. A binary tree node can never have more than two child nodes; this is where this type of tree gets its name. (There are other types of trees. For instance, the *n*-ary tree can have zero to *n* nodes for each node in the tree. This type of tree is defined in Recipe 11.7.)

A binary tree is very useful for storing objects and then efficiently searching for those objects. The following algorithm is used to store objects in a binary tree:

1. Start at the root node.
2. Is this node free?
   a. If yes, add the object to this node, and you are done.
   b. If no, continue.
3. Is the object to be added to the tree less than (*less than* is determined by the IComparable<T>.CompareTo method of the node being added) the current node?
   a. If yes, follow the branch to the node on the left side of the current node, and go to step 2.
   b. If no, follow the branch to the node of the right side of the current node, and go to step 2.

Basically, this algorithm states that the node to the left of the current node contains an object or value less than the current node, and the node to the right of the current node contains an object or value greater than (or equal to, if the binary tree can contain duplicates) the current node.

Searching for an object in a tree is easy. Just start at the root and ask yourself, "Is the object I am searching for less than the current node's object?" If it is, follow the left branch to the next node in the tree. If it is not, check the current node to determine whether it contains the object you are searching for. If this is still not the correct object, continue down the right branch to the next node. When you get to the next node, start the process over again.

The binary tree used in this recipe is made up of two classes. The BinaryTree<T> class is not a part of the actual tree; rather, it acts as a starting point from which you can create a tree, add nodes to it, search the tree for items, and retrieve the root node to perform other actions.

The second class, BinaryTreeNode<T>, is the heart of the binary tree and represents a single node in the tree. This class contains all the members that are required to create and work with a binary tree.

The BinaryTreeNode<T> class contains a protected field, nodeValue, that contains an object implementing the IComparable<T> interface. This structure allows you to perform searches and add nodes in the correct location in the tree. The CompareTo method of the IComparable<T> interface is used in searching and adding methods to determine whether you need to follow the left or right branch. See the AddNode, AddUniqueNode, and DepthFirstSearch methods—discussed in the following paragraphs—to see this in action.

There are two methods to add nodes to the tree, AddNode and AddUniqueNode. The AddNode method allows duplicates to be introduced to the tree, whereas the AddUniqueNode allows only unique nodes to be added.

The DepthFirstSearch method allows the tree to be searched by first checking the current node to see whether it contains the value searched for; if not, recursion is used to check the left or the right node. If no matching value is found in any node, this method returns null.

It is interesting to note that even though the BinaryTree<T> class is provided to create and manage the tree of BinaryTreeNode<T> objects, you can merely use the BinaryTreeNode<T> class as long as you keep track of the root node yourself. The code shown in Example 11-13 creates and manages the tree without the use of the BinaryTree<T> class.

Example 11-13. Creating and managing a binary tree without using the BinaryTree class

```
public static void TestManagedTreeWithNoBinaryTreeClass()
{
    // Create the root node.
    BinaryTreeNode<string> topLevel = new BinaryTreeNode<string>("d");

    // Create all nodes that will be added to the tree.
    BinaryTreeNode<string> one = new BinaryTreeNode<string>("b");
    BinaryTreeNode<string> two = new BinaryTreeNode<string>("c");
    BinaryTreeNode<string> three = new BinaryTreeNode<string>("a");
    BinaryTreeNode<string> four = new BinaryTreeNode<string>("e");
    BinaryTreeNode<string> five = new BinaryTreeNode<string>("f");
    BinaryTreeNode<string> six = new BinaryTreeNode<string>("g");

    // Add nodes to tree through the root.
    topLevel.AddNode(three);
    topLevel.AddNode(one);
    topLevel.AddNode(five);
    topLevel.AddNode(four);
    topLevel.AddNode(two);
    topLevel.AddNode(six);

    // Print the tree starting at the root node.
    topLevel.PrintDepthFirst();

    // Print the tree starting at node 'Three'.
    three.PrintDepthFirst();

    // Display the number of child nodes of various nodes in the tree.
    Console.WriteLine("topLevel.Children: " + topLevel.Children);
    Console.WriteLine("one.Children: " + one.Children);
    Console.WriteLine("three.Children: " + three.Children);
    Console.WriteLine("six.Children: " + six.Children);

    // Search the tree using the depth-first searching method.
    Console.WriteLine("topLevel.DepthFirstSearch(a): " +
                    topLevel.DepthFirstSearch("a").Value.ToString());
    Console.WriteLine("topLevel.DepthFirstSearch(b): " +
                    topLevel.DepthFirstSearch("b").Value.ToString());
    Console.WriteLine("topLevel.DepthFirstSearch(c): " +
                    topLevel.DepthFirstSearch("c").Value.ToString());
```

```
    Console.WriteLine("topLevel.DepthFirstSearch(d): " +
                  topLevel.DepthFirstSearch("d").Value.ToString( ));
    Console.WriteLine("topLevel.DepthFirstSearch(e): " +
                  topLevel.DepthFirstSearch("e").Value.ToString( ));
    Console.WriteLine("topLevel.DepthFirstSearch(f): " +
                  topLevel.DepthFirstSearch("f").Value.ToString( ));

    // Remove the left child node from the root node and display the entire tree.
    topLevel.RemoveLeftNode( );
    topLevel.PrintDepthFirst( );

    // Remove all nodes from the tree except for the root and display the tree.
    topLevel.RemoveRightNode( );
    topLevel.PrintDepthFirst( );
}
```

The output for this method is shown here:

```
a
    Contains Left:  NULL
    Contains Right: b
b
    Contains Left:  NULL
    Contains Right: c
c
    Contains Left:  NULL
    Contains Right: NULL
d
    Contains Left: a
    Contains Right: f
e
    Contains Left:  NULL
    Contains Right: NULL
f
    Contains Left: e
    Contains Right: g
g
    Contains Left:  NULL
    Contains Right: NULL
a
    Contains Left:  NULL
    Contains Right: b
b
    Contains Left:  NULL
    Contains Right: c
c
    Contains Left:  NULL
    Contains Right: NULL
topLevel.Children: 6
one.Children: 1
three.Children: 2
six.Children: 0
topLevel.DepthFirstSearch(a): a
```

```
topLevel.DepthFirstSearch(b): b
topLevel.DepthFirstSearch(c): c
topLevel.DepthFirstSearch(d): d
topLevel.DepthFirstSearch(e): e
topLevel.DepthFirstSearch(f): f
d
    Contains Left:  NULL
    Contains Right: f
e
    Contains Left:  NULL
    Contains Right: NULL
f
    Contains Left: e
    Contains Right: g
g
    Contains Left:  NULL
    Contains Right: NULL
d
    Contains Left:  NULL
    Contains Right: NULL
```

See Also

See the "Queue Class" and "IComparable<T> Interface" topics in the MSDN documentation.

11.7   Creating an n-ary Tree

Problem

You need a tree that can store a number of child nodes in each of its nodes. A binary tree will work if each node needs to have only two children, but in this case each node needs to have a fixed number of child nodes greater than two.

Solution

Use the NTree<T> class shown in Example 11-14 to create the root node for the *n*-ary tree.

Example 11-14. Generic NTree class

```
using System;
using System.Collections;
using System.Collections.Generic;


public class NTree<T> : IEnumerable<T>
    where T : IComparable<T>
{
    public NTree( )
    {
```

Example 11-14. Generic NTree class (continued)

```
        maxChildren = int.MaxValue;
    }

    public NTree(int maxNumChildren)
    {
        maxChildren = maxNumChildren;
    }


    // The root node of the tree
    protected NTreeNode<T> root = null;
    // The maximum number of child nodes that a parent node may contain
    protected int maxChildren = 0;


    public void AddRoot(NTreeNode<T> node)
    {
        root = node;
    }

    public NTreeNode<T> GetRoot()
    {
        return (root);
    }

    public int MaxChildren
    {
        get {return (maxChildren);}
    }

    IEnumerator<T> System.Collections.Generic.IEnumerable<T>.GetEnumerator()
    {
        List<T> nodes = new List<T>();

        nodes = GetRoot().IterateDepthFirst();
        nodes.Add(GetRoot().Value());

        foreach (T t in nodes)
            yield return (t);
    }

    IEnumerator System.Collections.IEnumerable.GetEnumerator()
    {
        throw (new NotSupportedException("This operation is not " +
 "supported use the GetEnumerator() that returns an IEnumerator<T>."));
    }
}
```

The methods defined in Table 11-6 are of particular interest to using an NTree<T> object.

Table 11-6. Members of the NTree<T> class

Member	Description
Overloaded constructor	This constructor creates an NTree<T> object. Its syntax is: NTree(int *maxNumChildren*) where *maxNumChildren* is the maximum number of children that one node may have at any time.
MaxChildren property	A read-only property to retrieve the maximum number of children any node may have. Its syntax is: int *MaxChildren* {get;} The value this property returns is set in the constructor.
AddRoot method	Adds a node to the tree. Its syntax is: AddRoot(NTreeNodeFactory<T>.NTreeNode<U> *node*) where *node* is the node to be added as a child to the current node.
GetRoot method	Returns the root node of this tree. Its syntax is: GetRoot( )

The NTreeNodeFactory<T> class is used to create nodes for the *n*-ary tree. These nodes are defined in the class NTreeNode<U>, which is nested inside of the NTreeNodeFactory<T> class. You are not able to create an NTreeNode<U> without the use of this factory class, as shown in Example 11-15.

Example 11-15. Using the class to create the nodes for an n-ary tree

```
public class NTreeNodeFactory<T>
    where T : IComparable<T>
{
    public NTreeNodeFactory(NTree<T> root)
    {
        maxChildren = root.MaxChildren;
    }


    private int maxChildren = 0;


    public int MaxChildren
    {
        get {return (maxChildren);}
    }

    public NTreeNode<T> CreateNode(T value)
    {
        return (new NTreeNode<T>(value, maxChildren));
    }
}

// Node class
public class NTreeNode<U>
    where U : IComparable<U>
{
```

```
public NTreeNode(U value, int maxChildren)
{
    if (value != null)
    {
        nodeValue = value;
    }

    childNodes = new NTreeNode<U>[maxChildren];
}


protected U nodeValue = default(U);
protected NTreeNode<U>[] childNodes = null;


public int CountChildren
{
    get
    {
        int currCount = 0;


        for (int index = 0; index <= childNodes.GetUpperBound(0); index++)
        {
            if (childNodes[index] != null)
            {
                ++currCount;
                currCount += childNodes[index].CountChildren;
            }
        }

        return (currCount);
    }
}

public int CountImmediateChildren
{
    get
    {
        int currCount = 0;

        for (int index = 0; index <= childNodes.GetUpperBound(0); index++)
        {
            if (childNodes[index] != null)
            {
                ++currCount;
            }
        }

        return (currCount);
    }
}
```

Example 11-15. Using the class to create the nodes for an n-ary tree (continued)

```
public NTreeNode<U>[] Children
{
    get {return (childNodes);}
}

public NTreeNode<U> GetChild(int index)
{
    return (childNodes[index]);
}

public U Value()
{
    return (nodeValue);
}

public void AddNode(NTreeNode<U> node)
{
    int numOfNonNullNodes = CountImmediateChildren;
    if (numOfNonNullNodes < childNodes.Length)
    {
        childNodes[numOfNonNullNodes] = node;
    }
    else
    {
        throw (new Exception("Cannot add more children to this node."));
    }
}

public NTreeNode<U> DepthFirstSearch(U targetObj)
{
    NTreeNode<U> retObj = default(NTreeNode<U>);

    if (targetObj.CompareTo(nodeValue) == 0)
    {
        retObj = this;
    }
    else
    {
        for (int index=0; index<=childNodes.GetUpperBound(0); index++)
        {
            if (childNodes[index] != null)
            {
                retObj = childNodes[index].DepthFirstSearch(targetObj);
                if (retObj != null)
                {
                    break;
                }
            }
        }
    }
    return (retObj);
}
```

```
public NTreeNode<U> BreadthFirstSearch(U targetObj)
{
    Queue<NTreeNode<U>> row = new Queue<NTreeNode<U>>( );
    row.Enqueue(this);

    while (row.Count > 0)
    {
        // Get next node in queue.
        NTreeNode<U> currentNode = row.Dequeue( );

        // Is this the node we are looking for?
        if (targetObj.CompareTo(currentNode.nodeValue) == 0)
        {
            return (currentNode);
        }

        for (int index = 0;
             index < currentNode.CountImmediateChildren;
             index++)
        {
            if (currentNode.Children[index] != null)
            {
                row.Enqueue(currentNode.Children[index]);
            }
        }
    }

    return (null);
}

public void PrintDepthFirst( )
{
    Console.WriteLine("this: " + nodeValue.ToString( ));

    for (int index = 0; index < childNodes.Length; index++)
    {
        if (childNodes[index] != null)
        {
            Console.WriteLine("\tchildNodes[" + index + "]:  " +
            childNodes[index].nodeValue.ToString( ));
        }
        else
        {
            Console.WriteLine("\tchildNodes[" + index + "]:  NULL");
        }
    }

    for (int index = 0; index < childNodes.Length; index++)
    {
        if (childNodes[index] != null)
        {
            childNodes[index].PrintDepthFirst( );
```

Example 11-15. Using the class to create the nodes for an n-ary tree (continued)

```
            }
        }
    }

    public List<U> IterateDepthFirst()
    {
        List<U> tempList = new List<U>();

        for (int index = 0; index < childNodes.Length; index++)
        {
            if (childNodes[index] != null)
            {
                tempList.Add(childNodes[index].nodeValue);
            }
        }

        for (int index = 0; index < childNodes.Length; index++)
        {
            if (childNodes[index] != null)
            {
                tempList.AddRange(childNodes[index].IterateDepthFirst());
            }
        }

        return (tempList);
    }

    public void RemoveNode(int index)
    {
        // Remove node from array and compact the array.
        if (index < childNodes.GetLowerBound(0) ||
            index > childNodes.GetUpperBound(0))
        {
            throw (new ArgumentOutOfRangeException("index", index,
                "Array index out of bounds."));
        }
        else if (index < childNodes.GetUpperBound(0))
        {
            Array.Copy(childNodes, index + 1, childNodes, index,
                    childNodes.Length - index - 1);
        }

        childNodes.SetValue(null, childNodes.GetUpperBound(0));
    }
}
```

The methods defined in Table 11-7 are of particular interest to using an NTreeNodeFactory<T> object.

Table 11-7. Members of the NTreeNodeFactory<T> class

Member	Description
Constructor	Creates a new NTreeNodeFactory<T> object that will create NTreeNode<U> objects with the same number of MaxChildren that the NTree<T> object passed in supports. Its syntax is: `NTreeNodeFactory(NTree<T> root)` where *root* is an NTree<T> object.
MaxChildren property	Read-only property that returns the maximum number of children that the NTree<T> object supports. Its syntax is: `int MaxChildren {get;}`

CreateNode method	Overloaded. Returns a new NTreeNode object. Its syntax is:
	 `CreateNode( )`
	 `CreateNode(IComparable value)`
	 where *value* is the IComparable object this new node object will contain.

The methods defined in Table 11-8 are of particular interest to using the nested NTreeNode<U> object.

Table 11-8. Members of the NTreeNode<U> class

Member	Description
Constructor	Creates a new NTreeNode<U> object from the NTreeNodeFactory<T> object passed in to it. Its syntax is: `NTreeNode(T value, int maxChildren)` where *value* is an IComparable<T> object and *maxChildren* is the total number of children allowed by this node.
NumOfChildren property	Read-only property that returns the total number of children below this node. Its syntax is: `int NumOfChildren {get;}`
Children property	Read-only property that returns all of the non-null child-node objects in an array that the current node contains. Its syntax is: `NTreeNode<U>[] Children {get;}`
CountChildren property	Recursively counts the number of non-null child nodes below the current node and returns this value as an integer. Its syntax is: `CountChildren`
CountImmediateChildren property	Counts only the non-null child nodes contained in the current node. Its syntax is: `CountImmediateChildren`
GetChild method	Uses an index to return the NTreeNode<U> contained by the current node. Its syntax is: `GetChild(int index)` where *index* is the array index where the child object is stored.
Value method	Returns an object of type T that the current node contains. Its syntax is: `Value( )`

Table 11-8. Members of the NTreeNode<U> class (continued)

Member	Description
AddNode method	Adds a new child node to the current node. Its syntax is: AddNode(NTreeNode<U> *node*) where *node* is the child node to be added.
DepthFirstSearch method	Attempts to locate an NTreeNode<U> by the IComparable<T> object that it contains. An NTreeNode<U> is returned if the IComparable<T> object is located or a null if it is not. Its syntax is: DepthFirstSearch(IComparable<T> *targetObj*) where *targetObj* is the IComparable<T> object to locate in the tree. Note that this search starts with the current node, which may or may not be the root of the tree. The tree traversal is done in a depth-first manner.
BreadthFirstSearch method	Attempts to locate an NTreeNode<U> by the IComparable<T> object that it contains. An NTreeNode<U> is returned if the IComparable<T> object is located or a null if it is not. Its syntax is: BreadthFirstSearch(IComparable<T> *targetObj*) where *targetObj* is the IComparable<T> object to locate in the tree. Note that this search starts with the current node, which may or may not be the root of the tree. The tree traversal is done in a breadth-first manner.
PrintDepthFirst method	Displays the tree structure on the console window starting with the current node. Its syntax is: PrintDepthFirst( ) This method uses recursion to display each node in the tree.
RemoveNode method	Removes the child node at the specified *index* on the current node. Its syntax is: RemoveNode(int *index*) where *index* is the array index where the child object is stored. Note that when a node is removed, all of its children nodes are removed as well.

The code shown in Example 11-16 illustrates the use of the NTree<T>, NTree-NodeFactory<T>, and NTreeNode<U> classes to create and manipulate an *n*-ary tree.

Example 11-16. Using the NTree<T>, NTreeNodeFactory<T>, and NTreeNode<U> classes

```
public static void TestNTree( )
{
    NTree<string> topLevel = new NTree<string>(3);
    NTreeNodeFactory<string> nodeFactory =
                new NTreeNodeFactory<string>(topLevel);

    NTreeNode<string> one = nodeFactory.CreateNode("One");
    NTreeNode<string> two = nodeFactory.CreateNode("Two");
    NTreeNode<string> three = nodeFactory.CreateNode("Three");
    NTreeNode<string> four = nodeFactory.CreateNode("Four");
    NTreeNode<string> five = nodeFactory.CreateNode("Five");
    NTreeNode<string> six = nodeFactory.CreateNode("Six");
    NTreeNode<string> seven = nodeFactory.CreateNode("Seven");
```

```
    NTreeNode<string> eight = nodeFactory.CreateNode("Eight");
    NTreeNode<string> nine = nodeFactory.CreateNode("Nine");

    topLevel.AddRoot(one);
    Console.WriteLine("topLevel.GetRoot( ).CountChildren: " +
            topLevel.GetRoot( ).CountChildren);

    topLevel.GetRoot( ).AddNode(two);
    topLevel.GetRoot( ).AddNode(three);
    topLevel.GetRoot( ).AddNode(four);

    topLevel.GetRoot( ).Children[0].AddNode(five);
    topLevel.GetRoot( ).Children[0].AddNode(eight);
    topLevel.GetRoot( ).Children[0].AddNode(nine);
    topLevel.GetRoot( ).Children[1].AddNode(six);
    topLevel.GetRoot( ).Children[1].Children[0].AddNode(seven);

    Console.WriteLine("Display Entire tree:");
    topLevel.GetRoot( ).PrintDepthFirst( );

    Console.WriteLine("Display tree from node [two]:");
    topLevel.GetRoot( ).Children[0].PrintDepthFirst( );

    Console.WriteLine("Depth First Search:");
    Console.WriteLine("topLevel.DepthFirstSearch(One): " +
            topLevel.GetRoot().DepthFirstSearch("One").Value( ).ToString( ));
    Console.WriteLine("topLevel.DepthFirstSearch(Two): " +
            topLevel.GetRoot().DepthFirstSearch("Two").Value( ).ToString( ));
    Console.WriteLine("topLevel.DepthFirstSearch(Three): " +
            topLevel.GetRoot().DepthFirstSearch("Three").Value( ).ToString( ));
    Console.WriteLine("topLevel.DepthFirstSearch(Four): " +
            topLevel.GetRoot().DepthFirstSearch("Four").Value( ).ToString( ));
    Console.WriteLine("topLevel.DepthFirstSearch(Five): " +
            topLevel.GetRoot().DepthFirstSearch("Five").Value( ).ToString( ));

    Console.WriteLine("\r\n\r\nBreadth First Search:");
    Console.WriteLine("topLevel.BreadthFirstSearch(One): " +
            topLevel.GetRoot().BreadthFirstSearch("One").Value( ).ToString( ));
    Console.WriteLine("topLevel.BreadthFirstSearch(Two): " +
            topLevel.GetRoot().BreadthFirstSearch("Two").Value( ).ToString( ));
    Console.WriteLine("topLevel.BreadthFirstSearch(Three): " +
            topLevel.GetRoot().BreadthFirstSearch("Three").Value( ).ToString( ));
    Console.WriteLine("topLevel.BreadthFirstSearch(Four): " +
            topLevel.GetRoot().BreadthFirstSearch("Four").Value( ).ToString( ));
}
```

The output for this method is shown here:

```
    topLevel.GetRoot( ).CountChildren: 0
    Display Entire tree:
    this: One
```

```
        childNodes[0]:    Two
        childNodes[1]:    Three
        childNodes[2]:    Four
this: Two
        childNodes[0]:    Five
        childNodes[1]:    Eight
        childNodes[2]:    Nine
this: Five
        childNodes[0]:    NULL
        childNodes[1]:    NULL
        childNodes[2]:    NULL
this: Eight
        childNodes[0]:    NULL
        childNodes[1]:    NULL
        childNodes[2]:    NULL
this: Nine
        childNodes[0]:    NULL
        childNodes[1]:    NULL
        childNodes[2]:    NULL
this: Three
        childNodes[0]:    Six
        childNodes[1]:    NULL
        childNodes[2]:    NULL
this: Six
        childNodes[0]:    Seven
        childNodes[1]:    NULL
        childNodes[2]:    NULL
this: Seven
        childNodes[0]:    NULL
        childNodes[1]:    NULL
        childNodes[2]:    NULL
this: Four
        childNodes[0]:    NULL
        childNodes[1]:    NULL
        childNodes[2]:    NULL
Display tree from node [two]:
this: Two
        childNodes[0]:    Five
        childNodes[1]:    Eight
        childNodes[2]:    Nine
this: Five
        childNodes[0]:    NULL
        childNodes[1]:    NULL
        childNodes[2]:    NULL
this: Eight
        childNodes[0]:    NULL
        childNodes[1]:    NULL
        childNodes[2]:    NULL
this: Nine
        childNodes[0]:    NULL
        childNodes[1]:    NULL
        childNodes[2]:    NULL
Depth First Search:
topLevel.DepthFirstSearch(One): One
```

```
topLevel.DepthFirstSearch(Two): Two
topLevel.DepthFirstSearch(Three): Three
topLevel.DepthFirstSearch(Four): Four
topLevel.DepthFirstSearch(Five): Five


Breadth First Search:
topLevel.BreadthFirstSearch(One): One
topLevel.BreadthFirstSearch(Two): Two
topLevel.BreadthFirstSearch(Three): Three
topLevel.BreadthFirstSearch(Four): Four
```

Discussion

An *n*-ary tree is one that has no limitation on the number of children each parent node may contain. This is in contrast to the binary tree in Recipe 11.6, in which each parent node may contain only two children nodes.

NTree<T> is a simple class that contains only a constructor and three public methods. Through this object, you can create an *n*-ary tree, set the root node, and obtain the root node in order to navigate and manipulate the tree. An NTree<T> object that can contain at most three children is created in the following manner:

```
NTree<string> topLevel = new NTree<string>(3);
```

An NTree<T> object that can contain at most int.MaxValue children, which allows greater flexibility, is created in the following manner:

```
NTree<string> topLevel = new NTree<string>();
```

The real work is done in the NTreeNodeFactory<T> object and the NTreeNode<U> object, which is nested in the NTreeNodeFactory<T> class. The NTreeNodeFactory<T> class is an object factory that facilitates the construction of all NTreeNode<U> objects. When the factory object is created, the NTree<T> object is passed in to the constructor, as shown here:

```
NTreeNodeFactory<string> nodeFactory = new NTreeNodeFactory<string>(topLevel);
```

Therefore, when the factory object is created, it knows the maximum number of children that a parent node may have. The factory object provides a public method, CreateNode, that allows for the creation of an NTreeNode<U> object. If an IComparable<T> type object is passed into this method, the IComparable<T> object will be contained within this new node in the nodeValue field. If a null is passed in, the new NTreeNode<U> object will contain the object U with it initialized using the default keyword. The String object can be passed in to this parameter with no modifications. Node creation is performed in the following manner:

```
NTreeNode<string> one = nodeFactory.CreateNode("One");
NTreeNode<string> two = nodeFactory.CreateNode("Two");
NTreeNode<string> three = nodeFactory.CreateNode("Three");
NTreeNode<string> four = nodeFactory.CreateNode("Four");
NTreeNode<string> five = nodeFactory.CreateNode("Five");
```

```
NTreeNode<string> six = nodeFactory.CreateNode("Six");
NTreeNode<string> seven = nodeFactory.CreateNode("Seven");
NTreeNode<string> eight = nodeFactory.CreateNode("Eight");
NTreeNode<string> nine = nodeFactory.CreateNode("Nine");
```

The NTreeNode<U> class is nested within the factory class; it is not supposed to be used directly to create a node object. Instead, the factory will create a node object and return it to the caller. NTreeNode<U> has one constructor that accepts two parameters: value, which is an object of type U used to store an object implementing the IComparable<T> interface; and an integer value, maxChildren, which is used to define the total number of child nodes allowed. It is the nodeValue field that you use when you are searching the tree for a particular item.

Adding a root node to the TopLevel NTree<T> object is performed using the AddRoot method of the NTree<T> object:

```
topLevel.AddRoot(one);
```

Each NTreeNode<U> object contains a field called childNodes. This field is an array containing all child nodes attached to this parent node object. The maximum number of children—obtained from the factory class—provides this number, which is used to create the fixed-size array. This array is initialized in the constructor of the NTreeNode<U> object.

The following code shows how to add nodes to this tree:

```
// Add nodes to root.
topLevel.GetRoot().AddNode(two);
topLevel.GetRoot().AddNode(three);
topLevel.GetRoot().AddNode(four);

// Add node to the first node Two of the root.
topLevel.GetRoot().Children[0].AddNode(five);

// Add node to the previous node added, node five.
topLevel.GetRoot().BreadthFirstSearch("Five").AddNode(six);
```

The searching method BreadthFirstSearch is constructed similarly to the way the same method was constructed for the binary tree in Recipe 11.6. The DepthFirstSearch method is constructed a little differently from the same method in the binary tree. This method uses recursion to search the tree, but it uses a for loop to iterate over the array of child nodes, searching each one in turn. In addition, the current node is checked first to determine whether it matches the targetObj parameter to this method. This is a better performing design, as opposed to moving this test to the end of the method.

If the RemoveNode method is successful, the array containing all child nodes of the current node is compacted to prevent fragmentation, which allows nodes to be added later in a much simpler manner. The AddNode method only has to add the child node to the end of this array as opposed to searching the array for an open element. The following code shows how to remove a node:

```
// Remove all nodes below node 'Two'.
// Nodes 'Five' and 'Six' are removed.
topLevel.GetRoot().BreadthFirstSearch("Two").RemoveNode(0);

// Remove node 'Three' from the root node.
topLevel.GetRoot().RemoveNode(1);
```

See Also

See the "Queue<T> Class" and "IComparable Interface" topics in the MSDN documentation.

11.8 Creating a Set Object

Problem

You need an object that contains a group of unordered objects. This object must be able to be compared to other objects containing sets of data. In addition, the two must be able to have the following actions performed on them:

- Union of the items contained by the two objects containing sets of data
- Intersection of the items contained by the two objects containing sets of data
- Difference of the items contained by the two objects containing sets of data

Solution

Create a Set<T> object, the code for which is shown in Example 11-17.

Example 11-17. Set class

```
using System;
using System.Collections;
using System.Collections.Generic;
using System.Text;


public class Set<T> : IEnumerable<T>
{
    private List<T> internalSet = new List<T>();

    public int Count
    {
        get {return (internalSet.Count);}
    }

    public T this[int index]
    {
        get
        {
            return (internalSet[index]);
```

Example 11-17. Set class (continued)

```
        }
        set
        {
            if (internalSet.Contains(value))
            {
                throw (new ArgumentException(
                        "Duplicate object cannot be added to this set.", "index"));
            }
            else
            {
                internalSet[index] = value;
            }
        }
    }

    public void Add(T obj)
    {
        if (internalSet.Contains(obj))
        {
            throw (new ArgumentException(
                    "Duplicate object cannot be added to this set.", "obj"));
        }
        else
        {
            internalSet.Add(obj);
        }
    }

    public void Remove(T obj)
    {
        if (!internalSet.Contains(obj))
        {
            throw (new ArgumentException("Object cannot be removed from " +
                    "this set because it does not exist in this set.", "obj"));
        }
        else
        {
            internalSet.Remove(obj);
        }
    }

    public void RemoveAt(int index)
    {
        internalSet.RemoveAt(index);
    }

    public bool Contains(T obj)
    {
        return (internalSet.Contains(obj));
    }

    public static Set<T> operator |(Set<T> lhs, Set<T> rhs)
```

Example 11-17. Set class (continued)

```
{
    return (lhs.UnionOf(rhs));
}

public Set<T> UnionOf(Set<T> set)
{
    Set<T> unionSet = new Set<T>( );
    Set<T> sourceSet = null;
    Set<T> mergeSet = null;

    if (set.Count > this.Count)   // An optimization
    {
        sourceSet = set;
        mergeSet = this;
    }
    else
    {
        sourceSet = this;
        mergeSet = set;
    }

    // Initialize unionSet with the entire SourceSet.
    for (int index = 0; index < sourceSet.Count; index++)
    {
        unionSet.Add(sourceSet.internalSet[index]);
    }

    // mergeSet OR sourceSet
    for (int index = 0; index < mergeSet.Count; index++)
    {
        if (!sourceSet.Contains(mergeSet.internalSet[index]))
        {
            unionSet.Add(mergeSet.internalSet[index]);
        }
    }

    return (unionSet);
}

public static Set<T> operator &(Set<T> lhs, Set<T> rhs)
{
    return (lhs.IntersectionOf(rhs));
}

public Set<T> IntersectionOf(Set<T> set)
{
    Set<T> intersectionSet = new Set<T>( );
    Set<T> sourceSet = null;
    Set<T> mergeSet = null;

    if (set.Count > this.Count)   // An optimization
    {
```

Example 11-17. Set class (continued)

```
            sourceSet = set;
            mergeSet = this;
        }
        else
        {
            sourceSet = this;
            mergeSet = set;
        }

        // mergeSet AND sourceSet
        for (int index = 0; index < mergeSet.Count; index++)
        {
            if (sourceSet.Contains(mergeSet.internalSet[index]))
            {
                intersectionSet.Add(mergeSet.internalSet[index]);
            }
        }

        return (intersectionSet);
    }

    public static Set<T> operator ^(Set<T> lhs, Set<T> rhs)
    {
        return (lhs.DifferenceOf(rhs));
    }

    public Set<T> DifferenceOf(Set<T> set)
    {
        Set<T> differenceSet = new Set<T>();

        // mergeSet XOR sourceSet
        for (int index = 0; index < set.Count; index++)
        {
            if (!this.Contains(set.internalSet[index]))
            {
                differenceSet.Add(set.internalSet[index]);
            }
        }

        for (int index = 0; index < this.Count; index++)
        {
            if (!set.Contains(internalSet[index]))
            {
                differenceSet.Add(internalSet[index]);
            }
        }

        return (differenceSet);
    }

    public static bool operator ==(Set<T> lhs, Set<T> rhs)
    {
```

Example 11-17. Set class (continued)

```
        return (lhs.Equals(rhs));
    }

    public static bool operator !=(Set<T> lhs, Set<T> rhs)
    {
        return (!lhs.Equals(rhs));
    }

    public override bool Equals(object obj)
    {
        bool isEquals = false;

        if (obj != null)
        {
            if (obj is Set<T>)
            {
                if (this.Count == ((Set<T>)obj).Count)
                {
                    if (this.IsSubsetOf((Set<T>)obj) &&
                        ((Set<T>)obj).IsSubsetOf(this))
                    {
                        isEquals = true;
                    }
                }
            }
        }

        return (isEquals);
    }

    public override int GetHashCode( )
    {
        return (internalSet.GetHashCode( ));
    }

    public bool IsSubsetOf(Set<T> set)
    {
        for (int index = 0; index < this.Count; index++)
        {
            if (!set.Contains(internalSet[index]))
            {
                return (false);
            }
        }

        return (true);
    }

    public bool IsSupersetOf(Set<T> set)
    {
        for (int index = 0; index < set.Count; index++)
        {
```

Example 11-17. Set class (continued)

```
            if (!this.Contains(set.internalSet[index]))
            {
                return (false);
            }
        }

        return (true);
    }

    public string DisplaySet( )
    {
        if (this.Count == 0)
        {
            return ("{}");
        }
        else
        {
            StringBuilder displayStr = new StringBuilder("{ ");

            for (int index = 0; index < (this.Count - 1); index++)
            {
                displayStr.Append(internalSet[index]);
                displayStr.Append(", ");
            }

            displayStr.Append(internalSet[internalSet.Count - 1]);
            displayStr.Append(" }");

            return (displayStr.ToString( ));
        }
    }

    public IEnumerator GetEnumerator( )
    {
        for (int cntr = 0; cntr < internalSet.Count; cntr++)
        {
            yield return (internalSet[cntr]);
        }
    }

    IEnumerator<T> IEnumerable<T>.GetEnumerator( )
    {
        for (int cntr = 0; cntr < internalSet.Count; cntr++)
        {
            yield return (internalSet[cntr]);
        }
    }
}
```

The methods defined in Table 11-9 are of particular interest to using a Set<T> object.

Table 11-9. Members of the Set<T> class

Member	Description
Count property	Read-only property to return the number of objects within this Set<T> object. Its syntax is: `int Count {get;}`
Indexer	Allows the Set<T> object to operate in a manner similar to an array. Its syntax is: `this[int index] {get; set;}`
Add method	Add a new object to the current Set<T> object. Its syntax is: `Add(T obj)` where *obj* is the object of type T to add to this Set.
Remove method	Removes an existing object from the current Set<T> object. Its syntax is: `Remove(T obj)` where *obj* is the object of type T to remove from this Set.
RemoveAt method	Removes an existing object from the current Set<T> object using an index. Its syntax is: `Add(int index)` where *index* is the index where the object to be removed is stored.
Contains method	Returns a Boolean indicating whether the object passed in exists within this Set<T> object. If a true is returned, the object exists; otherwise, it does not. Its syntax is: `Contains(T obj)` where *obj* is the object of type T to be searched for.
UnionOf method	Performs a union operation on the current Set<T> object and a second Set<T> object. A new Set<T> object is returned containing the union of these two Set<T> objects. Its syntax is: `UnionOf(Set<T> set)` where *set* is the second Set<T> object.
Overloaded | operator	This operator delegates its work to the UnionOf method.
IntersectionOf method	Performs an intersection operation on the current Set<T> object and a second Set<T> object. A new Set<T> object is returned containing the intersection of these two Set<T> objects. Its syntax is: `IntersectionOf(Set<T> set)` where *set* is the second Set<T> object.
Overloaded & operator	This operator delegates its work to the IntersectionOf method.
DifferenceOf method	Performs a difference operation on the current Set<T> object and a second Set<T> object. A new Set<T> object is returned containing the difference of these two Set<T> objects. Its syntax is: `DifferenceOf(Set<T> set)` where *set* is the second Set<T> object.
Overloaded ^ operator	This operator delegates its work to the DifferenceOf method.
Overloaded Equals method	Returns a Boolean indicating whether a second Set<T> object is equal to the current Set<T> object. Its syntax is: `Equals(object obj)` where *obj* is the second Set<T> object.
Overloaded == operator	This operator delegates its work to the Equals method.

Table 11-9. Members of the Set<T> class (continued)

Member	Description
Overloaded != operator	This operator delegates its work to the Equals method. However, this operator takes the inverse of the Boolean returned from the Equals method and returns this new value.
Overridden GetHashCode method	Returns the hash code of the internal List<T> used to hold the objects contained in this Set<T> object. Its syntax is: `GetHashCode( )`
IsSubsetOf method	Returns a Boolean indicating whether the current Set<T> object is a subset of a second Set<T> object. Its syntax is: `IsSubsetOf(Set<T> set)` where *set* is the second Set<T> object.
IsSupersetOf method	Returns a Boolean indicating whether the current Set<T> object is a superset of a second Set<T> object. Its syntax is: `IsSupersetOf(Set<T> set)` where *set* is the second Set<T> object.

DisplaySet method	Displays all objects within the current Set<T> object in the following format:
	
	`{Obj1, Obj2, Obj3, ...}`
	
	Its syntax is:
	
	`DisplaySet( )`

Example 11-18 illustrates the use of the Set <T> class.

Example 11-18. Using the Set <T> class

```
public static void TestSet( )
{
    Set<int> set1 = new Set<int>( );
    Set<int> set2 = new Set<int>( );
    Set<int> set3 = new Set<int>( );

    set1.Add(1);
    set1.Add(2);
    set1.Add(3);
    set1.Add(4);
    set1.Add(5);
    set1.Add(6);

    set2.Add(-10);
    set2.Add(2);
    set2.Add(40);

    set3.Add(3);
    set3.Add(6);

    foreach (int o in set2)
    {
        Console.WriteLine(o.ToString( ));
    }
```

Example 11-18. Using the Set <T> class (continued)

```
    Console.WriteLine("set1.Contains(2): " + set1.Contains(2));
    Console.WriteLine("set1.Contains(0): " + set1.Contains(0));

    Console.WriteLine("\r\nset1.Count: " + set1.Count);
    Console.WriteLine();

    Console.WriteLine("set1.DisplaySet: " + set1.DisplaySet());
    Console.WriteLine("set2.DisplaySet: " + set2.DisplaySet());
    Console.WriteLine("set3.DisplaySet: " + set3.DisplaySet());
    Console.WriteLine();

    Console.WriteLine("set1.UnionOf(set2): " +
                      set1.UnionOf(set2).DisplaySet());
    Console.WriteLine("set1.IntersectionOf(set2): " +
                      set1.IntersectionOf(set2).DisplaySet());
    Console.WriteLine("set1.DifferenceOf(set2): " +
                      set1.DifferenceOf(set2).DisplaySet());
    Console.WriteLine("set1 | set2: " + (set1 | set2).DisplaySet());
    Console.WriteLine("set1 & set2: " + (set1 & set2).DisplaySet());
    Console.WriteLine("set1 ^ set2: " + (set1 ^ set2).DisplaySet());
    Console.WriteLine("set1.Equals(set2): " + set1.Equals(set2));
    Console.WriteLine("set1 == set2: " + (set1 == set2));
    Console.WriteLine("set1 != set2: " + (set1 != set2));
    Console.WriteLine("set1.IsSubsetOf(set2): " + set1.IsSubsetOf(set2));
    Console.WriteLine("set1.IsSupersetOf(set2): " + set1.IsSupersetOf(set2));
    Console.WriteLine();

    Console.WriteLine("set2.UnionOf(set1): " +
                      set2.UnionOf(set1).DisplaySet());
    Console.WriteLine("set2.IntersectionOf(set1): " +
                      set2.IntersectionOf(set1).DisplaySet());
    Console.WriteLine("set2.DifferenceOf(set1): " +
                      set2.DifferenceOf(set1).DisplaySet());
    Console.WriteLine("set2.Equals(set1): " + set2.Equals(set1));
    Console.WriteLine("set2 == set1: " + (set2 == set1));
    Console.WriteLine("set2 != set1: " + (set2 != set1));
    Console.WriteLine("set2.IsSubsetOf(set1): " + set2.IsSubsetOf(set1));
    Console.WriteLine("set2.IsSupersetOf(set1): " + set2.IsSupersetOf(set1));
    Console.WriteLine();

    Console.WriteLine("set3.UnionOf(set1): " +
                      set3.UnionOf(set1).DisplaySet());
    Console.WriteLine("set3.IntersectionOf(set1): " +
                      set3.IntersectionOf(set1).DisplaySet());
    Console.WriteLine("set3.DifferenceOf(set1): " +
                      set3.DifferenceOf(set1).DisplaySet());
    Console.WriteLine("set3.Equals(set1): " + set3.Equals(set1));
    Console.WriteLine("set3 == set1: " + (set3 == set1));
    Console.WriteLine("set3 != set1: " + (set3 != set1));
    Console.WriteLine("set3.IsSubsetOf(set1): " + set3.IsSubsetOf(set1));
```

Example 11-18. Using the Set <T> class (continued)

```
    Console.WriteLine("set3.IsSupersetOf(set1): " + set3.IsSupersetOf(set1));
    Console.WriteLine("set1.IsSubsetOf(set3): " + set1.IsSubsetOf(set3));
    Console.WriteLine("set1.IsSupersetOf(set3): " + set1.IsSupersetOf(set3));

    Console.WriteLine();
    Console.WriteLine("set3.UnionOf(set2): " +
                        set3.UnionOf(set2).DisplaySet());
    Console.WriteLine("set3.IntersectionOf(set2): " +
                        set3.IntersectionOf(set2).DisplaySet());
    Console.WriteLine("set3.DifferenceOf(set2): " +
                        set3.DifferenceOf(set2).DisplaySet());
    Console.WriteLine("set3 | set2: " + (set3 | set2).DisplaySet());
    Console.WriteLine("set3 & set2: " + (set3 & set2).DisplaySet());
    Console.WriteLine("set3 ^ set2: " + (set3 ^ set2).DisplaySet());
    Console.WriteLine("set3.Equals(set2): " + set3.Equals(set2));
    Console.WriteLine("set3 == set2: " + (set3 == set2));
    Console.WriteLine("set3 != set2: " + (set3 != set2));
    Console.WriteLine("set3.IsSubsetOf(set2): " + set3.IsSubsetOf(set2));
    Console.WriteLine("set3.IsSupersetOf(set2): " + set3.IsSupersetOf(set2));
    Console.WriteLine();

    Console.WriteLine("set3.Equals(set3): " + set3.Equals(set3));
    Console.WriteLine("set3 == set3: " + (set3 == set3));
    Console.WriteLine("set3 != set3: " + (set3 != set3));
    Console.WriteLine("set3.IsSubsetOf(set3): " + set3.IsSubsetOf(set3));
    Console.WriteLine("set3.IsSupersetOf(set3): " + set3.IsSupersetOf(set3));

    Console.WriteLine("set1[1]: " + set1[1].ToString());
    set1[1] = 100;

    set1.RemoveAt(1);
    set1.RemoveAt(2);
    Console.WriteLine("set1: " + set1.DisplaySet());
}
```

The output for this method is shown here:

```
 -10
2
40
set1.Contains(2): True
set1.Contains(0): False

set1.Count: 6

set1.DisplaySet: { 1, 2, 3, 4, 5, 6 }
set2.DisplaySet: { -10, 2, 40 }
set3.DisplaySet: { 3, 6 }

set1.UnionOf(set2): { 1, 2, 3, 4, 5, 6, -10, 40 }
set1.IntersectionOf(set2): { 2 }
```

```
set1.DifferenceOf(set2): { -10, 40, 1, 3, 4, 5, 6 }
set1 | set2: { 1, 2, 3, 4, 5, 6, -10, 40 }
set1 & set2: { 2 }
set1 ^ set2: { -10, 40, 1, 3, 4, 5, 6 }
set1.Equals(set2): False
set1 == set2: False
set1 != set2: True
set1.IsSubsetOf(set2): False
set1.IsSupersetOf(set2): False

set2.UnionOf(set1): { 1, 2, 3, 4, 5, 6, -10, 40 }
set2.IntersectionOf(set1): { 2 }
set2.DifferenceOf(set1): { 1, 3, 4, 5, 6, -10, 40 }
set2.Equals(set1): False
set2 == set1): False
set2 != set1): True
set2.IsSubsetOf(set1): False
set2.IsSupersetOf(set1): False

set3.UnionOf(set1): { 1, 2, 3, 4, 5, 6 }
set3.IntersectionOf(set1): { 3, 6 }
set3.DifferenceOf(set1): { 1, 2, 4, 5 }
set3.Equals(set1): False
set3 == set1: False
set3 != set1: True
set3.IsSubsetOf(set1): True
set3.IsSupersetOf(set1): False
set1.IsSubsetOf(set3): False
set1.IsSupersetOf(set3): True

set3.UnionOf(set2): { -10, 2, 40, 3, 6 }
set3.IntersectionOf(set2): {}
set3.DifferenceOf(set2): { -10, 2, 40, 3, 6 }
set3 | set2: { -10, 2, 40, 3, 6 }
set3 & set2: {}
set3 ^ set2: { -10, 2, 40, 3, 6 }
set3.Equals(set2): False
set3 == set2: False
set3 != set2: True
set3.IsSubsetOf(set2): False
set3.IsSupersetOf(set2): False

set3.Equals(set3): True
set3 == set3: True
set3 != set3: False
set3.IsSubsetOf(set3): True
set3.IsSupersetOf(set3): True
set1[1]: 2
set1: { 1, 3, 5, 6 }
```

Discussion

Sets are containers that hold a group of homogeneous object types. Various mathematical operations can be performed on sets, including the following:

Union

  (A ∪ B)

  Combines all elements of set A and set B into a resulting Set<T> object. If an object exists in both sets, the resulting unioned Set<T> object contains only one of those elements, not both.

Intersection

  (A ∩ B)

  Combines all elements of set A and set B that are common to both A and B into a resulting Set<T> object. If an object exists in one set and not the other, the element is not added to the intersectioned Set<T> object.

Difference

  (A-B)

  Combines all elements of set A, except for the elements that are also members of set B, into a resulting Set<T> object. If an object exists in both sets A and B, it is not added to the final differenced Set<T> object. The difference is equivalent to taking the union of both sets and the intersection of both sets and then removing all elements in the unioned set that exist in the intersectioned set.

Subset

  (A ⊂ B)

  Returns true if all elements of set A are contained in a second set B; otherwise, it returns false. Set B may contain elements not found in A.

Superset

  (A ⊃ B)

  Returns true if all elements of set A are contained in a second set B; otherwise, it returns false. Set A may contain elements not found in B.

Equivalence

  (A == B)

  Returns true if both Set<T> objects contain the same number of elements and the same value for each element; otherwise, it returns false. This is equivalent to stating that (A ⊂ B) and (B ⊂ A). Nonequivalence is defined by the != operator. Note that the .NET Equals method can be used to test for equivalence.

The Set<T> class wraps a List<T> (internalSet), which contains all elements of that set. Many of the methods exposed by the Set<T> class are delegated to the internalSet List<T>. Of these wrapped methods, the Add method requires some discussion. This method prevents a duplicate object from being added to the Set<T> object. This is a property of sets—no set may contain duplicate elements at any time.

Calling the Contains method of the internalSet List<T>, to determine whether the new object is already contained in this Set<T> object, performs this check. This check is also performed in the set accessor of the indexer.

The following code creates and populates two Set<T> objects:

```
Set<int> set1 = new Set<int>();
Set<int> set2 = new Set<int>();

set1.Add(1);
set1.Add(2);
set1.Add(3);
set1.Add(4);
set1.Add(5);
set1.Add(6);

set2.Add(-10);
set2.Add(2);
set2.Add(40);
```

The union operation can be performed in one of two ways. The first is to use the UnionOf method and pass in a Set<T> with which to union this Set<T>. The Set<T> class also overrides the | operator to provide this same functionality. Notice that the OR operator is shorthand for the union operation. Essentially, the resulting set contains elements that exist in either of the two Set<T> objects or both Set<T> objects. The following code shows how both of these operations are performed:

```
Set<int> resultingUnionSet = set1.UnionOf(set2);
resultingUnionSet = set1 | set2;
```

The intersection operation is set up similarly to the union operation. There are two ways to perform an intersection between two Set<T> objects: the first is to use the IntersectionOf method; the second is to use the overloaded & operator. Once again, notice that the logic of the AND operator is the same as the intersection operation. Essentially, an element must be in both Set<T> A and Set<T> B in order for it to be placed in the resulting Set<T> object. The following code demonstrates the intersection operation:

```
Set<int> resultingIntersectSet = set1.IntersectionOf(set2);
resultingIntersectSet = set1 & set2;
```

The difference operation is performed either through the overloaded ^ operator or the DifferenceOf method. Notice that the XOR operation is similar to taking the difference of two sets. Essentially, only elements in either set, but not both, are placed in the resulting set. The following code demonstrates the difference operation:

```
Set<int> resultingDiffSet = set1.DifferenceOf(set2);
resultingDiffSet = set1 ^ set2;
```

The subset operation is performed only through a single method called IsSubsetOf. The superset operation is also performed using a single method called IsSupersetOf. The following code demonstrates these two operations:

```
bool isSubset = set1.IsSubsetOf(set2);
bool isSuperset = set1.IsSupersetOf(set2);
```

The equivalence operation is performed using either the overloaded == operator or the Equals method. Since the == operator was overloaded, the != operator must also be overloaded. The != operator returns the inverse of the == operator or Equals method. The following code demonstrates these three operations:

```
bool isEqual = set1.Equals(set2);
isEqual = set1 == set2;
bool isNotEqual = set1 != set2;
```

See Also

See the "List<T> Class," "Overloadable Operators," and "Operator Overloading Tutorial" topics in the MSDN documentation.

CHAPTER 12

Filesystem I/O

12.0 Introduction

This chapter deals with the filesystem in four distinct ways. The first set of recipes looks at typical file interactions like:

- Creation
- Reading and writing
- Deletion
- Attributes
- Encoding methods for character data
- Selecting the correct way (based on usage) to access files via streams

The second set looks at directory- or folder-based programming tasks such as file creation as well as renaming, deleting, and determining attributes. The third set deals with the parsing of paths and the use of temporary files and paths. The fourth set deals with more advanced topics in filesystem I/O, such as:

- Asynchronous reads and writes
- Monitoring for certain filesystem actions
- Version information in files
- Using P/Invoke to perform file I/O

The file-interactions section comes first since it sets the stage for many of the recipes in the temporary file and advanced sections. This is fundamental knowledge that will help you understand the other file I/O recipes and how to modify them for your purposes. The various file and directory I/O techniques are used throughout the more advanced examples to help show a couple of different ways to approach the problems you will encounter working with filesystem I/O.

Unless otherwise specified, you need the following using statements in any program that uses snippets or methods from this chapter:

```
using System;
using System.IO;
```

12.1 Creating, Copying, Moving, or Deleting a File

Problem

You need to create a new file, copy an existing file, move an existing file, or delete a file.

Solution

The System.IO namespace contains two classes to perform these actions: the File and FileInfo classes. The File class contains only static methods, while the FileInfo class contains only instance methods.

File's static Create method returns an instance of the FileStream class, which you can use to read from or write to the newly created file. For example, the following code uses the static Create method of the File class to create a new file:

```
FileStream fileStream = null;
if (!File.Exists(@"c:\delete\test\test.txt"))
{
    using(fileStream = File.Create(@"c:\delete\test\test.txt"))
    {
        // Use the fileStream var here...
    }
}
```

The Create instance method of the FileInfo class takes no parameters. You should supply the path with a filename as the only parameter to the FileInfo class constructor. The method returns an instance of the FileStream class that you can use to read from or write to the newly created file. For example, the following code uses the Create instance method of the FileInfo class to create a new file:

```
FileInfo fileInfo = null;
FileStream fileStream = null;
if (!File.Exists (@"c:\delete\test\test.txt"))
{
    fileInfo = new FileInfo(@"c:\delete\test\test.txt");
    using(fileStream = fileInfo.Create( ))
    {
        // Use the fileStream var here...
    }
}
```

You can copy a file using the overloaded static `File.Copy` method that returns void. The third parameter of one of the overrides for this function allows you to pass `true` or `false` depending upon whether you want to overwrite an existing destination file, as shown in the following code, which uses the static `Copy` method of the `File` class to copy a file:

```
if (File.Exists(@"c:\delete\test\test.txt"))
{
    File.Copy(@"c:\delete\test\test.txt ",
             Path.Combine(Directory.GetCurrentDirectory( ), @"\test.txt"),
             true);
}
```

The overloaded `CopyTo` instance method returns a `FileInfo` object that represents the newly copied file. This method can also take a Boolean in one of the overrides to signify your intent to overwrite an existing file. For example, the following code uses the `CopyTo` instance method of the `FileInfo` class to copy a file:

```
FileInfo fileInfo = new FileInfo(@"c:\delete\test\test.txt");
fileInfo.CopyTo(@"c:\test.txt", true);
```

You can move a file using the static `Move` method of the `File` class, which returns void. For example, the following code uses the static `Move` method to move a file after checking for its existence:

```
if (!File.Exists(Path.Combine(Directory.GetCurrentDirectory( ),
    @"\test.txt")))
{
    File.Move(@"c:\delete\test\test.txt",
        Path.Combine(Directory.GetCurrentDirectory( ), @"\test.txt"));
}
```

The `MoveTo` instance method is the way to move a file using the `FileInfo` class. For example, the following code moves a file using the `MoveTo` instance method of the `FileInfo` class after checking for the file's existence:

```
FileInfo fileInfo = new FileInfo(@"c:\delete\test\test.txt");
if (!File.Exists(@"c:\test.txt"))
{
    fileInfo.MoveTo(@"c:\test.txt");
}
```

You can delete a file using the static `Delete` method of the `File` class that returns void. For example, the following code uses the static `Delete` method to delete a file:

```
if (File.Exists(Path.Combine(Directory.GetCurrentDirectory( ),
    @"\test.txt")))
{
    File.Delete(Path.Combine(Directory.GetCurrentDirectory( ),
             @"\test.txt"));
}
```

The Delete instance method on the FileInfo class takes no parameters and returns void. For example, the following code uses the Delete instance method of the FileInfo class to delete a file:

```
if(File.Exists(@"c:\delete\test\test.txt"))
{
    FileInfo fileInfo = new FileInfo(@"c:\delete\test\test.txt");
    fileInfo.Delete( );
}
```

Discussion

Whether you choose to call the static or instance file-operation methods depends on what you are trying to accomplish. If you need a quick way of creating, moving, copying, or deleting a file, consider using the static methods. If you will be performing multiple operations on a file, such as creating, moving, and changing its attributes, you should consider the instance methods of the FileInfo class. Another consideration is that static methods on a class do not require an object to be created on the managed heap and subsequently destroyed by the garbage collector. Instance methods require an object to be created before the methods can be called. If you are trying to minimize the number of objects the garbage collector has to manage, consider using static methods.

A few items to note when using the file functions:

- If the directory doesn't exist, the method won't create it and you'll get an exception. See how to check whether a directory exists in Recipe 12.4.
- If no path is provided, the file will land in the current working directory. If the user does not have permission to write to the current working directory (as with a normal user writing to the *Program Files* directory), this will result in an UnauthorizedAccessException.
- If a relative path is provided (for example, *C:\dir1\dir2\..\..\file.txt*), it will be evaluated properly.
- If an absolute path is provided, the method will succeed as expected.

When creating a new file, you should first determine whether that file already exists. The default creation behavior of the file classes is either to overwrite the existing file silently or, if the file is read-only, to throw an exception. The File and FileInfo classes both contain a method, Exists, to test for a file's existence. Once it is determined that the file does not exist, we can create it using either the static or instance Create methods. Note that this does leave a small window open between the time you checked and the time that the creation starts, so it is not a replacement for proper exception and error handling of the Create call.

See Also

See the "File Class" and "FileInfo Class" topics in the MSDN documentation.

12.2   Manipulating File Attributes

Problem

You need to display or manipulate a file's attributes or timestamps.

Solution

To display a file's timestamps, you can use either the static methods of the File class or the instance properties of the FileInfo class. The static methods are GetCreationTime, GetLastAccessTime, and GetLastWriteTime. Each has a single parameter, the path and name of the file for which timestamp information is to be returned, and returns a DateTime value containing the relevant timestamp. For example:

```
public static void DisplayFileAttr(string path)
{
    Console.WriteLine(File.GetCreationTime(path));
    Console.WriteLine(File.GetLastAccessTime(path));
    Console.WriteLine(File.GetLastWriteTime(path));
}
```

The instance properties of the FileInfo class are CreationTime, LastAccessTime, and LastWriteTime. Each returns a DateTime value containing the respective timestamp of the file represented by the FileInfo object. The following code illustrates their use:

```
public static void DisplayFileAttr(string path)
{
    FileInfo fileInfo = new FileInfo(path);

    Console.WriteLine(fileInfo.CreationTime);
    Console.WriteLine(fileInfo.LastAccessTime);
    Console.WriteLine(fileInfo.LastWriteTime);
}
```

Using an instance of the FileInfo class is preferable to using the equivalent methods on the static File class (i.e., File.GetCreationTime, File.GetLastAccessTime, and File. GetLastWriteTime) as far as performance is concerned. This is because of the extra time it takes for the underlying implementation of the static methods to get information about the file handle each time a static method is called, as opposed to one time for the FileInfo instance object, which already holds this file handle information.

To modify a file's timestamps, you can use either the static methods of the File class or the instance properties of the FileInfo class. The static methods are SetCreationTime, SetLastAccessTime, and SetLastWriteTime. All of them take the path and name of the file for which the timestamp is to be modified as the first parameter and a DateTime value containing the new timestamp as the second, and each returns void. For example:

```
public static void ModifyFileAttr(string path)
{
    File.SetCreationTime(path, DateTime.Parse(@"May 10, 2003"));
```

```
    File.SetLastAccessTime(path, DateTime.Parse(@"May 10, 2003"));
    File.SetLastWriteTime(path, DateTime.Parse(@"May 10, 2003"));
}
```

The instance properties are the same as the properties used to display timestamp information: CreationTime, LastAccessTime, or LastWriteTime. To set the timestamp, assign a value of type DateTime to the relevant timestamp property. For example:

```
public static void ModifyFileAttr(string path)
{
    FileInfo fileInfo  = new FileInfo(path);

    DateTime dt = new DateTime(2001,2,8);
    fileInfo.CreationTime = dt;
    fileInfo.LastAccessTime = dt;
    fileInfo.LastWriteTime = dt;
}
```

To display or modify a file's attributes, use the instance Attributes property. The property's value is a bit mask consisting of one or more members of the FileAttributes enumeration. For example, the following code:

```
public static void ViewModifyFileAttr(string path)
{
    if (File.Exists(path))
    {
        FileInfo fileInfo = new FileInfo(path);

        // Display this file's attributes.
        Console.WriteLine(fileInfo.Attributes);

        // Display whether this file is hidden.
        Console.WriteLine("Is file hidden? = {0}",
            ((fileInfo.Attributes & FileAttributes.Hidden) == FileAttributes.Hidden));

        // Modify this file's attributes.
        fileInfo.Attributes |= FileAttributes.Hidden;
    }
}
```

Discussion

One of the easier methods of creating a DateTime object is to use the static DateTime. Parse method. This method accepts a string defining a particular date and is converted to a DateTime object.

In addition to timestamp information, a file's attributes may also be obtained and modified. This is accomplished through the use of the public instance Attributes property found on a FileInfo object. This property returns or modifies a FileAttributes enumeration. The FileAttributes enumeration is made up of bit flags that can be turned on or off through the use of the bitwise operators &, |, or ^.

Table 12-1 lists each of the flags in the FileAttributes enumeration.

Table 12-1. *FileAttributes enumeration values*

Member name	Description
Archive	Represents the file's archive status that marks the file for backup or removal.
Compressed	Indicates that the file is compressed.
Device	This option is reserved for future use.
Directory	Indicates that this is a directory.
Encrypted	Indicates that a file or directory is encrypted. In the case of a file, its contents are encrypted. In the case of a directory, newly created files will be encrypted by default.
Hidden	Indicates a hidden file.
Normal	Indicates that the file has no other attributes; as such, this attribute cannot be used in combination with others.
NotContentIndexed	Indicates that the file is excluded from the content index service.
Offline	Indicates that the state of the file is offline and its contents will be unavailable.
ReadOnly	Indicates that the file is read-only.
ReparsePoint	Indicates a *reparse point*, a block of data associated with a directory or file.
SparseFile	Indicates a sparse file, which may take up less space on the filesystem than its reported size because zeros in the file are not actually allocated on-disk.
System	Indicates that the file is a system file.
Temporary	Indicates a temporary file. It may reside entirely in memory.

In many cases, more than one of these flags can be set at one time, but see the description for the Normal flag, which must be used alone.

See Also

See the "File Class," "FileInfo Class," and "FileAttributes Enumeration" topics in the MSDN documentation.

12.3 Renaming a File

Problem

You need to rename a file.

Solution

With all of the bells and whistles hanging off the .NET Framework, you would figure that renaming a file is easy. Unfortunately, there is no specific rename method that can be used to rename a file. Instead, you can use the static Move method of the

File class or the instance MoveTo method of the FileInfo class. The static File.Move method can be used to rename a file in the following manner:

```
public static void RenameFile(string originalName, string newName)
{
    File.Move(originalName, newName);
}
```

This code has the effect of renaming the *originalName* file to *newName*.

The FileInfo.MoveTo instance method can also be used to rename a file in the following manner:

```
public static void RenameFile(FileInfo originalFile, string newName)
{
    originalFile.MoveTo(newName);
}
```

Discussion

The Move and MoveTo methods allow a file to be moved to a different location, but they can also be used to rename files. For example, you could use RenameFile to rename a file from *foo.txt* to *bar.dat*:

```
RenameFile("foo.txt","bar.dat");
```

You could also use fully qualified paths to rename them:

```
RenameFile("c:\mydir\foo.txt","c:\mydir\bar.dat");
```

See Also

See the "File Class" and "FileInfo Class" topics in the MSDN documentation.

12.4 Determining Whether a File Exists

Problem

You need to determine whether a file exists prior to creating or performing an action on that file.

Solution

Use the static Exists method of the File class to determine whether a file currently exists:

```
if (File.Exists(@"c:\delete\test\test.txt"))
{
    // Operate on that file here.
}
```

Discussion

Determining whether a file exists is often critical to your code. If a file exists and you try to create it using one of the file-creation methods, one of three things will happen: the existing file will be overwritten, an exception will be thrown if the file is read-only, or an exception will be thrown indicating that the state of the filesystem is not what you think it is. There is a small window between the Exists call and the actions you take where another process could change the filesystem, so you should be prepared for that with proper exception handling.

See Also

See the "File Class" topic in the MSDN documentation.

12.5 Choosing a Method of Opening a File or Stream for Reading and/or Writing

Problem

When you are first learning the .NET Framework—and even for some time after—the proper way to read to, write from, or otherwise interact with files can be unclear because the framework provides so many different ways of attacking this problem. How should you determine which approach fits your scenario?

Solution

Use file streams to perform various file functions. There are five basic types of built-in file-stream manipulation classes that you can use to read from and/or write to a file stream:

FileStream
>   For the most fine-grained control, use FileStream for file manipulation since it provides the most low-level access to the file, and, therefore, the most complex actions become available. Some of these actions are reading and writing files in both synchronous and asynchronous fashions and methods to lock and unlock part or all of a file, seek a particular position in a file, or even read the file as a stream of either characters or bytes.

StreamReader
>   This type is derived from the abstract base class TextReader. The StreamReader class is designed for reading character or string input from a file. This class contains methods to read single characters, blocks of characters, lines of characters, or even the whole file into a single string variable.

StreamWriter

> This class derives from the TextWriter class. It is designed for writing character or string output to a file. This class contains methods to write single characters or lines of characters.

BinaryReader

> This type is derived from the Object class, as is the BinaryWriter class. It is designed for reading primitive data types—including byte or char data—from a file. This class contains methods to read any of the simple types (int, long, float, etc.), including char arrays and byte arrays.

BinaryWriter

> This type derives from the Object class. It is designed for writing primitive data types—including byte or char data—to a file. This class contains methods to write any of the primitive types (int, long, float, etc.), including char arrays and byte arrays.

There are other stream readers and writers (XmlTextReader/Writer, StringReader/Writer) that can also perform file-stream functions, but at a higher level. This recipe is meant to give you a more fundamental approach to file operations.

Example 12-1 shows a few ways of using the various built-in streams.

Example 12-1. Using built-in .NET streams

```
// Create a temp file to work with.
string tempFile = Path.GetTempFileName( );

// FileStream
// Open the file.
using (FileStream fileStream = File.Open(tempFile,FileMode.Append))
{

    string text = "Hello World ";
    byte [] bytes = Encoding.ASCII.GetBytes(text.ToCharArray( ));

    // Write to the file.
    fileStream.Write(bytes,0,bytes.Length);
}

// StreamReader
using (StreamReader streamReader = new StreamReader(tempFile))
{
    char[] chars = new char[64];
    // Read a block of characters.
    streamReader.Read(chars,0,64);
    string charsFound = new string(chars);
    Console.WriteLine("Chars in stream {0}",charsFound);
}

// StreamWriter
StreamWriter streamWriter = null;
```

Example 12-1. Using built-in .NET streams (continued)

```
// Open for append.
streamWriter = new StreamWriter(tempFile,true);
// Append some text.
streamWriter.WriteLine(", It's the StreamWriter!");

// BinaryWriter
long pos = 0;
int twentyFive = 25;

// Start up the binaryWriter with the base stream from the streamWriter
// since it is open.
using (BinaryWriter binaryWriter = new BinaryWriter(streamWriter.BaseStream))
{
    // Move to end.
    pos = binaryWriter.Seek(0, SeekOrigin.End);
    // Write out 25.
    binaryWriter.Write(twentyFive);
}

// Cannot call Close on the streamWriter since the
// using stmt on the binaryWriter causes the binaryWriter.Dispose
// method to be called, which in turn calls Dispose on the internal
// reference to the streamWriter object that was passed in to the
// binaryWriter's constructor.

// BinaryReader
Using (StreamReader streamReader2 = new StreamReader(tempFile))
{
    using (BinaryReader binaryReader = new BinaryReader(streamReader2.BaseStream))
    {
        //long pos = 0;
        //int twentyFive = 25;

        // Advance the stream to the number we stored.
        for(long i=0;i<pos;i++)
            binaryReader.ReadByte();
        // Read our number (should be 25).
        int num = binaryReader.ReadInt32();
        // Is this the same number...?
        if(num == twentyFive)
            Console.WriteLine("Successfully read 25 back from stream");
        else
            Console.WriteLine("Failed to successfully read 25 back from stream");
    }
}
```

Discussion

There are many different ways to create a stream. First, we will examine the
FileStream class, referring to useful recipes that will help create objects of this type.
We will then look at the StreamWriter and StreamReader classes, followed by the
BinaryWriter and BinaryReader classes.

The most straightforward method of creating an object is to use the new keyword. The FileStream class has several overloaded class constructors that enable creating a new FileStream from scratch. The FileStream's constructor enables a new FileStream object to be created from either a filename or a file handle. See Recipe 12.19.

The FileStream constructor can also accept a FileMode, FileAccess, and/or FileShare enumeration value. These enumeration values are defined in Tables 12-2, 12-3, and 12-4, respectively.

Table 12-2. FileMode enumeration values

Value name	Definition	Specifics
Append	Opens an existing file and prepares it to be written to, starting at the end of the file. If the file does not exist, a new zero-length file is created.	This value can be used only in tandem with the FileAccess.Write enumeration value; otherwise, an ArgumentException is thrown.
Create	Creates a new file. If the specified file exists, it is truncated.	If you do not wish to lose data, consider employing the CreateNew enumeration value instead. This value can be used only in tandem with the FileAccess.Write or FileAccess.ReadWrite enumeration values; otherwise, an ArgumentException is thrown.
CreateNew	Creates a new file.	An IOException is thrown if the file already exists. This prevents accidental data loss. This value can be used only in tandem with the FileAccess.Write or FileAccess.ReadWrite enumeration values; otherwise, an ArgumentException is thrown.
Open	Opens an existing file.	A FileNotFoundException is thrown if the file does not exist. Use OpenOrCreate if it is possible that the file might not already exist.
OpenOrCreate	Opens a file if it exists or creates a new one if it does not exist.	Consider using Open if you expect the file to always exist before it is opened. An ArgumentException is *not* thrown if this enumeration value is used in tandem with the FileAccess.Read enumeration value.
Truncate	Opens an existing file and deletes all information in that file.	A FileNotFoundException is thrown if the file does not exist. This value can be used in tandem with the FileAccess.Write or FileAccess.ReadWrite enumeration values; otherwise, an ArgumentException is thrown.

Table 12-3. FileAccess enumeration values

Value name	Definition
Read	Allows data to only be read from a file.
ReadWrite	Allows data to be read from and written to a file. Same as FileAccess.Read	FileAccess.Write.
Write	Allows data to only be written to a file.

Table 12-4. FileShare enumeration values

Value name	Definition
Inheritable	Allows the file handle to be inherited by a child process.
None	The file cannot be accessed (read from or written to) or deleted by any other process.
Read	The file cannot be written to or deleted by this or any other process. It can be read from.
ReadWrite	The file can be read from or written to by this or any other process. The file still cannot be deleted while it is being shared in this mode. Same as using FileShare.Read | FileShare.Write.
Write	The file cannot be read from or deleted by this or any other process. It can be written to.

In addition to these enumerations that define how a file is opened, the FileStream constructor allows you to define whether this stream will be opened in a synchronous or asynchronous manner. This is the only class—of the ones discussed in this chapter—that allows a file to be opened in an asynchronous manner.

The FileStream class also has methods for seeking to a point within a file stream, as well as locking or unlocking a portion or an entire file; *locking* will prevent other processes or threads from modifying the file. The other stream types discussed in this chapter do not have the ability to lock or unlock portions or an entire file. This locking/unlocking functionality cannot even be accessed through the BaseStream property of any of these types. Seeking within a file can be done directly using the BinaryReader or BinaryWriter classes. The StreamReader and StreamWriter classes cannot directly access the seek functionality. However, by using the BaseStream property of either the StreamReader or StreamWriter classes, the base stream's seek functionality can be used.

FileStreams can also be created using the static methods of the File class. Table 12-5 shows these methods, along with their equivalent FileStream object constructor parameters.

Table 12-5. Static methods of the File class and their equivalent FileStream constructor calls

Static methods in File class	Equivalent FileStream constructor call
FileStream fileStream = File.Create("File.txt");	FileStream fileStream = new FileStream("File.txt", FileMode.Create, FileAccess.ReadWrite, FileShare.None);
FileStream fileStream = File.Open("File.txt");	FileStream fileStream = new FileStream("File.txt");
FileStream fileStream = File.OpenRead("File.txt");	FileStream fileStream = new FileStream("File.txt", FileMode.Open, FileAccess.Read, FileShare.Read);
FileStream fileStream = File.OpenWrite("File.txt");	FileStream fileStream = new FileStream("File.txt", FileMode.OpenOrCreate, FileAccess.Write, FileShare.None);

The File.Open method is overloaded to accept FileMode, FileAccess, and FileShare enumeration values. The FileStream constructor is also overloaded to accept these same parameters.

The File class has a complementary class called FileInfo that contains similar methods, but these methods are instance, not static, methods. Table 12-6 shows the FileInfo methods, which are similar to the File static methods, along with their equivalent FileStream object constructor parameters.

Table 12-6. Instance methods of the FileInfo class and equivalent FileStream constructor calls

Instance methods in FileInfo class	Equivalent FileStream constructor call

FileInfo fileInfo =
new FileInfo("File.txt");
 	
FileStream fileStream =
fileInfo.Create( );
	FileStream fileStream = new
	FileStream("File.txt",
	FileMode.Create, FileAccess.ReadWrite,
	FileShare.None);

FileInfo fileInfo =
new FileInfo("File.txt");
 	
FileStream fileStream =
fileInfo.Open(FileMode.open);
	FileStream fileStream = new
	FileStream("File.txt");

FileInfo fileInfo =
new FileInfo("File.txt");
 	
FileStream fileStream =
fileInfo.OpenRead( );
	FileStream fileStream = new
	FileStream("File.txt",
	FileMode.Open, FileAccess.Read, FileShare.
	Read);

FileInfo fileInfo =
new FileInfo("File.txt");
 	
FileStream fileStream =
fileInfo.OpenWrite( );
	FileStream fileStream = new
	FileStream("File.txt",
	FileMode.OpenOrCreate, FileAccess.Write,
	FileShare.
	None);

The FileInfo.Open instance method is overloaded to accept FileMode, FileAccess, and FileShare enumeration values.

The StreamReader and StreamWriter objects can be created using their overloaded constructors. These overloaded constructors accept as parameters either a file path and name or a FileStream object. Therefore, we can use any of the previously mentioned ways of creating a FileStream object in the construction of either a StreamReader or StreamWriter object.

In addition, we can use three of the static methods in the File class or three of the instance methods in the FileInfo class to create a StreamReader or StreamWriter object. Table 12-7 describes the static methods of the File class used to create StreamReader and StreamWriter objects and their equivalent StreamReader and StreamWriter object constructor parameters.

Table 12-7. Static methods of the File class and their equivalent StreamReader/StreamWriter constructor calls

Static methods in File class	Equivalent StreamReader/StreamWriter constructor calls
`StreamReader streamReader = File.OpenText("File.txt");`	`StreamReader streamReader = new StreamReader("File. txt");`
`StreamWriter streamWriter = File.AppendText("File.txt");`	`StreamWriter streamWriter = new StreamWriter("File. txt", true);`
`StreamWriter streamWriter = File.CreateText("File.txt");`	`StreamWriter streamWriter = new StreamWriter("File. txt", false);`

Table 12-8 describes the instance methods of the `FileInfo` class used to create `StreamReader` and `StreamWriter` objects and their equivalent `StreamReader` and `StreamWriter` object constructor parameters.

Table 12-8. Instance methods of the FileInfo class and their equivalent StreamReader/StreamWriter constructor calls

Instance methods in FileInfo class	Equivalent StreamReader/StreamWriter constructor calls
`FileInfo fileInfo = new FileInfo("File.txt");` `StreamReader streamReader = fileInfo.OpenText( );`	`StreamReader streamReader = new StreamReader("File.txt");`
`FileInfo fileInfo = new FileInfo("File.txt");` `StreamWriter streamWriter = fileInfo.AppendText( );`	`StreamWriter streamWriter = new StreamWriter("File.txt", true);`

The methods of the `File` and `FileInfo` classes do not return `BinaryReader` and `BinaryWriter` classes; therefore, we rely on their constructors to create these types of objects. The overloaded `BinaryReader` and `BinaryWriter` class constructors accept only a `Stream` object; they do not accept a filename.

To create a `BinaryReader` or `BinaryWriter` object, we first need to create a `Stream`-type object. Since `Stream` is an abstract class, we need to create one of its derived classes, such as the `FileStream` class. Any of the prior ways of creating a `FileStream` object may be employed as a parameter in the constructor of either a `BinaryReader` or `BinaryWriter`. The following code creates both a `BinaryReader` and a `BinaryWriter` object from a single `FileStream` object:

```
fileStream = File.Create("filename.file");
BinaryWriter binaryWriter1 = new BinaryWriter(fileStream);
BinaryReader binaryReader1 = new BinaryReader(fileStream);
```

There are many different ways of combining the techniques discussed in this recipe to create and open files. For example, if you require file locking and/or asynchronous file processing, you will need a FileStream object. If you are dealing with text streams in memory and on disk, perhaps StreamReader and StreamWriter might be a better choice. Finally, if you are dealing with binary data or mixed binary and text data in different encodings, you should consider BinaryReader and BinaryWriter.

See Also

See Recipe 12.19; see the "FileStream Class," "StreamReader Class," "StreamWriter Class," "BinaryReader," and "BinaryWriter" topics in the MSDN documentation.

12.6 Accessing Part of a File Randomly

Problem

When reading a file, you sometimes need to move from the current position in a file to a position some number of characters before or after the current position, including to the beginning or the end of a file. After moving to this point, you can add, modify, or read the information at this new point in the file.

Solution

To move around in a stream, use the Seek method. The following method writes the string contained in the variables theFirstLine and theSecondLine to a file in this same order. The stream is then flushed to the file on disk:

```
public static void CreateFile(string theFirstLine, int theSecondLine)
{
    using (FileStream fileStream = new FileStream("data.txt",
            FileMode.Create,
            FileAccess.ReadWrite,
            FileShare.None))
    {
        using (StreamWriter streamWriter = new StreamWriter(fileStream))
        {
            streamWriter.WriteLine(theFirstLine);
            streamWriter.WriteLine(theSecondLine);
            streamWriter.Flush( );
        }
    }
}
```

If the following code is used to call this method:

```
CreateFile("This is the first line.", 1020304050);
```

the resulting *data.txt* file will contain the following text:

```
This is the first line.
1020304050
```

The `ModifyFile` method, shown in Example 12-2, uses the Seek method to reposition the current file position at the end of the first line. A new line of text is then added between the first and second lines of text in the file. Finally, the Seek method is used to place the current position pointer in the file to the end, and a final line of text is written to this file.

Example 12-2. ModifyFile method

```
public static void ModifyFile(int theSecondLine)
{
    // Open the file for read/write.
    using (FileStream fileStream =
               File.Open("data.txt",
                   FileMode.Open,
                   FileAccess.ReadWrite,
                   FileShare.None))
    {
        Using (StreamWriter streamWriter = new StreamWriter(fileStream))
        {
            // Backup over the newline.
            int offset = streamWriter.NewLine.Length;
            // Backup over the second line.
            offset += (theSecondLine.ToString( ).Length);
            // Make negative.
            offset = -offset;
            // Move file pointer to just after first line.
            streamWriter.BaseStream.Seek(offset, SeekOrigin.End);

            StringBuilder stringBuilder
                = new StringBuilder("This line added by seeking ");
            stringBuilder.AppendFormat(
                "{0} chars from the end of this file.",offset);

            streamWriter.WriteLine(stringBuilder);
            streamWriter.Flush( );

            streamWriter.BaseStream.Seek(0, SeekOrigin.End);
            streamWriter.WriteLine("This is the last line" +
                ", added by seeking to the end of the file.");
        }
    }
}
```

If the following code is used to call this method:

```
ModifyFile(1020304050);
```

the resulting *data.txt* file will contain the following text:

```
This is the first line.
This line added by seeking -12 chars from the end of this file.
This is the last line, added by seeking to the end of the file.
```

The next method, ReadFile, reads the file that we just created. First, the current position pointer in the file is moved to the end of the first line (this line contains the string in the variable theFirstLine). The ReadToEnd method is invoked reading the rest of the file (the second and third lines in the file) and the results are displayed:

```
public static void ReadFile(string theFirstLine)
{
    using (StreamReader streamReader = new StreamReader("data.txt"))
    {
        streamReader.BaseStream.Seek(
            theFirstLine.Length + Environment.NewLine.Length, SeekOrigin.Begin);

        Console.WriteLine(streamReader.ReadToEnd( ));
    }
}
```

The following text is displayed:

```
This line added by seeking -12 chars from the end of this file.
This is the last line, added by seeking to the end of the file.
```

If you are wondering where the line of text that reads:

```
1020304050
```

is located, it was overwritten when we did the first Seek while writing data to this file.

Discussion

File seeking is the placement of the pointer to the current location in an opened file anywhere between—and including—the beginning and ending bytes of a file. Seeking is performed through the use of the Seek method.

This method returns the new location of the file pointer in the file.

Seeking is performed in one of three ways: as an offset from the beginning of the file, as an offset from the end of the file, or as an offset from the current location in the file, as shown here:

```
public static void MoveInFile(int offsetValue)
{
    Using (FileStream fileStream =
            File.Open("data.txt",
                FileMode.Open,
                FileAccess.ReadWrite,
                FileShare.None));
    {
        Using (StreamWriter streamWriter = new StreamWriter(fileStream))
        {
            // Move from the beginning of the file.
            streamWriter.BaseStream.Seek(offsetValue, SeekOrigin.Begin);

            // Move from the end of the file.
            streamWriter.BaseStream.Seek(offsetValue, SeekOrigin.End);
```

```
                // Move from the current file pointer location in the file.
                streamWriter.BaseStream.Seek(offsetValue, SeekOrigin.Current);
        }
    }
}
```

offsetValue may be any positive or negative number as long as it does not attempt to
force the file pointer before the beginning of the file or after the end. The SeekOrigin.
Begin enumeration value starts the offset at the beginning of the file; likewise, the
SeekOrigin.End value starts the offset at the end of the file. The SeekOrigin.Current
value starts the offset at the current location of the file pointer. You must take extra
care not to force the file pointer to a point before the start of the file when using the
seek method with a negative offset, since this action could move the file pointer
before the beginning of the file. If you think about it logically, you should be giving
positive values when specifying SeekOrigin.Begin and negative values when specifying SeekOrigin.End; any value makes sense for SeekOrigin.Current, so long as it
doesn't cause the pointer to roll past the beginning of the file. To prevent an
IOException from being thrown in this circumstance, you can test for this condition
in the manner shown in Example 12-3.

Example 12-3. Testing for the beginning or end of a file

```
long offsetValue = -20;
using (FileStream fileStream =
            File.Open("data.txt",
                FileMode.Open,
                FileAccess.ReadWrite,
                FileShare.None))
{
    using (StreamWriter streamWriter = new StreamWriter(fileStream))
    {
        if ((offsetValue + streamWriter.BaseStream.Position) >= 0)
        {
            streamWriter.BaseStream.Seek(offsetValue, SeekOrigin.Current);
        }
        else
        {
            Console.WriteLine("Cannot seek outside of the file.");
        }

        if ((offsetValue + streamWriter.BaseStream.Length) >= 0)
        {
            streamWriter.BaseStream.Seek(offsetValue, SeekOrigin.End);
        }
        else
        {
            Console.WriteLine("Cannot seek outside of the file.");
        }

        if (offsetValue >= 0)
        {
            streamWriter.BaseStream.Seek(offsetValue, SeekOrigin.Begin);
        }
```

Example 12-3. Testing for the beginning or end of a file (continued)

```
    else
    {
        Console.WriteLine("Cannot seek outside of the file.");
    }
  }
}
```

To seek to the beginning of a file, use the following code:

```
    streamWriter.BaseStream.Seek(0, SeekOrigin.Begin);
```

To seek to the end of a file, use the following code:

```
    streamWriter.BaseStream.Seek(0, SeekOrigin.End);
```

In these calls, the SeekOrigin enumeration value sets the file pointer to the beginning or end of a file. The offset, which is zero, does not force the file pointer to move. With this in mind, realize that using zero as an offset to SeekOrigin.Current is pointless because you don't move the pointer at all, and you are killing clock cycles to no effect.

See Also

See the "FileStream Class," "StreamReader Class," "StreamWriter Class," "Binary-Reader Class," "BinaryWriter Class," and "SeekOrigin Enumeration" topics in the MSDN documentation.

12.7 Outputting a Platform-Independent EOL Character

Problem

Your application will run on more than one platform. Each platform uses a different end-of-line (EOL) character. You want your code to output the correct EOL character without having to write code to handle the EOL character specially for each platform.

Solution

The .NET Framework provides the Environment.NewLine constant, which represents a newline on the given platform. This is the newline string used by all of the framework-provided WriteLine methods internally (including Console, Debug, and Trace).

There are a few different scenarios in which this could be useful:

- Formatting a block of text with newlines embedded within it:

```
    // Remember to use Environment.NewLine on every block of text
    // we format where we want platform-correct newlines inside of.
    string line;
```

```
line = String.Format("FirstLine {0} SecondLine {0} ThirdLine {0}",
            Environment.NewLine);

// Get a temp file to work with.
string file = Path.GetTempFileName( );
using (FileStream stream = File.Create(file))
{
    byte[] bytes = Encoding.Unicode.GetBytes(line);
    stream.Write(bytes,0,bytes.Length);
}

// Remove the file (good line to set a breakpoint to check out the file
// we created).
File.Delete(file);
```

1. You need to use a different newline character than the default one used by StreamWriter (which happens to be Environment.NewLine). You can set the newline that a StreamWriter will use once so that all WriteLines performed by the StreamWriter use that newline instead of having to manually do it each time:

```
// Set up a text writer and tell it to use a certain newline
// string.
// Get a new temp file.
file = Path.GetTempFileName( );
line = "Double spaced line";
using (StreamWriter streamWriter = new StreamWriter(file))
{
    // Make this always write out double lines.
    streamWriter.NewLine = Environment.NewLine + Environment.NewLine;
    // WriteLine on this stream will automatically use the newly specified
    // newline sequence (double newline in our case).
    streamWriter.WriteLine(line);
    streamWriter.WriteLine(line);
    streamWriter.WriteLine(line);
}

// Remove the file (good line to set a breakpoint to check out the file
// we created).
File.Delete(file);
```

2. Normal WriteLine calls:

```
// Just use any of the normal WriteLine methods as they use the
// Environment.NewLine by default.
line = "Default line";
Console.WriteLine(line);
```

Discussion

Environment.NewLine allows you to have peace of mind, whether the platform is using \n or \r\n as the newline or possibly something else. Your code will be doing things the right way for each platform.

One word of caution here: if you are interoperating with a non-Windows operating system via SOAP and Web Services, the Environment.NewLine defined here might not be accurate for a stream you send to or receive from that other operating system. Of course, if you are doing Web Services, newlines aren't your biggest concern.

See Also

See the "Environment Class" topic in the MSDN documentation.

12.8 Creating, Writing to, and Reading from a File

Problem

You need to create a file—possibly for logging information to or for storing temporary information—and then write information to it. You also need to be able to read the information that you wrote to this file.

Solution

To create, write to, and read from a logfile, we will use the FileStream and its reader and writer classes. For example, we will create methods to allow construction, reading to, and writing from a logfile. To create a logfile, you can use the following code:

```
FileStream fileStream = new FileStream(logFileName,
                       FileMode.Append,
                       FileAccess.Write,
                       FileShare.None);
```

To write text to this file, you can create a StreamWriter object wrapper around the previously created FileStream object (fileStream). You can then use the WriteLine method of the StreamWriter object. The following code writes three lines to the file: a string, followed by an integer, followed by a second string:

```
public static void WriteToLog(string logFileName, string data)
{
    using (FileStream fileStream = new FileStream(logFileName,
            FileMode.Append,
            FileAccess.Write,
            FileShare.None))
    {
        using (StreamWriter streamWriter = new StreamWriter(fileStream))
        {
            streamWriter.WriteLine(data);
        }
    }
}
```

Now that the file has been created and data has been written to it, you can read the data from this file. To read text from a file, create a StreamReader object wrapper around the file. If the code has not closed the FileStream object (fileStream), it can use that object in place of the filename used to create the StreamReader. To read the entire file in as a single string, use the ReadToEnd method:

```
public static string ReadAllLog(string logFileName)
{
    if (!File.Exists(logFileName))
    {
        throw (new FileNotFoundException(
          "logfile cannot be read since it does not exist.", logFileName));
    }

    string contents = "";

    using (FileStream fileStream = new FileStream(logFileName,
                FileMode.Open,
                FileAccess.Read,
                FileShare.None))
    {
        using (StreamReader streamReader = new StreamReader(fileStream))
        {
            contents = streamReader.ReadToEnd( );
        }
    }

    return contents;
}
```

If you need to read the lines in one by one, use the Peek method, as shown in
ReadLogPeeking or the ReadLine method, as shown in ReadLogByLines, both of which
appear in Example 12-4.

Example 12-4. ReadLogPeeking and ReadLogByLines methods

```
public static void ReadLogPeeking(string logFileName)
{
    if (!File.Exists(logFileName))
    {
        throw (new FileNotFoundException(
          "logfile cannot be read since it does not exist.", logFileName));
    }

    using (FileStream fileStream = new FileStream(logFileName,
                FileMode.Open,
                FileAccess.Read,
                FileShare.None))
    {
        Console.WriteLine("Reading file stream peeking at next line:");
        using (StreamReader streamReader = new StreamReader(fileStream))
        {
            while (streamReader.Peek( ) != -1)
            {
                Console.WriteLine(streamReader.ReadLine( ));
            }
        }
    }
}
```

or:

```
public static void ReadLogByLines(string logFileName)
{
    if (!File.Exists(logFileName))
    {
        throw (new FileNotFoundException(
            "Logfile cannot be read since it does not exist.", logFileName));
    }

    using (FileStream fileStream = new FileStream(logFileName,
                FileMode.Open,
                FileAccess.Read,
                FileShare.None))
    {
        Console.WriteLine("Reading file stream as lines:");
        using (StreamReader streamReader = new StreamReader(fileStream))
        {
            string text = streamReader.ReadLine();
            while (text != null)
            {
                Console.WriteLine(text);
                text = streamReader.ReadLine();
            }
        }
    }
}
```

If you need to read in each character of the file as a byte value, use the Read method, which returns a byte value:

```
public static void ReadAllLogAsBytes(string logFileName)
{
    if (!File.Exists(logFileName))
    {
        throw (new FileNotFoundException(
            "Logfile cannot be read since it does not exist.", logFileName));
    }

    using (FileStream fileStream = new FileStream(logFileName,
                FileMode.Open,
                FileAccess.Read,
                FileShare.None))
    {
        Console.WriteLine("Reading file stream as bytes:");
        using (StreamReader streamReader = new StreamReader(fileStream))
        {
            while (streamReader.Peek() != -1)
            {
                Console.Write(streamReader.Read());
            }
        }
    }
}
```

This method displays numeric byte values instead of the characters that they represent. For example, if the logfile contained the following text:

```
This is the first line.
100
This is the third line.
```

it would be displayed by the ReadAllLogAsBytes method as follows:

```
84104105115321051153211610410132102105114115116321081 0
5110101461310494848131084104105115321051153211610410 13
21161041051141003210810511010146131 0
```

If you need to read in the file by chunks, create and fill a buffer of an arbitrary length based on your performance needs. This buffer can then be displayed or manipulated as needed:

```csharp
public static void ReadAllBufferedLog(string logFileName)
{
    if (!File.Exists(logFileName))
    {
        throw (new FileNotFoundException(
          "Logfile cannot be read since it does not exist.", logFileName));
    }

    using (FileStream fileStream = new FileStream(logFileName,
                FileMode.Open,
                FileAccess.Read,
                FileShare.None))
    {
        Console.WriteLine("Reading file stream as buffers of bytes:");
        using (StreamReader streamReader = new StreamReader(fileStream))
        {
            while (streamReader.Peek( ) != -1)
            {
                char[] buffer = new char[10];
                int bufferFillSize = streamReader.Read(buffer, 0, 10);
                foreach (char c in buffer)
                {
                    Console.Write(c);
                }
                Console.WriteLine(bufferFillSize);
            }
        }
    }
}
```

This method displays the logfile's characters in 10-character chunks, followed by the number of characters actually read. For example, if the logfile contained the following text:

```
This is the first line.
100
This is the third line.
```

it would be displayed by the ReadAllBufferedLog method as follows:

```
This is th10
e first li10
ne.
100
10
This is th10
e third li10
ne.
    5
```

Notice that at the end of every 10th character (the buffer is a char array of size 10), the number of characters read in is displayed. During the last read performed, only five characters were left to read from the file. In this case, a 5 is displayed at the end of the text, indicating that the buffer was not completely filled.

Discussion

There are many mechanisms for recording state information about applications, other than creating a file full of the information. One example of this type of mechanism is the Windows Event Log, where informational, security, and error states can be logged during an application's progress. One of the primary reasons for creating a log is to assist in troubleshooting or to debug your code in the field. If you are shipping code without some sort of debugging mechanism for your support staff (or possibly for you in a small company), we suggest you consider adding some logging support. Any developer who has spent a late night debugging a problem on a QA machine or, worse yet, at a customer site, can tell you the value of a log of the program's actions.

If you are writing character information to a file, the simplest method is to use the Write and WriteLine methods of the StreamWriter class to write data to the file. These two methods are overloaded to handle any of the primitive values (except for the byte data type), as well as character arrays. These methods are also overloaded to handle various formatting techniques discussed in Recipe 2.16. All of this information is written to the file as character text, not as the underlying primitive type.

If you need to write byte data to a file, consider using the Write and WriteByte methods of the FileStream class. These methods are designed to write byte values to a file. The WriteByte method accepts a single byte value and writes it to the file, after which the pointer to the current position in the file is advanced to the next location after this byte. The Write method accepts an array of bytes that can be written to the file, after which the pointer to the current position in the file is advanced to the next location after this array of bytes. The Write method can also choose a range of bytes in the array to write to the file.

The Write method of the BinaryWriter class is overloaded in a similar fashion to the Write method of the StreamWriter class. The main difference is that the BinaryWriter class's Write method does not allow formatting. This forces the BinaryReader to read the information written by the BinaryWriter as its underlying type, not as a character or a byte. See Recipe 12.5 for an example of the `BinaryReader` and `BinaryWriter` classes in action.

Once we have the data written to the file, we can read it back out. The first concern when reading data from a file is to not go past the end of the file. The `StreamReader` class provides a Peek method that looks—but does not retrieve—the next character in the file. If the end of the file has been reached, a -1 is returned. Likewise, the Read method of this class also returns a -1 if it has reached the end of the file. The Peek and Read methods can be used in the following manner to make sure that you do not go past the end of the file:

```
using (StreamReader streamReader = new StreamReader("data.txt"))
{
    while (streamReader.Peek( ) != -1)
    {
        Console.WriteLine(streamReader.ReadLine( ));
    }
}
```

or:

```
using (StreamReader streamReader = new StreamReader("data.txt"))
{
    int nextChar = streamReader.Read( );
    while (nextChar > -1)
    {
        Console.WriteLine((char)nextChar);
        nextChar = streamReader.Read( );
    }
}
```

The main differences between the Read and Peek methods are that the Read method actually retrieves the next character and increments the pointer to the current position in the file by one character, and the Read method is overloaded to return an array of characters instead of just one. If you use the Read method that returns a buffer of characters and the buffer is larger than the file, the extra elements in the buffer array are untouched.

The `StreamReader` also contains a method to read an entire line up to and including the newline character. This method is called `ReadLine`. This method returns a null if it goes past the end of the file. The `ReadLine` method can be used in the following manner to make sure that you do not go past the end of the file:

```
using (StreamReader streamReader = new StreamReader("data.txt"))
{
    string text = streamReader.ReadLine( );
    while (text != null)
    {
        Console.WriteLine(text);
        text = streamReader.ReadLine( );
    }
}
```

If you simply need to read the whole file in at one time, use the ReadToEnd method to read the entire file into a string. If the current position in the file is moved to a point other than the beginning of the file, the ReadToEnd method returns a string of characters starting at that position in the file and ending at the end of the file.

The FileStream class contains two methods, Read and ReadByte, which read one or more bytes of the file. The Read method reads a byte value from the file and casts that byte to an int before returning the value. If you are explicitly expecting a byte value, consider casting the return type to a byte:

```
FileStream fileStream = new FileStream("data.txt", FileMode.Open);
byte retVal = (byte) fileStream.ReadByte( );
```

However, if retVal is being used to determine whether the end of the file has been reached (i.e., retVal == -1 or retVal == 0xffffffff in hexadecimal), you will run into problems. When the return value of ReadByte is cast to a byte, a -1 is cast to 0xff, which is not equal to -1 but is equal to 255 (the byte data type is not signed). If you are going to cast this return type to a byte value, you cannot use this value to determine whether you are at the end of the file. You must instead rely on the Length Property. The following code block shows the use of the return value of the ReadByte method to determine when we are at the end of the file:

```
using (FileStream fileStream = new FileStream("data.txt", FileMode.Open))
{
    int retByte = fileStream.ReadByte( );
    while (retByte != -1)
    {
        Console.WriteLine((byte)retByte);
        retByte = fileStream.ReadByte( );
    }
}
```

This code block shows the use of the Length property to determine when to stop reading the file:

```
using (FileStream fileStream = new FileStream("data.txt", FileMode.Open))
{
    long currPosition = 0;
    while (currPosition < fileStream.Length)
    {
        Console.WriteLine((byte) fileStream.ReadByte( ));
        currPosition++;
    }
}
```

The BinaryReader class contains several methods for reading specific primitive types, including character arrays and byte arrays. These methods can be used to read specific data types from a file. All of these methods, except for the Read method, indicate that the end of the file has been reached by throwing the EndOfStreamException. The Read method will return a -1 if it is trying to read past the end of the file. This class contains a PeekChar method that is very similar to the Peek method in the StreamReader class. The PeekChar method is used as follows:

```
using (FileStream fileStream = new FileStream("data.txt", FileMode.Open))
{
    BinaryReader binaryReader = new BinaryReader(fileStream);
    while (binaryReader.PeekChar( ) != -1)
    {
        Console.WriteLine(binaryReader.ReadChar( ));
    }
}
```

In this code, the PeekChar method is used to determine when to stop reading values in the file. This will prevent a costly EndOfStreamException from being thrown by the ReadChar method if it tries to read past the end of the file.

See Also

See the "FileStream Class," "StreamReader Class," "StreamWriter Class," "Binary-Reader Class," and "BinaryWriter Class" topics in the MSDN documentation.

12.9   Determining Whether a Directory Exists

Problem

You need to determine whether a directory exists prior to creating or performing an action on that directory.

Solution

Use the static Exists method on the Directory class to determine whether a directory currently exists:

```
if (Directory.Exists(@"c:\delete\test"))
{
    // Operate on that directory here
}
```

Discussion

If you try to delete a directory that no longer exists, a System.IO. DirectoryNotFoundException will be thrown. This can be handled by catching the exception and reporting the failure accordingly for your application.

This method returns a bool indicating whether the directory was found (true) or not (false).

See Also

See the "Directory Class" topic in the MSDN documentation.

12.10 Creating, Moving, or Deleting a Directory

Problem

You need to create a new directory, move an existing directory, or delete a directory.

Solution

The System.IO namespace contains two classes to perform these actions: the Directory and DirectoryInfo classes. The Directory class contains only static methods, while the DirectoryInfo class contains only instance methods.

To create a directory, you can use the static CreateDirectory method of the Directory class. The return value for this method is an instance of the DirectoryInfo class. This class can be used to invoke instance methods on the newly created directory. For example:

```
DirectoryInfo dirInfo = null;
if (!Directory.Exists(@"c:\delete\test"))
{
    dirInfo = Directory.CreateDirectory(@"c:\delete\test");
}
```

You can also use the instance Create method of the DirectoryInfo class—a method that takes no parameters and returns void. For example:

```
DirectoryInfo dirInfo = null;
if (!Directory.Exists(@"c:\delete\test"))
{
    dirInfo = new DirectoryInfo(@"c:\delete\test");
    dirInfo.Create( );
}
```

To move a directory, you can use the static Move method of the Directory class, which returns void. For example:

```
if (!Directory.Exists(@"c:\MovedDir"))
{
    Directory.Move(@"c:\delete", @"c:\MovedDir");
}
```

You can also use the instance MoveTo method of the DirectoryInfo class, which returns void. For example:

```
DirectoryInfo dirInfo = null;
if (!Directory.Exists(@"c:\MovedDir"))
{
    dirInfo = new DirectoryInfo(@"c:\delete\test");
    dirInfo.MoveTo(@"c:\MovedDir");
}
```

To delete a directory, you can use the static `Delete` method of the `Directory` class, which returns void. There are two overloads for this method: one that will attempt to delete just the directory and one that you can pass a Boolean value to tell it to delete recursively. If you elect to delete the directory recursively, all subdirectories and files will be deleted as well. If you do not use the recursive flag, the `Delete` method will throw an exception if you attempt to delete a directory that has either files or subdirectories still in it:

```
if (Directory.Exists(@"c:\MovedDir"))
{
    Directory.Delete(@"c:\MovedDir", true);
}
```

You can also use the instance `Delete` method of the `DirectoryInfo` class, which returns a void. For example:

```
DirectoryInfo dirInfo = null;
if (Directory.Exists(@"c:\MovedDir"))
{
    dirInfo = new DirectoryInfo(@"c:\delete\test");
    // This will delete all subdirectories and the files therein.
    dirInfo.Delete(true);
}
```

Discussion

Creating, moving, and deleting are the basic operations that you can perform on directories. It makes sense that there are specific methods to address each of these operations. In fact, there are two methods to perform each of these actions: one static and one instance method.

Which method you choose depends on what you are trying to accomplish. If you need a quick way of creating, moving, or deleting a directory, use the static methods since you don't incur the overhead of instantiating an object before performing the operation. If you will be performing multiple operations on a directory, you should use instance methods. Another consideration is that static methods on a class do not require an object to be created on the managed heap. Instance methods require an object to be created before the methods can be called. If you are trying to minimize the number of objects the garbage collector has to manage, consider using static methods.

Before creating a new directory, you should first determine whether that directory already exists. If you attempt to create a directory that already exists, an `IOException` is thrown. The `Directory` class contains a static method, `Exists`, to perform this operation (note that there are no instance classes to do this).

To move a directory, you must first determine whether the destination directory exists. If it does exist, the move operation will fail and throw an exception.

To delete a directory, you must first determine whether it exists. If it does not exist, the delete operation will fail and throw an exception.

See Also

See the "Directory Class" and "DirectoryInfo Class" topics in the MSDN documentation.

12.11 Manipulating Directory Attributes

Problem

You need to display or manipulate a directory's attributes or timestamps.

Solution

To display a directory's timestamps, you can use either the set of static methods from the Directory object or the set of instance properties from the DirectoryInfo object. The static methods are GetCreationTime, GetLastAccessTime, or GetLastWriteTime. For example:

```
public static void DisplayDirAttr(string path)
{
    Console.WriteLine(Directory.GetCreationTime(path));
    Console.WriteLine(Directory.GetLastAccessTime(path));
    Console.WriteLine(Directory.GetLastWriteTime(path));
}
```

In each case, *path* is the path to the directory with a timestamp you wish to retrieve, and the method returns a DateTime value containing the relevant timestamp. The instance properties are CreationTime, LastAccessTime, or LastWriteTime. For example:

```
public static void DisplayDirAttr(string path)
{
    DirectoryInfo dirInfo = Directory.CreateDirectory(path);

    Console.WriteLine(dirInfo.CreationTime);
    Console.WriteLine(dirInfo.LastAccessTime);
    Console.WriteLine(dirInfo.LastWriteTime);
}
```

Each property returns a DateTime value containing the timestamp from the directory represented by the DirInfo object. It should be noted that the static counterparts to these properties (i.e., the Directory.GetCreationTime, Directory.GetLastAccessTime, and Directory.GetLastWriteTime methods) perform slower than the instance properties of the DirectoryInfo class. This is because of the extra time it takes for the underlying implementation of the static methods to get information about the file handle each time a static method is called, as opposed to one time for the DirectoryInfo instance object, which already holds this file handle information.

To modify a directory's timestamps, you can use either the static methods of the Directory class or the instance properties of the DirectoryInfo class. The static methods are SetCreationTime, SetLastAccessTime, or SetLastWriteTime. For example:

```
public static void ModifyDirAttr(string path)
{
    DateTime dt = new DateTime(2003,5,10);
    Directory.SetCreationTime(path, dt);
    Directory.SetLastAccessTime(path, dt);
    Directory.SetLastWriteTime(path, dt);
}
```

Each method has two parameters: the first is the path to the directory with a timestamp that is to be set, and the second is a DateTime value containing the new timestamp. Each method returns void. The instance properties, all of which are of type DateTime, are CreationTime, LastAccessTime, and LastWriteTime. For example:

```
public static void ModifyDirAttr(string path)
{
    DirectoryInfo dirInfo = Directory.CreateDirectory(path);

    DateTime dt = new DateTime(2001,2,8);
    dirInfo.CreationTime = dt;
    dirInfo.LastAccessTime = dt;
    dirInfo.LastWriteTime = dt;
}
```

To display or modify a directory's attributes, use the instance property Attributes:

```
public static void ViewModifyDirAttr(string path, FileAttributes fileAttributes)
{
    DirectoryInfo dirInfo = new DirectoryInfo(@"C:\SomeDir");
    // Display this directory's attributes.
    Console.WriteLine(dirInfo.Attributes);

    // Display whether this directory is hidden.
    Console.WriteLine("Is directory hidden? = " +
        ((dirInfo.Attributes & FileAttributes.Hidden) == FileAttributes.Hidden));

    // Modify this directory's attributes.
    dirInfo.Attributes |= fileAttributes;
    // Display whether this directory is hidden.
    Console.WriteLine("Is directory hidden? = " +
        ((dirInfo.Attributes & FileAttributes.Hidden) == FileAttributes.Hidden));
}
```

The output of this code is shown here:

```
Directory
Is directory hidden? = False
Is directory hidden? = True
```

Discussion

There are three distinct timestamps associated with any directory. These timestamps are its creation time, its last access time, and its last write time.

In addition to timestamp information, a directory's attributes may also be obtained and modified. This is accomplished through the use of the public instance `Attributes` property found on a `DirectoryInfo` object. This property returns the `FileAttributes` enumeration value (see Table 12-9). The `FileAttributes` enumeration is made up of bit flags that can be turned on or off through the use of the bitwise operators &, |, or ^.

Table 12-9. Definitions of each bit flag in the FileAttributes enumeration

Flag name	Definition
Archive	Typically, backup applications will use this to indicate the archive status of the file.
Compress	The current directory uses compression.
Directory	The current item is a directory.
Encrypted	The current directory is encrypted.
Hidden	The current directory is hidden.
Normal	The current directory has no other attributes set. When this attribute is set, no others can be set.
NotContentIndexed	The current directory is not being indexed by the indexing service.
Offline	The current directory is offline, and its contents are not accessible unless it is online.
ReadOnly	The current directory is read-only.
ReparsePoint	The current directory contains a reparse point.
SparseFile	The current directory contains large files consisting mostly of zeros.
System	The current directory is used by the system.
Temporary	The current directory is classified as a temporary directory.

In many cases, more than one of these flags may be set at one time. The `Normal` flag is the exception; when this flag is set, no other flag may be set.

See Also

See the "Directory Class," "DirectoryInfo Class," and "FileAttributes Enumeration" topics in the MSDN documentation.

12.12 Renaming a Directory

Problem

You need to rename a directory.

Solution

Unfortunately, there is no specific rename method that can be used to rename a directory. However, you can use the instance MoveTo method of the DirectoryInfo class or the static Move method of the Directory class instead. The static Move method can be used to rename a directory in the following manner:

```
public static void DemonstrateRenameDir(string originalName, string newName)
{
    try
    {
        Directory.CreateDirectory(originalName);
        // "Rename" it.
        Directory.Move(originalName, newName);
    }
    catch(IOException ioe)
    {
        // Most likely given the directory exists or isn't empty
        Console.WriteLine(ioe.ToString( ));
    }
    catch(Exception e)
    {
        // Catch any other exceptions.
        Console.WriteLine(e.ToString( ));
    }
}
```

This code creates a directory using the *originalName* parameter and renames it to the value supplied in the *newName* parameter.

The instance MoveTo method of the DirectoryInfo class can also be used to rename a directory in the following manner:

```
public static void DemonstrateRenameDir (string originalName, string newName)
{
    try
    {
        DirectoryInfo dirInfo = new DirectoryInfo(originalName);
        // Create the dir.
        dirInfo.Create( );
        // "Rename" it.
        dirInfo.MoveTo(newName);
    }
    catch(IOException ioe)
    {
        // Most likely because the directory exists or isn't empty
        Console.WriteLine(ioe.ToString( ));
    }
    catch(Exception e)
    {
        // Catch any other exceptions.
        Console.WriteLine(e.ToString( ));
    }
}
```

This code creates a directory using the *originalName* parameter and renames it to the value supplied in the *newName* parameter.

Discussion

The Move and MoveTo methods allow a directory to be moved to a different location. However, when the path remains unchanged up to the directory that will have its name changed, the Move methods act as Rename methods.

See Also

See the "Directory Class" and "DirectoryInfo Class" topics in the MSDN documentation.

12.13 Searching for Directories or Files Using Wildcards

Problem

You are attempting to find one or more specific files or directories that might or might not exist within the current filesystem. The search might need to use wildcard characters in order to widen the search, for example, searching for all user-mode dump files in a filesystem. These files have a *.dmp* extension.

Solution

There are several methods of obtaining this information. The first three methods return a string array containing the full path of each item. The next three methods return an object that encapsulates a directory, a file, or both.

The static GetFileSystemEntries method on the Directory class returns a string array containing the names of all files and directories within a single directory, for example:

```
public static void DisplayFilesDirs(string path)
{
    string[] items = Directory.GetFileSystemEntries(path);
    foreach (string item in items)
    {
        Console.WriteLine(item);
    }
}
```

The static GetDirectories method on the Directory class returns a string array containing the names of all directories within a single directory. The following method, DisplayDirs, shows how you might use it:

```
public static void DisplayDirs(string path)
{
    string[] items = Directory.GetDirectories(path);
    foreach (string item in items)
    {
```

```
            Console.WriteLine(item);
        }
    }
```

The static GetFiles method on the Directory class returns a string array containing the names of all files within a single directory. The following method is very similar to DisplayDirs, but calls Directory.GetFiles instead of Directory.GetDirectories:

```
    public static void DisplayFiles(string path)
    {
        string[] items = Directory.GetFiles(path);
        foreach (string item in items)
        {
            Console.WriteLine(item);
        }
    }
```

These next three methods return an object instead of simply a string. The GetFileSystemInfos method of the DirectoryInfo object returns a strongly typed array of FileSystemInfo objects (that is, of DirectoryInfo and FileInfo objects) representing the directories and files within a single directory. The following example calls the GetFileSystemInfos method to retrieve an array of FileSystemInfo objects representing all the items in a particular directory and then lists the Name property of each item to the console window:

```
    public static void DisplayFilesDirs(string path)
    {
        DirectoryInfo mainDir = new DirectoryInfo(path);
        FileSystemInfo[] items = mainDir.GetFileSystemInfos( );
        foreach (FileSystemInfo item in items)
        {
            if (item is DirectoryInfo)
            {
                Console.WriteLine("DIRECTORY: " + ((DirectoryInfo)item).Name);
            }
            else if (item is FileInfo)
            {
                Console.WriteLine("FILE: " + item.Name);
            }
            else
            {
                Console.WriteLine("Unknown");
            }
        }
    }
```

The output for this code is shown here:

```
DIRECTORY: MyNestedTempDir
DIRECTORY: MyNestedTempDirPattern
FILE: MyTempFile.PDB
FILE: MyTempFile.TXT
```

The GetDirectories instance method of the DirectoryInfo object returns an array of DirectoryInfo objects representing only subdirectories in a single directory. For example, the following code calls the GetDirectories method to retrieve an array of DirectoryInfo objects, then displays the Name property of each object to the console window:

```
public static void DisplayDirs(string path)
{
    DirectoryInfo mainDir = new DirectoryInfo(path);
    DirectoryInfo[] items = mainDir.GetDirectories( );
    foreach (DirectoryInfo item in items)
    {
        Console.WriteLine("DIRECTORY: " + ((DirectoryInfo)item).Name);
    }
}
```

The GetFiles instance method of the DirectoryInfo object returns an array of FileInfo objects representing only the files in a single directory. For example, the following code calls the GetFiles method to retrieve an array of FileInfo objects, then it displays the Name property of each object to the console window:

```
public static void DisplayFiles(string path)
{
    DirectoryInfo mainDir = new DirectoryInfo(path);
    FileInfo[] items = mainDir.GetFiles( );
    foreach (FileInfo item in items)
    {
        Console.WriteLine("FILE: " + item.Name);
    }
}
```

The static GetFileSystemEntries method on the Directory class returns all files and directories in a single directory that match pattern:

```
public static void DisplayFilesDirs(string path, string pattern)
{
    string[] items = Directory.GetFileSystemEntries(path, pattern);
    foreach (string item in items)
    {
        Console.WriteLine(item);
    }
}
```

The static GetDirectories method on the Directory class returns only those directories in a single directory that match pattern:

```
public static void DisplayDirs(string path, string pattern)
{
    string[] items = Directory.GetDirectories(path, pattern);
    foreach (string item in items)
    {
        Console.WriteLine(item);
    }
}
```

The static `GetFiles` method on the `Directory` class returns only those files in a single directory that match pattern:

```
public static void DisplayFiles(string path, string pattern)
{
    string[] items = Directory.GetFiles(path, pattern);
    foreach (string item in items)
    {
        Console.WriteLine(item);
    }
}
```

These next three methods return an object instead of simply a string. The first instance method is `GetFileSystemInfos`, which returns both directories and files in a single directory that match pattern:

```
public static void DisplayFilesDirs(string path, string pattern)
{
    DirectoryInfo mainDir = new DirectoryInfo(path);
    FileSystemInfo[] items = mainDir.GetFileSystemInfos(pattern);
    foreach (FileSystemInfo item in items)
    {
        if (item is DirectoryInfo)
        {
            Console.WriteLine("DIRECTORY: " + ((DirectoryInfo)item).Name);
        }
        else if (item is FileInfo)
        {
            Console.WriteLine("FILE: " + item.Name);
        }
        else
        {
            Console.WriteLine("Unknown");
        }
    }
}
```

The `GetDirectories` instance method returns only directories (contained in the `DirectoryInfo` object) in a single directory that match pattern:

```
public static void DisplayDirs(string path, string pattern)
{
    DirectoryInfo mainDir = new DirectoryInfo(@"C:\TEMP ");
    DirectoryInfo[] items = mainDir.GetDirectories(pattern);
    foreach (DirectoryInfo item in items)
    {
        Console.WriteLine("DIRECTORY: " + ((DirectoryInfo)item).Name);
    }
}
```

The `GetFiles` instance method returns only file information (contained in the `FileInfo` object) in a single directory that matches pattern:

```
public static void DisplayFiles(string path, string pattern)
{
```

```
        DirectoryInfo mainDir = new DirectoryInfo(@"C:\TEMP ");
        FileInfo[] items = mainDir.GetFiles(pattern);
        foreach (FileInfo item in items)
        {
            Console.WriteLine("FILE: " + item.Name);
        }
    }
}
```

Discussion

If you need just an array of strings containing paths to both directories and files, you can use the static method `Directory.GetFileSystemEntries`. The string array returned does not include any information about whether an individual element is a directory or a file. Each string element contains the entire path to either a directory or file contained within the specified path.

To quickly and easily distinguish between directories and files, use the `Directory.GetDirectories` and `Directory.GetFiles` static methods. These methods return arrays of directory names and filenames. These methods return an array of string objects. Each element contains the full path to the directory or file.

Returning a string is fine if you do not need any other information about the directory or file returned to you or if you are going to need more information for only one of the files returned. It is more efficient to use the static methods to get the list of filenames and just retrieve the `FileInfo` for the ones you need than to have all of the `FileInfos` constructed for the directory, as the instance methods will do. If you are going to have to access attributes, lengths, or times on every one of the files, you should consider using the instance methods described here.

The instance method `GetFileSystemInfos` returns an array of strongly typed `FileSystemInfo` objects. (The `FileSystemInfo` object is the base class to the `DirectoryInfo` and `FileInfo` objects.) Therefore, you can test whether the returned type is a `DirectoryInfo` or `FileInfo` object using the is or as keywords. Once you know what subclass this object really is, you can cast it to that type and begin using it.

To get only `DirectoryInfo` objects, use the overloaded `GetDirectories` instance method. To get only `FileInfo` objects, use the overloaded `GetFiles` instance method. These methods return an array of `DirectoryInfo` and `FileInfo` objects, respectively; each element of which encapsulates a directory or file.

See Also

See the "DirectoryInfo Class," "FileInfo Class," and "FileSystemInfo Class" topics in the MSDN documentation.

12.14 Obtaining the Directory Tree

Problem

You need to get a directory tree, potentially including filenames, extending from any point in the directory hierarchy. In addition, each directory or file returned must be in the form of an object encapsulating that item. This will allow you to perform operations on the returned objects, such as deleting the file, renaming the file, or examining/changing its attributes. Finally, you potentially need the ability to search for a specific subset of these items based on a pattern, such as finding only files with the .*pdb* extension.

Solution

By placing a call to the GetFileSystemInfos instance method in a recursive method, you can iterate down the directory hierarchy from any starting point and get all files and directories:

```
public static void GetAllDirFilesRecurse(string dir)
{
    DirectoryInfo mainDir = new DirectoryInfo(dir);
    FileSystemInfo[] items = mainDir.GetFileSystemInfos( );
    foreach (FileSystemInfo item in items)
    {
        if (item is DirectoryInfo)
        {
            Console.WriteLine("DIRECTORY: " + ((DirectoryInfo)item).FullName);
            GetAllDirFilesRecurse(((DirectoryInfo)item).FullName);
        }
        if (item is FileInfo)
        {
            Console.WriteLine("FILE: " + ((FileInfo)item).FullName);
        }
        else
        {
            Console.WriteLine("Unknown");
        }
    }
}
```

It isn't necessarily true that you have to use recursion to retrieve information about *all* files and directories. The following recursive method uses a case-insensitive comparison to obtain a listing of all files with the extension of .*pdb* that exist in directories that begin with *Chapter 1*:

```
public static void GetAllFilesInPatternRecurse(string dir)
{
    DirectoryInfo mainDir = new DirectoryInfo(dir);
    FileSystemInfo[] items = mainDir.GetFileSystemInfos("Chapter 1*");
    foreach (FileSystemInfo item in items)
    {
        if (item is DirectoryInfo)
```

```
        {
            GetAllFilesInPatternRecurse(((DirectoryInfo)item).FullName);
        }
        if (item is FileInfo)
        {
            FileInfo fileInfo = item as FileInfo;
            if(fileInfo.Extension.ToUpper( ).CompareTo(".PDB")==0)
                Console.WriteLine("FILE: " + (fileInfo.FullName));
        }
    }
}
```

Discussion

To obtain a tree representation of a directory and the files it contains, you can use a simple recursive method. This recursive method first creates a DirectoryInfo object that begins in the directory with which you wish to start creating a hierarchy; in the first code example in the Solution section, this directory is represented by the mainDir object.

Next, it can call the GetFileSystemInfos method on the mainDir object to obtain both DirectoryInfo and FileInfo objects representing the files and directories in that initial folder. Alternatively, it could call both the GetFiles and GetDirectories methods on the mainDir object; the latter two methods return string arrays containing the paths and names of files and directories.

Simply calling the GetFileSystemInfos method is easy enough, but you need to cast the returned FileSystemInfo objects to their correct subtype, which is either a DirectoryInfo or a FileInfo object. Once cast to the correct type, you can perform operations on that object.

The final step is to add a recursive method call every time you find a DirectoryInfo object. This ((DirectoryInfo)item).FullName string is then passed as an argument to this same function, making it the starting directory for the new function call. This continues on until every directory under the initial directory has been returned along with its contents.

See Also

See the "DirectoryInfo Class," "FileInfo Class," and "FileSystemInfo Class" topics in the MSDN documentation.

12.15 Parsing a Path

Problem

You need to separate the constituent parts of a path and place them into separate variables.

Solution

Use the static methods of the Path class:

```
public static void ParsePath(string path)
{
    string root = Path.GetPathRoot(path);
    string dirName = Path.GetDirectoryName(path);
    string fullFileName = Path.GetFileName(path);
    string fileExt = Path.GetExtension(path);
    string fileNameWithoutExt = Path.GetFileNameWithoutExtension(path);
    StringBuilder format = new StringBuilder( );
    format.Append("ParsePath of {0} breaks up into the following pieces:" +
            Environment.NewLine + "\tRoot: {1}" +
            Environment.NewLine + "\t");
    format.Append("Directory Name: {2}" +
            Environment.NewLine + "\tFull File Name: {3}" +
            Environment.NewLine + "\t");
    format.Append("File Extension: {4}" +
            Environment.NewLine + "\tFile Name Without Extension: {5}" +
            Environment.NewLine + "");
    Console.WriteLine(format.ToString( ),path,root,dirName,
            fullFileName,fileExt,fileNameWithoutExt);
}
```

If the string @C:\test\tempfile.txt is passed to this method, the output looks like this:

```
ParsePath of C:\test\tempfile.txt breaks up into the following pieces:
        Root: C:\
        Directory Name: C:\test
        Full File Name: tempfile.txt
        File Extension: .txt
        File Name Without Extension: tempfile
```

Discussion

The Path class contains methods that can be used to parse a given path. Using these classes is much easier and less error-prone than writing path- and filename-parsing code. There are five main methods used to parse a path: GetPathRoot, GetDirectoryName, GetFileName, GetExtension, and GetFileNameWithoutExtension. Each has a single parameter, *path*, which represents the path to be parsed:

GetPathRoot

This method returns the root directory of the path. If no root is provided in the path, such as when a relative path is used, this method returns an empty string, not null.

GetDirectoryName

This method returns the complete path for the directory that the file is in.

GetFileName

This method returns the filename, including the file extension. If no filename is provided in the path, this method returns an empty string, not null.

GetExtension

This method returns the file's extension. If no extension is provided for the file or no file exists in the path, this method returns an empty string, not null.

GetFileNameWithoutExtension

This method returns the root filename without the file extension.

Be aware that these methods do not actually determine whether the drives, directories, or even files exist on the system that runs these methods. These methods are string parsers and if you pass one of them a string in some strange format (such as \\ZY:\foo), it will try to do what it can with it anyway:

```
ParsePath of \\ZY:\foo breaks up into the following pieces:
        Root: \\ZY:\foo
        Directory Name:
        Full File Name: foo
        File Extension:
        File Name Without Extension: foo
```

These methods will, however, throw an exception if illegal characters are found in the path.

To determine whether files or directories exist, use the static `Directory.Exists` or `File.Exists` method.

See Also

See the "Path Class" topic in the MSDN documentation.

12.16 Parsing Paths in Environment Variables

Problem

You need to parse multiple paths contained in environment variables, such as PATH or Include.

Solution

You can use the `Path.PathSeparator` field or the `;` character to extract individual paths from an environment variable with a value that consists of multiple paths and place them in an array. Then you can use a `foreach` loop to iterate over each individual path in the PATH environment variable and parse each path. This process is illustrated by the `ParsePathEnvironmentVariable` method:

```
public static void ParsePathEnvironmentVariable( )
{
    string originalPathEnv = Environment.GetEnvironmentVariable("PATH");
    string[] paths = originalPathEnv.Split(new char[1] {Path.PathSeparator});
    foreach (string s in paths)
    {
        string pathEnv = Environment.ExpandEnvironmentVariables(s);
        Console.WriteLine("Path = " + pathEnv);
        if(pathEnv.Length > 0)
        {
            Console.WriteLine("Individual Path = " + pathEnv);
        }
        else
        {
            Console.WriteLine("Skipping blank environment path details " +
                    " as it causes exceptions...");
        }
    }
}
```

If the PATH environment variable contains the following:

```
PATH=Path=C:\WINDOWS\system32;C:\WINDOWS
```

then the output of the ParsePathEnvironmentVariable method is as follows:

```
Individual Path = C:\WINDOWS\system32
Individual Path = C:\WINDOWS
```

Discussion

When working with environment variables in particular, there are a number of cases in which several paths may be concatenated and you need to parse each one individually. To distinguish each individual path from the others, Microsoft Windows uses the semicolon character. (Other operating systems might use a different character; Unix, Linux, and Mac OS X use a colon.) To make sure that we always use the correct path-separation character, the Path class contains a public static field called PathSeparator. This field contains the character used to separate paths in the current platform. This field is marked as read-only, so it cannot be modified.

To obtain each individual path contained in a single string, use the Split instance method from the String class. This method accepts a param array of character values that are used to break apart the string instance. These individual strings containing the paths are returned in a string array. Then we simply use the foreach loop construct to iterate over each string in this string array and use the static method ExpandEnvironmentVariables of the Environment class to operate on each individual path string. This static method ensures that any environment variables such as %SystemDrive% are converted to their equivalent value, in this case C:.

See Also

See the "Path Class" and "Environment Class" topics in the MSDN documentation.

12.17 Verifying a Path

Problem

You have a path—possibly entered by the user—and you need to verify that it has no illegal characters and that a filename and extension have been provided.

Solution

We use several of the static fields and methods in the Path class. We begin by writing a method called CheckUserEnteredPath, as shown in Example 12-5. It accepts a string containing a path entered by the user and a Boolean value to decide whether we want to find all illegal characters or just the occurrence of any illegal character. Just finding any illegal character is much faster if you don't care which illegal characters are present. This method first calls another method, either FindAnyIllegalChars or FindAllIllegalChars, each of which are described later in the Solution. If there are no illegal characters in this path, it is then checked for the presence of a filename and extension.

Example 12-5. CheckUserEnteredPath method

```
public static bool CheckUserEnteredPath(string path, bool any)
{
    try
    {
        Console.WriteLine("Checking path {0}",path);

        // Verify that the path parameter is not null.
        if (path == null)
        {
            throw (new ArgumentNullException("path",
                                    "The path passed in cannot be null"));
        }

        bool illegal = false;
        List<char> invalidChars = new List<char>();

        // Two ways to do the search, one more expensive than the other...
        if(any == true)
            illegal = FindAnyIllegalChars(path);    // Cheap
        else
            invalidChars = FindAllIllegalChars(path);    // Expensive

        if (!illegal && invalidChars.Count == 0)
        {
            // Now make sure the path is not an empty string
            // and its filename has an extension.
            if (Path.GetFileName(path).Length == 0)
            {
                Console.WriteLine("A file name must be entered");
```

Example 12-5. CheckUserEnteredPath method (continued)

```
            }
            else if (!Path.HasExtension(path))
            {
                Console.WriteLine("The file name must have an extension");
            }
            else
            {
                Console.WriteLine("Path is correct");
                return (true);
            }
        }
        else if (invalidChars.Count > 0)
        {
            foreach(char c in invalidChars)
                Console.WriteLine(c);
        }
    }
    catch(Exception e)
    {
        Console.WriteLine(e.ToString( ));
    }

    return (false);
}
```

The `FindAllIllegalChars` method, which is shown in Example 12-6 and which is called by the `CheckUserEnteredPath` method, accepts a string containing a path. This path is checked for illegal characters by using the `IndexOfAny` method on the string class. The `IndexOfAny` method finds the first occurrence of one of the characters supplied to it in the string being examined. This method uses the `Path.InvalidPathChars` static field to determine if any illegal characters exist in this path.

Example 12-6. FindAllIllegalChars method

```
private static List<char> FindAllIllegalChars(string path)
{
    // Get directory portion of the path.
    string dirName = path;
    string fullFileName = "";
    int pos = path.LastIndexOf( Path.DirectorySeparatorChar);
    if (pos >= 0)
    {
        dirName = path.Substring(0, pos);

        // Get filename portion of the path.
        if (pos >= 0 && (pos + 1) < path.Length)
            fullFileName = path.Substring(pos + 1);
    }

    int  invalidCharPos = 0;
    bool endOfPath = false;
```

Example 12-6. FindAllIllegalChars method (continued)

```csharp
    List<char> invalidChars = new List<char>( );

    // Find any characters in the directory that are illegal.
    while (!endOfPath)
    {
        invalidCharPos = dirName.IndexOfAny(Path.GetInvalidPathChars( ),
        invalidCharPos++);
        if (invalidCharPos == -1)
        {
            endOfPath = true;
        }
        else
        {
            Console.WriteLine(
                "Invalid char {0} found at position {1} in directory path.",
                            dirName[invalidCharPos], invalidCharPos);

            invalidChars.Add(dirName[invalidCharPos]);

            if (invalidCharPos >= dirName.Length - 1)
            {
                endOfPath = true;
            }
            else
            {
                invalidCharPos++;
            }
        }
    }

    bool endOfFileName = false;
    invalidCharPos = 0;

    // Find any characters in the filename that are illegal.
    while (!endOfFileName)
    {
        invalidCharPos = fullFileName.IndexOfAny(Path.GetInvalidFileNameChars( ),
                                        invalidCharPos++);
        if (invalidCharPos == -1)
        {
            endOfFileName = true;
        }
        else
        {
            Console.WriteLine(
                "Invalid char {0} found at position {1} in file name.",
                fullFileName[invalidCharPos], invalidCharPos);

            invalidChars.Add(fullFileName[invalidCharPos]);

            if (invalidCharPos >= fullFileName.Length - 1)
            {
```

Example 12-6. FindAllIllegalChars method (continued)

```
                endOfFileName = true;
            }
            else
            {
                invalidCharPos++;
            }
        }
    }

    return (invalidChars);
}
```

Notice that we did not use the `Path.GetDirectoryName` and `Path.GetFileName` methods to parse the directory and filename, respectively, from the entire path string. If we did use these methods on a `path` string containing invalid characters, they would throw an exception too early in the processing.

The `FindAnyIllegalChars` method shown in Example 12-7, which is also called by the `CheckUserEnteredPath` method, accepts a string containing a user-entered path. This path is checked for the existence of any illegal characters by using the `IndexOfAny` method on the string class. If the `IndexOfAny` method finds anything, we have an illegal path and we return false.

Example 12-7. FindAnyIllegalChars method

```
private static bool FindAnyIllegalChars(string path)
{
    // Get directory portion of the path.
    string dirName = path;
    string fullFileName = "";
    int pos = path.LastIndexOf(Path.DirectorySeparatorChar);
    if (pos >= 0)
    {
        dirName = path.Substring(0, pos);

        // Get filename portion of the path.
        if (pos >= 0 && (pos + 1) < path.Length)
            fullFileName = path.Substring(pos + 1);
    }

    // Find any characters in the directory that are illegal.
    int invalidCharPos = dirName.IndexOfAny(Path.GetInvalidPathChars());
    if (invalidCharPos == -1)
    {
        // Find any characters in the filename that are illegal.
        invalidCharPos = fullFileName.IndexOfAny(Path.GetInvalidFileNameChars());
        if (invalidCharPos == -1)
        {
            return (false);
        }
        else
```

Example 12-7. FindAnyIllegalChars method (continued)

```
    {
        Console.WriteLine(
            "Invalid char {0} found at position {1} in filename.",
            fullFileName[invalidCharPos], invalidCharPos);
        return (true);
    }
}
else
{
    Console.WriteLine(
        "Invalid char {0} found at position {1} in directory path.",
        dirName[invalidCharPos], invalidCharPos);
    return (true);
}
}
```

Discussion

This recipe provides a way of screening a path for invalid characters before it can be used in your application. This recipe does not verify that the directory or path exists; use the `Directory.Exists` or `File.Exists` methods to perform this verification.

The `CheckUserEnteredPath` method starts by calling the `FindAnyIllegalChars` or `FindAllIllegalChars` methods and passing the chosen one a path string. The path is validated against the set of characters supplied by both the `Path.GetInvalidPathChars` and the `Path.GetInvalidFileNameChars` static methods. These methods return character arrays that contain all of the invalid characters that could be entered into a path or filename string, respectively.

The `CheckUserEnteredPath` and `FindAnyIllegalChars` methods return true if there are illegal characters found. `FindAnyIllegalChars` prints information to the console for only the first one found, whereas `FindAllIllegalChars` returns a `List<char>` containing all illegal characters found.

See Also

See the "String Class" and "Path Class" topics in the MSDN documentation.

12.18 Using a Temporary File in Your Application

Problem

You need a temporary file in which to store information. This file should exist only as long as the process that created it remains running.

Solution

Use the static `GetTempPath` and `GetTempFileName` methods on the `Path` class. To create the temporary file in the directory set as the temporary directory and get the full path to it, use the following line of code:

```
string tempFilePathWithFileName = Path.GetTempFileName( );
```

Before the application terminates, you should delete this temporary file. The following line of code deletes this file:

```
File.Delete(tempFilePathWithFileName);
```

The `GetTempFileName` method creates the temporary file and returns the path, including the name of the file and its extension. To create and obtain just the path without the filename, use the following line of code:

```
string tempFilePathWithoutFileName = Path.GetTempPath( );
```

Discussion

You should use a temporary file whenever you need to store information temporarily for later retrieval. The one thing you must remember is to delete this temporary file before the application that created it is terminated. If it is not deleted, it will remain in the user's temporary directory until the user manually deletes it.

The `Path` class provides two methods for working with temporary files. The first is the static `GetTempPath` method, which returns the path to the temporary directory. The temporary directory is found by searching the `TMP`, then the `TEMP`, then the `USERPROFILE` environment variables, and finally the `Windows` directory.

The second static method, `GetTempFileName`, will automatically generate a temporary filename, create a zero-length file in the user's temporary directory, and return a string containing this filename and its path.

See Also

See the "Directory Class," "File Class," and "Path Class" topics in the MSDN documentation.

12.19 Opening a File Stream with Just a File Handle

Problem

When interoperating with unmanaged code, you encounter a situation in which you are provided a file handle and no other information. This file handle must be used to open its corresponding file.

Solution

In order to use an unmanaged file handle to access a file, use the `FileStream` class. The unmanaged file handle could have been generated using P/Invoke to open a file and get the file handle. The code would then use a `FileStream` object for writing data, then flush and close the unmanaged file handle. This setup is illustrated by the `UsingAnUnmanagedFileHandle` method shown in Example 12-8.

Example 12-8. UsingAnUnmanagedFileHandle method

```
public static void UsingAnUnmanagedFileHandle( )
{
    IntPtr hFile = IntPtr.Zero;
    // Create a file using unmanaged code.
    hFile = FileInteropFunctions.CreateFile("data.txt",
        FileInteropFunctions.GENERIC_WRITE,
        0,
        IntPtr.Zero,
        FileInteropFunctions.CREATE_ALWAYS,
        0,
        0);

    if(hFile.ToInt64( ) > 0)
    {
        // Write to the file using managed code.
        // Wrap our file handle in a safe handle wrapper object.
        Microsoft.Win32.SafeHandles.SafeFileHandle safeHFile =
            new Microsoft.Win32.SafeHandles.SafeFileHandle(hFile, true);

        // Open a FileStream object using the passed in safe file handle.
        using (FileStream fileStream =
                new FileStream(safeHFile, FileAccess.ReadWrite))
        {
            // Flush before we start to clear any pending unmanaged actions.
            fileStream.Flush( );
            // Operate on file here...
            string line = "Managed code wrote this line!";
            // Write to the file.
            byte[] bytes = Encoding.ASCII.GetBytes(line);
            fileStream.Write(bytes,0,bytes.Length);
        }

        // Remove the file.
        File.Delete("data.txt");
    }
}
```

In the `UsingAnUnmanagedFileHandle` method, we wrap the file handle in a `SafeFileHandle` object and pass it as the first parameter, in a `FileStream`. Once we have the file stream, we use its capabilities to write to the file handle. We get the bytes from a string in ASCII-encoding format and call `Write` on the file stream, as shown here:

```
byte[] bytes = Encoding.ASCII.GetBytes(line);
fileStream.Write(bytes,0,bytes.Length);
```

In order to perform the unmanaged functions of creating, flushing, and closing the file handle, we have wrapped the unmanaged Win32 API functions for these functions in the `FileInteropFunctions` class shown in Example 12-9. The `DllImport` attribute says that these functions are being used from *kernel32.dll* and the `SetLastError` attribute is set to true, so that we can see if anything went wrong. A few of the #defines used with file creation have been brought over from unmanaged code for readability.

Example 12-9. FileInteropFunctions class

```
class FileInteropFunctions
{
    public const uint GENERIC_READ = (0x80000000);
    public const uint GENERIC_WRITE = (0x40000000);
    public const uint GENERIC_EXECUTE = (0x20000000);
    public const uint GENERIC_ALL = (0x10000000);

    public const uint CREATE_NEW        = 1;
    public const uint CREATE_ALWAYS     = 2;
    public const uint OPEN_EXISTING     = 3;
    public const uint OPEN_ALWAYS       = 4;
    public const uint TRUNCATE_EXISTING = 5;

    [DllImport("kernel32.dll", SetLastError=true)]
    public static extern bool CloseHandle(IntPtr hObject);

    [DllImport("kernel32.dll", SetLastError=true)]
    public static extern IntPtr CreateFile(
        String lpFileName,              // Filename
        uint dwDesiredAccess,              // Access mode
        uint dwShareMode,              // Share mode
        IntPtr attr,                 // Security Descriptor
        uint dwCreationDisposition,          // How to create
        uint dwFlagsAndAttributes,          // File attributes
        uint hTemplateFile);              // Handle to template file

    [DllImport("kernel32.dll", SetLastError=true)]
    public static extern bool FlushFileBuffers(IntPtr hFile);
}
```

Discussion

You can open a file using one of the overloaded constructors of the `FileStream` class and passing a file handle into it. The `FileStream` constructors in Version 2.0 of the .NET Framework have been enhanced to accept a `Microsoft.Win32.SafeHandles.SafeFileHandle` object instead of an `IntPtr` for the file handle. The `SafeFileHandle` wraps the IntPtr file handle and allows the system to handle the releasing of this file handle automatically. To automatically release this wrapped file handle, you must pass true as the second argument to the SafeFileHandle constructor. Microsoft recommends letting the system handle the releasing of this wrapped file handle.

Keep your code short when opening a file using a file handle. Call the FileStream. Close method as soon as possible or use the using statement as in the Solution for this recipe. One reason for this recommendation is that another object might also have this file open, and operating on that file through both FileStream objects can corrupt the data in the file.

See Also

See the "DllImport Attribute," "File Class," and "FileStream Class" topics in the MSDN documentation.

12.20 Writing to Multiple Output Files at One Time

Problem

Any output that is written to one file must also be written to at least one other file. Essentially, you want to end up with at least the original file and a duplicate file.

Solution

Create a class called MultiWriter with the ability to write to multiple files from a single WriteLine call.

To create a set of files, just pass the file paths you would like to use to the constructor like this:

```
// Create a list of three filenames.
string[] names = new string[3];
for (int i=0;i<3;i++)
{
    names[i] = Path.GetTempFileName( );
}
MultiWriter multi = new MultiWriter(names);
```

Next, perform the writes and close the instance:

```
multi.WriteLine("First Line");
multi.WriteLine("Second Line");
multi.WriteLine("Third Line");
multi.Close( );
```

Example 12-10 is the implementation of the MultiWriter class.

Example 12-10. MultiWriter class

```csharp
class MultiWriter : IDisposable
{
    FileStream[] _streams;
    string [] _names;
    int _streamCount = 0;
    bool _disposed = false;

    public MultiWriter(string[] fileNames)
    {
        try
        {
            // Copy the names.
            _names = (string[])fileNames.Clone( );
            // Set the number of streams.
            _streamCount = fileNames.Length;
            // Make the stream array.
            _streams = new FileStream[_streamCount];
            for(int i = 0; i < _streams.Length; i++)
            {
                // Create this file stream.
                _streams[i] = new FileStream(_names[i],
                    FileMode.Create,
                    FileAccess.ReadWrite,
                    FileShare.None);
            }
        }
        catch(IOException ioe)
        {
            Console.WriteLine(ioe.ToString( ));
        }
    }

    public void WriteLine(string text)
    {
        // Add a newline.
        text += Environment.NewLine;
        // Get the bytes in unicode format...
        byte[] bytes = Encoding.ASCII.GetBytes(text);
        // Roll over the streams.
        for(int i = 0; i < _streams.Length; i++)
        {
            // Write the text.
            _streams[i].Write(bytes,0,bytes.Length);
        }
    }

    public void Close( )
    {
        Dispose( );
    }

    public void Dispose( )
```

Example 12-10. MultiWriter class (continued)

```
    {
        Dispose(true);
        // Prevent refinalizing.
        GC.SuppressFinalize(this);
    }

    protected void Dispose(bool disposing)
    {
        try
        {
            // Only close out once.
            if(_disposed == false && disposing == true)
            {
                // Close each stream.
                for(int i=0;i<_streams.Length;i++)
                {
                    _streams[i].Close( );
                }

                // Indicate we have done this already.
                _disposed = true;
            }
        }
        catch(IOException ioe)
        {
            Console.WriteLine(ioe);
        }
    }

    ~MultiWriter( )
    {
        Dispose(false);
    }
}
```

Discussion

MultiWriter implements the IDisposable interface, which helps the users remember to close the files this will create. Ultimately, if the user forgets to call Close (a thin wrapper around Dispose for semantic convenience), the finalizer (~MultiWriter) will call Dispose anyway and close the files when the garbage collector finalizes the instance. Note that in the public Dispose method, we call the protected Dispose method, which closes the file streams we created internally and calls the GC. SuppressFinalize method. This is an optimization to keep the garbage collector from having to call our finalizer.

See Also

See the "FileStream Class," "GC Class," and "IDisposable Interface" topics in the MSDN documentation.

12.21 Launching and Interacting with Console Utilities

Problem

You have an application that you need to automate and that takes input only from the standard input stream. You need to drive this application via the commands it will take over the standard input stream.

Solution

Say we needed to drive the *cmd.exe* application to display the current time with the TIME /T command (it is possible to just run this command from the command line, but this way we can demonstrate an alternative method to drive an application that responds to standard input). The way to do this is to launch a process that is looking for input on the standard input stream. This is accomplished via the Process class StartInfo property, which is an instance of a ProcessStartInfo class. The Process. Start method will launch a new process, but the StartInfo property controls many of the details of what sort of environment that process executes in.

First, make sure that the StartInfo.RedirectStandardInput property is set to true. This setting notifies the process that it should read from standard input. Then set the StartInfo.UseShellExecute property to false, because if you were to let the shell launch the process for you, it would prevent you from redirecting standard input.

Once this is done, launch the process and write to its standard input stream as shown in Example 12-11.

Example 12-11. RunProcessToReadStdIn method

```
public static void RunProcessToReadStdIn( )
{
    Process application = new Process( );
    // Run the command shell.
    application.StartInfo.FileName = @"cmd.exe";

    // Turn on standard extensions.
    application.StartInfo.Arguments = "/E:ON";

    application.StartInfo.RedirectStandardInput = true;

    application.StartInfo.UseShellExecute = false;

    // Start it up.
    application.Start( );

    // Get stdin.
    StreamWriter input = application.StandardInput;
```

Example 12-11. RunProcessToReadStdIn method (continued)

```
    // Run the command to display the time.
    input.WriteLine("TIME /T");

    // Stop the application we launched.
    input.WriteLine("exit");
}
```

Discussion

Once the input has been redirected, you can write into the standard input stream of the process by reading the `Process.StandardInput` property, which returns a `StreamWriter`. Once you have that, you can send things to the process via `WriteLine` calls, as shown earlier.

In order to use `StandardInput`, you have to specify true for the `StartInfo` property's `RedirectStandardInput` property. Otherwise, reading the `StandardInput` property throws an exception.

When `UseShellExecute` is false, you can use `Process` only to create executable processes. Normally the `Process` class can be used to perform operations on the file, like printing a Microsoft Word document. Another difference when `UseShellExecute` is set to false is that the working directory is not used to find the executable, so you should be mindful to pass a full path or have the executable on your `PATH` environment variable.

See Also

See the "Process Class," "ProcessStartInfo Class," "RedirectStandardInput Property," and "UseShellExecute Property" topics in the MSDN documentation.

12.22 Locking Subsections of a File

Problem

You need to read or write data from or to a section of a file, and you want to make sure that no other processes or threads can access, modify, or delete the file until you have finished with it.

Solution

Locking out other processes from accessing your file while you are using it is accomplished through the `Lock` method of the `FileStream` class. The following code creates a file from the *fileName* parameter and writes two lines to it. The entire file is then locked using the `Lock` method. While the file is locked, the code goes off and does some other processing; when this code returns, the file is closed, thereby unlocking it:

```
public static void CreateLockedFile(string fileName)
{
    using (FileStream fileStream = new FileStream(fileName,
            FileMode.Create,
            FileAccess.ReadWrite,
            FileShare.ReadWrite))
    {
        using (StreamWriter streamWriter = new StreamWriter(fileStream))
        {
            streamWriter.WriteLine("The First Line");
            streamWriter.WriteLine("The Second Line");
            streamWriter.Flush( );

            // Lock all of the file.
            fileStream.Lock(0, fileStream.Length);

            // Do some lengthy processing here...
            Thread.Sleep(1000);

            // Make sure we unlock the file.
            // If a process terminates with part of a file locked or closes a file
            // that has outstanding locks, the behavior is undefined which is MS
            // speak for bad things....
            fileStream.Unlock(0, fileStream.Length);

            streamWriter.WriteLine("The Third Line");
        }
    }
}
```

Discussion

If a file is opened within your application and the FileShare parameter of the
FileStream.Open call is set to FileShare.ReadWrite or FileShare.Write, other code in
your application can view or alter the contents of the file while you are using it. To
handle file access with more granularity, use the Lock method of the FileStream
object to prevent other code from overwriting all or a portion of your file. Once you
are done with the locked portion of your file, you can call the Unlock method on the
FileStream object to allow other code in your application to write data to that portion of the file.

To lock an entire file, use the following syntax:

```
fileStream.Lock(0, fileStream.Length);
```

To lock a portion of a file, use the following syntax:

```
fileStream.Lock(4, fileStream.Length - 4);
```

This line of code locks the entire file except for the first four characters. Note that
you can lock an entire file and still open it multiple times, as well as write to it.

If another thread is accessing this file, it is possible to see an IOException thrown during the call to either the Write, Flush, or Close methods. For example, the following code is prone to such an exception:

```
public static void CreateLockedFile(string fileName)
{
    using (FileStream fileStream = new FileStream(fileName,
                                    FileMode.Create,
                                    FileAccess.ReadWrite,
                                    FileShare.ReadWrite))
    {
        using (StreamWriter streamWriter = new StreamWriter(fileStream))
        {
            streamWriter.WriteLine("The First Line");
            streamWriter.WriteLine("The Second Line");
            streamWriter.Flush( );

            // Lock all of the file.
            fileStream.Lock(0, fileStream.Length);

            using (StreamWriter streamWriter2 = new StreamWriter(
                        new FileStream(fileName,
                                    FileMode.Open,
                                    FileAccess.Write,
                                    FileShare.ReadWrite)))
            {
                streamWriter2.Write("foo ");
                try
                {
                    streamWriter2.Close( );   // --> Exception occurs here!
                }
                catch
                {
                    Console.WriteLine(
                "The streamWriter2.Close call generated an exception.");
                }
                streamWriter.WriteLine("The Third Line");
            }
        }
    }
}
```

This code produces the following output:

```
The streamWriter2.Close call generated an exception.
```

Even though streamWriter2, the second StreamWriter object, writes to a locked file, it is when the streamWriter2.Close method is executed that the IOException is thrown.

If the code for this recipe were rewritten as follows:

```
public static void CreateLockedFile(string fileName)
{
    using (FileStream fileStream = new FileStream(fileName,
                                    FileMode.Create,
```

```
                       FileAccess.ReadWrite,
                       FileShare.ReadWrite))
   {
      using (StreamWriter streamWriter = new StreamWriter(fileStream))
      {
          streamWriter.WriteLine("The First Line");
          streamWriter.WriteLine("The Second Line");
          streamWriter.Flush( );

          // Lock all of the file.
          fileStream.Lock(0, fileStream.Length);

          // Try to access the locked file...
          using (StreamWriter streamWriter2 = new StreamWriter(
                   new FileStream(fileName,
                                  FileMode.Open,
                                  FileAccess.Write,
                                  FileShare.ReadWrite)))
          {
              streamWriter2.Write("foo");
              fileStream.Unlock(0, fileStream.Length);
              streamWriter2.Flush( );
          }
      }
   }
}
```

no exception is thrown. This is due to the fact that the code closed the FileStream object that initially locked the entire file. This action also freed all of the locks on the file that this FileStream object was holding onto. Since the streamWriter2. Write("Foo") method had written Foo to the stream's buffer (but had not flushed it), the string Foo was still waiting to be flushed and written to the actual file. Keep this situation in mind when interleaving the opening, locking, and closing of streams. Mistakes in code sometimes manifest themselves a while after they are written. This leads to some bugs that are more difficult to track down, so tread carefully when using file locking.

See Also

See the "StreamWriter Class" and "FileStream Class" topics in the MSDN documentation.

12.23 Watching the Filesystem for Specific Changes to One or More Files or Directories

Problem

You want to be notified when a file and/or directory is created, modified, or deleted. In addition, you might need to be notified of any of these actions for a group of files

---

and/or directories. This can aid in alerting your application when a file, such as a log-file, grows to a certain size, after which it must be truncated.

Solution

To be notified when an action takes place in the filesystem, you need to employ the FileSystemWatcher class. The TestWatcher method shown in Example 12-12 sets up a FileSystemWatcher object to watch the entire *C:* drive for any changes. The changes are limited to any file with the extension *.txt*. At the end of this method, the events are wired up for each one of the changes listed in the NotifyFilter property.

Example 12-12. Using the FileSystemWatcher class

```
public static void TestWatcher( )
{
    using (FileSystemWatcher fsw = new FileSystemWatcher( ))
    {
        fsw.Path = @"c:\";
        fsw.Filter = @"*.txt";
        fsw.IncludeSubdirectories = true;

        fsw.NotifyFilter = NotifyFilters.FileName    |
            NotifyFilters.Attributes   |
            NotifyFilters.LastAccess   |
            NotifyFilters.LastWrite    |
            NotifyFilters.Security     |
            NotifyFilters.Size         |
            NotifyFilters.CreationTime |
            NotifyFilters.DirectoryName;

        fsw.Changed += new FileSystemEventHandler(OnChanged);
        fsw.Created += new FileSystemEventHandler(OnCreated);
        fsw.Deleted += new FileSystemEventHandler(OnDeleted);
        fsw.Renamed += new RenamedEventHandler(OnRenamed);
        fsw.Error += new ErrorEventHandler(OnError);

        fsw.EnableRaisingEvents = true;

        string file = @"c:\myfile.txt";
        string newfile = @"c:\mynewfile.txt";

        using (FileStream stream = File.Create(file))
        {
            // Use stream var...
            byte[] bytes = new byte[5] {32,33,34,35,36};
            stream.Write(bytes, 0, bytes.Length);
        }

        using (FileStream stream = File.Create(newfile))
        {
            // Use stream var...
            byte[] bytes = new byte[5] {32,33,34,35,36};
```

Example 12-12. Using the FileSystemWatcher class (continued)

```
            stream.Write(bytes, 0, bytes.Length);
    }

    File.Delete(file);
    File.Delete(newfile);

    // Wait to allow the event handlers to catch up
    // to the events raised by the filesystem.
    Thread.Sleep(1000);
    }
}
```

The following code implements the event handlers to handle the events raised by the FileSystemWatcher object, which we created and initialized in the TestWatcher method:

```
public static void OnChanged(object source, FileSystemEventArgs e)
{
    Console.WriteLine("File " + e.FullPath + " --> " + e.ChangeType);
}

public static void OnDeleted(object source, FileSystemEventArgs e)
{
    Console.WriteLine("File " + e.FullPath + " --> " + e.ChangeType);
}

public static void OnCreated(object source, FileSystemEventArgs e)
{
    Console.WriteLine("File " + e.FullPath + " --> " + e.ChangeType);
}

public static void OnRenamed(object source, RenamedEventArgs e)
{
    Console.WriteLine("File " + e.OldFullPath + " (renamed to)--> " + e.FullPath);
}

public static void OnError(object source, ErrorEventArgs e)
{
    Console.WriteLine("Error " + e.ToString( ));
}
```

The output of the TestWatcher method is shown here:

```
File c:\myfile.txt --> Created
File c:\myfile.txt --> Changed
File c:\mynewfile.txt --> Created
File c:\mynewfile.txt --> Changed
File c:\myfile.txt --> Deleted
```

Discussion

Watching for changes in the filesystem centers around the FileSystemWatcher class. This class can watch for filesystem changes on the local machine, a networked drive, and even a remote machine. The limitations of watching files on a remote machine are that the watching machine must be running versions of Windows starting from Windows NT 4.0 through 2000, XP, Server 2003, and Windows Vista. The one caveat for Windows NT 4.0 is that a Windows NT 4.0 machine cannot watch another remote Windows NT 4.0 machine.

The FileSystemWatcher object cannot watch directories or files on a CD or DVD drive (including rewritables) in the current versions of the Framework. This limitation might be revisited in a future version. This object does watch files regardless of whether their hidden property is set.

To start watching a filesystem, we need to create an instance of the FileSystemWatcher class. After creating the FileSystemWatcher object, we can set its properties in order to focus our efforts in watching a filesystem. Table 12-10 examines the various properties that can be set on this object.

Table 12-10. Properties that can be set on the FileSystemWatcher object

Property name	Description

Path	A path to a directory to watch. The following are some examples of valid values for this property:
	
	`@"C:\temp"`
	`@"C:\Program Files"`
	`@"C:\Progra~1"`
	`@"..\..\temp"`
	`@"\\MyServer\temp"`
	`@"."`
	`@""`
	
	Note that if a directory is specified, changes to it, such as deleting it or changing its attributes, are not watched. Only changes within the directory are watched. Assigning an empty string forces the current directory to be watched.

IncludeSubdirectories	Set to `true` to monitor all subdirectories as well, or `false` to watch only the specified directory.

Filter	Specifies a specific subset of files to watch. The following are some examples of valid values for this property:
	
	`// Watch only .exe files`
	`@"*.exe"`
	`// Watch all files`
	`@"*"`
	`// Watch all files`
	`@""`
	`// Watch all files beginning // with the letter 'a'`
	`@"a*"`
	`// Watch all files with the // name "test" and // having a`
	`three-letter // extension starting // with the letter 'd'`
	`@"test.d??"`

Table 12-10. Properties that can be set on the FileSystemWatcher object (continued)

Property name	Description
NotifyFilter	One or more NotifyFilters enumeration values. This enumeration is marked with the FlagsAttribute, so each enumeration value can be ORed together using the | operator. By default, this property is set to FileName, DirectoryName, and LastWrite. The members of the NotifyFilters enumeration are shown in Table 12-11.
EnableRaisingEvents	When this property is set to true, the FileSystemWatcher object starts watching the filesystem. To stop this object from watching the filesystem, set this property to false.
InternalBufferSize	The internal buffer size in bytes for this object. It is used to store information about the raised filesystem events. This buffer defaults in size to 8192 bytes. See additional information about this property next.

The NotifyFilters enumeration values in Table 12-11 determine which events the FileSystemWatcher object watches. For example, the OnChanged event can be raised when any of the following NotifyFilters enumeration values are passed to the NotifyFilter property:

```
NotifyFilters.Attributes
NotifyFilters.Size
NotifyFilters.LastAccess
NotifyFilters.LastWrite
NotifyFilters.Security
NotifyFilters.CreationTime
```

Table 12-11. NotifyFilters enumeration value definitions

Enumeration name	Description
Attributes	Watches for changes to a file or directory's attributes.
CreationTime	Watches for changes to a file or directory's creation time.
DirectoryName	Watches for changes to a directory's name.
FileName	Watches for changes to a file's name.
LastAccess	Watches for changes to a file or directory's last-accessed property.
LastWrite	Watches for changes to a file or directory's last-written-to property.
Security	Watches for changes to a file or directory's security settings.
Size	Watches for changes to a file or directory's size.

The OnRenamed event can be raised when any of the following NotifyFilters enumeration values are passed to the NotifyFilter property:

```
NotifyFilters.DirectoryName
NotifyFilters.FileName
```

The OnCreated and OnDeleted events can be raised when any of the following NotifyFilters enumeration values are passed to the NotifyFilter property:

```
NotifyFilters.DirectoryName
NotifyFilters.FileName
```

There are times when the FileSystemWatcher object cannot handle the number of raised events coming from the filesystem. In this case, the Error event is raised, informing you that the buffer has overflowed and specific events may have been lost. To reduce the likelihood of this problem, we can limit the number of raised events by minimizing the number of events watched for in the NotifyFilter property. Limiting the filter on the Filter property, however, will not affect the number of raised events. To decrease the number of raised events further, you can set the IncludeSubdirectories property to false. You might also consider increasing the InternalBufferSize property. To estimate what size to increase this buffer to, Microsoft provides the following tips:

- A 4k-byte buffer can keep track of changes for about 80 files in a directory.
- Every event consumes 16 bytes of buffer space.
- In addition to these 16 bytes, the filename is stored as Unicode characters.
- If you are using Windows 2000, consider increasing/decreasing the buffer size by a multiple of 4k bytes. This is the same size as a default memory page.
- If you do not know your operating system's page size, use the following code to increase the FileSystemWatcher's buffer size:

```
FileSystemWatcher fsw = new FileSystemWatcher( );
fsw.InternalBufferSize *= Multiplier;
```

where Multiplier is an integer used to increase the size of the buffer. This makes the most efficient use of the buffer space.

You should increase the InternalBufferSize only as a last resort. This is an expensive operation, because the buffer space is created in nonpaged memory. Nonpaged memory is memory available to the process that will always be in physical memory. It is a limited resource and is shared across all processes on the machine, so it is possible to affect the operation of other processes using this pool if too much is requested.

In many cases, a single action performed by the user produces many filesystem events. Creating a text file on the desktop yields the following changes:

```
File c:\documents and settings\administrator\ntuser.dat.log --> Changed
File c:\documents and settings\administrator\ntuser.dat.log --> Changed
File c:\documents and settings\administrator\ntuser.dat.log --> Changed
File c:\documents and settings\administrator\ntuser.dat.log --> Changed
File c:\documents and settings\administrator\ntuser.dat.log --> Changed
File c:\documents and settings\administrator\ntuser.dat.log --> Changed
File c:\documents and settings\administrator\ntuser.dat.log --> Changed
File c:\documents and settings\administrator\ntuser.dat.log --> Changed
File c:\documents and settings\administrator\ntuser.dat --> Changed
File c:\documents and settings\administrator\ntuser.dat --> Changed
File c:\documents and settings\administrator\ntuser.dat --> Changed
File c:\documents and settings\administrator\ntuser.dat --> Changed
File c:\documents and settings\administrator\ntuser.dat.log --> Changed
File c:\winnt\system32\config\software.log --> Changed
```

```
File c:\winnt\system32\config\software.log --> Changed
File c:\winnt\system32\config\software.log --> Changed
File c:\winnt\system32\config\software --> Changed
File c:\winnt\system32\config\software --> Changed
File c:\winnt\system32\config\software --> Changed
File c:\winnt\system32\config\software --> Changed
File c:\winnt\system32\config\software.log --> Changed
File c:\documents and settings\administrator\desktop\newdoc.txt Created
```

Much of this work is simply registry access. Not until the end of this listing is the text file actually created.

Another example of multiple filesystem events firing for a single action is when this newly created text file is opened by double-clicking on it. The following events are raised by this action:

```
File c:\winnt\system32\notepad.exe --> Changed
File c:\winnt\system32\notepad.exe --> Changed
File c:\documents and settings\administrator\recent\newdoc.txt.lnk --> Deleted
File c:\documents and settings\administrator\recent\newdoc.txt.lnk --> Created
File c:\documents and settings\administrator\recent\newdoc.txt.lnk --> Changed
File c:\winnt\system32\config\software.log --> Changed
File c:\winnt\system32\shell32.dll --> Changed
File c:\winnt\system32\shell32.dll --> Changed
```

Of course, your results may vary, especially if another application accesses the registry or another file while the text file is being opened. Even more events may be raised if a background process or service, such as a virus checker, is accessing the filesystem.

See Also

See the "FileSystemWatcher Class" and "NotifyFilters Enumeration" topics in the MSDN documentation.

12.24 Waiting for an Action to Occur in the Filesystem

Problem

You need to be notified when a particular event occurs in the filesystem, such as the renaming of a file or directory, the increasing or decreasing of the size of a file, the user deleting a file or directory, the creation of a file or directory, or even the changing of a file or directory's attribute(s). However, this notification must occur synchronously. In other words, the application cannot continue unless a specific action occurs to a file or directory.

Solution

The WaitForChanged method of the FileSystemWatcher class can be called to wait synchronously for an event notification. This is illustrated by the WaitForZipCreation method shown in Example 12-13, which waits for an action—more specifically, the action of creating the *Backup.zip* file somewhere on the *C:\ drive*—to be performed before proceeding on to the next line of code, which is the WriteLine statement. Finally, we spin off a thread from the ThreadPool to execute the PauseAndCreateFile method, which does the actual work of creating the file. By doing this in a background thread, we allow the FileSystemWatcher to detect the file creation.

Example 12-13. WaitForZipCreation method

```
public void WaitForZipCreation(string path, string fileName)
{
    FileSystemWatcher fsw = null;
    try
    {
        using (fsw = new FileSystemWatcher( ))
        {
            string [] data = new string[] {path,fileName};
            fsw.Path = path;
            fsw.Filter = fileName;
            fsw.NotifyFilter = NotifyFilters.LastAccess | NotifyFilters.LastWrite
                | NotifyFilters.FileName | NotifyFilters.DirectoryName;

            // Run the code to generate the file we are looking for.
            // Normally you wouldn't do this as another source is creating
            // this file.
            if(ThreadPool.QueueUserWorkItem(new WaitCallback(PauseAndCreateFile),
                                                    data))
            {
                // Block waiting for change.
                WaitForChangedResult result =
                            fsw.WaitForChanged(WatcherChangeTypes.Created);
                Console.WriteLine("{0} created at {1}.",result.Name,path);
            }
        }
    }
    catch(Exception e)
    {
        Console.WriteLine(e.ToString( ));
        throw;
    }
    // Clean it up.
    File.Delete(fileName);
}
```

The code for PauseAndCreateFile is listed here. It is in the form of a WaitCallback to be used as an argument to QueueUserWorkItem on the ThreadPool class. QueueUserWorkItem will run PauseAndCreateFile on a thread from the .NET thread pool:

```
void PauseAndCreateFile(Object stateInfo)
{
    try
    {
```

```
        string[] data = (string[])stateInfo;
        // Wait a sec...
        Thread.Sleep(1000);
        // Create a file in the temp directory.
        string path = data[0];
        string file = path + data[1];
        Console.WriteLine("Creating {0} in PauseAndCreateFile...",file);
        using (FileStream fileStream = File.Create(file))
        {
            // Use fileStream var...
        }
    }
    catch(Exception e)
    {
        Console.WriteLine(e.ToString( ));
        throw;
    }
}
```

Discussion

The WaitForChanged method returns a WaitForChangedResult structure that contains the properties listed in Table 12-12.

Table 12-12. WaitForChangedResult properties

Property	Description
ChangeType	Lists the type of change that occurred. This change is returned as a WatcherChangeTypes enumeration. The values of this enumeration can possibly be ORed together.
Name	Holds the name of the file or directory that was changed. If the file or directory was renamed, this property returns the changed name. Its value is set to null if the operation method call times out.
OldName	The original name of the modified file or directory. If this file or directory was not renamed, this property will return the same value as the Name property. Its value is set to null if the operation method call times out.
TimedOut	Holds a Boolean indicating whether the WaitForChanged method timed out (true) or not (false).

The way we are currently making the WaitForChanged call could possibly block indefinitely. To prevent you from hanging forever on the WaitForChanged call, you can specify a timeout value of 3 seconds as follows:

```
WaitForChangedResult result =
        fsw.WaitForChanged(WatcherChangeTypes.Created, 3000);
```

See Also

See the "FileSystemWatcher Class," "NotifyFilters Enumeration," and "Wait-ForChangedResult Structure" topics in the MSDN documentation.

12.25 Comparing Version Information of Two Executable Modules

Problem

You need to programmatically compare the version information of two executable modules. An executable module is a file that contains executable code such as an *.exe* or *.dll* file. The ability to compare the version information of two executable modules can be very useful to an application in situations such as:

- Trying to determine if it has all of the "right" pieces present to execute
- Deciding on an assembly to dynamically load through reflection
- Looking for the newest version of a file or *.dll* from many files spread out in the local filesystem or on a network

Solution

Use the CompareFileVersions method to compare executable module version information. This method accepts two filenames, including their paths, as parameters. The version information of each module is retrieved and compared. This file returns a FileComparison enumeration, defined as follows:

```
public enum FileComparison
{
    Same = 0,
    Newer = 1,    // File1 is newer than File2
    Older = 2,    // File1 is older than File2
    Error = 3
}
```

The code for the CompareFileVersions method is shown in Example 12-14.

Example 12-14. CompareFileVersions method

```
public static FileComparison CompareFileVersions(string file1, string file2)
{
    FileComparison retValue = FileComparison.Error;
    // Do both files exist?
    if (!File.Exists(file1))
    {
        Console.WriteLine(file1 + " does not exist");
    }
    else if (!File.Exists(file2))
    {
        Console.WriteLine(file2 + " does not exist");
    }
    else
    {
        // Get the version information.
        FileVersionInfo file1Version = FileVersionInfo.GetVersionInfo(file1);
```

Example 12-14. CompareFileVersions method (continued)

```
        FileVersionInfo file2Version = FileVersionInfo.GetVersionInfo(file2);

// Check major.
if (file1Version.FileMajorPart > file2Version.FileMajorPart)
{
    Console.WriteLine(file1 + " is a newer version");
    retValue = FileComparison.Newer;
}
else if (file1Version.FileMajorPart < file2Version.FileMajorPart)
{
    Console.WriteLine(file2 + " is a newer version");
    retValue = FileComparison.Older;
}
else // Major version is equal, check next...
{
    // Check minor.
    if (file1Version.FileMinorPart > file2Version.FileMinorPart)
    {
        Console.WriteLine(file1 + " is a newer version");
        retValue = FileComparison.Newer;
    }
    else if (file1Version.FileMinorPart < file2Version.FileMinorPart)
    {
        Console.WriteLine(file2 + " is a newer version");
        retValue = FileComparison.Older;
    }
    else // Minor version is equal, check next...
    {
        // Check build.
        if (file1Version.FileBuildPart > file2Version.FileBuildPart)
        {
            Console.WriteLine(file1 + " is a newer version");
            retValue = FileComparison.Newer;
        }
        else if (file1Version.FileBuildPart < file2Version.FileBuildPart)
        {
            Console.WriteLine(file2 + " is a newer version");
            retValue = FileComparison.Older;
        }
        else // Build version is equal, check next...
        {
            // Check private.
            if (file1Version.FilePrivatePart >
                    file2Version.FilePrivatePart)
            {
                Console.WriteLine(file1 + " is a newer version");
                retValue = FileComparison.Newer;
            }
            else if (file1Version.FilePrivatePart <
                    file2Version.FilePrivatePart)
            {
                Console.WriteLine(file2 + " is a newer version");
```

Example 12-14. CompareFileVersions method (continued)

```
                retValue = FileComparison.Older;
            }
            else
            {
                // Identical versions
                Console.WriteLine("The files have the same version");
                retValue = FileComparison.Same;
            }
        }
    }
}
    return retValue;
}
```

Discussion

Not all executable modules have version information. If you load a module with no version information using the `FileVersionInfo` class, you will not provoke an exception, nor will you get `null` back for the object reference. Instead, you will get a valid `FileVersionInfo` object with all data members in their initial state (which is `null` for .NET objects).

Assemblies actually have two sets of version information: the version information available in the assembly manifest and the PE (Portable Executable) file version information. `FileVersionInfo` reads the assembly manifest version information.

The first action this method takes is to determine whether the two files passed in to the *file1* and *file2* parameters actually exist. If so, the static `GetVersionInfo` method of the `FileVersionInfo` class is called to get version information for the two files.

The `CompareFileVersions` method attempts to compare each portion of the file's version number using the following properties of the `FileVersionInfo` object returned by `GetVersionInfo`:

`FileMajorPart`
    The first 2 bytes of the version number

`FileMinorPart`
    The second 2 bytes of the version number

`FileBuildPart`
    The third 2 bytes of the version number

`FilePrivatePart`
    The final 2 bytes of the version number

The full version number is comprised of these four parts, making up an 8-byte number representing the file's version number.

The CompareFileVersions method first compares the FileMajorPart version information of the two files. If these are equal, the FileMinorPart version information of the two files is compared. This continues through the FileBuildPart and finally the FilePrivatePart version information values. If all four parts are equal, the files are considered to have the same version number. If either file is found to have a higher number than the other file, it is considered to be the latest version.

See Also

See the "FileVersionInfo Class" topic in the MSDN documentation.

12.26 Querying Information for All Drives on a System

Problem

Your application needs to know if a drive (HDD, CD drive, DVD drive, etc.) is available and ready to be written to and/or read from. Additionally, it would be nice to know if you have enough available free space on the drive to write information to.

Solution

Use the various properties in the DriveInfo class as shown here:

```
public static void DisplayAllDriveInfo()
{
    foreach (DriveInfo drive in DriveInfo.GetDrives())
    {
        if (drive.IsReady)
        {
            Console.WriteLine("Drive " + drive.Name + " is ready.");
            Console.WriteLine("AvailableFreeSpace: " + drive.AvailableFreeSpace);
            Console.WriteLine("DriveFormat: " + drive.DriveFormat);
            Console.WriteLine("DriveType: " + drive.DriveType);
            Console.WriteLine("Name: " + drive.Name);
            Console.WriteLine("RootDirectory.FullName: " +
                drive.RootDirectory.FullName);
            Console.WriteLine("TotalFreeSpace: " + drive.TotalFreeSpace);
            Console.WriteLine("TotalSize: " + drive.TotalSize);
            Console.WriteLine("VolumeLabel: " + drive.VolumeLabel);
        }
        else
        {
            Console.WriteLine("Drive " + drive.Name + " is not ready.");
        }
    }
}
```

This code will display something like the following, though of course each system is different and the results will vary:

```
Drive C:\ is ready.
AvailableFreeSpace: 143210795008
DriveFormat: NTFS
DriveType: Fixed
Name: C:\
RootDirectory.FullName: C:\
TotalFreeSpace: 143210795008
TotalSize: 159989886976
VolumeLabel: Vol1

Drive D:\ is ready.
AvailableFreeSpace: 0
DriveFormat: UDF
DriveType: CDRom
Name: D:\
RootDirectory.FullName: D:\
TotalFreeSpace: 0
TotalSize: 3305965568
VolumeLabel: Vol2

Drive E:\ is ready.
AvailableFreeSpace: 4649025536
DriveFormat: UDF
DriveType: CDRom
Name: E:\
RootDirectory.FullName: E:\
TotalFreeSpace: 4649025536
TotalSize: 4691197952
VolumeLabel: Vol3

Drive F:\ is not ready.
```

Of particular interest are the IsReady and AvailableFreeSpace properties. The IsReady property determines if the drive is ready to be queried, written to, or read from. The AvailableFreeSpace property returns the free space on that drive in bytes.

Discussion

The DriveInfo class has been added to the .NET Framework to allow you to easily query information on one particular drive or on all drives in the system. To query the information from a single drive you would use the code in Example 12-15.

Example 12-15. Getting information from a specific drive

```
DriveInfo drive = new DriveInfo("D");
if (drive.IsReady)
    Console.WriteLine("The space available on the D:\\ drive: " +
                      drive.AvailableFreeSpace);
else
    Console.WriteLine("Drive D:\\ is not ready.");
```

Notice that only the drive letter is passed in to the Driveinfo constructor. This drive letter can be either uppercase or lowercase—it does not matter. The next thing you will notice with the code in Example 12-15 and the code in the Solution to this recipe is that the IsReady property is always tested for true before either using the drive or querying its properties. If we did not test this property for true and for some reason the drive was not ready (e.g., a CD was not in the drive at that time), a System.IO.IOException would be returned stating that "The device is not ready." To prevent this exception from being thrown (since it is an expensive operation), simply test the IsReady property to determine if it is true or not.

For the Solution to this recipe, the DriveInfo constructor was not used. Instead, the static GetDrives method of the DriveInfo class was used to return an array of DriveInfo objects. Each DriveInfo object in this array corresponds to one drive on the current system.

The DriveType property of the DriveInfo class returns an enumeration value from the DriveType enumeration (yes, they have the same name, unfortunately). This enumeration value identifies what type of drive the current DriveInfo object represents. Table 12-13 identifies the various values of the DriveType enumeration.

Table 12-13. DriveType enumeration values

Enum value	Description
CDRom	This can be a CD-ROM, CD writer, DVD-ROM, or DVD writer drive.
Fixed	This is the fixed drive such as an HDD. Note that USB HDDs fall into this category.
Network	A network drive.
NoRootDirectory	No root directory was found on this drive.
Ram	A RAM disk.
Removable	A removable storage device.
Unknown	Some other type of drive than those listed here.

In the DriveInfo class there are two very similar properties, AvailableFreeSpace and TotalFreeSpace. Each of these properties will return the same value in most cases. However, AvailableFreeSpace also takes into account any disk-quota information for a particular drive. Disk-quota information can be found by right-clicking a drive in Windows Explorer and selecting the Properties pop-up menu item. This displays the Properties page for this drive. On this Properties page, click on the Quota tab to view the quota information for that drive. If the Enable Quota Management checkbox is unchecked, then disk-quota management is disabled, and both the AvailableFreeSpace and TotalFreeSpace properties should be equal.

See Also

See the "DriveInfo Class" topic in the MSDN documentation.

12.27 Encrypting/Decrypting an Existing File

Problem

You need a simple way to encrypt an existing file on the filesystem so that only the account used to encrypt the file can decrypt it.

Solution

Use the Decrypt and Encrypt methods of the File class:

```
public static void EncryptFile(string fileName)
{
    File.Encrypt(fileName);
}

public static void DecryptFile(string fileName)
{
    File.Decrypt(fileName);
}
```

Discussion

Both the Encrypt and Decrypt methods of the File class accept a single parameter, a file path/name, and return a void. The filename parameter must be a valid path and name. The result of calling the Encrypt method is an encrypted file that can be unencrypted only by the user who encrypted it in the first place. Calling the Decrypt method decrypts the file.

The Encrypt method is a wrapper around the EncryptFile method in the unmanaged *Advapi32.dll*, and the Decrypt method is a wrapper around the DecryptFile method, also in *Advapi32.dll*. These underlying methods require exclusive access to the file that is being encrypted/decrypted. This means that no other process may be currently accessing this file when the Encrypt/Decrypt methods are called. Also be aware that the filesystem must be NTFS or a NotSupportedException will be thrown by the Encrypt/Decrypt method. If the operating system is not Microsoft Windows NT or later, a PlatformNotSupportedException will be thrown and the operation will fail.

Note that before encrypting or decrypting a file, the method will first determine if the file is compressed. If so, the file is decompressed before the encryption/decryption operation can proceed. If you are encrypting/decrypting many compressed files (or files on a compressed disk) you should be aware that this will take more time than if the files are uncompressed.

See Also

See the "File Class" topic in the MSDN documentation.

12.28 Compressing and Decompressing Your Files

Problem

You need a way to compress the data you write to a file using one of the stream-based classes. In addition, you need a way to decompress the data from this compressed file when you read it back in.

Solution

Use the `System.IO.Compression.DeflateStream` or the `System.IO.Compression.GZip-Stream` classes to read and write compressed data to a file. The `CompressFile`, `DeCompressFile`, and `DeCompress` methods shown in Example 12-16 demonstrate how to use these classes to compress and expand data on the fly.

Example 12-16. The CompressFile, DeCompressFile, and DeCompress methods

```
public static void CompressFile(Stream strm, byte[] data,
                                CompressionType compressionType)
{
    // Determine how to compress the file.
    Stream deflate = null;
    if (compressionType == CompressionType.Deflate)
    {
        using (deflate = new DeflateStream(strm, CompressionMode.Compress))
        {
            // Write compressed data to the file.
            deflate.Write(data, 0, data.Length);
        }
    }
    else
    {
        using (deflate = new GZipStream(strm, CompressionMode.Compress))
        {
            // Write compressed data to the file.
            deflate.Write(data, 0, data.Length);
        }
    }
}

public static byte[] DeCompressFile(Stream strm,
                                    CompressionType compressionType)
{
    // Determine how to decompress the file.
    Stream reInflate = null;

    if (compressionType == CompressionType.Deflate)
    {
        using (reInflate = new DeflateStream(strm, CompressionMode.Decompress))
        {
            return (Decompress(reInflate));
```

```
        }
    }
    else
    {
        using (reInflate = new GZipStream(strm, CompressionMode.Decompress))
        {
            return (Decompress(reInflate));
        }
    }
}

public static byte[] Decompress(Stream reInflate)
{
    List<byte> data = new List<byte>();
    int retVal = 0;

    // Read all data in and uncompress it.
    while (retVal >= 0)
    {
        retVal = reInflate.ReadByte();
        if (retVal != -1)
            data.Add((byte)retVal);
    }

    return (data.ToArray());
}
```

The CompressionType enumeration is defined as follows:

```
public enum CompressionType
{
    Deflate,
    GZip
}
```

Discussion

The CompressFile method accepts a Stream object, data in the form of a byte array, and a CompressionType enumeration value indicating which type of compression algorithm to use (Deflate or GZip). This method produces a file containing the compressed data.

The DeCompressFile method accepts a Stream object and a CompressionType enumeration value indicating which type of decompression algorithm to use (Deflate or GZip). This method calls the Decompress method, which reads from a compressed file and places the data, uncompressed and in the form of bytes, into a generic List<byte> collection object. This collection object is then converted to a byte[] and returned with the data to the calling method.

The TestCompressNewFile method shown in Example 12-17 exercises the CompressFile and DeCompressFile methods defined in the Solution section of this recipe. It also uses another method, NormalFile (shown first), that creates an uncompressed file to show how the file sizes differ.

Example 12-17. Using the CompressFile and DecompressFile methods

```
// Method to write out an uncompressed file to compare sizes
public static void NormalFile(Stream strm, byte[] data)
{
    BinaryWriter normal = new BinaryWriter(strm);
    normal.Write(data);
    normal.Close( );
}

public static void TestCompressNewFile( )
{
    byte[] data = new byte[10000000];
    for (int i = 0; i < 10000000; i++)
        data[i] = 254;

    using (FileStream fs = new FileStream(@"C:\NewNormalFile.txt",
            FileMode.OpenOrCreate, FileAccess.ReadWrite, FileShare.None))
        NormalFile(fs, data);

    using (FileStream fs = new FileStream(@"C:\NewCompressedFile.txt",
            FileMode.OpenOrCreate, FileAccess.ReadWrite, FileShare.None))
        CompressFile(fs, data, CompressionType.Deflate);

    using (FileStream fs = new FileStream(@"C:\NewCompressedFile.txt",
            FileMode.OpenOrCreate, FileAccess.ReadWrite, FileShare.None))
    {
        byte[] retData = DeCompressFile(fs, CompressionType.Deflate);
        Console.WriteLine("Deflated file bytes count == " + retData.Length);
    }

    using (FileStream fs = new FileStream(@"C:\NewGZCompressedFile.txt",
            FileMode.OpenOrCreate, FileAccess.ReadWrite, FileShare.None))
        CompressFile(fs, data, CompressionType.GZip);

    using (FileStream fs = new FileStream(@"C:\NewGzCompressedFile.txt",
            FileMode.OpenOrCreate, FileAccess.ReadWrite, FileShare.None))
    {
        byte[] retData = DeCompressFile(fs, CompressionType.GZip);
        Console.WriteLine("GZipped file bytes count == " + retData.Length);
    }
}
```

When this test code is run, we get three files with different sizes. The first file, *NewNormalFile.txt*, is 10,000,000 bytes in size. The *NewCompressedFile.txt* file is 85,095 bytes. The final file, *NewGzCompressedFile.txt* file is 85,113 bytes. As you can see, there is not much difference between the sizes for the files compressed with the DeflateStream class and the GZipStream class. The reason for this is that both compression classes use the same compression/decompression algorithm (i.e., the lossless Deflate algorithm as described in the RFC 1951: Deflate 1.3 specification).

You may be wondering why you would pick one class over the other if they use the same algorithm. There is one good reason; the `GZipStream` class adds a CRC check to the file to determine if it has been corrupted. If the file has been corrupted, an `InvalidDataException` is thrown with the statement "The CRC in GZip footer does not match the CRC calculated from the decompressed data." By catching this exception, you can determine if your data is corrupted.

See Also

See the "DeflateStream Class" and "GZipStream" topics in the MSDN documentation.

CHAPTER 13

Reflection

13.0 Introduction

Reflection is the mechanism provided by the .NET Framework to allow you to inspect how a program is constructed. Using reflection, you can obtain information such as the name of an assembly and what other assemblies a given assembly imports. You can even dynamically call methods on a type in a given assembly. Reflection also allows you to create code dynamically and compile it to an in-memory assembly or to build a symbol table of type entries in an assembly.

Reflection is a very powerful feature of the Framework and, as such, is guarded by the runtime. The ReflectionPermission must be granted to assemblies that are going to access the protected or private members of a type. If you are going to access only the public members of a public type, you will not need to be granted the ReflectionPermission. Code Access Security has only two permission sets that give all reflection access by default: FullTrust and Everything. The LocalIntranet permission set allows for the ReflectionEmit privilege that allows for emitting metadata and creating assemblies or the MemberAccess privilege for performing dynamic invocation of methods on types in assemblies.

In this chapter, you will see how you can use reflection to dynamically invoke members on types, figure out all of the assemblies a given assembly is dependent on, and inspect assemblies for different types of information. Reflection is a great way to understand how things are put together in .NET; this chapter provides a starting point.

13.1 Listing Referenced Assemblies

Problem

You need to determine each assembly imported by a particular assembly. This information can show you if this assembly is using one or more of your assemblies or if your assembly is using another specific assembly.

Solution

Use the `Assembly.GetReferencedAssemblies` method, as shown in Example 13-1, to obtain the imported assemblies of an assembly.

Example 13-1. Using the Assembly.GetReferencedAssemblies method

```
using System;
using System.Reflection;
using System.Collections.Specialized;

public static string[] BuildDependentAssemblyList(string path,
                                                  List<string> assemblies)
{
    // Maintain a list of assemblies the original one needs.
    if (assemblies == null)
        assemblies = new List<string>();

    // Have we already seen this one?
    if (assemblies.Contains(path) == true)
        return (new string[0]);

    Assembly asm = null;
    // Look for common path delimiters in the string
    // to see if it is a name or a path.
    if ((path.IndexOf(Path.DirectorySeparatorChar, 0, path.Length) != -1) ||
        (path.IndexOf(Path.AltDirectorySeparatorChar, 0, path.Length) != -1))
    {
        // Load the assembly from a path.
        asm = Assembly.ReflectionOnlyLoadFrom(path);
    }
    else
    {
        // Try as assembly name.
        asm = Assembly.ReflectionOnlyLoad(path);
    }

    // Add the assembly to the list.
    if (asm != null)
    {
        assemblies.Add(path);
    }
```

```
    // Get the referenced assemblies.
    AssemblyName[] imports = asm.GetReferencedAssemblies();

    // Iterate.
    foreach (AssemblyName asmName in imports)
    {
        // Now recursively call this assembly to get the new modules
        // it references.
        BuildDependentAssemblyList(asmName.FullName, assemblies);
    }

    string[] temp = new string[assemblies.Count];
    assemblies.CopyTo(temp, 0);
    return (temp);
}
```

This code returns a `string[]` containing the original assembly, all imported assemblies, and the dependent assemblies of the imported assemblies.

If you ran this method against the assembly *C:\CSharpRecipes\bin\Debug\CSharpRecipes. exe*, you'd get the following dependency tree:

```
C:\CSharpRecipes\bin\Debug\CSharpRecipes.exe

mscorlib, Version=2.0.3600.0, Culture=neutral, PublicKeyToken=b77a5c561934e089

System, Version=2.0.3600.0, Culture=neutral, PublicKeyToken=b77a5c561934e089

System.Configuration, Version=2.0.3600.0, Culture=neutral,
    PublicKeyToken=b03f5f7f11d50a3a

System.Xml, Version=2.0.3600.0, Culture=neutral, PublicKeyToken=b77a5c561934e089

System.Security, Version=2.0.3600.0, Culture=neutral, PublicKeyToken=b03f5f7f11d50a3a

System.Web.RegularExpressions, Version=2.0.3600.0, Culture=neutral,
    PublicKeyToken=b03f5f7f11d50a3a

System.Runtime.Serialization.Formatters.Soap, Version=2.0.3600.0, Culture=neutral,
    PublicKeyToken=b03f5f7f11d50a3a
```

Discussion

Obtaining the imported types in an assembly is useful in determining what assemblies another assembly is using. This knowledge can greatly aid in learning to use a new assembly. This method can also help determine dependencies between assemblies for shipping purposes.

The `GetReferencedAssemblies` method of the `System.Reflection.Assembly` class obtains a list of all the imported assemblies. This method accepts no parameters and returns an array of `AssemblyName` objects instead of an array of `Types`. The

AssemblyName type is made up of members that allow access to the information about an assembly, such as the name, version, culture information, public/private key pairs, and other data.

Note that this method does not account for assemblies loaded using the `Assembly.ReflectionOnlyLoad*` methods, as it is inspecting for only compile-time references.

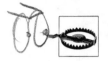 When loading assemblies for inspection using reflection, you should use the `ReflectionOnlyLoad*` methods. These methods do not allow you to execute code from the loaded assembly.

See Also

See the "Assembly Class" topic in the MSDN documentation.

13.2 Listing Exported Types

Problem

You need to obtain all the exported types of an assembly. This information allows you to see what types are usable from outside of this assembly.

Solution

Use `Assembly.GetExportedTypes` to obtain the exported types of an assembly:

```
using System;
using System.Reflection;

public static void ListExportedTypes(string path)
{
    // Load the assembly.
    Assembly asm = Assembly. ReflectionOnlyLoadFrom(path);
    Console.WriteLine("Assembly: {0} imports:",path);
    // Get the exported types.
    Type[] types = asm.GetExportedTypes( );
    foreach (Type t in types)
    {
        Console.WriteLine ("\tExported Type: {0}",t.FullName);
    }
}
```

The previous example will display all exported, or public, types:

```
Assembly: C:\C#Cookbook\CSharpRecipes.exe imports:
        Exported Type: CSharpRecipes.ClassAndStructs
        Exported Type: CSharpRecipes.Line
        Exported Type: CSharpRecipes.Square
        Exported Type: CSharpRecipes.CompareHeight
        Exported Type: CSharpRecipes.Foo
        Exported Type: CSharpRecipes.ObjState
```

Discussion

Obtaining the exported types in an assembly is useful when determining the public interface to that assembly. This ability can greatly aid in learning to use a new assembly or can aid the developer of that assembly in determining all access points to the assembly to verify that they are adequately secure from malicious code. To get these exported types, use the GetExportedTypes method on the System.Reflection.Assembly type. The exported types consist of all of the types that are publicly accessible from outside of the assembly. A type may have public accessibility but not be accessible from outside of the assembly. Take, for example, the following code:

```
public class Outer
{
    public class Inner {}
    private class SecretInner {}
}
```

The exported types are Outer and Outer.Inner; the type SecretInner is not exposed to the world outside of this assembly. If you change the Outer accessibility from public to private, you now have no types accessible to the outside world—the Inner class access level is downgraded because of the private on the Outer class.

See Also

See the "Assembly Class" topic in the MSDN documentation.

13.3 Finding Overridden Methods

Problem

You have an inheritance hierarchy that is several levels deep and has many virtual and overridden methods. You need a list of the base class method(s) that are overridden by methods within a derived class.

Solution

Use the MethodInfo.GetBaseDefinition method to determine which method is overridden in what base class. The overloaded FindMethodOverrides method shown in Example 13-2 examines all of the public instance methods in a class and displays which methods override their respective base class methods. This method also determines which base class the overridden method is in. This overloaded method accepts an assembly path and name along with a type name in which to find overriding methods. Note that the *typeName* parameter must be the fully qualified type name (i.e., the complete namespace hierarchy, followed by any containing classes, followed by the type name you are querying).

Example 13-2. Overloaded FindMethodOverrides methods

```
public class ReflectionUtils
{
    public static void FindMethodOverrides(string asmPath, string typeName)
    {
        Assembly asm = Assembly.ReflectionOnlyLoadFrom(asmPath);
        Type type = asm.GetType(typeName);
        FindMethodOverrides(type);
    }

    public static void FindMethodOverrides(Type type)
    {
        Console.WriteLine("---[" + type.FullName + "]---");

        // Get the methods defined by this type.
        MethodInfo[] methods = type.GetMethods(BindingFlags.Instance |
            BindingFlags.NonPublic | BindingFlags.Public |
            BindingFlags.DeclaredOnly);
        foreach (MethodInfo method in methods)
        {
            Console.WriteLine("Current Method:  " + method.ToString( ));

            // Get the base method.
            MethodInfo baseDef = method.GetBaseDefinition( );
            if (baseDef != method)
            {
                Console.WriteLine("Base Type FullName:  " +
                    baseDef.DeclaringType.FullName);
                Console.WriteLine("Base Method:  " + baseDef.ToString( ));

                // List the types of this method.
                Type[] paramTypes = new Type[method.GetParameters( ).Length];
                int counter = 0;
                foreach (ParameterInfo param in method.GetParameters( ))
                {
                    paramTypes[counter] = param.ParameterType;
                    Console.WriteLine("\tParam {0}: {1}",
                        param.Name,param.ParameterType.ToString( ));
                    counter++;
                }
            }
            Console.WriteLine( );
        }
    }
}
```

see p. 762-(A)

The second overloaded method allows you to determine whether a particular method overrides a method in its base class. It accepts the same two arguments as the first overloaded method, along with the full method name and an array of Type objects representing its parameter types:

```
public class ReflectionUtils
{
```

```
public static void FindMethodOverrides(string asmPath, string typeName,
    string methodName, Type[] paramTypes)
{
    Console.WriteLine("For [Type] Method:  [" + typeName + "] " + methodName);

    Assembly asm = Assembly.ReflectionOnlyLoadFrom(asmPath);
    Type type = asm.GetType(typeName,true,true);
    MethodInfo method = type.GetMethod(methodName, paramTypes);
    FindMethodOverrides(method, paramTypes);
}
public static void FindMethodOverrides(MethodInfo method,
        Type[] paramTypes)
{
    if (method != null)
    {
        MethodInfo baseDef = method.GetBaseDefinition( );
        if (baseDef != method)
        {
            Console.WriteLine("Base Type FullName:  " +
                baseDef.DeclaringType.FullName);
            Console.WriteLine("Base Method:  " + baseDef.ToString( ));

            foreach (ParameterInfo param in baseDef.GetParameters( ))
            {
                // List the params so we can see which one we got.
                Console.WriteLine("\tParam {0}: {1}",
                    param.Name,param.ParameterType.ToString( ));
            }
            // We found the one we were looking for.
            Console.WriteLine("Found Match!");
        }
        Console.WriteLine( );
    }
}
```

a lot of duplicate code

The following code shows how to use each of these overloaded methods:

```
public static void FindOverriddenMethods( )
{
    Process current = Process.GetCurrentProcess( );
    // Get the path of the current module.
    string path = current.MainModule.FileName;

    // Try the easier one.
    ReflectionUtils.FindMethodOverrides.
        (path,"CSharpRecipes.ReflectionUtils+DerivedOverrides");

    // Try the signature FindMethodOverrides.
    ReflectionUtils.FindMethodOverrides(path,
        "CSharpRecipes.ReflectionUtils+DerivedOverrides",
        "Foo",
        new Type[3] {typeof(long), typeof(double), typeof(byte[])});
}
```

The output of this method, using the BaseOverrides and DerivedOverrides classes defined afterward, is shown here:

```
---[CSharpRecipes.ReflectionUtils+DerivedOverrides]---
Current Method:  Void Foo(System.String, Int32)
Base Type FullName:  CSharpRecipes.ReflectionUtils+BaseOverrides
Base Method:  Void Foo(System.String, Int32)
        Param str: System.String
        Param i: System.Int32

Current Method:  Void Foo(Int64, Double, Byte[])
Base Type FullName:  CSharpRecipes.ReflectionUtils+BaseOverrides
Base Method:  Void Foo(Int64, Double, Byte[])
        Param l: System.Int64
        Param d: System.Double
        Param bytes: System.Byte[]

For [Type] Method:  [CSharpRecipes.ReflectionUtils+DerivedOverrides] Foo
Base Type FullName:  CSharpRecipes.ReflectionUtils+BaseOverrides
Base Method:  Void Foo(Int64, Double, Byte[])
        Param l: System.Int64
        Param d: System.Double
        Param bytes: System.Byte[]
Found Match!
```

In the usage code, you get the path to the test code assembly (*CSharpRecipes.exe*) via the Process class. You then use that to find a class that has been defined in the ReflectionUtils class, called DerivedOverrides. DerivedOverrides derives from BaseOverrides, and they are both shown here:

```
public abstract class BaseOverrides
{
    public abstract void Foo(string str, int i);

    public abstract void Foo(long l, double d, byte[] bytes);
}

public class DerivedOverrides : BaseOverrides
{
    public override void Foo(string str, int i)
    {
    }

    public override void Foo(long l, double d, byte[] bytes)
    {
    }
}
```

The first method passes in only the assembly path and the fully qualified type name. This method returns every overridden method for each method that it finds in the Reflection.DerivedOverrides type. If you want to display all overriding methods and their corresponding overridden methods, you can remove the `BindingFlags.DeclaredOnly` binding enumeration from the `GetMethods` method call:

```
MethodInfo[] methods = asmType.GetMethods(BindingFlags.Instance |
                            BindingFlags.NonPublic | BindingFlags.Public);
```

This change now produces the following output using the same classes, `BaseOverrides` and `DerivedOverrides`:

```
---[CSharpRecipes.ReflectionUtils+DerivedOverrides]---
Current Method:  Void Foo(System.String, Int32)
Base Type FullName:  CSharpRecipes.ReflectionUtils+BaseOverrides
Base Method:  Void Foo(System.String, Int32)
        Param str: System.String
        Param i: System.Int32

Current Method:  Void Foo(Int64, Double, Byte[])
Base Type FullName:  CSharpRecipes.ReflectionUtils+BaseOverrides
Base Method:  Void Foo(Int64, Double, Byte[])
        Param l: System.Int64
        Param d: System.Double
        Param bytes: System.Byte[]

Current Method:  System.Type GetType()

Current Method:  System.Object MemberwiseClone()

Current Method:  System.String ToString()
Base Type FullName:  System.Object
Base Method:  System.String ToString()

Current Method:  Boolean Equals(System.Object)
Base Type FullName:  System.Object
Base Method:  Boolean Equals(System.Object)
        Param obj: System.Object

Current Method:  Int32 GetHashCode()
Base Type FullName:  System.Object
Base Method:  Int32 GetHashCode()

Current Method:  Void Finalize()
Base Type FullName:  System.Object
Base Method:  Void Finalize()

For [Type] Method:  [CSharpRecipes.ReflectionUtils+DerivedOverrides] Foo
Base Type FullName:  CSharpRecipes.ReflectionUtils+BaseOverrides
Base Method:  Void Foo(Int64, Double, Byte[])
        Param l: System.Int64
        Param d: System.Double
        Param bytes: System.Byte[]
Found Match!
```

The second method passes in the assembly path, the fully qualified type name, a method name, and the parameters for this method to find the override that specifically matches the signature based on the parameters. In this case, the parameter types of method Foo are long, double, and byte[]. This method displays the method that CSharpRecipes.ReflectionUtils+DerivedOverrides.Foo overrides. The + in the type name represents a nested class.

Discussion

Determining which methods override their base class methods would be a tedious chore if it were not for the GetBaseDefinition method of the System.Reflection.MethodInfo type. This method takes no parameters and returns a MethodInfo object that corresponds to the overridden method in the base class. If this method is used on a MethodInfo object representing a method that is not being overridden—as is the case with a virtual or abstract method—GetBaseDefinition returns the original MethodInfo object.

The code for the FindMethodOverrides methods first loads the assembly using the *asmPath* parameter and then gets the type that is specified by the *typeName* parameter.

Once the type is located, its Type object's GetMethod or GetMethods method is called. GetMethod is used when both the method name and its parameter array are passed in to FindMethodOverrides; otherwise, GetMethods is used. If the method is correctly located and its MethodInfo object obtained, the GetBaseDefinition method is called on that MethodInfo object to get the first overridden method in the nearest base class in the inheritance hierarchy. This MethodInfo type is compared to the MethodInfo type that the GetBaseDefinition method was called on. If these two objects are the same, it means that there were no overridden methods in any base classes; therefore, nothing is displayed. This code will display only the overridden methods; if no methods are overridden, then nothing is displayed.

See Also

See Recipe 13.10; see the "Process Class," "Assembly Class," "MethodInfo Class," and "ParameterInfo Class" topics in the MSDN documentation.

13.4   Finding Members in an Assembly

Problem

You need to find one or more members of types in an assembly with a specific name or containing part of a name. This partial name could be, for example, any member starting with the letter *A* or the string "Test."

Solution

Use the `Type.GetMember` method, which returns all members that match a specified criteria:

```csharp
public static void FindMemberInAssembly(string asmPath, string memberName)
{
    Assembly asm = Assembly.LoadFrom(asmPath);
    foreach(Type type in asm.GetTypes( ))
    {
        // Check for static ones first.
        MemberInfo[] members = type.GetMember(memberName, MemberTypes.All,
            BindingFlags.Public | BindingFlags.NonPublic |
            BindingFlags.Static | BindingFlags.Instance);

        foreach (MemberInfo member in members)
        {
            Console.WriteLine("Found " + member.MemberType + ":  " +
                member.ToString( ) + " IN " +
                member.DeclaringType.FullName);
        }
    }
}
```

The *memberName* argument can contain the wildcard character * to indicate any character or characters. So to find all methods starting with the string "Test", pass the string "Test*" to the *memberName* parameter. Note that the *memberName* argument is case-sensitive, but the *asmPath* argument is not. If you'd like to do a case-insensitive search for members, add the `BindingFlags.IgnoreCase` flag to the other `BindingFlags` in the call to `Type.GetMember`.

Discussion

The `GetMember` method of the `System.Type` class is useful for finding one or more methods within a type. This method returns an array of `MemberInfo` objects that describe any members that match the given parameters.

 The * character may be used as a wildcard character only at the end of the *name* parameter string. If placed anywhere else in the string, it will not be treated as a wildcard character. In addition, it may be the only character in the *name* parameter; if this is so, all members are returned. No other wildcard characters, such as ?, are supported.

Once you obtain an array of `MemberInfo` objects, you need to examine what kind of members they are. To do this, the `MemberInfo` class contains a `MemberType` property that returns a `System.Reflection.MemberTypes` enumeration value. This can be any of the values defined in Table 13-1, except for the `All` value.

Table 13-1. MemberTypes enumeration values

Enumeration value	Definition
All	All member types
Constructor	A constructor member
Custom	A custom member type
Event	An event member
Field	A field member
Method	A method member
NestedType	A nested type
Property	A property member
TypeInfo	A type member that represents a `TypeInfo` member

See Also

See Recipe 13.10; see the "Assembly Class," "BindingFlags Enumeration," and "MemberInfo Class" topics in the MSDN documentation.

13.5   Finding Members Within an Interface

Problem

You need to find one or more members with a specific name, or a part of a name, that belong to an interface.

Solution

Use the same technique outlined in Recipe 13.4, but filter out all types except interfaces. The first overloaded version of the `FindIFaceMemberInAssembly` method finds a member specified by the *memberName* parameter in all interfaces contained in an assembly. Its source code is:

```
public static void FindIFaceMemberInAssembly(string asmPath, string memberName)
{
    // Delegates to the overloaded FindIFaceMemberInAssembly method
    // passing in a wildcard character as the interfaceName param.
    FindIFaceMemberInAssembly(asmPath, memberName, "*");
}
```

The second overloaded version of the `FindIFaceMemberInAssembly` method finds a member in the interface specified by the *interfaceName* parameter. Its source code is:

```
public static void FindIFaceMemberInAssembly(string asmPath, string memberName,
    string interfaceName)
{
    Assembly asm = Assembly.LoadFrom(asmPath);
    foreach(Type type in asm.GetTypes( ))
```

```
    {
        if (type.IsInterface &&
            (type.Name.Equals(interfaceName) ||
                            interfaceName.Equals("*")))
        {
            MemberInfo[] members = type.GetMember(memberName, MemberTypes.All,
                    BindingFlags.Instance | BindingFlags.NonPublic |
                    BindingFlags.Public | BindingFlags.Static |
                    BindingFlags.IgnoreCase);

            if (members.Length > 0)
            {
                foreach(MemberInfo iface in members)
                {
                    Console.WriteLine("Found member {0}.{1}",
                        type.ToString( ),iface.ToString( ));
                }
            }
        }
    }
}
```

Discussion

The FindIFaceMemberInAssembly method operates very similarly to the FindMemberInAssembly method of Recipe 13.4. The main difference between this recipe and the one in Recipe 13.4 is that this method uses the IsInterface property of the System.Type class to determine whether this type is an interface. If this property returns true, the type is an interface; otherwise, it is a noninterface type.

This recipe also makes use of the GetMember method of the System.Type class. This name may contain an * wildcard character at the end of the string only. If the * wildcard character is the only character in the name parameter, all members are returned.

If you'd like to do a case-sensitive search, you can omit the BindingFlags.IgnoreCase flag from the call to Type.GetMember.

See Also

See Recipes 13.4 and 13.10; see the "Assembly Class," "BindingFlags Enumeration," and "MemberInfo Class" topics in the MSDN documentation.

13.6 Determining and Obtaining Nested Types Within an Assembly

Problem

You need to determine which types have nested types contained within them in your assembly. Determining the nested types allows you to programmatically examine various aspects of some design patterns. Various design patterns may specify that a type will contain another type; for example, the *Decorator* and *State* design patterns make use of object containment.

not really.
Involves containment

Solution

Use the DisplayNestedTypes method to iterate through all types in your assembly and list all of their nested types. Its code is:

```
public static void DisplayNestedTypes(string asmPath)
{
    bool output = false;
    string line;
    Assembly asm = Assembly.LoadFrom(asmPath);
    foreach(Type type in asm.GetTypes( ))
    {
        line = type.FullName + " Contains:\n" ;
        output = false;

        // Get all nested types.
        Type[] nestedTypes = type.GetNestedTypes(
                BindingFlags.Public |
                BindingFlags.NonPublic);

        // Roll over the nested types.
        foreach (Type t in nestedTypes)
        {
            line += "    " + t.FullName + "\n";
            output = true;
        }

        if (output)
            Console.WriteLine(line);
    }
}
```

Discussion

The DisplayNestedTypes method uses an outer foreach loop to iterate over all types in the assembly specified by the asmPath parameter. Within this loop the GetNestedTypes method of the Type class is called to obtain the nested types of the type specified in the type variable.

Usually the dot operator is used to delimit namespaces and types; however, nested types are somewhat special. Nested types are set apart from other types by the + operator in their fully qualified name when dealing with them in the reflection APIs. By passing this fully qualified name in to the static GetType methods, the actual type that it represents can be acquired.

These methods return a Type object that represents the type identified by the *typeName* parameter.

Calling Type.GetType to retrieve a type defined in a dynamic assembly (one that is created using the types defined in the System.Reflection. Emit namespace) returns a null if that assembly has not already been persisted to disk. Typically you would use the static Assembly.GetType method on the dynamic assembly's Assembly object.

See Also

See Recipe 13.10; see the "Assembly Class" and "BindingFlags Enumeration" topics in the MSDN documentation.

13.7   Displaying the Inheritance Hierarchy for a Type

Problem

You need to determine all of the base types that make up a specific type. Essentially, you need to determine the inheritance hierarchy of a type starting with the base (least derived) type and ending with the specified (most derived) type.

Solution

Use the DisplayInheritanceChain method to display the entire inheritance hierarchy for all types existing in an assembly specified by the asmPath parameter. Its source code is:

```
public static void DisplayInheritanceChain(string asmPath)
{
    Assembly asm = Assembly.LoadFrom(asmPath);
    foreach(Type type in asm.GetTypes())
    {
        DisplayInheritanceChain(type);
    }
}

public static void DisplayInheritanceChain(Type type)
{
    // Recurse over all base types.
    Console.WriteLine ("Derived Type: " + type.FullName);
    Console.WriteLine ("Base Type List: " + GetBaseTypeList(type));
    Console.WriteLine ();
}
```

DisplayInheritanceChain, in turn, calls GetBaseTypeList, a private method that uses recursion to get all base types. Its source code is:

```
private static string GetBaseTypeList(Type type)
{
    if (type != null)
    {
```

```
    // Recursive method call
    string baseTypeName = GetBaseTypeList(type.BaseType);
    if (baseTypeName.Length <= 0)
    {
        return (type.Name);
    }
    else
    {
        return (baseTypeName + "<-" + type.Name);
    }
}
else
{
    return ("");
}
}
```

If you want to obtain only the inheritance hierarchy of a specific type as a string, use
the following DisplayInheritanceChain overload:

```
public static void DisplayInheritanceChain(string asmPath, string baseType)
{
    Assembly asm = Assembly.LoadFrom(asmPath);
    DisplayInheritanceChain(asm, baseType);
}

public static void DisplayInheritanceChain(Assembly asm, string baseType)
{
    string typeHierarchy = GetBaseTypeList(asm.GetType(baseType));
    Console.WriteLine(typeHierarchy);
}
```

To display the inheritance hierarchy of all types within an assembly, use the first
instance of the DisplayInheritanceChain method call. To obtain the inheritance hierarchy of a single type as a string, use the second instance of the DisplayInheritanceChain
method call. In this instance, you are looking for the type hierarchy of the
CSharpRecipes.ReflectionUtils+DerivedOverrides nested class:

```
public static void DisplayInheritanceHierarchyType( )
{
    Process current = Process.GetCurrentProcess( );
    // Get the path of the current module.
    string asmPath = current.MainModule.FileName;
    // A specific type
    DisplayInheritanceChain(asmPath,
        "CSharpRecipes.ReflectionUtils+DerivedOverrides");
    // All types in the assembly
    DisplayInheritanceChain(asmPath);
}
```

These methods result in output like the following:

```
Derived Type: CSharpRecipes.Reflection
Base Type List: Object<-Reflection
```

```
Derived Type: CSharpRecipes.ReflectionUtils+BaseOverrides
Base Type List: Object<-BaseOverrides

Derived Type: CSharpRecipes.ReflectionUtils+DerivedOverrides
Base Type List: Object<-BaseOverrides <-DerivedOverrides
```

This output shows that when looking at the Reflection class in the CSharpRecipes namespace, its base-type list (or inheritance hierarchy) starts with Object (like all types in .NET). The nested class BaseOverrides also shows a base-type list starting with Object. The nested class DerivedOverrides shows a more interesting base-type list, where DerivedOverrides derives from BaseOverrides, which derives from Object.

Discussion

Unfortunately, no property of the Type class exists to obtain the inheritance hierarchy of a type. The DisplayInheritanceChain methods in this recipe allow you to obtain the inheritance hierarchy of a type. All that is required is the path to an assembly and the name of the type with the inheritance hierarchy that is to be obtained. The DisplayInheritanceChain method requires only an assembly path since it displays the inheritance hierarchy for all types within that assembly.

The core code of this recipe exists in the GetBaseTypeList method. This is a recursive method that walks each inherited type until it finds the ultimate base class—which is always the object class. Once it arrives at this ultimate base class, it returns to its caller. Each time the method returns to its caller, the next base class in the inheritance hierarchy is added to the string until the final GetBaseTypeList method returns the completed string.

See Also

See the "Assembly Class" and "Type.BaseType Method" topics in the MSDN documentation.

13.8   Finding the Subclasses of a Type

Problem

You have a type and you need to find out whether it is subclassed anywhere in an assembly.

Solution

Use the Type.IsSubclassOf method to test all types within a given assembly, which determines whether each type is a subclass of the type specified in the argument to IsSubClassOf:

```
public static Type[] GetSubClasses(string asmPath, Type baseClassType)
{
    Assembly asm = Assembly.LoadFrom(asmPath);
```

```
        return (GetSubClasses(asm, baseClassType));
    }

    public static Type[] GetSubClasses(Assembly asm, Type baseClassType)
    {
        List<Type> subClasses = new List<Type>();

        foreach(Type type in asm.GetTypes())
        {
            if (type.IsSubclassOf(baseClassType))
            {
                subClasses.Add(type);
            }
        }

        return (subClasses.ToArray());
    }
```

The GetSubClasses method accepts an assembly path string and a second string containing a fully qualified base class name. This method returns a Type[] of Types representing the subclasses of the type passed to the *baseClass* parameter.

Discussion

The IsSubclassOf method on the Type class allows you to determine whether the current type is a subclass of the type passed in to this method.

The following code shows how to use this method:

```
    public static void FindSubClassOfType()
    {
        Assembly asm = Assembly.GetExecutingAssembly();
        Type type = Type.GetType("CSharpRecipes.ReflectionUtils+BaseOverrides");
        Type[] subClasses = GetSubClasses(asm,type);

        // Write out the subclasses for this type.
        if(subClasses.Length > 0)
        {
            Console.WriteLine("{0} is subclassed by:",type.FullName);
            foreach(Type t in subClasses)
            {
                Console.WriteLine("\t{0}",t.FullName);
            }
        }
    }
```

First you get the assembly path from the current process, and then you set up use of CSharpRecipes.ReflectionUtils+BaseOverrides as the type to test for subclasses. You call GetSubClasses, and it returns a Type[] that you use to produce the following output:

```
    CSharpRecipes.ReflectionUtils+BaseOverrides is subclassed by:
            CSharpRecipes.ReflectionUtils+DerivedOverrides
```

See Also

See the "Assembly Class" and "Type Class" topics in the MSDN documentation.

13.9 Finding All Serializable Types Within an Assembly

Problem

You need to find all the serializable types within an assembly.

Solution

Instead of testing the implemented interfaces and attributes on every type, you can query the Type.IsSerialized property to determine whether it is marked as serializable, as the following method does:

```
public static Type[] GetSerializableTypes(Assembly asm)
{
    List<Type> serializableTypes = new List<Type>();

    // Look at all types in the assembly.
    foreach(Type type in asm.GetTypes())
    {
        if (type.IsSerializable)
        {
            // Add the name of the serializable type.
            serializableTypes.Add(type);
        }
    }

    return (serializableTypes.ToArray());
}
```

The GetSerializableTypes method accepts an Assembly through its *asm* parameter. This assembly is searched for any serializable types, and their full names (including namespaces) are returned in a Type[].

In order to use this method to display the serializable types in an assembly, run the following code:

```
public static void FindSerializable()
{
    Assembly asm = Assembly.GetExecutingAssembly();
    Type[] serializable = GetSerializableTypes(asm);
    // Write out the serializable types in the assembly.
    if(serializable.Length > 0)
    {
        Console.WriteLine("{0} has serializable types:",asm.Location);
        foreach (Type t in serializable)
```

```
        {
            Console.WriteLine("\t{0}", t.FullName);
        }
    }
}
```

The output of this method is shown here:

```
C:\CSharp Recipes 2nd Edition\Code\CSharpRecipes\bin\Debug\CSharpRecipes.exe has
serializable types:
        CSharpRecipes.ExceptionHandling+RemoteComponentException
        CSharpRecipes.DelegatesEventsAnonymousMethods+HashtableEventHandler
        CSharpRecipes.Collections+MaxMinSizeDictionary`2
        CSharpRecipes.Collections+MaxMinValueHashtable
        CSharpRecipes.DataStructsAndAlgorithms+DblQueue`1
        CSharpRecipes.ClassAndStructs+DeepClone
        CSharpRecipes.ClassAndStructs+MultiClone
        CSharpRecipes.ClassAndStructs+Serializer`1
```

Discussion

A type may be marked as serializable using the SerializableAttribute attribute. Testing for the SerializableAttribute attribute on a type can turn into a fair amount of work. This is because the SerializableAttribute is a magic attribute that the C# compiler actually strips off your code at compile time. Using ildasm you will see that this custom attribute just isn't there—normally you see a .custom entry for each custom attribute, but not with SerializableAttribute. The C# compiler removes it, and instead sets a flag in the metadata of the class. In source code, it looks like a custom attribute, but it compiles into one of a small set of attributes that gets a special representation in metadata. That's why it gets special treatment in the reflection APIs. Fortunately, you do not have to do all of this work. The IsSerializable property on the Type class returns a true if the current type is marked as serializable with the SerializableAttribute; otherwise, this property returns false.

See Also

See the "Assembly Class" and "TypeAttributes Enumeration" in the MSDN documentation.

13.10 Filtering Output When Obtaining Members

Problem

You want to get information about one or more members, but you want to retrieve only a subset of members. For example, you need to obtain only the static constructor of a type, or you need to obtain only the noninherited nonpublic fields of a type.

Solution

Use the `BindingFlags` enumeration together with the appropriate `Type.Get`*xxx* methods to find out about the type, as in the code shown here in Example 13-3.

Example 13-3. Filtering members

```
public static void FilteringOutputObtainingMembers( )
{
    Type reflection = typeof(Reflection);
    ConstructorInfo[] constructors =
        reflection.GetConstructors(BindingFlags.Public |
                                   BindingFlags.NonPublic |
                                   BindingFlags.Instance |
                                   BindingFlags.Static);

    Console.WriteLine("Looking for All Constructors");
    foreach(ConstructorInfo c in constructors)
    {
        Console.WriteLine("\tFound Constructor {0}",c.Name);
    }

    constructors =
        reflection.GetConstructors(BindingFlags.Public |
                                   BindingFlags.Instance);
    Console.WriteLine("Looking for Public Instance Constructors");
    foreach(ConstructorInfo c in constructors)
    {
        Console.WriteLine("\tFound Constructor {0}",c.Name);
    }

    constructors =
        reflection.GetConstructors(BindingFlags.NonPublic |
                                   BindingFlags.Instance |
                                   BindingFlags.Static);
    Console.WriteLine("Looking for NonPublic Constructors");
    foreach(ConstructorInfo c in constructors)
    {
        Console.WriteLine("\tFound Constructor {0}",c.Name);
    }

    FieldInfo[] fields =
        reflection.GetFields(BindingFlags.Static |
                             BindingFlags.Public);
    Console.WriteLine("Looking for Public, Static Fields");
    foreach(FieldInfo f in fields)
    {
        Console.WriteLine("\tFound Field {0}",f.Name);
    }

    fields =
        reflection.GetFields(BindingFlags.Public |
                             BindingFlags.Static |
                             BindingFlags.Instance);
```

Example 13-3. Filtering members (continued)

```
    Console.WriteLine("Looking for Public Fields");
    foreach(FieldInfo f in fields)
    {
        Console.WriteLine("\tFound Field {0}",f.Name);
    }

    fields =
        reflection.GetFields(BindingFlags.NonPublic |
                             BindingFlags.Static );
    Console.WriteLine("Looking for NonPublic, Static Fields");
    foreach(FieldInfo f in fields)
    {
        Console.WriteLine("\tFound Field {0}",f.Name);
    }

}
```

This example examines the CSharpRecipes.Reflection type for constructors and fields. The constructors and fields are listed here:

```
#region Fields
    int i = 0;
    public int pi = 0;
    static int si = 0;
    public static int psi = 0;
    object o = null;
    public object po = null;
    static object so = null;
    public static object pso = null;
#endregion

#region Constructors
    static Reflection( )
    {
        si++;
        psi = 0;
        so = new Object( );
        pso = new Object( );
    }

    Reflection( )
    {
        i = 0;
        pi = 0;
        o = new Object( );
        po = new Object( );
    }

    public Reflection(int index)
    {
        i = index;
        pi = index;
```

```
            o = new Object( );
            po = new Object( );
        }
    #endregion
```

The output this generates is listed here:

```
Looking for All Constructors
        Found Constructor .cctor
        Found Constructor .ctor
        Found Constructor .ctor
Looking for Public Instance Constructors
        Found Constructor .ctor
Looking for NonPublic Constructors
        Found Constructor .cctor
        Found Constructor .ctor
Looking for Public, Static Fields
        Found Field psi
        Found Field pso
Looking for Public Fields
        Found Field pi
        Found Field po
        Found Field psi
        Found Field pso
Looking for NonPublic, Static Fields
        Found Field si
        Found Field so
```

Discussion

The following methods of the Type object accept a BindingFlags enumerator to filter output:

```
Type.GetConstructor
Type.GetConstructors
Type.GetMethod
Type.GetMethods
Type.GetField
Type.GetFields
Type.GetProperty
Type.GetProperties
Type.Event
Type.Events
Type.GetMember
Type.GetMembers
Type.FindMembers
```

The following are also methods that accept a BindingFlags enumerator to filter members and types to invoke or instantiate:

```
Type.InvokeMember
Type.CreateInstance
```

BindingFlags allows the list of members on which these methods operate to be expanded or limited. For example, if the BindingFlags.Public flag is passed to the

Type.GetFields method, only public fields are returned. If both the BindingFlags.Public and BindingFlags.NonPublic flags are passed to the Type.GetFields method, the list of fields is expanded to include the protected, internal, protected internal, and private fields of a type. Table 13-2 lists and describes each flag in the BindingFlags enumeration.

Table 13-2. Relevant binding flag definitions

Flag name	Definition
IgnoreCase	Case sensitivity is turned off.
Instance	Include all instance members when obtaining members of a type.
NonPublic	Include all nonpublic members when obtaining members of a type.
Public	Include all public members when obtaining members of a type.
Static	Include all static members when obtaining members of a type.

Be aware that to examine or invoke nonpublic members, your assembly must have the correct reflection permissions. The reflection permission flags, and what PermissionSets they are included in by default, are listed in Table 13-3.

Table 13-3. Reflection permission flags

Permission flag	Description	Permission sets including these rights
AllFlags	TypeInformation, MemberAccess, and ReflectionEmit are set.	FullTrust, Everything
MemberAccess	Invocation of operations on all type members is allowed. If this flag is not set, only invocation of operations on visible type members is allowed.	FullTrust, Everything
NoFlags	No reflection is allowed on types that are not visible.	All permission sets
ReflectionEmit	Use of System.Reflection.Emit is allowed.	FullTrust, Everything, LocalIntranet
TypeInformation	Reflection is allowed on members of a type that is not visible.	FullTrust, Everything

One other item to note is that when supplying a BindingFlags set of flags for one of the Get* methods, you must always pass either BindingFlags.Instance or BindingFlags.Static in order to get any results back. If you pass just BindingFlags.Public, for example, you will not find any results. You need to pass BindingFlags.Public | BindingFlags.Instance to get public instance results.

See Also

See the "BindingFlags Enumeration," "Type Class," "ConstructorInfo Class," and "FieldInfo Class" topics in the MSDN documentation.

➡️13.11 Dynamically Invoking Members

Problem

You have a list of method names that you wish to invoke dynamically within your application. As your code executes, it will pull names off this list and attempt to invoke these methods. This technique might be useful to create a test harness for components that reads in the methods to execute from an XML file and executes them with the given parameters.

Solution

The TestDynamicInvocation method shown in Example 13-4 calls the DynamicInvocation method, which opens the XML configuration file, reads out the test information, and executes each test method dynamically.

Example 13-4. Invoking members dynamically

```
public static void TestExecuteTests()
{
    ExecuteTests(@"..\..\SampleClassLibrary\SampleClassLibraryTests.xml",
             @"SampleClassLibrary.dll");
}

public static void ExecuteTests(string xmlFile, string path)
{
    // Read in the methods to run from the XML file.
    XmlDocument doc = new XmlDocument();
    doc.Load(xmlFile);

    // Get the tests to run.
    XmlNodeList nodes = doc.SelectNodes(@"Tests/Test");

    // Run each test method.
    foreach(XmlNode node in nodes)
    {
        // Get the name of the type from the className attribute on Test.
        string typeName = node.Attributes.GetNamedItem("className").Value;

        // Get the name of the method from the methodName attribute on Test.
        string methodName = node.Attributes.GetNamedItem("methodName").Value;

        // Get all the parameter types.
        int index = 0;
        object[] parameters = new object[node.ChildNodes.Count];
        foreach(XmlNode n in node.ChildNodes)
        {
            parameters[index] = n.InnerText;
            index++;
        }
```

Example 13-4. Invoking members dynamically (continued)

```
        object obj = InvokeMethod(path, typeName, methodName,
                                  node.ChildNodes.Count, parameters);

      // Print out the return.
      Console.WriteLine("\tReturned object: " + obj);
      Console.WriteLine("\tReturned object: " + obj.GetType().FullName);
   }
}
```

The XML document in which the test method information is contained looks like this:

```
    <?xml version="1.0" encoding="utf-8" ?>
    <Tests>
        <Test className='SampleClassLibrary.SampleClass' methodName='TestMethod1'>
            <Parameter>Running TestMethod1</Parameter>
        </Test>
        <Test className='SampleClassLibrary.SampleClass' methodName='TestMethod2'>
            <Parameter>Running TestMethod2</Parameter>
            <Parameter>27</Parameter>
        </Test>
    </Tests>
```

InvokeMethod, shown in Example 13-5, dynamically invokes the method that is passed to it using the information contained in the XmlNode. The parameter's types are determined by examining the ParameterInfo items on the MethodInfo, and then the values provided are converted to the actual type from a string via the Convert. ChangeType method. Finally, the return value of the invoked method is returned by this method.

Example 13-5. InvokeMethod method

```
public static object InvokeMethod(string asmPath, string typeName,
                                  string methodName, int paramCount,
                                  object[] parameters)
{
    // Load the assembly.
    Assembly asm = Assembly.LoadFrom(asmPath);

    // Create the actual type.
    Type dynClassType = asm.GetType(typeName, true, false);

    // Create an instance of this type and verify that it exists.
    object dynObj = Activator.CreateInstance(dynClassType);
    if (dynObj != null)
    {
        // Verify that the method exists and get its MethodInfo obj.
        MethodInfo invokedMethod = dynClassType.GetMethod(methodName);
        if (invokedMethod != null)
        {
            // Create the parameter list for the dynamically invoked methods.
            int index = 0;
```

Example 13-5. InvokeMethod method (continued)

```
            // For each parameter, add it to the list.
            foreach (object parameter in parameters)
            {
                // Get the type of the parameter.
                Type paramType =
                    invokedMethod.GetParameters()[index].ParameterType;

                // Change the value to that type and assign it.
                parameters[index] =
                    Convert.ChangeType(parameter, paramType);
                index++;
            }

            // Invoke the method with the parameters.
            object retObj = invokedMethod.Invoke(dynObj, parameters);
            // Return the returned object.
            return (retObj);
        }
    }

    return (null);
}
```

These are the dynamically invoked methods located on the `SampleClass` type in the `SampleClassLibrary` assembly:

```
public bool TestMethod1(string text)
{
    Console.WriteLine(text);
    return (true);
}

public bool TestMethod2(string text, int n)
{
    Console.WriteLine(text + " invoked with {0}",n);
    return (true);
}
```

The output from these methods looks like this:

```
Running TestMethod1
        Returned object: True
        Returned object: System.Boolean
Running TestMethod2 invoked with 27
        Returned object: True
        Returned object: System.Boolean
```

Discussion

Reflection gives you the ability to dynamically invoke both static and instance methods within a type in either the same assembly or in a different one. This can be a very powerful tool to allow your code to determine at runtime which method to call. This determination can be based on an assembly name, a type name, or a method name, though the assembly name is not required if the method exists in the same assembly as the invoking code, if you already have the Assembly object, or if you have a Type object for the class the method is on.

This technique may seem similar to delegates since both can dynamically determine at runtime which method is to be called. Delegates, on the whole, require you to know signatures of methods you might call at runtime, whereas with reflection, you can invoke methods when you have no idea of the signature, providing a much looser binding. More dynamic invocation can be achieved with Delegate. DynamicInvoke, but this is more of a reflection-based method than the traditional delegate invocation.

The InvokeMethod method shown in the Solution section contains all the code required to dynamically invoke a method. This code first loads the assembly using its assembly name (passed in through the *asmPath* parameter). Next, it gets the Type object for the class containing the method to invoke (the class name is gotten from the Test element's className attribute). The method name is then retrieved (from the Test element's methodName attribute). Once you have all of the information from the Test element, an instance of the Type object is created, and you then invoke the specified method on this created instance:

- First, the static Activator.CreateInstance method is called to actually create an instance of the Type object contained in the local variable dynClassType. The method returns an object reference to the instance of *type* that was created or throws an exception if the object cannot be created.

- Once you have successfully obtained the instance of this class, the MethodInfo object of the method to be invoked is acquired through a call to GetMethod on the Type object.

The instance of the object created with the CreateInstance method is then passed as the first parameter to the MethodInfo.Invoke method. This method returns an object containing the return value of the invoked method. This object is then returned by InvokeMethod. The second parameter to MethodInfo.Invoke is an object array containing any parameters to be passed to this method. This array is constructed based on the number of Parameter elements under each Test element in the XML. You then look at the ParameterInfo of each parameter (gotten from MethodInfo.GetParameters( )) and use the Convert.ChangeType method to coerce the string value from the XML to the proper type.

The ExecuteTests method finally displays each returned object value and its type. Note that there is no extra logic required to return different return values from the invoked methods since they are all returned as an object, unlike passing differing arguments to the invoked methods.

See Also

See the "Activator Class," "MethodInfo Class," "Convert.ChangeType Method," and "ParameterInfo Class" topics in the MSDN documentation.

13.12 Providing Guidance to Obfuscators

Problem

You need to configure Dotfuscator (or another type of compatible obfuscator utility) to operate independently on a number of assemblies, but you do not want to manually have to create a configuration file for each unique assembly configuration.

Solution

Use the ObfuscateAssembly and/or Obfuscation attributes in the System.Reflection namespace. The ObfuscateAssembly attribute can be used to indicate how to obfuscate the entire assembly:

```
[assembly: ObfuscateAssembly(true)]
```

Use the Obfuscation attribute on an assembly, on a type, or on the members of a type to gain a fine-grained control over what is obfuscated and what is not:

```
// Obfuscate this class and all of its members.
[Obfuscation(ApplyToMembers = true, Exclude = false)]
public class ObfuscatedCls() {...}
```

You can use this attribute at the assembly level, but you lose the ability to indicate whether or not this assembly is public or private, which affects how the obfuscator will handle the types and members of those types in the assembly. It is better to use the ObfuscateAssembly attribute at the assembly level and indicate whether or not this is a public or private assembly in its constructor. The Obfuscation attribute can then be used to tweak how the obfuscator utility will handle individual types and members of the assembly.

When using these attributes, you will typically want to add the ObfuscateAssembly attribute to each assembly that will be obfuscated. Next, you will want to add any Obfuscation attributes to indicate which types and/or members will be excluded from obfuscation.

Discussion

The true value that is passed in to the ObfuscateAssembly attribute's constructor indicates that this assembly is a private assembly, one that will be used by a single application only. Setting this option to true indicates to the Dotfuscator utility to do the following:

- Everything is renamed except for methods that override methods that exist outside this assembly.
- Property and event metadata is removed.

- Pruning rules for the professional version:
  — Included classes, methods, and fields are not removed.
  — Methods that act as entry points to your *.exe* or *.dll* are not removed.
  — Classes, members, and fields that will not be renamed will also not be removed.
  — Unreachable classes, fields, and methods are removed.

Setting this value to `false` indicates to the Dotfuscator utility to do the following:

- Public outer and nested class names are not modified.
- Public, protected, and internal protected member names of public classes are not modified.
- No virtual methods are modified.
- No property and event metadata is modified.
- Pruning rules for the professional version:
  — Public classes are never removed.
  — Public, protected, and internal protected fields of public classes are not removed.
  — Public, protected, and internal protected methods of public classes are not removed.
  — Entry points and their called methods are not removed.

You can force the `ObfuscateAssembly` attribute to not be removed after obfuscation occurs by setting a named parameter `StripAfterObfuscation` to `false` (by default it is set to `true`):

```
[assembly: ObfuscateAssembly(true, StripAfterObfuscation=false)]
```

Typically you want to set this parameter to `false` only when this attribute is applied to a *.dll* that will be obfuscated as part of an application that uses this *.dll*.

The `ApplyToMembers` named parameter on the `Obfuscation` attribute indicates whether or not this attribute is also applied to the members within this type. The following code will obfuscate the `ObfuscatedCls` class and all of its members.

```
[Obfuscation(ApplyToMembers = true, Exclude = false)]
public class ObfuscatedCls() {...}
```

However, you can place this same attribute on a member of the `ObfuscatedCls` class with the `Exclude` named parameter set to `true` to override the outer `Obfuscation` attribute.

You should be aware that by applying these attributes you are only providing configuration information to the obfuscator utility. These attributes will not actually obfuscate your assembly.

If you are using Dotfuscator, you need to allow it to use these attributes by setting the Honor Obfuscation Attributes button to enabled.

See Also

See the "ObfuscationAssemblyAttribute Class," "ObfuscationAttribute Class," and "Declarative Obfuscation" topics in the MSDN documentation.

13.13 Determining if a Type or Method Is Generic

Problem

You need to test a type and/or a method to determine whether it is generic.

Solution

Use the `IsGenericType` method of the `Type` class and the `IsGenericMethod` method of the `MethodInfo` class:

```
public static bool IsGenericType(Type type)
{
    return (type.IsGenericType);
}

public static bool IsGenericMethod(MethodInfo mi)
{
    return (mi.IsGenericMethod);
}
```

Discussion

The `IsGenericType` method examines objects and the `IsGenericMethod` method examines methods. These methods will return a `true` indicating that this object or method accepts type arguments and `false` indicating that it does not. One or more type arguments indicate that this type is a generic type.

To call these methods, use code like the following:

```
Assembly asm = Assembly.GetExecutingAssembly();
// Get the type.
Type t = typeof(CSharpRecipes.DataStructsAndAlgorithms.PriorityQueue<int>);

bool genericType = IsGenericType(t);

bool genericMethod = false;
foreach (MethodInfo mi in t.GetMethods())
    genericMethod = IsGenericMethod(mi);
```

This code first obtains an Assembly object for the currently executing assembly. Next, the Type object is obtained using the typeof method. For this method call, you pass in a fully qualified name of an object to this method. In this case you pass in CSharpRecipes.DataStructsAndAlgorithms.PriorityQueue<int>. Notice at the end is the string <int>. This indicates that this type is a generic type with a single type parameter of type int. In other words, this type is defined as follows:

```
public class PriorityQueue<T> {...}
```

If this type were defined with two type parameters, it would look like this:

```
public class PriorityQueue<T, U> {...}
```

and its fully qualified name would be CSharpRecipes.DataStructsAndAlgorithms. PriorityQueue<int, int>.

This Type object t is then passed into the IsGenericType method and the return value is true indicating that this type is indeed generic.

Next, you collect all the MethodInfo objects for this type t using the GetMethods method of the Type t object. Each MethodInfo object is passed into the IsGenericMethod method to determine if it is generic or not.

See Also

See the "Type.HasGenericArguments Method" and "MethodInfo.HasGenericArguments Method" topics in the MSDN documentation.

13.14 Reading Manifest Resources Programmatically

Problem

You need to obtain information about manifest resources.

Solution

Use the GetManifestResourceInfo and GetManifestResourceNames methods of the Assembly class:

```
public static void DisplayManifestResourceInfo(string asmPath)
{
    Assembly asm = Assembly.LoadFrom(asmPath);

    foreach (string resName in asm.GetManifestResourceNames())
    {
        Console.WriteLine("Resource Name: " + resName);

        ManifestResourceInfo mri = asm.GetManifestResourceInfo(resName);
        Console.WriteLine("\rFileName: " + mri.FileName);
```

```
                Console.WriteLine("\rResourceLocation: " + mri.ResourceLocation);
                if (mri.ReferencedAssembly != null)
                    Console.WriteLine("\rReferencedAssembly: " +
                                        mri.ReferencedAssembly.FullName);
        }
    }
```

Discussion

To obtain a ManifestResourceInfo object or objects, you must first call the
GetManifestResourceNames method on an Assembly object. This method returns an
array of string objects, which contain the resource name. This resource name is then
passed in to the GetManifestResourceInfo method to obtain the ManifestResourceInfo
object. The ManifestResourceInfo object is what contains all the information about
the manifest resource.

The ManifestResourceInfo.FileName property returns a fully qualified string describing the file that contains the manifest resource. This property will return an empty
string if the resource is embedded in the same assembly on which the GetManifestResourceInfo
was called.

The ManifestResourceInfo.ResourceLocation property returns all the ResourceLocation flags
for this resource. These flags can be one or a combination of three values described
in Table 13-4.

Table 13-4. ResourceLocation enumeration flags

Enumeration value	Definition
ContainedInAnotherAssembly	This resource exists in a separate assembly.
ContainedInManifestFile	This resource exists in the manifest file.
Embedded	This resource is an embedded resource, as opposed to a linked resource from a separate assembly.

The final property of use in the ManifestResourceInfo class is the ReferencedAssembly
property. This property returns an Assembly object that contains the resource. This
property returns null when the resource is embedded in the assembly on which this
property was called.

See Also

See the "GetManifestResourceInfo Method" and "GetManifestResourceNames
Method" topics in the MSDN documentation.

13.15 Accessing Local Variable Information

Problem

You are building a tool that examines code and you need to get access to the local variables within a method.

Solution

Use the LocalVariables property on the MethodBody class to return an IList of LocalVariableInfo objects, each of which describes a local variable within the method:

```
public static IList<LocalVariableInfo> GetLocalVars(string asmPath,
                                    string typeName, string methodName)
{
    Assembly asm = Assembly.LoadFrom(asmPath);
    Type asmType = asm.GetType(typeName);
    MethodInfo mi = asmType.GetMethod(methodName);
    MethodBody mb = mi.GetMethodBody();

    IList<LocalVariableInfo> vars = mb.LocalVariables;

    // Display information about each local variable.
    foreach (LocalVariableInfo lvi in vars)
    {
        Console.WriteLine("IsPinned: " + lvi.IsPinned);
        Console.WriteLine("LocalIndex: " + lvi.LocalIndex);
        Console.WriteLine("LocalType.Module: " + lvi.LocalType.Module);
        Console.WriteLine("LocalType.FullName: " + lvi.LocalType.FullName);
        Console.WriteLine("ToString(): " + lvi.ToString());
    }

    return (vars);
}
```

The GetLocalVars method can be called using the following code:

```
public static void TestGetLocalVars()
{
    Process current = Process.GetCurrentProcess();

    // Get the path of the current module.
    string path = current.MainModule.FileName;

    // Get all local var info for the CSharpRecipes.Reflection.GetLocalVars method.
    System.Collections.ObjectModel.ReadOnlyCollection<LocalVariableInfo> vars =
        (System.Collections.ObjectModel.ReadOnlyCollection<LocalVariableInfo>)
        GetLocalVars(path, "CSharpRecipes.Reflection", "GetLocalVars");
}
```

The output of this method is shown here:

```
IsPinned: False
LocalIndex: 0
LocalType.Module: CommonLanguageRuntimeLibrary
LocalType.FullName: System.Reflection.Assembly
ToString(): System.Reflection.Assembly (0)
IsPinned: False
LocalIndex: 1
LocalType.Module: CommonLanguageRuntimeLibrary
LocalType.FullName: System.Type
ToString(): System.Type (1)
IsPinned: False
LocalIndex: 2
LocalType.Module: CommonLanguageRuntimeLibrary
LocalType.FullName: System.Reflection.MethodInfo
ToString(): System.Reflection.MethodInfo (2)
IsPinned: False
LocalIndex: 3
LocalType.Module: CommonLanguageRuntimeLibrary
LocalType.FullName: System.Reflection.MethodBody
ToString(): System.Reflection.MethodBody (3)
IsPinned: False
LocalIndex: 4
LocalType.Module: CommonLanguageRuntimeLibrary
LocalType.FullName: System.Collections.ObjectModel.ReadOnlyCollection`1[[System.
Reflection.LocalVariableInfo, mscorlib, Version=2.0.0.0, Culture=neutral, Public
KeyToken=b77a5c561934e089]]
ToString(): System.Collections.ObjectModel.ReadOnlyCollection`1[System.Reflectio
n.LocalVariableInfo] (4)
```

The LocalVariableInfo objects for each local variable found in the CSharpRecipes.
Reflection.GetLocalVars method will be returned in the vars IList collection.

Discussion

The LocalVariables property can give you a good amount of information about variables within a method. The LocalVariables property returns an IList<LocalVariableInfo> collection. Each LocalVariableInfo object contains the information described in Table 13-5.

Table 13-5. LocalVariableInfo information

Member	Definition
IsPinned	Returns a bool indicating if the object that this variable refers to is pinned in memory (true) or not (false)
LocalIndex	Returns the index of this variable within this method's body
LocalType	Returns a Type object that describes the type of this variable
ToString	Returns the LocalType.FullName, a space, and then the LocalIndex value surrounded by parentheses

See Also

See the "MethodInfo Class," "MethodBody Class," "ReadOnlyCollection<T> Class," and "LocalVariableInfo Class" topics in the MSDN documentation.

13.16 Creating a Generic Type

Problem

You want to create a generic type using only the reflection APIs.

Solution

You create a generic type similarly to how a nongeneric type is created; however, there is an extra step of creating the type arguments you want to use in creating this generic type and binding these type arguments to the generic type's type parameters at construction. To do this, you will use a new method added to the Type class called BindGenericParameters:

```
public static void CreateMultiMap(Assembly asm)
{
    // Get the type we want to construct.
    Type typeToConstruct = asm.GetType(
        "CSharpRecipes.DataStructsAndAlgorithms+MultiMap`2");
    // Get the type arguments we want to construct our type with.
    Type[] typeArguments = new Type[2] {Type.GetType("System.Int32"),
                                        Type.GetType("System.String")};
    // Bind these type arguments to our generic type.
    Type newType = typeToConstruct.MakeGenericType(typeArguments);
    // Construct our type.
    DataStructsAndAlgorithms.MultiMap<int, string> mm = (
        DataStructsAndAlgorithms.MultiMap<int,
                string>)Activator.CreateInstance(newType);

    // Test our newly constructed type.
    Console.WriteLine("Count == " + mm.Count);
    mm.Add(1, "test1");
    Console.WriteLine("Count == " + mm.Count);
}
```

[handwritten annotation: ? BindGenericParameters]

The code to test the CreateMultiMap method is shown here:

```
public static void TestCreateMultiMap()
{
    Assembly asm = Assembly.LoadFrom("C:\\CSharp Recipes 2nd Edition" +
            "\\Code\\CSharpRecipes\\bin\\Debug\\CSharpRecipes.exe");
    CreateMultiMap(asm);
}
```

The output of this method is shown here:

```
Count == 0
Count == 1
```

Discussion

Type parameters are defined on a class and indicate that any type is allowed to be substituted for this type parameter (unless of course there are constraints placed on this type parameter using the where keyword). For example, the following class has two type parameters, T and U:

```
public class Foo<T, U> {...}
```

Of course you do not have to use T and U; you can instead use another letter or even a full name such as TypeParam1 and TypeParam2.

A type argument is defined as the actual type that will be substituted for the type parameter. In the previously defined class Foo, you can replace type parameter T with the type argument int and type parameter U with the type argument string.

The BindGenericParameters method allows you to substitute type parameters with actual type arguments. This method accepts a single Type array parameter. This Type array consists of each type argument that will be substituted for each type parameter of the generic type. These type arguments must be added to this Type array in the same order as they are defined on the class. For example, the Foo class defines type parameters T and U, in that order. The Type array that you define contains an int type and a string type, in that order. This means that the type parameter T will be substituted for the type argument int and U will be replaced with a string type. The BindGenericParameters method returns a Type object of the type you specified along with the type arguments.

See Also

See the "Type.BindGenericParameters method" topic in the MSDN documentation.

CHAPTER 14

Web

14.0 Introduction

The World Wide Web has worked its way into every nook and cranny of what most .NET developers encounter when building their solutions today. Web services are on the rise, and ASP.NET is one of the main players in the web application space. Because of the general needs to deal with HTML and TCP/IP name resolution and because uniform resource indicators and uniform resource locators are being used for more and more purposes, developers need tools to help them concentrate on building the best web-interactive applications they can. This chapter is dedicated to taking care of some of the grunge that comes along with programming when the Web is involved. This is not an ASP.NET tutorial chapter but rather some functionality that developers can use in both ASP.NET and other C#-based applications. For more on ASP.NET, see the *ASP.NET Cookbook* and *Programming ASP.NET,* Second Edition (both from O'Reilly).

14.1 Converting an IP Address to a Hostname

Problem

You have an IP address that you need to resolve into a hostname.

Solution

Use the `Dns.GetHostEntry` method to get the hostname for an IP address. In the following code, an IP address is resolved, and the hostname is accessible from the `HostName` property of the `IPHostEntry`:

```
using System;
using System.Net;

//...
```

```
// Use the Dns class to resolve the address.
IPHostEntry iphost = Dns.GetHostEntry("127.0.0.1");

// HostName property holds the hostname.
string hostName = iphost.HostName;

// Print out name.
Console.WriteLine(hostName);
```

Discussion

The System.Net.Dns class is provided for simple DNS resolution functionality. The GetHostEntry method returns an IPHostEntry that can be used to access the hostname via the HostName property. If the entry cannot be resolved, the IPHostEntry will have a HostName that has a string representation of the IP address that was passed in (assuming it is a valid IP address). If the first member of the AddressList ([0]) is accessed and the IPAddress.ScopeId property is checked for these entries, it will throw a SocketException.

See Also

See the "DNS Class" and "IPHostEntry Class" topics in the MSDN documentation.

14.2 Converting a Hostname to an IP Address

Problem

You have a string representation of a host (such as *www.oreilly.com*), and you need to obtain the IP address from this hostname.

Solution

Use the Dns.GetHostEntry method to get the IP addresses. In the following code, a hostname is provided to the GetHostEntry method, which returns an IPHostEntry from which a string of addresses can be constructed. If the hostname does not resolve, a SocketException stating "No such host is known" is thrown.

```
using System;
using System.Net;
using System.Text;

// ...

public static string HostName2IP(string hostname)
{
    // Resolve the hostname into an iphost entry using the Dns class.
    IPHostEntry iphost = System.Net.Dns.GetHostEntry(hostname);
    // Get all of the possible IP addresses for this hostname.
    IPAddress[] addresses = iphost.AddressList;
    // Make a text representation of the list.
```

```
            StringBuilder addressList = new StringBuilder( );
            // Get each IP address.
            foreach(IPAddress address in addresses)
            {
                // Append it to the list.
                addressList.AppendFormat("IP Address: {0};", address.ToString( ));
            }
            return addressList.ToString( );
        }

    // ...

    // Writes "IP Address: 208.201.239.37;IP Address: 208.201.239.36;"
    Console.WriteLine(HostName2IP("www.oreilly.com"));
```

Discussion

An IPHostEntry can associate multiple IP addresses with a single hostname via the AddressList property. AddressList is an array of IPAddress objects, each of which holds a single IP address. Once the IPHostEntry is resolved, the AddressList can be looped over using foreach to create a string that shows all of the IP addresses for the given hostname. If the entry cannot be resolved, a SocketException is thrown.

See Also

See the "DNS Class," "IPHostEntry Class," and "IPAddress" topics in the MSDN documentation.

14.3 Parsing a URI

Problem

You need to split a uniform resource identifier (URI) into its constituent parts.

Solution

Construct a System.Net.Uri object and pass the URI to the constructor. This class constructor parses out the constituent parts of the URI and allows access to them via the Uri properties. You can then display the URI pieces individually, as shown in Example 14-1.

Example 14-1. ParseURI method

```
public static void ParseUri(string uriString)
{
    try
    {
        // Use just one of the constructors for the System.Net.Uri class.
        // This will parse it for us.
        Uri uri = new Uri(uriString);
        // Look at the information we can get at now...
```

Example 14-1. ParseURI method (continued)

```
StringBuilder uriParts = new StringBuilder( );
uriParts.AppendFormat("AbsoluteURI: {0}{1}",
                    uri.AbsoluteUri,Environment.NewLine);
uriParts.AppendFormat("AbsolutePath: {0}{1}",
                    uri.AbsolutePath,Environment.NewLine);
uriParts.AppendFormat("Scheme: {0}{1}",
                    uri.Scheme,Environment.NewLine);
uriParts.AppendFormat("UserInfo: {0}{1}",
                    uri.UserInfo,Environment.NewLine);
uriParts.AppendFormat("Authority: {0}{1}",
                    uri.Authority,Environment.NewLine);
uriParts.AppendFormat("DnsSafeHost: {0}{1}",
                    uri.DnsSafeHost,Environment.NewLine);
uriParts.AppendFormat("Host: {0}{1}",
                    uri.Host,Environment.NewLine);
uriParts.AppendFormat("HostNameType: {0}{1}",
                    uri.HostNameType.ToString( ),Environment.NewLine);
uriParts.AppendFormat("Port: {0}{1}",uri.Port,Environment.NewLine);
uriParts.AppendFormat("Path: {0}{1}",uri.LocalPath,Environment.NewLine);
uriParts.AppendFormat("QueryString: {0}{1}",uri.Query,Environment.NewLine);
uriParts.AppendFormat("Path and QueryString: {0}{1}",
                    uri.PathAndQuery,Environment.NewLine);
uriParts.AppendFormat("Fragment: {0}{1}",uri.Fragment,Environment.NewLine);
uriParts.AppendFormat("Original String: {0}{1}",
                    uri.OriginalString,Environment.NewLine);
uriParts.AppendFormat("Segments: {0}",Environment.NewLine);
for (int i = 0; i < uri.Segments.Length; i++)
    uriParts.AppendFormat("    Segment {0}:{1}{2}",
                    i, uri.Segments[i], Environment.NewLine);


// GetComponents can be used to get commonly used combinations
// of URI information.
uriParts.AppendFormat("GetComponents for specialized combinations: {0}",
                    Environment.NewLine);
uriParts.AppendFormat("Host and Port (unescaped): {0}{1}",
                    uri.GetComponents(UriComponents.HostAndPort,
                    UriFormat.Unescaped),Environment.NewLine);
uriParts.AppendFormat("HttpRequestUrl (unescaped): {0}{1}",
                    uri.GetComponents(UriComponents.HttpRequestUrl,
                    UriFormat.Unescaped),Environment.NewLine);
uriParts.AppendFormat("HttpRequestUrl (escaped): {0}{1}",
                    uri.GetComponents(UriComponents.HttpRequestUrl,
                    UriFormat.UriEscaped),Environment.NewLine);
uriParts.AppendFormat("HttpRequestUrl (safeunescaped): {0}{1}",
                    uri.GetComponents(UriComponents.HttpRequestUrl,
                    UriFormat.SafeUnescaped),Environment.NewLine);
uriParts.AppendFormat("Scheme And Server (unescaped): {0}{1}",
                    uri.GetComponents(UriComponents.SchemeAndServer,
                    UriFormat.Unescaped),Environment.NewLine);
uriParts.AppendFormat("SerializationInfo String (unescaped): {0}{1}",
                    uri.GetComponents(UriComponents.SerializationInfoString,
                    UriFormat.Unescaped),Environment.NewLine);
```

Example 14-1. ParseURI method (continued)

```
        uriParts.AppendFormat("StrongAuthority (unescaped): {0}{1}",
                        uri.GetComponents(UriComponents.StrongAuthority,
                        UriFormat.Unescaped),Environment.NewLine);
        uriParts.AppendFormat("StrongPort (unescaped): {0}{1}",
                        uri.GetComponents(UriComponents.StrongPort,
                        UriFormat.Unescaped),Environment.NewLine);

        // Write out our summary.
        Console.WriteLine(uriParts.ToString( ));
    }
    catch(ArgumentNullException e)
    {
        // UriString is a null reference (Nothing in Visual Basic).
        Console.WriteLine("URI string object is a null reference: {0}",e);
    }
    catch(UriFormatException e)
    {
        Console.WriteLine("URI formatting error: {0}",e);
    }
}
```

Discussion

The Solution code uses the Uri class to do the heavy lifting. The constructor for the Uri class can throw two types of exceptions: an ArgumentNullException and a UriFormatException. The ArgumentNullException is thrown when the uri argument passed is null. The UriFormatException is thrown when the uri argument passed is of an incorrect or indeterminate format. Here are the error conditions that can throw a UriFormatException:

- An empty URI was passed in.
- The scheme specified in the Uri is not correctly formed. See CheckSchemeName.
- The URI passed in contains too many slashes.
- The password specified in the passed-in URI is invalid.
- The hostname specified in the passed-in URI is invalid.
- The filename specified in the passed-in URI is invalid.
- The username specified in the passed-in URI is invalid.
- The host or authority name specified in the passed-in URI cannot be terminated by backslashes.
- The port number specified in the passed-in URI is invalid or cannot be parsed.
- The length of the passed-in URI exceeds 65,534 characters.
- The length of the scheme specified in the passed-in URI exceeds 1023 characters.
- There is an invalid character sequence in the passed-in URI.

There is no actual validation that occurs for the username, host or authority name, password or port number to insure that they exist or are correct. The validation is simply that they are in the correct format according to the URI specification (RFC 2396).

System.Net.Uri provides methods to compare URIs, parse URIs, and combine URIs. It is all you should ever need for URI manipulation and is used by other classes in the Framework when a URI is called for. The syntax for the pieces of a URI is this:

```
[scheme]://[user]:[password]@[host/authority]:[port]/[path];[params]?
[query string]#[fragment]
```

If you pass the following URI to ParseURI:

http://user:password@localhost:8080/www.abc.com/home.htm?item=1233#stuff

it will display the following items:

```
AbsoluteURI: http://user:password@localhost:8080/www.abc.com/home%20page.htm?
item=1233#stuff
AbsolutePath: /www.abc.com/home%20page.htm
Scheme: http
UserInfo: user:password
Authority: localhost:8080
DnsSafeHost: localhost
Host: localhost
HostNameType: Dns
Port: 8080
Path: /www.abc.com/home page.htm
QueryString: ?item=1233
Path and QueryString: /www.abc.com/home%20page.htm?item=1233
Fragment: #stuff
Original String: http://user:password@localhost:8080/www.abc.com/home%20page.htm?
item=1233#stuff
Segments:
    Segment 0: /
    Segment 1: www.abc.com/
    Segment 2: home%20page.htm
GetComponents for specialized combinations:
Host and Port (unescaped): localhost:8080
HttpRequestUrl (unescaped): http://localhost:8080/www.abc.com/home page.htm?
item=1233
HttpRequestUrl (escaped): http://localhost:8080/www.abc.com/home%20page.htm?
item=1233
HttpRequestUrl (safeunescaped): http://localhost:8080/www.abc.com/home page.htm?
item=1233
Scheme And Server (unescaped): http://localhost:8080
SerializationInfo String (unescaped): http://user:password@localhost:8080/
www.abc.com/home page.htm?item=1233#stuff
StrongAuthority (unescaped): user:password@localhost:8080
StrongPort (unescaped): 8080
```

See Also

See the "Uri Class," "ArgumentNullException Class," and "UriFormatException Class" topics in the MSDN documentation.

14.4 Forming and Validating an Absolute URI

Problem

You have a base URI of the form *http://www.oreilly.com* and a relative URI of the form *hello%20world.htm*; you want to form an absolute URI from them and ensure it is correctly formed.

Solution

Use the `Uri` class to combine a base URI and a relative URI via a constructor overload that takes the base and relative paths and then use the functions on the `Uri` class to validate it, as shown in Example 14-2.

Example 14-2. CreateAndVerifyAbsoluteUri method

```
public static Uri CreateAndVerifyAbsoluteUri(string uriBaseString,
                      string uriRelativeString)
{
    try
    {
        // Make the base URI.
        Uri baseUri = new Uri(uriBaseString,UriKind.Absolute);
        // Make the relative URI.
        Uri relativeUri = new Uri(uriRelativeString, UriKind.Relative);
        // Create the full URI by combining the base and relative.
        Uri absoluteUri = new Uri(baseUri, relativeUri);

        // Verify we did make an absolute URI.
        if(absoluteUri.IsAbsoluteUri==false)
            throw new UriFormatException(
                "Could not form absolute Uri from " +
                baseUri.OriginalString + " and " +
                relativeUri.OriginalString);

        // Make sure our original base URI is a base URI for the new
        // absolute URI.
        if(baseUri.IsBaseOf(absoluteUri)==false)
            throw new UriFormatException(
                "Base Uri was invalid for newly formed Absolute Uri: " +
                baseUri.OriginalString + " and " +
                absoluteUri.OriginalString);

        // Get the relative URI from the difference between the base
        // and the absolute URIs.
```

Example 14-2. CreateAndVerifyAbsoluteUri method (continued)

```
        Uri relCheckUri = baseUri.MakeRelativeUri(absoluteUri);
        // This new relative URI should equal our previous URI.
        if(relCheckUri != relativeUri)
            throw new UriFormatException(
                "Could not make equivalent relative Uri from new " +
                "Absolute Uri: " +
                relCheckUri.OriginalString + " and " +
                absoluteUri.OriginalString);

        Uri newAbsoluteUri = new Uri(baseUri, relCheckUri);
        // Check that the new and the original match.
        if(Uri.Compare(absoluteUri, newAbsoluteUri,
            UriComponents.AbsoluteUri, UriFormat.Unescaped,
            StringComparison.InvariantCulture) != 0)
        {
            throw new UriFormatException(
                "New Absolute Uri did not equal originally formed " +
                "Absolute Uri: " +
                baseUri.OriginalString + " and " +
                absoluteUri.OriginalString);
        }

        // It's OK, send it.
        return absoluteUri;
    }
    catch (ArgumentNullException e)
    {
        // uriString is a null reference (Nothing in Visual Basic).
        Console.WriteLine("URI string object is a null reference: {0}", e);
    }
    catch (UriFormatException e)
    {
        Console.WriteLine("URI formatting error: {0}", e);
    }
    return null;
}


// ...

Uri myUri = CreateAndVerifyAbsoluteUri("http://www.oreilly.com",
                    "hello%20world.htm");

// Displays http://www.oreilly.com/hello world.htm.
Console.WriteLine(myUri.AbsoluteUri);
```

Discussion

The System.Net.Uri class has a constructor overload that allows you to create a URI from a base Uri and a relative Uri. This creates the absolute URI and places it in the Uri.AbsoluteUri property. If there are two strings for the base path and relative path, escaping/unescaping can also be controlled through another overload of the Uri constructor that takes a UriKind as the last parameter (UriKind), but care needs to be taken here: if you unescape the Uri, it will put the URI into a form more readable by a human but no longer usable as a URI (this is because any spaces that were escaped as %20 will now be considered whitespace).

Here are the error conditions that can cause a UriFormatException to be thrown when using the Uri constructor that takes a string for the path and a UriKind to control escaping:

- The passed string contains a relative URI, and the UriKind is Absolute.
- The passed string contains an absolute URI, and the UriKind is Relative.

There are various ways that URI creation can fail. A URI might fail the IsAbsoluteUri check if the authority is not provided as part of the base URI. The IsBaseOf method on a URI might fail if the current URI is not identical to the internal base URI, given that all items after the last slash are ignored on the full URI.

See Also

See the "Uri Class" topic in the MSDN documentation.

14.5   Handling Web Server Errors

Problem

You have obtained a response from a web server and you want to make sure that there were no errors in processing the initial request, such as failing to connect, being redirected, timing out, or failing to validate a certificate. You don't want to have to monitor for all of the different response codes available.

Solution

Check the StatusCode property of the HttpWebResponse class to determine what category of status this StatusCode falls into, and return an enumeration value (ResponseCategories) representing the category. This technique will allow you to use a broader approach to dealing with response codes.

```
public static ResponseCategories VerifyResponse(HttpWebResponse httpResponse)
{
    // Just in case there are more success codes defined in the future
    // by HttpStatusCode, we will check here for the "success" ranges
    // instead of using the HttpStatusCode enum as it overloads some
    // values.
    int statusCode = (int)httpResponse.StatusCode;
    if((statusCode >= 100)&& (statusCode <= 199))
    {
        return ResponseCategories.Informational;
    }
```

```
    else if((statusCode >= 200)&& (statusCode <= 299))
    {
        return ResponseCategories.Success;
    }
    else if((statusCode >= 300)&& (statusCode <= 399))
    {
        return ResponseCategories.Redirected;
    }
    else if((statusCode >= 400)&& (statusCode <= 499))
    {
        return ResponseCategories.ClientError;
    }
    else if((statusCode >= 500)&& (statusCode <= 599))
    {
        return ResponseCategories.ServerError;
    }
    return ResponseCategories.Unknown;
}
```

The ResponseCategories enumeration is defined like this:

```
public enum ResponseCategories
{
    Unknown = 0,        // Unknown code  ( < 100 or > 599)
    Informational = 1,  // Informational codes (100 <= 199)
    Success = 2,        // Success codes (200 <= 299)
    Redirected = 3,     // Redirection code (300 <= 399)
    ClientError = 4,    // Client error code (400 <= 499)
    ServerError = 5     // Server error code (500 <= 599)
}
```

Discussion

There are five different categories of status codes on an HTTP response, as shown in Table 14-1.

Table 14-1. Categories of HTTP response status codes

Category	Available range	HttpStatusCode defined range
Informational	100-199	100-101
Successful	200-299	200-206
Redirection	300-399	300-307
Client Error	400-499	400-417
Server Error	500-599	500-505

Each of the status codes defined by Microsoft in the .NET Framework is assigned an enumeration value in the HttpStatusCode enumeration. These status codes reflect what can happen when a request is submitted. The web server is free to return a status code in the available range, even if it is not currently defined for most commercial web servers. The defined status codes are listed in RFC 2616—Section 10 for HTTP/1.1.

You are trying to figure out the broad category of the status of the request. You achieve this by inspecting the `HttpResponse.StatusCode` property, comparing it to the defined status code ranges for HTTP, and returning the appropriate `ResponseCategories` value.

When dealing with `HttpStatusCode`, you will notice that there are certain `HttpStatusCode` flags that map to the same status code value. An example of this is `HttpStatusCode.Ambiguous` and `HttpStatusCode.MultipleChoices`, which both map to HTTP status code 300. If you try to use both of these in a switch statement on the `HttpStatusCode`, you will get the following error because the C# compiler cannot tell the difference:

```
error CS0152: The label 'case 300:' already occurs in this switch statement.
```

See Also

See *HTTP: The Definitive Guide* (O'Reilly); see the "HttpStatusCode Enumeration" topic in the MSDN documentation; and see HTTP/1.1 RFC 2616—Section 10 Status Codes: *http://www.w3.org/Protocols/rfc2616/rfc2616-sec10.html*.

14.6 Communicating with a Web Server

Problem

You want to send a request to a web server in the form of a GET or POST request. After you send the request to a web server, you want to get the results of that request (the response) from the web server.

Solution

Use the `HttpWebRequest` class in conjunction with the `WebRequest` class to create and send a request to a server.

Take the URI of the resource, the method to use in the request (GET or POST), and the data to send (only for POST requests), and use this information to create an `HttpWebRequest`, as shown in Example 14-3.

Example 14-3. Communicating with a web server

```
using System.Net;
using System.IO;
using System.Text;


// ...

// GET overload
public static HttpWebRequest GenerateHttpWebRequest(string uriString)
{
```

Example 14-3. Communicating with a web server (continued)

```
    // Get a URI object.
    Uri uri = new Uri(uriString);
    // Create the initial request.
    HttpWebRequest httpRequest = (HttpWebRequest)WebRequest.Create(uri);
    // Return the request.
    return httpRequest;
}

// POST overload
public static HttpWebRequest GenerateHttpWebRequest(string uriString,
    string postData,
    string contentType)
{
    // Get a URI object.
    Uri uri = new Uri(uriString);
    // Create the initial request.
    HttpWebRequest httpRequest = (HttpWebRequest)WebRequest.Create(uri);

    // Get the bytes for the request; should be pre-escaped.
    byte[] bytes = Encoding.UTF8.GetBytes(postData);

    // Set the content type of the data being posted.
    httpRequest.ContentType = contentType;
        //"application/x-www-form-urlencoded"; for forms

    // Set the content length of the string being posted.
    httpRequest.ContentLength = postData.Length;

    // Get the request stream and write the post data in.
    using (Stream requestStream = httpRequest.GetRequestStream())
    {
        requestStream.Write(bytes, 0, bytes.Length);
    }
    // Return the request.
    return httpRequest;
}
```

Once you have an HttpWebRequest, you send the request and get the response using the GetResponse method. It takes the newly created HttpWebRequest as input and returns an HttpWebResponse. The following example performs a GET for the *index.aspx* page from the *http://localhost/mysite* web site:

```
HttpWebRequest request =
 GenerateHttpWebRequest(http://localhost/mysite/index.aspx);

using(HttpWebResponse response = (HttpWebResponse) request.GetResponse())
{
    // This next line uses VerifyResponse from Recipe 14.5.
    if(VerifyResponse(response)==ResponseCategories.Success)
    {
        Console.WriteLine("Request succeeded");
    }
}
```

You generate the HttpWebRequest, send it and get the HttpWebResponse, then check the success using the VerifyResponse method from Recipe 14.5.

Discussion

The WebRequest and WebResponse classes encapsulate all of the functionality to perform basic web communications. HttpWebRequest and HttpWebResponse are derived from these classes and provide the HTTP-specific support.

At the most fundamental level, to perform an HTTP-based web transaction, you use the Create method on the WebRequest class to get a WebRequest that can be cast to an HttpWebRequest (so long as the scheme is http:// or https://). This HttpWebRequest is then submitted to the web server in question when the GetResponse method is called, and it returns an HttpWebResponse that can then be inspected for the response data.

See Also

See the "WebRequest Class," "WebResponse Class," "HttpWebRequest Class," and "HttpWebResponse Class" topics in the MSDN documentation.

14.7   Going Through a Proxy

Problem

Many companies have a web proxy that allows employees to access the Internet, while at the same time preventing outsiders from accessing the company's internal network. The problem is that to create an application that accesses the Internet from within your company, you must first connect to your proxy and then send information through it, rather than directly out to an Internet web server.

Solution

In order to get an HttpWebRequest successfully through a specific proxy server, you need to set up a WebProxy object with the settings to validate your specific request to a given proxy. Since this function is generic for any request, you can create the AddProxyInfoToRequest method:

```
public static HttpWebRequest AddProxyInfoToRequest(HttpWebRequest httpRequest,
                        string proxyUri,
                        string proxyID,
                        string proxyPwd,
                        string proxyDomain)
{
    if(httpRequest != null)
    {
        // Create the proxy object.
        WebProxy proxyInfo = new WebProxy();
        // Add the address of the proxy server to use.
```

```
        proxyInfo.Address = new Uri(proxyUri);
        // Tell it to bypass the proxy server for local addresses.
        proxyInfo.BypassProxyOnLocal = true;
        // Add any credential information to present to the proxy server.
        proxyInfo.Credentials = new NetworkCredential(proxyID,
                                                      proxyPwd,
                                                      proxyDomain);

        // Assign the proxy information to the request.
        httpRequest.Proxy = proxyInfo;
    }
    // Return the request.
    return httpRequest;
}
```

If all requests are going to go through the same proxy, in the 1.x versions of the Framework, you used the static Select method on the GlobalProxySelection class to set up the proxy settings for all WebRequests. In Version 2.0, the WebRequest.Default-WebProxy property should be used:

```
Uri proxyURI = new Uri("http://webproxy:80");
WebRequest.DefaultWebProxy = new WebProxy(proxyURI);

// Old v1.x way of doing this...
//GlobalProxySelection.Select = new WebProxy(proxyURI);
```

Discussion

AddProxyInfoToRequest takes the URI of the proxy and creates a Uri object, which is used to construct the WebProxy object. The WebProxy object is set to bypass the proxy for local addresses and then the credential information is used to create a NetworkCredential object. The NetworkCredential object represents the authentication information necessary for the request to succeed at this proxy and is assigned to the WebProxy.Credentials property. Once the WebProxy object is completed, it is assigned to the Proxy property of the HttpWebRequest and the request is ready to be submitted.

See Also

See the "WebProxy Class," "NetworkCredential Class," and "HttpWebRequest Class" topics in the MSDN documentation.

14.8 Obtaining the HTML from a URL

Problem

You need to get the HTML returned from a web server in order to examine it for items of interest. For example, you could examine the returned HTML for links to other pages or for headlines from a news site.

Solution

You can use the methods for web communication that were set up in Recipes 14.5 and 14.6 to make the HTTP request and verify the response; then, you can get at the HTML via the ResponseStream property of the HttpWebResponse object:

```
public static string GetHtmlFromUrl(string url)
{
    if (string.IsNullOrEmpty(url))
        throw new ArgumentNullException("url","Parameter is null or empty");

    string html = "";
    HttpWebRequest request = GenerateHttpWebRequest(url);
    using(HttpWebResponse response = (HttpWebResponse)request.GetResponse())
    {
        if (VerifyResponse(response) == ResponseCategories.Success)
        {
            // Get the response stream.
            Stream responseStream = response.GetResponseStream();
            // Use a stream reader that understands UTF8.
            using(StreamReader reader =
            new StreamReader(responseStream, Encoding.UTF8))
            {
                html = reader.ReadToEnd();
            }
        }
    }
    return html;
}
```

Discussion

The GetHtmlFromUrl method gets a web page using the GenerateHttpWebRequest and GetResponse methods, verifies the response using the VerifyResponse method, and then, once it has a valid response, starts looking for the HTML that was returned.

The GetResponseStream method on the HttpWebResponse provides access to the body of the message that was returned in a System.IO.Stream object. In order to read the data, instantiate a StreamReader with the response stream and the UTF8 property of the Encoding class to allow for the UTF8-encoded text data to be read correctly from the stream. Then call the StreamReader's ReadToEnd method, which puts all of the content in the string variable called html, and return it.

See Also

See the "HttpWebResponse.GetResponseStream Method," "Stream Class," and "String-Builder Class" topics in the MSDN documentation.

14.9 Using the New Web Browser Control

Problem

You need to display HTML-based content in a WinForms-based application.

Solution

Use the `System.Windows.Forms.WebBrowser` class to embed web browser functionality into your application. The Cheapo-Browser seen in Figure 14-1 shows some of the capabilities of this control.

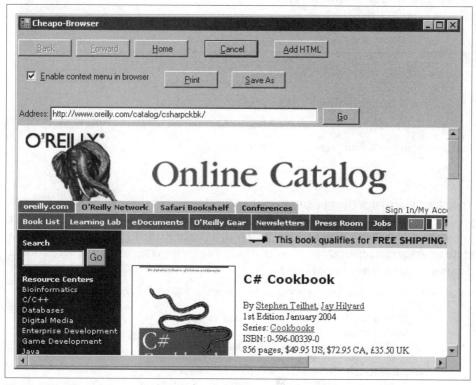

Figure 14-1. The web browser control

While this is not a production quality user interface, it is called Cheapo-Browser for a reason. It can be used to select a web address, display the content, navigate forward and backward, cancel the request, go to the home page, add HTML directly to the control, print the HTML or save it, and finally enable or disable the context menu inside of the browser window. The `WebBrowser` control is capable of much more, but this recipe is meant to give you a flavor of what is possible. It would be well worth exploring its capabilities further to see what other needs it might fill.

When you add your HTML (`<h1>Hey you added some HTML!</h1>`), it is displayed as shown in Figure 14-2.

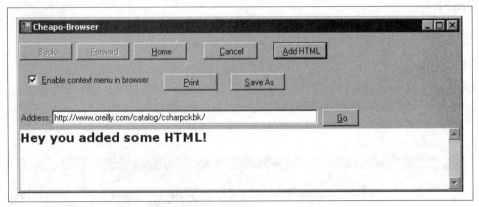

Figure 14-2. Adding HTML to the Cheapo-Browser

The code to accomplish this is rather simple:

```
this._webBrowser.Document.Body.InnerHtml = "<h1>Hey you added some HTML!</h1>";
```

The navigation to a web page is equally trivial:

```
Uri uri = new Uri(this._txtAddress.Text);
this._webBrowser.Navigate(uri);
```

The nice thing about the navigation is the `Navigated` event that can be subscribed so you are notified when the navigation has completed. This allows code to spin this off in a thread and then come back to it once it is fully loaded. The event provides a `WebBrowserNavigatedEventArgs` class that has a `Url` property to tell the URL of the document that has been navigated to.

```
private void _webBrowser_Navigated(object sender, WebBrowserNavigatedEventArgs e)
{
    // Update with where we ended up in case of redirection
    // from the original URI.
    this._txtAddress.Text = e.Url.ToString();
    // Set up the buttons if we can go back or forth.
    this._btnBack.Enabled = this._webBrowser.CanGoBack;
    this._btnForward.Enabled = this._webBrowser.CanGoForward;
}
```

Discussion

In the 1.x versions of the .NET Framework, embedding a web browser in your Win-Forms application was much more difficult and error-prone. With the advent of the 2.0 Framework, there is finally a .NET-based web browser control. You no longer have to struggle with some of the COM interop issues that could arise while trying to hook up to browser events. This is a good opportunity to make the line between your desktop and web applications blur even further and use the power of a rich client combined with web flexibility.

See Also

See the "WebBrowser Class" topic in the MSDN documentation.

14.10 Tying Database Tables to the Cache

Problem

You want to cache datasets you create from a database to help the performance of your ASP.NET application, but you want changes to the data in the database to be reflected in your pages.

Solution

Use the SqlCacheDependency class to expire data in the cache when the underlying database data changes. A SqlCacheDependency sets up a relationship with the database so that, if the data changes, the item in the cache that has this dependency is released from the cache, and the code that established the item can fetch the values from the database again.

To demonstrate this, a SqlCacheDependency object is created for the Authors table in the pubs database in Microsoft SQL Server using the CreateSqlCacheDependency method. The pubs database is a sample database that ships with SQL Server 2000.

```
public SqlCacheDependency CreateSqlCacheDependency(string connStr)
{
    // Make a dependency on the authors database table so that
    // if it changes, the cached data will also be disposed of.

    // Make sure we are enabled for notifications for the db.
    // Note that the parameter has to be the actual connection
    // string NOT the connection string NAME from web.config.
    SqlCacheDependencyAdmin.EnableNotifications(connStr);

    // Make sure we are enabled for notifications for the table.
    SqlCacheDependencyAdmin.EnableTableForNotifications(connStr, "Authors");

    // This is case-sensitive so make sure the first entry
    // matches the entry in the web.config file exactly.
    // The first parameter here must be the connection string
    // NAME not the connection string itself...
    return new SqlCacheDependency("pubs", "Authors");
}
```

The SqlCacheDependencyAdmin class is responsible for talking to SQL Server to set up the necessary infrastructure (triggers and the like for SQL Server 2000, Cache Sync for SQL Server 2005) for the SqlCacheDependency to fire correctly. The SqlCacheDependency has a section in the application's *web.config* file under *configuration/system.web/caching* defining the parameters that the dependency operates under. There are timeout settings for the polling time (for SQL Server 2000 as SQL Server 2005 doesn't poll) and the connection time, as well as a link to the connection string to use via its name. This connection string can be found in the *web.config* file in the *configuration/connectionStrings* section. The two entries are shown here:

```
<caching>
  <sqlCacheDependency enabled="True" pollTime="60000">
    <databases>
      <add name="pubs" connectionStringName="LocalPubs" pollTime="9000000" />
    </databases>
  </sqlCacheDependency>
</caching>

<connectionStrings>
  <add name="LocalPubs" connectionString="Server=(local);Integrated
Security=True;Database=pubs;Persist Security Info=True"
providerName="System.Data.SqlClient"/>
</connectionStrings>
```

Discussion

The main scenario for using SqlDependencyCache is for data that is read frequently but changes very infrequently. The data should be reasonably static as there is overhead associated with keeping the cache in sync with the database table. While the SqlDependencyCache is for use with Microsoft SQL Server, it is just a derived implementation of a CacheDependency class. CacheDependency-based classes could be written for any other database provider, but surprisingly (or perhaps not so) Microsoft SQL Server is the only database with one provided.

When using the SqlCacheDependency class, the first thing to do is insure that Notifications have been enabled for both the database and the table being monitored for changes. If either of these notifications is not enabled for the database and/or table, a DatabaseNotEnabledForNotificationException will be thrown when constructing the SqlCacheDependency. A SqlCacheDependency can also be created directly from a SqlCommand object.

See Also

See Recipe 14.11; see the "SqlCacheDependency," "SqlCacheDependencyAdmin," and "CacheDependency" topics in the MSDN documentation.

14.11 Caching Data with Multiple Dependencies

Problem

A dataset you are using in an ASP.NET page is comprised of data from multiple data sources. You want to use caching for performance, but only one dependency object can be added with the cache item.

Solution

Use the AggregateCacheDependency class to tie multiple cache dependencies together. AggregateCacheDependency has an Add method that takes an array of CacheDependency objects. This lets you write code that takes ordinary CacheDependency, SqlCacheDependency, and even custom CacheDependency objects, and the cached item is removed when any of these dependencies changes.

For example, suppose that data for an author tracking system was being pulled from an XML file with royalty information and from a database for the author addresses and contact information. This data is combined into a single DataSet that is used by the ASP.NET code to produce a web page of author information. To make sure that the page gets a DataSet quickly, it is put in the cache once it is created.

First a CacheDependency is created for the XML file with the royalty information:

```
// Make a dependency on the author royalties file
// so if someone updates it, the cached data will
// be disposed of.
string file = this.Server.MapPath("author_royalties.xml");
CacheDependency fileDep = new CacheDependency(file);
```

Next a SqlCacheDependency is created for the pubs database and the Authors table using the method from Recipe 14.10:

```
// Use our method from 14.10 to make a SqlCacheDependency.
SqlCacheDependency sqlDep = CreateSqlCacheDependency(connStr);
```

Then a DataSet reference is created and the code looks in the cache for it. If there is no DataSet already cached for this, a new DataSet is created and filled from the database, then populated from the XML file:

```
// Set up data table to get.
DataSet authorInfo = null;

// Look for the pubs key in the cache.
// If it isn't there, create it with a dependency
// on a SQL Server table using the SqlCacheDependency class.
// The "this" pointer refers to a Page class for a web page and
// it accesses the System.Web.UI.Page.Cache property.
if (this.Cache["authorInfo"] == null)
{
    // The data wasn't there so go get it and put it in the cache.
    authorInfo = new DataSet("AuthorInfo");
```

```
using (SqlConnection sqlConn = new SqlConnection(connStr))
{
    using (SqlDataAdapter adapter =
        new SqlDataAdapter("SELECT * FROM AUTHORS", sqlConn))
    {
        adapter.Fill(authorInfo);

        // Now add the royalty info.
        authorInfo.ReadXml(file, XmlReadMode.InferSchema);
```

Finally, an AggregateCacheDependency is created for the DataSet from the CacheDependency (fileDep) and the SqlCacheDependency (sqlDep). The DataSet is added to the cache with the AggregateCacheDependency (aggDep) and the cache takes care of managing the DataSet from this point forward. If a DataSet is in the cache already and the dependencies have not been triggered, the DataSet from the cache is returned.

```
        // Make the aggregate dependency so that if either the
        // db or file changes, we toss this out of the cache.
        AggregateCacheDependency aggDep = new AggregateCacheDependency();
        // Add the two dependencies to the aggregate.
        aggDep.Add(new CacheDependency[] { sqlDep, fileDep });

        // Add author info dataset to cache with the aggregate
        // dependency so that if either changes the cache will refetch.
        this.Cache.Insert("authorInfo", authorInfo, aggDep);
    }
    }
}
else
{
    authorInfo = (DataSet)this.Cache["authorInfo"];
}
```

Discussion

The AggregateCacheDependency class is new in the 2.0 Framework, and it is a welcome addition to an already strong caching arsenal for the ASP.NET cache. Almost the same effect could be accomplished in the 1.x Frameworks by adding a cache entry for each dependency, but then the data is being stored twice as well. AggregateCacheDependency allows for the user to specify more clearly what the dependencies are for a given item being cached. By not having to have a one-to-one ratio of dependencies to cache items anymore, the cache can be even leaner and perform better.

See Also

See Recipe 14.10; see the "AggregateCacheDependency Class," "CacheDependency Class," "SqlCacheDependency Class," and "DataSet" topics in the MSDN documentation.

14.12 Prebuilding an ASP.NET Web Site Programmatically

Problem

You want to prebuild your web site to avoid compilation delays and to avoid the hosting scenario in which source code needs to be on the server.

Solution

Use the `ClientBuildManager` to prebuild your web site into an assembly. In order to prebuild the web site, you must specify:

- The virtual directory for the web application
- The physical path to the web application directory
- The location where you want to build the web application
- Flags that help control the compilation

To prebuild the web application in the sample code for the book, first retrieve the directory where the web application is located, then provide a virtual directory name and a location for the web application to build to:

```
// Get the path to the web app shipping with this code...
string cscbWebPath = GetWebAppPath( );

// Make sure we have a web path.
if(cscbWebPath.Length>0)
{
    string appVirtualDir = @"CSCBWeb";
    string appPhysicalSourceDir = cscbWebPath;

    // Make the target an adjacent directory as it cannot be in the same tree
    // or the build manager screams...
    string appPhysicalTargetDir = Path.GetDirectoryName(cscbWebPath) + @"\BuildCSCB";
```

Next, set up the flags for the compile using the `PrecompilationFlags` enumeration. The `PrecompilationFlags` values are listed in Table 14-2.

Table 14-2. PrecompilationFlags enumeration values

Flag value	Purpose
AllowPartiallyTrustedCallers	Add the APTC attribute to the built assembly.
Clean	Remove any existing compiled image.
CodeAnalysis	Build for code analysis.
Default	Use the default compile options.
DelaySign	DelaySign the assembly.

Table 14-2. *PrecompilationFlags enumeration values (continued)*

Flag value	Purpose
FixedNames	Assembly generated with fixed names for pages. No batch compilation is performed, just individual compilation.
ForceDebug	Ensure that the assembly is compiled for Debug.
OverwriteTarget	The target assembly should be overwritten if it exists.
Updateable	Insure the assembly is updateable.

To build a debug image and make sure it is created successfully if the compilation is good, the ForceDebug and OverwriteTarget flags are used:

```
PrecompilationFlags flags = PrecompilationFlags.ForceDebug |
                PrecompilationFlags.OverwriteTarget;
```

The PrecompilationFlags are then stored in a new instance of the ClientBuildManagerParameter class, and the ClientBuildManager is created with the parameters that have been set up for it. To accomplish the prebuild, the PrecompileApplication method is called. Notice that there is an instance of a class called MyClientBuildManagerCallback that is passed to the PrecompileApplication method.

```
ClientBuildManagerParameter cbmp = new ClientBuildManagerParameter( );
cbmp.PrecompilationFlags = flags;

ClientBuildManager cbm =
            new ClientBuildManager(appVirtualDir,
                    appPhysicalSourceDir,
                    appPhysicalTargetDir,
                                cbmp);

MyClientBuildManagerCallback myCallback = new MyClientBuildManagerCallback( );
cbm.PrecompileApplication(myCallback);
```

The MyClientBuildManagerCallback class is derived from the ClientBuildManagerCallback class and allows the code to receive notifications during the compilation of the web application. Compiler errors, parsing errors, and progress notifications are all available. In the MyClientBuildManagerCallback class, they are all implemented to write to the debug stream and the console.

```
public class MyClientBuildManagerCallback : ClientBuildManagerCallback
{
    public MyClientBuildManagerCallback( )
        : base( )
    {
    }

    public override void ReportCompilerError(CompilerError error)
```

```
    {
        string msg = "Report Compiler Error: " + error.ToString();
        Debug.WriteLine(msg);
        Console.WriteLine(msg);
    }

    public override void ReportParseError(ParserError error)
    {
        string msg = "Report Parse Error: " + error.ToString();
        Debug.WriteLine(msg);
        Console.WriteLine(msg);
    }

    public override void ReportProgress(string message)
    {
        string msg = "Report Progress: " + message;
        Debug.WriteLine(msg);
        Console.WriteLine(msg);
    }
}
```

The output from a successful compilation of the CSCB web site looks like this:

```
Report Progress: Building directory '/CSCBWeb/App_Data'.
Report Progress: Building directory '/CSCBWeb/Role_Database'.
Report Progress: Building directory '/CSCBWeb'.
```

Discussion

ClientBuildManager is actually a thin wrapper around the BuildManager class, which does most of the heavy lifting of the compilation. ClientBuildManager makes it more straightforward to ensure that all the important parts of the web application are addressed, while BuildManager gives a bit more fine-grained control. The ClientBuildManager also allows for subscribing to AppDomain notification events such as start, shutdown, and unload, allowing for error handling in the event that the AppDomain is going away during a prebuild.

To prebuild applications in ASP.NET 2.0 without resorting to the ClientBuildManager, an HTTP request can be posted to the web site in the format of *http://server/webapp/precompile.axd*. The *precompile.axd* "document" triggers an ASP.NET HttpHandler for this that will prebuild the web site for you. This is handled by the *aspnet_compiler.exe* module that essentially wraps the ClientBuildManager functionality.

See Also

See the "ClientBuildManager," "ClientBuildManagerParameters," "BuildManager," and "ASP.NET Web Site Precompilation" topics in the MSDN documentation.

14.13 Escaping and Unescaping Data for the Web

Problem

You need to transform data for use in web operations from escaped to unescaped format or vice versa for proper transmission. This escaping and unescaping should follow the format outlined in RFC 2396—Uniform Resource Identifiers (URI): Generic Syntax.

Solution

Use the Uri class static methods for escaping and unescaping data and Uris.

To escape data, use the static Uri.EscapeDataString method as shown here:

```
string data = "<H1>My html</H1>";
Console.WriteLine("Original Data: {0}",data);
Console.WriteLine();
// public static string EscapeDataString(string stringToEscape);
string escapedData = Uri.EscapeDataString(data);
Console.WriteLine("escaped Data: {0}",escapedData);
Console.WriteLine();



// Output from above code is
//
// Original Data: <H1>My html</H1>
//
// Escaped Data: %3CH1%3EMy%20html%3C%2FH1%3E
```

To unescape the data, use the static Uri.UnescapeDataString method:

```
// public static string UnescapeDataString(    string stringToUnescape);
string unescapedData = Uri.UnescapeDataString(escapedData);
Console.WriteLine("unescaped Data: {0}",data);
Console.WriteLine();



// Output from above code is
//
// Unescaped Data: <H1>My html</H1>
```

To escape a Uri, use the static Uri.EscapeUriString method:

```
string uriString = "http://user:password@localhost:8080/www.abc.com/" +
    "home page.htm?item=1233;html=<h1>Heading</h1>#stuff";
Console.WriteLine("Original Uri string: {0}",uriString);
Console.WriteLine();

// public static string EscapeUriString(string stringToEscape);
string escapedUriString = Uri.EscapeUriString(uriString);
Console.WriteLine("Escaped Uri string: {0}",escapedUriString);
Console.WriteLine();
```

```
// Output from above code is
//
//Original Uri string:
http://user:password@localhost:8080/www.abc.com/home
//page.htm?item=1233;html=<h1>Heading</h1>#stuff
//
//Escaped Uri string:
//http://user:password@localhost:8080/www.abc.com/home%20page.
//htm?item=1233;
//html=%3Ch1%3EHeading%3C/h1%3E#stuff
```

In case you are wondering why escaping a Uri has its own method (EscapeUriString), take a look at what the escaped Uri looks like if you use Uri.EscapeDataString and Uri.UnescapeDataString on it:

```
// Why not just use EscapeDataString to escape a Uri?  It's not picky enough...
string escapedUriData = Uri.EscapeDataString(uriString);
Console.WriteLine("Escaped Uri data: {0}",escapedUriData);
Console.WriteLine();

Console.WriteLine(Uri.UnescapeDataString(escapedUriString));


// Output from above code is
//
//
//Escaped Uri data:
//http%3A%2F%2Fuser%3Apassword%40localhost%3A8080%2Fwww.abc.
//com%2Fhome%20page.htm
//%3Fitem%3D1233%3Bhtml%3D%3Ch1%3EHeading%3C%2Fh1%3E%23stuff
//
//http://user:password@localhost:8080/www.abc.com/home
//page.htm?item=1233;html=<h1>Heading</h1>#stuff
```

Notice that the :, /, :, @, and ? characters get escaped when they shouldn't, which is why you use the EscapeUriString method for Uris.

Discussion

EscapeUriString assumes that there are no escape sequences already present in the string being escaped. The escaping follows the convention set down in RFC 2396 for converting all reserved characters and characters with a value greater than 128 to their hexadecimal format.

In section 2.2 of RFC 2396, it states that the reserved characters are:

; | / | ? | : | @ | & | = | + | $ | ,

The EscapeUriString method is useful when creating a System.Uri object to ensure that the Uri is escaped correctly.

See Also

See the "EscapeUriString Method," "EscapeUriData Method," and "Unescape-
DataString Method" topics in the MSDN documentation.

14.14 Using the UriBuilder Class

Problem

You want to avoid making URI syntax errors when creating a URI.

Solution

Use the UriBuilder class to add each piece without worrying about syntax or placement in the string.

Building a URI programmatically can be challenging to do correctly in all instances.
Using the UriBuilder can help to simplify it. For instance, if you needed to assemble
an HTTP URI that looked like this:

> *http://user:password@localhost:8080/www.abc.com/home page
> htm?item=1233;html=<h1>Heading</h1>#stuff*

you would need to understand the layout of the HTTP uri, which is this:

> *[scheme]://[user]:[password]@[host/authority]:[port]/[path];[params]?[query
> string]#[fragment]*

It is very possible that information could come in that has only some of these pieces,
or all of the pieces might be present. The UriBuilder allows the code to set properties for each of the components of the URI. This is great except for one small glitch.
Every time you set the Query property, the UriBuilder class appends a ? to the front
of the query string information. This means if code is written in this manner:

```
UriBuilder ub = new UriBuilder();
ub.Query = "item=1233";
ub.Query += "html-<h1>heading</h1>";
```

the resulting query string looks like this with two question marks:

```
??item=1233;html=<h1>heading</h1>
```

To correct this sad state of affairs, use the UriBuilderFix which overloads the Query
property and deals with this in a more reasonable manner. UriBuilderFix is a light
wrapper for UriBuilder that cleans up the Query property behavior.

```
public class UriBuilderFix : UriBuilder
{
    public UriBuilderFix() : base()
    {
    }
```

```
        public new string Query
        {
            get
            {
                return base.Query;
            }
            set
            {
             if (!string.IsNullOrEmpty(value))
               {
                    if (value[0] == '?')
                        // Trim off the leading ? as the underlying
                        // UriBuilder class will add one to the
                        // query string.  Also prepend ; for additional items.
                        base.Query = value.Substring(1);
                    else
                        base.Query = value;
               }
            else
                    base.Query = string.Empty;
            }
        }
    }
```

The UriBuilderFix is used just like the UriBuilder, except you now get the expected output from adding to the query string:

```
UriBuilderFix ubf = new UriBuilderFix( );
ubf.Scheme = "http";
ubf.UserName = "user";
ubf.Password = "password";
ubf.Host = "localhost";
ubf.Port = 8080;
ubf.Path = "www.abc.com/home page.htm";

//The Query property contains any query information included in the URI.
//Query information is separated from the path information by a question mark (?) and //
//continues to the end of the URI. The query information returned includes the /////
//leading question mark.
//The query information is escaped according to RFC 2396.
//Setting the Query property to null or to System.String.Empty clears the property.
//Note:   Do not append a string directly to this property.
//Instead retrieve the property value as a string, remove the leading question mark,
//append the new query string, and set the property with the combined string.

ubf.Query = "item=1233";
ubf.Query += ";html=<h1>heading</h1>";

ubf.Fragment = "stuff";

Console.WriteLine("Absolute Composed Uri: " + ubf.Uri.AbsoluteUri);
Console.WriteLine("Composed Uri: " + ubf.ToString( ));
```

This example produces the following output:

```
Absolute Composed Uri: http://user:password@localhost:8080/www.abc.com/home%20page.
htm?item=1233;html=%3Ch1%3Eheading%3C/h1%3E

Composed Uri:
http://user:password@localhost:8080/www.abc.com/home%20page.htm?item=1233;html=
%3Ch1%3Eheading%3C/h1%3E
```

Discussion

Even without the addition of the `Query` behavior in `BetterUriBuilder`, `UriBuilder` is a great way to build up `Uris` without resorting to assembling the whole string yourself. Once the construction of the `Uri` is complete, get the `Uri` object from the `UriBuilder.Uri` property to use it.

See Also

See Recipes 14.3 and 14.4; see the "UriBuilder Class" and "Uri Class" topics in the MSDN documentation.

14.15 Inspect and Change Your Web Application Configuration

Problem

You want to be able to modify some settings in your web application configuration file from within a web page.

Solution

Use the `System.Configuration.WebConfigurationManager` and `System.Configuration.Configuration` classes to access elements of your web application's configuration settings.

First get a `Configuration` object for the configuration settings by calling the `OpenWebConfiguration` method on the `WebConfigurationManager`:

```
System.Configuration.Configuration cfg =
    WebConfigurationManager.OpenWebConfiguration(@"/CSCBWeb");
```

Now use the `Configuration` object to get a specific section of the settings. The following code retrieves the `sqlCacheDependencySection` of the configuration:

```
// Get the sqlCacheDependencySection.
SqlCacheDependencySection sqlCacheDep = (SqlCacheDependencySection)cfg.GetSection(
    "system.web/caching/sqlCacheDependency");
```

The `SqlCacheDependencySection` allows for creating a new `SqlCacheDependencyDatabase` and adding it to the configuration, then saving the new configuration:

```
// Create a database entry for the sql cache.
SqlCacheDependencyDatabase sqlCacheDb = new
        SqlCacheDependencyDatabase("pubs","LocalPubs",9000000);
// Add our database entry for the caching.
sqlCacheDep.Databases.Add(sqlCacheDb);
// Enable it.
sqlCacheDep.Enabled = true;
// Poll once a minute.
sqlCacheDep.PollTime = 60000;
// Save our new settings to the cfg file.
cfg.Save(ConfigurationSaveMode.Modified);
```

This creates the following section in the *web.config* file for the application:

```
<sqlCacheDependency enabled="True" pollTime="60000">
  <databases>
    <add name="pubs" connectionStringName="LocalPubs" pollTime="9000000" />
  </databases>
</sqlCacheDependency>
```

Now the application is configured to allow a SqlCacheDependency to be created.

Discussion

This may seem like a lot of work at first. It would be pretty easy to rip through the *web.config* file using an XmlTextReader/Writer combination or an XmlDocument. But that would get the settings in only that *web.config* file, not all of the other *web.config* files that merge with the application-level one to make up the true configuration. The WebConfigurationManager allows for accessing the current settings at runtime, not just the static ones on disk in the multiple files.

> One of the results of changing the configuration of a web application programmatically is that it can result in the restart of the application domain for the application. This can cause performance issues on your server. The other major area to consider is security. If the page that executes this code is not secured properly, the application/server hosting the page could be open to attack.

When the configuration is modified during the processing of the web page, the changes are not immediately reflected in the current configuration, as the page needs to finish processing before the configuration can be updated. In the earlier case in which a SqlCacheDependency is configured, the attempt to immediately construct the SqlCacheDependency object will throw an exception stating that the application is not configured to do this. To get around this, you can do the configuration setting work, then redirect back to the same page with a parameter in the query string that bypasses this setup code and moves right into the code that uses the new configuration (the creation of the SqlCacheDependency in this case):

```
// If the initial request.
if (Request.QueryString.Count == 0)
```

```
{
    // Add the sqlCache database entry
    // to web.config.
    TestConfig();
    // Now redirect to ourselves adding a query string.
    // We do this so that the change we made to
    // web.config gets picked up for the code in
    // CreateSqlCacheDependency and SetupCacheDependencies.
    // as it depends on that configuration being present.

    // If you just create the entry and call the setup
    // code in the same page instance, the internal
    // configuration stuff doesn't refresh and you get
    // an exception when the code can't find the sqlCache
    // section it needs.
    Response.Redirect(Request.RawUrl + "?run=1");
}
else
{
    // Run 14.10.
    CreateSqlCacheDependency();
    // Run 14.11.
    SetupCacheDependencies();
}
```

See Also

See Recipes 14.10 and 14.11; see the "WebConfigurationManager Class" and "System.Configuration Namespace" topics in the MSDN documentation.

14.16 Working with HTML

Problem

You need to parse some HTML to get certain values from it, but you don't want to write all of the HTML parsing logic yourself.

Solution

Use the Microsoft.MSHTML Primary Interop Assembly wrapper and let the Internet Explorer parsing engine do the work. The first thing that has to happen is to establish a reference to the MSHTML control, which is located in the *Program Files\Microsoft. NET\Primary Interop Assemblies* directory in the *Microsoft.mshtml.dll* assembly. Once this reference has been made, just use the mshtml namespace like so:

```
using mshtml;
```

Now that the code is set up properly, you can use the MSHTML control to do your HTML parsing. First declare an instance of the HTMLDocument class, then declare an instance of the IHTMLDocument2 interface and fill a string with some HTML to parse:

```
HTMLDocument htmlDoc = new HTMLDocument( );
IHTMLDocument2 iHtmlDoc2 = null;

string html =
    "<!DOCTYPE html PUBLIC \"-//W3C//DTD XHTML 1.1//EN\"" +
    "\"http://www.w3.org/TR/xhtml11/DTD/xhtml11.dtd\">" +
    "<html xmlns=\"http://www.w3.org/1999/xhtml\" >" +
    "<head><title>Test Page</title></head>" +
    "<body><form method=\"post\" action=\"Default.aspx\" id=\"form1\">" +
    "<div><input id=\"Text1\" type=\"text\" />" +
    "<input id=\"Checkbox1\" type=\"checkbox\" />" +
    "<input id=\"Radio1\" type=\"radio\" />" +
    "<select id=\"Select1\">" +
    "<option selected=\"selected\"></option></select>" +
    "<input name=\"TextBox1\" type=\"text\" id=\"TextBox1\" />" +
    "</div></form></body></html>";
```

The `IHTMLDocument2` interface reference is set by casting the `HTMLDocument` to the
`IHTMLDocument2` interface. Then the design mode is turned on so that any script that is
embedded in the HTML does not execute while the HTML loads and is parsed. Place
the HTML into the `iHtmlDoc2` using the `write` method and close it to finish loading
the HTML:

```
// Get the IHTMLDocument2 interface.
iHtmlDoc2 = (IHTMLDocument2)htmlDoc;

// Put the document in design mode so we don't execute scripts
// while loading.
iHtmlDoc2.designMode = "On";

// Have to put some HTML in the DOM before using it.
iHtmlDoc2.write(html);

// Close it.
iHtmlDoc2.close( );
```

Now that the HTML is loaded and parsed, look for items of interest in it. Do this by
casting the iHtmlDoc2 interface to the `HTMLDocumentClass`, then look at each `IHTMLElement` in
the `IHTMLElementCollection` exposed by the `all` property on the body property for the
`HTMLDocumentClass`.

Roll over each of the `IHTMLElements` and check against the various type classes for various HTML elements like form, input, text areas, and more as shown in Example 14-4.

Example 14-4. Parsing HTML

```
//Roll over every element in the HTML.
foreach (IHTMLElement htmlElem in (IHTMLElementCollection)iHtmlDoc2.body.all)
{
    // Note: every time we do the is and as, it does a COM call to the
    // MSHTML object. This can be rather expensive so you would want to cache
    // the results elsewhere once you have them, not just keep calling
    // properties on it as those end up making a round-trip as well.
```

Example 14-4. Parsing HTML (continued)

```csharp
    if (htmlElem is HTMLAnchorElementClass)
    {
        HTMLAnchorElementClass anchor = htmlElem as HTMLAnchorElementClass;
        if (anchor != null)
            Console.WriteLine("Anchor element found: " + anchor.href);
    }
    else if (htmlElem is HTMLFormElementClass)
    {
        HTMLFormElementClass form = htmlElem as HTMLFormElementClass;
        if (form != null)
            Console.WriteLine("Form element found: " + form.id);
    }
    else if (htmlElem is HTMLGenericElementClass)
    {
        HTMLGenericElementClass genElem = htmlElem as HTMLGenericElementClass;
        if (genElem != null)
            Console.WriteLine("Input Element found: " + genElem.scopeName +
                "." + genElem.tagName);
    }
    else if (htmlElem is HTMLInputElementClass)
    {
        HTMLInputElementClass input = htmlElem as HTMLInputElementClass;
        if (input != null)
            Console.WriteLine("Input Element found: " + input.id);
    }
    else if (htmlElem is HTMLTextAreaElementClass)
    {
        HTMLTextAreaElementClass text = htmlElem as HTMLTextAreaElementClass;
        if (text != null)
            Console.WriteLine("Text Area Element found: " + text.name);
    }
}
```

This code will have the following output:

```
Form element found: form1
Input Element found: Text1
Input Element found: Checkbox1
Input Element found: Radio1
Input Element found: TextBox1
```

Discussion

There are many ways that HTML can be parsed: regular expressions, straight text parsing, or even third-party product offerings. The MSHTML parser is free and prevalent but it is COM-based. Being COM-based in a .NET world carries a price tag of having to have all calls go through the COM interop layer and have items marshaled back and forth. MSHTML can be made to perform decently in many situations, but this is not a solution for high-end HTML parsing due to the overhead that will be incurred each time the COM interop layer is traversed. This should be considered a client-side operation only. The overhead would quickly degrade performance in a server-side scenario like an HttpHandler or in a high-traffic web page.

That being said, if you are looking for a quick way to parse HTML in your application and it is not a potential performance hotspot, this method will do quite nicely. Like many other things in .NET, if you know what you are using it for and the scope of the work it will do, many alternatives become acceptable.

See Also

See the "IHtmlDocument2 Interface" and "MSHTML" topics in the MSDN documentation.

14.17 Using Cached Results When Working with HTTP for Faster Performance

Problem

You are looking for a way to speed up code that reaches out to the Web via HTTP for content.

Solution

Use the RequestCachePolicy class to determine how your HttpWebRequests react in the presence of a caching entity. RequestCachePolicy has seven levels defined by the RequestCacheLevel enumeration, as shown in Table 14-3.

Table 14-3. RequestCacheLevel enumeration values

Flag value	Purpose
BypassCache	Get content only directly from the server (default setting in .NET).
CacheIfAvailable	Accept the requested item from any cache between the request and the server of the content.
CacheOnly	Accept the request to be fulfilled from only the local cache; throws a WebException if not found in the cache.
Default	Accept content from intermediate caches or from the server directly, subject to the current cache policy and content age (recommended level for most apps even though it is not the default setting).
NoCacheNoStore	Content will not be accepted from caches nor added to any. Equivalent to the HTTP no-cache directive.
Reload	Get content directly from the server but store response in the cache.
Revalidate	Check the content timestamp on the server against the cache and take the most recent one.

The RequestCachePolicy is set up using the CacheIfAvailable RequestCacheLevel so that the request will always take the "closest" content to enhance retrieval speed. If Default is used, the request is still subject to the underlying cache policy of the system, and that can prevent the use of intermediate caches.

To assign the cache policy, set the CachePolicy property on the HttpWebRequest to the newly created RequestCachePolicy. Once the policy is in place, get the response. The HttpWebResponse object has a property called IsFromCache that tells if the response came from a cache.

```
string html = "";
string url = "http://www.oreilly.com";

// Set up the request (Recipe 14.6 has GenerateHttpWebRequest).
HttpWebRequest request = GenerateHttpWebRequest(url);

// Make a cache policy to use cached results if available.
// The default is to bypass the cache in machine.config.
RequestCachePolicy rcpCheckCache =
    new RequestCachePolicy(RequestCacheLevel.CacheIfAvailable);

// Assign the new policy to the request.
request.CachePolicy = rcpCheckCache;

// Execute the request.
HttpWebResponse response = null;
try
{
    response = (HttpWebResponse)request.GetResponse();
}
catch (WebException we)
{
    Console.WriteLine(we.ToString());
}

// Check if we hit the cache.
if(response.IsFromCache==false)
{
    Console.WriteLine("Didn't hit the cache");
}
```

Discussion

The default request cache policy for an AppDomain can be set by using the HttpWebRequest.DefaultCachePolicy property. The CachePolicy property shown in the solution sets the policy for a particular request.

The default caching policy is specified in the *machine.config* file in the system.net/ requestCaching element as shown here:

```
<requestCaching defaultPolicyLevel="BypassCache" isPrivateCache="true"
unspecifiedMaximumAge="1.00:00:00" >
```

See Also

See the "RequestCachePolicy Class," "RequestCacheLevel Enumeration," and "Default-CachePolicy Property" topics in the MSDN documentation.

14.18 Checking out a Web Server's Custom Error Pages

Problem

You have an application that needs to know what custom error pages are set up for the various HTTP error return codes on a given IIS server.

Solution

Use the System.DirectoryServices.DirectoryEntry class to talk to the Internet Information Server (IIS) metabase to find out which custom error pages are set up. The metabase holds the configuration information for the web server. DirectoryEntry uses the Active Directory IIS service provider to communicate with the metabase by specifying the "IIS" scheme in the constructor for the DirectoryEntry.

```
// This is a case-sensitive entry in the metabase.
// You'd think it was misspelled but you would be mistaken...
const string WebServerSchema = "IIsWebServer";

// Set up to talk to the local IIS server.
string server = "localhost";

// Create a dictionary entry for the IIS server with a fake
// user and password.  Credentials would have to be provided
// if you are running as a regular user.
using (DirectoryEntry w3svc =
    new DirectoryEntry(
        string.Format("IIS://{0}/w3svc", server),
            "Domain/UserCode", "Password"))
{
```

Once the connection is established, the web server schema entry is specified to show where the IIS settings are kept (IIsWebServer). The DirectoryEntry has a property that allows access to its children (Children) and the SchemaClassName is checked for each entry to see if it is in the web server settings section. Once the web server settings are found, the web root node is located, and from there the HttpErrors property is retrieved. HttpErrors is a comma-delimited string that indicates the HTTP error code, the HTTP suberror code, the message type, and the path to the HTML file to serve when this error occurs. Using the Split method to break this into a string array allows the code to access the individual values and write them out. The code for carrying out these operations is shown in Example 14-5.

Example 14-5. Finding custom error pages

```
// Can't talk to the metabase for some reason: bail.
if (w3svc != null)
{
    foreach (DirectoryEntry site in w3svc.Children)
    {
```

Example 14-5. Finding custom error pages (continued)

```
            if (site != null)
            {
                using (site)
                {
                    // Check all web servers on this box.
                    if (site.SchemaClassName == WebServerSchema)
                    {
                        // Get the metabase entry for this server.
                        string metabaseDir =
                            string.Format("/w3svc/{0}/ROOT", site.Name);

                        if (site.Children != null)
                        {
                            // Find the root directory for each server.
                            foreach (DirectoryEntry root in site.Children)
                            {
                                using (root)
                                {
                                    // Did we find the root dir for this site?
                                    if (root != null &&
                                        root.Name.Equals("ROOT",
                                            StringComparison.OrdinalIgnoreCase))
                                    {
                                        // Get the HttpErrors.
                                        if (root.Properties.Contains("HttpErrors")
                                          == true)
                                        {
                                            // Write them out.
                                            PropertyValueCollection httpErrors =
                                            root.Properties["HttpErrors"];
                                            if (httpErrors != null)
                                            {
                                                for (int i = 0; i < httpErrors.Count; i++)
                                                {
//400,*,FILE,C:\WINDOWS\help\iisHelp\common\400.htm
                                                    string[] errorParts = httpErrors[i].
                                                      ToString( ).Split(',');
                                                    Console.WriteLine("Error Mapping
                                                      Entry:");
                                                    Console.WriteLine("\tHTTP error code:
                                                      {0}", errorParts[0]);
                                                    Console.WriteLine("\tHTTP sub-error
                                                      code: {0}", errorParts[1]);
                                                    Console.WriteLine("\tMessage Type:
                                                      {0}", errorParts[2]);
                                                    Console.WriteLine("\tPath to error
                                                      HTML file: {0}", errorParts[3]);
                                                }
                                            }
                                        }
                                    }
                                }
                            }
                        }
```

Example 14-5. Finding custom error pages (continued)

```
                    }
                }
            }
        }
    }
}
// End using initial DirectoryEntry.
```

At this point, an application could cache these settings for mapping its own error results, or it could dynamically modify the error pages to provide customized content. The important thing to take away is that the settings information for the web server is readily available to all applications with a bit of coding.

Discussion

`System.DirectoryServices.DirectoryEntry` is usually used for Active Directory programming, but it is able to use any of the providers that are available for Active Directory as well. This approach allows code to examine the IIS metabase for both the older style IIS 5.x metabases as well as the newer IIS 6.0 metabase that ships with Windows Server 2003.I

See Also

See Recipe 14.19; see the "HttpErrors [IIS]," "IIS Metabase Properties," and "DirectoryEntry Class" topics in the MSDN documentation.

14.19 Determining the Application Mappings for ASP.NET Set Up on IIS

Problem

You want to determine what application mappings are set up on a given web server for ASP.NET.

Solution

Use the `System.DirectoryServices.DirectoryEntry` class to examine the IIS metabase for the application mappings (also known as extension mappings) for the given web server. This is accomplished by creating a `DirectoryEntry` that talks to the IIS service provider for Active Directory and using it to locate the web server root node. The root node contains a `ScriptMaps` property that holds all extension mappings for the web server. Filter out the set of items that are redirected to the *aspnet_isapi.dll* (this

ISAPI is the connector between IIS and the ASP.NET worker process) and the list of ASP.NET application mappings is created. The code for carrying out these operations is shown in Example 14-6.

Example 14-6. Determining the application settings for ASP.NET on a given web server

```
// This is a case-sensitive entry in the metabase.
// You'd think it was misspelled but you would be mistaken...
const string WebServerSchema = "IIsWebServer";

// Set up to talk to the local IIS server.
string server = "localhost";

// Create a dictionary entry for the IIS server with a fake
// user and password. Credentials would have to be provided
// if you are running as a regular user.
using (DirectoryEntry w3svc =
  new DirectoryEntry(string.Format("IIS://{0}/w3svc", server),
    "Domain/UserCode", "Password"))
{
  // Can't talk to the metabase for some reason: bail.
  if (w3svc != null)
  {
    foreach (DirectoryEntry site in w3svc.Children)
    {
      using (site)
      {
        if (site != null)
        {
          // Check all web servers on this box.
          if (site.SchemaClassName == WebServerSchema)
          {
            // Get the metabase entry for this server.
            string metabaseDir =
              string.Format("/w3svc/{0}/ROOT", site.Name);

            if (site.Children != null)
            {
              // Find the root directory for each server.
              foreach (DirectoryEntry root in site.Children)
              {
                using (root)
                {
                  // Did we find the root dir for this site?
                  if (root != null &&
                      root.Name.Equals("ROOT", StringComparison.OrdinalIgnoreCase))
                  {
                    // Get the application mappings in the ScriptMaps property.
                    if (root.Properties.Contains("ScriptMaps") == true)
                    {
```

```
                // Write them out.
                PropertyValueCollection scriptMaps = root.Properties["ScriptMaps"];
                if (scriptMaps != null)
                {
                    for (int i = 0; i < scriptMaps.Count; i++)
                    {
                      //.aspx,
                      //C:\WINDOWS\Microsoft.NET\Framework\v2.0.50110\
                          aspnet_isapi.dll
                      //,1,GET,HEAD,POST,DEBUG
                      string[] mappingParts = scriptMaps[i].ToString().Split(',');

                      // The ASP.NET redirector is implemented in the
                      // aspnet_isapi.dll file so any extensions mapped to it
                      // will be processed by ASP.NET.
                      if (mappingParts[1].ToUpper().IndexOf("ASPNET_ISAPI") != -1)
                      {
                        // Write out details for the ASP.NET mappings.
                        Console.WriteLine("Extension Mappings:");
                          Console.WriteLine("\tMapped Extension: {0}",
                            mappingParts[0]);
                        Console.WriteLine("\tHandler: {0}", mappingParts[1]);
                        for (int j = 3; j < mappingParts.Length; j++)
                          Console.WriteLine("\tHTTP VERB: {0}", mappingParts[j]);
                      }
                      else
                      {
                        // Write out those unmapped items.
                          Console.WriteLine("Skipping {0} as it is not processed by
                            ASP.NET",
                            mappingParts[0]);
                      }
                    }
                }
              }
            }
          }
        }
      }
    }
  }
}
```

Discussion

The metabase in IIS contains many properties of interest to web application developers, and it is easily explored using the MetaEdit tool available from Microsoft (search on support knowledge base article 232068). MetaEdit is like RegEdit for the IIS metabase and allows for easy exploration of the settings in IIS. As with RegEdit, much harm can be done while editing, so care should be taken when performing any modifications. All web and virtual directory settings are located in the appropriate web site folder on the server.

See Also

See Recipe 14.18; see the "ScriptMaps [IIS]" and "IIS Metabase Properties" topics in the MSDN documentation.

CHAPTER 15

XML

15.0 Introduction

Extensible Markup Language (XML) is a simple, portable, and flexible way to represent data in a structured format. XML is used in a myriad of ways, from acting as the foundation of web-based messaging protocols such as SOAP, to being one of the more popular ways to store configuration data (such as the *web.config*, *machine.config*, or *security.config* files in the .NET Framework). Microsoft recognized the usefulness of XML to developers and has done a nice job of giving you choices concerning the trade-offs involved. Sometimes you want to simply run though an XML document looking for a value in a read-only cursorlike fashion, and other times you need to be able to randomly access various pieces of the document. Microsoft provides classes like XmlReader and XmlWriter for lighter access and XmlDocument for full Document Object Model (DOM) processing support. In the 1.x versions of the Framework, the XmlTextReader, XmlTextWriter, and XmlValidatingReader classes were provided as concrete instances to be used. Microsoft is now recommending using the factory methods on the XmlReader and XmlWriter classes, in conjunction with the XmlReaderSettings and XmlWriterSettings classes to work with XML.

It is likely that you will be dealing with XML in .NET to one degree or another. So this chapter explores some of the uses for XML and XML-based technologies such as XPath and XSLT. It also explores topics such as XML validation and transformation of XML to HTML.

15.1 Reading and Accessing XML Data in Document Order

Problem

You need to read in all the elements of an XML document and obtain information about each element, such as its name and attributes.

Solution

Create an XmlReader and use its Read method to process the document as shown in Example 15-1.

Example 15-1. Reading an XML document

```
using System;
using System.Xml;

// ...

public static void Indent(int level)
{
    for (int i = 0; i < level; i++)
      Console.Write(" ");
}

public static void AccessXML( )
{
    string xmlFragment = "<?xml version='1.0'?>" +
        "<!-- My sample XML -->" +
        "<?pi myProcessingInstruction?>" +
        "<Root>" +
        "<Node1 nodeId='1'>First Node</Node1>" +
        "<Node2 nodeId='2'>Second Node</Node2>" +
        "<Node3 nodeId='3'>Third Node</Node3>" +
        "</Root>";

    byte[] bytes = Encoding.UTF8.GetBytes(xmlFragment);
    using (MemoryStream memStream = new MemoryStream(bytes))
    {
        XmlReaderSettings settings = new XmlReaderSettings( );
        // Check for any illegal characters in the XML.
        settings.CheckCharacters = true;

        using (XmlReader reader = XmlReader.Create(memStream, settings))
        {
            int level = 0;
            while (reader.Read( ))
            {
                switch (reader.NodeType)
                {
                    case XmlNodeType.CDATA:
                        Indent(level);
                        Console.WriteLine("CDATA: {0}", reader.Value);
                        break;
                    case XmlNodeType.Comment:
                        Indent(level);
                        Console.WriteLine("COMMENT: {0}", reader.Value);
                        break;
                    case XmlNodeType.DocumentType:
                        Indent(level);
```

Example 15-1. Reading an XML document (continued)

```
                        Console.WriteLine("DOCTYPE: {0}={1}",
                            reader.Name, reader.Value);
                        break;
                    case XmlNodeType.Element:
                        Indent(level);
                        Console.WriteLine("ELEMENT: {0}", reader.Name);
                        level++;
                        while (reader.MoveToNextAttribute())
                        {
                            Indent(level);
                            Console.WriteLine("ATTRIBUTE: {0}='{1}'",
                                reader.Name, reader.Value);
                        }
                        break;
                    case XmlNodeType.EndElement:
                        level--;
                        break;
                    case XmlNodeType.EntityReference:
                        Indent(level);
                        Console.WriteLine("ENTITY: {0}", reader.Name);
                        break;
                    case XmlNodeType.ProcessingInstruction:
                        Indent(level);
                        Console.WriteLine("INSTRUCTION: {0}={1}",
                            reader.Name, reader.Value);
                        break;
                    case XmlNodeType.Text:
                        Indent(level);
                        Console.WriteLine("TEXT: {0}", reader.Value);
                        break;
                    case XmlNodeType.XmlDeclaration:
                        Indent(level);
                        Console.WriteLine("DECLARATION: {0}={1}",
                            reader.Name, reader.Value);
                        break;
                }
            }
        }
    }
}
```

This code dumps the XML document in a hierarchical format:

```
DECLARATION: xml=version='1.0'
COMMENT:  My sample XML
INSTRUCTION: pi=myProcessingInstruction
ELEMENT: Root
 ELEMENT: Node1
  ATTRIBUTE: nodeId='1'
  TEXT: First Node
 ELEMENT: Node2
  ATTRIBUTE: nodeId='2'
  TEXT: Second Node
```

```
ELEMENT: Node3
 ATTRIBUTE: nodeId='3'
 TEXT: Third Node
```

Discussion

Reading existing XML and identifying different node types is one of the fundamental actions that you will need to perform when dealing with XML. The code in the Solution creates an XmlReader from a string (it could also have used a stream), then iterates over the nodes while re-creating the formatted XML for output to the console window.

The Solution shows creating a MemoryStream from an XML fragment in a string like this:

```
string xmlFragment = "<?xml version='1.0'?>" +
    "<!-- My sample XML -->" +
    "<?pi myProcessingInstruction?>" +
    "<Root>" +
    "<Node1 nodeId='1'>First Node</Node1>" +
    "<Node2 nodeId='2'>Second Node</Node2>" +
    "<Node3 nodeId='3'>Third Node</Node3>" +
    "</Root>";

byte[] bytes = Encoding.UTF8.GetBytes(xmlFragment);
MemoryStream memStream = new MemoryStream(bytes);
```

Once the MemoryStream has been established, the settings for the XmlReader need to be set up on an XmlReaderSettings object instance. These settings tell the XmlReader to check for any illegal characters in the XML fragment:

```
XmlReaderSettings settings = new XmlReaderSettings();
// Check for any illegal characters in the XML.
settings.CheckCharacters = true;
```

The while loop iterates over the XML by reading one node at a time and examining the NodeType property of the current node that the reader is on to determine what type of XML node it is:

```
while (reader.Read())
{
    switch (reader.NodeType)
    {
```

The NodeType property is an XmlNodeType enumeration value that specifies the types of XML nodes that can be present. The XmlNodeType enumeration values are shown in Table 15-1.

Table 15-1. The XmlNodeType enumeration values

Name	Description
Attribute	An attribute node of an element.
CDATA	A marker for sections of text to escape that would usually be treated as markup.

Table 15-1. The XmlNodeType enumeration values (continued)

Name	Description
Comment	A comment in the XML: `<!--my comment -->`.
Document	The root of the XML document tree.
DocumentFragment	Document fragment node.
DocumentType	The document type declaration.
Element	An element tag: `<myelement>`.
EndElement	An end element tag: `</myelement>`.
EndEntity	Returned at the end of an entity after calling `ResolveEntity`.
Entity	Entity declaration.
EntityReference	A reference to an entity.
None	This is the node returned if Read has not yet been called on the XmlReader.
Notation	A notation in the DTD (document type definition).
ProcessingInstruction	The processing instruction: `<?pi myProcessingInstruction?>`.
SignificantWhitespace	Whitespace when mixed content model is used or when whitespace is being preserved.
Text	Text content for a node.
Whitespace	The whitespace between markup entries.
XmlDeclaration	The first node in the document that cannot have children: `<?xml version='1.0'?>`.

See Also

See the "XmlReader Class," "XmlNodeType Enumeration," and "MemoryStream Class" topics in the MSDN documentation.

15.2   Reading XML on the Web

Problem

Given a URL that points to an XML document, you need to grab the XML.

Solution

Use the XmlReader constructor that takes a URL as a parameter:

```
string url = "http://localhost/xml/sample.xml";

using (XmlReader reader = XmlReader.Create(url))
{
```

```
        while (reader.Read())
        {
            switch (reader.NodeType)
            {
                case XmlNodeType.Element:
                    Console.Write("<{0}>", reader.Name);
                    break;
            }
        }
    }
```

Discussion

Using the `XmlReader.Create` method with a URI is a quick way to access XML documents that are stored remotely without writing all of the connectivity code. This uses an instance of the `XmlUrlResolver` class to check the URI passed in and then opens a stream to the XML document indicated by the URI. To specify settings on the reader, there is a second overload of `Create` that also takes an `XmlReaderSettings` instance to facilitate this.

The *sample.xml* file being referenced in this code is set up in a virtual directory named *xml* on the local system. The code retrieves the *sample.xml* file from the web server and displays all of the elements in the XML.

sample.xml contains the following XML data:

```
<?xml version='1.0'?>
<!-- My sample XML -->
<?pi myProcessingInstruction?>
<Root>
    <Node1 nodeId='1'>First Node</Node1>
    <Node2 nodeId='2'>Second Node</Node2>
    <Node3 nodeId='3'>Third Node</Node3>
    <Node4><![CDATA[<>\&']]></Node4>
</Root>
```

See Also

See the "XmlReader Class" topic in the MSDN documentation.

15.3   Querying the Contents of an XML Document

Problem

You have a large and complex XML document and you need to find various pieces of information, such as all the information contained within a specific element and having a particular attribute setting. You want to query the XML structure without having to iterate through all the nodes in the XML document and search for a particular item by hand.

Solution

To query a database, you normally use SQL. To query an XML document, you currently use XPath or with SQL Server 2005 possibly XQuery (as .NET 2.0 does not support it as part of the Base Class Library [BCL.NET]). In .NET, this means using the System.Xml.XPath namespace and classes like XPathDocument, XPathNavigator, and XPathNodeIterator.

In the following example, you use these classes to select nodes from an XML document that holds members from the board game Clue (or Cluedo, as it is known abroad) and their various roles. You want to be able to select the married female participants who were witnesses to the crime. In order to do this, pass an XPath expression to query the XML dataset as shown in Example 15-2.

Example 15-2. Querying an XML document

```
public static void QueryXML( )
{
    string xmlFragment = "<?xml version='1.0'?>" +
        "<Clue>" +
        "<Participant type='Perpetrator'>Professor Plum</Participant>" +
        "<Participant type='Witness'>Colonel Mustard</Participant>" +
        "<Participant type='Witness'>Mrs. White</Participant>" +
        "<Participant type='Witness'>Mrs. Peacock</Participant>" +
        "<Participant type='Witness'>Mr. Green</Participant>" +
        "</Clue>";

    using (StringReader reader = new StringReader(xmlFragment))
    {
        // Instantiate an XPathDocument using the StringReader.
        XPathDocument xpathDoc = new XPathDocument(reader);

        // Get the navigator.
        XPathNavigator xpathNav = xpathDoc.CreateNavigator( );

        // Get up the query looking for the married female participants
        // who were witnesses.
        string xpathQuery =
            "/Clue/Participant[attribute::type='Witness'][contains(text( ),'Mrs.')]";
        XPathExpression xpathExpr = xpathNav.Compile(xpathQuery);

        // Get the nodeset from the compiled expression.
        XPathNodeIterator xpathIter = xpathNav.Select(xpathExpr);

        // Write out the nodes found (Mrs. White and Mrs.Peacock in this instance).
        while (xpathIter.MoveNext( ))
        {
            Console.WriteLine(xpathIter.Current.Value);
        }
    }
}
```

This outputs the following:

```
Mrs. White
Mrs. Peacock
```

Discussion

XPath is a very versatile language for performing queries on XML-based data. In order to accomplish this goal, you first create an XML fragment that looks like this:

```
<?xml version='1.0'?>
<Clue>
    <Participant type='Perpetrator'>Professor Plum</Participant>
    <Participant type='Witness'>Colonel Mustard</Participant>
    <Participant type='Witness'>Mrs. White</Participant>
    <Participant type='Witness'>Mrs. Peacock</Participant>
    <Participant type='Witness'>Mr. Green</Participant>
</Clue>;
```

You then load this fragment into a `StringReader`, then construct an `XPathDocument` to allow you to create an `XPathNavigator`. This lets you use XPath syntax to query the XML document shown in the preceding listing. The `XPathDocument` instance wraps the `MemoryStream` so you can use XPath to locate nodes (as well as perform XSLT transforms directly), and the `XPathNavigator` gets the set of nodes selected by the XPath expression.

```
byte[] bytes = Encoding.UTF8.GetBytes(xmlFragment);
MemoryStream memStream = new MemoryStream(bytes);

// Instantiate an XPathDocument using the MemoryStream.
XPathDocument xpathDoc = new XPathDocument(memStream);

// Get the navigator.
XPathNavigator xpathNav = xpathDoc.CreateNavigator();
```

Now you have to determine the XPath-based query to get all of the married female participants who were witnesses. This is set up in the xpathQuery string like this:

```
// Get up the query looking for the married female participants
// who were witnesses.
string xpathQuery =
  "/Clue/Participant[attribute::type='Witness'][contains(text( ),'Mrs.')]";
```

To help you grasp what is going on here, let's look at the syntax:

- `/Clue/Participant` says "Get all of the Participants under the root-level node Clue."

- `Participant[attribute::type='Witness']` says "Select only Participants with an attribute called type with a value of Witness."

- `Participant[contains(text( ),'Mrs.')]` says "Select only Participants with a value that contains 'Mrs.'"

Put them all together and you get all of the married female participants who were witnesses.

Once you have an XPathNavigator, call the Select method on it, passing the XPath-based query to select the nodes you are looking for. These are returned via the XPathNodeIterator. You use the XPathNodeIterator to write out the names of the participants you found and close the MemoryStream.

See Also

See the "XPathDocument Class," "XPathNavigator Enumeration," and "XPathNode-Iterator Class" topics in the MSDN documentation.

15.4 Validating XML

Problem

You are accepting an XML document created by another source and you want to verify that it conforms to a specific schema. This schema may be in the form of an XML schema (XSD or XML—XDR); alternatively, you want the flexibility to use a document type definition (DTD) to validate the XML.

Solution

Use the XmlReaderSettings to create an XmlReader that can validate XML documents against any descriptor document, such as an XSD, a DTD, or an XDR, as shown in Example 15-3.

Example 15-3. Validating XML

```
public static void ValidateXml()
{
    // Create XSD schema collection with book.xsd.
    XmlReaderSettings settings = new XmlReaderSettings();
    // Wire up handler to get any validation errors.
    settings.ValidationEventHandler += settings_ValidationEventHandler;

    // Set the validation type to schema.
    settings.ValidationType = ValidationType.Schema;

    // Add book.xsd.
    settings.Schemas.Add(null, XmlReader.Create(@"..\..\Book.xsd"));
    // Make sure we added.
    if (settings.Schemas.Count > 0)
    {
        // Open the bookbad.xml file.
        using (XmlReader reader = XmlReader.Create(@"..\..\BookBad.xml", settings))
        {
            // Replace validReader with reader for the whole loop.
```

Example 15-3. Validating XML (continued)

```csharp
        while (reader.Read())
        {
            if (reader.NodeType == XmlNodeType.Element)
            {
                Console.Write("<{0}", reader.Name);
                while (reader.MoveToNextAttribute())
                {
                    Console.Write(" {0}='{1}'", reader.Name,
                        reader.Value);
                }
                Console.Write(">");
            }
            else if (reader.NodeType == XmlNodeType.Text)
            {
                Console.Write(reader.Value);
            }
            else if (reader.NodeType == XmlNodeType.EndElement)
            {
                Console.WriteLine("</{0}>", reader.Name);
            }
        }
    }
  }
}

private static void settings_ValidationEventHandler(object sender,
                        ValidationEventArgs e)
{
    Console.WriteLine("Validation Error Message: {0}", e.Message);
    Console.WriteLine("Validation Error Severity: {0}", e.Severity);
    if (e.Exception != null)
    {
        Console.WriteLine("Validation Error Line Number: {0}",
                e.Exception.LineNumber);
        Console.WriteLine("Validation Error Line Position: {0}",
                e.Exception.LinePosition);
        Console.WriteLine("Validation Error Source: {0}",
                e.Exception.Source);
        Console.WriteLine("Validation Error Source Schema: {0}",
                e.Exception.SourceSchemaObject);
        Console.WriteLine("Validation Error Source Uri: {0}",
                e.Exception.SourceUri);
        Console.WriteLine("Validation Error thrown from: {0}",
                e.Exception.TargetSite);
        Console.WriteLine("Validation Error callstack: {0}",
                e.Exception.StackTrace);
    }
}
```

Discussion

The Solution illustrates how to use the XmlReader to validate the *book.xml* document against a *book.xsd* XSD definition file. DTDs were the original way to specify the structure of an XML document, but it has become more common to use XSD since it reached W3C Recommendation status in May 2001. XDR was a predecessor of XSD provided by Microsoft, and, while it might be encountered in existing systems, it should not be used for new development.

The first thing to do is create an XmlReader to hold your XSD (*book.xsd*). Add it to the XmlSchemaSet (Schemas property) on the XmlReaderSettings object settings:

```
// Wire up handler to get any validation errors.
settings.ValidationEventHandler += settings_ValidationEventHandler;

// Set the validation type to schema.
settings.ValidationType = ValidationType.Schema;

// Add book.xsd.
settings.Schemas.Add(null, XmlReader.Create(@"..\..\Book.xsd"));
```

The preceding code also hooks up the schema-collection event handler for validation errors to the settings_ValidationEventHandler function. It also sets the ValidationType to Schema. Setting XmlReaderSettings.ValidationType to ValidationType. Schema tells the XmlReader to perform XML Schema validation.

> To perform DTD validation, use a DTD and ValidationType.DTD, and to perform XDR validation, use an XDR schema and ValidationType. XDR.

The settings_ValidationEventHandler function then examines the ValidationEventArgs object passed when a validation error occurs and writes the pertinent information to the console:

```
private static void settings_ValidationEventHandler(object sender,
                            ValidationEventArgs e)
{
    Console.WriteLine("Validation Error Message: {0}", e.Message);
    Console.WriteLine("Validation Error Severity: {0}", e.Severity);
    if (e.Exception != null)
    {
        Console.WriteLine("Validation Error Line Number: {0}",
                e.Exception.LineNumber);
        Console.WriteLine("Validation Error Line Position: {0}",
                e.Exception.LinePosition);
        Console.WriteLine("Validation Error Source: {0}",
                e.Exception.Source);
        Console.WriteLine("Validation Error Source Schema: {0}",
                e.Exception.SourceSchemaObject);
        Console.WriteLine("Validation Error Source Uri: {0}",
                e.Exception.SourceUri);
```

```
            Console.WriteLine("Validation Error thrown from: {0}",
                    e.Exception.TargetSite);
            Console.WriteLine("Validation Error callstack: {0}",
                    e.Exception.StackTrace);
    }
}
```

Once you have the schema collection, create an XmlReader to load the *BookBad.xml* file:

```
// Open the book.xml file.
using(XmlReader reader = XmlReader.Create(@"..\..\BookBad.xml", settings))
```

You then proceed to roll over the XML document and write out the elements and attributes:

```
// Read all nodes and print out.
while (reader.Read( ))
{
    if(reader.NodeType == XmlNodeType.Element)
    {
        Console.Write("<{0}", reader.Name);
        while (reader.MoveToNextAttribute( ))
        {
            Console.Write(" {0}='{1}'", reader.Name,
                        reader.Value);
        }
        Console.Write(">");
    }
    else if (reader.NodeType == XmlNodeType.Text)
    {
        Console.Write(reader.Value);
    }
    else if (reader.NodeType == XmlNodeType.EndElement)
    {
        Console.WriteLine("</{0}>", reader.Name);
    }
}
```

The *BookBad.xml* file contains the following:

```
<?xml version="1.0" encoding="utf-8"?>
<Book xmlns="http://tempuri.org/Book.xsd" name="C# Cookbook">
    <Chapter>File System IO</Chapter>
    <Chapter>Security</Chapter>
    <Chapter>Data Structures and Algorithms</Chapter>
    <Chapter>Reflection</Chapter>
    <Chapter>Threading and Synchronization</Chapter>
    <Chapter>Numbers and Enumerations</Chapter>
    <BadElement>I don't belong here</BadElement>
    <Chapter>Strings and Characters</Chapter>
    <Chapter>Classes And Structures</Chapter>
    <Chapter>Collections</Chapter>
    <Chapter>XML</Chapter>
    <Chapter>Delegates, Events, and Anonymous Methods</Chapter>
```

```
        <Chapter>Diagnostics</Chapter>
        <Chapter>Toolbox</Chapter>
        <Chapter>Unsafe Code</Chapter>
        <Chapter>Regular Expressions</Chapter>
        <Chapter>Generics</Chapter>
        <Chapter>Iterators and Partial Types</Chapter>
        <Chapter>Exception Handling</Chapter>
        <Chapter>Web</Chapter>
        <Chapter>Networking</Chapter>
    </Book>
```

The *book.xsd* file contains the following:

```
<?xml version="1.0" ?>
<xs:schema id="NewDataSet" targetNamespace="http://tempuri.org/Book.xsd"
xmlns:mstns="http://tempuri.org/Book.xsd"
    xmlns="http://tempuri.org/Book.xsd"
    xmlns:xs="http://www.w3.org/2001/XMLSchema"
    xmlns:msdata="urn:schemas-microsoft-com:xml-msdata"
    attributeFormDefault="qualified" elementFormDefault="qualified">
    <xs:element name="Book">
        <xs:complexType>
            <xs:sequence>
                <xs:element name="Chapter" nillable="true"
                        minOccurs="0" maxOccurs="unbounded">
                    <xs:complexType>
                        <xs:simpleContent
                            msdata:ColumnName="Chapter_Text" msdata:Ordinal="0">
                            <xs:extension base="xs:string">
                            </xs:extension>
                        </xs:simpleContent>
                    </xs:complexType>
                </xs:element>
            </xs:sequence>
            <xs:attribute name="name" form="unqualified" type="xs:string"/>
        </xs:complexType>
    </xs:element>
</xs:schema>
```

When this is run, the following output is generated, showing the validation failure occurring on BadElement:

```
<Book xmlns='http://tempuri.org/Book.xsd' name='C# Cookbook'><Chapter>File System
IO</Chapter>
<Chapter>Security</Chapter>
<Chapter>Data Structures and Algorithms</Chapter>
<Chapter>Reflection</Chapter>
<Chapter>Threading and Synchronization</Chapter>
<Chapter>Numbers and Enumerations</Chapter>
Validation Error Message: The element 'Book' in namespace 'http://tempuri.org/Book.
xsd' has invalid child element 'BadElement' in namespace 'http://tempuri.org/Book.
xsd'. List of possible elements expected: 'Chapter' in namespace 'http://tempuri.org/
Book.xsd'.
Validation Error Severity: Error
Validation Error Line Number: 9
```

```
Validation Error Line Position: 6
Validation Error Source:
Validation Error Source Schema:
Validation Error Source Uri: file:///C:/PRJ32/Book_2_0/C%23Cookbook2/Code/
CSharpRecipes/BookBad.xml
Validation Error thrown from:
Validation Error callstack:
<BadElement>I don't belong here</BadElement>
<Chapter>Strings and Characters</Chapter>
<Chapter>Classes And Structures</Chapter>
<Chapter>Collections</Chapter>
<Chapter>XML</Chapter>
<Chapter>Delegates, Events, and Anonymous Methods</Chapter>
<Chapter>Diagnostics</Chapter>
<Chapter>Toolbox</Chapter>
<Chapter>Unsafe Code</Chapter>
<Chapter>Regular Expressions</Chapter>
<Chapter>Generics</Chapter>
<Chapter>Iterators and Partial Types</Chapter>
<Chapter>Exception Handling</Chapter>
<Chapter>Web</Chapter>
<Chapter>Networking</Chapter>
</Book>
```

See Also

See the "XmlReader Class," "XmlSchemaSet Class," "ValidationEventHandler Class," "ValidationType Enumeration," and "XmlReaderSettings Class" topics in the MSDN documentation.

15.5   Creating an XML Document Programmatically

Problem

You have data that you want to put into a more structured form, such as an XML document.

Solution

Suppose you have the information shown in Table 15-2 for an address book that you want to turn into XML.

Table 15-2. Sample address book data

Name	Phone
Tim	999-888-0000
Newman	666-666-6666
Harold	777-555-3333

Use the XmlWriter to create XML for this table:

```
XmlWriterSettings settings = new XmlWriterSettings( );
settings.Indent = true;
using (XmlWriter writer = XmlWriter.Create(Console.Out, settings))
{
    writer.WriteStartElement("AddressBook");
    writer.WriteStartElement("Contact");
    writer.WriteAttributeString("name", "Tim");
    writer.WriteAttributeString("phone", "999-888-0000");
    writer.WriteEndElement( );
    writer.WriteStartElement("Contact");
    writer.WriteAttributeString("name", "Newman");
    writer.WriteAttributeString("phone", "666-666-6666");
    writer.WriteEndElement( );
    writer.WriteStartElement("Contact");
    writer.WriteAttributeString("name", "Harold");
    writer.WriteAttributeString("phone", "777-555-3333");
    writer.WriteEndElement( );
    writer.WriteEndElement( );
}
```

This method will give you output like this:

```
<AddressBook>
    <Contact name="Tim" phone="999-888-0000" />
    <Contact name="Newman" phone="666-666-6666" />
    <Contact name="Harold" phone="777-555-3333" />
</AddressBook>
```

Or you can use the XmlDocument class to programmatically construct the XML:

```
public static void CreateXml( )
{
    // Start by making an XmlDocument.
    XmlDocument xmlDoc = new XmlDocument( );
    // Create a root node for the document.
    XmlElement addrBook = xmlDoc.CreateElement("AddressBook");
    xmlDoc.AppendChild(addrBook);
    // Create the Tim contact.
    XmlElement contact = xmlDoc.CreateElement("Contact");
    contact.SetAttribute("name","Tim");
    contact.SetAttribute("phone","999-888-0000");
    addrBook.AppendChild(contact);
    // Create the Newman contact.
    contact = xmlDoc.CreateElement("Contact");
    contact.SetAttribute("name","Newman");
    contact.SetAttribute("phone","666-666-6666");
    addrBook.AppendChild(contact);
    // Create the Harold contact.
    contact = xmlDoc.CreateElement("Contact");
    contact.SetAttribute("name","Harold");
    contact.SetAttribute("phone","777-555-3333");
    addrBook.AppendChild(contact);
```

```
    // Display XML.
    Console.WriteLine("Generated XML:\r\n{0}",addrBook.OuterXml);
    Console.WriteLine( );
}
```

This method gives the output like this:

```
Generated XML:
<AddressBook><Contact name="Tim" phone="999-888-0000" /><Contact name="Newman"
phone="666-666-6666" /><Contact name="Harold" phone="777-555-3333" /></AddressBook>
```

Both methods produce the same XML, but the first method is formatted with indents.

Discussion

Now that you have seen two ways to do this, the question arises: "Which one to use?" The XmlDocument uses the traditional DOM method of interacting with XML, while the XmlReader/XmlWriter combination deals with XML in a stream. If you are dealing with larger documents, you are probably better off using the XmlReader/XmlWriter combination than the XmlDocument. The XmlReader/XmlWriter combination is the better-performing of the two when you do not need the whole document in memory. If you need the power of being able to traverse back over what you have written already or write items out of order, use XmlDocument.

XmlDocument is the class that implements the DOM model for XML processing in the .NET Framework. The DOM holds all of the nodes in the XML in memory at the same time, which enables tree traversal both forward and backward. DOM also allows for a writable interface to the whole XML document, which other XML classes do not provide in .NET. XmlDocument allows you to manipulate any aspect of the XML tree. It is also eligible to be used for XSLT transformations via the XslCompiledTransform class, through its support of the IXPathNavigable interface. It allows you to run XPath queries against the document without having to create an XPathDocument first.

See Also

See the "XmlDocument Class," "XML Document Object Model (DOM)," "XslCompiledTransform Class," and "IXPathNavigable Interface" topics in the MSDN documentation.

15.6 Detecting Changes to an XML Document

Problem

You need to inform one or more classes or components that a node in an XML document has been inserted or removed or had its value changed.

Solution

In order to track changes to an active XML document, subscribe to the events published by the XmlDocument class. XmlDocument publishes events for node creation, insertion, and removal for both the pre- and post-conditions of these actions.

Example 15-4 shows a number of event handlers defined in the same scope as the DetectXMLChanges method, but they could just as easily be callbacks to functions on other classes that are interested in the manipulation of the live XML document.

DetectXMLChanges loads an XML fragment you define in the method; wires up the event handlers for the node events; adds, changes, and removes some nodes to trigger the events; then writes out the resulting XML.

Example 15-4. Detecting changes to an XML document

```
public static void DetectXmlChanges( )
{
    string xmlFragment = "<?xml version='1.0'?>" +
        "<!-- My sample XML -->" +
        "<?pi myProcessingInstruction?>" +
        "<Root>" +
        "<Node1 nodeId='1'>First Node</Node1>" +
        "<Node2 nodeId='2'>Second Node</Node2>" +
        "<Node3 nodeId='3'>Third Node</Node3>" +
        @"<Node4><![CDATA[<>\&']]></Node4>" +
        "</Root>";

    XmlDocument doc = new XmlDocument( );
    doc.LoadXml(xmlFragment);

    //Create the event handlers.
    doc.NodeChanging += new XmlNodeChangedEventHandler(NodeChangingEvent);
    doc.NodeChanged += new XmlNodeChangedEventHandler(NodeChangedEvent);
    doc.NodeInserting += new XmlNodeChangedEventHandler(NodeInsertingEvent);
    doc.NodeInserted += new XmlNodeChangedEventHandler(NodeInsertedEvent);
    doc.NodeRemoving += new XmlNodeChangedEventHandler(NodeRemovingEvent);
    doc.NodeRemoved += new XmlNodeChangedEventHandler(NodeRemovedEvent);

    // Add a new element node.
    XmlElement elem = doc.CreateElement("Node5");
    XmlText text = doc.CreateTextNode("Fifth Element");
    doc.DocumentElement.AppendChild(elem);
    doc.DocumentElement.LastChild.AppendChild(text);

    // Change the first node.
    doc.DocumentElement.FirstChild.InnerText = "1st Node";

    // Remove the fourth node.
    XmlNodeList nodes = doc.DocumentElement.ChildNodes;
    foreach(XmlNode node in nodes)
    {
        if(node.Name == "Node4")
        {
```

Example 15-4. Detecting changes to an XML document (continued)

```
        doc.DocumentElement.RemoveChild(node);
        break;
    }
  }

  // Write out the new xml.
  Console.WriteLine(doc.OuterXml);
}
```

Example 15-5 shows the event handlers from the XmlDocument, along with one formatting method, WriteNodeInfo. This method takes an action string and gets the name and value of the node being manipulated. All of the event handlers invoke this formatting method, passing the corresponding action string.

Example 15-5. XMLDocument event handlers and WtiteNodeInfo method

```
private static void WriteNodeInfo(string action, XmlNode node)
{
    if (node.Value != null)
    {
        Console.WriteLine("Element: <{0}> {1} with value {2}",
            node.Name,action,node.Value);
    }
    else
        Console.WriteLine("Element: <{0}> {1} with null value",
            node.Name,action);
}

public static void NodeChangingEvent(object source, XmlNodeChangedEventArgs e)
{
    WriteNodeInfo("changing",e.Node);
}

public static void NodeChangedEvent(object source, XmlNodeChangedEventArgs e)
{
    WriteNodeInfo("changed",e.Node);
}

public static void NodeInsertingEvent(object source, XmlNodeChangedEventArgs e)
{
    WriteNodeInfo("inserting",e.Node);
}

public static void NodeInsertedEvent(object source, XmlNodeChangedEventArgs e)
{
    WriteNodeInfo("inserted",e.Node);
}

public static void NodeRemovingEvent(object source, XmlNodeChangedEventArgs e)
{
    WriteNodeInfo("removing",e.Node);
}
```

```
public static void NodeRemovedEvent(object source, XmlNodeChangedEventArgs e)
{
    WriteNodeInfo("removed",e.Node);
}
```

The `DetectXmlChanges` method results in the following output:

```
Element: <Node5> inserting with null value
Element: <Node5> inserted with null value
Element: <#text> inserting with value Fifth Element
Element: <#text> inserted with value Fifth Element
Element: <#text> changing with value First Node
Element: <#text> changed with value 1st Node
Element: <Node4> removing with null value
Element: <Node4> removed with null value
<?xml version="1.0"?><!-- My sample XML --><?pi myProcessingInstruction?><Root><
Node1 nodeId="1">1st Node</Node1><Node2 nodeId="2">Second Node</Node2><Node3 nod
eId="3">Third Node</Node3><Node5>Fifth Element</Node5></Root>
```

Discussion

With an `XmlDocument`, you can traverse both forward and backward in the XML stream, as well as use `XPath` navigation to find nodes. If you are just reading XML and not modifying it, and you have no need for traversing backward through the nodes, you should avoid using `XmlDocument`, since `XmlReader` is faster for reading and `XmlWriter` is faster for writing (both have less overhead than `XmlDocument`). The .NET Framework team did a nice job of giving XML processing flexibility, but if you use a class with more functionality than you need, you will pay the resulting performance penalty.

See Also

See the "XmlDocument Class" and "XmlNodeChangedEventHandler Class" topics in the MSDN documentation.

15.7 Handling Invalid Characters in an XML String

Problem

You are creating an XML string. Before adding a tag containing a text element, you want to check it to determine whether the string contains any of the following invalid characters:

<

>

"

'

&

If any of these characters are encountered, you want them to be replaced with their escaped form:

    <
    >
    "
    '
    &

Solution

There are different ways to accomplish this, depending on which XML-creation approach you are using. If you are using XmlWriter, the WriteCData, WriteString, WriteAttributeString, WriteValue, and WriteElementString methods take care of this for you. If you are using XmlDocument and XmlElements, the XmlElement.InnerText method will handle these characters.

The two ways to handle this using an XmlWriter work like this. The WriteCData method will wrap the invalid character text in a CDATA section, as shown in the creation of the InvalidChars1 element in the example that follows. The other method, using XmlWriter, is to use the WriteElementString method that will automatically escape the text for you, as shown while creating the InvalidChars2 element.

```
// Set up a string with our invalid chars.
string invalidChars = @"<>\&'";
XmlWriterSettings settings = new XmlWriterSettings();
settings.Indent = true;
using (XmlWriter writer = XmlWriter.Create(Console.Out, settings))
{
    writer.WriteStartElement("Root");
    writer.WriteStartElement("InvalidChars1");
    writer.WriteCData(invalidChars);
    writer.WriteEndElement();
    writer.WriteElementString("InvalidChars2", invalidChars);
    writer.WriteEndElement();
}
```

The output from this is:

```
<?xml version="1.0" encoding="IBM437"?>
<Root>
  <InvalidChars1><![CDATA[<>\&']]></InvalidChars1>
  <InvalidChars2>&lt;&gt;\&amp;'</InvalidChars2>
</Root>
```

There are two ways you can handle this problem with XmlDocument and XmlElement. The first way is to surround the text you are adding to the XML element with a CDATA section and add it to the InnerXML property of the XmlElement:

```
// Set up a string with our invalid chars.
string invalidChars = @"<>\&'";
XmlElement invalidElement1 = xmlDoc.CreateElement("InvalidChars1");
invalidElement1.AppendChild(xmlDoc.CreateCDataSection(invalidChars));
```

The second way is to let the XmlElement class escape the data for you by assigning the text directly to the InnerText property like this:

```
// Set up a string with our invalid chars.
string invalidChars = @"<>\&'";
XmlElement invalidElement2 = xmlDoc.CreateElement("InvalidChars2");
invalidElement2.InnerText = invalidChars;
```

The whole XmlDocument is created with these XmlElements in this code:

```
public static void HandlingInvalidChars( )
{
    // Set up a string with our invalid chars.
    string invalidChars = @"<>\&'";

    XmlDocument xmlDoc = new XmlDocument( );
    // Create a root node for the document.
    XmlElement root = xmlDoc.CreateElement("Root");
    xmlDoc.AppendChild(root);

    // Create the first invalid character node.
    XmlElement invalidElement1 = xmlDoc.CreateElement("InvalidChars1");
    // Wrap the invalid chars in a CDATA section and use the
    // InnerXML property to assign the value as it doesn't
    // escape the values, just passes in the text provided.
    invalidElement1.InnerXml = "<![CDATA[" + invalidChars + "]]>";
    // Append the element to the root node.
    root.AppendChild(invalidElement1);

    // Create the second invalid character node.
    XmlElement invalidElement2 = xmlDoc.CreateElement("InvalidChars2");
    // Add the invalid chars directly using the InnerText
    // property to assign the value as it will automatically
    // escape the values.
    invalidElement2.InnerText = invalidChars;
    // Append the element to the root node.
    root.AppendChild(invalidElement2);

    Console.WriteLine("Generated XML with Invalid Chars:\r\n{0}",xmlDoc.OuterXml);
    Console.WriteLine( );
}
```

The XML created by this procedure (and output to the console) looks like this:

```
Generated XML with Invalid Chars:
<Root><InvalidChars1><![CDATA[<>\&']]></InvalidChars1><InvalidChars2>&lt;&gt;\
&amp;'</InvalidChars2></Root>
```

Discussion

The CDATA node allows you to represent the items in the text section as character data, not as escaped XML, for ease of entry. Normally these characters would need to be in their escaped format (< for < and so on), but the CDATA section allows you to enter them as regular text.

When the CDATA tag is used in conjunction with the InnerXml property of the XmlElement class, you can submit characters that would normally need to be escaped first. The XmlElement class also has an InnerText property that will automatically escape any markup found in the string assigned. This allows you to add these characters without having to worry about them.

See Also

See the "XmlDocument Class," "XmlWriter Class," "XmlElement Class," and "CDATA Sections" topics in the MSDN documentation.

15.8 Transforming XML

Problem

You have a raw XML document that you need to convert into a more readable format. For example, you have personnel data that is stored as an XML document and you need to display it on a web page or place it in a comma-delimited text file for legacy system integration. Unfortunately, not everyone wants to sort through reams of XML all day; they would rather read the data as a formatted list or within a grid with defined columns and rows. You need a method of transposing the XML data into a more readable form as well as into the comma-delimited format.

Solution

The solution for this is to use an XSLT stylesheet to transform the XML into another format using the XslCompiledTransform class. In the example code, you transform some personnel data from a fictitious business stored in *Personnel.xml*. First, load the stylesheet for generating HTML output, then perform the transformation to HTML via XSLT using the *PersonnelHTML.xsl* stylesheet. After that, transform the data to comma-delimited format using the *PersonnelCSV.xsl* stylesheet:

```
public static void TransformXML( )
{
    // Create a resolver with default credentials.
    XmlUrlResolver resolver = new XmlUrlResolver( );
    resolver.Credentials = System.Net.CredentialCache.DefaultCredentials;

    // Transform the personnel.xml file to html.
    XslCompiledTransform transform = new XslCompiledTransform( );
    XsltSettings settings = new XsltSettings( );
    // Disable both of these (the default) for security reasons.
    settings.EnableDocumentFunction = false;
    settings.EnableScript = false;
    // Load up the stylesheet.
    transform.Load(@"..\..\PersonnelHTML.xsl",settings,resolver);
    // Perform the transformation.
    transform.Transform(@"..\..\Personnel.xml",@"..\..\Personnel.html");
```

```
        // Or transform the Personnel.xml file to comma-delimited format.

        // Load up the stylesheet.
        transform.Load(@"..\..\PersonnelCSV.xsl",settings,resolver);
        // Perform the transformation.
        transform.Transform(@"..\..\Personnel.xml",
            @"..\..\Personnel.csv");
    }
```

The *Personnel.xml* file contains the following items:

```
<?xml version="1.0" encoding="utf-8"?>
<Personnel>
    <Employee name="Bob" title="Customer Service" companyYears="1"/>
    <Employee name="Alice" title="Manager" companyYears="12"/>
    <Employee name="Chas" title="Salesman" companyYears="3"/>
    <Employee name="Rutherford" title="CEO" companyYears="27"/>
</Personnel>
```

The *PersonnelHTML.xsl* stylesheet looks like this:

```
<?xml version="1.0" encoding="UTF-8"?>
<xsl:stylesheet version="1.0"
    xmlns:xsl="http://www.w3.org/1999/XSL/Transform"
    xmlns:xs="http://www.w3.org/2001/XMLSchema">
    <xsl:template match="/">
      <html>
        <head />
          <body title="Personnel">
            <xsl:for-each select="Personnel">
              <p>
                <xsl:for-each select="Employee">
                    <xsl:if test="position( )=1">
                        <table border="1">
                            <thead>
                                <tr>
                                    <td>Employee Name</td>
                                    <td>Employee Title</td>
                                    <td>Years with Company</td>
                                </tr>
                            </thead>
                            <tbody>
                              <xsl:for-each select="../Employee">
                                <tr>
                                  <td>
                                    <xsl:for-each select="@name">
                                        <xsl:value-of select="." />
                                    </xsl:for-each>
                                  </td>
                                  <td>
                                    <xsl:for-each select="@title">
                                        <xsl:value-of select="." />
                                    </xsl:for-each>
                                  </td>
                                  <td>
```

```
                              <xsl:for-each select="@companyYears">
                                  <xsl:value-of select="." />
                              </xsl:for-each>
                          </td>
                      </tr>
                  </xsl:for-each>
              </tbody>
          </table>
        </xsl:if>
      </xsl:for-each>
    </p>
  </xsl:for-each>
</body>
</html>
</xsl:template>
</xsl:stylesheet>
```

To generate the HTML screen in Figure 15-1, use the *PersonnelHTML.xsl* stylesheet and the *Personnel.xml* file.

Employee Name	Employee Title	Years with Company
Bob	Customer Service	1
Alice	Manager	12
Chas	Salesman	3
Rutherford	CEO	27

Figure 15-1. Personnel HTML table generated from Personnel.xml

Here is the HTML source:

```
<html xmlns:xs="http://www.w3.org/2001/XMLSchema">
  <head>
    <META http-equiv="Content-Type" content="text/html; charset=utf-8">
  </head>
  <body title="Personnel">
    <p>
      <table border="1">
        <thead>
          <tr>
            <td>Employee Name</td>
            <td>Employee Title</td>
            <td>Years with Company</td>
          </tr>
        </thead>
        <tbody>
          <tr>
            <td>Bob</td>
            <td>Customer Service</td>
            <td>1</td>
          </tr>
          <tr>
```

```
            <td>Alice</td>
            <td>Manager</td>
            <td>12</td>
          </tr>
          <tr>
            <td>Chas</td>
            <td>Salesman</td>
            <td>3</td>
          </tr>
          <tr>
            <td>Rutherford</td>
            <td>CEO</td>
            <td>27</td>
          </tr>
        </tbody>
      </table>
    </p>
  </body>
</html>
```

To generate comma-delimited output, use *PersonnelCSV.xsl* and *Personnel.xml*; the stylesheet is shown here:

```
<?xml version="1.0" encoding="UTF-8"?>
<xsl:stylesheet version="1.0" xmlns:xsl="http://www.w3.org/1999/XSL/Transform"
xmlns:xs="http://www.w3.org/2001/XMLSchema">
<xsl:output method="text" encoding="UTF-8"/>
    <xsl:template match="/">
                <xsl:for-each select="Personnel">
                    <xsl:for-each select="Employee">
                        <xsl:for-each select="@name">
                            <xsl:value-of select="." />
                        </xsl:for-each>,<xsl:for-each select="@title">
                            <xsl:value-of select="." />
                        </xsl:for-each>,<xsl:for-each select="@companyYears">
                            <xsl:value-of select="." />
                        </xsl:for-each>
                <xsl:text> &#xd;&#xa;</xsl:text>
            </xsl:for-each>
            </xsl:for-each>
    </xsl:template>
</xsl:stylesheet>
```

The output from the *PersonnelCSV.xsl* stylesheet is shown here:

```
Bob,Customer Service,1
Alice,Manager,12
Chas,Salesman,3
Rutherford,CEO,27
```

Discussion

There are many overrides for the XslCompiledTransform.Transform method. Since XmlResolver is an abstract class, you need to use either the XmlUrlResolver or the

XmlSecureResolver or pass null as the XmlResolver-typed argument. The XmlUrlResolver will resolve URLs to external resources, such as schema files, using the FILE, HTTP, and HTTPS protocols. The XmlSecureResolver restricts the resources that you can access by requiring you to pass in evidence, which helps prevent cross-domain redirection in XML. If you are accepting XML from the Internet, it could easily have a redirection to a site where malicious XML would be waiting to be downloaded and executed if you were not using the XmlSecureResolver. If you pass null for the XmlResolver, you are saying you do not want to resolve any external resources. Microsoft has declared the null option to be obsolete, and it shouldn't be used anyway since you should always use some type of XmlResolver.

XSLT is a very powerful technology that allows you to transform XML into just about any format you can think of, but it can be frustrating at times. The simple need of a carriage return/line feed combination in the XSLT output was such a trial that we were able to find more than 20 different message board requests for help on how to do this! After looking at the W3C spec for XSLT, we found you could do this using the xsl:text element like this:

```
<xsl:text> &#xd;&#xa;</xsl:text>
```

The  stands for a hexadecimal 13, or a carriage return, and the
 stands for a hexadecimal 10, or a line feed. This is output at the end of each employee's data from the XML.

See Also

See the "XslCompiledTransform Class," "XmlResolver Class," "XmlUrlResolver Class," "XmlSecureResolver Class," and "xsl:text" topics in the MSDN documentation.

15.9   Tearing Apart an XML Document

Problem

You have an XML document that needs to be broken apart into multiple parts. Each part can then be sent to a different destination (possibly a web service) to be processed individually. This solution is useful when you have a large document, such as an invoice, in XML form. For example, with an invoice, you would want to tear off the billing information and send this to Accounting, while sending the shipping information to Shipping, and then send the invoice items to Fulfillment to be processed.

Solution

In order to separate the invoice items, load an XmlDocument with the invoice XML from the *Invoice.xml* file shown in Example 15-6.

Example 15-6. Invoice.xml

```xml
<?xml version="1.0" encoding="UTF-8"?>
<Invoice invoiceDate='2003-10-05' invoiceNumber='INV-01'>
    <shipInfo>
        <name>Beerly Standing</name>
        <attn>Receiving</attn>
        <street>47 South Street</street>
        <city>Intox</city>
        <state>NH</state>
    </shipInfo>
    <billInfo>
        <name>Beerly Standing</name>
        <attn>Accounting</attn>
        <street>98 North Street</street>
        <city>Intox</city>
        <state>NH</state>
    </billInfo>
    <Items>
        <item partNum="98745">
            <productName>Brown Eyed Stout</productName>
            <quantity>12</quantity>
            <price>23.99</price>
            <shipDate>2003-12-20</shipDate>
        </item>
        <item partNum="34987">
            <productName>Diamond Pearl Lager</productName>
            <quantity>22</quantity>
            <price>35.98</price>
            <shipDate>2003-12-20</shipDate>
        </item>
        <item partNum="AK254">
            <productName>Job Site Ale</productName>
            <quantity>50</quantity>
            <price>12.56</price>
            <shipDate>2003-11-12</shipDate>
        </item>
    </Items>
</Invoice>
```

The code to tear this invoice apart and send the various information pieces to their respective departments is shown in Example 15-7.

Example 15-7. Tearing apart an XML document (Invoice.xml)

```csharp
public static void ProcessInvoice()
{
    XmlDocument xmlDoc = new XmlDocument();
    // Pick up invoice from deposited directory.
    xmlDoc.Load(@"..\..\Invoice.xml");
    // Get the Invoice element node.
    XmlNode Invoice = xmlDoc.SelectSingleNode("/Invoice");

    // Get the invoice date attribute.
    XmlAttribute invDate =
```

Example 15-7. Tearing apart an XML document (Invoice.xml) (continued)

```
            (XmlAttribute)Invoice.Attributes.GetNamedItem("invoiceDate");
        // Get the invoice number attribute.
        XmlAttribute invNum =
            (XmlAttribute)Invoice.Attributes.GetNamedItem("invoiceNumber");

        // Process the billing information to Accounting.
        WriteInformation(@"..\..\BillingEnvelope.xml",
                         "BillingEnvelope",
                         invDate, invNum, xmlDoc,
                         "/Invoice/billInfo");

        // Process the shipping information to Shipping.
        WriteInformation(@"..\..\ShippingEnvelope.xml",
                         "ShippingEnvelope",
                         invDate, invNum, xmlDoc,
                         "/Invoice/shipInfo");

        // Process the item information to Fulfillment.
        WriteInformation(@"..\..\FulfillmentEnvelope.xml",
                         "FulfillmentEnvelope",
                         invDate, invNum, xmlDoc,
                         "/Invoice/Items/item");

        // Now send the data to the web services ...
    }

    private static void WriteInformation(string path,
                         string rootNode,
                         XmlAttribute invDate,
                         XmlAttribute invNum,
                         XmlDocument xmlDoc,
                         string nodePath)
    {
        XmlWriterSettings settings = new XmlWriterSettings();
        settings.Indent = true;
        using (XmlWriter writer =
            XmlWriter.Create(path, settings))
        {
            writer.WriteStartDocument();
            writer.WriteStartElement(rootNode);
            writer.WriteAttributeString(invDate.Name, invDate.Value);
            writer.WriteAttributeString(invNum.Name, invNum.Value);
            XmlNodeList nodeList = xmlDoc.SelectNodes(nodePath);
            // Add the billing information to the envelope.
            foreach (XmlNode node in nodeList)
            {
                writer.WriteRaw(node.OuterXml);
            }
            writer.WriteEndElement();
            writer.WriteEndDocument();
        }
    }
}
```

The "envelopes" containing the various pieces of XML data for the web services are listed below.

BillingEnvelope *XML*

```
<BillingEnvelope invoiceDate="2003-10-05" invoiceNumber="INV-01">
    <billInfo>
        <name>Beerly Standing</name>
        <attn>Accounting</attn>
        <street>98 North Street</street>
        <city>Intox</city>
        <state>NH</state>
    </billInfo>
</BillingEnvelope>
```

ShippingEnvelope *XML*

```
<ShippingEnvelope invoiceDate="2003-10-05" invoiceNumber="INV-01">
    <shipInfo>
        <name>Beerly Standing</name>
        <attn>Receiving</attn>
        <street>47 South Street</street>
        <city>Intox</city>
        <state>NH</state>
    </shipInfo>
</ShippingEnvelope>
```

FulfillmentEnvelope *XML*

```
<FulfillmentEnvelope invoiceDate="2003-10-05" invoiceNumber="INV-01">
    <item partNum="98745">
        <productName>Brown Eyed Stout</productName>
        <quantity>12</quantity>
        <price>23.99</price>
        <shipDate>2003-12-20</shipDate>
    </item>
    <item partNum="34987">
        <productName>Diamond Pearl Lager</productName>
        <quantity>22</quantity>
        <price>35.98</price>
        <shipDate>2003-12-20</shipDate>
    </item>
    <item partNum="AK254">
        <productName>Job Site Ale</productName>
        <quantity>50</quantity>
        <price>12.56</price>
        <shipDate>2003-11-12</shipDate>
    </item>
</FulfillmentEnvelope>
```

Discussion

In order to tear apart the invoice, you need to establish what pieces go to which departments. The breakdown of this is that each of the envelopes gets the invoice date and invoice number from the main invoice to give context to the information in the envelope. The billInfo element and children go to the BillingEnvelope, the shipInfo element and children go to the ShippingEnvelope, and the item elements go to the FulfillmentEnvelope. Once these envelopes are constructed, they are sent to the web services for each department to perform its function for this invoice.

In the example program from the Solution, you first load the *Invoice.xml* file and get the attributes you are going to give to each of the envelopes:

```
XmlDocument xmlDoc = new XmlDocument( );
// Pick up invoice from deposited directory.
xmlDoc.Load(@"..\..\Invoice.xml");
// Get the Invoice element node.
XmlNode Invoice = xmlDoc.SelectSingleNode("/Invoice");

// Get the invoice date attribute.
XmlAttribute invDate =
    (XmlAttribute)Invoice.Attributes.GetNamedItem("invoiceDate");
// Get the invoice number attribute.
XmlAttribute invNum =
    (XmlAttribute)Invoice.Attributes.GetNamedItem("invoiceNumber");
```

Then you establish each envelope with the sections of the invoice that matter to the respective functions (the BillingEnvelope is handled by Accounting, the ShippingEnvelope is handled by Shipping, and the FulfillmentEnvelope is handled by Fulfillment) by calling the WriteInformation method, starting with the BillingEnvelope:

```
// Process the billing information to Accounting.
WriteInformation(@"..\..\BillingEnvelope.xml",
                "BillingEnvelope",
                invDate, invNum, xmlDoc,
                "/Invoice/billInfo");
```

Then the ShippingEnvelope is created:

```
// Process the shipping information to Shipping.
WriteInformation(@"..\..\ShippingEnvelope.xml",
                "ShippingEnvelope",
                invDate, invNum, xmlDoc,
                "/Invoice/shipInfo");
```

Finally, the FulfillmentEnvelope is created:

```
// Process the item information to Fulfillment.
WriteInformation(@"..\..\FulfillmentEnvelope.xml",
                "FulfillmentEnvelope",
                invDate, invNum, xmlDoc,
                "/Invoice/Items/item");
```

At this point, each of the envelopes can be posted to the respective web services interfaces.

 When you append the attributes from the Invoice to the envelopes, you call the XmlNode.Clone method on the XmlAttributes. This is done so that each of the elements has its own separate copy. If you do not do this, then the attribute will appear only on the last element it is assigned to.

See Also

See the "XmlDocument Class," "XmlElement Class," and "XmlAttribute Class" topics in the MSDN documentation.

15.10 Putting Together an XML Document

Problem

You have various pieces of a document in XML form that need to be put together to form a single XML document—the opposite of what was done in Recipe 15.9. In this case, you have received various pieces of an invoice in XML form. For example, one department sent the shipping information as an XML document, one sent the billing information in XML, and another sent invoice line items, also as an XML document. You need a way to put these XML pieces together to form a single XML invoice document.

Solution

In order to reconstitute the original invoice, you need to reverse the process used to create the pieces of the invoice using multiple XmlDocuments. There are three parts being sent back to you to help in re-forming the original invoice XML: *BillingEnvelope.xml*, *ShippingEnvelope.xml*, and *Fulfillment.xml*. These are listed below:

BillingEnvelope *XML*

```
<BillingEnvelope invoiceDate="2003-10-05" invoiceNumber="INV-01">
    <billInfo>
        <name>Beerly Standing</name>
        <attn>Accounting</attn>
        <street>98 North Street</street>
        <city>Intox</city>
        <state>NH</state>
    </billInfo>
</BillingEnvelope>
```

ShippingEnvelope *XML*

```
<ShippingEnvelope invoiceDate="2003-10-05" invoiceNumber="INV-01">
    <shipInfo>
        <name>Beerly Standing</name>
        <attn>Receiving</attn>
        <street>47 South Street</street>
        <city>Intox</city>
        <state>NH</state>
    </shipInfo>
</ShippingEnvelope>
```

FulfillmentEnvelope *XML*

```
<FulfillmentEnvelope invoiceDate="2003-10-05" invoiceNumber="INV-01">
    <item partNum="98745">
        <productName>Brown Eyed Stout</productName>
        <quantity>12</quantity>
```

```
        <price>23.99</price>
        <shipDate>2003-12-20</shipDate>
    </item>
    <item partNum="34987">
        <productName>Diamond Pearl Lager</productName>
        <quantity>22</quantity>
        <price>35.98</price>
        <shipDate>2003-12-20</shipDate>
    </item>
    <item partNum="AK254">
        <productName>Job Site Ale</productName>
        <quantity>50</quantity>
        <price>12.56</price>
        <shipDate>2003-11-12</shipDate>
    </item>
</FulfillmentEnvelope>
```

To put these back together as a single invoice, reverse the process you went through to break it apart, while inferring the invoice date and invoice number from the BillingEnvelope to help reestablish the invoice, as shown in Example 15-8.

Example 15-8. Reconstructing an XML document

```
public static void ReceiveInvoice( )
{
    XmlDocument invoice = new XmlDocument( );
    XmlDocument billing = new XmlDocument( );
    XmlDocument shipping = new XmlDocument( );
    XmlDocument fulfillment = new XmlDocument( );

    // Get up root invoice node.
    XmlElement invoiceElement = invoice.CreateElement("Invoice");
    invoice.AppendChild(invoiceElement);

    // Load the billing.
    billing.Load(@"..\..\BillingEnvelope.xml");
    // Get the invoice date attribute.
    XmlAttribute invDate = (XmlAttribute)
      billing.DocumentElement.Attributes.GetNamedItem("invoiceDate");
    // Get the invoice number attribute.
    XmlAttribute invNum = (XmlAttribute)
      billing.DocumentElement.Attributes.GetNamedItem("invoiceNumber");
    // Set up the invoice with this info.
    invoice.DocumentElement.Attributes.SetNamedItem(invDate.Clone( ));
    invoice.DocumentElement.Attributes.SetNamedItem(invNum.Clone( ));
    // Add the billInfo back in.
    XmlNodeList billList = billing.SelectNodes("/BillingEnvelope/billInfo");
    foreach(XmlNode billInfo in billList)
    {
        invoice.DocumentElement.AppendChild(invoice.ImportNode(billInfo,true));
    }

    // Load the shipping.
    shipping.Load(@"..\..\ShippingEnvelope.xml");
    // Add the shipInfo back in.
```

Example 15-8. Reconstructing an XML document (continued)

```
    XmlNodeList shipList = shipping.SelectNodes("/ShippingEnvelope/shipInfo");
    foreach(XmlNode shipInfo in shipList)
    {
        invoice.DocumentElement.AppendChild(invoice.ImportNode(shipInfo,true));
    }

    // Load the items.
    fulfillment.Load(@"..\..\FulfillmentEnvelope.xml");

    // Create an Items element in the Invoice to add these under.
    XmlElement items = invoice.CreateElement("Items");

    // Add the items back in under Items.
    XmlNodeList itemList = fulfillment.SelectNodes("/FulfillmentEnvelope/item");
    foreach(XmlNode item in itemList)
    {
        items.AppendChild(invoice.ImportNode(item,true));
    }

    // Add it in.
    invoice.DocumentElement.AppendChild(items.Clone( ));

    // Display Invoice XML.
    Console.WriteLine("Invoice:\r\n{0}",invoice.OuterXml);

    // Save our reconstitued invoice.
    invoice.Save(@"..\..\ReceivedInvoice.xml");
}
```

The code reconstitutes the invoice and saves it as *ReceivedInvoice.xml*, the contents of which are shown here:

```
<Invoice invoiceDate="2003-10-05" invoiceNumber="INV-01"><billInfo><name>Beerly
Standing</name><attn>Accounting</attn><street>98 North Street</street><city>Intox</
city><state>NH</state></billInfo><shipInfo><name>Beerly Standing</name><attn>
Receiving</attn><street>47 South Street</street><city>Intox</city><state>NH</state></
shipInfo><Items><item partNum="98745"><productName>Brown Eyed Stout</productName>
<quantity>12</quantity><price>23.99</price><shipDate>2003-12-20</shipDate></item>
<item partNum="34987"><productName>Diamond Pearl Lager</productName><quantity>22</
quantity><price>35.98</price><shipDate>2003-12-20</shipDate></item><item
partNum="AK254"><productName>Job Site Ale</productName><quantity>50</quantity><price>
12.56</price><shipDate>2003-11-12</shipDate></item></Items></Invoice>
```

Discussion

In the Solution code, the first step is to create a set of XmlDocuments for the Invoice, BillingEnvelope, ShippingEnvelope, and FulfillmentEnvelope. Then you create the new root Invoice element in the invoice XmlDocument:

```
XmlDocument invoice = new XmlDocument( );
XmlDocument billing = new XmlDocument( );
```

```
XmlDocument shipping = new XmlDocument( );
XmlDocument fulfillment = new XmlDocument( );

// Set up root invoice node.
XmlElement invoiceElement = invoice.CreateElement("Invoice");
invoice.AppendChild(invoiceElement);
```

Next, you process the BillingEnvelope, taking the invoice date and number from it and adding it to the Invoice. Then you add the billing information back in to the invoice:

```
// Load the billing.
billing.Load(@"..\..\BillingEnvelope.xml");
// Get the invoice date attribute.
XmlAttribute invDate = (XmlAttribute)
 billing.DocumentElement.Attributes.GetNamedItem("invoiceDate");
// Get the invoice number attribute.
XmlAttribute invNum = (XmlAttribute)
 billing.DocumentElement.Attributes.GetNamedItem("invoiceNumber");
// Set up the invoice with this info.
invoice.DocumentElement.Attributes.SetNamedItem(invDate.Clone( ));
invoice.DocumentElement.Attributes.SetNamedItem(invNum.Clone( ));
// Add the billInfo back in.
XmlNodeList billList = billing.SelectNodes("/BillingEnvelope/billInfo");
foreach(XmlNode billInfo in billList)
{
    invoice.DocumentElement.AppendChild(invoice.ImportNode(billInfo,true));
}
```

The ShippingEnvelope came next:

```
// Load the shipping.
shipping.Load(@"..\..\ShippingEnvelope.xml");
// Add the shipInfo back in.
XmlNodeList shipList = shipping.SelectNodes("/ShippingEnvelope/shipInfo");
foreach(XmlNode shipInfo in shipList)
{
    invoice.DocumentElement.AppendChild(invoice.ImportNode(shipInfo,true));
}
```

And finally, the items from the FulfillmentEnvelope were placed back under an Items element under the main Invoice element:

```
// Load the items.
fulfillment.Load(@"..\..\FulfillmentEnvelope.xml");

// Create an Items element in the Invoice to add these under
XmlElement items = invoice.CreateElement("Items");

// Add the items back in under Items.
XmlNodeList itemList = fulfillment.SelectNodes("/FulfillmentEnvelope/item");
foreach(XmlNode item in itemList)
{
    items.AppendChild(invoice.ImportNode(item,true));
```

```
}

// Add it in.
invoice.DocumentElement.AppendChild(items.Clone( ));
```

One item to be aware of when dealing with multiple XmlDocuments is that when you take a node from one XmlDocument, you cannot just append it as a child to a node in a different XmlDocument because the node has the context of the original XmlDocument. If you try to do this, you will get the following exception message:

```
The node to be inserted is from a different document context.
```

To fix this, use the XmlDocument.ImportNode method, which will make a copy (deep or shallow) of the node you are bringing over to the new XmlDocument. For instance, when you add the shipping information like so:

```
invoice.DocumentElement.AppendChild(invoice.ImportNode(shipInfo,true));
```

this line takes the shipInfo node, clones it deeply, then appends it to the main invoice node.

See Also

See the "XmlDocument Class," "XmlElement Class," and "XmlAttribute Class" topics in the MSDN documentation.

15.11 Validating Modified XML Documents Without Reloading

Problem

You are using the XmlDocument to modify an XML document loaded in memory. Once the document has been modified, the modifications need to be verified and schema defaults need to be enforced.

Solution

Use the XmlDocument.Validate method to perform the validation and apply schema defaults and type information.

Create an XmlSchemaSet with the XML Schema document (*book.xsd*) and an XmlReader, and point the Schemas property of the XmlDocument to it:

```
string xmlFile = @"..\..\Book.xml";
string xsdFile = @"..\..\Book.xsd";

// Create the schema set.
XmlSchemaSet schemaSet = new XmlSchemaSet( );
```

```
// Add the new schema with the target namespace
// (could add all the schema at once here if there are multiple).
schemaSet.Add("http://tempuri.org/Book.xsd", XmlReader.Create(xsdFile));

// Load up the XML file.
XmlDocument xmlDoc = new XmlDocument();
// Add the schema.
xmlDoc.Schemas = schemaSet;
```

Load the *book.xml* file into the XmlDocument, set up a ValidationEventHandler to catch any errors, then call Validate with the event handler to validate *book.xml* against the *book.xsd* schema:

```
// Validate after load.
xmlDoc.Load(xmlFile);
ValidationEventHandler eventHandler = ValidationEventHandler_15_11;
xmlDoc.Validate(eventHandler);
```

Add a new element node that is not in the schema into the XmlDocument and then call Validate again with the event handler to revalidate the changed XmlDocument. If the document triggers any validation events, then bValidXml is set to false by the ValidationEventHandler.

```
// Set the initial check for validity to true at the class level.
static bool bValidXml = true;

// Add in a new node that is not in the schema.
// Since we have already validated, no callbacks fire during the add...
XmlNode newNode = xmlDoc.CreateElement("BogusElement");
newNode.InnerText = "Totally";
// Add the new element.
xmlDoc.DocumentElement.AppendChild(newNode);
// Now we will do validation of the new stuff we added.
xmlDoc.Validate(eventHandler);

if (bValidXml == true)
{
    Console.WriteLine("Successfully validated modified XML");
}
else
{
    Console.WriteLine("Modified XML did not validate successfully");
}
```

The ValidationEventHandler looks like the one from Recipe 15.4:

```
private static void ValidationEventHandler_15_11(object sender,
                          ValidationEventArgs e)
{
    // We got called so this isn't valid.
    bValidXml = false;
    Console.WriteLine("Validation Error Message: {0}", e.Message);
    Console.WriteLine("Validation Error Severity: {0}", e.Severity);
    if (e.Exception != null)
```

```
    {
        Console.WriteLine("Validation Error Line Number: {0}",
                e.Exception.LineNumber);
        Console.WriteLine("Validation Error Line Position: {0}",
                e.Exception.LinePosition);
        Console.WriteLine("Validation Error Source: {0}",
                e.Exception.Source);
        Console.WriteLine("Validation Error Source Schema: {0}",
                e.Exception.SourceSchemaObject);
        Console.WriteLine("Validation Error Source Uri: {0}",
                e.Exception.SourceUri);
        Console.WriteLine("Validation Error thrown from: {0}",
                e.Exception.TargetSite);
        Console.WriteLine("Validation Error callstack: {0}",
                e.Exception.StackTrace);
    }
}
```

Discussion

There is an override to the XmlDocument.Validate method that allows you to pass a specific XmlNode to validate. If the XmlDocument is large, this override to Validate should be used:

```
public void Validate(
    ValidationEventHandler validationEventHandler,
    XmlNode nodeToValidate
);
```

One other approach to this problem is to instantiate an instance of the XmlNodeReader with the XmlDocument and then create an XmlReader with validation settings as shown in Recipe 15.4. This would allow for continual validation while the reader navigated through the underlying XML.

The output from running the code is listed here:

```
Validation Error Message: The element 'Book' in namespace 'http://tempuri.org/Book.
xsd' has invalid child element 'BogusElement'. List of possible elements expected:
'Chapter' in namespace 'http://tempuri.org/Book.xsd'.
Validation Error Severity: Error
Validation Error Line Number: 0
Validation Error Line Position: 0
Validation Error Source:
Validation Error Source Schema:
Validation Error Source Uri: file:///C:/PRJ32/Book_2_0/C%23Cookbook2/Code/
CSharpRecipes/Book.xml
Validation Error thrown from:
Validation Error callstack:
Modified XML did not validate successfully
```

Notice that the BogusElement element that you added was not part of the schema for the Book element so you got a validation error along with the information about where the error occurred. Finally, you got a report that the modified XML did not validate correctly.

See Also

See Recipe 15.4 and the "XmlDocument.Validate" topic in the MSDN documentation.

15.12 Extending XSLT Transformations

Problem

You want to perform operations that are outside the scope of XSLT to include data in the transformed result.

Solution

Add an extension object to the transformation that can perform the operations necessary based on the node it is passed. This can be accomplished by using the `XsltArgumentList.AddExtensionObject` method. This object you've created (`XslExtensionObject`) can then be accessed in the XSLT and a method called on it to return the data you want included in the final transformed result:

```
string xmlFile = @"..\..\publications.xml";
string xslt = @"..\..\publications.xsl";

//Create the XslTransform and load the stylesheet.
// This is not XslCompiledTransform because it gives a different empty node.
//Create the XslCompiledTransform and load the stylesheet.
XslCompiledTransform transform = new XslCompiledTransform();
transform.Load(xslt);

// Load the XML.
XPathDocument xPathDoc = new XPathDocument(xmlFile);

// Make up the args for the stylesheet with the extension object.
XsltArgumentList xslArg = new XsltArgumentList();
// Create our custom extension object.
XSLExtensionObject xslExt = new XSLExtensionObject();
xslArg.AddExtensionObject("urn:xslext", xslExt);

// Send output to the console and do the transformation.
using (XmlWriter writer = XmlWriter.Create(Console.Out))
{
    transform.Transform(xPathDoc, xslArg, writer);
}
```

Note that when the extension object is added to the `XsltArgumentList`, it supplies a namespace of `urn:xslext`. This namespace is used in the XSLT stylesheet to reference the object. The `XSLExtensionObject` is defined here:

```
// Our extension object to help with functionality
public class XslExtensionObject
{
```

```
public XPathNodeIterator GetErrata(XPathNodeIterator nodeChapter)
{
    try
    {
        // In here we could go do other lookup calls
        // (XML, database, web service) to get information to
        // add back in to the transformation result.
        string errata =
            string.Format("<Errata>{0} has {1} errata</Errata>",
                nodeChapter.Current.Value, nodeChapter.Current.Value.Length);
        XmlDocument xDoc = new XmlDocument();
        xDoc.LoadXml(errata);
        XPathNavigator xPathNav = xDoc.CreateNavigator();
        xPathNav.MoveToChild(XPathNodeType.Element);
        XPathNodeIterator iter = xPathNav.Select(".");
        return iter;
    }
    catch (Exception e)
    {
        // Eat the exception, as we were unable to use the extension.
        // So just return the original iterator.
        return nodeChapter;
    }
}
```

The GetErrata method is called during the execution of the XSLT stylesheet to provide data in XPathNodeIterator format to the transformation. The xmlns:xslext namespace is declared as urn:xslext, which matches the namespace value you passed as an argument to the transformation. In the processing of the Book template for each Chapter, an xsl:value-of is called with the select criteria containing a call to the xslext:GetErrata method. The stylesheet makes the call as shown here:

```
<xsl:stylesheet version="1.0" xmlns:xsl="http://www.w3.org/1999/XSL/Transform"
    xmlns:xslext="urn:xslext">
    <xsl:template match="/">
        <xsl:element name="PublishedWorks">
            <xsl:apply-templates/>
        </xsl:element>
    </xsl:template>
    <xsl:template match="Book">
        <Book>
            <xsl:attribute name="name">
                <xsl:value-of select="@name"/>
            </xsl:attribute>
            <xsl:for-each select="Chapter">
                <Chapter>
                    <xsl:value-of select="xslext:GetErrata(/)"/>
                </Chapter>
            </xsl:for-each>
        </Book>
    </xsl:template>
</xsl:stylesheet>
```

Discussion

The ability to call custom code from inside of an XSLT stylesheet is a very powerful one, but one that should be used cautiously. Adding code like this into stylesheets usually renders them less useful in other environments. If the stylesheet never has to be used to transform XML in another parser, this can be a good way to offload work that is either difficult or impossible to accomplish in regular XSLT syntax.

The sample data used in the Solution is presented here:

```xml
<?xml version="1.0" encoding="utf-8"?>
<Publications>
    <Book name="Subclassing and Hooking with Visual Basic">
        <Chapter>Introduction</Chapter>
        <Chapter>Windows System-Specific Information</Chapter>
        <Chapter>The Basics of Subclassing and Hooks</Chapter>
        <Chapter>Subclassing and Superclassing</Chapter>
        <Chapter>Subclassing the Windows Common Dialog Boxes</Chapter>
        <Chapter>ActiveX Controls and Subclassing</Chapter>
        <Chapter>Superclassing</Chapter>
        <Chapter>Debugging Techniques for Subclassing</Chapter>
        <Chapter>WH_CALLWNDPROC</Chapter>
        <Chapter>WH_CALLWNDPROCRET</Chapter>
        <Chapter>WH_GETMESSAGE</Chapter>
        <Chapter>WH_KEYBOARD and WH_KEYBOARD_LL</Chapter>
        <Chapter>WH_MOUSE and WH_MOUSE_LL</Chapter>
        <Chapter>WH_FOREGROUNDIDLE</Chapter>
        <Chapter>WH_MSGFILTER</Chapter>
        <Chapter>WH_SYSMSGFILTER</Chapter>
        <Chapter>WH_SHELL</Chapter>
        <Chapter>WH_CBT</Chapter>
        <Chapter>WH_JOURNALRECORD</Chapter>
        <Chapter>WH_JOURNALPLAYBACK</Chapter>
        <Chapter>WH_DEBUG</Chapter>
        <Chapter>Subclassing .NET WinForms</Chapter>
        <Chapter>Implementing Hooks in VB.NET</Chapter>
    </Book>
    <Book name="C# Cookbook">
        <Chapter>Numbers</Chapter>
        <Chapter>Strings and Characters</Chapter>
        <Chapter>Classes And Structures</Chapter>
        <Chapter>Enums</Chapter>
        <Chapter>Exception Handling</Chapter>
        <Chapter>Diagnostics</Chapter>
        <Chapter>Delegates and Events</Chapter>
        <Chapter>Regular Expressions</Chapter>
        <Chapter>Collections</Chapter>
        <Chapter>Data Structures and Algorithms</Chapter>
        <Chapter>File System IO</Chapter>
        <Chapter>Reflection</Chapter>
        <Chapter>Networking</Chapter>
        <Chapter>Security</Chapter>
        <Chapter>Threading</Chapter>
```

```
        <Chapter>Unsafe Code</Chapter>
        <Chapter>XML</Chapter>
    </Book>
    <Book name="C# Cookbook 2.0">
        <Chapter>Numbers and Enumerations</Chapter>
        <Chapter>Strings and Characters</Chapter>
        <Chapter>Classes And Structures</Chapter>
        <Chapter>Generics</Chapter>
        <Chapter>Collections</Chapter>
        <Chapter>Iterators and Partial Types</Chapter>
        <Chapter>Exception Handling</Chapter>
        <Chapter>Diagnostics</Chapter>
        <Chapter>Delegates, Events, and Anonymous Methods</Chapter>
        <Chapter>Regular Expressions</Chapter>
        <Chapter>Data Structures and Algorithms</Chapter>
        <Chapter>File System IO</Chapter>
        <Chapter>Reflection</Chapter>
        <Chapter>Web</Chapter>
        <Chapter>XML</Chapter>
        <Chapter>Networking</Chapter>
        <Chapter>Security</Chapter>
        <Chapter>Threading and Synchronization</Chapter>
        <Chapter>Unsafe Code</Chapter>
        <Chapter>Toolbox</Chapter>
    </Book>
</Publications>
```

See Also

See the "XsltArgumentList Class" topic in the MSDN documentation.

15.13 Getting Your Schema in Bulk from Existing XML Files

Problem

You have come on to a new project in which XML was used for data transmission, but the programmers who came before you didn't use an XSD for one reason or another. You need to generate beginning schema files for each of the XML examples.

Solution

Use the XmlSchemaInference class to infer schema from the XML samples. The GenerateSchemaForDirectory function in Example 15-9 enumerates all of the XML files in a given directory and processes each of them using the XmlSchemaInference. InferSchema method. Once the schemas have been determined, it rolls over the collection and saves out each schema to an XSD file using a FileStream.

Example 15-9. Generating an XML Schema

```
public static void GenerateSchemaForDirectory(string dir)
{
    // Make sure the directory exists.
    if (Directory.Exists(dir))
    {
        // Get the files in the directory.
        string[] files = Directory.GetFiles(dir, "*.xml");
        foreach (string file in files)
        {
            // Set up a reader for the file.
            using (XmlReader reader = XmlReader.Create(file))
            {
                XmlSchemaSet schemaSet = new XmlSchemaSet();
                XmlSchemaInference schemaInference =
                            new XmlSchemaInference();

                // Get the schema.
                schemaSet = schemaInference.InferSchema(reader);

                string schemaPath = "";
                foreach (XmlSchema schema in schemaSet.Schemas())
                {
                    // Make schema file path.
                    schemaPath = Path.GetDirectoryName(file) + @"\" +
                                Path.GetFileNameWithoutExtension(file) + ".xsd";
                    using (FileStream fs =
                        new FileStream(schemaPath, FileMode.OpenOrCreate))
                    {
                        schema.Write(fs);
                    }
                }
            }
        }
    }
}
```

The GenerateSchemaForDirectory method can be called like this:

```
// Get the directory two levels up from where we are running.
DirectoryInfo di = new DirectoryInfo(@"..\..");
string dir = di.FullName;
// Generate the schema.
GenerateSchemaForDirectory(dir);
```

Discussion

Having an XSD for the XML files in an application allows for a number of things:

1. Validation of XML presented to the system

2. Documentation of the semantics of the data

3. Programmatic discovery of the data structure through XML reading methods

Using the GenerateSchemaForDirectory method can jump-start the process of developing schema for your XML, but each schema should be reviewed by the team member responsible for producing the XML. This will help to ensure that the rules as stated in the schema are correct and also to make sure that additional items like schema default values and other relationships are added. Any relationships that were not present in the example XML files would be missed by the schema generator.

See Also

See the "XmlSchemaInference Class" and "XML Schemas (XSD) Reference" topics in the MSDN documentation.

15.14 Passing Parameters to XSLT Transformations

Problem

You need to use XSLT to produce information that has a few data items that could change between transformations and you don't want to have a separate XSLT stylesheet for each variation.

Solution

Use the XsltArgumentList class to pass arguments to the XSLT transformation. This technique allows the program to generate an object for the stylesheet to access (such as a dynamic string) and use while it transforms the given XML file. The storeTitle and pageDate arguments are passed in to the transformation in the following example. The storeTitle is for the title of the comic store and pageDate is the date the report is run for. These are added using the AddParam method of the XsltArgumentList object instance args.

```
XsltArgumentList args = new XsltArgumentList();
args.AddParam("storeTitle", "", "Hero Comics Inventory");
args.AddParam("pageDate", "", DateTime.Now.ToString("F"));

// Create a resolver with default credentials.
XmlUrlResolver resolver = new XmlUrlResolver();
resolver.Credentials = System.Net.CredentialCache.DefaultCredentials;
```

The XsltSettings class allows changing the behavior of the transformation. If you use the XsltSettings.Default instance, the transformation will be done without allowing scripting or the use of the document( ) XSLT function, as they can be security risks. If the stylesheet is from a trusted source, you can just create an XsltSettings object and use it, but it is better to be safe. Further changes to the code could open it up to use with untrusted XSLT stylesheets.

```
XslCompiledTransform transform = new XslCompiledTransform();
// Load up the stylesheet.
transform.Load(@"..\..\ParameterExample.xslt", XsltSettings.Default, resolver);
```

```
    // Perform the transformation.
    FileStream fs = null;
    using (fs = new FileStream(@"..\..\ParameterExample.htm",
        FileMode.OpenOrCreate, FileAccess.Write))
    {
        transform.Transform(@"..\..\ParameterExample.xml", args, fs);
    }
```

To show the different parameters in action, now you change storeTitle and pageDate again and run the transformation again:

```
    // Now change the parameters and reprocess.
    args = new XsltArgumentList();
    args.AddParam("storeTitle", "", "Fabulous Adventures Inventory");
    args.AddParam("pageDate", "", DateTime.Now.ToString("D"));
    using (fs = new FileStream(@"..\..\ParameterExample2.htm",
        FileMode.OpenOrCreate, FileAccess.Write))
    {
        transform.Transform(@"..\..\ParameterExample.xml", args, fs);
    }
```

The *ParameterExample.xml* file contains the following:

```
    <?xml version="1.0" encoding="utf-8" ?>
    <ParameterExample>
        <ComicBook name="The Amazing Spider-Man" edition="1"/>
        <ComicBook name="The Uncanny X-Men" edition="2"/>
        <ComicBook name="Superman" edition="3"/>
        <ComicBook name="Batman" edition="4"/>
        <ComicBook name="The Fantastic Four" edition="5"/>
    </ParameterExample>
```

The *ParameterExample.xslt* file contains the following:

```
    <?xml version="1.0" encoding="UTF-8" ?>
    <xsl:stylesheet version="1.0" xmlns:xsl="http://www.w3.org/1999/XSL/Transform">
      <xsl:output method="html" indent="yes" />
      <xsl:param name="storeTitle"/>
        <xsl:param name="pageDate"/>

        <xsl:template match="ParameterExample">
        <html>
          <head/>
          <body>
            <h3><xsl:text>Brought to you by </xsl:text>
            <xsl:value-of select="$storeTitle"/><br/>
            <xsl:text> on </xsl:text>
            <xsl:value-of select="$pageDate"/>
            <xsl:text> &#xd;&#xa;</xsl:text>
            </h3>
            <br/>
            <table border="2">
              <thead>
                <tr>
                  <td>
                    <b>Heroes</b>
```

```
          </td>
          <td>
            <b>Edition</b>
        </td>
        </tr>
      </thead>
      <tbody>
        <xsl:apply-templates/>
      </tbody>
    </table>
  </body>
</html>
</xsl:template>

<xsl:template match="ComicBook">
<tr>
  <td>
    <xsl:value-of select="@name"/>
  </td>
  <td>
    <xsl:value-of select="@edition"/>
  </td>
</tr>
</xsl:template>
</xsl:stylesheet>
```

The output from the first transformation to *ParameterExample.htm* is shown in Figure 15-2.

Brought to you by Hero Comics Inventory on Sunday, August 07, 2005 12:38:51 PM

Heroes	Edition
The Amazing Spider-Man	1
The Uncanny X-Men	2
Superman	3
Batman	4
The Fantastic Four	5

Figure 15-2. Output from the first set of parameters

Output from the second transformation to *ParameterExample2.htm* is shown in Figure 15-3.

Discussion

The ability to pass information to the XSLT stylesheet allows a much greater degree of flexibility when designing reports or user interfaces via XSLT transformations.

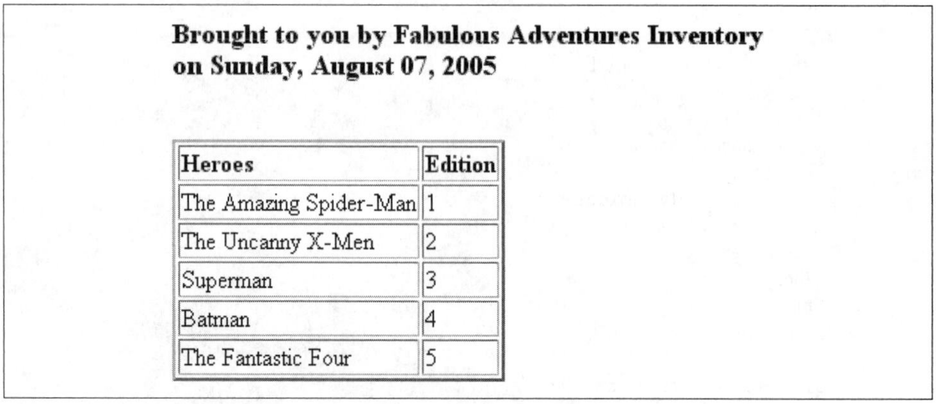

Brought to you by Fabulous Adventures Inventory on Sunday, August 07, 2005

Heroes	Edition
The Amazing Spider-Man	1
The Uncanny X-Men	2
Superman	3
Batman	4
The Fantastic Four	5

Figure 15-3. Output from the second set of parameters

This capability can help customize the output based on just about any criteria you can think of, as the data being passed in is totally controlled by your program. Once you get the hang of using parameters with XSLT, a whole new level of customization becomes possible. As an added bonus, it is portable between environments (.NET, Xalan, etc.).

See Also

See the "XsltArgumentList Class" and "XsltSettings Class" topics in the MSDN documentation.

CHAPTER 16

Networking

16.0 Introduction

.NET provides many classes to help make network programming easier than many environments that preceded it. There is a great deal of functionality to assist you with tasks like:

- Building network-aware applications
- Downloading files via FTP
- Sending and receiving HTTP requests
- Getting a higher degree of control using TCP/IP and sockets directly

In the areas in which Microsoft has not provided managed classes to access networking functionality (such as named pipes or some of the methods exposed by the WinInet API for Internet connection settings), there is always P/Invoke so you can code to the Win32 API; you'll explore this in this chapter. With all of the functionality at your disposal in the System.Net namespaces, you can write network utilities very quickly. Let's take a closer look at just a few of the things this section of .NET provides you access to.

16.1 Writing a TCP Server

Problem

You need to create a server that listens on a port for incoming requests from a TCP client. These client requests can then be processed at the server, and any responses can be sent back to the client. Recipe 16.2 shows how to write a TCP client to interact with this server.

Solution

Use the MyTcpServer class created here to listen on a TCP-based endpoint for requests arriving on a given port:

```
class MyTcpServer
{
    #region Private Members
    private TcpListener _listener = null;
    private IPAddress _address;
    private int _port;
    private bool _listening = false;
    #endregion

    #region CTORs

    public MyTcpServer(IPAddress address, int port)
    {
        _port = port;
        _address = address;
    }
    #endregion // CTORs
```

The TCPServer class has two properties:

- Address, an IPAddress
- Port, an int

These return the current address and port on which the server is listening and the listening state:

```
#region Properties
public IPAddress Address
{
    get { return _address; }
}

public int Port
{
    get { return _port; }
}

public bool Listening
{
    get { return _listening; }
}
#endregion
```

The Listen method tells the MyTcpServer class to start listening on the specified address and port combination. You create and start a TcpListener, then call its AcceptTcpClient method to wait for a client request to arrive. Once the client connects, a request is sent to the thread pool to service the client and that runs the ProcessClient method.

The listener shuts down after serving the client:

```
#region Public Methods
public void Listen( )
{
    try
    {
        lock (_syncRoot)
        {
            _listener = new TcpListener(_address, _port);

            // Fire up the server.
            _listener.Start( );

            // Set _listening bit.
            _listening = true;
        }

        // Enter the _listening loop.
        do
        {
            Trace.Write("Looking for someone to talk to... ");

            // Wait for connection.
            TcpClient newClient = _listener.AcceptTcpClient( );
            Trace.WriteLine("Connected to new client");

            // Queue a request to take care of the client.
            ThreadPool.QueueUserWorkItem(new WaitCallback(ProcessClient),
            newClient);
        }
        while (_listening);
    }
    catch (SocketException se)
    {
        Trace.WriteLine("SocketException: " + se.ToString( ));
    }
    finally
    {
        // Shut it down.
        StopListening( );
    }
}
```

The StopListening method is called to stop the TCPServer from listening for requests:

```
public void StopListening( )
{
    if (_listening)
    {
        lock (_syncRoot)
        {
            // Set listening bit.
            _listening = false;
            // Shut it down.
```

```
                _listener.Stop();
            }
        }
    }
}
#endregion
```

The ProcessClient method shown in Example 16-1 executes on a thread-pool thread to serve a connected client. It gets the NetworkStream from the client using the TcpClient.GetStream method, then reads the whole request. After sending back a response, it shuts down the client connection.

Example 16-1. ProcessClient method

```
#region Private Methods
private void ProcessClient(object client)
{
    TcpClient newClient = (TcpClient)client;
    try
    {
        // Buffer for reading data.
        byte[] bytes = new byte[1024];
        StringBuilder clientData = new StringBuilder();

        // Get the stream to talk to the client over.
        using (NetworkStream ns = newClient.GetStream())
        {
            // Set initial read timeout to 1 minute to allow for connection.
            ns.ReadTimeout = 60000;
            // Loop to receive all the data sent by the client.
            int bytesRead = 0;
            do
            {
                // Read the data.
                try
                {
                    bytesRead = ns.Read(bytes, 0, bytes.Length);
                    if (bytesRead > 0)
                    {
                        // Translate data bytes to an ASCII string and append.
                        clientData.Append(
                            Encoding.ASCII.GetString(bytes, 0, bytesRead));
                        // Decrease read timeout to 1 second now
                        // that data is coming in.
                        ns.ReadTimeout = 1000;
                    }
                }
                catch (IOException ioe)
                {
                    // Read timed out; all data has been retrieved.
                    Trace.WriteLine("Read timed out: " + ioe.ToString());
                    bytesRead = 0;
                }
            }
```

Example 16-1. ProcessClient method (continued)

```
                while (bytesRead > 0);

                Trace.WriteLine("Client says: " + clientData.ToString());

                // Thank them for their input.
                bytes = Encoding.ASCII.GetBytes("Thanks call again!");

                // Send back a response.
                ns.Write(bytes, 0, bytes.Length);
            }
        }
        finally
        {
            // Stop talking to client.
            if(newClient != null)
                newClient.Close();
        }
    }
    #endregion
}
```

A simple server that listens for clients until the Escape key is pressed might look like the following code:

```
class Program
{
    static MyTcpServer server = null;
    static void Main(string[] args)
    {
        // Run the server on a different thread.
        ThreadPool.QueueUserWorkItem(RunServer);

        Console.WriteLine("Press Esc to stop the server...");
        ConsoleKeyInfo cki;
        while(true)
        {
            cki = Console.ReadKey();
            if (cki.Key == ConsoleKey.Escape)
                break;
        }
    }

    static void RunServer( object stateInfo )
    {
        // Fire it up.
        server = new MyTcpServer(IPAddress.Loopback,55555);
        server.Listen();
    }
}
```

When talking to the MyTcpClient class in Recipe 16.2, the output for the server looks like this:

```
Press Esc to stop the server...
Looking for someone to talk to... Connected to new client
Looking for someone to talk to... Client says: Just wanted to say hi
Connected to new client
Looking for someone to talk to... Client says: Just wanted to say hi again
Connected to new client
Looking for someone to talk to... Client says: Are you ignoring me?
Connected to new client
Looking for someone to talk to... Connected to new client
Looking for someone to talk to... Client says: I'll not be ignored! (round 0)
Client says: I'll not be ignored! (round 1)
Connected to new client
Looking for someone to talk to... Connected to new client
Looking for someone to talk to... Client says: I'll not be ignored! (round 2)
Client says: I'll not be ignored! (round 3)
Connected to new client
Looking for someone to talk to... Client says: I'll not be ignored! (round 4)
Connected to new client
Looking for someone to talk to... Client says: I'll not be ignored! (round 5)
Connected to new client
Looking for someone to talk to... Client says: I'll not be ignored! (round 6)
Connected to new client
Looking for someone to talk to... Client says: I'll not be ignored! (round 7)
Connected to new client
Looking for someone to talk to... Client says: I'll not be ignored! (round 8)
[more output follows...]
```

Discussion

The Transmission Control Protocol (TCP) is the protocol used by the majority of traffic on the Internet today. TCP is responsible for the correct delivery of data packets from one endpoint to another. It uses the Internet Protocol (IP) to make the delivery. IP handles getting the packets from node to node; TCP detects when packets are not correct, are missing, or are sent out of order, and it arranges for missing or damaged packets to be resent. The TCPServer class is a basic server mechanism for dealing with requests that come from clients over TCP.

MyTcpServer takes the IP address and port passed in then in the Listen method and creates a TcpListener on that IPAddress and port. Once created, the TcpListener. Start method is called to start up the server. The blocking AcceptTcpClient method is called to listen for requests from TCP-based clients. Once the client connects, the ProcessClient method is executed. In this method, the server reads request data from the client and returns a brief acknowledgment. The server disconnects from the client by calling NetworkStream.Close and TcpClient.Close. The server stops listening when the StopListening method is called. StopListening takes the server offline by calling TcpListener.Stop.

See Also

See the "IPAddress Class," "TcpListener Class," and "TcpClient Class" topics in the MSDN documentation.

16.2 Writing a TCP Client

Problem

You want to interact with a TCP-based server.

Solution

Use the `MyTcpClient` class shown in Example 16-2 to connect to and converse with a TCP-based server by passing the address and port of the server to talk to, using the `System.Net.TcpClient` class. This example will talk to the server from Recipe 16.1.

Example 16-2. MyTcpClient class

```
class MyTcpClient
{
    private TcpClient _client = null;
    private IPAddress _address;
    private int _port;
    private IPEndPoint _endPoint = null;

    public MyTcpClient(IPAddress address, int port)
    {
        _address = address;
        _port = port;
        _endPoint = new IPEndPoint(_address, _port);
    }


    public void ConnectToServer(string msg)
    {
        try
        {
            _client = new TcpClient();
            _client.Connect(_endPoint);

            // Get the bytes to send for the message.
            byte[] bytes = Encoding.ASCII.GetBytes(msg);
            // Get the stream to talk to the server on.
            using (NetworkStream ns = _client.GetStream())
            {
                // Send message.
                Trace.WriteLine("Sending message to server: " + msg);
                ns.Write(bytes, 0, bytes.Length);
```

Example 16-2. MyTcpClient class (continued)

```
                    // Get the response.
                    // Buffer to store the response bytes.
                    bytes = new byte[1024];

                    // Display the response.
                    int bytesRead = ns.Read(bytes, 0, bytes.Length);
                    string serverResponse = Encoding.ASCII.GetString(bytes, 0, bytesRead);
                    Trace.WriteLine("Server said: " + serverResponse);
                }
            }
            catch (SocketException se)
            {
                Trace.WriteLine("There was an error talking to the server: " +
                    se.ToString());
            }
            finally
            {
                // Close everything.
                if(_client != null)
                    _client.Close();
            }
        }
    }
}
```

To use the `MyTcpClient` in a program, you can simply create an instance of it and call `ConnectToServer` to send a request. In this program, you first make three calls to the server to test the basic mechanism. Next, you enter a loop to really pound on it and make sure you force it over the default `ThreadPool` limit. This verifies that the server's mechanism for handling multiple requests is sound.

```
static void Main(string[] args)
{

    MakeClientCallToServer("Just wanted to say hi");
    MakeClientCallToServer("Just wanted to say hi again");
    MakeClientCallToServer("Are you ignoring me?");

    // Now send a bunch of messages...
    string msg;
    for (int i = 0; i < 100; i++)
    {
        msg = string.Format("I'll not be ignored! (round {0})", i);
        ThreadPool.QueueUserWorkItem(new WaitCallback(MakeClientCallToServer), msg);
    }

    Console.WriteLine("\n Press any key to continue... (if you can find it...)");
    Console.Read();
}

static void MakeClientCallToServer(object objMsg)
{
    string msg = (string)objMsg;
```

```
        MyTcpClient client = new MyTcpClient(IPAddress.Loopback,55555);
        client.ConnectToServer(msg);
}
```

The output on the client side for this exchange of messages is:

```
Sending message to server: Just wanted to say hi
Server said: Thanks call again!
Sending message to server: Just wanted to say hi again
Server said: Thanks call again!
Sending message to server: Are you ignoring me?
Server said: Thanks call again!
 Press any key to continue... (if you can find it...)
Sending message to server: I'll not be ignored! (round 0)
Sending message to server: I'll not be ignored! (round 1)
Server said: Thanks call again!
Server said: Thanks call again!
Sending message to server: I'll not be ignored! (round 2)
Server said: Thanks call again!
Sending message to server: I'll not be ignored! (round 3)
Sending message to server: I'll not be ignored! (round 4)
Server said: Thanks call again!
Server said: Thanks call again!
Sending message to server: I'll not be ignored! (round 5)
Sending message to server: I'll not be ignored! (round 6)
Server said: Thanks call again!
Server said: Thanks call again!
Sending message to server: I'll not be ignored! (round 7)
Sending message to server: I'll not be ignored! (round 8)
Server said: Thanks call again!
[more output follows...]
```

Discussion

MyTcpClient.ConnectToServer is designed to send one message, get the response, display it as a string, then close the connection. To accomplish this, it creates a System.Net.TcpClient and connects to the server by calling the TcpClient.Connect method. Connect targets the server using an IPEndPoint built from the address and port that you passed to the MyTcpClient constructor.

MyTcpClient.ConnectToServer then gets the bytes for the string using the Encoding.ASCII.GetBytes method. Once it has the bytes to send, it gets the NetworkStream from the underlying System.Net.TcpClient by calling its GetStream method, then sends the message using the TcpClient.Write method.

In order to receive the response from the server, the blocking TcpClient.Read method is called. Once Read returns, the bytes are decoded to get the string that contains the response from the server. The connections are then closed and the client ends.

See Also

See the "TcpClient Class," "NetworkStream Class," and "Encoding.ASCII Property" topics in the MSDN documentation.

16.3   Simulating Form Execution

Problem

You need to send a collection of name-value pairs to simulate a form being executed on a browser to a location identified by a URL.

Solution

Use the `System.Net.WebClient` class to send a set of name-value pairs to the web server using the `UploadValues` method. This class enables you to masquerade as the browser executing a form by setting up the name-value pairs with the input data. The input field ID is the name, and the value to use in the field is the value:

```
using System;
using System.Net;
using System.Text;
using System.Collections.Specialized;

Uri uri = new Uri("http://localhost/FormSim/WebForm1.aspx");
WebClient client = new WebClient( );

// Create a series of name-value pairs to send.
NameValueCollection collection = new NameValueCollection( );

// Add necessary parameter-value pairs to the name-value container.
collection.Add("Identity","foo@bar.com");
collection.Add("Item","Books");
collection.Add("Quantity","5");
Console.WriteLine("Uploading name/value pairs to URI {0} ...",
                  uri.AbsoluteUri);

// Upload the NameValueCollection.
byte[] responseArray =
    client.UploadValues(uri.AbsoluteUri,"POST",collection);
// Decode and display the response.
Console.WriteLine("\nResponse received was {0}",
    Encoding.ASCII.GetString(responseArray));
```

The *webform1.aspx* page, which receives and processes this data, looks like this:

```
<%@ Page language="c#" Codebehind="WebForm1.aspx.cs" AutoEventWireup="false"
Inherits="FormSim.WebForm1" %>
<!DOCTYPE HTML PUBLIC "-//W3C//DTD HTML 4.0 Transitional//EN" >
<HTML>
    <HEAD>
        <title>WebForm1</title>
        <meta name="GENERATOR" Content="Microsoft Visual Studio .NET 7.1">
        <meta name="CODE_LANGUAGE" Content="C#">
        <meta name="vs_defaultClientScript" content="JavaScript">
        <meta name="vs_targetSchema"
              content="http://schemas.microsoft.com/intellisense/ie5">
    </HEAD>
    <body MS_POSITIONING="GridLayout">
```

```
            <form id="Form1" method="post" runat="server">
                <asp:TextBox id="Identity" style="Z-INDEX: 101; LEFT: 194px;
                        POSITION: absolute; TOP: 52px" runat="server"></asp:TextBox>
                <asp:TextBox id="Item" style="Z-INDEX: 102; LEFT: 193px;
                        POSITION: absolute; TOP: 93px" runat="server"></asp:TextBox>
                <asp:TextBox id="Quantity" style="Z-INDEX: 103; LEFT: 193px;
                        POSITION: absolute; TOP: 132px"
                    runat="server"></asp:TextBox>
                <asp:Button id="Button1" style="Z-INDEX: 104; LEFT: 203px;
                        POSITION: absolute; TOP: 183px" runat="server"
                    Text="Submit"></asp:Button>
                <asp:Label id="Label1" style="Z-INDEX: 105; LEFT: 58px;
                        POSITION: absolute; TOP: 54px" runat="server"
                    Width="122px" Height="24px">Identity:</asp:Label>
                <asp:Label id="Label2" style="Z-INDEX: 106; LEFT: 57px;
                        POSITION: absolute; TOP: 94px" runat="server"
                    Width="128px" Height="25px">Item:</asp:Label>
                <asp:Label id="Label3" style="Z-INDEX: 107; LEFT: 57px;
                        POSITION: absolute; TOP: 135px" runat="server"
                    Width="124px" Height="20px">Quantity:</asp:Label>
            </form>
        </body>
</HTML>
```

The *webform1.aspx* code-behind looks like this. The added code is highlighted.

```
using System;
using System.Collections;
using System.ComponentModel;
using System.Data;
using System.Drawing;
using System.Web;
using System.Web.SessionState;
using System.Web.UI;
using System.Web.UI.WebControls;
using System.Web.UI.HtmlControls;

namespace FormSim
{
    /// <summary>
    /// Summary description for WebForm1
    /// </summary>
    public class WebForm1 : System.Web.UI.Page
    {
        protected System.Web.UI.WebControls.Button Button1;
        protected System.Web.UI.WebControls.TextBox Item;
        protected System.Web.UI.WebControls.Label Label1;
        protected System.Web.UI.WebControls.Label Label2;
        protected System.Web.UI.WebControls.Label Label3;
        protected System.Web.UI.WebControls.TextBox Identity;
        protected System.Web.UI.WebControls.TextBox Quantity;

        private void Page_Load(object sender, System.EventArgs e)
        {
            // Put user code to initialize the page here.
```

```
        }

        #region Web Form Designer generated code
        override protected void OnInit(EventArgs e)
        {
            //
            // CODEGEN: This call is required by the ASP.NET Web Form Designer.
            //
            InitializeComponent( );
            base.OnInit(e);
        }

        /// <summary>
        /// Required method for Designer support - do not modify
        /// the contents of this method with the code editor
        /// </summary>
        private void InitializeComponent( )
        {
            this.Button1.Click +=
                    new System.EventHandler(this.Button1_Click);
            this.Load += new System.EventHandler(this.Page_Load);
        }

        }
        #endregion

        private void Button1_Click(object sender, System.EventArgs e)
        {
            string response = "Thanks for the order!<br/>";
            response += "Identity: " + Request.Form["Identity"] + "<br/>";
            response += "Item: " + Request.Form["Item"] + "<br/>";
            response += "Quantity: " + Request.Form["Quantity"] + "<br/>";
            Response.Write(response);
        }
    }
}
```

The output from the form execution looks like this:

```
Uploading name-value pairs to URI http://localhost/FormSim/WebForm1.aspx ...
Response received was
<!DOCTYPE HTML PUBLIC "-//W3C//DTD HTML 4.0 Transitional//EN" >
<HTML>
    <HEAD>
        <title>WebForm1</title>
        <meta name="GENERATOR" Content="Microsoft Visual Studio .NET 7.1">
        <meta name="CODE_LANGUAGE" Content="C#">
        <meta name="vs_defaultClientScript" content="JavaScript">
        <meta name="vs_targetSchema"
content="http://schemas.microsoft.com/intellisense/ie5">
    </HEAD>
    <body MS_POSITIONING="GridLayout">
        <form name="Form1" method="post" action="WebForm1.aspx" id="Form1">
<input type="hidden" name="__VIEWSTATE"
value="dDwtMTI3ODA2MzE3NDs7PqEOyO3ljfXs5tGC+P86HObF9IMA" />
```

```
            <input name="Identity" type="text" id="Identity" style="Z-INDEX: 101;
LEFT: 194px; POSITION: absolute; TOP: 52px" />
            <input name="Item" type="text" id="Item" style="Z-INDEX: 102; LEFT:
193px; POSITION: absolute; TOP: 93px" />
            <input name="Quantity" type="text" id="Quantity" style="Z-INDEX: 103;
LEFT: 193px; POSITION: absolute; TOP: 132px" />
            <input type="submit" name="Button1" value="Submit" id="Button1" style="Z-
INDEX: 104; LEFT: 203px; POSITION: absolute; TOP: 183px" />
            <span id="Label1" style="Z-INDEX: 105; LEFT: 58px; POSITION: absolute;
TOP: 54px">Identity:</span>
            <span id="Label2" style="Z-INDEX: 106; LEFT: 57px; POSITION: absolute;
TOP: 94px">Item:</span>
            <span id="Label3" style="Z-INDEX: 107; LEFT: 57px; POSITION: absolute;
TOP: 135px">Quantity:</span>
        </form>
    </body>
</HTML>
```

Discussion

The WebClient class makes it easy to upload form data to a web server in the common
format of a set of name-value pairs. You can see this technique in the call to
UploadValues that takes an absolute URI (*http://localhost/FormSim/WebForm1.aspx*),
the HTTP method to use (POST), and the NameValueCollection you created
(collection). The NameValueCollection is populated with the data for each of the fields
on the form by calling its Add method, passing the id of the input field as the name and
the value to put in the field as the value. In this example, you fill in the Identity field
with *foo@bar.com*, the Item field with Book, and the Quantity field with 5. You then
print out the resulting response from the POST to the console window.

See Also

See the "WebClient Class" topic in the MSDN documentation.

16.4 Downloading Data from a Server

Problem

You need to download data from a location specified by a URL; this data can be
either an array of bytes or a file.

Solution

Use the WebClient.DownloadData method to download data from a URL:

```
string uri = "http://localhost/mysite/index.aspx";

// Make a client.
using (WebClient client = new WebClient())
{
    // Get the contents of the file.
```

```
        Console.WriteLine("Downloading {0} " + uri);
        // Download the page and store the bytes.
        byte[] bytes;
        try
        {
            bytes = client.DownloadData(uri);
        }
        catch (WebException we)
        {
            Console.WriteLine(we.ToString( ));
            return;
        }
        // Write the content out.
        string page = Encoding.ASCII.GetString(bytes);
        Console.WriteLine(page);
}
```

This will produce the following output:

```
Downloading {0} http://localhost/mysite/index.aspx

<!DOCTYPE HTML PUBLIC "-//W3C//DTD HTML 4.0 Transitional//EN" >
<HTML>
    <HEAD>
        <title>WebForm1</title>
        <meta name="GENERATOR" Content="Microsoft Visual Studio .NET 7.1">
        <meta name="CODE_LANGUAGE" Content="C#">
        <meta name="vs_defaultClientScript" content="JavaScript">
        <meta name="vs_targetSchema"
content="http://schemas.microsoft.com/intellisense/ie5">
    </HEAD>
    <body MS_POSITIONING="GridLayout">
        <form name="Form1" method="post" action="index.aspx" id="Form1">
<input type="hidden" name="__VIEWSTATE"
value="dDwyMDQwNjUzNDY2Ozs+kS9hguYm9369sybDqmIowOAvxBg=" />

            <span id="Label1" style="Z-INDEX: 101; LEFT: 142px; POSITION: absolute;
TOP: 164px">This is index.aspx!</span>
        </form>
    </body>
</HTML>
```

You can also download data to a file using DownloadFile:

```
// Make a client.
using (WebClient client = new WebClient( ))
{
    // Go get the file.
    Console.WriteLine("Retrieving file from {0}...\r\n", uri);
    // Get file and put it in a temp file.
    string tempFile = Path.GetTempFileName( );
    client.DownloadFile(uri,tempFile);
    Console.WriteLine("Downloaded {0} to {1}",uri,tempFile);
}
```

This will produce the following output:

```
Retrieving file from http://localhost/mysite/index.aspx...

Downloaded http://localhost/mysite/index.aspx to C:\Documents and Settings\[user]\
Local Settings\Temp\tmp17C.tmp
```

Discussion

`WebClient` simplifies downloading of files and bytes in files, as these are common tasks when dealing with the Web. The more traditional stream-based method for downloading can also be accessed via the `OpenRead` method on the `WebClient`.

See Also

See the "WebClient Class" topic in the MSDN documentation.

16.5 Using Named Pipes to Communicate

Problem

You need a way to use named pipes to communicate with another application across the network.

Solution

Create a P/Invoke wrapper class for the named-pipe APIs in *Kernel32.dll*. You can then create a managed client and managed server class to work with named pipes.

Example 16-3 shows the named-pipe interop wrappers in a class called `NamedPipeInterop`.

Example 16-3. NamedPipeInterop class

```
namespace NamedPipes
{
    /// <summary>
    /// Imported named-pipe entry points for P/Invoke into native code
    /// </summary>
    public class NamedPipeInterop
    {
        // #defines related to named-pipe processing
        public const int PIPE_ACCESS_OUTBOUND = 0x00000002;
        public const int PIPE_ACCESS_DUPLEX = 0x00000003;
        public const int PIPE_ACCESS_INBOUND = 0x00000001;

        public const int PIPE_WAIT = 0x00000000;
        public const int PIPE_NOWAIT = 0x00000001;
        public const int PIPE_READMODE_BYTE = 0x00000000;
        public const int PIPE_READMODE_MESSAGE = 0x00000002;
        public const int PIPE_TYPE_BYTE = 0x00000000;
        public const int PIPE_TYPE_MESSAGE = 0x00000004;
```

Example 16-3. NamedPipeInterop class (continued)

```csharp
        public const int PIPE_CLIENT_END = 0x00000000;
        public const int PIPE_SERVER_END = 0x00000001;

        public const int PIPE_UNLIMITED_INSTANCES = 255;

        public const uint NMPWAIT_WAIT_FOREVER = 0xffffffff;
        public const uint NMPWAIT_NOWAIT = 0x00000001;
        public const uint NMPWAIT_USE_DEFAULT_WAIT = 0x00000000;

        public const uint GENERIC_READ = (0x80000000);
        public const uint GENERIC_WRITE = (0x40000000);
        public const uint GENERIC_EXECUTE = (0x20000000);
        public const uint GENERIC_ALL = (0x10000000);

        public const int CREATE_NEW = 1;
        public const int CREATE_ALWAYS = 2;
        public const int OPEN_EXISTING = 3;
        public const int OPEN_ALWAYS = 4;
        public const int TRUNCATE_EXISTING = 5;

        public static IntPtr INVALID_HANDLE_VALUE = (IntPtr)(-1);
        public const int ERROR_PIPE_BUSY = 231;
        public const int ERROR_NO_DATA = 232;
        public const int ERROR_PIPE_NOT_CONNECTED = 233;
        public const int ERROR_MORE_DATA = 234;
        public const int ERROR_PIPE_CONNECTED = 535;
        public const int ERROR_PIPE_LISTENING = 536;

        [DllImport("kernel32.dll", SetLastError = true)]
        public static extern bool CallNamedPipe(
            string lpNamedPipeName,
            byte[] lpInBuffer,
            uint nInBufferSize,
            byte[] lpOutBuffer,
            uint nOutBufferSize,
            byte[] lpBytesRead,
            uint nTimeOut);

        [DllImport("kernel32.dll", SetLastError = true)]
        public static extern bool CloseHandle(SafeFileHandle hObject);

        [DllImport("kernel32.dll", SetLastError = true)]
        public static extern bool ConnectNamedPipe(
            SafeFileHandle hNamedPipe,          // Handle to named pipe
            IntPtr lpOverlapped    // Overlapped structure
            );

        [DllImport("kernel32.dll", SetLastError = true)]
        public static extern SafeFileHandle CreateNamedPipe(
            String lpName,         // Pipe name
            uint dwOpenMode,      // Pipe open mode
            uint dwPipeMode,      // Pipe-specific modes
```

Example 16-3. NamedPipeInterop class (continued)

```
            uint nMaxInstances,     // Maximum number of instances
            uint nOutBufferSize,    // Output buffer size
            uint nInBufferSize,     // Input buffer size
            uint nDefaultTimeOut,   // Time-out interval
            //SecurityAttributes attr
            IntPtr pipeSecurityDescriptor // Security descriptor
            );


        [DllImport("kernel32.dll", SetLastError = true)]
        public static extern SafeFileHandle CreatePipe(
            SafeFileHandle hReadPipe,
            SafeFileHandle hWritePipe,
            IntPtr lpPipeAttributes,
            uint nSize);

        [DllImport("kernel32.dll", SetLastError = true)]
        public static extern SafeFileHandle CreateFile(
            String lpFileName,        // File name
            uint dwDesiredAccess,        // Access mode
            uint dwShareMode,         // Share mode
            IntPtr attr,     // Security descriptor
            uint dwCreationDisposition,     // How to create
            uint dwFlagsAndAttributes,    // File attributes
            uint hTemplateFile);        // Handle to template file

        [DllImport("kernel32.dll", SetLastError = true)]
        public static extern bool DisconnectNamedPipe(SafeFileHandle hNamedPipe);

        [DllImport("kernel32.dll", SetLastError = true)]
        public static extern bool FlushFileBuffers(SafeFileHandle hFile);

        [DllImport("kernel32.dll", SetLastError = true)]
        public static extern bool GetNamedPipeHandleState(
            SafeFileHandle hNamedPipe,
            IntPtr lpState,
            IntPtr lpCurInstances,
            IntPtr lpMaxCollectionCount,
            IntPtr lpCollectDataTimeout,
            string lpUserName,
            uint nMaxUserNameSize);

        [DllImport("KERNEL32.DLL", SetLastError = true)]
        public static extern bool GetNamedPipeInfo(
            SafeFileHandle hNamedPipe,
            out uint lpFlags,
            out uint lpOutBufferSize,
            out uint lpInBufferSize,
            out uint lpMaxInstances);

        [DllImport("KERNEL32.DLL", SetLastError = true)]
        public static extern bool PeekNamedPipe(
```

Example 16-3. NamedPipeInterop class (continued)

```
            SafeFileHandle hNamedPipe,
            byte[] lpBuffer,
            uint nBufferSize,
            byte[] lpBytesRead,
            out uint lpTotalBytesAvail,
            out uint lpBytesLeftThisMessage);

    [DllImport("KERNEL32.DLL", SetLastError = true)]
    public static extern bool SetNamedPipeHandleState(
            SafeFileHandle hNamedPipe,
            ref int lpMode,
            IntPtr lpMaxCollectionCount,
            IntPtr lpCollectDataTimeout);

    [DllImport("KERNEL32.DLL", SetLastError = true)]
    public static extern bool TransactNamedPipe(
            SafeFileHandle hNamedPipe,
            byte[] lpInBuffer,
            uint nInBufferSize,
            [Out] byte[] lpOutBuffer,
            uint nOutBufferSize,
            IntPtr lpBytesRead,
            IntPtr lpOverlapped);

    [DllImport("kernel32.dll", SetLastError = true)]
    public static extern bool WaitNamedPipe(
            string name,
            uint timeout);

    [DllImport("kernel32.dll", SetLastError = true)]
    public static extern bool ReadFile(
            SafeFileHandle hFile,            // Handle to file
            byte[] lpBuffer,        // Data buffer
            uint nNumberOfBytesToRead,    // Number of bytes to read
            byte[] lpNumberOfBytesRead,    // Number of bytes read
            uint lpOverlapped        // Overlapped buffer
            );


    [DllImport("kernel32.dll", SetLastError = true)]
    public static extern bool WriteFile(
            SafeFileHandle hFile,                // Handle to file
            byte[] lpBuffer,            // Data buffer
            uint nNumberOfBytesToWrite,        // Number of bytes to write
            byte[] lpNumberOfBytesWritten,  // Number of bytes written
            uint lpOverlapped            // Overlapped buffer
            );
}
```

Now, using the interop wrappers, you can create a named-pipe client class named
NamedPipeClient, as shown in Example 16-4.

Example 16-4. NamedPipeClient class

```csharp
using System;
using System.Collections.Generic;
using System.Text;
using System.Runtime.InteropServices;
using System.Diagnostics;
using System.ComponentModel;
using System.IO;
using System.Threading;
using Microsoft.Win32.SafeHandles;

namespace NamedPipes
{
    /// <summary>
    /// NamedPipeClient - An implementation of a synchronous, message-based,
    /// named pipe client
    ///
    /// </summary>
    public class NamedPipeClient : IDisposable
    {
        #region Private Members
        /// <summary>
        ///     The full name of the pipe being connected to
        /// </summary>
        private string _pipeName = "";

        /// <summary>
        /// The pipe handle once connected
        /// </summary>
        private SafeFileHandle _handle =
                new SafeFileHandle(NamedPipeInterop.INVALID_HANDLE_VALUE,true);

        /// <summary>
        /// Default response buffer size (1K)
        /// </summary>
        private int _responseBufferSize = 1024;

        /// <summary>
        /// Track if dispose has been called
        /// </summary>
        private bool disposed = false;

        /// <summary>
        /// Timeout for the retry after first failed connect
        /// </summary>
        private int _retryTimeout = 20000;

        /// <summary>
        /// Number of times to retry connecting
        /// </summary>
        private int _retryConnect = 5;
        #endregion
```

Example 16-4. NamedPipeClient class (continued)

```
#region Construction / Cleanup
/// <summary>
/// CTOR
/// </summary>
/// <param name="pipeName">name of the pipe</param>
public NamedPipeClient(string pipeName)
{
    _pipeName = pipeName;
    Trace.WriteLine("NamedPipeClient using pipe name of " + _pipeName);
}

/// <summary>
/// Finalizer
/// </summary>
~NamedPipeClient()
{
    Dispose(false);
}

public void Dispose()
{
    Dispose(true);
    GC.SuppressFinalize(this);
}

private void Dispose(bool disposing)
{
    // Check to see if Dispose has already been called.
    if (!this.disposed)
    {
        ClosePipe();
    }
    disposed = true;
}

private void ClosePipe()
{
    if (!_handle.IsInvalid)
    {
        _handle.Close();
    }
}

/// <summary>
/// Close - because it is more intuitive than Dispose...
/// </summary>
public void Close()
{
    ClosePipe();
}
#endregion
```

Example 16-4. NamedPipeClient class (continued)

```csharp
#region Properties
/// <summary>
/// ResponseBufferSize Property - the size used to create response buffers
/// for messages written using WriteMessage
/// </summary>
public int ResponseBufferSize
{
    get
    {
        return _responseBufferSize;
    }
    set
    {
        _responseBufferSize = value;
    }
}


/// <summary>
/// The number of milliseconds to wait when attempting to retry a connection
/// </summary>
public int RetryConnectCount
{
    get
    {
        return _retryConnect;
    }
    set
    {
        _retryConnect = value;
    }
}


/// <summary>
/// The number of milliseconds to wait when attempting to retry a connection
/// </summary>
public int RetryConnectTimeout
{
    get
    {
        return _retryTimeout;
    }
    set
    {
        _retryTimeout = value;
    }
}
#endregion

#region Public Methods
/// <summary>
/// Connect - connect to an existing pipe.
/// </summary>
```

Example 16-4. NamedPipeClient class (continued)

```csharp
/// <returns>true if connected</returns>
public void Connect()
{
    if (!_handle.IsInvalid)
        throw new InvalidOperationException("Pipe is already connected!");

    string errMsg = "";
    int errCode = 0;
    int retryAttempts = _retryConnect;
    // Keep trying to connect.
    while (retryAttempts > 0)
    {
        // Mark off one attempt.
        retryAttempts--;

        // Connect to existing pipe.
        _handle = NamedPipeInterop.CreateFile(_pipeName,
            NamedPipeInterop.GENERIC_READ |
            NamedPipeInterop.GENERIC_WRITE,
            0,
            IntPtr.Zero,
            NamedPipeInterop.OPEN_EXISTING,
            0,
            0);

        // Check to see if we connected.
        if (!_handle.IsInvalid)
            break;

        // The pipe could not be opened as all instances are busy.
        // Any other error we bail for.
        errCode = Marshal.GetLastWin32Error();
        if (errCode !=
            NamedPipeInterop.ERROR_PIPE_BUSY)
        {
            errMsg = string.Format("Could not open pipe {0} with error {1}"_
                pipeName,errCode);
            Trace.WriteLine(errMsg);
            throw new Win32Exception(errCode, errMsg);
        }
        // If it was busy, see if we can wait it out.
        else if (!NamedPipeInterop.WaitNamedPipe(_pipeName, (uint)_retryTimeout))
        {
            errCode = Marshal.GetLastWin32Error();
            errMsg =
                string.Format("Wait for pipe {0} timed out after {1} milliseconds
                    with error code {2}.",
                        _pipeName, _retryTimeout,errCode);
            Trace.WriteLine(errMsg);
            throw new Win32Exception(errCode, errMsg);
        }
    }
```

Example 16-4. NamedPipeClient class (continued)

```
            // Indicate connection in debug.
            Trace.WriteLine("Connected to pipe: " + _pipeName);

            // The pipe connected; change to message-read mode
            bool success = false;
            int mode = (int)NamedPipeInterop.PIPE_READMODE_MESSAGE;

            // Set to message mode.
            success = NamedPipeInterop.SetNamedPipeHandleState(
                _handle,      // Pipe handle
                ref mode,  // New pipe mode
                IntPtr.Zero,      // Don't set maximum bytes.
                IntPtr.Zero);     // Don't set maximum time.

            // Currently implemented for just synchronous, message-based pipes
            // so bail if we couldn't set the client up properly.
            if (false == success)
            {
                errCode = Marshal.GetLastWin32Error();
                errMsg =
                    string.Format("Could not change pipe mode to message with error code
                        {0}",
                            errCode);
                Trace.WriteLine(errMsg);
                Dispose();
                throw new Win32Exception(errCode, errMsg);
            }
        }


        /// <summary>
        /// WriteMessage - write an array of bytes and return the response from the
        /// server.
        /// </summary>
        /// <param name="buffer">bytes to write</param>
        /// <param name="bytesToWrite">number of bytes to write</param>
        /// <returns>true if written successfully</returns>
        public MemoryStream WriteMessage(byte[] buffer,  // the write buffer
            uint bytesToWrite)  // Number of bytes in the write buffer
        // Message responses
        {
            // Buffer to get the number of bytes read/written back
            byte[] _numReadWritten = new byte[4];
            MemoryStream responseStream = null;

            bool success = false;
            // Write the byte buffer to the pipe.
            success = NamedPipeInterop.WriteFile(_handle,
                buffer,
                bytesToWrite,
                _numReadWritten,
                0);
```

Example 16-4. NamedPipeClient class (continued)

```
if (success)
{
    byte[] responseBuffer = new byte[_responseBufferSize];
    responseStream = new MemoryStream(_responseBufferSize);
    {
        do
        {
            // Read the response from the pipe.
            success = NamedPipeInterop.ReadFile(
                _handle,      // Pipe handle
                responseBuffer,     // Buffer to receive reply
                (uint)_responseBufferSize,     // Size of buffer
                _numReadWritten,  // Number of bytes read
                0);     // Not overlapped

            // Failed, not just more data to come
            if (!success && Marshal.GetLastWin32Error() != NamedPipeInterop.
ERROR_MORE_DATA)
                break;

            // Concat response to stream.
            responseStream.Write(responseBuffer,
                0,
                responseBuffer.Length);

        } while (!success);

    }
}
return responseStream;
}
#endregion
}
}
```

Then you need to create a server class for testing, which you can call NamedPipeServer, as shown in Example 16-5.

Example 16-5. NamedPipeServer class

```
using System;
using System.Collections.Generic;
using System.Text;
using System.Runtime.InteropServices;
using System.Diagnostics;
using System.ComponentModel;
using System.IO;
using System.Threading;
using Microsoft.Win32.SafeHandles;

namespace NamedPipes
{
```

Example 16-5. NamedPipeServer class (continued)

```
/// <summary>
/// NamedPipeServer - An implementation of a synchronous, message-based,
/// named-pipe server
///
/// </summary>
public class NamedPipeServer : IDisposable
{
    #region Private Members
    /// <summary>
    /// The pipe handle
    /// </summary>
    private SafeFileHandle _handle =
            new SafeFileHandle(NamedPipeInterop.INVALID_HANDLE_VALUE, true);

    /// <summary>
    /// The name of the pipe
    /// </summary>
    private string _pipeName = "";

    /// <summary>
    /// Default size of message buffer to read
    /// </summary>
    private int _receiveBufferSize = 1024;

    /// <summary>
    /// Track if dispose has been called.
    /// </summary>
    private bool disposed = false;

    /// <summary>
    /// PIPE_SERVER_BUFFER_SIZE set to 8192 by default
    /// </summary>
    private const int PIPE_SERVER_BUFFER_SIZE = 8192;
    #endregion

    #region Construction / Cleanup
    /// <summary>
    /// CTOR
    /// </summary>
    /// <param name="pipeBaseName">the base name of the pipe</param>
    /// <param name="msgReceivedDelegate">delegate to be notified when
    /// a message is received</param>.
    public NamedPipeServer(string pipeBaseName)
    {
        // Assemble the pipe name.
        _pipeName = "\\\\.\\PIPE\\" + pipeBaseName;
        Trace.WriteLine("NamedPipeServer using pipe name " + _pipeName);
    }

    /// <summary>
    /// Finalizer
    /// </summary>
```

Example 16-5. NamedPipeServer class (continued)

```
~NamedPipeServer( )
{
    Dispose(false);
}

public void Dispose( )
{
    Dispose(true);
    GC.SuppressFinalize(this);
}

private void Dispose(bool disposing)
{
    // Check to see if Dispose has already been called.
    if (!this.disposed)
    {
        ClosePipe( );
    }
    disposed = true;
}

private void ClosePipe( )
{
    Trace.WriteLine("NamedPipeServer closing pipe");

    if (!_handle.IsInvalid)
    {
        _handle.Close( );
    }
}

/// <summary>
/// Close - because it is more intuitive than Dispose...
/// </summary>
public void Close( )
{
    ClosePipe( );
}
#endregion

#region Properties
/// <summary>
/// PipeName
/// </summary>
/// <returns>the composed pipe name</returns>
public string PipeName
{
    get
    {
        return _pipeName;
    }
}
```

Example 16-5. NamedPipeServer class (continued)

```csharp
/// <summary>
/// ReceiveBufferSize Property - the size used to create receive buffers
/// for messages received using WaitForMessage
/// </summary>
public int ReceiveBufferSize
{
    get
    {
        return _receiveBufferSize;
    }
    set
    {
        _receiveBufferSize = value;
    }
}
#endregion

#region Public Methods
/// <summary>
/// CreatePipe - create the named pipe
/// </summary>
/// <returns>true is pipe created</returns>
public bool CreatePipe()
{
    // Make a named pipe in message mode.
    _handle = NamedPipeInterop.CreateNamedPipe(_pipeName,
        NamedPipeInterop.PIPE_ACCESS_DUPLEX,
        NamedPipeInterop.PIPE_TYPE_MESSAGE | NamedPipeInterop.PIPE_READMODE_
    MESSAGE |
        NamedPipeInterop.PIPE_WAIT,
        NamedPipeInterop.PIPE_UNLIMITED_INSTANCES,
        PIPE_SERVER_BUFFER_SIZE,
        PIPE_SERVER_BUFFER_SIZE,
        NamedPipeInterop.NMPWAIT_WAIT_FOREVER,
        IntPtr.Zero);

    // Make sure we got a good one.
    if (_handle.IsInvalid)
    {
        Debug.WriteLine("Could not create the pipe (" +
            _pipeName + ") - os returned " +
            Marshal.GetLastWin32Error());

        return false;
    }
    return true;
}

/// <summary>
/// WaitForClientConnect - wait for a client to connect to this pipe
/// </summary>
/// <returns>true if connected, false if timed out</returns>
```

Example 16-5. NamedPipeServer class (continued)

```csharp
public bool WaitForClientConnect( )
{
    // Wait for someone to talk to us.
    return NamedPipeInterop.ConnectNamedPipe(_handle, IntPtr.Zero);
}

/// <summary>
/// WaitForMessage - have the server wait for a message
/// </summary>
 /// <returns>a non-null MessageStream if it got a message, null if timed out or
        error
/// </returns>
public MemoryStream WaitForMessage( )
{
    bool fullyRead = false;
    string errMsg = "";
    int errCode = 0;
    // They want to talk to us, read their messages and write
    // replies.
    MemoryStream receiveStream = new MemoryStream( );
    byte[] buffer = new byte[_receiveBufferSize];
    byte[] _numReadWritten = new byte[4];

    // Need to read the whole message and put it in one message
    // byte buffer.
    do
    {
        // Read the response from the pipe.
        if (!NamedPipeInterop.ReadFile(
            _handle,     // Pipe handle
            buffer,     // Buffer to receive reply
            (uint)_receiveBufferSize,      // Size of buffer
            _numReadWritten,  // Number of bytes read
            0))    // Not overlapped
        {
            // Failed, not just more data to come
            errCode = Marshal.GetLastWin32Error( );
            if (errCode != NamedPipeInterop.ERROR_MORE_DATA)
                break;
            else
            {
                errMsg = string.Format("Could not read from pipe with error {0}",
                                    errCode);
                Trace.WriteLine(errMsg);
                throw new Win32Exception(errCode, errMsg);
            }
        }
        else
        {
            // We succeeded and no more data is coming.
            fullyRead = true;
        }
```

Example 16-5. NamedPipeServer class (continued)

```
                // Concat the message bytes to the stream.
                receiveStream.Write(buffer, 0, buffer.Length);

        } while (!fullyRead);

        if (receiveStream.Length > 0)
        {
            // Now set up response with a polite response using the same
            // Unicode string protocol.
            string reply = "Thanks for the message!";
            byte[] msgBytes = Encoding.Unicode.GetBytes(reply);

            uint len = (uint)msgBytes.Length;
            // Write the response message provided
            // by the delegate.
            if (!NamedPipeInterop.WriteFile(_handle,
                msgBytes,
                len,
                _numReadWritten,
                0))
            {
                errCode = Marshal.GetLastWin32Error();
                errMsg = string.Format("Could not write response with error {0}",
                  errCode);
                Trace.WriteLine(errMsg);
                throw new Win32Exception(errCode, errMsg);
            }

            // Return the message we received.
            return receiveStream;
        }
        else // Didn't receive anything.
            return null;
    }
    #endregion
    }
}
```

In order to use the `NamedPipeClient` class, you need some code like that shown in Example 16-6.

Example 16-6. Using the NamedPipeClient class

```
using System;
using System.Collections.Generic;
using System.Text;
using System.IO;
using System.Diagnostics;

namespace NamedPipes
{
```

Example 16-6. Using the NamedPipeClient class (continued)

```
class NamedPipeClientConsole
{
    static void Main(string[] args)
    {
        // Client test code - commented out as it should go in a separate
        // console test app

        // Create our pipe client.
        NamedPipeClient _pc =
            new NamedPipeClient("\\\\.\\PIPE\\mypipe");

        if (_pc != null)
        {
            using (_pc)
            {
                // Connect to the server.
                _pc.Connect();
                // Set up a dummy message.
                string testString = "This is my message!";

                // Turn it into a byte array.
                byte[] writebuffer = Encoding.Unicode.GetBytes(testString);
                uint len = Convert.ToUInt32(writebuffer.Length);

                // Write the message ten times.
                for (int i = 0; i < 10; i++)
                {
                    MemoryStream response = _pc.WriteMessage(writebuffer, len);
                    if (response == null)
                    {
                        Debug.Assert(false,
                            "Failed to write message!");
                    }
                    else
                    {
                        WriteMessageResponse(response);
                    }
                }
            }
        }
        Console.WriteLine("Press Enter to exit...");
        Console.ReadLine();
    }

    static void WriteMessageResponse(MemoryStream responseStream)
    {
        string response =
            Encoding.Unicode.GetString(responseStream.ToArray());
        Console.WriteLine("Received response: {0}", response);
    }
}
}
```

Then, to set up a server for the client to talk to, you use the `NamedPipeServer` class as shown in Example 16-7.

Example 16-7. Setting up a server for the client

```
using System;
using System.Collections.Generic;
using System.Text;
using System.IO;
using System.ComponentModel;

namespace NamedPipes
{
    class NamedPipeServerConsole
    {
        static void Main(string[] args)
        {
            // Server test code - commented out as it should go in a separate
            // console test app as shown in the book

            // Create pipe server.
            using (NamedPipeServer _ps =
                new NamedPipeServer("mypipe"))
            {
                // Create pipe.
                if (_ps.CreatePipe())
                {
                    // I get the name of the pipe here just to show you can.
                    // Normally we would then have to get this name to the client
                    // so it knows the name of the pipe to open but hey, I wrote
                    // the client to so for now I'm just hardcoding it in the
                    // client so we can ignore it.
                    string pipeName = _ps.PipeName;

                    // Wait for clients to connect.
                    if (_ps.WaitForClientConnect())
                    {
                        // Process messages until the read fails.
                        // (client goes away...)
                        bool success = true;
                        while (success)
                        {
                            try
                            {
                                // Wait for a message from the client.
                                MemoryStream messageStream = _ps.WaitForMessage();
                                if (messageStream != null)
                                {
                                    // Get the bytes of the message from the stream.
                                    byte[] msgBytes = messageStream.ToArray();
                                    string messageText;
```

Example 16-7. Setting up a server for the client (continued)

```
                                   // I know in the client I used a Unicode encoding
                                   // for the string to turn it into a series of bytes
                                   // for transmission so just reverse that.
                                   messageText = Encoding.Unicode.GetString(msgBytes);

                                   // Write out our string message from the client.
                                   Console.WriteLine(messageText);
                               }
                               else
                                   success = false;
                           }
                           catch (Win32Exception)
                           {
                               success = false;
                           }
                       }
                   }
               }
           }
           // Make our server hang around so you can see the messages sent.
           Console.WriteLine("Press Enter to exit...");
           Console.ReadLine();
       }
   }
}
```

Discussion

Named pipes are a mechanism to allow interprocess or intermachine communications in Windows. The .NET Framework currently has not provided managed access to named pipes, so the first thing you need to do is to wrap the functions in *Kernel32.dll* for direct access from managed code in your `NamedPipesInterop` class.

Once you have this foundation, you can then build a client for using named pipes to talk to a server, as in the `NamedPipeClient` class. The methods on `NamedPipeClient` are listed in Table 16-1 with a description for each.

Table 16-1. NamedPipeClient methods

Method	Description
Close	Close method, which calls the Dispose method.
Connect	Connects to a named-pipe server.
Dispose	Dispose method for the named-pipe client so that the pipe handle is not held any longer than necessary.
NamedPipeClient	Constructor for the named-pipe client.
~NamedPipeClient	Finalizer for the named-pipe client. This makes sure the pipe handle is closed.
WriteMessage	Writes a message to the connected server.

You then create the NamedPipeServer class to be able to have something for the NamedPipeClient to connect to. The methods on the NamedPipeServer are listed in Table 16-2 with a description for each as well.

Table 16-2. NamedPipeServer methods

Method	Description
Close	Close method that calls the Dispose method. Many developers use Close, so it is provided for completeness.
CreatePipe	Creates a listener pipe on the server.
Dispose	Dispose method for the named-pipe server so that pipe handles are not held any longer than necessary.
NamedPipeServer	Constructor for the named-pipe server.
~NamedPipeServer	Finalizer for the named-pipe server. This makes sure the pipe handle is closed.
PipeName	Returns the composed pipe name.
WaitForClientConnect	Wait on the pipe handle for a client to talk to.
WaitForMessage	Have the server wait for a message from the client.

Finally, you create some code to use NamedPipeClient and NamedPipeServer. The interaction between these two goes like this:

1. The server process is started; it fires up a NamedPipeServer, calls CreatePipe to make a pipe, then calls WaitForClientConnect to wait for the NamedPipeClient to connect:

```
using (NamedPipeServer _ps =
    new NamedPipeServer("mypipe"))
{
    // Create pipe.
    if (_ps.CreatePipe())
    {
        // Wait for clients to connect.
        if (_ps.WaitForClientConnect())
        {
```

2. The client process is created; it fires up a NamedPipeClient, calls Connect, and connects to the server process:

```
// Create our pipe client.
NamedPipeClient _pc =
    new NamedPipeClient("\\\\.\\PIPE\\mypipe");

if (_pc != null)
{
    using (_pc)
    {
        // Connect to the server.
        _pc.Connect();
```

3. The server process sees the connection from the client and then calls WaitForMessage in a loop. WaitForMessage starts reading the pipe, which blocks until a message is written to the pipe by the client.

```
// Process messages until the read fails.
// (client goes away...)
bool success = true;
while (success)
{
    try
    {
        // Wait for a message from the client.
        MemoryStream messageStream = _ps.WaitForMessage();

        // More processing code in here....
    }
    catch (Win32Exception)
    {
        success = false;
    }
}
```

4. The client process then writes a number of messages to the server process using WriteMessage:

```
// Set up a dummy message.
string testString = "This is my message!";

// Turn it into a byte array.
byte[] writebuffer = Encoding.Unicode.GetBytes(testString);
uint len = Convert.ToUInt32(writebuffer.Length);

// Write the message ten times.
for (int i = 0; i < 10; i++)
{
    MemoryStream response = _pc.WriteMessage(writebuffer, len);
    if (response == null)
    {
        Debug.Assert(false,
            "Failed to write message!");
    }
    else
    {
        WriteMessageResponse(response);
    }
}
```

5. In WaitForMessage, shown in Example 16-8, the server process sees the message, processes it, writes a response to the client, returns a MemoryStream with the received message in it, then goes back to waiting.

Example 16-8. WaitForMessage method

```csharp
public MemoryStream WaitForMessage( )
{
    bool fullyRead = false;
    string errMsg = "";
    int errCode = 0;
    // They want to talk to us, read their messages and write
    // replies.
    MemoryStream receiveStream = new MemoryStream( );
    byte[] buffer = new byte[_receiveBufferSize];
    byte[] _numReadWritten = new byte[4];

    // Need to read the whole message and put it in one message.
    // byte buffer
    do
    {
        // Read the response from the pipe.
        if (!NamedPipeInterop.ReadFile(
            _handle,       // Pipe handle
            buffer,        // Buffer to receive reply
            (uint)_receiveBufferSize,       // Size of buffer
            _numReadWritten,  // Number of bytes read
            0))     // Not overlapped
        {
            // Failed, not just more data to come
            errCode = Marshal.GetLastWin32Error( );
            if (errCode != NamedPipeInterop.ERROR_MORE_DATA)
                break;
            else
            {
                errMsg = string.Format("Could not read from pipe with error {0}",
                    errCode);
                Trace.WriteLine(errMsg);
                throw new Win32Exception(errCode, errMsg);
            }
        }
        else
        {
            // We succeeded and no more data is coming.
            fullyRead = true;
        }
        // Concat the message bytes to the stream.
        receiveStream.Write(buffer, 0, buffer.Length);

    } while (!fullyRead);

    if (receiveStream.Length > 0)
    {
        // Now set up response with a polite response using the same
        // Unicode string protocol.
        string reply = "Thanks for the message!";
        byte[] msgBytes = Encoding.Unicode.GetBytes(reply);
```

Example 16-8. WaitForMessage method (continued)

```
                uint len = (uint)msgBytes.Length;
                // Write the response message provided
                // by the delegate.
                if (!NamedPipeInterop.WriteFile(_handle,
                    msgBytes,
                    len,
                    _numReadWritten,
                    0))
                {
                    errCode = Marshal.GetLastWin32Error();
                    errMsg = string.Format("Could not write response with error {0}",
                    errCode);
                    Trace.WriteLine(errMsg);
                    throw new Win32Exception(errCode, errMsg);
                }

                // Return the message we received.
                return receiveStream;
            }
            else // Didn't receive anything.
                return null;
    }
```

6. When the client process receives the response from the server, it returns a MemoryStream with the response for processing. If the message sending is complete, the NamedPipeClient goes out of the scope of the using statement and closes (thereby closing the connection on the client side) and then waits to go away when the user presses Enter.

```
                // Write a message and get a response stream.
                MemoryStream response = _pc.WriteMessage(writebuffer, len);
                if (response == null)
                {
                    Debug.Assert(false,
                        "Failed to write message!");
                }
                else
                {
                    // Process response message to console.
                    WriteMessageResponse(response);
                }

        static void WriteMessageResponse(MemoryStream responseStream)
        {
            string response =
                Encoding.Unicode.GetString(responseStream.ToArray());
            Console.WriteLine("Received response: {0}", response);
        }
```

7. The server process notes that the client has closed the pipe connection via the failed NamedPipesInterop.ReadFile call in WaitForMessage. It calls Close to clean up, then waits for the user to press Enter to terminate the process.

The client output looks like this:

```
Received response: Thanks for the message!
Received response: Thanks for the message!
Received response: Thanks for the message!
Received response: Thanks for the message!
Received response: Thanks for the message!
Received response: Thanks for the message!
Received response: Thanks for the message!
Received response: Thanks for the message!
Received response: Thanks for the message!
Received response: Thanks for the message!
Press Enter to exit...
```

The server output looks like this:

```
This is my message!
This is my message!
This is my message!
This is my message!
This is my message!
This is my message!
This is my message!
This is my message!
This is my message!
This is my message!
Press Enter to exit...
```

See Also

See the "Named Pipes," "DllImport Attribute," "IDisposable Interface," and "GC.
SuppressFinalize Method" topics in the MSDN documentation.

16.6   Pinging Programmatically

Problem

You want to check a computer's availability on the network.

Solution

Use the System.Net.NetworkInformation.Ping class to determine if a machine is available. In the TestPing method, an instance of the Ping class is created. A ping request
is sent to *www.oreilly.com* using the Send method. The Send method is synchronous
and returns a PingReply that can be examined for the result of the ping. You perform
the second ping request asynchronously using the SendAsync method, after hooking
up to the Ping class for the PingCompleted event.

```
public static void TestPing( )
{
    System.Net.NetworkInformation.Ping pinger =
        new System.Net.NetworkInformation.Ping( );
```

```
    PingReply reply = pinger.Send("www.oreilly.com");
    DisplayPingReplyInfo(reply);

    pinger.PingCompleted += new PingCompletedEventHandler(pinger_PingCompleted);
    pinger.SendAsync("www.oreilly.com", "oreilly ping");
}
```

The DisplayPingReplyInfo method shows some of the more common items you want
to know from a ping, such as the RoundtripTime and the Status of the reply. These
can be accessed from those properties on the PingReply.

```
private static void DisplayPingReplyInfo(PingReply reply)
{
    Console.WriteLine("Results from pinging " + reply.Address);
    Console.WriteLine("\tFragmentation allowed?: {0}", !reply.Options.DontFragment);
    Console.WriteLine("\tTime to live: {0}", reply.Options.Ttl);
    Console.WriteLine("\tRoundtrip took: {0}", reply.RoundtripTime);
    Console.WriteLine("\tStatus: {0}", reply.Status.ToString());
}
```

The event handler for the PingCompleted event is the pinger_PingCompleted method.
This event handler follows the usual EventHandler convention of the sender object
and event arguments. The argument type for this event is PingCompletedEventArgs.
The PingReply can be accessed in the Reply property of the event arguments. If the
ping was canceled or an exception was thrown, that information can be accessed via
the Cancelled and Error properties.

```
private static void pinger_PingCompleted(object sender, PingCompletedEventArgs e)
{
    PingReply reply = e.Reply;
    DisplayPingReplyInfo(reply);

    if(e.Cancelled)
    {
        Console.WriteLine("Ping for " + e.UserState.ToString() + " was cancelled");
    }
    else if (e.Error != null)
    {
        Console.WriteLine("Exception thrown during ping: {0}", e.Error.ToString());
    }
}
```

The output from DisplayPingReplyInfo looks like this:

```
Results from pinging 208.201.239.37
    Fragmentation allowed?: True
    Time to live: 39
    Roundtrip took: 103
    Status: Success
```

Discussion

Ping uses an Internet Control Message Protocol (ICMP) echo request message as
defined in RFC 792. If a computer is not reached successfully by the ping request, it

---

does not necessarily mean that the computer is unreachable. Many factors can prevent a ping from succeeding aside from the machine being offline. Network topology, firewalls, packet filters, and proxy servers all can interrupt the normal flow of a ping request. By default, the Windows Firewall installed with Windows XP Service Pack 2 disables ICMP traffic, so if you are having difficulty pinging a machine running XP, check the firewall settings on that machine.

See Also

See the "Ping Class," "PingReply Class," and "PingCompleted Event" topics in the MSDN documentation.

16.7   Send SMTP Mail Using the SMTP Service

Problem

You want to be able to send email via SMTP from your program, but you don't want to learn the SMTP protocol and hand-code a class to implement it.

Solution

Use the System.Net.Mail namespace, which contains classes to take care of the harder parts of constructing an SMTP-based email message. The System.Net.Mail. MailMessage class encapsulates constructing an SMTP-based message, and the System.Net.Mail.SmtpClient class provides the sending mechanism for sending the message to an SMTP server. SmtpClient does depend on there being an SMTP server set up somewhere for it to relay messages through. Attachments are added by creating instances of System.Net.Mail.Attachment and providing the path to the file as well as the media type.

```
// Send a message with attachments.
string from = "hilyard@comcast.net";
string to = "hilyard@comcast.net";
MailMessage attachmentMessage = new MailMessage(from, to);
attachmentMessage.Subject = "Hi there!";
attachmentMessage.Body = "Check out this cool code!";
// Many systems filter out HTML mail that is relayed.
attachmentMessage.IsBodyHtml = false;
// Set up the attachment.
string pathToCode = @"..\..\16_Networking.cs";
Attachment attachment =
    new Attachment(pathToCode,
        MediaTypeNames.Application.Octet);
attachmentMessage.Attachments.Add(attachment);
```

To send a simple email with no attachments, call the `System.Net.Mail.MailMessage` constructor with just the to, from, subject, and body information. This version of the `MailMessage` constructor simply fills in those items and then you can pass it to `SmtpClient.Send` to send it along.

```
// Bounce this off the local SMTP service. The local SMTP service needs to
// have relaying set up to go through a real email server...
// This could also set up to go against an SMTP server available to
// you on the network.
SmtpClient client = new SmtpClient("localhost");
client.Send(attachmentMessage);


// Or just send text.
MailMessage textMessage = new MailMessage("hilyard@comcast.net",
                    "hilyard@comcast.net",
                    "Me again",
                    "You need therapy, talking to yourself is one thing but " +
                    "writing code to send email is a whole other thing...");
client.Send(textMessage);
```

Discussion

SMTP stands for the Simple Mail Transfer Protocol, defined in RFC 821. To take advantage of the support for SMTP mail in the .NET Framework using the `System.Net.Mail.SmtpClient` class, an SMTP server must be specified to relay the messages through. Since Windows 2000, the operating system has come with an SMTP server that can be installed as part of IIS. In the Solution, the `SmtpClient` takes advantage of this by specifying `"localhost"` for the server to connect to, which indicates the local machine is the SMTP relay server. Setting up the SMTP service may not be possible in your network environment and you may need to use the `SmtpClient` class to set up credentials to connect to the SMTP server on the network directly.

To set up SMTP relaying after installing the SMTP service via Add/Remove Windows Components in the Control Panel, open the Internet Information Services applet and right-click on the Default SMTP Virtual Server entry. Next, choose Properties. When you select the Delivery tab, you will see the dialog shown in Figure 16-1.

Now click the Advanced button to display the Advanced Delivery dialog that you will use to set the relay parameters, as shown in Figure 16-2.

Supply your domain name and the SMTP address for a valid SMTP host, then email away. Once you have the SMTP service set up, you should configure it to respond to requests from only the local machine, or you could become a target for spammers. To do this, go to the Access tab of the Default SMTP Virtual Server Properties dialog, shown in Figure 16-3, and select Connection.

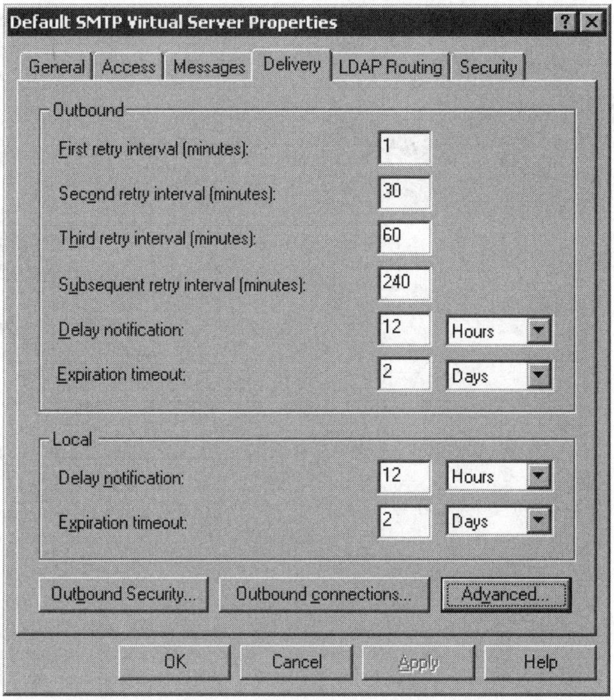

Figure 16-1. Configuring SMTP relaying

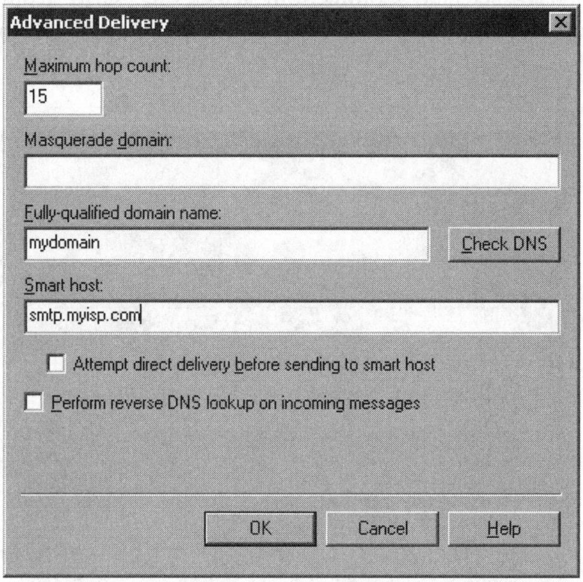

Figure 16-2. SMTP relaying, Advanced Delivery options

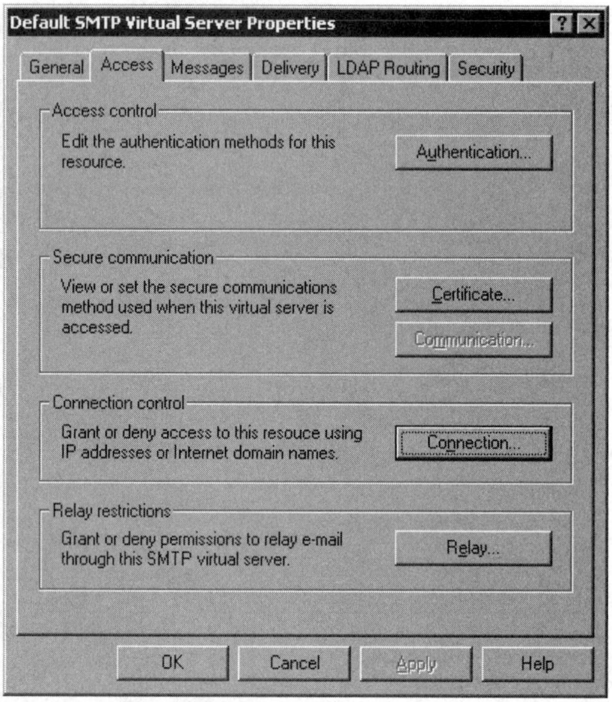

Figure 16-3. Setting the SMTP server properties

Then once you have selected Connection, select the "Only from the list below" option in the Connection dialog, shown in Figure 16-4, and click the Add button to add an IP address.

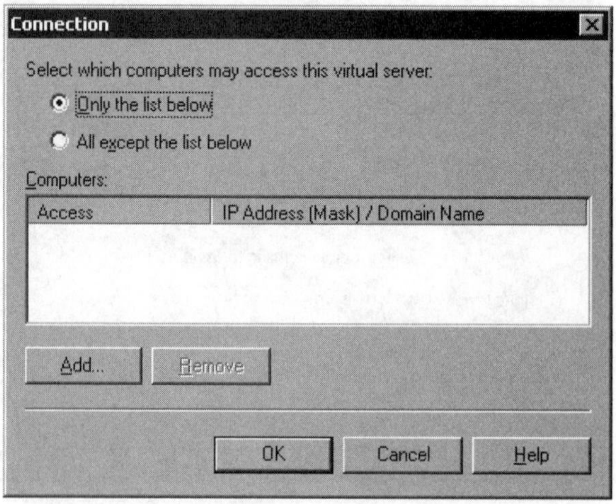

Figure 16-4. Allowing an IP address to access the SMTP server

Finally, enter the IP address 127.0.0.1 to give access to only this machine, as shown in Figure 16-5.

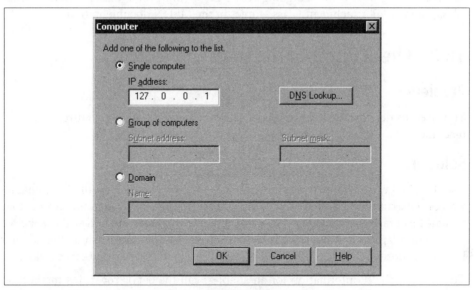

Figure 16-5. Allowing access to local machine (IP address 127.0.0.1)

You list will now look like Figure 16-6.

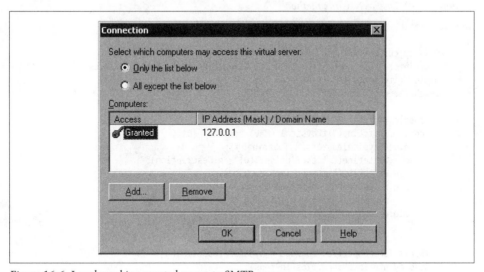

Figure 16-6. Local machine granted access to SMTP server

See Also

See the "Using SMTP for Outgoing Messages," "SmtpMail Class," "MailMessage Class," and "MailAttachment Class" topics in the MSDN documentation.

16.8   Check Out Your Network Connectivity

Problem

You need to determine the characteristics of the network adapters currently on the machine.

Solution

Use the `DisplayNICInfo` method shown in Example 16-9 to display all of the characteristics of the currently existing network adapters using the `System.Net.NetworkInformation.NetworkInterface` class. Calling the `GetAllNetworkInterfaces` method will get the list of current adapters as `NetworkInterface` instances. Information such as the adapter ID, MAC address, status, and NIC type is available on the `NetworkInterface` class.

To see all of the IP information for an adapter, call the `GetIPProperties` method on the `NetworkAdapter` instance and pass the `IPInterfaceProperties` collection to the `DisplayInterfaceProperties` method (implemented shortly).

Example 16-9. DisplayNICInfo method

```
private static void DisplayNICInfo( )
{
    //Display current network adapter states
    NetworkInterface[] adapters = NetworkInterface.GetAllNetworkInterfaces( );
    Console.WriteLine("Network Adapter Information:");
    foreach (NetworkInterface n in adapters)
    {
        Console.WriteLine("\tId: {0}", n.Id);
        Console.WriteLine("\tPhysical (MAC) Address: {0}",
            n.GetPhysicalAddress( ).ToString( ));
        Console.WriteLine("\tDescription: {0}", n.Description);
        Console.WriteLine("\tName: {0}", n.Name);
        Console.WriteLine("\tOperationalStatus: {0}",
                n.OperationalStatus.ToString( ));
        Console.WriteLine("\tInterface type: {0}",
                n.NetworkInterfaceType.ToString( ));
        Console.WriteLine("\tSpeed: {0}", n.Speed);
        IPInterfaceProperties ipProps = n.GetIPProperties( );
        DisplayInterfaceProperties(ipProps);

    }
    Console.WriteLine("");
}
```

The DisplayInterfaceProperties method shown in Example 16-10 breaks down and displays all of the IP configuration information, such as DHCP and WINS addresses, gateway and DNS addresses, assigned IP addresses for the adapter, as well as multicast and unicast information.

Example 16-10. DisplayInterfaceProperties method

```
private static void DisplayInterfaceProperties(IPInterfaceProperties props)
{
    Console.WriteLine("\t\tDns Suffix : {0}", props.DnsSuffix);
    Console.WriteLine("\t\tAnycast Addresses:");
    foreach (IPAddressInformation ipInfo in props.AnycastAddresses)
    {
        Console.WriteLine("\t\t\t{0}", ipInfo.Address.ToString( ));
        Console.WriteLine("\t\t\tIsDnsEligible: {0}", ipInfo.IsDnsEligible);
        Console.WriteLine("\t\t\tIsTransient: {0}", ipInfo.IsTransient);
    }

    Console.WriteLine("\t\tDHCP Server Addresses:");
    foreach (IPAddress ipAddr in props.DhcpServerAddresses)
    {
        Console.WriteLine("\t\t\t{0}", ipAddr.ToString( ));
    }

    Console.WriteLine("\t\tDNS Addresses:");
    foreach (IPAddress ipAddr in props.DnsAddresses)
    {
        Console.WriteLine("\t\t\t{0}", ipAddr.ToString( ));
    }

    Console.WriteLine("\t\tGateway Addresses:");
    foreach (GatewayIPAddressInformation gatewayIPInfo in props.GatewayAddresses)
    {
        Console.WriteLine("\t\t\t{0}", gatewayIPInfo.Address.ToString( ));
    }

    Console.WriteLine("\t\tUnicast Addresses:");
    foreach (UnicastIPAddressInformation uniIPInfo in props.UnicastAddresses)
    {
        Console.WriteLine("\t\t\tAddress: {0}",
                uniIPInfo.Address.ToString( ));
        Console.WriteLine("\t\t\tPreferred Lifetime: {0}",
                uniIPInfo.AddressPreferredLifetime);
        Console.WriteLine("\t\t\tValid Lifetime: {0}",
                uniIPInfo.AddressValidLifetime);
        Console.WriteLine("\t\t\tDHCP Lease Lifetime: {0}",
                uniIPInfo.DhcpLeaseLifetime);
        Console.WriteLine("\t\t\tPrefix Origin: {0}",
                uniIPInfo.PrefixOrigin.ToString( ));
        Console.WriteLine("\t\t\tSuffix Origin: {0}",
                uniIPInfo.SuffixOrigin.ToString( ));
    }
```

Example 16-10. DisplayInterfaceProperties method (continued)

```
Console.WriteLine("\t\tMulticast Addresses:");
foreach (MulticastIPAddressInformation multiIPInfo in props.MulticastAddresses)
{
    Console.WriteLine("\t\t\tAddress: {0}", multiIPInfo.Address.ToString());
    Console.WriteLine("\t\t\tPreferred Lifetime: {0}",
                multiIPInfo.AddressPreferredLifetime);
    Console.WriteLine("\t\t\tValid Lifetime: {0}",
                multiIPInfo.AddressValidLifetime);
    Console.WriteLine("\t\t\tDHCP Lease Lifetime: {0}",
                multiIPInfo.DhcpLeaseLifetime);
    Console.WriteLine("\t\t\tPrefix Origin: {0}",
                multiIPInfo.PrefixOrigin.ToString());
    Console.WriteLine("\t\t\tSuffix Origin: {0}",
                multiIPInfo.SuffixOrigin.ToString());
}

Console.WriteLine("\t\tWINS Server Addresses:");
foreach (IPAddress ipAddr in props.WinsServersAddresses)
{
    Console.WriteLine("\t\t\t{0}", ipAddr.ToString());
}
Console.WriteLine("");

}
```

The .NET runtime also provides event notifications when the network address changes
for an adapter or the network availability state changes, through the NetworkChange.
NetworkAddressChanged and NetworkChange.NetworkAvailabilityChanged events. In the
TestNetInfo method, you hook up for these events, then handle them in the
NetworkChange_NetworkAddressChanged and NetworkChange_NetworkAvailability-
Changed methods. When the availability event fires, the NetworkAvailabilityEventArgs
object can be accessed to see if the network is available through the IsAvailable property. The network address event does not supply information about what address
changed, so you simply call DisplayNICInfo again.

```
public static void TestNetInfo()
{
    // Hook up for network events.
    NetworkChange.NetworkAddressChanged += new
NetworkAddressChangedEventHandler(NetworkChange_NetworkAddressChanged);

    NetworkChange.NetworkAvailabilityChanged += new
NetworkAvailabilityChangedEventHandler(NetworkChange_NetworkAvailabilityChanged);

    DisplayNICInfo();
}

static void NetworkChange_NetworkAddressChanged(object sender, EventArgs e)
{
    // A network address changed; redisplay the info.
    Console.WriteLine("*** NEW NETWORK INFORMATION IS AVAILABLE *** ");
```

```
        DisplayNICInfo( );
    }

    static void NetworkChange_NetworkAvailabilityChanged(object sender,
        NetworkAvailabilityEventArgs e)
    {
        if(e.IsAvailable)
            Console.WriteLine("Network is now available");
        else
            Console.WriteLine("Network is no longer available");
    }
```

The output is shown here:

```
Network Adapter Information:
    Id: {XXXXXXXX-XXXX-XXXX-XXXX-XXXXXXXXXXXX}
    Physical (MAC) Address: XXXXXXXXXXXX
    Description: Broadcom NetXtreme 57xx Gigabit Controller - Packet Scheduler
Miniport
    Name: Local Area Connection
    OperationalStatus: Up
    Interface type: Ethernet
    Speed: 100000000
        Dns Suffix :
        Anycast Addresses:
        DHCP Server Addresses:
            255.0.0.1
        DNS Addresses:
            255.0.0.1
        Gateway Addresses:
            255.0.0.1
        Unicast Addresses:
            Address: 255.0.0.101
            Preferred Lifetime: 52434
            Valid Lifetime: 52434
            DHCP Lease Lifetime: 52434
            Prefix Origin: Dhcp
            Suffix Origin: OriginDhcp
        Multicast Addresses:
            Address: 224.0.0.1
            Preferred Lifetime: 0
            Valid Lifetime: 0
            DHCP Lease Lifetime: 24
            Prefix Origin: 48
            Suffix Origin: WellKnown
            Address: 255.255.255.250
            Preferred Lifetime: 0
            Valid Lifetime: 0
            DHCP Lease Lifetime: 24
            Prefix Origin: Other
            Suffix Origin: WellKnown
        WINS Server Addresses:
            0.0.0.0
            0.0.0.0
```

```
       Id: MS TCP Loopback interface
       Physical (MAC) Address:
       Description: MS TCP Loopback interface
       Name: MS TCP Loopback interface
       OperationalStatus: Up
       Interface type: Loopback
       Speed: 10000000
           Dns Suffix :
           Anycast Addresses:
           DHCP Server Addresses:
           DNS Addresses:
           Gateway Addresses:
           Unicast Addresses:
               Address: 127.0.0.1
               Preferred Lifetime: 3170812643
               Valid Lifetime: 3170812643
               DHCP Lease Lifetime: 3170812643
               Prefix Origin: Manual
               Suffix Origin: Manual
           Multicast Addresses:
               Address: 224.0.0.1
               Preferred Lifetime: 0
               Valid Lifetime: 0
               DHCP Lease Lifetime: 7733284
               Prefix Origin: 110
               Suffix Origin: WellKnown
           WINS Server Addresses:
```

Discussion

Knowing the configuration of the network you are running on can come in handy when attempting to troubleshoot connectivity issues. Being able to get an event notification when connectivity is lost or an adapter changes its IP address is a great benefit, as it allows you to write code that can recover gracefully and instruct the user what has happened. However you want to use it, there is a lot of valuable information provided in the NetworkInformation namespace that can make life a bit better for developers working in a connected environment.

See Also

See the "System.Net.NetworkInformation Namespace," "Network Interface Class," and "IPInterfaceProperties Class" topics in the MSDN documentation.

16.9   Use Sockets to Scan the Ports on a Machine

Problem

You want to determine the open ports on a machine to see where the security risks are.

Solution

Use the CheapoPortScanner class constructed for your use; its code is shown in Example 16-11. CheapoPortScanner uses the Socket class to attempt to open a socket and connect to an address on a given port. The OpenPortFound event is available for a callback when an open port is found in the range supplied to the CheapoPortScanner constructor or in the default range (1 to 65535). By default, CheapoPortScanner will scan the local machine.

Example 16-11. CheapoPortScanner class

```
class CheapoPortScanner
{
    #region Private consts and members
    const int PORT_MIN_VALUE = 1;
    const int PORT_MAX_VALUE = 65535;

    private int _minPort = PORT_MIN_VALUE;
    private int _maxPort = PORT_MAX_VALUE;
    private List<int> _openPorts = null;
    private List<int> _closedPorts = null;
    private string _host = "127.0.0.1"; // localhost
    #endregion

    #region Event
    public class OpenPortEventArgs : EventArgs
    {
        int _portNum;
        public OpenPortEventArgs(int portNum) : base()
        {
            _portNum = portNum;
        }

        public int PortNum
        {
         get { return _portNum; }
        }
    }

    public delegate void OpenPortFoundEventHandler(object sender, OpenPortEventArgs args);
    public event OpenPortFoundEventHandler OpenPortFound;
    #endregion // Event

    #region CTORs & Init code
    public CheapoPortScanner()
    {
        // Defaults are already set for ports and localhost.
        SetupLists();
    }

    public CheapoPortScanner(string host, int minPort, int maxPort)
    {
        if (minPort > maxPort)
```

Example 16-11. CheapoPortScanner class (continued)

```
        throw new
            ArgumentException("Min port cannot be greater than max port");
    if (minPort < PORT_MIN_VALUE || minPort > PORT_MAX_VALUE)
        throw new ArgumentOutOfRangeException("Min port cannot be less than "+
                    PORT_MIN_VALUE + " or greater than " + PORT_MAX_VALUE);
    if (maxPort < PORT_MIN_VALUE || maxPort > PORT_MAX_VALUE)
        throw new ArgumentOutOfRangeException("Max port cannot be less than "+
                    PORT_MIN_VALUE + " or greater than " + PORT_MAX_VALUE);

    _host = host;
    _minPort = minPort;
    _maxPort = maxPort;
    SetupLists();
}

private void SetupLists()
{
    // Set up lists with capacity to hold half of range.
    // Since we can't know how many ports are going to be open,
    // we compromise and allocate enough for half.

    // rangeCount is max - min + 1
    int rangeCount = (_maxPort - _minPort) + 1;

    // If there are an odd number, bump by one to get one extra slot.
    if (rangeCount % 2 != 0)
        rangeCount += 1;

    // Reserve half the ports in the range for each.
    _openPorts = new List<int>(rangeCount / 2);
    _closedPorts = new List<int>(rangeCount / 2);
}
#endregion // CTORs & Init code
```

There are two properties on CheapoPortScanner that bear mentioning. The OpenPorts
and ClosedPorts properties return a ReadOnlyCollection of type int that is a list of the
ports that are open and closed, respectively. Their code is shown in Example 16-12.

Example 16-12. OpenPorts and ClosedPorts properties

```
#region Properties
public ReadOnlyCollection<int> OpenPorts
{
    get { return new ReadOnlyCollection<int>(_openPorts); }
}

public ReadOnlyCollection<int> ClosedPorts
{
    get { return new ReadOnlyCollection<int>(_closedPorts); }
}
#endregion // Properties
```

Example 16-12. OpenPorts and ClosedPorts properties (continued)

```
#region Private Methods
private void CheckPort(int port)
{
    if (IsPortOpen(port))
    {
        // If we got here it is open.
        _openPorts.Add(port);

        // Notify anyone paying attention.
        OpenPortFoundEventHandler openPortFound = OpenPortFound;
        if (openPortFound != null)
            openPortFound(this, new OpenPortEventArgs(port));
    }
    else
    {
        // Server doesn't have that port open.
        _closedPorts.Add(port);
    }
}

private bool IsPortOpen(int port)
{
    Socket sock = null;
    try
    {
        // Make a TCP-based socket.
        sock = new Socket(AddressFamily.InterNetwork,
                        SocketType.Stream,
                        ProtocolType.Tcp);
        // Connect.
        sock.Connect(_host, port);
        return true;

    }
    catch (SocketException se)
    {
        if (se.SocketErrorCode == SocketError.ConnectionRefused)
        {
            return false;
        }
        else
        {
            // An error occurred when attempting to access the socket.
            Debug.WriteLine(se.ToString());
            Console.WriteLine(se.ToString());
        }
    }
    finally
    {
        if (sock != null)
        {
            if (sock.Connected)
```

Example 16-12. OpenPorts and ClosedPorts properties (continued)

```
                    sock.Disconnect(false);
                sock.Close( );
            }
        }
        return false;
    }
    #endregion
```

The trigger method for the CheapoPortScanner is Scan. Scan will check all of the ports
in the range specified in the constructor. The ReportToConsole method will dump the
pertinent information about the last scan to the console output stream:

```
#region Public Methods
public void Scan( )
{
    for (int port = _minPort; port <= _maxPort; port++)
    {
        CheckPort(port);
    }
}

public void ReportToConsole( )
{
    Console.WriteLine("Port Scan for host at {0}:", _host.ToString( ));
    Console.WriteLine("\tStarting Port: {0}; Ending Port: {1}",
                        _minPort, _maxPort);
    Console.WriteLine("\tOpen ports:");
    foreach (int port in _openPorts)
    {
        Console.WriteLine("\t\tPort {0}", port);
    }
    Console.WriteLine("\tClosed ports:");
    foreach (int port in _closedPorts)
    {
        Console.WriteLine("\t\tPort {0}", port);
    }
}

#endregion // Public Methods
```

The PortScan method demonstrates how to use CheapoPortScanner by scanning ports
1–30 on the local machine. It first subscribes to the OpenPortFound event. The handler method for this event, cps_OpenPortFound, writes out the number of any port
found open. Next, PortScan calls the Scan method. Finally, it calls ReportToConsole to
show the full results of the scan, including the closed ports as well as the open ones.

```
public static void PortScan ( )
{
    // Do a specific range.
    Console.WriteLine("Checking ports 1-30 on localhost...");
    CheapoPortScanner cps = new CheapoPortScanner("127.0.0.1",1,30);
    cps.OpenPortFound +=
```

```
        new CheapoPortScanner.OpenPortFoundEventHandler(cps_OpenPortFound);
    cps.Scan();
    Console.WriteLine("Found {0} ports open and {1} ports closed",
            cps.OpenPorts.Count, cps.ClosedPorts.Count);

    // Do the local machine, whole port range 1-65535.
    cps = new CheapoPortScanner();
    cps.Scan();
    cps.ReportToConsole();
}

static void cps_OpenPortFound(object sender, CheapoPortScanner.OpenPortEventArgs
args)
{
    Console.WriteLine("OpenPortFound reported port {0} was open",args.PPortNumP);
}
```

The output for the port scanner as shown appears here:

```
Checking ports 1-30 on localhost...
OpenPortFound reported port 22 was open
OpenPortFound reported port 26 was open
Found 2 ports open and 28 ports closed
```

Discussion

Open ports on a machine are significant because they indicate the presence of a program listening on those ports. Hackers look for "open" ports as ways to enter your systems without permission. CheapoPortScanner is an admittedly rudimentary mechanism for checking for open ports, but it demonstrates the principle well enough to provide a good starting point.

 If you run this on a corporate network, you may quickly get a visit from your network administrator, as you may set off alarms in some intrusion-detection systems. Be judicious in your use of this code.

See Also

See the "Socket Class" and "Sockets" topics in the MSDN documentation.

16.10 Use the Current Internet Connection Settings

Problem

Your program wants to use the current Internet connection settings without forcing the user to add them to your application manually.

Solution

Read the current Internet connectivity settings with the InternetSettingsReader class provided for you in Example 16-13. InternetSettingsReader calls some methods of the WinINet API via P/Invoke to retrieve current Internet connection information. The majority of the work is done in setting up the structures that WinINet uses and then marshaling the structure pointers correctly to retrieve the values.

Example 16-13. InternetSettingsReader class

```csharp
public class InternetSettingsReader
{
    #region WinInet structures
    [StructLayout(LayoutKind.Sequential, CharSet = CharSet.Auto)]
    public struct InternetPerConnOptionList
    {
        public int dwSize; // size of the INTERNET_PER_CONN_OPTION_LIST struct
        public IntPtr szConnection;    // Connection name to set/query options
        public int dwOptionCount;    // Number of options to set/query
        public int dwOptionError;        // On error, which option failed
        public IntPtr options;
    };

    [StructLayout(LayoutKind.Sequential, CharSet = CharSet.Auto)]
    public struct InternetConnectionOption
    {
        static readonly int Size;
        public PerConnOption m_Option;
        public InternetConnectionOptionValue m_Value;
        static InternetConnectionOption( )
        {
            InternetConnectionOption.Size =
              Marshal.SizeOf(typeof(InternetConnectionOption));
        }

        // Nested Types
        [StructLayout(LayoutKind.Explicit)]
        public struct InternetConnectionOptionValue
        {
            // Fields
            [FieldOffset(0)]
            public System.Runtime.InteropServices.ComTypes.FILETIME m_FileTime;
            [FieldOffset(0)]
            public int m_Int;
            [FieldOffset(0)]
            public IntPtr m_StringPtr;
        }
    }
    #endregion

    #region WinInet enums
```

Example 16-13. InternetSettingsReader class (continued)

```csharp
// Options used in INTERNET_PER_CONN_OPTON struct
//
public enum PerConnOption
{
// Sets or retrieves the connection type. The Value member will contain one
// or more of the values from PerConnFlags.
        INTERNET_PER_CONN_FLAGS = 1,
// Sets or retrieves a string containing the proxy servers.
    INTERNET_PER_CONN_PROXY_SERVER = 2,
// Sets or retrieves a string containing the URLs that do not use the
// proxy server.
        INTERNET_PER_CONN_PROXY_BYPASS = 3,
// Sets or retrieves a string containing the URL to the automatic
// configuration script.
    INTERNET_PER_CONN_AUTOCONFIG_URL = 4,
}


//
// PER_CONN_FLAGS
//
[Flags]
public enum PerConnFlags
{
    PROXY_TYPE_DIRECT = 0x00000001,  // Direct to net
    PROXY_TYPE_PROXY = 0x00000002,   // Via named proxy
    PROXY_TYPE_AUTO_PROXY_URL = 0x00000004,  // Autoproxy URL
    PROXY_TYPE_AUTO_DETECT = 0x00000008    // Use autoproxy detection.
}


#region P/Invoke defs
[DllImport("WinInet.dll", EntryPoint = "InternetQueryOption",
    SetLastError = true)]

public static extern bool InternetQueryOption(
    IntPtr hInternet,
    int dwOption,
    ref InternetPerConnOptionList optionsList,
    ref int bufferLength
    );
#endregion

#region Private Members
string _proxyAddr = "";
int _proxyPort = -1;
bool _bypassLocal = false;
string _autoConfigAddr = "";
string[] _proxyExceptions = null;
PerConnFlags _flags;
#endregion
```

Example 16-13. InternetSettingsReader class (continued)

```
#region CTOR
public InternetSettingsReader( )
{
}
#endregion
```

Each of the properties of InternetSettingsReader shown in Example 16-14 call into the GetInternetConnectionOption method, which returns an InternetConnectionOption. The InternetConnectionOption structure holds all of the pertinent data for the value being returned, and that value is then retrieved based on what type of value was asked for by the specific properties.

Example 16-14. InternetSettingsReader properties

```
#region Properties
public string ProxyAddr
{
    get
    {
        InternetConnectionOption ico =
            GetInternetConnectionOption(
                PerConnOption.INTERNET_PER_CONN_PROXY_SERVER);
        // Parse out the addr and port.
        string proxyInfo = Marshal.PtrToStringUni(
                            ico.m_Value.m_StringPtr);
        ParseProxyInfo(proxyInfo);
        return _proxyAddr;
    }
}
public int ProxyPort
{
    get
    {
        InternetConnectionOption ico =
            GetInternetConnectionOption(
                PerConnOption.INTERNET_PER_CONN_PROXY_SERVER);
        // Parse out the addr and port.
        string proxyInfo = Marshal.PtrToStringUni(
                            ico.m_Value.m_StringPtr);
        ParseProxyInfo(proxyInfo);
        return _proxyPort;
    }
}
public bool BypassLocalAddresses
{
    get
    {
        InternetConnectionOption ico =
            GetInternetConnectionOption(
                PerConnOption.INTERNET_PER_CONN_PROXY_BYPASS);
        // Bypass is listed as <local> in the exceptions list.
```

Example 16-14. InternetSettingsReader properties (continued)

```
            string exceptions =
                Marshal.PtrToStringUni(ico.m_Value.m_StringPtr);

            if (exceptions.IndexOf("<local>") != -1)
                _bypassLocal = true;
            else
                _bypassLocal = false;
            return _bypassLocal;
        }
    }
    public string AutoConfigurationAddr
    {
        get
        {
            InternetConnectionOption ico =
                GetInternetConnectionOption(
                    PerConnOption.INTERNET_PER_CONN_AUTOCONFIG_URL);
            // Get these straight.
            _autoConfigAddr =
                Marshal.PtrToStringUni(ico.m_Value.m_StringPtr);
            if (_autoConfigAddr == null)
                _autoConfigAddr = "";
            return _autoConfigAddr;
        }
    }
    public string[] ProxyExceptions
    {
        get
        {
            InternetConnectionOption ico =
                GetInternetConnectionOption(
                    PerConnOption.INTERNET_PER_CONN_PROXY_BYPASS);
            // Exceptions are separated by semicolon.
            string exceptions =
                Marshal.PtrToStringUni(ico.m_Value.m_StringPtr);
            if (!string.IsNullOrEmpty(exceptions))
            {
                _proxyExceptions = exceptions.Split(';');
            }
            return _proxyExceptions;
        }
    }
    public PerConnFlags ConnectionType
    {
        get
        {
            InternetConnectionOption ico =
                GetInternetConnectionOption(
                    PerConnOption.INTERNET_PER_CONN_FLAGS);
            _flags = (PerConnFlags)ico.m_Value.m_Int;
```

Example 16-14. InternetSettingsReader properties (continued)

```
        return _flags;
    }
}

#endregion
private void ParseProxyInfo(string proxyInfo)
{
    if(!string.IsNullOrEmpty(proxyInfo))
    {
        string [] parts = proxyInfo.Split(':');
        if (parts.Length == 2)
        {
            _proxyAddr = parts[0];
            try
            {
                _proxyPort = Convert.ToInt32(parts[1]);
            }
            catch (FormatException)
            {
                // No port
                _proxyPort = -1;
            }
        }
        else
        {
            _proxyAddr = parts[0];
            _proxyPort = -1;
        }
    }
}
```

The GetInternetConnectionOption method shown in Example 16-15 does the heavy lifting as far as communicating with WinINet. First an InternetPerConnOptionList is created as well as an InternetConnectionOption structure to hold the returned value. The InternetConnectionOption structure is then pinned so that the garbage collector does not move the structure in memory and the PerConnOption value is assigned to determine what Internet option to retrieve. The InternetPerConnOptionList is initialized to hold the option values and then the WinINet function IntrenetQueryOption is called. The InternetConnectionOption is filled using the Marshal.PtrToStructure method and returned with the value.

Example 16-15. GetInternetConnectionOption method

```
private InternetConnectionOption GetInternetConnectionOption(PerConnOption pco)
{
    // Allocate the list and option.
    InternetPerConnOptionList perConnOptList = new InternetPerConnOptionList();
    InternetConnectionOption ico = new InternetConnectionOption();
    // Pin the option structure.
    GCHandle gch = GCHandle.Alloc(ico, GCHandleType.Pinned);
```

Example 16-15. GetInternetConnectionOption method (continued)

```
        // Initialize the option for the data we want.
        ico.m_Option = pco;
        //Initialize the option list for the default connection or LAN
        int listSize = Marshal.SizeOf(perConnOptList);
        perConnOptList.dwSize = listSize;
        perConnOptList.szConnection = IntPtr.Zero;
        perConnOptList.dwOptionCount = 1;
        perConnOptList.dwOptionError = 0;
        // Figure out sizes and offsets.
        int icoSize = Marshal.SizeOf(ico);
        int optionTotalSize = icoSize;
        // Alloc enough memory for the option.
        perConnOptList.options =
            Marshal.AllocCoTaskMem(icoSize);

        long icoOffset = (long)perConnOptList.options + (long)icoSize;
        // Make pointer from the structure.
        IntPtr optionListPtr = perConnOptList.options;
        Marshal.StructureToPtr(ico, optionListPtr, false);

        // Make the query.
        if (InternetQueryOption(
            IntPtr.Zero,
            75, //(int)InternetOption.INTERNET_OPTION_PER_CONNECTION_OPTION,
            ref perConnOptList,
            ref listSize) == true)
        {
            // Retrieve the value.
            ico =
(InternetConnectionOption)Marshal.PtrToStructure(perConnOptList.options,
                               typeof(InternetConnectionOption));
        }
        // Free the COM memory.
        Marshal.FreeCoTaskMem(perConnOptList.options);

        // Unpin the structs.
        gch.Free();

        return ico;
    }
```

Using the `InternetSettingsReader` is demonstrated in the `GetInternetSettings` method shown in Example 16-16. The proxy information is retrieved and displayed to the console here, but could easily be stored in another program for use as proxy information when connecting. See Recipe 14.7 for details on setting up the proxy information for a `WebRequest`.

Example 16-16. Using the InternetSettingsReader

```
public static void GetInternetSettings()
{
    InternetSettingsReader isr = new InternetSettingsReader();
    Console.WriteLine("Current Proxy Address: {0}",isr.ProxyAddr);
```

Example 16-16. Using the InternetSettingsReader (continued)

```
        Console.WriteLine("Current Proxy Port: {0}",isr.ProxyPort);
        Console.WriteLine("Current ByPass Local Address setting: {0}",
                            isr.BypassLocalAddresses);
        Console.WriteLine("Exception addresses for proxy (bypass):");
        if(isr.ProxyExceptions != null)
        {
            foreach(string addr in isr.ProxyExceptions)
            {
                Console.WriteLine("\t{0}",addr);
            }
        }
        Console.WriteLine("Proxy connection type: {0}",isr.ConnectionType.ToString());
}
```

Output for the Solution:

```
Current Proxy Address: CORPORATEPROXY
Current Proxy Port: 8080
Current ByPass Local Address setting: True
Exception addresses for proxy (bypass):
    corporate.com
    <local>
Proxy connection type: PROXY_TYPE_DIRECT, PROXY_TYPE_PROXY
```

Discussion

The WinInet Windows Internet (WinInet) API is the unmanaged API for interacting with the FTP, HTTP, and Gopher protocols. This API can be used fill in where managed code leaves off, such as with the Internet configuration settings shown in the Solution. It can also be used for downloading files, working with cookies, and participating in Gopher sessions. You need to understand that WinInet is meant to be a client-side API and is not suited for server-side or service applications; issues could arise in your application from improper usage.

There is a huge amount of information available to the C# programmer directly through the FCLFramework class FCLibrary, but at times you still need to roll up your sleeves and talk to the Win32 API. Even in situations in which restricted privileges are the norm, it is not always out of bounds to create a small assembly that needs enhanced access to do P/Invoke. It can have its access locked down so as not to become a risk to the system.

See Also

See the "InternetQueryOption Function [WinInet]" topic in the MSDN documentation.

16.11 Download a File Using FTP

Problem

You want to programmatically download files using the File Transfer Protocol (FTP).

Solution

Use the `System.Net.FtpWebRequest` class to download the files. `FtpWebRequests` are created from the `WebRequest` class `Create` method by specifying the URI for the FTP download. In the example that follows, the source code from the first edition of the *C# Cookbook* is the target for the download. A `FileStream` is opened for the target and then is wrapped by a `BinaryWriter`. A `BinaryReader` is created with the response stream from the `FtpWebRequest`. Then the stream is read and the target is written until the entire file has been downloaded. This series of operations is demonstrated in Example 16-17.

Example 16-17. Using the System.Net.FtpWebRequest class

```
// Go get the same code from edition 1.
FtpWebRequest request =
    (FtpWebRequest)WebRequest.Create(
    "ftp://ftp.oreilly.com/pub/examples/csharpckbk/CSharpCookbook.zip");

request.Credentials = new NetworkCredential("anonymous", "hilyard@oreilly.com");
using (FtpWebResponse response = (FtpWebResponse)request.GetResponse( ))
{
    Stream data = response.GetResponseStream( );
    string targetPath = "CSharpCookbook.zip";
    if (File.Exists(targetPath))
        File.Delete(targetPath);

    byte[] byteBuffer = new byte[4096];
    using (FileStream output = new FileStream(targetPath, FileMode.CreateNew))
    {
        int bytesRead = 0;
        do
        {
            bytesRead = data.Read(byteBuffer, 0, byteBuffer.Length);
            if (bytesRead > 0)
            {
                output.Write(byteBuffer, 0, bytesRead);
            }
        }
        while (bytesRead > 0);
    }
}
```

Discussion

The File Transfer Protocol (FTP) is defined in RFC 959 and is one of the main ways files are distributed over the Internet. The port number for FTP is usually 21. Happily, you don't have to really know much about how FTP works in order to use it. This could be useful to your applications in automatic download of information from a dedicated FTP site or in providing automatic update capabilities.

See Also

See the "FtpWebRequest Class," "FtpWebResponse Class," "WebRequest Class," and "WebResponse Class" topics in the MSDN documentation.

CHAPTER 17

Security

17.0 Introduction

There are many ways to secure different parts of your application. The security of running code in .NET revolves around the concept of Code Access Security (CAS). CAS determines the trustworthiness of an assembly based upon its origin and the characteristics of the assembly itself, such as its hash value. For example, code installed locally on the machine is more trusted than code downloaded from the Internet. The runtime will also validate an assembly's metadata and type safety before that code is allowed to run.

There are many ways to write secure code and protect data using the .NET Framework. In this chapter, we explore such things as controlling access to types, encryption and decryption, random numbers, securely storing data, and using programmatic and declarative security.

17.1 Controlling Access to Types in a Local Assembly

Problem

You have an existing class that contains sensitive data and you do not want clients to have direct access to any objects of this class. Instead, you want an intermediary object to talk to the clients and to allow access to sensitive data based on the client's credentials. What's more, you would also like to have specific queries and modifications to the sensitive data tracked, so that if an attacker manages to access the object, you will have a log of what the attacker was attempting to do.

Solution

Use the *proxy design pattern* to allow clients to talk directly to a proxy object. This proxy object will act as gatekeeper to the class that contains the sensitive data. To keep malicious users from accessing the class itself, make it private, which will at least keep code without the ReflectionPermissionFlag.TypeInformation access (which is currently given only in fully trusted code scenarios like executing code interactively on a local machine) from getting at it.

The namespaces we will be using are:

```
using System;
using System.IO;
using System.Security;
using System.Security.Permissions;
using System.Security.Principal;
```

Let's start this design by creating an interface, shown in Example 17-1, that will be common to both the proxy objects and the object that contains sensitive data.

Example 17-1. ICompanyData interface

```
internal interface ICompanyData
{
    string AdminUserName
    {
        get;
        set;
    }

    string AdminPwd
    {
        get;
        set;
    }

    string CEOPhoneNumExt
    {
        get;
        set;
    }

    void RefreshData( );
    void SaveNewData( );
}
```

The CompanyData class shown in Example 17-2 is the underlying object that is "expensive" to create.

Example 17-2. CompanyData class

```
internal class CompanyData : ICompanyData
{
    public CompanyData( )
    {
        Console.WriteLine("[CONCRETE] CompanyData Created");
        // Perform expensive initialization here.
    }
```

Example 17-2. CompanyData class (continued)

```
    private string adminUserName = "admin";
    private string adminPwd = "password";
    private string ceoPhoneNumExt = "0000";

    public string AdminUserName
    {
        get {return (adminUserName);}
        set {adminUserName = value;}
    }

    public string AdminPwd
    {
        get {return (adminPwd);}
        set {adminPwd = value;}
    }

    public string CEOPhoneNumExt
    {
        get {return (ceoPhoneNumExt);}
        set {ceoPhoneNumExt = value;}
    }

    public void RefreshData( )
    {
        Console.WriteLine("[CONCRETE] Data Refreshed");
    }

    public void SaveNewData( )
    {
        Console.WriteLine("[CONCRETE] Data Saved");
    }
}
```

The code shown in Example 17-3 for the security proxy class checks the caller's permissions to determine whether the CompanyData object should be created and its methods or properties called.

Example 17-3. CompanyDataSecProxy security proxy class

```
public class CompanyDataSecProxy : ICompanyData
{
    public CompanyDataSecProxy( )
    {
        Console.WriteLine("[SECPROXY] Created");

        // Must set principal policy first.
        AppDomain.CurrentDomain.SetPrincipalPolicy(PrincipalPolicy.
            WindowsPrincipal);
    }

    private ICompanyData coData = null;
    private PrincipalPermission admPerm =
```

Example 17-3. CompanyDataSecProxy security proxy class (continued)

```
        new PrincipalPermission(null, @"BUILTIN\Administrators", true);
    private PrincipalPermission guestPerm =
        new PrincipalPermission(null, @"BUILTIN\Guest", true);
    private PrincipalPermission powerPerm =
        new PrincipalPermission(null, @"BUILTIN\PowerUser", true);
    private PrincipalPermission userPerm =
        new PrincipalPermission(null, @"BUILTIN\User", true);

    public string AdminUserName
    {
        get
        {
            string userName = "";
            try
            {
                admPerm.Demand( );
                Startup( );
                userName = coData.AdminUserName;
            }
            catch(SecurityException e)
            {
                Console.WriteLine("AdminUserName_get failed! {0}",e.ToString( ));
            }
            return (userName);
        }
        set
        {
            try
            {
                admPerm.Demand( );
                Startup( );
                coData.AdminUserName = value;
            }
            catch(SecurityException e)
            {
                Console.WriteLine("AdminUserName_set failed! {0}",e.ToString( ));
            }
        }
    }

    public string AdminPwd
    {
        get
        {
            string pwd = "";
            try
            {
                admPerm.Demand( );
                Startup( );
                pwd = coData.AdminPwd;
            }
            catch(SecurityException e)
```

Example 17-3. CompanyDataSecProxy security proxy class (continued)

```
            {
                Console.WriteLine("AdminPwd_get Failed! {0}",e.ToString( ));
            }

            return (pwd);
        }
        set
        {
            try
            {
                admPerm.Demand( );
                Startup( );
                coData.AdminPwd = value;
            }
            catch(SecurityException e)
            {
                Console.WriteLine("AdminPwd_set Failed! {0}",e.ToString( ));
            }
        }
    }

    public string CEOPhoneNumExt
    {
        get
        {
            string ceoPhoneNum = "";
            try
            {
                admPerm.Union(powerPerm).Demand( );
                Startup( );
                ceoPhoneNum = coData.CEOPhoneNumExt;
            }
            catch(SecurityException e)
            {
                Console.WriteLine("CEOPhoneNum_set Failed! {0}",e.ToString( ));
            }
            return (ceoPhoneNum);
        }
        set
        {
            try
            {
                admPerm.Demand( );
                Startup( );
                coData.CEOPhoneNumExt = value;
            }
            catch(SecurityException e)
            {
                Console.WriteLine("CEOPhoneNum_set Failed! {0}",e.ToString( ));
            }
        }
    }
```

Example 17-3. CompanyDataSecProxy security proxy class (continued)

```
    public void RefreshData( )
    {
        try
        {
            admPerm.Union(powerPerm.Union(userPerm)).Demand( );
            Startup( );
            Console.WriteLine("[SECPROXY] Data Refreshed");
            coData.RefreshData( );
        }
        catch(SecurityException e)
        {
            Console.WriteLine("RefreshData Failed! {0}",e.ToString( ));
        }
    }

    public void SaveNewData( )
    {
        try
        {
            admPerm.Union(powerPerm).Demand( );
            Startup( );
            Console.WriteLine("[SECPROXY] Data Saved");
            coData.SaveNewData( );
        }
        catch(SecurityException e)
        {
            Console.WriteLine("SaveNewData Failed! {0}",e.ToString( ));
        }
    }

    // DO NOT forget to use [#define DOTRACE] to control the tracing proxy.
    private void Startup( )
    {
        if (coData == null)
        {
#if (DOTRACE)
            coData = new CompanyDataTraceProxy( );
#else
            coData = new CompanyData( );
#endif
            Console.WriteLine("[SECPROXY] Refresh Data");
            coData.RefreshData( );
        }
    }
}
```

When creating the `PrincipalPermissions` as part of the object construction, you are using string representations of the built-in objects ("BUILTIN\Administrators") to set up the principal role. However, the names of these objects may be different depending on the locale the code runs under. It would be appropriate to use the `WindowsAccountType.Administrator` enumeration value to ease localization since this

value is defined to represent the administrator role as well. We used text here to clarify what was being done and also to access the PowerUsers role, which is not available through the WindowsAccountType enumeration.

If the call to the CompanyData object passes through the CompanyDataSecProxy, then the
user has permissions to access the underlying data. Any access to this data may be
logged so the administrator can check for any attempt to hack the CompanyData
object. The code shown in Example 17-4 is the tracing proxy used to log access to
the various method and property access points in the CompanyData object (note that
the CompanyDataSecProxy contains the code to turn this proxy object on or off).

Example 17-4. CompanyDataTraceProxy tracing proxy class

```
public class CompanyDataTraceProxy : ICompanyData
{
    public CompanyDataTraceProxy( )
    {
        Console.WriteLine("[TRACEPROXY] Created");
        string path = Path.GetTempPath( ) + @"\CompanyAccessTraceFile.txt";
        fileStream = new FileStream(path, FileMode.Append,
            FileAccess.Write, FileShare.None);
        traceWriter = new StreamWriter(fileStream);
        coData = new CompanyData( );
    }

    private ICompanyData coData = null;
    private FileStream fileStream = null;
    private StreamWriter traceWriter = null;

    public string AdminPwd
    {
        get
        {
            traceWriter.WriteLine("AdminPwd read by user.");
            traceWriter.Flush( );
            return (coData.AdminPwd);
        }
        set
        {
            traceWriter.WriteLine("AdminPwd written by user.");
            traceWriter.Flush( );
            coData.AdminPwd = value;
        }
    }

    public string AdminUserName
    {
        get
        {
            traceWriter.WriteLine("AdminUserName read by user.");
            traceWriter.Flush( );
            return (coData.AdminUserName);
```

Example 17-4. CompanyDataTraceProxy tracing proxy class (continued)

```
        }
        set
        {
            traceWriter.WriteLine("AdminUserName written by user.");
            traceWriter.Flush( );
            coData.AdminUserName = value;
        }
    }

    public string CEOPhoneNumExt
    {
        get
        {
            traceWriter.WriteLine("CEOPhoneNumExt read by user.");
            traceWriter.Flush( );
            return (coData.CEOPhoneNumExt);
        }
        set
        {
            traceWriter.WriteLine("CEOPhoneNumExt written by user.");
            traceWriter.Flush( );
            coData.CEOPhoneNumExt = value;
        }
    }

    public void RefreshData( )
    {
        Console.WriteLine("[TRACEPROXY] Refresh Data");
        coData.RefreshData( );
    }

    public void SaveNewData( )
    {
        Console.WriteLine("[TRACEPROXY] Save Data");
        coData.SaveNewData( );
    }
}
```

The proxy is used in the following manner:

```
    // Create the security proxy here.
    CompanyDataSecProxy companyDataSecProxy = new CompanyDataSecProxy( );

    // Read some data.
    Console.WriteLine("CEOPhoneNumExt: " + companyDataSecProxy.CEOPhoneNumExt);

    // Write some data.
    companyDataSecProxy.AdminPwd = "asdf";
    companyDataSecProxy.AdminUserName = "asdf";

    // Save and refresh this data.
    companyDataSecProxy.SaveNewData( );
    companyDataSecProxy.RefreshData( );
```

Note that as long as the `CompanyData` object was accessible, you could have also written this to access the object directly:

```
// Instantiate the CompanyData object directly without a proxy.
CompanyData companyData = new CompanyData( );

// Read some data.
Console.WriteLine("CEOPhoneNumExt: " + companyData.CEOPhoneNumExt);

// Write some data.
companyData.AdminPwd = "asdf";
companyData.AdminUserName = "asdf";

// Save and refresh this data.
companyData.SaveNewData( );
companyData.RefreshData( );
```

If these two blocks of code are run, the same fundamental actions occur: data is read, data is written, and data is updated/refreshed. This shows you that your proxy objects are set up correctly and function as they should.

Discussion

The *proxy design pattern* is useful for several tasks. The most notable—in COM, COM+, and .NET remoting—is for marshaling data across boundaries such as AppDomains or even across a network. To the client, a proxy looks and acts exactly the same as its underlying object; fundamentally, the proxy object is just a wrapper around the object.

A proxy can test the security and/or identity permissions of the caller before the underlying object is created or accessed. Proxy objects can also be chained together to form several layers around an underlying object. Each proxy can be added or removed depending on the circumstances.

For the proxy object to look and act the same as its underlying object, both should implement the same interface. The implementation in this recipe uses an ICompanyData interface on both the proxies (CompanyDataSecProxy and CompanyDataTraceProxy) and the underlying object (CompanyData). If more proxies are created, they, too, need to implement this interface.

The CompanyData class represents an expensive object to create. In addition, this class contains a mixture of sensitive and nonsensitive data that requires permission checks to be made before the data is accessed. For this recipe, the CompanyData class simply contains a group of properties to access company data and two methods for updating and refreshing this data. You can replace this class with one of your own and create a corresponding interface that both the class and its proxies implement.

The CompanyDataSecProxy object is the object that a client must interact with. This object is responsible for determining whether the client has the correct privileges to access the method or property that it is calling. The get accessor of the `AdminUserName` property shows the structure of the code throughout most of this class:

```csharp
public string AdminUserName
{
    get
    {
        string userName = "";
        try
        {
            admPerm.Demand( );
            Startup( );
            userName = coData.AdminUserName;
        }
        catch(SecurityException e)
        {
            Console.WriteLine("AdminUserName_get Failed!: {0}",e.ToString( ));
        }
        return (userName);
    }
    set
    {
        try
        {
            admPerm.Demand( );
            Startup( );
            coData.AdminUserName = value;
        }
        catch(SecurityException e)
        {
            Console.WriteLine("AdminUserName_set Failed! {0}",e.ToString( ));
        }
    }
}
```

Initially, a single permission (AdmPerm) is demanded. If this demand fails, a SecurityException, which is handled by the catch clause, is thrown. (Other exceptions will be handed back to the caller.) If the Demand succeeds, the Startup method is called. It is in charge of instantiating either the next proxy object in the chain (CompanyDataTraceProxy) or the underlying CompanyData object. The choice depends on whether the DOTRACE preprocessor symbol has been defined. You may use a different technique, such as a registry key to turn tracing on or off, if you wish.

This proxy class uses the private field coData to hold a reference to an ICompanyData type, which can be either a CompanyDataTraceProxy or the CompanyData object. This reference allows you to chain several proxies together.

The CompanyDataTraceProxy simply logs any access to the CompanyData object's information to a text file. Since this proxy will not attempt to prevent a client from accessing the CompanyData object, the CompanyData object is created and explicitly called in each property and method of this object.

See Also

See *Design Patterns* (Addison-Wesley).

17.2 Encrypting and Decrypting a String

Problem

You have a string you want to be able to encrypt and decrypt—perhaps a password or software key—which will be stored in some form accessible by users, such as in a file, the registry, or even a field, that may be open to attack from malicious code.

Solution

Encrypting the string will prevent users from being able to read and decipher the information. The CryptoString class shown in Example 17-5 contains two static methods to encrypt and decrypt a string and two static properties to retrieve the generated key and inititialization vector (IV—a random number used as a starting point to encrypt data) after encryption has occurred.

Example 17-5. CryptoString class

```
using System;
using System.Security.Cryptography;

public sealed class CryptoString
{
    private CryptoString( ) {}

    private static byte[] savedKey = null;
    private static byte[] savedIV = null;

    public static byte[] Key
    {
     get { return savedKey; }
     set { savedKey = value; }
    }

    public static byte[] IV
    {
     get { return savedIV; }
     set { savedIV = value; }
    }

    private static void RdGenerateSecretKey(RijndaelManaged rdProvider)
    {
        if (savedKey == null)
        {
            rdProvider.KeySize = 256;
            rdProvider.GenerateKey( );
```

Example 17-5. CryptoString class (continued)

```
            savedKey = rdProvider.Key;
        }
    }

    private static void RdGenerateSecretInitVector(RijndaelManaged rdProvider)
    {
        if (savedIV == null)
        {
            rdProvider.GenerateIV( );
            savedIV = rdProvider.IV;
        }
    }

    public static string Encrypt(string originalStr)
    {
        // Encode data string to be stored in memory.
        byte[] originalStrAsBytes = Encoding.ASCII.GetBytes(originalStr);
        byte[] originalBytes = {};

        // Create MemoryStream to contain output.
        using (MemoryStream memStream = new
                MemoryStream(originalStrAsBytes.Length))
        {
            using (RijndaelManaged rijndael = new RijndaelManaged( ))
            {
                // Generate and save secret key and init vector.
                RdGenerateSecretKey(rijndael);
                RdGenerateSecretInitVector(rijndael);

                if (savedKey == null || savedIV == null)
                {
                    throw (new NullReferenceException(
                        "savedKey and savedIV must be non-null."));
                }

                // Create encryptor and stream objects.
                using (ICryptoTransform rdTransform =
                    rijndael.CreateEncryptor((byte[])savedKey.
                    Clone( ),(byte[])savedIV.Clone( )))
                {
                    using (CryptoStream cryptoStream = new CryptoStream(memStream,
                        rdTransform, CryptoStreamMode.Write))
                    {
                        // Write encrypted data to the MemoryStream.
                        cryptoStream.Write(originalStrAsBytes, 0,
                                originalStrAsBytes.Length);
                        cryptoStream.FlushFinalBlock( );
                        originalBytes = memStream.ToArray( );
                    }
                }
            }
        }
```

Example 17-5. CryptoString class (continued)

```
    // Convert encrypted string.
    string encryptedStr = Convert.ToBase64String(originalBytes);
    return (encryptedStr);
}

public static string Decrypt(string encryptedStr)
{
    // Unconvert encrypted string.
    byte[] encryptedStrAsBytes = Convert.FromBase64String(encryptedStr);
    byte[] initialText = new Byte[encryptedStrAsBytes.Length];

    using (RijndaelManaged rijndael = new RijndaelManaged( ))
    {
        using (MemoryStream memStream = new MemoryStream(encryptedStrAsBytes))
        {
            if (savedKey == null || savedIV == null)
            {
                throw (new NullReferenceException(
                        "savedKey and savedIV must be non-null."));
            }

            // Create decryptor, and stream objects.
            using (ICryptoTransform rdTransform =
                rijndael.CreateDecryptor((byte[])savedKey.
                Clone( ),(byte[])savedIV.Clone( )))
            {
                using (CryptoStream cryptoStream = new CryptoStream(memStream,
                rdTransform, CryptoStreamMode.Read))
                {
                // Read in decrypted string as a byte[].
                cryptoStream.Read(initialText, 0, initialText.Length);
                }
            }
        }
    }

    // Convert byte[] to string.
    string decryptedStr = Encoding.ASCII.GetString(initialText);
    return (decryptedStr);
}
}
```

Discussion

The CryptoString class contains only static members, except for the private instance constructor, which prevents anyone from directly creating an object from this class.

This class uses the *Rijndael algorithm* to encrypt and decrypt a string. This algorithm is found in the System.Security.Cryptography.RijndaelManaged class. This algorithm requires a secret key and an initialization vector; both are byte arrays. A random secret key can be generated for you by calling the GenerateKey method on the

RijndaelManaged class. This method accepts no parameters and returns void. The generated key is placed in the Key property of the RijndaelManaged class. The GenerateIV method generates a random initialization vector and places this vector in the IV property of the RijndaelManaged class.

The byte array values in the Key and IV properties must be stored for later use and not modified. This is due to the nature of private-key encryption classes, such as RijndaelManaged. The Key and IV values must be used by both the encryption and decryption routines to successfully encrypt and decrypt data.

The SavedKey and SavedIV private static fields contain the secret key and initialization vector, respectively. The secret key is used by both the encryption and decryption methods to encrypt and decrypt data. This is why there are public properties for these values, so they can be stored somewhere secure for later use. This means that any strings encrypted by this object must be decrypted by this object. The initialization vector is used to prevent anyone from attempting to decipher the secret key.

Two methods in the CryptoString class, RdGenerateSecretKey and RdGenerateSecretInitVector, are used to generate a secret key and initialization vector when none exists. The RdGenerateSecretKey method generates the secret key, which is placed in the SavedKey field. Likewise, the RdGenerateSecretInitVector generates the initialization vector, which is placed in the SavedIV field. There is only one key and one IV generated for this class. This enables the encryption and decryption routines to have access to the same key and IV information at all times.

The Encrypt and Decrypt methods of the CryptoString class do the actual work of encrypting and decrypting a string. The Encrypt method accepts a string that you want to encrypt and returns an encrypted string. The following code calls this method and passes in a string to be encrypted:

```
string encryptedString = CryptoString.Encrypt("MyPassword");
Console.WriteLine("encryptedString: {0}", encryptedString);
// Get the key and IV used so you can decrypt it later.
byte [] key = CryptoString.Key;
byte [] IV = CryptoString.IV;
```

Once the string is encrypted, the key and IV are stored for later decryption. This method displays:

```
encryptedString: Ah4vkmVKpwMYRT97Q8cVgQ==
```

Note that your output may differ since you will be using a different key and IV value. The following code sets the key and IV used to encrypt the string, then calls the Decrypt method to decrypt the previously encrypted string:

```
CryptoString.Key = key;
CryptoString.IV = IV;
string decryptedString = CryptoString.Decrypt(encryptedString);
Console.WriteLine("decryptedString: {0}", decryptedString);
```

This method displays:

```
decryptedString: MyPassword
```

There does not seem to be any problem with using escape sequences such as \r, \n, \r\n, or \t in the string to be encrypted. In addition, using a quoted string literal, with or without escaped characters, works without a problem:

```
@"MyPassword"
```

See Also

See Recipe 17.3; see the "System.Cryptography Namespace," "MemoryStream Class," "ICryptoTransform Interface," and "RijndaelManaged Class" topics in the MSDN documentation.

17.3 Encrypting and Decrypting a File

Problem

You have sensitive information that must be encrypted before it is written to a file that might be in a nonsecure area. This information must also be decrypted before it is read back in to the application.

Solution

Use multiple cryptography providers and write the data to a file in encrypted format. This is accomplished in the following class, which has a constructor that expects an instance of the System.Security.Cryptography.SymmetricAlgorithm class and a path for the file. The SymmetricAlgorithm class is an abstract base class for all cryptographic providers in .NET, so you can be reasonably assured that this class could be extended to cover all of them. This example implements support for TripleDES and Rijndael. It is easily be extended for Data Encryption Standard (DES) and RC2, which are also provided by the Framework.

The following namespaces are needed for this solution:

```
using System;
using System.Text;
using System.IO;
using System.Security.Cryptography;
```

The class SecretFile (implemented in this recipe) can be used for TripleDES as shown:

```
// Use TripleDES.
using (TripleDESCryptoServiceProvider tdes = new TripleDESCryptoServiceProvider( ))
{
    SecretFile secretTDESFile = new SecretFile(tdes,"tdestext.secret");

    string encrypt = "My TDES Secret Data!";
```

```
        Console.WriteLine("Writing secret data: {0}",encrypt);
        secretTDESFile.SaveSensitiveData(encrypt);
        // Save for storage to read file.
        byte [] key = secretTDESFile.Key;
        byte [] IV = secretTDESFile.IV;

        string decrypt = secretTDESFile.ReadSensitiveData( );
        Console.WriteLine("Read secret data: {0}",decrypt);
    }
```

To use SecretFile with Rijndael, just substitute the provider in the constructor like this:

```
    // Use Rijndael.
    using (RijndaelManaged rdProvider = new RijndaelManaged( ))
    {
        SecretFile secretRDFile = new SecretFile(rdProvider,"rdtext.secret");

        string encrypt = "My Rijndael Secret Data!";

        Console.WriteLine("Writing secret data: {0}",encrypt);
        secretRDFile.SaveSensitiveData(encrypt);
        // Save for storage to read file.
        byte [] key = secretRDFile.Key;
        byte [] IV = secretRDFile.IV;

        string decrypt = secretRDFile.ReadSensitiveData( );
        Console.WriteLine("Read secret data: {0}",decrypt);
    }
```

Example 17-6 shows the implementation of SecretFile.

Example 17-6. SecretFile class

```
public class SecretFile
{
    private byte[] savedKey = null;
    private byte[] savedIV = null;
    private SymmetricAlgorithm symmetricAlgorithm;
    string path;

    public byte[] Key
    {
        get { return savedKey; }
        set { savedKey = value; }
    }

    public byte[] IV
    {
        get { return savedIV; }
        set { savedIV = value; }
    }

    public SecretFile(SymmetricAlgorithm algorithm, string fileName)
    {
```

Example 17-6. SecretFile class (continued)

```
        symmetricAlgorithm = algorithm;
        path = fileName;
    }

    public void SaveSensitiveData(string sensitiveData)
    {
        // Encode data string to be stored in encrypted file.
        byte[] encodedData = Encoding.Unicode.GetBytes(sensitiveData);

        // Create FileStream and crypto service provider objects.
        using (FileStream fileStream = new FileStream(path,
                                             FileMode.Create,
                                             FileAccess.Write))
        {
            // Generate and save secret key and init vector.
            GenerateSecretKey( );
            GenerateSecretInitVector( );

            // Create crypto transform and stream objects.
            using (ICryptoTransform transform =
                    symmetricAlgorithm.CreateEncryptor(savedKey,
                    savedIV))
            {
                using (CryptoStream cryptoStream =
              new CryptoStream(fileStream, transform, CryptoStreamMode.Write))
                {
                    // Write encrypted data to the file.
                    cryptoStream.Write(encodedData, 0, encodedData.Length);
                }
            }
        }
    }

    public string ReadSensitiveData( )
    {
        string decrypted = "";

        // Create file stream to read encrypted file back.
        using (FileStream fileStream = new FileStream(path,
                                               FileMode.Open,
                                               FileAccess.Read))
        {
            // Print out the contents of the encrypted file.
            using (BinaryReader binReader = new BinaryReader(fileStream))
            {
                Console.WriteLine("---------- Encrypted Data ---------");
                int count = (Convert.ToInt32(binReader.BaseStream.Length));
                byte [] bytes = binReader.ReadBytes(count);
                char [] array = Encoding.Unicode.GetChars(bytes);
                string encdata = new string(array);
                Console.WriteLine(encdata);
                Console.WriteLine("---------- Encrypted Data ---------\r\n");
```

Example 17-6. SecretFile class (continued)

```
                // Reset the file stream.
                fileStream.Seek(0,SeekOrigin.Begin);

                // Create decryptor.
                using (ICryptoTransform transform =
                    symmetricAlgorithm.CreateDecryptor(savedKey, savedIV))
                {
                    using (CryptoStream cryptoStream = new CryptoStream(fileStream,
                                                    transform,
                                                    CryptoStreamMode.Read))
                    {
                        // Print out the contents of the decrypted file.
                        StreamReader srDecrypted = new StreamReader(cryptoStream,
                                                    new UnicodeEncoding( ));
                        Console.WriteLine("---------- Decrypted Data ---------");
                        decrypted = srDecrypted.ReadToEnd( );
                        Console.WriteLine(decrypted);
                        Console.WriteLine("---------- Decrypted Data ---------");
                    }
                }
            }

        return decrypted;
    }

    private void GenerateSecretKey( )
    {
        if (null != (symmetricAlgorithm as TripleDESCryptoServiceProvider))
        {
            TripleDESCryptoServiceProvider tdes;
            tdes = symmetricAlgorithm as TripleDESCryptoServiceProvider;
            tdes.KeySize = 192; //  Maximum key size
            tdes.GenerateKey( );
            savedKey = tdes.Key;
        }
        else if (null != (symmetricAlgorithm as RijndaelManaged))
        {
            RijndaelManaged rdProvider;
            rdProvider = symmetricAlgorithm as RijndaelManaged;
            rdProvider.KeySize = 256; // Maximum key size
            rdProvider.GenerateKey( );
            savedKey = rdProvider.Key;
        }
    }

    private void GenerateSecretInitVector( )
    {
        if (null != (symmetricAlgorithm as TripleDESCryptoServiceProvider))
        {
            TripleDESCryptoServiceProvider tdes;
            tdes = symmetricAlgorithm as TripleDESCryptoServiceProvider;
```

Example 17-6. SecretFile class (continued)

```
            tdes.GenerateIV( );
            savedIV = tdes.IV;
        }
        else if (null != (symmetricAlgorithm as RijndaelManaged))
        {
            RijndaelManaged rdProvider;
            rdProvider = symmetricAlgorithm as RijndaelManaged;
            rdProvider.GenerateIV( );
            savedIV = rdProvider.IV;
        }
    }
}
```

If the SaveSensitiveData method is used to save the following text to a file:

```
This is a test
This is sensitive data!
```

the ReadSensitiveData method will display the following information from this same file:

```
---------- Encrypted Data ---------
??????????????????????????????????????????????
---------- Encrypted Data ---------

---------- Decrypted Data ---------
This is a test
This is sensitive data!
---------- Decrypted Data ---------
```

Discussion

Encrypting data is essential to many applications, especially ones that store information in easily accessible locations. Once data is encrypted, a decryption scheme is required to restore the data back to an unencrypted form without losing any information. The same underlying algorithms can be used to authenticate the source of a file or message.

The encryption schemes used in this recipe are TripleDES and Rijndael. The reasons for using Triple DES are:

- TripleDES employs symmetric encryption, meaning that a single private key is used to encrypt and decrypt data. This process allows much faster encryption and decryption, especially as the streams of data become larger.

- TripleDES encryption is much harder to crack than the older DES encryption.

- If you wish to use another type of encryption, this recipe can be easily converted using any provider derived from the SymmetricAlgorithm class.

The main drawback to TripleDES is that both the sender and receiver must use the same key and initialization vector (IV) in order to encrypt and decrypt the data successfully. If you wish to have an even more secure encryption scheme, use the Rijndael scheme. This type of encryption scheme is highly regarded as a solid encryption scheme, since it is fast and can use larger key sizes than TripleDES. However, it is still a symmetric cryptosystem, which means that it relies on shared secrets. Use an asymmetric cryptosystem, such as RSA or DSA, for a cryptosystem that uses shared public keys with private keys that are never shared between parties.

See Also

See the "SymmetricAlgorithm Class," "TripleDESCryptoServiceProvider Class," and "RijndaelManaged Class" topics in the MSDN documentation.

17.4   Cleaning up Cryptography Information

Problem

You will be using the cryptography classes in the FCL to encrypt and/or decrypt data. In doing so, you want to make sure that no data (e.g., seed values or keys) is left in memory for longer than you are using the cryptography classes. Hackers can sometimes find this information in memory and use it to break your encryption or, worse, to break your encryption, modify the data, and then reencrypt the data and pass it on to your application.

Solution

In order to clear out the key and initialization vector (or seed), you need to call the Clear method on whichever SymmetricAlgorithm- or AsymmetricAlgorithm-derived class you are using. Clear reinitializes the Key and IV properties, preventing them from being found in memory. This is done after saving the key and IV so that you can decrypt later. Example 17-7 encodes a string, then cleans up immediately afterward to provide the smallest window possible for potential attackers.

Example 17-7. Cleaning up cryptography information

```
using System;
using System.Text;
using System.IO;
using System.Security.Cryptography;

string originalStr = "SuperSecret information";
// Encode data string to be stored in memory.
byte[] originalStrAsBytes = Encoding.ASCII.GetBytes(originalStr);

// Create MemoryStream to contain output.
MemoryStream memStream = new MemoryStream(originalStrAsBytes.Length);
```

Example 17-7. Cleaning up cryptography information (continued)

```
RijndaelManaged rijndael = new RijndaelManaged( );

// Generate secret key and init vector.
rijndael.KeySize = 256;
rijndael.GenerateKey( );
rijndael.GenerateIV( );

// Save the key and IV for later decryption.
byte [] key = rijndael.Key;
byte [] IV = rijndael.IV;

// Create encryptor, and stream objects.
ICryptoTransform transform = rijndael.CreateEncryptor(rijndael.Key,
    rijndael.IV);
CryptoStream cryptoStream = new CryptoStream(memStream, transform,
    CryptoStreamMode.Write);

// Write encrypted data to the MemoryStream.
cryptoStream.Write(originalStrAsBytes, 0, originalStrAsBytes.Length);
cryptoStream.FlushFinalBlock( );

// Release all resources as soon as we are done with them
// to prevent retaining any information in memory.
memStream.Close( );
cryptoStream.Close( );
transform.Dispose( );
// This clear statement regens both the key and the init vector so that
// what is left in memory is no longer the values you used to encrypt with.
rijndael.Clear( );
```

You can also make your life a little easier by taking advantage of the using statement, instead of having to remember to manually call each of the Close methods individually. This code block shows how to use the using statement:

```
public static void CleanUpCryptoWithUsing( )
{
    string originalStr = "SuperSecret information";
    // Encode data string to be stored in memory.
    byte[] originalStrAsBytes = Encoding.ASCII.GetBytes(originalStr);
    byte[] originalBytes = { };

    // Create MemoryStream to contain output.
    using (MemoryStream memStream = new MemoryStream(originalStrAsBytes.Length))
    {
        using (RijndaelManaged rijndael = new RijndaelManaged( ))
        {
            // Generate secret key and init vector.
            rijndael.KeySize = 256;
            rijndael.GenerateKey( );
            rijndael.GenerateIV( );

            // Save off the key and IV for later decryption.
```

```
            byte[] key = rijndael.Key;
            byte[] IV = rijndael.IV;

            // Create encryptor, and stream objects.
            using (ICryptoTransform transform =
                rijndael.CreateEncryptor(rijndael.Key, rijndael.IV))
            {
                using (CryptoStream cryptoStream = new
                        CryptoStream(memStream, transform,
                         CryptoStreamMode.Write))
                {
                    // Write encrypted data to the MemoryStream.
                    cryptoStream.Write(originalStrAsBytes, 0,
                            originalStrAsBytes.Length);
                    cryptoStream.FlushFinalBlock();
                }
            }
        }
    }
}
```

Discussion

To make sure your data is safe, you need to close the MemoryStream and CryptoStream objects as soon as possible, as well as calling Dispose on the ICryptoTransform implementation to clear out any resources used in this encryption. The using statement makes this process much easier, makes your code easier to read, and leads to fewer programming mistakes.

See Also

See the "SymmetricAlgorithm.Clear Method" and "AsymmetricAlgorithm.Clear Method" topics in the MSDN documentation.

17.5 Verifying that a String Remains Uncorrupted Following Transmission

Problem

You have some text that will be sent across a network to another machine for processing. It is critical for you to verify that this text remains intact and unmodified when it arrives at its destination.

Solution

Calculate a hash value from the string and append it to the string before it is sent to its destination. Once the destination receives the string, it can remove the hash value and determine whether the string is the same one that was initially sent. The

CreateStringHash method takes a string as input, adds a hash value to the end of it, and returns the new string, as shown in Example 17-8.

Example 17-8. Verifying that a string remains uncorrupted following transmission

```
public class HashOps
{
  // The number 44 is the exact length of the base64 representation
  // of the hash value, which was appended to the string.
  private const int HASH_LENGTH = 44;

  public static string CreateStringHash(string unHashedString)
  {
      byte[] encodedUnHashedString = Encoding.Unicode.GetBytes(unHashedString);
      string stringWithHash = "";

      using (SHA256Managed hashingObj = new SHA256Managed( ))
      {
        byte[] hashCode = hashingObj.ComputeHash(encodedUnHashedString);

        string hashBase64 = Convert.ToBase64String(hashCode);
        stringWithHash = unHashedString + hashBase64;
      }

      return (stringWithHash);
  }

  public static bool TestReceivedStringHash(string stringWithHash,
                                            out string originalStr)
  {
      // Code to quickly test the handling of a tampered string.
      //stringWithHash = stringWithHash.Replace('a', 'b');

      if (stringWithHash.Length <= HASH_LENGTH)
      {
          originalStr = null;
          return (true);
      }

      string hashCodeString =
        stringWithHash.Substring(stringWithHash.Length - HASH_LENGTH);
      string unHashedString =
        stringWithHash.Substring(0, stringWithHash.Length - HASH_LENGTH);

      byte[] hashCode = Convert.FromBase64String(hashCodeString);

      byte[] encodedUnHashedString = Encoding.Unicode.GetBytes(unHashedString);

      bool hasBeenTamperedWith = false;
      using (SHA256Managed hashingObj = new SHA256Managed( ))
      {
        byte[] receivedHashCode = hashingObj.ComputeHash(encodedUnHashedString);
```

```
        for (int counter = 0; counter < receivedHashCode.Length; counter++)
        {
          if (receivedHashCode[counter] != hashCode[counter])
          {
              hasBeenTamperedWith = true;
              break;
          }
        }

        if (!hasBeenTamperedWith)
        {
          originalStr = unHashedString;
        }
        else
        {
          originalStr = null;
        }
      }

    return (hasBeenTamperedWith);
  }
}
```

The TestReceivedStringHash method is called by the code that receives a string with a hash value appended. This method removes the hash value, calculates a new hash value for the string, and checks to see whether both hash values match. If they match, both strings are exactly the same, and the method returns false. If they don't match, the string has been tampered with, and the method returns true.

Since the CreateStringHash and TestReceivedStringHash methods are static members of a class named HashOps, you can call these methods with code like the following:

```
    public static void VerifyNonStringCorruption( )
    {
        string testString = "This is the string that we'll be testing.";
        string unhashedString;
        string hashedString = HashOps.CreateStringHash(testString);

        bool result = HashOps.TestReceivedStringHash(hashedString, out unhashedString);
        Console.WriteLine(result);
        if (!result)
            Console.WriteLine("The string sent is: " + unhashedString);
        else
            Console.WriteLine("The string: " + unhashedString +
                " has become corrupted.");
    }
```

The output of this method is shown here when the string is uncorrupted:

```
    False
    The string sent is: This is the string that we'll be testing.
```

The output of this method is shown here when the string is corrupted:

```
False
The string: This is the string that we'll #$%^(&&*2 be testing.
has become corrupted.
```

Discussion

You can use a hash, checksum, or *cyclic redundancy check* (CRC) to calculate a value based on a message. This value is then used at the destination to determine whether the message has been modified during transmission between the source and destination.

This recipe uses a hash value as a reliable method of determining whether a string has been modified. The hash value for this recipe is calculated using the SHA256Managed class. This hash value is 256 bits in size and produces greatly differing results when calculated from strings that are very similar, but not exactly the same. In fact, if a single letter is removed or even capitalized, the resulting hash value will change.

By appending this value to the string, both the string and hash values can be sent to their destination. The destination then removes the hash value and calculates a hash value of its own based on the received string. These two hash values are then compared. If they are equal, the strings are exactly the same. If they are not equal, you can be sure that somewhere between the source and destination, the string was corrupted. This technique is great for verifying that transmission succeeded without errors, but it does not guarantee against malicious tampering. To protect against malicious tampering, use an asymmetric algorithm: sign the string with a private key and verify the signature with a public key.

The CreateStringHash method first converts the unhashed string into a byte array using the GetBytes method of the UnicodeEncoding class. This byte array is then passed to the ComputeHash method of the SHA256Managed class.

Once the hash value is calculated, the byte array containing the hash code is converted to a string containing base64 digits, using the Convert.ToBase64String method. This method accepts a byte array, converts it to a string of base64 digits, and returns that string. The reason for doing this is to convert all unsigned integers in the byte array to values that can be represented in a string data type. The last thing that this method does is to append the hash value to the end of the string and return the newly hashed string.

The TestReceivedStringHash method accepts a hashed string and an out parameter that will return the unhashed string. This method returns a Boolean; as previously mentioned, true indicates that the string has been modified, false indicates that the string is unmodified.

This method first removes the hash value from the end of the StringWithHash variable. Next, a new hash is calculated using the string portion of the StringWithHash variable. These two hash values are compared. If they are the same, the string has been received, unmodified. Note that if you change the hashing algorithm used, you must change it in both this method and the CreateStringHash method. You must also change the HASH_LENGTH constant in the TestReceivedStringHash method to an appropriate size for the new hashing algorithm. This number is the exact length of the base64 representation of the hash value, which was appended to the string.

See Also

See the "SHA256Managed Class," "Convert.ToBase64String Method," and "Convert.FromBase64String Method" topics in the MSDN documentation.

17.6 Wrapping a String Hash for Ease of Use

Problem

You need to create a class to isolate other developers on your team from the details of adding a hash to a string, as well as the details of using the hash to verify if the string has been modified or corrupted.

Solution

The following classes decorate the StringWriter and StringReader classes to handle a hash added to its contained string. The WriterDecorator and StringWriterHash classes allow the StringWriter class to be decorated with extra functionality to add a hash value to the StringWriter's internal string. Note that the CreateStringHash method that creates the hash value is defined in Recipe 17.5.

The code for the WriterDecorator abstract base class is shown in Example 17-9.

Example 17-9. WriterDecorator class

```
using System;
using System.Text;
using System.IO;

[Serializable]
public abstract class WriterDecorator : TextWriter
{
    public WriterDecorator( ) {}

    public WriterDecorator(StringWriter stringWriter)
    {
        internalStringWriter = stringWriter;
    }

    protected bool isHashed = false;
```

Example 17-9. WriterDecorator class (continued)

```
    protected StringWriter internalStringWriter = null;

    public void SetWriter(StringWriter stringWriter)
    {
        internalStringWriter = stringWriter;
    }
}
```

The StringWriterHash class shown in Example 17-10 is a concrete implementation of
the WriterDecorator class.

Example 17-10. StringWriterHash class

```
[Serializable]
public class StringWriterHash : WriterDecorator
{
    public StringWriterHash( ) : base( ) {}

    public StringWriterHash(StringWriter stringWriter) : base(stringWriter)
    {
    }

    public override Encoding Encoding
    {
        get {return (internalStringWriter.Encoding);}
    }

    public override void Close( )
    {
        internalStringWriter.Close( );
        base.Dispose(true);            // Completes the cleanup.
    }

    public override void Flush( )
    {
        internalStringWriter.Flush( );
        base.Flush( );
    }

    public virtual StringBuilder GetStringBuilder( )
    {
        return (internalStringWriter.GetStringBuilder( ));
    }

    public override string ToString( )
    {
        return (internalStringWriter.ToString( ));
    }

    public void WriteHash( )
    {
        int originalStrLen = internalStringWriter.GetStringBuilder( ).Length;
```

Example 17-10. StringWriterHash class (continued)

```csharp
            // Call hash generator here for whole string.
            string hashedString = HashOps.CreateStringHash(this.ToString( ));
            internalStringWriter.Write(hashedString.Substring(originalStrLen));

            isHashed = true;
        }

        public override void Write(char value)
        {
            if (isHashed)
            {
                throw (new Exception("A hash has already been added to this string"+
                                    ", it cannot be modified."));
            }
            else
            {
                internalStringWriter.Write(value);
            }
        }

        public override void Write(string value)
        {
            if (isHashed)
            {
                throw (new Exception("A hash has already been added to this string"+
                                    ", it cannot be modified."));
            }
            else
            {
                internalStringWriter.Write(value);
            }
        }

        public override void Write(char[] buffer, int index, int count)
        {
            if (isHashed)
            {
                throw (new Exception("A hash has already been added to this string"+
                                    ", it cannot be modified."));
            }
            else
            {
                internalStringWriter.Write(buffer, index, count);
            }
        }

        protected override void Dispose(bool disposing)
        {
            base.Dispose(disposing);
        }
    }
```

The `ReaderDecorator` and `StringReaderHash` classes shown in Examples 17-11 and 17-12 allow the `StringReader` class to be decorated with extra functionality to handle the verification of a string's hash value. Note that the `TestReceivedStringHash` method that verifies the hash value is defined in Recipe 17.5.

Example 17-11. ReaderDecorator class

```
[Serializable]
public abstract class ReaderDecorator : TextReader
{
    public ReaderDecorator( ) {}

    public ReaderDecorator(StringReader stringReader)
    {
        internalStringReader = stringReader;
    }

    protected StringReader internalStringReader = null;

    public void SetReader(StringReader stringReader)
    {
        internalStringReader = stringReader;
    }
}
```

`StringReaderHash`, shown in Example 17-12, is the concrete implementation of the `ReaderDecorator` class.

Example 17-12. StringReaderHash class

```
[Serializable]
public class StringReaderHash : ReaderDecorator
{
    public StringReaderHash( ) : base( ) {}

    public StringReaderHash(StringReader stringReader) : base(stringReader)
    {
    }

    public override void Close( )
    {
        internalStringReader.Close( );
        base.Dispose(true); // Completes the cleanup.
    }

    public string ReadToEndHash( )
    {
        string hashStr = internalStringReader.ReadToEnd( );

        string originalStr = "";
        // Call hash reader here.
        bool isInvalid = HashOps.TestReceivedStringHash(hashStr,
                                                        out originalStr);
```

Example 17-12. StringReaderHash class (continued)

```
        if (isInvalid)
        {
            throw (new Exception("This string has failed its hash check."));
        }

        return (originalStr);
    }

    public override int Read( )
    {
        return (internalStringReader.Read( ));
    }

    public override int Read(char[] buffer, int index, int count)
    {
        return (internalStringReader.Read(buffer, index, count));
    }

    public override string ReadLine( )
    {
        return (internalStringReader.ReadLine( ));
    }

    public override string ReadToEnd( )
    {
        return (internalStringReader.ReadToEnd( ));
    }

    protected override void Dispose(bool disposing)
    {
        base.Dispose(disposing);
    }
}
```

The following code creates a `StringWriter` object (`stringWriter`) and decorates it with a `StringWriterHash` object:

```
StringWriter stringWriter = new StringWriter(new StringBuilder("Initial Text"));
StringWriterHash stringWriterHash = new StringWriterHash( );
stringWriterHash.SetWriter(stringWriter);
stringWriterHash.Write("-Extra Text-");
stringWriterHash.WriteHash( );
Console.WriteLine("stringWriterHash.ToString( ): " + stringWriterHash.ToString( ));
```

The string "Initial Text" is added to the `StringWriter` on initialization, and later the string "-Extra Text-" is added. Next, the `WriteHash` method is called to add a hash value to the end of the complete string. Notice that if the code attempts to write more text to the `StringWriterHash` object after the `WriteHash` method has been called, an exception will be thrown. The string cannot be modified once the hash has been calculated and added.

The following code takes a `StringReader` object (`stringReader`) that was initialized with the string and hash produced by the previous code and decorates it with a `StringReaderHash` object:

```
StringReader stringReader = new StringReader(stringWriterHash.ToString( ));
StringReaderHash stringReaderHash = new StringReaderHash( );
stringReaderHash.SetReader(stringReader);
Console.WriteLine("stringReaderHash.ReadToEndHash( ): " +
                  stringReaderHash.ReadToEndHash( ));
```

If the original string is modified after the hash is added, the `ReadToEndHash` method throws an exception.

Discussion

The *decorator design pattern* provides the ability to modify individual objects without having to modify or subclass the object's class. This allows for the creation of both decorated and undecorated objects. The implementation of a decorator pattern is sometimes hard to understand at first. An abstract decorator class is created that inherits from the same base class as the class you will decorate. In the case of this recipe, you will decorate the `StringReader`/`StringWriter` classes to allow a hash to be calculated and used. The `StringReader` class inherits from `TextReader`, and the `StringWriter` class inherits from `TextWriter`. Knowing this, you create two abstract decorator classes: `ReaderDecorator`, which inherits from `TextReader`, and `WriterDecorator`, which inherits from `TextWriter`.

The abstract decorator classes contain two constructors, a private field named `internalStreamReader\internalStreamWriter` and a method named `SetReader\SetWriter`. Basically, the field stores a reference to the contained `StringReader` or `StringWriter` object that is being decorated. This field can be set through either a constructor or the `SetReader\SetWriter` method. The interesting thing about this pattern is that each of the decorator objects must also contain an instance of the class that they decorate. The `StringReaderHash` class contains a `StringReader` object in its `internalStreamReader` field, and the `StringWriterHash` class contains a `StringWriter` object in its `internalStreamWriter` field.

A concrete decorator class that inherits from the abstract decorator classes is created. The `StringReaderHash` class inherits from `ReaderDecorator`, while the `StringWriterHash` inherits from `WriterDecorator`. This pattern allows you the flexibility to add concrete decorator classes without having to touch the existing code.

Most of the methods in the `StringReaderHash` and `StringWriterHash` classes simply act as wrappers to the `internalStreamReader` or `internalStreamWriter` objects, respectively. The method that actually decorates the `StringReader` object with a hash is the `StringReaderHash.ReadToEndHash` method, and the method that actually decorates the `StringWriter` object is `StringWriterHash.WriteHash`. These two methods allow the hash to be attached to a string and later used to determine whether the string contents have changed.

The attractiveness of the decorator pattern is that you can add any number of concrete decorator classes that derive from either ReaderDecorator or WriterDecorator. If you need to use a different hashing algorithm, or even a quick and dirty hash algorithm, you can subclass the ReaderDecorator or WriterDecorator classes and add functionality to use these new algorithms. Now you have more choices of how to decorate these classes.

See Also

See the "StringWriter Class" and "StringReader Class" topics in the MSDN documentation.

17.7 A Better Random Number Generator

Problem

You need a random number with which to generate items such as a sequence of session keys. The random number must be as unpredictable as possible so that the likelihood of predicting the sequence of keys is as low as possible.

Solution

Use the class System.Security.Cryptography.RNGCryptoServiceProvider.

The RNGCryptoServiceProvider is used to populate a random byte array using the GetBytes method that is then printed out as a string in the following example:

```
public static void BetterRandomString( )
{
    // Create a stronger hash code using RNGCryptoServiceProvider.
    byte[] random = new byte[64];
    RNGCryptoServiceProvider rng = new RNGCryptoServiceProvider( );
    // Populate with random bytes.
    rng.GetBytes(random);

    // Convert random bytes to string.
    string randomBase64 = Convert.ToBase64String(random);
    // Display.
    Console.WriteLine("Random string: {0} ",randomBase64);
}
```

The output of this method is shown here:

```
Random string:
xDNitrreUpMml07Opd6AFvMC8VIG9+sAGfyvdZr2lEY1M3n2v3Ap4JIkYfJWW+sZaJjJMxj475VlVQFoRKvFI
g==
```

Discussion

Random provides methods like Next, NextBytes, and NextDouble to generate random information for integers, arrays of bytes, and doubles, respectively. These methods can produce a moderate level of unpredictability, but to truly generate a more unpredictable random series, you need to use the RNGCryptoServiceProvider.

RNGCryptoServiceProvider can be customized to use any of the underlying Win32 Crypto API providers. You pass a CspParameters class in the constructor to determine exactly which provider is responsible for generating the random byte sequence. CspParameters allows you to customize items such as the key container name, the provider type code, the provider name, and the key number used.

The GetBytes method populates the entire length of the byte array with random bytes.

See Also

See the "RNGCryptoServiceProvider Class," "CspParameters Class," and "Cryptographic Provider Types" topics in the MSDN documentation.

17.8   Storing Data Securely

Problem

You need to store settings data about individual users for use by your application and keep this data isolated from other instances of your application run by different users.

Solution

You can use isolated storage to establish per-user data stores for your application data and then use hashed values for critical data.

To illustrate how to do this for settings data, you create the following UserSettings class. UserSettings holds only two pieces of information: the user identity (current WindowsIdentity) and the password for your application. The user identity is accessed via the User property, and the password is accessed via the Password property. Note that the password field is created the first time and is stored as a salted hashed value to keep it secure. The combination of the isolated storage and the hashing of the password value helps to strengthen the security of the password by using the *defense in depth* principle. The settings data is held in XML that is stored in the isolated storage scope and accessed via an XmlDocument instance.

This solution uses the following namespaces:

```
using System;
using System.IO;
```

```
using System.IO.IsolatedStorage;
using System.Xml;
using System.Text;
using System.Diagnostics;
using System.Security.Principal;
using System.Security.Cryptography;
```

The UserSettings class is shown in Example 17-13.

Example 17-13. UserSettings class

```
// Class to hold user settings
public class UserSettings
{
    isoFileStream = null;
    XmlDocument settingsDoc = null;
    const string storageName = "SettingsStorage.xml";

    // Constructor
    public UserSettings(string password)
    {
        // Get the isolated storage.
        using (IsolatedStorageFile isoStorageFile =
            IsolatedStorageFile.GetUserStoreForDomain( ))
        {
            // Create an internal DOM for settings.
            settingsDoc = new XmlDocument( );
            // If no settings, create default.
            if(isoStorageFile.GetFileNames(storageName).Length == 0)
            {
                using (IsolatedStorageFileStream isoFileStream =
                    new IsolatedStorageFileStream(storageName,
                                                  FileMode.Create,
                                                  isoStorageFile))
                {
                    using (XmlTextWriter writer = new
                        XmlTextWriter(isoFileStream,Encoding.UTF8))
                    {
                        writer.WriteStartDocument( );
                        writer.WriteStartElement("Settings");
                        writer.WriteStartElement("User");
                        // Get current user.
                        WindowsIdentity user = WindowsIdentity.GetCurrent( );
                        writer.WriteString(user.Name);
                        writer.WriteEndElement( );
                        writer.WriteStartElement("Password");

                        // Pass null to CreateHashedPassword as the salt
                        // to establish one.
                        // CreateHashedPassword appears shortly.
                        string hashedPassword =
                                CreateHashedPassword(password,null);
                        writer.WriteString(hashedPassword);
                        writer.WriteEndElement( );
```

Example 17-13. UserSettings class (continued)

```
                writer.WriteEndElement( );
                writer.WriteEndDocument( );
                Console.WriteLine("Creating settings for " + user.Name);
            }
        }
    }

    // Set up access to settings store.
    using (IsolatedStorageFileStream isoFileStream =
        new IsolatedStorageFileStream(storageName,
                                FileMode.Open,
                                isoStorageFile))
    {
        // Load settings from isolated filestream.
        settingsDoc.Load(isoFileStream);
        Console.WriteLine("Loaded settings for " + User);
    }
}
}
```

The User property provides access to the WindowsIdentity of the user that this set of settings belongs to:

```
// User property
public string User
{
    get
    {
        XmlNode userNode = settingsDoc.SelectSingleNode("Settings/User");
        if(userNode != null)
        {
            return userNode.InnerText;
        }
        return "";
    }
}
```

The Password property gets the salted and hashed password value from the XML store and, when updating the password, takes the plain text of the password and creates the salted and hashed version, which is then stored:

```
// Password property
public string Password
{
    get
    {
        XmlNode pwdNode =
                settingsDoc.SelectSingleNode("Settings/Password");
        if(pwdNode != null)
        {
            return pwdNode.InnerText;
        }
        return "";
```

```
    }
    set
    {
        XmlNode pwdNode =
                settingsDoc.SelectSingleNode("Settings/Password");

        string hashedPassword = CreateHashedPassword(value,null);
        if(pwdNode != null)
        {
            pwdNode.InnerText = hashedPassword;
        }
        else
        {
            XmlNode settingsNode =
                    settingsDoc.SelectSingleNode("Settings");
            XmlElement pwdElem =
                    settingsDoc.CreateElement("Password");
            pwdElem.InnerText=hashedPassword;
            settingsNode.AppendChild(pwdElem);
        }
    }
}
```

The CreateHashedPassword method creates the salted and hashed password. The password parameter is the plain text of the password; the existingSalt parameter is the salt to use when creating the salted and hashed version. If no salt exists, such as the first time a password is stored, existingSalt should be passed as null, and a random salt will be generated.

Once you have the salt, it is combined with the plain text password and hashed using the SHA512Managed class. The salt value is then appended to the end of the hashed value and returned. The salt is appended so that when you attempt to validate the password, you know what salt was used to create the hashed value. The entire value is then base64-encoded and returned:

```
// Make a hashed password.
private string CreateHashedPassword(string password,
                                    byte[] existingSalt)
{
    byte [] salt = null;
    if(existingSalt == null)
    {
        // Make a salt of random size.
        // Create a stronger hash code using RNGCryptoServiceProvider.
        byte[] random = new byte[1];
        RNGCryptoServiceProvider rngSize = new RNGCryptoServiceProvider();
        // Populate with random bytes.
        rngSize.GetBytes(random);

        // Convert random bytes to string.
        int size = Convert.ToInt32(random[0]);
```

```
        // Create salt array.
        salt = new byte[size];

        // Use the better random number generator to get
        // bytes for the salt.
        RNGCryptoServiceProvider rngSalt =
            new RNGCryptoServiceProvider( );
        rngSalt.GetNonZeroBytes(salt);
    }
    else
        salt = existingSalt;

    // Turn string into bytes.
    byte[] pwd = Encoding.UTF8.GetBytes(password);

    // Make storage for both password and salt.
    byte[] saltedPwd = new byte[pwd.Length + salt.Length];

    // Add pwd bytes first.
    pwd.CopyTo(saltedPwd,0);
    // now add salt
    salt.CopyTo(saltedPwd,pwd.Length);

    // Use SHA512 as the hashing algorithm.
    byte[] hashWithSalt = null;
    using (SHA512Managed sha512 = new SHA512Managed( ))
    {
        // Get hash of salted password.
        byte[] hash = sha512.ComputeHash(saltedPwd);

        // Append salt to hash so we have it.
        hashWithSalt = new byte[hash.Length + salt.Length];

        // Copy in bytes.
        hash.CopyTo(hashWithSalt,0);
        salt.CopyTo(hashWithSalt,hash.Length);
    }

    // Return base64-encoded hash with salt.
    return Convert.ToBase64String(hashWithSalt);
}
```

To check a given password against the stored value (which is salted and hashed), you call CheckPassword and pass in the plain text password to check. First, the stored value is retrieved using the Password property and converted from base64. Since you know you used SHA512, there are 512 bits in the hash. But you need the byte size, so you do the math and get that size in bytes. This allows you to figure out where to get the salt from in the value, so you copy it out of the value and call CreateHashedPassword using that salt and the plain text password parameter. This gives you the hashed value for the password that was passed in to verify. Once you have that, you just compare it to the Password property to see whether you have a match and return true or false as appropriate.

```
            // Check the password against our storage.
            public bool CheckPassword(string password)
            {
                // Get bytes for password.
                // This is the hash of the salted password and the salt.
                byte[] hashWithSalt = Convert.FromBase64String(Password);

                // We used 512 bits as the hash size (SHA512).
                int hashSizeInBytes = 512 / 8;

                // Make holder for original salt.
                int saltSize = hashWithSalt.Length - hashSizeInBytes;
                byte[] salt = new byte[saltSize];

                // Copy out the salt.
                Array.Copy(hashWithSalt,hashSizeInBytes,salt,0,saltSize);

                // Figure out hash for this password.
                string passwordHash = CreateHashedPassword(password,salt);

                // If the computed hash matches the specified hash,
                // the plain text value must be correct.
                // See if Password (stored) matched password passed in.
                return (Password == passwordHash);
            }
        }
```

Code that uses the UserSettings class is shown here:

```
    class IsoApplication
    {
      static void Main(string[] args)
      {
            if(args.Length > 0)
            {
                UserSettings settings = new UserSettings(args[0]);
                if(settings.CheckPassword(args[0]))
                {
                    Console.WriteLine("Welcome");
                    return;
                }
            }
            Console.WriteLine("The system could not validate your credentials");
      }
    }
```

The way to use this application is to pass the password on the command line as the
first argument. This password is then checked against the UserSettings, which is
stored in the isolated storage for this particular user. If the password is correct, the
user is welcomed; if not, the user is shown the door.

Discussion

Isolated storage allows an application to store data that is unique to the application and the user running it. This storage allows the application to write out state information that is not visible to other applications or even other users of the same application. Isolated storage is based on the code identity as determined by the CLR, and it stores the information either directly on the client machine or in isolated stores that can be opened and roam with the user. The storage space available to the application is directly controllable by the administrator of the machine on which the application operates.

The Solution uses isolation by User, AppDomain, and Assembly by calling IsolatedStorageFile.GetUserStoreForDomain. This creates an isolated store that is accessible by only this user in the current assembly in the current AppDomain:

```
// Get the isolated storage.
isoStorageFile = IsolatedStorageFile.GetUserStoreForDomain( );
```

The *Storeadm.exe* utility will allow you to see which isolated-storage stores have been set up on the machine by running the utility with the /LIST command-line switch. *Storeadm.exe* is part of the .NET Framework SDK and can be located in your Visual Studio installation directory under the *\SDK\v2.0\Bin* subdirectory.

The output after using the UserSettings class would look like this:

```
C:\>storeadm /LIST
Microsoft (R) .NET Framework Store Admin 1.1.4322.573
Copyright (C) Microsoft Corporation 1998-2002. All rights reserved.

Record #1
[Domain]
<System.Security.Policy.Url version="1">
    <Url>file://D:/PRJ32/Book/IsolatedStorage/bin/Debug/IsolatedStorage.exe</Url>

</System.Security.Policy.Url>

[Assembly]
<System.Security.Policy.Url version="1">
    <Url>file://D:/PRJ32/Book/IsolatedStorage/bin/Debug/IsolatedStorage.exe</Url>

</System.Security.Policy.Url>

        Size : 1024
```

Passwords should never be stored in plain text, period. It is a bad habit to get into, so in the UserSettings class, you have added the salting and hashing of the password value via the CreateHashedPassword method and verification through the CheckPassword method. Adding a salt to the hash helps to strengthen the protection on the value being hashed so that the isolated storage, the hash, and the salt now protect the password you are storing.

See Also

See the "IsolatedStorageFile Class," "IsolatedStorageStream Class," "About Isolated Storage," and "ComputeHash Method" topics in the MSDN documentation.

17.9   Making a Security Assert Safe

Problem

You want to assert that at a particular point in the call stack, a given permission is available for all subsequent calls. However, doing this can easily open a security hole to allow other malicious code to spoof your code or to create a back door into your component. You want to assert a given security permission, but you want to do so in a secure and efficient manner.

Solution

In order to make this approach secure, you need to call Demand on the permissions that the subsequent calls need. This makes sure that code that doesn't have these permissions can't slip by due to the Assert. The Demand is done to ensure that you have indeed been granted this permission before using the Assert to short-circuit the stackwalk. This is demonstrated by the function CallSecureFunctionSafelyAndEfficiently, which performs a Demand and an Assert before calling SecureFunction, which in turn does a Demand for a ReflectionPermission.

The code listing for CallSecureFunctionSafelyAndEfficiently is shown in Example 17-14.

Example 17-14. CallSecureFunctionSafelyAndEfficiently function

```
public static void CallSecureFunctionSafelyAndEfficiently( )
{

    // Set up a permission to be able to access nonpublic members
    // via reflection.
    ReflectionPermission perm =
        new ReflectionPermission(ReflectionPermissionFlag.MemberAccess);

    // Demand the permission set we have compiled before using Assert
    // to make sure we have the right before we Assert it.  We do
    // the Demand to ensure that we have checked for this permission
    // before using Assert to short-circuit stackwalking for it, which
    // helps us stay secure, while performing better.
    perm.Demand( );

    // Assert this right before calling into the function that
    // would also perform the Demand to short-circuit the stack walk
    // each call would generate.  The Assert helps us to optimize
    // our use of SecureFunction.
    perm.Assert( );
```

```
    // We call the secure function 100 times but only generate
    // the stackwalk from the function to this calling function
    // instead of walking the whole stack 100 times.
    for(int i=0;i<100;i++)
    {
        SecureFunction( );
    }
}
```

The code listing for SecureFunction is shown here:

```
public static void SecureFunction( )
{
    // Set up a permission to be able to access nonpublic members
    // via reflection.
    ReflectionPermission perm =
        new ReflectionPermission(ReflectionPermissionFlag.MemberAccess);

    // Demand the right to do this and cause a stackwalk.
    perm.Demand( );

    // Perform the action here...
}
```

Discussion

In the demonstration function CallSecureFunctionSafelyAndEfficiently, the function you are calling (SecureFunction) performs a Demand on a ReflectionPermission to ensure that the code can access nonpublic members of classes via reflection. Normally, this would result in a stackwalk for every call to SecureFunction. The Demand in CallSecureFunctionSafelyAndEfficiently is there only to protect against the usage of the Assert in the first place. To make this more efficient, you can use Assert to state that all functions issuing Demands that are called from this one do not have to stackwalk any further. The Assert says stop checking for this permission in the call stack. In order to do this, you need the permission to call Assert.

The problem comes in with this Assert as it opens up a potential luring attack where SecureFunction is called via CallSecureFunctionSafelyAndEfficiently, which calls Assert to stop the Demand stackwalks from SecureFunction. If unauthorized code without this ReflectionPermission were able to call CallSecureFunctionSafelyAndEfficiently, the Assert would prevent the SecureFunction Demand call from determining that there is some code in the call stack without the proper rights. This is the power of the call stack checking in the CLR when a Demand occurs.

In order to protect against this, you issue a Demand for the ReflectionPermission needed by SecureFunction in CallSecureFunctionSafelyAndEfficiently to close this hole before issuing the Assert. The combination of this Demand and the Assert causes you to do one stack walk instead of the original 100 that would have been caused by the Demand in SecureFunction but to still maintain secure access to this functionality.

Security optimization techniques, such as using Assert in this case (even though it isn't the primary reason to use Assert), can help class library as well as control developers who are trusted to perform Asserts in order to speed the interaction of their code with the CLR; but if used improperly, these techniques can also open up holes in the security picture. This example shows that you can have both performance and security where secure access is concerned.

If you are using Assert, be mindful that stackwalk overrides should never be made in a class constructor. Constructors are not guaranteed to have any particular security context, nor are they guaranteed to execute at a specific point in time. This lack leads to the call stack not being well defined, and Assert used here can produce unexpected results.

One other thing to remember with Assert is that you can have only one active Assert in a function at a given time. If you Assert the same permission twice, a SecurityException is thrown by the CLR. You must revert the original Assert first using RevertAssert. Then you can declare the second Assert.

See Also

See the "CodeAccessSecurity.Assert Method," "CodeAccessSecurity.Demand Method," "CodeAccessSecurity.RevertAssert Method," and "Overriding Security Checks" topics in the MSDN documentation.

17.10 Preventing Malicious Modifications to an Assembly

Problem

You are distributing an assembly, but you want to ensure that nobody can tamper with the internals of that assembly. This tampering could result in its use to gather sensitive information from a user or to act as a backdoor mechanism in attacking a network. Additionally, you do not want other malicious assemblies that look like yours but operate in malevolent ways (e.g., stealing passwords, reformatting a disk drive) to be created. In effect, this malevolent assembly is created to spoof your benevolent assembly.

Solution

This can be averted to a certain degree by using a strong name for your assembly. A strong-named assembly has a digital signature that is generated from a public-private-key pair. The public key is the part of the pair that identifies your assembly as being from you. The private key is the part of the pair that you keep secret. It ensures that the assembly came from you and hasn't been tampered with.

In order to generate a key pair, you use the *SN.exe* from the Framework SDK:

```
SN -k MyKeys.snk
```

This line creates your key pair in a file called *MyKeys.snk*. Since this file contains both your public and private keys, you need to guard it carefully; store it only on a machine that's locked down enough to be considered highly trusted. Never make copies of this key, and store it only on a highly trusted machine or on media that are easy to secure.

Now that you have a key pair, you can get the public key from the pair in order to be able to delay-sign your assemblies. Delay-signing allows day-to-day development to continue on the assemblies while a trusted system holds the public-private-key pair file (*MyKeys.snk*) for final signing of the assemblies.

In order to extract the public key from your key pair, use the -p switch on *SN.exe* to produce the *MyPublicKey.snk* file that holds your public key:

```
SN -p MyKeys.snk MyPublicKey.snk
```

Now you can delay-sign the assembly using the public key. You should not place the public key in two assembly-level attributes shown here, as you would have done in previous versions of VS.NET:

```
[assembly: System.Reflection.AssemblyKeyFile("MyPublicKey.snk")]
[assembly: System.Reflection.AssemblyDelaySign(true)]
```

Microsoft has deemed this a security risk. Instead, there is now a tab on the project properties that allows you to add the public key to the project. To add the public key, right-click on the project in the Solution Explorer tab in the IDE and choose Properties. The project properties will be displayed in the IDE in its own window. Click on the Signing tab on the lefthand side of this window; see Figure 17-1. This is the tab that allows you to add the public key to this project. To finish this process, check the Sign the Assembly checkbox and select the public key file that you created by clicking on "<Browse...>" in the "Choose a strong name" key file drop-down box. If this assembly will be delay-signed, check the Delay Sign Only checkbox.

In order to finish the signing process, once you are ready to deploy your assembly, use *SN.exe* again to add the final signing piece, using the -R option like this:

```
SN -R SignedAssembly.dll MyKeys.snk
```

This line results in SignedAssembly being fully signed using the private key in *MyKeys.snk*. This step is normally performed on a secure system that has access to the private key.

Discussion

Note that in Visual Studio .NET 2005, the private-key file location needs to be relative to the *.exe* or *.dll* or you will get an error when you try to sign the resulting assembly.

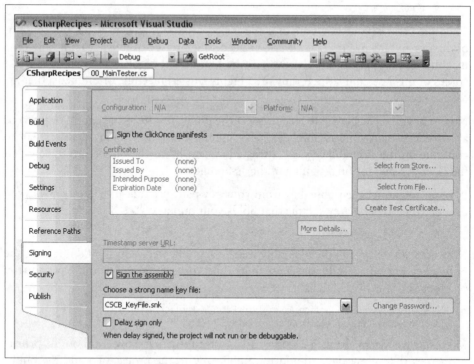

Figure 17-1. The Signing tab of the project properties

In order to use delay-signing, you need to prepare the development environments for assemblies that are only partially signed. To do this, instruct the CLR to skip verification of assemblies using a given public key. Once again, use *SN.exe* to accomplish this:

```
SN -Vr *,d15f821006850b34
```

One other approach is to have separate keys for development and final release versions, which allows for fully signed development versions without compromising the signed assemblies that you ship to customers.

Note that this solution will protect your assembly only as long as the machine it is running on is secure. If a malicious user can access the code that uses the assembly and the assembly itself, he can simply replace them with his own copies.

See Also

See the "AssemblyKeyFile Attribute" and "AssemblyDelaySign Attribute" topics in the MSDN documentation.

17.11 Verifying That an Assembly Has Been Granted Specific Permissions

Problem

When your assembly requests optional permissions (such as asking for disk access to enable users to export data to disk as a product feature) using the `SecurityAction.RequestOptional` flag, it might or might not get those permissions. Regardless, your assembly will still load and execute. You need a way to verify whether your assembly actually obtained those permissions. This can help prevent many security exceptions from being thrown. For example, if you optionally requested read/write permissions on the registry but did not receive them, you could disable the user interface controls that are used to read and store application settings in the registry.

Solution

Check to see if your assembly received the optional permissions using the `SecurityManager.IsGranted` method like this:

```
using System;
using System.Text.RegularExpressions;
using System.Web;
using System.Net;
using System.Security;

Regex regex = new Regex(@"http://www\.oreilly\.com/.*");
WebPermission webConnectPerm = new WebPermission(NetworkAccess.Connect,regex);
if(SecurityManager.IsGranted(webConnectPerm))
{
    // Connect to the O'Reilly site.
}
```

This code sets up a `Regex` for the O'Reilly web site, then uses it to create a `WebPermission` for connecting to that site and all sites containing the *www.oreilly.com* string. You then check the `WebPermission` by calling `SecurityManager.IsGranted` to see whether you have permission to do this.

Discussion

The `IsGranted` method is a lightweight way of determining whether permission is granted for an assembly without incurring the full stackwalk that a `Demand` gives you. The downside to this approach is that the code is still subject to a luring attack if `Assert` is misused, so you need to consider where the call to `IsGranted` is being made in the overall scheme of your security.

Some of the reasons you might design an assembly to have optional permissions is for deployment in different customer scenarios. In some scenarios (like desktop applications), it might be acceptable to have an assembly that can perform more robust actions (talk to a database, create network traffic via HTTP, etc.). In other scenarios, you can defer these actions if the customer does not wish to grant enough permissions for these extra services to function.

See Also

See the "WebPermission Class," "SecurityManager Class," and "IsGranted Method" topics in the MSDN documentation.

17.12 Minimizing the Attack Surface of an Assembly

Problem

Someone attacking your assembly will first attempt to find out as many things as possible about your assembly and then use this information in constructing the attack(s). The more surface area you give to attackers, the more they have to work with. You need to minimize what your assembly is allowed to do so that, if an attacker is successful in taking it over, the attacker will not have the necessary privileges to do any damage to the system.

Solution

Use the SecurityAction.RequestRefuse enumeration member to indicate, at an assembly level, the permissions that you do not wish this assembly to have. This will force the CLR to refuse these permissions to your code and will ensure that, even if another part of the system is compromised, your code cannot be used to perform functions that it does not need the rights to do.

The following example allows the assembly to perform file I/O as part of its minimal permission set but explicitly refuses to allow this assembly to have permissions to skip verification:

```
[assembly: FileIOPermission(SecurityAction.RequestMinimum,Unrestricted=true)]
[assembly: SecurityPermission(SecurityAction.RequestRefuse,
          SkipVerification=false)]
```

Discussion

Once you have determined what permissions your assembly needs as part of your normal security testing, you can use RequestRefuse to lock down your code. If this seems extreme, think of scenarios in which your code could be accessing a data store containing sensitive information, such as Social Security numbers or salary information. This proactive step can help you show your customers that you take security seriously and can help defend your interests in case a break-in occurs on a system that your code is part of.

One serious consideration with this approach is that the use of RequestRefuse marks your assembly as partially trusted. This in turn prevents it from calling any strong-named assembly that hasn't been marked with the AllowPartiallyTrustedCallers attribute.

See Also

See Chapter 8 of Microsoft Patterns & Practices Group: *http://msdn.microsoft.com/library/default.asp?url=/library/en-us/dnnetsec/html/THCMCh08.asp*; see the "SecurityAction Enumeration" and "Global Attributes" topics in the MSDN documentation.

17.13 Obtaining Security/Audit Information

Problem

You need to obtain the security rights and/or audit information for a file or registry key.

Solution

When obtaining security/audit information for a file, use the static GetAccessControl method of the File class to obtain a System.Security.AccessControl.FileSecurity object. Use the FileSecurity object to access the security and audit information for the file. These steps are demonstrated in Example 17-15.

Example 17-15. Obtaining security audit information

```
public static void ViewFileRights()
{
    // Get security information from a file.
    string file = @"c:\FOO.TXT";
    FileSecurity fileSec = File.GetAccessControl(file);
    DisplayFileSecurityInfo(fileSec);
}

public static void DisplayFileSecurityInfo(FileSecurity fileSec)
{
    Console.WriteLine("GetSecurityDescriptorSddlForm: {0}",
        fileSec.GetSecurityDescriptorSddlForm(AccessControlSections.All));

    foreach (FileSystemAccessRule ace in
            fileSec.GetAccessRules(true, true, typeof(NTAccount)))
    {
        Console.WriteLine("\tIdentityReference.Value: {0}",
                        ace.IdentityReference.Value);
        Console.WriteLine("\tAccessControlType: {0}", ace.AccessControlType);
        Console.WriteLine("\tFileSystemRights: {0}", ace.FileSystemRights);
        Console.WriteLine("\tInheritanceFlags: {0}", ace.InheritanceFlags);
        Console.WriteLine("\tIsInherited: {0}", ace.IsInherited);
```

Example 17-15. Obtaining security audit information (continued)

```
        Console.WriteLine("\tPropagationFlags: {0}", ace.PropagationFlags);


        Console.WriteLine("-----------------\r\n\r\n");
    }


    foreach (FileSystemAuditRule ace in
            fileSec.GetAuditRules(true, true, typeof(NTAccount)))
    {
        Console.WriteLine("\tIdentityReference.Value: {0}",
                        ace.IdentityReference.Value);
        Console.WriteLine("\tAuditFlags: {0}", ace.AuditFlags);
        Console.WriteLine("\tFileSystemRights: {0}", ace.FileSystemRights);
        Console.WriteLine("\tInheritanceFlags: {0}", ace.InheritanceFlags);
        Console.WriteLine("\tIsInherited: {0}", ace.IsInherited);
        Console.WriteLine("\tPropagationFlags: {0}", ace.PropagationFlags);

        Console.WriteLine("-----------------\r\n\r\n");
    }

    Console.WriteLine("GetGroup(typeof(NTAccount)).Value: {0}",
                    fileSec.GetGroup(typeof(NTAccount)).Value);
    Console.WriteLine("GetOwner(typeof(NTAccount)).Value: {0}",
                    fileSec.GetOwner(typeof(NTAccount)).Value);

    Console.WriteLine("---------------------------------------\r\n\r\n\r\n");
}
```

These methods produce the following output:

```
GetSecurityDescriptorSddlForm:   O:BAG:SYD:PAI(A;;FA;;;SY)(A;;FA;;;BA)
    IdentityReference.Value: NT AUTHORITY\SYSTEM
    AccessControlType: Allow
    FileSystemRights: FullControl
    InheritanceFlags: None
    IsInherited: False
    PropagationFlags: None
-----------------


    IdentityReference.Value: BUILTIN\Administrators
    AccessControlType: Allow
    FileSystemRights: FullControl
    InheritanceFlags: None
    IsInherited: False
    PropagationFlags: None
-----------------


GetGroup(typeof(NTAccount)).Value: NT AUTHORITY\SYSTEM
GetOwner(typeof(NTAccount)).Value: BUILTIN\Administrators
---------------------------------------
```

When obtaining security/audit information for a registry key, use the GetAccess-Control instance method of the Microsoft.Win32.RegistryKey class to obtain a System.Security.AccessControl.RegistrySecurity object. Use the RegistrySecurity object to access the security and audit information for the registry key. These steps are demonstrated in Example 17-16.

Example 17-16. Getting security or audit information for a registry key

```
public static void ViewRegKeyRights( )
{
    // Get security information from a registry key.
    using (RegistryKey regKey =
        Registry.LocalMachine.OpenSubKey(@"SOFTWARE\MyCompany\MyApp"))
    {
        RegistrySecurity regSecurity = regKey.GetAccessControl( );
        DisplayRegKeySecurityInfo(regSecurity);
    }
}


public static void DisplayRegKeySecurityInfo(RegistrySecurity regSec)
{
    Console.WriteLine("GetSecurityDescriptorSddlForm:  {0}",
        regSec.GetSecurityDescriptorSddlForm(AccessControlSections.All));

    foreach (RegistryAccessRule ace in
            regSec.GetAccessRules(true, true, typeof(NTAccount)))
    {
        Console.WriteLine("\tIdentityReference.Value: {0}",
                        ace.IdentityReference.Value);
        Console.WriteLine("\tAccessControlType: {0}", ace.AccessControlType);
        Console.WriteLine("\tRegistryRights: {0}", ace.RegistryRights.ToString( ));
        Console.WriteLine("\tInheritanceFlags: {0}", ace.InheritanceFlags);
        Console.WriteLine("\tIsInherited: {0}", ace.IsInherited);
        Console.WriteLine("\tPropagationFlags: {0}", ace.PropagationFlags);

        Console.WriteLine("----------------\r\n\r\n");
    }


    foreach (RegistryAuditRule ace in
            regSec.GetAuditRules(true, true, typeof(NTAccount)))
    {
        Console.WriteLine("\tIdentityReference.Value: {0}",
                        ace.IdentityReference.Value);
        Console.WriteLine("\tAuditFlags: {0}", ace.AuditFlags);
        Console.WriteLine("\tRegistryRights: {0}", ace.RegistryRights.ToString( ));
        Console.WriteLine("\tInheritanceFlags: {0}", ace.InheritanceFlags);
        Console.WriteLine("\tIsInherited: {0}", ace.IsInherited);
        Console.WriteLine("\tPropagationFlags: {0}", ace.PropagationFlags);

        Console.WriteLine("----------------\r\n\r\n");
    }
```

Example 17-16. Getting security or audit information for a registry key (continued)

```
        Console.WriteLine("GetGroup(typeof(NTAccount)).Value: {0}",
                          regSec.GetGroup(typeof(NTAccount)).Value);
        Console.WriteLine("GetOwner(typeof(NTAccount)).Value: {0}",
                          regSec.GetOwner(typeof(NTAccount)).Value);

        Console.WriteLine("--------------------------------------\r\n\r\n\r\n");
    }
```

These methods produce the following output:

```
GetSecurityDescriptorSddlForm:  O:S-1-5-21-329068152-1383384898-682003330-1004G:S-1-
5-21-329068152-1383384898-682003330-513D:
AI(A;ID;KR;;;BU)(A;CIIOID;GR;;;BU)(A;ID;KA;;;BA)(A;CIIOID;GA;;;BA)(A;ID;KA;;;SY)(A;CI
IOID;GA;;;SY)(A;ID;KA;;;S-1-5-21-329068152-1383384898-682003330-
1004)(A;CIIOID;GA;;;CO)
        IdentityReference.Value: BUILTIN\Users
        AccessControlType: Allow
        RegistryRights: ReadKey
        InheritanceFlags: None
        IsInherited: True
        PropagationFlags: None
        -----------------


        IdentityReference.Value: BUILTIN\Users
        AccessControlType: Allow
        RegistryRights: -2147483648
        InheritanceFlags: ContainerInherit
        IsInherited: True
        PropagationFlags: InheritOnly
        -----------------


        IdentityReference.Value: BUILTIN\Administrators
        AccessControlType: Allow
        RegistryRights: FullControl
        InheritanceFlags: None
        IsInherited: True
        PropagationFlags: None
        -----------------


        IdentityReference.Value: BUILTIN\Administrators
        AccessControlType: Allow
        RegistryRights: 268435456
        InheritanceFlags: ContainerInherit
        IsInherited: True
        PropagationFlags: InheritOnly
        -----------------


        IdentityReference.Value: NT AUTHORITY\SYSTEM
        AccessControlType: Allow
```

```
    RegistryRights: FullControl
    InheritanceFlags: None
    IsInherited: True
    PropagationFlags: None
    -----------------


    IdentityReference.Value: NT AUTHORITY\SYSTEM
    AccessControlType: Allow
    RegistryRights: 268435456
    InheritanceFlags: ContainerInherit
    IsInherited: True
    PropagationFlags: InheritOnly
    -----------------


    IdentityReference.Value: OPERATOR-C1EFE0\Admin
    AccessControlType: Allow
    RegistryRights: FullControl
    InheritanceFlags: None
    IsInherited: True
    PropagationFlags: None
    -----------------


    IdentityReference.Value: CREATOR OWNER
    AccessControlType: Allow
    RegistryRights: 268435456
    InheritanceFlags: ContainerInherit
    IsInherited: True
    PropagationFlags: InheritOnly
    -----------------


GetGroup(typeof(NTAccount)).Value: OPERATOR-C1EFE0\None
GetOwner(typeof(NTAccount)).Value: OPERATOR-C1EFE0\Admin
----------------------------------------
```

Discussion

The essential method that is used to obtain the security information for a file or registry key is the GetAccessControl method. When this method is called on the
RegistryKey object, a RegistrySecurity object is returned. However, when this
method is called on a File class, a FileSecurity object is returned. The
RegistrySecurity and FileSecurity objects essentially represent a Discretionary
Access Control List (DACL), which is what developers writing code in unmanaged
languages such as C++ are used to working with.

The RegistrySecurity and FileSecurity objects each contains a list of security rules
that has been applied to the system object that it represents. The RegistrySecurity
object contains a list of RegistryAccessRule objects, and the FileSecurity object contains a list of FileSystemAccessRule objects. These rule objects are the equivalent of

the Access Control Entries (ACE) that make up the list of security rules within a DACL.

System objects other than just the File class and RegistryKey object allow security privileges to be queried. Table 17-1 lists all the .NET Framework classes that return a security object type and what that type is. In addition, the rule-object type that is contained in the security object is also listed.

Table 17-1. List of all *Security and *AccessRule objects and the types to which they apply

Class	Object returned by the GetAccessControl method	Rule-object type contained within the security object
Directory	DirectorySecurity	FileSystemAccessRule
DirectoryInfo	DirectorySecurity	FileSystemAccessRule
EventWaitHandle	EventWaitHandleSecurity	EventWaitHandleAccessRule
File	FileSecurity	FileSystemAccessRule
FileInfo	FileSecurity	FileSystemAccessRule
FileStream	FileSecurity	FileSystemAccessRule
Mutex	MutexSecurity	MutexAccessRule
RegistryKey	RegistrySecurity	RegistryAccessRule
Semaphore	SemaphoreSecurity	SemaphoreAccessRule

The abstraction of a system object's DACL through the *Security objects and the abstraction of a DACL's ACE through the *AccessRule objects allows easy access to the security privileges of that system object. In previous versions of the .NET Framework, these DACLs and their ACEs would have been accessible only in unmanaged code. With the latest .NET Framework, you now have access to view and program these objects.

See Also

See Recipe 17.14; see the "System.IO.File.GetAccessControl Method," "System.Security.AccessControl.FileSecurity Class," "Microsoft.Win32.RegistryKey.GetAccessControl Method," and "System.Security.AccessControl.RegistrySecurity Class" topics in the MSDN documentation.

17.14 Granting/Revoking Access to a File or Registry Key

Problem

You need to change the security privileges of either a file or registry key programmatically.

Solution

The code shown in Example 17-17 grants and then revokes the ability to perform write actions on a registry key.

Example 17-17. Granting and revoking the right to perform write actions on a registry key

```
public static void GrantRevokeRegKeyRights()
{
    NTAccount user = new NTAccount(@"WRKSTN\ST");

    using (RegistryKey regKey = Registry.LocalMachine.OpenSubKey(
                        @"SOFTWARE\MyCompany\MyApp"))
    {
        GrantRegKeyRights(regKey, user, RegistryRights.WriteKey,
            InheritanceFlags.None, PropagationFlags.None, AccessControlType.Allow);
        RevokeRegKeyRights(regKey, user, RegistryRights.WriteKey,
                    InheritanceFlags.None, PropagationFlags.None,
                    AccessControlType.Allow)
    }
}

public static void GrantRegKeyRights(RegistryKey regKey,
                                NTAccount user,
                                RegistryRights rightsFlags,
                                InheritanceFlags inherFlags,
                                PropagationFlags propFlags,
                                AccessControlType actFlags)
{
    RegistrySecurity regSecurity = regKey.GetAccessControl();

    RegistryAccessRule rule = new RegistryAccessRule(user, rightsFlags, inherFlags,
                                            propFlags, actFlags);
    regSecurity.AddAccessRule(rule);
    regKey.SetAccessControl(regSecurity);
}

public static void RevokeRegKeyRights(RegistryKey regKey,
                                NTAccount user,
                                RegistryRights rightsFlags,
                                InheritanceFlags inherFlags,
                                PropagationFlags propFlags,
                                AccessControlType actFlags)
{
    RegistrySecurity regSecurity = regKey.GetAccessControl();

    RegistryAccessRule rule = new RegistryAccessRule(user, rightsFlags, inherFlags,
                                            propFlags, actFlags);
    regSecurity.RemoveAccessRuleSpecific(rule);

    regKey.SetAccessControl(regSecurity);
}
```

The code shown in Example 17-18 grants and then revokes the ability to delete a file.

Example 17-18. Granting and revoking the right to delete a file

```
public static void GrantRevokeFileRights()
{
    NTAccount user = new NTAccount(@"WRKSTN\ST");

    string file = @"c:\FOO.TXT";
    GrantFileRights(file, user, FileSystemRights.Delete, InheritanceFlags.None,
                    PropagationFlags.None, AccessControlType.Allow);
    RevokeFileRights(file, user, FileSystemRights.Delete, InheritanceFlags.None,
                     PropagationFlags.None, AccessControlType.Allow);
}

public static void GrantFileRights(string file,
                                   NTAccount user,
                                   FileSystemRights rightsFlags,
                                   InheritanceFlags inherFlags,
                                   PropagationFlags propFlags,
                                   AccessControlType actFlags)
{
    FileSecurity fileSecurity = File.GetAccessControl(file);

    FileSystemAccessRule rule = new FileSystemAccessRule(user, rightsFlags,
                                                         inherFlags, propFlags,
                                                         actFlags);
    fileSecurity.AddAccessRule(rule);
    File.SetAccessControl(file, fileSecurity);
}

public static void RevokeFileRights(string file,
                                    NTAccount user,
                                    FileSystemRights rightsFlags,
                                    InheritanceFlags inherFlags,
                                    PropagationFlags propFlags,
                                    AccessControlType actFlags)
{
    FileSecurity fileSecurity = File.GetAccessControl(file);

    FileSystemAccessRule rule = new FileSystemAccessRule(user, rightsFlags,
                                                         inherFlags, propFlags,
                                                         actFlags);
    fileSecurity.RemoveAccessRuleSpecific(rule);
    File.SetAccessControl(file, fileSecurity);
}
```

Discussion

When granting or revoking access rights on a file or registry key, you need two things. The first is a valid NTAccount object. This object essentially encapsulates a user or group account. A valid NTAccount object is required in order to create either a new RegistryAccessRule or a new FileSystemAccessRule. The NTAccount identifies the user or group this access rule will apply to. Note that the string passed in to the

NTAccount constructor must be changed to a valid user or group name that exists on your machine. If you pass in the name of an existing user or group account that has been disabled, an `IdentityNotMappedException` will be thrown with the message "Some or all identity references could not be translated."

The second item that is needed is either a valid `RegistryKey` object, if you are modifying security access to a registry key or a string containing a valid path and filename to an existing file. These objects will have security permissions either granted to them or revoked from them.

Once these two items have been obtained, you can use the second item to obtain a security object, which contains the list of access-rule objects. For example, the following code obtains the security object for the registry key HKEY-LOCAL_MACHINE\SOFTWARE\MyCompany\MyApp:

```
RegistryKey regKey = Registry.LocalMachine.OpenSubKey(
                        @"SOFTWARE\MyCompany\MyApp");
RegistrySecurity regSecurity = regKey.GetAccessControl();
```

The following code obtains the security object for the *FOO.TXT* file:

```
string file = @"c:\FOO.TXT";
FileSecurity fileSecurity = File.GetAccessControl(file);
```

Now that you have your particular security object, you can create an access-rule object that will be added to this security object. To do this, you need to create a new access rule. For a registry key, you have to create a new `RegistryAccessRule` object, and for a file, you have to create a new `FileSystemAccessRule` object. To add this access rule to the correct security object, you call the `SetAccessControl` method on the security object. Note that `RegistryAccessRule` objects can be added only to `RegistrySecurity` objects and `FileSystemAccessRule` objects can be added only to `FileSecurity` objects.

To remove an access-rule object from a system object, you follow the same set of steps, except that you call the `RemoveAccessRuleSpecific` method instead of `AddAccessRule`. `RemoveAccessRuleSpecific` accepts an access-rule object and attempts to remove the rule that exactly matches this rule object from the security object. As always, you must remember to call the `SetAccessControl` method to apply any changes to the actual system object.

For a list of other classes that allow security permissions to be modified programmatically, see Recipe 17.13.

See Also

See Recipe 17.13; see the "System.IO.File.GetAccessControl Method," "System.Security.AccessControl.FileSecurity Class," "System.Security.AccessControl.FileSystemAccessRule Class," "Microsoft.Win32.RegistryKey.GetAccessControl Method," "System.Security.AccessControl.RegistrySecurity Class," and "System.Security.AccessControl.RegistryAccessRule Class" topics in the MSDN documentation.

17.15 Protecting String Data with Secure Strings

Problem

You need to store sensitive information, such as a Social Security number, in a string. However, you do not want prying eyes to be able to view this data in memory.

Solution

Use the `SecureString` object. To place text from a stream object within a SecureString object, use the following method:

```
public static SecureString CreateSecureString(StreamReader secretStream)
{
    SecureString secretStr = new SecureString( );
    char buf;

    while (secretStream.Peek( ) >= 0)
    {
        buf = (char)secretStream.Read( );
        secretStr.AppendChar(buf);
    }

    // Make the secretStr object read-only.
    secretStr.MakeReadOnly( );

    return (secretStr);
}
```

To pull the text out of a SecureString object, use the following method:

```
public static void ReadSecureString(SecureString secretStr)
{
    // In order to read back the string, you need to use some special methods.
    IntPtr secretStrPtr = Marshal.SecureStringToBSTR(secretStr);
    string nonSecureStr = Marshal.PtrToStringBSTR(secretStrPtr);

    // Use the unprotected string.
    Console.WriteLine("nonSecureStr = {0}", nonSecureStr);

    Marshal.ZeroFreeBSTR(secretStrPtr);

    if (!secretStr.IsReadOnly( ))
    {
        secretStr.Clear( );
    }
}
```

Discussion

A SecureString object is designed specifically to contain string data that you want to keep secret. Some of the data you may want to store in a SecureString object would be a Social Security number, a credit card number, a PIN number, a password, an employee ID, or any other type of sensitive information.

This string data is automatically encrypted immediately upon being added to the SecureString object, and it is automatically decrypted when the string data is extracted from the SecureString object. The encryption is one of the highlights of using this object. In addition to encryption, there will be only one copy of a SecureString object in memory at any one time. This is in direct contrast to a String object, which creates multiple copies in memory whenever the text in the String object is modified.

Another feature of a SecureString object is that when the MakeReadOnly method is called, the SecureString becomes immutable. Any attempt to modify the string data within the read-only SecureString object causes an InvalidOperationException to be thrown. Once a SecureString object is made read-only, it cannot go back to a read/write state. However, you need to be careful when calling the Copy method on an existing SecureString object. This method will create a new instance of the SecureString object on which it was called, with a copy of its data. However, this new SecureString object is now readable and writable. You should review your code to determine if this new SecureString object should be made read-only similarly to its original SecureString object.

 The SecureString object can be used only on Windows 2000 (with Service Pack 3 or greater) or later operating systems.

In this recipe you create a SecureString object from data read in from a stream. This data could also come from a char* using unsafe code. The SecureString object contains a constructor that accepts a parameter of this type in addition to an integer parameter that takes a length value, which determines the number of characters to pull from the char*.

Getting data out of a SecureString object is not obvious at first glance. There are no methods to return the data contained within a SecureString object. In order to accomplish this, you must use two static methods on the Marshal class. The first is the SecureStringToBSTR, which accepts your SecureString object and returns an IntPtr. This IntPtr is then passed into the PtrToStringBSTR method, also on the Marshal class. The PtrToStringBSTR method then returns an unsecure String object containing your decrypted string data.

Once you are done using the SecureString object, you should call the static ZeroFreeBSTR method on the Marshal class to zero out any memory allocated when extracting the data from the SecureStirng. As an added safeguard, you should call the Clear method of the SecureString object to zero out the encrypted string from memory. If you have made your SecureString object read-only, you will not be able to call the Clear method to wipe out its data. In this situation, you must either call the Dispose method on the SecureString object or rely on the garbage collector to remove the SecureString object and its data from memory.

Notice that when you pull a SecureString object into an unsecure String, its data becomes viewable by a malicious hacker. So it may seem pointless to go through the trouble of using a SecureString when you are just going to convert it into an unsecure String. However, by using a SecureString, you narrow the window of opportunity for a malicious hacker to view this data in memory. In addition, some APIs accept a SecureString as a parameter so that you don't have to convert it to an unsecure String. The ProcessStartInfo, for example, accepts a password in its Password property as a SecureString object.

 The SecureString object is not a silver bullet for securing your data. It is, however, another layer of defense you can add to your application.

See Also

See the "SecureString Class" topic in the MSDN documentation.

17.16 Securing Stream Data

Problem

You want to use the TCP server in Recipe 16.1 to communicate with the TCP client in Recipe 16.2. However, you need the communication to be secure.

Solution

Replace the NetworkStream class with the more secure SslStream class on both the client and the server. The code for the more secure TCP client, TCPClient_SSL, is shown in Example 17-19 (changes are highlighted).

Example 17-19. TCPClient_SSL class

```
class TCPClient_SSL
{
    private TcpClient _client = null;
    private IPAddress _address = IPAddress.Parse("127.0.0.1");
    private int _port = 5;
    private IPEndPoint _endPoint = null;

    public TCPClient_SSL(string address, string port)
    {
        _address = IPAddress.Parse(address);
        _port = Convert.ToInt32(port);
```

Example 17-19. TCPClient_SSL class (continued)

```csharp
        _endPoint = new IPEndPoint(_address, _port);
    }

    public void ConnectToServer(string msg)
    {
        try
        {
            using (client = new TcpClient( ))
            {
                client.Connect(_endPoint);

                using (SslStream sslStream = new SslStream(_client.GetStream( ),
                            false, new RemoteCertificateValidationCallback(
                                CertificateValidationCallback)))
                {
                    sslStream.AuthenticateAsClient("MyTestCert2");

                    // Get the bytes to send for the message.
                    byte[] bytes = Encoding.ASCII.GetBytes(msg);

                    // Send message.
                    Console.WriteLine("Sending message to server: " + msg);
                    sslStream.Write(bytes, 0, bytes.Length);

                    // Get the response.
                    // Buffer to store the response bytes.
                    bytes = new byte[1024];

                    // Display the response.
                    int bytesRead = sslStream.Read(bytes, 0, bytes.Length);
                    string serverResponse = Encoding.ASCII.GetString(bytes, 0,
                        bytesRead);
                    Console.WriteLine("Server said: " + serverResponse);
                }
            }
        }
        catch (SocketException e)
        {
            Console.WriteLine("There was an error talking to the server: {0}",
            e.ToString( ));
        }
    }

    private bool CertificateValidationCallback(object sender,
                                    X509Certificate certificate,
                                    X509Chain chain,
                                    SslPolicyErrors sslPolicyErrors)
    {
        if (sslPolicyErrors == SslPolicyErrors.None)
        {
            return true;
        }
```

Example 17-19. TCPClient_SSL class (continued)

```
        else
        {
            if (sslPolicyErrors == SslPolicyErrors.RemoteCertificateChainErrors)
            {
                Console.WriteLine("The X509Chain.ChainStatus returned an array " +
                    "of X509ChainStatus objects containing error information.");
            }
            else if (sslPolicyErrors ==
                    SslPolicyErrors.RemoteCertificateNameMismatch)
            {
                Console.WriteLine("There was a mismatch of the name " +
                    "on a certificate.");
            }
            else if (sslPolicyErrors ==
                    SslPolicyErrors.RemoteCertificateNotAvailable)
            {
                Console.WriteLine("No certificate was available.");
            }
            else
            {
                Console.WriteLine("SSL Certificate Validation Error!");
            }
        }

        Console.WriteLine(Environment.NewLine +
                        "SSL Certificate Validation Error!");
        Console.WriteLine(sslPolicyErrors.ToString());

        return false;
    }
}
```

The new code for the more secure TCP server, TCPServer_SSL, is shown in Example 17-20 (changes are highlighted).

Example 17-20. TCPServer_SSL class

```
class TCPServer_SSL
{
    private TcpListener _listener = null;
    private IPAddress _address = IPAddress.Parse("127.0.0.1");
    private int _port = 55555;

    #region CTORs
    public TCPServer_SSL()
    {
    }

    public TCPServer_SSL(string address, string port)
    {
        _port = Convert.ToInt32(port);
        _address = IPAddress.Parse(address);
```

Example 17-20. TCPServer_SSL class (continued)

```
    }
    #endregion // CTORs

    #region Properties
    public IPAddress Address
    {
        get { return _address; }
        set { _address = value; }
    }

    public int Port
    {
        get { return _port; }
        set { _port = value; }
    }
    #endregion

    public void Listen()
    {
        try
        {
            _using_(listener = new TcpListener(_address, _port))
            {
                // Fire up the server.
                listener.Start();

                // Enter the listening loop.
                while (true)
                {
                    Console.Write("Looking for someone to talk to... ");

                    // Wait for connection.
                    TcpClient newClient = _listener.AcceptTcpClient();
                    Console.WriteLine("Connected to new client");

                    // Spin a thread to take care of the client.
                    ThreadPool.QueueUserWorkItem(new WaitCallback(ProcessClient),
                                        newClient);
                }
            }
        }
        catch (SocketException e)
        {
            Console.WriteLine("SocketException: {0}", e);
        }
        finally
        {
            // Shut it down.
            _listener.Stop();
        }

        Console.WriteLine("\nHit any key (where is ANYKEY?) to continue...");
```

Example 17-20. TCPServer_SSL class (continued)

```
        Console.Read( );
    }

    private void ProcessClient(object client)
    {
        using (TcpClient newClient = (TcpClient)client)
        {
            // Buffer for reading data.
            byte[] bytes = new byte[1024];
            string clientData = null;

            using (SslStream sslStream = new SslStream(newClient.GetStream( )))
            {
                sslStream.AuthenticateAsServer(GetServerCert("MyTestCert2"), false,
                                        SslProtocols.Default, true);

                // Loop to receive all the data sent by the client.
                int bytesRead = 0;
                while ((bytesRead = sslStream.Read(bytes, 0, bytes.Length)) != 0)
                {
                    // Translate data bytes to an ASCII string.
                    clientData = Encoding.ASCII.GetString(bytes, 0, bytesRead);
                    Console.WriteLine("Client says: {0}", clientData);

                    // Thank them for their input.
                    bytes = Encoding.ASCII.GetBytes("Thanks call again!");

                    // Send back a response.
                    sslStream.Write(bytes, 0, bytes.Length);
                }
            }
        }
    }

    private static X509Certificate GetServerCert(string subjectName)
    {
        X509Store store = new X509Store(StoreName.My, StoreLocation.LocalMachine);
        store.Open(OpenFlags.ReadOnly);
        X509CertificateCollection certificate =
                store.Certificates.Find(X509FindType.FindBySubjectName,
                                        subjectName, true);

        if (certificate.Count > 0)
            return (certificate[0]);
        else
            return (null);
    }
}
```

Discussion

For more information about the inner workings of the TCP server and client and how to run these applications, see Recipes 16.1 and 16.2. In this recipe, you will cover only the changes needed to convert the TCP server and client to use the SslStream object for secure communication.

The SslStream object uses the SSL protocol to provide a secure encrypted channel on which to send data. However, encryption is just one of the security features built into the SslStream object. Another feature of SslStream is that it prevents malicious or even accidental modification to the data. Even though the data is encrypted, it may become modified during transit. To determine if this has occurred, the data is signed with a hash before it is sent. When it is received, the data is rehashed and the two hashes are compared. If both hashes are equivalent, the message arrived intact; if the hashes are not equivalent, then something modified the data during transit.

The SslStream object also has the ability to use client and/or server certificates to authenticate the client and/or the server. These certificates are used to prove the identity of the issuer. For example, if a client attaches to a server using SSL, the server must provide a certificate to the client that is used to prove that the server is who it says it is. The SslStream object also allows the client to pass a certificate to the server if the client also needs to prove who it is to the server.

To allow the TCP server and client to communicate successfully, you need to set up an X.509 certificate that will be used to authenticate the TCP server. To do this, you set up a test certificate using the *makecert.exe* utility. This utility can be found in the *<drive>:\Program Files\Microsoft Visual Studio 8\SDK\v2.0\Bin* directory. The syntax for creating a simple certificate is as follows:

```
makecert -r -pe -n "CN=MyTestCert2" -e 01/01/2036
        -sr localMachine c:\MyAppTestCert.cer
```

The options are defined as follows:

-r

The certificate will be self-signed.

-pe

The certificate's private key will be exportable so that it can be included in the certificate.

-n "CN=MyTestCert2"

The publisher's certificate name. The name follows the "CN=" text.

-e 01/01/2036

The date at which this certificate expires.

-sr localMachine

The store where this certificate will be located. In this case, it is localMachine. However, you can also specify currentUser (which is the default if this switch is omitted).

The final argument to the *makecert.exe* utility is the output filename, in this case *c:\MyAppTestCert.cer*. This will create the certificate in the *c:\MyAppTestCert.cer* file on the hard drive.

The next step involves opening Windows Explorer and right-clicking on the *c:\MyAppTestCert.cer* file. This will display a pop-up menu with the Install Certificate menu item. Click this menu item and a wizard will be started to allow you to import this *.cer* file into the certificate store. The first dialog box of the wizard is shown in Figure 17-2. Click the Next button to go to the next step in the wizard.

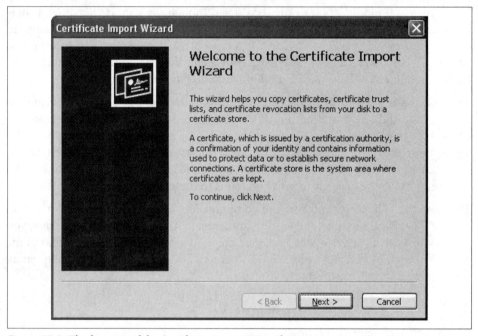

Figure 17-2. The first step of the Certificate Import Wizard

The next step in the wizard allows you to choose the certificate store in which you want to install your certificate. This dialog is shown in Figure 17-3. Keep the defaults and click the Next button.

The final step in the wizard is shown in Figure 17-4. On this dialog, click the Finish button.

After you click the Finish button, the message box shown in Figure 17-5 is displayed, warning you to verify the certificate that you wish to install. Click the Yes button to install the certificate.

Finally, the message box in Figure 17-6 is displayed, indicating that the import was successful.

At this point you can run the TCP server and client and they should communicate successfully.

Figure 17-3. Specifying a certificate store in the Certificate Import Wizard

Figure 17-4. The last step of the Certificate Import Wizard

To use the SslStream in the TCP server project, you need to create a new SslStream object to wrap the TcpClient object:

```
SslStream sslStream = new SslStream(newClient.GetStream());
```

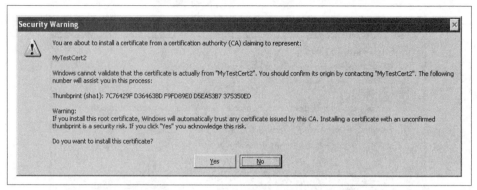

Figure 17-5. The security warning

Figure 17-6. The import successful message

Before you can use this new stream object, you must authenticate the server using the following line of code:

```
sslStream.AuthenticateAsServer(GetServerCert("MyTestCert2"),
                               false, SslProtocols.Default, true);
```

The GetServerCert method finds the server certificate used to authenticate the server. Notice the name passed in to this method; it is the same as the publisher's certificate name switch used with the *makecert.exe* utility (see the *–n* switch). This certificate is returned from the GetServerCert method as an X509Certificate object. The next argument to the AuthenticateAsServer method is false, indicating that a client certificate is not required. The SslProtocols.Default argument indicates that the authentication mechanism (SSL 2.0, SSL 3.0, TLS 1.0, or PCT 1.0) is chosen based on what is available to the client and server. The final argument indicates that the certificate will be checked to see whether it has been revoked.

To use the SslStream in the TCP client project, you create a new SslStream object, a bit differently from how it was created in the TCP server project:

```
SslStream sslStream = new SslStream(_client.GetStream( ), false,
    new RemoteCertificateValidationCallback(CertificateValidationCallback));
```

This constructor accepts a stream from the _client field, a false indicating that the stream associated with the _client field will be closed when the Close method of the SslStream object is called, and a delegate that validates the server certificate. The

CertificateValidationCallback method is called whenever a server certificate needs to be validated. The server certificate is checked and any errors are passed into this delegate method to allow you to handle them as you wish.

The AuthenticateAsClient method is called next to authenticate the server:

```
sslStream.AuthenticateAsClient("MyTestCert2");
```

As you can see, with a little extra work, you can replace the current stream type you are using with the SslStream to gain the benefits of the SSL protocol.

See Also

See the "SslStream Class" topic in the MSDN documentation.

17.17 Encrypting web.config Information

Problem

You need to encrypt data within a *web.config* file programmatically.

Solution

To encrypt data within a *web.config* file section, use the following method:

```
public static void EncryptWebConfigData(string appPath,
                                        string protectedSection,
                                        string dataProtectionProvider)
{
    System.Configuration.Configuration webConfig =
                WebConfigurationManager.OpenWebConfiguration(appPath);
    ConfigurationSection webConfigSection = webConfig.GetSection(protectedSection);

    if (!webConfigSection.SectionInformation.IsProtected)
    {
        webConfigSection.SectionInformation.ProtectSection(dataProtectionProvider);
        webConfig.Save();
    }
}
```

To decrypt data within a *web.config* file section, use the following method:

```
public static void DecryptWebConfigData(string appPath, string protectedSection)
{
    System.Configuration.Configuration webConfig =
                WebConfigurationManager.OpenWebConfiguration(appPath);
    ConfigurationSection webConfigSection = webConfig.GetSection(protectedSection);

    if (webConfigSection.SectionInformation.IsProtected)
    {
        webConfigSection.SectionInformation.UnprotectSection();
        webConfig.Save();
    }
}
```

You will need to add the System.Web and System.Configuration DLLs to your project before this code will compile.

Discussion

To encrypt data, you can call the EncryptWebConfigData method with the following arguments:

```
EncryptWebConfigData("/WebApplication1", "appSettings",
                    "DataProtectionConfigurationProvider");
```

The first argument is the virtual path to the web application, the second argument is the section that you want to encrypt, and the last argument is the data protection provider that you want to use to encrypt the data.

The EncryptWebConfigData method uses the virtual path passed into it to open the *web.config* file. This is done using the OpenWebConfiguration static method of the WebConfigurationManager class:

```
System.Configuration.Configuration webConfig =
    WebConfigurationManager.OpenWebConfiguration(appPath);
```

This method returns a System.Configuration.Configuration object, which you use to get the section of the *web.config* file that you wish to encrypt. This is accomplished through the GetSection method:

```
ConfigurationSection webConfigSection = webConfig.GetSection(protectedSection);
```

This method returns a ConfigurationSection object that you can use to encrypt the section. This is done through a call to the ProtectSection method:

```
webConfigSection.SectionInformation.ProtectSection(dataProtectionProvider);
```

The dataProtectionProvider argument is a string identifying which data protection provider you want to use to encrypt the section information. The two available providers are DpapiProtectedConfigurationProvider and RsaProtectedConfigurationProvider. The DpapiProtectedConfigurationProvider class makes use of the Data Protection API (DPAPI) to encrypt and decrypt data. The RsaProtectedConfigurationProvider class makes use of the RsaCryptoServiceProvider class in the .NET Framework to encrypt and decrypt data.

The final step to encrypting the section information is to call the Save method of the System.Configuration.Configuration object. This saves the changes to the *web.config* file. If this method is not called, the encrypted data will not be saved.

To decrypt data within a *web.config* file, you can call the DecryptWebConfigData method with the following parameters:

```
DecryptWebConfigData("/WebApplication1", "appSettings");
```

The first argument is the virtual path to the web application; the second argument is the section that you want to encrypt.

The `DecryptWebConfigData` method operates very similarly to the `EncryptWebConfigData` method, except that it calls the `UnprotectSection` method to decrypt the encrypted data in the *web.config* file:

```
webConfigSection.SectionInformation.UnprotectSection( );
```

If you encrypt data in the *web.config* file using this technique, the data will automatically be decrypted when the web application accesses the encrypted data in the *web. config* file.

See Also

See the "System.Configuration.Configuration Class" topic in the MSDN documentation.

17.18 Obtaining the Full Reason a SecurityException Was Thrown

Problem

You need more information as to why a `SecurityException` was thrown.

Solution

Use the new properties available on the `SecurityException` object, shown in Table 17-2.

Table 17-2. SecurityException Properties

Property	Description
Action	This property returns a `SecurityAction` enumeration value indicating the cause of the security check failure. Possible values can be any of the following:
	Assert
	Demand
	DemandChoice
	Deny
	InheritanceDemand
	InheritanceDemandChoice
	LinkDemand
	LinkDemandChoice
	PermitOnly
	RequestMinimum
	RequestOptional
	RequestRefuseusing
Data	An `IDictionary` of user-defined key-value pairs.

Table 17-2. SecurityException Properties (continued)

Property	Description
Demanded	Returns the permission(s) that caused the Demand to fail. The returned object needs to be cast to a Permission, PermissionSet, or PermissionSetCollection type in order to access its information. You can use the is keyword to determine which one of these types this property returned.
DenySetInstance	Returns the denied permission(s) that caused the Demand to fail. This property contains a value whenever a Deny higher up in the stack causes a Demand to fail. The returned object needs to be cast to a Permission, PermissionSet, or PermissionSetCollection type in order to access its information. You can use the is keyword to determine which one of these types this property returned.
FailedAssemblyInfo	Returns an AssemblyName object for the assembly where this exception occurred (i.e., the assembly where the Demand that failed was called).
FirstPermission ThatFailed	Returns an IPermission object of the first permission that failed. This is useful when several permissions in a permission set were demanded at one time. This property identifies which permission caused the exception to occur.
Method	Returns a MethodInfo object for the method where this exception originated. If the cause of the exception was due to a Deny or PermitOnly, the method containing the Deny or PermitOnly will be returned by this property. From this object you can also obtain information on the type and assembly that contain this method.
PermitOnlySetIn stance	Returns the permission(s) that were set by a PermitOnly at the point where the security exception was thrown. The returned object needs to be cast to a Permission, PermissionSet, or PermissionSetCollection type in order to access its information. You can use the is keyword to determine which one of these types this property returned.
URL	Returns a string representing the URL of the assembly where this exception originated.
Zone	Returns a SecurityZone enumeration value indicating the zone of the assembly where this exception originated. Possible values can be any of the following: Internet Intranet MyComputer NoZone Trusted Untrusted

Discussion

These new properties on the SecurityException class provide much more insight into what caused the exception to be thrown. For example, if you think a Demand has failed, you can examine the Action property to determine that it was in fact the Demand. Next you can use the Demanded property to find out exactly what permission(s) the Demand attempted to demand. You can compare this to the GrantedSet property, which contains the permission(s) that were granted to the assembly. Now that you know what caused the Demand to fail, you can use the Method, FailedAssemblyInfo, and URL properties to determine where the failure occurred.

The Data property can be a very useful property to a developer. This property contains key-value pairs that the developer creates and fills with information concerning why this exception occurred. In this property, you can place variable names and the data they contained at the time of the exception. This can give you even more clues as to why this exception was thrown. See Recipe 7.18 for more information on the Exception.Data property.

See Also

See the "SecurityException" topic in the MSDN documentation.

17.19 Achieving Secure Unicode Encoding

Problem

You want to make sure that your UnicodeEncoding or UTF8Encoding class detects any errors, such as an invalid sequence of bytes.

Solution

Use the constructor for the UnicodeEncoding class that accepts three parameters:

```
UnicodeEncoding encoding = new UnicodeEncoding(false, true, true);
```

Or use the constructor for the UTF8Encoding class that accepts two parameters:

```
UTF8Encoding encoding = new UTF8Encoding(true, true);
```

Discussion

The final argument to both these constructors should be true. This turns on error detection for this class. Error detection will help when an attacker somehow is able to access and modify a Unicode- or a UTF8-encoded stream of characters. If the attacker is not careful she can invalidate the encoded stream. If error detection is turned on, it will be a first defense in catching these invalid encoded streams.

When error detection is turned on, errors such as the following are dealt with by throwing an ArgumentException:

- Leftover bytes that do not make up a complete encoded character sequence exist.
- An invalid encoded start character was detected. For example, a UTF8 character does not fit into one of the following classes: Single-Byte, Double-Byte, Three-Byte, Four-Byte, Five-Byte, or Six-Byte.
- Extra bits are found after processing an extra byte in a multibyte sequence.
- The leftover bytes in a sequence could not be used to create a complete character.

- A high surrogate value is not followed by a low surrogate value.
- In the case of the GetBytes method, the byte[] that is used to hold the resulting bytes is not large enough.
- In the case of the GetChars method, the char[] that is used to hold the resulting characters is not large enough.

If you use a constructor other than the one shown in this recipe or if you set the last parameter in this constructor to false, any errors in the encoding sequence are ignored and no exception is thrown.

See Also

See the "UnicodeEncoding Class" and "UTF8Encoding Class" topic in the MSDN documentation.

17.20 Obtaining a Safer File Handle

Problem

You want more security when manipulating an unmanaged file handle than a simple IntPtr can provide.

Solution

Use the Microsoft.Win32.SafeHandles.SafeFileHandle object to wrap an existing unmanaged file handle:

```
public static void WriteToFileHandle(IntPtr hFile)
{
    // Wrap our file handle in a safe handle wrapper object.
    using (Microsoft.Win32.SafeHandles.SafeFileHandle safeHFile =
        new Microsoft.Win32.SafeHandles.SafeFileHandle(hFile, true))
    {
        // Open a FileStream object using the passed-in safe file handle.
        using (FileStream fileStream = new FileStream(safeHFile,
            FileAccess.ReadWrite))
        {
            // Flush before we start to clear any pending unmanaged actions.
            fileStream.Flush();

            // Operate on file here.
            string line = "Using a safe file handle object";

            // Write to the file.
            byte[] bytes = Encoding.ASCII.GetBytes(line);
            fileStream.Write(bytes,0,bytes.Length);
        }
    }
    // Note that the hFile handle is invalid at this point.
}
```

The SafeFileHandle constructor takes two arguments. The first is an IntPtr that contains a handle to an unmanaged resource. The second argument is a Boolean value, where true indicates that the handle will always be released during finalization and false indicates that the safeguards that force the handle to be released during finalization are turned off. Unless you have an extremely good reason to turn off these safeguards, it is recommended that you always set this Boolean value to true.

Discussion

A SafeFileHandle object contains a single handle to an unmanaged file resource. This class has two major benefits over using an IntPtr to store a handle—critical finalization and prevention of handle recycling attacks. The SafeFileHandle is seen by the garbage collector as a critical finalizer, due to the fact that one of the SafeFileHandle's base classes is CriticalFinalizerObject. The garbage collector separates finalizers into two categories: critical and noncritical. The noncritical finalizers are run first, followed by the critical finalizers. If a FileStream's finalizer flushes any data, it can assume that the SafeFileHandle object is still valid, because the SafeFileHandle finalizer is guaranteed to run after the FileStream's.

 The Close method on the FileStream object will also close its underlying SafeFileHandle object.

Since the SafeFileHandle falls under critical finalization, it means that the underlying unmanaged handle is always released (i.e., the SafeFileHandle.ReleaseHandle method is always called), even in situations in which the AppDomain is corrupted and/or shutting down or the thread is being aborted. This will prevent resource handle leaks.

The SafeFileHandle object also helps to prevent handle recycling attacks. The operating system aggressively tries to recycle handles, so it is possible to close one handle and open another soon afterward and get the same value for the new handle. One way an attacker will take advantage of this is by forcing an accessible handle to close on one thread while it is possibly still being used on another in the hope that the handle will be recycled quickly and used as a handle to a new resource, possibly one that the attacker does not have permission to access. If the application still has this original handle and is actively using it, data corruption could be an issue.

Since this class inherits from the SafeHandleZeroOrMinusOneIsInvalid class, a handle value of zero or minus one is considered an invalid handle.

See Also

See the "Microsoft.Win32.SafeHandles.SafeFileHandle Class" topic in the MSDN documentation.

CHAPTER 18

Threading and Synchronization

18.0 Introduction

A *thread* represents a single flow of execution logic in a program. Some programs never need more than a single thread to execute efficiently, but many do, and that is what this chapter is about. Threading in .NET allows you to build responsive and efficient applications. Many applications have a need to perform multiple actions at the same time (such as user interface interaction and processing data) and threading provides the capability to achieve this. Being able to have your application perform multiple tasks is a very liberating and yet complicating factor in your application design. Once you have multiple threads of execution in your application, you need to start thinking about what data in your application needs to be protected from multiple accesses, what data could cause threads to develop an interdependency that could lead to deadlocking (Thread A has a resource that Thread B is waiting for and Thread B has a resource that Thread A is waiting for), and how to store data you want to associate with the individual threads. You will explore some of these issues to help you take advantage of this wonderful capability of the .NET Framework. You will also see the areas where you need to be careful and items to keep in mind while designing and creating your multithreaded application.

18.1 Creating Per-Thread Static Fields

Problem

Static fields, by default, are shared between threads within an application domain. You need to allow each thread to have its own nonshared copy of a static field, so that this static field can be updated on a per-thread basis.

Solution

Use ThreadStaticAttribute to mark any static fields as not shareable between threads:

```
using System;
using System.Threading;

public class Foo
{
    [ThreadStaticAttribute( )]
    public static string bar = "Initialized string";
}
```

Discussion

By default, static fields are shared between all threads that access these fields in the same application domain. To see this, you'll create a class with a static field called bar and a static method to access and display the value contained in this field:

```
using System;
using System.Threading;

public class ThreadStaticField
{
    public static string bar = "Initialized string";

    public static void DisplayStaticFieldValue( )
    {
        string msg =
            string.Format("{0} contains static field value of: {1}",
                Thread.CurrentThread.GetHashCode( ),
                ThreadStaticField.bar);
        Console.WriteLine(msg);
    }
}
```

Next, create a test method that accesses this static field both on the current thread and on a newly spawned thread:

```
public static void TestStaticField( )
{
    ThreadStaticField.DisplayStaticFieldValue( );

    Thread newStaticFieldThread =
        new Thread(ThreadStaticField.DisplayStaticFieldValue);

    newStaticFieldThread.Start( );

    ThreadStaticField.DisplayStaticFieldValue( );
}
```

This code displays output that resembles the following:

```
9 contains static field value of: Initialized string
10 contains static field value of: Initialized string
9 contains static field value of: Initialized string
```

In the preceding example, the current thread's hash value is 9 and the new thread's hash value is 10. These values will vary from system to system. Notice that both threads are accessing the same static bar field. Next, add the ThreadStaticAttribute to the static field:

```
public class ThreadStaticField
{
    [ThreadStaticAttribute( )]
    public static string bar = "Initialized string";

    public static void DisplayStaticFieldValue( )
    {
        string msg =
            string.Format("{0} contains static field value of: {1}",
                Thread.CurrentThread.GetHashCode( ),
                ThreadStaticField.bar);
        Console.WriteLine(msg);
    }
}
```

Now, output resembling the following is displayed:

```
9 contains static field value of: Initialized string
10 contains static field value of:
9 contains static field value of: Initialized string
```

Notice that the new thread returns a null for the value of the static bar field. This is the expected behavior. The bar field is initialized only in the first thread that accesses it. In all other threads, this field is initialized to null. Therefore, it is imperative that you initialize the bar field in all threads before it is used.

 Remember to initialize any static field that is marked with ThreadStaticAttribute before it is used in any thread. That is, this field should be initialized in the method passed in to the ThreadStart delegate. You should make sure to not initialize the static field using a field initializer as shown in the prior code, since only one thread gets to see that initial value.

The bar field is initialized to the "Initialized string" string literal before it is used in the first thread that accesses this field. In the previous test code, the bar field was accessed first, and, therefore, it was initialized, in the current thread. Suppose you were to remove the first line of the TestStaticField method, as shown here:

```
public static void TestStaticField( )
{
//  ThreadStaticField.DisplayStaticFieldValue( );
```

```
    Thread newStaticFieldThread =
        new Thread(ThreadStaticField.DisplayStaticFieldValue);

    newStaticFieldThread.Start( );

    ThreadStaticField.DisplayStaticFieldValue( );
}
```

This code now displays similar output to the following:

```
10 contains static field value of: Initialized string
9 contains static field value of:
```

The current thread does not access the bar field first and therefore does not initialize it. However, when the new thread accesses it first, it does initialize it.

Note that adding a static constructor to initialize the static field marked with this attribute will still follow the same behavior. Static constructors are executed only one time per application domain.

See Also

See the "ThreadStaticAttribute Attribute" and "Static Modifier (C#)" topics in the MSDN documentation.

18.2 Providing Thread-Safe Access to Class Members

Problem

You need to provide thread-safe access through accessor functions to an internal member variable.

The following NoSafeMemberAccess class shows three methods: ReadNumericField, IncrementNumericField, and ModifyNumericField. While all of these methods access the internal numericField member, the access is currently not safe for multithreaded access:

```
public static class NoSafeMemberAccess
{
    private static int numericField = 1;

    public static void IncrementNumericField( )
    {
        ++numericField;
    }

    public static void ModifyNumericField(int newValue)
    {
        numericField = newValue;
    }

    public static int ReadNumericField( )
```

```
    {
        return (numericField);
    }
}
```

Solution

NoSafeMemberAccess could be used in a multithreaded application, and therefore it must be made thread-safe. Consider what would occur if multiple threads were calling the IncrementNumericField method at the same time. It is possible that two calls could occur to IncrementNumericField while the numericField is updated only once. In order to protect against this, you will modify this class by creating an object that you can lock against in critical sections of the code:

```
public static class SaferMemberAccess
{
    private static int numericField = 1;
    private static object syncObj = new object( );

    public static void IncrementNumericField( )
    {
        lock(syncObj)
        {
            ++numericField;
        }
    }

    public static void ModifyNumericField(int newValue)
    {
        lock(syncObj)
        {
            numericField = newValue;
        }
    }

    public static int ReadNumericField( )
    {
        lock (syncObj)
        {
            return (numericField);
        }
    }

}
```

Using the lock statement on the syncObj object lets you synchronize access to the numericField member. This now makes all three methods safe for multithreaded access.

Discussion

Marking a block of code as a critical section is done using the lock keyword. The lock keyword should not be used on a public type or on an instance out of the control of the program as this can contribute to deadlocks. Examples of this are using the "this" pointer, the type object for a class (typeof(MyClass)), or a string literal ("MyLock"). If you are attempting to protect code in only public static methods, the System.Runtime.CompilerServices.MethodImpl attribute could also be used for this purpose with the MethodImplOption.Synchronized value:

```
[MethodImpl (MethodImplOptions.Synchronized)]
public static void MySynchronizedMethod( )
{
}
```

There is a problem with synchronization using an object such as syncObj in the SaferMemberAccess example. If you lock an object or type that can be accessed by other objects within the application, other objects may also attempt to lock this same object. This will manifest itself in poorly written code that locks itself, such as the following code:

```
public class DeadLock
{
    public void Method1( )
    {
        lock(this)
        {
            // Do something.
        }
    }
}
```

When Method1 is called, it locks the current DeadLock object. Unfortunately, any object that has access to the DeadLock class may also lock it. This is shown here:

```
using System;
using System.Threading;

public class AnotherCls
{
    public void DoSomething( )
    {
        DeadLock deadLock = new DeadLock( );
        lock(deadLock)
        {
            Thread thread = new Thread(deadLock.Method1);
            thread.Start( );

            // Do some time-consuming task here.
        }
    }
}
```

The DoSomething method obtains a lock on the deadLock object and then attempts to call the Method1 method of the deadLock object on another thread, after which a very long task is executed. While the long task is executing, the lock on the deadLock object prevents Method1 from being called on the other thread. Only when this long task ends, and execution exits the critical section of the DoSomething method, will the Method1 method be able to acquire a lock on the this object. As you can see, this can become a major headache to track down in a much larger application.

Jeffrey Richter has come up with a relatively simple method to remedy this situation, which he details quite clearly in the article "Safe Thread Synchronization" in the January 2003 issue of *MSDN Magazine*. His solution is to create a private field within the class on which to synchronize. Only the object itself can acquire this private field; no outside object or type may acquire it. This solution is also now the recommended practice in the MSDN documentation for the lock keyword. The DeadLock class can be rewritten, as follows, to fix this problem:

```
public class DeadLock
{
    private object syncObj = new object( );

    public void Method1( )
    {
        lock(syncObj)
        {
            // Do something.
        }
    }
}
```

Now in the DeadLock class, you are locking on the internal syncObj, while the DoSomething method locks on the DeadLock class instance. This resolves the deadlock condition, but the DoSomething method still should not lock on a public type. Therefore, change the AnotherCls class like so:

```
public class AnotherCls
{
    private object deadLockSyncObj = new object( );

    public void DoSomething( )
    {
        DeadLock deadLock = new DeadLock( );
        lock(deadLockSyncObj)
        {
            Thread thread = new Thread(deadLock.Method1);
            thread.Start( );

            // Do some time-consuming task here.
        }
    }
}
```

Now the AnotherCls class has an object of its own to protect access to the DeadLock class instance in DoSomething instead of locking on the public type.

To clean up your code, you should stop locking any objects or types except for the synchronization objects that are private to your type or object, such as the syncObj in the fixed DeadLock class. This recipe makes use of this pattern by creating a static syncObj object within the SaferMemberAccess class. The IncrementNumericField, ModifyNumericField, and ReadNumericField methods use this syncObj to synchronize access to the numericField field. Note that if you do not need a lock while the numericField is being read in the ReadNumericField method, you can remove this lock block and simply return the value contained in the numericField field.

 Minimizing the number of critical sections within your code can significantly improve performance. Use what you need to secure resource access, but no more.

If you require more control over locking and unlocking of critical sections, you might want to try using the overloaded static Monitor.TryEnter methods. These methods allow more flexibility by introducing a timeout value. The lock keyword will attempt to acquire a lock on a critical section indefinitely. However, with the TryEnter method, you can specify a timeout value in milliseconds (as an integer) or as a TimeSpan structure. The TryEnter methods return true if a lock was acquired and false if it was not. Note that the overload of the TryEnter method that accepts only a single parameter does not block for any amount of time. This method returns immediately, regardless of whether the lock was acquired.

The updated class using the Monitor methods is shown in Example 18-1.

Example 18-1. Using Monitor methods

```
using System;
using System.Threading;

public static class MonitorMethodAccess
{
    private static int numericField = 1;
    private static object syncObj = new object( );

    public static object SyncRoot
    {
        get { return syncObj; }
    }

    public static void IncrementNumericField( )
    {
        if (Monitor.TryEnter(syncObj, 250))
        {
            try
            {
                ++numericField;
            }
            finally
            {
                Monitor.Exit(syncObj);
```

Example 18-1. Using Monitor methods (continued)

```
            }
        }
    }

    public static void ModifyNumericField(int newValue)
    {
        if (Monitor.TryEnter(syncObj, 250))
        {
            try
            {
                numericField = newValue;
            }
            finally
            {
                Monitor.Exit(syncObj);
            }
        }
    }

    public static int ReadNumericField( )
    {
        if (Monitor.TryEnter(syncObj, 250))
        {
            try
            {
                return (numericField);
            }
            finally
            {
                Monitor.Exit(syncObj);
            }
        }

        return (-1);
    }

}
```

Note that with the TryEnter methods, you should always check to see whether the lock was in fact acquired. If not, your code should wait and try again or return to the caller.

You might think at this point that all of the methods are thread-safe. Individually, they are, but what if you are trying to call them and you expect synchronized access between two of the methods? If ModifyNumericField and ReadNumericField are used one after the other by Class 1 on Thread 1 at the same time Class 2 is using these methods on Thread 2, locking or Monitor calls will not prevent Class 2 from modifying the value before Thread 1 reads it. Here is a series of actions that demonstrates this:

Class 1 Thread 1
    Calls `ModifyNumericField` with 10

Class 2 Thread 2
    Calls `ModifyNumericField` with 15

Class 1 Thread 1
    Calls `ReadNumericField` and gets 15, not 10

Class 2 Thread 2
    Calls `ReadNumericField` and gets 15, which it expected

In order to solve this problem of synchronizing reads and writes, the calling class needs to manage the interaction. The external class can accomplish this by using the `Monitor` class to establish a lock on the exposed synchronization object `SyncRoot` from `MonitorMethodAccess`, as shown here:

```
int num = 0;
if(Monitor.TryEnter(MonitorMethodAccess.SyncRoot,250))
{
    MonitorMethodAccess.ModifyNumericField(10);
    num = MonitorMethodAccess.ReadNumericField();
    Monitor.Exit(MonitorMethodAccess.SyncRoot);
}
Console.WriteLine(num);
```

See Also

See the "Lock Statement," "Thread Class," and "Monitor Class" topics in the MSDN documentation; see the "Safe Thread Synchronization" article in the January 2003 issue of *MSDN Magazine*.

18.3 Preventing Silent Thread Termination

Problem

An exception thrown in a spawned worker thread will cause this thread to be silently terminated if the exception is unhandled. You need to make sure all exceptions are handled in all threads. If an exception happens in this new thread, you want to handle it and be notified of its occurrence.

Solution

You must add exception handling to the method that you pass to the `ThreadStart` delegate with a `try-catch`, `try-finally`, or `try-catch-finally` block. The code to do this is shown in Example 18-2 in bold.

Example 18-2. Preventing silent thread termination

```
using System;
using System.Threading;

public class MainThread
{
    public void CreateNewThread( )
    {
        // Spawn new thread to do concurrent work.
        Thread newWorkerThread = new Thread(Worker.DoWork);
        newWorkerThread.Start( );
    }
}

public class Worker
{
    // Method called by ThreadStart delegate to do concurrent work
    public static void DoWork ( )
    {
        try
        {
            // Do thread work here.
        }
        catch
        {
            // Handle thread exception here.
            // Do not re-throw exception.
        }
        finally
        {
            // Do thread cleanup here.
        }
    }
}
```

Discussion

If an unhandled exception occurs in the main thread of an application, the main thread terminates, along with your entire application. An unhandled exception in a spawned worker thread, however, will terminate only that thread. This will happen without any visible warnings, and your application will continue to run as if nothing happened.

Simply wrapping an exception handler around the Start method of the Thread class will not catch the exception on the newly created thread. The Start method is called within the context of the current thread, not the newly created thread. It also returns immediately once the thread is launched, so it isn't going to wait around for the thread to finish. Therefore, the exception thrown in the new thread will not be caught since it is not visible to any other threads.

If the exception is rethrown from the catch block, the finally block of this structured exception handler will still execute. However, after the finally block is finished, the rethrown exception is, at that point, rethrown. The rethrown exception cannot be handled and the thread terminates. If there is any code after the finally block, it will not be executed, since an unhandled exception occurred.

 Never rethrow an exception at the highest point in the exception-handling hierarchy within a thread. Since no exception handlers can catch this rethrown exception, it will be considered unhandled and the thread will terminate after all finally blocks have been executed.

What if you use the ThreadPool and QueueUserWorkItem? This method will still help you because you added the handling code that will execute inside the thread. Just make sure you have the finally block set up so that you can notify yourself of exceptions in other threads as shown earlier.

In order to provide a last-chance exception handler for your WinForms application, you need to hook up to two separate events. The first event is the System.AppDomain.CurrentDomain.UnhandledException event, which will catch all unhandled exceptions in the current AppDomain on worker threads; it will not catch exceptions that occur on the main UI thread of a WinForms application. See Recipe 7.10 for more information on the System.AppDomain.UnhandledException event. In order to catch those, you also need to hook up to the System.Windows.Forms.Application.ThreadException, which will catch unhandled exceptions in the main UI thread. See Recipe 7.20 for more information about the ThreadException event.

See Also

See the "Thread Class" and "Exception Class" topics in the MSDN documentation.

18.4   Polling an Asynchronous Delegate

Problem

While an asynchronous delegate is executing, you need to continuously poll it to see whether it has completed. This ability is useful when you need to monitor the length of time it takes the asynchronous delegate to execute. It can also be helpful if you need to monitor other objects in the system in parallel with this asynchronous delegate, possibly to determine which object finishes first, second, third, and so on. It can also be useful when performing a continuous task, such as displaying an indicator to the user that the asynchronous operation is still running.

Solution

Use the IsCompleted property of the IAsyncResult interface to determine when the
asynchronous call has completed. Note that the BeginInvoke method call on the delegate passes null for the callback setup parameters. Example 18-3 shows how this is
accomplished.

Example 18-3. Polling an asynchronous delegate

```
using System;
using System.Threading;

public class AsyncAction
{
    public void PollAsyncDelegate( )
    {
        // Set up the delegate.
        AsyncInvoke method1 = TestAsyncInvoke.Method1;
        // Since we are not using a callback here, we pass null for the
        // callback and null for the object data for the callback.
        Console.WriteLine("Calling BeginInvoke on Thread {0}",
            Thread.CurrentThread.ManagedThreadId);
        IAsyncResult asyncResult = method1.BeginInvoke(null, null);

        Console.WriteLine("Starting Polling on Thread {0}",
            Thread.CurrentThread.ManagedThreadId);
        while (!asyncResult.IsCompleted)
        {
            // Give up the CPU for 1 second.
            Thread.Sleep(1000);
            Console.Write('.');
        }
        Console.WriteLine("Finished Polling on Thread {0}",
            Thread.CurrentThread.ManagedThreadId);

        try
        {
            int retVal = method1.EndInvoke(asyncResult);
            Console.WriteLine("retVal: " + retVal);
        }
        catch (Exception e)
        {
            Console.WriteLine(e.ToString( ));
        }
    }
}
```

The following code defines the AsyncInvoke delegate and the asynchronously invoked
static method TestAsyncInvoke.Method1:

```
public delegate int AsyncInvoke( );

public class TestAsyncInvoke
```

```
    {
        public static int Method1( )
        {
            Console.WriteLine("Invoked Method1 on Thread {0}",
                Thread.CurrentThread.ManagedThreadId );
            return (1);
        }
    }
```

To run the asynchronous invocation, create an instance of the AsyncAction class and
call the PollAsyncDelegate method like so:

```
AsyncAction aa = new AsyncAction( );
aa.PollAsyncDelegate( );
```

The output for this code is shown next. Note that the Method1 thread ID is different:

```
Calling BeginInvoke on Thread 9
Starting Polling on Thread 9
Invoked Method1 on Thread 10
.Finished Polling on Thread 9
retVal: 1
```

Discussion

The delegate, AsyncInvoke, is invoked asynchronously using its BeginInvoke method.
The BeginInvoke method returns an IAsyncResult object, which allows access to the
result information from an asynchronous operation.

If the delegate accepts a string and an int, in this order, the BeginInvoke method is
defined as this:

```
public IAsyncResult BeginInvoke(string s, int i, AsyncCallback callback,
                                object state)
```

For this recipe, the method that the delegate will call takes no arguments, and the
callback and *state* parameters are set to null. The *callback* parameter could call
back at completion into the code that invoked it, but for this example, it is a no-op.

To poll for the completion of the method1 delegate, you get the IsCompleted property
of the IAsyncResult object that is returned by the BeginInvoke method. The
IsCompleted property returns true if the method1 delegate has completed its operation or false if it has not. This property can be called continuously within a loop to
check whether the delegate has finished.

Once the method1 delegate has finished its asynchronous processing, the results of the
operation can be retrieved through a call to the EndInvoke method. The compiler also
creates this method dynamically, so that the return value of the delegate can be
accessed through the EndInvoke method—as well as any out or ref parameters that
the delegate accepts as parameters.

The way that EndInvoke works in general is that it returns an object of the same type as the return value of the delegate and has the same out and ref parameters as the initial delegate. An EndInvoke method called on a delegate of the following signature:

```
public delegate long Foo(ref int i, out string s, bool b);
```

will be defined as follows:

```
public long EndInvoke(ref int i, out string s, IAsyncResult result)
```

Notice that the return type is a long and only the ref and out parameters of the original delegate are in the signature for this method. The EndInvoke method parameters contain only those original method parameters marked as ref or out. The IAsyncResult (result) is the context handed back from the initial call to BeginInvoke.

 If the asynchronous delegate throws an exception, the only way to obtain that exception object is through the EndInvoke method. The EndInvoke method should be wrapped in an exception handler.

Once the while loop of the PollAsyncDelegate method in this recipe is exited—meaning that the asynchronous delegate has completed—the EndInvoke method can be safely called to retrieve the return value of the delegate as well as any ref or out parameter values. If you want to obtain these values, you must call the EndInvoke method; however, if you do not need any of these values, you may leave out the call to the EndInvoke method.

See Also

See the "IAsyncResult Interface," "AsyncResult Class," "BeginInvoke Method," and "EndInvoke Method" topics in the MSDN documentation.

18.5   Timing Out an Asynchronous Delegate

Problem

You want an asynchronous delegate to operate only within an allowed time span. If it is not finished processing within this time frame, the operation will time out. If the asynchronous delegate times out, it must perform any cleanup before the thread it is running on is terminated.

Solution

The WaitHandle.WaitOne method can indicate when an asynchronous operation times out. The code on the invoking thread needs to periodically wake up to do some work along with timing out after a specific period of time. Use the approach shown in the following code, which will wake up every 20 milliseconds to do some processing. This method also times out after a specific number of wait/process cycles (note that this code will actually time out after more than 2 seconds of operation since work is being done between the wait cycles):

```
public class AsyncAction
{
    public void TimeOutWakeAsyncDelegate( )
    {
        // Set up the delegate.
        AsyncInvoke method1 = TestAsyncInvoke.Method1;
        // Since we are not using a callback here, we pass null for the
        // callback and null for the object data for the callback.
        Console.WriteLine("Calling BeginInvoke on Thread {0}",
            Thread.CurrentThread.ManagedThreadId);
        IAsyncResult asyncResult = method1.BeginInvoke(null, null);

        int counter = 0;
        while (counter <= 25 &&
            !asyncResult.AsyncWaitHandle.WaitOne(20, true))
        {
            counter++;
            Console.WriteLine("Processing...");
        }

        if (asyncResult.IsCompleted)
        {
            int retVal = method1.EndInvoke(asyncResult);
            Console.WriteLine("retVal (TimeOut): " + retVal);
        }
        else
        {
            Console.WriteLine("TimedOut");
        }
    }
}
```

The following code defines the AsyncInvoke delegate and the asynchronously invoked static method TestAsyncInvoke.Method1:

```
public delegate int AsyncInvoke( );

public class TestAsyncInvoke
{
    public static int Method1( )
    {
        Console.WriteLine("Invoked Method1 on Thread {0}",
            Thread.CurrentThread.ManagedThreadId );
        return (1);
    }
}
```

To run the asynchronous invocation, create an instance of the AsyncAction class and call the TimeOutWakeAsyncDelegate method like so:

```
AsyncAction aa1 = new AsyncAction( );
aa1.TimeOutWakeAsyncDelegate( );
```

The output for this code looks like this:

```
Calling BeginInvoke on Thread 9
Invoked Method1 on Thread 10
retVal (TimeOut): 1
```

Discussion

The asynchronous delegates in this recipe are created and invoked in the same fashion as the asynchronous delegate in Recipe 18.4. However, instead of using the IsCompleted property to determine whether the asynchronous delegate is finished processing, WaitHandle.WaitOne is used. This method blocks the thread that it is called on either indefinitely or for a specified length of time. This method will stop blocking the thread when it is signaled by the ThreadPool that the thread has completed or timed out and returns a true indicating that the asynchronous processing is finished. If the processing is not finished before the allotted time-out value expires, WaitOne returns false. Note that the WaitOne method that accepts no parameters will block the calling thread indefinitely.

 It is usually a better idea to include a time-out value when using the WaitOne method, as this will prevent the calling thread from being blocked forever if a deadlock situation occurs (in which case the thread on which the WaitOne method waits is never signaled) or if the thread running the asynchronous delegate never returns, such as when entering into an infinite loop.

The TimeOutWakeAsyncDelegate method in this recipe will periodically wake up (after 20 milliseconds) and perform some task on the calling thread; unlike the TimeOutAsyncDelegate method, which will continue blocking for the allotted time frame and not wake up. After 25 wait cycles, if the asynchronous delegate has not finished processing, the while loop will be exited, essentially timing out the delegate. If the delegate finishes processing before the 25 wait cycles have completed, the while loop is exited.

The IsCompleted property is checked next to determine whether the asynchronous delegate has finished its processing at this time. If it has finished, the EndInvoke method is called using the IAsyncResult from the initial BeginInvoke call to obtain any return value, ref parameter values, or out parameter values. Otherwise, the delegate has not completed within the allotted time span and the application should be informed that this thread has timed out.

See Also

See the "WaitOne Method" and "AsyncResult Class" topics in the MSDN documentation.

18.6 Being Notified of the Completion of an Asynchronous Delegate

Problem

You need a way of receiving notification from an asynchronously invoked delegate that it has finished. However, it must be more flexible than the notification schemes in the previous two recipes (Recipes 18.4 and 18.5). This scheme must allow your code to continue processing without having to constantly call IsCompleted in a loop or to rely on the WaitOne method. Since the asynchronous delegate will return a value, you must be able to pass this return value back to the invoking thread.

Solution

Use the BeginInvoke method to start the asynchronous delegate, but use the first parameter to pass a callback delegate to the asynchronous delegate, as shown in Example 18-4.

Example 18-4. Getting notification on completion of an anonymous delegate

```
using System;
using System.Threading;

public class AsyncAction2
{
    public void CallbackAsyncDelegate()
    {
        AsyncCallback callBack = DelegateCallback;

        AsyncInvoke method1 = TestAsyncInvoke.Method1;
        Console.WriteLine("Calling BeginInvoke on Thread {0}",
            Thread.CurrentThread.ManagedThreadId);
        IAsyncResult asyncResult = method1.BeginInvoke(callBack, method1);

        // No need to poll or use the WaitOne method here, so return to the calling
// method.
        return;
    }

    private static void DelegateCallback(IAsyncResult iresult)
    {
        Console.WriteLine("Getting callback on Thread {0}",
            Thread.CurrentThread.ManagedThreadId);
        AsyncResult asyncResult = (AsyncResult)iresult;
        AsyncInvoke method1 = (AsyncInvoke)asyncResult.AsyncDelegate;

        int retVal = method1.EndInvoke(asyncResult);
        Console.WriteLine("retVal (Callback): " + retVal);
    }
}
```

This callback delegate will call the `DelegateCallback` method on the thread the method was invoked on when the asynchronous delegate is finished processing.

The following code defines the `AsyncInvoke` delegate and the asynchronously invoked static method `TestAsyncInvoke.Method1`:

```
public delegate int AsyncInvoke( );

public class TestAsyncInvoke
{
    public static int Method1( )
    {
        Console.WriteLine("Invoked Method1 on Thread {0}",
            Thread.CurrentThread.ManagedThreadId );
        return (1);
    }
}
```

To run the asynchronous invocation, create an instance of the `AsyncAction` class and call the `CallbackAsyncDelegate` method like so:

```
AsyncAction aa2 = new AsyncAction( );
aa2.CallbackAsyncDelegate( );
```

The output for this code is shown next. Note that the thread ID for `Method1` is different:

```
Calling BeginInvoke on Thread 9
Invoked Method1 on Thread 10
Getting callback on Thread 10
retVal (Callback): 1
```

Discussion

The asynchronous delegates in this recipe are created and invoked in the same fashion as the asynchronous delegate in Recipe 18.4. Instead of using the `IsCompleted` property to determine when the asynchronous delegate is finished processing (or the `WaitOne` method to block for a specified time while the asynchronous delegate continues processing), this recipe uses a callback to indicate to the calling thread that the asynchronous delegate has finished processing and that its return value, `ref` parameter values, and out parameter values are available.

Invoking a delegate in this manner is much more flexible and efficient than simply polling the `IsCompleted` property to determine when a delegate finishes processing. When polling this property in a loop, the polling method cannot return and allow the application to continue processing. A callback is also better than using a `WaitOne` method, since the `WaitOne` method will block the calling thread and allow no processing to occur. You can break up the `WaitOne` method into a limited number of wait cycles as in Recipe 18.5, but this is simply a merging of the polling technique with the `WaitOne` operation.

The `CallbackAsyncDelegate` method in this recipe makes use of the first parameter to the `BeginInvoke` method of the asynchronous delegate to pass in another delegate. This contains a callback method to be called when the asynchronous delegate finishes processing. After calling `BeginInvoke`, this method can now return and the application can continue processing; it does not have to wait in a polling loop or be blocked while the asynchronous delegate is running.

The `AsyncInvoke` delegate that is passed into the first parameter of the `BeginInvoke` method is defined as follows:

```
public delegate void AsyncCallback(IAsyncResult ar)
```

When this delegate is created, as shown here, the callback method passed in, `DelegateCallback`, will be called as soon as the asynchronous delegate completes:

```
AsyncCallback callBack = new AsyncCallback(DelegateCallback);
```

`DelegateCallback` will not run on the same thread as `BeginInvoke` but rather on a `Thread` from the `ThreadPool`. This callback method accepts a parameter of type `IAsyncResult`. You can cast this parameter to an `AsyncResult` object within the method and use it to obtain information about the completed asynchronous delegate, such as its return value, any `ref` parameter values, and any `out` parameter values. If the delegate instance that was used to call `BeginInvoke` is still in scope, you can just pass the `IAsyncResult` to the `EndInvoke` method. In addition, this object can obtain any state information passed into the second parameter of the `BeginInvoke` method. This state information can be any object type.

The `DelegateCallback` method casts the `IAsyncResult` parameter to an `AsyncResult` object and obtains the asynchronous delegate that was originally called. The `EndInvoke` method of this asynchronous delegate is called to process any return value, `ref` parameters, or `out` parameters. If any state object was passed in to the `BeginInvoke` method's second parameter, it can be obtained here through the following line of code:

```
object state = asyncResult.AsyncState;
```

See Also

See the "AsyncCallback Delegate" topic in the MSDN documentation.

18.7 Determining Whether a Request for a Pooled Thread Will be Queued

Problem

Your application will be creating many threads from the thread pool. When creating a thread from this pool, you want to be informed as to whether a thread in the pool is available or if the request for a new thread will have to be queued. Basically, you want to know whether a thread is available for immediate use from the thread pool.

Solution

Use the ThreadPool.GetAvailableThreads method to get the number of worker threads currently available in the ThreadPool. This allows you to determine whether you should queue another request to launch a thread via ThreadPool.QueueUserWorkItem or should take an alternate action.

The Main method shown here calls a method (SpawnManyThreads) to spawn lots of threads from the ThreadPool, then waits for a bit to simulate processing:

```
public class TestThreads
{
    public static void Run( )
    {
        SpawnManyThreads( );
        // Have to wait here or the background threads in the thread
        // pool would not run before the main thread exits.
        Console.WriteLine("Main Thread waiting to complete...");
        Thread.Sleep(2000);
        Console.WriteLine("Main Thread completing...");
    }
```

The SpawnManyThreads method launches threads and pauses between each launch to allow the ThreadPool to register the request and act upon it. The isThreadAvailable method is called with the parameter set to true to determine whether there is a worker thread available for use in the ThreadPool:

```
public static bool SpawnManyThreads( )
{
    try
    {
        for(int i=0;i<500;i++)
        {
            // Have to wait or thread pool never gives out threads to
            // requests.
            Thread.Sleep(100);
            // Check to see if worker threads are available in the pool.
            if(true == IsThreadAvailable(true))
            {
                // Launch thread if queue isn't full.
                Console.WriteLine("Worker Thread was available...");
                ThreadPool.QueueUserWorkItem(ThreadProc,i);
            }
            else
                Console.WriteLine("Worker Thread was NOT available...");
        }
    }
    catch(Exception e)
```

```
    {
        Console.WriteLine(e.ToString( ));
        return false;
    }
    return true;
}
```

The `IsThreadAvailable` method calls `ThreadPool.GetAvailableThreads` to determine whether the `ThreadPool` has any available worker threads left. If you pass `false` as the `checkWorkerThreads` parameter, it also sees whether there are any completion port threads available. The `GetAvailableThreads` method compares the current number of threads allocated from the pool against the maximum `ThreadPool` threads. The worker thread maximum is 25 per CPU, regardless of the number of CPUs, in v1.1 of the CLR. In v2.0 of the CLR, the maximum number of worker threads is actually settable. The maximum number of worker threads applies to each CPU, so if it is set to 25 on a two-processor machine, the maximum will actually be 50.

```
public static bool IsThreadAvailable(bool checkWorkerThreads)
{
    int workerThreads = 0;
    int completionPortThreads = 0;
    // Get available threads.
    ThreadPool.GetAvailableThreads(out workerThreads,
        out completionPortThreads);

    // Indicate how many work threads are available.
    Console.WriteLine("{0} worker threads available in thread pool.",
        workerThreads);

    if(checkWorkerThreads)
    {
        if(workerThreads > 0)
            return true;
    }
    else // Check completion port threads.
    {
        if(completionPortThreads > 0)
            return true;
    }
    return false;
}
```

This is a simple method to call in a threaded fashion:

```
static void ThreadProc(Object stateInfo)
{
    // Show we did something with this thread.
    Console.WriteLine("Thread {0} running...",stateInfo);
    Thread.Sleep(1000);
}
}
```

Discussion

The ThreadPool is a great way to perform background tasks without having to manage all aspects of the thread yourself. It can be handy to know when the ThreadPool itself is going to become a bottleneck to your application, and the GetAvailableThreads method can help you. However, you might want to check your application design if you are consistently using this many threads, as you might be losing performance due to contention or context switching. Queuing up work when the ThreadPool is full simply queues it up for execution once one of the threads comes free; the request isn't lost, just postponed.

See Also

See the "ThreadPool Class" topic in the MSDN documentation; see *Applied Microsoft .NET Framework Programming* (Wintellect).

18.8   Configuring a Timer

Problem

You have one of the following timer configuration needs:

- You want to use a timer to call a timer callback method at a fixed time after the timer object has been created. Once this callback method has been called the first time, you want to call this same callback method at a specified interval (this interval might be different from the time interval between the creation of the timer and the first time the timer callback method is called).

- You want to use a timer to call a timer callback method immediately upon creation of the System.Threading.Timer object, after which the callback method is called at a specified interval.

- You want to use a timer to call a timer callback method one time only.

- You have been using a System.Threading.Timer object and need to change the intervals at which its timer callback method is called.

Solution

To fire a System.Threading.Timer after an initial delay, and then at a specified period after that, use the System.Threading.Timer constructor to set up different times for the initial and following callbacks, as shown in Example 18-5.

Example 18-5. Configuring a timer

```
using System;
using System.Threading;
```

Example 18-5. Configuring a timer (continued)

```
public class TestTimers
{
    public static int count = 0;
    public static Timer timerRef = null;
    private static bool limitHit = false;
    private static object syncRoot = new object( );

    public static bool LimitHit
    {
        get
        {
            lock (syncRoot)
            {
                return limitHit;
            }
        }
        set
        {
            lock (syncRoot)
            {
                limitHit = value;
            }
        }
    }

    public static void Run( )
    {
        TimerCallback callback = TimerMethod;

        // Create a timer that waits one half second, then invokes
        // the callback every second thereafter.
        Timer timer = new Timer(callback, null,500, 1000);

        // Store a reference to this timer so the callback can use it.
        timerRef = timer;

        // The main thread does nothing until the timer is disposed.
        while (true)
        {
            if (LimitHit == false)
                Thread.Sleep(0);
            else
                break;
        }
        Console.WriteLine("Timer example done.");
    }

    static void TimerMethod(Object state)
    {
        count++;
        if(count == 5)
```

Example 18-5. Configuring a timer (continued)

```
        {
            LimitHit = true;
            timerRef.Dispose( );
        }
    }
}
```

The previous method showed how to fire the callback after 500 milliseconds. To fire the initial callback immediately, change the value to zero:

```
// Create a timer that doesn't wait, then invokes
// the callback every second thereafter.
Timer timer = new Timer(callback, null,0, 1000);
```

To have the timer call the callback only once, change the constructor to pass `Timeout.Infinite` for the second callback interval. You also have to change the current scheme that waits for five callbacks before disposing of the timer to do it the first time. If you didn't do this, the program will hang, since the `Main` function is still waiting for the timer to have `Dispose` called, but the fifth callback will never trigger the `Dispose` call:

```
// Create a timer that waits for half a second, then is disposed.
Timer timer = new Timer(callback, null,500, Timeout.Infinite);

    static void TimerMethod(Object state)
    {
            timerRef.Dispose( );
    }
```

To change the interval of a running `System.Threading.Timer`, call the `Change` method specifying the delay before the next callback and the new callback interval, like this:

```
    static void TimerMethod(Object state)
    {
        count++;
        if(count == 5)
        {
            timerRef.Change(1000,2000);
        }
        if(count == 10)
        {
            timerRef.Dispose( );
        }
    }
```

This code now checks for the fifth callback and changes the interval from 1 second to 2 seconds. The sixth callback will happen 1 second after, and then callbacks through 10 will happen 2 seconds apart.

Discussion

One item to be aware of when using System.Threading.Timers and TimerCallbacks is that they are serviced from the ThreadPool. This means that if you have other work being farmed out to the ThreadPool in your application, it could be contending with the Timer callbacks for an available worker thread. The basic timer is enough to serve the earlier scenarios, but if you are doing UI work and want to use timers, you should investigate the System.Windows.Forms.Timer class. If you are doing server work, you might also want to look at System.Timers.Timer as well. Both of these classes add events for when the timers are disposed and when the timer "ticks"; they also add properties that expose the settings.

See Also

See the "System.Threading.Timer Class," "TimerCallback Delegate," "System.Windows. Forms.Timer Class," and "System.Timers.Timer" topics in the MSDN documentation.

18.9   Storing Thread-Specific Data Privately

Problem

You want to store thread-specific data discovered at runtime. This data should be accessible only to code running within that thread.

Solution

Use the AllocateDataSlot, AllocateNamedDataSlot, or GetNamedDataSlot method on the Thread class to reserve a *thread local storage* (TLS) slot. Using TLS, a large object can be stored in a data slot on a thread and used in many different methods. This can be done without having to pass the structure as a parameter.

For this example, a structure called Data here represents a structure that can grow to be very large in size:

```
public class Data
{
    // Application data is stored here.
}
```

Before using this structure, a data slot has to be created in TLS to store the structure. GetNamedDataSlot is called to get the appDataSlot. Since that doesn't exist, the default behavior for GetNamedDataSlot is to just create it. The following code creates an instance of the Data structure and stores it in the data slot named appDataSlot:

```
Data appData = new Data( );
Thread.SetData(Thread.GetNamedDataSlot("appDataSlot"), appData);
```

Whenever this structure is needed, it can be retrieved with a call to `Thread.GetData`. The following line of code gets the `appData` structure from the data slot named `appDataSlot`:

```
Data storedAppData = (Data)Thread.GetData(Thread.GetNamedDataSlot("appDataSlot"));
```

At this point, the `storedAppData` structure can be read or modified. After the action has been performed on the `storedAppData` structure, `storedAppData` must be placed back into the data slot named `appDataSlot`:

```
Thread.SetData(Thread.GetNamedDataSlot("appDataSlot"), appData);
```

Once the application is finished using this structure, the data slot can be released from memory using the following method call:

```
Thread.FreeNamedDataSlot("appDataSlot");
```

The `HandleClass` class in Example 18-6 shows how TLS can be used to store a structure.

Example 18-6. Using TLS to store a structure

```
using System;
using System.Threading;

public class HandleClass
{
    public static void Main( )
    {
        // Create structure instance and store it in the named data slot.
        Data appData = new Data( );
        Thread.SetData(Thread.GetNamedDataSlot("appDataSlot"), appData);

        // Call another method that will use this structure.
        HandleClass.MethodB( );

        // When done, free this data slot.
        Thread.FreeNamedDataSlot("appDataSlot");
    }

    public static void MethodB( )
    {
        // Get the structure instance from the named data slot.
        Data storedAppData = (Data)Thread.GetData(
          Thread.GetNamedDataSlot("appDataSlot"));

        // Modify the StoredAppData structure.

        // When finished modifying this structure, store the changes back
        // into the named data slot.
        Thread.SetData(Thread.GetNamedDataSlot("appDataSlot"),
                        storedAppData);

        // Call another method that will use this structure.
```

Example 18-6. Using TLS to store a structure (continued)

```
        HandleClass.MethodC( );
    }

    public static void MethodC( )
    {
        // Get the structure instance from the named data slot.
        Data storedAppData =
            (Data)Thread.GetData(Thread.GetNamedDataSlot("appDataSlot"));

        // Modify the storedAppData structure.

        // When finished modifying this structure, store the changes back into
        // the named data slot.
        Thread.SetData(Thread.GetNamedDataSlot("appDataSlot"), storedAppData);
    }
}
```

Discussion

Thread local storage is a convenient way to store data that is usable across method calls without having to pass the structure to the method or even without knowledge about where the structure was actually created.

Data stored in a named TLS data slot is available only to that thread; no other thread can access a named data slot of another thread. The data stored in this data slot is accessible from anywhere within the thread. This setup essentially makes this data global to the thread.

To create a named data slot, use the static Thread.GetNamedDataSlot method. This method accepts a single parameter, *name*, that defines the name of the data slot. This name should be unique; if a data slot with the same name exists, then the contents of that data slot will be returned and a new data slot will not be created. This action occurs silently; there is no exception thrown or error code available to inform you that you are using a data slot someone else created. To be sure that you are using a unique data slot, use the Thread.AllocateNamedDataSlot method. This method throws a System.ArgumentException if a data slot already exists with the same name. Otherwise, it operates similarly to the GetNamedDataSlot method.

It is interesting to note that this named data slot is created on every thread in the process, not just the thread that called this method. This fact should not be much more than an inconvenience to you, though, since the data in each data slot can be accessed only by the thread that contains it. In addition, if a data slot with the same name was created on a separate thread and you call GetNamedDataSlot on the current thread with this name, none of the data in any data slot on any thread will be destroyed.

GetNamedDataSlot returns a LocalDataStoreSlot object that is used to access the data slot. Note that this class is not creatable through the use of the new keyword. It must be created through one of the AllocateDataSlot or AllocateNamedDataSlot methods on the Thread class.

To store data in this data slot, use the static Thread.SetData method. This method takes the object passed in to the *data* parameter and stores it in the data slot defined by the *dataSlot* parameter.

The static Thread.GetData method retrieves the object stored in a data slot. This method retrieves a LocalDataStoreSlot object that is created through the Thread. GetNamedDataSlot method. The GetData method then returns the object that was stored in that particular data slot. Note that the object returned might have to be cast to its original type before it can be used.

The static method Thread.FreeNamedDataSlot will free the memory associated with a named data slot. This method accepts the name of the data slot as a string and, in turn, frees the memory associated with that data slot. Remember that when a data slot is created with GetNamedDataSlot, a named data slot is also created on all of the other threads running in that process. This is not really a problem when creating data slots with the GetNamedDataSlot method because, if a data slot exists with this name, a LocalDataStoreSlot object that refers to that data slot is returned, a new data slot is not created, and the original data in that data slot is not destroyed.

This situation becomes more of a problem when using the FreeNamedDataSlot method. This method will free the memory associated with the data slot name passed in to it for all threads, not just the thread that it was called on. Freeing a data slot before all threads have finished using the data within that data slot can be disastrous to your application.

A way to work around this problem is to not call the FreeNamedDataSlot method at all. When a thread terminates, all of its data slots in TLS are freed automatically. The side effect of not calling FreeNamedDataSlot is that the slot is taken up until the garbage collector determines that the thread the slot was created on has finished and the slot can be freed.

If you know the number of TLS slots you need for your code at compile time, consider using the ThreadStaticAttribute on a static field of your class to set up TLS-like storage.

See Also

See the "Thread Local Storage and Thread Relative Static Fields," "ThreadStatic-Attribute Attribute," and "Thread Class" topics in the MSDN documentation.

18.10 Granting Multiple Access to Resources with a Semaphore

Problem

You have a resource you want only a certain number of clients to access at a given time.

Solution

Use a semaphore to enable resource-counted access to the resource. For example, if you have an Xbox and a copy of Halo2 (the resource) and a development staff eager to blow off some steam (the clients), you have to synchronize access to the Xbox. Since the Xbox has four controllers, up to four clients can be playing at any given time. The rules of the house are that when you die, you give up your controller.

To accomplish this, create a class called Halo2Session with a Semaphore called _Xbox like this:

```
public class Halo2Session
{
    // A semaphore that simulates a limited resource pool
    //
    private static Semaphore _Xbox;

    // Player handles for Xbox
    private static string [] _handles = new string [9]{"Igor",
                            "AxeMan",
                            "Frosty",
                            "Dr. Death",
                            "HaPpyCaMpEr",
                            "Executioner",
                            "FragMan",
                            "Beatdown",
                            "Stoney"
                            };
```

The _handles array is an array of player names that will be used. In order to get things rolling, you need to call the Play method, shown in Example 18-7, on the Halo2Session class.

Example 18-7. Play method

```
public static void Play( )
{
    // An Xbox has four controller ports so four people can play at a time.
    // We use 4 as the max and zero to start with as we want players
    // to queue up at first until the Xbox boots and loads the game.
    //
    _Xbox = new Semaphore(0, 4, "Xbox");
    ManualResetEvent GameOver = new ManualResetEvent(false);
```

Example 18-7. Play method (continued)

```
    //
    // Nine players log in to play.
    //
    for(int i = 0; i < 9; i++)
    {
        Thread t = new Thread(new ParameterizedThreadStart(XboxPlayer.JoinIn));

        XboxPlayer.Data playerData = new XboxPlayer.Data( );
        // Set the handle.
        playerData._handle = _handles[i];
        // Set the game over event.
        playerData._GameOver = GameOver;

        // Put a name on the thread.
        t.Name = _handles[i];
        // Fire up the player with the data.
        t.Start(playerData);
    }

    // Wait for the Xbox to spin up and load Halo2 (3 seconds).
    Console.WriteLine("Xbox initializing...");
    Thread.Sleep(3000);
    Console.WriteLine("Halo2 loaded & ready, allowing 4 players in now...");

    // The Xbox has the whole semaphore count.  We call
    // Release(4) to open up four slots and
    // allow the waiting players to enter the Xbox(semaphore)
    // up to four at a time.
    //
    _Xbox.Release(4);

    // Wait for the game to end...
    GameOver.WaitOne( );
}
```

The first thing the Play method does is to create a new semaphore that has a maximum resource count of 4 and a name of Xbox. This is the semaphore that will be used by all of the player threads to gain access to the game. A ManualResetEvent called GameOver is created to track when the game has ended.

```
public class XboxPlayer
{
    public class Data
    {
        public ManualResetEvent _GameOver;
        public string _handle;
    }
    //... more class
}
```

To simulate the nine developers, you create nine threads, each with its own XboxPlayer.Data class instance to contain the player name and a reference to the GameOver ManualResetEvent. The thread creation is using the new (in the .NET Framework Version 2.0) ParameterizedThreadStart delegate, which takes the method to execute on the new thread in the constructor, but also allows you to pass the data object directly to a new overload of the Thread.Start method.

Once the players are in motion, the Xbox "initializes" and then calls Release on the semaphore to open four slots for player threads to grab onto, then waits until it detects that the game is over from the firing of the GameOver event.

The players initialize on separate threads and run the JoinIn method, shown in Example 18-8. First they open the Xbox semaphore by name and get the data that was passed to the thread. Once they have the semaphore, they call WaitOne to queue up to play. Once the initial four slots are opened or another player "dies," then the call to WaitOne unblocks and the player "plays" for a random amount of time, then dies. Once the players are dead, they call Release on the semaphore to indicate their slot is now open. If the semaphore reaches its maximum resource count, the GameOver event is set.

Example 18-8. JoinIn method

```
public static void JoinIn(object info)
{
    // Open up the semaphore by name so we can act on it.
    Semaphore Xbox = Semaphore.OpenExisting("Xbox");

    // Get the data object.
    Data data = (Data)info;

    // Each player notifies the Xbox he wants to play
    Console.WriteLine("{0} is waiting to play!", data._handle);

    // They wait on the Xbox (semaphore) until it lets them
    // have a controller.
    Xbox.WaitOne();

    // The Xbox has chosen the player! (Or the semaphore has
    // allowed access to the resource...)
    Console.WriteLine("{0} has been chosen to play. " +
        "Welcome to your doom {0}. >:)", data._handle);

    // Figure out a random value for how long the player lasts.
    System.Random rand = new Random(500);
    int timeTillDeath = rand.Next(100, 1000);

    // Simulate the player as busy playing till they die.
    Thread.Sleep(timeTillDeath);

    // Figure out how they died.
    rand = new Random();
```

Example 18-8. JoinIn method (continued)

```
    int deathIndex = rand.Next(6);

    // Notify of the player's passing.
    Console.WriteLine("{0} has {1} and gives way to another player",
        data._handle, _deaths[deathIndex]);

    // If all ports are open, everyone has played and the game is over.
    int semaphoreCount = Xbox.Release();
    if (semaphoreCount == 3)
    {
        Console.WriteLine("Thank you for playing, the game has ended.");
        // Set the GameOver event.
        data._GameOver.Set();
        // Close out the semaphore.
        Xbox.Close();
    }
}
```

When the Play method is run, output similar to the following is generated:

```
Igor is waiting to play!
AxeMan is waiting to play!
Frosty is waiting to play!
Dr. Death is waiting to play!
HaPpyCaMpEr is waiting to play!
FragMan is waiting to play!
Executioner is waiting to play!
Stoney is waiting to play!
Beatdown is waiting to play!
Xbox initializing...
Halo2 loaded & ready, allowing 4 players in now...
Frosty has been chosen to play. Welcome to your doom Frosty. >:)
HaPpyCaMpEr has been chosen to play. Welcome to your doom HaPpyCaMpEr. >:)
FragMan has been chosen to play. Welcome to your doom FragMan. >:)
Dr. Death has been chosen to play. Welcome to your doom Dr. Death. >:)
Frosty has fallen to their death and gives way to another player.
Executioner has been chosen to play. Welcome to your doom Executioner. >:)
HaPpyCaMpEr has died of lead poisoning and gives way to another player.
Beatdown has been chosen to play. Welcome to your doom Beatdown. >:)
FragMan has shot their own foot and gives way to another player.
AxeMan has been chosen to play. Welcome to your doom AxeMan. >:)
Dr. Death has was captured and gives way to another player.
Stoney has been chosen to play. Welcome to your doom Stoney. >:)
Executioner has choked on a rocket and gives way to another player.
Igor has been chosen to play. Welcome to your doom Igor. >:)
Beatdown has fallen to their death and gives way to another player.
AxeMan has died of lead poisoning and gives way to another player.
Stoney has bought the farm and gives way to another player.
Igor has choked on a rocket and gives way to another player.
Thank you for playing, the game has ended.
```

Discussion

Semaphores are a new piece of the Framework in 2.0 and a welcome one. They are primarily used for resource counting and are available cross-process when named (as they are based on the underlying kernel semaphore object). *Cross-process* may not sound too exciting to many .NET developers until they realize that cross-process also means *cross-AppDomain*. If you are creating additional AppDomains to perform work in, say, for instance, to hold assemblies you are loading dynamically that you don't want to stick around for the whole life of your main AppDomain, the semaphore can help you keep track of how many are loaded at a time. Being able to control access up to a certain number of users can be useful in many scenarios (socket programming, custom thread pools, etc.).

See Also

See the "Semaphore," "ManualResetEvent," and "ParameterizedThreadStart" topics in the MSDN documentation.

18.11 Synchronizing Multiple Processes with the Mutex

Problem

You have two processes or AppDomains that are running code with actions that you need to coordinate.

Solution

Use a named `Mutex` as a common signaling mechanism to do the coordination. A named `Mutex` can be accessed from both pieces of code even when running in different processes or AppDomains.

One situation in which this can be useful is when you are using shared memory to communicate between processes. The `SharedMemoryManager` class presented in this recipe will show the named `Mutex` in action by setting up a section of shared memory that can be used to pass serializable objects between processes. The "server" process creates a `SharedMemoryManager` instance which sets up the shared memory and then creates the `Mutex` as the initial owner. The "client" process then also creates a `SharedMemoryManager` instance that finds the shared memory and hooks up to it. Once this connection is established, the "client" process then sets up to receive the serialized objects and waits until one is sent by waiting on the `Mutex` the "server" process created. The "server" process then takes a serializable object, serializes it into the shared memory, and releases the `Mutex`. It then waits on it again so that when the "client" is done receiving the object, it can release the `Mutex` and give control back to the "server." The "client" process that was waiting on the `Mutex` then deserializes the object from the shared memory and releases the `Mutex`.

In the example, you will send the Contact structure, which looks like this:

```
[StructLayout(LayoutKind.Sequential)]
[Serializable()]
public struct Contact
{
    public string _name;
    public int _age;
}
```

The "server" process code to send the Contact looks like this:

```
// Create the initial shared memory manager to get things set up.
using(SharedMemoryManager<Contact> sm =
    new SharedMemoryManager<Contact>("Contacts",8092))
{
    // This is the sender process.

    // Launch the second process to get going.
    string processName = Process.GetCurrentProcess().MainModule.FileName;
    int index = processName.IndexOf("vshost");
    if (index != -1)
    {
        string first = processName.Substring(0, index);
        int numChars = processName.Length - (index + 7);
        string second = processName.Substring(index + 7, numChars);

        processName = first + second;
    }
    Process receiver = Process.Start(
        new ProcessStartInfo(
            processName,
            "Receiver"));

    // Give it 5 seconds to spin up.
    Thread.Sleep(5000);

    // Make up a contact.
    Contact man;
    man._age = 23;
    man._name = "Dirk Daring";

    // Send it to the other process via shared memory.
    sm.SendObject(man);
}
```

The "client" process code to receive the Contact looks like this:

```
// Create the initial shared memory manager to get things set up.
using(SharedMemoryManager<Contact> sm =
    new SharedMemoryManager<Contact>("Contacts",8092))
{

    // Get the contact once it has been sent.
```

```
        Contact c = (Contact)sm.ReceiveObject();

        // Write it out (or to a database...)
        Console.WriteLine("Contact {0} is {1} years old.",
                          c._name, c._age);

        // Show for 5 seconds.
        Thread.Sleep(5000);
    }
```

The way this usually works is that one process creates a section of shared memory backed by the paging file using the unmanaged Win32 APIs CreateFileMapping and MapViewOfFile. Currently there is no purely managed way to do this, so you have to use P/Invoke, as you can see in Example 18-9 in the constructor code for the SharedMemoryManager and the private SetupSharedMemory method. The constructor takes a name to use as part of the name of the shared memory and the base size of the shared memory block to allocate. It is the base size because the SharedMemoryManager has to allocate a bit extra for keeping track of the data moving through the buffer.

Example 18-9. Constructor and SetupSharedMemory private method

```
public SharedMemoryManager(string name,int sharedMemoryBaseSize)
{
    if (string.IsNullOrEmpty(name))
        throw new ArgumentNullException("name");

    if (sharedMemoryBaseSize <= 0)
        throw new ArgumentOutOfRangeException("sharedMemoryBaseSize",
            "Shared Memory Base Size must be a value greater than zero");

    // Set name of the region.
    _memoryRegionName = name;
    // Save base size.
    _sharedMemoryBaseSize = sharedMemoryBaseSize;
    // Set up the memory region size.
    _memRegionSize = (uint)(_sharedMemoryBaseSize + sizeof(int));
    // Set up the shared memory section.
    SetupSharedMemory();
}

private void SetupSharedMemory()
{
    // Grab some storage from the page file.
    _handleFileMapping =
        PInvoke.CreateFileMapping((IntPtr)INVALID_HANDLE_VALUE,
                        IntPtr.Zero,
                        PInvoke.PageProtection.ReadWrite,
                        0,
                        _memRegionSize,
                        _memoryRegionName);

    if (_handleFileMapping == IntPtr.Zero)
```

Example 18-9. Constructor and SetupSharedMemory private method (continued)

```
    {
        throw new Win32Exception(
            "Could not create file mapping");
    }

    // Check the error status.
    int retVal = Marshal.GetLastWin32Error();
    if (retVal == ERROR_ALREADY_EXISTS)
    {
        // We opened one that already existed.
        // Make the mutex not the initial owner
        // of the mutex since we are connecting
        // to an existing one.
        _mtxSharedMem = new Mutex(false,
            string.Format("{0}mtx{1}",
                typeof(TransferItemType), _memoryRegionName));
    }
    else if (retVal == 0)
    {
        // We opened a new one.
        // Make the mutex the initial owner.
        _mtxSharedMem = new Mutex(true,
            string.Format("{0}mtx{1}",
                typeof(TransferItemType), _memoryRegionName));
    }
    else
    {
        // Something else went wrong.
        throw new Win32Exception(retVal, "Error creating file mapping");
    }

    // Map the shared memory.
    _ptrToMemory = PInvoke.MapViewOfFile(_handleFileMapping,
                                FILE_MAP_WRITE,
                                0, 0, IntPtr.Zero);

    if (_ptrToMemory == IntPtr.Zero)
    {
        retVal = Marshal.GetLastWin32Error();
        throw new Win32Exception(retVal, "Could not map file view");
    }

    retVal = Marshal.GetLastWin32Error();
    if (retVal != 0 && retVal != ERROR_ALREADY_EXISTS)
    {
        // Something else went wrong.
        throw new Win32Exception(retVal, "Error mapping file view");
    }
}
```

The code to send an object through the shared memory is contained in the
SendObject method, shown in Example 18-10. First it checks to see if the object

being sent is indeed serializable by checking the IsSerializable property on the type of the object. If the object is serializable, an integer with the size of the serialized object and the serialized object content are written out to the shared memory section. Then the Mutex is released to indicate that there is an object in the shared memory. It then waits on the Mutex again to wait until the "client" has received the object.

Example 18-10. SendObject method

```
public void SendObject(TransferItemType transferObject)
{
    // Can send only Seralizable objects.
    if (!transferObject.GetType( ).IsSerializable)
        throw new ArgumentException(
            string.Format("Object {0} is not serializeable.",
                transferObject));

    // Create a memory stream, initialize size.
    using (MemoryStream ms = new MemoryStream( ))
    {
        // Get a formatter to serialize with.
        BinaryFormatter formatter = new BinaryFormatter( );
        try
        {
            // Serialize the object to the stream.
            formatter.Serialize(ms, transferObject);

            // Get the bytes for the serialized object.
            byte[] bytes = ms.GetBuffer( );

            // Check that this object will fit.
            if(bytes.Length + sizeof(int) > _memRegionSize)
            {
                string fmt =
                    "{0} object instance serialized to {1} bytes " +
                    "which is too large for the shared memory region";

                string msg =
                    string.Format(fmt,
                        typeof(TransferItemType),bytes.Length);

                throw new ArgumentException(msg, "transferObject");
            }

            // Write out how long this object is.
            Marshal.WriteInt32(this._ptrToMemory, bytes.Length);

            // Write out the bytes.
            Marshal.Copy(bytes, 0, this._ptrToMemory, bytes.Length);
        }
        finally
        {
            // Signal the other process using the mutex to tell it
            // to do receive processing.
```

Example 18-10. SendObject method (continued)

```
            _mtxSharedMem.ReleaseMutex();

            // Wait for the other process to signal it has received
            // and we can move on.
            _mtxSharedMem.WaitOne();
        }
    }
}
```

The ReceiveObject method shown in Example 18-11 allows the client to wait until there is an object in the shared memory section, then read the size of the serialized object and deserialize it to a managed object. It then releases the Mutex to let the sender know to continue.

Example 18-11. ReceiveObject method

```
public TransferItemType ReceiveObject()
{
    // Wait on the mutex for an object to be queued by the sender.
    _mtxSharedMem.WaitOne();

    // Get the count of what is in the shared memory.
    int count = Marshal.ReadInt32(_ptrToMemory);
    if (count <= 0)
    {
        throw new InvalidDataException("No object to read");
    }

    // Make an array to hold the bytes.
    byte[] bytes = new byte[count];

    // Read out the bytes for the object.
    Marshal.Copy(_ptrToMemory, bytes, 0, count);

    // Set up the memory stream with the object bytes.
    using (MemoryStream ms = new MemoryStream(bytes))
    {
        // Set up a binary formatter.
        BinaryFormatter formatter = new BinaryFormatter();

        // Get the object to return.
        TransferItemType item;
        try
        {
            item = (TransferItemType)formatter.Deserialize(ms);
        }
        finally
        {
            // Signal that we received the object using the mutex.
            _mtxSharedMem.ReleaseMutex();
        }
        // Give them the object.
```

Example 18-11. ReceiveObject method (continued)

```
        return item;
    }
}
```

Discussion

A `Mutex` is designed to give mutually exclusive (thus the name) access to a single resource. A `Mutex` can be thought of as a cross-process, named `Monitor` where the `Mutex` is "entered" by waiting on it and becoming the owner, then "exited" by releasing the `Mutex` for the next thread that is waiting on it. If a thread that owns a `Mutex` ends, the `Mutex` is released automatically.

Using a `Mutex` is slower than using a `Monitor` as a `Monitor` is a purely managed construct whereas a `Mutex` is based on the `Mutex` kernel object. A `Mutex` cannot be "pulsed" as can a `Monitor`, but it can be used across processes which a `Monitor` cannot. Finally, the `Mutex` is based on `WaitHandle`, so it can be waited on with other objects derived from `WaitHandle`, like `Semaphore` and the event classes.

The `SharedMemoryManager` and `PInvoke` classes are listed in their entirety in Example 18-12.

Example 18-12. SharedMemoryManager and PInvoke classes

```
/// <summary>
/// Class for sending objects through shared memory using a mutex
/// to synchronize access to the shared memory
/// </summary>
public class SharedMemoryManager<TransferItemType> : IDisposable
{
    #region Consts
    const int INVALID_HANDLE_VALUE = -1;
    const int FILE_MAP_WRITE = 0x0002;
    /// <summary>
    /// Define from Win32 API.
    /// </summary>
    const int ERROR_ALREADY_EXISTS = 183;
    #endregion

    #region Private members
    IntPtr _handleFileMapping = IntPtr.Zero;
    IntPtr _ptrToMemory = IntPtr.Zero;
    uint _memRegionSize = 0;
    string _memoryRegionName;
    bool disposed = false;
    int _sharedMemoryBaseSize = 0;
    Mutex _mtxSharedMem = null;

    #endregion

    #region Construction / Cleanup
```

Example 18-12. SharedMemoryManager and PInvoke classes (continued)

```
public SharedMemoryManager(string name,int sharedMemoryBaseSize)
{
    // Can be built for only Seralizable objects
    if (!typeof(TransferItemType).IsSerializable)
        throw new ArgumentException(
            string.Format("Object {0} is not serializeable.",
                typeof(TransferItemType)));

    if (string.IsNullOrEmpty(name))
        throw new ArgumentNullException("name");

    if (sharedMemoryBaseSize <= 0)
        throw new ArgumentOutOfRangeException("sharedMemoryBaseSize",
            "Shared Memory Base Size must be a value greater than zero");

    // Set name of the region.
    _memoryRegionName = name;
    // Save base size.
    _sharedMemoryBaseSize = sharedMemoryBaseSize;
    // Set up the memory region size.
    _memRegionSize = (uint)(_sharedMemoryBaseSize + sizeof(int));
    // Set up the shared memory section.
    SetupSharedMemory();
}

private void SetupSharedMemory()
{
    // Grab some storage from the page file.
    _handleFileMapping =
        PInvoke.CreateFileMapping((IntPtr)INVALID_HANDLE_VALUE,
                            IntPtr.Zero,
                            PInvoke.PageProtection.ReadWrite,
                            0,
                            _memRegionSize,
                            _memoryRegionName);

    if (_handleFileMapping == IntPtr.Zero)
    {
        throw new Win32Exception(
            "Could not create file mapping");
    }

    // Check the error status.
    int retVal = Marshal.GetLastWin32Error();
    if (retVal == ERROR_ALREADY_EXISTS)
    {
        // We opened one that already existed.
        // Make the mutex not the initial owner
        // of the mutex since we are connecting
        // to an existing one.
        _mtxSharedMem = new Mutex(false,
            string.Format("{0}mtx{1}",
```

Example 18-12. SharedMemoryManager and PInvoke classes (continued)

```
                    typeof(TransferItemType), _memoryRegionName));
    }
    else if (retVal == 0)
    {
        // We opened a new one.
        // Make the mutex the initial owner.
        _mtxSharedMem = new Mutex(true,
            string.Format("{0}mtx{1}",
                typeof(TransferItemType), _memoryRegionName));
    }
    else
    {
        // Something else went wrong.
        throw new Win32Exception(retVal, "Error creating file mapping");
    }

    // Map the shared memory.
    _ptrToMemory = PInvoke.MapViewOfFile(_handleFileMapping,
                                FILE_MAP_WRITE,
                                0, 0, IntPtr.Zero);

    if (_ptrToMemory == IntPtr.Zero)
    {
        retVal = Marshal.GetLastWin32Error();
        throw new Win32Exception(retVal, "Could not map file view");
    }

    retVal = Marshal.GetLastWin32Error();
    if (retVal != 0 && retVal != ERROR_ALREADY_EXISTS)
    {
        // Something else went wrong.
        throw new Win32Exception(retVal, "Error mapping file view");
    }
}

~SharedMemoryManager()
{
    // Make sure we close.
    Dispose(false);
}

public void Dispose()
{
    Dispose(true);
    GC.SuppressFinalize(this);
}

private void Dispose(bool disposing)
{
    // Check to see if Dispose has already been called.
    if (!this.disposed)
    {
```

Example 18-12. SharedMemoryManager and PInvoke classes (continued)

```
            CloseSharedMemory();
        }
        disposed = true;
    }

    private void CloseSharedMemory()
    {
        if (_ptrToMemory != IntPtr.Zero)
        {
            // Close map for shared memory.
            PInvoke.UnmapViewOfFile(_ptrToMemory);
            _ptrToMemory = IntPtr.Zero;
        }
        if (_handleFileMapping != IntPtr.Zero)
        {
            // Close handle.
            PInvoke.CloseHandle(_handleFileMapping);
            _handleFileMapping = IntPtr.Zero;
        }
    }

    public void Close()
    {
        CloseSharedMemory();
    }
    #endregion

    #region Properties
    public int SharedMemoryBaseSize
    {
        get { return _sharedMemoryBaseSize; }
    }
    #endregion

    #region Public Methods
    /// <summary>
    /// Send a serializable object through the shared memory
    /// and wait for it to be picked up.
    /// </summary>
    /// <param name="transferObject"></param>
    public void SendObject(TransferItemType transferObject)
    {
        // Create a memory stream, initialize size.
        using (MemoryStream ms = new MemoryStream())
        {
            // Get a formatter to serialize with.
            BinaryFormatter formatter = new BinaryFormatter();
            try
            {
                // Serialize the object to the stream.
                formatter.Serialize(ms, transferObject);
```

Example 18-12. SharedMemoryManager and PInvoke classes (continued)

```
            // Get the bytes for the serialized object.
            byte[] bytes = ms.ToArray( );

            // Check that this object will fit.
            if(bytes.Length + sizeof(int) > _memRegionSize)
            {
                string fmt =
                    "{0} object instance serialized to {1} bytes " +
                    "which is too large for the shared memory region";

                string msg =
                    string.Format(fmt,
                        typeof(TransferItemType),bytes.Length);

                throw new ArgumentException(msg, "transferObject");
            }

            // Write out how long this object is.
            Marshal.WriteInt32(this._ptrToMemory, bytes.Length);

            // Write out the bytes.
            Marshal.Copy(bytes, 0, this._ptrToMemory, bytes.Length);
        }
        finally
        {
            // Signal the other process using the mutex to tell it
            // to do receive processing.
            _mtxSharedMem.ReleaseMutex( );

            // Wait for the other process to signal it has received
            // and we can move on.
            _mtxSharedMem.WaitOne( );
        }
    }
}

/// <summary>
/// Wait for an object to hit the shared memory and then deserialize it.
/// </summary>
/// <returns>object passed</returns>
public TransferItemType ReceiveObject( )
{
    // Wait on the mutex for an object to be queued by the sender.
    _mtxSharedMem.WaitOne( );

    // Get the count of what is in the shared memory.
    int count = Marshal.ReadInt32(_ptrToMemory);
    if (count <= 0)
    {
        throw new InvalidDataException("No object to read");
    }
```

Example 18-12. SharedMemoryManager and PInvoke classes (continued)

```csharp
            // Make an array to hold the bytes.
            byte[] bytes = new byte[count];

            // Read out the bytes for the object.
            Marshal.Copy(_ptrToMemory, bytes, 0, count);

            // Set up the memory stream with the object bytes.
            using (MemoryStream ms = new MemoryStream(bytes))
            {
                // Set up a binary formatter.
                BinaryFormatter formatter = new BinaryFormatter();

                // Get the object to return.
                TransferItemType item;
                try
                {
                    item = (TransferItemType)formatter.Deserialize(ms);
                }
                finally
                {
                    // Signal that we received the object using the mutex.
                    _mtxSharedMem.ReleaseMutex();
                }
                // Give them the object.
                return item;
            }
        }
        #endregion
    }

    public class PInvoke
    {
        #region PInvoke defines
        [Flags]
        public enum PageProtection : uint
        {
            NoAccess = 0x01,
            Readonly = 0x02,
            ReadWrite = 0x04,
            WriteCopy = 0x08,
            Execute = 0x10,
            ExecuteRead = 0x20,
            ExecuteReadWrite = 0x40,
            ExecuteWriteCopy = 0x80,
            Guard = 0x100,
            NoCache = 0x200,
            WriteCombine = 0x400,
        }

        [DllImport("kernel32.dll", SetLastError = true)]
        public static extern IntPtr CreateFileMapping(IntPtr hFile,
            IntPtr lpFileMappingAttributes, PageProtection flProtect,
```

Example 18-12. SharedMemoryManager and PInvoke classes (continued)

```
            uint dwMaximumSizeHigh,
            uint dwMaximumSizeLow, string lpName);

    [DllImport("kernel32.dll", SetLastError = true)]
    public static extern IntPtr MapViewOfFile(IntPtr hFileMappingObject, uint
        dwDesiredAccess, uint dwFileOffsetHigh, uint dwFileOffsetLow,
        IntPtr dwNumberOfBytesToMap);

    [DllImport("kernel32.dll", SetLastError = true)]
    public static extern bool UnmapViewOfFile(IntPtr lpBaseAddress);

    [DllImport("kernel32.dll", SetLastError = true)]
    public static extern bool CloseHandle(IntPtr hObject);
    #endregion
}
```

See Also

See the "Mutex" and "Mutex Class" topics in the MSDN documentation and *Programming Applications for Microsoft Windows*, Fourth Edition.

18.12 Using Events to Make Threads Cooperate

Problem

You have multiple threads that need to be served by a server but only one can be served at a time.

Solution

Use an AutoResetEvent to notify each thread when it is going to be served. For example, a diner has a cook and multiple waitresses. The waitresses can keep bringing in orders, but the cook can serve up only one at a time. You can simulate this with the Cook class shown in Example 18-13.

Example 18-13. Using events to make threads cooperate

```
public class Cook
{
    public static AutoResetEvent OrderReady = new AutoResetEvent(false);

    public void CallWaitress()
    {
        // We call Set on the AutoResetEvent and don't have to
        // call Reset like we would with ManualResetEvent to fire it
        // off again.  This sets the event that the waitress is waiting for
        // in PlaceOrder.
        OrderReady.Set();
```

Example 18-13. Using events to make threads cooperate (continued)

```
        }
    }
```

The Cook class has an AutoResetEvent called OrderReady that the cook will use to tell the waiting waitresses that an order is ready. Since there is only one order ready at a time and this is an equal opportunity diner, the waitress who has been waiting longest gets her order first. The AutoResetEvent allows for just signaling the single thread when you call Set on the OrderReady event.

The Waitress class has the PlaceOrder method that is executed by the thread. PlaceOrder takes an object parameter, which is passed in from the call to t.Start in the next code block. The Start method uses a ParameterizedThreadStart delegate, which takes an object parameter. PlaceOrder has been set up to be compatible with it. It takes the AutoResetEvent passed in and calls WaitOne to wait until the order is ready. Once the Cook fires the event enough times that this waitress is at the head of the line, the code finishes.

```
public class Waitress
{
    public static void PlaceOrder(object signal)
    {
        // Cast the AutoResetEvent so the waitress can wait for the
        // order to be ready.
        AutoResetEvent OrderReady = (AutoResetEvent)signal;
        // Wait for the order...
        OrderReady.WaitOne( );
        // Order is ready....
        Console.WriteLine("Waitress got order!");
    }
}
```

The code to run the "diner" creates a Cook and spins off the Waitress threads, then calls all waitresses when their orders are ready by calling Set on the AutoResetEvent:

```
// We have a diner with a cook who can serve up only one meal at a time.
Cook Mel = new Cook( );

// Make up five waitresses and tell them to get orders.
for (int i = 0; i < 5; i++)
{
    Thread t = new Thread(Waitress.PlaceOrder);
    // The Waitress places the order and then waits for the order.
    t.Start(Cook.OrderReady);
}

// Now we can go through and let people in.
for (int i = 0; i < 5; i++)
{
    // Make the waitresses wait...
    Thread.Sleep(2000);
    // OK, next waitress, pickup!
```

```
        Mel.CallWaitress();
    }
```

Discussion

There are two types of events, AutoResetEvent and ManualResetEvent. There are two main differences between the events. The first is that AutoResetEvents release only one of the threads that are waiting on the event while a ManualResetEvent will release all of them when Set is called. The second difference is that when Set is called on an AutoResetEvent, it is automatically reset to a nonsignaled state while the ManualResetEvent is left in a signaled state until the Reset method is called.

See Also

See the "AutoResetEvent" and "ManualResetEvent" topics in the MSDN documentation and *Programming Applications for Microsoft Windows*, (Fourth Edition).

18.13 Get the Naming Rights for Your Events

Problem

You want to have code running in worker threads, or in other processes or AppDomains, to be able to wait on an event.

Solution

Use the EventWaitHandle class, new to the 2.0 Framework. With it, you can create a named event that will allow any code running on the local machine to find and wait on the event. AutoResetEvent and ManualResetEvent are excellent for signaling events in threaded code and even between AppDomains if you are willing to go through the hassle of passing the event reference around. Why bother? Both of them derive from EventWaitHandle, but neither exposes the naming facility. EventWaitHandle can not only take the name of the event, but also can take an EventResetMode parameter to indicate if it should act like a ManualResetEvent (EventResetMode.ManualReset) or an AutoResetEvent (EventResetMode.AutoReset). Named events have been available to Windows developers for a long time, and the EventWaitHandle class can serve as a named version of either an AutoResetEvent or a ManualResetEvent.

To set up a named EventWaitHandle that operates as a ManualResetEvent, do this:

```
// Make a named manual reset event.
EventWaitHandle ewhSuperBowl =
    new EventWaitHandle(false, // Not initially signaled
                        EventResetMode.ManualReset,
                        @"Champs");

// Spin up three threads to listen for the event.
for (int i = 0; i < 3; i++)
```

```
    {
        Thread t = new Thread(ManualFan);
        // The fans wait anxiously...
        t.Name = "Fan " + i;
        t.Start( );
    }
    // Play the game.
    Thread.Sleep(10000);
    // Notify people.
    Console.WriteLine("Patriots win the SuperBowl!");
    // Signal all fans.
    ewhSuperBowl.Set( );
    // Close the event.
    ewhSuperBowl.Close( );
```

The ManualFan method is listed here:

```
public static void ManualFan( )
{
    // Open the event by name.
    EventWaitHandle ewhSuperBowl =
        new EventWaitHandle(false,
                            EventResetMode.ManualReset,
                            @"Champs");

    // Wait for the signal.
    ewhSuperBowl.WaitOne( );
    // Shout out.
    Console.WriteLine("\"They're great!\" says {0}",Thread.CurrentThread.Name);
    // Close the event.
    ewhSuperBowl.Close( );
}
```

The output from the manual event code will resemble the listing here (the ManualFan
threads might be in a different order):

```
Patriots win the SuperBowl!
"They're great!" says Fan 2
"They're great!" says Fan 1
"They're great!" says Fan 0
```

To set up a named EventWaitHandle to operate as an AutoResetEvent, do this:

```
// Make a named auto reset event.
EventWaitHandle ewhSuperBowl =
    new EventWaitHandle(false, // Not initially signalled
                        EventResetMode.AutoReset,
                        @"Champs");

// Spin up three threads to listen for the event.
for (int i = 0; i < 3; i++)
{
    Thread t = new Thread(AutoFan, i);
    // The fans wait anxiously...
    t.Name = "Fan " + i;
    t.Start( );
```

```
    }
    // Play the game.
    Thread.Sleep(10000);
    // Notify people.
    Console.WriteLine("Patriots win the SuperBowl!");
    // Signal one fan at a time.
    for (int i = 0; i < 3; i++)
    {
        Console.WriteLine("Notify fans");
        ewhSuperBowl.Set();
    }
    // Close the event.
    ewhSuperBowl.Close();
```

The AutoFan method is listed here:

```
public static void AutoFan()
{
    // Open the event by name.
    EventWaitHandle ewhSuperBowl =
        new EventWaitHandle(false,
                            EventResetMode.AutoReset,
                            @"Champs");

    // Wait for the signal.
    ewhSuperBowl.WaitOne();
    // Shout out.
    Console.WriteLine("\"Yahoo!\" says {0}", Thread.CurrentThread.Name);
    // Close the event.
    ewhSuperBowl.Close();
}
```

The output from the automatic event code will resemble the listing here (the AutoFan threads might be in a different order):

```
Patriots win the SuperBowl!
Notify fans
"Yahoo!" says Fan 0
Notify fans
"Yahoo!" says Fan 2
Notify fans
"Yahoo!" says Fan 1
```

Discussion

EventWaitHandle is defined as deriving from WaitHandle, which in turn derives from MarshalByRefObject. EventWaitHandle implements the IDisposable interface.

```
public class EventWaitHandle : WaitHandle
```

```
public abstract class WaitHandle : MarshalByRefObject, IDisposable
```

WaitHandle derives from MarshalByRefObject so you can use it across AppDomains, and it implements IDisposable to make sure the event handle gets released properly.

The EventWaitHandle class can also open an existing named event by calling the OpenExisting method and get the event's access-control security from GetAccessControl.

When naming events, one consideration is how it will react in the presence of terminal sessions. *Terminal sessions* are the underlying technology behind Fast User switching and Remote Desktop, as well as Terminal Services. The consideration is due to how kernel objects (such as events) are created with respect to the terminal sessions. If a kernel object is created with a name and no prefix, it belongs to the Global namespace for named objects and is visible across terminal sessions. By default, EventWaitHandle creates the event in the Global namespace. A kernel object can also be created in the Local namespace for a given terminal session, in which case the named object belongs to the specific terminal session namespace. If you pass the *Local* namespace prefix (*Local\[EventName]*), then the event will be created in the local session for events that should be visible from only one terminal session.

```
// Open the event by local name.
EventWaitHandle ewhSuperBowl =
    new EventWaitHandle(false,
                        EventResetMode.ManualReset,
                        @"Local\Champs");
```

Named events can be quite useful not only when communicating between processes, AppDomains, or threads, but also when debugging code that uses events, as the name will help you identify which event you are looking at if you have a number of them.

See Also

See the "EventWaitHandle," "AutoResetEvent," "ManualResetEvent," and "Kernel Object Namespaces (Platform SDK Help)" topics in the MSDN documentation.

18.14 Performing Atomic Operations Among Threads

Problem

You are operating on data from multiple threads and want to insure that each operation is carried out fully before performing the next operation from a different thread.

Solution

Use the Interlocked family of functions to insure atomic access. Interlocked has methods to increment and decrement values, add a specific amount to a given value, exchange an original value for a new value, compare the current value to the original value, and exchange the original value for a new value if it is equal to the current value.

To increment or decrement an integer value, use the Increment or Decrement methods, respectively:

```
int i = 0;
long l = 0;

Interlocked.Increment(ref i); // i = 1
Interlocked.Decrement(ref i); // i = 0
Interlocked.Increment(ref l); // l = 1
Interlocked.Decrement(ref i); // l = 0
```

To add a specific amount to a given integer value, use the Add method:

```
Interlocked.Add(ref i, 10); // i = 10;
Interlocked.Add(ref l, 100); // l = 100;
```

To replace an existing value, use the Exchange method:

```
string name = "Mr. Ed";
Interlocked.Exchange(ref name, "Barney");
```

To check if another thread has changed a value out from under the existing code before replacing the existing value, use the CompareExchange method:

```
int i = 0;
double runningTotal = 0.0;
double startingTotal = 0.0;
double calc = 0.0;
for (i = 0; i < 10; i++)
{
    do
    {
        // Store of the original total
        startingTotal = runningTotal;

        // Do an intense calculation.
        calc = runningTotal + i * Math.PI * 2 / Math.PI;
    }
    // Check to make sure runningTotal wasn't modified
    // and replace it with calc if not.  If it was,
    // run through the loop until we get it current.
    while (startingTotal !=
        Interlocked.CompareExchange(
            ref runningTotal, calc, startingTotal));
}
```

Discussion

In an operating system like Microsoft Windows, with its ability to perform preemptive multitasking, certain considerations must be given to data integrity when working with multiple threads. There are many synchronization primitives to help secure sections of code, as well as signal when data is available to be modified. To this list is added the capability to perform operations that are guaranteed to be atomic in nature.

If there has not been much threading or assembly language in your past, you might wonder what the big deal is and why you need these atomic functions at all. The basic reason is that the line of code written in C# ultimately has to be translated down to a machine instruction and along the way the one line of code written in C# can turn into multiple instructions for the machine to execute. If the machine has to execute multiple instructions to perform a task and the operating system allows for preemption, it is possible that these instructions may not be executed as a block. They could be interrupted by other code that modifies the value being changed by the original line of C# code in the middle of the C# code being executed. As you can imagine, this could lead to some pretty spectacular errors, or it might just round off the lottery number that keeps a certain C# programmer from winning the big one.

Threading is a powerful tool, but like most "power" tools, you have to understand its operation to use it effectively and safely. Threading bugs are notorious for being some of the most difficult to debug, as the runtime behavior is not constant. Trying to reproduce them can be a nightmare. Recognizing that working in a multithreaded environment imposes a certain amount of forethought about protecting data access and understanding when to use the Interlocked class will go a long way toward preventing long frustrating evenings with the debugger.

See Also

See the "Interlocked" and "Interlocked Class" topics in the MSDN documentation.

CHAPTER 19

Unsafe Code

19.0 Introduction

Visual C# .NET allows you to step outside of the safe environment of managed code and write code that is considered "unsafe" by the CLR. Running unsafe code presents a certain set of restrictions in exchange for opening up possibilities, like accessing memory-mapped data or implementing time-critical algorithms that use pointers directly. These restrictions are mainly based in the CAS system of the CLR and are in place to draw a distinct line between code the CLR knows to be playing by the rules (or "safe") and code that needs to do a bit outside of the traditional sandbox of the CLR (and is thus "unsafe" code). In order to run code that is marked as unsafe by the CLR, you need to have the CAS `SkipVerification` privilege granted to the assembly where the unsafe code is implemented. This tells the CLR to not bother verifying the code and to allow it to run, whereas normally unverified code would not run. This is a highly privileged operation and is not to be done lightly, as you increase the permissions your application will require in order to operate correctly on a user's system. If you use unsafe types in a method signature, you also make the code non-CLS-compliant. This means that interoperability with other .NET-based languages, like VB.NET or Managed C++, for this assembly is compromised.

Even though unsafe code allows you to easily write potentially unstable code, it does have several safeguards. You can create only pointers to value types or value types inside of reference types; you cannot create pointers to reference types. This forces pointer types to be created solely on the stack, so you do not have to use the new and delete operations to allocate and release the memory to which the variable points. You only have to wait for the method that declared the pointer type to return, forcing the pointer to go out of scope and clearing any stack space devoted to this method. You can get into a bit of trouble if you are doing exotic things with unsafe code, such as pointing to a value type inside of a reference type. This behavior allows access to heap-based memory, thereby opening up the possibility for pointer pitfalls, such as those seen in C++.

19.1 Controlling Changes to Pointers Passed to Methods

Problem

You must pass a pointer variable to a method; however, you do not want to allow the called method to change the address that the pointer points to. For example, a developer wants to assume that, after passing a pointer parameter to a method, the parameter is still pointing to the same address when the method returns. If the called method were to change what the pointer pointed to, bugs could be introduced into the code.

In other cases, the converse may be true: the developer *wants* to allow the address to be changed in the method she passes the pointer to. Consider a developer who might create a method that accepts two pointers and switches those pointers by switching the memory locations to which each pointer points to, rather than swapping the values each pointer points to.

Solution

You must decide whether to pass a pointer by value, by reference, or as an out parameter. There are several ways to pass pointers to methods. These include using or not using the ref or out keyword to define how the parameters are to be handled.

To make sure that a method does not modify the pointer itself, pass the pointer by value, as shown here:

```
unsafe
{
    int num = 1;
    int* numPtr = &num;
    ModifyValue(numPtr);
    // Continue using numPtr...
}
```

The method ModifyValue can still change the value in the memory location to which numPtr points to, but it cannot force numPtr to point to a different memory location after the method ModifyValue returns.

To allow the method to modify the pointer, pass it by reference:

```
public unsafe void TestSwitchXY( )
{
    int x = 100;
    int y = 20;
    int* ptrx = &x;
    int* ptry = &y;

    Console.WriteLine(*ptrx + "\t" + (int)ptrx);
    Console.WriteLine(*ptry + "\t" + (int)ptry);
```

```
SwitchXY(ref ptrx, ref ptry);

Console.WriteLine(*ptrx + "\t" + (int)ptrx);
Console.WriteLine(*ptry + "\t" + (int)ptry);
}

public unsafe void SwitchXY(ref int* x, ref int* y)
{
    int* temp = x;
    x = y;
    y = temp;
}
```

The SwitchXY method switches the values of the x and y pointers so that they point to the memory location originally pointed to by the other parameter. In this case, you must pass the pointers in to the SwitchXY method by reference (ref). This allows the SwitchXY method to actually change the pointers and to return these modified pointers.

Discussion

In safe code, passing a value type to a method *by value* means that the value, not the reference to that value, is passed in. Therefore, the called method cannot modify the value that the calling method's reference points to; it can modify only the copy that it receives.

It works the same way with unsafe code. When an unsafe pointer is passed in to a method by value, the value of the pointer (which is a memory location) cannot be modified; however, the value that this pointer points to can be modified.

To examine the difference between passing a pointer by reference and by value, you first need to set up a pointer to an integer:

```
int x = 5;
int* ptrx = &x;
```

Next, write the method that attempts to modify the pointer parameter:

```
private unsafe void CallByValue(int* x)
{
    int newNum = 7;
    x = &newNum;
}
```

Finally, call the method and pass in ptrx to this method:

```
CallByValue(ptrx);
```

If you examine the pointer variable ptrx before the call to CallByValue, you'll see that it points to the value 5. The called method CallByValue changes the passed-in parameter to point to a different memory location. However, when the CallByValue returns, the ptrx pointer still points to the original memory location that contains the value 5. The reason for this is that CallByValue accepts the pointer ptrx by value. This means that whatever value ptrx holds, a memory location in this case, it cannot be modified.

At other times, you need to allow a called method to modify the memory location that a pointer points to. Passing a pointer *by reference* does this. This means that the called method may, in fact, modify the memory location to which a pointer parameter points. To see this, again set up a pointer:

```
int x = 5;
int* ptrx = &x;
```

Next, write the method that attempts to modify the parameter:

```
private unsafe void CallByRef(ref int* x)
{
    int newNum = 7;
    x = &newNum;
}
```

Finally, call the method and pass the pointer by reference:

```
CallByRef(ref ptrx);
```

Now if you examine the value that the pointer ptrx points to, before and after the call is made to CallByRef, you'll see that it has indeed changed from 5 to 7. Not only this, but the ptrx pointer is actually pointing to a different memory location. Essentially, the ref keyword allows the method CallByRef to modify the value contained in the ptrx variable.

Let's consider the use of the out or ref keywords with pointers. A method that accepts a pointer as an out or ref parameter is called like this:

```
public unsafe void TestOut( )
{
    int* ptrx;
    CallUsingOut(out ptrx);

    Console.WriteLine(*ptrx + "\t" + (int)ptrx);
}
```

The CallUsingOut method is written as follows:

```
public unsafe void CallUsingOut(out int* ptrx)
{
    int x = 7;
    ptrx = &x;
}
```

The ptrx variable is initially a null pointer. After the call is made to the CallUsingOut method, the ptrx variable points to the value 0. There is a serious flaw in the design of this example code (the code in the Solution section does not contain this flaw).

The problem is that the temp variable, pointed to by the out parameter ptrx in the CallUsingOut method, is in the stack frame of the CallUsingOut method. The stack frame to the CallUsingOut method is promptly overwritten when this method returns, thereby causing the value in ptrx to be undefined.

This mistake is easy to make, especially as the code gets more and more complex. This error can also occur when returning a pointer from a method as a return value. To solve this, you need to not assign local variables that are created on the stack in the scope of the method to the pointer, since the value being pointed to can "go away" once the scope is exited, creating a dangling pointer.

 Be very careful that you do not create dangling pointers (a pointer that doesn't point at anything valid, such as by assigning a pointer to memory that is collected before leaving the function) when passing pointer parameters as ref or out. This warning also applies to pointers used as return values.

See Also

See the "Method Parameters," "out Parameter," and "ref Parameter" topics in the MSDN documentation.

19.2   Comparing Pointers

Problem

You need to know whether two pointers point to the same memory location. If they don't, you need to know which of the two pointers points to a higher or lower element in the same block of memory.

Solution

Using the == and != operators, you can determine if two pointers point to the same memory location. For example, the code:

```
unsafe
{
    int[] arr = new int[5] {1,2,3,4,5};
    fixed(int* ptrArr = &arr[0])
    {
        int* p1 = (ptrArr + 1);
        int* p2 = (ptrArr + 3);

        Console.WriteLine("p2 > p1");
        Console.WriteLine("(p2 == p1) = " + (p2 == p1));
        Console.WriteLine("(p2 != p1) = " + (p2 != p1));

        p2 = p1;
        Console.WriteLine("p2 == p1");
        Console.WriteLine("(p2 == p1) = " + (p2 == p1));
        Console.WriteLine("(p2 != p1) = " + (p2 != p1));
    }
}
```

displays the following:

```
p2 > p1
(p2 == p1) = False
(p2 != p1) = True


p2 == p1
(p2 == p1) = True
(p2 != p1) = False
```

Using the >, <, >=, or <= comparison operators, you can determine whether two pointers are pointing to a higher, a lower, or the same element in an array. For example, the code:

```
unsafe
{
    int[] arr = new int[5] {1,2,3,4,5};
    fixed(int* ptrArr = &arr[0])
    {
        int* p1 = (ptrArr + 1);
        int* p2 = (ptrArr + 3);

        Console.WriteLine("p2 > p1");
        Console.WriteLine("(p2 > p1) = " + (p2 > p1));
        Console.WriteLine("(p2 < p1) = " + (p2 < p1));
        Console.WriteLine("(p2 >= p1) = " + (p2 >= p1));
        Console.WriteLine("(p2 <= p1) = " + (p2 <= p1));

        p2 = p1;
        Console.WriteLine("p2 == p1");
        Console.WriteLine("(p2 > p1) = " + (p2 > p1));
        Console.WriteLine("(p2 < p1) = " + (p2 < p1));
        Console.WriteLine("(p2 >= p1) = " + (p2 >= p1));
        Console.WriteLine("(p2 <= p1) = " + (p2 <= p1));
    }
}
```

displays the following:

```
p2 > p1
(p2 > p1) = True
(p2 < p1) = False
(p2 >= p1) = True
(p2 <= p1) = False


p2 == p1
(p2 > p1) = False
(p2 < p1) = False
(p2 >= p1) = True
(p2 <= p1) = True
```

Discussion

When manipulating the addresses that pointers point to, it is sometimes necessary to compare their addresses. The ==, !=, >, <, >=, and <= operators have been overloaded to operate on pointer-type variables. These comparison operators do not compare the value pointed to by the pointers; instead, they compare the addresses pointed to by the pointers.

To compare the values pointed to by two pointers: dereference the pointers and then use a comparison operator on them. For example:

```
*intPtr == *intPtr2
```

will compare the values pointed to by these pointers, rather than their addresses.

See Also

See the "C# Operators," "== Operator," and "!= Operator" topics in the MSDN documentation.

19.3   Navigating Arrays

Problem

You need to iterate through the elements of a single-dimensional, multidimensional, or jagged array using a pointer to that array.

Solution

To enable iteration, create an unsafe pointer that points to an array. The manipulation of the array can then be performed through this pointer.

To create a pointer to a single-dimensional array, declare and initialize the array:

```
int[] intArray = new int[5] {1, 2, 3, 4, 5};
```

and then set a pointer, arrayPtr, to the address of the first element in this array (you must use the fixed keyword to pin the array in the managed heap so that the garbage collector does not move it):

```
fixed(int* arrayPtr = &intArray[0])
```

Note that this line could also be written as:

```
fixed(int* arrayPtr = intArray)
```

without any address of (&) operator or indexer. This is because the array variable always points to the first element, similarly to how C/C++ array pointers operate.

The following code creates and initializes a pointer to a single-dimensional array and then displays the last item in that array:

```
unsafe
{
    int[] intArray = new int[5] {1, 2, 3, 4, 5};
    fixed(int* arrayPtr = intArray)
    {
```

```
        Console.WriteLine(*(arrayPtr + 4)); //Display the last value '5'
    }
}
```

Creating a pointer to an array of enumeration values is very similar:

```
unsafe
{
    Colors[] intArray = new Colors[2] {Colors.Red, Colors.Blue};
    fixed(Colors* arrayPtr = intArray)
    {
        // Use arrayPtr here.
    }
}
```

where Colors is declared as follows:

```
public enum Colors{Red, Green, Blue}
```

Creating a pointer to a multidimensional array is performed by declaring and initializing a multidimensional array:

```
int[,] intMultiArray = new int[2,5] {{1,2,3,4,5},{6,7,8,9,10}};
```

You then set a pointer to the address of the first element in this array:

```
fixed(int* arrayPtr = intMultiArray)
```

For example, the following code creates and initializes a pointer to a multidimensional array, then displays the last item in that array:

```
unsafe
{
    int[,] intMultiArray = new int[2,5] {{1,2,3,4,5},{6,7,8,9,10}};
    fixed(int* arrayPtr = intMultiArray)
    {
        Console.WriteLine(*(arrayPtr + 9)); //Display the last value '10'
    }
}
```

See Also

See the "Multidimensional Arrays" and "Jagged Arrays" topics and the "Unsafe at the Limit" article in the MSDN documentation.

19.4   Manipulating a Pointer to a Fixed Array

Problem

One limitation of a pointer to a fixed array is that you cannot reassign this pointer to any other element of that array using pointer arithmetic. The following code will not compile since you are attempting to modify where the fixed pointer, arrayPtr, is pointing. The line of code in error is highlighted; it results in a compile-time error, as shown next.

```
unsafe
{
    int[] intArray = new int[5] {1,2,3,4,5};
    fixed(int* arrayPtr = &intArray[0])
    {
        arrayPtr++;
    }
}
```

You need a way to increment the address stored in the arrayPtr to access other elements in the array.

Solution

To allow this operation, create a new temporary pointer to the fixed array, shown here:

```
unsafe
{
    int[] intArray = new int[5] {1,2,3,4,5};
    fixed(int* arrayPtr = &intArray[0])
    {
        int* tempPtr = arrayPtr;
        tempPtr++;
    }
}
```

By assigning a pointer that points to the fixed pointer (arrayPtr), you now have a variable (tempPtr) that you can manipulate as you wish.

Discussion

Any variables declared in a fixed statement cannot be modified or passed as ref or out parameters to other methods. This can pose a problem when attempting to move a pointer of this type through the elements of an array. Getting around this involves creating a temporary variable, tempPtr, that points to the same memory locations as the pointer declared in the fixed statement. Pointer arithmetic can then be applied to this temporary variable to move the pointer to any of the elements in the array.

See Also

See the "unsafe Keyword" and "fixed Keyword" topics in the MSDN documentation.

19.5 Returning a Pointer to a Particular Element in an Array

Problem

You need to create a method that accepts a pointer to an array, searches that array for a particular element, and returns to the location of the found element in the array.

Solution

The FindInArray method, used in the following example, will return the position of the element found in the array given a fixed integer pointer. To see FindInFixedArray in action, look at the TestFind method shown here:

```
public void TestFind( )
{
    unsafe
    {
        int[] numericArr = new int[3] {2,4,6};
        fixed(int* ptrArr = numericArr)
        {
            int foundPos = FindInFixedArray(ptrArr, numericArr.Length, 4);
            if (foundPos > -1)
            {
                Console.WriteLine("Position in array: " + foundPos);
            }
            else
            {
                Console.WriteLine("Not Found");
            }
        }
    }
}
```

The TestFind method creates an array of integers (numericArr), then uses the fixed statement to create a pointer (ptrArr) and to make sure the array will not be moved in memory by the garbage collector. The ptrArr pointer variable is passed to the FindInFixedArray method shown here to get the position of the element for the value being searched for:

```
public unsafe int FindInFixedArray(int* theArray, int arrayLength,
int valueToFind)
{
    for (int counter = 0; counter < arrayLength; counter++)
    {
        if (theArray[counter] == valueToFind)
        {
            return (counter);
        }
    }

    // Return -1 if the value is not found in the array.
    return (-1);
}
```

Notice that the FindInFixedArray method requires that the int* be fixed to be effective. If the pointer passed in to the FindInFixedArray method is not fixed, the garbage collector could move the array being searched at any time. To avoid this, use the fixed statement as shown in the TestFind example. This method is strongly typed for arrays that contain integers. To modify this method to use another type, change

---

the int* types to the pointer type of your choice. Note that if no elements are found in the array, a value of -1 is returned.

Discussion

The FindInArray method accepts three parameters. The first parameter, theArray, is a pointer to the first element in the array that will be searched. The second parameter, arrayLength, is the length of the array, and the final parameter, valueToFind, is the value you wish to find in the array theArray.

The second parameter, arrayLength, informs the for loop of the length of the array. You cannot determine the length of an array from just a pointer to that array, so this parameter is needed. Many unmanaged APIs that accept a pointer to an array also require that the length of the array be passed.

 You could pass a pointer to any element in the array through the theArray parameter, but if you do so, you must calculate the remaining length by subtracting the element location from the length of the array and passing the result to the arrayLength parameter.

The loop iterates over each element in the array and looks for the element that has a value equal to the parameter valueToFind. Once this element is found, the location of this element in the array is returned to the caller.

See Also

See the "unsafe Keyword" in the MSDN documentation.

19.6   Creating and Using an Array of Pointers

Problem

You need to create, initialize, and use an array containing pointers.

Solution

The following code creates three pointers to a NewBrush structure (theNewBrush1, theNewBrush2, and theNewBrush3) that are inserted as elements in an array. The NewBrush structure used here is defined like this:

```
public struct NewBrush
{
    public int BrushType;
}
```

The array of pointers is created and set to a size of 3 so that it can hold each element. This newly defined array now contains undefined pointers. These undefined pointers should be initialized either to point to a value or to point to null. Here, all of the pointers in the array are initialized as null pointers. Finally, each NewBrush structure is added to the array. Now you have a fully initialized array of pointers. From here you can use this array as you wish:

```
unsafe
{
    NewBrush theNewBrush1 = new NewBrush( );
    NewBrush theNewBrush2 = new NewBrush( );
    NewBrush theNewBrush3 = new NewBrush( );

    NewBrush*[] arrayOfNewBrushPtrs = new NewBrush*[3];

    arrayOfNewBrushPtrs[0] = &theNewBrush1;
    arrayOfNewBrushPtrs[1] = &theNewBrush2;
    arrayOfNewBrushPtrs[2] = &theNewBrush3;
}
```

This array of pointers to NewBrush objects must be referenced as a pointer to a pointer in unsafe code. The following code shows how to dereference each pointer within the array arrayOfNewBrushPtrs:

```
unsafe
{
    fixed(NewBrush** ptrArrayOfNewBrushPtrs = arrayOfNewBrushPtrs)
    {
        for (int counter = 0; counter < 3; counter++)
        {
            ptrArrayOfNewBrushPtrs[counter]->BrushType = counter;
            Console.WriteLine(ptrArrayOfNewBrushPtrs[counter]->BrushType);
            Console.WriteLine((int)ptrArrayOfNewBrushPtrs[counter]);
        }
    }
}
```

The for loop initializes the BrushType field of each of the pointers to NewBrush objects in the array. This field is initialized to the current value of the loop counter (counter). The next two lines display this newly initialized field and the address of the structure in memory. This code displays the following output (note that the addresses will be different on different machines):

```
0
1243292
1
1243284
2
1243276
```

Discussion

When using an array of pointers, the fixed statement pins the array in memory. Even though this array consists of pointers to value types, the array itself is created on the managed heap. Notice that ptrArrayOfNewBrushPtrs is defined as a pointer to a pointer. This stems from having created a pointer (ptrArrayOfNewBrushPtrs) that initially points to the first element in an array of pointers. To be able to dereference this pointer to get to the value that the array element is pointing to, you must dereference it once to get to the array element and then a second time to get the value that the element is pointing to.

See Also

See the "Unsafe Code Tutorial" topic in the MSDN documentation.

19.7   Switching Unknown Pointer Types

Problem

You need a generic method that accepts two pointers and switches the addresses that each pointer points to. In other words, if x points to an integer variable Foo and y points to an integer variable Bar, you want to switch x so that it points to Bar and switch y so that it points to Foo.

Solution

Create a method that accepts two void pointers. The following method accepts two pointers to void by reference. The *by reference* is required since you are actually switching the values contained in the pointer variables, not the value that the pointer is pointing to:

```
public unsafe void Switch(ref void* x, ref void* y)
{
    void* temp = x;
    x = y;
    y = temp;
}
```

The following test code calls the Switch method with two integer variables that point to different memory locations:

```
public unsafe void TestSwitch( )
{
    int x = 100;
    int y = 20;
    int* ptrx = &x;
    int* ptry = &y;

    Console.WriteLine(*ptrx + "\t" + (int)ptrx);
    Console.WriteLine(*ptry + "\t" + (int)ptry);

    // Convert int* to void*.
    void* voidx = (void*)ptrx;
    void* voidy = (void*)ptry;
```

```
    // Switch pointer values.
    Switch(ref voidx, ref voidy);

    // Convert returned void* to a usable int*.
    ptrx = (int*)voidx;
    ptry = (int*)voidy;

    Console.WriteLine(*ptrx + "\t" + (int)ptrx);
    Console.WriteLine(*ptry + "\t" + (int)ptry);
}
```

The following is displayed (note that the addresses will be different on different machines):

```
100      1243108
20       1243104
20       1243104
100      1243108
```

The TestSwitch method could have been written just as easily with another data type, such as a byte, shown here:

```
public unsafe void TestSwitch( )
{
    byte x = 100;
    byte y = 20;
    byte* ptrx = &x;
    byte* ptry = &y;

    Console.WriteLine(*ptrx + "\t" + (int)ptrx);
    Console.WriteLine(*ptry + "\t" + (int)ptry);

    // Convert byte* to void*.
    void* voidx = (void*)ptrx;
    void* voidy = (void*)ptry;

    // Switch pointer values.
    Switch(ref voidx, ref voidy);

    // Convert returned void* to a usable byte*.
    ptrx = (byte*)voidx;
    ptry = (byte*)voidy;

    Console.WriteLine(*ptrx + "\t" + (int)ptrx);
    Console.WriteLine(*ptry + "\t" + (int)ptry);
}
```

All that had to be done is to change the int* types to byte* types. The problem here is that there are no safeguards against passing in pointers to different types. This can be a big problem, if you swap out, say, a byte and an integer.

Discussion

A void pointer has no type and therefore cannot be dereferenced, nor can pointer arithmetic be applied to this type of pointer. A void pointer does have one very useful function, though; it can be cast to a pointer of any other type. Notice that the Switch method, used in the Solution for this recipe, takes two parameters of type void* by reference. You are declaring that any pointer type may be passed to these two parameters. Once inside the Switch method, you can manipulate the value contained in the void pointers. However, since you do not know the original type that the void* was cast from, you cannot dereference the void*.

The one drawback to this technique is that before the Switch method is called in the TestSwitch method, the int* or byte* pointers must be cast to a void*. When the Switch method returns, the void* pointers must be cast back to their original types before they can be used. The reason for this casting is that you are passing the void* pointers by reference instead of by value.

You could pass the void* pointers by value instead and simply switch the values pointed to, rather than the memory locations pointed to, in the Switch method. This new SwitchValues method would look something like this:

```
public unsafe void SwitchValues(void* x, void* y)
{
    void* temp = x;
    *x = *y;
    *y = *temp;
}
```

Unfortunately, this code will not compile, since you cannot dereference a void*. The void* must be cast to its original type before it can be dereferenced. To do this, you must also pass along the type information to the SwitchValues method. This can become very cumbersome, and it reduces the generic character of this method as well.

See Also

See the section "A.4 Pointer Conversions" in the C# specification.

19.8   Converting a String to a char*

Problem

You have a string that you want to convert to a char*, which is essentially a pointer to the first element in a character array.

Solution

Use the ToCharArray method of the string type to create a char* character array:

```
public static void ConvertStringToCharPtr(string str)
{
    unsafe
    {
        fixed (char* pStr = str.ToCharArray())
        {
            // Display some of the characters.
            Console.WriteLine(pStr->ToString());    // Could also have been
                                                    // written as pStr[0].ToString().

            Console.WriteLine(pStr[1].ToString());
            Console.WriteLine(pStr[2].ToString());
            Console.WriteLine(pStr[3].ToString());
        }
    }
}
```

Discussion

To get a character array from a string object, you can use the overloaded ToCharArray method on the string object. This method is overloaded to accept no arguments and convert the entire string to a character array or to take two integer arguments and convert only a substring of the entire string to a character array. These two integer parameters hold a startIndex value and a length value. The substring starting at the startIndex position in the string and ending at the (startIndex + length) position in the string is converted to a character array.

See Also

See Recipes 19.3–19.7; see the "Unsafe Code Tutorial" and the "Fixed Statement" topics in the MSDN documentation.

19.9 Declaring a Fixed-Size Structure with an Embedded Array

Problem

You require a structure to contain a fixed-size array in which the array is not stored on the managed heap; rather, the array needs to be stored inside the structure on the stack. This type of structure is useful when an unmanaged method that requires a fixed-size structure as a parameter is called from managed code.

Solution

Use a fixed array inside of a structure:

```
public unsafe struct UnsafeByteArray
{
    public fixed byte Data[254];
}
```

Discussion

A fixed type can be one of the following built-in types: bool, byte, sbyte, char, short, ushort, int, uint, long, ulong, float, or double. In addition, the array must be a fixed size. For example, the following code will not compile:

```
public unsafe struct UnsafeByteArray
{
    public fixed byte Data1[];    // Needs to be a fixed size.
    public fixed byte[] Data2;    // Needs to be one of the
                                  // aforementioned built-in types.
}
```

A fixed-size buffer has a few other limitations, including:

- You can use it only in an unsafe context.
- You cannot declare it as a static field, only as an instance field.
- It can be only a one-dimensional array with a lower bound of zero (i.e., a vector array).

Declaring a structure with an embedded array in the following manner:

```
public struct SafeByteArray
{
    public SafeByteArray(int size)
    {
        // Create the byte array.
        Data = new byte[254];
    }

    public byte[] Data;
}
```

simply creates a structure that is 8 bytes in size. This is because arrays are reference types and are created on the managed heap while the structure, SafeByteArray, is created on the stack with a 4-byte pointer to the array on the managed heap. The UnsafeByteArray structure created in the Solution to this recipe has a size of 254 bytes in memory. This is because of the fixed keyword, which fixes the array inside of the structure as opposed to creating a pointer to an array on the managed heap. Since structures typically exist on the stack, unless they are referenced inside of a reference type, the fixed data will also reside in the stack.

See Also

See the "Unsafe Code Tutorial," the "Fixed-Size Buffers," and the "Fixed Statement" topics in the MSDN documentation.

CHAPTER 20

Toolbox

20.0 Introduction

Every programmer has a certain set of routines that he refers back to and uses over and over again. These utility functions are usually bits of code that are not provided by any particular language or framework. This chapter is a compilation of utility routines that we have gathered during our time with C# and the .NET Framework. The type of things found in this chapter are:

- Determining the path for various locations in the operating system
- Interacting with services
- Inspecting the Global Assembly Cache
- Message queuing

It is a grab bag of code that can help to solve a specific need while you are working on a larger set of functionality in your application.

20.1 Dealing with Operating System Shutdown, Power Management, or User Session Changes

Problem

You want to be notified whenever the operating system or a user has initiated an action that requires your application to shut down or be inactive (user logoff, remote session disconnect, system shutdown, hibernate/restore, etc.). This notification will allow you have your application respond gracefully to the changes.

Solution

Use the `Microsoft.Win32.SystemEvents` class to get notification of operating system, user session change, and power management events. The `RegisterForSystemEvents` method shown next hooks up the five event handlers necessary to capture these events and would be placed in the initialization section for your code:

```
public static void RegisterForSystemEvents()
{
    // Always get the final notification when the event thread is shutting down
    // so we can unregister.
    SystemEvents.EventsThreadShutdown +=
        new EventHandler(OnEventsThreadShutdown);
    SystemEvents.PowerModeChanged +=
        new PowerModeChangedEventHandler(OnPowerModeChanged);
    SystemEvents.SessionSwitch +=
        new SessionSwitchEventHandler(OnSessionSwitch);
    SystemEvents.SessionEnding +=
        new SessionEndingEventHandler(OnSessionEnding);
    SystemEvents.SessionEnded +=
        new SessionEndedEventHandler(OnSessionEnded);
}
```

The EventsThreadShutdown event notifies you of when the thread that is distributing the events from the SystemEvents class is shutting down so that you can unregister the events on the SystemEvents class if you have not already done so. The PowerModeChanged event triggers when the user suspends or resumes the system from a suspended state. The SessionSwitch event is triggered by a change in the logged-on user. The SessionEnding event is triggered when the user is trying to log off or shut down the system, and the SessionEnded event is triggered when the user is actually logging off or shutting down the system.

The events can be unregistered using the UnregisterFromSystemEvents method. UnregisterFromSystemEvents should be called from the termination code of your Windows Form, user control, or any other class that may come and go, as well as from one other area shown later in the recipe:

```
private static void UnregisterFromSystemEvents()
{
    SystemEvents.EventsThreadShutdown -=
        new EventHandler(OnEventsThreadShutdown);
    SystemEvents.PowerModeChanged -=
        new PowerModeChangedEventHandler(OnPowerModeChanged);
    SystemEvents.SessionSwitch -=
        new SessionSwitchEventHandler(OnSessionSwitch);
    SystemEvents.SessionEnding -=
        new SessionEndingEventHandler(OnSessionEnding);
    SystemEvents.SessionEnded -=
        new SessionEndedEventHandler(OnSessionEnded);
}
```

Since the events exposed by SystemEvents are static, if you are using them in a section of code that could be invoked multiple times (secondary Windows Form, user control, monitoring class, etc.), you *must* unregister your handlers or you will cause memory leaks in the application.

The SystemEvents handler methods are the individual event handlers for each of the events that have been subscribed to in RegisterForSystemEvents. The first handler to cover is the OnEventsThreadShutdown handler. It is essential that your handlers are unregistered if this event fires, as the notification thread for the SystemEvents class is going away and the class may be gone before your application is. If you haven't unregistered before that point, you will cause memory leaks, so add a call to UnregisterFromSystemEvents into this handler as shown here:

```
private static void OnEventsThreadShutdown(object sender, EventArgs e)
{
    Debug.WriteLine("System event thread is shutting down, no more notifications.");

    // Unregister all our events as the notification thread is going away.
    UnregisterFromSystemEvents();
}
```

The next handler to explore is the OnPowerModeChanged method. This handler can report the type of power management event through the Mode property of the PowerModeEventChangedArgs parameter. The Mode property has the PowerMode enumeration type and specifies the event type through the enumeration value contained therein.

```
private static void OnPowerModeChanged(object sender, PowerModeChangedEventArgs e)
{
    // Power mode is changing.
    switch (e.Mode)
    {
        case PowerModes.Resume:
            Debug.WriteLine("PowerMode: OS is resuming from suspended state");
            break;
        case PowerModes.StatusChange:
            Debug.WriteLine("PowerMode: There was a change relating to the power" +
                " supply (weak battery, unplug, etc..)");
            break;
        case PowerModes.Suspend:
            Debug.WriteLine("PowerMode: OS is about to be suspended");
            break;
    }
}
```

The next three handlers all deal with operating system session states. They are OnSessionSwitch, OnSessionEnding, and OnSessionEnded. Handling all three of these events covers all of the operating system session state transitions that your application may need to worry about. In OnSessionEnding, there is a SessionEndingEventArgs parameter, which has a Cancel member. This Cancel member allows you to request that the session not end if set to false. Code for the three handlers is shown in Example 20-1.

Example 20-1. OnSessionSwitch, OnSessionEnding, and OnSessionEnded handlers

```
private static void OnSessionSwitch(object sender, SessionSwitchEventArgs e)
{
    // Check reason.
    switch (e.Reason)
    {
        case SessionSwitchReason.ConsoleConnect:
            Debug.WriteLine("Session connected from the console");
            break;
        case SessionSwitchReason.ConsoleDisconnect:
            Debug.WriteLine("Session disconnected from the console");
            break;
        case SessionSwitchReason.RemoteConnect:
            Debug.WriteLine("Remote session connected");
            break;
        case SessionSwitchReason.RemoteDisconnect:
            Debug.WriteLine("Remote session disconnected");
            break;
        case SessionSwitchReason.SessionLock:
            Debug.WriteLine("Session has been locked");
            break;
        case SessionSwitchReason.SessionLogoff:
            Debug.WriteLine("User was logged off from a session");
            break;
        case SessionSwitchReason.SessionLogon:
            Debug.WriteLine("User has logged on to a session");
            break;
        case SessionSwitchReason.SessionRemoteControl:
            Debug.WriteLine("Session changed to or from remote status");
            break;
        case SessionSwitchReason.SessionUnlock:
            Debug.WriteLine("Session has been unlocked");
            break;
    }
}

private static void OnSessionEnding(object sender, SessionEndingEventArgs e)
{
    // True to cancel the user request to end the session, false otherwise
    e.Cancel = false;
    // Check reason.
    switch(e.Reason)
    {
        case SessionEndReasons.Logoff:
            Debug.WriteLine("Session ending as the user is logging off");
            break;
        case SessionEndReasons.SystemShutdown:
            Debug.WriteLine("Session ending as the OS is shutting down");
```

Example 20-1. OnSessionSwitch, OnSessionEnding, and OnSessionEnded handlers (continued)

```
            break;
    }
}

private static void OnSessionEnded(object sender, SessionEndedEventArgs e)
{
    switch (e.Reason)
    {
        case SessionEndReasons.Logoff:
            Debug.WriteLine("Session ended as the user is logging off");
            break;
        case SessionEndReasons.SystemShutdown:
            Debug.WriteLine("Session ended as the OS is shutting down");
            break;
    }
}
```

Discussion

The .NET Framework provides many opportunities to get feedback from the system when there are changes due to either user or system interactions. The SystemEvents class exposes more events than just the ones used in this recipe. For a full listing, see Table 20-1.

Table 20-1. The SystemEvents events

Value	Description
DisplaySettingsChanged	User changed display settings.
DisplaySettingsChanging	Display settings are changing.
EventsThreadShutdown	Thread listening for system events is terminating.
InstalledFontsChanged	User added or removed fonts.
PaletteChanged	User switched to an application with a different palette.
PowerModeChanged	User suspended or resumed the system.
SessionEnded	User shut down the system or logged off.
SessionEnding	User is attempting to shut down the system or log off.
SessionSwitch	The currently logged-in user changed.
TimeChanged	User changed system time.
TimerElapsed	A Windows timer interval expired.
UserPreferenceChanged	User changed a preference in the system.
UserPreferenceChanging	User is trying to change a preference in the system.

 Keep in mind that these are system events. Therefore, the amount of work done in the handlers should be kept to a minimum so the system can move on to the next task.

The notifications from SystemEvents come on a dedicated thread for raising these events. In a Windows Forms application, you will need to get back on to the correct user interface thread before updating a UI with any of this information, using one of the various methods for doing so (Control.BeginInvoke, Control.Invoke, BackgroundWorker).

See Also

See the "SystemEvents Class," "PowerModeChangedEventArgs Class," "Session-EndedEventArgs Class," "SessionEndingEventArgs Class," "SessionSwitchEvent-Args Class," "TimerElapsedEventArgs Class," "UserPreferenceChangingEventArgs Class," and "UserPreferenceChangedEventArgs Class" topics in the MSDN documentation.

20.2 Controlling a Service

Problem

You need to programmatically manipulate a service that your application interacts with.

Solution

Use the System.ServiceProcess.ServiceController class to control the service. ServiceController allows you to interact with an existing service and to read and change its properties. In the example, it will be used to manipulate the ASP.NET State Service. The name, the service type, and the display name are easily available from the ServiceName, ServiceType, and DisplayName properties.

```
ServiceController scStateService = new ServiceController("COM+ Event System");
Console.WriteLine("Service Name: " + scStateService.ServiceName);
Console.WriteLine("Service Type: " + scStateService.ServiceType.ToString());
Console.WriteLine("Display Name: " + scStateService.DisplayName);
```

The ServiceType enumeration has a number of values, shown in Table 20-2.

Table 20-2. The ServiceType enumeration values

Value	Description
Adapter	Service that serves a hardware device
FileSystemDriver	Driver for the filesystem (kernel level)
InteractiveProcess	Service that communicates with the desktop
KernelDriver	Low-level hardware device driver
RecognizerDriver	Driver for identifying filesystems on startup
Win32OwnProcess	Win32 program that runs as a service in its own process
Win32ShareProcess	Win32 program that runs as a service in a shared process like SvcHost

One useful task is to determine a service's dependents. The services that depend on the current service are accessed through the DependentServices property, an array of ServiceController instances (one for each dependent service):

```
foreach (ServiceController sc in scStateService.DependentServices)
{
    Console.WriteLine(scStateService.DisplayName + " is depended on by: " +
            sc.DisplayName);
}
```

To see the services that the current service does depend on, the ServicesDependedOn array contains ServiceController instances for each of those:

```
foreach (ServiceController sc in scStateService.ServicesDependedOn)
{
    Console.WriteLine(scStateService.DisplayName + " depends on: " +
            sc.DisplayName);
}
```

One of the most important things about services is what state they are in. A service doesn't do much good if it is supposed to be running and it isn't—or worse yet, it is supposed to be disabled (perhaps as a security risk) and isn't. To find out the current status of the service, check the Status property. For this example, the original state of the service will be saved so it can be restored later in the originalState variable.

```
Console.WriteLine("Status: " + scStateService.Status);
// Save original state.
ServiceControllerStatus originalState = scStateService.Status;
```

If a service is stopped, it can be started with the Start method. First, check if the service is stopped, then once Start has been called on the ServiceController instance, the WaitForStatus method should be called to make sure that the service started. WaitForStatus can take a timeout value so that the application is not waiting forever for the service to start in the case of a problem.

```
// If it is stopped, start it.
TimeSpan serviceTimeout = TimeSpan.FromSeconds(60);
if (scStateService.Status == ServiceControllerStatus.Stopped)
{
    scStateService.Start();
    // Wait up to 60 seconds for start.
    scStateService.WaitForStatus(ServiceControllerStatus.Running, serviceTimeout);
}
Console.WriteLine("Status: " + scStateService.Status);
```

Services can also be paused. If the service is paused, the application needs to check if it can be continued by looking at the CanPauseAndContinue property. If so, the Continue method will get the service going again, and the WaitForStatus method should be called to wait until it does:

```
// If it is paused, continue.
if (scStateService.Status == ServiceControllerStatus.Paused)
```

```
{
    if(scStateService.CanPauseAndContinue)
    {
        scStateService.Continue();
        // Wait up to 60 seconds for running.
        scStateService.WaitForStatus(ServiceControllerStatus.Running,
                            serviceTimeout);
    }
}
Console.WriteLine("Status: " + scStateService.Status);

// Should be running at this point.
```

Determining if a service can be stopped is done through the CanStop property. If it can be stopped, then stopping it is a matter of calling the Stop method followed by WaitForStatus:

```
// Can we stop it?
if (scStateService.CanStop)
{
    scStateService.Stop();
    // Wait up to 60 seconds for stop.
    scStateService.WaitForStatus(ServiceControllerStatus.Stopped, serviceTimeout);
}
Console.WriteLine("Status: " + scStateService.Status);
```

Now it is time to set the service back to how you found it. The originalState variable has the original state, and the switch statement holds actions for taking the service from the current stopped state to its original state:

```
// Set it back to the original state.
switch (originalState)
{
    case ServiceControllerStatus.Stopped:
        if (scStateService.CanStop)
        {
            scStateService.Stop();
        }
        break;
    case ServiceControllerStatus.Running:
        scStateService.Start();
        // Wait up to 60 seconds for stop.
        scStateService.WaitForStatus(ServiceControllerStatus.Running,
                        serviceTimeout);
        break;
    case ServiceControllerStatus.Paused:
        // If it was paused and is stopped, need to restart so we can pause.
        if (scStateService.Status == ServiceControllerStatus.Stopped)
        {
            scStateService.Start();
            // Wait up to 60 seconds for start.
            scStateService.WaitForStatus(ServiceControllerStatus.Running,
                        serviceTimeout);
        }
```

```
        // Now pause.
        if (scStateService.CanPauseAndContinue)
        {
            scStateService.Pause();
            // Wait up to 60 seconds for stop.
            scStateService.WaitForStatus(ServiceControllerStatus.Paused,
                        serviceTimeout);
        }
        break;
}
```

In order to be sure that the Status property is correct on the service, the application should call Refresh to update it before testing the value of the Status property. Once the application is done with the service, call the Close method.

```
scStateService.Refresh();
Console.WriteLine("Status: " + scStateService.Status.ToString());

// Close it.
scStateService.Close();
```

Discussion

Services run many of the operating system functions today. They usually run under a system account (LocalSystem, NetworkService, LocalService) or a specific user account that has been granted specific permissions and rights. If your application uses a service, then this is a good way to determine if everything for the service to run is set up and configured properly before your application attempts to use it. Not all applications depend on services directly. But if your application does, or you have written a service as part of your application, it can be handy to have an easy way to check the status of your service and possibly correct the situation.

See Also

See the "ServiceController Class" and "ServiceControllerStatus Enumeration" topics in the MSDN documentation.

20.3 List What Processes an Assembly Is Loaded In

Problem

You want to know what current processes have a given assembly loaded.

Solution

Use the GetProcessesAssemblyIsLoadedIn method that we've created for this purpose to return a list of processes that a given assembly is loaded in. GetProcessesAssemblyIsLoadedIn takes the filename of the assembly to look for (like *System.Data.dll*), then gets a list of the currently running processes on the machine by calling `Process.GetProcesses`. It then searches the processes to see if the assembly is loaded into any of them. When found in a process, that `Process` object is added to a `List<Process>`. The entire `List<Process>` is returned once all the processes have been examined.

```
public static List<Process> GetProcessesAssemblyIsLoadedIn(string assemblyFileName)
{
    List<Process> processList = new List<Process>();
    Process[] processes = Process.GetProcesses();
    foreach (Process p in processes)
    {
        foreach (ProcessModule module in p.Modules)
        {
            if (module.ModuleName.Equals(assemblyFileName,
                StringComparison.OrdinalIgnoreCase))
            {
                processList.Add(p);
                break;
            }
        }
    }
    return processList;
}
```

Discussion

In some circumstances, such as when uninstalling software or debugging version conflicts, it is beneficial to know if an assembly is loaded into more than one process. By quickly getting a list of the `Process` objects that the assembly is loaded in, you can narrow the scope of your investigation.

The following code uses this routine:

```
string searchAssm = "System.Data.dll";
List<Process> processes = Toolbox.GetProcessesAssemblyIsLoadedIn(searchAssm);
foreach (Process p in processes)
{
    Console.WriteLine("Found {0} in {1}",searchAssm, p.MainModule.ModuleName);
}
```

The preceding code might produce output like this (you may see more if you have other applications running):

```
Found System.Data.dll in WebDev.WebServer.EXE
Found System.Data.dll in devenv.exe
Found System.Data.dll in CSharpRecipes.vshost.exe
```

Since this is a diagnostic function, you will need `FullTrust` security access to use this method.

See Also

See the "Process Class," "ProcessModule Class," and "GetProcesses Method" topics in the MSDN documentation.

20.4 Using Message Queues on a Local Workstation

Problem

You need a way to disconnect two components of your application (like a web service endpoint and processing logic) so that the first component has to worry about only formatting the instructions and the bulk of the processing occurs in the second component.

Solution

Use the MQWorker class shown here in both the first and second components to write and read messages to and from a message queue. MQWorker uses the local message-queuing services to do this. The queue pathname is supplied in the constructor, and the existence of the queue is checked in the SetUpQueue method.

```
class MQWorker
{
    private string _mqPathName;
    MessageQueue _queue = null;

    public MQWorker(string queuePathName)
    {
        if (string.IsNullOrEmpty(queuePathName))
            throw new ArgumentNullException("queuePathName");

        _mqPathName = queuePathName;

        SetUpQueue();
    }
```

SetUpQueue creates a message queue of the supplied name using the MessageQueue class if none exists. It accounts for the scenario in which the message-queuing services are running on a workstation computer. In that situation, it makes the queue private, as that is the only type of queue allowed on a workstation.

```
    private void SetUpQueue()
    {
        // See if the queue exists, create it if not.
        if (!MessageQueue.Exists(_mqPathName))
        {
            try
            {
                _queue = MessageQueue.Create(_mqPathName);
            }
            catch (MessageQueueException mqex)
            {
                // See if we are running on a workgroup computer.
                if (mqex.MessageQueueErrorCode ==
                    MessageQueueErrorCode.UnsupportedOperation)
                {
```

```
                  string origPath = _mqPathName;
                  // Must be a private queue in workstation mode.
                  int index = _mqPathName.ToLower().IndexOf("private$");
                  if (index == -1)
                  {
                      // Get the first \.
                      index = _mqPathName.IndexOf(@"\");
                      // Insert private$\ after server entry.
                      _mqPathName = _mqPathName.Insert(index + 1, @"private$\");

                      if (!MessageQueue.Exists(_mqPathName))
                          _queue = MessageQueue.Create(_mqPathName);
                      else
                          _queue = new MessageQueue(_mqPathName);
                  }
              }
          }
      }
      else
      {
          _queue = new MessageQueue(_mqPathName);
      }
  }
```

The SendMessage method sends a message to the queue set up in the constructor. The body of the message is supplied in the body parameter, and then an instance of System.Messaging.Message is created and populated. The BinaryMessageFormatter is used to format the message, as it enables larger volumes of messages to be sent with fewer resources than does the default XmlMessageFormatter. Messages are set to be persistent by setting the Recoverable property to true. Finally, the Body is set and the message is sent.

```
  public void SendMessage(string label, string body)
  {
      if (_queue != null)
      {
          Message msg = new Message();
          // Label our message.
          msg.Label = label;

          // Override the default XML formatting with binary
          // as it is faster (at the expense of legibility while debugging).
          msg.Formatter = new BinaryMessageFormatter();
          // Make this message persist (causes message to be written
          // to disk).
          msg.Recoverable = true;
          msg.Body = body;
          _queue.Send(msg);
      }
  }
```

The ReadMessage method reads messages from the queue set up in the constructor by creating a Message object and calling its Receive method. The message formatter is set to the `BinaryMessageFormatter` for the `Message`, since that is how we write to the queue. Finally, the body of the message is returned from the method.

```
public string ReadMessage( )
{
 Message msg = null;
 msg = _queue.Receive( );
 msg.Formatter = new BinaryMessageFormatter( );
 return (string)msg.Body;
}

}
```

To show how the `MQWorker` class is used, the following example creates an `MQWorker`. It then sends a message (a small blob of XML) using `SendMessage`, then retrieves it using `ReadMessage`:

```
// NOTE: Message Queue services must be set up for this to work.
// This can be added in Add/Remove Windows Components.

// This is the right syntax for workstation queues.
//MQWorker mqw = new MQWorker(@".\private$\MQWorkerQ");
MQWorker mqw = new MQWorker(@".\MQWorkerQ");
string xml = "<MyXml><InnerXml location=\"inside\"/></MyXml>";
Console.WriteLine("Sending message to message queue: " + xml);
mqw.SendMessage("Message Label",xml);

// This could also be in a separate component.
string retXml = mqw.ReadMessage( );
Console.WriteLine("Read message from message queue: " + retXml);
```

Discussion

Message queues are very useful when you are attempting to distribute the processing load for scalability purposes. Without question, using a message queue adds overhead to the processing, as the messages must travel through the infrastructure of MSMQ, overhead would not incur without it. One benefit is that MSMQ allows your application to spread out across multiple machines, so there can be a net gain in production. Another advantage is that this supports reliable asynchronous handling of the messages so that the sending side can be confident that the receiving side will get the message without the sender having to wait for confirmation. The Message Queue services are not installed by default, but can be installed through the Add/Remove Windows Components applet in Control Panel. Using a message queue to buffer your processing logic from high volumes of requests (such as in the web service scenario presented earlier) can lead to more stability and ultimately can produce more throughput for your application through using multiple reader processes on multiple machines.

See Also

See the "Message Class" and "MessageQueue Class" topics in the MSDN documentation.

20.5 Finding the Path to the Current Framework Version

Problem

You need the path to where the version of the .NET Framework you are running on is located.

Solution

Use the GetRuntimeDirectoryRuntimeDirectory method (implemented in System. Runtime.InteropServices.RuntimeEnvironment) to return the full path to the folder that the current version of .NET is installed in:

```
public static string GetCurrentFrameworkPath()
{
    return
System.Runtime.InteropServices.RuntimeEnvironment.GetRuntimeDirectory();
}
```

Discussion

There are many reasons why you might want to know the current framework path, including:

- Manually loading the configuration files in the *config* directory to check settings
- Dynamically adding references for system components in a code generator

The list could go on and on. Since the method to get to the path is pretty far down a namespace chain (System.Runtime.InteropServices.RuntimeEnvironment), it is provided for your programming convenience.

See Also

See the "Version Class" and "Version.ToString Method" topics in the MSDN documentation.

20.6 Determining the Versions of an Assembly That Are Registered in the Global Assembly Cache (GAC)

Problem

You need to determine all of the versions of an assembly that are currently installed in the GAC.

Solution

Use the `PrintGACRegisteredVersions` method (implemented here) to display all of the versions (both native and managed) of an assembly in the GAC. In order to be complete, the code looks for *.dll*, *.exe*, and the native versions of *.dll* and *.exe* files in the Global Assembly Cache.

```
public static void PrintGACRegisteredVersions(string assmFileName)
{
    Console.WriteLine("Searching for GAC Entries for {0}\r\n", assmFileName);
    // Get the filename without the extension as that is the subdirectory
    // name in the GAC where it would be registered.
    string assmFileNameNoExt = Path.GetFileNameWithoutExtension(assmFileName);

    // Need to look for both the native images as well as "regular" .dlls and .exes.
    string searchDLL = assmFileNameNoExt + ".dll";
    string searchEXE = assmFileNameNoExt + ".exe";
    string searchNIDLL = assmFileNameNoExt + ".ni.dll";
    string searchNIEXE = assmFileNameNoExt + ".ni.exe";
```

The `Directory.GetFiles` method is used to determine if any of those versions are present in the GAC, which is located in the *[Windows]\ASSEMBLY* folder.

> The *ASSEMBLY* folder is not visible through Windows Explorer, as the GAC shell extension gets in the way. But if you run a Command Prompt window, you can maneuver to the *[Windows]\ASSEMBLY* folder and see how things are stored in the GAC.

Finally, all of the files are combined into a master `ArrayList` using the `AddRange` method:

```
// Get the path to the GAC using GetWinDir from 20.7.
string gacPath = GetWinDir() + @"\ASSEMBLY\";

// Go get all of the possible file derivatives in the GAC.
string [] dllFiles = Directory.GetFiles(gacPath, searchDLL,
                        SearchOption.AllDirectories);
string [] exeFiles = Directory.GetFiles(gacPath, searchEXE,
                        SearchOption.AllDirectories);
string [] niDllFiles = Directory.GetFiles(gacPath, searchNIDLL,
```

```
                        SearchOption.AllDirectories);
        string [] niExeFiles = Directory.GetFiles(gacPath, searchNIEXE,
                        SearchOption.AllDirectories);

    ArrayList files = new ArrayList(5);
    files.AddRange(dllFiles);
    files.AddRange(exeFiles);
    files.AddRange(niDllFiles);
    files.AddRange(niExeFiles);
```

Now that you have a master list of the versions of this file in the GAC, you display the information for each individual item by examining the FileVersionInfo and writing it out to the console:

```
    foreach (string file in files)
    {
        // Grab the version info and print.
        FileVersionInfo fileVersion = FileVersionInfo.GetVersionInfo(file);
        if (file.IndexOf("NativeImage") != -1)
        {
            Console.WriteLine("Found {0} in the GAC under {1} as a native image",
                assmFileNameNoExt, Path.GetDirectoryName(file));
        }
        else
        {
            Console.WriteLine("Found {0} in the GAC under {1} with version " +
                    "information:\r\n{2}",
                        assmFileNameNoExt, Path.GetDirectoryName(file),
                    fileVersion.ToString());
        }
    }
}
```

The output from this when looking for *mscorlib* looks like this:

```
Found mscorlib in the GAC under C:\WINDOWS\ASSEMBLY\NativeImages1_v1.1.4322\mscorlib\
1.0.5000.0__b77a5c561934e089_a4b3b51f as a native image
Found mscorlib in the GAC under C:\WINDOWS\ASSEMBLY\NativeImages1_v1.1.4322\mscorlib\
1.0.5000.0__b77a5c561934e089_605b23c2 as a native image
Found mscorlib in the GAC under C:\WINDOWS\ASSEMBLY\NativeImages1_v1.0.3705\MSCORLIB\
1.0.3300.0__b77a5c561934e089_22016492 as a native image
Found mscorlib in the GAC under C:\WINDOWS\ASSEMBLY\GAC_32\mscorlib\2.0.0.0__
b77a5c561934e089 with version information:
File:             C:\WINDOWS\ASSEMBLY\GAC_32\mscorlib\2.0.0.0__b77a5c561934e089\
mscorlib.dll
InternalName:     mscorlib.dll
OriginalFilename: mscorlib.dll
FileVersion:      2.0.50712.6 (lab23df.050712-0600)
FileDescription:  Microsoft Common Language Runtime Class Library
Product:          Microsoftr .NET Framework
ProductVersion:   2.0.50712.6
Debug:            False
Patched:          False
PreRelease:       False
PrivateBuild:     False
```

```
SpecialBuild:       False
Language:           English (United States)

Found mscorlib in the GAC under C:\WINDOWS\ASSEMBLY\NativeImages_v2.0.50712_32\
mscorlib\043d0388db36f94390f023725a82a5e4 as a native image
Found mscorlib in the GAC under C:\WINDOWS\ASSEMBLY\NativeImages_v2.0.50601_32\
mscorlib\e56acc8ebce07f4db51f6f98c84419c2 as a native image
Found mscorlib in the GAC under C:\WINDOWS\ASSEMBLY\NativeImages_v2.0.50215_32\
mscorlib\5259bd1f47da3e329e6706b9d018132f as a native image
Found mscorlib in the GAC under C:\WINDOWS\ASSEMBLY\NativeImages_v2.0.50110_32\
mscorlib\1958e0d8502fff3f9b6b032a1e517867 as a native image
Found mscorlib in the GAC under C:\WINDOWS\ASSEMBLY\NativeImages_v2.0.50110_32\
mscorlib\07185e97384cd23eb6c91147f5db32ce as a native image
Found mscorlib in the GAC under C:\WINDOWS\ASSEMBLY\NativeImages_v2.0.41115_32\
mscorlib\ce295c2bd5b3d53cbcdca987ec346d99 as a native image
```

Discussion

The ability to have multiple versions of assemblies on a machine and having absolute binding mechanisms to the specific version of an assembly, were proclaimed as
the cure to *.dll hell*. *.dll hell* was the case in which two applications linked to a *.dll* of
the same name in a common folder (like *System32*), but each application needed a
different version of the *.dll*. Problems occurred when you attempted to run one or the
other application, depending upon which version was present. With assemblies and
the GAC, this scenario occurs only when the application is improperly configured by
allowing it to use newer versions of an assembly automatically or via publisher policy issues. Perhaps things are better now. In any case, they are different, and the
starting point for debugging assembly loads is to figure out what is on the system.
This can be helped by looking at the Assembly Binding Log Viewer (*FUSLOGVW.
exe*). But having a way to just see what is on the system with a particular filename
and what versions are included can be a very useful thing.

See Also

See the "Directory Class," "ArrayList Class," and "FileVersionInfo Class" topics in
the MSDN documentation.

20.7 Getting the Windows Directory

Problem

You need to know the full path to the Windows directory.

Solution

Call the GetWinDir method created for your use here to return the Windows directory path in a string:

```
public static string GetWinDir( )
{
    string sysDir = Environment.GetFolderPath(Environment.SpecialFolder.System);
    return Path.GetFullPath(sysDir + @"\..");
}
```

Discussion

There is an enumeration to describe almost every significant operating system folder (Environment.SpecialFolder). But for some reason, since the inception of .NET, the Windows directory has been deemed unacceptably off-limits. This recipe exists for want of an Environment.SpecialFolder.Windows value. Another way to get at this value is to use the Environment.GetEnvironmentVariable function, passing in "windir" as the value.

Table 20-3 shows all of the other places in the OS you can get through Environment. SpecialFolder.

Table 20-3. The Environment.SpecialFolder enumeration values

Value	Description
ApplicationData	Roaming user's application data directory
CommonApplicationData	Application data directory for all roaming users
CommonProgramFiles	Folder for common application components
Cookies	Directory where cookies are stored
Desktop	The logical desktop folder
DesktopDirectory	The physical desktop folder
Favorites	Where favorites are stored on disk
History	Internet history items folder
InternetCache	Where temporary Internet files are stored
LocalApplicationData	Nonroaming user's application data directory
MyComputer	Physical location of My Computer folder
MyDocuments	Physical location of My Documents folder
MyMusic	Physical location of My Music folder
MyPictures	Physical location of My Pictures folder
Personal	Physical location of personal documents
ProgramFiles	Physical location of the official Program Files directory
Programs	Folder where Program Groups are stored
Recent	Folder containing most recently used documents
SendTo	Send To menu item folder
StartMenu	Folder containing the Start menu structure and items
Startup	Folder corresponding to the Startup Program Group location
System	The system directory
Templates	Common location for document templates

See Also

See the "Environment.SpecialFolder Enumeration" and "Environment.GetFolderPath Method" topics in the MSDN documentation.

20.8 Capturing Output from the Standard Output Stream

Problem

You want to capture output that is going to the standard output stream from within your C# program.

Solution

Use the `Console.SetOut` method to capture and release the standard output stream. `SetOut` sets the standard output stream to whatever `System.IO.TextWriter`-based stream it is handed. To capture the output to a file, create a `StreamWriter` to write to it, and set that writer using `SetOut`. Now when `Console.WriteLine` is called, the output goes to the `StreamWriter`, not to stdout as shown here:

```
try
{
    Console.WriteLine("Stealing standard output!");
    using (StreamWriter writer = new StreamWriter(@"c:\log.txt"))
    {
        // Steal stdout for our own purposes...
        Console.SetOut(writer);

        Console.WriteLine("Writing to the console... NOT!");

        for (int i = 0; i < 10; i++)
            Console.WriteLine(i);
    }
}
catch(IOException e)
{
    Debug.WriteLine(e.ToString());
    return ;
}
```

To restore writing to the standard output stream, create another `StreamWriter`. This time, call the `Console.OpenStandardOutput` method to acquire the standard output stream and use `SetOut` to set it once again. Now calls to `Console.WriteLine` appear on the console again.

```
// Recover the standard output stream so that a
// completion message can be displayed.
    using (StreamWriter standardOutput =
                    new StreamWriter(Console.OpenStandardOutput( )))
```

```
    {
        standardOutput.AutoFlush = true;
        Console.SetOut(standardOutput);
        Console.WriteLine("Back to standard output!");
    }
```

The console output from this code looks like this:

```
Stealing standard output!
Back to standard output!
```

log.txt contains the following after the code is executed:

```
Writing to the console... NOT!
0
1
2
3
4
5
6
7
8
9
```

Discussion

Redirecting the standard output stream inside of the program may seem a bit anti-quated. But consider the situation when you're using another class that writes information to this stream. You don't want the output to appear in your application, but you have to use the class. This could also be useful if you create a small launcher application to capture output from a console application.

See Also

See the "Console.SetOut Method," "Console.OpenStandardOutput Method," and "StreamWriter Class" topics in the MSDN documentation.

20.9   Running Code in Its Own AppDomain

Problem

You want to run code isolated from the main part of your application.

Solution

Create a separate AppDomain to run the code using the AppDomain.CreateDomain method. CreateDomain allows the application to control many aspects of the AppDomain being created like the security environment, the AppDomain settings, and base paths for the AppDomain. To demonstrate this, the code creates an instance of the RunMe class (shown in full later in this recipe) and calls the PrintCurrentAppDomainName method. This prints the name of the AppDomain where the code is running.

```
public static void RunCodeInNewAppDomain( )
{
    AppDomain myOwnAppDomain = AppDomain.CreateDomain("MyOwnAppDomain");
    // Print out our current AppDomain name.
    RunMe rm = new RunMe( );
    rm.PrintCurrentAppDomainName( );
```

Now you create an instance of the RunMe class in the "MyOwnAppDomain" AppDomain by
calling CreateInstance on the AppDomain. We pass CreateInstance the module and
type information necessary for constructing the type, and it returns an ObjectHandle.
We can then retrieve a proxy to the instance running in the AppDomain by taking the
returned ObjectHandle and casting it to a RunMe reference using the Unwrap method.

```
    // Create our RunMe class in the new AppDomain.
    Type adType = typeof(RunMe);
    ObjectHandle objHdl =
        myOwnAppDomain.CreateInstance(adType.Module.Assembly.FullName,
                        adType.FullName);

    // Unwrap the reference.
    RunMe adRunMe = (RunMe)objHdl.Unwrap( );
```

The PrintCurrentAppDomainName method is called on the RunMe instance in the
"MyOwnAppDomain" AppDomain and it prints out "Hello from MyOwnAppDomain!". The
AppDomain is unloaded using AppDomain.Unload and the program terminates.

```
    // Make a call on the toolbox.
    adRunMe.PrintCurrentAppDomainName( );

    // Now unload the AppDomain.
    AppDomain.Unload(myOwnAppDomain);
}
```

The RunMe class is defined here. It inherits from MarshalByRefObject, as that allows
you to retrieve the proxy reference when you call Unwrap on the ObjectHandle and
have the calls on the class remoted into the new AppDomain. The PrintCurrentApp-
DomainName method simply accesses the FriendlyName property on the current
AppDomain and prints out the "Hello from {*AppDomain*}!" message.

```
public class RunMe : MarshalByRefObject
{
    public RunMe( )
    {
        PrintCurrentAppDomainName( );
    }

    public void PrintCurrentAppDomainName( )
    {
        string name = AppDomain.CurrentDomain.FriendlyName;
        Console.WriteLine("Hello from {0}!", name);
    }
}
```

The output from this example is shown here:

```
Hello from CSharpRecipes.vshost.exe!
Hello from CSharpRecipes.vshost.exe!
Hello from MyOwnAppDomain!
Hello from MyOwnAppDomain!
```

Discussion

Isolating code in a separate AppDomain is overkill for something as trivial as this example, but it demonstrates that code can be executed remotely in an AppDomain created by your application. There are six overloads for the CreateDomain method and each adds a bit more complexity to the AppDomain creation. In situations in which the isolation or configuration benefits outweigh the complexities of not only setting up a separate AppDomain but debugging code in it as well, it is a useful tool. A good real-world example is hosting a separate AppDomain to run ASP.NET pages outside of the normal ASP.NET environment though this is truly a nontrivial usage.

See Also

See the "AppDomain Class," "AppDomain.CreateDomain Method," and "ObjectHandle Class" topics in the MSDN documentation.

20.10 Determining the Operating System and Service Pack Version of the Current Operating System

Problem

You want to know the current operating system and service pack.

Solution

Use the GetOSAndServicePack method shown in Example 20-2 to get a string representing the current operating system and service pack. GetOSAndServicePack uses the Environment.OSVersion property to get the version information for the operating system, then determines the "official" name of the OS from that. The OperatingSystem class retrieved from Environment.OSVersion has a property for the service pack called ServicePack. The two strings are then merged together and returned as the OS and service pack string.

Example 20-2. GetOSAndServicePack method

```
public static string GetOSAndServicePack( )
{
    // Get the current OS info.
    OperatingSystem os = Environment.OSVersion;
    string osText = "";
    // If version is 5, then it is Win2K, XP, or 2003
```

Example 20-2. GetOSAndServicePack method (continued)

```
    if (os.Version.Major == 5)
    {
        switch (os.Version.Minor)
        {
            case 0: osText = "Windows 2000";
                break;
            case 1: osText = "Windows XP";
                break;
            case 2: osText = "Windows Server 2003";
                break;
            // This is the default but it usually reports "Microsoft Windows NT"
            //   due to relying on the PlatformID.
            default: osText = os.ToString();
                break;
        }
    }
    else
    {
        // Probably NT4 as .NET doesn't run on Win9X...
        osText = os.VersionString;
    }

    // Get the text for the service pack.
    string spText = os.ServicePack;
    // Build the whole string.
    return string.Format("{0} {1}", osText, spText);
}
```

Discussion

Enabling your application to know the current operating system and service pack allows you to include that information in debugging reports and in the about box (if you have one) for your application. The simple knowledge of the correct operating system and service pack transmitted through your support department can save you hours in debugging time. It is well worth making available so your support department can easily direct your clients to it in case they cannot otherwise locate it.

See Also

See the "Environment.OSVersion Property" and "OperatingSystem Class" topics in the MSDN documentation.

Index

Symbols

- (hyphen)
    in regular expression patterns, 586
    on command line, 168

!= (inequality operator)
    comparing pointers with, 1069
    overriding, 401
    Set<T> class, 666, 672

" (quotes, double), on command line, 169

(comment character), 589

$ (dollar sign), end of line matching in
    regular expressions, 588

& (bitwise AND) operator, 125, 665, 671
    determining if flag turned on in
        enumeration value, 28
    high word and low word of a number,
        getting, 9
    overloaded, implemented as
        operator, 343–350
    testing if bit flags are on or off, 31
    turning on/of FileAttributes
        enumeration, 678

&& (logical AND) operator, indirectly
    overloading, 120–122

( ) (cast operator), 138

( ) (parentheses)
    balanced, 619
    in equations, 126–128

* (wildcard character), 763

*= (assignment operator), 116–119

+ (addition) operator
    overloaded, implemented as
        iterator, 343–350

+= (assignment operator), 116–119

/ (slash), on command line, 168

// (comment characters), 589

//... (omitted C# code in examples), xxv

/= (assignment operator), 116–119

/main compiler switch, 160

: (colon), path-separation character, 717

; (semicolon)
    on command line, 168
    path-separation character, 717

< (less-than operator), 1070

< > (angle brackets), determining if
        balanced, 619

<!--...--> (omitted XML code in
        examples), xxv

<= (less than or equal operator), 1070

-= (assignment operator), 116–119

== (equality operator)
    comparing pointers with, 1069
    comparing strings with, 72
    overriding, 401
    Set<T> class, 665, 672

> (greater-than operator), 1070

>= (greater-than or equal operator), 1070

?: (conditional) operator
    indirectly overloading, 120–122
    nested, problems with precedence, 127

[ ] (brackets), determinining if balanced, 619

\ (backslash)
    in regular expression patterns, 586
    on command line, 169

^ (bitwise XOR) operator, 125, 665, 671
    turning on/off FileAttributes
        enumeration, 678

We'd like to hear your suggestions for improving our indexes. Send email to *index@oreilly.com*.

B

backslash (\)
    in regular expression patterns, 586
    on command line, 169
BadImageFormatException exception, 385,
        387
Balance class, 619–623
    Check methods, 619–621
    testing, 621
base classes, overridden methods in, listing
        for derived class, 757–762
base counter, 469
base keyword, 163, 293
base10, converting numbers in other bases
        to, 10
base64 data
    decoding into byte array, 56
    encoding binary data as, 55
Base64DecodeString method, 56
Base64EncodeBytes method, 55
BaseOverrides class, 760, 769
BeforeAddItem event, 526
BeforeAddListener method, 527
BeforeChangeItem event, 526
BeforeChangeListener method, 527
BeginInvoke method, 498, 1024, 1025, 1028,
        1029
BetterRandomString method, 970
big-endian encoding, 60
binary data
    converting numbers to base10, 10
    decoding Base64 data into, 56
binary functions, 555
binary operators, numeric promotion and, 7
binary predicates, 556
binary trees, 632–646
    algorithm for storing objects, 643
    creating and managing without
        BinaryTree<T> class, 644–646
    defined, 642
    using BinaryTree<T> and
        BinaryTreeNode<T>
        classes, 640–642
BinaryMessageFormatter class, 1094, 1095
BinaryPredicate<T> delegate, 556
BinaryReader class, 682, 687, 698, 937
    PeekChar method, 701
    Read method, 700
BinarySearch method
    Array class, 112
    ArrayList class, 112

List<T> class, 238, 295, 298, 304, 306
ListEx<T> class, 296
PriorityQueue<T> class, 607
BinarySearchCountAll method, 295, 296,
        297
BinarySearchGetAll method, 298, 299
BinaryTree<T> class, 633–634, 643
    members, listed, 638
BinaryTreeNode<T> class, 634–638, 643
    members, listed, 639
BinaryWriter class, 682, 687, 698, 937
BindGenericParameters method, Type
        class, 788
BindingFlags enumeration, 515, 773, 775
    flags, listing of, 776
bit flags
    turning on or off, 122–126
    (see also flags enumeration)
bit masks, 124
    using enumerated members in, 27–30
BitArray class, 280
bitmaps, 56
bitwise AND operator (&), 125, 665, 671
bitwise binary operators, numeric promotion
        and, 7
bitwise complement operator (~), 6, 306
bitwise operators, turning on/off
        FileAttributes enumeration, 678
bitwise OR operator (|), 125, 665, 671
bitwise XOR operator (^), 125, 665, 671
blittable objects, 77
books
    about C#, xxiv
    about design patterns, 949
    about Visual Studio .NET, xxiv
bool data type, 1100
Boolean class, Parse method, 63
Boolean equations
    ensuring correctness of, 126
    simplifying, 128–131
Boolean equations, ensuring correctness
        of, 126–128
Boolean logic, overloading, 120–122
boolean values, conversions to, 60, 134, 135
BooleanSwitch class, controlling tracing
        with, 437, 439
boxing, 87
    avoiding with generic Queue and Stack
        types, 233
    finding where it occurs, 214–216
    in standard .NET type, 223
    preventing, 215

email, sending via SMTP, 915–920
empty strings, testing for, 78
EnableRaisingEvents property, 462
Encoder class, Convert method, 80, 82
Encoding class
    ASCII property, 885
    GetBytes method, 59
    GetString method, 58
    Unicode encoding, 84
    UTF8 property, 804
Encrypt method
    CryptoString class, 952
    File class, 748
encryption, 957
    clearing key and initialization
        vector, 958–960
    digital signatures for assemblies, 980
    encrypting files, 953–958
    encrypting strings, 949–953
    of strings, 949
    random number generator for, 970
    secure strings, 995
    SSL protocol, 1001
    web.config data, 1005–1007
EncryptWebConfigData method, 1005, 1006
EndInvoke method, 420, 421, 424, 498,
        1025, 1026, 1028
EndOfStreamException exception, 387, 700
EndsWith method, String class, 50
EndTagRegex class, 593
EnhancedLog class, 162
Enqueue method, PriorityQueue<T>
        class, 606, 607
EnqueueHead method, DblQueue<T>
        class, 615
EnqueueTail method, DblQueue<T>
        class, 615
EnsureCapacity method, StringBuilder
        class, 76
entry points, application
    parsed arguments passed to, 169
    using multiple for versioning, 159–161
EntryPointNotFoundException
        exception, 387
EntryWrittenEventArgs class, 462
EntryWrittenEventHandler delegate, 462
Enum class, 2
    IsDefined method, 24, 372
        Flags enumerations, 26
    Parse method, 22, 63
    ToString method, 21

enumerations, 2
    converting strings to, 60
    determining if flags are set, 30–33
    displaying a value as a string, 20–22
    exceptions for, 376
    numeric values for items, 2
    testing for valid enumeration
        value, 23–25
    testing for valid Flags enumeration, 25
    textual value, converting to enumeration
        value, 22
    using bitwise complement (~) operator
        with, 6
    using members in bit mask, 27–30
Environment class, 484
    CommandLine property, 169
    ExpandEnvironmentVariables
        method, 717
    GetCommandLineArgs method, 169
    NewLine constant, 692–694
    OSVersion property, 1104
    SpecialFolder enumeration, 1100
    StackTrace method, 412
    StackTrace property, 411, 485
environment variables
    parsing multiple paths in, 716–717
    viewing and manipulating, 484
EOL (end-of-line) characters, 692–694
epsilon value, 4
equality operator (==)
    comparing pointers with, 1069
    comparing strings with, 72
    overriding, 401
    Set<T> class, 665, 672
Equals method
    GetHashCode method as alternative
        to, 595
    overridden, using with GetHashCode
        method, 602
    Set<T> class, 665, 672
    String class, 39, 40, 72
equations
    balanced, determining, 619
    complex, ensuring correctness of, 126
    complex, simplifying, 128–131
Error event, 738
error handling
    code examples in this book, xxv
    web server errors, 798
    (see also exception handling)

POST request, sending to web
server, 800–802
PowerModeChanged event, 1084
PowerModeEventChangedArgs class, 1085
PowerUsers role, 945
PrecompilationFlags enumeration, 811
PrecompileApplication method, 812
Predicate<T> class, 318, 555, 556
predicates, 556
preprocessor directives, allowing or
preventing compilation
with, 445–447
PreventLossOfException method, 379
PrincipalPermissions class, 944
Print method, BinaryTree<T> class, 639
PrintCurrentAppDomainName
method, 1103
PrintDepthFirst method
BinaryTreeNode<T> class, 640
NTreeNode<U> class, 654
PrintGACRegisteredVersions method, 1097
priority queue, 603
priority, boosting for a process
programmatically, 483
PriorityClass property, Process class, 483
PriorityQueue class, 603
PriorityQueue<T> class, 603–611
members, listed, 607
special comparer object
(CompareLen), 610
testing, 608
Process class, 476, 483
GetProcesses, 1092
MainWindowHandle property, 448
Responding property, 448
StandardInput property, 730
Start method, 729
StartInfo property, 476, 729
static methods to get process
information, 449
ProcessClient method, 878, 880, 882
processes
amount of physical memory being used
by, 485
boosting priority programmatically, 483
capturing standard output for, 475–478
launching console utilities with, 729
listing processes an assembly is loaded
in, 1091
not responding, determining, 447
ProcessInfo class, 476

ProcessInvoice method, 857
processors, number of, 484
ProcessPriorityClass, enumeration
values, 483
ProcessRespondingState enumeration, 448
ProcessSomething method, 151
ProcessStartInfo class, 483, 729
profiling tools, 214, 216
ProgIdAttribute, 175
properties
called on object already disposed, 371
parameters for, verifying correctness
of, 371–373
protected virtual methods, 526
protected visibility, methods, 24
protocol, pluggable, exceptions for, 376
proxies
accessing Internet through, 802
information about, 935
interface implementation, 947
security proxy classes, 941–949
proxy design pattern, 939, 947
PtrToStringBSTR method, Marshal
class, 995
PtrToStructure method, Marshal class, 934
public visibility
methods, 24
punctuation, determining if character is, 34
Pythagorean theorem, 18

Q

Query property, UriBuilder class, 816–818
QueryXML method, 837
Queue class, 280
replacing Queue objects with generic
Queue
benefits of, 233
replacing Queue objects with generic
Queue<T>, 231–235
snapshot of, 314
Queue<T> class, 280
snapshot of current state, 314
queues
double queue, 612–618
priority, 603–611
QueueUserWorkItem method, ThreadPool
class, 740
quotes, double ("), on command line, 169

R

\r (carriage return), line termination in Macintosh files, 579
\r\n (carriage return followed by line feed), 579
radians
    angles of right triangle, 19
    converting degrees to, 4
    converting to degrees, 5
random number generator, 970
range, determining if character is in, 37–39
RankException exception, 388
RateOfCountsPerSecond32 counter, 468
RateOfCountsPerSecond64 counter, 468
RawFraction counter, 472
RawValue property (PerformanceCounter), 468
RCW (runtime callable wrapper) of a COM object, 189
    garbage collection, 212
RdGenerateSecretInitVector method, CryptoString class, 952
RdGenerateSecretKey method, CryptoString class, 952
Read method
    BinaryReader class, 700
    FileStream class, 700
    StreamReader class, 696, 699
    TcpClient class, 885
    XmlReader class, 835
    XMLTextReader class, 832
ReadAllBufferedLog method, 697
ReadAllLog method, 694
ReadAllLogAsBytes method, 696
ReadByte method, FileStream class, 700
ReaderDecorator class, 967, 969
ReadFile method, 690
ReadLine method, StreamReader class, 578, 580, 695, 699
ReadLogByLines method, 695, 696
ReadLogPeeking method, 695
ReadMessage method, 1094
readonly field, 178
    initializing, 179
    instance readonly field, using, 181
ReadOnlyCollection<T> class, 269–270
ReadSensitiveData method, SecretFile class, 957
ReadToEnd method, StreamReader class, 694, 700

ReadToEndHash method, StringReaderHash class, 969
Receive method, Message class, 1094
ReceiveInvoice method, 862
redirecting standard output, 477
RedirectStandardOutput property (Process.StartInfo class), 476
ref parameter, 165
    passing pointers as, 1068
    use with anonymous methods, 545–547
reference types
    performance, structures vs., 86
    type arguments narrowed down to, 277
    unsafe code and, 1065
ReferencedAssembly property, ManifestResourceInfo class, 785
Reflect class, 382
reflection, 753–789
    configuring obfuscators on assemblies, 781–783
    dynamically invoking members, 777–780
    finding members in an assembly, 762–764
    finding members in an interface, 764
    generic type or method, determining, 783
    generic type, creating, 788
    handling exceptions generated by methods using, 382–385
    inheritance hierarchy for a type, 767–769
    IsDefined method, Enum class, 372
    listing assemblies imported by an assembly, 754–756
    listing exported types of an assembly, 756
    local variable information, 786
    manifest resources, reading programmatically, 784
    member information, filtering, 772–776
    nested types within an assembly, 765–767
    overridden methods, listing, 757–762
    permissions for, 753, 776, 978, 979
    serializable types in an assembly, 771
    subclasses of a type, 769–771
ReflectionEmit privilege, 753, 776
ReflectionException method, 382
ReflectionOnlyLoad* methods, Assembly class, 756
ReflectionPermissionFlag class, TypeInformation access, 940
ReflectionTypeLoadException exception, 388

About the Authors

Jay Hilyard has been developing applications for the Windows platform for over 12 years and for .NET for more than 4 years. Jay has published multiple articles in *MSDN Magazine* and he currently works on the New Product Development team at Newmarket International in Portsmouth, NH. When not immersed in .NET, Jay spends his time with his family and rooting for the Patriots.

Stephen Teilhet earned a degree in electrical engineering, but soon afterward began to write software for the Windows platform. For the last 11 years, he's worked for several consulting firms on a wide range of projects, specializing in Visual Basic, Visual C++, MTS, COM, MSMQ, and SQL Server. Stephen currently is employed at Compuware Numega Labs in Nashua, NH, where he has worked on several award-winning products, including DevPartner CodeReview and, most recently, DevPartner SecurityChecker.

Colophon

The animal on the cover of *C# Cookbook* is a garter snake (*Thamnophis sirtalis*). Named because their longitudinal stripes resemble those on garters once used to hold up men's socks, garter snakes are easily identified by their distinctive stripes: a narrow stripe down the middle of the back with a broad stripe on each side of it. Color and pattern variations enable them to blend into their native environments, helping them evade predators. They are the most common snake in North America and the only species of snake found in Alaska.

Garter snakes have keeled scales—one or more ridges down the central axis of the scales—giving them a rough texture and lackluster appearance. Adult garter snakes generally range in length between 46 and 130 centimeters (one and a half feet to over four feet). Females are usually larger than males, with shorter tails and a bulge where the body and tail meet.

Female garters are ovoviviparous, meaning they deliver "live" young that have gestated in soft eggs. Upon delivery, most of the eggs and mucous membranes have broken, which makes their births appear live. Occasionally, a baby will be born still inside its soft shell. A female will usually deliver 10 to 40 babies: the largest recorded number of live babies birthed by a garter snake is 98. Once emerging from their mothers, baby garters are completely independent and must begin fending for themselves. During this time they are most susceptible to predation, and over half of all baby garters die before they are one year old.

Garter snakes are one of the few animals able to eat toads, newts, and other amphibians with strong chemical defenses. Although diets vary depending on their environments, garter snakes mostly eat earthworms and amphibians; however, they occasionally dine on baby birds, fish, and small rodents. Garter snakes have toxic saliva (harmless to humans), which they use to stun or kill their prey before swallowing them whole.

The cover image is from a 19th-century engraving from the Dover Pictorial Archive. The cover font is Adobe ITC Garamond. The text font is Linotype Birka; the heading font is Adobe Myriad Condensed; and the code font is LucasFont's TheSans Mono Condensed.

Better than e-books

Buy *C# Cookbook*, 2nd Edition, and access
the digital edition FREE on Safari for 45 days.

Go to www.oreilly.com/go/safarienabled
and type in coupon code ITL7-HS4N-NSUI-76NX-CEGK

Search
thousands of
top tech books

Download
whole chapters

Cut and Paste
code examples

Find
answers fast

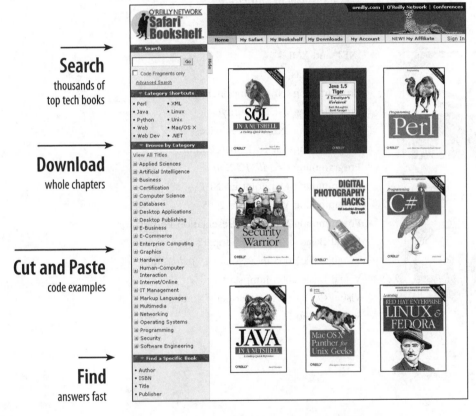

Search Safari! The premier electronic reference
library for programmers and IT professionals.

Related Titles from O'Reilly

.NET

ADO.NET Cookbook

ASP.NET Cookbook

ASP.NET 2.0 Cookbook

ASP.NET 2.0: A Developer's Notebook

C# Cookbook, *2nd Edition*

C# in a Nutshell, *2nd Edition*

C# Language Pocket Guide

Learning C#

.NET and XML

.NET Gotchas

Programming .NET Components, *2nd Edition*

Programming .NET Security

Programming .NET Web Services

Programming ASP.NET, *3rd Edition*

Programming C#, *4th Edition*

Programming MapPoint in .NET

Programming Visual Basic 2005

Programming Windows Presentation Foundation

Visual Basic 2005: A Developer's Notebook

Visual Basic 2005 in a Nutshell, *3rd Edition*

Visual Basic 2005 Jumpstart

Visual C# 2005: A Developer's Notebook

Visual Studio Hacks

O'REILLY®

Our books are available at most retail and online bookstores.

To order direct: 1-800-998-9938 • *order@oreilly.com* • *www.oreilly.com*

Online editions of most O'Reilly titles are available by subscription at *safari.oreilly.com*